In Praise of *Memory Systems: Cache, DRAM, Disk*

Memory Systems: Cache, DRAM, Disk *is the first book that takes on the whole hierarchy in a way that is consistent, covers the complete memory hierarchy, and treats each aspect in significant detail. This book will serve as a definitive reference manual for the expert designer, yet it is so complete that it can be read by a relative novice to the computer design space. While memory technologies improve in terms of density and performance, and new memory device technologies provide additional properties as design options, the principles and methodology presented in this amazingly complete treatise will remain useful for decades. I only wish that a book like this had been available when I started out more than three decades ago. It truly is a landmark publication. Kudos to the authors.*

—Al Davis, University of Utah

Memory Systems: Cache, DRAM, Disk *fills a huge void in the literature about modern computer architecture. The book starts by providing a high level overview and building a solid knowledge basis and then provides the details for a deep understanding of essentially all aspects of modern computer memory systems including architectural considerations that are put in perspective with cost, performance and power considerations. In addition, the historical background and politics leading to one or the other implementation are revealed. Overall, Jacob, Ng, and Wang have created one of the truly great technology books that turns reading about bits and bytes into an exciting journey towards understanding technology.*

—Michael Schuette, Ph.D., VP of Technology Development at OCZ Technology

This book is a critical resource for anyone wanting to know how DRAM, cache, and hard drives really work. It describes the implementation issues, timing constraints, and trade-offs involved in past, present, and future designs. The text is exceedingly well-written, beginning with high-level analysis and proceeding to incredible detail only for those who need it. It includes many graphs that give the reader both explanation and intuition. This will be an invaluable resource for graduate students wanting to study these areas, implementers, designers, and professors.

—Diana Franklin, California Polytechnic University, San Luis Obispo

Memory Systems: Cache, DRAM, Disk *fills an important gap in exploring modern disk technology with accuracy, lucidity, and authority. The details provided would only be known to a researcher who has also contributed in the development phase. I recommend this comprehensive book to engineers, graduate students, and researchers in the storage area, since details provided in computer architecture textbooks are woefully inadequate.*

—Alexander Thomasian, IEEE Fellow, New Jersey Institute of Technology and Thomasian and Associates

Memory Systems: Cache, DRAM, Disk *offers a valuable state of the art information in memory systems that can only be gained through years of working in advanced industry and research. It is about time that we have such a good reference in an important field for researchers, educators and engineers.*

—Nagi Mekhiel, Department of Electrical and Computer Engineering, Ryerson University, Toronto

This is the only book covering the important DRAM and disk technologies in detail. Clear, comprehensive, and authoritative, I have been waiting for such a book for long time.

—Yiming Hu, University of Cincinnati

Memory is often perceived as the performance bottleneck in computing architectures. Memory Systems: Cache, DRAM, Disk, *sheds light on the mystical area of memory system design with a no-nonsense approach to what matters and how it affects performance. From historical discussions to modern case study examples this book is certain to become as ubiquitous and used as the other Morgan Kaufmann classic textbooks in computer engineering including Hennessy and Patterson's* Computer Architecture: A Quantitative Approach.

—R. Jacob Baker, Micron Technology, Inc. and Boise State University.

Memory Systems: Cache, DRAM, Disk *is a remarkable book that fills a very large void. The book is remarkable in both its scope and depth. It ranges from high performance cache memories to disk systems. It spans circuit design to system architecture in a clear, cohesive manner. It is the memory architecture that defines modern computer systems, after all. Yet, memory systems are often considered as an appendage and are covered in a piecemeal fashion. This book recognizes that memory systems are the heart and soul of modern computer systems and takes a 'holistic' approach to describing and analyzing memory systems.*

The classic book on memory systems was written by Dick Matick of IBM over thirty years ago. So not only does this book fill a void, it is a long-standing void. It carries on the tradition of Dick Matick's book extremely well, and it will doubtless be the definitive reference for students and designers of memory systems for many years to come. Furthermore, it would be easy to build a top-notch memory systems course around this book. The authors clearly and succinctly describe the important issues in an easy-to-read manner. And the figures and graphs are really great—one of the best parts of the book.

When I work at home, I make coffee in a little stove-top espresso maker I got in Spain. It makes good coffee very efficiently, but if you put it on the stove and forget it's there, bad things happen—smoke, melted gasket—'burned coffee meltdown.' This only happens when I'm totally engrossed in a paper or article. Today, for the first time, it happened twice in a row—while I was reading the final version of this book.

—Jim Smith, University of Wisconsin—Madison

Memory Systems

Cache, DRAM, Disk

Memory Systems
Cache, DRAM, Disk

Bruce Jacob
University of Maryland at College Park

Spencer W. Ng
Hitachi Global Storage Technologies

David T. Wang
MetaRAM

With Contributions By

Samuel Rodriguez
Advanced Micro Devices

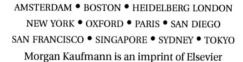

AMSTERDAM • BOSTON • HEIDELBERG LONDON
NEW YORK • OXFORD • PARIS • SAN DIEGO
SAN FRANCISCO • SINGAPORE • SYDNEY • TOKYO
Morgan Kaufmann is an imprint of Elsevier

Publisher	Denise E.M. Penrose
Acquisitions Editor	Chuck Glaser
Publishing Services Manager	George Morrison
Senior Production Editor	Paul Gottehrer
Developmental Editor	Nate McFadden
Assistant Editor	Kimberlee Honjo
Cover Design	Joanne Blank
Text Design	Dennis Schaefer
Composition	diacriTech
Interior printer	Maple-Vail Book Manufacturing Group
Cover printer	Phoenix Color

Morgan Kaufmann Publishers is an imprint of Elsevier.
30 Corporate Drive, Suite 400, Burlington, MA 01803, USA

This book is printed on acid-free paper.

Library of Congress Cataloging-in-Publication Data
Application submitted

ISBN: 978-0-12-379751-3

For information on all Morgan Kaufmann publications,
visit our Web site at *www.mkp.com* or *www.books.elsevier.com*

Printed in the United States of America
Transferred to Digital Printing, 2010

Dedication

Jacob   *To my parents, Bruce and Ann Jacob, my wife, Dorinda, and my children, Garrett, Carolyn, and Nate*

Ng   *Dedicated to the memory of my parents Ching-Sum and Yuk-Ching Ng*

Wang   *Dedicated to my parents Tu-Sheng Wang and Hsin-Hsin Wang*

You can tell whether a person plays or not by the way he carries the instrument, whether it means something to him or not.

Then the way they talk and act. If they act too hip, you know they can't play [jack].

—Miles Davis

[...] in connection with musical continuity, Cowell remarked at the New School before a concert of works by Christian Wolff, Earle Brown, Morton Feldman, and myself, that here were four composers who were getting rid of glue. That is: Where people had felt the necessity to stick sounds together to make a continuity, we four felt the opposite necessity to get rid of the glue so that sounds would be themselves.

Christian Wolff was the first to do this. He wrote some pieces vertically on the page but recommended their being played horizontally left to right, as is conventional. Later he discovered other geometrical means for freeing his music of intentional continuity. Morton Feldman divided pitches into three areas, high, middle, and low, and established a time unit. Writing on graph paper, he simply inscribed numbers of tones to be played at any time within specified periods of time.

There are people who say, "If music's that easy to write, I could do it." Of course they could, but they don't. I find Feldman's own statement more affirmative. We were driving back from some place in New England where a concert had been given. He is a large man and falls asleep easily. Out of a sound sleep, he awoke to say, "Now that things are so simple, there's so much to do." And then he went back to sleep.

—John Cage, *Silence*

Contents

Chapter 13 DRAM Memory Controller 497

Preface

"It's the Memory, Stupid!"

If you develop an ear for sounds that are musical it is like developing an ego. You begin to refuse sounds that are not musical and that way cut yourself off from a good deal of experience.

—John Cage

In 1996, Richard Sites, one of the fathers of computer architecture and lead designers of the DEC Alpha, had the following to say about the future of computer architecture research:

> *Across the industry, today's chips are largely able to execute code faster than we can feed them with instructions and data. There are no longer performance bottlenecks in the floating-point multiplier or in having only a single integer unit. The real design action is in memory subsystems—caches, buses, bandwidth, and latency.*

> *An anecdote: in a recent database benchmark study using TPC-C, both 200-MHz Pentium Pro and 400MHz 21164 Alpha systems were measured at 4.2–4.5 CPU cycles per instruction retired. In other words, three out of every four CPU cycles retired zero instructions: most were spent waiting for memory. Processor speed has seriously outstripped memory speed.*

> *Increasing the width of instruction issue and increasing the number of simultaneous instruction streams only makes the memory bottleneck worse. If a CPU chip today needs to move 2 GBytes/s (say, 16 bytes every 8 ns) across the pins to keep itself busy, imagine a chip in the foreseeable future with twice the clock rate, twice the issue width, and two instruction*

> *streams. All these factors multiply together to require about 16 GBytes/s of pin bandwidth to keep this chip busy. It is not clear whether pin bandwidth can keep up—32 bytes every 2ns?*

> *I expect that over the coming decade memory subsystems design will be the **only** important design issue for microprocessors.* [Sites 1996, emphasis Sites']

The title of Sites' article is "It's the Memory, Stupid!" Sites realized in 1996 what we as a community are only now, more than a decade later, beginning to digest and internalize fully: *uh, guys, it really **is** the memory system ... little else matters right now, so stop wasting time and resources on other facets of the design.* Most of his colleagues designing next-generation Alpha architectures at Digital Equipment Corp. ignored his advice and instead remained focused on building ever faster microprocessors, rather than shifting their focus to the building of ever faster *systems*. It is perhaps worth noting that Digital Equipment Corp. no longer exists.

The increasing gap between processor and memory speeds has rendered the organization, architecture, and design of memory subsystems an increasingly important part of computer-systems design. Today, the divide is so severe we are now in one of those down-cycles where the processor is so good at number-crunching it has completely sidelined itself; it is too fast for its own good, in a sense. Sites' prediction came true: memory subsystems design is now and has been for several years the *only* important design issue for microprocessors and systems. Memory-hierarchy parameters affect system performance *significantly* more than processor parameters (e.g., they are responsible for 2–10× changes in execution time, as opposed to 2–10%), making it absolutely essential for any designer of computer systems to exhibit an in-depth knowledge of the memory system's organization, its operation, its not-so-obvious behavior, and its range of performance characteristics. This is true now, and it is likely to remain true in the near future.

Thus this book, which is intended to provide exactly that type of in-depth coverage over a wide range of topics.

Topics Covered

In the following chapters we address the logical design and operation, the physical design and operation, the performance characteristics (i.e., design trade-offs), and, to a limited extent, the energy consumption of modern memory hierarchies.

In the cache section, we present topics and perspectives that will be new (or at least interesting) to even veterans in the field. What this implies is that the cache section is *not* an overview of processor-cache organization and its effect on performance—instead, we build up the concept of cache from first principles and discuss topics that are incompletely covered in the computer-engineering literature. The section discusses a significant degree of historical development in cache-management techniques, the physical design of modern SRAM structures, the operating system's role in cache coherence, and the continuum of cache architectures from those that are fully transparent (to application software and/or the operating system) to those that are fully visible.

DRAM and disk are interesting technologies because, unlike caches, they are not typically integrated onto the microprocessor die. Thus any discussion of these topics necessarily deals with the issue of communication: e.g., channels, signalling, protocols, and request scheduling.

DRAM involves one or more chip-to-chip crossings, and so signalling and signal integrity are as fundamental as circuit design to the technology. In the DRAM section, we present an intuitive understanding of exactly what happens inside the DRAM so that the ubiquitous parameters of the interface (e.g., t_{RC}, t_{RCD}, t_{CAS}, etc.) will make sense. We survey the various DRAM architectures that have appeared over the years and give an in-depth description of the technologies in the next generation memory-system architecture. We discuss memory-controller issues and investigate performance issues of modern systems.

The disk section builds from the bottom up, providing a view of the disk from physical recording principles to the configuration and operation of disks within system settings. We discuss the operation of the disk's read/write heads; the arrangement of recording media within the enclosure; and the organization-level view of blocks, sectors, tracks, and cylinders, as well as various protocols used to encode data. We discuss performance issues and techniques used to improve performance, including caching and buffering, prefetching, request scheduling, and data reorganization. We discuss the various disk interfaces available today (e.g., ATA, serial ATA, SCSI, fibre channel, etc.) as well as system configurations such as RAID, SAN, and NAS.

The last section of the book, *Cross-Cutting Issues*, covers topics that apply to all levels of the memory hierarchy, such as the tools of analysis and how to use them correctly, subthreshold leakage power in CMOS devices and circuits, a look at power breakdowns in future SRAMs, codes for error detection and error correction, the design and operation of virtual memory systems, and the hardware mechanisms that are required in microprocessors to support virtual memory.

Goals and Audience

The primary goal of this book is to bring the reader to a level of understanding at which the physical design and/or detailed software emulation of the entire hierarchy is possible, from cache to disk. As we argue in the initial chapter, this level of understanding is important now and will become increasingly necessary over time. Another goal of the book is to discuss techniques of analysis, so that the next generation of design engineers is prepared to tackle the nontrivial multidimensional optimization problems that result from considering detailed side-effects that can manifest themselves at any point in the entire hierarchy.

Accordingly, our target audience are those planning to build and/or optimize memory systems: i.e., computer-engineering and computer-science faculty and graduate students (and perhaps advanced undergraduates) and developers in the computer design, peripheral design, and embedded systems industries.

As an educational textbook, this is targeted at graduate and undergraduate students with a solid background in computer organization and architecture. It could serve to support an advanced senior-level undergraduate course or a second-year graduate course specializing in computer-systems design. There is clearly far too much material here for any single course; the book provides depth on enough topics to support two to three separate courses. For example, at the University of Maryland we use the DRAM section to teach a graduate class called *High-Speed Memory Systems*, and we supplement both our general and advanced architecture classes with material from the sections on *Caches* and *Cross-Cutting Issues*. The *Disk* section could support a class focused solely on disks, and it is also possible to create for advanced students a survey class that lightly touches on all the topics in the book.

As a reference, this book is targeted toward both academics and professionals alike. It provides the breadth necessary to understand the wide scope of behaviors that appear in modern memory systems, and most of the topics are addressed in enough depth that a reader should be able to build (or at least model in significant detail) caches, DRAMs, disks, their controllers, their subsystems ... and understand their interactions.

What this means is that the book should not only be useful to developers, but it should also be useful to those responsible for long-range planning and forecasting for future product developments and their issues.

Acknowledgments and Thanks

Beyond the kind folks named in the book's Dedication, we have a lot of people to thank. The following people were enormously helpful in creating the contents of this book:

- Prof. Rajeev Barua, ECE Maryland, provided text to explain scratch-pad memories and their accompanying partitioning problem (see Chapter 3).

- Dr. Brinda Ganesh, a former graduate student in Bruce Jacob's research group, now at Intel DAP, wrote the latency-oriented section of the DRAM-performance chapter (see Section 15.5).

- Joseph Gross, a graduate student in Bruce Jacob's research group, updated the numbers in David Wang's Ph.D. proposal to produce the tables comparing the characteristics of modern DRAMs in the book's *Overview* chapter.

- Dr. Ed Growchowski, formerly of Hitachi Global Storage Technologies and currently a consultant for IDEMA, provided some of the disk recording density history charts.

- Dr. Martin Hassner, Dr. Bruce Wilson, Dr. Matt White, Chuck Cox (now with IBM), Frank Chu, and Tony Dunn of Hitatchi Global Storage Technologies provided important consultation on various details of disk drive design.

- Dr. Windsor Hsu, formerly of IBM Almaden Research Center and now with Data Domain, Inc., provided important consultation on system issues related to disk drives.

- Dr. Aamer Jaleel, a former graduate student in Bruce Jacob's research group, now at Intel VSSAD, is responsible for Chapter 4's sections on cache coherence.

- Michael Martin, a graduate student in Bruce Jacob's research group, executed simulations for the final table (Ov. 5) and formatted the four large time-sequence graphs in the *Overview* chapter.

- Rami Nasr, a graduate student at Maryland who wrote his M.S. thesis on the Fully

Buffered DIMM architecture, provided much of the contents of Chapter 14.

- Prof. Marty Peckerar, ECE Maryland, provided brilliant text and illustrations to explain the subthreshold leakage problem (see the book's *Overview* and Section 29.2).

- Profs. Yan Solihin, ECE NCSU, and Donald Yeung, ECE Maryland, provided much of the material on hardware and software prefetching (Sections 3.1.2 and 3.2.2); this came from a book chapter on the topic written by the pair for Kaeli and Yew's *Speculative Execution in High Performance Computer Architectures* (CRC Press, 2005).

- Sadagopan Srinivasan, a graduate student in Bruce Jacob's research group, performed the study at the end of Chapter 1 and provided much insight on the memory behavior of both streaming applications and multi-core systems.

- Dr. Nuengwong Tuaycharoen, a former graduate student in Bruce Jacob's research group, now at Thailand's Dhurakijpundit University, performed the experiments, and wrote the example holistic analysis at the end of the book's *Overview* chapter, directly relating to the behavior of caches, DRAMs, and disks in a single study.

- Patricia Wadkins and others in the Rochester SITLab of Hitachi Global Storage Technologies provided test results and measurement data for the book's Section III on *Disks*.

- Mr. Yong Wang, a signal integrity expert, formerly of HP and Intel, now with Meta-RAM, contributed extensively to the Chapter on *DRAM System Signaling and Timing* (Chapter 9).

- Michael Xu at Hitachi Global Storage Technologies drew the beautiful, complex illustrations, as well as provided some of the photographs, in the book's Section III on Disks.

In addition, several students involved in tool support over the years deserve special recognition:

- Brinda Ganesh took the reins from David Wang to maintain *DRAMsim*; among other things, she is largely responsible for the FB-DIMM support in that tool.

- Joseph Gross also supports *DRAMsim* and is leading the development of the second generation version of the software, which is object-oriented and significantly streamlined.

- Nuengwong Tuaycharoen integrated the various disparate software modules to produce *SYSim*, a full-system simulator that gave us the wonderful time-sequence graphs at the end of the *Overview*.

Numerous reviewers spent considerable time reading early drafts of the manuscript and providing excellent critiques or our direction, approach, and raw content. The following reviewers directly contributed to the book in this way: Ashraf Aboulnaga, *University of Waterloo*; Al Davis, *University of Utah*; Diana Franklin, *California Polytechnic University, San Luis Obispo*; Yiming Hu, *University of Cincinnati*; David Kaeli, *Northeastern University*; Nagi Mekhiel, *Ryerson University, Toronto*; Michael Schuette, Ph.D., VP of Technology Development at *OCZ Technology*; Jim Smith, *University of Wisconsin—Madison*; Yan Solin, *North Carolina State University*; and Several Anonymous reviewers (i.e., we the authors were told not to use their names).

The editorial and production staff at Morgan Kaufmann/Elsevier was amazing to work with: Denise Penrose pitched the idea to us in the first place (and enormous thanks go to Jim Smith, who pointed her in our direction) and Nate McFadden and Paul Gottehrer made the process of writing, editing, and proofing go incredibly smoothly.

Lastly, Dr. Richard Matick, the author of the original memory-systems book (*Computer Storage Systems and Technology*, John Wiley & Sons, 1976) and currently a leading researcher in embedded DRAM at IBM T. J. Watson, provided enormous help in direction, focus, and approach.

Dave, Spencer, Sam, and I are indebted to all of these writers, illustrators, coders, editors, and reviewers alike; they all helped to make this book what it is. To those contributors: thank you. You rock.

Bruce Jacob, Summer 2007
College Park, Maryland

On Memory Systems and Their Design

Memory is essential to the operation of a computer system, and nothing is more important to the development of the modern memory system than the concept of the memory hierarchy. While a flat memory system built of a single technology is attractive for its simplicity, a well-implemented hierarchy allows a memory system to approach simultaneously the performance of the fastest component, the cost per bit of the cheapest component, and the energy consumption of the most energy-efficient component.

For years, the use of a memory hierarchy has been very convenient, in that it has simplified the process of designing memory systems. The use of a hierarchy allowed designers to treat system design as a modularized process—to treat the memory system as an abstraction and to optimize individual subsystems (caches, DRAMs [dynamic RAM], disks) in isolation.

However, we are finding that treating the hierarchy in this way—as a set of disparate subsystems that interact only through well-defined functional interfaces and that can be optimized in isolation—no longer suffices for the design of modern memory systems. One trend becoming apparent is that many of the underlying implementation issues are becoming significant. These include the physics of device and interconnect scaling, the choice of signaling protocols and topologies to ensure signal integrity, design parameters such as granularity of access and support for concurrency, and communication-related issues such as scheduling algorithms and queueing. These low-level details have begun to affect the higher level design process

quite dramatically, whereas they were considered transparent only a design-generation ago. Cache architectures are appearing that play to the limitations imposed by interconnect physics in deep submicron processes; modern DRAM design is driven by circuit-level limitations that create system-level headaches; and modern disk performance is dominated by the on-board caching and scheduling policies. This is a non-trivial environment in which to attempt optimal design.

This trend will undoubtedly become more important as time goes on, and even now it has tremendous impact on design results. As hierarchies and their components grow more complex, *systemic* behaviors—those arising from the complex interaction of the memory system's parts—have begun to dominate. The real loss of performance is not seen in the CPU or caches or DRAM devices or disk assemblies themselves, but in the subtle interactions between these subsystems and in the manner in which these subsystems are connected. Consequently, it is becoming increasingly foolhardy to attempt system-level optimization by designing/optimizing each of the parts in isolation (which, unfortunately, is often the approach taken in modern computer design). No longer can a designer remain oblivious to issues "outside the scope" and focus solely on designing a subsystem. It has now become the case that a memory-systems designer, wishing to build a properly behaved memory hierarchy, must be intimately familiar with issues involved at all levels of an implementation, from cache to DRAM to disk. Thus, we wrote this book.

Ov.1 Memory Systems

A memory hierarchy is designed to provide multiple functions that are seemingly mutually exclusive. We start at random-access memory (RAM): all microprocessors (and computer systems in general) expect a random-access memory out of which they operate. This is fundamental to the structure of modern software, built upon the von Neumann model in which code and data are essentially the same and reside in the same place (i.e., memory). All requests, whether for instructions or for data, go to this random-access memory. At any given moment, any particular datum in memory may be needed; there is no requirement that data reside next to the code that manipulates it, and there is no requirement that two instructions executed one after the other need to be adjacent in memory. Thus, the memory system must be able to handle randomly addressed[1] requests in a manner that favors no particular request. For instance, using a tape drive for this primary memory is unacceptable for performance reasons, though it might be acceptable in the Turing-machine sense.

Where does the mutually exclusive part come in? As we said, all microprocessors are built to expect a random-access memory out of which they can operate. Moreover, this memory must be *fast*, matching the machine's processing speed; otherwise, the machine will spend most of its time tapping its foot and staring at its watch. In addition, modern software is written to expect gigabytes of storage for data, and the modern consumer expects this storage to be cheap. How many memory technologies provide both tremendous speed and tremendous storage capacity at a low price? Modern processors execute instructions both out of order and speculatively—put simply, they execute instructions that, in some cases, are not meant to get executed—and system software is typically built to expect that certain changes to memory are permanent. How many memory technologies provide non-volatility and an *undo* operation?

While it might be elegant to provide all of these competing demands with a single technology (say,

for example, a gigantic battery-backed SRAM [static RAM]), and though there is no engineering problem that cannot be solved (if ever in doubt about this, simply query a room full of engineers), the reality is that building a full memory system out of such a technology would be prohibitively expensive today.[2] The good news is that it is not necessary. Specialization and division of labor make possible all of these competing goals simultaneously. Modern memory systems often have a terabyte of storage on the desktop and provide instruction-fetch and data-access bandwidths of 128 GB/s or more. Nearly all of the storage in the system is non-volatile, and speculative execution on the part of the microprocessor is supported. All of this can be found in a memory system that has an average cost of roughly 1/100,000,000 pennies per bit of storage.

The reason all of this is possible is because of a phenomenon called *locality of reference* [Belady 1966, Denning 1970]. This is an observed behavior that computer applications tend to exhibit and that, when exploited properly, allows a small memory to serve in place of a larger one.

Ov.1.1 Locality of Reference Breeds the Memory Hierarchy

We think linearly (in steps), and so we program the computer to solve problems by working in steps. The practical implications of this are that a computer's use of the memory system tends to be non-random and highly predictable. Thus is born the concept of *locality of reference*, so named because memory references tend to be localized in time and space:

- If you use something once, you are likely to use it again.
- If you use something once, you are likely to use its neighbor.

The first of these principles is called *temporal locality*; the second is called *spatial locality*. We will discuss them (and another type of locality) in more detail in *Part I: Cache* of this book, but for now it suffices to

---

[1]Though "random" addressing is the commonly used term, authors actually mean *arbitrarily* addressed requests because, in most memory systems, a *randomly* addressed sequence is one of the most efficiently handled events.
[2]Even Cray machines, which were famous for using SRAM as their main memory, today are built upon DRAM for their main memory.

say that one can exploit the locality principle and render a single-level memory system, which we just said was expensive, unnecessary. If a computer's use of the memory system, given a small time window, is both predictable and limited in spatial extent, then it stands to reason that a program does not need all of its data immediately accessible. A program would perform nearly as well if it had, for instance, a *two-level* store, in which the first level provides immediate access to a subset of the program's data, the second level holds the remainder of the data but is slower and therefore cheaper, and some appropriate heuristic is used to manage the movement of data back and forth between the levels, thereby ensuring that the most-needed data is usually in the first-level store.

This generalizes to the *memory hierarchy*: multiple levels of storage, each optimized for its assigned task. By choosing these levels wisely a designer can produce a system that has the best of all worlds: performance approaching that of the fastest component, cost per bit approaching that of the cheapest component, and energy consumption per access approaching that of the least power-hungry component.

The modern hierarchy is comprised of the following components, each performing a particular function or filling a functional niche within the system:

- **Cache (SRAM):** Cache provides access to program instructions and data that has very low latency (e.g., 1/4 nanosecond per access) and very high bandwidth (e.g., a 16-byte instruction block and a 16-byte

data block per cycle => 32 bytes per 1/4 nanosecond, or 128 bytes per nanosecond, or 128 GB/s). It is also important to note that cache, on a per-access basis, also has relatively low energy requirements compared to other technologies.

- **DRAM:** DRAM provides a random-access storage that is relatively large, relatively fast, and relatively cheap. It is large and cheap compared to cache, and it is fast compared to disk. Its main strength is that it is just fast enough and just cheap enough to act as an operating store.

- **Disk:** Disk provides permanent storage at an ultra-low cost per bit. As mentioned, nearly all computer systems expect *some* data to be modifiable yet permanent, so the memory system must have, at some level, a permanent store. Disk's advantage is its very reasonable cost (currently less than 50¢ per gigabyte), which is low enough for users to buy enough of it to store thousands of songs, video clips, photos, and other memory hogs that users are wont to accumulate in their accounts (authors included).

Table Ov.1 lists some rough order-of-magnitude comparisons for access time and energy consumption per access.

Why is it not feasible to build a flat memory system out of these technologies? Cache is far too expensive to be used as permanent storage, and its cost to store a single album's worth of audio would exceed that of the

TABLE Ov.1 Cost-performance for various memory technologies

Technology	Bytes per Access (typ.)	Latency per Access	Cost per Megabyte[a]	Energy per Access
On-chip Cache	10	100 of picoseconds	$1–100	1 nJ
Off-chip Cache	100	Nanoseconds	$1–10	10–100 nJ
DRAM	1000 (internally fetched)	10–100 nanoseconds	$0.1	1–100 nJ (per device)
Disk	1000	Milliseconds	$0.001	100–1000 mJ

[a]Cost of semiconductor memory is extremely variable, dependent much more on economic factors and sales volume than on manufacturing issues. In particular, on-chip caches (i.e., those integrated with a microprocessor core) can take up half of the die area, in which case their "cost" would be half of the selling price of that microprocessor. Depending on the market (e.g., embedded versus high end) and sales volume, microprocessor costs cover an enormous range of prices, from pennies per square millimeter to several dollars per square millimeter.

original music CD by several orders of magnitude. Disk is far too slow to be used as an operating store, and its average seek time for random accesses is measured in milliseconds. Of the three, DRAM is the closest to providing a flat memory system. DRAM is sufficiently fast enough that, without the support of a cache front-end, it can act as an operating store for many embedded systems, and with battery back-up it can be made to function as a permanent store. However, DRAM alone is not cheap enough to serve the needs of human users, who often want nearly a terabyte of permanent storage, and, even with random access times in the tens of nanoseconds, DRAM is not quite fast enough to serve as the only memory for modern general-purpose microprocessors, which would prefer a new block of instructions every fraction of a nanosecond.

So far, no technology has appeared that provides every desired characteristic: low cost, non-volatility, high bandwidth, low latency, etc. So instead we build a system in which each component is designed to offer one or more characteristics, and we manage the operation of the system so that the poorer characteristics of the various technologies are "hidden." For example, if most of the memory references made by the microprocessor are handled by the cache and/or DRAM subsystems, then the disk will be used only rarely, and, therefore, its extremely long latency will contribute very little to the average access time. If most of the data resides in the disk subsystem, and very little of it is needed at any given moment in time, then the cache and DRAM subsystems will not need much storage, and, therefore, their higher costs per bit will contribute very little to the average cost of the system. If done right, a memory system has an average cost approaching that of bottommost layer and an average access time and bandwidth approaching that of topmost layer.

The memory hierarchy is usually pictured as a pyramid, as shown in Figure Ov.1. The higher levels in the

FIGURE Ov.1: A memory hierachy.

hierarchy have better performance characteristics than the lower levels in the hierarchy; the higher levels have a higher cost per bit than the lower levels; and the system uses fewer bits of storage in the higher levels than found in the lower levels.

Though modern memory systems are comprised of SRAM, DRAM, and disk, these are simply technologies chosen to serve particular needs of the system, namely permanent store, operating store, and a fast store. Any technology set would suffice if it (a) provides permanent and operating stores and (b) satisfies the given computer system's performance, cost, and power requirements.

Permanent Store

The system's permanent store is where everything lives … meaning it is home to data that can be modified (potentially), but whose modifications must be remembered across invocations of the system (power-ups and power-downs). In general-purpose systems, this data typically includes the operating system's files, such as boot program, OS (operating system) executable, libraries, utilities, applications, etc., and the users' files, such as graphics, word-processing documents, spreadsheets, digital photographs, digital audio and video, email, etc. In embedded systems, this data typically includes the system's executable image and any installation-specific configuration information that it requires. Some embedded systems also maintain in permanent store the state of any partially completed transactions to withstand worst-case scenarios such as the system going down before the transaction is finished (e.g., financial transactions).

These all represent data that should not disappear when the machine shuts down, such as a user's saved email messages, the operating system's code and configuration information, and applications and their saved documents. Thus, the storage must be *non-volatile*, which in this context means not susceptible to power outages. Storage technologies chosen for permanent store include magnetic disk, flash memory, and even EEPROM (electrically erasable programmable read-only memory), of which flash memory is a special type. Other forms of programmable ROM (read-only memory) such as ROM, PROM (programmable ROM), or EPROM (erasable programmable ROM) are suitable for non-writable permanent information such as the executable image of an embedded system or a general-purpose system's boot code and BIOS.[3] Numerous exotic non-volatile technologies are in development, including magnetic RAM (MRAM), FeRAM (ferroelectric RAM), and phase-change RAM (PCRAM).

In most systems, the cost per bit of this technology is a very important consideration. In general-purpose systems, this is the case because these systems tend to have an enormous amount of permanent storage. A desktop can easily have more than 500 GB of permanent store, and a departmental server can have one hundred times that amount. The enormous number of bits in these systems translates even modest cost-per-bit increases into significant dollar amounts. In embedded systems, the cost per bit is important because of the significant number of units shipped. Embedded systems are often consumer devices that are manufactured and sold in vast quantities, e.g., cell phones, digital cameras, MP3 players, programmable thermostats, and disk drives. Each embedded system might not require more than a handful of megabytes of storage, yet a tiny 1¢ increase in the cost per megabyte of memory can translate to a $100,000 increase in cost per million units manufactured.

Operating (Random-Access) Store

As mentioned earlier, a typical microprocessor expects a new instruction or set of instructions on every clock cycle, and it can perform a data-read or data-write every clock cycle. Because the addresses of these instructions and data need not be sequential (or, in fact, related in any detectable way), the memory system must be able to handle *random access*—it must be able to provide instant access to any datum in the memory system.

The machine's operating store is the level of memory that provides random access at the microprocessor's data granularity. It is the storage level out of which the microprocessor could conceivably operate, i.e., it is the storage level that can provide random access to its

storage, one data word at a time. This storage level is typically called "main memory." Disks cannot serve as main memory or operating store and cannot provide random access for two reasons: instant access is provided for only the data underneath the disk's head at any given moment, and the granularity of access is not what a typical processor requires. Disks are block-oriented devices, which means they read and write data only in large chunks; the typical granularity is 512 B. Processors, in contrast, typically operate at the granularity of 4 B or 8 B data words. To use a disk, a microprocessor must have additional buffering memory out of which it can read one instruction at a time and read or write one datum at a time. This buffering memory would become the *de facto* operating store of the system.

Flash memory and EEPROM (as well as the exotic non-volatile technologies mentioned earlier) are potentially viable as an operating store for systems that have small permanent-storage needs, and the non-volatility of these technologies provides them with a distinct advantage. However, not all are set up as an ideal operating store; for example, flash memory supports word-sized reads but supports only block-sized writes. If this type of issue can be handled in a manner that is transparent to the processor (e.g., in this case through additional data buffering), then the memory technology can still serve as a reasonable hybrid operating store.

Though the non-volatile technologies seem positioned perfectly to serve as operating store in all manner of devices and systems, DRAM is the most commonly used technology. Note that the only requirement of a memory system's operating store is that it provide random access with a small access granularity. Non-volatility is not a requirement, so long as it is provided by another level in the hierarchy. DRAM is a popular choice for operating store for several reasons: DRAM is faster than the various non-volatile technologies (in some cases *much* faster); DRAM supports an unlimited number of writes, whereas some non-volatile technologies start to fail after being erased and rewritten too many times (in some technologies, as few as 1–10,000 erase/write cycles); and DRAM processes are very similar to those used to build logic devices.

---

[3]BIOS = basic input/output system, the code that provides to software low-level access to much of the hardware.

DRAM can be fabricated using similar materials and (relatively) similar silicon-based process technologies as most microprocessors, whereas many of the various non-volatile technologies require new materials and (relatively) different process technologies.

Fast (and Relatively Low-Power) Store

If these storage technologies provide such reasonable operating store, why, then, do modern systems use cache? Cache is inserted between the processor and the main memory system whenever the access behavior of the main memory is not sufficient for the needs or goals of the system. Typical figures of merit include performance and energy consumption (or power dissipation). If the performance when operating out of main memory is insufficient, cache is interposed between the processor and main memory to decrease the average access time for data. Similarly, if the energy consumed when operating out of main memory is too high, cache is interposed between the processor and main memory to decrease the system's energy consumption.

The data in Table Ov.1 should give some intuition about the design choice. If a cache can reduce the number of accesses made to the next level down in the hierarchy, then it potentially reduces both execution time and energy consumption for an application. The gain is only potential because these numbers are valid only for certain technology parameters. For example, many designs use large SRAM caches that consume much more energy than several DRAM chips combined, but because the caches can reduce execution time they are used in systems where performance is critical, even at the expense of energy consumption.

It is important to note at this point that, even though the term "cache" is usually interpreted to mean SRAM, a cache is merely a concept and as such imposes no expectations on its implementation. Caches are best thought of as compact databases, as shown in Figure Ov.2. They contain data and, optionally, metadata such as the unique ID (address) of each data block in the array, whether it has been updated recently, etc. Caches can be built from SRAM, DRAM, disk, or virtually any storage technology. They can be managed completely in hardware and thus can be transparent to the running application and even to the memory system itself; and at the other extreme they can be explicitly managed by the running application. For instance, Figure Ov.2 shows that there is an optional block of metadata, which if implemented in hardware would be called the cache's *tags*. In that instance, a key is passed to the tags array, which produces either the location of the corresponding item in the data array (a *cache hit*) or an indication that the item is not in the data array (a *cache miss*). Alternatively, software can be written to index the array explicitly, using direct cache-array addresses, in which case the key lookup (as well as its associated tags array) is unnecessary. The configuration chosen for the cache is called its *organization*. Cache organizations exist at all spots along the continuum between these two extremes. Clearly, the choice of organization will significantly impact the cache's performance and energy consumption.

Predictability of access time is another common figure of merit. It is a special aspect of performance that is very important when building real-time systems or systems with highly orchestrated data movement. DRAM is occasionally in a state where it needs to ignore external requests so that it can guarantee the integrity of its stored data (this is called *refresh* and will be discussed in detail in Part II of the book). Such hiccups in data movement can be disastrous for some applications. For this reason, many microprocessors, such as digital signal processors (DSPs) and processors used in embedded control applications (called *microcontrollers*), often

Metadata Data

Input Key → Entry in Data Array → Data Available

FIGURE Ov.2: An idealized cache lookup. A cache is logically comprised of two elements: the data array and some management information that indicates what is in the data array (labeled "metadata"). Note that the key information may be virtual, i.e., data addresses can be embedded in the software using the cache, in which case there is no explicit key lookup, and only the data array is needed.

have special caches that look like small main memories. These are *scratch-pad RAMs* whose implementation lies toward the end of the spectrum at which the
running application manages the cache explicitly. DSPs
typically have two of these scratch-pad SRAMs so that
they can issue on every cycle a new *multiply-accumu-
late (MAC)* operation, an important DSP instruction
whose repeated operation on a pair of data arrays produces its dot product. Performing a new MAC operation every cycle requires the memory system to load
new elements from two different arrays simultaneously
in the same cycle. This is most easily accomplished
by having two separate data busses, each with its own
independent data memory and each holding the elements of a different array.

Perhaps the most familiar example of a software-
managed memory is the processor's *register file*, an
array of storage locations that is indexed directly by bits
within the instruction and whose contents are dictated
entirely by software. Values are brought into the register
file explicitly by software instructions, and old values
are only overwritten if done so explicitly by software.
Moreover, the register file is significantly smaller than
most on-chip caches and typically consumes far less
energy. Accordingly, software's best bet is often to optimize its use of the register file [Postiff & Mudge 1999].

Ov.1.2 Important Figures of Merit

The following issues have been touched on during
the previous discussion, but at this point it would be
valuable to formally present the various figures of merit
that are important to a designer of memory systems.
Depending on the environment in which the memory
system will be used (supercomputer, departmental
server, desktop, laptop, signal-processing system,
embedded control system, etc.), each metric will carry
more or less weight. Though most academic studies
tend to focus on one axis at a time (e.g., performance),
the design of a memory system is a multi-dimensional
optimization problem, with all the adherent complexities of analysis. For instance, to analyze something in
this design space or to consider one memory system

over another, a designer should be familiar with concepts such as Pareto optimality (described later in this
chapter). The various figures of merit, in no particular order other than performance being first due to
its popularity, are performance, energy consumption
and power dissipation, predictability of behavior (i.e.,
real time), manufacturing costs, and system reliability.
This section describes them briefly, collectively. Later
sections will treat them in more detail.

Performance

The term "performance" means many things to
many people. The performance of a system is typically
measured in the time it takes to execute a task (i.e., task
latency), but it can also be measured in the number of
tasks that can be handled in a unit time period (i.e.,
task *bandwidth*). Popular figures of merit for performance include the following:[4]

- Cycles per Instruction (CPI)
$$= \frac{\text{Total execution cycles}}{\text{Total user-level instructions committed}}$$

- Memory-system CPI overhead
$$= \text{Real CPI} - \text{CPI assuming perfect memory}$$

- Memory Cycles per Instruction (MCPI)
$$= \frac{\text{Total cycles spent in memory system}}{\text{Total user-level instructions committed}}$$

- Cache miss rate $= \frac{\text{Total cache misses}}{\text{Total cache accesses}}$

- Cache hit rate $= 1 - \text{Cache miss rate}$

- Average access time
$$= \text{(hit rate} \cdot \text{average to service hit)} + \text{(miss rate} \cdot \text{average to service miss)}$$

- Million Instructions per Second (MIPS)
$$= \frac{\text{Instructions executed (seconds)}}{10^6 \cdot \text{Average required for execution}}$$

[4]Note that the MIPS metric is easily abused. For instance, it is inappropriate for comparing different instruction-set
architectures, and marketing literature often takes the definition of "instructions executed" to mean any particular given
window of time as opposed to the full execution of an application. In such cases, the metric can mean the highest possible
issue rate of instructions that the machine can achieve (but not necessarily sustain for any realistic period of time).

A cautionary note: using a metric of performance for the memory system that is independent of a processing context can be very deceptive. For instance, the MCPI metric does not take into account how much of the memory system's activity can be overlapped with processor activity, and, as a result, memory system A which has a worse MCPI than memory system B might actually yield a computer system with better total performance. As Figure Ov.5 in a later section shows, there can be significantly different amounts of overlapping activity between the memory system and CPU execution.

How to average a set of performance metrics correctly is still a poorly understood topic, and it is very sensitive to the weights chosen (either explicitly or implicitly) for the various benchmarks considered [John 2004]. Comparing performance is always the least ambiguous when it means the amount of time saved by using one design over another. When we ask the question *this machine is how much faster than that machine?* the implication is that we have been using *that* machine for some time and wish to know how much time we would save by using *this* machine instead. The true measure of performance is to compare the total execution time of one machine to another, with each machine running the benchmark programs that represent the user's typical workload as often as a user expects to run them. For instance, if a user compiles a large software application ten times per day and runs a series of regression tests once per day, then the total execution time should count the compiler's execution ten times more than the regression test.

Energy Consumption and Power Dissipation

Energy consumption is related to work accomplished (e.g., how much computing can be done with a given battery), whereas power dissipation is the rate of consumption. The instantaneous power dissipation of CMOS (complementary metal-oxide-semiconductor) devices, such as microprocessors, is measured in watts (W) and represents the sum of two components: *active power*, due to switching activity, and *static power*, due primarily to subthreshold leakage. To a first approximation, average power

dissipation is equal to the following (we will present a more detailed model later):

$$P_{avg} = (P_{dynamic} + P_{static}) \equiv C_{tot} V^2_{dd} f + I_{leak} V_{dd} \quad \text{(EQ Ov.1)}$$

where C_{tot} is the total capacitance switched, V_{dd} is the power supply, f is the switching frequency, and I_{leak} is the leakage current, which includes such sources as subthreshold and gate leakage. With each generation in process technology, active power is decreasing on a device level and remaining roughly constant on a chip level. Leakage power, which used to be insignificant relative to switching power, increases as devices become smaller and has recently caught up to switching power in magnitude [Grove 2002]. In the future, leakage will be the primary concern.

Energy is related to power through time. The energy consumed by a computation that requires T seconds is measured in joules (J) and is equal to the integral of the instantaneous power over time T. If the power dissipation remains constant over T, the resultant energy consumption is simply the product of power and time.

$$E = (P_{avg} \cdot T) \equiv C_{tot} V^2_{dd} N + I_{leak} V_{dd} T \quad \text{(EQ Ov.2)}$$

where N is the number of switching events that occurs during the computation.

In general, if one is interested in extending battery life or reducing the electricity costs of an enterprise computing center, then *energy* is the appropriate metric to use in an analysis comparing approaches. If one is concerned with heat removal from a system or the thermal effects that a functional block can create, then *power* is the appropriate metric. In informal discussions (i.e., in common-parlance prose rather than in equations where units of measurement are inescapable), the two terms "power" and "energy" are frequently used interchangeably, though such use is technically incorrect. Beware, because this can lead to ambiguity and even misconception, which is usually unintentional, but not always so. For instance, microprocessor manufacturers will occasionally claim to have a "low-power" microprocessor that beats its predecessor by a factor of, say, two. This is easily accomplished by running the microprocessor at half the clock rate, which does reduce its power dissipation, but remember that power is the rate at which energy is consumed. However, to a first order, doing so doubles the time over which the processor dissipates that power. The net result is a processor that consumes the same amount of *energy* as before, though it is branded as having lower *power*, which is technically not a lie.

Popular figures of merit that incorporate both energy/power and performance include the following:

- Energy-Delay Product

$$= \left(\begin{array}{c} \text{Energy required} \\ \text{to perform task} \end{array} \right) \cdot \left(\begin{array}{c} \text{Time required} \\ \text{to perform task} \end{array} \right)$$

- Power-Delay Product

$$= \left(\begin{array}{c} \text{Power required} \\ \text{to perform task} \end{array} \right)^{m} \cdot \left(\begin{array}{c} \text{Time required} \\ \text{to perform task} \end{array} \right)^{n}$$

- MIPS per watt

$$= \frac{\text{Performance of benchmark in MIPS}}{\text{Average power dissipated by benchmark}}$$

The second equation was offered as a generalized form of the first (note that the two are equivalent when $m = 1$ and $n = 2$) so that designers could place more weight on the metric (time or energy/power) that is most important to their design goals [Gonzalez & Horowitz 1996, Brooks et al. 2000a].

Predictable (Real-Time) Behavior

Predictability of behavior is extremely important when analyzing real-time systems, because correctness of operation is often the primary design goal for these systems (consider, for example, medical equipment, navigation systems, anti-lock brakes, flight control systems, etc., in which failure to perform as predicted is not an option).

Popular figures of merit for expressing predictability of behavior include the following:

- Worst-Case Execution Time (WCET), taken to mean the longest amount of time a function could take to execute
- Response time, taken to mean the time between a stimulus to the system and the system's response (e.g., time to respond to an external interrupt)

- Jitter, the amount of deviation from an average timing value

These metrics are typically given as single numbers (average or worst case), but we have found that the probability density function makes a valuable aid in system analysis [Baynes et al. 2001, 2003].

Design (and Fabrication and Test) Costs

Cost is an obvious, but often unstated, design goal. Many consumer devices have cost as their primary consideration: if the cost to design and manufacture an item is not low enough, it is not worth the effort to build and sell it. Cost can be represented in many different ways (note that energy consumption is a measure of cost), but for the purposes of this book, by "cost" we mean the cost of producing an item: to wit, the cost of its design, the cost of testing the item, and/or the cost of the item's manufacture. Popular figures of merit for cost include the following:

- Dollar cost (best, but often hard to even approximate)
- Design size, e.g., die area (cost of manufacturing a VLSI (very large scale integration) design is proportional to its area cubed or more)
- Packaging costs, e.g., pin count
- Design complexity (can be expressed in terms of number of logic gates, number of transistors, lines of code, time to compile or synthesize, time to verify or run DRC (design-rule check), and many others, including a design's impact on clock cycle time [Palacharla et al. 1996])

Cost is often presented in a relative sense, allowing differing technologies or approaches to be placed on equal footing for a comparison.

- Cost per storage bit/byte/KB/MB/etc. (allows cost comparison between different storage technologies)
- Die area per storage bit (allows size-efficiency comparison within same process technology)

In a similar vein, cost is especially informative when combined with performance metrics. The following are variations on the theme:

- Bandwidth per package pin (total sustainable bandwidth to/from part, divided by total number of pins in package)
- Execution-time-dollars (total execution time multiplied by total cost; note that cost can be expressed in other units, e.g., pins, die area, etc.)

An important note: cost should incorporate *all* sources of that cost. Focusing on just one source of cost blinds the analysis in two ways: first, the true cost of the system is not considered, and second, solutions can be unintentionally excluded from the analysis. If cost is expressed in pin count, then all pins should be considered by the analysis; the analysis should not focus solely on data pins, for example. Similarly, if cost is expressed in die area, then all sources of die area should be considered by the analysis; the analysis should not focus solely on the number of banks, for example, but should also consider the cost of building control logic (decoders, muxes, bus lines, etc.) to select among the various banks.

Reliability

Like the term "performance," the term "reliability" means many things to many different people. In this book, we mean reliability of the data stored within the memory system: how easily is our stored data corrupted or lost, and how can it be protected from corruption or loss? Data integrity is dependent upon physical devices, and physical devices can fail.

Approaches to guarantee the integrity of stored data typically operate by storing redundant information in the memory system so that in the case of device failure, some but not all of the data will be lost or corrupted. If enough redundant information is stored, then the missing data can be reconstructed. Popular figures of merit for measuring reliability

characterize both device fragility and robustness of a proposed solution. They include the following:

- Mean Time Between Failures (MTBF): [5] given in time (seconds, hours, etc.) or number of uses
- Bit-error tolerance, e.g., how many bit errors in a data word or packet the mechanism can correct, and how many it can detect (but not necessarily correct)
- Error-rate tolerance, e.g., how many errors per second in a data stream the mechanism can correct
- Application-specific metrics, e.g., how much radiation a design can tolerate before failure, etc.

Note that values given for MTBF often seem astronomically high. This is because they are not meant to apply to individual devices, but to system-wide device use, as in a large installation. For instance, if the expected service lifetime of a device is several years, then that device is expected to fail in several years. If an administrator swaps out devices every few years (before the service lifetime is up), then the administrator should expect to see failure frequencies consistent with the MTBF rating.

Ov.1.3 The Goal of a Memory Hierarchy

As already mentioned, a well-implemented hierarchy allows a memory system to approach simultaneously the performance of the fastest component, the cost per bit of the cheapest component, and the energy consumption of the most energy-efficient component. A modern memory system typically has performance close to that of on-chip cache, the fastest component in the system. The rate at which microprocessors fetch and execute their instructions is measured in nanoseconds or fractions of a nanosecond. A modern low-end desktop machine has several hundred gigabytes of storage and sells for under $500, roughly half of which goes to the on-chip caches, off-chip caches, DRAM, and disk. This represents an average cost of

---

[5]A common variation is "Mean Time To Failure (MTTF)."

several dollars per gigabyte—very close to that of disk, the cheapest component. Modern desktop systems have an energy cost that is typically in the low tens of nanojoules per instruction executed—close to that of on-chip SRAM cache, the least energy-costly component in the system (on a per-access basis).

The goal for a memory-system designer is to create a system that behaves, on average and from the point of view of the processor, like a big cache that has the price tag of a disk. A successful memory hierarchy is much more than the sum of its parts; moreover, successful memory-system design is non-trivial.

How the system is built, how it is used (and what parts of it are used more heavily than others), and on which issues an engineer should focus most of his effort at design time—all these are highly dependent on the target application of the memory system. Two common categories of target applications are (a) general-purpose systems, which are characterized by their need for universal applicability for just about any type of computation, and (b) embedded systems, which are characterized by their tight design restrictions along multiple axes (e.g., cost, correctness of design, energy consumption, reliability) and the fact that each executes only a single, dedicated software application its entire lifespan, which opens up possibilities for optimization that are less appropriate for general-purpose systems.

General-Purpose Computer Systems

General-purpose systems are what people normally think of as "computers." These are the machines on your desktop, the machines in the refrigerated server room at work, and the laptop on the kitchen table. They are designed to handle any and all tasks thrown at them, and the software they run on a day-to-day basis is radically different from machine to machine.

General-purpose systems are typically overbuilt. By definition they are expected by the consumer to run all possible software applications with acceptable speed, and therefore, they are built to handle the average case very well and the worst case at least tolerably well. Were they optimized for any particular task, they could easily become less than optimal for all dissimilar tasks. Therefore, general-purpose

systems are optimized for everything, which is another way of saying that they are actually optimized for nothing in particular. However, they make up for this in raw performance, pure number-crunching. The average notebook computer is capable of performing orders of magnitude more operations per second than that required by a word processor or email client, tasks to which the average notebook is frequently relegated, but because the general-purpose system may be expected to handle virtually anything at any time, it must have significant spare number-crunching ability, just in case.

It stands to reason that the memory system of this computer must also be designed in a Swiss-army-knife fashion. Figure Ov.3 shows the organization of a typical personal computer, with the components of the memory system highlighted in grey boxes. The cache levels are found both on-chip (i.e., integrated on the same die as the microprocessor core) and off-chip (i.e., on a separate die). The DRAM system is comprised of a memory controller and a number of DRAM chips organized into DIMMs (dual in-line memory modules, printed circuit boards that contain a handful of DRAMs each). The memory controller can be located on-chip or off-chip, but the DRAMs are always separate from the CPU to allow memory upgrades. The disks in the system are considered peripheral devices, and so their access is made through one or more levels of controllers, each representing a potential chip-to-chip crossing (e.g., here a disk request passes through the system controller to the PCI (peripheral component interconnect) bus controller, to the SCSI (small computer system interface) controller, and finally to the disk itself).

The software that runs on a general-purpose system typically executes in the context of a robust operating system, one that provides virtual memory. Virtual memory is a mechanism whereby the operating system can provide to all running user-level software (i.e., email clients, web browsers, spreadsheets, word-processing packages, graphics and video editing software, etc.) the illusion that the user-level software is in direct control of the computer, when in fact its use of the computer's resources is managed by the operating system. This is a very effective way for an operating system to provide simultaneous access by

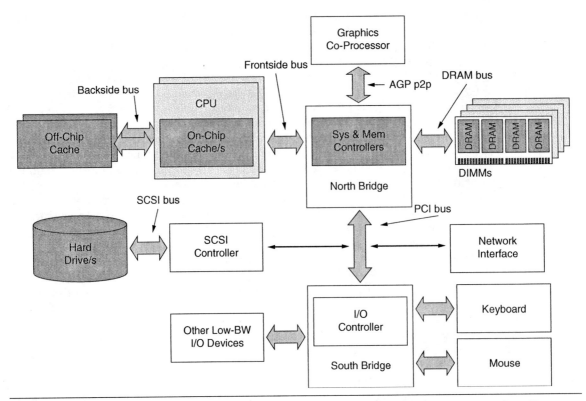

FIGURE Ov.3: Typical PC organization. The memory subsystem is one part of a relatively complex whole. This figure illustrates a two-way multiprocessor, with each processor having its own dedicated off-chip cache. The parts most relevant to this text are shaded in grey: the CPU and its cache system, the system and memory controllers, the DIMMs and their component DRAMs, and the hard drive/s.

large numbers of software packages to small numbers of limited-use resources (e.g., physical memory, the hard disk, the network, etc.).

The virtual memory system is the primary constituent of the memory system, in that it is the primary determinant of the manner/s in which the memory system's components are used by software running on the computer. Permanent data is stored on the disk, and the operating store, DRAM, is used as a cache for this permanent data. This DRAM-based cache is explicitly managed by the operating system. The operating system decides what data from the disk should be kept, what should be discarded, what should be sent back to the disk, and, for data retained,

where it should be placed in the DRAM system. The primary and secondary caches are usually transparent to software, which means that they are managed by hardware, not software (note, however, the use of the word "usually"—later sections will delve into this in more detail). In general, the primary and secondary caches hold *demand-fetched* data, i.e., running software demands data, the hardware fetches it from memory, and the caches retain as much of it as possible. The DRAM system contains data that the operating system deems worthy of keeping around, and because fetching data from the disk and writing it back to the disk are such time-consuming processes, the operating system can exploit that lag time (during

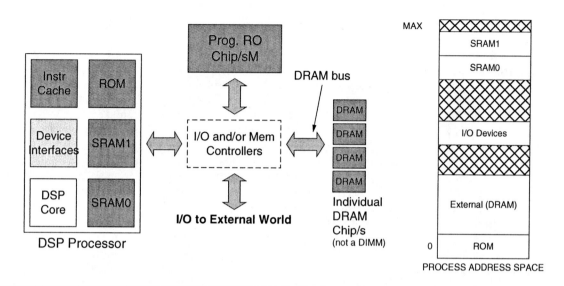

FIGURE Ov.4: DSP-style memory system. Example based on Texas Instruments' TMS320C3x DSP family.

which it would otherwise be stalled, doing nothing) to use sophisticated heuristics to decide what data to retain.

Embedded Computer Systems

Embedded systems differ from general-purpose systems in two main aspects. First and foremost, the two are designed to suit very different purposes. While general-purpose systems run a myriad of unrelated software packages, each having potentially very different performance requirements and dynamic behavior compared to the rest, embedded systems perform a single function their entire lifetime and thus execute the same code day in and day out until the system is discarded or a software upgrade is performed. Second, while performance is the primary (in many instances, the only) figure of merit by which a general-purpose system is judged, optimal embedded-system designs usually represent trade-offs between several goals, including manufacturing cost (e.g., die area), energy consumption, and performance.

As a result, we see two very different design strategies in the two camps. As mentioned, general-purpose systems are typically overbuilt; they are optimized for nothing in particular and must make up for this in raw performance. On the other hand, embedded systems are expected to handle only one task that is known at design time. Thus, it is not only possible, but highly beneficial to optimize an embedded design for its one suited task. If general-purpose systems are *overbuilt*, the goal for an embedded system is to be *appropriately* built. In addition, because effort spent at design time is amortized over the life of a product, and because many embedded systems have long lifetimes (tens of years), many embedded design houses will expend significant resources up front to optimize a design, using techniques not generally used in general-purpose systems (for instance, compiler optimizations that require many days or weeks to perform).

The memory system of a typical embedded system is less complex than that of a general-purpose system.[6] Figure Ov.4 illustrates an average digital signal-processing system with dual tagless SRAMs on-chip,

---

[6]Note that "less complex" does not necessarily imply "small," e.g., consider a typical iPod (or similar MP3 player), whose primary function is to store gigabytes' worth of a user's music and/or image files.

an off-chip programmable ROM (e.g., PROM, EPROM, flash ROM, etc.) that holds the executable image, and an off-chip DRAM that is used for computation and holding variable data. External memory and device controllers can be used, but many embedded microprocessors already have such controllers integrated onto the CPU die. This cuts down on the system's die count and thus cost. Note that it would be possible for the entire hierarchy to lie on the CPU die, yielding a single-chip solution called a *system-on-chip*. This is relatively common for systems that have limited memory requirements. Many DSPs and microcontrollers have programmable ROM embedded within them. Larger systems that require megabytes of storage (e.g., in Cisco routers, the instruction code alone is more than a 12 MB) will have increasing numbers of memory chips in the system.

On the right side of Figure Ov.4 is the software's view of the memory system. The primary distinction is that, unlike general-purpose systems, is that the SRAM caches are visible as separately addressable memories, whereas they are transparent to software in general-purpose systems.

Memory, whether SRAM or DRAM, usually represents one of the more costly components in an embedded system, especially if the memory is located on-CPU because once the CPU is fabricated, the memory size cannot be increased. In nearly all system-on-chip designs and many microcontrollers as well, memory accounts for the lion's share of available die area. Moreover, memory is one of the primary consumers of energy in a system, both on-CPU and off-CPU. As an example, it has been shown that, in many digital signal-processing applications, the memory system consumes more of both energy and die area than the processor datapath. Clearly, this is a resource on which significant time and energy is spent performing optimization.

Ov.2 Four Anecdotes on Modular Design

It is our observation that computer-system design in general, and memory-hierarchy design in particular, has reached a point at which it is no longer sufficient to design and optimize subsystems in isolation. Because memory systems and their subsystems are so complex, it is now the rule, and not the exception, that the subsystems we thought to be independent actually interact in unanticipated ways. Consequently, our traditional design methodologies no longer work because their underlying assumptions no longer hold. Modular design, one of the most widely adopted design methodologies, is an oft-praised engineering design principle in which clean functional interfaces separate subsystems (i.e., modules) so that subsystem design and optimization can be performed independently and in parallel by different designers. Applying the principles of modular design to produce a complex product can reduce the time and thus the cost for system-level design, integration, and test; optimization at the modular level guarantees optimization at the system level, provided that the system-level architecture and resulting module-to-module interfaces are optimal.

That last part is the sticking point: the principle of modular design assumes no interaction between module-level implementations and the choice of system-level architecture, but that is exactly the kind of interaction that we have observed in the design of modern, high-performance memory systems. Consequently, though modular design has been a staple of memory-systems design for decades, allowing cache designers to focus solely on caches, DRAM designers to focus solely on DRAMs, and disk designers to focus solely on disks, we find that, going forward, modular design is no longer an appropriate methodology.

Earlier we noted that, in the design of memory systems, many of the underlying implementation issues have begun to affect the higher level design process quite significantly: cache design is driven by interconnect physics; DRAM design is driven by circuit-level limitations that have dramatic system-level effects; and modern disk performance is dominated by the on-board caching and scheduling policies. As hierarchies and their components grow more complex, we find that the bulk of performance is lost not in the CPUs or caches or DRAM devices or disk assemblies themselves, but in the subtle interactions between these subsystems and in the manner in which these subsystems are connected. The bulk of lost performance is due to poor configuration of system-level parameters such as bus widths, granularity of access, scheduling policies, queue organizations, and so forth.

This is extremely important, so it bears repeating: the bulk of lost performance is not due to the number of CPU pipeline stages or functional units or choice of branch prediction algorithm or even CPU clock speed; the bulk of lost performance is due to poor configuration of system-level parameters such as bus widths, granularity of access, scheduling policies, queue organizations, etc. Today's computer-system performance is dominated by the manner in which data is moved between subsystems, i.e., the scheduling of transactions, and so it is not surprising that seemingly insignificant details can cause such a headache, as scheduling is known to be highly sensitive to such details.

Consequently, one can no longer attempt system-level optimization by designing/optimizing each of the parts in isolation (which, unfortunately, is often the approach taken in modern computer design). In subsystem design, nothing can be considered "outside the scope" and thus ignored. Memory-system design must become the purview of architects, and a subsystem designer must consider the system-level ramifications of even the slightest low-level design decision or modification. In addition, a designer must understand the low-level implications of system-level design choices. A simpler form of this maxim is as follows:

A designer must consider the system-level ramifications of circuit- and device-level decisions as well as the circuit- and device-level ramifications of system-level decisions.

To illustrate what we mean and to motivate our point, we present several anecdotes. Though they focus on the DRAM system, their message is global, and we will show over the course of the book that the relationships they uncover are certainly not restricted to the DRAM system alone. We will return to these anecdotes and discuss them in much more detail in Chapter 27, *The Case for Holistic Design*, which follows the technical section of the book.

Ov.2.1 Anecdote I: Systemic Behaviors Exist

In 1999–2001, we performed a study of DRAM systems in which we explicitly studied only system-level effects—those that had nothing to do with the CPU architecture, DRAM architecture, or even DRAM interface protocol. In this study, we held constant the CPU and DRAM architectures and considered only a handful of parameters that would affect how well the two communicate with each other. Figure Ov.5 shows some of the results [Cuppu & Jacob 1999, 2001, Jacob 2003]. The varied parameters in Figure Ov.5 are all seemingly innocuous parameters, certainly not the type that would account for up to 20% differences in system performance (execution time) if one parameter was increased or decreased by a small amount, which is indeed the case. Moreover, considering the top two graphs, all of the choices represent intuitively "good" configurations. None of the displayed values represent strawmen, machine configurations that one would avoid putting on one's own desktop. Nonetheless, the performance variability is significant. When the analysis considers a wider range of bus speeds and burst lengths, the problematic behavior increases. As shown in the bottom graph, the ratio of best to worst execution times can be a factor of three, and the local optima are both more frequent and more exaggerated. Systems with relatively low bandwidth (e.g., 100, 200, 400 MB/s) and relatively slow bus speeds (e.g., 100, 200 MHz), if configured well, can match or exceed the performance of system configurations with much faster hardware that is poorly configured.

Intuitively, one would expect the design space to be relatively smooth: as system bandwidth increases, so should system performance. Yet the design space is far from smooth. Performance variations of 20% or more can be found in design points that are immediately adjacent to one another. The variations from best-performing to worst-performing design exceed a factor of three across the full space studied, and local minima and maxima abound. Moreover, the behaviors are related. Increasing one parameter by a factor of two toward higher expected performance (e.g., increasing the channel width) can move the system off a local optimum, but local optimality can be restored by changing other related parameters to follow suit,

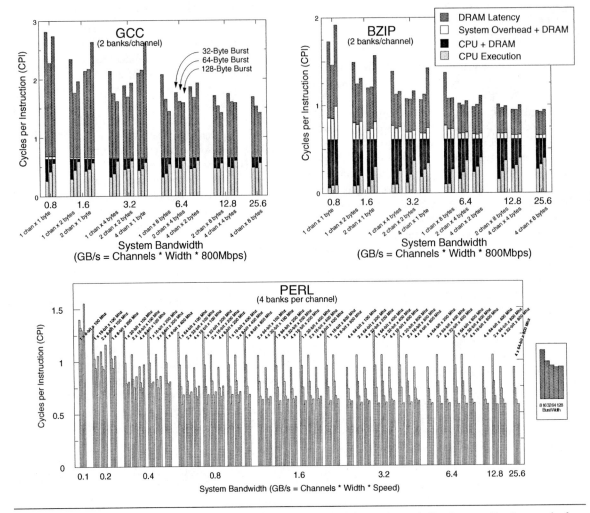

FIGURE Ov.5: Execution time as a function of bandwidth, channel organization, and granularity of access. Top two graphs from Cuppu & Jacob [2001] (© 2001 *IEEE*); bottom graph from Jacob [2003] (© 2003 *IEEE*).

such as increasing the burst length and cache block size to match the new channel width. This complex interaction between parameters previously thought to be independent arises because of the complexity of the system under study, and so we have named these "systemic" behaviors.[7] This study represents the moment we realized that systemic behaviors exist and that they are significant. Note that the behavior

---

[7]There is a distinction between this type of behavior and what in complex system theory is called "emergent system" behaviors or properties. Emergent system behaviors are those of individuals within a complex system, behaviors that an individual may perform in a group setting that the individual would never perform alone. In our environment, the behaviors are observations we have made of the design space, which is derived from the system as a whole.

is not restricted to the DRAM system. We have seen it in the disk system as well, where the variations in performance from one configuration to the next are even more pronounced.

Recall that this behavior comes from the varying of parameters that are seemingly unimportant in the grand scheme of things—at least they would certainly seem to be far less important than, say, the cache architecture or the number of functional units in the processor core. The bottom line, as we have observed, is that systemic behaviors—unanticipated interactions between seemingly innocuous parameters and mechanisms—cause significant losses in performance, requiring in-depth, detailed design-space exploration to achieve anything close to an optimal design given a set of technologies and limitations.

Ov.2.2 Anecdote II: The DLL in DDR SDRAM

Beginning with their first generation, DDR (double data rate) SDRAM devices have included a circuit-level mechanism that has generated significant controversy within JEDEC (Joint Electron Device Engineering Council), the industry consortium that created the DDR SDRAM standard. The mechanism is a delay-locked loop (DLL), whose purpose is to more precisely align the output of the DDR part with the clock on the system bus. The controversy stems from the cost of the technology versus its benefits.

The system's global clock signal, as it enters the chip, is delayed by the DLL so that the chip's internal clock signal, after amplification and distribution across the chip, is exactly in-phase with the original system clock signal. This more precisely aligns the DRAM part's output with the system clock. The trade-off is extra latency in the datapath as well as a higher power and heat dissipation because the DLL, a dynamic control mechanism, is continuously running. By aligning each DRAM part in a DIMM to the system clock, each DRAM part is effectively de-skewed with respect to the other parts, and the DLLs cancel out timing differences due to process variations and thermal gradients.

Figure Ov.6 illustrates a small handful of alternative solutions considered by JEDEC, who ultimately chose Figure Ov.6(b) for the standard. The interesting thing is that the data strobe is not used to capture data at the memory controller, bringing into question its purpose if the DLL is being used to help with data transfer to the memory controller. There is significant disagreement over the value of the chosen design; an anonymous JEDEC member, when

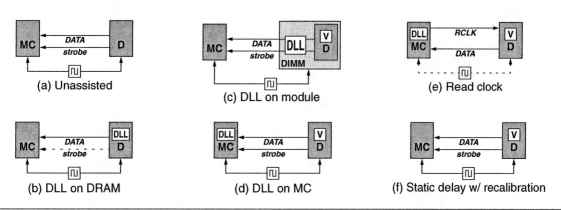

(a) Unassisted

(b) DLL on DRAM

(c) DLL on module

(d) DLL on MC

(e) Read clock

(f) Static delay w/ recalibration

FIGURE Ov.6: Several alternatives to the per-DRAM DLL. The figure illustrates a half dozen different timing conventions (a dotted line indicates a signal is unused for capturing data): (a) the scheme in single data rate SDRAM; (b) the scheme chosen for DDR SDRAM; (c) moving the DLL onto the module, with a per-DRAM static delay element (Vernier); (d) moving the DLL onto the memory controller, with a per-DRAM static delay; (e) using a separate read clock per DRAM or per DIMM; and (f) using only a static delay element and recalibrating periodically to address dynamic changes.

asked "what is the DLL doing on the DDR chip?" answered with a grin, "burning power." In applications that require low latency and low power dissipation, designers turn off the DLL entirely and use only the data strobe for data capture, ignoring the system clock (as in Figure Ov.6(a)) [Kellogg 2002, Lee 2002, Rhoden 2002].

The argument for the DLL is that it de-skews the DRAM devices on a DIMM and provides a path for system design that can use a global clocking scheme, one of the simplest system designs known. The argument against the DLL is that it would be unnecessary if a designer learned to use the data strobe—this would require a more sophisticated system design, but it would achieve better performance at a lower cost. At the very least, it is clear that a DLL is a circuit-oriented solution to the problem of system-level skew, which could explain the controversy.

Ov.2.3 Anecdote III: A Catch-22 in the Search for Bandwidth

With every DRAM generation, timing parameters are added. Several have been added to the DDR specification to address the issues of power dissipation and synchronization.

- t_{FAW} (*Four-bank Activation Window*) and t_{RRD} (*Row-to-Row activation Delay*) put a ceiling on the maximum current draw of a single DRAM part. These are protocol-level limitations whose values are chosen to prevent a memory controller from exceeding circuit-related thresholds.

- t_{DQS} is our own name for the DDR system-bus turnaround time; one can think of it as the DIMM-to-DIMM switching time that has implications only at the system level (i.e., it has no meaning or effect if considering read requests in a system with but a single DIMM). By obeying t_{DQS}, one can ensure that a second DIMM will not drive

the data bus at the same time as a first when switching from one DIMM to another for data output.

These are per-device timing parameters that were chosen to improve the behavior (current draw, timing uncertainty) of individual devices. However, they do so at the expense of a significant loss in system-level performance. When reading large amounts of data from the DRAM system, an application will have to read, and thus will have to *activate*, numerous DRAM rows. At this point, the t_{FAW} and t_{RRD} timing parameters kick in and limit the available read bandwidth. The t_{RRD} parameter specifies the minimum time between two successive row activation commands to the same DRAM device (which implies the same DIMM, because all the DRAMs on a DIMM are slaved together[8]). The t_{FAW} parameter represents a sliding window of time during which no more than four row activation commands to the same device may appear.

The parameters are specified in nanoseconds and not bus cycles, so they become increasingly problematic at higher bus frequencies. Their net effect is to limit the bandwidth available from a DIMM by limiting how quickly one can get the data out of the DRAM's storage array, irrespective of how fast the DRAM's I/O circuitry can ship the data back to the memory controller. At around 1 GBps, sustainable bandwidth hits a ceiling and remains flat no matter how fast the bus runs because the memory controller is limited in how quickly it can activate a new row and start reading data from it.

The obvious solution is to interleave data from different DIMMs on the bus. If one DIMM is limited in how quickly it can read data from its arrays, then one should populate the bus with many DIMMs and move through them in a round-robin fashion. This should bring the system bandwidth up to maximum. However, the function of t_{DQS} is to prevent exactly that: t_{DQS} is the bus turnaround time, inserted to account for skew on the bus and to prevent different bus masters from driving the bus at the same time.

---

[8]This is a minor oversimplification. We would like to avoid having to explain details of DRAM-system organization, such as the concept of *rank*, at this point.

To avoid such collisions, a second DIMM must wait at least t_{DQS} after a first DIMM has finished before driving the bus. So we have a catch:

- One set of parameters limits device-level bandwidth and expects a designer to go to the system level to reclaim performance.
- The other parameter limits system-level bandwidth and expects a designer to go to the device level to reclaim performance.

The good news is that the problem is solvable (see Chapter 15, Section 15.4.3, *DRAM Command Scheduling Algorithms*), but this is nonetheless a very good example of low-level design decisions that create headaches at the system level.

Ov.2.4 Anecdote IV: Proposals to Exploit Variability in Cell Leakage

The last anecdote is an example of a system-level design decision that ignores circuit- and device-level implications. Ever since DRAM was invented, it has been observed that different DRAM cells exhibit different data-retention time characteristics, typically ranging between hundreds of milliseconds to tens of seconds. DRAM manufacturers typically set the refresh requirement conservatively and require that every row in a DRAM device be refreshed at least once every 64 or 32 ms to avoid losing data. Though refresh might not seem to be a significant concern, in mobile devices researchers have observed that refresh can account for one-third of the power in otherwise idle systems, prompting action to address the issue. Several recent papers propose moving the refresh function into the memory controller and refreshing each row only when needed. During an initialization phase, the controller would characterize each row in the memory system, measuring DRAM data-retention time on a row-by-row basis, discarding leaky rows entirely, limiting its DRAM use to only those rows deemed non-leaky, and refreshing once every tens of seconds instead of once every tens of milliseconds.

The problem is that these proposals ignore another, less well-known phenomenon of DRAM cell variability, namely that a cell with a long retention time can suddenly (in the time frame of seconds) exhibit a short retention time [Yaney et al. 1987, Restle et al. 1992, Ueno et al. 1998, Kim 2004]. Such an effect would render these power-efficient proposals functionally erroneous. The phenomenon is called *variable retention time* (VRT), and though its occurrence is infrequent, it is non-zero. The occurrence rate is low enough that a system using one of these reduced-refresh proposals could protect itself against VRT by using error correcting codes (ECC, described in detail in Chapter 30, *Memory Errors and Error Correction*), but none of the proposals so far discuss VRT or ECC.

Ov.2.5 Perspective

To summarize so far:

Anecdote I: Systemic behaviors exist and are significant (they can be responsible for factors of two to three in execution time).

Anecdote II: The DLL in DDR SDRAM is a circuit-level solution chosen to address system-level skew.

Anecdote III: t_{DQS} represents a circuit-level solution chosen to address system-level skew in DDR SDRAM; t_{FAW} and t_{RRD} are circuit-level limitations that significantly limit system-level performance.

Anecdote IV: Several research groups have recently proposed system-level solutions to the DRAM-refresh problem, but fail to account for circuit-level details that might compromise the correctness of the resulting system.

Anecdotes II and III show that a common practice in industry is to focus at the level of devices and circuits, in some cases ignoring their system-level ramifications. Anecdote IV shows that a common practice in research is to design systems that have device- and circuit-level ramifications while abstracting away the details of the devices and circuits involved. Anecdote I illustrates that both approaches are doomed to failure in future memory-systems design.

It is clear that in the future we will have to move away from modular design; one can no longer safely abstract away details that were previously considered "out of scope." To produce a credible analysis, a designer must consider many different subsystems of a design and many different levels of abstraction—one must consider the forest when designing trees and consider the trees when designing the forest.

Ov.3 Cross-Cutting Issues

Though their implementation details might apply at a local level, most design decisions must be considered in terms of their system-level effects and side-effects before they become part of the system/hierarchy. For instance, power is a cross-cutting, system-level phenomenon, even though most power optimizations are specific to certain technologies and are applied locally; reliability is a system-level issue, even though each level of the hierarchy implements its own techniques for improving it; and, as we have shown, performance optimizations such as widening a bus or increasing support for concurrency rarely result in system performance that is globally optimal. Moreover, design decisions that locally optimize along one axis (e.g., power) can have even larger effects on the system level when all axes are considered. Not only can the global power dissipation be thrown off optimality by blindly making a local decision, it is even easier to throw the system off a global optimum when more than one axis is considered (e.g., power/performance).

Designing the best system given a set of constraints requires an approach that considers multiple axes simultaneously and measures the system-level effects of all design choices. Such a holistic approach requires an understanding of many issues, including cost and performance models, power, reliability, and software structure. The following sections provide overviews of these cross-cutting issues, and Part IV of the book will treat these topics in more detail.

Ov.3.1 Cost/Performance Analysis

To perform a cost/performance analysis correctly, the designer must define the problem correctly, use the appropriate tools for analysis, and apply those tools in the manner for which they were designed. This section provides a brief, intuitive look at the problem. Herein, we will use *cost* as an example of problem definition, *Pareto optimality* as an example of an appropriate tool, and *sampled averages* as an example to illustrate correct tool usage. We will discuss these issues in more detail with more examples in Chapter 28, *Analysis of Cost and Performance*.

Problem Definition: Cost

A designer must think in an all-inclusive manner when accounting for cost. For example, consider a cost-performance analysis of a DRAM system wherein performance is measured in sustainable bandwidth and cost is measured in pin count.

To represent the cost correctly, the analysis should consider *all* pins, including those for control, power, ground, address, and data. Otherwise, the resulting analysis can incorrectly portray the design space, and workable solutions can get left out of the analysis. For example, a designer can reduce latency in some cases by increasing the number of address and command pins, but if the cost analysis only considers data pins, then these optimizations would be cost-free. Consider DRAM addressing, which is done half of an address at a time. A 32-bit physical address is sent to the DRAM system 16 bits at a time in two different commands; one could potentially decrease DRAM latency by using an SRAM-like wide address bus and sending the entire 32 bits at once. This represents a *real* cost in design and manufacturing that would be higher, but an analysis that accounts only for data pins would not consider it as such.

Power and ground pins must also be counted in a cost analysis for similar reasons. High-speed chip-to-chip interfaces typically require more power and ground pins than slower interfaces. The extra power and ground signals help to isolate the I/O drivers from each other and the signal lines from each other, both improving signal integrity by reducing crosstalk, ground bounce, and related effects. I/O systems with higher switching speeds would have an unfair advantage over those with lower switching speeds (and thus fewer power/ground pins) in a cost-performance analysis if power and ground pins were to be excluded from the analysis. The inclusion of these pins would provide for an effective and easily quantified trade-off between cost and bandwidth.

Failure to include address, control, power, and ground pins in an analysis, meaning failure to be all-inclusive at the conceptual stages of design, would tend to blind a designer to possibilities. For example, an architecturally related family of solutions that at first glance gives up total system bandwidth so as to be more cost-effective might be thrown out at the conceptual stages for its intuitively lower performance. However, considering all sources of cost in the analysis would allow a designer to look more closely at this family and possibly to recover lost bandwidth through the addition of pins.

Comparing SDRAM and Rambus system architectures provides an excellent example of consid-ering cost as the total number of pins leading to a continuum of designs. The Rambus memory system is a narrow-channel architecture, compared to SDRAM's wide-channel architecture, pictured in Figure Ov.7 Rambus uses fewer address and command pins than SDRAM and thus incurs an additional latency at the command level. Rambus also uses fewer data pins and occurs an additional latency when transmitting data as well. The trade-off is the ability to run the bus at a much higher bus frequency, or *pin-bandwidth* in bits per second per pin, than SDRAM. The longer channel of the DRDRAM (direct Rambus DRAM) memory system contributes directly to longer read-command latencies and longer bus turnaround times. However, the longer channel also allows for more devices to be connected to the memory system and reduces the likelihood that consecutive commands access the same device. The width and depth of the memory channels impact the bandwidth, latency, pin count, and various cost components of the respective memory systems. The effect that these organizational differences have on the DRAM access protocol is shown in Figure Ov.8 which illustrates a row activation and column read

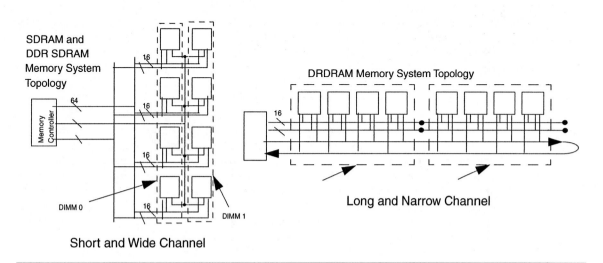

FIGURE Ov.7: Difference in topology between SDRAM and Rambus memory systems.

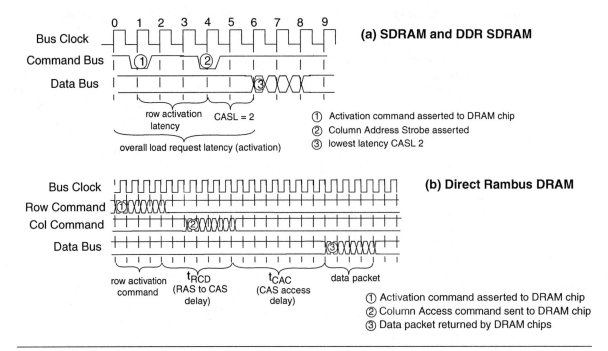

FIGURE Ov.8: Memory access latency in SDRAM and DDR SDRAM memory systems (top) and DRDRAM (bottom).

command for both DDR SDRAM and Direct Rambus DRAM.

Contemporary SDRAM and DDR SDRAM memory chips operating at a frequency of 200 MHz can activate a row in 3 clock cycles. Once the row is activated, memory controllers in SDRAM or DDR SDRAM memory systems can retrieve data using a simple column address strobe command with a latency of 2 or 3 clock cycles. In Figure Ov.8(a), Step 1 shows the assertion of a row activation command, and Step 2 shows the assertion of the column address strobe signal. Step 3 shows the relative timing of a high-performance DDR SDRAM memory module with a CASL (CAS latency) of 2 cycles. For a fair comparison against the DRDRAM memory system, we include the bus cycle that the memory controller uses to assert the load command to the memory chips. With this additional cycle included, a DDR SDRAM memory system has a read latency of 6 clock cycles (to critical data). In a SDRAM or DDR SDRAM memory system that operates at 200 MHz, 6 clock cycles translate to 30 ns of latency for a memory load command with row activation latency

inclusive. These latency values are the same for high-performance SDRAM and DDR SDRAM memory systems.

The DRDRAM memory system behaves very differently from SDRAM and DDR SDRAM memory systems. Figure Ov.8(b) shows a row activation command in Step 1, followed by a column access command in Step 2. The requested data is then returned by the memory chip to the memory controller in Step 3. The row activation command in Step 1 is transmitted by the memory controller to the memory chip in a packet format that spans 4 clock cycles. The minimum delay between the row activation and column access is 7 clock cycles, and, after an additional (also minimum) CAS (column address strobe) latency of 8 clock cycles, the DRDRAM chip begins to transmit the data to the memory controller. One caveat to the computation of the access latency in the DRDRAM memory system is that CAS delay in the DRDRAM memory system is a function of the number of devices on a single DRDRAM memory channel. On a DRDRAM memory system with a full load of 32 devices

TABLE Ov.2   Peak bandwidth statistics of SDRAM, DDR SDRAM, and DRDRAM memory systems

	Operating Frequency (Data)	Data Channel Pin Count	Data Channel Bandwidth	Control Channel Pin Count	Command Channel Bandwidth	Address Channel Pin Count	Address Channel Bandwidth
SDRAM controller	133	64	1064 MB/s	28	465 MB/s	30	500 MB/s
DDR SDRAM controller	2 * 200	64	3200 MB/s	42	1050 MB/s	30	750 MB/s
DRDRAM controller	2 * 600	16	2400 MB/s	9	1350 MB/s	8	1200 MB/s
x16 SDRAM chip	133	16	256 MB/s	9	150 MB/s	15	250 MB/s
x16 DDR SDRAM chip	2 *200	16	800 MB/s	11	275 MB/s	15	375 MB/s

TABLE Ov.3   Cross-comparison of SDRAM, DDR SDRAM, and DRDRAM memory systems

DRAM Technology	Operating Frequency (Data Bus)	Pin Count per Channel	Peak Band-width	Sustained BW on StreamAdd	Bits per Pin per Cycle (Peak)	Bits per Pin per Cycle (Sustained)
SDRAM	133	152	1064 MB/s	540 MB/s	0.4211	0.2139
DDR SDRAM	2 * 200	171	3200 MB/s	1496 MB/s	0.3743	0.1750
DRDRAm	2 * 600	117	2400 MB/s	1499 MB/s	0.1368	0.0854

on the data bus, the CAS-latency delay may be as large as 12 clock cycles. Finally, it takes 4 clock cycles for the DRDRAM memory system to transport the data packet. Note that we add half the transmission time of the data packet in the computation of the latency of a memory request in a DRDRAM memory system due to the fact that the DRDRAM memory system does not support critical word forwarding, and the critically requested data may exist in the latter parts of the data packet; on average, it will be somewhere in the middle. This yields a total latency of 21 cycles, which, in a DRDRAM memory system operating at 600 MHz, translates to a latency of 35 ns.

The Rambus memory system trades off a longer latency for fewer pins and higher pin bandwidth (in this example, three times higher bandwidth). How do the systems compare in performance?

Peak bandwidth of any interface depends solely on the channel width and the operating frequency of the channel. In Table Ov.2, we summarize the statistics of the interconnects and compute the peak bandwidths of the memory systems at the interface

of the memory controller and at the interface of the memory chips as well.

Table Ov.3 compares a 133-MHz SDRAM, a 200-MHz DDR SDRAM system, and a 600-MHz DRDRAM system. The 133-MHz SDRAM system, as represented by a PC-133 compliant SDRAM memory system on an AMD Athlon-based computer system, has a theoretical peak bandwidth of 1064 MB/s. The maximum sustained bandwidth for the single channel of SDRAM, as measured by the use of the add kernel in the STREAM benchmark, reaches 540 MB/s. The maximum sustained bandwidth for DDR SDRAM and DRDRAM was also measured on STREAM, yielding 1496 and 1499 MB/s, respectively. The pin cost of each system is factored in, yielding bandwidth per pin on both a per-cycle basis and a per-nanosecond basis.

Appropriate Tools: Pareto Optimality

It is convenient to represent the "goodness" of a design solution, a particular system configuration, as a single number so that one can readily compare the number with the goodness ratings of other candidate design solutions and thereby quickly find the "best" system configuration. However, in the design of memory systems, we are inherently dealing with a multi-dimensional design space (e.g., one that encompasses performance, energy consumption, cost, etc.), and so using a single number to represent a solution's worth is not really appropriate, unless we can assign exact weights to the various figures of merit (which is dangerous and will be discussed in more detail later) or we care about one aspect to the exclusion of all others (e.g., performance at any cost).

Assuming that we do not have exact weights for the figures of merit and that we do care about more than one aspect of the system, a very powerful tool to aid in system analysis is the concept of *Pareto optimality* or *Pareto efficiency*, named after the Italian economist Vilfredo Pareto, who invented it in the early 1900s.

Pareto optimality asserts that one candidate solution to a problem is better than another candidate solution only if the first *dominates* the second, i.e., if the first is better than or equal to the second in *all* figures of merit. If one solution has a better value in one dimension but a worse value in another, then the two candidates are Pareto equivalent. The best solution is actually a set

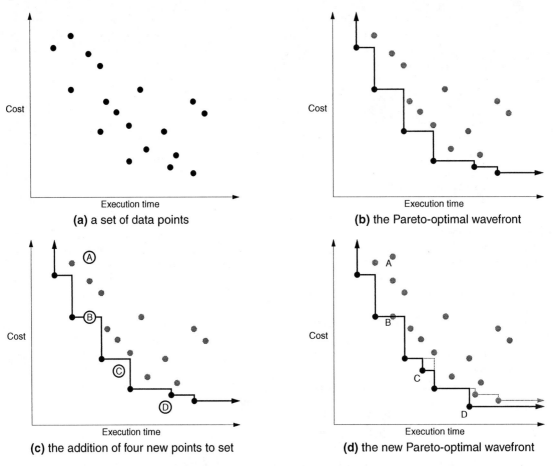

(a) a set of data points

(b) the Pareto-optimal wavefront

(c) the addition of four new points to set

(d) the new Pareto-optimal wavefront

FIGURE Ov.9: Pareto optimality. Members of the Pareto-optimal set are shown in solid black; non-optimal points are grey.

of candidate solutions: the set of Pareto-equivalent solutions that is not dominated by any solution.

Figure Ov.9(a) shows a set of candidate solutions in a two-dimensional space that represent a cost/performance metric. The x-axis represents system performance in execution time (smaller numbers are better), and the y-axis represents system cost in dollars (smaller numbers are better). Figure Ov.9(b) shows the Pareto-optimal set in solid black and connected by a line; non-optimal data points are shown in grey. The Pareto-optimal set forms a wavefront that approaches both axes simultaneously. Figures Ov.9(c) and (d) show the effect of adding four new candidate solutions to the space: one lies inside the wavefront, one lies on the wavefront, and two lie outside the wavefront. The first two new additions, A and B, are both dominated by at least one member of the Pareto-optimal set, and so neither is considered Pareto optimal. Even though B lies on the wavefront, it is not considered Pareto optimal. The point to the left of B has better performance than B at equal cost. Thus, it dominates B.

Point C is not dominated by any member of the Pareto-optimal set, nor does it dominate any member of the Pareto-optimal set. Thus, candidate-solution C is added to the optimal set, and its addition changes the shape of the wavefront slightly. The last of the additional points, D, is dominated by no members of the optimal set, but it *does* dominate several members of the optimal set, so D's inclusion in the optimal set excludes those dominated members from the set. As a result, candidate-solution D changes the shape of the wave front more significantly than candidate-solution C.

Tool Use: Taking Sampled Averages Correctly

In many fields, including the field of computer engineering, it is quite popular to find a *sampled average*, i.e., the average of a sampled set of numbers, rather than the average of the entire set. This is useful when the entire set is unavailable, difficult to obtain, or expensive to obtain. For example, one might want to use this technique to keep a running performance average for a real microprocessor, or one might want to sample several windows of execution in a terabyte-size trace file. Provided that the sampled subset is representative of the set as a whole, and provided that the technique used to collect the samples is correct, this mechanism provides a low-cost alternative that can be very accurate.

The discussion will use as an example a mechanism that samples the miles-per-gallon performance of an automobile under way. The trip we will study is an out and back trip with a brief pit stop, as shown in Figure Ov.10. The automobile will follow a simple course that is easily analyzed:

1. The auto will travel over even ground for 60 miles at 60 mph, and it will achieve 30 mpg during this window of time.

2. The auto will travel uphill for 20 miles at 60 mph, and it will achieve 10 mpg during this window of time.

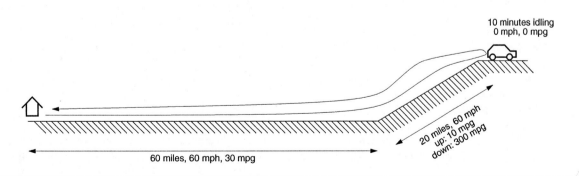

FIGURE Ov.10: Course taken by the automobile in the example.

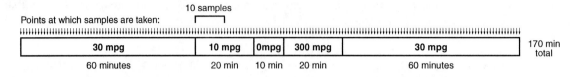

FIGURE Ov.11: Sampling miles-per-gallon (mpg) over time. The figure shows the trip in time, with each segment of time labeled with the average miles-per-gallon for the car during that segment of the trip. Thus, whenever the sampling algorithm samples miles-per-gallon during a window of time, it will add that value to the running average.

3. The auto will travel downhill for 20 miles at 60 mph, and it will achieve 300 mpg during this window of time.

4. The auto will travel back home over even ground for 60 miles at 60 mph, and it will achieve 30 mpg during this window of time.

5. In addition, before returning home, the driver will sit at the top of the hill for 10 minutes, enjoying the view, with the auto idling, consuming gasoline at the rate of 1 gallon every 5 hours. This is equivalent to 1/300 gallon per minute or 1/30 of a gallon during the 10-minute respite. Note that the auto will achieve 0 mpg during this window of time.

Our car's algorithm samples evenly in time, so for our analysis we need to break down the segments of the trip by the amount of time that they take:

- Outbound: 60 minutes
- Uphill: 20 minutes
- Idling: 10 minutes
- Downhill: 20 minutes
- Return: 60 minutes

This is displayed graphically in Figure Ov.11, in which the time for each segment is shown to scale. Assume, for the sake of simplicity, that the sampling algorithm samples the car's miles-per-gallon every minute and adds that sampled value to the running average (it could just as easily sample every second or millisecond). Then the algorithm will sample the value 30 mpg 60 times during the first segment of the trip, the value 10 mpg 20 times during the second segment of the trip, the value 0 mpg 10 times during

the third segment of the trip, and so on. Over the trip, the car is operating for a total of 170 minutes. Thus, we can derive the sampling algorithm's results as follows:

$$\tfrac{60}{170}30 + \tfrac{20}{170}10 + \tfrac{10}{170}0 + \tfrac{20}{170}300 + \tfrac{60}{170}30 = 57.5\text{mpg}$$

(EQ Ov.3)

The sampling algorithm tells us that the auto achieved 57.5 mpg during our trip. However, a quick reality check will demonstrate that this cannot be correct; somewhere in our analysis we have made an invalid assumption. What is the correct answer, the correct approach? In Part IV of the book we will revisit this example and provide a complete picture. In the meantime, the reader is encouraged to figure the answer out for him- or herself.

Ov.3.2 Power and Energy

Power has become a "first-class" design goal in recent years within the computer architecture and design community. Previously, low-power circuit, chip, and system design was considered the purview of specialized communities, but this is no longer the case, as even high-performance chip manufacturers can be blindsided by power dissipation problems.

Power Dissipation in Computer Systems

Power dissipation in CMOS circuits arises from two different mechanisms: *static power*, which is primarily *leakage power* and is caused by the transistor not completely turning off, and *dynamic power*, which is largely the result of switching capacitive loads between two different voltage states. Dynamic power is dependent on frequency of circuit activity, since no power is dissipated if the node values do not change, while static power is independent of the frequency of activity and exists whenever the chip is powered on. When CMOS circuits were first used, one of their main advantages was the negligible leakage current flowing with the gate at DC or steady state. Practically all of the power consumed by CMOS gates was due to dynamic power consumed during the transition of the gate. But as transistors become increasingly smaller, the CMOS leakage current starts to become significant and is projected to be larger than the dynamic power, as shown in Figure Ov.12.

In charging a load capacitor C up ΔV volts and discharging it to its original voltage, a gate pulls an amount of current equal to $C \cdot \Delta V$ from the V_{dd} supply to charge up the capacitor and then sinks this charge to ground discharging the node. At the end of a charge/discharge cycle, the gate/capacitor combination has moved $C \cdot \Delta V$ of charge from V_{dd} to ground, which uses an amount of energy equal to $C \cdot \Delta V \cdot V_{dd}$ that is independent of the cycle time. The average dynamic power of this node, the average rate of its energy consumption, is given by the following equation [Chandrakasan & Brodersen 1995]:

$$P_{dynamic} = C \cdot \Delta V \cdot V_{dd} \cdot \alpha \cdot f \qquad \textbf{(EQ Ov.4)}$$

Dividing by the charge/discharge period (i.e., multiplying by the clock frequency f) produces the rate of energy consumption over that period. Multiplying by the expected *activity ratio* α, the probability that the node will switch (in which case it dissipates dynamic power; otherwise, it does not), yields an average power dissipation over a larger window of time for which the activity ratio holds (e.g., this can yield average power for an entire hour of computation, not just a nanosecond). The dynamic power for the whole chip is the sum of this equation over all nodes in the circuit.

It is clear from EQ Ov.4 what can be done to reduce the dynamic power dissipation of a system. We can either reduce the capacitance being switched, the voltage swing, the power supply voltage, the activity ratio, or the operating frequency. Most of these options are available to a designer at the architecture level.

Note that, for a specific chip, the voltage swing ΔV is usually proportional to V_{dd}, so EQ Ov.4 is often simplified to the following:

$$P_{dynamic} = C \cdot V^2_{dd} \cdot \alpha \cdot f \qquad \textbf{(EQ Ov.5)}$$

Moreover, the activity ratio α is often approximated as 1/2, giving the following form:

$$P_{dynamic} = \tfrac{1}{2} \cdot C \cdot V^2_{dd} \cdot f \qquad \textbf{(EQ Ov.6)}$$

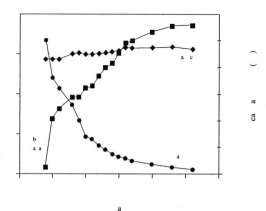

FIGURE Ov.12: Projections for dynamic and leakage, along with gate length. (Figure taken from Kim et al. [2004a]).

Static leakage power is due to our inability to completely turn off the transistor, which leaks current in the subthreshold operating region [Taur & Ning 1998]. The gate couples to the active channel mainly through the gate oxide capacitance, but there are other capacitances in a transistor that couple the gate to a "fixed charge" (charge which cannot move) present in the bulk and not associated with current flow [Peckerar et al. 1979, 1982]. If these extra capacitances are large (note that they increase with each process generation as physical dimensions shrink), then changing the gate bias merely alters the densities of the fixed charge and will not turn the channel off. In this situation, the transistor becomes a leaky faucet; it does not turn off no matter how hard you turn it.

Leakage power is proportional to V_{dd}. It is a linear, not a quadratic, relationship. For a particular process technology, the per-device leakage power is given as follows [Butts & Sohi 2000]:

$$P_{static} = I_{leakage} \cdot V^2_{dd} \qquad \text{(EQ Ov.7)}$$

Leakage energy is the product of leakage power times the duration of operation.

It is clear from EQ Ov.7 what can be done to reduce the leakage power dissipation of a system: reduce leakage current and/or reduce the power supply voltage. Both options are available to a designer at the architecture level.

Heat in VLSI circuits is becoming a significant and related problem. The rate at which physical dimensions such as gate length and gate oxide thickness have been reduced is faster than for other parameters, especially voltage, resulting in higher power densities on the chip surface. To lower leakage power and maintain device operation, voltage levels are set according to the silicon bandgap and intrinsic built-in potentials, in spite of the conventional scaling algorithm. Thus, power densities are increasing exponentially for next-generation chips. For instance, the power density of Intel's Pentium chip line has already surpassed that of a hot plate with the introduction of the Pentium Pro [Gelsinger 2001]. The problem of power and heat dissipation now extends to the DRAM system, which traditionally has represented low power densities and low costs. Today, higher end DRAMs are dynamically throttled when, due to repeated high-speed access to the same devices, their operating temperatures surpass design thresholds. The next-generation memory system embraced by the DRAM community, the Fully Buffered DIMM architecture, specifies a per-module controller that, in many implementations, requires a heatsink. This is a cost previously unthinkable in DRAM-system design.

Disks have many components that dissipate power, including the spindle motor driving the platters, the actuator that positions the disk heads, the bus interface circuitry, and the microcontroller/s and memory chips. The spindle motor dissipates the bulk of the power, with the entire disk assembly typically dissipating power in the tens of watts.

Schemes for Reducing Power and Energy

There are numerous mechanisms in the literature that attack the power dissipation and/or energy consumption problem. Here, we will briefly describe three: dynamic voltage scaling, the powering down of unused blocks, and circuit-level approaches for reducing leakage power.

Dynamic Voltage Scaling Recall that total energy is the sum of switching energy and leakage energy, which, to a first approximation, is equal to the following:

$$E_{tot} = [(C_{tot} \cdot V^2_{dd} \cdot \alpha \cdot f)$$
$$+ (N_{tot} \cdot I_{leakage} \cdot V_{dd})] \cdot T \qquad \text{(EQ Ov.8)}$$

T is the time required for the computation, and N_{tot} is the total number of devices leaking current. Variations in processor utilization affect the amount of switching activity (the activity ratio α). However, a light workload produces an idle processor that wastes clock cycles and energy because the clock signal continues propagating and the operating voltage remains the same. Gating the clock during idle cycles reduces the switched capacitance C_{tot} during idle cycles. Reducing the frequency f during periods of low workload eliminates most idle cycles altogether.

None of the approaches, however, affects $C_{tot}V^2_{dd}$ for the actual computation or substantially reduces the energy lost to leakage current. Instead, reducing the supply voltage V_{dd} in conjunction with the frequency f achieves savings in switching energy and reduces leakage energy. For high-speed digital CMOS, a reduction in supply voltage increases the circuit delay as shown by the following equation [Baker et al. 1998, Baker 2005]:

$$T_d = \frac{C_L V_{dd}}{\mu C_{ox}(W/L)(V_{dd} - V_t)^2} \qquad \text{(EQ Ov.9)}$$

where

- T_d is the delay or the reciprocal of the frequency f
- V_{dd} is the supply voltage
- C_L is the total node capacitance
- μ is the carrier mobility
- C_{ox} is the oxide capacitance
- V_t is the threshold voltage
- W/L is the width-to-length ratio of the transistors in the circuit

This can be simplified to the following form, which gives the maximum operating frequency as a function of supply and threshold voltages:

$$f_{MAX} \sim \frac{(V_{dd} - V_t)^2}{V_{dd}} \qquad \text{(EQ Ov.10)}$$

As mentioned earlier, the threshold voltage is closely tied to the problem of leakage power, so it cannot be arbitrarily lowered. Thus, the right-hand side of the relation ends up being a constant proportion of the operating voltage for a given process technology. Microprocessors typically operate at the maximum speed at which their operating voltage level will allow, so there is not much headroom to arbitrarily lower V_{dd} by itself. However, V_{dd} can be lowered if the clock frequency is also lowered in the same proportion. This mechanism is called *dynamic voltage scaling (DVS)* [Pering & Broderson 1998] and

is appearing in nearly every modern microprocessor. The technique sets the microprocessor's frequency to the most appropriate level for performing each task at hand, thus avoiding hurry-up-and-wait scenarios that consume more energy than is required for the computation (see Figure Ov.13). As Weiser points out,

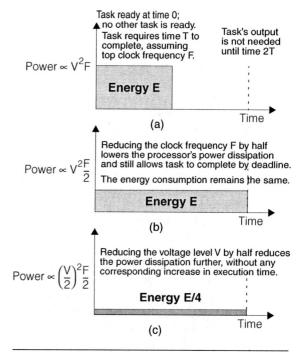

FIGURE Ov.13: Dynamic voltage scaling. Not every task needs the CPU's full computational power. In many cases, for example, the processing of video and audio streams, the only performance requirement is that the task meet a deadline, see (a). Such cases create opportunities to run the CPU at a lower performance level and achieve the same perceived performance while consuming less energy. As (b) shows, reducing the clock frequency of a processor reduces power dissipation but simply spreads a computation out over time, thereby consuming the same total energy as before. As (c) shows, reducing the voltage level as well as the clock frequency achieves the desired goal of reduced energy consumption and appropriate performance level. Figure and caption from Varma et al. [2003].

idle time represents wasted energy, even if the CPU is stopped [Weiser et al. 1994].

Note that it is not sufficient to merely have a chip that *supports* voltage scaling. There must be a heuristic, either implemented in hardware or software, that decides when to scale the voltage and by how much to scale it. This decision is essentially a prediction of the near-future computational needs of the system and is generally made on the basis of the recent computing requirements of all tasks and threads running at the time. The development of good heuristics is a tricky problem (pointed out by Weiser et al. [1994]). Heuristics that closely track performance requirements save little energy, while those that save the most energy tend to do so at the expense of performance, resulting in poor response time, for example.

Most research quantifies the effect that DVS has on reducing dynamic power dissipation because dynamic power follows V_{dd} in a quadratic relationship: reducing V_{dd} can significantly reduce dynamic power. However, lowering V_{dd} also reduces leakage power, which is becoming just as significant as dynamic power. Though the reduction is only linear, it is nonetheless a reduction.

Note also that even though DVS is commonly applied to microprocessors, it is perfectly well suited to the memory system as well. As a processor's speed is decreased through application of DVS, it requires less speed out of its associated SRAM caches, whose power supply can be scaled to keep pace. This will reduce both the dynamic and the static power dissipation of the memory circuits.

Powering-Down Unused Blocks A popular mechanism for reducing power is simply to turn off functional blocks that are not needed. This is done at both the circuit level and the chip or I/O-device level.

At the circuit level, the technique is called *clock gating*. The clock signal to a functional block (e.g., an adder, multiplier, or predictor) passes through a gate, and whenever a control circuit determines that the functional block will be unused for several cycles, the gate halts the clock signal and sends a non-oscillating voltage level to the functional block instead. The latches in the functional block retain their information; do not change their outputs; and, because the data is held constant to the combinational logic in the circuit, do not switch. Therefore, it does not draw current or consume energy.

Note that, in the naïve implementation, the circuits in this instance are still powered up, so they still dissipate static power; clock gating is a technique that only reduces dynamic power. Other gating techniques can reduce leakage as well. For example, in caches, unused blocks can be powered down using Gated-V_{dd} [Powell et al. 2000] or Gated-ground [Powell et al. 2000] techniques. Gated-V_{dd} puts the power supply of the SRAM in a series with a transistor as shown in Figure Ov.14. With the stacking effect introduced by this transistor, the leakage current is reduced drastically. This technique benefits from having both low-leakage current and a simpler fabrication process requirement since only a single threshold voltage is conceptually required (although, as shown in Figure Ov.14, the gating transistor can also have a high threshold to decrease the leakage even further at the expense of process complexity).

At the device level, for instance in DRAM chips or disk assemblies, the mechanism puts the device into a low-activity, low-voltage, and/or low-frequency mode such as *sleep* or *doze* or, in the case of disks, *spin-down*. For example, microprocessors can dissipate anywhere from a fraction of a watt to over 100 W of power; when not in use, they can be put into a low-power sleep or doze mode that consumes milli-watts. The processor typically expects an interrupt to cause it to resume normal operation, for instance, a clock interrupt, the interrupt output of a watchdog timer, or an external device interrupt. DRAM chips typically consume on the order of 1 W each; they have a low-power mode that will reduce this by more than an order of magnitude. Disks typically dissipate power in the tens of watts, the bulk of which is in the spindle motor. When the disk is placed in the "spin-down" mode (i.e., it is not rotating, but it is still responding to the disk controller),

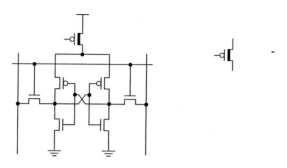

FIGURE Ov.14: Gated-V_{dd} technique using a high-V_t transistor to gate V_{dd}.

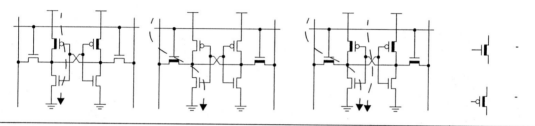

FIGURE Ov.15: Different multi-V_t configurations for the 6T memory cell showing which leakage currents are reduced for each configuration.

the disk assembly consumes a total of a handful of watts [Gurumurthi et al. 2003].

Leakage Power in SRAMs Low-power SRAM techniques provide good examples of approaches for lowering leakage power. SRAM designs targeted for low power have begun to account for the increasingly larger amount of power consumed by leakage currents.

One conceptually simple solution is the use of multi-threshold CMOS circuits. This involves using process-level techniques to increase the threshold voltage of transistors to reduce the leakage current. Increasing this threshold serves to reduce the gate overdrive and reduces the gate's drive strength, resulting in increased delay. Because of this, the technique is mostly used on the non-critical paths of the logic, and fast, low-V_t transistors

are used for the critical paths. In this way the delay penalty involved in using higher V_t transistors can be hidden in the non-critical paths, while reducing the leakage currents drastically. For example, multi-V_t transistors are selectively used for memory cells since they represent a majority of the circuit, reaping the most benefit in leakage power consumption with a minor penalty in the access time. Different multi-V_t configurations are shown in Figure Ov.15, along with the leakage current path that each configuration is designed to minimize.

Another technique that reduces leakage power in SRAMs is the Drowsy technique [Kim et al. 2004a]. This is similar to gated-V_{dd} and gated-ground techniques in that it uses a transistor to conditionally enable the power supply to a given part of the SRAM. The difference is that this technique puts infrequently accessed parts of the SRAM into a

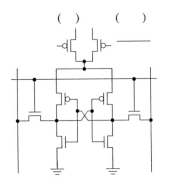

FIGURE Ov.16: A drowsy SRAM cell containing the transistors that gate the desired power supply.

state-preserving, low-power mode. A second power supply with a lower voltage than the regular supply provides power to memory cells in the "drowsy" mode. Leakage power is effectively reduced because of its dependence on the value of the power supply. An SRAM cell of a drowsy cache is shown in Figure Ov.16.

Ov.3.3 Reliability

Like performance, reliability means many things to many people. For example, embedded systems are computer systems, typically small, that run dedicated software and are embedded within the context of a larger system. They are increasingly appearing in the place of traditional electromechanical systems, whose function they are replacing because one can now find chip-level computer systems which can be programmed to perform virtually any function at a price of pennies per system. The reliability problem stems from the fact that the embedded system is a state machine (piece of software) executing within the context of a relatively complex state machine (real-time operating system) executing within the context of an extremely complex state machine (microprocessor and its memory system). We are replacing simple electromechanical systems with ultra-complex systems whose correct function cannot be guaranteed. This presents an enormous problem for the future, in which systems will only get more

complex and will be used increasingly in safety-critical situations, where incorrect functioning can cause great harm.

This is a very deep problem, and one that is not likely to be solved soon. A smaller problem that we *can* solve right now—one that engineers currently do—is to increase the reliability of data within the memory system. If a datum is stored in the memory system, whether in a cache, in a DRAM, or on disk, it is reasonable to expect that the next time a processor reads that datum, the processor will get the value that was written.

How could the datum's value change? Solid-state memory devices (e.g., SRAMs and DRAMs) are susceptible to both hard failures and soft errors in the same manner that other semiconductor-based electronic devices are susceptible to both hard failures and soft failures. Hard failures can be caused by electromigration, corrosion, thermal cycling, or electrostatic shock. In contrast to hard failures, soft errors are failures where the physical device remains functional, but random and transient electronic noises corrupt the value of the stored information in the memory system. Transient noise and upset comes from a multitude of sources, including circuit noise (e.g., crosstalk, ground bounce, etc.), ambient radiation (e.g., even from sources within the computer chassis), clock jitter, or substrate interactions with high-energy particles. Which of these is the most common is obviously very dependent on the operating environment.

Figure Ov.17 illustrates the last of these examples. It pictures the interactions between high-energy alpha particles and neutrons with the silicon lattice. The figure shows that when high-energy alpha particles pass through silicon, the alpha particle leaves an ionized trail, and the length of that ionized trail depends on the energy of the alpha particle. The figure also illustrates that when high-energy neutrons pass through silicon, some neutrons pass through without affecting operations of the semiconductor device, but some neutrons collide with nuclei in the silicon lattice. The atomic collision can result in the creation of multiple ionized trails as the secondary particles generated in the collision scatter in the silicon lattice. In the presence of an electric field, the ionized trails of

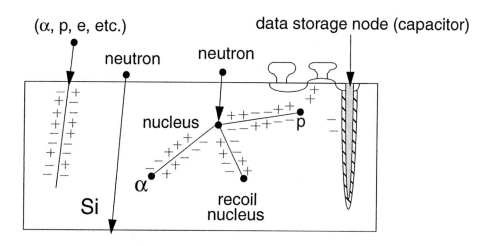

FIGURE Ov.17: Generation of electron-hole pairs in silicon by alpha particles and high-energy neutrons.

TABLE Ov.4   Cross-comparison of failure rates for SRAM, DRAM, and disk

Technology	Failure Rate[a] (SRAM & DRAM: at 0.13 μm)	Frequency of Multi-bit Errors (Relative to Single-bit Errors)	Expected Service Life
SRAM	100 per million device-hours		Several years
DRAM	1 per million device-hours	10–20%	Several years
Disk	1 per million device-hours		Several years

[a]Note that failure rate, i.e., a variation of mean-time-between-failures, says nothing about the expected performance of a single device. However, taken with the expected service life of a device, it can give a designer or administrator an idea of expected performance. If the service life of a device is 5 years, then the part will last about 5 years. A very large installation of those devices (e.g., in the case of disks or DRAMs, hundreds or more) will collectively see the expected failure rate: i.e., several hundred disks will collectively see several million device hours of operation before a single disk fails.

electron-hole pairs behave as temporary surges in current or as charges that can change the data values in storage cells. In addition, charge from the ionized trails of electron-hole pairs can impact the voltage level of bit lines as the value of the stored data is resolved by the sense amplifiers. The result is that the *soft error rate (SER)* of a memory-storage device depends on a combination of factors including the type, number, and energy distribution of the incident particles as well as the process technology design of the storage cells, design of the bit lines and sense

amplifiers, voltage level of the device, as well as the design of the logic circuits that control the movement of data in the DRAM device.

Table Ov.4 compares the failure rates for SRAM, DRAM, and disk. SRAM device error rates have historically tracked DRAM devices and did so up until the 180-nm process generation. The combination of reduced supply voltage and reduced critical cell charge means that SRAM SERs have climbed dramatically for the 180-nm and 130-nm process generations. In a recent publication, Monolithic System

Technology, Inc. (MoSys) claimed that for the 250-nm process generation, SRAM SERs were reported to be in the range of 100 failures per million device-hours per megabit, while SERs were reported to be in the range of 100,000 failures per megabit for the 130-nm process generation. The generalized trend is expected to continue to increase as the demand for low power dissipation forces a continued reduction in supply voltage and reduced critical charge per cell.

Solid-state memory devices (SRAMs and DRAMs) are typically protected by error detection codes and/or ECC. These are mechanisms wherein data redundancy is used to detect and/or recover from single- and even multi-bit errors. For instance, parity is a simple scheme that adds a bit to a protected word, indicating the number of even or odd bits in the word. If the read value of the word does not match the parity value, then the processor knows that the read value does not equal the value that was initially written, and an error has occurred. Error correction is achieved by encoding a word such that a bit error moves the resulting word some distance away from the original word (in the Hamming-distance sense) into an invalid encoding. The encoding space is chosen such that the new, invalid word is closest in the space to the original, valid word. Thus, the original word can always be derived from an invalid codeword, assuming a maximum number of bit errors.

Due to SRAM's extreme sensitivity to soft errors, modern processors now ship with parity and single-bit error correction for the SRAM caches. Typically, the tag arrays are protected by parity, whereas the data arrays are protected by single-bit error correction. More sophisticated multi-bit ECC algorithms are typically not deployed for on-chip SRAM caches in modern processors since the addition of sophisticated computation circuitry can add to the die size and cause significant delay relative to the timing demands of the on-chip caches. Moreover, caches store frequently accessed data, and in case an uncorrectable error is detected, a processor simply has to re-fetch the data from memory. In this sense, it can be considered unnecessary to detect and correct multi-bit errors, but sufficient to simply detect multi-bit errors. However, in the

physical design of modern SRAMs, often designers will intentionally place capacitors above the SRAM cell to improve SER.

Disk reliability is a more-researched area than data reliability in disks, because data stored in magnetic disks tends to be more resistant to transient errors than data stored in solid-state memories. In other words, whereas reliability in solid-state memories is largely concerned with correcting soft errors, reliability in hard disks is concerned with the fact that disks occasionally die, taking most or all of their data with them. Given that the disk drive performs the function of permanent store, its reliability is paramount, and, as Table Ov.4 shows, disks tend to last several years. This data is corroborated by a recent study from researchers at Google [Pinheiro et al. 2007]. The study tracks the behavior and environmental parameters of a fleet of over 100,000 disks for five years.

Reliability in the disk system is improved in much the same manner as ECC: data stored in the disk system is done so in a redundant fashion. RAID (redundant array of inexpensive disks) is a technique wherein encoded data is striped across multiple disks, so that even in the case of a disk's total failure the data will always be available.

Ov.3.4 Virtual Memory

Virtual memory is the mechanism by which the operating system provides executing software access to the memory system. In this regard, it is the primary consumer of the memory system: its procedures, data structures, and protocols dictate how the components of the memory system are used by all software that runs on the computer. It therefore behooves the reader to know what the virtual memory system does and how it does it. This section provides a brief overview of the mechanics of virtual memory. More detailed treatments of the topic can also be found on-line in articles by the author [Jacob & Mudge 1998a–c].

In general, programs today are written to run on no particular hardware configuration. They have no knowledge of the underlying memory system. Processes execute in imaginary address spaces that are mapped onto the memory system (including the DRAM system and disk system) by the operating system. Processes generate instruction fetches and loads and stores using imaginary or "virtual" names for their instructions and data. The ultimate home for the process's address space is nonvolatile *permanent store*, usually a disk drive; this is where the process's instructions and data come from and where all of its permanent changes go to. Every hardware memory structure between the CPU and the permanent store is a cache for the instructions and data in the process's address space. This includes main memory—main memory is really nothing more than a cache for a process's virtual address space. A cache operates on the prin-

ciple that a small, fast storage device can hold the most important data found on a larger, slower storage device, effectively making the slower device look fast. The large storage area in this case is the process address space, which can range from kilobytes to gigabytes or more in size. Everything in the address space initially comes from the program file stored on disk or is created on demand and defined to be zero. This is illustrated in Figure Ov.18.

Address Translation

Translating addresses from virtual space to physical space is depicted in Figure Ov.19. Addresses are mapped at the granularity of *pages*. Virtual memory is

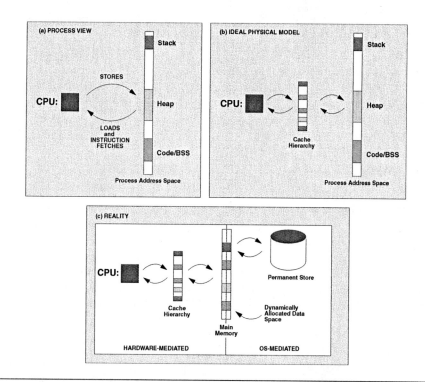

FIGURE Ov.18: Caching the process address space. In the first view, a process is shown referencing locations in its address space. Note that all loads, stores, and fetches use virtual names for objects. The second view illustrates that a process references locations in its address space indirectly through a hierarchy of caches. The third view shows that the address space is not a linear object stored on some device, but is instead scattered across hard drives and dynamically allocated when necessary.

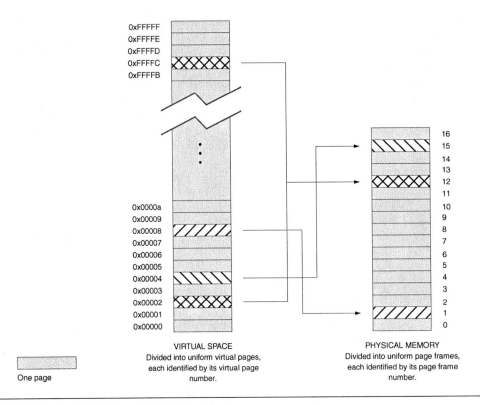

FIGURE Ov.19: Mapping virtual pages into physical page frames.

essentially a mapping of *virtual page numbers* (*VPNs*) to *page frame numbers* (*PFNs*). The mapping is a function, and any virtual page can have only one location. However, the inverse map is not necessarily a function. It is possible and sometimes advantageous to have several virtual pages mapped to the same page frame (to share memory between processes or threads or to allow different views of data with different protections, for example). This is depicted in Figure Ov.19 by mapping two virtual pages (0x00002 and 0xFFFFC) to PFN 12.

If DRAM is a cache, what is its organization? For example, an idealized *fully associative* cache (one in which any datum can reside at any location within the cache's data array) is pictured in Figure Ov.20. A data tag is fed into the cache. The first stage compares the input tag to the tag of every piece of data in the cache. The matching tag points to the data's location in the cache. However, DRAM is not physically built like a cache. For example, it has no inherent concept of a tags array: one merely tells memory what data location one wishes to read or write, and the datum at that location is read out or overwritten. There is no attempt to match the address against a tag to verify the contents of the data location. However, if main memory is to be an effective cache for the virtual address space, the tags mechanism must be implemented *somewhere*. There is clearly a myriad of possibilities, from special DRAM designs that include a hardware tag feature to software algorithms that make several memory references to look up one datum. Traditional virtual memory has the tags array implemented in software, and this software structure often holds more entries than there are entries in the data array (i.e., pages in main memory). The software structure is called a *page table;* it is a database of mapping information.

The page table performs the function of the tags array depicted in Figure Ov.20. For any given memory reference, it indicates where in main memory (corresponding to "data array" in the figure) that page can be found. There are many different possible organizations for page tables, most of which require only a few memory references to find the appropriate tag entry. However, requiring more than one memory reference for a page table lookup can be very costly, and so access to the page table is sped up by caching its entries in a special cache called the *transla-*

tion lookaside buffer (TLB) [Lee 1960], a hardware structure that typically has far fewer entries than there are pages in main memory. The TLB is a hardware cache which is usually implemented as a content addressable memory (CAM), also called a fully associative cache.

The TLB takes as input a VPN, possibly extended by an address-space identifier, and returns the corresponding PFN and protection information. This is illustrated in Figure Ov.21. The address-space identifier, if used, extends the virtual address to distinguish it from similar virtual addresses produced by other processes. For a load or store to complete successfully, the

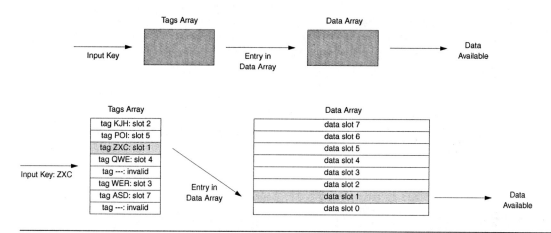

FIGURE Ov.20: An idealized cache lookup. A cache is comprised of two parts: the tag's array and the data array. In the example organization, the tags act as a database. They accept as input a key (an address) and output either the location of the item in the data array or an indication that the item is not in the data array.

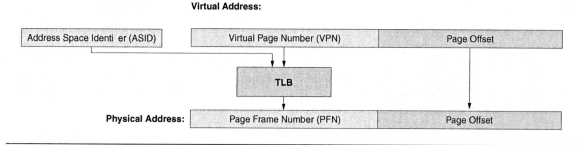

FIGURE Ov.21: Virtual-to-physical address translation using a TLB.

TLB must contain the mapping information for that virtual location. If it does not, a *TLB miss* occurs, and the system[9] must search the page table for the appropriate entry and place it into the TLB. If the system fails to find the mapping information in the page table, or if it finds the mapping but it indicates that the desired page is on disk, a *page fault* occurs. A page fault interrupts the OS, which must then retrieve the page from disk and place it into memory, create a new page if the page does not yet exist (as when a process allocates a new stack frame in virgin territory), or send the process an error signal if the access is to illegal space.

Shared Memory

Shared memory is a feature supported by virtual memory that causes many problems and gives rise to cache-management issues. It is a mechanism whereby two address spaces that are normally protected from each other are allowed to intersect at points, still retaining protection over the non-intersecting regions. Several processes sharing portions of their address spaces are pictured in Figure Ov.22. The shared memory mechanism only opens up a pre-defined portion of a process's address space; the rest of the address space is still protected, and even the shared portion is only unprotected for those processes sharing the memory. For instance, in Figure Ov.22, the region of A's address space that is shared with process B is unprotected from whatever actions B might want to take, but it is safe from the actions of any other processes. It is therefore useful as a simple, secure means for inter-process communication. Shared memory also reduces requirements for physical memory, as when the text regions of processes are shared whenever multiple instances of a single program are run or when multiple instances of a common library are used in different programs.

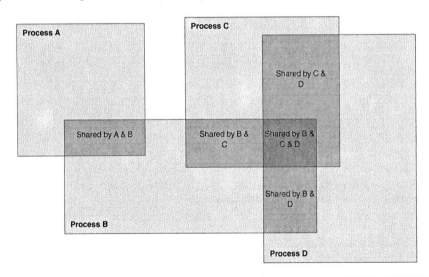

FIGURE Ov.22: Shared memory. Shared memory allows processes to overlap portions of their address space while retaining protection for the nonintersecting regions. This is a simple and effective method for inter-process communication. Pictured are four process address spaces that have overlapped. The darker regions are shared by more than one process, while the lightest regions are still protected from other processes.

---

[9]In the discussions, we will use the generic term "system" when the acting agent is implementation-dependent and can refer to either a hardware state machine or the operating system. For example, in some implementations, the page table search immediately following a TLB miss is performed by the operating system (MIPS, Alpha); in other implementations, it is performed by the hardware (PowerPC, x86).

The mechanism works by ensuring that shared pages map to the same physical page. This can be done by simply placing the same PFN in the page tables of two processes sharing a page. An example is shown in Figure Ov.23. Here, two very small address spaces are shown overlapping at several places, and one address space overlaps with itself; two of its virtual pages map to the same physical page. This is not just a contrived example. Many operating systems allow this, and it is useful, for example, in the implementation of user-level threads.

Some Commercial Examples

A few examples of what has been done in industry can help to illustrate some of the issues involved.

MIPS Page Table Design MIPS [Heinrich 1995, Kane & Heinrich 1992] eliminated the page table-walking hardware found in traditional memory management units and, in doing so, demonstrated that software can table-walk with reasonable efficiency. It also presented a simple hierarchical page table design, shown in Figure Ov.24. On a TLB miss, the VPN of the

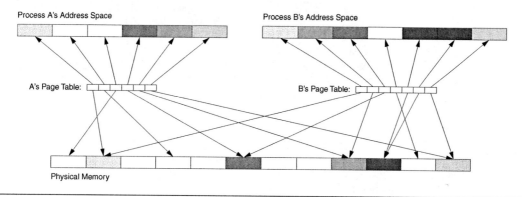

FIGURE Ov.23: An example of shared memory. Two process address spaces—one comprised of six virtual pages and the other of seven virtual pages—are shown sharing several pages. Their page tables maintain information on where virtual pages are located in physical memory. The darkened pages are mapped to several locations; note that the darkest page is mapped at two locations in the same address space.

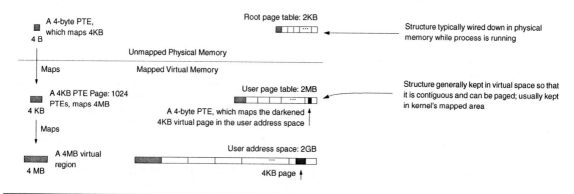

FIGURE Ov.24: The MIPS 32-bit hierarchical page table. MIPS hardware provides support for a 2-MB linear virtual page table that maps the 2-GB user address space by constructing a virtual address from a faulting virtual address that indexes the mapping PTE (page-table entry) in the user page table. This 2-MB page table can easily be mapped by a 2-KB user root page table.

address that missed the TLB is used as an index into the user page table, which is accessed using a virtual address. The architecture provides hardware support for this activity, storing the virtual address of the base of the user-level page table in a hardware register and forming the concatenation of the base address with the VPN. This is illustrated in Figure Ov.25. On a TLB miss, the hardware creates a virtual address for the mapping PTE in the user page table, which must be aligned on a 2-MB virtual boundary for the hardware's lookup address to work. The base pointer, called *PTEBase*, is stored in a hardware register and is usually changed on context switch.

PowerPC Segmented Translation   The IBM 801 introduced a segmented design that persisted through the POWER and PowerPC architectures [Chang & Mergen 1988, IBM & Motorola 1993, May et al. 1994, Weiss & Smith 1994]. It is illustrated in Figure Ov.26. Applications generate 32-bit "effective" addresses that are mapped onto a larger "virtual" address space at the granularity of *segments*, 256-MB virtual regions. Sixteen segments comprise an application's address space. The top four bits of the effective address select a segment identifier from a set of 16 registers. This segment ID is concatenated with the bottom 28 bits of the effective address to form an extended virtual address. This extended address is used in the TLB and page table. The operating system performs data movement and relocation at the granularity of pages, not segments.

The architecture does not use explicit address-space identifiers; the segment registers ensure address space protection. If two processes duplicate an identifier in their segment registers, they share that virtual segment by definition. Similarly, protection is guaranteed if identifiers are *not* duplicated. If memory is shared through global addresses, the TLB and cache need not be flushed on context switch[10] because the system behaves like a single address space operating system. For more details, see Chapter 31, Section 31.1.7, *Perspective: Segmented Addressing Solves the Synonym Problem.*

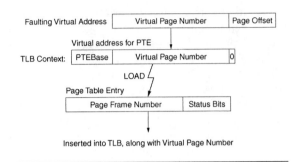

FIGURE Ov.25: The use of the MIPS TLB context register. The VPN of the faulting virtual address is placed into the context register, creating the virtual address of the mapping PTE. This PTE goes directly into the TLB.

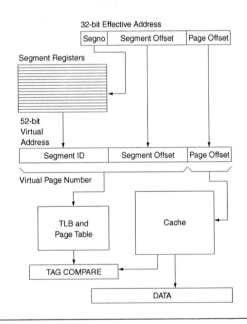

FIGURE Ov.26: PowerPC segmented address translation. Processes generate 32-bit effective addresses that are mapped onto a 52-bit address space via 16 segment registers, using the top 4 bits of the effective address as an index. It is this extended virtual address that is mapped by the TLB and page table. The segments provide address space protection and can be used for shared memory.

---

[10]Flushing is avoided until the system runs out of identifiers and must reuse them. For example, the address-space identifiers on the MIPS R3000 and Alpha 21064 are six bits wide, with a maximum of 64 active processes [Digital 1994, Kane & Heinrich 1992]. If more processes are desired, identifiers must be constantly reassigned, requiring TLB and virtual-cache flushes.

Ov.4 An Example Holistic Analysis

Disk I/O accounts for a substantial fraction of an application's execution time and power dissipation. A new DRAM technology called *Fully Buffered DIMM* (*FB-DIMM*) has been in development in the industry [Vogt 2004a, b, Haas & Vogt 2005], and, though it provides storage scalability significantly beyond the current DDRx architecture, FB-DIMM has met with some resistance due to its high power dissipation. Our modeling results show that the energy consumed in a moderate-size FB-DIMM system is indeed quite large, and it can easily approach the energy consumed by a disk.

This analysis looks at a trade-off between storage in the DRAM system and in the disk system, focusing on the disk-side write buffer; if configured and managed correctly, the write buffer enables a system to approach the performance of a large DRAM installation at half the energy. Disk-side caches and write buffers have been proposed and studied, but their effect upon total system behavior has not been studied. We present the impact on total system execution time, CPI, and memory-system power, including the effects of the operating system. Using a full-system, execution-based simulator that combines Bochs, Wattch, CACTI, DRAMsim, and DiskSim and boots the RedHat Linux 6.0 kernel, we have investigated the memory-system behavior of the SPEC CPU2000 applications. We study the disk-side cache in both single-disk and RAID-5 organizations. Cache parameters include size, organization, whether the cache supports write caching or not, and whether it prefetches read blocks or not. Our results are given in terms of L1/L2 cache accesses, power dissipation, and energy consumption; DRAM-system accesses, power dissipation, and energy consumption; disk-system accesses, power dissipation, and energy consumption; and execution time of the application plus operating system, in seconds. The results are not from sampling, but rather from a simulator that calculates these values on a cycle-by-cycle basis over the entire execution of the application.

Ov.4.1 Fully-Buffered DIMM vs. the Disk Cache

It is common knowledge that disk I/O is expensive in both power dissipated and time spent waiting on it. What is less well known is the system-wide breakdown of disk power versus cache power versus DRAM power, especially in light of the newest DRAM architecture adopted by industry, the FB-DIMM. This new DRAM standard replaces the conventional memory bus with a narrow, high-speed interface between the memory controller and the DIMMs. It has been shown to provide performance similar to that of DDRx systems, and thus, it represents a relatively low-overhead mechanism (in terms of execution time) for scaling DRAM-system capacity. FB-DIMM's latency degradation is not severe. It provides a noticeable bandwidth improvement, and it is relatively insensitive to scheduling policies [Ganesh et al. 2007].

FB-DIMM was designed to solve the problem of storage scalability in the DRAM system, and it provides scalability well beyond the current JEDEC-style DDRx architecture, which supports at most two to four DIMMs in a fully populated dual-channel system (DDR2 supports up to two DIMMs per channel; proposals for DDR3 include limiting a channel to a single DIMM). The daisy-chained architecture of FB-DIMM supports up to eight DIMMs per channel, and its narrow bus requires roughly one-third the pins of a DDRx SDRAM system. Thus, an FB-DIMM system supports an order of magnitude more DIMMs than DDRx. This scalability comes at a cost, however. The DIMM itself dissipates almost an order of magnitude more power than a traditional DDRx DIMM. Couple this with an order-of-magnitude increase in DIMMs per system, and one faces a serious problem.

To give an idea of the problem, Figure Ov.27 shows the simulation results of an entire execution of the *gzip* benchmark from SPEC CPU2000 on a complete-system simulator. The memory system is only moderate in size: one channel and four DIMMs, totalling a half-gigabyte. The graphs demonstrate numerous important issues, but in this book we are concerned with two items in particular:

- Program initialization is lengthy and represents a significant portion of an application's run time. As the CPI graph shows, the first two-thirds of execution time are spent dealing with the disk, and the corresponding CPI (both average and instantaneous) ranges from the 100s to the 1000s. After this initialization phase, the application settles into a

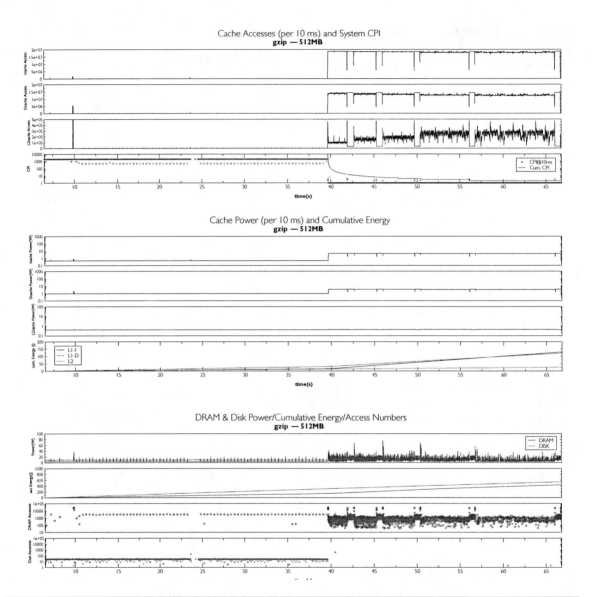

FIGURE Ov.27: Full execution of Gzip. The figure shows the entire run of gzip. System configuration is a 2-GHz Pentium processor with 512 MB of DDR2-533 FB-DIMM main memory and a 12k-RPM disk drive with built-in disk cache. The figure shows the interaction between all components of the memory system, including the L1 instruction and data caches, the unified L2 cache, the DRAM system, and the disk drive. All graphs use the same x-axis, which represents execution time in seconds. The x-axis does not start at zero; the measurements exclude system boot time, invocation of the shell, etc. Each data point represents aggregated (not sampled) activity within a 10-ms epoch. The CPI graph shows two system CPI values: one is the average CPI for each 10-ms epoch, and the other is the cumulative average CPI. A duration with no CPI data point indicates that no instructions were executed due to I/O latency. During such a window the CPI is essentially infinite, and thus, it is possible for the cumulative average to range higher than the displayed instantaneous CPI. Note that the CPI, the DRAM accesses, and the disk accesses are plotted on log scales.

more compute-intensive phase in which the CPI asymptotes down to the theoretical sustainable performance, the single-digit values that architecture research typically reports.

- By the end of execution, the total energy consumed in the FB-DIMM DRAM system (a half a kilojoule) almost equals that of the energy consumed by the disk, and it is twice that of the L1 data cache, L1 instruction cache, and unified L2 cache combined.

Currently, there is substantial work happening in both industry and academia to address the latter issue, with much of the work focusing on access scheduling, architecture improvements, and data migration. To complement this work, we look at a wide range of organizational approaches, i.e., attacking the problem from a parameter point of view rather than a system-redesign, component-redesign, or new-proposed-mechanism point of view, and find significant synergy between the disk cache and the memory system. Choices in the disk-side cache affect both system-level performance and system-level (in particular, DRAM-subsystem-level) energy consumption. Though disk-side caches have been proposed and studied, their effect upon the total system behavior, namely execution time or CPI or total memory-system power including the effects of the operating system, is as yet unreported. For example, Zhu and Hu [2002] evaluate disk built-in cache using both real and synthetic workloads and report the results in terms of average response time. Smith [1985a and b] evaluates a disk cache mechanism with real traces collected in real IBM mainframes on a disk cache simulator and reports the results in terms of miss rate. Huh and Chang [2003] evaluate their RAID controller cache organization with a synthetic trace. Varma and Jacobson [1998] and Solworth and Orji [1990] evaluate destaging algorithms and write caches, respectively, with synthetic workloads. This study represents the first time that the effects of the disk-side cache can be viewed at a system level (considering both application and operating-system effects) and compared directly to all the other components of the memory system.

We use a full-system, execution-based simulator combining Bochs [Bochs 2006], Wattch [Brooks et al. 2000], CACTI [Wilton & Jouppi 1994], DRAMsim [Wang et al. 2005, September], and DiskSim [Ganger et al. 2006]. It boots the RedHat Linux 6.0 kernel and therefore can capture all application behavior, and all operating-system behavior, including I/O activity, disk-block buffering, system-call overhead, and virtual memory overhead such as translation, table walking, and page swapping. We investigate the disk-side cache in both single-disk and RAID-5 organizations. Cache parameters include size, organization, whether the cache supports write caching or not, and whether it prefetches read blocks or not. Additional parameters include disk rotational speed and DRAM-system capacity.

We find a complex trade-off between the disk cache, the DRAM system, and disk parameters like rotational speed. The disk cache, particularly its write-buffering feature, represents a very powerful tool enabling significant savings in both energy and execution time. This is important because, though the cache's support for write buffering is often enabled in desktop operating systems (e.g., Windows and some but not all flavors of Unix/Linux [Ng 2006]), it is typically disabled in enterprise computing applications [Ng 2006], and these are the applications most likely to use FB-DIMMs [Haas & Vogt 2005]. We find substantial improvement between existing implementations and an ideal write buffer (i.e., this is a limit study). In particular, the disk cache's write-buffering ability can offset the total energy consumption of the memory system (including caches, DRAMs, and disks) by nearly a factor of two, while sacrificing a small amount of performance.

Ov.4.2 Fully Buffered DIMM: Basics

The relation between a traditional organization and a FB-DIMM organization is shown in Figure Ov.28, which motivates the design in terms of a graphics-card organization. The first two drawings show a multi-drop DRAM bus next to a DRAM bus organization typical of graphics cards, which use point-to-point soldered connections between the DRAM and memory controller to achieve higher speeds. This arrangement is used in FB-DIMM.

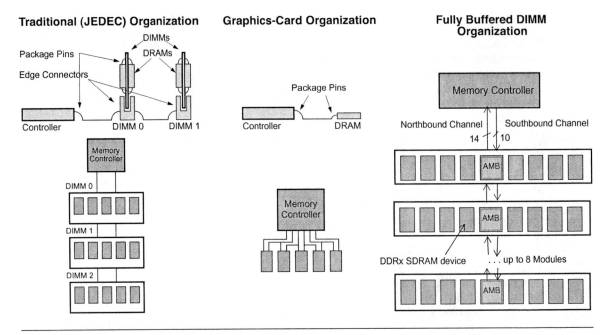

Traditional (JEDEC) Organization **Graphics-Card Organization** **Fully Buffered DIMM Organization**

FIGURE Ov.28: FB-DIMM and its motivation. The first two pictures compare the memory organizations of a JEDEC SDRAM system and a graphics card. Above each design is its side-profile, indicating potential impedance mismatches (sources of reflections). The organization on the far right shows how the FB-DIMM takes the graphics-card organization as its *de facto* DIMM. In the FB-DIMM organization, there are no multi-drop busses; DIMM-to-DIMM connections are point to point. The memory controller is connected to the nearest AMB via two unidirectional links. The AMB is, in turn, connected to its southern neighbor via the same two links.

A slave memory controller has been added onto each DIMM, and all connections in the system are point to point. A narrow, high-speed channel connects the master memory controller to the DIMM-level memory controllers (called *Advanced Memory Buffers* or AMBs). Since each DIMM-to-DIMM connection is a point-to-point connection, a channel becomes a *de facto* multi-hop store and forward network. The FB-DIMM architecture limits the channel length to eight DIMMs, and the narrower inter-module bus requires roughly one-third as many pins as a traditional organization. As a result, an FB-DIMM organization can handle roughly 24 times the storage capacity of a single-DIMM DDR3-based system, without sacrificing any bandwidth and even leaving headroom for increased intra-module bandwidth.

The AMB acts like a pass-through switch, directly forwarding the requests it receives from the controller

to successive DIMMs and forwarding frames from southerly DIMMs to northerly DIMMs or the memory controller. All frames are processed to determine whether the data and commands are for the local DIMM. The FB-DIMM system uses a serial packet-based protocol to communicate between the memory controller and the DIMMs. Frames may contain data and/or commands. Commands include DRAM commands such as row activate (RAS), column read (CAS), refresh (REF) and so on, as well as channel commands such as write to configuration registers, synchronization commands, etc. Frame scheduling is performed exclusively by the memory controller. The AMB only converts the serial protocol to DDRx-based commands without implementing any scheduling functionality.

The AMB is connected to the memory controller and/or adjacent DIMMs via unidirectional links: the southbound channel which transmits both data and commands and the northbound channel which transmits data and status information. The southbound and northbound datapaths are 10 bits and 14 bits wide, respectively. The FB-DIMM channel clock operates at six times the speed of the DIMM clock; i.e., the link speed is 4 Gbps for a 667-Mbps DDRx system. Frames on the north- and southbound channel require 12 transfers (6 FB-DIMM channel clock cycles) for transmission. This 6:1 ratio ensures that the FB-DIMM frame rate matches the DRAM command clock rate.

Southbound frames comprise both data and commands and are 120 bits long; northbound frames are data only and are 168 bits long. In addition to the data and command information, the frames also carry header information and a frame CRC (cyclic redundancy check) checksum that is used to check for transmission errors. A northbound read-data frame transports 18 bytes of data in 6 FB-DIMM clocks or 1 DIMM clock. A DDRx system can burst back the same amount of data to the memory controller in two successive beats lasting an entire DRAM clock cycle. Thus, the read bandwidth of an FB-DIMM system is the same as that of a single channel of a DDRx system. Due to the narrower southbound channel, the write bandwidth in FB-DIMM systems is one-half that available in a DDRx system. However, this makes the *total* bandwidth available in an FB-DIMM system 1.5 times that of a DDRx system.

Figure Ov.29 shows the processing of a read transaction in an FB-DIMM system. Initially, a command frame is used to transmit a command that will perform row activation. The AMB translates the request and relays it to the DIMM. The memory controller schedules the CAS command in a following frame. The AMB relays the CAS command to the DRAM devices which burst the data back to the AMB. The AMB bundles two consecutive bursts of data into a single northbound frame and transmits it to the memory controller. In this example, we assume a burst length of four corresponding to two FB-DIMM data frames. Note that although the figures do not identify parameters like t_CAS, t_RCD, and t_CWD, the memory controller must ensure that these constraints are met.

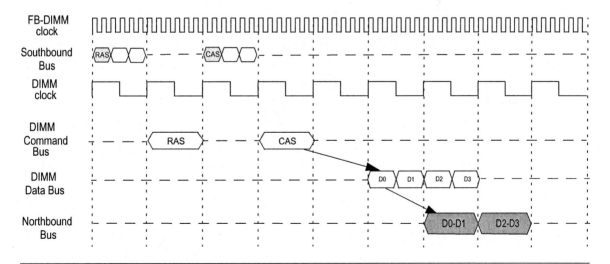

FIGURE Ov.29: Read transaction in an FB-DIMM system. The figure shows how a read transaction is performed in an FB-DIMM system. The FB-DIMM serial busses are clocked at six times the DIMM busses. Each FB-DIMM frame on the southbound bus takes six FB-DIMM clock periods to transmit. On the northbound bus a frame comprises two DDRx data bursts.

The primary dissipater of power in an FB-DIMM channel is the AMB, and its power depends on its position within the channel. The AMB nearest to the memory controller must handle its own traffic and repeat all packets to and from all downstream AMBs, and this dissipates the most power. The AMB in DDR2-533 FB-DIMM dissipates 6 W, and it is currently 10 W for 800 Mbps DDR2 [Staktek 2006]. Even if one averages out the activity on the AMB in a long channel, the eight AMBs in a single 800-Mbps channel can easily dissipate 50 W. Note that this number is for the AMBs only; it does not include power dissipated by the DRAM devices.

Ov.4.3 Disk Caches: Basics

Today's disk drives all come with a built-in cache as part of the drive controller electronics, ranging in size from 512 KB for the micro-drive to 16 MB for the largest server drives. Figure Ov.30 shows the cache and its place within a system. The earliest drives had no cache memory, as they had little control electronics. As the control of data transfer migrated from the host-side control logic to the drive's own controller, a small amount of memory was needed to act as a speed-matching buffer, because the disk's media data rate is different from that of the interface. Buffering is also needed because when the head is at a position ready to do data transfer, the host or the interface may be busy and not ready to receive read data. DRAM is usually used as this buffer memory.

In a system, the host typically has some memory dedicated for caching disk data, and if a drive is attached to the host via some external controller, that controller also typically has a cache. Both the system cache and the external cache are much larger than the disk drive's internal cache. Hence, for most workloads, the drive's cache is not likely to see too many reuse cache hits. However, the disk-side cache is very effective in opportunistically prefetching data, as only the controller inside the drive knows the state the drive is in and when and how it can prefetch without adding any cost in time. Finally, the drive needs cache memory if it is to support write caching/buffering.

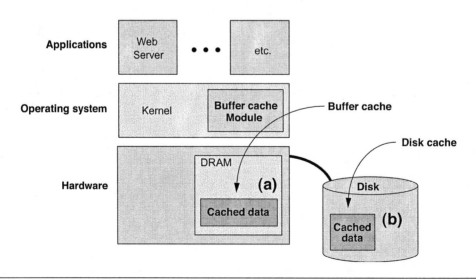

FIGURE Ov.30: Buffer caches and disk caches. Disk blocks are cached in several places, including (a) the operating system's *buffer cache* in main memory and (b), on the disk, in another DRAM buffer, called a *disk cache*.

With write caching, the drive controller services a write request by transferring the write data from the host to the drive's cache memory and then reports back to the host that the write is "done," even though the data has not yet been written to the disk media (data not yet written out to disk is referred to as *dirty*). Thus, the service time for a cached write is about the same as that for a read cache hit, involving only some drive controller overhead and electronic data transfer time but no mechanical time. Clearly, write caching does not need to depend on having the right content in the cache memory for it to work, unlike read caching. Write caching will always work, i.e., a write command will always be a cache hit, as long as there is available space in the cache memory. When the cache becomes full, some or all of the dirty data are written out to the disk media to free up space. This process is commonly referred to as *destage*.

Ideally, destage should be done while the drive is idle so that it does not affect the servicing of read requests. However, this may not be always possible. The drive may be operating in a high-usage system with little idle time ever, or the writes often arrive in bursts which quickly fill up the limited memory space of the cache. When destage must take place while the drive is busy, such activity adds to the load of drive at that time, and a user will notice a longer response time for his requests. Instead of providing the full benefit of cache hits, write caching in this case merely delays the disk writes.

Zhu and Hu [2002] have suggested that large disk built-in caches will not significantly benefit the overall system performance because all modern operating systems already use large file system caches to cache reads and writes. As suggested by Przybylski [1990], the reference stream missing a first-level cache and being handled by a second-level cache tends to exhibit relatively low locality. In a real system, the reference stream to the disk system has missed the operating system's buffer cache, and the locality in the stream tends to be low. Thus, our simulation captures all of this activity. In our experiments, we investigate the disk cache, including the full effects of the operating system's file-system caching.

Ov.4.4 Experimental Results

Figure Ov.27 showed the execution of the GZIP benchmark with a moderate-sized FB-DIMM DRAM system: half a gigabyte of storage. At 512 MB, there is no page swapping for this application. When the storage size is cut in half to 256 MB, page swapping begins but does not affect the execution time significantly. When the storage size is cut to one-quarter of its original size (128 MB), the page swapping is significant enough to slow the application down by an order of magnitude. This represents the hard type of decision that a memory-systems designer would have to face: if one can reduce power dissipation by cutting the amount of storage and feel negligible impact on performance, then one has too much storage to begin with.

Figure Ov.31 shows the behavior of the system when storage is cut to 128 MB. Note that all aspects of system behavior have degraded; execution time is longer, *and* the system consumes more energy. Though the DRAM system's energy has decreased from 440 J to just under 410 J, the execution time has increased from 67 to 170 seconds, the total cache energy has increased from 275 to 450 J, the disk energy has increased from 540 to 1635 J, and the total energy has doubled from 1260 to 2515 J. This is the result of swapping activity—not enough to bring the system to its knees, but enough to be relatively painful.

We noticed that there exists in the disk subsystem the same sort of activity observed in a microprocessor's load/store queue: reads are often stalled waiting for writes to finish, despite the fact that the disk has a 4-MB read/write cache on board. The disk's cache is typically organized to prioritize prefetch activity over write activity because this tends to give the best performance results and because the write buffering is often disabled by the operating system. The solution to the write-stall problem in microprocessors has been to use write buffers; we therefore modified DiskSim to implement an ideal write buffer on the disk side that would not interfere with the disk cache. Figure Ov.32 indicates that the size of the cache seems to make little difference to the behavior of the system. The important thing is that a cache is present. Thus, we should not expect read performance to suddenly increase as a result of moving writes into a separate write buffer.

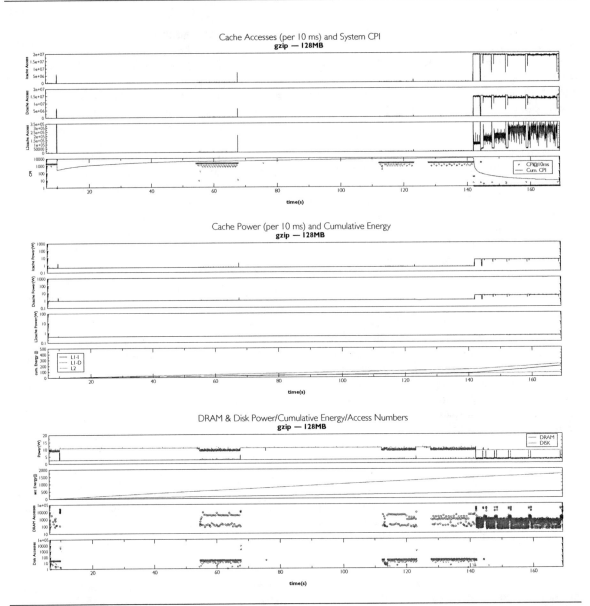

FIGURE Ov.31: Full execution of GZIP, 128 MB DRAM. The figure shows the entire run of GZIP. System configuration is a 2 GHz Pentium processor with 128 MB of FB-DIMM main memory and a 12 K-RPM disk drive with built-in disk cache. The figure shows the interaction between all components of the memory system, including the L1 instruction cache, the L1 data cache, the unified L2 cache, the DRAM system, and the disk drive. All graphs use the same x-axis, which represents the execution time in seconds. The x-axis does not start at zero; the measurements exclude system boot time, invocation of the shell, etc. Each data point represents aggregated (not sampled) activity within a 10-ms epoch. The CPI graph shows 2 system CPI values: one is the average CPI for each 10-ms epoch, the other is the cumulative average CPI. A duration with no CPI data point indicates that no instructions were executed due to I/O latency. The application is run in single-user mode, as is common for SPEC measurements; therefore, disk delay shows up as stall time. Note that the CPI, the DRAM accesses, and the Disk accesses are plotted on log scales.

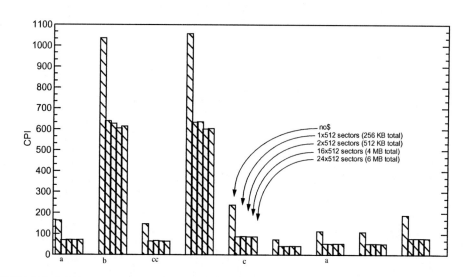

FIGURE Ov.32: The effects of disk cache size by varying the number of segments. The figure shows the effects of a different number of segments with the same segment size in the disk cache. The system configuration is 128 MB of DDR SDRAM with a 12k-RPM disk. There are five bars for each benchmark, which are (1) no cache, (2) 1 segment of 512 sectors each, (3) 2 segments of 512 sectors each, (4) 16 segment of 512 sectors each, and (5) 24 segment of 512 sectors each. Note that the CPI values are for the disk-intensive portion of application execution, not the CPU-intensive portion of application execution (which could otherwise blur distinctions).

Figure Ov.33 shows the behavior of the system with 128 MB and an ideal write buffer. As mentioned, the performance increase and energy decrease is due to the writes being buffered, allowing read requests to progress. Execution time is 75 seconds (compared to 67 seconds for a 512 MB system); and total energy is 1100 J (compared to 1260 J for a 512-MB system). For comparison, to show the effect of faster read and write throughput, Figure Ov.34 shows the behavior of the system with 128 MB and an 8-disk RAID-5 system. Execution time is 115 seconds, and energy consumption is 8.5 KJ. This achieves part of the performance effect as write buffering by improving write time, thereby freeing up read bandwidth sooner. However, the benefit comes at a significant cost in energy.

Table Ov.5 gives breakdowns for **gzip** in tabular form, and the graphs beneath the table give the breakdowns for **gzip**, **bzip2**, and **ammp** in graphical form and for a wider range of parameters (different disk RPMs). The applications all demonstrate the same trends: to cut down the energy of a 512-MB system by reducing the memory to 128 MB which

causes both the performance and the energy to get worse. Performance degrades by a factor of 5–10; energy increases by 1.5× to 10×. Ideal write buffering can give the best of both worlds (performance of a large memory system and energy consumption of a small memory system), and its benefit is independent of the disk's RPM. Using a RAID system does not gain significant performance improvement, but it consumes energy proportionally to the number of disks. Note, however, that this is a uniprocessor model running in single-user mode, so RAID is not expected to shine.

Figure Ov.35 shows the effects of disk caching and prefetching on both single-disk and RAID systems. In RAID systems, disk caching has only marginal effects to both the CPI and the disk average response time. However, disk caching with prefetching has significant benefits. In a slow disk system (i.e., 5400 RPM), RAID has more tangible benefits over a non-RAID system. Nevertheless, the combination of using RAID, disk cache, and fast disks can improve the overall performance up to a factor of 10. For the

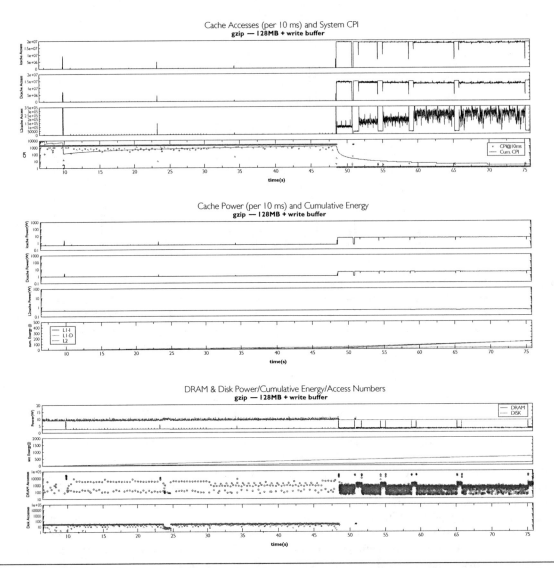

FIGURE Ov.33: Full execution of GZIP, 128 MB DRAM and ideal write buffer. The figure shows the entire run of GZIP. System configuration is a 2 GHz Pentium processor with 128 MB of FB-DIMM main memory and a 12 K-RPM disk drive with built-in disk cache. The figure shows the interaction between all components of the memory system, including the L1 instruction cache, the L1 data cache, the unified L2 cache, the DRAM system, and the disk drive. All graphs use the same x-axis, which represents the execution time in seconds. The x-axis does not start at zero; the measurements exclude system boot time, invocation of the shell, etc. Each data point represents aggregated (not sampled) activity within a 10-ms epoch. The CPI graph shows two system CPI values: one is the average CPI for each 10-ms epoch, the other is the cumulative average CPI. A duration with no CPI data point indicates that no instructions were executed due to I/O latency. The application is run in single-user mode, as is common for SPEC measurements; therefore, disk delay shows up as stall time. Note that the CPI, the DRAM accesses, and the Disk accesses are plotted on log scales.

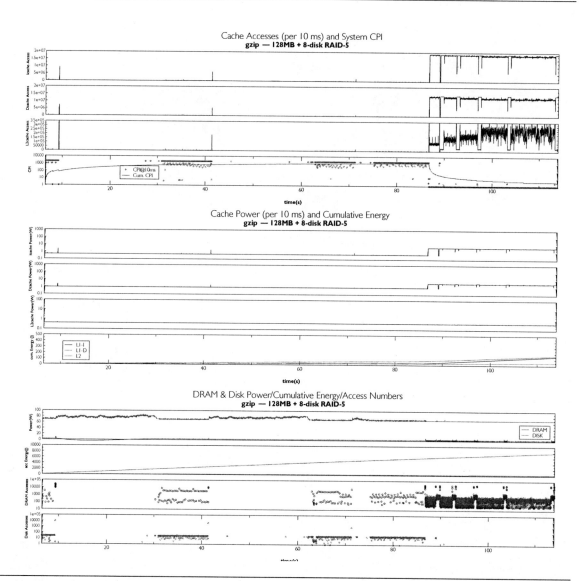

FIGURE Ov.34: Full execution of GZIP, 128 MB DRAM and RAID-5 disk system. The figure shows the entire run of GZIP. System configuration is a 2 GHz Pentium processor with 128 MB of FB-DIMM main memory and a RAID-5 system of eight 12-K-RPM disk drives with built-in disk cache. The figure shows the interaction between all components of the memory system, including the L1 instruction cache, the L1 data cache, the unified L2 cache, the DRAM system, and the disk drive. All graphs use the same x-axis, which represents the execution time in seconds. The x-axis does not start at zero; the measurements exclude system boot time, invocation of the shell, etc. Each data point represents aggregated (not sampled) activity within a 10-ms epoch. The CPI graph shows two system CPI values: one is the average CPI for each 10-ms epoch, the other is the cumulative average CPI. A duration with no CPI data point indicates that no instructions were executed due to I/O latency. The application is run in single-user mode, as is common for SPEC measurements; therefore, disk delay shows up as stall time. Note that the CPI, the DRAM accesses, and the Disk accesses are plotted on log scales.

TABLE Ov.5   Execution time and energy breakdowns for GZIP and BZIP2

System Configuration (DRAM Size - Disk RPM - Option)	Ex. Time (sec)	L1-I Energy (J)	L1-D Energy (J)	L2 Energy (J)	DRAM Energy (J)	Disk Energy (J)	Total Energy (J)
GZIP							
512 MB–12 K	66.8	129.4	122.1	25.4	440.8	544.1	1261.8
128 MB–12 K	169.3	176.5	216.4	67.7	419.6	1635.4	2515.6
128 MB–12 K-WB	75.8	133.4	130.2	28.7	179.9	622.5	1094.7
128 MB–12 K-RAID	113.9	151	165.5	44.8	277.8	7830	8469.1

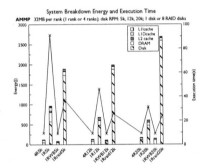
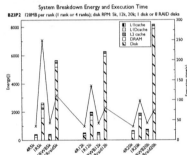
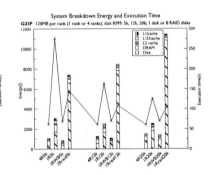

average response time, even though the write response time in a RAID system is much higher than the write response time in a single-disk system, this trend does not translate directly into the overall performance. The write response time in a RAID system is higher due to parity calculations, especially the benchmarks with small writes. Despite the improvement in performance, care must be taken in applying RAID because RAID increases the energy proportionally to the number of the disks.

Perhaps the most interesting result in Figure Ov.35 is that the CPI values (top graph) track the disk's *average read* response time (bottom graph) and not the disk's *average response time* (which includes both reads and writes, also bottom graph). This observation holds true for both read-dominated applications and applications with significant write activity (as are **gzip** and **bzip2**). The reason this is interesting is that the disk community tends to report performance numbers in terms of average response time and not average *read* response

time, presumably believing the former to be a better indicator of system-level performance than the latter. Our results suggest that the disk community would be better served by continuing to model the effects of write traffic (as it affects read latency) by reporting performance as the average *read* response time.

Ov.4.5   Conclusions

We find that the disk cache can be an effective tool for improving performance at the system level. There is a significant interplay between the DRAM system and the disk's ability to buffer writes and prefetch reads. An ideal write buffer homed within the disk has the potential to move write traffic out of the way and begin working on read requests far sooner, with the result that a system can be made to perform nearly as well as one with four times the amount of main memory, but with roughly half the energy consumption of the configuration with more main memory.

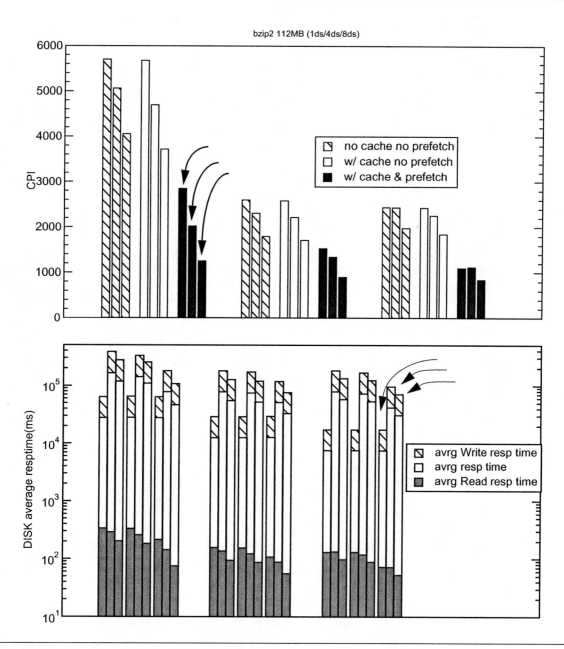

FIGURE Ov.35: The effects of disk prefetching. The experiment tries to identify the effects of prefetching and caching in the disk cache. The configuration is 112 MB of DDR SDRAM running bzip2. The three bars in each group represent a single-disk system, 4-disk RAID-5 system, and 8-disk RAID-5 system. The figure above shows the CPI of each configuration, and the figure below shows the average response time of the disk requests. Note that the CPI axis is in linear scale, but the disk average response time axis is in log scale. The height of the each bar in the average response time graph is the absolute value.

This is extremely important, because FB-DIMM systems are likely to have significant power-dissipation problems, and because of this they will run at the cutting edge of the storage-performance trade-off. Administrators will configure these systems to use the least amount of storage available to achieve the desired performance, and thus a simple reduction in FB-DIMM storage will result in an unacceptable hit to performance. We have shown that an ideal write buffer in the disk system will solve this problem, transparently to the operating system.

Ov.5 What to Expect

What are the more important architecture-level issues in store for these technologies? On what problems should a designer concentrate?

For caches and SRAMs in particular, power dissipation and reliability are primary issues. A rule of thumb is that SRAMs typically account for at least one-third of the power dissipated by microprocessors, and the reliability for SRAM is the worst of the three technologies.

For DRAMs, power dissipation is becoming an issue with the high I/O speeds expected of future systems. The FB-DIMM, the only proposed architecture seriously being considered for adoption that would solve the capacity-scaling problem facing DRAM systems, dissipates roughly two orders of magnitude more power than a traditional organization (due to an order of magnitude higher per DIMM power dissipation and the ability to put an order of magnitude more DIMMs into a system).

For disks, miniaturization and development of heuristics for control are the primary consider-

ations, but a related issue is the reduction of power dissipation in the drive's electronics and mechanisms. Another point is that some time this year, the industry will be seeing the first generation of hybrid disk drives: those with flash memory to do write caching. Initially, hybrid drives will be available only for mobile applications. One reason for a hybrid drive is to be able to have a disk drive in spin-down mode longer (no need to spin up to do a write). This will save more power and make the battery of a laptop last longer.

For memory systems as a whole, a primary issue is optimization in the face of subsytems that have unanticipated interactions in their design parameters.

From this book, a reader should expect to learn the details of operation and tools of analysis that are necessary for understanding the intricacies and optimizing the behavior of modern memory systems. The designer should expect of the future a memory-system design space that will become increasingly difficult to analyze simply and in which alternative figures of merit (e.g., energy consumption, cost, reliability) will become increasingly important. Future designers of memory systems will have to perform design-space explorations that consider the effects of design parameters in all subsystems of the memory hierarchy, and they will have to consider multiple dimensions of design criteria (e.g., performance, energy consumption, cost, reliability, and real-time behavior).

In short, a holistic approach to design that considers the whole hierarchy is warranted, but this is very hard to do. Among other things, it requires in-depth understanding at all the levels of the hierarchy. It is our goal that this book will enable just such an approach.

PART I

Cache

So, we can never reach a Final Understanding of anything because it will change as we develop understanding. If we did reach a Final Understanding, simultaneously the "subject" would have changed, rendering our understanding as past tense ... .

— Robert Fripp

CHAPTER 1

An Overview of Cache Principles

A cache (also called "look-aside" [Bloom et al. 1962] or "slave memory" [Wilkes 1965]) can speed up accesses to all manners of storage devices, including tape drives, disk drives, main memory, servers on the network (e.g., web servers are a type of storage device), and even other caches. It works on the principle of *locality of reference*, the tendency of applications to reference a predictably small amount of data within a given window of time [Belady 1966, Denning 1970]. Any storage device can be characterized by its access time and cost per bit, where faster storage technologies tend to have a lower access time and cost more per bit than slower technologies. A cache fronting a given storage device would be built from a technology that is faster than that of the storage device in question; the cache technology would typically cost more on a per-bit basis, but to be effective the cache would only need to be large enough to hold the application's *working set*—the set of instructions and/or data items the application is currently using to perform its computations [Denning 1967]. Due to locality of reference, most of the application accesses will be satisfied out of the cache, and so most of the time the access characteristics will be that of the cache: far faster and often consuming less energy than the larger storage device behind the cache.

As far as implementation technologies, caches can be built of anything that holds state. Hardware caches are used widely in computer systems (SRAM can act as a cache for DRAM; DRAM can act as a cache for disk; fast DRAM can act as a cache for slow DRAM; disk can act as a cache for tape; etc.), and software caches abound as well (the operating system caches disk blocks and network addresses; web proxies cache popular web-based documents; even

hardware devices such as disk drives cache data locally, implementing the cache algorithm in software executing on a control processor). In addition, what is logically a single cache may, in fact, be comprised of many distinct entities that operate in concert. For instance, the separate last-level caches belonging to the different processors in a symmetric multiprocessor can be thought of (and even managed) as a distributed but logically monolithic entity. Conversely, some cache organizations described as a single cache are, in fact, multi-level hierarchies [Kim et al. 2002]. Neither of these scenarios are erroneous or should be taken as misleading. Any set of multiple storage units can be labeled and analyzed as a single "cache," and any monolithic cache can be labeled and analyzed as a set of multiple, independent entities. The choice of how to portray a particular cache is often made out of necessity (e.g., to make an algorithm feasible, as in Wheeler and Bershad's treatment of a single cache as a collection of logically independent partitions [1992]) or out of convenience (e.g., to simplify an explanation, as in Kim's NUCA [Non-Uniform Cache Architecture]). The bottom line is that the term *cache* means many things to many different fields of discipline, and rather than treat some uses as "correct" and others as "incorrect," we consider it quite useful to develop a framework that encompasses most, if not all, uses of the term. The primary contribution of Part I of the book is the presentation of just such a framework.

Caches can be *transparent*, meaning that they work independently of the client making the request (e.g., the application software executing on the computer) and therefore have built-in heuristics that determine what data to retain. Caches can also be managed explicitly by the client making the request (these are often called *scratch-pads*) or can represent some hybrid of the two extremes. Examples of transparent caches include the processor caches found in general-purpose systems, the file caches found in most distributed file systems, and nearly all forms of web cache given that the "client" of a web cache is typically the person using the web browser. Examples of scratch-pads include the ubiquitous register file as well as the tagless SRAMs found in nearly all microcontrollers and digital signal processors. The former (transparent cache) operates autonomously with respect to the client; the cached version can be deleted, lost, or invalidated, and the original is still available in the backing store. The latter (scratch-pad) requires the direct control of the client to move data in and out; working with the *cached* version of a datum means one is, in fact, working with the *only* version—the cache is not autonomous and therefore makes no attempt to propagate changes back to the original.

Hybrid caches incorporate aspects of both autonomy and client-directed management. Examples include Cheriton's software-controlled caches in the VMP multiprocessor system [Cheriton et al. 1986, 1988, 1989], as well as modern "snarfing" caches found in many commercial multiprocessors. A slightly different hybrid example is the operating system's buffer cache, a section of main memory that is managed by the operating system to store disk blocks. The software that manages the buffer cache operates independently of application software, but the buffer cache can also serve the operating system itself, i.e., the operating system can be a client of the buffer cache, just like application software, and in this case there is no distinction between the manager of the cache and the client of the cache, just like a software-managed cache or a scratch-pad memory.

The reason it is important to identify who or what is responsible for managing the cache contents is that, if given little direct input from the running application, a cache must infer the application's intent, i.e., it must attempt to predict the future behavior of the client (e.g., the application currently executing). Thus, the cache's heuristics for deciding what to retain, when to retain it, where to store it, and when to get rid of it are

extremely important. The heuristics for a transparent cache, which are embodied in its organization and various fetch, eviction, and placement strategies, fundamentally determine the cache's effectiveness. By contrast, purely client-managed caches incorporate no cache-based heuristics whatsoever. For example, solid-state caches managed by application software embody no hardware-based heuristics at all; the cache's effectiveness is determined entirely by choices made by the application itself.

This leads us to the three primary components of our framework. Every cache, whether implemented in hardware or software, whether transparent or client managed, whether distributed or monolithic, embodies instances of the following three items:

- The cache's **organization** is the logical arrangement of data stored within its context. For example, an operating system's buffer cache could be organized as an array of queues, with each queue loosely representing the last time a stored object was referenced (e.g., queue1 holds items just arrived, queue2 holds items recently referenced, queue3 holds items not referenced in a while, etc.); a solid-state cache could be organized as an array of sets, each of which contains a handful of cache blocks maintained in a time-ordered manner.

- **Content-management heuristics** represent the decision to cache or not to cache a particular item at a particular time during execution. These can be implemented either at design time by the programmer and/or compiler—or at run time by application software and/or the cache itself. The heuristics can be static in nature, in which case the cache's contents do not change significantly over time, or dynamic in nature, in which case the cache's contents could change radically from moment to moment.

- **Consistency-management heuristics** ensure that the instructions and data that application software expects to receive are the ones the software does, indeed, receive. Like cache contents, consistency can be managed by any of several different entities, including the operating system, the application software, or the cache itself.

These components appear in every cache, and they are present even if not explicitly chosen or implemented. For example, a simple array of blocks is an organization. Even *fetch-nothing* can be considered a simple, if ineffectual, content-management heuristic; and, similarly, having no consistency heuristic at all is still a design choice. At first glance, these mechanisms are all independent; they are largely orthogonal in that the choice made for one component typically does not restrict significantly a designer's available choices for the other components. For instance, one can freely change cache size and associativity simultaneously with the prefetch and write-back policies and also simultaneously with the choice of cache-coherence protocol. Upon deeper inspection, however, many of the issues are heavily interconnected: choices made for one component can make the problems easier or harder to solve for other components. For example, the use of a virtual cache organization places an enormous burden on consistency management that is not present with physical caches (for more detail, see Chapter 4, Section 4.2.1, "Virtual Cache Management).

For further in-depth reading on the topic of transparent processor caches, we suggest as starting points the thorough discussion by Hennessy and Patterson [2003] and Alan J. Smith's excellent survey [1982], which is as pertinent today as it was when it was written (i.e., don't let the publication date fool you). For further reading on both hardware and software techniques for scratch-pad memories specifically and embedded memory systems generally, we suggest as a starting point the inaugural, two-part issue of *ACM Transactions on Embedded Computing Systems* [Jacob & Bhattacharyya 2002].

1.1 Caches, 'Caches,' and "Caches"

Nearly every field imaginable, or at least every field that deals with data in some form or another, has adapted the concept of cache, and every field uses the same term (i.e., cache) to describe what it is that they have built. For example, the digital signal processor (DSP) community uses the word *cache* to describe the dual SRAM scratch-pads found on DSP chips that enable simultaneous access to two data operands [Lapsley et al. 1997], and the high-performance computing community uses the same word to describe the largely autonomous and increasingly complex processor caches that are completely transparent to software and resemble small hardware databases more than anything else. These are both built-in hardware. Software caches are just as prevalent: the world-wide web uses file caching extensively in web proxies [Luotonen & Altis 1994]; network routers cache domain name system (DNS) entries to speed translation from domain names to Internet Protocol (IP) addresses; the operating system stores disk data in its buffer cache (an in-memory cache of disk buffers) to reduce the time spent going to the disk system; and even the disk itself caches buffers in its own local storage.

This is illustrated in Figure 1.1, which shows numerous different caches. The top row presents various configurations of solid-state hardware caches, and the bottom row presents examples of software caches.

- Figure 1.1(a) shows a general-purpose core with its cache. The cache is transparent in that the software executing on the core makes what it believes to be a request to the backing store (the DRAM behind the cache), and the cache intercepts the request. This requires the cache to be aware of its own contents so it can determine if the requested data is stored locally or not.

- Figure 1.1(b) shows another configuration of a general-purpose cache, in which the cache is logically and/or physically split into two separate partitions: one that holds only instructions and one that holds only data. Partitioning caches can improve behavior. For instance, providing a separate bus to each partition potentially doubles the bandwidth to the cache, and devoting one partition to fixed-length instructions can simplify read-out logic by obviating support for variable-sized reads.

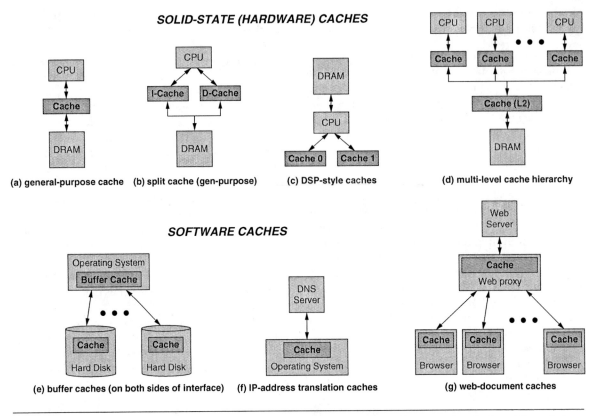

FIGURE 1.1: Examples of caches. The caches are divided into two main groups: solid-state caches (top), and those that are implemented by software mechanisms, typically storing the cached data in main memory (e.g., DRAM) or disk.

- Figure 1.1(c) shows another partitioned configuration, one that is found in most DSP architectures. As we will discuss in more detail later, these caches are an extension of the memory space, and, unlike the previous two organizations, they are not transparent to software. The main item to note is that the two partitions both hold data. This configuration is desirable in DSPs because of the high data bandwidth required by many DSP algorithms (e.g., dot-product calculations such as finite impulse response [FIR] filters), which fetch two different data operands from memory on every cycle.
- Figure 1.1(d) shows a typical cache hierarchy for a multiprocessor organization. Each

processor core has its own private cache, and the last-level cache before the backing store (DRAM) is shared by all cores.
- Figure 1.1(e) shows two different types of caches. First, the operating system stores the blocks it has fetched from disk in main memory as part of a *buffer cache*. When an application reads and writes data from/to files on disk, those requests are not serviced by the disk directly but are instead serviced out of the buffer cache. In addition, modern disks implement their own caches as well; these caches are not under the control of the operating system, but instead operate autonomously. We discuss disk caches in more detail in Chapter 22.

- Figure 1.1(f) shows another cache maintained by the operating system. When a translation is needed from domain name to IP address, the operating system may or may not actually ask a DNS server directly. Translations may be cached locally to avoid network requests. Similarly, routing information for hosts and subnets is typically cached locally.
- Figure 1.1(g) shows two different types of caches. First, each web browser typically maintains its own local cache of downloaded web documents. These documents are usually stored on the local disk and buffered in main memory as part of the operating system's buffer cache (Figure 1.1(e)). In addition, a request that is sent to a particular web server may or may not actually reach the web server. A web proxy, which behaves like the transparent caches in Figures 1.1(a), (b), and (d), may intercept the request and reply on behalf of the server [Luotonen & Altis 1994].

One of the most important distinctions between different types of cache is their method of addressing. Some caches do not hold a *copy* of a datum; they hold the datum itself. These are often called *scratch-pad memory* and use a separate namespace from the backing store (i.e., the primary memory). A scratch-pad is *non-transparent* in that a program addresses it explicitly. A datum is brought into the scratch-pad by an explicit move that does not destroy the original copy. Therefore, two equal versions of the data remain; there is no attempt by the hardware to keep the versions consistent (to ensure that they always have the same value) because the semantics of the mechanism suggest that the two copies are not, in fact, copies of the same datum, but are instead two independent data. If they are to remain consistent, it is up to software. By contrast, the typical general-purpose cache uses the same namespace as the primary memory system. It is transparent in that a program addresses main memory to access the cache—a program does not explicitly access the cache or even need to know that the cache exists.

How each of these two mechanisms (transparent cache and scratch-pad memory) fits into the microprocessor's memory model is shown in Figure 1.2, using solid-state memories (processor caches and tagless SRAMs) for examples. A general-purpose memory model has a single namespace[1] that is shared by all memory structures. Any datum from any part of the namespace can be found in any of the caches. By contrast, a scratch-pad uses the namespace to directly address the caches. For instance, the DSP memory model shown on the right explicitly places the system's memory structures at specific disjunct locations in the namespace. A particular address corresponds to a particular physical storage device, and unlike a transparently addressed cache, a single address in the scratch-pad's namespace cannot refer to both a cached datum and its copy in the backing store.

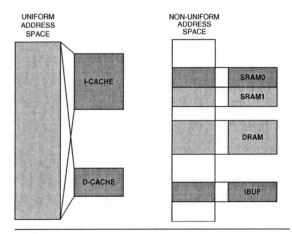

FIGURE 1.2: Transparent caches in a uniform space versus scratch-pad SRAMs in a non-uniform space. Any datum in the memory space can also reside in a cache (thus the designation "transparent"). Only items in certain segments of the memory space can reside in a scratch-pad memory.

---

[1]Assumes physically indexed caches.

As mentioned earlier, what one terms a single cache, or what one terms a set of multiple independent caches, is entirely a matter of convenience and/or need. For instance, the caches in Figure 1.1(b) can be labeled and analyzed as a single cache. One can always analyze the multiple caches at the same "level" in the hierarchy as a single unit (e.g., the L1 caches in Figure 1.1(d), the disk caches in Figure 1.1(e), or the browser caches in Figure 1.1(g)), even though they operate independently. Similarly, one can group the caches in Figures 1.1(d), (e), and (g), which all incorporate entire hierarchies. Depending on the analysis, it may be convenient to treat all levels of cache as a single entity separate from the backing store, but not separate from each other. Going the other way, it is just as correct to treat what appears to be a single cache as a set of independent units. For instance, the caches in Figures 1.1(a) and (f) could each be treated as a collection of independently analyzed blocks.

Finally, embracing all of these different mechanisms as caches, as different aspects of the same thing, enables the solutions developed in different fields of study to cross-pollinate. The goal and point of the formalism, which is presented in detail in the following chapters, are to enable such an analysis. First, the remainder of this chapter presents many of the underlying principles that are common to the caches found across disciplines.

1.2 Locality Principles

Over the decades that the computer has been used and studied, computer engineers have measured program behavior and have made the following observations:

- The memory-access patterns of programs are not random.
- Accesses tend to repeat themselves in time and/or be near each other in the memory address space.

An important note is that these are not guarantees, they are merely observations. The implication of their being observations, as opposed to provably inherent behaviors, is that, unless we can show that new program behaviors will never appear, we need to continue measuring and observing programs and should expect to discover new behaviors occasionally.

As mentioned in the *Overview* chapter, the phenomenon of exhibiting predictable, non-random memory-access behavior is called *locality of reference*. The behavior is so named[2] because we have observed that a program's memory *references* tend to be *localized* in time and space:

- If the program references a datum once, it is likely in the near future to reference that datum again.
- If the program references a datum once, it is likely in the near future to reference nearby data as well.

The first of these phenomena is called *temporal locality*, and the second is called *spatial locality*.

This begs the question: is there nothing else? We have "temporal" and "spatial" aspects of locality. These are brilliantly chosen terms because they imply completeness: time and space cover all possibilities, giving one the distinct if, perhaps, subconscious impression that no other form of locality could possibly exist. It may come as a surprise to some readers that this impression would be wrong.

Remember that these phenomena, these aspects of locality that programs exhibit, are merely observations. They are not inherent to programs, and there is no reason to believe that they are required attributes of a particular program or that they perfectly describe every program that exists. They are merely descriptions of the way that most observed programs tend to behave. Lately, computer engineers have observed a new type of phenomenon.

In the past decade, another class of behavior has sprung up, a consequence of the widespread use of

---

[2]The term "locality" was put forth by Belady [1966] and was later formalized, in terms of the *working set* model, by Denning [1970].

computer graphics algorithms and similar algorithms in other domains, including computer simulation, circuit emulation, interpretation of HDL[3] code, etc. These programs typically walk down dynamic data structures and access the same data in the same order time and time again (e.g., walking through the components of a 3D scene each time a new video frame is created), so their behavior is inherently predictable. However, the time between two successive accesses to the same data is large (thus, the program exhibits no significant temporal locality), and the data objects are generally nowhere near each other in the memory space (thus, the program exhibits no significant spatial locality). According to our existing definitions of locality, these programs exhibit no significant locality,[4] but, nonetheless, the programs of this type exhibit regular, predictable, exploitable behavior. It is hard to categorize this type of behavior because, between time and space, we seem to have everything covered. So it is easy to overlook the fact that this behavior even exists. But exist it clearly does, even if we have no term for it and even if our naming continuum seems to allow no room for a new term to exist.

For lack of a better term, we will call this behavior *algorithmic locality*.

The following sections describe these phenomena in more detail.

1.2.1 Temporal Locality

Temporal locality is the tendency of programs to use data items over and again during the course of their execution. This is the founding principle behind caches and gives a clear guide to an appropriate data-management heuristic. If a program uses an instruction or data variable, it is probably a good idea to keep that instruction or data item nearby in case the program wants it again in the near future.

One corresponding data-management policy or heuristic that exploits this type of locality is *demand-fetch*. In this policy, when the program *demands* (references) an instruction or data item, the cache hardware or software *fetches* the item from memory and retains it in the cache. The policy is easily implemented in hardware. As a side effect of bringing any data (either instructions or program variables and constants) into the processor core from memory, a copy of that data is stored into the cache. Before looking to memory for a particular data item, the cache is searched for a local copy.

The only real limitation in exploiting this form of locality is cache storage size. If the cache is large enough, no data item ever need be fetched from the backing store or written to the backing store more than once. Note that the *backing store* is the term for the level of storage beneath the cache, whether that level is main memory, the disk system, or another level of cache. The term can also be used to mean, collectively, the remainder of the memory hierarchy below the cache level in question.

1.2.2 Spatial Locality

Spatial locality arises because of the tendency of programmers and compilers to cluster related objects together in the memory space. As a result of this, and also because of the human-like way that programs tend to work on related data items one right after the other, memory references within a narrow range of time tend to be clustered together in the memory space. The classic example of this behavior is array processing, in which the elements of an array are processed one right after the other: elements i and $i+1$ are adjacent in the memory space, and element $i+1$ is usually processed immediately after element i.

This behavior, like temporal locality, also points to an obvious data-management policy, typically called *lookahead*: when instruction i or data item i is requested by the program, that datum should be brought into the processor core and, in addition,

---

[3]HDLs are *Hardware Description Languages* such as Verilog or VHDL, which are commonly used in the specification and design of computer circuits and systems.
[4]Another way of looking at this is that the programs exhibit temporal and/or spatial locality on scales so large that the terms become meaningless.

instruction or data item *i+1* should be brought in as well. The simplest form of this policy is to choose judiciously the data-access granularity: to build caches in atomic units called *cache blocks* that are larger than a single data item. For example, a processor in which the fundamental data unit is a 4-byte word might use a 16-byte cache block containing 4 data words, or a 32-byte cache block containing 8 data words, and so on. Because the cache block is *atomic* (meaning that this is the granularity of data access between the cache and memory—the amount of data that is moved for every[5] read or write), a program's request for a single data item will result in the surrounding data items all being fetched from memory as a matter of course.

The use of a cache block that is larger than a single data word is very effective, leads to a simple implementation, and can be thought of as a *passive* form of exploiting spatial locality. Another very effective way to exploit spatial locality is *prefetching*, which, by comparison, is an *active* form. Prefetching (which can be done in hardware, software, or a combination of the two) is a mechanism in which the program's request for an instruction or data item causes more data than just the requested cache block to be fetched from memory. An algorithm uses the memory address with the associated recent history of requested addresses to speculate on which cache block or cache blocks might be used next. An obvious hardware algorithm would be something like fetch-next-block, called *one-block lookahead* prefetching [Smith 1982], which can be seen as a simple extension of the cache block granularity of access. An obvious software algorithm would be something like fetch-next-array-element, which cannot be performed in hardware alone because it requires information about the size of each data element. Much more sophisticated (and complex) algorithms have been explored as well.

The limit on exploiting this type of locality is due to program behavior and the algorithm's accuracy of prediction. If the program tends to access instructions and data in a largely sequential manner, then a simple mechanism is all that is necessary, and the performance results can be extremely good. If the program behavior is more complex (say, for example, the program jumps around from cache block to cache block, but in a predictable manner), a static algorithm will not be capable of adapting and will therefore do poorly. In this case, a more sophisticated prefetching algorithm might be able to track program behavior and correctly predict which block to fetch next.

1.2.3 Algorithmic Locality

The last discussion leads us into algorithmic locality. Algorithmic locality arises when a program repeatedly accesses data items or executes code blocks that are distributed widely across the memory space. The net result is program behavior that tends to be predictable, but, nonetheless, cannot be captured by using granularity of access or simple lookahead-prefetching mechanisms because the data items referenced by the program are nowhere near each other. Similarly, this behavior cannot be captured by simply increasing the cache size by a factor of two or three because the data and code sizes involved are typically very large.

Many applications that exhibit this aspect of locality perform repeated operations on very large data sets that are stored in dynamic data structures that do not change shape radically over short periods of time. Example applications of this sort include graphics processing, computer simulation, circuit emulation, and various forms of HDL processing (interpretation, synthesis, validation, verification, rule-checking, regression testing, etc.).

Many of the steps in 3D computer-graphics processing find the program repeatedly traversing a large dynamic data structure representing the shape of the physical object being rendered. One example is the *Z-buffer algorithm*, in which the depth of each object

---

[5]However, there are always exceptions (see "Other Policies and Strategies for Transparent (Processor) Caches" in Section 3.1).

in the 3D scene is used to paint the two-dimensional (2D) image of the scene:

```
for each polygon P in scene {
    for each pixel p in P {
        if (depth of p at i,j < image[i,j].depth) {
            image[i,j].color = p.color
            image[i,j].depth = depth of p at i,j
        }
    }
}
```

The algorithm walks through a list of polygons, performing a number of calculations on each polygon. As a scene is portrayed using an increasingly fine mesh of polygons, the more realistic the rendered scene tends to look. Thus, in practice, the number of polygons tends to be large, and the number of pixels per polygon tends to be small.

This algorithm will walk through the polygon list over and over for each frame of a video sequence. The polygon list is typically a dynamic data structure such as a linked list, not a static array. Because there can be no guarantee about the physical placement in memory for any particular element in the list, one cannot expect to see this algorithm exhibit significant spatial locality. Because the polygon list is large, significant time will pass before any polygon is revisited by the algorithm, and thus, the algorithm will not exhibit significant temporal locality either. The algorithm is highly predictable in terms of its memory-access patterns. It is largely because of this predictability that graphics coprocessors have been able to make such an enormous impact on the computing industry.

Because the predictability is exploitable, it most certainly represents a type of locality, and it arises from the behavior of the algorithm (thus, the name). To exploit this locality, one must know the algorithm's behavior, which means the optimization could be a run-time mechanism that observes program behavior and adapts to it, or it could be a relatively simple prefetching code inserted by the compiler or programmer at design time. For instance, the algorithm could be rewritten as follows to prefetch polygons into the processor core before they are actually needed for processing (the primary difference is in

bold and assumes some form of linked-list representation for polygons):

```
for each polygon P in scene {
    prefetch P.next
    for each pixel p in P {
        if (depth of p at i,j < image[i,j].depth) {
            image[i,j].color = p.color
            image[i,j].depth = depth of p at i,j
        }
    }
}
```

This is but a simple, obvious example (for more discussion on prefetching, see Chapter 3, Section 3.1.2, "On-Line Prefetching Heuristics," and Section 3.2.2, "Off-Line Prefetching Heuristics"). Exploiting this type of locality is limited only by the imagination of the algorithm's writers and/or the hardware's designers. For instance, more sophisticated software algorithms can prefetch more than one polygon ahead (i.e., further out into the program's "future" execution), and larger prefetch buffers can accommodate more data fetched. Both would allow the algorithm to tolerate very long memory latencies.

1.2.4 Geographical Locality? Demographical Locality?

As we will discuss in more detail later, designers continue to refine cache performance (as well as power dissipation, timeliness, predictability, etc.), often by the divide-and-conquer approach of classification, to wit:

1. Identify classes of application/algorithm behavior or data types that exhibit recognizable behavior.
2. Exploit the (predictable) behaviors that are exhibited.

This applies very well to locality principles: demand-fetch caches exploit temporal locality; large block sizes and/or simple prefetching schemes exploit spatial locality; and software-directed prefetching schemes and hardware prefetching schemes that use dynamic pattern recognition exploit algorithmic locality. As new applications emerge that can benefit from caching, new forms of behavior are seen, and new mechanisms to exploit that behavior are used. Web caching (and content delivery in the general sense) is but one example that introduces radically different new forms of behavior; entire geographical regions and/or demographical subsets within those regions can exhibit recognizable, exploitable behavior. Consider, for example, a prefetching heuristic for proxy caches that would improve North American network traffic and browser latency on Superbowl Sunday. Attempting to think about such problems without considering the cause of the behavior, e.g., trying to optimize a content-delivery system by treating data traffic in terms of only temporal and spatial locality and ignoring the human element behind the traffic, is guaranteed to produce a second-rate result.

1.3 What to Cache, Where to Put It, and How to Maintain It

As illustrated in Figure 1.3, there are five orthogonal components comprising a cache design: the decision of what to put into the cache, a content-management heuristic that can be made either dynamically or statically by the programmer, by the compiler, by the running application, by the operating system, or by the cache itself; the decision of where and how to store

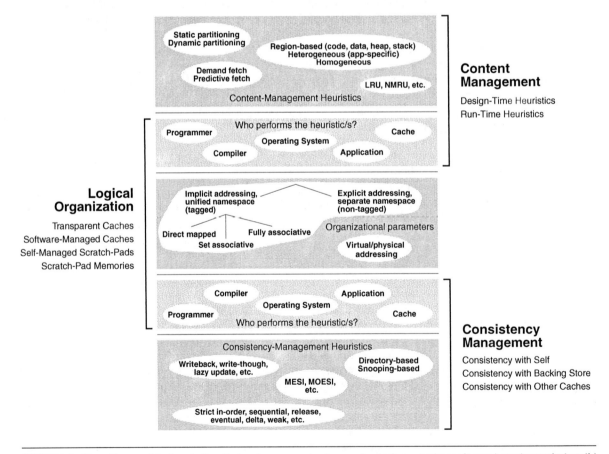

FIGURE 1.3: The orthogonal design choices that make up a cache. Any cache design, whether software based or entirely solid state, comprises a logical storage organization, one or more content-management heuristics, and one or more consistency-management heuristics.

cached data within the cache's physical extent and/or logical arrangement (its logical organization); and the mechanism by which the cache (together with any executing software) ensures the consistency of data stored within it, a heuristic that can be performed by any of several entities, including the application code, the operating system, or the cache itself. A cache can be built by combining essentially any logical organization with essentially any set of management heuristics.

This section sets up the next three chapters of the book. The three primary issues illustrated in Figure 1.3 (Logical Organization, Content Management, and Consistency Management) will be discussed here in an overview fashion, and the next three chapters will go into each in more detail.

1.3.1 Logical Organization Basics: Blocks, Tags, Sets

A cache stores chunks of data (called *cache blocks* or *cache lines*) that come from the backing store. A consequence of this block-oriented arrangement is that we logically divide the backing store into equal, cache-block-sized chunks. A useful side effect of this is the provision for a simple and effective means to identify a particular block: the *block ID*. A subset of the address, the block ID is illustrated in Figure 1.4, which shows a 32-bit byte main memory address as a bit vector divided into two components: the cache block ID and the byte's offset within that cache block. Note that the "byte in block" component is given as 4 bits. This example, therefore, represents a cache block of size 16 bytes. If a cache were to contain disk blocks, with several disk blocks to a cache block, then this arrangement would be the same, except that the 32-bit physical memory address would become a disk block number.

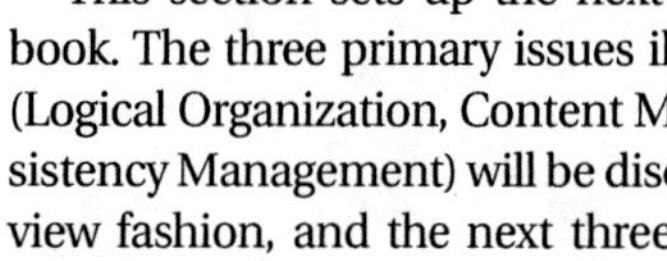

Because a cache is typically much smaller than the backing store, there is a good possibility that any particular requested datum is not in the cache. Therefore, some mechanism must indicate whether any particular datum is present in the cache or not. The *cache tags* fill this purpose. The tags, a set of block IDs, comprise a list of valid entries in the cache, with one tag per data entry. The basic structure is illustrated in Figure 1.5, which shows a cache as a set of cache entries [Smith 1982]. This can take any form: a solid-state array (e.g., an SRAM implementation) or, if the cache is implemented in software, a binary search tree or even a short linked list.

If a cache's size is but one block, then its organization should be relatively obvious: data goes into the one block, displacing whatever was previously there. However, as soon as a cache has more than one block, its organization becomes an issue: where should that second block be placed? The data corresponding to a particular block ID can only be found in one cache entry at a time, but there is still flexibility in the choice of which entry in the cache to choose. We will use the vertical and horizontal dimensions in our figures to denote a group of equivalence classes; each row is an equivalence class called a cache *set*. The single, unique set to which a particular chunk of

32-bit address:

28 bits	4 bits
Block ID	**byte in block**

FIGURE 1.4: A 32-bit address.

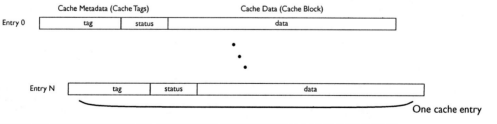

	Cache Metadata (Cache Tags)		Cache Data (Cache Block)
Entry 0	tag	status	data

• • •

| Entry N | tag | status | data |

One cache entry

FIGURE 1.5: Basic cache structure. A cache is composed of two main parts: The cache metadata (or, simply, tags) and the cache data. Each data entry is termed a *cache line* or *cache block*. The tag entries identify the contents of their corresponding data entries. Status information includes a valid bit.

data belongs is typically determined by a subset of bits taken from its block ID, as shown in Figure 1.6. Once the set is determined, the data chunk may be placed within any block in that set.

There are three basic cache organizations that arise from this equivalence-class mechanism: *direct-mapped, fully associative,* and *set associative.* Direct-mapped caches have sets with only one block in each set; each block is its own equivalence class. Fully associative caches (also called *content-addressable memories*) have only one set that encompasses all blocks; thus, all blocks in the cache are in the same equivalence class. Set-associative caches strike a balance between these two choices. A set-associate cache has more than one set (if only one, the cache would be fully associative), and each set in the cache incorporates more than one block in its equivalence class (if only one, the cache would be direct-mapped). Figure 1.7 illustrates the three cache organizations by demonstrating the various ways a cache of eight blocks can be organized.

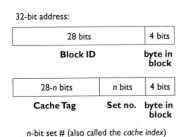

FIGURE 1.6: Different address views.

1.3.2 Content Management: To Cache or Not to Cache

As an application executes over time, it makes a sequence of references to memory (or, more generally, the backing store), each of which is a potential candidate for caching. The purpose of a content-management solution is to determine which references are the best candidates for caching and to ensure that their corresponding data values are in the cache at the time the application requests them. Simultaneously, it must consider the currently cached items and decide which should be evicted to make room for more important data not yet cached. The optimal algorithm is one that can look into the future and determine what will be needed and ensure that all important data words, up to the limits of the cache's capacity and organization, are in the cache when requested. This is similar in spirit to Belady's MIN algorithm for disk block replacement [Belady 1966]. Both schemes rely upon an oracle to guarantee optimal performance.

Given the absence of an oracle, one is left with sub-optimal approaches, i.e., heuristics that can, at best, approximate the optimal approach, making do with imperfect and/or incomplete information. These heuristics take as input anything that might describe a data item: e.g., who is using it, how it is being used, how important it is, and at what point in the application's execution is the item being considered. Using this, the heuristic makes a "yes/no" decision to cache the item. Note that the decision can be made at any of several different times, by any of several different entities. The time can be relatively early on in the process—for instance, when the programmer writes and compiles the application code—or

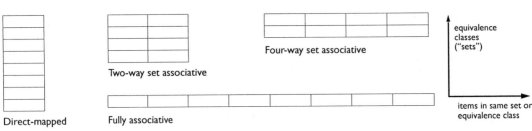

FIGURE 1.7: Four organizations for a cache of eight blocks. Eight blocks can be configured in a direct-mapped organization, a fully associative organization, or any of two different set-associative organizations.

it can be made relatively late in the process—for instance, while the application code is executing. The decision can be made by the programmer, the compiler, the operating system, the application code, or the cache itself. In addition, some decisions will be inherently *predictive* in nature (e.g., a design-time heuristic embedded in the compiler determines that a particular reference should hit the cache, so proactive steps such as prefetching should be performed to ensure that the data is in the cache at the time the reference is made), while other decisions will be inherently *reactive* in nature (e.g., a run-time heuristic in the cache determines that a requested item is valuable and therefore should remain in the cache once fetched from the backing store).

An important thing to bear in mind when considering the role of the content-management solution (i.e., the set of design-time and/or run-time heuristics) is that the logical organization of the cache has the final word on whether something a heuristic decides to cache will, in fact, remain cached. The logical organization defines how and where cached data is stored, and if a heuristic chooses to cache two items that the logical organization cannot hold simultaneously, then one of the two must go. For example, consider two back-to-back references made to items deemed important by some heuristic, but positioned in the backing store's namespace such that they are assigned to the same set in the cache (this would happen if the two items were stored in memory exactly 1 MB apart, given a cache of 1 MB in size or less), and, further, assume that the cache is not set associative (each set can hold only one data item). The cache can hold only one of these items, and so the second reference would displace the first, irrespective of the heuristic's wishes.

1.3.3 Consistency Management: Its Responsibilities

Consistency management comprises three main charges:

1. Keep the cache consistent with itself
2. Keep the cache consistent with the backing store
3. Keep the cache consistent with other caches

In many cases, these goals can be accomplished simply. In most cases, the choice of logical organization can complicate things tremendously.

Keep the Cache Consistent with Itself

There should never be two copies of a single item in different places of the cache, unless it is guaranteed that they will always have the same value. In general, this tends not to be a problem, provided the cache is physically indexed and physically tagged.

Many operating systems allow two completely unrelated virtual addresses to map to the same physical address, creating a *synonym*. The synonym problem is non-trivial and is discussed in more detail in Chapter 4. It creates a problem by allowing the physical datum to lie in two different virtually indexed cache sets at the same time, immediately creating an inconsistency as soon as one of those copies is written. If the cache's sets are referenced using a physical address (i.e., an address corresponding to the backing store, which would uniquely identify the datum), then there is no problem.

Using tags that correspond to the backing store solves another problem. Even if some mechanism ensures that two synonyms map to the same set in the cache, the cache could nonetheless hold the two different copies if the cache is set associative and the two cache blocks are not tagged with an ID taken from the backing store. For example, if the cache uses virtual tags or if the cache fails to ensure that the blocks held in a set all have unique tags, then an inconsistency could occur.

Keep the Cache Consistent with the Backing Store

The value kept in the backing store should be up-to-date with any changes made to the version stored in the cache, but only to the point that it is possible to ensure that any read requests to the version in the backing store (e.g., from another processor) return the most recently written value stored in the cache.

Two typical mechanisms used in general-purpose caches to effect this responsibility are *write-back* and *write-through* policies. When writing to a cache, the backing store is implicitly updated, but when? Two obvious choices are *immediately* and *later*; the first is write-through, and the second is write back. Write-through offers the advantage of having a very small window in which the backing store has an outdated ("stale") copy of a datum. Write-back takes advantage of locality in that, if a block is written, the block will likely be written again in the near future, in which case it would make no sense to transmit both values to the backing store. A write-back cache keeps track of blocks that have been written (called "dirty") and writes their contents to memory only upon block replacement, potentially saving significant bandwidth to the backing store.

The disadvantage of write-through is its cost: shoveling every write to the cache into the backing store at the same time becomes expensive, because the backing store typically cannot provide the same bandwidth as the cache. The solution is to provide an additional fast memory of some sort that is physically part of the cache, but logically part of the backing store. Popular choices for this fast memory are FIFO (first-in first-out) write buffers, coalescing write buffers, or searchable write buffers, a.k.a. write caches. The point of this hardware is to decouple the bursty nature of the microprocessor's write operations from the backing store and to dribble the written data to the backing store at whatever speed it can handle. The simple write buffer must be drained if it fills or if a cache miss occurs. More complex write buffers are capable of much more sophisticated behavior.

The primary disadvantage of write-back caches is their interaction with other *processors* and other *processes*. In the first case, in a multiprocessor organization, having a long window of time wherein the backing store can have the wrong value for a particular datum increases the likelihood that another processor sharing the backing store will read that (wrong) datum. We will discuss this later in Chapter 4. In the second case, the virtual memory system's synonym problem complicates things tremendously. Consider, for example, the case when a process writes into its address space, exits, and part of its data space is reused when another process is created or dynamically allocates memory in its heap or stack segments. Nothing prevents a write-back

virtually indexed cache from overwriting the new process's address space when those cache blocks are finally replaced. Even if the operating system wipes the data pages clean, the old written data from the first process can still be found in the cache if the operating system uses different virtual addresses or a different address-space identifier than the original process.

Keep the Cache Consistent with Other Caches

Other caches in the system should all be treated much like the backing store in terms of keeping the various copies of a datum up-to-date, as in Item #2 above.

Note that we are using the term *consistent* here in the normal, Merriam-Webster sense; we are not talking about *memory consistency*, a mechanism to specify the ordering of reads and writes that a (multiprocessor) system as a whole sees.

1.3.4 Inclusion and Exclusion

Before we move on, an aspect of cache organization and operation needs discussion: inclusion. The concept of *inclusion* combines all three aspects of caching just described. Inclusion can be defined by a cache's logical organization, and it is enforced by the cache's content- and consistency-management policies.

Figure 1.8 gives a picture of the canonical memory hierarchy. The hierarchy is *vertically partitioned* into separate storage levels, and each level can be *horizontally partitioned* further [Lee & Tyson 2000]. This horizontal partitioning is also called a *multi-lateral cache* [Rivers et al. 1997]. Partitioning is a powerful mechanism. For instance, Lee and Tyson [2000] note that much work in cache-level energy reduction has been to exploit these divisions. One can use vertical partitioning and move more frequently accessed data into storage units that are closer to the microprocessor—units that can be made significantly smaller than units further out from the microprocessor (e.g., the line buffer [Wilson et al. 1996]), and thus typically consume less energy per reference [Kin et al. 1997, 2000]. Similarly, one can use horizontal partitioning and slice a logically monolithic cache into smaller

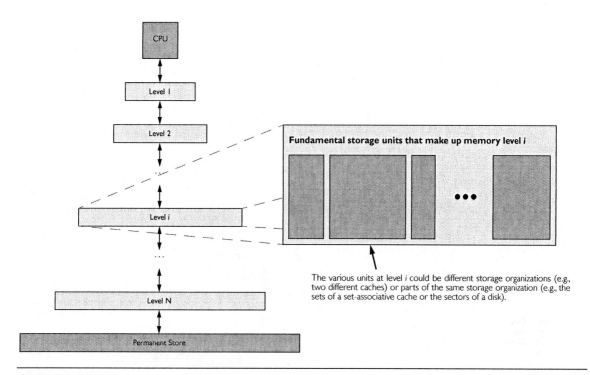

FIGURE 1.8: A canonical memory hierarchy. As one moves down through the hierarchy, from the central processor toward the permanent store, the levels are larger but slower. At each level, the storage may be a monolithic organization, or it may be partitioned into multiple segments we have called generically "units." Every fundamental unit has an exclusive or inclusive relationship with every other unit in the hierarchy.

segments (e.g., subbanks [Ghose & Kamble 1999]), each of which consumes a fraction of the whole cache's energy and is only driven when a reference targets it directly.

The principles of *inclusion* and *exclusion* define a particular class of relationship that exists between any two partitions in a cache system. Whether the two partitions or "units" are found at the same level in the hierarchy or at different levels in the hierarchy, there is a relationship that defines what the expected intersection of those two units would produce. That relationship is either exclusive or inclusive (or a hybrid of the two). Figure 1.9 illustrates a specific memory hierarchy with many of its relationships indicated.

An inclusive relationship between two fundamental units is one in which every cached item found in one of the units has a copy found in the other. For example, this is the relationship that is found in many

(but not all) general-purpose, processor cache hierarchies. Every cache level maintains an inclusive relationship with the cache level immediately beneath it, and the lowest level cache maintains an inclusive relationship with main memory. When data is moved from main memory into the cache hierarchy, a copy of it remains in main memory, and this copy is kept *consistent* with the copy in the caches; i.e., when the cached copy is modified, those modifications are propagated at some point in time to main memory. Similarly, copies of a datum held within lower levels of the cache hierarchy are kept consistent with the copies in the higher cache levels. All this is done transparently, without any explicit direction by the cache system's client.

Keeping all of these additional copies spread around the memory system would seem wasteful. Why is it done? It is done for simplicity of design and

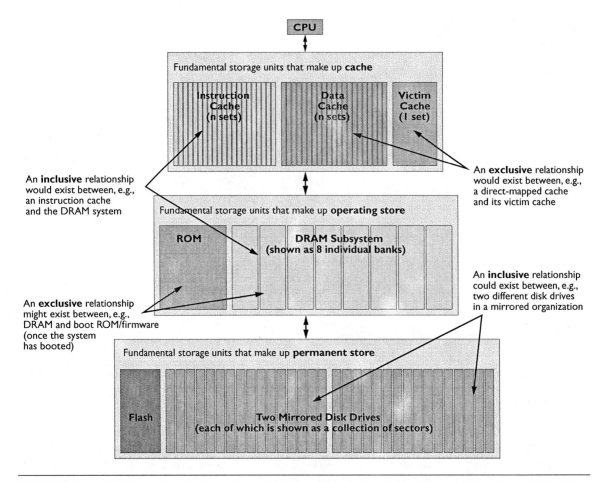

FIGURE 1.9: A specific memory hierarchy. A specific example of a memory system shows various vertical and horizontal partitions that can exist, as well as the inclusive/exclusive relationship between many of the fundamental storage units.

correctness of design. If an inclusive relationship exists between partitions A and B (everything in A is also held in B, and B is kept consistent with the copy in A), then A can be considered nothing more than an optimized lookup: the contents of A could be lost forever, and the only significant effect on the system would be a momentary lapse of performance, a slightly higher energy drain, until A is refilled from B with the data it lost. This is not a hypothetical situation. Low-power caching strategies exist that temporarily power-down portions of the cache when the cache seems underutilized (e.g., a bank at a time). Similarly, the arrangement

simplifies eviction: a block can be discarded from a cache at any time if it is known that the next level in the hierarchy has a consistent copy.

An exclusive relationship between two units is one in which the expected intersection between those units is the null set: an exclusive relationship between A and B specifies that any given item is either in A or B or in neither, but it absolutely should not be in both. The content- and consistency-management protocols, whether implemented by the application software, the operating system, the cache, or some other entity, are responsible for maintaining exclusion between the two partitions. In particular, in many designs, when an item is moved from A to B, the item must be swapped with another item on the other side (which is moved from B to A). This is required because, unlike inclusive relationships in which a replaced item can be simply and safely discarded, there are no "copies" of data in an exclusive relationship. All instances of data are, in a sense, *originals*—loss of a data item is not recoverable; it is an error situation.

Note that there are many examples of cache units in which this swapping of data never happens because data items are never moved between units. For example, the sets of a direct-mapped or set-associative cache exhibit an exclusive relationship with each other; they are partitions of a cache level, and when data is brought into that cache level, the data goes to the one partition to which it is assigned, and it never gets placed into any other set, ever.[6]

1.4 Insights and Optimizations

1.4.1 Perspective

Using general terms, we intentionally describe traditional concepts such as locality, inclusion/exclusion, coherence/consistency, cache organization, protocols, policies, heuristics, etc. to make it clear that they are universally applicable to all manners of cache implementation. One item that should follow from this general treatment is for the reader to recognize potential relationships between mechanisms that are not usually considered related or even compatible. This general treatment should make obvious to the reader potentially interesting avenues for research. As an example,

- Figure 1.3 makes it clear that having different entities perform the same type of heuristic is a complementary action. For instance, both hardware and software could perform content management simultaneously, much in line with hybrid branch predictors or as is already done with software-prefetching schemes (where both cache and software can decide to store items in the cache).

- Considering the sets of a transparent cache as having an exclusive relationship with each other begs the question, *why?* Why not allow some things to reside in multiple sets of a direct-mapped or set-associative cache? Perhaps naming can be a way to accomplish this simply, i.e., through the compiler or virtual memory system (using a virtually indexed cache). Note that this would complicate consistency management.

- Similarly, if one looks at a (set-associative) cache as just a collection of equivalence classes, there is no reason to require each set to have the same cardinality, i.e., to have the same degree of set associativity. Some sets could be large, and others could be small, just as a cache partition could be large or small. Some could have different organizations entirely, with naming schemes used to assign items to different sets or equivalence classes. This is already done in file caching (e.g., see Chapter 2, Section 2.6.2, "A Software Implementation: BSD's Buffer Cache"), and in a solid-state implementation it would be similar in spirit to the work done by Farrens, Rivers, Tyson, and others [Tyson et al. 1995, Rivers & Davidson 1996, Johnson & Hwu 1997] in their work on alternative content-management strategies (discussed in more detail in Chapter 3, Section 3.1.1, "On-Line Partitioning Heuristics").

- Given that content management is orthogonal to cache organization (clear from Figure 1.3), one can start to combine traditionally separated heuristics and organizations. For instance, one could use scratch-pad placement solutions to solve the problems of cache-set assignment.

---

[6]This is mostly, but not completely, true. See the discussion of problems in virtual caches (Chapter 4, Section 4.2.1, "Virtual Cache Management"), and the section on trace caches (Chapter 2, Section 2.6.3, "Another Dynamic Cache Block: Trace Caches").

The list goes on. The whole point of starting from the basics and using general terms is to facilitate novel applications of the tremendous amount of work done in cache design (across many different areas) into new areas.

Reconsidering Bandwidth and Block Size: DSP Caches

One example of the types of opportunities that become available when traditional lines are crossed is a study originally done several years ago [Srinivasan et al. 2001], the idea for which only came about because the traditional line between DSP caches and general-purpose caches had been crossed by the DSP community in their desire to compile C code for DSP architectures. The following is a brief excerpt[7] of the study.

As mentioned earlier, DSPs typically use a non-uniform addressing model in which the primary components of the memory system, the DRAM and dual tagless SRAMs, are referenced through separate segments of the address space (see Figure 1.2). The recent trend of programming DSPs in high-level languages instead of assembly code has exposed this memory model as a potential weakness, as the model makes for a poor compiler target. In many of today's high-performance DSPs, this non-uniform model is being replaced by a uniform model, a transparent organization like that of most general-purpose systems, in which all memory structures share the same address space as the DRAM system.

This opens up an interesting design space to study—how best to build transparent caches for DSPs, perhaps exploiting the regular behavior exhibited by many applications on DSP processors (similar in vein to vector apps on vector processors), as well as their use of memory resources (ports), a behavior that resembles an exclusive partition and is very predictable. For example, DSPs might be able to make good use of large cache blocks, particularly block sizes where a general-purpose application might exhibit high degrees of cache pollution. An obvious downside of doing so is the long fill-time for large blocks, but this can be offset with increased memory bandwidth.

We look at two different organizations illustrated in Figure 1.10. The first is an extremely simple organization: two blocks, each one dedicated to a different load/store unit. The second adds a single-block *victim cache* [Jouppi 1990] to each of the blocks in the first organization. In this organization, each victim cache block holds only victims taken from its associated cache block. Note that in all organizations, cache reads may be satisfied out of any block in the cache. The tying of a block to a particular load/store unit is simply used in the replacement policy; it does not affect the cache lookup mechanism. Any load/store unit can read a value from any block in the cache, which makes the cache effectively fully associative.

This is a rather non-traditional cache organization, but it follows from our observations of the behavior of 'C6000 DSP applications. In particular, we found that the C compiler tends to assign load and store instructions to particular ports in a manner that does not change dynamically: to wit, if the DSP reads a particular datum from a particular port, the DSP is less than 50% likely to read that datum from the other port in the near future, and it is *far* less than 50% likely to *write* that datum to the other port in the near future. We exploit the observed behavior by constraining which blocks can be replaced and written from which ports, thereby creating a simpler cache. Note that this behavior is specific to compiled applications, as opposed to DSP applications written by hand in assembly code, but it is also likely that the observed behavior would be seen in any DSP with a unified memory space and a high-level language compiler.

Figure 1.11 shows the performance of the two organizations, compared to the performance of the 64-KB scratch-pad SRAM at 400 MB/s. Note that the vertical scales of the various graphs differ.

---

[7]This work is based on an earlier work: "Transparent data-memory organizations for digital signal processors," by S. Srinivasan, V. Cuppu, and B. Jacob, in *Proc. International Conference on Compilers, Architecture, and Synthesis for Embedded Systems (CASES 2001)*, November 2001. © ACM, 2001. http://doi.acm.org/10.1145/502217.502224

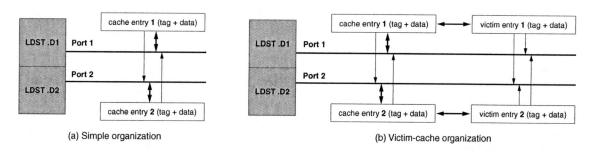

(a) Simple organization   (b) Victim-cache organization

FIGURE 1.10: Slightly non-traditional cache organizations. Each load/store unit can read from any block in the cache, but it can only write to the primary block that is assigned to it. Similarly, load misses only fill the cache block assigned to a load/store unit. The victim cache organization adds two blocks to the cache that are only filled by blocks replaced from the corresponding primary blocks.

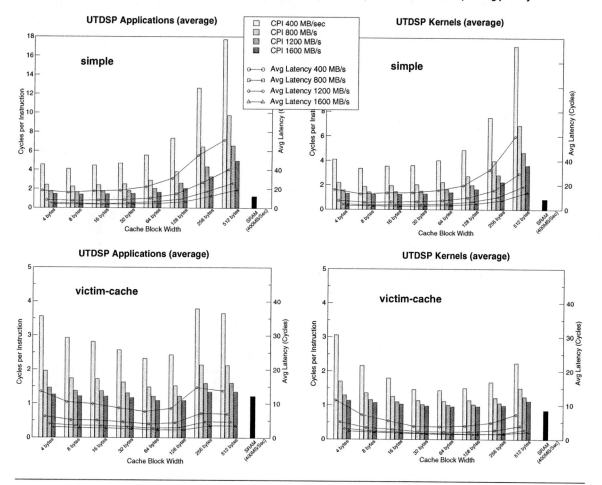

FIGURE 1.11: Performance graphs. The top two graphs give results for the "simple" organization. The bottom two give results for the "victim cache" organization.

Execution time (in CPI) is given on the left side of each graph, corresponding to the histograms; average latency per memory instruction is given on the right side of each graph, corresponding to the line graphs. Memory bandwidth and cache block size are the variables (note that total cache capacity is not kept constant and instead grows as block size grows).

In general, if one is willing to pay for more bandwidth, one can get away with significantly less on-chip storage and reach the same levels of performance. This represents an interesting trade-off between chip costs in on-chip storage and system costs in memory bandwidth. That one can approach the performance of the traditional DSP memory organization with such a simple structure is a natural consequence of the fact that DSP applications typically stream data, obviating large cache structures and making stream buffers more attractive.

Reconsidering Permanent Store: Plan 9's File System

Another example of interesting cache designs is Plan 9's file system,[8] in which the designers re-defined the concept of "permanent store" [Quinlan 1991]. The operating system treats the entire magnetic disk system as a mere cache for the backup system (the WORM [write once, read many] jukebox, a jukebox of write-once/read-many optical disks[9]), which is considered the repository of the true file system and thus the ultimate in permanent backing store.

The work is based upon earlier explorations in the same general direction. For instance, Garfinkel [1986] describes a file-system API (application programming interface) that moves copies of files to backup whenever those files are written. The File Motel [Hume 1988] uses the WORM drive as a transparent backup for the file system, which resides as normal on the magnetic disk system. A separate magnetic-disk-resident database maps files to locations on the WORM drive, and the design is such that the mapping database can be reconstructed from the WORM-resident permanent data if the magnetic disk ever crashes. The disadvantage of the design is that copies to backup (the WORM system) can take significant time, resulting in snapshots that are far from atomic (e.g., one can still modify the file system while it is being backed up to the WORM drive, which creates the potential for inconsistency).

Tektronix's Optical File Cabinet [Gait 1988, Laskodi et al. 1988] addresses this issue by placing the file system into the WORM drive itself, so there is always an atomic snapshot of the system. The file system uses a logical namespace that is different from the WORM's physical namespace, because the file system transparently maps files to the WORM space, creating a new WORM-resident block and remapping the logical block every time a block is updated by application or Operating System software. Because every block-write allocates a new block in the WORM drive, the files system's logical namespace must necessarily be significantly smaller than the WORM's physically available namespace. It is possible to write a logical block many times, creating many backups of the block on the WORM drive.

In the design described by Quinlan [1991], the best of both worlds is reached by combining the full namespace of the backing store with the magnetic-disk storage medium. The Operating System's file system resides on the backup device, because the file system identifies its blocks using the namespace offered by the backup device. The operating system uses the faster magnetic-disk space as a transparent cache. Instead of creating a new WORM block on every write, the Plan 9 file system creates one on every backup event (e.g., once every night), holding the newly written data on magnetic disk until that point. This is similar in nature to a write-back cache, whereas the Optical File Cabinet is more akin to a write-through cache.

---

[8]Plan 9 is the (whimsical) name given to version 9 of the Unix operating system.
[9]This research occurred at a time when WORM disks were available, cost roughly the same as magnetic tape, were significantly faster than tape, had a longer shelf-life than magnetic tape, and offered storage densities an order of magnitude larger than rewritable optical media [Hume 1988].

1.4.2 Important Issues, Future Directions

Research in cache design is by no means at a stand still, and the future holds numerous avenues for interesting work. For SRAM-based caches in particular, power dissipation and reliability are primary issues. A rule of thumb is that SRAMs typically account for at least one-third of the power dissipated by microprocessors, and the reliability for SRAM is the worst of the technologies surveyed in this book.

On the power-dissipation front, the decline in importance of dynamic power with respect to leakage power changes some traditional rules. For instance, fully associative caches have long been a staple for applications that require high hit rate with a minimum of storage, but they are often avoided due to their high dynamic power dissipation. As leakage power comes to dominate total power, these caches are likely to become more popular, as they can require significantly less storage (and thus fewer transistors) than an equivalently performing direct-mapped or set-associative cache. Fewer transistors means less leakage power.

Taking a different approach, building on-chip caches out of alternative technologies, such as embedded DRAM (eDRAM), is also a promising direction. Though studies in the past have dismissed eDRAM as having unacceptable performance in general-purpose environments, there are several factors at work to counter these initial results, given enough time.

1. The working sets of many high-end applications are growing at a phenomenal pace, making DRAM-based solutions attractive due to their density.
2. The performance of eDRAM technologies is improving to the point that eDRAM matches the performance of off-chip SRAM caches.
3. Embedded DRAM is available in many logic-based processes and even there has a higher reliability than SRAM.
4. Embedded DRAM is expected to dissipate significantly less power, both dynamic and static, compared to SRAM caches.

Another issue for future study is the incredible opportunity for exploring significantly more sophisticated algorithms for content and consistency management as multiple cores and their associated last-level cache controller all move onto the same die. When the last-level cache controller was off-chip (e.g., as part of the system controller), it ran at a significantly slower speed than the microprocessors it served. Moving it onto the same die can increase tenfold the amount of work it can do during the same request. In addition, moving the controller on-chip opens up possibilities for information sharing, giving the controller more access to system state than it ever had before.

Finally, the application of cache principles to new areas that have not traditionally used caches is always a promising area, one that should become very interesting as the sophistication of the various heuristics that can be built grows. For example, the original development of complex block-replacement algorithms, such as least-recently-used (LRU), was done in the context of the operating system's buffer cache, which could afford high-complexity heuristics as the heuristics would be performed in the background of a disk block fetch, a relatively lengthy operation. Such complexity was unthinkable for heuristics in other areas such as solid-state processor caches. Nonetheless, as the technologies from which caches were built in other disciplines grew in capability, these disciplines adopted the same type of analysis and heuristics as the operating system's buffer cache. Currently, the computer-architecture world has explored numerous sophisticated heuristics for prefetching data and dynamic classification of loads. It is only a matter of time before these mechanisms appear elsewhere.

CHAPTER 2

Logical Organization

A cache's logical organization embodies two primary concepts:

1. Physical parameters that determine how the cache is addressed, how it is searched, and what it can store
2. Whether the cache is responsible for performing the various management heuristics on the client's behalf, or whether the client (e.g., a software application using the cache) is responsible

The logical organization of a cache influences how the data is stored in the cache and how it is retrieved from the cache. Deciding *what* to store is a different issue and will be covered in following chapters, as will the topic of maintaining the data's consistency. However, and this is an extremely important point, though the determination of *what to store* is made by a set of heuristics executed at design time and/or run time, the logical organization of the cache also indirectly determines what to cache. While the content-management heuristics make *explicit* choices of what to cache, the logical organization makes *implicit* choices; to wit, the determination of *what to store* can be, and often is, overridden by the cache's logical organization, because the logical organization determines how and where data is stored in the cache. If the organization is incapable of storing two particular data items simultaneously, then, regardless of how important those two data items may be, one of them must remain uncached while the other is in the cache.

Thus, a cache's logical organization is extremely important, and over the years many exhaustive research studies have been performed to choose the "best" organization for a particular cache, given a particular technology and a particular set of benchmarks. In general, a cache organization that places no restrictions on what can be stored and where it can be placed would be best (i.e., a fully associative cache), but this is a potentially expensive design choice.

2.1 Logical Organization: A Taxonomy

The previous chapter introduced transparent caches and scratch-pad memories. Because they are used differently, transparent caches and scratch-pad memories have different implementations and, more importantly, different ramifications. Because they lie at opposite ends of a continuum of design architectures, they define a taxonomy, a range of hybrid cache architectures that lie between them based on their most evident characteristics, including their methods of addressing and content management.

- *Addressing Scheme:* Transparent caches use the naming scheme of the backing store: a program references the cache implicitly and does not even need to know that the cache exists. The scratch-pad, by contrast, uses a separate namespace from the backing store: a program must reference the scratch-pad explicitly. Note that, because they could potentially hold anything in the space, transparent caches require keys or tags to indicate what data is currently cached. Scratch-pad memories require no tags.
- *Management Schemes:* The contents of traditional caches are managed in a manner that is transparent to the application

software: if a data item is touched by the application, it is brought into the cache, and the consistency of the cached data is ensured by the cache. Scratch-pad random-access memories (RAMs) require explicit management: nothing is brought into the scratch-pad unless it is done so intentionally by the application software through an explicit load and store, and hardware makes no attempt to keep the cached version consistent with main memory.

These two parameters define a taxonomy of four[1] basic cache types, shown in Table 2.1:

- **Transparent Cache:** An application can be totally unaware of a transparent cache's existence. Examples include nearly all general-purpose processor caches.
- **Scratch-Pad Memory:** When using a scratch-pad memory, the application is in control of everything. Nothing is stored in the cache unless the application puts it there, and the memory uses a separate namespace disjoint from the backing store. Examples include the tagless SRAMs used in DSPs and microcontrollers.
- **Software-Managed Cache:** In a software-managed cache, the application software controls the cache's contents, but the cache's

addressing scheme is transparent—the cache uses the same namespace as the backing store, and thus, the cache can automatically keep its contents consistent with the backing store. Examples include the software-controlled caches in the VMP multiprocessor [Cheriton et al. 1986], in which a software handler is invoked on cache misses and other events that require cache-coherence actions.

- **Self-Managed Scratch-Pad:** In a self-managed scratch-pad, the cache contents are managed by the cache itself (e.g., in a demand-fetch manner or some other heuristic), and the cache's storage uses a separate namespace from the backing store, addressed explicitly by application software. Examples include implementations of distributed memory, especially those with migrating objects (e.g., Emerald [Jul et al. 1988]).

Figure 2.1 shows the four different types of cache organization. Each has its own implementation and design issues, and each expects different things of the software running on the machine. For purposes of discussion in this chapter, the primary classification will be the addressing mechanism (transparent or non-transparent); within this classification, the cache's contents can either be managed explicitly by the client or by the cache itself.

TABLE 2.1 A taxonomy of cache types

Cache Type	Addressing Scheme	Management Scheme
Transparent cache	Transparent	Implicit (by cache)
Software-managed cache	Transparent	Explicit (by application)
Self-managed scratch-pad	Non-transparent	Implicit (by cache)
Scratch-pad memory	Non-transparent	Explicit (by application)

---

[1]An aside: one could attempt to pull apart the use of tags and the choice of transparent or non-transparent addressing, giving eight different types instead of four. For example, one could in theory build a transparently addressed scratch-pad in which the cache contents are explicitly managed by the application software. The cache has no tag store, but the addressing scheme is transparent. This could be done, for example, if an address translation step was performed before cache index, such as inserting a TLB before indexing an SRAM. However, the TLB in this scheme would become a *de facto* tags array, yielding a software-managed cache.

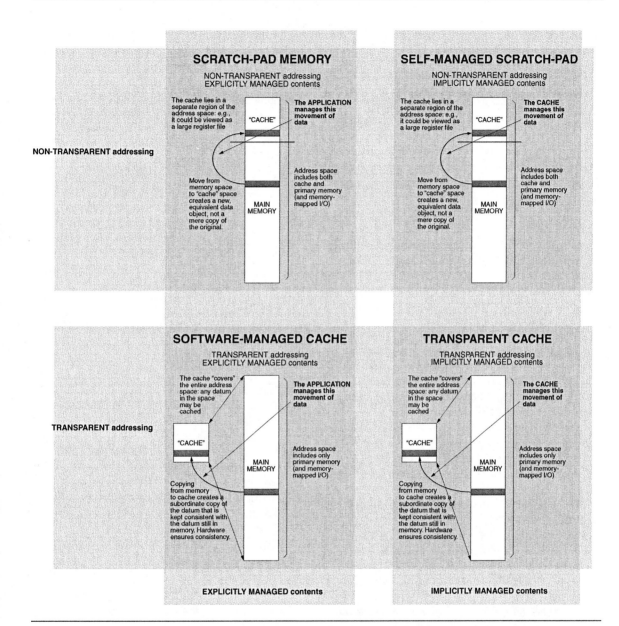

FIGURE 2.1: Examples of several different cache organizations. Though this illustrates "cache" in the context of solid-state memories (e.g., SRAM cache and DRAM main memory), the concepts are applicable to all manners of storage technologies, including SRAM, DRAM, disk, and even tertiary (backup) storage such as optical disk and magnetic tape.

2.2 Transparently Addressed Caches

A transparently addressed cache uses the same namespace as the backing store; that is, a cache lookup for the desired data object uses the same object name one would use when accessing the backing store. For example, if the backing store is the disk drive, then the disk block number would be used to search (or "probe") the cache. If the backing store is main memory, then the physical memory address would be used to search the cache. If the backing store is a magneto-optical or tape jukebox, then its associated identifier would be used. The mechanism extends to software caches as well. For example, if the backing store is the operating system's file system, then the file name would be used to search the cache. If the backing store is the world-wide web, then the URL would be used, and so on. The point is that the client (e.g., application software or even an operating system) need not know anything about the cache's organization or operation to benefit from it. The client simply makes a request to the backing store, and the cache is searched for the requested object implicitly.

Because the cache must be *searched* (a consequence of the fact that it is addressed transparently and not explicitly), there must be a way to determine the cache's contents, and thus, an implicitly addressed cache must have keys or tags, most likely taken from the backing store's namespace as object identifiers. For instance, a software cache could be implemented as a binary search tree, a solid-state cache could be implemented with a tag store that matches the organization of the data store, or a DRAM-based cache fronting a disk drive could have a CAM lookup preceding data access to find the correct physical address [Braunstein et al. 1989]. Note that this is precisely what the TLB does.

Because the cost of searching can be high (consider, for example, a large cache in which every single key or tag is checked for every single lookup), different logical organizations have been developed that try to accomplish simultaneously two goals:

1. Reduce the number of tags checked
2. Keep the likelihood of a cache hit high

Note that these goals tend to pull a cache design in opposite directions. For instance, an easy way to satisfy Goal 1 is to assign a particular data object a single space in the cache, kind of like assigning the parking spaces outside a company's offices. The problem with this is that, unless the cache is extremely large, one can quickly run out of spaces to assign, in which case the cache might have to start throwing out useful data (as an analogy, a company might have to reassign to a new employee a parking spot belonging to the company's CEO).

Basic organization for implicitly addressed caches has already been discussed briefly in Chapter 1. The main point is that a transparent cache typically divides its storage into equivalence classes, or *sets*, and assigns blocks to sets based on the block ID. The single, unique set to which a particular chunk of data belongs is typically determined by a subset of bits taken from its block ID, as shown in Figure 2.2. Once the set is determined, the block may be placed anywhere within that set. Because a block's ID, taken from its location in the memory space, does not change over the course of its lifetime (exceptions including virtually indexed caches), a block will not typically migrate between cache sets. Therefore, one can view these sets as having an exclusive relationship with each other, and so *any* heuristic that chooses a partitioning of data between exclusive storage units would be just as appropriate as the simple bit-vector method shown in Figure 2.2.

A cache can comprise one or more sets; each set can comprise one or more storage slots. This gives rise to the following organizations for solid-state designs.

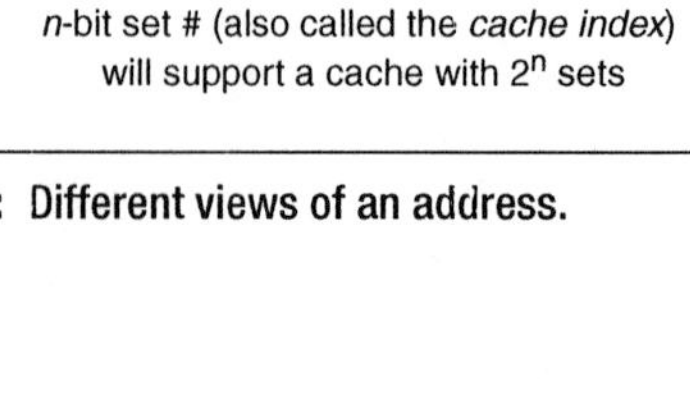

32-bit address:

28 bits	4 bits
Block ID	**byte in block**

28-n bits	n bits	4 bits
Cache Tag	**Set no.**	**byte in block**

n-bit set # (also called the *cache index*) will support a cache with 2^n sets

FIGURE 2.2: Different views of an address.

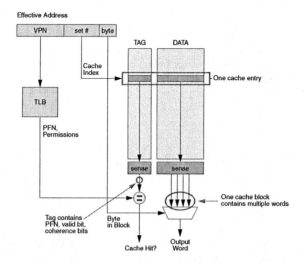

FIGURE 2.3: Block diagram for a direct-mapped cache. Note that data read-out is controlled by tag comparison with the TLB output as well as the block-valid bit (part of the tag or metadata entry) and the page permissions (part of the TLB entry). Data is not read from the cache if the valid bit is not set or if the permissions indicate an invalid access (e.g., writing a read-only block). Note also that the cache size is equal to the virtual memory page size (the cache index does not use bits from the VPN).

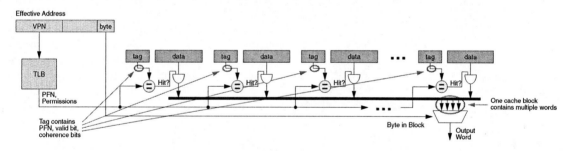

FIGURE 2.4: Fully associative lookup mechanism. This organization is also called a CAM, for content-addressable memory. It is similar to a database in that any entry that has the same tag as the lookup address matches, no matter where it is in the cache. This organization reduces cache contention, but the lookup can be expensive, since the tag of every entry is matched against the lookup address.

- **Direct-Mapped Organization:** Figure 2.3 illustrates a read operation in a *direct-mapped* cache organization. In this organization, a given datum can only reside in one entry of the cache, usually determined by a subset of the datum's address bits. Though the most common index is the low-order bits of the tag field, other indexing schemes exist that use a different set of bits or hash the address to compute an index value bearing

no obvious correspondence to the original address. Whereas in the associative scheme there are *n* tag matches, where *n* is the number of cache lines, in this scheme there is only one tag match because the requested datum can only be found at one location: it is either there or nowhere in the cache.

- **Fully Associative Organization:** Figure 2.4 demonstrates a *fully associative* lookup. In a fully associative organization, the cache is truly a small hardware database. A datum can be placed anywhere in the cache; the tag field identifies the data contents. A search checks the tag of every datum stored in the cache. If any one of the tags matches the tag of the requested address, it is a *cache hit:* the cache contains the requested data.

The benefit of a direct-mapped cache is that it is extremely quick to search and dissipates relatively little power, since there can only be one place that any particular datum can be found. However, this introduces the possibility that several different data might need to reside in the cache at the same place, causing what is known as *contention* for the desired data entry. This results in poor performance, with entries in the cache being replaced frequently; these are *conflict misses.* The problem can be solved by using a fully associative cache, a design choice traditionally avoided due to its high dynamic power dissipation (in a typical lookup, every single tag is compared to the search tag). However, as dynamic power decreases in significance relative to leakage power, this design choice will become more attractive.

- **Set-Associative Organization:** As a compromise between the two extremes, a set-associative cache lies in between direct-mapped and fully associative designs and often reaps the benefits of both designs—fast lookup and lower contention. Figures 2.5 and 2.6 illustrate two set-associative organizations. Figure 2.5 shows an implementation built of a small number of direct-mapped caches, typically used for low levels of set associativity, and Figure 2.6 shows an implementation built of a small number of content-addressable memories, typically used for higher degrees of set associativity.

These are the basic choices of organization for transparently addressed caches. They are applicable to solid-state implementations (evident from the diagrams) as well as software implementations. For instance, an operating system's buffer cache or distributed memory system's object cache could be implemented as a large array of blocks, indexed by a hash of the block ID or object ID, which would correspond to a direct-mapped organization as in Figure 2.3; it could be implemented as a binary search tree, which would correspond to a fully associative organization, because the search tree is simply software's way to "search all tags in parallel" as in Figure 2.4; or it could be implemented as a set of equivalence classes, each of which maintains its own binary search tree, an arrangement that would correspond to a set-associative organization as in Figure 2.6 (each row in the figure is a separate equivalence class). The last organization of software

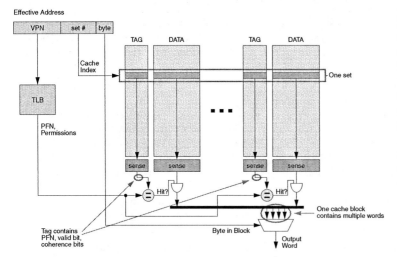

FIGURE 2.5: Block diagram for an n-way set-associative cache. A set-associative cache can be made of several direct-mapped caches operated in parallel. Note that data read-out is controlled by tag comparison with the TLB output as well as the block-valid bit (part of the tag or metadata entry) and the page permissions (part of the TLB entry). Note also that the cache column size is equal to the virtual memory page size (the cache index does not use bits from the VPN).

cache could significantly reduce the search time for any given object, assuming that the assignment of objects to equivalence classes is evenly distributed.

An important point to note is that, because the transparently addressed cache uses the same namespace as the backing store, it is possible (and this is indeed the typical case) for the cache to maintain only a *copy* of the datum that is held in the backing store. In other words, caching an object does not necessarily supersede or invalidate the original. The original stays where it is, and it is up to the consistency-management solution to ensure that the original is kept consistent with the cached copy.

What does this have to do with logical organization? Because the transparently addressed cache maintains a copy of the object's identifier (e.g., its physical address, if the backing store is main memory), it is possible for the cache to keep the copy in the backing store consistent transparently. Without this information, the application software must be responsible for maintaining consistency between the cache and the backing store. This is a significant issue for processor caches: if the cache does not maintain a physical tag for each cached item, then the cache hardware is not capable of ensuring the consistency of the copy in main memory.

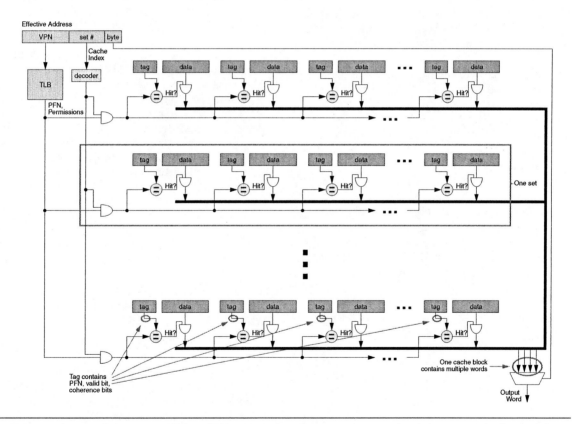

FIGURE 2.6: Set-associative cache built from CAMs. The previous figure showed a set-associative cache built of several direct-mapped caches, which is appropriate when the degree of associativity is low. When the degree of associativity is high, it is more appropriate to build the cache out of CAMs (content-addressable memories, i.e., fully associative caches), where each CAM represents one data set or equivalence class. For example, the Strong ARM's 32-way set-associative cache is built this way.

From this point, transparently addressed caches are further divided, depending on whether their contents are managed implicitly (i.e., by the cache itself) or explicitly (i.e., by the application software).

2.2.1 Implicit Management: Transparent Caches

Transparent caches are the most common form of general-purpose processor caches. Their advantage is that they will typically do a reasonable job of improving performance even if unoptimized and even if the software is totally unaware of their presence. However, because software does not handle them directly and does not dictate their contents, these caches, above all other cache organizations, must successfully *infer application intent* to be effective at reducing accesses to the backing store. At this, transparent caches do a remarkable job.

Cache design and optimization is the process of performing a design-space exploration of the various parameters available to a designer by running example benchmarks on a parameterized cache simulator. This is the "quantitative approach" advocated by Hennessy and Patterson in the late 1980s and early 1990s [Hennessy & Patterson 1990]. The latest edition of their book is a good starting point for a thorough discussion of how a cache's performance is affected when the various organizational parameters are changed. Just a few items are worth mentioning here (and note that we have not even touched the dynamic aspects of caches, i.e., their various policies and strategies):

- Cache misses decrease with cache size, up to a point where the application fits into the cache. For large applications, it is worth plotting cache misses on a logarithmic scale because a linear scale will tend to downplay the true effect of the cache. For example, a cache miss rate that decreases from 1% to 0.1% to 0.01% as the cache increases in size will be shown as a flat line on a typical linear scale, suggesting no improvement whatsoever, whereas a log scale will indicate the true point of diminishing returns, wherever that might be. If the cost of missing the cache is small, using the wrong knee of the curve will likely make little difference, but if the cost of missing the cache is high (for example, if studying TLB misses or consistency misses that necessitate flushing the processor pipeline), then using the wrong knee can be very expensive.

- Comparing two cache organizations on miss rate alone is only acceptable these days if it is shown that the two caches have the same access time. For example, processor caches have a tremendous impact on the achievable cycle time of the microprocessor, so a larger cache with a lower miss rate might require a longer cycle time that ends up yielding worse execution time than a smaller, faster cache. Pareto-optimality graphs plotting miss rate against cycle time work well, as do graphs plotting total execution time against power dissipation or die area.

- As shown at the end of the previous chapter, the cache block size is an extremely powerful parameter that is worth exploiting. Large block sizes reduce the size and thus the cost of the tags array and decoder circuit. The familiar saddle shape in graphs of block size versus miss rate indicates when cache pollution occurs, but this is a phenomenon that scales with cache size. Large cache sizes can and should exploit large block sizes, and this couples well with the tremendous bandwidths available from modern DRAM architectures.

2.2.2 Explicit Management: Software-Managed Caches

We return to the difference between transparent caches and scratch-pad memories. A program addresses a transparent cache implicitly, and the cache holds but a copy of the referenced datum. A program references a scratch-pad explicitly, and a datum is brought into the scratch-pad by an operation that effectively gives the item a new name. In essence, a load from the backing store, followed by a store into a scratch-pad, creates a new datum, but does not destroy the original. Therefore, two equal versions of the datum remain. However, there is no attempt by the hardware to keep the versions consistent (to ensure that they always have the same value) because the semantics of the mechanism suggest that the two copies are not, in fact, copies of the same datum, but instead two independent data. If they are to remain consistent, it is up to the application software to perform the necessary updates. As mentioned earlier, this makes scratch-pad memories less-than-ideal compiler targets, especially when compared to transparent caches. Round one to the transparent cache.

Because they could potentially hold anything in the backing store, transparent caches require tags to indicate what data is currently cached; scratch-pad memories require no tags. In solid-state implementations, tags add significant die area and power dissipation: a scratch-pad SRAM can have 34% smaller area and 40% lower power dissipation than a transparent cache of the same capacity [Banakar et al. 2002]. Round two to the scratch-pad.

General-purpose processor caches are managed by the cache hardware in a manner that is transparent to the application software. In general, any data item touched by the application is brought into the cache. In contrast, nothing is brought into the scratch-pad unless it is done so intentionally by the application software through an explicit load and store. The flip side of this is interesting. Whereas any reference can potentially cause important information to be removed from a traditional cache, data is never removed from a scratch-pad unless it is done so intentionally. This is why scratch-pads have more predictable behavior than transparent caches and why transparent caches are almost universally disabled in real-time systems, which value predictability over raw performance. Round three to the scratch-pad, at least for embedded applications.

A hybrid solution that could potentially draw together two of the better aspects of caches and scratch-pads is an explicitly managed, transparently addressed cache, or *software-managed cache* [Jacob 1998]. Such a cache organization uses transparent addressing, which offers a better compiler target than explicit addressing, but the organization relies upon software for content management,

an arrangement that allows one to ensure at design time what the cache's contents will be at run time. In addition, the cache uses the same namespace as the backing store, and thus the cache can automatically keep its contents consistent with the backing store. As will be discussed in the next chapter, the cache can rely upon the programmer and/or compiler to decide what to cache and when to cache it, similar to scratch-pad memories. Note that this organization is not an all-around total-win situation because it still requires a tag store or similar function, and thus it is more expensive than a scratch-pad SRAM, at least in a solid-state implementation.

The following are examples of software-managed processor caches.

VMP: Software-Controlled Virtual Caches

The VMP multiprocessor [Cheriton et al. 1986, 1988, 1989] places the content and consistency management of its virtual caches under software control, providing its designers an extremely flexible and powerful tool for exploring coherence protocols. The design uses large cache blocks and a high degree of associativity to reduce the number of cache misses and therefore the frequency of incurring the potentially high costs of a software-based cache fill.

Each VMP processor node contains several hardware structures, including a central processing unit, a software-controlled virtual cache, a cache controller, and special memory (see Figure 2.7). Objects the system cannot afford to have causing faults, such as root page tables and fault-handling code, are kept in a separate area called *local memory*, distinguished by the high-order bits of the virtual address. Local memory is essentially a scratch-pad memory. Like SPUR (symbolic processing using RISCs) [Ritchie 1985, Hill et al. 1986], VMP eliminates the TLB, but instead of using a hardware table-walker, VMP relies upon a software handler maintained in this local memory. A cache miss invokes a fault handler that locates the requested data, possibly causes other caches on the bus to invalidate their copies, and loads the cache. Note that, even though the cache-miss handler is maintained in a separate cache namespace, it is capable of interacting with other software modules in the system.

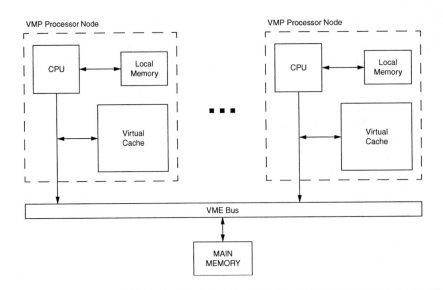

FIGURE 2.7: The VMP multiprocessor. Each VMP processor node contains a microprocessor (68020), local cache outside the namespace of main memory, and a software-controlled virtual cache. The software-controlled cache made the design space for multiprocessor cache coherency easier to explore, as the protocols could be rewritten at will.

An interesting development in VMP is the use of a directory structure for implementing cache coherence. Moreover, because the directory maintains both virtual and physical tags for objects (so that main memory can be kept consistent transparently), the directory structure also effectively acts as a cache for the page table. The VMP software architecture uses the directory structure almost to the exclusion of the page table for providing translations because it is faster, and using it instead of the page table can reduce memory traffic significantly. This enables the software handler to perform address translation as part of cache fill without the aid of a TLB, but yet quickly enough for high-performance needs. A later enhancement to the architecture [Cheriton et al., 1988] allowed the cache to do a hardware-based cache refill automatically, i.e., without vectoring to a software handler, in instances where the virtual-physical translation is found in the directory structure.

SoftVM: A Cache-Fill Instruction

Another software-managed cache design was developed for the University of Michigan's PUMA project [Jacob & Mudge 1996, 1997, 2001]. It is very similar to Cheriton's software-controlled virtual caches, with the interesting difference being the mechanism provided by the architecture for cache fill. The software cache-fill handler in VMP is given by the hardware a cache slot as a suggestion, and the hardware moves the loaded data to that slot on behalf of the software. PUMA's SoftVM mechanism was an experiment to see how little hardware one could get away with (e.g., it maintains the handler in regular memory and not a separate memory, and like SPUR and VMP, it eliminates the TLB); the mechanism provides the bare necessities to the software in the form of a single instruction.[2]

When a virtual address fails to hit in the bottommost cache level, a *cache-miss* exception is raised. The address that fails to hit in the lowest level cache is the

---

[2]Portions reprinted, with permission, from "Uniprocessor virtual memory without TLBs," by B. Jacob and T. Mudge. *IEEE Transactions on Computers*, 50(5), 482–499, May 2001. Copyright © 2001 IEEE.

failing address, and the data it references is the *failing data*. On a cache-miss exception, the hardware saves the program counter of the instruction causing the cache miss and invokes the miss handler. The miss handler loads the data at the failing address on behalf of the user thread. The operating system must therefore be able to load a datum using one address and place it in the cache tagged with a different address. It must also be able to reference memory virtually or physically, cached or uncached. For example, to avoid causing a cache-miss exception, the cache-miss handler must execute using physical addresses. These may be cacheable, provided that a cacheable physical address that misses the cache causes no exception and that a portion of the virtual space can be directly mapped onto physical memory.

When a virtual address misses the cache, the failing data, once loaded, must be placed in the cache at an index derived from the failing address and tagged with the failing address's virtual tag; otherwise, the original thread will not be able to reference its own data. A new load instruction is defined, in which the operating system specifies a virtual tag and set of protection bits to apply to the incoming data, as well as a physical address from which to load the data. The incoming data is inserted into the caches with the specified tag and protection information. This scheme requires a privileged instruction to be added to the instruction-set architecture: *mapped-load*, depicted in Figure 2.8.

The mapped-load instruction is simply a load-to-cache instruction that happens to tell the virtual cache explicitly what bits to use for the tag and protection information. It does *not* load to the register file. It has two operands, as shown in the following syntax:

```
mapld rP, rV  # register P contains physical address
              # register V contains VADDR and
                protection bits
```

The protection bits in **rV** come from the mapping PTE. The VADDR portion of **rV** comes from the failing virtual address; it is the topmost bits of the virtual address minus the size of the protection information (which should be no more than the bits needed to identify a byte within a cache block). Both the cache index and cache tag are recovered from

VADDR (virtual address); note that this field is larger than the virtual page number. The hardware should not assume *any* overlap between virtual and physical addresses beyond the cache line offset. This is essential to allow a software-defined (i.e., operating-system-defined) page size.

The **rP** operand is used to fetch the requested datum, so it can contain a virtual or physical address. The datum identified by the **rP** operand is obtained from memory (or perhaps the cache itself) and then inserted into the cache at the cache block determined by the VADDR bits and tagged with the specified virtual tag. Thus, an operating system can translate data that misses the cache; load it from memory (or even another location in the cache); and place it in any cache block, tagged with any value. When the original thread is restarted, its data is in the cache at the correct line with the correct tag. To restart the thread, the failing load or store instruction is retried.

```
MAPPED-LOAD:   mapld rP, rV

               VCache.data[ rV.index ] <- Memory[ rP ]
               VCache.tag[ rV.index ] <- rV.tag
               VCache.prot[ rV.index ] <- rV.prot
```

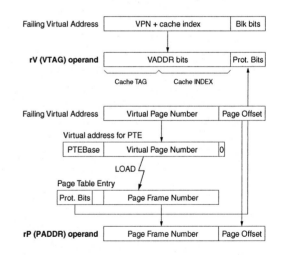

FIGURE 2.8: Mapped-load instruction. The top portion gives the syntax and semantics of the instruction. The bottom portion illustrates the source of the rV (VTAG+prot bits) and rP (physical address) operands. The example assumes an MIPS-like page table.

The single mapped-load instruction is an atomic operation. The fact that the load is not binding (i.e., no data is brought into the register file) means that it does not actually change the processor state. Protections are not checked until the failing load or store instruction is retried, at which point it could be found that a protection violation occurred. This simplifies the hardware requirements. Because the data is not transferred to the register file until a failing load is retried, different forms of the mapped-load for load word, load halfword, load byte, etc. are not necessary. There is no compiler impact on adding the mapped-load to an instruction set because the instruction is privileged and will not be used by user-level instructions; it will be found only in the cache-miss handler which will most likely be written in assembly code.

2.3 Non-Transparently Addressed Caches

A non-transparently addressed cache is one that the application software must know about to use. The cache data lies in a separate namespace from the backing store, and the application must be aware of this namespace if it is to use the cache. The advantage of this arrangement is that a cache access requires no search, no lookup. There is no question whether the item requested is present in the cache because the item being requested is not an object from the backing store, but instead is a storage unit within the cache itself, e.g., the cache would be explicitly asked by application software for the contents of its nth storage block, which the cache would return without the need for a tag compare or key lookup. This has a tremendous impact on implementation. For instance, in solid-state technologies (e.g., SRAMs) this type of cache does not require the tag bits, dirty bits, and comparison logic found in transparently addressed caches.

A common example of non-transparently addressed caches is SRAM that is memory-mapped to a part of the address space (e.g., the SRAM0 and SRAM1 segments shown in Chapter 0, Figure 0.4) or storage that is accessed based on context (e.g., the internal and external data segments of the 8051 microcontroller, shown in Figure 2.9). Note that these arrangements exhibit an exclusive relationship with the backing store: an item is either in the scratch-pad or in the backing store, but it cannot be in both because their namespaces (enforced by requiring different access mechanisms) are disjoint.

Because there is no need for a potentially expensive search in this type of cache, many of the different

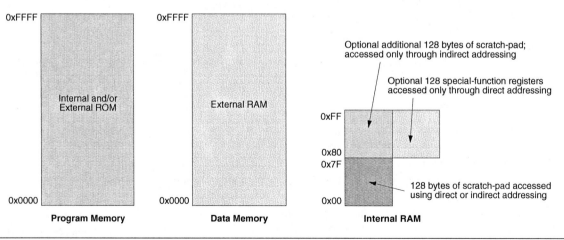

FIGURE 2.9: Memory map for the 8051 microcontroller. Program memory, which is either internal or external ROM, is accessed on instruction-fetch; data memory, external RAM, is accessed through MOVX instructions; and internal RAM is accessed using indirect and/or direct addressing [Synopsys 2002].

choices of organization for transparently addressed caches become obviated, and in practice, many nontransparent caches are simply large arrays of storage blocks. However, because the cost of reading the cache can be significant both in access time and in power dissipation as the cache gets large, the cache is typically partitioned into subordinate banks, only one of which is activated on a read or write. This partitioning can be transparent or exposed to the application software. A transparent example would be an SRAM divided in 2^n banks, one of which is chosen by an n-bit vector taken from the cache address. On the other hand, one would want to expose the partition to software if, for example, the partitions are not all equal in size or cost of access, in which case a compiler-based heuristic could arrange cached data among the various partitions according to weights derived from the partitions' associated costs.

An important point to note is that, because the cache uses a namespace that is separate from the backing store, the cache exhibits an exclusive relationship with the backing store; that is, the cache, by definition, does not maintain a *copy* of the datum in the backing store, but instead holds a separate datum entirely. Moving data into an explicitly addressed cache creates a brand-new data item, and unless the cache is given a pointer to the original in the backing store, the cache cannot automatically maintain consistency between the version in the cache and the version in the backing store.

From this point, explicitly addressed caches are further divided, depending on whether their contents are managed explicitly (i.e., by the application software) or implicitly (i.e., by the cache itself).

2.3.1 Explicit Management: Scratch-Pad Memories

Scratch-pad memory (SPM) offers the ultimate in application control. It is explicitly addressed, and its contents are explicitly managed by the application software. Its data allocation is meant to be done by the software, usually the compiler, and thus, like software-managed caches, it represents a more predictable form of caching that is more appropriate for real-time systems than caches using implicit management.

The major challenge in using SPMs is to allocate explicitly to them the application program's frequently used data and/or instructions. The traditional approach has been to rely on the programmer, who writes annotations in source code that assign variables to different memory regions. Program annotations, however, have numerous drawbacks.

- They are tedious to derive and, like all things manual in programming, are fraught with the potential for introducing bugs.
- A corollary to the previous point: they increase software development time and cost.
- They are not portable across memory sizes (they require manual rewriting for different memory sizes).
- They do not adapt to dynamically changing program behavior.

For these reasons, programmer annotations are increasingly being replaced by automated, compile-time methods. We will discuss such methods in the next chapter.

Perspective: Embedded vs. General-Purpose Systems

As mentioned earlier, transparent caches can improve code even if that code has not been designed or optimized specifically for the given cache's organization. Consequently, transparent caches have been a big success for general-purpose systems, in which backward compatibility between next-generation processors and previous-generation code is extremely important (i.e., modern processors are expected to run legacy code that was written with older hardware in mind). Continuing with this logic, using SPM is usually not even feasible in general-purpose systems due to binary-code portability: code compiled for the scratch-pad is usually fixed for one SRAM size. Binary portability is valuable for desktops, where independently distributed binaries must work on any cache size. In many embedded systems, however, the software is usually considered part of the co-design of the system: it resides in ROM and cannot be changed. Thus, there is really no harm to having embedded binaries customized to a particular memory size. Note that source code is portable even though a specific executable is optimized for a particular SRAM size; recompilation with a different memory size is always possible.

Though transparent caches are a mainstay of general-purpose systems, their overheads are less defensible for use in embedded systems. Transparent caches incur significant penalties in area cost, energy, hit latency, and real-time guarantees. Other than hit latency, all of these are more important for embedded systems than for general-purpose systems. A detailed recent study compares transparent caches with SPMs. Among other things, they show that a scratch-pad has 34% smaller area and 40% lower power consumption than a cache of the same capacity [Banakar et al. 2002]. These savings are significant since the on-chip cache typically consumes 25–50% of the processor's area and energy consumption, a fraction that is increasing with time. More surprisingly, Banakar compares performance of a transparent cache to that of a scratch-pad using a simple static knapsack-based allocation algorithm and measures a run-time cycle count that is 18% better for the scratch-pad. Defying conventional wisdom, they found no advantage to using a transparent cache, even in high-end embedded systems in which performance is important.

Given the power, cost, performance, and real-time advantages of a scratch-pad, it is not surprising that scratch-pads are the most common form of SRAM in embedded CPUs today. Examples of embedded processors with a scratch-pad include low-end chips such as the Motorola MPC500, Analog Devices ADSP-21XX, and Motorola Coldfire 5206E; mid-grade chips such as the ARMv6, Analog Devices ADSP-21160m, Atmel AT91-C140, ARM 968E-S, Hitachi M32R-32192, and Infineon XC166; and high-end chips such as Analog Devices ADSP-TS201S, Hitachi SuperH-SH7050, IBM's PowerPC 405/440, and Motorola Dragonball. In addition, high-performance chips for games and other media applications, such as IBM's new Cell Architecture, and network processors, such as the Intel's IXP network processor family, all include SPM.

Trends in recent embedded designs indicate that the dominance of a scratch-pad will likely consolidate further in the future [LCTES Panel 2003, Banakar et al. 2002] for regular processors as well as network processors.

2.3.2 Implicit Management: Self-Managed Scratch-Pads

The implicitly managed, non-transparent memory, or *self-managed scratch-pad*, is an odd beast. Due to the cache's non-transparent addressing scheme, the cache data lies in its own namespace, and therefore, the cache exhibits an exclusive relationship with the backing store. It does not hold copies of the data, but the actual data themselves. This could be useful in a secure setting or one in which storage space is at a premium. The cache contents are decided by the cache's heuristics, not the application software. This provides cross-compatibility to support software not explicitly written for the cache in question, and it makes for a better compiler target than an explicitly managed cache.

Such a cache model would make sense, for example, in a distributed shared memory system in which objects are not allowed to have multiple copies lying around the system (e.g., Emerald's mobile objects [Jul et al. 1988]), the local space and global storage use different namespaces (e.g., permanent object stores that perform *swizzling* [Hosking & Moss 1990]), and the underlying caching architecture performs the cache fill automatically on behalf of the application.

2.4 Virtual Addressing and Protection

Virtual addressing is available for solid-state cache implementations in systems with virtual memory support. Generally, the concept is also applicable beyond solid-state implementations and simply implies that one can create a new namespace orthogonal to that of the backing store and local cache storage and perform some mapping between. However, we will stick to the solid-state version, largely because this serves as a foundation for the many problems that virtual memory creates and must be solved.

By "protection" we are referring to the general mechanism that the operating system uses to protect data from misuse, e.g., overwriting text pages, gaining access to the data of another process, etc. The operating system cannot be involved in every memory access, and one efficient alternative is to provide the appropriate support in the cache system.

Note that these mechanisms are not specific to explicit/implicit addressing or explicit/implicit management. Virtual caches, address-space identifiers (ASIDs), and/or protection bits can all be used in any of the cache organizations described in this chapter.

2.4.1 Virtual Caches

As mentioned earlier, a transparent cache is an implementation in which the stored object retains the same identifier as is used to access it from the backing store. Virtual caches offer a slight twist on this idea. The backing store for a processor cache is usually taken to be main memory, physically addressed; therefore, one would expect all processor caches to use the physical address to identify a cached item. However, virtual memory offers a completely different address for use, one which might be even more convenient to use than the physical address. Recall that on each cache access, the cache is *indexed*, and the *tags* are compared. For each of these actions,

either the data block's virtual address or the data block's physical address may be used. Thus, we have four choices for cache organization.

Physically indexed, physically tagged: The cache is indexed and tagged by its physical address. Therefore, the virtual address must be translated before the cache can be accessed. The advantage of the design is that since the cache uses the same namespace as physical memory, it can be entirely controlled by hardware, and the operating system need not concern itself with managing the cache. The disadvantage is that address translation is in the critical path. This becomes a problem as clock speeds increase, as application data sets increase with increasing memory sizes, and as larger TLBs are needed to map the larger data sets (it is difficult and expensive to make a large TLB fast). Two different physically indexed, physically tagged organizations are illustrated in Figure 2.10. The difference between the two is that the second

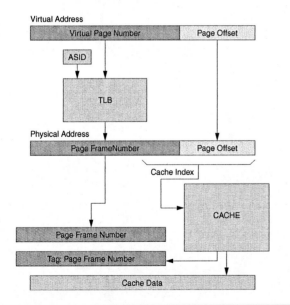

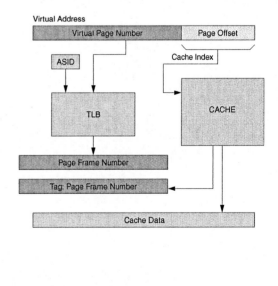

FIGURE 2.10: Two physically indexed, physically tagged cache organizations. The cache organization on the right uses only bits from the page offset to index the cache, and so it is technically still a virtually indexed cache. The benefit of doing so is that its TLB lookup is not in the critical path for cache indexing (as is the case in the organization on the left). The disadvantage is that the cache index cannot grow, and so cache capacity can only grow by increasing the size of each cache block and/or increasing set associativity.

uses only bits from the page offset to index the cache, and therefore its TLB lookup is not in the critical path for cache indexing (as it is in the first organization).

Physically indexed, virtually tagged: The cache is indexed by its physical address, but the tag contains the virtual address. This is traditionally considered an odd combination, as the tag is read out as a result of indexing the cache. If the physical address is available at the start of the procedure (implying that address translation has been performed), then why not use the physical address as a tag? If a single physical page is being shared at two different virtual addresses, then there will be contention for the cache line, since both arrangements cannot be satisfied at the same time. However, if the cache is the size of a virtual page, or if the size of the *cache bin* (the size of the cache divided by its associativity [Kessler & Hill 1992])

is no more than a virtual page, then the cache is effectively indexed by the physical address since the page offset is identical in the virtual and physical addresses. This organization is pictured in Figure 2.11 on the left. The advantage of the physically indexed, virtually tagged cache organization is that, like the physically indexed/physically tagged organization, the operating system need not perform explicit cache management. On the right is an optimization that applies to this organization as well as the previous organization. To index the cache with a physical address, not all of the virtual page bits need translation; only those that index the cache need translation. The MIPS R6000 used what they called a *TLB Slice* to translate only the small number of bits needed for cache access [Taylor et al. 1990]. The "translation" obtained is only a hint and not guaranteed to be correct. Thus, it uses only part of the VPN and does not require an ASID.

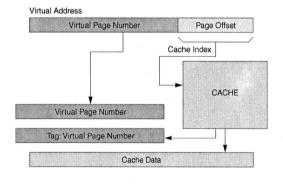

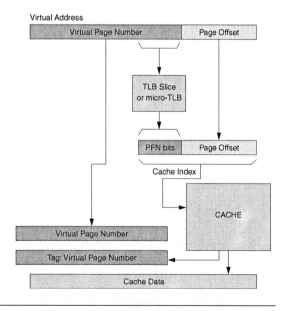

FIGURE 2.11: Two physically indexed, virtually tagged cache organizations. The cache organization on the left uses only bits from the page offset to index the cache. It is technically still a virtually indexed cache. As shown on the right, one need not incur the cost of accessing the entire TLB to get a physical index; one need only translate enough bits to index the cache.

Virtually indexed, physically tagged: The cache is indexed by the virtual address, which is available immediately since it needs no translation, and the cache is tagged by the physical address, which does require translation. Since the tag compare happens after indexing the cache, the translation of the virtual address can happen at the same time as the cache index; the two can be done in parallel. Though address translation is necessary, it is not in the critical path. The advantages of the scheme are a much faster access time than a physically indexed cache and a reduced need for management as compared to a virtually indexed, virtually tagged cache (e.g., hardware can ensure that multiple aliases to the same physical block do not reside in multiple entries of a set). However, management is still necessary, as opposed to physically indexed caches, because the cache is virtually indexed. The cache organization is illustrated in Figure 2.12.

Virtually indexed, virtually tagged: The cache is indexed and tagged by the virtual address. The advantage of this design is that address translation is not needed anywhere in the process. A translation lookaside buffer is not needed, and if one is used, it only needs to be accessed when a requested datum is not in the cache. On such a cache miss, the operating system must translate the virtual address and load the datum from physical memory. A TLB would speed up the translation if the translation had been performed previously and the mapping was still to be found in the TLB. Since the TLB is not in the critical path, it could be very large; though this would imply a slow access time, a larger TLB would hold much more mapping information, and its slow access time would be offset by its infrequency of access. The cache organization is illustrated in Figure 2.13.

Why might one of these organizations be more convenient than another? One can clearly see that the TLB, if involved, is an essential component of cache lookup. In a large, physically indexed cache, the TLB lookup is on the critical path to cache access: the cache cannot be accessed until the TLB returns the

physical translation. Either both lookups (TLB probe and cache probe) must be fast enough to fit together, sequentially, in a single clock cycle or the two must be pipelined on successive cycles, which pushes cache access out a cycle later than when the target address first becomes available. Using the virtual index (or constraining the size of the cache so that the cache index is the same bit vector in both the virtual and physical addresses, as in the right-hand side of Figure 2.10) moves the TLB lookup off the critical path, thereby speeding up the cache access.

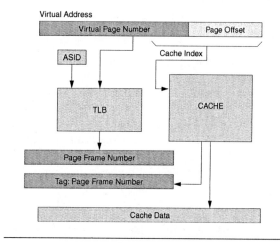

FIGURE 2.12: A virtually indexed, physically tagged cache organization.

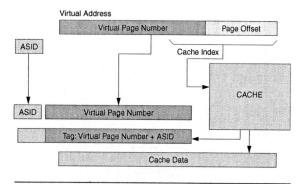

FIGURE 2.13: A virtually indexed, virtually tagged cache organization.

For another example, note that a cache hit relies upon a TLB hit (for the tag as well as page-level access permissions). Instances exist in which the requested data is found in the cache, but its corresponding mapping information is not found in the TLB. These cases represent *de facto* cache misses because, in these cases, the cache access cannot proceed until the TLB is refilled [Jacob & Mudge 1997, 2001]. In virtually tagged caches (Figures 2.11 and 2.13), the TLB probe is not needed until a cache miss occurs, an event that is infrequent for large caches. These cache organizations can accept a TLB that is expensive (i.e., slow and/or power inefficient) because the TLB is rarely probed—as opposed to cache organizations with physical tags, in which the TLB is probed on every cache access.

However, removing the TLB from the equation is very tricky. For instance, if the cache uses a virtual tag, then the cache must be direct-mapped or managed by the client (e.g., the operating system). The use of a virtual tag implies that the cache itself will not be able to distinguish between multiple copies of the same datum if each copy is labeled with a different virtual address. If a physical region is accessed through multiple virtual addresses, then a set-associative cache with only virtual tags would allow the corresponding cache data to reside in multiple locations within the cache—even within multiple blocks of the same set.

Note that, though virtual addressing is compatible with both explicit and implicit cache management, if a virtual cache is expected to maintain data consistency with the backing store, the cache's organization must contain for each stored block its identifier from the backing store (e.g., a physical tag for a solid-state implementation). If the cache has no back-pointer, it will be incapable of transparently updating the backing store, and such consistency management will necessarily be the software's responsibility.

2.4.2 ASIDs and Protection Bits

ASIDs and protection bits are means for the cache to enforce the operating system's protection designation for blocks of data. An operating system that implements multi-tasking will assign different IDs to different tasks to keep their associated data structures (e.g., process control blocks) separate and distinct. Operating systems also keep track of page-level protections, such as enforcing read-only status for text pages and allowing data pages to be marked as read-only, read/write, or write-only, for example, to implement safely a unidirectional communication pipe between processes through shared memory segments.

Some issues that arise include distinguishing the data of one process from the data belonging to another process once the data are cached. Numerous simple solutions exist, but the simple solutions are often inefficient. For example, one could use no ASIDs in the cache system and flush the caches on context switches and operating-system traps. One could use no protection bits in the cache system and avoid caching writable data, instead flushing all write data immediately to the backing store. Obviously, using the cache system to perform these functions is appropriate, and if the cache system is to enforce protection, it must maintain ASIDs and protection bits.

Address space identification within the cache is implicit if the cache is physically tagged—using physical tags pushes the burden of differentiating processes onto the shoulders of the virtual memory system (e.g., via the TLB, which takes an ASID as input, or via the page table, which effectively does the same). However, if the cache is virtually tagged, an ASID must be present, for example, in each tag.

Protection bits are necessary for both virtual and physical caches, unless the function is provided by the TLB. If so, note that read/write protection is provided at a page-level granularity, which precludes a block- or sub-block-level protection mechanism, both of which have been explored in multiprocessor systems to reduce false sharing.

2.4.3 Inherent Problems

Virtual caches complicate support for virtual-address aliasing and protection-bit modification. Aliasing can give rise to the *synonym problem* when memory is shared at different virtual addresses [Goodman 1987], and this has been shown to cause significant overhead [Wheeler & Bershad 1992].

Protection-bit modification is used to implement such features as copy-on-write [Anderson et al. 1991, Rashid et al. 1988] and can also cause significant overhead when used frequently.

The synonym problem has been solved in hardware using schemes such as dual tag sets [Goodman 1987] or back-pointers [Wang et al. 1989]. Synonyms can be avoided completely by setting policy in the operating system. For example, OS/2 requires all shared segments to be located at identical virtual addresses in all processes so that processes use the same address for the same data [Deitel 1990]. SunOS requires shared pages to be aligned in virtual space on extremely large boundaries (at least the size of the largest cache) so that aliases will map to the same cache line[3] [Cheng 1987]. Single address space operating systems such as Opal [Chase et al. 1992a and b] or Psyche [Scott et al. 1988] solve the problem by eliminating the need for virtual-address aliasing entirely. In a single address space, all shared data is referenced through global addresses. As in OS/2, this allows pointers to be shared freely across process boundaries.

Protection-bit modification in virtual caches can also be problematic. A virtual cache allows one to "lazily" access the TLB only on a cache miss. If this happens, protection bits must be stored with each cache line or in an associated page-protection structure accessed every cycle, or else protection is ignored. When one replicates protection bits for a page across several cache lines, changing the page's protection can be costly. Obvious but expensive solutions include flushing the entire cache or sweeping through the entire cache and modifying the affected lines.

A problem also exists with ASIDs. An operating system can maintain hundreds or thousands of active processes simultaneously, and in the course of an afternoon, it can sweep through many times that amount. Each one of these processes will be given a unique identifier, because operating systems typically use 32-bit or 64-bit numbers to identify processes. In contrast, many hardware architectures only recognize tens to hundreds of different processes [Jacob & Mudge 1998b]—MIPS R2000/3000 has a 6-bit ASID; MIPS R10000 has an 8-bit ASID; and Alpha 21164 has a 7-bit ASID. In these instances, the operating system will be forced to perform frequent remapping of ASIDs to process IDs, with TLB and cache flushes required for every remap (though, depending on implementation, these flushes could be specific to the ASID involved and not a whole-scale flush of the entire TLB and/or cache). Architectures that use IBM 801-style segmentation [Chang & Mergen 1988] and/or larger ASIDs tend to have an easier time of this.

2.5 Distributed and Partitioned Caches

Numerous cache organizations exist that are not monolithic entities. As mentioned earlier, the primary concern is convenience when analyzing these caches. For example, a level-1 cache may comprise a dedicated instruction cache and another dedicated data cache. In some instances, it is convenient to refer to "the level-1 cache" as a whole (e.g., "the chip has a 1MB L1 cache"), while in other instances it conveys more information to refer to each individual part of the cache (e.g., "the L1 i-cache has a 10% hit rate, while the L1 d-cache has a 90% hit rate," suggesting a rebalancing of resources). Note that the constituent components ganged together for the sake of convenience need not lie at the same horizontal "level" in the memory hierarchy (as illustrated in Chapter 1, Figures 1.8 and 1.9). A hierarchical web cache can be described and analyzed as "a cache" when, in fact, it is an entire subnetwork of servers organized in a tiered fashion and covering a large physical/geographical expanse.

Generally speaking, the smallest thing that can be called a cache is the smallest addressable unit of storage—a unit that may or may not be exposed externally to the cache's client. For example, within a multi-banked, solid-state cache, the bank is the smallest

---

[3]Note that the SunOS scheme only solves the problem for direct-mapped virtual caches or set-associative virtual caches with physical tags. Shared data can still exist in two different blocks of the same set in an associative, virtually indexed, virtually tagged cache.

addressable unit of storage (note that a common metric for measuring cache behavior is the degree of "bank conflicts"), but the bank is usually not directly addressable by the cache's client. As another example, web proxies can be transparent to client software, in which case the client makes a request to the primary server and the request is caught by or redirected to a different server entirely. The bottom line is that the constituent components of a cache or cache system may or may not be addressable by the cache's clients. In other words, the various internal partitions of the cache are typically treated as implementation details and are not usually exposed to client software. However, one might *want* to expose the internal partitions to client software if, for example, the partitions are not all equal in size or cost of access. Note that web caching comes in several different flavors. Proxy servers can be hidden, as described above, but they can just as easily be exposed to client software and even to the human using the web browser, as in the case of mirror sites for downloads, in which case the human typically chooses the nearest source for the desired data. The process can be automated. For instance, if a solid-state cache's partitions are exposed to software and exhibit different behaviors (cost of access, cost of storage, etc.), a compiler-based heuristic could arrange cached data among the various partitions according to weights derived from the partitions' associated costs. An extremely diverse range of heuristics has been explored in both software and hardware to do exactly this (see Chapter 3, "Management of Cache Contents").

The following sections describe briefly some common distributed and/or partitioned cache organizations.

2.5.1 UMA and NUMA

UMA and NUMA stand for *uniform memory access* and *non-uniform memory access*, respectively. The terms are most often used in the context of higher order memory systems and not specifically cache systems, but they are useful designations in the discussion of distributed/partitioned caches because UMA/NUMA systems illustrate the main issues of dealing with physically disjoint memories. A *NUMA* architecture is one in which all memory accesses have nominally the same latency; a *NUMA* architecture is one in which references to different addresses may have different latencies due to the nature of where the data is stored. The implication behind the deceptively simple "where the data is stored" is that an item's identity is tied to its location. For instance, in a solid-state setting, an item's physical address determines the memory partition in which it can be found. As an example, in a system of 16 memory nodes, the physical memory space could be divided into 16 regions, and the top 4 bits of the address would determine which node owns the data in question.

Figure 2.14(a) shows an organization in which a CPU's requests all go to the same memory system (which could be a cache, the DRAM system, or a disk; the details do not matter for purposes of this discussion). Thus, all memory requests have nominally the same latency—any observed variations in latency will be due to the specifics of the memory technology and not the memory organization. This organization is typical of shared cache organizations (e.g., the last-level cache of a chip-level multiprocessor) and symmetric multiprocessors.

Figure 2.14(b) shows an organization in which a CPU's memory request may be satisfied by one of

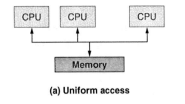

(a) Uniform access

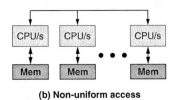

(b) Non-uniform access

FIGURE 2.14: UMA and NUMA organizations.

many possible sub-memories. In particular, a request to any non-local memory (any memory not directly attached to the CPU making the request) is likely to exhibit a higher latency than a request to a local memory. This organization is used in many commercial settings, such as those based on AMD Opteron or Alpha 21364 (EV7) processors. The ccNUMA variant (for *cache-coherent NUMA*) is one in which each processor or processor cluster maintains a cache or cache system that caches requests to reduce inter-node traffic and average latency to non-local data.

The concepts embodied in the terms UMA and NUMA extend to cache systems and memory systems in general because the issues are those of data partitioning and placement, cost/benefit analysis, etc., which are universal. The Fully Buffered DIMM is a prime example of a non-uniform memory architecture which can be configured to behave as a uniform architecture by forcing all DIMMs in the system to stall and emulate the latency of the slowest DIMM in the system. For more detail, see Chapter 14, "The Fully Buffered DIMM Memory System."

2.5.2 COMA

COMA stands for *cache-only memory architecture*, an organization designed to address the issues of UMA and NUMA and ccNUMA machines [Hagersten et al. 1992]. UMA organizations are not scalable beyond a relatively small number of nodes per memory; the shared-bus traffic quickly becomes a limiter to system performance. In NUMA organizations, the static assignment of data to partition creates unnecessary network traffic in the (frequent) case that the software working on the data happens to be running on a non-local processor. Even with caches at each compute node in a NUMA organization (ccNUMA), the problem is not necessarily solved. In high-performance applications, data sets can easily exceed the limited cache space.

COMA organizations were proposed to solve the problem by blurring the distinction between cache and backing store, making the local cache effectively the same size as the local backing store (DRAM system). A COMA organization is a distributed system of compute nodes that treats the DRAM space as a large

cache, called an *attraction memory*. The idea is that the organization does the job of data partitioning for the software dynamically: as software threads run on different compute nodes, they *attract* to their node's local memory all code they need and data on which they are working. In instances with little write-sharing of data, after an initial flurry of network activity, there is little memory traffic on the network.

There are two primary implications of this organization: one an advantage, the other a disadvantage. The advantage is a dramatically increased local cache space, which potentially reduces latency significantly. The disadvantage is that, by definition ("cache *only*"), there is no backing store, and thus, the system must keep track of extant cached copies so that they are not all deleted from the system. This complicates the cache-coherence mechanism. In addition, the fact that DRAM is treated as a cache implies that a tag feature must be added. This can be done through the virtual memory system (as pointed out, the virtual memory system treats main memory as an associative cache for the disk space), but it is limited by the *reach* of the TLB, meaning that if the TLB maps 4 KB per entry and has 256 entries, then at any given moment it can *map* a total of 1 MB of space (i.e., translate to physical addresses, or in the context of COMA, perform the tag-compare function). Anything outside of that space will require a page table traversal and TLB refill. Alternatively, the tag-compare function can be performed by special hardware (e.g., use a non-standard DRAM bus and store tag information with every block of memory), but this would increase the cost of the system.

2.5.3 NUCA and NuRAPID

Figure 2.15 illustrates some recent perspectives on distributed/partitioned caches. The NUCA and NuRAPID (non-uniform access with replacement and placement using distance associativity) [Kim et al. 2002, Chishti et al. 2003] organizations gather together a set of storage nodes on a network-on-chip that is collectively called a monolithic cache, but which behaves as a *de facto* cache hierarchy, exhibiting different access latencies depending on the distance from the central access point and supporting

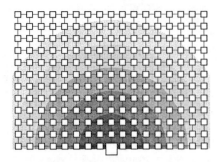

FIGURE 2.15: NUCA and NuRAPID cache architectures. The cache is an explicit network of storage blocks, each of which has a different network latency that scales with the block's distance from the central access point. The varying shades of grey represent distance from central point and thus latency.

the migration of data within the cache. The argument for treating the cache as a monolothic entity is that large on-chip caches already exhibit internal latencies that differ depending on the block being accessed. Another treatment of the cache would be to consider it as an explicit non-inclusive partition and use naming of objects for assignment to different sets within the cache, with the sets being grouped by similar latencies. One could locate data within the cache and schedule accesses to the cache using schemes similar to Abraham et al. [1993].

2.5.4 Web Caches

A good example of a distributed cache is the increasingly common web cache [Luotonen & Altis 1994] pictured in Figure 2.16 (note that the figure shows several different types of caches within a larger context of web infrastructure). First, each browser typically manages its own local cache in the client machine's file system (which itself is cached by the operating system in an in-memory buffer cache). Second, the web server's files are cached within the buffer cache of *its* operating system (and there is even a cache within the disk drive pictured). Finally, two different web caches are pictured. Web cache (a) is a server-side network of proxies put in place to reduce

load on the main web server. The server-side cache increases system throughput and reduces average latency to clients of the system (i.e., customers). This type of cache can also reduce exposure to security problems by allowing the main bulk of an organization's computing facilities, including the primary web server, to remain behind a firewall. Web cache (b) is a client-side cache put in place to reduce the traffic on an organization's outgoing link to the network, thereby improving all traffic in general—queries satisfied by the cache appear to have very low latency, and, if the web cache has a high hit rate, other queries (including non-web traffic) see improved latency and bandwidth because they face less competition for access to the network.

As Figure 2.16 shows, web caches are installed at various levels in the network, function at several different granularities, and provide a wide range of different services. Thus, it should be no surprise that each distinct type of web cache has its own set of issues. The universal issues include the following:

- The data is largely read-only. Inclusive caches have an advantage here because read-only data can be removed from the cache at any time without fear of consistency problems. All lessons learned from instruction-delivery in very large multiprocessor machines are applicable (e.g., broadcast, replication, etc.), but the issue is complicated by the possibility of data becoming invalid from the server side when documents are updated with new content.

- The variable document size presents a serious problem in that a heuristic must address two orthogonal issues: (i) should the document in question be cached? and (ii) how best to allocate space for it? There is no unit-granularity "block size" to consider other than "byte," and therefore replacement may involve removing more than one document from the cache to make room for an incoming document. Given that simple replacement (as in solid-state caches and buffer caches) is not an entirely closed question, complicating it further with additional variables is certain to make things

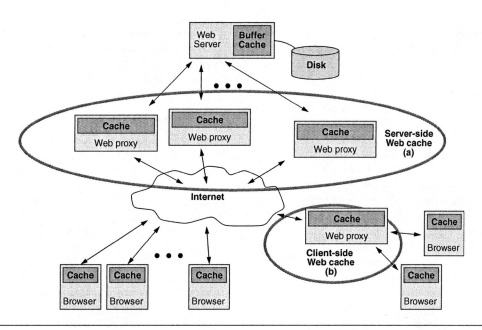

FIGURE 2.16: Web cache organization. Web cache (a) is put in place by the administrator of the server to reduce exposure to security issues (e.g., to put only proxies outside a firewall) and/or to distribute server load across many machines. Web cache (b) is put in place by the administrator of a subnet to reduce the traffic on its Internet link; the cache satisfies many of the local web requests and decreases the likelihood that a particular browser request will leave the local subnet.

difficult: witness the extremely large number of replacement policies that have been explored for web caches, and the issue is still open [Podlipnig & Böszörményi 2003].

Furthermore, the issues for client-side and server-side web caches can be treated separately.

Client-Side Web Caches

Client-side caches are transparent caches: they are transparently addressed and implicitly managed. The client-side web cache is responsible for managing its own contents by observing the stream of requests coming from the client side. All lessons learned from the design of transparent caches (e.g., the solid-state caches used in microprocessors and general-purpose computing systems) are applicable, including the wide assortment of partitioning and prefetching heuristics explored in the literature

(see, for example, Chapter 3, Section 3.1.1, "On-Line Partitioning Heuristics," and Section 3.1.2, "On-Line Prefetching Heuristics").

Invalidation of data is an issue with these caches, but because the primary web server does not necessarily know of the existence of the cache, invalidation is either done through polling or timestamps. In a polling scenario, the client-side cache, before serving a cached document to a requesting browser, first queries the server on the freshness of its copy of the document. The primary server informs the proxy of the latest modification date of the primary copy, and the proxy then serves the client with the cached copy or a newly downloaded copy. In a timestamp scenario, the primary server associates a *time-to-live* (*TTL*) value with each document that indicates the point in time when the document's contents become invalid, requiring a proxy to download a new copy. During the window between the first download and TTL expiration, the proxy assumes that the cached copy is valid, even if the copy at the primary server is, in fact, a newer updated version.

Server-Side Web Caches

Like client-side caches, server-side web caches are also transparently addressed, but their contents can be explicitly managed by the (administrators of the) primary web server. Thus, server-side web caches can be an example of a software-managed cache. Not all server-side web caches are under the same administrative domain as the primary server. For example, *country caches* service an entire domain name within the Internet namespace (e.g., *.it or *.ch or *.de), and because they cache documents from all web servers within the domain name, they are by definition independent from the organizations owning the individual web servers. Thus, server-side web caches can also be transparent.

In these organizations, the issue of document update and invalidation is slightly more complicated because, when the web cache and primary server *are* under the same administrative domain, mechanisms are available that are not possible otherwise. For instance, the cache can be entirely under the control of the server, in which case the server pushes content out to the caches, and the cache need not worry about document freshness. Otherwise, the issues are much the same as in client-side caches.

2.5.5 Buffer Caches

Figure 2.16 illustrates software caching of data. Figure 2.17 shows in more detail how the operating system is involved. Note that data is cached on both the operating system side and the disk side, which implements its own DRAM-resident cache for data. This can be thought of as a client-side cache (at the operating system level) and a server-side cache (at the disk level); the issues of partitioning the management heuristics are very similar to those in web cache design. Note that this is easily analyzed as a distributed cache, even though the constituent components are currently implemented independently. It is always possible (and, indeed, it has been proposed) to merge the management of the two caches into a single control point. Chapter 22 will go into the details of disk caching, and the next section gives a case study of the buffer cache in BSD (Berkeley Software Distributions) Unix.

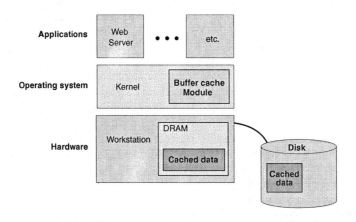

FIGURE 2.17: Buffer caches and disk caches. Disk data is cached in two places: (a) in main memory in the operating system's buffer cache and (b) on the disk in another DRAM buffer.

2.6 Case Studies

The following sections present some well-known examples of cache organizations to illustrate the principles described in this chapter.

2.6.1 A Horizontal-Exclusive Organization: Victim Caches, Assist Caches

As an example of an exclusive partition on a horizontal level, consider Jouppi's *victim cache* [1990], a small cache with a high degree of associativity that sits next to another, larger cache that has limited set associativity. The addition of a victim cache to a larger main cache allows the main cache to approach the miss rate of a cache with higher associativity. For example, Jouppi's experiments show that a direct-mapped cache with a small fully associative victim cache can approach the miss rate of a two-way set associative cache.

The two caches in a main-cache-victim-cache pair exhibit an exclusive organization: a block is found in either the main cache or in the victim cache, but not in both. In theory, the exclusive organization gives rise to a non-trivial mapping problem of deciding which cache should hold a particular datum, but the mechanism is actually very straightforward as well as effective. The victim cache's contents are defined by the replacement policy of the main cache; that is, the only data items found within the victim cache are those that have been thrown out of the main cache at some point in the past. When a cache probe, which looks in both caches, finds the requested block in the victim cache, that block is swapped with the block it replaces in the main cache. This swapping ensures the exclusive relationship. One of many variations on this theme is the HP-7200 *assist cache* [Chan et al. 1996], whose design was motivated by the processor's automatic stride-based prefetch engine: if too aggressive, the engine would prefetch data that would victimize soon-to-be-used cache entries. In the assist cache, the incoming prefetch block is loaded not into the main cache, but instead into the highly associative cache and is then promoted into the main cache only if it exhibits temporal locality by being referenced again soon. Blocks exhibiting only spatial locality are not moved to the main cache and are replaced

to main memory in a FIFO fashion. These two management heuristics are compared later in Chapter 3 (see "Jouppi's Victim Cache, HP-7200 Assist Cache" in Section 3.1).

By adding a fully associative victim cache, a direct-mapped cache can approach the performance of a two-way set-associative cache, but because the victim cache is probed in parallel with the main cache, this performance boost comes at the expense of performing multiple tag comparisons (more than just two), which can potentially dissipate more dynamic power than a simple two-way set-associative cache. However, the victim cache organization uses fewer transistors than an equivalently performing set-associative cache, and leakage is related to the total number of transistors in the design (scales roughly with die area). Leakage power in caches is quickly outpacing dynamic power, so the victim cache is likely to become even more important in the future.

As we will see in later sections, an interesting point on the effectiveness of the victim cache is that there have been numerous studies of sophisticated dynamic heuristics that try to partition references into multiple use-based streams (e.g., those that exhibit locality and so should be cached, and those that exhibit streaming behavior and so should go to a different cache or no cache at all). The victim cache, a simpler organization embodying a far simpler heuristic, tends to keep up with the other schemes to the point of outperforming them in many instances [Rivers et al. 1998].

A cache organization (and management heuristic) similar to the victim cache is implemented in the virtual memory code of many operating systems. A virtual memory system maintains a pool of physical pages, similar to the I/O system's buffer cache (see discussion of BSD below). The primary distinction between the two caches is that the I/O system is invoked directly by an application and thus observes all user activity to a particular set of pages, whereas the virtual memory system is transparent—invoked only indirectly when translations are needed—and thus sees almost no user-level activity to a given set of pages. Any access to the disk system is handled through a system call: the user application explicitly invokes a software routine within the operating system to read or write the disk system. In the virtual memory system, a user application accesses the physical memory directly without any assistance from the operating system, except in the case of TLB misses, protection violations, or page faults. In such a scenario, the operating system must be very clever about inferring application intent because, unlike the I/O system, the virtual memory system has no way of maintaining page-access statistics to determine each page's suitability for replacement (e.g., how recently and/or frequently has each page been referenced).

Solutions to this problem include the *clock* algorithm and other similar algorithms [Corbato 1968, Bensoussan et al. 1972, Carr & Hennessy 1981], in which pages are maintained in an LRU fashion based upon hardware providing a *use* bit for each page, a per-page indicator set by hardware whenever its corresponding page has been accessed. The clock algorithm periodically walks the list of pages and marks them ready for replacement if they have not been used recently. Modern processor architectures do not typically support a *use* bit because the per-page reference information has traditionally been communicated to the operating system by the hardware modifying the page table directly (e.g., Bensoussan et al. [1972]), which is currently considered an extravagant overhead. However, modern architectures do support protection bits, and so the clock algorithm is often approximated in modern operating systems by tagging a page as non-readable and setting an appropriate bit when the operating system's page-protection-violation handler is invoked upon the page's first reference. If, within a period of time, the page has not been accessed, the handler is not invoked, and the corresponding bit does not get set. In the MIPS R2000 port of Mach, this mechanism is implemented through a set of queues: a page in the system is found on one of several queues based upon how recently it has been referenced on each period (execution of the clock algorithm), all unused pages are migrated one hop toward the *available* queue, and all referenced pages are moved onto the *in-use* queue. Thus, a physical page has several periods to prove its usefulness by being referenced before its time expires and it becomes available for replacement. This mechanism

provides the same second-chance behavior to data that the victim cache does: blocks that are identified as unused or tagged to be replaced are not thrown out immediately, but instead move through a series of victim caches (queues) before being thrown out.

2.6.2 A Software Implementation: BSD's Buffer Cache

The buffer cache in 4.3BSD Unix [Leffler et al. 1989] is a good example to illustrate organizational choices in a non-solid-state cache implementation. The buffer cache is the portion of the operating system that manages disk blocks and attempts to keep in main memory the most useful data read in from disk. In general, successfully buffering disk I/O is at least as important to a system as ensuring that one's processor caches hide the latency of main memory.

The BSD buffer cache provides a straightforward example of a set-associative cache organization, but it also provides an example of a cache organization whose block size is determined dynamically. Another example of a variable-sized cache block is the modern disk cache (see Chapter 22, Section 22.2, "Cache Organizations"), as well as the *trace cache*, described in the next section.

A Set-Associative Software-Managed Cache

Figure 2.18 shows the organization of the buffer cache (also called the *buffer pool*). A block contains a variable amount of data (the *sz* and *ptr* fields), an identification of which disk and which block it corresponds to, and status bits indicating such things as whether the block is dirty or not, whether it is awaiting data from disk, etc.

Every block in the cache can be found on exactly two queues. Queues coming in from the left side are hash queues and facilitate quick lookup of a given block, given its ID. Queues coming down from the top are used to determine *replacement* (a content-management heuristic that will be discussed in more detail in the next chapter) and designate the degree to which a particular block on that list can be replaced without affecting performance. The *locked* queue holds cache blocks that must not be flushed

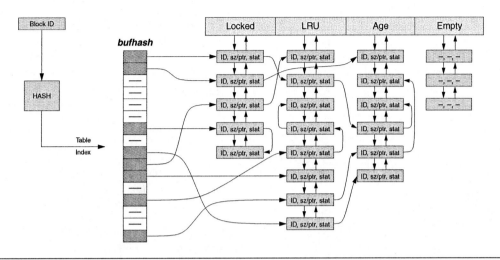

FIGURE 2.18: The buffer cache in 4.3BSD Unix. Cache block lookups based on the block's ID use the queues anchored in the *bufhash* array. The array can be sized appropriately to minimize the length of the search queues. Context-based searches use the four queues at the top of the diagram: *locked* holds important blocks that must not be thrown out (e.g., superblocks); LRU holds blocks in a time-ordered list; *age* holds blocks that are available for reuse; and *empty* holds blocks that have had their assigned physical storage stripped from them.

from the cache (an implementation choice that was later abandoned due to deadlock problems). The *LRU* queue holds valuable disk blocks in a time-ordered sequence based on last use. The *age* queue holds blocks of two types: blocks that are not-yet-proven-valuable (i.e., speculatively fetched data) and blocks that have outlived their usefulness and are not expected to be reused any time soon. Items on the *age* queue are in order of predicted usefulness. The *empty* queue holds cache blocks that have no available storage left; this is a side effect of having a dynamically determined block size and will be discussed shortly. Cache blocks in this queue are unusable and are waiting for memory space to be freed up.

To find a cached block within the buffer pool, first its identifier is hashed to produce an index into the *bufhash* array of queue heads. Then the corresponding queue is located and searched, linearly, for the requested cache block. The requested block, once found, is moved to the back of the *LRU* queue, whether it was on the *LRU* or *age* queue to begin with (this is how items are moved from *age* to *LRU* when they prove their usefulness by being requested).

A block is *not* moved from one hash queue to another; it is always to be found in the queue identified by the hash product of its identifier (which does not change, because the ID does not change). This represents a clear example of a set-associative organization: each hash queue represents an equivalence class with a dynamically determined cardinality (i.e., some hash queues may contain many cache blocks, while others may be empty; a queue's contents are determined by the stream of requests serviced by the buffer cache).

To find a suitable block for reuse to hold incoming disk data, the cache is searched from the top queues. The *age* queue is searched first, as it contains data of questionable usefulness. If it contains a buffer, that buffer is reused for the incoming data. If the *age* queue is empty, or if it does not contain enough storage to hold the incoming data, the *LRU* queue is searched next. The cache block at the front of the *LRU* queue is taken, with it being the least recently used block since all blocks, when used, are put at the back of the queue. As with the cache's lookup mechanism, this also represents a set-associative organization, one in which different heuristics apply to different sets. The *LRU* set is managed in a time-ordered manner, and the *age* set is managed in a completely different manner (e.g., prefetched blocks are put at the back of the queue, newly created empty blocks are put at the front of the queue, and blocks are extracted from the front).

The cache is transparently addressed: the cache is actively searched and not merely indexed; the disk block number, an ID from the backing store, is the key used to search the cache. Because the cache is managed by the same entity that is one of the cache's clients (i.e., the operating system uses the buffer cache and manages it as well), it is an explicitly managed cache. Thus, this, like the buffer caches in most operating systems, is an example of a software-managed cache.

A Dynamically Defined Cache Block

Even though the preceding discussion called the units of storage within the cache "cache blocks," BSD's buffer cache does not hold *disk* blocks, which are 512 bytes apiece, but rather it holds fragments of files. Because files range significantly in size, and requests to those files also range significantly in size, the buffer cache is designed to accommodate this variability by not using a fixed block size. A block's size can be as small as the disk block size (512 bytes), or it can range in multiples of 512 B up to 8 KB. At initialization, all buffers are allocated 2 KB of physical space.

If a requested disk block or range of disk blocks is not found in the buffer cache, space is allocated for it by grabbing cache blocks from the *age* and *LRU* queues as necessary, and their contents are written back to disk if their status indicates that they are dirty. Assume an example request is for 3 KB of data. If the first acquired block has exactly 3 KB assigned to it, then the process is done. The more interesting scenarios are when this is not the case:

- If the first block acquired has *less* than 3 KB assigned to it (e.g., say, 2 KB), then a second block is acquired. If the second has less than or is equal to 1 KB, then its storage is added to that of the first, and the second block, now empty of storage, is placed on the *empty* queue. If the second has more than 1 KB of space, then 1 KB of its storage is added to

that of the first block, and the second block is moved to the front of *age* queue, as it is now available for a new request (its contents having been written back to disk, and it having non-zero space allocated to it).

- If, on the other hand, the first block acquired has *more* than 3 KB assigned to it, the excess is given to a block on the *empty* queue, which is then moved to the front of the *age* queue. If the *empty* queue holds no blocks, the excess storage remains attached to the block in question and is just wasted until that block is reclaimed for another use.

One way to look at this is that the cache supports a single, atomic cache block size of 512 B, but the fundamental cache organization and operation are centered around a *logical* block size that is dynamically determined on a request-by-request basis, with a logical block being assembled dynamically from an integral number of atomic blocks.

2.6.3 Another Dynamic Cache Block: Trace Caches

A similar example to the dynamic cache block of BSD's buffer cache is the familiar *trace cache*, a solid-state cache that implements a dynamically assembled cache block. The cache block contents can represent several non-contiguous streams of bytes in the backing store. While the BSD buffer cache changes the cache's block size to match each incoming request's size but takes its data from a single stream of bytes from the backing store, the trace cache dynamically redefines not only the block size, but the block contents as well. On a block-by-block basis, the trace cache assembles into a single block (which holds a contiguous array of instructions) data from up to three disjoint locations, i.e., past one or more branches.

The trace cache mechanism directly addresses the problem of providing high-bandwidth instruction-fetch. The issues in instruction-fetch today include the following:

- Basic blocks are small, and conditional branches are frequent.

- To match issue and execute bandwidths, the required bandwidths of instruction-fetch are high, and to match these one must successfully predict multiple branches in a single cycle.
- Assuming one can predict multiple branches per cycle, multiple corresponding fetch addresses must be produced. Instructions from more than one cache block must be fetched in a single clock cycle, and these disjoint instruction streams (each of which may comprise a full cache block or a partial cache block) must be rearranged and reassembled into the desired execution order.

The trace cache addresses these issues by placing into a single cache block instructions from different basic blocks: the control-flow path has been predicted, so each cache block represents a *trace* [Fisher 1981] through the control-flow graph. This addresses the issues above by placing multiple basic blocks into a single fetch unit, obviating any need for fetching multiple cache blocks or rearranging fetched instructions.

The trace cache mechanism is particularly interesting because it represents a dynamic redefinition of the cache block itself. Remember that a cache block is generally considered to be a set of data items that are contiguous in the backing store and therefore make up a convenient unit to fetch from the backing store—the convenience is from the point of view of the mechanism responsible for fetching data from the backing store (the memory and/or cache controller). The trace cache completely redefines the concept of a cache block: by dynamically assembling together the instructions that a processor core needs (as opposed to a collection of items that a compiler placed together), this turns the cache-resident block into a convenient unit of instruction-fetch from the processor core's point of view. The mechanism really strides the line between an unorthodox cache organization and a hybrid of cache organization and content-management heuristic. Allowing a cache block to contain instructions from disjoint streams (i.e., past branches) is an interesting twist on cache organization. Dynamically assembling the cache blocks is a form of content-management heuristic.

The following sections describe the various forms of trace cache that have been proposed and built (e.g., fetch mechanisms in *ELI* and *ROPE*, *tree-VLIW* structures, the *fill unit*, the *shadow cache*, the *dynamic flow instruction cache*, and the *trace cache*) plus a few additional studies that help put its development into historical perspective. The two primary concepts embodied in the trace cache—a cache block holding disjoint streams and its dynamic assembly—both find their roots in the late 1970s and 1980s. Briefly, the history discussed goes as follows:

- Early research in very long instruction word (VLIW) architecture identifies the instruction-fetch problem (1980).
- Several architectures (ELI, ROPE) provide support for multiple simultaneous branch instructions and simultaneous instruction-fetch from non-contiguous streams (1980–1985).
- Tree-VLIW puts non-contiguous instruction streams into the same cache block (1987).
- The *fill unit* dynamically assembles a cache block from a sequential stream, reordering instructions as necessary (1988).
- Multiple branches are predicted in a single cycle (1993).
- The *shadow cache* dynamically assembles a cache block, combining instructions from non-contiguous streams (1994).
- Called the *dynamic flow instruction cache*, the trace cache is patented by Peleg and Weiser (1995).
- A significant range of instruction-fetch solutions is explored, underscoring the difficulty of fetching non-contiguous streams (1995).
- The *trace cache* appears, which dynamically combines instructions past two branches (i.e., from three non-contiguous streams), using a generic cache block structure (1996).

VLIW and the Instruction-Fetch Problem

The problem of providing enough fetch bandwidth to feed the execution units is not new. Early research in VLIW architectures (also called *horizontal micro-code*) identified this as a primary performance-limiting issue, citing explicitly the density of branches, the need to operate on multiple potentially non-contiguous streams, and the requirement of performing (which would today be predicting) multiple conditional branches simultaneously:

> *The designs of all very wide microengines we have seen to date have what we consider to be a serious defect: in essence, only one test [i.e., conditional branch] instruction may be scheduled per wide instruction. ... Thus no matter how many FU's and data paths are thrown at the algorithm, a serious bottleneck will occur while awaiting the tests to be resolved one at a time. [Fisher 1980, p. 65]*

> *Since the instructions within a basic block usually have serial dependencies, code rearrangement has to range over several basic blocks. In horizontal microcode, several data path operations can often be started simultaneously. Unless several conditional jumps are evaluated at once, the ratio of jumps to straight-line code becomes unacceptably high. Furthermore, the density of conditional jumps foils the effectiveness of the traditional pre-fetch mechanism in which the next instruction is pre-fetched sequentially. [Karplus & Nicolau 1985, p. 12]*

To combat the problem, researchers developed sophisticated scheduling and instruction-packing techniques to ensure that a constant stream of multiple instructions per cycle was being fed to the back-end processor core, designed to work hand-in-hand with the compiler and supporting scheduling software (e.g., Fisher [1980, 1981, 1983], Fisher et al. [1984], Karplus and Nicolau [1985], Ebcioglu [1987, 1988], Aiken and Nicolau [1988]). Two schemes that resemble the modern trace cache are the ELI and ROPE mechanisms, both of which implement multi-way branches and fetch instructions from logically non-contiguous code locations. ELI is an explicit VLIW architecture; ROPE is a general instruction-fetch mechanism explicitly targeted for both VLIW and serial (RISC and/or CISC) processing architectures.

Multi-way Branches and Disjoint I-Fetch in ELI and ROPE. Fisher puts the problem well, an argument that is still applicable to the architectures of today:

> *Comparing VLIWs with vector machines illustrates the problems to be solved. VLIWs put fine-grained, tightly coupled, but logically unrelated operations in single instructions. Vector machines do many fine-grained, tightly coupled, logically related operations at once to the elements of a vector. Vector machines can do many parallel operations between tests; VLIWs cannot. Vector machines can structure memory references to entire arrays or slices of arrays; VLIWs cannot. We've argued, of course, that vector machines fail on general scientific code for other reasons. How do we get their virtues without their vices?*

> *VLIWs need clever jump mechanisms.*

> *Short basic blocks impl[y] a lack of local parallelism. They also imply a low ratio of operations to tests. If we are going to pack a great many operations into each cycle, we had better be prepared to make more than one test per cycle. [Fisher 1983, pp. 145–146]*

ELI: Extremely Long Instructions. The solution of the day was to perform multi-way branches, and ELI's mechanism differed from previous schemes in that it performed independent branches simultaneously: ELI put multiple conditional branches into the same VLIW instruction and executed them simultaneously [Fisher 1980, 1983].

However, performing a multi-way branch implies that, to avoid stalling, *all* of the possible target instruction streams must be prefetched simultaneously. The solution offered in ELI, pictured in Figure 2.19, is a multi-banked instruction memory, interleaved to the same degree as the degree of multi-branching, with the instruction streams at the various target code blocks mapped to the same offset in different banks. All n banks are accessed simultaneously with the same index (effectively representing a single, logical cache block), yielding n target instruction streams, one of which is ultimately selected by the branch-resolution hardware.

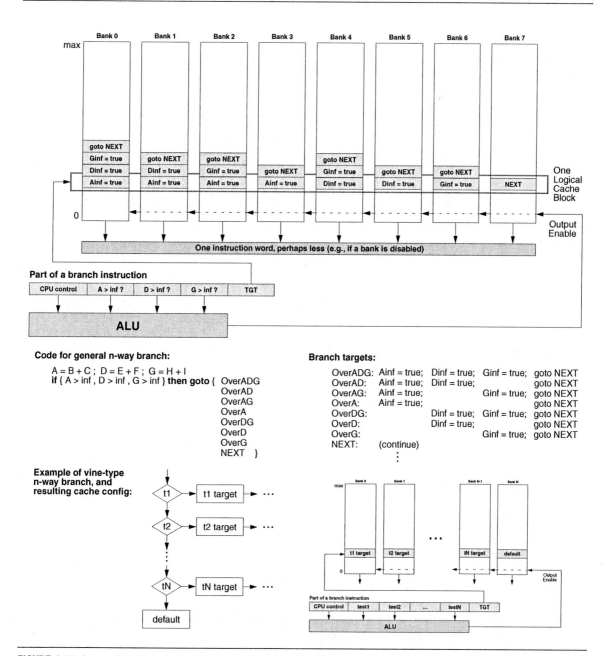

FIGURE 2.19: Instruction-fetch in Fisher's ELI architecture. This illustrates the mechanism for resolving an *n*-way branch instruction, which has 2^n possible branch targets; all targets point to independent instruction streams housed in the same VLIW instruction. At the bottom of the figure is the code that the microinstruction arrangement would implement. Later implementations of ELI simplified this branch architecture to support a linear if-then-else chain called a vine, pictured at the bottom.

ROPE: Ring Of Prefetch Elements Karplus and Nicolau [1985] use a similar multi-banked scheme to implement a general high-bandwidth fetch engine called ROPE, illustrated in Figure 2.20. ROPE is targeted at supporting any back-end processor architecture that requires high instruction-fetch bandwidth, whether VLIW or serial RISC/CISC. Like ELI, ROPE executes a multi-way branch and fetches simultaneously out of multiple banks to avoid stalling. The primary difference between ROPE and the fetch engine in ELI is that the banks in ROPE are not slaved to one another as they are in ELI; ROPE's prefetch engines operate independently, each passing a follow-on target address to the next element in the ring. Thus, each element can be fetching simultaneously, producing at the output of the fetch unit a large number of non-contiguous instruction streams.

Tree-VLIW Instructions

ELI can be said to support a logical cache block made up of multiple, logically non-contiguous instruction streams. However, the instruction streams are, in fact, contiguous in terms of physical addresses. A fair amount of compiler and hardware support packs these logically non-contiguous instructions together into the same physical instruction word to support the multi-way branch.

A similar mechanism that moves closer to the trace cache concept (i.e., the idea of allowing a cache block to contain atomic instructions that span a break in sequential control flow) is the tree-VLIW instruction word, described by Ebcioglu in 1987 and 1988, but not named so until later. The basic premise of the architecture is that, unlike the previous VLIW architectures that support multiple exit points out of an instruction word in which every atomic instruction is executed, this architecture supports conditional execution of the atomic instructions within the long instruction word. This is illustrated in Figure 2.21. The DAG represents a single instruction, 500–1800 bits wide, in which multiple paths of control exist. Only those atomic instructions on the *taken* control path are executed. Because the instruction word contains

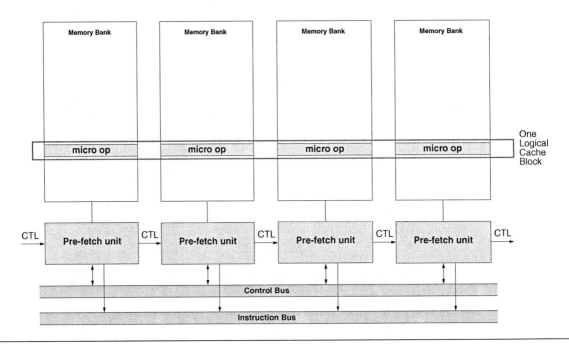

FIGURE 2.20: Karplus's ROPE mechanism.

multiple paths of control, it defines a cache design that explicitly holds multiple disjoint instruction streams, each potentially fairly long, given even the smallest targeted word size (500 bits). Note that the structure of this multi-branch operation is an *n* = 2 organization of Fisher's *vine* structure [Fisher 1983].

The Fill Unit

The idea of dynamically assembling a cache block's contents originates with Melvin's *fill unit* [Melvin et al. 1988], which dynamically reorders and repacks fetched microoperations (e.g., RISC-like instructions) into the decoded instruction cache's blocks, taking its instructions from either a non-decoded instruction cache or main memory. In cooperation with the prefetch buffer, microoperation generator, address re-alias unit, and decoded instruction cache (see Figure 2.22), the fill unit interprets incoming instructions, reorders them, renames their register operands, and reformats them to use the format that the back-end processing core expects, which may differ

significantly from the compiler's target. The fill unit dynamically redefines the instruction stream, checks inter-instruction dependences, and only *finalizes* a group of instructions (stops filling an i-cache block, thus defining the boundaries of instruction-fetch) when a branch is detected or the capacity of the i-cache block is exceeded. The combined portions of the design, shown highlighted by the grey blob in the figure, are very similar to the modern trace cache, with the significant difference being that the design does not attempt to create long sequences of instructions that span a change in control flow.

Multi-Branch Predictor and Branch-Address Cache

As Fisher points out [1983], VLIWs need clever jump mechanisms, and the observation extends to any scalar architecture that executes multiple instructions simultaneously. Modern architectures do not typically use the multi-way branch instructions and architectures of the 1980s, largely due to the development of accurate branch prediction (i.e., the *two-level adaptive*

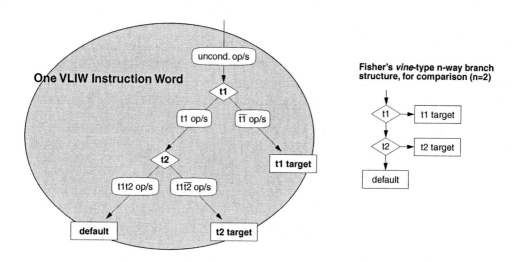

FIGURE 2.21: Ebcioglu's tree-like instruction word. On each edge of the control-flow graph (which represents a single VLIW instruction), multiple conditional operations can be placed. These are only conditional upon being on the dynamically executed path through the control-flow graph. The figure illustrates this, showing the logic value of tests 1 and 2 that is required for each operation or set of operations to be performed: e.g., "t1t̄2 op/s" means 0 or more operations that will be executed if, when the block is executed, t1 dynamically evaluates to *true* and t2 dynamically evaluates to *false*.

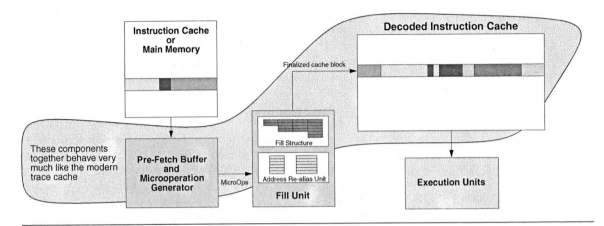

FIGURE 2.22: Melvin's fill unit and related mechanisms.

training branch predictor [sic][Yeh & Patt 1991], a hybrid of Jim Smith's *dynamic* predictors [1981b], which introduced adaptive state machines such as a table of *n*-bit saturating up/down counters, and *prediction based on branch history*, the mechanism described by Lee and Smith [1984] and represented as *static training* by Yeh & Patt, which introduced the two-level approach of using a per-branch *n*-bit history of outcomes as an index). Successful prediction of single two-way branches supports the same degree of instruction-fetch bandwidth available in the 1980s with multi-way branches. However, even this is insufficient for architectures of the mid-1990s, which require more than just two basic blocks of instructions per cycle.

To increase the visible window of instructions to fetch, Yeh presents a branch predictor design that predicts two branches per cycle and a branch-address cache that provides multiple target addresses per cycle [Yeh et al. 1993]. Coupled with these mechanisms is an instruction cache reminiscent of ELI and ROPE: a highly banked, pseudo-multi-ported cache that can produce multiple (four) non-contiguous cache blocks per cycle. The multiple-branch-predictor-cum-branch-address-cache mechanism is similar to the trace cache in its goal of delivering a stream of instructions that are potentially non-contiguous in memory. Like Melvin's fill unit, the mechanism does not put into a single cache block, either physical or

logical, sequences of instructions that span a change in control flow.

The Shadow Cache

In this regard—to wit, dynamically creating cache blocks filled with instructions that are non-contiguous in the memory space and that represent multiple streams of instructions that lie on different sides of a control-flow decision—Franklin and Smotherman [1994] present the first real trace cache, called the *shadow cache*. Using a modified fill unit (see Figure 2.23), the shadow cache dynamically assembles shadow cache blocks from disjoint regions in the code space. The shadow cache is operated in parallel with the instruction cache and is filled from the instruction cache (like both Melvin's fill unit and Rotenberg's trace cache). The design creates a linear array of instructions that can extend past (at most) one branch. The scheme does not lend itself well to an extension of handling arbitrary numbers of branches, because, at least in the experimental implementation evaluated in the paper, the shadow cache's block holds instructions from both taken *and* non-taken paths past the branch.

One of the disadvantages of dynamically defining the cache block in this way is that two different paths dynamically taken through a basic block (e.g., two vectors into a basic block) can produce two different

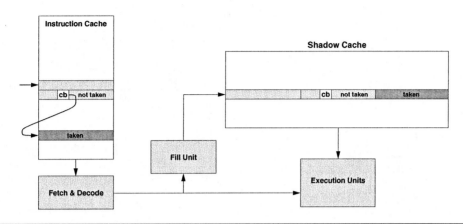

FIGURE 2.23: Franklin's shadow cache mechanism.

cache blocks, thereby effectively lowering the cache's capacity due to the cache holding replicated instructions. This is not specific to the shadow cache; it is generally true of the trace cache concept, a function of dynamically assembling a multi-instruction trace.

The shadow cache implementation represents an execution architecture that lies somewhere between out-of-order superscalar and VLIW. One of the goals of the work is to provide the implementation simplicity of VLIW with the programming and compiler-target simplicity of a sequential architecture. To this end, the shadow cache maintains a block structure that is targeted for a specific back-end implementation, and its fill unit does a modicum of rearranging instructions to match the back-end execution hardware's expectations. Compared to a modern trace cache, the shadow cache holds instructions in *issued* order rather than *fetched* order. It is more or less a *de facto* VLIW back-end, with the fill unit and shadow cache effectively hiding implementation details from the program and compiler.

A Range of Fetch and Align Strategies

Conte explores a wide range of instruction-fetch implementations using a traditional cache design, focusing on the mask-and-reorder circuitry that is required to handle non-contiguous streams of instructions that span more than one basic block

[Conte et al. 1995]. The study explores schemes that range from lower bound (fetch a single cache block and extract instructions, stopping at first branch) to upper bound (fetch enough instructions from as many cache blocks as required to fill the fetch buffer) and includes the following:

- Interleaved sequential: fetch two cache blocks, sequentially ordered, and stop filling buffer at first branch
- Banked sequential: fetch two cache blocks, the second based on branch target buffer output (i.e., not necessarily sequential blocks, and so the scheme effectively handles inter-block branches), and stop filling buffer on first intra-block branch
- Collapsing buffer: fetch two cache blocks, the second based on branch target buffer output (i.e., not necessarily sequential blocks, and so the scheme effectively handles inter-block branches), and handle intra-block branches by "collapsing" the buffer (i.e., masking out jumped-over instructions and compacting the remainder)

The experimental results show that, as complexity is added to the fetch design, the various schemes improve upon the lower bound and approach the performance of the upper bound, but one of the most important contributions is to demonstrate just how much work is involved in handling non-contiguous instruction streams and how expensive it can be in both cases of branches jumping to instructions within the same cache block and branches jumping to instructions in different cache blocks.

The Patented Design

This brings us to Peleg and Weiser's *dynamic flow instruction cache*, a mechanism that solves the problem of mask and reorder (among other issues) by keeping the masked-and-reordered instruction stream in the cache. Peleg, a student at Technion in Israel, and Weiser of Intel, also an adjunct professor at Technion and Peleg's advisor, patented their invention in 1995 [Peleg & Weiser 1995], shown in Figure 2.24. This patent forms the basis of Intel's commercialized trace cache. The motivation of the design:

> With prior art instruction cache memories, when a branch is taken, the next requested instruction may be on another line. Therefore, some of the instructions stored in the cache memory may never be used and moreover, the organization on each line is independent of branching. In contrast, with the present invention, the organization of the cache memory is dynamically built on the order of execution of the instructions. [Peleg & Weiser 1995]

The main contribution of the design is that the data layout stored in the cache is more generic than previous designs. Melvin's fill unit and Franklin's shadow cache both tie the cache block structure to the back-end processing core's implementation, whereas Peleg's design puts no such restriction on the cache block format. Though the patent description above suggests that the instruction ordering represents instruction execution (which would imply an invention similar to the fill unit and shadow cache), the instruction stream is only reordered at the basic-block level: a cache block can hold up to two non-contiguous basic blocks, and instructions within each basic block are stored in the cache in program order.

The mechanism trades off space for instruction-fetch bandwidth: at any given moment, the cache contains potentially significant excess or unused space (e.g., 32 bytes per block, all of which may or may not be filled). In addition, like the fill unit and shadow cache, the dynamic flow cache suffers the overhead of storing a given static instruction multiple times at multiple locations in the cache (every basic block is considered to be a follow-on from the previous basic block, as well as the beginning of a new trace). The bandwidth is achieved by eliminating the need to predict multiple cache blocks for fetch (the predictions are implicit in the trace stored within a block) and eliminating the need to mask and reorder a stream of fetched instructions that span multiple basic blocks (such alignment is implicit in the instruction stream stored within a block).

The "Trace Cache"

Rotenberg's *trace cache* extends the number of basic blocks represented in a single cache block, something very important given the amount of attention paid to predicting more than one branch in a single cycle. The authors describe the problem well:

> The job of the fetch unit is to feed the dynamic instruction stream to the decoder. A problem is that instructions are placed in the cache in their compiled order. Storing programs in static form favors fetching code that does not branch or code with large basic blocks. Neither of these cases is typical of integer code. [Rotenberg et al. 1996, p. 25]

The trace cache extends Franklin and Smotherman's shadow cache and Peleg's design to handle non-contiguous streams spanning two branches (i.e., up to three basic blocks), and it does so in a generic and scalable manner that would support even more basic blocks. Like Peleg's design, the trace cache stores instructions in program order within a basic block, as opposed to storing reordered instructions. The cache has a fixed maximum block size of 16 instructions and fills this block from the dynamic instruction-execution stream (i.e., from disjoint regions in the code space), up to 16 instructions or a third conditional branch, whichever comes first (see Figure 2.25). Like the dynamic flow cache, the trace

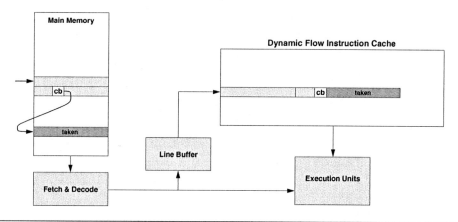

FIGURE 2.24: The Intel trace cache patent.

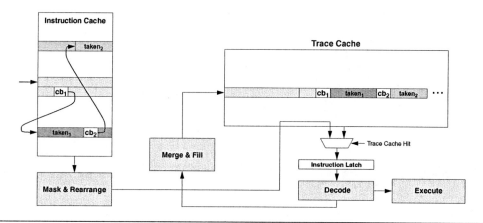

FIGURE 2.25: Rotenberg's trace cache mechanism.

cache trades off storage for bandwidth; a cache block may or may not be completely filled, and a given instruction may reside in multiple locations within the cache, corresponding to multiple traces.

Note that the sets of the cache maintain a non-exclusive relationship with each other, if a given instruction can be found within multiple cache blocks (this is potentially true of the fill unit, shadow cache, and dynamic flow cache as well). This is not considered a problem because most operating systems treat the code space as a non-writable region. Note, how-ever, that some "operating systems" are, in fact, just program loaders and do not enforce or guarantee this form of resource management and protection.

In a similar vein, the trace cache, like the fill unit and shadow cache, maintains a non-inclusive rela-tionship with the traditional instruction cache with which it operates in parallel. A given static instruction can be found in both caches, but it need not be. This is not considered a problem because most operat-ing systems treat the code space as a non-writable region.

CHAPTER 3

Management of Cache Contents

Now that we have seen a sampling of cache organizations (albeit weighted toward solid-state implementations), it makes sense to look at how the decision is made to put something into a cache. A cache's content-management solution has several responsibilities. First, it must identify important instructions and data and decide where in the memory hierarchy they should be at any given point in time. Second, it must ensure, or at least increase the likelihood, that the envisioned state of affairs actually happens. These responsibilities are addressed by actions taken by three different components:

- Partitioning heuristics
- (Pre)fetching heuristics
- Locality optimizations

Partitioning heuristics determine what items to cache. They assign data objects to storage units, and this assignment may change over time. Storage units could be caches, prefetch buffers, the different sets of a cache, different banks of the same logical unit, or different explicitly addressed partitions. The partitioning heuristics divide instructions and data vertically and horizontally over the memory system.

Once some heuristic decides "yes" for a given data item, additional mechanisms ensure that the item is actually in the appropriate place at the moment it is needed. This job is handled by (pre)fetching heuristics, the simplest of which is *demand-fetch*, and by locality optimizations that rearrange code, data, and the algorithms that operate on data to better exploit the cache hierarchy's logical organization and management policies. Fetching data and instructions before they are referenced can increase the cache's effective

capacity (in other words, with prefetching one can achieve the same performance using a smaller cache) and can reduce average latency. Locality optimizations exploit knowledge of the cache organization and operation; they either change the layout of data in memory or change the algorithm itself (and thus the order of accesses to the data), thereby improving the reuse of data and/or code in the cache.

Consider a memory system of multiple storage units, each exhibiting different access characteristics (latency, power dissipation, etc.). Leaving to chance the assignment of instructions and data to storage units will obviously yield performance, power dissipation, and/or real-time behaviors that are non-optimal. In contrast, a deliberate mechanism must classify instructions and data by their impact upon the system (e.g., their contribution to execution time and/or energy consumption) and partition them accordingly into the various storage units that are available, for instance, by assigning the most heavily accessed items to the storage unit that dissipates the least power. Assuming that the assignment is *dynamic*—assuming the heuristic determines that the best achievable behavior is such that a particular item should reside in different storage units at different points in time, i.e., close to the processor when it is needed and out in the backing store when it is not needed—then another mechanism must actively or passively schedule the movement of data during application execution to ensure that instructions and data are at the right place at the right time. That mechanism can reside within the application itself, or it can be an independent heuristic, embodied, for example, in the cache or operating system. Finally, whether the assignment is dynamic or not, the scheme will almost

117

certainly benefit from optimization techniques that help exploit available locality. For instance, if the initial partitioning heuristic determines that 100 KB of instructions and data should be cached, but the cache is only 64 KB, one can address the problem in any of a number of ways: one can compress the instructions and/or data so that the entire application fits, one can rearrange the data and/or reorder access to the data so that the data streams sequentially into the processor (thus requiring less cache space), one can use tiling and explicit memory overlays, etc.

A distinction we will make is that of design time versus run time; some of the management heuristics are invoked during application design and development, and others are invoked at the time of the application's execution. Heuristics in each of these categories are all related, even if they perform very different functions, because they all share the same view of the application.

- *Off-line heuristics* involve the programmer and/or compiler at some level. Thus, the heuristics can exploit knowledge about the semantics of the application code. These heuristics are often embodied in the software itself and thus have a *de facto* run-time counterpart, such as a prefetch instruction that begins loading data many cycles before it is needed or an initialization sequence that moves regions of code and/or data into a scratch-pad memory.
- *On-line heuristics* have no design-time analysis counterpart and thus operate at run time without direct knowledge of the application's code or semantics. If these heuristics are to react to application behavior, they must either make static assumptions about application behavior and/or structure (e.g., *predict-not-taken* is such a heuristic) or must infer application intent from dynamic observations of its behavior.

Many of these schemes are orthogonal and can be used independently of each other (e.g., code compression and either hardware or software prefetching), and many are synergistic and benefit from cooperative design (e.g., tiling and software prefetch-

ing). Additionally, a particular implementation may make use of multiple off-line and on-line heuristics embodied in many different entities (the compiler, the operating system, the cache, etc.). However, though they might be complementary, multiple heuristics could just as easily compete with each other. For example, a cache's replacement policy may strive to keep certain data items around, and this may compete with a prefetch mechanism that brings in more data than each set can handle.

A concept that we will revisit periodically is that of divide and conquer: to continually improve upon previous management solutions, designers separate different classes of memory references and exploit each behavior separately. One of the most obvious classifications is that of instructions/code versus data. References to each exhibit very distinctive behaviors that are identifiable and recognizable. Each has its own forms of analysis, optimization, and scheduling, and each has its own form of on-line management such as behavior tracking and prediction.

This is important because classification tends to scale well: the more tightly one can identify a class of data or behavior or memory access, the more specific a heuristic can be at exploiting that particular behavior. For example, sub-classifications within the larger class of *code* include function calls and other unconditional branches, long-distance branches, short-distance branches, forward-vs.-backward branches, straight-line code, etc. Sub-classifications within data are even more varied. Classes the data-prefetching community have identified include sequential access exhibited by walking through an array one element at a time, interleaved sequential access in which one walks multiple arrays simultaneously, (interleaved) stride access in which one uses potentially different non-unit strides to walk the arrays, non-stride repeating access, and non-repeating access. Data references are also classified by their use within the application (e.g., stack data, heap data, global data, and read-only data such as strings) and by the type of locality that they display. To each of these sub-classes one can apply a different solution specific to the behaviors of that sub-class.

Obviously, this scaling does not come for free; the more tightly one can tailor a heuristic to improve a particular behavior, the larger the number of heuristics one needs to cover the many varied behaviors that applications exhibit. This increases the cost of the system, in that more heuristics will be needed, but it also increases the time and cost of system verification to guarantee that the work done by one heuristic doesn't undo the optimizations of another.

In many cases, the classifications serve as designations for structural partitions, i.e., different branch predictors that handle different classes of branch and different partitions of the cache that handle different classes of data. In other cases, different off-line algorithms and heuristics are applied to each classification: tiling optimizes data layout and access, Mowry's algorithm is used to prefetch array-based computations, trace scheduling is used to optimize code, etc.

One example of an early comprehensive cache-management scheme is Abraham's control of the memory hierarchy in the PlayDoh architecture [Abraham et al. 1993, Kathail et al. 2000], a content-management solution combining both hardware and software support and both off-line and on-line mechanisms. The authors write:

> In most systems, caches are entirely managed by the hardware. But in order to control the placement of data in hardware managed caches, the programmer/compiler must second-guess the hardware. Furthermore, since the cache management decisions are not directly evident to the software, the load/store latencies are non-deterministic. At the other extreme, local or secondary memory is entirely managed by the program. The main disadvantage of an explicitly managed local memory is that the software is forced to make all management decisions.
>
> We describe a mixed implicit-explicit managed cache that captures most of the advantages of the two extremes [citation: HPL PlayDoh]. A mixed cache provides software mechanisms to explicitly control the cache as well as simple default hardware policies. The software mechanisms are utilized when the compiler has sufficient knowledge of the program's memory accessing behavior and when significant

> performance improvements are obtainable through software control Otherwise, the cache is managed using the default hardware policies. [Abraham et al. 1993, p. 141]

PlayDoh supports a full complement of level-directed load instructions; a load instruction can specify as an ultimate destination any storage unit in the memory system, including the register file, L1 or L2 cache, prefetch buffer, etc. Abraham profiles the application and schedules load instructions accordingly. We describe this particular scheme in more detail in Section 3.3.1. Note that the HPL PlayDoh architecture has been renamed the HPL-PD architecture, of which the IA-64 (Itanium) is a high-profile commercial example [Kathail et al. 2000].

The case studies section is divided into three parts.

- *On-line heuristics* require no input or information from the programmer or compiler and make use of values only available at time of execution.
- *Off-line heuristics* exploit inside information about application code and/or semantics.
- *Combined approaches* try to combine the best of both worlds.

Using different terminology, the first two divisions could just as easily be called *run-time* and *compile-time/design-time* heuristics. As mentioned earlier, heuristics in each of these categories are all related because they all share the same view of the application. Describing them together in this manner should highlight similarities and suggest future directions of study and development. Within each section, schemes are further classified into three categories.

- *Partitioning heuristics* are those mechanisms that decide whether to cache an object or not (in particular, with respect to all other objects) and/or in which cache an object should be placed.
- *Prefetching heuristics* are those mechanisms that decide whether and when to bring an item into a cache (the least interesting of

which is *demand-fetch*, i.e., waiting until the item is actually requested).

- *Locality optimizations* are those mechanisms that (re-)organize code, data, and their references to best exploit cache behavior.

A caveat: few papers in the last half-dozen years are covered in this chapter. This is intentional. It is far easier to assess the impact of older papers, and omission should not be interpreted to mean that the omitted research is not worthwhile.

3.1 Case Studies: On-Line Heuristics

We begin with a discussion of on-line or run-time techniques, those in which the program's semantics and/or structure are unknown to the heuristic. To optimize program execution, the heuristic must either make blanket choices that are good in the average case or tailor its choices to the observed behavior of the program.

3.1.1 On-Line Partitioning Heuristics

Partitioning heuristics are those that classify items. Obvious classifications include *cache-this* versus *don't-cache-this* or *put-this-into-cache* versus *put-this-into-prefetch-buffer*, but less obvious classifications are the decisions to cache *part* of an object as opposed to caching the entire object or the decision about what to throw out of a cache when it is full and more data is coming in (an implicit distinction between *cache-this* and *don't-cache-this*). At the most fundamental level, every partitioning heuristic is essentially a replacement strategy, and every replacement strategy is a partitioning heuristic. The following sections present just a handful of the many implementations that have been developed.

Replacement Strategies

Historically, this is one of the most heavily researched areas in cache design. Much research on replacement strategies has targeted the operating system's buffer cache, due to the fact that the

heuristics there can be significantly more complex than those in processor caches. The basic question is what to throw out when a new block is fetched from the backing store: the steady-state of a typical cache is *full*, and so something old must go if something new is to be brought in. The algorithm used to determine what to throw out is the cache's *replacement strategy* or *policy*.

The number of blocks to choose from is equal to the cache's associativity. If the cache's organization is direct-mapped, then the choice is trivial; there is but one block that can be replaced. With N-way set associativity, any of N blocks could be replaced. Obvious strategies are *random, FIFO* (i.e., a round-robin approach), *least-recently used* (LRU, i.e., throw out the block that has sat unreferenced for the longest period of time), *not most-recently used* (NMRU, i.e., randomly choose between all blocks but the one most recently referenced, an implementation that is typically less expensive than LRU), and *least-frequently used* (LFU, i.e., throw out the block that has been referenced the fewest number of times). As the web community has shown, the list only *begins* at that point. Podlipnig and Böszörményi survey several dozen different strategies used in web caching [2003], including LRU-Threshold, SIZE, Value-Aging, Pyramidal Selection, Partitioned Caching, LFU-Aging, LRU-Hot, HYPER-G, M-Metric, Cubic Selection, Greedy Dual, Logistic Regression, LNC-R-W3, Taylor Series Prediction, and many, many others.

Perhaps the most famous replacement strategy is Belady's MIN [1966], which uses an oracle to replace the block that will be referenced the furthest out into the future (clearly, it is not implementable as an on-line or run-time strategy). What should not be surprising is that MIN yields optimal performance—all else being equal, such as the cost of replacing different blocks, etc. Therefore, MIN is the expected ceiling function on performance and the gold standard against which other strategies are (or at least should be) measured. What might be surprising is that, though it is proven to be optimal, MIN does not actually yield the *best* performance, i.e., MIN is not OPT [McFarling 1989]. Implicit in the assumptions behind MIN is the decision to replace a block that is in the cache (a perfectly reasonable assumption, given the domain of virtual memory buffer caching, for which MIN was developed and in which the block must be loaded into the cache to be used—i.e., unlike the situation in solid-state processor caches, cache-bypass is not really an option in buffer caches). Note that it is quite possible that the incoming block is the one destined to be referenced furthest out into the future, in which case *it* should be the block that gets replaced, or "replaced," because in this case the incoming block should *bypass* the cache: the referenced word should go into the register file, but the remainder of the incoming block should be discarded, the cache contents undisturbed. The best-performing strategy is one that considers for replacement the incoming block as well as all cache-resident blocks in the set. When comparing one's scheme to an "optimal" strategy, this is the scheme to use.

Williams offers an *extremely* interesting perspective on replacement policies [Williams et al. 1996], in which replacement is defined as a two-phase process:

1. Sort the cached documents (blocks) according to one or more keys: first by a primary key, ties broken by a secondary key, etc.

2. Remove zero or more documents (blocks) from the head of the sorted list until some criteria are satisfied (usually, the process stops when the cache has enough free space to hold incoming block/s).

This definition is offered in the domain of web-document caching, in which making replacement decisions is a bit more involved than in processor caches because of the larger number of variables involved. For instance, document arrival, size, creation time, and other characteristics are kept with each cached document. The size issue alone makes replacement non-trivial in these caches, because it might not be the case that removing a single cached item is sufficient to guarantee enough free space for an incoming document.

Williams' replacement-policy definition is very powerful. It provides a partial taxonomy of possibilities (the authors note that it does not cover all existing replacement strategies), exposing numerous avenues

for further exploration. Clearly, the mechanism applies equally well to solid-state processor caches. For instance, the primary key in all transparent processor caches is set associativity: the first "sort" operation divides cached blocks into equivalence classes denoted by the cache's sets. From there another key (usually time based such as LRU, pseudo-LRU, or NMRU) is used to rank the blocks in order of preference. This provides a satisfying, formal explanation of why the cache's organization takes precedence over other heuristics in deciding matters of cacheability; it represents the primary key.

Other Policies and Strategies for Transparent (Processor) Caches

This section gives but a flavor of the choices that are available to a designer. A. J. Smith's survey [1982] is an ideal place to start for more details on the topic, followed by Hennessy and Patterson's discussion [2003], which brings later developments into the picture. For details on write policies, see Jouppi's work [1993].

As mentioned earlier, a transparent cache's implicit heuristics are determined by its logical organization, but they are also determined by its policies and strategies for handling various events, such as the handling of write data, read and write misses, block replacement, etc. For instance, on a write miss, should the entire block be read from the backing store, only to be partially overwritten by the store instruction? When a store instruction writes its data to the cache, should it also write that data immediately to the backing store, or should it wait a while? On a read miss, should the entire block be fetched from the backing store, or should the block be subdivided, with each sub-block filled separately? When a new block is brought into a set-associative cache, which block in the set, if any, should be replaced by the incoming data? These are questions that could be answered more easily with the aid of the programmer or compiler, but a transparent cache by definition is self-managed, and so these questions are usually answered by architectural design-space exploration.

Specifically, consider the handling of read and write misses. When a cache miss occurs, what should happen? On reads that miss the cache, it is likely that data will be fetched from the backing store. How much data should be fetched? It may be simplest to fetch the entire block, but it is possible to fragment a block into multiple sub-blocks, which are fetched separately or, perhaps, are fetched together but each of which is replaced separately (which is the case in early MIPS R2000 caches, which had blocks of one word wide, and several contiguous words/blocks were fetched from the backing store simultaneously). This all goes against the notion we put forward earlier in Chapter 1 that a cache block is an atomic unit; as all things engineering, many of the best ideas start out as exceptions to the rule.

On a write, things are slightly more complex, because it is not at all clear that *any* data should be fetched from the backing store. Many caches are *non-allocating* on write misses, which means that they predict a write miss will be soon followed by another write to a different word in the same block (e.g., if initializing or overwriting an array or large data structure), in which case it makes no sense to bring an entire block from memory, which will only be overwritten. The same sub-blocking concepts apply here as well.

Note that some of these issues would require unorthodox support for use in file caches. For instance, a typical file cache cannot be non-allocating because a file cache has no concept of cache-bypass for reads or direct-to-backing-store for writes: operations on file cache objects are not as atomic as single load/store instructions. With buffering, however, many of these mechanisms could potentially find their way into standard file caches.

Jouppi's Victim Cache, HP-7200 Assist Cache

In the preceding chapter, we used Jouppi's *victim cache* [1990] as an example of an exclusive horizontal (or lateral) partition. We revisit the design, as well as the HP-7200 *assist cache* [Chan et al. 1996], to illustrate how these hardware mechanisms effectively partition/isolate data references according to the type of locality that they exhibit.

Figure 3.1 illustrates how the two caches work. In both organizations, a cache lookup probes both partitions (main cache and victim/assist cache). Figure 3.1(a) shows the victim cache's management strategy:

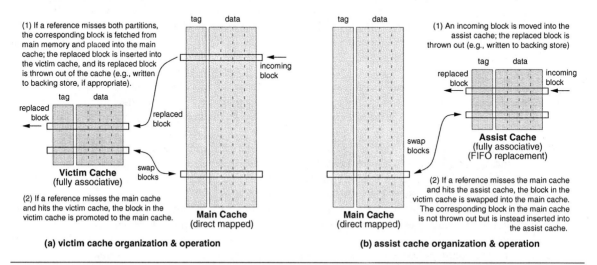

(a) victim cache organization & operation

(1) If a reference misses both partitions, the corresponding block is fetched from main memory and placed into the main cache; the replaced block is inserted into the victim cache, and its replaced block is thrown out of the cache (e.g., written to backing store, if appropriate).

Victim Cache (fully associative)

(2) If a reference misses the main cache and hits the victim cache, the block in the victim cache is promoted to the main cache.

Main Cache (direct mapped)

(b) assist cache organization & operation

(1) An incoming block is moved into the assist cache; the replaced block is thrown out (e.g., written to backing store)

Assist Cache (fully associative) (FIFO replacement)

(2) If a reference misses the main cache and hits the assist cache, the block in the victim cache is swapped into the main cache. The corresponding block in the main cache is not thrown out but is instead inserted into the assist cache.

Main Cache (direct mapped)

FIGURE 3.1: Victim cache and assist cache organization and operation. The assist cache operation shown is one possibility. Other schemes include moving a replaced block from the assist cache to main cache, especially when the main cache is very large and off-chip.

1. An incoming block is placed into the main cache, and the replaced block is inserted into the victim cache.
2. On a main cache miss but a victim cache hit, the referenced block is swapped out of the victim cache into the main cache, and the block replaced from the main cache is moved into the victim cache.

Figure 3.1(b) shows the assist cache's management strategy:

1. An incoming (prefetched) block is placed into the assist cache, which is managed using a FIFO replacement strategy.
2. On a main cache miss but an assist cache hit, the referenced block is swapped out of the assist cache into the main cache, and the block replaced from the main cache is moved into the assist cache.

The victim cache captures temporal locality: blocks that are accessed frequently within a given time period, even if replaced from the main cache, remain within the larger cache organization. The cache organization addresses the limitation of the direct-mapped/limited-associativity main cache by giving blocks a second chance if they exhibit conflict with one or more blocks vying for the same set. Note that the replacement policy of the victim cache can be very simple: given the scheme's operation, a FIFO replacement policy effectively achieves *true-LRU* behavior. Any reference to the victim cache pulls the referenced block out of the victim cache; thus, the LRU block in the victim cache will, by definition, be the oldest one there (assuming that aging begins when a block enters the victim cache).

The assist cache, on the other hand, separates blocks exhibiting spatial locality from those exhibiting temporal locality. Because incoming blocks are placed in the assist cache first, and because the assist cache is managed using a FIFO heuristic, the scheme has the potential to discard blocks that exhibit streaming behavior once they have been used, without moving them into the main cache. Such a partition would guarantee that only blocks exhibiting

temporal locality get promoted to the main cache, especially if coupled with the re-reference detector described by Rivers and Davidson [1996] in the NTS (non-temporal streaming) cache, described later. The primary difference is that the fully associative buffer in the NTS cache is managed in an LRU fashion rather than a FIFO fashion.

McFarling's Dynamic Exclusion

McFarling [1991] presents one of the earliest hardware schemes that uses a predictor to dynamically partition the address space, in this case deciding whether or not to exclude certain instructions from being cached.

McFarling notes several scenarios of loop-based code in which instructions conflict with each other in the (direct-mapped) instruction cache and in which the optimal scenario can be achieved with hardware conflict detection. To address conflicts without disturbing scenarios in which the direct-mapped cache already performs as well as can be expected, McFarling adds a *sticky* bit to each cache entry, indicating that the block currently held there is valuable and should not be replaced by incoming instructions. To each cache block (i.e., group of instructions or region of the backing store), he adds a *hit-last* bit indicating that the block was used the last time it was in the cache (caused a cache hit). The *sticky* bit stays with the cache; the *hit-last* information travels with the block if it is evicted from the cache.

A finite state machine, shown in Figure 3.2, operates in conjunction with the two state bits associated with each cache entry and the *hit-last* bit of any incoming block. For instance, if the currently cached block is a and the cache entry's *sticky* bit is set (state A,s, upper left-hand corner), block a will be replaced if a conflicting instruction is requested and the incoming block has its *hit-last* bit set (a transition to state B,s); otherwise, if the incoming block does not have its *hit-last* bit set, a reference to a conflicting instruction only clears the cache entry's *sticky* bit (to state $A,\bar{s}$), at which point a request to a resets the sticky bit (to state A,s) and a request to any conflicting instruction causes a to be replaced (state B,s).

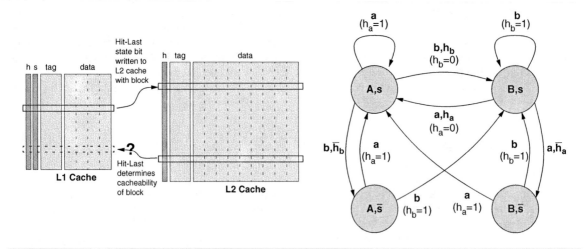

FIGURE 3.2: Finite state machine for McFarling's dynamic exclusion. Upper-case labels (A or B) indicate the cached block; lower-case labels (a or b) indicate the requested block; overbars represent negated logic; s is the value of the cache entry's sticky bit; and h_x is the hit-last bit of the incoming block. Conditionals are shown in bold with the form requested-block{, state}, and actions are shown in parentheses.

The scheme extends to data caches as well as instruction caches [McFarling 1991], and it clearly extends to software implementations as well (e.g., file caches). Note that any block in the backing store is potentially cacheable or non-cacheable, and the partition between those items to be cached and those items to exclude from the cache changes dynamically with application behavior.

Tyson's Modified Approach

Tyson gives an example of an on-line mechanism that classifies load/store instructions as being problematic (causing more than their fair share of cache misses) and thus chooses not to cache them [Tyson et al. 1995]. The on-line mechanism creates a dynamic partition because a datum's cacheability can change from moment to moment.

As pointed out by Abraham [Abraham et al. 1993], in many applications a small number of load instructions tend to be responsible for a disproportionately large number of cache misses. Tyson investigates what would happen if those

load instructions are identified, either at compile time or at run time, and are tagged *cacheable/non-allocatable*, meaning that these instructions should not cause data allocation in the cache, but their requested data might nonetheless be found in the cache, if it was loaded by a different instruction [Tyson et al. 1995].

The authors first investigate a simple static partition in which the tagging is done at compile time after profiling and a load instruction's characterization does not change over the execution of the application. This tends to increase the cache miss rate slightly, but it decreases memory bandwidth requirements significantly. Note that it requires hardware support in the instruction set. The authors also investigate a dynamic on-line mechanism that requires no application profiling and no instruction-set support. As shown in Figure 3.3, a table similar to a branch predictor is indexed by the load instruction's program counter and tracks whether the load instruction causes a miss in the data cache. After enough consecutive misses, the load instruction is marked *cacheable/non-allocatable*.

Rivers' Non-Temporal Streaming Cache

A similar dynamic-partition/on-line mechanism is explored by Rivers [Rivers & Davidson 1996, Rivers et al. 1997]: the *NTS* cache places in parallel with the primary cache a fully associative buffer (an arrangement like that of victim- and assist-cache organizations) whose purpose is to hold items that would otherwise disrupt the temporal locality of items held in the primary cache. The organization is shown in Figure 3.4. The fully associative NT buffer is managed in an LRU fashion.

A predictor similar to those of McFarling [1991] and Tyson [Tyson et al. 1995] tracks data use and identifies "nontemporal" blocks, i.e., those that display either no locality or streaming behavior, and maps those blocks to the fully associative buffer and not the primary cache. Like McFarling's scheme, the predictor observes application behavior and tags each block

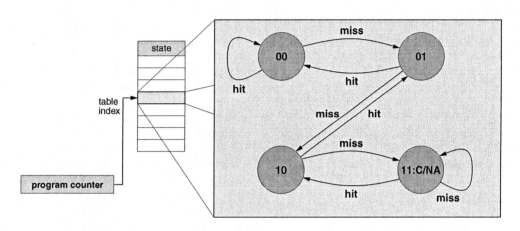

FIGURE 3.3: Tyson's modified approach to cache management. A (potentially tagged) prediction table, indexed by the program counter, contains two-bit saturating counters that are incremented on cache misses and decremented on cache hits. A load instruction is marked cacheable/*non-allocatable (C/NA)* if its predictor tracks three misses in a row. Conditionals are shown in bold.

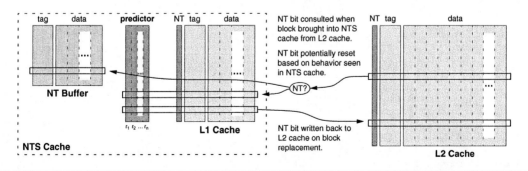

FIGURE 3.4: Rivers' non-temporal streaming cache with predictor bits. The figure shows a generic cache block structure with n data words in the L1 cache block. Predictor maintains n re-reference bits r_1-r_n that track the access behavior of the individual words in each block.

of data with a characteristic that stays with the block while it is in the cache system (and could conceivably be stored with the block when it is written out to the backing store). When the block is resident in the L1 cache, a bit vector keeps track of the word reuse within the block. If a word within the block is referenced more than once while the block is in the cache, the block is labeled as exhibiting temporal locality; otherwise, it is labeled as being non-temporal. The label, embodied in the *NT bit* shown in Figure 3.4, is written back to the L2 cache when the block is evicted. If the block is brought again into the L1 cache, the label in the NT bit determines whether the block is placed into the main cache or the fully associative non-temporal buffer. The scheme reduces miss ratio, memory traffic, and the average access penalty.

Johnson's Frequency Tracking

Another technique uses frequency of access to identify blocks to cache. Johnson and Hwu [1997] propose a memory address table (MAT), shown in Figure 3.5. The MAT is a separate cache of saturating counters, each of which tracks how frequently the blocks within a "macroblock" are referenced while their data is resident in the primary cache. A macroblock is a region of memory larger than a single cache block; all cache blocks within a macroblock update the same counter. So, for instance, a macroblock

exhibiting streaming behavior and containing four cache blocks would report the same number of references as another macroblock in which one of its blocks was referenced four times and the other blocks went unreferenced.

Any reference to a macroblock causes its MAT entry to be incremented. If the corresponding cache block is cache resident, nothing further happens. If the block is *not* cache resident, its counter value is compared to that of the cache block that *is* resident. The higher cache block is given priority. If a cache-resident block wins over a non-resident block, its counter is decremented—an attempt to guarantee some sort of fairness.

Note that to be effective the MAT must be large enough to cover macroblocks not currently in the cache. Like McFarling's and Rivers' schemes, the state of a cache-resident block is compared to that of an incoming block, which implies that state is retained for a (macro)block when it is evicted from the cache. The authors do not explicitly investigate distributed schemes such as McFarling's or Rivers'. Note also that there are two different mechanisms at work: (1) the aggregation of data (encoding in a single state variable the behavior of an entire region, as opposed to the behavior of a single block) and (2) the use of a frequency metric, as opposed to tracking spatial or temporal locality. It is not clear which is the more important mechanism.

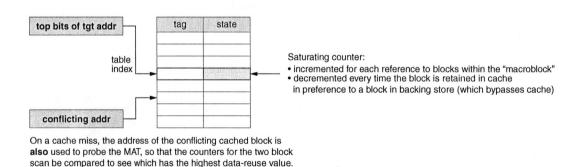

On a cache miss, the address of the conflicting cached block is **also** used to probe the MAT, so that the counters for the two block scan be compared to see which has the highest data-reuse value.

FIGURE 3.5: Johnson's memory-address table. The MAT can be direct-mapped, fully associative, or set associative. It typically does not mirror the cache organization. A system would typically use a separate MAT each for L1, L2, … caches.

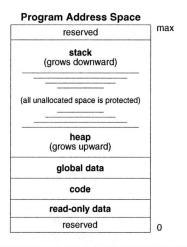

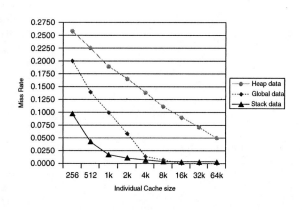

FIGURE 3.6: Average miss rates for segregated caches. References are divided between stack, heap, and globals (shown on left, MIPS ISA). Figures used with permission from Lee and Tyson [2000].

Lee's Region-Based Division

Lee and Tyson present an on-line mechanism that enforces a static partition of data references into stack, global, and everything else [2000]. This is similar in spirit to Murta's *partitioned web caching* that divides all cached objects into three different groups, *small*, *medium*, and *large*, with each group using its own space managed separately from the others [Murta et al. 1998]. Both are dynamic mechanisms that enforce a statically defined partition of the space.

Lee and Tyson note that data references to the different regions of a process's address space can exhibit dramatically different hit rates. This is illustrated in Figure 3.6. They explore a static, exclusive partitioning of the address space to exploit this difference in behavior: each region is assigned its own partition of the L1 cache. Figure 3.7 shows an example implementation with separate partitions placed alongside the L1 cache. Note that the partitions can be made much smaller than the L1 cache (and thus can dissipate less power), because the storage requirements for the stack and global data of the studied applications tend to be smaller

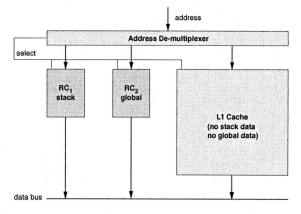

FIGURE 3.7: Region-based cache partitioning. A cache's partition is only activated (thus dissipating power) if an address references it. Figure used with permission from Lee and Tyson [2000].

than the requirements for the applications' heaps. As the authors point out, this mechanism requires slightly more decode circuitry than a simple non-partitioned cache, but the net result is a reduction in energy consumption.

On-Line Low-Power Schemes: Kaxiras' Cache Decay

Proposals have apppeared for transparently managing the power of processor caches; one example is the *cache-decay* mechanism proposed by Kaxiras [Kaxiras et al. 2001]. Other mechanisms are described in Chapter 5, Section 5.3.1, "Low-Leakage Operation." Cache decay is discussed here because it has a relatively complex control heuristic compared to other schemes.

Cache decay reduces leakage power in caches by disabling (disconnecting from the power supply) those blocks the heuristic believes to be no longer needed. This comes from the observation that data blocks brought into a cache are often used frequently within a short window of time and then go unused for a relatively long window of time preceding their replacement by another incoming block. The heuristic exploits this behavior by disabling blocks as soon as it detects a significant slow-down in the frequency

with which they are accessed. Note that this is *not* a state-preserving operation: disabling a block implies that the contents of the block are discarded. If the contents are dirty (e.g., in a write-back cache), they need to be written to the memory system first. Figure 3.8 (from Kaxiras et al. [2001, Figures 1 and 2]) shows the time that fetched blocks spend in this interim "dead" state, not being used and merely awaiting replacement. If this dead time were eliminated—if the cache blocks holding the data could be disabled during this dead time—cache leakage power could be reduced by roughly 70%.

Kaxiras' cache-decay mechanism maintains a countdown timer for each block in the cache. Whenever the block is read or written, the timer is reset. If the timer reaches zero, the block's data is removed from the cache (flushed to memory if dirty; discarded otherwise), and the block is disconnected from the power supply. Because the observed inactivity intervals tend to

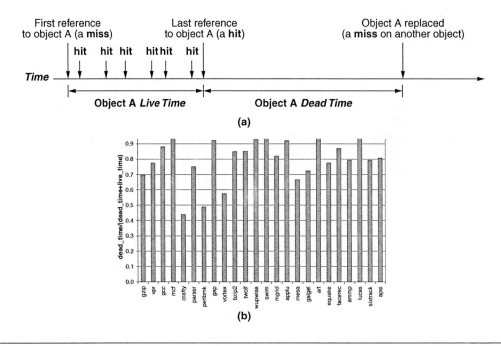

(a)

(b)

FIGURE 3.8: Fraction of time cache data are dead. (a) Illustrates the definition of dead time as the window between last reference and replacement. (b) Illustrates the fraction of time an application data spends in dead state; on average, leakage power could be reduced significantly by eliminating dead time.

be large (either hundreds or thousands of processor cycles), there is only one fine-grained counter that drives the heuristic: with each block is associated a lower resolution 2-bit counter that is driven by a high-order bit of the high-resolution counter. This significantly reduces the active power overhead of the system, as compared to using a high-resolution counter for each cache block, and the authors note that it achieves very reasonable behavior. Not surprisingly, the heuristic exposes a trade-off between performance (cache miss rate) and leakage power. Setting the cache's *decay interval* to be short, i.e., choosing to discard the contents of a cache block after it has been inactive for a relatively short period of time, reduces the cache's leakage power significantly, but increases the cache miss rate just as significantly by throwing out data prematurely. On the other hand, using long decay intervals tends to avoid discarding data prematurely, but it also leaves cache blocks active for long intervals and thus fails to reduce leakage power significantly. Clearly, an adaptive or per-block heuristic is worth investigating; Kaxiras explores a mechanism whereby the predicted dead time is tracked once a block is discarded. Noting that a cache miss seen soon after discarding a block is likely an indication of a premature block-flush, the mechanism is augmented to adjust the decay interval dynamically.

3.1.2 On-Line Prefetching Heuristics[1]

As mentioned, spatial locality leads to a simple heuristic: use larger cache blocks. Though effective, this does not scale indefinitely because not all referenced data exhibits spatial locality. Thus, the use of extremely large blocks leads to cache pollution, reduced cache hit rates, and excessive memory traffic. Therefore, more sophisticated mechanisms are warranted. Because a purely on-line heuristic has no inside knowledge of the application's behavior (i.e., it does not rely upon off-line code analysis), it must be proactive and/or predictive to some degree—it must observe and track application

behavior to decide what to prefetch and/or when to fetch it. The simplest possible (pre)fetch mechanism is demand-fetch, in which blocks are fetched when requested. Moving beyond demand-fetch to *prefetch* can increase effective cache capacity and decrease average latency. This is not totally free, because if the mechanism is not 100% accurate, the memory bus carries useless prefetches (thus reducing the effective memory bandwidth), and the cache can be forced to throw out otherwise useful code/data to store the uselessly fetched blocks.

Note that prefetching can be initiated at any of several levels in the memory hierarchy, and the prefetched block can be placed in any level. Prefetching can be initiated in the L1 cache level, the L2 cache level, the memory controller, or even in the memory chips. The prefetched data is usually stored at the level where the prefetch is initiated, either in the prefetch-initiating cache or in a separate prefetch buffer at the same level as the prefetch-initiating cache (the latter mechanism avoids polluting the cache with prefetched data). In some cases, the initiating level is not the same as the destination. For example, a memory-side prefetching may be initiated near the memory, but the prefetched data is pushed into the L2 cache.

Prefetching Instructions, i.e., Branch Prediction

Fetching memory blocks ahead of time is intuitively attractive and also, just as intuitively, very difficult. As suggested earlier, the problem has proven tractable largely because designers have separated out different classes of items to prefetch. One of the most obvious classifications is that of instructions/code versus data. To predict what instructions to fetch ahead of time, one requires either foreknowledge of application behavior (which is possible for many regular applications) or the ability to observe branch behavior and predict future outcomes (which is possible for all types of applications, including irregular

---

[1]The following contains some material from "Data Cache Prefetching" by Yan Solihin and Donald Yeung, in *Speculative Execution in High Performance Computer Architectures*, CRC Press, Chapman and Hall, D. Kaeli and P. Yew, editors, ISBN-1-58488-447-9, 2005. Copyright © 2005 CRC Press. Used with permission.

ones). Branch prediction is a heavily researched field, because the closer one's miss rate approaches zero, the larger one's window of instructions available for high-confidence prefetch becomes.

Further sub-classification is exploited heavily in branch prediction. Consider the sub-classes already listed: function calls and other unconditional branches, long-distance branches, short-distance branches, forward-vs.-backward branches, straight-line code; each has its own heuristic. Return address stacks improve function calls [Webb 1988, Kaeli & Emma 1991]; branch-target buffers improve long-distance branches [Lee & Smith 1984]; mechanisms such as the trace cache and collapsing buffer (see Chapter 2, Section 2.6.3, "Another Dynamic Cache Block: Trace Caches") address short-distance branches; loop caches address tight loops (short, backward branches) [Lee & Smith 1984]; etc.

Early Work in Prefetching Sequential Data Accesses

As mentioned, increasing block size exploits spatial locality, but the solution does not scale very far. Rather than increasing the block size indiscriminately, one can, perhaps conditionally, fetch block $i+1$ (possibly block $i+2$ or 3 as well) whenever block i is fetched by the application. Early work, surveyed by Smith [1982], includes the following: (a) prefetch on every application reference, (b) prefetch only on cache miss, and (c) *tagged prefetch*, in which a bit associated with each cache entry identifies references that would have caused cache misses were their corresponding cache blocks not prefetched. A cache entry's tag bit is set to one whenever the application references it; the cache entry's tag bit is set to zero when an incoming *prefetched* block is placed in the entry. Thus, any zero-to-one transition indicates a reference to a block that is only present because of a prefetch and thus should count as a cache miss in terms of initiating another lookahead prefetch.

Prefetching is also studied in the context of software-based caches (e.g., the operating system's virtual memory paging system and/or file system), which can support more sophisticated algorithms. A good example is Baer and Sager's "spatial lookahead" mechanism [1976], a *de facto* correlation table

used by the operating system to speculatively prefetch pages of an application's virtual-address space.

Other contemporary cache research is concerned with prioritizing access to resources given the different classes of request, including instruction fetches and prefetches and data fetches and prefetches. What should be the order of priority when there is contention for the cache port or for the memory port and memory bus? What type of data should have the higher priority in determining placement and replacement within the cache? This is similar in spirit to using the classification of load instructions versus store instructions to determine block allocation (e.g., caches that fetch the entire block on read misses, but fetch nothing or a partial block on write misses).

The literature on solid-state processor caches typically dismisses the *fetch-always* heuristic as being unrealistic (scheme (a) above; it generates an enormous amount of memory traffic but does produce low miss rates). The reason for this is lack of bandwidth: an L1 processor cache has an extremely high access rate compared to the sustainable bandwidth to the backing store, and, due to this imbalance, a fetch-always scheme can generate significantly many more prefetches in a time period than the backing store could possibly service. The heuristic is viable for cache implementations that exhibit no such imbalance, such as buffer caches, disk caches, some web caches, proactive DRAM bank activation, and even potentially the lowest level of processor cache before the main memory system, if its request traffic is slow enough: i.e., if, as in the Itanium's L3 cache, the main purpose of the cache is not to provide significant access bandwidth, but is instead to provide enough capacity to hide the latency to the backing store (see Chapter 6).

Jouppi's Stream Buffers

On a related note, Jouppi notes that the reactive lookahead scheme is not aggressive enough for modern multi-issue cores; it requires a miss before a new prefetch can be initiated, which introduces significant delay due to the large and growing imbalance between high execution rates, high L1 cache bandwidth, and the relatively long latencies to the backing store [1990]. Jouppi proposes *stream buffers* to solve the problem, a mechanism similar to the sliding window used in networking protocols [Jacobsen et al. 1992].

A stream buffer is a FIFO buffer. Each of its entries contains a cache block, the block's tag, and an *available* bit. Figure 3.9 illustrates the organization and operation of three stream buffers. Multiple buffers support the prefetching of multiple streams in parallel, where each buffer prefetches from one stream. On a cache access, the cache and the head entries of the stream buffers are checked for a match (Jouppi's original mechanism uses a single tag comparator per stream; one can envision more complex mechanisms). If the requested block is found in the cache, no action on the stream buffers is performed. If the block is not found in the cache, but is found at the head of a stream buffer, the block is moved into the cache. The head pointer of the stream buffer moves to the next entry, and the buffer prefetches the last entry's successor into the freed entry, i.e., if the last entry's block address is L, then block L+1 is prefetched. If the block is found in neither cache nor stream buffer, a new stream buffer is allocated, and the block's successors are prefetched to fill the stream buffers. While a prefetch is in flight, the *available* bit

is set to '0' and is set to '1' only when the prefetch has completed.

A simple mechanism that detects sequential streaming (i.e., indicates when to allocate a new stream buffer) is described by Palacharla and Kessler [1994]. The idea is to start streaming when a cache sees misses to blocks A and $A+1$ in succession, suggesting that a miss to block $A+2$ cannot be far off. The scheme maintains a history buffer of miss addresses and places into the buffer address $A+1$ whenever block A misses the cache. A reference (e.g., to $A+1$) that misses the cache but hits the history buffer indicates sequential streaming behavior (at least potentially). A reference that misses both the cache and the history buffer should not allocate a new stream buffer, as it indicates either (a) no locality or (b) non-unit strides. The issue of non-unit strides brings us to the next section.

Baer's Reference Prediction Table: Stride Prefetching

Figure 3.9 illustrates a problem in simple sequential prefetching, a scenario in which the block-address reference stream is $A, B, A+2, B+1, A+4, B+2, \ldots$. The access to block A results in a cache miss, which results

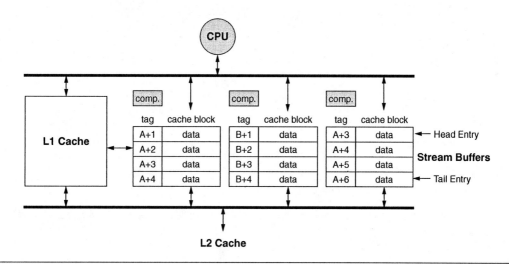

FIGURE 3.9: Stream buffer organization and operation. Each stream is maintained in a FIFO order, and each has a comparator associated with the head entry's tag.

in allocating a stream buffer for A's successors: $A + 1$, $A + 2$, $A + 3$, $A + 4$. Similarly, the access to block B results in a cache miss, which results in allocating a stream buffer and initiates prefetches for $B + 1$, $B + 2, B + 3, B + 4$. On the next access, to block $A + 2$, the cache and the head entries of the stream buffers both yield a miss; consequently, a new stream buffer is allocated for $A + 2$'s successors: $A + 3, A + 4, A + 5, A + 6$.

At this point, two separate stream buffers are allocated for A's successors and $A + 2$'s successors, and some entries overlap ($A + 3$ and $A + 4$). This is due to two factors: the single comparator per stream buffer and the mechanism's inability to identify the non-unit stride of A's stream. Note that simply increasing the number of comparators is not a complete solution. While it would eliminate the allocation of multiple buffers to a logically single stream and the resultant duplication of blocks across stream buffers, it would not eliminate the useless prefetches (those for blocks $A + 1, A + 3, ...$) that increase memory traffic and reduce the effective capacity of the stream buffers.

A better solution is a mechanism[2] that handles non-unit strides.

Baer and Chen describe such a mechanism: a hardware prefetching scheme that detects and adapts to non-sequential access [1991]. It detects and prefetches non-unit strides, and it detects and avoids prefetches for non-repeating accesses. As shown in Figure 3.10, the program counter probes the Reference Prediction Table, a cache in which each entry identifies its corresponding load/store instruction, the previous address used, the most recently observed stride, and a two-bit state value (to be used by an associated FSM (finite state machine), shown in the figure) that tracks accuracy and enables a prediction. On every reference from a load/store instruction, the new target address is compared to the predicted address (*prev_addr* + *stride*), and the result is used to update state and other fields in the entry. The scheme tracks strides and generates prefetches when stride accesses are detected; when it detects non-stride accesses it ensures that no prefetches are initiated.

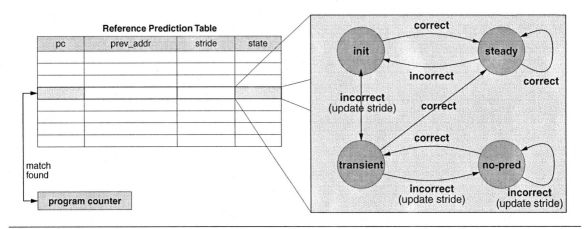

FIGURE 3.10: Baer and Chen's PC-based stride predictor. In the finite state machine, conditionals are shown in bold, and actions are shown in parentheses.

---

[2]Note that increasing the cache block size creates *de facto* sequential accesses out of small-stride accesses.

Palacharla's Elimination of the Program Counter

An important aspect of Baer and Chen's mechanism is that it uses the program counter to separate different address streams coming from different load and store instructions. When multiple streams are interleaved, the net result can look random even if the individual streams are regular and easily predicted. Thus, the program counter is a powerful tool that separates different streams with different behaviors, each of which can be more predictable individually than the total stream. This is similar in spirit to applying different heuristics to different classifications of behavior. However, in the absence of special hardware support, the use of the program counter necessitates an on-core, hardware-based prefetching solution: the PC-based mechanism cannot be used to generate prefetches from the off-chip caches to memory; it cannot be used in the disk cache; it cannot be used in web caches; etc. On the other hand, the operating system's buffer cache can potentially make use of a PC-based prefetching scheme, because the operating system does have access to the program counter of the trap instruction that invoked the I/O system. However, if the trap instruction is in a shared library (e.g., *fread()* or *fwrite()*), then it cannot be used to distinguish activity coming from different regions of the application code.

The net result is that it would be very valuable to have a mechanism that can recognize patterns within a larger stream without the need for a program counter. Such a mechanism could be used at any point in the memory system (on-chip, off-chip, in the DRAM system, in the disk system, in hardware, in software, etc.). Palacharla and Kessler present such a mechanism [1994], shown in Figure 3.11. The scheme dynamically partitions the memory space into statically defined equal-sized regions (defined by the *tag/czone* partition shown in the figure), each of which is tracked for stride behavior. Instead of separating streams from each other by identifying each with its program counter, the scheme exploits the fact that stream behavior is likely to be localized (consider, for example, a vector operation on two large arrays A and B with non-sequential behavior $A + 1, A + 3, A + 5, \ldots$ and $B, B + 2, B + 4, \ldots$; note that $A + 3$ and $A + 5$ are nearby in the memory space, as are $B + 2$ and $B + 4$, but $A + 3$ and $B + 2$ are relatively distant). Judicious choice of the partition between tag and czone (stands for "concentration zone") enables one to separate the A stream from the B stream. If the *czone* partition is no larger than the array size, references to A and B will have different *tag* values, but if the tag bit vector is made too small (if *czone* is large enough to encompass both A and B), then references to A and B will appear to be in the same stream.

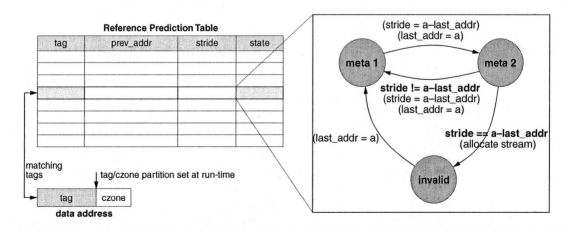

FIGURE 3.11: Palacharla and Kessler's non-PC-based stride predictor. In the finite state machine, state-transition conditions are shown in bold, and actions are shown in parentheses.

The finite state machine shown in Figure 3.11 requires three references that miss the cache and sequential stream buffers (which capture sequential streaming behavior). The state machine ensures that the delta between the first two references is the same as the delta between the second two references.

Note that the scheme typically requires off-line code analysis to set the tag/czone partition appropriately. Alternatively, the scheme can be used in conjunction with a closed-loop feedback mechanism that dynamically adjusts the partition and tracks the accuracy of the resultant prefetches. Note also that the scheme is easily extended to other domains: for instance, the partition in file caching can be set by any combination of memory address or object ID, process ID, machine ID, network domain, file name prefix ("/usr" or "/bin" or "/usr/local," etc.), and so on.

Prefetching Non-Stride Accesses

Overall, prefetching for sequential and strided accesses is achievable with relatively simple hardware. Several recent machines, such as the Intel Pentium 4 and IBM Power4 architectures, implement a hardware prefetcher that is similar to stream buffers at the L2 cache level [Hinton et al. 2001, IBM 2002c]. The L2 cache in the Power4 can detect up to eight sequential streams. The L2 cache line is 128 bytes, and therefore a sequential stream detector can catch most strided accesses. On a cache miss to a line in the L2 cache, the fifth successor line is prefetched. The L3 cache block is four times larger than the L2 (512 bytes), and therefore it only prefetches the next successive line on an L3 miss.

Some accesses that are not strided but that do have repeated patterns may appear random to the prefetcher and are therefore not easy to detect and prefetch. A good example includes applications that exhibit algorithmic locality, but not spatial or temporal locality. These accesses may result from a linked data structure traversal, or they may result from indirect array references, such as in $A[B[i]]$. One technique to address these sequences records one or more successor miss addresses for references that miss the cache and is therefore able to correlate misses. This type of technique is called *correlation prefetching*. Another technique, called *content-directed prefetching*, tries to identify addresses in fetched data and use them to fetch more data. For example, this can address the pointer-chasing problem if the mechanism can identify the *next* pointer in a fetched data structure.

Though these schemes are not widely used in commercial hardware systems, they are valuable as examples because they can be suitable (and have been explored) in other domains such as paging and file caching—scenarios in which the fetch latency is long enough to hide the operation of a complex heuristic and in which the request-traffic bandwidth might be low enough to allow an aggressive prefetch heuristic that might have less-than-ideal accuracy.

Ramamoorthy's Look-ahead Unit: Continual Optimization in 1966

An early example in which the dividing line between compiler techniques and on-line heuristics is deliberately obscured is Ramamoorthy's use of a *connectivity matrix* and *reachability matrix* to drive a "look-ahead unit" [1966]. This is one of the earliest attempts to prefetch logically related and/or temporally related blocks as opposed to sequential or stride-related blocks. The scheme is also important in its support of profiling program behavior for off-line mechanisms, and we will return to it (briefly) in Section 3.3.

Figure 3.12 shows an example program fragment and its corresponding connectivity and reachability matrices. A directed edge from node i to node j in the connectivity graph (i.e., connectivity matrix element $C_{ij} = 1$) indicates that one can reach code block j from code block i directly. This information can be used at compile time to pack the application's procedures (or basic blocks—whatever is appropriate, given the chosen granularity for the graph representation) into virtual pages or cache blocks with the goal of minimizing page faults or cache misses. This will be described in more detail later in Section 3.3.3. The connectivty matrix is used at run time by the look-ahead unit, in conjunction with information on each code block's data needs (for example, as encoded in the *data-reference matrix* P [Lowe 1969]), to prefetch program code and its requisite data. For

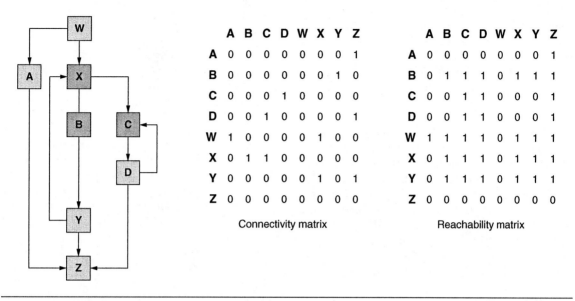

FIGURE 3.12: The connectivity and reachability matrices.

instance, when program execution reaches node X in the figure, the look-ahead unit would fetch blocks B and C [Ramamoorthy 1966]. The mechanism is similar in spirit to Pierce's wrong-path prefetching in this regard, in that it prefetches logically related blocks that will likely be used in the near future even if not used in the immediate future [Pierce 1995, Pierce & Mudge 1996].

A directed edge from node i to node j in the reachability graph (i.e., reachability matrix element $R_{ij} = 1$) indicates that one can reach code block j from code block i either directly or indirectly. Thus, though $C_{XY} = 0$, $R_{XY} = 1$. This information is used by the look-ahead unit to make cache-replacement decisions: at the time of a page fault, the reachability matrix is used to identify any sections of the code that are no longer useful because they can no longer be reached by the currently executing code block; if such blocks are found, they are marked for replacement. Knuth gives an algorithm that would generate the connectivity matrix C [1963]; the reachability matrix R is derived from C. These matrices can be produced at or before compile time.

Ramamoorthy discusses how the connectivity graph can be augmented by attaching to each directed edge weights representing the probability of the edge being taken, based on the results of profiling instrumented code. This would provide better insight and predictive abilities for both code/data packing at compile time (i.e., locality optimization) and code/data prefetching at run time. Ramamoorthy even suggests a continual optimization approach in which an application updates the probabilities in its connectivity matrix every time it is run.

Correlation Prefetching in Processor Caches

Correlation prefetching uses past sequences of reference or miss addresses to predict and prefetch future misses (early examples: Baer and Sager [1976], Rechstschaffen [1983], Pomerene et al. [1989], Charney and Reeves [1995], Alexander and Kedem [1996], and Joseph and Grunwald [1997]; Sazeides and Smith use a similar mechanism to predict data values as opposed to data addresses [1997]). A typical implementation uses a *correlation table* to record miss addresses and one or more successor misses. Later, when a miss is observed, the addresses that are correlated with the miss address are prefetched. Correlation prefetching has general applicability in that it works for any access or miss pattern as long as the miss address sequences repeat. The drawbacks are that the table needs to be trained to record the first appearance of the sequences, and, to be effective, the table size needs to scale with the program's working set.

The earliest appearance of a correlation predictor is within the context of a cache other than a solid-state processor cache. Baer and Sager propose two different correlation mechanisms to prefetch pages of instructions and/or data on behalf of a running application [1976]. The mechanisms are implemented within the operating system as part of virtual memory paging, and because they are invoked at the time of a page fault, they can be considerably more sophisticated than contemporaneous prefetching techniques implemented in hardware for processor caches. Baer and Sager consider three algorithms: *one-block lookahead, spatial lookahead, and temporal lookahead*, with the latter two being examples of correlation predictors. Each uses a prediction table, PRED, indexed by the virtual page number, and a usage stack, LRU, representing the order in which the memory's n pages have been referenced. LAST is the last page causing a page fault. The prefetch arrays work as follows. Note that the discussions leave out regular paging activity: i.e., on a fault to page q, remove page LRU[n] from memory, fetch page q, set LRU[1] <– q. The discussions also leave out the obvious prefetching activity: i.e., on a fault to page q, if PRED[q] is not resident, prefetch it and set LRU[n] <– PRED[q] (with the latter expression ensuring that the prefetched page will be the first page considered for replacement unless it is referenced before another page fault occurs).

- *One-block lookahead*: PRED[i] = i + 1.
- *Spatial lookahead*: PRED[i] is initialized to i + 1. On a fault to page q, if no prefetching was done for previous fault, or if a page was prefetched but was not referenced, set PRED[LAST] <– q. Set LAST <– q. Note that if a prefetch occurred for page LAST, and the

prefetched page was referenced, then setting PRED[LAST] <– q would overwrite correct predictive information.
- *Temporal lookahead*: PRED[i] is initialized to i + 1. On a fault to page q, update the value PRED[LRU[1]] <– q (obviously, before updating LRU[1] <– q).

In both spatial and temporal lookahead schemes, PRED[] is a correlation table of the form shown in Figure 3.13(a); the difference between the two is the choice of page numbers (i.e., cache blocks) that they correlate. In the "spatial" scheme, which actually correlates temporal page faults (or cache misses, in a processor cache scenario), faulting page q is correlated with faulting page LAST, and no faults occur in between the two fault events (i.e., missing block q is correlated with missing block LAST, and no cache misses occur between the two cache-miss events). In the "temporal" scheme, page q is correlated with the page most recently used (but not necessarily causing a fault) before the fault to page q. In a processor cache scenario, missing block q is correlated with the most recently referenced block in the cache, whether that reference was a cache miss or a cache hit. Baer and Sager find that the spatial scheme, which corresponds more closely to modern correlation schemes correlating cache misses, performs the most accurately out of the three surveyed.

In the 1980s, IBM researchers applied correlation prefetching in the context of the processor cache [Rechstschaffen 1983, Pomerene et al. 1989]. Rechstschaffen's *cache-miss history table* [1983] has the form shown in Figure 3.13(a), with *NumSucc*=1; the table (a four-way set-associative cache in the original report) maintains for each entry a miss address and the most recent address that follows it. This was extended in Pomerene's patent application (on which Rechstschaffen is listed as a co-inventor) to provide a "shadow directory" next to a cache (the term "directory" refers to what is commonly called a cache's "tags" today). The shadow directory is larger than the cache in number of sets, so as to include information on both cached blocks and recently cached blocks (perhaps eight times larger [Pomerene et al. 1989]). Its format is virtually

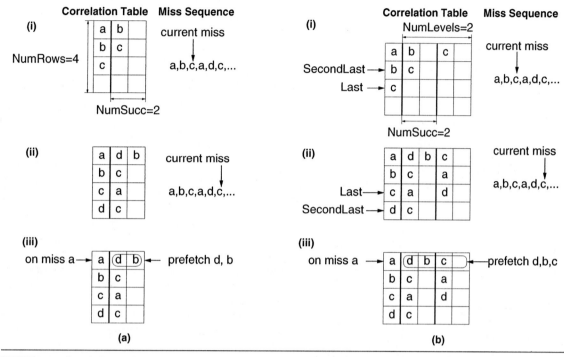

FIGURE 3.13: Correlation prefetching algorithms: (a) base and (b) replicated.

identical to Rechstschaffen's cache-miss history table: the table retains the most recent correlated miss, in its fundamental implementation. To wit, if item Q causes a cache miss after item P causes a cache miss, then the shadow directory holds an entry of the form "P:Q," where P is the tag and Q is its corresponding data. A later miss to P followed by a miss to X causes the P:Q entry to be replaced by a P:X entry. The directory is managed in an LRU fashion, and each entry maintains status such as a confidence bit indicating that the following address was seen more than once. The patent description also describes an extension in which an entry in the directory can maintain information on more than one subsequent reference address (similar to having *NumSucc* > 1).

Figure 3.13(a) illustrates in a bit more detail how a typical correlation table is organized and operated

(e.g., by Baer and Sager, Rechstschaffen and Pomerene, but also by Charney and Reeves [1995], Joseph and Grunwald [1997], and Sherwood et al. [2000]). Each row stores the tag of an address that missed and the addresses of a set of *NumSucc* immediate successor misses—misses that have been seen to immediately follow the first one at different points in the application. The figure shows two snapshots of the table at different points in the miss stream (*i* and *ii*). Within a row, successors are listed in MRU order from left to right. At any time, the hardware keeps a pointer to the row of the last miss observed. On a miss, the table places the miss address as one of the immediate successors of the last miss, and a new row is allocated for the new miss unless it already exists. When the table is used to prefetch (*iii*), it reacts to an observed miss by finding the corresponding row and prefetching all *NumSucc* successors, starting from the MRU one. In the figure, since the table has observed miss pairs *a,b* and *a,d* in the past, when *a* is observed, both *b* and *d* are prefetched.

Proposed schemes typically need a 1–2 MB on-chip table [Joseph & Grunwald 1997, Lai et al. 2001], while some applications with large footprints can require tables an order of magnitude larger [Lai et al. 2001]. Alexander and Kedem propose maintaining the table in the DRAM system, which addresses this issue [1996], and software-based implementations (e.g., buffer caches, disk caches, and web caches) would be less constrained than processor-core-resident implementations. The idea can be expanded even further: the Alpha EV7 set a precedent by storing a cache block's metadata—cache-coherence directory information—out into the memory system with each block (this was due to the use of five Rambus channels to provide ECC, which left extra bits available for storage). One can easily envision a memory system in which each block or superblock stores metadata, including its likely successor block/s—a scheme similar to correlation prefetching as implemented in file caches (e.g., see Griffioen and Appleton [1994], described in the next section).

Another limitation is that prefetching only the immediate successors for each miss limits the prefetcher's performance; the mechanism must wait until a *trigger* miss occurs before it can prefetch immediate successors, and the immediate successor prefetch may not be timely enough to hide its full memory latency. One proposed solution is to store not just immediate successor addresses, but indirect miss addresses as well. This is illustrated in Figure 3.13(b).

The "replicated" scheme [Solihin et al. 2002] maintains more than one pointer into the table, representing the most recent miss addresses, in order (Figure 3.13 shows two addresses: *Last* and *SecondLast*). On a miss, the mechanism inserts the new miss address as the immediate successor of the *Last* miss address, the once-removed immediate successor of the *Second-Last* miss address (and so on, if the scheme maintains more pointers). When a miss is seen, all the entries from different successor levels in the corresponding row are prefetched.

Correlation Prefetching in File Caches: Overcoming State-Table Limits

Before it was rediscovered for use with processor caches [Charney & Reeves 1995], correlation prefetching was adapted for use in the operating system's buffer cache. For instance, Korner [1990] describes an expert system that correlates files and their access behavior, partitioning the blocks from those files in different segments of the buffer cache, each of which is managed with its own replacement policy. The mechanism is also able to preload caches based on hints gleaned from observed behavior. Tait and Duchamp [1991] build a *working graph* based on file accesses seen in the buffer cache. This is a directed graph of actions such as executing a file (through the *exec()* system call), accessing a file, or creating a file, with directed arcs representing who acted upon what. The graph is then used to predict sequences of file accesses when repeated patterns are detected. Note that a set of working graphs is maintained for each program (all activity begins with the execution of a program, which represents the root of a tree). The authors deal with issues that arise, such as dealing with overly large graphs that fail to fit in the cache, etc.

An interesting approach is when the entire state table is moved into the file system itself. Griffioen and Appleton [1994] observe in their studies of file-system behavior on a Sun/SPARC-based departmental file server that roughly 95% of file-system accesses follow logically from the previous access, even in a multi-programming environment with multiple users and background daemons sharing the file system. They instrument the file system to maintain information on file *open()* actions, as their own studies, which confirm previous studies, show that file contents are typically read immediately after opening a file, if at all. With each file's inode is kept a table of successor files that are opened within a *lookahead window* (i.e., "soon thereafter"), and with each entry in the table is kept a count of times that successor file is opened within the lookahead window. The table gives weights for the likelihood of opening (and thus reading) additional files. The authors define the *chance* of opening file j after opening file i in terms of these weights:

$$\text{chance} = \frac{\text{count for file } j}{\sum_{\substack{\text{entries} \\ \text{in table}}} \text{entry count}} \qquad \textbf{(EQ 3.1)}$$

The buffer-cache-management software prefetches a file if its chance exceeds a *minimum chance*, a value that is varied for the study. A prediction is "correct" if the predicted file is, indeed, opened within the lookahead window. The authors find that using a low minimum chance (65%) yields roughly one prediction made for every two files opened and an 80% prediction accuracy (average correctness). Using a high minimum chance (90%) yields roughly one prediction made for every ten files opened and a near-perfect prediction accuracy. They find that the scheme can perform as well or better than an LRU-managed cache of twice the capacity.

Why this is particularly interesting is that the predictor's state (i.e., what corresponds to the predictor table shown in Figure 3.13) is distributed with the objects being predicted: with each object's metadata (file information) is held a small part of what is an enormous logical table. This arrangement has tremendous benefit over the limited table sizes in processor cache implementations. The table is persistent, meaning that an entry's state is not lost when the entry is replaced in favor of a new entry, and unlike previous file cache implementations, there are no conflict or capacity misses to worry about. Recall Alpha EV7's storing of cache block metadata in the memory system with the block; this would apply quite well.

Padmanabhan and Mogul [1996] adapt the mechanism to predictively fetch web pages. In this mechanism, the server maintains the predictor and informs the web client (i.e., browser application) when it would be a good idea to predictively prefetch one or more web pages into its local cache in anticipation of the user's future requests. The browser decides whether to initiate the prefetch, presumably based on available local storage or local network bandwidth (note, however, that a proxy could intercept the transmission and make its own independent decision). This is analogous to maintaining a backing-store-resident predictor and informing a cache of good

prefetch opportunities: e.g., holding the table in main memory with a memory-resident state machine, and returning to a processor core, along with any requested data, hints about future prefetches. Padmanabhan and Mogul's server-based hint (as opposed to server-based *push*) makes intuitive sense because of the imbalance between costs of sending requests and sending the corresponding data: a GET command is relatively inexpensive, while the corresponding data retrieval is not. A typical DRAM system might not fit this profile. On the other hand, it is a very good match for typical disk systems, and it is a fair match for narrow-channel DRAMs such as Rambus and FB-DIMM (see Chapter 7, Section 7.3.2, "Other Technologies, Rambus in Particular," and Chapter 14, "The Fully Buffered DIMM Memory System").

Even more sophisticated correlation algorithms have been explored in file caches. For instance, Kroeger and Long [1996] implement a scheme based on the *prediction by partial match* compression algorithm [Bell et al. 1989] that supports matching on higher order contexts, meaning that if the sequence "ABCD" has been seen previously, though less frequently than the sequence "BCE," the predictor can use the longer sequence to predict what comes after event "C" if it is preceded by "AB," as opposed to just "B." This is similar to the data-address and data-value predictors evaluated in processor cache environments by Sazeides and Smith [1997] and Joseph and Grunwald [1997]. Kroeger and Long find that a 4-MB buffer cache using PPM (prediction by partial match) can outperform, on average, an LRU-based buffer cache of 90 MB.

Content-Based Prefetching

Roth identifies a pointer load by tracking whether a consumer load instruction uses an address from a producer load instruction, as opposed to an address produced by an add or multiply instruction [Roth et al. 1998]. If the producer and consumer are the same static load instruction, which typically results from pointer chasing, for example, in the form of $p = p \rightarrow next$, the instruction is categorized as a *recurrent load*, and the data it loads is used to prefetch the next block of data.

Touch and Farber [1994] illustrate a similar concept in the file system. They show that the data loaded by an I/O operation can help determine what to fetch next when the semantics of the I/O operation are known. For instance, they prefetch/preload the contents of a directory whenever a user changes to that directory via a *cd* (change directory) operation. However, one cannot directly apply this to a transparent I/O cache that does not know why a particular block was fetched; there is no simple transformation from Roth's scheme because Roth exploits the fact that a load instruction typically produces a single register value—a relatively small datum easily tracked to identify it as the target address for a following load. I/O "loads," on the other hand, produce much larger blocks of data (two orders of magnitude larger). Thus it is harder to identify the data corresponding to a recurrent I/O load.

Cooksey describes a scheme that could address this issue [Cooksey et al. 2002]. In Cooksey's *content-directed* prefetching, pointers are identified and prefetched based on a set of heuristics applied to the contents of an entire memory block. The technique borrows from conservative garbage collection; when data is demand-fetched from memory, each address-sized word of the data is examined for its suitability as a likely address. Candidate addresses need to be translated from the virtual to the physical address space and then issued as prefetch requests. As prefetch requests return

data from memory, their contents are examined to retrieve subsequent candidates. The heuristics scan each 4-byte chunk on every loaded cache block. Each chunk is divided into several sections, as shown in Figure 3.14. The figure shows an L2 miss address that causes a block to be brought into the L2 cache and a 4-byte chunk from the incoming block to be considered as a candidate prefetch address. The first heuristic compares a few upper bits (the *compare* bits) of the candidate prefetch address with ones from the miss address. If they match, the candidate prefetch address may be an address that points to the same region of memory as the miss address. This heuristic relies on the fact that linked data structure traversal may dereference many pointers that are located nearby; pointers that jump across a large space, for example, a pointer from the stack to heap region, cannot be identified by the heuristic as recurrent-load addresses. The heuristics works well except for the two regions where the compare bits are all 0's or all 1's. Small non-address integers with 0's in their compare bits should not be confused as addresses, and small negative numbers may have all 1's in the compare bits; these instances need a different heuristic to distinguish them from addresses. One alternative would be to disregard prefetch addresses that have all 0's and all 1's in their compare bits. Unfortunately, these cases are too frequent to ignore because many operating systems allocate stack or heap data in those locations. To address this,

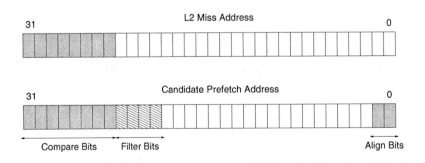

FIGURE 3.14: Heuristics for pointer identification.

additional heuristics complement the first. If the compare bits are all zeroes/ones, the next several bits (*filter* bits) are examined; if a non-zero/non-one bit is found within the filter bit range, the data value is deemed to be a likely address. Finally, a few lower bits (*align* bits) also help to identify pointers: due to memory alignment restrictions, pointer addresses typically align on 4- or 8-byte boundaries in memory. Therefore, the lower bits of the candidate pointer should be zero.

This is clearly applicable to file caches, but it requires a significantly more complex implementation with a relatively large state table and that would undoubtedly benefit from closed-loop feedback, e.g., accuracy tracking similar to correlation predictors that only use a miss address to make a prediction once the sequence has been seen more than once.

3.1.3 On-Line Locality Optimizations

Locality optimizations modify the structure of code and/or data to enhance the forms of locality most easily exploited by the cache system, namely temporal locality (e.g., by reordering operations to ensure those that are related to each other are performed near to each other in time) and spatial locality (e.g., by grouping together related items into the same or adjacent cache blocks or the same or adjacent virtual pages). The following sections give a few examples.

Dynamic (Re-)Grouping of Instructions and Data

As with many of the modern staples of processor cache research, such as replacement algorithms and various forms of data prefetching, many of the ideas in modern locality optimizations were first explored in the 1960s and 1970s in the context of the virtual memory system's paging behavior. In particular, the discovery that design optimization focusing solely on page-replacement strategies leads to memory systems that are good but nonetheless non-optimal[3] led to numerous studies that

rearrange the code and/or data of programs, both at compile time and at run time, to reduce the number of page faults.

Early work falling under the rubric "automatic segmentation" is exactly this: the compile-time decision-making of which code and data blocks should occupy which virtual pages—the grouping of instructions and data in the address space. Example work includes Ramamoorthy's connectivity matrix, potentially augmented with profile-generated probabilities on the graph edges [1966]; Comeau's study showing the connection between page layout and resulting application performance [1967]; Lowe's transformations on Boolean matrices (e.g., the connectivity matrix) to deduce timing information [1969]; and Lowe's enhancements to Ramamoorthy's methodology to handle common corner cases in code packing, such as when a page or segment is not large enough to hold all of the code objects that are deemed "connected" by the algorithm and should all reside in the same page or segment [1970]. Because these are really compile-time algorithms, we will treat them in detail in Section 3.2. Algorithms that exploit profiling will be treated in detail in Section 3.3.

Garbage Collection However, forms of object regrouping that are dynamic and performed at run time do exist in this time-frame. In particular, the garbage-collection schemes of early list-processing systems do exactly this. McCarthy describes the first LISP system as well as the algorithm used for garbage collection [1960]. Figure 3.15 illustrates several example list objects and their corresponding data structure representations. An interesting aspect of the programming system is that the programmer never deals directly with the data structure itself, but only with its abstract representation (the list). Due to this, the programmer is never responsible for data structure allocation or deallocation. Instead, data structures are allocated as needed, and a periodic mark-and-sweep garbage collector reclaims those data structures no

---

[3]Early work in paging systems explicitly states the futility of looking at anything but replacement strategies. For example, papers in the late 1960s flatly state that prefetching cannot be done. Thus, the early 1970s demonstration that it is, indeed, possible to outperform an LRU-based system is significant.

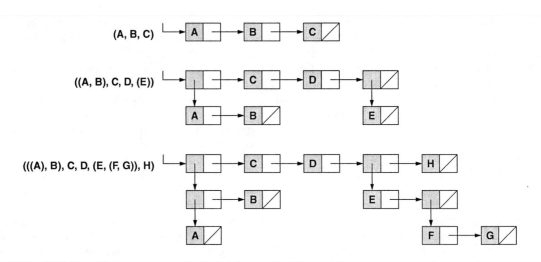

FIGURE 3.15: A list object and its corresponding data structure.

longer in use. When the system runs out of free space, the garbage collector walks the set of active lists and marks all reachable data objects. Once all active lists have been traversed, all unmarked data structures are reclaimed and placed on the free list.

The goal of early garbage-collection mechanisms is the reclamation of free space. With the late-1960s advent of commercial virtual memory systems, finding free space became less important than optimizing data placement for locality:

> With the coming of virtual-memory systems ... a [list-processing] system may run almost endlessly with no need for garbage-collection. As operation proceeds, however, performance degrades. This is because the active-list-storage becomes spread over a larger and larger region of virtual storage, and it becomes increasingly likely that a given reference to this virtual memory will require a reference to secondary storage. [Fenichel & Yochelson 1969]

Locality Optimization via Deadwood Removal
In other words, even in the early days of computing, the primary goal of garbage collection was the compaction of data (thus increasing data locality) and not the discovery of free space. Fenichel and Yochelson

[1969] characterize the problem of garbage collection in an "effectively infinite" memory space: "it is especially clear that a routine will not do if its gathering phase must scan all potential storage." They describe a generational collection scheme that divides the available space into two *semispaces*, only one of which is currently active at any given point. The collector walks all active data structures (lists) and copies each to the non-current semispace. When all lists are copied, the target semispace becomes the new active space, and the old is available as the next target for garbage collection. As a result, the spatial locality of the total working set (all active lists) is improved by periodically removing (i.e., failing to copy to the target semispace) the inactive lists. The question remains of when to initiate garbage collection; previous collectors ran when free space is exhausted, a situation unlikely to occur in a large enough memory space. The authors propose running the collector during periods of inactivity or in response to the observation of poor performance due to high page-fault rates.

Dynamic, Transparent Data Linearization Hansen [1969] takes the concept even further into the domain of locality optimization. He describes in detail a generational garbage collector whose goal is to generate from active lists "compact" representations. The scheme described by Fenichel and Yochelson improves inter-list locality by removing dead lists. The scheme described by Hansen improves intra-list locality significantly by explicitly linearizing lists, much in the same vein as *data linearization* proposed by Luk and Mowry [1996], except that Hansen's approach is dynamic, is performed by the system, and thus remains completely transparent to application software.

Figure 3.16 illustrates Hansen's mechanism. Figure 3.16(a) shows a typical list representation; in particular, elements added to a list are dynamically allocated and separately allocated structures. Thus, any newly added elements will be linked data structures. Figure 3.16(b) shows the result of list compaction; data structures logically adjacent in the list become physically contiguous in memory. Note that this is not a one-time fix that is run once and is never needed again. Any changes to the compacted list structure (e.g., element additions or deletions, list-element restructuring, etc.) will yield a linked-list organization of physically disjunct data structures. This type of dynamic, transparent data linearization is possible in a LISP system (or any similar system) because the linked nature of the data structures is not visible to the programmer. Therefore, if the system software works correctly, there can be no instances of dangling pointers when data structures are copied and old versions are deleted; the system can account for every pointer to an object because such pointers are under its direct control. Garbage collection is possible in such a system because the relocation of objects is provably non-deleterious—the relocation of an object cannot affect application-level program correctness. The same is *not* true of other programming systems and languages, particularly C—one cannot dynamically and transparently relocate linked structures out from under a C program because one cannot account for all possible pointers to an object. C exports the notion of a memory pointer to the programmer, which is both extremely powerful and extremely dangerous or at least extremely limiting in terms of what dynamic optimizations are possible and easily accomplished. This is precisely why memory allocation and deallocation are explicitly left to the programmer in C and C-like languages.

Nonetheless, transparent object relocation *has* been done for C-language programs. The trick is to provide a safety net that catches those instances where a dangling pointer is later used. Luk and Mowry

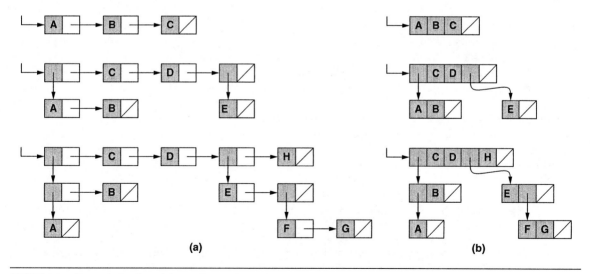

(a)   **(b)**

FIGURE 3.16: Hansen's list-linearizing garbage collector: (a) data structures for several typical lists; (b) corresponding compact representations produced by the garbage collector.

describe such a scheme they call *memory forwarding* [1998]. The basic idea is not to reclaim the space from which an object is moved, but instead to use it as a forwarding address, a pointer to the object's new location. This requires the ability to mark a memory space as "invalid" so that the loading of a datum will alert the application software that the loaded item is not a regular item of data, but instead a forwarding pointer. Because the item loaded could be any data type (e.g., signed/unsigned integer, floating point number, byte, pointer, etc.), the only way to tag it as invalid is to add another bit. For example, a 64-bit system would have an additional 65th bit, indicating the status of its corresponding oct-byte. For every 64 bits available to the programmer, a 65th bit would be stored in the memory system, loaded by the processor whenever the corresponding oct-byte is loaded, and checked by hardware and/or software before any of the 8 bytes covered are used in an operation.

Page Coloring and Careful Mappping

As we will discuss in Section 3.2.3, significant compile-time effort is directed toward choosing code and data layouts in the virtual space that yield good cache behavior (e.g., McFarling's instruction-cache-aware code placement [1989]). However, the use of physically indexed caches can largely undo this effort, because an application's layout in the memory space need not resemble its layout in the physical space; pages that are contiguous in virtual space may or may not be contiguous in physical space; and, more importantly, pages that would never conflict in a virtually indexed cache can map to the same set of cache blocks in a physically indexed cache. Thus, while a programmer- or compiler-chosen page assignment can ensure two objects to be conflict free in a virtually indexed cache (e.g., by placing the objects in adjacent virtual pages), its guarantee can be counteracted by the operating system if the operating system maps

those virtual pages to physical page frames separated by a large power-of-two distance. This is illustrated in Figure 3.17.

The issue of *page coloring* comes into play. Page coloring was proposed by Taylor et al. [1990] to increase the hit rate of MIPS's TLB slice, a mini-TLB used to move page translation off the critical path while retaining a physically indexed cache. The TLB slice translates just enough low-order bits of the virtual page number to create an index into a physical cache. The hit rate of the TLB slice is improved significantly when the bottom bits of the page frame number match the bottom bits of the virtual page number. Thus, the operating system's page-mapping policy is modified to prefer[4] such mappings. This preference is called *page coloring*.

Though page coloring was proposed to solve a completely different problem, it is clearly also a solution to the problem of an operating system potentially undermining the efforts of the compiler to minimize cache conflicts between code and data objects. An operating system written to prefer matching the bottom bits of the page frame number (PFN) to the bottom bits of the virtual page number (VPN) will only run into problems when the page cannot be colored appropriately (and, even in those instances, there may be no actual cache conflicts that arise). Kessler and Hill [1992] explore page coloring and other similar mechanisms as heuristics embedded within the operating system; none of the schemes rely upon application-specific compile-time knowledge, and none make use of application-specific run-time feedback. The "careful mapping" schemes described by Kessler and Hill include the following:

- **Page coloring:** This scheme prefers mappings in which the bottommost bits of the VPN and PFN match; it maintains a separate queue of page frames for each bin[5] of physical pages mapping to the same region of the

---

[4]Note that if the operating system can *guarantee* appropriately colored page mappings in all instances, the TLB slice becomes unnecessary; however, this is only reasonable (i.e., can be provided without significant degradation in performance) if the set of all virtual pages in use by all applications is evenly distributed over the virtual space—a requirement that cannot be guaranteed.

[5]A "bin" is defined to be the equivalence class of page frames mapping to the same page-sized region of the cache. In a system with 4-KB pages, a 64-KB direct-mapped cache has 16 bins, and a 64-KB two-way set-associative cache has 8 bins.

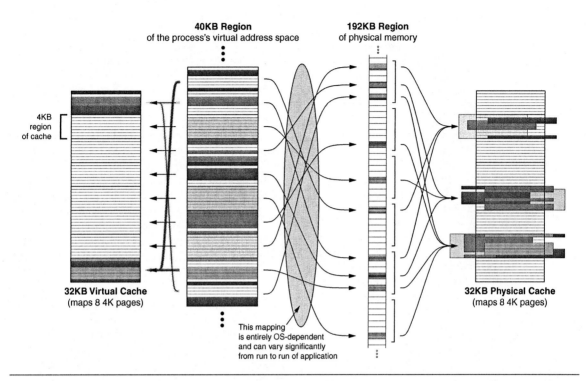

FIGURE 3.17: How virtual mapping can negate page placement. A compiler's page-placement heuristic ensures that objects used at the same time are placed in adjacent or non-conflicting locations, e.g., pages that do not map to the same region in a virtually indexed cache. This is shown on the left side of the Figure. For objects that cannot be placed in adjacent locations, such as a block of code and the data on which it operates, the page-placement heuristic ensures that even if the objects map to the same region of the cache, they will not map to the same cache blocks (as shown on the left: two instances where two pages co-reside in the cache without conflict). However, when a physically indexed cache is used, the compiler's efforts are completely undone, unless the kernel preserves contiguity of virtual data in the physical space (which it does not, in general, do). On the right is shown an arbitrary mapping of virtual pages to physical pages that results in numerous page and cache block conflicts that would not have occurred in a virtually indexed cache.

cache. A variant hashes the process ID with the VPN first to ensure that similar, commonly referenced address ranges in different processes map to different ranges in the cache (e.g., the beginning of the code section, the top of the stack, etc.).

- **Bin hopping:** This uses a round-robin page assignment in which the operating system maintains for each process a separate pointer into the set of bin queues, facilitating the same separation of process-

address spaces as the hashed version of page coloring, above. For example, the first virtual page mapped in address space UID is assigned to a page frame in bin number (last_bin[UID] = rand()), meaning that the initial placement is random. The second is assigned to a page frame in bin number (++last_bin[UID]), meaning that the bin number is one greater than the previous. If no pages are available in the desired bin, the next sequential bin is chosen.

- **Best bin:** For each equivalence class (each bin), the operating system maintains a counter pair <used[UID], free>. The *used* array of counters indicates the number of virtual pages assigned to this bin for a particular process. The *free* counter indicates the number of free page frames for this equivalence class. For the *best bin* heuristic, the operating system assigns a virtual page to the bin that has the smallest *used* value and the highest *free* value.
- **Hierarchical:** This heuristic approximates the *best bin* algorithm, but uses a tree-based search through the array of counter pairs instead of a linear search, thereby guaranteeing a O(log n) search time instead of O(n) in the size of the cache (n is the number of cache bins). The trade-off is that the two algorithms might choose different bins for a particular mapping; *hierarchical* may choose a locally optimal bin that is not the globally optimal bin.

The paper (Kessler & Hill [1992]) compares the performance of *Hierarchical* to that of a baseline.

- **Random:** This scheme uses the operating system's default page-mapping strategy, which is to map an incoming page to the first available free page or to the page at the bottom of the LRU list if no free pages are available.

The motivation is that a random mapping of virtual pages to physical pages can create unbalanced scenarios as the one shown in Figure 3.18. A "careful" mapping strategy, on the other hand, would tend to spread pages out across the physically indexed cache, thus reducing cache conflicts.

Note that the heuristics exploit no run-time information other than the status of the queues and availability of pages within. An interesting extension would combine as a direct feedback mechanism the modern performance counters available in most processor cores. For instance, the hardware could export an n-bit hot spot vector, where a '1' in a bit position indicates recent conflicts in that cache bin, for a cache of size n bins. At page-mapping time, the operating system could prefer to choose from those bins that have experienced fewer cache misses in recent history, i.e., the operating system would

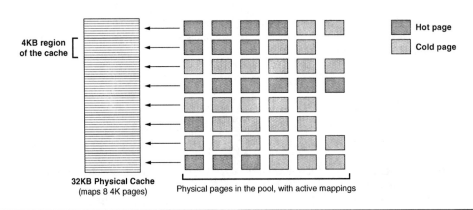

FIGURE 3.18: Random mapping can create hot spots in the cache. By definition, a "random" mapping policy maintains no correlation between page usage and page placement. Thus, even if the kernel does attempt to distribute pages in the physical memory in a manner that spreads pages out evenly over the cache (as in the illustrated example), the kernel will not be aware of any hot pages, and if the hot pages do not happen to be distributed evenly in space, hot spots in the cache will necessarily form.

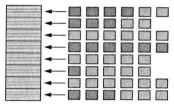

Page distribution from previous figure

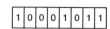

(a) an example hot-spot vector
with **one bit** per page-sized region

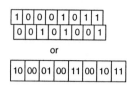

(b) an example hot-spot vector
with **two bits** per page-sized region

FIGURE 3.19: Example hot-spot vectors. The hardware can export to the kernel (via a control register, part of the PSW) a bit vector indicating the recent cache-miss status of page-size regions of the cache. The vector can represent the miss status with one or more bits per region; using more bits gives the kernel a higher likelihood of identifying the hot pages within each equivalence class.

choose not to allocate a virtual page to a page frame in a bin recently experiencing numerous cache misses (which would simply exacerbate the cache-miss problem). Another mechanism would be to consider recoloring pages dynamically if they exhibit high rates of conflict. Figure 3.19 illustrates that if a hardware-generated "hot-spot" vector (or any other mechanism) indicates a non-even distribution of hot and cold pages (with respect to cache activity), the operating system can swap one or more hot-page mappings with one or more cold-page mappings, thereby evening out the distribution of accesses to the cache. Note that this dynamic recoloring need not require the actual movement of page data if the system supports a second level of page indirection [Carter et al. 1999].

Dynamic Compression of Instructions and Data

Compression of instructions and data can increase the effective capacity of a cache, and it can reduce the latency and energy costs of transferring data between levels in a memory hierarchy. Automated compression has been proposed and used in the file system at least as far back as the 1950s and 1960s. For instance, the SQUOZE code-compression mechanism in SHARE 709 (a system environment for the IBM 709) automatically compresses a program into a form that is an order of magnitude smaller than the original executable program—a form claimed to be more suitable for execution and that requires less overhead to

transfer and load into core [Boehm & Steel 1959]. The mechanism is akin to a modern assembler/linker, but in the context of its time it represents a move toward automation.

The Self-Organizing Large Information Dissemination (SOLID) system represents perhaps the first true automation of compression and decompression: data files transferred between levels of the storage hierarchy are compressed and decompressed transparently to the user [de Maine & Marron 1966, Marron & de Maine 1967]. In accordance to the system's *mobile strategy* for managing file location and status, data is compressed when transferred out of "fast" memory (i.e., cache or DRAM in modern systems) into "slow" memory (i.e., DRAM or disk or backup storage in modern systems), and it is decompressed on its return.

It is not clear whether the ambitious proposal described by de Maine and Marron was ever implemented. The authors note that "while this component of the SOLID system [i.e., the mobile strategy] has not yet been implemented, the logical steps to be taken have been worked out. Details of the logic, together with cost studies [of] the mobile strategy component will be offered after its implementation" [de Maine & Marron 1966, p. 245]. Our inability to find later work describing the mechanism should not detract from the vision put forward by the authors at such an early date in the development of computer and information systems.

Representing a move toward the goal of automated compression are the automatic file-migration systems of the late 1970s, such as the CASHEW system at Lawrence Berkeley Lab [Knight 1976] and other systems from government labs and industry in 1977 and 1978 (e.g., IBM's MARC System (*MVS Archival System*) [Considine & Myers 1977]). Earlier systems perform migration of files to backup storage (e.g., IBM's TSS/360 system in 1969 [Considine & Myers 1969]), but these are not completely automated. The automatic systems manage the storage hierarchy as a cache system; the local disk space is a cache that holds only the most recently referenced files. Files that have not been referenced recently are migrated out to mass storage, which has a longer latency and much larger capacity than the local disk space; files are automatically migrated to tape backup as well. Any reference to a file causes the file-migration system to move the file into the local disk space, regardless of where the file is found within the hierarchy. The movement of files within the hierarchy is transparent to the user and/or user application software.

IBM's Information Management System (IMS), a database-management system, realizes the vision of de Maine and Marron by providing *de facto* automatic compression of files within the database: with each I/O action (e.g., read segment, store segment) an *exit* action may be associated. Possible exit actions include segment compression and/or decompression [IBM 1981]. Thus, IMS supports transparent compression on segment stores and transparent decompression on segment reads. In IMS, segments are typically small and can be presented to the I/O system in any order. This tends to preclude sophisticated adaptive coding schemes that span many bytes and/or multiple segments [Cormack 1985]. Thus, contemporary research aims at improving compression algorithms (e.g., Welch's fast implementation of Lempel-Ziv [1984]) as well as infrastructures for file migration to the backing store (e.g., replacement policies [Smith 1981a], compression within the tape-backup unit [Bell et al. 1989], efficient user-directed compression facilities [Pechura 1982], etc.).

Cate and Gross [1991] note that while it is relatively straightforward to compress files as they move to backup storage, it is not a trivial matter to apply the concept to the on-line file system. Backup storage typically uses a linear format, such as tape, which works well with the fact that the file size (i.e., its storage requirements) is not known until after compression. In contrast, the file system uses a fixed number of fixed-length disk sectors. On the surface, this would seem to present the same implementation issues as a web-object cache or any other cache with variable-sized blocks—issues typically addressed by reserving a block of temporary storage for moving blocks in and out of the cache and providing a replacement policy that can replace more than one cache-resident block to make room for the incoming data.

Cate and Gross explore an implementation along these lines that divides the local disk storage into two partitions: one that holds compressed data, and another that holds uncompressed data. The authors call this a "two-level" file system because the compressed partition has a larger effective capacity (or lower cost) per bit than the uncompressed partition and has a longer latency. Files are migrated to the compressed partition when unused and are returned upon reference. The authors find that, in theory, an implementation can cut storage needs in half without imposing a significant average delay to user files. They implement a prototype proof-of-concept in an NFS server (Sun's network file system): inactive files are compressed at night when the system activity is low; files are decompressed as soon as they are requested. The server puts the partition information into the file's inode (hidden within the group ID): any first access to a file requires reading that file's inode, which indicates whether the file is compressed or uncompressed. Because the mechanism applies to general storage technologies (i.e., it is not tailored to linear-format devices) and is purely transparent to the file cache's constituency, the mechanism is applicable to any form of cache organization, including solid-state processor cache hierarchies.

Burrows builds upon the linear-format concept and applies compression to Sprite LFS (a log-structured file system), which places all file data and almost all file metadata (e.g., directory information) in a sequentially written log [Burrows et al. 1992]. They improve upon Cate and Gross's mechanism by compressing at the granularity of 16-KB blocks as opposed to entire files. Thus, a file can be partially compressed, alleviating potential performance problems when dealing with large files (in the Cate and Gross scheme, a file is an atomic structure and resides entirely in one partition or the other). Burrows' choice of a compression granularity larger than a page size amortizes the cost of decompression for the common case, i.e., reading sequentially through (large) files.

Douglis [1993] shows the concept is indeed general by extending it further up the cache hierarchy: the *compression cache* applies Cate and Gross's mechansm to main memory. Douglis' mechanism exploits Sprite's virtual memory system to implement a variable-sized compressed partition: Sprite dynamically trades physical memory between the virtual memory page pool and the buffer cache, and this allows the compression cache to vary in size as needed. LRU pages are compressed to make room for new pages and decompressed if referenced. Compressed LRU pages are written to the backing store if more space is needed. Douglis reports mixed results and notes that performance should improve as compression gets faster relative to I/O (note that the study uses software compression).

Brooks' Dynamic Adjustment of Data Width

Much of the work to incorporate compression into the cache hierarchy is non-transparent; it is done at design time (e.g., compressing programs to reduce memory storage needs and decompressing them when fetching lines into the cache [Wolfe & Chanin 1992], or compressing programs in a manner so that they can reside in the cache in compressed form [Lefurgy et al. 1997]—these are described in more detail in Section 3.2.3). A related mechanism that can carry the concept of transparent compression into the cache hierarchy and processor core is described by Brooks and Martonosi [1999]. To reduce power dissipation (and potentially increase performance as well), the hardware can dynamically detect situations where a small data value is encoded in an unnecessarily large data word. For example, Figure 3.20 shows the cumulative percentage and probability densities for ALU (arithmetic logic unit) operations (ranging over the SPECint95 applications executed on a 64-bit Alpha architecture) in which *both* operands have the specified bitwidth or less. In the figure, a "0" bitwidth

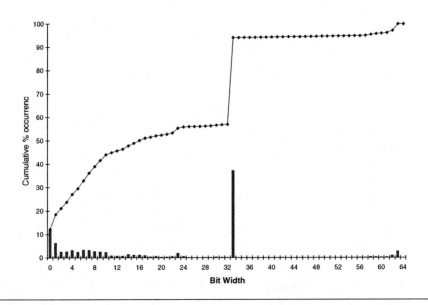

FIGURE 3.20: Bitwidths for SPECint95 on a 64-bit Alpha. Figure used with permission from Brooks and Martonosi [1999].

means that both operands were zeroes. A "1" bit-width mans that both operands had the value one or zero. For all other bitwidths, the meaning is that both operands have values of 2^x or less. The analysis does not include instructions without operands (e.g., *syscall, trap, return-from-interrupt*, etc.). Looking at the graph, one sees that roughly 10% of all operations use only zeroes as operands; another 5% use only ones or zeroes; and nearly 50% of all operations use operands that can be expressed in as few as 10 bits. Note the substantial jump at 33 bits, reflecting the large number of address calculations.

This observation leads Brooks and Martonosi to devise a mechanism that detects scenarios in which both operands have narrow bitwidths and, when detecting such scenarios, aggressively clock-gates the ALU circuitry to use only a fraction of the logic otherwise required. The net power savings is roughly 50% in the integer unit, including the extra power dissipated in the detection and multiplexing circuitry.

The same detection circuitry is evaluated in a performance-optimization scheme as well as the power-reduction mechanism. The authors explore packing operands together to exploit SIMD (single instruction multiple data) functional units when two instructions with the same opcode and narrow-width operands are in the dispatch queue. For instance, two different 64-bit ADD instructions, each with narrow-width operands, can be packed dynamically into a single 2x32-bit SIMD (single instruction multiple data) ADD instruction that performs both operations simultaneously on 32-bit operands. The control hardware would then de-multiplex the results off the result bus, sign-extend each value, and insert them back into their respective queue entries. As expected, the scheme performs better as the machine's issue width increases.

Though the study might not immediately seem related to the topic of locality in the cache system, it is. The study shows that significant opportunities exist for exploiting dynamic data packing in the cache (and register file) and that a detection mechanism can be built with low overhead. When roughly half of one's 64-bit operands can be expressed in 16 bits, simple schemes similar to the zero-encoding used in fax machine transmissions can be used to reduce the

overhead of transmitting values over the bus (potentially more energy efficient than compressing and decompressing the values). For example, an escape bit at the beginning of each data word could signifiy whether a 64-bit value or 16-bit value is being transmitted. This would be particularly valuable in high-speed, narrow-width memory busses such as Rambus or the FB DIMM architecture, where data is transferred over a sequence of cycles and thus resembles a network packet more than anything else (for more detail, see Chapter 7, Section 7.3.2, "Other Technologies, Rambus in Particular," and Chapter 14, "The Fully Buffered DIMM Memory System"). Similarly, the mechanism could be used within the cache or register file itself to conditionally drive the top 48 bit lines and sense amplifiers for each word, thereby reducing power dissipation. One could potentially use the mechanism to increase the cache's effective capacity by reclaiming unused operand space to store other data; the only issue would be to handle instances where a narrow-width operand is overwritten by a larger value (e.g., when incrementing a register holding the value 65,535).

Dynamic Reordering of Memory Requests

The memory controller can reorder requests dynamically to exploit locality within the DRAM system: namely, while a DRAM bank is open, the data is available with relatively low latency. If two successive requests to the same row within the same bank are serviced by the memory controller, only the first request incurs the latency of activating the bank; the second request incurs only the latency of reading data from the sense amplifiers. However, if an intervening request is for a different row in the same bank, it will destroy the locality offered by the sense amplifiers, and all three requests will incur the latency of activating the bank. As McKee shows [McKee & Wulf 1995], the following code can easily exhibit this behavior:

```
for (sum=0, i=1; i<n; i++)
    sum += A[i] * B[i];
```

because the memory request stream that the code produces is for alternating A[i] and B[i] vector elements, which can map to the same bank if separated by only a few tens of megabytes and which will almost certainly map to different rows. McKee and Wulf explore an off-line mechanism wherein the application informs the hardware about vector-access (i.e., streaming) behavior, thus improving performance significantly. A memory controller that queues requests and dynamically reorders them to exploit locality can dynamically improve performance in the same manner without support from the application, compiler, or programmer. Chapter 15, "Memory System Design Analysis," discusses this aspect in more detail.

3.2 Case Studies: Off-Line Heuristics

We continue illustrating the range of techniques that have been explored in the literature. This section presents design-time techniques, i.e., those in which the programmer and/or compiler perform some amount of analysis and realize within the application itself mechanisms that will manage the memory system directly at run time. Schemes in which hardware and application collaborate, in which there is no clear on-line/off-line division, will be addressed in Section 3.3.

3.2.1 Off-Line Partitioning Heuristics

Much work in off-line partitioning focuses on embedded systems, because the typical microcontroller or DSP used in embedded systems has an exposed memory system in which the various storage units in the system are directly addressable by software. Leaving to chance the assignment of code and data to the storage unit invariably leads to systems with less than optimal power dissipation, predictability, performance, and resource requirements.

Static methods are those in which the storage unit assignment for a datum does not change at run time; most are concerned with *scratch-pad memory* (SPM) allocation (i.e., partitioning the address space between scratch-pad and off-chip memory).

However, the solutions are generally applicable to any physical partition of memory. They apply to scratch-pads as well as exclusive caches as well as horizontally partitioned caches (e.g., real-time, thread-based, partitioned caches; the sets of a direct-mapped or set-associative cache; etc.). Dynamic methods to allocate SPM space change the allocation during run time. Some static methods allocate only global variables to SPM, while others allocate both global and stack variables to SPM. Some of these methods use greedy strategies to find a solution and others model the problem as a knapsack problem or an integer-linear programming problem to find a solution. Frequently, it is valuable to allocate to SPM code as well as data. Code allocation is valuable if the code is stored in slower memory such as DRAM or a slower variant of flash memory. If code is burned into a ROM that is much faster than the DRAM, then there is little advantage is placing code in SPM.

Programmer-Directed Partition Assignment

Figure 3.21 shows the types of compiler constructs available to programmers that allow one to specify ranges of addresses for both code and data. The code snippet in the figure, writtesn for the Analog Devices TS-101's ccts compiler, illustrates the use of the *section* identifier, directing the compiler to locate the indicated code/data object in the corresponding address range. In some cases, the ranges correspond to reserved keywords (e.g., *data1*, *data2*, and *program* in the figure). In other cases (e.g., *SDRAM)*, the corresponding address ranges are implementation-specific, identified in an associated configuration file the compiler reads.

The example places several arrays into various memories available on the DSP (including two data memories and an instruction memory). Interesting to note is the compiler's support for writing data into the program memory.

The same mechanism can be used to direct the compiler to place certain functions into the program memory, excluding others. For instance, the following

```
/************************ SDRAM TEST ************************/
/*                                                         */
/* BY: J S Smith                                           */
/*                                                         */
/* Write 0000FFFF to SDRAM from internal cache             */
/*                                                         */
/* This code is written for an Analog Devices TS-101       */
/* This chip has 3 internal caches(1 for program and 2 for data */
/*                                                         */
/* This will fill data cache 1 will a striding pattern.    */
/* It will copy this strided pattern to the same data cache 1, */
/* to the other data cache 2, to the program cache and finally */
/* to the external SDRAM.                                  */
/*                                                         */
/***********************************************************/

#define SIZE 512

section  ("data1")    float data_orig[SIZE];
section  ("SDRAM")    float data_external[SZE];
section  ("data1")    float data_int_1[SIZE];
section  ("data2")    float data_int_2[SIZE];
section  ("program")  float data_int_p[SIZE];

int main()
{
        int i;

        /* Fill the original array with the stride pattern. */
        for(i = 0; i < SIZE; i++)
            data_orig[i] = 0x0000FFFF;

        /* Copy from data cache 1 to data cache 1 */
        for(i = 0; i < SIZE; i++)
            data_int_1[i] = data_orig[i];

        /* Copy from data cache 1 to data cache 2 */
        for(i = 0; i < SIZE; i++)
            data_int_2[i] = data_orig[i];

        /* Copy from data cache 1 to program cache */
        for(i = 0; i < SIZE; i++)
            data_int_p[i] = data_orig[i];

        /* Copy from data cache 1 to SDRAM */
        for(i = 0; i < SIZE; i++)
            data_external[i] = data_orig[i];

        return 0;
}
```

FIGURE 3.21: Example of static partitioning of code and data into separate memories by the software engineer. The *ccts* compiler for the Analog Devices TS-101 recognizes the keywords *data1*, *data2*, and *program* as memory regions with specific addresses. The location "SDRAM" is specified with a starting address at 0x400000 in a separate configuration file.

syntax directs the compiler to locate a function *my_function* in the program memory:

```
section ("program") void my_function();
```

or even

```
section ("program")
void my_function (int a, char *b, float c) {
    // perform computation
    return;
}
```

Note that in these examples the compiler is given freedom to choose where in each of these caches the data or program code will be placed. A programmer could exercise more control by choosing specific addresses directly, using the same configuration-file mechanism used to map region SDRAM to address 0x400000.

Farrahi's Partitioning for Sleep Mode

As described in the *Overview* chapter, turning off (or down) unused blocks is a simple and effective means to reduce power in a circuit. Memories have many forms of low-power modes. For instance, both SRAMs and DRAMs can be shut down (in which case data may be lost) or put in drowsy or sleep mode (in which case data is retained, but the device requires time to come out of the low-power mode). For more detail on low-power SRAM implementations, see Chapter 5, Section 5.3.1, "Low-Leakage Operation." Farrahi explores the optimization problem of achieving simultaneously the following two goals [Farrahi et al. 1995]:

1. Maximize the time that a memory system (or each portion/bank of the memory system) spends in a low-power mode
2. Minimize the time that the memory system spends in transition between normal mode and low-power mode

This is illustrated in Figure 3.22, which shows an application of what is essentially *lifetime analysis* [Aho et al. 1988]. Figure 3.22(a) shows the sequences of reads and writes to a set of variables. The space of time between a read followed by a write is *idle* in the sense that the bank can be shut down either completely or partially without affecting the correctness of the computation. Figure 3.22(b) shows the idle sets from Figure 3.22(a) with the variables grouped into two different banks, B1 and B2, resulting in the total time that each bank can be placed into a low-power mode.

Farrahi shows that the problem is NP-complete. However, the authors show that it is solvable in pseudo-polynomial time if the number of transitions to/from low-power mode is bounded (a reasonable assumption).

Static Scratch-Pad Management: Panda, Banakar

Panda explores a static partition of data in a hybrid-memory embedded processor, i.e., one that has both an SPM and a transparent cache [Panda et al. 2000]. Only those items explicitly moved into the scratch-pad by the application software will be found there. The transparent cache holds a copy of any datum fetched from memory (i.e., anything referenced, cacheable, and not found in the scratch-pad).

Their motivating example, representative of a large class of algorithms with similar memory-conflict behavior, is the popular *histogram* application that takes as input a photograph and produces a histogram of the brightness

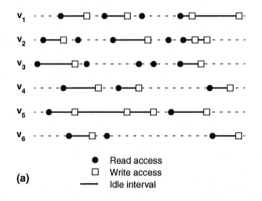

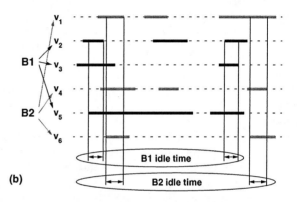

FIGURE 3.22: Lifetime analysis to maximize energy savings in low-power mode. Variables assigned to bank B1: v2, v3, v5. Their idle times are shown in black in (b). Variables assigned to bank B2: v1, v4, v6. Their idle times are shown in grey in (b).

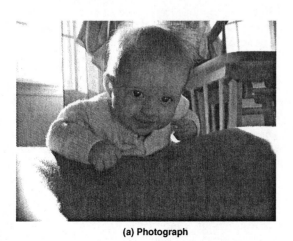

(a) Photograph

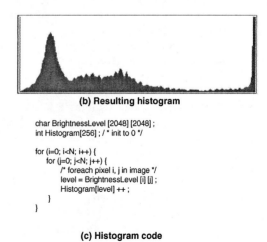

(b) Resulting histogram

```
char BrightnessLevel [2048] [2048] ;
int Histogram[256] ; / * init to 0 */

for (i=0; i<N; i++) {
    for (j=0; j<N; j++) {
        /* foreach pixel i, j in image */
        level = BrightnessLevel [i] [j] ;
        Histogram[level] ++ ;
    }
}
```

(c) Histogram code

FIGURE 3.23: Histogram example. (a) is a black and white photograph; (b) is the resulting histogram; and (c) is a code snippet that would produce the histogram given the image as input.

levels found within the photograph (see Figure 3.23). This application is used in nearly every digital camera and image-processing application available today. The image size is several megapixels, with each pixel encoding 24 bits of red/green/blue information. Unless the application is executed on a cache larger than the entire image (e.g., 8 MB or larger), performance of the application suffers from conflicts between the *BrightnessLevel* and *Histogram* arrays. As Panda points out, data layout techniques such as tiling cannot eliminate the conflicts because accesses to *Histogram* are data-dependent (they resemble A[B[i]] indirection which is difficult to predict). Moreover, for typical processor cache sizes, the problem occurs in direct-mapped as well as set-associative caches. Note that the problem can be solved by partitioning the cache and placing the two arrays in different partitions.

Panda's scheme first maps all scalars to the SPM. If there is space remaining, the scheme performs lifetime analysis [Aho et al. 1988] on those array variables small enough to fit in the remaining scratch-pad space and ranks those arrays by the largest intersection of lifetimes (i.e., those arrays that would conflict in the cache with other arrays are considered for placement in the scratch-pad). The study shows that the performance of the resulting hybrid system is better than the alternatives of using all storage resources for scratch-pad or all for cache (e.g., 2-KB scratch-pad versus 2-KB cache versus hybrid 1-KB scratch-pad + 1-KB cache).

A study by Banakar et al. [2002] performs a static packing of the scratch-pad based on frequency of use and provides not only performance numbers but detailed energy numbers. The study is intriguing because, even though it considers a limited set of applications, it finds that a scratch-pad using static management beats an equivalent-size, two-way set-associative cache, in both performance and energy consumption. The study reports an average energy reduction of 40%, die-area reduction of 30%, and performance improvement of 20% when a scratch-pad is used instead of a transparent cache. The applications considered include sorting and matrix multiplication. Further results from the same group of researchers [Steinke et al. 2002b] show that the dynamic management of the scratch-pad, i.e., the use of explicit memory overlays, performs even better than static

management in both execution time and energy consumption.

Dynamic Scratch-Pad Management: Cooper, Kandemir, Udayakumaran

Although static allocation methods for SPM are simple, their key drawback is that they cannot change the allocation to SPM at run time. Consider the following: let a program consist of three successive loops, not nested, the first of which makes repeated references to array A, the second to B, and the third to C. If only one of the three arrays can fit within the SRAM, then any static allocation suffers backing store accesses for two out of three loops. In contrast, a dynamic strategy can fit all three arrays in SRAM at different times. Although this example is oversimplified, it intuitively illustrates the benefits of dynamic allocation: unlike a static method, a dynamic method is able to change the location of a variable from SPM to off-chip memory or vice-versa during its lifetime. The dynamic method is nonetheless compiler-decided in that the transfers between memories are implemented using compiler-inserted code in the program.

Numerous dynamic mechanisms have been explored in the literature. Cooper and Harvey [1998] use a scratch-pad to store register spills. They argue that "the cache is the wrong place to spill," which is intuitively appealing: the partition created by the cache and CCM (*compiler-controlled memory*, a scratch-pad of 512–1024 bytes) effectively separates items that exhibit either temporal or spatial locality (i.e., the cached items) from those that, for the near future, are going to exhibit neither (data spilled from the register file). The mechanism is low cost (equal to or smaller than a 32x32 register file) and can reduce a non-trivial amount of memory overhead. Kandemir's management of embedded scratch-pads [Kandemir et al. 2001] investigates the optimization of matrix-based computations; the compiler explores tiling dimensions that fit within the scratch-pad and instruments the loop code to preload each tile into the scratch-pad before operating on it. The compiler automatically changes the memory addresses used to reference the array items while they are held within the scratch-pad. Udayakumaran and Barua explore a dynamic memory allocation method for global and stack variables [2003]. At compile time, the compiler inserts code into the application to copy variables from DRAM into the scratch-pad whenever it expects them to be used frequently thereafter, as predicted by previously collected profile data. Unlike software caching (e.g., maintaining a binary search tree of items), since the compiler knows exactly where each variable is at each program point, no run-time checks are needed to find the location of any given variable.

3.2.2 Off-Line Prefetching Heuristics[6]

Off-line prefetching techniques are application based and therefore rely on the programmer or compiler to insert explicit prefetch instructions into the application code for memory references that are likely to miss in the cache. At run time, the inserted prefetch instructions bring the data into the processor's cache in advance of its use, thus overlapping the cost of the memory access with useful work in the processor. Historically, software prefetching has been quite effective in reducing memory stalls for scientific programs that reference array-based data structures [Callahan et al. 1991, Chen et al. 1991, Klaiber & Levy 1991, Mowry & 1993, Gupta Mowry et al. 1992]. More recently, techniques have also been developed to apply software prefetching for non-numeric programs that reference pointer-based data structures as well [Luk & Mowry 1996, Roth & Sohi 1999, Karlsson et al. 2000].

Architectural Support

Although software prefetching is a software-centric technique, some hardware support is necessary. First, the architecture's instruction set must provide a *prefetch instruction*. Prefetch instructions are non-blocking memory loads (i.e., they do not wait for the reply from the memory system). They cause a cache

fill of the requested memory location on a cache miss, but have no other side effects. Since they are effectively NOPs (no operation) from the processor's standpoint, prefetch instructions can be ignored by the memory system (for example, at times when memory resources are scarce) without affecting program correctness. Hence, prefetch instructions enable software to provide "hints" to the memory system regarding the memory locations that should be loaded into cache.

In addition to prefetch instructions, software prefetching also requires lockup-free caches [Kroft 1981]. Since software prefetching tries to hide memory latency underneath useful computation, the cache must continue servicing normal memory requests from the microprocess or following cache misses triggered by prefetch instructions. For systems that prefetch aggressively, it is also necessary for the cache and memory subsystem to support multiple outstanding memory requests. This allows independent prefetch requests to overlap with each other.

Unless the compiler or programmer can guarantee the safety of all prefetches, another requirement from the architecture is support for ignoring memory faults caused by prefetch instructions, such as protection violations, page faults, bus errors, etc. (in which cases the instruction is ignored by the memory system). This support is particularly useful when instrumenting prefetch instructions speculatively, for example, to prefetch data accessed within conditional statements (e.g., Callahan et al. [1991]).

Finally, a few researchers have investigated software prefetching assuming support for *prefetch buffers* [Chen et al. 1991, Klaiber & Levy 1991]. Instead of prefetching directly into the L1 cache, these approaches place prefetched data in a special data buffer. On a memory request, the processor checks both the L1 cache and the prefetch buffer and moves prefetched data into the L1 cache only on a prefetch buffer hit. Hence, prefetched blocks that are never referenced by the processor do not evict potentially

---

[6]Portions reprinted, with permission, from "Data Cache Prefetching" by Yan Solihin and Donald Yeung, in *Speculative Execution in High Performance Computer Architectures*, CRC Press, Chapman and Hall, D. Kaeli and P. Yew, editors, ISBN-1-58488-447-9, 2005. Copyright © 2005 CRC Press.

useful blocks from the L1 cache. In addition, usefully prefetched blocks are filled into the L1 cache as late as possible—at the time of the processor's reference rather than the prefetch block's arrival—thus delaying the eviction of potentially useful blocks from the L1 cache. On the other hand, prefetch buffers consume memory that could have otherwise been used to build a larger L1 cache.

Mowry's Algorithm

Most software prefetching in practice focuses on array references performed within loops that give rise to regular memory-access patterns. These memory references employ array subscripts that are *affine*, i.e., linear combinations of loop index variables with constant coefficients and additive constants. Affine array references are quite common in a variety of applications, including dense-matrix linear algebra and finite-difference PDE (partial differential equation) solvers as well as image processing and scans/joins in relational databases. These programs can usually exploit long cache lines to reduce memory-access costs but may suffer poor performance due to cache conflict and capacity misses arising from the large amounts of data accessed. An important feature of these codes is that memory-access patterns can be identified exactly at compile time, assuming array dimension sizes are known. Consequently, programs performing affine array references are good candidates for software prefetching.

The best-known approach for instrumenting software prefetching of affine array references is the compiler algorithm proposed by Mowry [Mowry et al. 1992, Mowry 1998]. To illustrate the algorithm we use the two-dimensional (2D) Jacobi kernel in Figure 3.24(a) as an example, instrumenting it with software prefetching using Mowry's algorithm in Figure 3.24(b). The algorithm involves three major steps: locality analysis, cache-miss isolation, and prefetch scheduling.

Locality analysis determines the array references that will miss in the cache and thus require prefetching. The goal of this step is to avoid *unnecessary prefetches*, or prefetches that incur run-time overhead without improving performance because they hit in the cache. The analysis proceeds in two parts. First, reuse between dynamic instances of individual static array references is identified. In particular, locality analysis looks for three types of reuse: spatial,

```
a) for (j=2; j <= N-1; j++)
     for (i=2; i <= N-1; i++)
       A[j][i]=0.25*(B[j][i-1]+B[j][i+1]+B[j-1][i]+B[j+1][i]);


b) for (j=2; j <= N-1; j++) {
     for (i=2; i <= PD; i+=4) {        //    Prologue
       prefetch(&B[j][i]);
       prefetch(&B[j-1][i]);
       prefetch(&B[j+1][i]);
       prefetch(&A[j][i]);
     }
     for (i=2; i < N-PD-1; i+=4) {     //   Steady State
       prefetch(&B[j][i+PD]);
       prefetch(&B[j-1][i+PD]);
       prefetch(&B[j+1][i+PD]);
       prefetch(&A[j][i+PD]);

       A[j][i]=0.25*(B[j][i-1]+B[j][i+1]+B[j-1][i]+B[j+1][i]);
       A[j][i+1]=0.25*(B[j][i]+B[j][i+2]+B[j-1][i+1]+B[j+1][i+1]);
       A[j][i+2]=0.25*(B[j][i+1]+B[j][i+3]+B[j-1][i+2]+B[j+1][i+2]);
       A[j][i+3]=0.25*(B[j][i+2]+B[j][i+4]+B[j-1][i+3]+B[j+1][i+3]);
     }
     for (i=N-PD; i <= N-1; i++)       //    Epilogue
       A[j][i]=0.25*(B[j][i-1]+B[j][i+1]+B[j-1][i]+B[j+1][i]);
   }
```

FIGURE 3.24: Example illustrating Mowry's algorithm. (a) is 2D Jacobi kernel code; (b) is code instrumented with software prefetching using Mowry's algorithm [Mowry 1991].

temporal, and group. Spatial reuse occurs whenever a static array reference accesses locations close together in memory. For example, every array reference in Figure 3.24(a) exhibits spatial reuse. Since the *i* loop performs a unit-stride traversal of each inner array dimension, contemporaneous iterations access the same cache block. In contrast, temporal reuse occurs whenever a static array reference accesses the same memory location. (None of the array references in Figure 3.24(a) exhibits temporal reuse since all dynamic instances access distinct array elements.) Finally, group reuse occurs whenever two or more different static array references access the same memory location. In Figure 3.24(a), all four *B* array references exhibit group reuse since many of their dynamic instances refer to the same array elements.

After identifying reuse, locality analysis determines which reuses result in cache hits. The algorithm computes the number of loop iterations in between reuses and the amount of data referenced within these intervening iterations. If the size of this referenced data is smaller than the cache size, then the algorithm assumes the reuse is captured in the cache and the dynamic instances do not need to be prefetched. All other dynamic instances, however, are assumed to miss in the cache and require prefetching.

The next step in Mowry's algorithm, after locality analysis, is *cache-miss isolation*. For static array references that experience a mix of cache hits and misses (as determined by locality analysis), code transformations are performed to isolate the misses from the hits in separate static array references. This enables prefetching of the cache-missing instances while avoiding unnecessary prefetches fully statically, i.e., without predicating prefetch instructions with *IF* statements that incur run-time overhead.

The appropriate cache-miss isolation transformation depends on the type of reuse. For spatial reuse, *loop unrolling* is performed. Figure 3.24(b) illustrates loop unrolling for the 2D Jacobi kernel (see the second nested loop). As described earlier, the *i* loop of the Jacobi kernel performs a unit-stride traversal of the *A* and *B* inner array dimensions. Assuming 8-byte array elements and a 32-byte cache block, cache misses for each static array reference occur every ($32 \div 8 = 4$) iterations. By unrolling the loop four times, the lead-

ing array references incur cache misses every iteration, while the remaining unrolled references never miss, thus isolating the cache misses. For temporal reuse, cache misses are isolated via *loop peeling*. In this case, some subset of iterations (usually the first) incurs all the cache misses, and the remaining iterations hit in the cache. The cache-missing iteration(s) are peeled off and placed in a separate loop. Finally, for group reuse, no explicit transformation is necessary since cache misses already occur in separate static array references. Analysis is performed simply to identify which static array reference is the leading reference in each group and hence will incur all the cache misses on behalf of the other static references.

Once the cache misses have been isolated, prefetches are inserted for the static array references that incur them. Figure 3.24(b) illustrates the prefetch instrumentation for the 2D Jacobi kernel. Assuming the group reuse between $B[j][i+1]$ and $B[j][i-1]$ is captured by the cache, but the group reuse across outer loop iterations (i.e., the *j* subscripts) is not, there are four static array references that incur all the cache misses: $A[j][i]$, $B[j][i+1]$, $B[j-1][i]$, and $B[j+1][i]$. Prefetches are instrumented for these four array references, as illustrated in Figure 3.24(b) (again, see the second nested loop). Notice that prefetches are not instrumented for the remaining static array references, thus avoiding unnecessary prefetches and reducing prefetch overhead.

The last step in Mowry's algorithm is *prefetch scheduling*. Given the high memory latency of most modern memory systems, a single-loop iteration normally contains insufficient work under which to hide the cost of memory accesses. To ensure that data arrive in time, the instrumented prefetches must initiate multiple iterations in advance. The minimum number of loop iterations needed to fully overlap a memory access is known as the *prefetch distance*. Assuming the memory latency is l cycles and the work per loop iteration is w cycles, the prefetch distance, *PD*, is given by the following:

$$PD = \left\lceil \frac{l}{w} \right\rceil \qquad \text{(EQ 3.2)}$$

Figure 3.24(b) illustrates the indices of prefetched array elements that contain a *PD* term, providing the early prefetch initiation required.

By initiating prefetches *PD* iterations in advance, the first *PD* iterations are not prefetched, while the last *PD* iterations prefetch past the end of each array. These inefficiencies can be addressed by performing *software* pipelining to handle the first and last *PD* iterations separately. Software pipelining creates a *prologue loop* to execute *PD* prefetches for the first *PD* array elements and an *epilogue loop* to execute the last *PD* iterations without prefetching. Along with the original loop, called the *steady-state* loop, the transformed code initiates, overlaps, and completes all prefetches relative to the computation in a pipelined fashion. Figure 3.24(b) illustrates the prologue, steady-state, and epilogue loops created by software pipelining for the 2D Jacobi kernel.

Support for Indexed Arrays

In addition to affine arrays, another common type of array is *indexed* arrays. Indexed arrays take the form A[B[i]], in which a data array and index array are .composed to form an *indirect* array reference. While the inner array reference is affine and regular, the outer array reference is *irregular* due to memory indirection. Indexed arrays arise in scientific applications that attempt complex simulations. In computational fluid dynamics, meshes for modeling large problems are sparse to reduce memory and computation requirements. In *N*-body solvers for astrophysics and molecular dynamics, data structures are irregular because they model the positions of particles and their interactions. Indexed arrays are frequently used to express these complex data relationships since they are more efficient than pointers. Unfortunately, the cache performance of indexed arrays can be poor since both spatial and temporal locality is low due to the irregularity of the access pattern.

Software prefetching of indexed arrays was first studied by Callahan [Callahan et al. 1991]. Later, Mowry extended his algorithm for affine arrays to handle indexed arrays [Mowry 1994, 1998]. Mowry's extended algorithm follows the same steps discussed earlier, with some modifications. The modifications stem from two differences between indexed and affine array references. First, static analysis cannot determine locality information for consecutively accessed indexed array elements since their addresses depend on the index array values known only at run time. Hence, the algorithm conservatively assumes no reuse occurs between indexed array references, requiring prefetching for all dynamic instances. Moreover, since the algorithm assumes all dynamic instances miss in the cache, there is also no need for cache-miss isolation.

Second, before a data array reference can perform, the corresponding index array reference must complete since the index value is used to index into the data array. Hence, pairs of data and index array references are serialized. This affects prefetch scheduling. As in affine array prefetching, the computation of the prefetch distance uses Equation 3.2. However, the adjustment of array indices for indexed arrays must take into consideration the serialization of data and index array references. Since data array elements cannot be prefetched until the index array values they depend on are available, prefetches for index array elements should be initiated twice as early as data array elements. This ensures that an index array value is in cache when its corresponding data array prefetch is issued.

Pointer Prefetching

Pointer-chasing codes use linked data structures (LDS), such as linked lists, *n*-ary trees, and other graph structures, that are dynamically allocated at run time. They arise from solving complex problems where the amount and organization of data cannot be determined at compile time, requiring the use of pointers to dynamically manage both storage and linkage. They may also arise from high-level programming language constructs, such as those found in object-oriented programs.

Unlike array-based codes, pointer-based codes present a significant challenge to optimization. Chilimbi puts it well:

In general, software [data-]reference locality can be improved either by changing a program's data access pattern or its data organization and layout. The first approach has been successfully applied to improve the cache locality of scientific programs that manipulate dense matrices. Two properties of array structures are essential to this work: uniform, random access to elements, and a numer theoretic basis for statically analyzing data dependencies. These properties allow compilers to analyze array accesses completely and to reorder them in a way that increases cache locality (loop transformations) without affecting a program's result.

Unfortunately, pointer structures share neither property. [Chilimbi et al. 1999]

Due to the dynamic nature of LDS creation and modification, pointer-chasing codes commonly exhibit poor spatial and temporal locality and experience poor cache behavior. In addition, LDS traversal requires the sequential reference and dereference of the pointers stored inside visited nodes, thus serializing all memory operations performed along the traversal.

The pointer-chasing problem not only limits application performance, but it also potentially limits the effectiveness of prefetching. As discussed earlier, an important goal of software prefetching is to initiate prefetches sufficiently early to tolerate their latency. Doing so requires knowing the prefetch memory address in advance as well. This is straightforward for array data structures since the address of future array elements can be computed given the desired array indices. However, determining the address of a future link node in an LDS requires traversing the intermediate link nodes due to the pointer-chasing problem, thus preventing the early initiation of prefetches.

Natural Pointer Techniques

The simplest software prefetching technique for LDS traversal is greedy prefetching, proposed by Luk and Mowry [1996]. Greedy prefetching inserts software prefetch instructions immediately prior to visiting a node for all possible successor nodes that might be encountered by the traversal. To demonstrate the technique, Figure 3.25 shows the prefetch instrumentation for two types of LDS traversals. Figure 3.25(a) illustrates greedy prefetching for a loop-based, linked-list traversal in which a single prefetch is inserted at the top of the loop for the next link node in the list. Figure 3.25(b) illustrates greedy prefetching for a recursive tree traversal in which prefetches are inserted at the top of the recursive function for each child node in the sub-tree.

Greedy prefetching is attractive due to its simplicity. However, its ability to properly time prefetch initiation is limited. For the linked-list traversal in Figure 3.25(a), each prefetch overlaps with a single-loop iteration only. Greater overlap is not possible since the technique cannot prefetch nodes beyond the immediate successor due to the pointer-chasing problem described earlier. If the amount of work in a single-loop iteration is small compared to the prefetch latency, than greedy prefetching will not effectively tolerate the memory stalls. The situation is somewhat better for the tree traversal in Figure 3.25(b). Although the prefetch of *ptr->left* suffers a similar problem as the linked-list traversal (its latency overlaps with a single recursive call only), the prefetch of *ptr->right* overlaps with more work—the traversal of the entire left sub-tree. But the timing of prefetch initiation may

```
a)   struct node {data, next}
         *ptr, *list_head;

     ptr = list_head;
     while (ptr) {
        prefetch(ptr->next);
        ...
        ptr = ptr->next;
     }
```

```
b)   struct node {data, left, right}
         *ptr;

     void recurse(ptr){
        prefetch(ptr->left);
        prefetch(ptr->right);
        ...
        recurse(ptr->left);
        recurse(ptr->right);
     }
```

FIGURE 3.25: Example illustrating greedy pointer prefetching. Example pointer prefetching for (a) linked-list and (b) tree traversals using greedy prefetching.

not be ideal. The latency for prefetching *ptr->right* may still not be fully tolerated if the left sub-tree traversal contains insufficient work. Alternatively, the prefetched node may arrive too early and suffer eviction if the left sub-tree traversal contains too much work.

Another approach to prefetching LDS traversals is *data linearization* prefetching. Like greedy prefetching, this technique was proposed by Luk and Mowry [1996]. Data linearization prefetching makes the observation that if contemporaneously traversed link nodes in an LDS are laid out linearly in memory, then prefetching a future node no longer requires sequentially traversing the intermediate nodes to determine its address. Instead, a future node's memory address can be computed simply by offsetting from the current node pointer, much like indexing into an array. Hence, data linearization prefetching avoids the pointer-chasing problem altogether and can initiate prefetches as far in advance as necessary.

The key issue for data linearization prefetching is achieving the desired linear layout of LDS nodes. Linearization can occur either at LDS creation or after an LDS has been created. From a cost standpoint, the former is more desirable since the latter requires reorganizing an existing LDS via data copying at run time. Moreover, linearizing at LDS creation is feasible especially if the order of LDS traversal is known *a priori*. In this case, the allocation and linkage of individual LDS nodes should simply follow the order of node traversal. As long as the memory allocator places contemporaneously allocated nodes regularly in memory, the desired linearization can be achieved. Notice, however, that periodic "re-linearization" (via copying) may be necessary if link nodes are inserted and deleted frequently. Hence, data linearization prefetching is most effective for applications in which the LDS connectivity does not change significantly during program execution.

Jump Pointer Techniques

Both greedy and data linearization prefetching do not modify the logical structure of the LDS to perform prefetching. In contrast, another group of pointer prefetching techniques have been studied that insert special pointers into the LDS, called *jump pointers*, for the sole purpose of prefetching. Jump pointers connect non-consecutive link nodes, allowing prefetch instructions to name link nodes further down the pointer chain without traversing the intermediate link nodes and without performing linearization beforehand. Effectively, the jump pointers increase the dimensionality and reduce the diameter of an LDS, an idea borrowed from Skip Lists [Pugh 1990].

Several jump pointer techniques have been studied in the literature. The most basic approach is jump pointer prefetching as originally proposed by Luk and Mowry [1996]. Roth and Sohi [1999] also investigated jump pointer prefetching, introducing variations that use a combination of software and hardware support to pursue the jump pointers. Figure 3.26(a) illustrates the basic technique, applying jump pointer prefetching to the same linked-list traversal shown in Figure 3.25. Each linked-list node is augmented with a jump pointer field, called *jump*

```
a)    struct node {data, next, jump}
         *ptr, *list_head, *prefetch_array[PD], *history[PD];
      int i, head, tail;

      for (i = 0; i < PD; i++) //    Prologue Loop
         prefetch(prefetch_array[i]);

      ptr = list_head;
      while (ptr->next) { //  Steady State Loop
         prefetch(ptr->jump);
         ...
         ptr = ptr->next;
      }

b)    for (i = 0; i < PD; i++) history[i] = NULL;
      tail = 0;
      head = PD-1;

      ptr = list_head;
      while (ptr) { //    Prefetch Pointer Generation Loop
         history[head] = ptr;
         if (!history[tail])
            prefetch_array[tail] = ptr;
         else
            history[tail]->jump = ptr;
         head = (head+1)%PD;
         tail = (tail+1)%PD;
         ptr = ptr->next;
      }
```

FIGURE 3.26: Example illustrating jump pointer and prefetch array pointer prefetching. Example pointer prefetching for a linked, list traversal using jump pointers and prefetch arrays. (a) shows the traversal code instrumented with prefetching through jump pointers and prefetch arrays. (b) shows the prefetch pointer initialization code.

in Figure 3.26(a). During a separate initialization pass (discussed below), the jump pointers are set to point to a link node further down the linked list that will be referenced by a future loop iteration. The number of consecutive link nodes skipped by the jump pointers is the prefetch distance, *PD*, which is computed using the same approach described earlier for array prefetching. Once the jump pointers have been installed, prefetch instructions can prefetch through the jump pointers, as illustrated in Figure 3.26(a) by the loop labeled "Steady State."

Unfortunately, jump pointer prefetching cannot prefetch the first *PD* link nodes in a linked list because there are no jump pointers that point to these early nodes. In many pointer-chasing applications, this limitation significantly reduces the effectiveness of jump pointer prefetching because pointer chains are kept short by design. To enable prefetching of early nodes, jump pointer prefetching can be extended with prefetch arrays [Karlsson et al. 2000]. In this technique, an array of prefetch pointers is added to every linked list to point to the first *PD* link nodes. Hence, prefetches can be issued through the memory addresses in the prefetch arrays before traversing each linked list to cover the early nodes, much like the prologue loops for array prefetching prefetch the first *PD* array elements. Figure 3.26(b) illustrates the addition of a prologue loop that performs prefetching through a prefetch array.

As described earlier, the prefetch pointers must be installed before prefetching can commence. Figure 3.26(b) shows an example of prefetch pointer installation code that uses a history pointer array [Luk & Mowry 1996] to set the prefetch pointers. The history pointer array, called *history* in Figure 3.26, is a circular queue that records the last *PD* link nodes traversed by the initialization code. Whenever a new link node is traversed, it is added to the head of the circular queue, and the head is incremented. At the same time, the tail of the circular queue is tested. If the tail is NULL, then the current node is one of the first *PD* link nodes in the list since *PD* link nodes must be encountered before the circular queue fills. In this case, we set one of the *prefetch_array* pointers to point to the node. Otherwise, the tail's jump pointer is set to point to the current link node. Since the circular queue has depth *PD*, all jump

pointers are initialized to point *PD* link nodes *ahead*, thus providing that the proper prefetch distance. Normally, the compiler or programmer ensures that the prefetch pointer installation code gets executed prior to prefetching, for example, on the first traversal of an LDS. Furthermore, if the application modifies the LDS after the prefetch pointers have been installed, it may be necessary to update the prefetch pointers either by re-executing the installation code or by using other fix-up code.

3.2.3 Off-Line Locality Optimizations

Off-line locality optimizations rely only on the (static) information known about an application at compile time. Compile-time mechanisms that use application profiling are different; they exploit on-line knowledge of an application's behavior to make off-line decisions. Because they stride the boundary between on-line and off-line heuristics, profile-directed heuristics are treated in Section 3.3.

Ramamoorthy's Connectivity and Reachability Matrices

A significant consideration in the mid-1960s was the minimization of disk paging by choosing an optimal layout for a program's code and data. Ramamoorthy shows how a compile-time mechanism can pack program segments to exploit locality [1966]. Figure 3.27(a) depicts a program as a directed graph of *basic blocks* [Earnest et al. 1972]; Figure 3.27(b) shows several possible run-time sequences of blocks; and Figure 3.27(c) shows the connectivity matrix C obtained as a result of compile-time analysis of the program. Knuth gives an algorithm that would generate the matrix, given program code as input [1963].

The connectivity matrix gives information about what blocks are directly reachable from any given block and, at least potentially, the branching probabilities. Ramamoorthy notes [1966] that the matrix elements could be binary, indicating the presence of a directed arc, or they could contain weights representing the likelihood of a transition from one block to another. As he discusses in earlier work [Ramamoorthy 1965], the branching probabilities can be

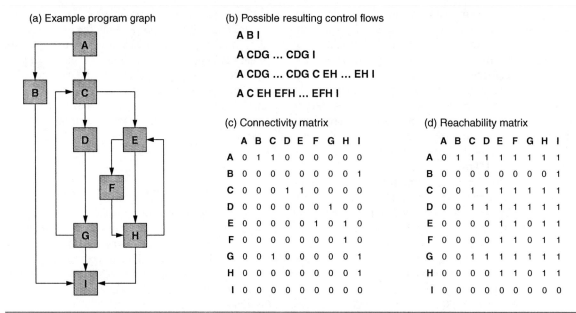

FIGURE 3.27: An example program and its connectivity matrix. (a) is an example program slightly different from the graph in Figure 3.12; (b) shows possible run-time sequences; (c) shows the resulting connectivity matrix; and (d) shows the resulting reachability matrix. Note that all possible runs of the program produce the same matrices.

calculated at compile time for deterministic events such as subroutine exits and fixed-iteration loop structures and for data-dependent branches as well, provided that the distribution of data values is known. Other probabilities, he notes, can be estimated or observed from test runs of the program.

Ramamoorthy's work is done in the context of *segmentation*, a virtual memory paradigm popular in the 1960s in which programs are divided into non-uniform-size regions called *segments*. These are atomic in the sense that they are moved in and out of the backing store as a unit: a segment is either present in main memory or not present. Ramamoorthy's packing algorithm chooses to place together into the same segment all members of each *maximal strongly connected* (MSC) *subgraph* [1966]. An MSC subgraph is one that includes all nodes that can reach each other and no other nodes. From the connectivity matrix C, the reachability matrix R is derived, which identifies all MSC subgraphs as well as all other leftover nodes (which occur as instances of the topology "link" subgraph, so named due to its shape). Figure 3.28

illustrates how the algorithm packs the example program into segments, given the block sizes and a maximum segment size of 4 KB. Branch probabilities are also shown to give an intuition behind program behavior and the appropriateness of the packing results: forward branches are 50/50, and backward branches are 90/10. When a given MSC subgraph is too large, the algorithm uses a greedy approach to pare the subgraph down by throwing out edges (and their corresponding nodes) that have the lowest transition probabilities. Note that this is the only instance in which the branching probabilities are used in Ramamoorthy's algorithm; if there is no limit on segment size, then Boolean matrices can be used.

Lowe's Incorporation of Data and a Notion of Time

Lowe extends Ramamoorthy's approach in two dimensions, capturing data-reference behavior as well as (an estimation of) the passage of time [Lowe 1969, 1970]. Note that the connectivity and reachability matrices do not distinguish between the following two

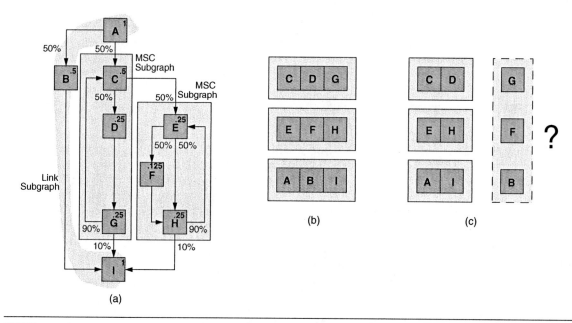

FIGURE 3.28: Ramamoorthy's packing algorithm at work. (a) is the example program DAG with branching probabilities and node-execution probabilities shown and MSC and link subgraphs identified; (b) shows the resulting program segments for a segment size of three units or larger; and (c) shows the program segments if a segment size is two units—the least likely visited node is thrown out greedily, and it is not clear which, if any, excised nodes would be recombined.

cases, assuming code blocks i and j are part of the same MSC subgraph:

- Code block i references code block j indirectly through 1 node
- Code block i references j indirectly through a sequence of 20 nodes

When paring down segment sizes, Ramamoorthy's algorithm does not necessarily throw out nodes that are separated from the rest of the subgraph by the largest number of "hops" (which translates to time). Lowe tries to capture this notion in his graph representation:

> ... it is useful to have some concept of the 'distance' of one program area from another. Connectivity information contained in a model can be analyzed in order to determine this, and if the second model is employed, such 'distance' is directly related to computation time. [Lowe 1969, p. 200]

Lowe's program representation builds upon Ramamoorthy's by considering not just the connectivity matrix C and the reachability matrix R, but, in essence, also the sequence of transformations from C to R. He augments the connectivity matrix with the concept of execution time for each code block, which is assumed to be equal to the number of instructions in the block, but just as easily could be an analytically or empirically derived number (i.e., the analysis does not depend on the source of the data). The augmentation produces a new connectivity matrix in which each time-step is represented as a separate node. In his analysis, the kth "power" of the augmented connectivity matrix represents the nodes that lie at a distance of k from each other. This value is easily derived iteratively.

Rather than trimming program segments that are too large (i.e., paring down MSC subgraphs that fail to fit into a single segment), Lowe's algorithm builds program segments up, block by block, until the segment size threshold is reached [Lowe 1970]. Like Ramamoorthy's algorithm, Lowe's algorithm considers MSC subgraphs; the algorithm examines, for each power of the augmented connectivity matrix, whether any of the new nodes reachable can be "merged" with any of the nodes to which it is connected and then merges any reachable nodes that are small enough to fit within the threshold. Figure 3.29(a) shows the same program as in the previous example with sizes and execution times for each block (for the sake of the example's simplicity, values are given in unit-time and unit-size instructions, i.e., a block of size 2 indicates two instructions

that take equal time to execute, but the mechanism is general enough to handle separate sizes and execution times). Figure 3.29(b) shows the augmented connectivity matrix and its 2nd and 3rd powers. Figure 3.30(a) shows the resulting code segmentation produced by Ramamoorthy's algorithm, given that one of the MSC subgraphs is too large to fit into a single segment. Figure 3.30(b) shows the segmentation produced by Lowe's algorithm. Ramamoorthy's algorithm chooses to remove block F from the third segment because (as shown in Figure 3.28), of all blocks in the segment, it has the lowest probability of being visited (12.5% as opposed to 25% for E and H). Lowe's algorithm builds the segment up from atomic pieces, greedily choosing those with the

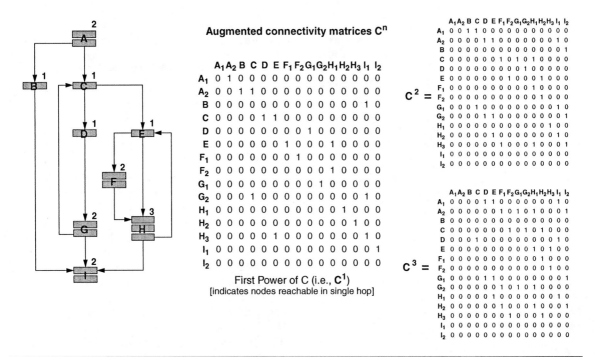

FIGURE 3.29: Lowe's algorithm and its notion of time. The graph shows the program structure as a collection of individual instructions, each of which (for the sake of simplicity) takes unit time to execute. Program time is approximated by the use of "powers" of the connectivity matrix: the nth power indicates what nodes are reachable in exactly n steps. The numbers at the top right of each block of instructions simply gives the size (and thus execution time) of that block.

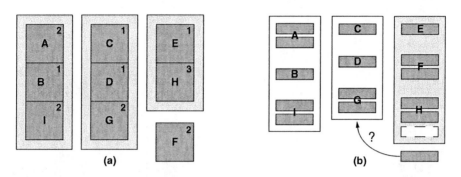

(a) (b)

FIGURE 3.30: Segmentation results for Ramamoorthy's and Lowe's algorithms. Results from (a) Ramamoorthy's and (b) Lowe's algorithms, both run on the program given in Figure 3.29, given a segment size of 5. Lowe's algorithm could integrate the last block of H into the CDG segment, depending on which segment is created first.

smallest edge distance: though E is one hop away from H_3, H_3 is three hops away from E (the start of the maximal subgraph), while all other blocks are, at most, two hops away.

Both schemes work well at identifying the closely related code blocks and grouping them together into the same segment. However, this relies upon the identification of small MSC subgraphs (small in relation to the size of a segment). This is not the case as the size of each MSC subgraph grows. For instance, as shown in Figure 3.31(a), a conditional loop back to the beginning of a program causes the entire program to be a single MSC subgraph (e.g., in the case of a program of the form "read next record in file and process it—repeat until the file is empty"). Note that, unlike previous versions of this graph, every node is reachable from every other node (the definition of an MSC subgraph). Figures 3.31(b) and (c) show the partitioning given by Ramamoorthy's algorithm and Lowe's algorithm, respectively, given a segment size of 10 units. The most important item to note is that large-scale program constructs obscure the smaller details, and the heuristics used by Ramamoorthy and Lowe cannot capture behavior exhibited at granularities smaller than an MSC subgraph. In particular, both fail to capture into a single segment the most relevant program behavior: the

EFH loop, which is executed very heavily. The identification of an "MSC sub-subgraph" would solve this problem, but is not clear that this is even possible using a purely static analysis. Analysis that captures the passage of time would solve the problem, but both algorithms use heuristics to approximate the passage of time. Later developments in the field incorporate profiling and thereby address exactly this issue (see Section 3.3.3).

Lowe also proposes a representation of a program's data needs that can support efficient data layout, in addition to packing code objects [1969]. Figure 3.32 shows a program graph in which data-reference behavior is captured as well as its corresponding (non-square) data-reference matrix. Directed edges represent transfer of control; undirected edges represent the consumption or production of data. Note that multiple code blocks may use the same block of data. Lowe suggests that this representation can be used to make intelligent page-replacement decisions at run time and that the scheme can be used to generate data layouts as well as code layouts, but no data-segmentation algorithm is presented. Note that the representation works well for contemporary programming languages such as FORTRAN, but does not handle modern languages and variants in which data can be dynamically allocated or deallocated.

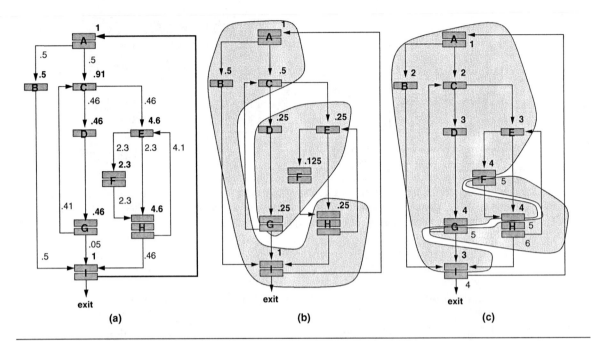

FIGURE 3.31: Sub-optimal program segmentation. (a) shows an example program with edges and nodes labeled (using regular and bold fonts, respectively) by their average expected number of executions per iteration through the loop—note that this is **not** the same as a probability of occurrence. Note also that numbers have been rounded to two significant digits. Segmentation results, given a segment size of 10, are shown for (b) Ramamoorthy's algorithm (with probabilities from Figure 3.28) and (c) Lowe's algorithm (with pseudo-time labeled at each node). The example assumes that node naming/numbering is used to break a tie.

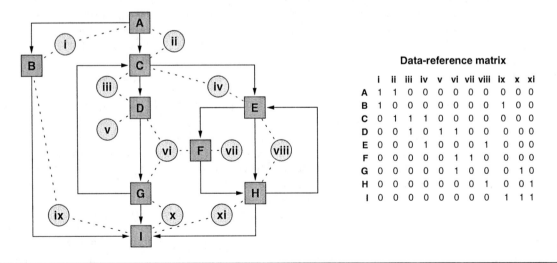

FIGURE 3.32: Lowe's representation of data-reference behavior. This is the same program graph as in earlier illustrations, with data references indicated by circular nodes and dashed, undirected arcs.

Tiling (or Blocking) and Interleaving

Tiling originates from the early days of virtual 1memory systems when the data structure to be manipulated (e.g., in a matrix multiplication) was too large to fit into the physical memory space at once [McKellar & Coffman 1969]. The idea is to restructure the algorithm to walk through the data in a fashion that exploits the available storage. For instance, a typical implementation of $n \times n$ matrix multiplication looks like the following:

```
for i := 1 step 1 until n do
  for j := 1 step 1 until n do
    for k := 1 step 1 until n do
      C[i,j] := C[i,j] + A[i,k] • B[k,j]
```

This algorithm exhibits the data-access pattern shown in Figure 3.33(a). A restructuring of the algorithm to "tile" the matrix into submatrices, each of which fits within a page, thereby reducing the number of page faults, is given by the following, where the original $n \times n$ matrix is subdivided into N^2 $r \times r$ submatrices [McKellar & Coffman 1969]:

```
for I := 1 step 1 until N do
  for J := 1 step 1 until N do
    for K := 1 step 1 until N do
      for i := r • (I − 1) step 1 until r • I do
        for j := r • (J − 1) step 1 until r • J do
          for k := r • (K − 1) step 1 until r • K do
            C[i,j] := C[i,j] + A[i,k] • B[k,j]
```

This algorithm has the data-access behavior shown in Figure 3.33(b).

Later work (e.g., Lam's study of cache blocking [Lam et al. 1991]) extends the concept to processor caches. Lam considers a version of the first original

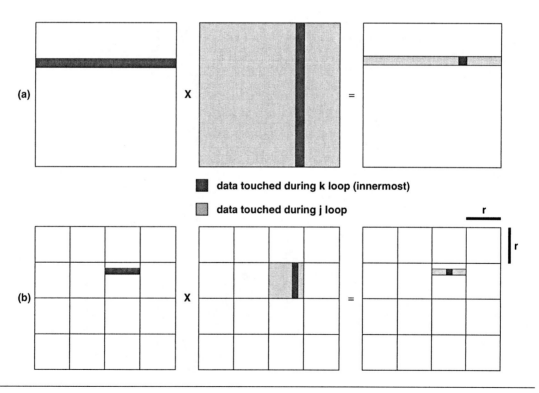

FIGURE 3.33: Data-access behavior of tiled matrix multiplication.

algorithm that walks through the matrices differently (the inner loop walks matrices C and B, not A and B):

```
for i := 1 step 1 until n do
    for k := 1 step 1 until n do
        for j := 1 step 1 until n do
            C[i,j] := C[i,j] + A[i,k] • B[k,j]
```

This has the data-access behavior shown in Figure 3.34(a). Lam subdivides the matrix by considering the size of the cache block and gives the following algorithm, where r is the *blocking factor*, chosen so that the r × r submatrix of B and a row of length r of C can both fit into the cache simultaneously (note this requires assurance that the two will not conflict in the cache):

```
for K := 1 step r until n do
    for J := 1 step r until n do
        for i := 1 step 1 until n do
            for k := K step 1 until min(n, K+r − 1) do
                for j := J step 1 until min(n, J+r − 1) do
                    C[i,j] := C[i,j] + A[i,k] • B[k,j]
```

This algorithm has the data-access behavior shown in Figure 3.34(b).

A similar optimization is to interleave arrays. For example, assume the computation is a typical vector operation, such as the following:

```
int A[ARRAY_SIZE], B[ARRAY_SIZE] ;

for (sum=0, i=1; i<ARRAY_SIZE; i++)
    sum += A[i] * B[i];
```

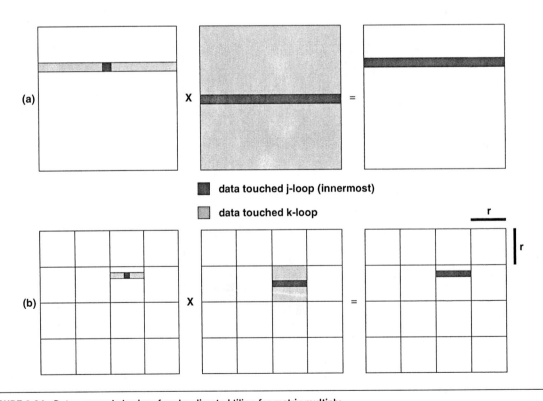

data touched j-loop (innermost)

data touched k-loop

FIGURE 3.34: Data-access behavior of cache-directed tiling for matrix multiply.

The locality of this can be improved by redefining A and B and their access methods as follows:

```
struct { int A; int B; } AB[ARRAY_SIZE];

for (sum=0, i=1; i<ARRAY_SIZE; i++)
    sum += AB[i].A * AB[i].B;
```

The data layouts of these two algorithms are shown in Figure 3.35.

Alternatively, when it is known that an array of structs is not used to its best advantage, e.g., if only one element in the struct is used at any given time, one can disaggregate some or all of the struct's elements into their own separate arrays (the reverse of what is shown in Figure 3.35). A controversial example of this optimization in use is the "ART hack" [Wolfe 2005], a scheme used in several commercial compilers to speed up the ART benchmark in the SPEC benchmark suite. It is controversial because it is not automatable; a programmer must inspect the code to ensure that such an optimization does not interfere with program correctness.

3.3 Case Studies: Combined Approaches

There are numerous examples of schemes that fashion a synergy between on-line and off-line mechanisms. These are schemes where the two cooperate

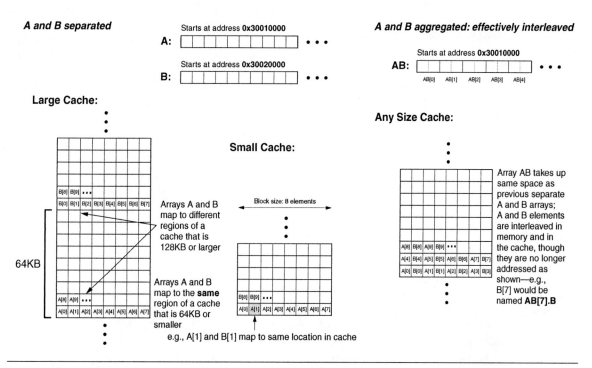

FIGURE 3.35: Data-access behavior for array aggregation. On the left is shown a typical arrangement for two vectors A and B, placed contiguously in memory and each 64 KB in size. The arrays do not conflict in large caches (128 KB and larger), and they do conflict in caches 64 KB and smaller. On the right is shown an aggregate array that combines into a single array both of the previous two arrays, and effectively interleaving the two on an element-by-element basis. This arrangement does not suffer from cache conflicts: elements A[i] and B[i] do not conflict in the cache (unless each is extremely large and the cache is extremely small), and, if considering primitive element types and most cache block sizes, both A[i] and B[i] are likely to reside in the same cache block at the same time.

to exploit the opportunities available on each side. The off-line mechanism exploits knowledge of the application code and provides information to the online mechanism, which can exploit dynamic information such as memory disambiguation.

A simple example is the PA-7200's *spatial locality only* cache hint for load/store instructions [Chan et al. 1996]. This mechanism indicates to the memory system that the corresponding data exhibits spatial locality, but not temporal locality; the data should not necessarily be found in or placed in the regular cache hierarchy. When operating in conjunction with the PA-7200's assist cache, the hint indicates to the hardware that the fetched data should be left in the assist cache and not moved into the main cache. Other, more complex, mechanisms have been proposed and/or built. This section describes a few of them.

Many of the mechanisms presented in this section are here because they use profiling—an approach that combines compiler knowledge of program structure and run-time knowledge of program behavior. As discussed previously (e.g., in Section 3.2.3), some early approaches are limited significantly by their static view of the program. Without a notion of the program's working set and how it changes over time, an algorithm trying to analyze the program's behavior is necessarily constrained by the program's structure, and even minor changes to the program's structure can expose or obscure important details in the program's run-time behavior. Researchers in the 1960s and early 1970s were well aware of profiling. They describe it as a straightforward optimization that may lead to better results for the profiled data set, but cannot guarantee improvements for different program inputs (e.g., Hatfield and Gerald [1971]). One of the first to validate the use of profiling is Babonneau, who demonstrates "the stability of program behavior with respect to the input-data" based on multiple executions of different programs using different input sets [Babonneau et al. 1977, p. 109].

3.3.1 Combined Approaches to Partitioning

Several examples of partitioning revolve around the PlayDoh architecture from Hewlett-Packard Labs.

HPL-PD, PlayDoh v1.1 — General Architecture

One content-management mechanism in which the hardware and software cooperate in interesting ways is the HPL PlayDoh architecture, renamed the HPL-PD architecture, embodied in the EPIC line of processors [Kathail et al. 2000]. Two facets of the memory system are exposed to the programmer and compiler through instruction-set hooks: (1) the memory-system structure and (2) the memory disambiguation scheme.

The HPL-PD architecture exposes its view or definition of the memory system, shown in Figure 3.36, to the programmer and compiler. The instruction-set architecture is aware of four components in the memory system: the L1 and L2 caches, an L1 streaming or data-prefetch cache (sits next to the L1 cache), and main memory. The exact organization of each structure is not exposed to the architecture. As with other mechanisms that have placed separately managed buffers adjacent to the L1 cache, the explicit

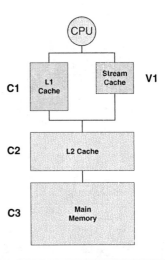

FIGURE 3.36: The memory system defined by the HPL-PD architecture. Each component in the memory system is shown with the assembly-code instruction modifier used by a load or store instruction to specify that component. The L1 cache is called C1, the streaming or prefetch cache is V1, the L2 cache is C2, and the main memory is C3.

goal of the streaming/prefetch cache is to partition data into disjoint sets: (1) data that exhibits temporal locality and should reside in the L1 cache, and (2) everything else (e.g., data that exhibits only spatial locality), which should reside in the streaming cache.

To manage data movement in this hierarchy, the instruction set provides several modifiers for the standard set of load and store instructions.

Load instructions have two modifiers:

1. *A latency and source cache specifier* hints to the hardware where the data is expected to be found (i.e., the L1 cache, the streaming cache, the L2 cache, main memory) and also specifies to the hardware the compiler's assumed latency for scheduling this particular load instruction. In machine implementations that require rigid timing (e.g., traditional VLIW), the hardware must stall if the data is not available with this latency; in machine implementations that have dynamic scheduling around cache misses (e.g., a superscalar implementation of the architecture), the hardware can ignore the value.

2. *A target cache specifier* indicates to hardware where the load data should be placed within the memory system (i.e., place it in the L1 cache, place it in the streaming cache, bring it no higher than the L2 cache, or leave it in main memory). Note that all loads specify a target register, but the target register may be r0, a read-only bit-bucket in both general-purpose and floating-point register files, providing a *de facto* form of non-binding prefetch. Presumably the processor core communicates the *binding/ non-binding* status to the memory system to avoid useless bus activity.

Store instructions have one modifier:

1. The *target cache specifier,* like that for load instructions, indicates to the hardware the highest component in the memory system in which the store data should be retained.

A store instruction's ultimate target is main memory, and the instruction can leave a copy in the cache system if the compiler recognizes that the value will be reused soon or can specify main memory as the highest level if the compiler expects no immediate reuse for the data.

Abraham's Profile-Directed Partitioning

Abraham describes a compiler mechanism to exploit the Play Doh facility [Abraham et al. 1993]. At first glance, the authors note that it seems to offer too few choices to be of much use: a compiler can only distinguish between short-latency loads (expected to be found in L1), long-latency loads (expected in L2), and very long-latency loads (in main memory). A simple cache-performance analysis of a blocked matrix multiply shows that all loads have relatively low miss rates, which would suggest using the expectation of short latencies to schedule all load instructions.

However, the authors show that by loop peeling one can do much better. Loop peeling is a relatively simple compiler transformation that extracts a specific iteration of a loop and moves it outside the loop body. This increases code size (the loop body is replicated), but it opens up new possibilities for scheduling. In particular, keeping in mind the facilities offered by the HPL-PD instruction set, many loops display the following behavior: the first iteration of the loop makes (perhaps numerous) data references that miss the cache; the main body of the loop enjoys reasonable cache hit rates; and the last iteration of the loop has high hit rates, but it represents the last time the data will be used.

The HPL-PD transformation of the loop peels off first and last iterations:

*   The first iteration of the loop uses load instructions that specify main memory as the likely source cache; the store instructions target the L1 cache.
*   The body of the loop uses load instructions that specify the L1 cache as the likely source; the store instructions also target the L1 cache.

- The last iteration of the loop uses load instructions that specify the L1 cache as the likely source; the store instructions target main memory.

The authors note that such a transformation is easily automated for regular codes, but irregular codes present a difficult challenge. The focus of the Abraham et al. study is to quantify the predictability of memory access in irregular applications. The study finds that, in most programs, a very small number of load instructions cause the bulk of cache misses. This is encouraging because if those instructions can be identified at compile time, they can be optimized by hand or perhaps by a compiler.

Hardware/Software Memory Disambiguation

The HPL-PD's memory disambiguation scheme comes from the *memory conflict buffer* in William Chen's Ph.D. thesis [1993]. The hardware provides to the software a mechanism that can detect and patch up memory conflicts, provided that the software identifies loads that are risky and then follows each up with an explicit invocation of a hardware check. The compiler/programmer can exploit the scheme to speculatively issue loads ahead of when it is safe to issue them, or it can ignore the scheme. The scheme by definition requires the cooperation of software and hardware to reap any benefits. The point of the scheme is to enable the compiler to improve its scheduling of code for which compile-time analysis of pointer addresses is not possible. For example, the following code uses pointer addresses in registers *a1*, *a2*, *a3*, and *a4* that cannot be guaranteed to be conflict free:

```
r1 = LD(a1);
r2 = ADD(r1, r5);
ST(a2,r2);
r3 = LD(a3);
r4 = ADD(r3, r5);
ST(a4,r4);
```

The code has the following conservative schedule (assuming 2-cycle load latencies—equivalent to a 1-cycle load-use penalty, as in separate EX and MEM pipeline stages in an in-order pipe—and 1-cycle latencies for all else):

```
1. r1 = LD(a1);
2. ---
3. r2 = ADD(r1, r5);
4. ST(a2,r2);
5. r3 = LD(a3);
6. ---
7. r4 = ADD(r3, r5);
8. ST(a4,r4);
```

A better schedule would be the following, which moves the second load instruction ahead of the first store:

```
1. r1 = LD(a1);
2. r3 = LD(a3);
3. r2 = ADD(r1, r5);
4. ST(a2,r2); r4 = ADD(r3, r5);
5. ST(a4,r4);
```

If we assume two memory ports, the following schedule is slightly better:

```
1. r1 = LD(a1);          r3 = LD(a3);
2. ---                   ---
3. r2 = ADD(r1, r5);     r4 = ADD(r3, r5);
4. ST(a2,r2);            ST(a4,r4);
```

However, the compiler cannot guarantee the safety of this code, because it cannot guarantee that *a3* and *a2* will contain different values at run time. Chen's solution, used in HPL-PD, is for the compiler to inform the hardware that a particular load is risky. This allows the hardware to make note of that load and to compare its run-time address to stores that follow it. The scheme also relies upon the compiler to perform a post-verification that can patch up errors if it turns out that there was indeed a conflict by aggressively scheduling the load ahead of the store.

The scheme centers around the *LDS log*, a record of speculatively issued load instructions that maintains in each of its entries the target register of the load and the memory address that the load uses. There are two types of instructions that the compiler uses to manage the log's state, and store instructions affect its state implicitly:

1. LDS instructions are *load-speculative* instructions that explicitly allocate a new entry in the log (remember an entry contains the target register and memory address). On executing an LDS instruction, the hardware creates a new entry and invalidates any old entries that have the same target register.

2. Store instructions modify the log implicitly. On executing a store, the hardware checks the log for a live entry that matches the same memory address and deletes any entries that match.

3. LDV instructions are *load-verification* instructions that must be placed conservatively in the code (after a potentially conflicting store instruction). They check to see if there was a conflict between the speculative load and the store. On executing an LDV instruction, the hardware checks the log for a valid entry with the matching target register. If an entry exists, the instruction can be treated as an NOP; if no entry matches, the LDV is treated as a load instruction (it computes a memory address, fetches the datum from memory, and places it into the target register).

The example code becomes the following, where the second LD instruction is replaced by an LDS/LDV pair:

```
r1 = LD(a1);
r2 = ADD(r1, r5);
ST(a2,r2);
r3 = LDS(a3);
r3 = LDV(a3);
r4 = ADD(r3, r5);
ST(a4,r4);
```

The compiler can schedule the LDS instruction aggressively, keeping the matching LDV instruction in the conservative spot behind the store instruction (note that in HPL-PD, memory operations are prioritized left

to right, so the LDV operation is technically "behind" the ST).

```
1. r1 = LD(a1);
2. r3 = LDS(a3);
3. r2 = ADD(r1, r5);
4. ST(a2,r2); r3 = LDV(a3);
5. r4 = ADD(r3, r5);
6. ST(a4,r4);
```

If we assume two memory ports, there is not much to be gained, because the LDV must be scheduled to happen after the potentially aliasing ST (store) instruction, which would yield effectively the same schedule as above. To address this type of issue (as well as many similar scenarios) the architecture also provides a BRDV instruction, a post-verification instruction similar to LDV that, instead of loading data, branches to a specified location on detection of a memory conflict. This instruction is used in conjunction with compiler-generated patch-up code to handle more complex scenarios. For instance, the following could be used for implementations with a single memory port:

```
1. r1 = LD(a1);
2. r3 = LDS(a3);
3. r2 = ADD(r1, r5);
4. ST(a2,r2); r4 = ADD(r3, r5); BRDV(a3,patchup);
5. ST(a4,r4);
   next: ...
```

The following can be used with multiple memory ports:

```
1. r1 = LD(a1);              r3 = LD(a3);
2. ---                       ---
3. r2 = ADD(r1, r5);         r4 = ADD(r3, r5);
4. ST(a2,r2);                ST(a4,r4);
5. BRDV(a3,patchup);
   next: ...
```

where the patch-up code is given as follows:

```
patchup:
1. r3 = LD(a3);
2. ---
3. r4 = ADD(r3, r5);
4. ST(a4,r4);
5. JUMP(next);
```

Using the BRDV instruction, the compiler can achieve optimal scheduling.

There are a number of issues that the HPL-PD mechanism must handle. For instance, the hardware must ensure that no virtual-address aliases can cause problems (e.g., different virtual addresses that map to the same physical address, if the operating system supports this). The hardware must also handle partial overwrites, for instance, a write instruction that writes a single byte to a four-byte word that was previously read speculatively (the addresses would not necessarily match). The compiler must ensure that every LDS is followed by a matching LDV that uses the same target register and address register (for obvious reasons), and the compiler also must ensure that no intervening operations disturb the log or the target register. The LDV instruction must block until complete to achieve effectively single-cycle latencies.

3.3.2 Combined Approaches to Prefetching

The following combine hardware and software mechanisms for prefetching.

Pipelined Vector Computers

One of the most straightforward examples of a hardware/software synergy in managing the memory system is the pipelined vector computer. Vector processing targets a specific application class—a class of algorithms that have the same function and properties as the types of code structure targeted by Mowry's prefetching algorithm (see Section 3.2.2). A vector computer can express in a single instruction an entire vector operation such as the following:

```
for (i=0; i<128; i++)
    A[i] = B[i] + C[i];
```

which, by the way, produces the following lightly optimized[7] PowerPC loop (via *cc -O*):

```
L2:   wzx r0,r9,r8
      lwzx r2,r9,r10
      add r0,r0,r2
      stwx r0,r9,r7
      addi r0,r11,1
      addi r9,r9,4
      bdz L3
      mr r11,r0
      b L2
L3:   // store to i
      ...
```

So, by encoding instructions to represent a specialized form of algorithm, one can reduce the amount of memory storage and bus traffic to handle instructions by an order of magnitude, even more compared to unoptimized code (note that this is the same approach taken in the instruction sets for DSPs). Essentially, all memory bandwidth is available for data, and there is no branch-instruction overhead, as the control-flow information is implicit in the vector operation.

The effect on data traffic is even more interesting, and this is where the management of the memory system becomes apparent. The vector operation walks through a linear sequence of data items, which is something most memory systems are readily capable of delivering. The instruction-set architecture is defined to exploit memory-system bandwidth and tolerate memory-system latency. Provided that the memory system can supply a stream of data, the vector processor can be kept completely busy. Each element in the vector stream arrives more or less exactly when it is needed. The data cache is almost superfluous, as it is relegated to the status of a buffer used to smooth out traffic. In addition, the cache need not be extremely large, provided that the backing store can deliver the vector processor's required bandwidth (the vector cache is often simply a register file). Vector processing is arguably the ultimate in a content-management mechanism because, by its very nature, it places every data access at the right place, at the right time.

---

[7]Note that most commercial code does not use anything beyond the *-O* compiler flag (if that).

An Argument for Application-Directed File Caches

Stonebreaker argues that general-purpose operating systems do not provide the appropriate file-I/O support needed by database-management systems, a narrow but important class of applications [1981]. In particular, Stonebreaker describes problems of performance, choice of buffer-pool replacement policy, prefetch heuristics, and support for crash recovery.

We focus on the cache-specific portion of the discussion. Stonebreaker states that the operating system's default replacement policy (LRU) is inimical when used to manage buffers on behalf of a DBMS (database management system):

> Database access in INGRES is a combination of:
>
> (1) sequential access to blocks which will not be rereferenced;
>
> (2) sequential access to blocks which will be cyclically rereferenced;
>
> (3) random access to blocks which will not be referenced again;
>
> (4) random access to blocks for which there is a nonzero probability of rereference.
>
> Although LRU works well for case 4, it is a bad strategy for other situations. Since a DBMS knows which blocks are in each category, it can use a composite strategy. For case 4 it should use LRU while for 1 and 3 it should use toss immediately. For blocks in class 3 the reference pattern is 1, 2, 3, ..., n, 1, 2, 3, ... Clearly, LRU is the worst possible replacement algorithm for this situation. [p. 413]

Stonebreaker identifies a similar problem in the operating system's prefetch policy:

> Although UNIX correctly prefetches pages when sequential [file I/O] access is detected, there are important instances in which it fails. Except in rare cases INGRES at (or very shortly after) the beginning of its examination of a block knows exactly which block it will access next. Unfortunately, this block is not necessarily the next one in logical file order. Hence, there is no way for an OS to implement the correct prefetch strategy. [p. 413]

Note that the problem is not unique to database-management systems. Nearly all caches (both file caches and processor caches) suffer from design that is driven by conflicting goals. A simple insight is that prefetch mechanisms are typically geared for sequential access, while the most common replacement policy (LRU) is geared for quite the opposite behavior (MRU should be used if sequential access is expected).

Stonebreaker challenges the systems community to provide the requisite support:

> In order for an OS to provide buffer management, some means must be found to allow it to accept "advice" from an application program (e.g., a DBMS) .... Although it is possible to provide an OS buffer manager with the required features, none currently exists, at least to our knowledge. Designing such a facility with prefetch advice, block management advice, and selected force out would be an interesting exercise. [pp. 413, 414]

In the early to mid-1990s, several research groups took up the challenge. Cao and others at Princeton implemented application-directed replacement policies [Cao et al. 1994b]; Patterson and others at Carnegie Mellon implemented application-directed prefetching and replacement [Patterson et al. 1995]; Cao also investigated the relatively complex relationship between replacement and prefetch policies [Cao et al. 1995, 1996]. The following sections describe each of these.

Cao's Application-Controlled File Caching

Cao provides means for an application to guide the operating system's replacement policy [Cao et al. 1994a, b]. The application's interface includes the following system calls:

- **set_priority(file, priority):** This allows an application to set the priority level of a given file. For each priority level, the operating system manages a separate buffer pool. Thus, the invocation of this system call causes the blocks of the indicated file to reside in the associated buffer pool.

- **set_policy(priority, policy):** This allows an application to set the replacement policy for its subset of the blocks at a given priority level. The invocation of this system call causes the operating system to manage the blocks in that buffer pool (that are owned by the corresponding process) in either MRU or LRU fashion (clearly, this can be extended to include any set of policies).

- **set_temppri(file, startblock, endblock, priority):** This allows an application to temporarily reassign a new priority level to a selected portion of a file's blocks. The change only affects blocks currently in the file cache, and the priority change to each block only lasts until the block is referenced or replaced, at which point its priority reverts to the original value indicated by set_priority().

The interface is two levels in the sense that responsibilities are shared between the application and operating-system kernel: the kernel allocates cache blocks to processes, and each process determines the replacement strategy to be used on its share of the cache blocks. Note that the application can override the kernel, and the kernel can also override the application. Allowing the kernel to override the application is necessary for the kernel to ensure the following stated goals:

1. A process that chooses not to use the mechanism does no worse than the default (global LRU) replacement policy.

2. A process cannot, through the use of the mechanism, degrade the performance of another process.

3. A process is not penalized for making a wise choice when overruling the operating system.

Consequently, if the heuristic's implementation achieves the stated goals, a process that makes intelligent decisions about its file-access behavior can only maintain or improve its level of performance by using the mechanism.

Cao proposes a file-cache-management implementation that satisfies the properties, called LRU-SP (for LRU with Swapping and Placeholders). At the time of block replacement, the kernel informs the application of the block it has chosen to replace and allows the application to choose a different block in its place. Though the application ostensibly has the final say in what block gets replaced, the kernel does override the application if it detects instances where the application has made poor choices in the past. Whenever the application overrides the kernel's choice for block replacement, the kernel first swaps the two blocks in the LRU list and then creates a placeholder for the replaced block that references the kernel's original choice. If, over the course of future requests, the kernel determines that the application's choice was poor, it will override the application (see Figure 3.37). Figure 3.37(a) shows the state of the buffer pool (managed as a global MRU/LRU doubly linked queue). The kernel has chosen to replace block A, as it is at the end of the list. The application overrides the decision and chooses to have block B replaced instead; the kernel swaps the two blocks in the list, making B the locally LRU block and promoting block A to the status that B previously had. Figure 3.37(b) shows the state of the queue after the swap. The operating system then makes note of the fact that block B was replaced in A's stead; a *placeholder* data structure references block A, shown in Figure 3.37(c), which indicates to the kernel the block that would have been in the buffer pool under the default-management policy. If the application later makes a request for block B, and block A is still in the queue, the kernel recognizes this fact and chooses to replace block A. If the application makes a request for block A before making a request to block B (in which case the application's overriding decision was good), the placeholder structure is removed. Consider the following request stream, with a cache of size 2:

ABCAB

This is essentially the situation illustrated in Figure 3.37. At the reference to C, the kernel would choose to discard block A; a wise application would choose block B. On the next reference (to A), it is important that the placeholder is deleted. Otherwise, when the second reference to B is made, the kernel would have a placeholder for it, referencing block A, which would cause the kernel to mistakenly

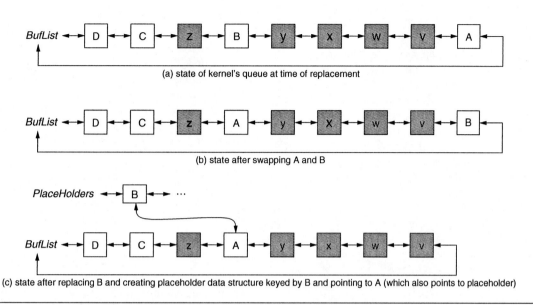

(a) state of kernel's queue at time of replacement

(b) state after swapping A and B

(c) state after replacing B and creating placeholder data structure keyed by B and pointing to A (which also points to placeholder)

FIGURE 3.37: The use of swapping and placeholders. (a) shows a global time-ordered list of buffers with grey boxes representing blocks from other processes. The LRU block is at the end and the MRU block is at the head. An example reference string (local to the application in question) creating the current list state would be ABABCBCD. (b) shows the state of the list after swapping priorities for blocks A and B. (c) shows the state of the list after discarding block B and creating a "placeholder" referencing block A. If A is referenced before B, the placeholder is deleted; if B is referenced before A, A is replaced by B.

believe the application's earlier override to be a poor choice.

The experimental results show improvement in performance. Note that the primary reason for swapping is to attempt to bring the kernel's management policy into accord with the application's policy: if a chosen block is at the end of the LRU list, and the application wants to keep it, then that same block will come up again at the next replacement decision (e.g., ahead of blocks v, w, x, and y in Figure 3.37), unless the block is somehow promoted in the ranks. Ergo swapping. However, given the actual implementation (the only choices to the application are LRU and MRU policies), it seems the kernel could simply keep the same list-maintenance code and dynamically choose the end of the queue from which to pick a candidate block. If a local management policy is desired, the kernel could create separate lists for each process. If a global policy is desired, the decision of which application's block to choose could be determined by a

global LRU list of process IDs that indicates the order in which processes access the I/O buffers, even if kept in separate lists. The trade-off would be that such an implementation might prevent the kernel from keeping track of how well or poorly an application-level heuristic performs compared to global LRU.

Note that this is the function of the placeholder mechanism. The primary reasons for maintaining placeholders are to protect an application from itself, to recognize when an application is making poor choices, and to protect other applications from its behavior. Applications that make poor file-caching choices tend to use the disk more heavily and thus, despite the best efforts of the kernel, can penalize other applications by creating a denial-of-service scenario. After observing this behavior even in the system just described, Cao proposes a more aggressive kernel approach wherein the kernel revokes an application's right to control caching when such scenarios are detected [Cao et al. 1994b].

Patterson's Informed Prefetching and Caching

Patterson investigates a modification to the file system that accepts advice from the application in the form of *disclosures* or *hints* [Patterson et al. 1995]. Patterson is quick to differentiate *advice*, in which an application tells the file system how to behave, from *disclosures*, in which the application informs the file system of its upcoming activity; the claim is that the latter is preferable as it is more portable and assumes nothing about the system's implementation or concurrent activities.

Examples of how the mechanism could be used are given by Patterson. In shell expansions such as "grep foobar *.txt," the operating system eventually opens and reads a potentially large number of files. The process could be sped up if, at the outset, either *grep* or the shell informs the operating system of the upcoming requests rather than opening and reading the files iteratively. A similar situation arises in *make*, a development tool on Unix platforms that orchestrates complex program compilations involving multiple files. In general, Patterson argues that there exists a large class of applications whose use of the disk appears as serial streams of non-sequential access [Patterson et al. 1995]. These applications exhibit no streaming (thus no obvious source of prefetching) and no parallelism; their service time tends to be dominated by the disk's seek and rotational latencies.

Informed prefetching and caching (or "TIP," for *transparent informed prefetching* [Patterson et al. 1993, 1995]) seeks to uncover parallelism in these applications. The main idea is to dynamically (and transparently) reschedule an application's file activity using foreknowledge of its future behavior. In this regard, it could be viewed as comparable to a file-I/O version of loop unrolling. Figure 3.38 illustrates TIP's effect on the scheduling of processing within an application. Because there is nothing speculative about the I/O fetch in TIP (the application discloses its upcoming file-I/O activity; the kernel decides whether or not to act on the information), it is somewhat of a misnomer to call it *prefetching*—a more appropriate term might be *scheduled fetching* or just *fetching*.

One could conceivably get comparable performance by rewriting an application to place its file-I/O requests up front (e.g., explicitly unrolling loop-structured I/O operations as in the grep foobar *.txt and make examples presented earlier), but doing so would require additional system-level support, for instance, a non-blocking *open()* system call or at least a non-blocking *fopen()* library call. However, by making the process transparent as in TIP, the kernel ultimately makes the decision to allocate resources, which would not be the case if the process were entirely application driven. In TIP, the kernel can decide how best to allocate buffers and how far ahead to prefetch; this would be analogous to a dynamic loop unrolling mechanism that determines at run time how much register pressure the system can tolerate and therefore to what degree one can unroll loops.

A Note on Prefetching and Caching

A problem with application-directed file cache behavior is that, as Cao shows [Cao et al. 1995] and as Patterson admits [Patterson et al. 1993, 1995], things

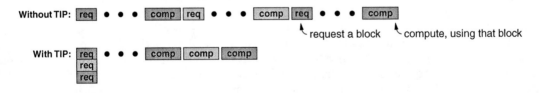

FIGURE 3.38: Request scheduling in transparent informed prefetching (TIP). Without TIP, an application makes requests as data is needed, e.g., opening a file right before reading it. With TIP, an application informs the kernel of its upcoming file needs without actually opening any files. If the kernel acts on this information and prefetches the data, the computation can be sped up significantly.

tend to go awry when an application's attempts at fetch-ahead conflict with the file cache's buffer-management policy. A problem is that buffer management in file caches requires temporal considerations that one can usually ignore in processor caches. Replacement and fetching can conflict because the act of fetching a block takes many cycles to complete and renders the target buffer invalid during (almost[8]) the entire operation. Cao explains:

The main complication is that prefetching file blocks into a cache can be harmful even if the blocks will be accessed in the near future. This is because a cache block needs to be reserved

for the block being prefetched at the time the prefetch is initiated. The reservation of a cache block requires performing a cache-block replacement earlier than it would otherwise have been done. [Cao et al. 1995, p. 188]

Due to the peculiarities of file caching, the prefetch strategy and block-replacement strategy can have significant deleterious interactions, even for relatively simple scenarios (see Figure 3.39). The figure shows that, for the request sequence ABCA and a two-block cache, a prefetching scenario with MIN block replacement (Belady's oracle [Belady 1966]) actually does worse than a non-prefetching scenario (also

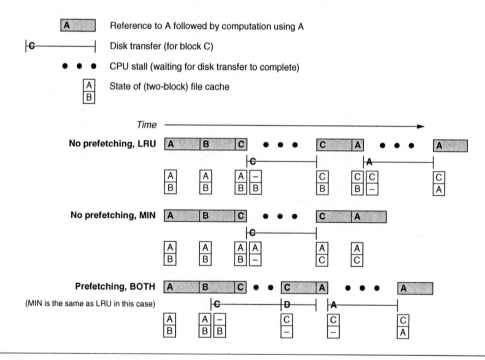

FIGURE 3.39: Problematic behavior in file caches not seen in processor caches. Shown are four instances of {no,yes} prefetching and {LRU,MIN} block-replacement heuristics, given the reference stream ABCA. Because a cache block must be reserved at the time a prefetch is initiated, that block is taken out of circulation for a significant length of time. This effectively causes a block replacement to occur earlier than otherwise, in this case causing block A to be replaced when C is fetched for both LRU and MIN policies, because block B is still in use.

---

[8]An obvious optimization is to have a separate status bit to distinguish replaced buffers that have not yet been overwritten by any data from the block-in-transit; e.g., a replaced block would still be valid for a period of time after the replacement decision equal to the seek time of the disk.

using MIN). The difference is not due to the prefetching heuristic fetching useless data (e.g., the regular prefetching heuristic fetches block D as soon as block C is referenced), as the process would take the same length of time were the prefetch to D removed and block B retained in the cache.

It is likely that more important work will be seen in this area, as it is clearly not a completely solved problem. As mentioned earlier, nearly all caches (both file caches and processor caches) suffer from a lack of synergy between these two components; prefetch mechanisms are typically geared for sequential access, while the most common replacement policy (LRU) is geared for non-sequential access.

3.3.3 Combined Approaches to Optimizing Locality

There are several ways to address locality optimization in a combined hardware/software approach. One is to statically compress program code and data and decompress it dynamically at run time (cf. Subsection "Dynamic Compression of Instructions and Data," in Section 3.1.3). For instance, Wolfe and Chanin [1992] compress programs to reduce memory storage needs; the programs are then decompressed by the hardware when fetching lines into the cache—the cache holds decompressed code and data, thereby requiring no changes to the processor core [Wolfe & Chanin 1992]. To improve the storage capacity of the cache in addition to main memory, Lefurgy provides a hardware mechanism whereby compressed programs can reside in the cache in compressed form [Lefurgy et al. 1997].

Another combined hardware/software approach to locality optimization is the use of profiling to direct otherwise static heuristics, an approach in which the compiler exploits both its own understanding of program structure as well as the results of application profiling (i.e., its understanding of program run-time behavior). This section describes several examples of this second approach.

Hatfield and Gerald's Program Restructuring

A 1967 study by Comeau underlines the importance of optimal page layout: by simply changing the ordering of program pages, the author demonstrates a fivefold decrease in page faults and resulting memory traffic [Comeau 1967]. Layouts investigated, from worst performing to best performing, include *alphabetic* (data is arranged in the executable image in order of the names of the program variables), 6500 page faults, i.e., cache misses; *random*, 4200 page faults; *aligned* (programmer directed, based on knowledge of the code structure), 2400 page faults; and *JAS* (programmer directed,[9] based on knowledge of the code structure and the run-time paging behavior of the *aligned* workload), 1200 page faults. In short, random placement of code and data does better than arbitrary placement (alphabetic); grouping related modules together does better than random placement; and grouping related modules using the results of profiling does the best.

Hatfield and Gerald [1971] address the two important issues demonstrated by Comeau's study. They investigate a mechanism for *automatic page layout* that is directed by *application profiling*. They note the potential weakness of their approach—that profiling may or may not generate a code layout appropriate for all data inputs[10]—but, given today's historical perspective, this potential is not realized, as Babonneau's later study (as well as others) answers the question [Babonneau et al. 1977].

Hatfield and Gerald group related modules using the results of application profiling. Analyzing the program at the level of what is essentially basic blocks ("sectors"), they extend the concept of the Boolean

---

[9]"JAS" are the initials of the programmer who structured the page layout.

[10]The authors are very conservative in their claims. They note this potential weakness even though their own results suggest an experimental validation of their approach (this is noted by others, e.g., "a high degree of input-data independence in all the programs they have examined" [Ferrari 1973 in reference to Hatfield and Gerald]).

connectivity matrix [Ramamoorthy 1966] to construct a *nearness matrix C*, in which element C_{ij} is incremented whenever there is a transfer of control from sector *i* to sector *j* or a use of data in sector *j* by code in sector *i*. A reordering of the program's code sectors produces a reordering of the rows and columns of the matrix; the authors note that the "best" code sector orderings produce clusterings of large values around the diagonals of their matrices. Figure 3.40 illustrates an example program (call graph weights taken from Figure 3.31(a)), two different page layouts, and the corresponding nearness matrices.

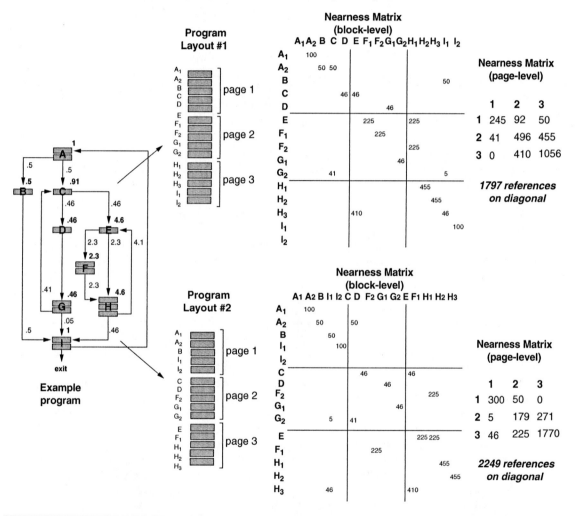

FIGURE 3.40: Example page layouts and the corresponding nearness matrices. The program from earlier examples is given two potential layouts, where the program has 15 code blocks and the page size is 5 blocks (see Figures 3.30 and 3.31). The graph weights represent expected executions per outer loop iteration; the nearness matrices assume 100 iterations of the outer loop. Each layout generates a different nearness matrix. Hatfield and Gerald's nearness matrix is page granularity; we show a block-granularity matrix as well to illustrate how the matrix corresponds to the inter-block behavior. Note that a graphical representation of these program layouts (grouping of blocks onto pages) is shown in Figure 3.42.

This produces a non-trivial optimization problem. Consider a simple case in which all sectors are the same size and equal to half the page size: two code sectors can fit on each page. The number of page faults (i.e., cache misses, were one to translate the analysis to processor caches) would be given by the following sum:

$$\sum_{i,j=1}^{m} C_{ij}P_{ij} \qquad \text{(EQ 3.3)}$$

where m is the number of sectors in the program and is thus the matrix dimension, C_{ij} is an element in the nearness matrix, and P_{ij} is the probability that sectors i and j are in memory (i.e., the cache) at the same time. When sectors i and j are chosen to reside in the same page, P_{ij} is 1; otherwise, P_{ij} depends on the state of the memory system (what pages are currently held in memory). The optimization problem is to choose a pairing of code sectors into pages that minimizes the sum.

Note that the solution to even this simple scenario is not easily determined, because the state of the memory system at any given moment is a data-dependent value, and few non-trivial programs have data dependencies that are fully analyzable at compile time. Given this, Hatfield and Gerald choose the simpler optimization problem, which maximizes the sum

$$\sum_{i,j \in \alpha} C_{ij} \qquad \text{(EQ 3.4)}$$

where the notation $i, j \in \alpha$ indicates that code sectors i and j are resident in the same page; the summation is over all pages, and the optimization chooses a page layout that maximizes the number of intra-page code transitions. The two different matrices in Figure 3.40 correspond to two different page layouts, yielding the summations given below each matrix.

The authors wrestle with the concept of time, noting that the nearness matrix does not really adequately represent a program's "local nearness requirements," i.e., the fact that a program's working set [Denning 1967] changes over time. Note that a program generating 1000 transfers of control from sector i to sector j at the beginning of program execution will produce

the same nearness matrix as (and will thus be indistinguishable from) a program generating those same 1000 transfers of control but distributing them evenly over the full course of program execution. The simpler optimization problem (which aims to maximize inter-page transfers of control) is only optimal in the absence of dynamic replacement; it produces a static packing that is optimal if pages are not moved in and out of main memory dynamically. Despite this limitation in the heuristic, it provides a reasonable approximation, and Hatfield and Gerald are able to report performance results that equal or better the results of a hand-optimized layout.

Interlude: The Importance of Considering Time

Ferrari points out a weakness of using an imperfect representation of time in Hatfield and Gerald's approach [1974]. Take, for example, the scenario described in the previous paragraph, in which program execution trace S_1 exhibits 1000 transfers of control from sector i to sector j at the beginning of program execution and program execution trace S_2 exhibits 1000 transfers of control from sector i to sector j distributed evenly over the full course of program execution. The value of C_{ij} is the same for both matrices: equal to 1000. The value of C_{ji} could be zero for both matrices, or it could be non-zero for S_1 if control ever passes back to node i from node j immediately (e.g., $ij\ ij\ ij$ versus $ij\ a\ ij\ b\ ij\ ...$). In any case, the probability that Hatfield and Gerald's clustering algorithm will put nodes i and j on the same page is either the same for the two traces or higher for trace S_1. However, the cost of failing to cluster the two sectors onto the same page is higher for trace S_2 than S_1, since the number of page faults due to references to j immediately following i will be, at most, 1 in trace S_1 (for a reasonable-sized cache), but it could be as high as 1000 in trace S_2. This is illustrated in Figure 3.41. When references are clustered in time, a single cache miss fetches the needed page, which remains in the cache during the execution of the code blocks. When the references are not clustered in time, the application may experience a cache miss for every sector reference.

Trace S$_1$: i j aaa i j aab i j aac i j aad i j aad i j … i j zzy i j zzz a b c d e b c e a f…

All references to i and j are at beginning of program execution,
and each is separated from the next by few unique items … next reference will likely hit in cache

Trace S$_2$: i j a b c d … i j x y z a … i j a a b z … i j x w d a … i j d b o f … i j z w…

References to i and j are spread evenly across entire program execution,
each separated from the next by many unique items … each reference is likely to miss in cache

Cache Behavior *(in terms of miss/hit references to i and j only)*

S_1	**i, j co-located:**	$M_i H_j H_i H_j H_i H_j H_i H_j H_i H_j … H_i H_j$	*(~100% hit rate)*
	i, j separate pages:	$M_i M_j H_i H_j H_i H_j H_i H_j H_i H_j … H_i H_j$	*(~100% hit rate)*
S_2	**i, j co-located:**	$M_i H_j M_i H_j M_i H_j M_i H_j M_i H_j … M_i H_j$	*(50% hit rate)*
	i, j separate pages:	$M_i M_j M_i M_j M_i M_j M_i M_j M_i M_j … M_i M_j$	*(0% hit rate)*

FIGURE 3.41: The passage of time and temporal locality.

In other words, in places where a program's structure exhibits good temporal locality, it is less important for the compiler to ensure good spatial locality for the corresponding code and data because this will naturally be provided by a typical cache. Conversely, in places where the application does *not* naturally display good temporal locality, it can become *critical* for the compiler to make up for this by ensuring good spatial locality.

The bottom line is that the passage of time is the essence of temporal locality. Therefore, an algorithm that fails to capture adequately the passage of time will be at a loss to analyze an application's temporal locality.

Ferrari's Critical Working Sets

Ferrari's analysis edges closer to capturing time-variant program behavior by dividing program execution into periods where the full working set is resident in memory and keeping track of the transitions between those periods. He defines a *critical working set* as the set of pages immediately preceding a page fault [1973]. A request to a new page that is non-resident in memory (and whose last reference lies outside the time-window defined by the working-set parameters) causes a transition from one working set to another. By maintaining a sequence of page addresses that cause these transitions (the pages are called *critical references*), Ferrari is able to track the behavior of the program over time. Using the two page layouts from Figure 3.40, this is illustrated in Figure 3.42.

Ferrari notes that, given a memory system managed under the working-set policy, the number of page faults can be no larger than the number of critical working sets; he concludes that a program (re-) structuring algorithm should focus on minimizing these [Ferrari 1974]. His algorithm maximizes the critical working sets that, due to the choice of block clustering, cause block faults but not page faults, i.e., instances in which a code or data block that would have otherwise caused a page fault is prefetched along with another block on the same page.

The algorithm constructs a *CWS matrix* based on the string of block references (a "block" is equivalent to Hatfield and Gerald's sector). The ij^{th} element in the matrix, C_{ij}, is the number of critical working sets that have block i as their critical reference and also contain block j. Thus, the sum

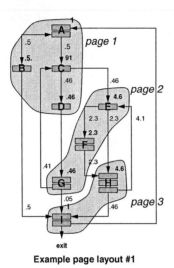
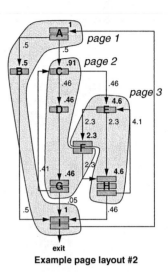

Example page layout #1   Example page layout #2

Macroblock:
$$A \; B \; I \; A \; C \; D \; G \; (C \; D \; G)^8 \; C \; E \; F_{1,2} \; H \; E \; H \; (E \; F_{1,2} \; H)^3 \; (E \; H)^2 E \; F_{1,2} \; H \; I \; A \; B \; I \; ...$$

Page-Level 1:
(5 page faults)
$$\underline{1} \; 1 \; \underline{3} \; 1 \; 1 \; 1 \; \underline{2} \; (1 \; 1 \; 2)^8 \; 1 \; 2 \; 2,2 \; \underline{3} \; 2 \; 3 \; (2 \; 2,2 \; 3)^3 \; (2 \; 3)^2 \; 2 \; 2,2 \; 3 \; 3 \; \underline{1} \; 1 \; 3 \; ...$$

Page-Level 2:
(4 page faults)
$$\underline{1} \; 1 \; 1 \; 1 \; \underline{2} \; 2 \; 2 \; (2 \; 2 \; 2)^8 \; 2 \; \underline{3} \; 3,2 \; 3 \; 3 \; 3 \; (3 \; 3,2 \; 3)^3 \; (3 \; 3)^2 \; 3 \; \underline{3},2 \; 3 \; \underline{1} \; 1 \; 1 \; 1 \; ...$$

FIGURE 3.42: Ferrari's CWS analysis of critical references. Two different page layouts from a previous example are compared in terms of critical references. An example reference stream is given ("macroblock" trace), and each page layout generates a different run-time behavior, because the blocks are in different pages. References that cause page faults in a cache of two pages (the program is three pages in size) are shown in bold and underlined. The example assumes cold cache (first two references miss) and a perfect replacement policy. Superscripts indicate repeated substrings (i.e., loop behavior). Note that references to macroblock F are split into two because in layout #2 it is spread out over two pages (2 and 3).

$C_{ij} + C_{ji}$ is the number of critical working sets that become non-critical working sets if blocks i and j are mapped to the same page. Figure 3.43 shows, for the block-level stream in Figure 3.42, two matrices corresponding to two different working-set window sizes.

There is an obvious trade-off inherent in scaling the window size: as window size increases, the absolute number of critical references decreases dramatically, allowing one to isolate the most important references. However, the algorithm necessarily spreads that information out over a larger number of matrix

entries. The increase in window size yields more i,jth entries incremented per critical reference.

Ferrari shows that the algorithm produces an optimal page clustering if there are no more than two blocks per page. This is good news if the algorithm is used to cluster basic blocks (on the order of 24 bytes) into cache blocks (typically 32 or 64 bytes, or 128 bytes for last-level caches); the news is not as good when clustering basic blocks into modern-size virtual pages (4 KB or larger). Ferrari also shows [1976] that his algorithm tends to do better than others as the cache size increases.

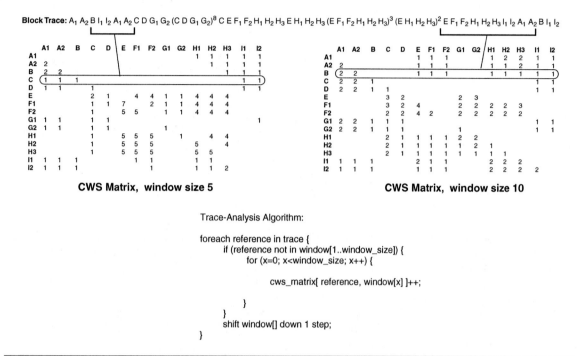

Block Trace: $A_1\,A_2\,B\,I_1\,I_2\,A_1\,A_2\,C\,D\,G_1\,G_2\,(C\,D\,G_1\,G_2)^8\,C\,E\,F_1\,F_2\,H_1\,H_2\,H_3\,E\,H_1\,H_2\,H_3\,(E\,F_1\,F_2\,H_1\,H_2\,H_3)^3\,(E\,H_1\,H_2\,H_3)^2\,E\,F_1\,F_2\,H_1\,H_2\,H_3\,I_1\,I_2\,A_1\,A_2\,B\,I_1\,I_2$

CWS Matrix, window size 5   **CWS Matrix, window size 10**

Trace-Analysis Algorithm:

```
foreach reference in trace {
    if (reference not in window[1..window_size]) {
        for (x=0; x<window_size; x++) {

            cws_matrix[ reference, window[x] ]++;

        }
    }
    shift window[] down 1 step;
}
```

FIGURE 3.43: Ferrari's CWS algorithm. The CWS algorithm steps through the address trace, maintaining a working-set window (FIFO) of most recently referenced items. If the next reference is not in the window, it is a critical reference, and the algorithm increments the count of the i,j[th] entries in the matrix, where i is the critical reference in question, and j ranges over every item in the current window. The two window sizes (5 and 10) are shown on the trace, with each indicating a critical reference and the elements in the matrix that are affected.

McFarling's Instruction Cache Optimization

McFarling's instruction cache optimization is one of the earlier studies that extends into the domain of caches the work done by others in page layout for virtual memory systems [McFarling 1989]. He works with a direct-mapped cache, as it provides an easier target for analysis, and his mechanism (re)structures compiled object files to achieve two goals: (i) the most often used segments of code are more likely to remain in the instruction cache (i.e., they are less likely to conflict with other, less often used segments), and (ii) code segments accessed nearby in time map to different cache sets.

To represent dynamic behavior (locality information), the algorithm uses a profiled object file: an object file with an accompanying profile file that contains execution counts for code blocks in the object

file. The stated advantages of working with object files include the following:

1. The mechanism is independent of any programming language (and the object file can represent a compilation from multiple languages and compilers).

2. The mechanism performs whole-program optimization, which is necessary given that code blocks related in both time and function can lie in modules in separate files compiled separately and can end up some distance from each other in the program.

3. The sizes of all basic blocks are known exactly, simplifying the analysis (note that the accompanying profile file contains execution counts for the basic blocks).

The advantages of working with block-execution counts as profile information are the relative ease of gathering profile data, simplicity of profile representation, and corresponding simplicity of the optimization algorithm. The disadvantage of working with execution counts is that, like much of the earlier work in the area, the mechanism fails to represent the passage of time (see Figure 3.44). McFarling admits the limitation and addresses it by overdesign: the algorithm conservatively interprets the execution counts as worst case, which, for the example in Figure 3.44, would result in optimizing the program layout assuming something similar to the last trace, which represents the least amount of temporal locality and the greatest potential for cache conflicts.

The algorithm begins with a routine *Label Structure* (pseudo-code given in Figure 3.45) that takes as input a weighted graph of code blocks indicating what instructions belong to what program structures. Among other things, the routine pares down code blocks that are too large to fit into the cache. For example, the algorithm will ignore (i.e., choose not to label) the least-frequently executed instructions

within a loop structure that exceeds the size of the cache.

Reconstructing the control-flow graph enables the distinction between those program subsets that are related (executed in the same region of time) from those program subsets that are unrelated. Related blocks must be positioned in the cache so that they do not conflict; unrelated blocks may be given conflicting addresses in the cache without fear of cache-thrashing. This is illustrated in Figure 3.46.

Hwu and Chang's Optimizing Compiler

Hwu and Chang [1989] integrate into the IMPACT compiler the same sort of instruction cache optimization that McFarling performs on object code. Their algorithm uses both a weighted call graph and weighted control graphs to represent the effects of time (i.e., the locality of the program). The steps of their algorithm are discussed below.

1. **Profiling.** The program is represented by a weighted call graph, with the weights

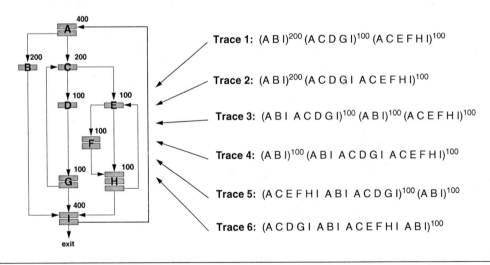

Trace 1: $(A\ B\ I)^{200}\ (A\ C\ D\ G\ I)^{100}\ (A\ C\ E\ F\ H\ I)^{100}$

Trace 2: $(A\ B\ I)^{200}\ (A\ C\ D\ G\ I\ \ A\ C\ E\ F\ H\ I)^{100}$

Trace 3: $(A\ B\ I\ \ A\ C\ D\ G\ I)^{100}\ (A\ B\ I)^{100}\ (A\ C\ E\ F\ H\ I)^{100}$

Trace 4: $(A\ B\ I)^{100}\ (A\ B\ I\ \ A\ C\ D\ G\ I\ \ A\ C\ E\ F\ H\ I)^{100}$

Trace 5: $(A\ C\ E\ F\ H\ I\ \ A\ B\ I\ \ A\ C\ D\ G\ I)^{100}\ (A\ B\ I)^{100}$

Trace 6: $(A\ C\ D\ G\ I\ \ A\ B\ I\ \ A\ C\ E\ F\ H\ I\ \ A\ B\ I)^{100}$

FIGURE 3.44: Basic-block execution count versus the passage of time. The use of simple block-execution counts can obscure temporal information, e.g., all of the traces on the right would produce the same block counts (graph on left).

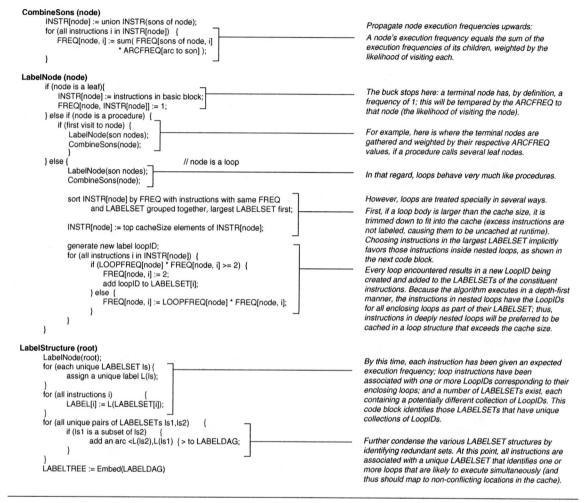

CombineSons (node)
```
    INSTR[node] := union INSTR(sons of node);
    for (all instructions i in INSTR[node])  {
        FREQ[node, i] := sum( FREQ[sons of node, i]
                            * ARCFREQ[arc to son] );
    }
```
Propagate node execution frequencies upwards:
A node's execution frequency equals the sum of the execution frequencies of its children, weighted by the likelihood of visiting each.

LabelNode (node)
```
    if (node is a leaf){
        INSTR[node] := instructions in basic block;
        FREQ[node, INSTR[node]] := 1;
    } else if (node is a procedure)  {
        if (first visit to node)  {
            LabelNode(son nodes);
            CombineSons(node);
        }
    } else {                          // node is a loop
        LabelNode(son nodes);
        CombineSons(node);

        sort INSTR[node] by FREQ with instructions with same FREQ
            and LABELSET grouped together, largest LABELSET first;

        INSTR[node] := top cacheSize elements of INSTR[node];

        generate new label loopID;
        for (all instructions i in INSTR[node])  {
            if (LOOPFREQ[node] * FREQ[node, i] >= 2)  {
                FREQ[node, i] := 2;
                add loopID to LABELSET[i];
            } else {
                FREQ[node, i] := LOOPFREQ[node] * FREQ[node, i];
            }
        }
    }
```
The buck stops here: a terminal node has, by definition, a frequency of 1; this will be tempered by the ARCFREQ to that node (the likelihood of visiting the node).

For example, here is where the terminal nodes are gathered and weighted by their respective ARCFREQ values, if a procedure calls several leaf nodes.

In that regard, loops behave very much like procedures.

However, loops are treated specially in several ways.
First, if a loop body is larger than the cache size, it is trimmed down to fit into the cache (excess instructions are not labeled, causing them to be uncached at runtime). Choosing instructions in the largest LABELSET implicitly favors those instructions inside nested loops, as shown in the next code block.
Every loop encountered results in a new LoopID being created and added to the LABELSETs of the constituent instructions. Because the algorithm executes in a depth-first manner, the instructions in nested loops have the LoopIDs for all enclosing loops as part of their LABELSET; thus, instructions in deeply nested loops will be preferred to be cached in a loop structure that exceeds the cache size.

LabelStructure (root)
```
    LabelNode(root);
    for (each unique LABELSET ls) {
        assign a unique label L(ls);
    }
    for (all instructions i)          {
        LABEL[i] := L(LABELSET[i]);
    }
    for (all unique pairs of LABELSETs ls1,ls2)     {
        if (ls1 is a subset of ls2)     {
            add an arc <L(ls2),L(ls1) { > to LABELDAG;
        }
    }
    LABELTREE := Embed(LABELDAG)
```
By this time, each instruction has been given an expected execution frequency; loop instructions have been associated with one or more LoopIDs corresponding to their enclosing loops; and a number of LABELSETs exist, each containing a potentially different collection of LoopIDs. This code block identifies those LABELSETs that have unique collections of LoopIDs.

Further condense the various LABELSET structures by identifying redundant sets. At this point, all instructions are associated with a unique LABELSET that identifies one or more loops that are likely to execute simultaneously (and thus should map to non-conflicting locations in the cache).

FIGURE 3.45: Pseudo-code for McFarling's LabelStructure.

being expected execution counts obtained from profiling (e.g., the execution counts in Figure 3.47(a), the same as shown in earlier examples). The nodes in the call graph represent functions, each of which has a corresponding weighted *control graph* that represents the basic blocks that make up the function (e.g., the example in Figure 3.47(b), which uses the same

general form as earlier but interpreted as a control graph). The control graph also uses expected execution counts as the node weights.

2. **Function in-line expansion.** The compiler increases the degree of spatial locality exhibited in the program by in-lining small functions when and where they are called frequently. Though this increases the

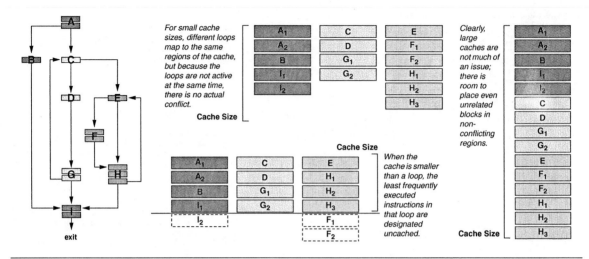

FIGURE 3.46: Cache layouts resulting from a program graph. Assume that blocks in graph correspond to cache block-size chunks of data. Related blocks should be mapped to non-conflicting regions of the cache. Unrelated blocks can map to conflicting blocks without fear of undue overhead at run time.

program's total memory footprint, it also has the stated potential to reduce cache conflicts between interacting functions by reducing the number of function invocations.

3. **Trace selection.** Like Josh Fisher's work [1981], the IMPACT compiler selects for sequential grouping in the cache those paths through the program (i.e., its control-flow graph) that are executed more heavily than others. The algorithm begins with the most often executed node within a block and greedily builds traces from the node's best successor, only looking to predecessor nodes once a deadend is reached. Figure 3.48 shows the pseudo-code. Hwu and Chang explore trace selection according to node weight and/or arc weight (i.e., they look at different implementations of the *best_successor_of()* and *best_predecessor_of()* functions). They also note that, should there be no obvious dominating arc out of a node, the performance gains by grouping the node with another could be overshadowed by those run-time instances in which the path is *not* taken and instead control flows to some other block

[Chang & Hwu 1988]. To illustrate the behavior of the algorithm in Figure 3.48, Figure 3.49 shows three different sets of traces for the control graph of Figure 3.49(b), where each is produced by a different trace-selection heuristic. Figure 3.49(a) shows traces generated by selection based on node weight; Figure 3.49(b) shows traces generated by selection based on arc weight; and Figure 3.49(c) shows traces generated by selection based on arc weight with termination if the most likely arc only has 50% probability or less.

4. **Function layout.** Starting with the function's entrance code and progressing outward, the compiler places in sequential order the chosen traces through the function. The selection algorithm is greedy (depth first). It first chooses from the traces whose headers are linked to the tail of the current trace, choosing the trace with the highest execution count. If there are no traces linked from the tail of the current trace, the algorithm selects the trace with the highest execution count and progresses from there. By design, the algorithm places

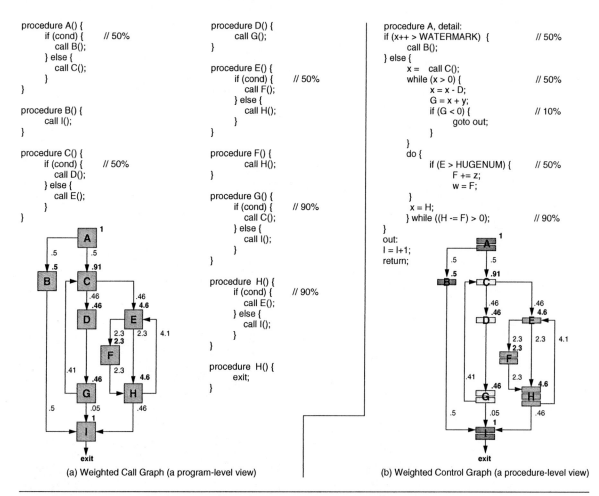

```
procedure A() {
    if (cond) {      // 50%
        call B();
    } else {
        call C();
    }
}

procedure B() {
    call I();
}

procedure C() {
    if (cond) {      // 50%
        call D();
    } else {
        call E();
    }
}
```

```
procedure D() {
    call G();
}

procedure E() {
    if (cond) {      // 50%
        call F();
    } else {
        call H();
    }
}

procedure F() {
    call H();
}

procedure G() {
    if (cond) {      // 90%
        call C();
    } else {
        call I();
    }
}

procedure H() {
    if (cond) {      // 90%
        call E();
    } else {
        call I();
    }
}

procedure H() {
    exit;
}
```

```
procedure A, detail:
if (x++ > WATERMARK) {        // 50%
    call B();
} else {
    x =   call C();
    while (x > 0) {           // 50%
        x = x - D;
        G = x + y;
        if (G < 0) {          // 10%
            goto out;
        }
    }
    do {
        if (E > HUGENUM) {    // 50%
            F += z;
            w = F;
        }
        x = H;
    } while ((H -= F) > 0);   // 90%
}
out:
I = I+1;
return;
```

(a) Weighted Call Graph (a program-level view)   (b) Weighted Control Graph (a procedure-level view)

FIGURE 3.47: Contrasting the weighted call graph and weighted control graph. Each block in the weighted call graph on the left represents a procedure; each block in the weighted control graph on the right represents a group of one or more instructions within a procedure. Boldface numbers at the top right of blocks indicate the expected number of executions per trip through the graph, assuming the entry point is block A. Non-boldface numbers represent the expected number of times the corresponding link is traversed. For example, in the call graph on the left, A is equivalent to main(), and the numbers represent the expected number of invocations per run of the program. In the control graph on the right, the graph represents a detailed view of one procedure (e.g., procedure A()), and the numbers also represent the expected block-execution counts per execution of the program. Branch probabilities (as profiled) are shown in the pseudo-code.

traces with a profiled zero execution count at the end of the function. In a sense, this is very similar to using heuristic #1 in Figure 3.49(a), but at the trace level (building up a function) rather than the block level

(building up traces). Figure 3.50 illustrates three different function layouts for the traces identified by the three heuristics in Figure 3.49. Note that additional instructions and numerous instances of

```
mark all nodes unvisited;
while (there are unvisited nodes){

        // select a seed
        seed = the node with the largest execution count among unvisited nodes;
        mark seed visited;

        // grow the trace forward
        current = seed;
        loop   {
                s = best_successor_of(current);
                if (s == NULL) exit loop;
                add s to the trace;
                mark s visited;
                current = s;
        }

        // grow the trace backward
        current = seed;
        loop   {
                s = best_predecessor_of(current);
                if (s == NULL) exit loop;
                add s to the trace;
                mark s visited;
                current = s;
        }

        perform trace compaction & bookkeeping;

}
```

FIGURE 3.48: Pseudo-code for trace selection. Adapted by Chang and Hwu [1988] from Ellis [1985]. Though it is not explicitly shown in the pseudo-code, the algorithm prohibits the crossing of loop back edges to ensure that loop headers become leading nodes in traces.

non-sequential control flow are not necessarily indicative of a bad function layout (e.g., the middle layout looks like it could be the "best" layout from that perspective). If the layout is correctly optimized for the most frequently executed sequential trace, then the other inefficiencies matter little.

5. **Global layout**. This step places into the same or adjacent virtual pages functions that are executed close in time. Using the weighted call graph, which represents the entire program, the functions are laid out in a manner similar in spirit to the function-layout algorithm described above and illustrated in Figure 3.50.

Hwu and Chang show that their algorithm can increase cache efficiency to the point that a direct-mapped instruction cache executing optimized code behaves much like a fully associative cache executing non-optimized code.

Pettis and Hansen's Profile-Guided Positioning

Pettis and Hansen [1990] take an approach similar to that of Hwu and Chang to represent locality and the passage of time. Their algorithm makes use of both weighted control and call graphs. In their 1990 paper, they present a code-positioning algorithm and specifically focus on the selection of blocks to aggregate with others. Like Hwu and Chang [1989], part of their optimization heuristic

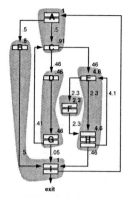

Trace 1 *(seed node = E @ 4.6)*
Forward growth: E –> H1 –> H2 –> H3 –> *(back-edge to E)*
Backward growth: E –> *(back-edge to H3)*
Result: E –> H1 –> H2 –> H3

Trace 2 *(seed node = F1 @ 2.3)*
Forward growth: F1 –> F2 –> *(already visited H1)*
Backward growth: F1 –> *(already visited E)*
Result: F1 –> F2

Trace 3 *(seed node = A1 @ 1)*
Forward growth: A1 –> A2 –> C –> *(already visited E)*
Backward growth: A1 –> *(back-edge to I2)*
Result: A1 –> A2 –> C

Trace 4 *(seed node = I1 @ 1)*
Forward growth: I1 –> I2 –> *(back-edge to A1)*
Backward growth: I1 –> B –> *(already visited A2)*
Result: B –> I1 –> I2

Trace 5 *(seed node = D @ 0.46)*
Forward growth: D –> G1 –> G2 –> *(already visited I1)*
Backward growth: D –> *(already visited C)*
Result: D –> G1 –> G2

(a) heuristic #1 selects greatest node weight

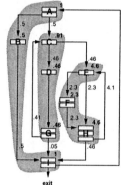

Trace 1 *(seed node = E @ 4.6)*
Forward growth: E –> F1 –> F2 –> H1 –> H2 –> H3 –> *(back-edge to E)*
Backward growth: E –> *(back-edge to H3)*
Result: E –> F1 –> F2 –> H1 –> H2 –> H3

Trace 2 *(seed node = A1 @ 1)*
Forward growth: A_1 –> A_2 –> B –> I_1 –> I_2 –> *(back-edge to A_1)*
Backward growth: A_1 –> *(back-edge to I_2)*
Result: A_1 –> A_2 –> B –> I_1 –> I_2

Trace 3 *(seed node = C @ 0.91)*
Forward growth: C –> D –> G_1 –> G_2 –> *(back-edge to C)*
Backward growth: C –> *(A_2 already visited & out of nodes)*
Result: C –> D –> G_1 –> G_2

(b) heuristic #2 selects greatest arc weight

Trace 1 *(seed node = E @ 4.6)*
Forward growth: E –> *(no dominant edge: all edges 50%)*
Backward growth: E –> *(back-edge to H_3; edge from C only 10%)*
Result: E

Trace 2 *(seed node = H_1 @ 4.6)*
Forward growth: H_1 –> H_2 –> H_3 –> *(back-edge to E; no dominant edge: edge to I_1 = 10%)*
Backward growth: H_1 –> *(no dominant edge: all edges 50%)*
Result: H_1 –> H_2 –> H_3

Trace 3 *(seed node = F_1 @ 2.3)*
Forward growth: F_1 –> F_2 –> *(already visited H_1)*
Backward growth: F_1 –> *(already visited E; edge also only 50%)*
Result: F_1 –> F_2

Trace 4 *(seed node = A_1 @ 1)*
Forward growth: A_1 –> A_2 –> *(no dominant edge: all edges 50%)*
Backward growth: A_1 –> *(back-edge to I_2)*
Result: A_1 –> A_2

Trace 5 *(seed node = I_1 @ 1)*
Forward growth: I_1 –> I_2 –> *(back-edge to A_1)*
Backward growth: I_1 –> *(no dominant edge: all edges 50%)*
Result: I_1 –> I_2

Trace 6 *(seed node = C @ 0.91)*
Forward growth: C –> *(no dominant edge: all edges 50%)*
Backward growth: C –> *(back-edge to G_2; edge from A_2 only 50%)*
Result: C

Trace 7 *(seed node = B @ 0.5)*
Forward growth: B –> *(already visited I_1)*
Backward growth: B –> *(already visited A_2)*
Result: B

Trace 7 *(seed node = D @ 0.46)*
Forward growth: D –> G_1 –> G_2 –> *(already visited I_1)*
Backward growth: D –> *(already visited C)*
Result: D –> G_1 –> G_2

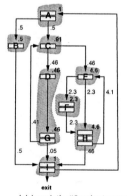

(c) heuristic #3 selects greatest arc weight, provided the arc probability is greater than 50%

FIGURE 3.49: Selection based on node weight versus arc weight. For later work, Chang & Hwu chose heuristic #3 (c).

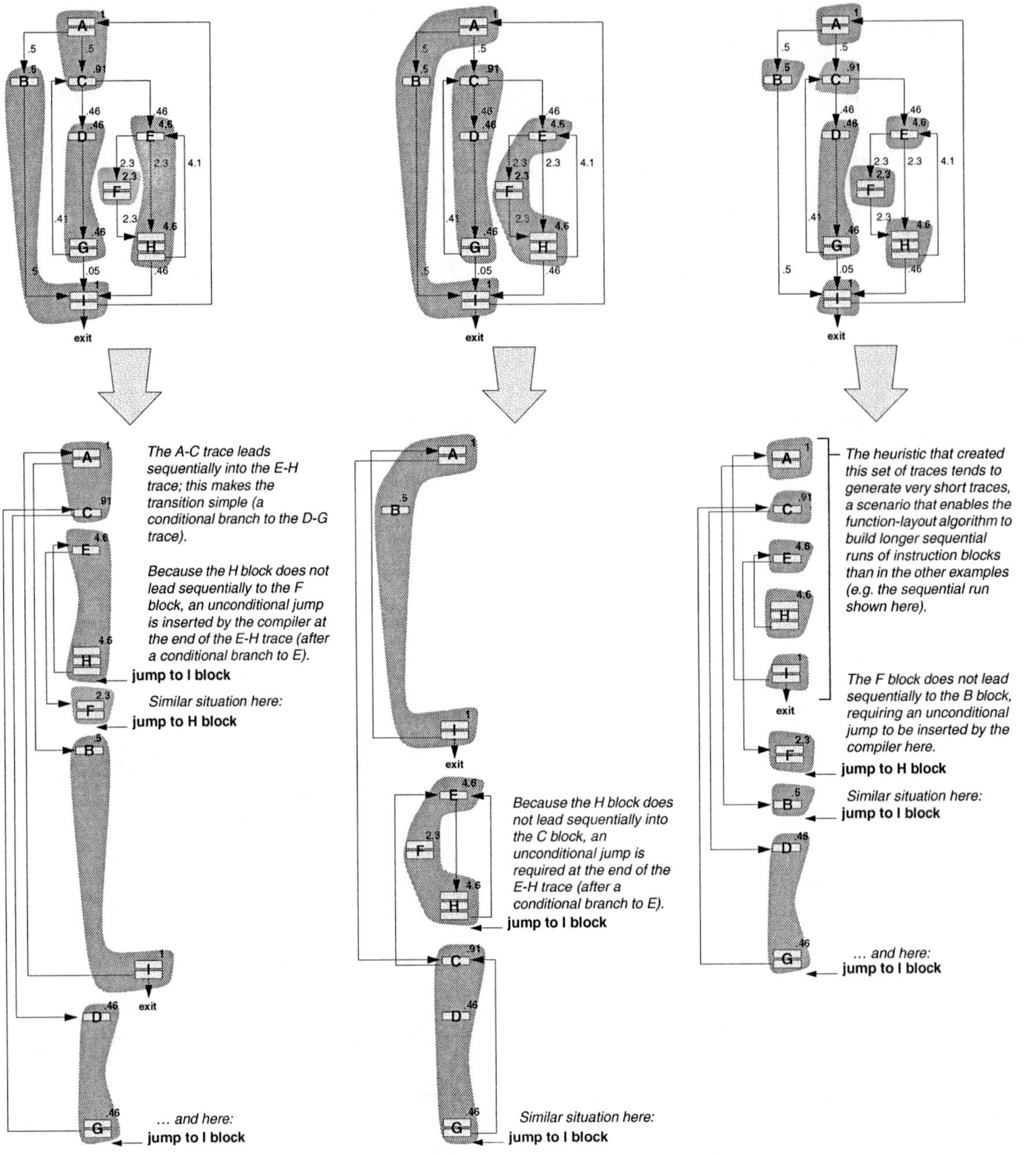

The A-C trace leads sequentially into the E-H trace; this makes the transition simple (a conditional branch to the D-G trace).

Because the H block does not lead sequentially to the F block, an unconditional jump is inserted by the compiler at the end of the E-H trace (after a conditional branch to E).
jump to I block

Similar situation here:
jump to H block

... and here:
jump to I block

Because the H block does not lead sequentially into the C block, an unconditional jump is required at the end of the E-H trace (after a conditional branch to E).
jump to I block

Similar situation here:
jump to I block

The heuristic that created this set of traces tends to generate very short traces, a scenario that enables the function-layout algorithm to build longer sequential runs of instruction blocks than in the other examples (e.g. the sequential run shown here).

The F block does not lead sequentially to the B block, requiring an unconditional jump to be inserted by the compiler here.
jump to H block

Similar situation here:
jump to I block

... and here:
jump to I block

FIGURE 3.50: Layout of functions from previous figure. Arcs for sequential code motion within and between traces are not shown. Arcs represent targets from conditional branches present in the original control graph (blocks A_2, C, E, G_2, H_3, and I_2). Jumps (in boldface) are new instructions not in the original graph, which contained only conditional branches.

resides in the compiler and rearranges procedures at the basic-block level. Like McFarling [1989], they also optimize at the object-code level, allowing the heuristic to rearrange procedures with respect to each other. Like Lowe [1969, 1970] and unlike Hwu and Chang, Pettis and Hansen's algorithm *merges* nodes together as the trace selection progresses, which leads to different behavior.

The heuristic takes the approach of "closest is best"—if procedure A calls procedure B, the heuristic prefers to locate the two procedures near each other in the memory space, thereby potentially reducing paging activity and/or TLB misses. Proximity of related functions also reduces the distance needed to jump between them; this can potentially support less expensive function-call implementations (e.g., single-instruction branches with small immediate values as opposed to the multi-instruction sequences typically required to set up long-distance jumps). The same approach is used for the basic-block-level positioning heuristic. Input to both heuristics is application profile information in the form of node and edge counts. Like Chang and Hwu [1988], Pettis and Hansen find edge counts more effective than node counts in determining the priority of merge ordering (which nodes to merge first).

Figure 3.51 illustrates the act of merging two nodes in a graph; Pettis and Hansen perform node merging at both the procedure level (i.e., merging nodes in the control graph when placing basic blocks relative to one another) and the program level (i.e., merging nodes in the call graph when placing procedures relative to one another). The algorithm uses edge weights, rather than node weights, to determine merge priority. This is like heuristics #2 and #3 in Figure 3.49, but the Pettis and Hansen algorithm begins with the largest edge weight instead of starting at the node with the largest execution weight and choosing as the best successor node the neighbor with the largest edge weight. A few items to note are the following:

- Merging two nodes creates a new node and (for the purposes of choosing the next node to merge) eliminates the previously existing nodes.

- As a result, arc weights change, readjusting merge priorities.
- Unlike Hwu and Chang's algorithm, which looks to the successor nodes of the most recently added node (the *current* node), this algorithm looks to the successor nodes of the newly created node, a potentially larger pool of candidates.
- The algorithm tries to create strings of sequential code; so what appear to be backward branches in the graph may, in fact, end up to be straight-line code.
- The original graph really does not go away with the creation of merged nodes; the arc weights from the original graph determine node ordering within a trace. For example, if node J is to be merged with node DI next in Figure 3.51, the resulting trace would be either JID or DIJ, because the arc between J and I is stronger than the arc between J and D.

Figure 3.52 shows the result of merging the nodes of the running example control graph. Note that several of the traces created have loop headers in the middle (nodes HEF and IAB), which is not allowed by the Chang and Hwu algorithm [1988, p. 23]. In step (e) of the example, the layout of the program in memory represents an ordering chosen by the algorithm to reduce the number of unlikely backward branches. This design choice accommodates many branch predictors that predict forward branches as untaken and backward branches as taken. Therefore, in this example, block IAB has the most incoming arcs (which are low-probability branches), and it is therefore placed at the end of the layout, even though its constituent block A is the entry point of the function. Putting CDG first is equivalent to putting HEF first, in that both choices end up creating one backward branch in the total order; the choice between the two is arbitrary.

Similar to Hwu and Chang's algorithm, the Pettis and Hansen algorithm moves unusual-case code to the periphery, where it stays out of the way. The difference is the degree of effort expended by the compiler to streamline the final layout. An an example

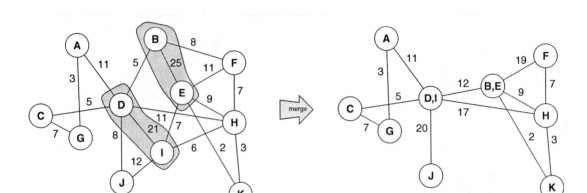

FIGURE 3.51: Merging nodes to form traces. The two largest weights are between D and I (which merge to form node D,I) and between B and E (which merge to form node B,E). Any arcs to the merged nodes are also merged: e.g., node J has arcs to both D and I (of weights 8 and 12, respectively), which after the merger of D and I become a single arc of the combined weight of 20. This serves to readjust merge priorities (by changing/increasing arc weights) and to increase the population of choices for the next node to merge (i.e., after merging I into D, all nodes connecting to both D and I are potential candidates, as opposed to only those nodes connected to I). The merge mechanism applies at both the call graph level and the control graph level.

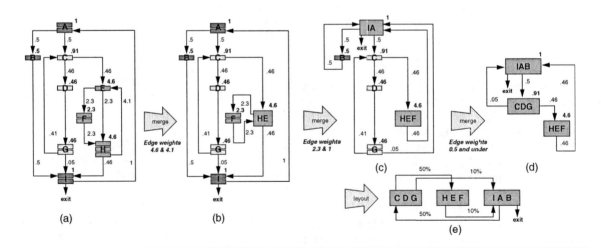

FIGURE 3.52: Pettis and Hansen's algorithm on the running example. The H_i blocks have edges between them with weight 4.6; they are merged first. The next highest edge weight is 4.1 (H->E), whose merger results in the second graph (b). After that, the nodes with edge weights of 2.3 are merged (producing node HEF), followed by those with edge weights of 1 (producing node IA); results are shown in graph (c). Graph (d) shows results after merging nodes with edge weights of 0.5, producing nodes IAB and CDG. The algorithm will not merge both B and C with A because, once either B or C is chosen, A is no longer at the end of the trace. The algorithm arbitrarily chooses one, leaving the other to start its own trace. Graph (e) shows the final total order (i.e., layout in memory), chosen to reduce backward branches that are not likely to be taken.

(also shown in Figure 3.53(a)), simple error-handling code such as the following can cause problems if handled in a naive manner:

```
llist_t *lp, *headp;

if ((lp = (llist_t *)malloc(sizeof(llist_t))) == NULL)
{
    /* perform error-handling code */
}
/* common-case code: use the pointer
(e.g., put it in a list) */
init_and_insert_element(lp, headp);
```

The most straightforward treatment of this code structure creates a conditional (forward) branch around the error-handling block (see Figure 3.53(b)). However, most simple pipelines, e.g., those found in embedded microprocessors, predict forward branches as not taken, while this type of code block will (almost) never be executed. Thus, simple pipelines will always mispredict this type of branch if the layout of this code structure is handled by the compiler in a naive manner.

Pettis and Hansen profile code to identify unused code blocks like this and gather them into a single, unorthodox function that at run time is never used and is therefore never loaded into the memory system. Figure 3.53(c) illustrates the mechanism: the little-used code blocks (called "fluff" by Pettis and Hansen and labeled "error handler" in the figure) are gathered together into a large block with multiple entry points (one for each segment of fluff). Within normal code, conditional branches to these blocks are turned into short-distance forward branches that target entries in a jump table located at the end of the function. The jump table then launches a long-distance jump to the little-used error-handling code in the large block. The mechanism represents high overhead in the case that the error-handling cases are actually used, but the more common cases of errors not occurring are streamlined.

```
llist_t *lp, *headp;

if ((lp = (llist_t *)malloc(sizeof(llist_t))) == NULL) {
        /* perform error-handling code */
}
/* common-case code: use the pointer (e.g., put it in a list) */
init_and_insert_element(lp, headp);
```

(a)

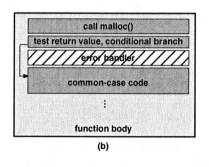

(b)

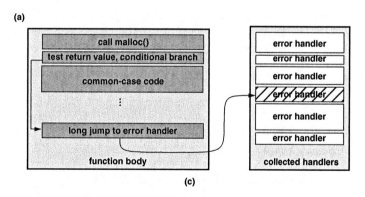

(c)

FIGURE 3.53: Pettis and Hansen's handling of uncommon-case code. (a) shows some example of little-used code. (b) shows the naive layout, which puts the error-handling code immediately after the conditional branch. (c) shows Pettis and Hansen's structure, which creates a jump table at the end of each function and moves the uncommon code blocks into a single lump at the end of the program; the jump tables target the "fluff" at the end of the program, which is rarely, if ever, used and is thus rarely brought into the memory and cache systems.

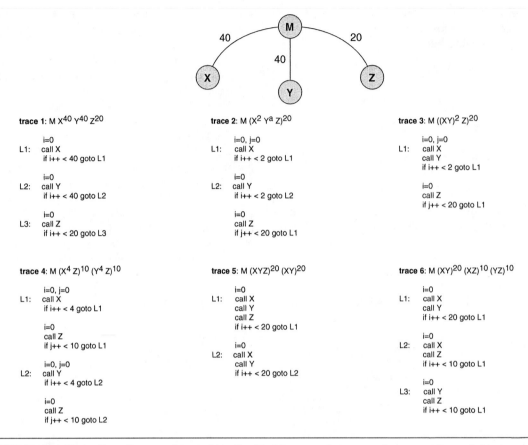

trace 1: M X^{40} Y^{40} Z^{20}

```
        i=0
L1:     call X
        if i++ < 40 goto L1

        i=0
L2:     call Y
        if i++ < 40 goto L2

        i=0
L3:     call Z
        if i++ < 20 goto L3
```

trace 2: M $(X^2 Y^a Z)^{20}$

```
        i=0, j=0
L1:     call X
        if i++ < 2 goto L1

        i=0
L2:     call Y
        if i++ < 2 goto L2

        i=0
        call Z
        if j++ < 20 goto L1
```

trace 3: M $((XY)^2 Z)^{20}$

```
        i=0, j=0
L1:     call X
        call Y
        if i++ < 2 goto L1

        i=0
        call Z
        if j++ < 20 goto L1
```

trace 4: M $(X^4 Z)^{10}$ $(Y^4 Z)^{10}$

```
        i=0, j=0
L1:     call X
        if i++ < 4 goto L1

        i=0
        call Z
        if j++ < 10 goto L1

        i=0, j=0
L2:     call Y
        if i++ < 4 goto L2

        i=0
        call Z
        if j++ < 10 goto L2
```

trace 5: M $(XYZ)^{20}$ $(XY)^{20}$

```
        i=0
L1:     call X
        call Y
        call Z
        if i++ < 20 goto L1

        i=0
L2:     call X
        call Y
        if i++ < 20 goto L2
```

trace 6: M $(XY)^{20}$ $(XZ)^{10}$ $(YZ)^{10}$

```
        i=0
L1:     call X
        call Y
        if i++ < 20 goto L1

        i=0
L2:     call X
        call Z
        if i++ < 10 goto L1

        i=0
L3:     call Y
        call Z
        if i++ < 10 goto L1
```

FIGURE 3.54: Weighted call graphs versus temporal locality. All of the example traces and corresponding code blocks produce the same weighted call graph (top), despite the fact that they display significantly different locality behaviors.

Hwu and Chang's mechanism is similar in that it moves little-used code to the end of functions (because the little-used code blocks will be the last blocks to be chosen by the placement algorithm), but it does not go to the extreme of moving the code into a separate function.

Gloy's Temporal Ordering Information

Since the 1960s, it has been noted that though the weighted call and control graphs identify call/return relationships between blocks of code, they do not give an indication of the timescales exhibited by those relationships. For instance, Figure 3.54 shows several different procedure traces, all of which result in the same weighted call graph.

To represent temporal locality directly, Gloy introduces an extension of the weighted call graph called the *temporal relationship graph* (TRG) [Gloy et al. 1997]. The TRG begins with the procedure-granularity weighted call graph and creates additional weighted edges indicating when two vertices, in this case procedures, are referenced in the manner of an *indirect* call/return within a short window of time. The algorithm passes over an application execution trace, maintaining a sliding window of procedure references and creating temporal edges between

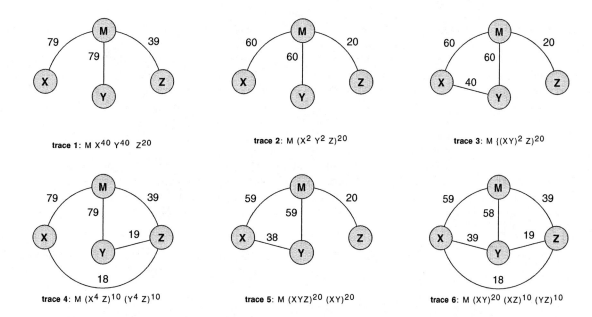

FIGURE 3.55: Temporal relationship graphs for various traces. TRGS are only meaningful in the context of the window size used to produce them. These graphs were produced with a window size of 3 procedure blocks. For instance, the beginning of trace 3 (M X Y X Y Z ...), when one includes the return to M between function calls, becomes M X M Y M X M Y M Z ... and at the time that Z is executed, Z, M, and Y are in the window (in that order).

all procedures executed within the same window.[11] Thus, the resulting edge weights provide a rough estimate of the expected number of cache conflicts that would arise if the two connected vertices were mapped to the same cache set.

The sliding window maintains an LRU-ordered list of the most recently executed procedures, where the total *size* of the procedures in the window is less than or equal to a watermark derived form the targeted cache size (the authors observe that, in practice, a watermark equal to twice the cache size "works quite well"). The algorithm thus embodies the LRU *stack-depth* metric for quantifying temporal locality [Mattson et al. 1970].

Figure 3.55 illustrates the form of Gloy's TRG, compared to the traditional weighted call graph; the same procedure traces as in Figure 3.54 are used, but they are presented in TRG form—each trace is distinct from the other. Note that the examples yield different graphs, but this is not generally true, i.e., it is possible to contrive different procedure traces that would have different cache behavior but similar TRG forms.

Importantly, Gloy notes that, by itself, the addition of this temporal locality information is insufficient to guarantee an improvement in instruction cache performance compared to that of Pettis and Hansen's algorithm. To achieve more consistent improvements, the authors combine the temporal-ordering information

---

[11]For instance, if the current window of procedure invocations is

$$M, X, Y, Z, M,$$

then the algorithm would recognize a call/return from M to (X, Y, Z) and back and would increment (non-directed) graph edges G_{MX}, G_{MY}, and G_{MZ}.

with a relative placement algorithm reminiscent of McFarling's [1989]. Each procedure is divided into 256-byte "chunks," and, while generating the procedure-granularity TRG already described, the algorithm simultaneously generates a *chunk*-granularity TRG. The coarse-grained graph is used to determine the order in which to place procedures relative to each other; the fine-grained graph is used to determine the relative placement. Unlike McFarling, however, Gloy's mechanism does not rearrange code at the basic-block or chunk granularity; a procedure's internal arrangement is taken as given and is not modified. The chunk-to-chunk temporal relationship information determines

the relative placement of procedures only. (See Figure 3.56.) However, there is nothing to prevent a compiler from using the algorithm to determine relative placement of basic blocks, which can be rearranged easily through well-placed branch instructions [McFarling 1989].

Zorn's Lifetime-Conscious Heap Management

The last few mechanisms described (McFarling, Hwu and Chang, Pettis and Hansen, and Gloy et al.) focus on placing instructions in the virtual memory space to achieve good instruction cache behavior.

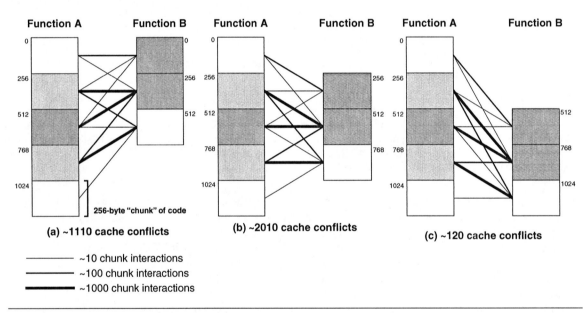

FIGURE 3.56: Using chunk information to place procedures. Two example functions are shown, each of which has an uneven distribution of activity across its 256-byte "chunks". Some chunks of a function will be passed over lightly, while others will see heavy execution (activity is represented by shades of grey). Moreover, each individual chunk can interact differently with another function, compared to the other chunks within the function. The chunk-granularity TRG edge weights are represented by the thickness of lines connecting the various chunks. The legend explains the approximate weights assigned to the three line thicknesses. Gloy's point is that one cannot simply choose either to colocate two functions in the cache or to avoid colocating them; there are numerous possibilities for partial or total overlap at a chunk granularity. Three different cache arrangements are shown, each of which is a complete overlap (all of the chunks of Function B map to the same part of the cache as a chunk in Function A). The alignments are shown by the modulo addresses assigned to each chunk. Note that not all alignments produce the same results: there is an order-of-magnitude difference in the expected number of cache conflicts between the different mappings. This observation gives the compiler much more flexibility in determining an appropriate relative mapping between two functions.

This section and the next focus on placing *data* in the memory space to achieve good *data* cache behavior.

Zorn's work uses profile-obtained lifetime prediction as a heuristic to segregate dynamically allocated objects into different physical regions [Barrett & Zorn 1993, Seidl & Zorn 1998]. While the mechanism reduces the execution overhead of storage allocation and deallocation, its effect on the cache system is ambiguous [Seidl & Zorn 1998]. Later cache-targeted studies use Zorn's profiling methodology for analyzing dynamically allocated objects [Barrett & Zorn 1993], so it is useful to understand what it does and why.

Barret and Zorn build upon earlier work that indicates an advantage to dividing the heap into disjunct regions, each of which aggregates objects of similar lifetimes, i.e., keep long-lived objects together, keep short-lived objects together, and keep the two regions separate. Previous work uses programmer-directed segregation; Barrett and Zorn attempt to automate the process [Barrett & Zorn 1993]. They show that it is possible to use the *allocation site* and *object size* of a dynamically allocated object to predict its lifetime (how long before the object is deallocated). The allocation site is a heuristic meant to approximate a location in a call graph. It is given by the *call chain*, an abstraction of the program's call stack at the time of allocation—an ordered list of functions with any recursive sequence collapsed to a single entry. The combination of allocation site and object size yields a reasonable correlation with expected object lifetime.

Seidl and Zorn evaluate the cache behavior of several heuristics, including one called *stack contents*—a mechanism similar to allocation site, but that does not include object size [Seidl & Zorn 1998]. Among other things, they show that this heuristic successfully identifies little-used and unused objects, and the segregation of objects with different access behavior significantly reduces overheads such as virtual memory paging. However, the mechanism shows variable cache behavior in terms of miss rate; in small caches, the *stack contents* heuristic outperforms all others, but in large caches it tends to do worse than unmodified *vmalloc()*. Note that the heuristic is not designed to improve cache performance. It is designed to classify dynamically allocated objects and thereby reduce

memory-management overhead, both of which it does quite well.

Calder's Cache-Conscious Data Placement

Other work in the area explicitly places data in the memory space aiming to reduce cache conflicts. Besides using Zorn's mechanism, Calder's work [Calder et al. 1998] builds upon Gloy's work [Gloy et al. 1997] in several aspects: Calder's compiler-resident algorithm begins by building a *TRG*, uses a threshold of two times the cache size for the window, and manages data at a 256-byte chunk granularity for the analysis and determination of cache conflicts. Beyond the placement of static data objects (e.g., global variables), Calder changes the various run-time data-allocation routines such as *malloc()* and *calloc()* to provide support for intelligent placement of dynamic data objects. The stack is treated as a single object (i.e., it is the object holding automatic variables) and is optimized in terms of its initial starting address. The heap is optimized more extensively at an object-allocation granularity.

As in Zorn's work, the difficult issue is to analyze and distinguish invocations of the dynamic allocation routines that come from different locations within the call graph and that occur at different times. In addition, to be effective, the mechanism must reduce cache conflicts for heap objects regardless of the data input set. Calder uses an object-identification method based on Zorn's [Barrett & Zorn 1993, Seidl & Zorn 1998], which combines several return addresses from the stack, all XOR-folded into a small data package (a single integer). During the application-profiling step, the TRG is created, wherein the vertices are (chunks of) objects identified in the manner just presented.

The placement algorithm takes as input the object-chunk-granularity TRG and performs a greedy algorithm that chooses cache offsets for the stack, global variables, and heap variables. The heap variables are first binned together according to temporal locality (i.e., according to edge weights). Then the stack is placed. The non-stack variables are then merged (placed relative to each other) in a manner similar in spirit to Gloy's code-chunk merging [Gloy et al.

1997]: nodes are merged one at a time, starting with nodes that have the highest edge weights, and a given merger need not be contiguous. Note that the results are specific to a given cache size.

At run time, the heap-variable bins are used to prefer adjacent memory locations for objects binned together—items in the same bin have been aggregated because they were found to exhibit high degrees of temporal locality during application profiling. When *malloc()* is called, it creates a tag from the most recent return addresses on the stack. If this tag is found to correspond to any of the allocation bins, the object is allocated from the free list associated with that bin; otherwise, or if the desired free list is empty, the object is allocated from the default free list.

The authors note the complexities created by the potential for multiple active objects to exist with the same ID. For example, consider the following pseudo-code, which reads in a file of data records and constructs a dynamically linked data structure wherein each element in the structure contains the corresponding information for a (different) single file record:

```
while (!end_of_file(fileptr)) {
    element_t *ep = malloc(sizeof(element_t));
    initialize_from_file(ep, fileptr);
    insert_element(ep, headptr, comparefunction);
}
```

Due to the iterative nature of memory allocation, the various invocations of *malloc()* cannot be distinguished using the return-address approach. Consequently, the resulting dynamic linked data structure would be comprised of numerous data structures all with the same, ostensibly unique, ID. Such a multiplicity of objects using the same identifier causes no correctness problems at run time, due to the free-list-based implementation, but one can easily see that it could skew the profile-based analysis by generating large edge weights between graph vertices that are supposed to represent single objects. Calder does state that the run-time implementation is designed to accommodate multiple objects with the same ID, but the paper does not address the profile-time issue.

Calder performs cache-conscious placement on the stack and global variables for a set of benchmarks

and reports good cache performance for these applications. The paper only applies the heap-variable placement for a small subset of the applications; Calder notes that, for the benchmarks given heap-variable optimization, the objects that exhibit high cache miss rates tend to be small, short lived, and only referenced a handful of times. Whether this is due to the shortcomings of the identification heuristic is unknown.

Chilimbi's Cache-Conscious Structure Layout

A different approach to handling dynamic data structures is presented by Chilimbi [Chilimbi et al. 1999]. Though the mechanism could arguably be classified as a purely off-line approach (e.g., the optimization is not based on profile information), it combines both design-time modifications to the code and run-time modifications to dynamic data structures.

Chilimbi offers two routines that a programmer inserts into the application code. One is a custom version of *malloc()* which, the authors point out, due to the nature of the changes, requires very little in-depth knowledge of the application code. The other is a routine that walks through a given tree structure and reorganizes it for better cache performance; this can be invoked periodically by the application to track dynamic changes to the data structure.

- **ccmalloc**—*cache-conscious allocation*. This is a modified version of *malloc()* that takes a single additional argument—a pointer to a heap-resident data structure that is likely to be used concurrently with the to-be-allocated object. The routine attempts to place the newly allocated object into the same L2 cache block if possible and avoids placing the new object in an address range that would cause cache conflicts with the old object. For example, in a linked list, the old object would be the predecessor node; in a tree structure, it would be the parent node. The study presents several different heuristics for choosing a starting address when there is not enough room in the L2 cache block for both new and old objects. The authors find that allocating a brand-new cache block for the new object works better than others (including first fit and closest fit).

- **ccmorph**—*cache-conscious reorganization.* This routine is given the root of a tree structure and a function that walks the tree. The routine dynamically relocates the nodes of the structure on the heap according to a set of heuristics. The heuristics investigated in the study include *clustering*, in which the routine attempts to place a parent node and its children into the same L2 cache block or nearby in the memory space (see Figure 3.57(a)), and *coloring*, in which the cache is partitioned into one region holding only the most heavily accessed elements (e.g., the nodes near the root of a tree) and another region holding all other data (see Figure 3.57(b)). The authors find that the combination of the two heuristics performs best. Chilimbi states that the routine only

works with tree-like structures; it does not apply to general graphs (e.g., DAGs [directed acyclic graph]). However, there is no reason to expect that the concept cannot be extended to cover more general forms, especially if profiling information is obtained (e.g., to show the most common paths through a DAG, etc.).

It should be clear that *ccmorph()* is meant to optimize "read-mostly" data structures, e.g., those that are created at program initialization and change relatively slowly from that point on. In addition, the use of *ccmorph()* requires a deeper understanding of the application code than does the use of *ccmalloc()*, because, whereas *ccmalloc()* simply provides a hint to the underlying memory-allocation infrastructure, *ccmorph()* can adversely affect the correctness of the code if the application exhibits any (ill-advised) exporting of pointers—a data structure

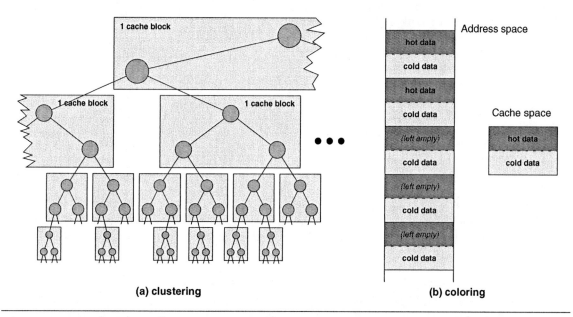

(a) clustering　　　　**(b) coloring**

FIGURE 3.57: Clustering and coloring in Chilimbi's ccmorph(). Clustering (a) attempts to put parents and children of dynamic data structures together into the same cache block if possible. Coloring (b) segregates hot and cold data items, placing each into the memory space so that they map to different partitions of the cache. Importantly, coloring only uses a small number of "hot" spots in the memory space. This ensures that "hot" items will experience less contention in the cache. The rest of the hot slots in memory are left empty, unused.

cannot be correctly relocated if any dangling pointers to it remain after it has been moved. Such exporting of pointers can be common in code that tries to optimize searches by retaining shortcuts to recently visited nodes (simple example: jump pointers). Note, however, that this is exactly the kind of problem that is solved by Luk and Mowry's *memory forwarding* [1999], which enables "aggressive, yet safe, data relocation." Memory forwarding is similar to the concept of pointer swizzling [Wilson 1991, Moss 1992] in that it recognizes at run time when a pointer to a non-resident or relocated object is dereferenced and transparently retargets the pointer to reference the correct object location.

An important distinction in Chilimbi's approach to heap/data cache optimization is that while typical (unoptimized) memory allocators create spatial locality based on the order in which nodes are *created*, Chilimbi's approach tries to create spatial locality based on the order in which nodes are *traversed*. Experiments show the mechanism to outperform both software prefetching (Luk and Mowry's jump pointers [1996]) and hardware prefetching. The latter should not be surprising, as linked data structures are known to confound such prefetchers.

DRAM Address Mappings

Another way to optimize locality that combines aspects of both design time and run time is the choice of what bits in a physical address correspond to what physical resources in the memory system. For example, one subset of the bits identifies the channel; another subset of the bits identifies a rank within that channel; another subset identifies a bank within that rank; another subset identifies a row within that bank; and so on. For more discussion of the resources in the memory system, see Chapter 10, Section 10.2, "Basic Nomenclature." Changing the bit assignments can have a significant effect on system performance. For instance, one can guarantee that simultaneous access to two different large matrices will be possible, or one can ensure that a reference to the first matrix will conflict with any contemporary reference to the second matrix. For more discussion on address mapping policies, see Chapter 13, Section 13.3, "Address Mapping (Translation)."

3.4 Discussions

The following sections put the case studies in perspective.

3.4.1 Proposed Scheme vs. Baseline

It is important to quantify how effectively the management solution satisfies its responsibilities. The prefetching community offers an excellent set of metrics for judging a particular scheme against a baseline: *coverage*, *accuracy*, and *timeliness*. These are (re-)defined here to apply to general management schemes.

- *Coverage* is defined as the fraction of original (baseline) backing store references that, in the new design, become cache hits or partial cache misses.
- *Accuracy* is defined as the fraction of "yes" decisions that are useful, i.e., they result in cache hits at the time of execution (note that should the decision interfere with another, for instance, in the case of two heuristics trying to place two different valuable data into the same cache block, accuracy declines, even though the data are, in fact, valuable).
- *Timeliness* indicates how much of the full cache-miss latency is hidden. In the case of a cache hit, the full latency is hidden, but in the case of a partial miss (e.g., a block is already *en route* from the backing store when its data is requested), only a part of the miss latency is hidden.

An ideal content-management solution should exhibit high coverage so that it eliminates most of the cache misses, high accuracy so that it does not increase memory bandwidth consumption, and reasonable timeliness so that the full latency of the backing store is seen as little as possible. However, achieving this ideal is a challenge. The baseline demand-fetch heuristic can provide good accuracy and timeliness if the application exhibits good spatial and/or temporal locality; each first reference will miss the cache, but follow-on references will typically exhibit high hit rates. By proactively moving data around the system in anticipation of software's needs, i.e., in the case of using a heuristic that prefetches data and/or instructions, one can achieve better timeliness than a purely reactive (i.e., demand-fetch) strategy and yet provide the same accuracy. However, if the prefetching heuristic is too aggressive, both timeliness and accuracy can suffer. If the scheme initiates prefetches too early, even if they are for correct addresses, it may pollute the cache, causing data to be replaced from the cache or prefetch buffer before it is used by the processor. If the prefetch scheme fetches too much data, it pollutes the cache and overburdens the memory bus. The demand-fetch strategy is simple but conservative; it moves into the cache only those items that the application requests at run time and may achieve high accuracy but low coverage. On the other hand, if the application's working set fits into the cache and changes slowly over time, the demand-fetch approach is ideal, as its performance is near-optimal, and it is simple and inexpensive to implement.

3.4.2 Prefetching vs. Locality Optimizations

Although both software prefetching and data locality optimizations improve memory performance, they do so in very different ways. Prefetching initiates memory operations early to hide their latency underneath useful computation, whereas data locality optimizations improve reuse in the data cache. The former is a *latency tolerance* technique, while the latter is a *latency reduction technique*.

Because prefetching only tolerates memory latency, it requires adequate memory bandwidth to be effective. As software prefetches bring required data to the processor increasingly early, the computation executes faster, causing a higher rate of data requests. If memory bandwidth saturates, prefetching will not provide further performance gains, and the application will become limited by the speed of the memory system. In contrast, data locality optimizations reduce the average memory latency by eliminating a portion of the application's cache misses. Hence, it not only reduces memory stalls, it also reduces traffic to lower levels of the memory hierarchy as well as the memory contention this traffic causes.

Compared to data locality optimizations, software prefetching can potentially remove more memory stalls since it can target *all* cache misses. Provided that

ample memory bandwidth exists, software prefetching can potentially remove the performance degradation of the memory system entirely. Data locality optimizations cannot remove all stalls, for example, those arising from cold misses. Another advantage of software prefetching is software transformations are purely speculative; they do not change the semantics of the program code. In contrast, data locality optimizations can affect program correctness. Hence, compilers must prove the correctness of transformations before they can be applied. In some cases, this can reduce the applicability of data locality optimizations compared to software prefetching.

3.4.3 Application-Directed Management vs. Transparent Management

Advantages of software-directed management center around its ability to exploit application semantics in ways that are obscured at run time. For instance, the information needed to generate accurate prefetches is often there in the source code for regular applications whose branches are easily predicted. By performing analysis and instrumentation off-line, software mechanisms off-load these tasks from the cache (usually hardware) onto software, reducing the investment necessary to support partitioning and prefetching. This can lower system complexity and cost, thereby reducing design and test times, and it may enable a faster, more streamlined implementation.

Working against application-directed management is the fact that legacy code must be instrumented (perhaps recompiled, or even rewritten) to exploit the mechanisms. To exploit some off-line heuristics, the application programmer must learn a new set of compiler and/or operating-system directives (e.g., the hints in informed prefetching [Patterson et al. 1995]) that must be "strategically deployed" throughout the program [Griffioen & Appleton 1994]. This can be fraught with problems; directives improperly used or poorly placed can easily degrade performance rather than improve it. Relying on the compiler or some other form of automated code analysis is often unrealistic. For instance, Abraham notes that for irregular programs such as *gcc* and *spice*, compile-time techniques "have not been developed" that can accurately predict run-time memory latencies

[Abraham et al. 1993]. Note that many of the software-directed prefetching mechanisms proposed in the literature have not been implemented in compilers; compiler-based heuristics include array-based algorithms and only the simplest of pointer-based mechanisms.

Advantages of transparent (e.g., hardware-directed or cache-directed) management center around its ability to exploit application behavior in ways that are obscured at design or compile time. For instance, conditional branches make data-driven computation inherently unpredictable. A simple study by Brooks and Martonosi [1999, fig. 2] shows that it is difficult to predict at compile time even the *magnitude* of an operand—the number of bits required to represent that operand at run time—let alone its actual value. Similarly, pointer analysis runs into problems. On-line optimizations can exploit knowledge of actual run-time values. For instance, run-time hardware can differentiate pointer addresses and identify appropriate bitwidths. Hardware-directed cache management can use that knowledge to correctly predict objects to prefetch and to exploit data compaction.

Working against cache-directed management is the complexity of the heuristics that are needed. Data prefetching tables can require megabytes of storage; branch predictors can dissipate tremendous amounts of power; and web cache replacement policies can require software implementations and data structures for storage that one would never want to implement in hardware.

For general applications, there is clearly no "better" choice between application-directed management and cache-directed (or hardware-directed, for solid-state caches) management. An appealing thought is that a synergistic implementation strategically combining both mechanisms will do better than either mechanism in isolation, but none of the "combined heuristics" described in the previous section has emerged as a dominating mechanism. The jury is still out on this one.

3.4.4 Real Time vs. Average Case

It has long been recognized that, for good performance, applications require fast access to their data and instructions. Accordingly, general-purpose processors have offered (transparent) caches to speed up computations in general-purpose applications. Caches hold only a small fraction of a program's total data or instructions, but they are designed to retain the most important items, so that at any given moment it is likely the cache holds the desired item. However, hardware-managed caching has been found to be detrimental to real-time applications, and as a result, real-time applications often disable any hardware caches in the system.

Why is this so? The emphasis in general-purpose systems is typically speed, which is related to the *average-case* behavior of a system. In contrast, real-time designers are concerned with the accuracy and reliability of a system, which are related to the *worst-case* behavior of a system. When a real-time system is controlling critical equipment, execution time must lie within predesigned constraints, without fail. Variability in execution time is completely unacceptable when the function is a critical component, such as in the flight control system of an airplane or the antilock brake system of an automobile.

The problem with using traditional hardware-managed caches in real-time systems is that they provide a probabilistic performance boost; a cache may or may not contain the desired data at any given time. If the data is present in the cache, access is very fast. If the data is *not* present in the cache, access is very slow. Typically, the first time a memory item is requested, it is not in the cache. Further accesses to the item are likely to find the data in the cache; therefore, access will be fast. However, later memory requests to other locations might displace this item from the cache. Analysis that guarantees when a particular item will or will not be in the cache has proven difficult, so many real-time systems simply disable caching to enable schedulability analysis based on worst-case execution time.

It is difficult for software to make up for hardware's inadequacy. One solution is to pin down lines in the cache, when hardware systems support it. System software can load data and instructions into the cache and instruct the cache to disable their replacement. Another solution is to guarantee at design time the number of cache misses that will occur at run time, even if the code and data are not pinned. There have been numerous studies rearranging code and data to better fit into a cache. Examples include tiling, page coloring, cache-conscious data placement, loop interchange, unroll-and-jam, etc. [McFarling 1989, Carr 1993, Bershad et al. 1994a, Carr et al. 1994a, Calder et al. 1998]. Additionally, it has long been known that increasing set associativity decreases cache misses, particularly conflict misses. However, these mechanisms, both hardware and software, have the goal of *decreasing* the number of cache misses, not *guaranteeing* the number of cache misses. Not surprisingly, guaranteeing cache performance requires considerably more work. In fact, as we will show in the next section, the task of assigning memory addresses to code and data objects so as to eliminate cache conflicts is NP-complete.

3.4.5 Naming vs. Cache Conflicts

As should be obvious by now, the placement of data within the memory system determines the data's cache block ID, which determines its location within a transparently addressed cache (either a traditional "cache" or a software-managed cache). An item's location within the cache is what causes it to cause conflict misses with other blocks. Thus, the placement of data within the memory system, or virtual memory system (depending on whether the caches are physically indexed or virtually indexed), is crucial to reducing the number of conflict misses to the minimum possible. The problem is that *doing* this—placing data in memory in a manner that is guaranteed to yield no conflict misses—is intractable. Nonetheless, in practice, it can be done, given that the programs in question are well behaved.

Though this is important for general-purpose systems, because it (at least potentially) increases performance and reduces energy consumption, reducing cache misses is particularly important for embedded systems (if the designer wishes to use caches). The difficult problem really is eliminating conflict misses. Even if we eliminate capacity misses by judiciously selecting the items to cache so that we do not exceed the cache's storage, the task is still intractable. Assume that through code inspection or application profiling or compiler optimization it is possible to identify a subset of the program (chosen at a cache block granularity) that should be cached; the rest of the program will remain non-cached for the duration of application execution. To guarantee that there will be no cache conflict problems during execution it is necessary to arrange the cached items in memory such that the maximum degree of overlap in the cache is less than the cache's degree of associativity.

The intuitive picture is shown in Figure 3.58. The program contains a number of atomic objects that cannot be broken up any further, labeled *A, B, C, … .*

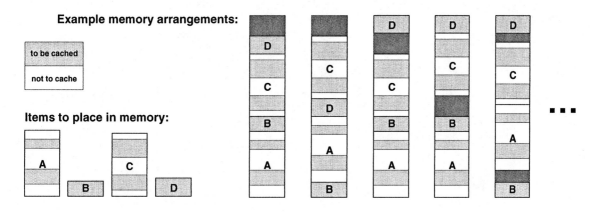

FIGURE 3.58: Possible layouts in the memory space of objects with cached and uncached regions.

These are, for example, C-language *structs* or *arrays*. Portions of these objects may be designated *to-be-cached* or *not-to-be-cached*; this is identified by shading within each object. Assuming that the total size of the regions to be cached does not exceed the cache size, there exist many potential arrangements of the objects in the memory space, each of which might yield a conflict-free cache arrangement. Finding such a conflict-free arrangement of code and data objects is a non-trivial problem. The following is a summary of the problem and NP-completeness proof. The interested reader can find the proof in its entirety on-line [Jacob & Bhattacharyya 2000].

An initial scenario is that of direct-mapped caches and programs whose code and data just fit into the available memory space. Consider an instance of the placement problem in which all of the objects to be placed into memory have the same size, which is one-third of the cache size. This means that there are only three places in the cache to which any object can map, since the sum of the objects' sizes equals the memory size, and the cache is direct-mapped. The problem instance is illustrated in Figure 3.59

The mapping is extremely restricted by this arrangement and effectively defines three equivalence classes for objects, which correspond to the three-thirds of the cache to which an object can map. Two objects must not be in the same equivalence class, i.e., they must not map to the same third of the cache, if any of their cacheable blocks would overlap in the cache. This is shown in Figure 3.60, where objects A and B have blocks in common positions that are to be cached, and thus they cannot map to the same third of the cache. This restricts where in memory they may be placed relative to each other. Object C also has cached blocks, but these blocks do not align with cached blocks in A or B. Object C can therefore be placed anywhere in memory relative to A and B.

It should come as no surprise that 3-COLOR, a well-known NP-complete problem, can be transformed to this problem instance in polynomial time. The problem even intuitively resembles 3-COLOR (see Figure 3.61, which gives a picture of the transformation, where memory object o_x corresponds to vertex v_x in the graph). Any legal coloring of the vertices corresponds to a legal mapping of the objects to the memory space, and any legal mapping of the objects in the memory space corresponds to a legal coloring of the vertices in the graph.

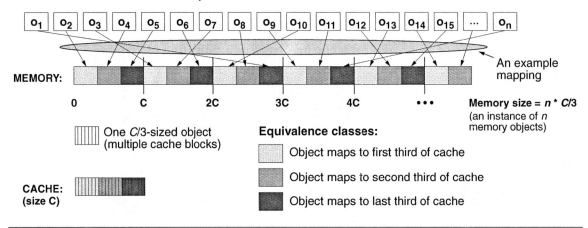

A collection of *n* OBJECTS to be placed into MEMORY:

FIGURE 3.59: Special case in which all objects are equal in size, with each size C/3, where C is the size of the cache.

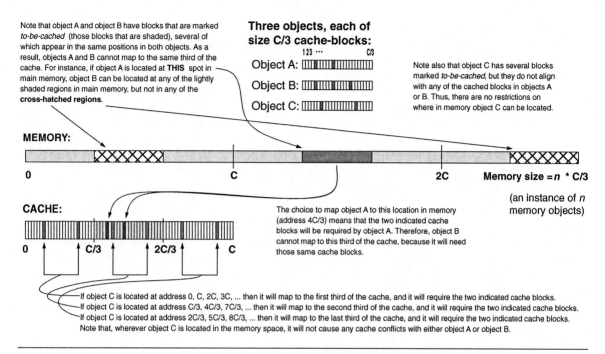

FIGURE 3.60: Cache conflicts and conflict avoidance by judicious placement in memory.

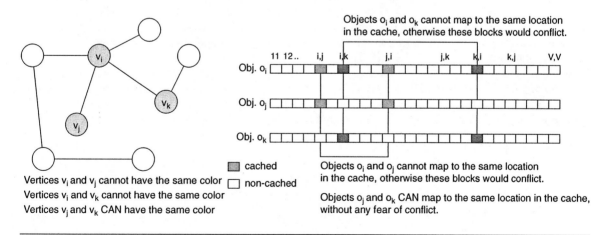

FIGURE 3.61: Correspondence between graph vertices and memory objects.

However, the fact that the memory size equals the sum of the individual object sizes is not what makes the problem intractable; increasing the size of the memory space does not make the problem solvable in polynomial time. Consider an instance of the placement problem in which there are $(k-1)$ extra blocks in the memory space, above and beyond the amount needed to hold the memory objects. Moreover, the memory objects are all uniform in size; they are all the same size as the cache, which would intuitively seem to make the problem easier to solve. Nonetheless, this instance can be mapped to the NP-*complete* *k*-COLOR problem: the equivalence classes to which the memory objects are assigned correspond to whether the object is located at memory location 0 (mod C), 1 (mod C), ..., or (*k*−1) (mod C). These equivalence classes are illustrated in Figure 3.62 for *k* = 3; there are three regions of memory objects laid out in the memory space, defined by where the two blank spaces are positioned (the empty blocks are assumed to be aligned on cache-block-sized boundaries). After each empty block, the subsequent memory objects are all offset from the previous memory objects by one cache block (mod C). There are *n* memory objects in the memory space. Those in the lower address space are aligned on cache-sized boundaries, and the dotted lines in Figure 3.62 indicate the locations of memory objects that are found at higher addresses in the memory space. Figure 3.63 shows how this corresponds to the graph-coloring problem, again with *k* = 3. The figure gives two example placement results: one invalid (the algorithm would not return this as a result) and one valid.

Eliminating conflict misses in traditional, hardware-managed caches is intractable. The problem is solvable in polynomial time, however, assuming that the cached/non-cached regions have a simple organization (for example, one cached region per atomic object): if *M* is large enough, then we can simply choose mappings from {s_{il}} to Z^+ such that each cached region begins exactly one cache block beyond the previous object's cached region. This fails to work when we have odd organizations, such as two arrays, one in which every other block should be cached and the other in which every third block should be cached. However, if the application has well-behaved cached/non-cached regions, *M* can be increased to (almost) arbitrary size by using virtual addressing. Hardware support includes a software-managed cache or a traditional TLB+cache, provided that the TLB is software managed and fully maps the cache with at least one slot to spare, using the uppermost TLB slots for cached data and the remaining TLB slot/s for translating the rest of the application in memory. This scheme requires translation for *all* memory locations, not just *cached* memory locations, which means we need a small memory space, a large TLB, a large page size, or a well-thought-out translation scheme.

3.4.6 Dynamic vs. Static Management

Using an analytical approach to cache models similar to that presented in previous work [Jacob et al. 1996], we show that, for many applications, a perfect statically managed CAM performs worse than a simple LRU-managed CAM. The static-CAM results represent an upper bound on realistic scratch-pad RAM performance, given a fixed arrangement of the most important or highly referenced items. A dynamically managed CAM can be used to solve the problem of capacity misses. This analysis compares the static management of a scratch-pad RAM

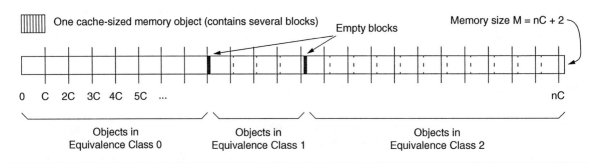

FIGURE 3.62: An example memory arrangement corresponding to *k*-COLOR in which *k* = 3, *n* = |V|.

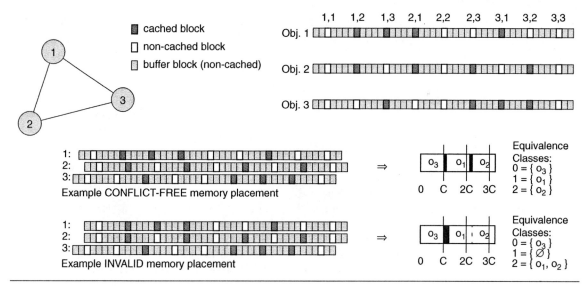

FIGURE 3.63: Simple example of *k*-COLOR transformation for *k* = 3.

(a hardware mechanism used in nearly all DSPs [Lapsley et al. 1994 and 1997]) to the dynamic management of a fully associative cache. The scratch-pad is modeled as a CAM, yielding an upper bound on performance. The analysis shows that somewhere between no locality and perfect locality there is a crossover where it becomes more efficient to manage the cache dynamically. The analysis also shows that as the application footprint grows relative to the cache size, the appeal of static management shrinks.

Assume that we have a running application that generates a stream of references to locations in its address space. Let us say that a function $f(x')$ yields the number of times the application referenced address x'. Note that we have not specified the granularity of access; it could be at a byte, word, or block granularity. The only restriction for this analysis is that all references have the same granularity.

Suppose that we sort the pairs $\{ x', f(x') \}$ from highest $f(x')$ value to lowest $f(x')$ value, thereby creating a new relation. If we map the reordered x' domain onto the integers via mapping $x : Z^+ \varnothing x'$, we can imagine the new function $f(x)$ yielding the frequency of access

of the xth most commonly referenced item. That is, $f(1)$ is the number of times the most commonly referenced item was referenced; $f(2)$ is the number of times the second most commonly referenced item was referenced; $f(3)$ is the number of times the third most commonly referenced item was referenced; etc. Then, assuming the following,

- Perfect static management
- No constraints on contiguity

we can organize our code and data such that the most often referenced code and data are assigned to the scratch-pad, up to the point that the scratch-pad is filled, and all other code and data reside in DRAM. Then the number of hits to a scratch-pad RAM of size S is given by

$$\int_0^S f(x)\,dx \qquad \text{(EQ 3.5)}$$

The total access time is then given by the following, which ignores the cost of compulsory misses (the cost of first copying everything from DRAM or ROM into the scratch-pad RAM). Note that t_S and t_D represent the access times for the scratch-pad RAM and DRAM, respectively.

$$T_{STAT} = t_s \int_0^S f(x)dx + t_D \int_S^\infty f(x)dx \qquad \text{(EQ 3.6)}$$

This is the best performance that one can possibly achieve with a statically managed scratch-pad RAM. This performance number is very aggressive, because it assumes that one can juggle code and data around without fear of addressing conflicts in the scratch-pad RAM and without having to preserve contiguity. As described previously, this is not the case. It is difficult and often impossible to cache only portions of a data structure or to place code and data at arbitrary locations in the cache. Equation (3.6) therefore represents the upper bound on performance for a statically managed scratch-pad RAM.

We compare this to the cost of managing a similar-sized memory in an LRU fashion. From the original application's dynamic execution, we can also derive a function $g(x)$ which represents for each address x the average stack depth at which x is found. This is similar to, but not equal to, the stack-depth function used in previous work [Jacob et al. 1996]. Like $f(x)$, the function $g(x)$ is sorted, but it is sorted from least to highest value. Then the number of hits to a cache managed in an LRU fashion is given by the following:

$$\int_0^{g^{-1}(S)} f(x)dx \qquad \text{(EQ 3.7)}$$

The limits of integration cover all addresses that have an average stack depth of S or less. By definition, references to these addresses will hit in the cache, on average. From this, we can calculate the total access time, as before:

$$T_{DYN} = t_s \int_0^{g^{-1}(S)} f(x)dx + t_D \int_{g^{-1}(S)}^\infty f(x)dx \qquad \text{(EQ 3.8)}$$

The dynamic scheme is better than the perfect static scheme whenever $T_{DYN} < T_{STAT}$, i.e., whenever we have the following:

$$\left[t_s \int_0^{g^{-1}(S)} f(x)dx + t_D \int_{g^{-1}(S)}^\infty f(x)dx \right]$$

$$< \left[t_s \int_0^S f(x)dx + t_D \int_S^\infty f(x)dx \right] \qquad \text{(EQ 3.9)}$$

Because $t_S \ll t_D$, the dynamic scheme is better whenever $g^{-1}(S) > S$ or, assuming g is invertible, whenever $g(S) < S$. The next step is to find $g(x)$.

In the best possible scenario, there is total locality, e.g., focusing on one location at a time. An example (MRU, not LRU) address stream would be the following:

AAAAABBBBBBCCCCCCCDDDDEEFFGGGGHHHHHHHH ...

Here, if we ignore compulsory misses (as in the previous analysis), every access to every location will be found at a stack depth of zero (there are zero intervening unique addresses). Thus, for this example, we find the following:

$$g(x) = 0 \qquad \text{(EQ 3.10)}$$

Clearly, in this scenario, because S (cache size) is greater than zero by definition, $g(S) < S$ for all S. Therefore, for an address stream displaying this degree of locality, one should always manage the cache dynamically, not statically.

In the worst-case scenario, there is as little locality as possible. This happens when references to each address are spread out as distantly as possible so that there is as much intervening data as possible. If we take every reference and spread it evenly across the address stream, we get the greatest average stack depth, and we can define $g(x)$ as follows. First, we can define the average distance between successive references to the same item by simply dividing the total number of references in the dynamic execution by the number of references to address x:

$$\frac{\int_0^\infty f(y)dy}{f(x)} \qquad \text{(EQ 3.11)}$$

This does not give us the stack distance, however, because the stack distance is the number of unique *items between* successive references to the same item. Equation (3.11) gives us the number of *total items* between successive references. Given a particular address x, for every $z < x$, there will be exactly one unique occurrence of z between successive references to x. For every $z > x$, the average number of occurrences between successive references to x will be given by

$$\frac{f(z)}{f(x)} \qquad \text{(EQ 3.12)}$$

What we want is the following summation of a discrete function:

$$g(x) = \sum_{z=0}^\infty \begin{cases} z \le x & 1 \\ z > x & \frac{f(z)}{f(x)} \end{cases} \qquad \text{(EQ 3.13)}$$

This translates well to our continuous-function framework, yielding the following for $g(x)$:

$$g(x) = x + \frac{\int_x^\infty f(z)dz}{f(x)} \qquad \text{(EQ 3.14)}$$

Clearly, for all realistic S, $g(S) > S$, and we obtain the predictable result that when there is no locality, it is best to manage the scratch-pad RAM statically (assuming that our static management policy is perfect).

As a result, we have two bounds: to a first-order approximation, $g(x)$ can never be better than Equation (3.10) and can never be worse than Equation (3.14). We have observed numerous benchmarks and have found that $f(x)$ is typically a decreasing function with a polynomial shape (for a small sample, see processor traces and AFS disk traces in Jacob et al. [1996]). This gives us a wide range of possibilities that are illustrated in Figure 3.64. The graph shows two things. First, there are quite a few realistic ranges for $g(x)$ that exhibit better performance using dynamic management than with static management.

Second, and more importantly, Equation (3.14) gives a form for $g(x)$ that is a decreasing polynomial added to the line $y = x$ and is illustrated in Figure 3.64.

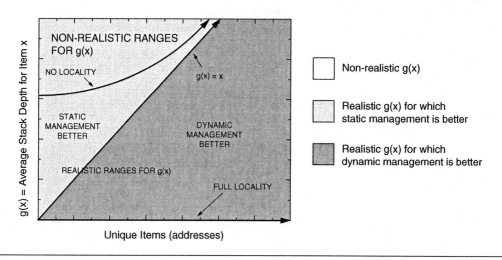

FIGURE 3.64: Static management versus dynamic management of local memory.

There is a decreasing difference between static management and dynamic management as x increases, which means that as application footprints increase in size relative to the scratch-pad size, the difference between worst-case dynamic management and best-case static management narrows. This correlates well with other studies, notably results from Banakar et al. [2002] and Steinke et al. [2002 a and b], which show that static management of the scratch-pad outperforms a hardware-managed cache, and dynamic management of the scratch-pad outperforms static management. One of the reasons that the cache does so poorly relative to scratch-pads is that its management heuristic is *on-line*—it fails to adapt intelligently to the changing needs of the application. The embedded applications chosen for these studies lend themselves to *off-line* heuristics that can exploit knowledge of the changing behavior of the program, e.g., one can anticipate when the application is going through different phases of execution and load the scratch-pad with an entirely different set of code and data.

3.5 Building a Content-Management Solution

Several aspects must be considered when designing one's own content-management solution.

3.5.1 Degree of Dynamism

The content-management scheme decides, for every item in an application's memory space, whether to cache the item, where to put it, how to (re)arrange the item, and when to get it from the backing store. How dynamic is this decision, and how dynamic is the heuristic that makes the decision?

Static Decision

In a static partitioning, regions are either cached or uncached, and the "cache/not-cache" designation for a particular item does not change over time. The prime example of a static partition is the processor cache design found in nearly every general-purpose core. Every single item in the memory system is considered

a "to-cache" item: *any* item brought into the core, whether an instruction or datum, is placed into the cache unless explicitly labeled otherwise. Labeling an item *do not cache* is typically done through the page table and/or TLB—for example, to identify I/O registers that should not be cached or to temporarily disable caching of a DMA target (a region within the memory space into which a *direct-memory-access* controller is actively reading or writing data).

Another form of static partitioning is illustrated in Figure 3.21, which shows the types of compiler constructs available to programmers that allow one to specify ranges of addresses for both code and data. A third form of static partitioning is the region-based caching work of Lee and Tyson [2000], in which the functional region to which a data item belongs (e.g., the stack, the heap, the initialized data, etc.) determines its assignment to one of several partitions of the cache.

Static prefetching decisions include those in Mowry's algorithm (see "Mowry's Algorithm" in Section 3.3.3) because the same sequence of prefetch instructions happens on each iteration of the loop; no dynamic decisions are made. Similarly, jump pointers [Luk & Mowry 1996, Roth & Sohi 1999] are another static prefetch mechanism. They are statically placed in the data structure (which implies their availability every time a new data structure is loaded), and, unless guarded by a dynamic decision such as a branch instruction or predicated load, they are invoked whenever encountered. Branch prediction is the primary heuristic enabling instruction prefetch; static mechanisms include predict-not-taken and similar schemes.

Static locality optimizations include code and data compression [Cate & Gross 1991, Wolfe & Chanin 1992, Lefurgy et al. 1997, Brooks & Martonosi 1999] and the reordering mechanisms in the memory controllers by McKee [McKee & Wulf 1995, McKee et al. 1996] and the Impulse group [Carter et al. 1999].

Dynamic Decision

The cache/not-cache decision for a particular item can change over time and is typically made at run time in response to application behavior, for example, in the same manner as adaptive training branch predictors [Yeh & Patt 1991] or adaptive filters [Haykin 2002]. One of the earliest schemes using hardware predictors to dynamically partition data is McFarling's modification to direct-mapped caches that dynamically detects scenarios in which memory requests competing for the same cache set exhibit different degrees of locality. In such scenarios, the scheme chooses not to cache the item exhibiting poor locality. It is also possible to have a dynamic partition with software-managed memories. For instance, Kandemir's dynamic management of scratch-pad memories [Kandemir et al. 2001] changes the contents of the scratch-pad over time.

Dynamic data-prefetching heuristics include correlation and content-based schemes [Rechstschaffen 1983, Pomerene et al. 1989, Korner 1990, Tait & Duchamp 1991, Griffioen & Appleton 1994, Charney & Reeves 1995, Alexander & Kedem 1996]. Instruction-prefetching heuristics include all forms of branch predictors [Smith 1981b, Lee & Smith 1984, Yeh & Patt 1991, Yeh et al. 1993, Lee et al. 1997a].

Dynamic locality optimizations include reordering memory transactions, for instance, at the memory-controller level (see, for example, Cuppu et al. [1999], Rixner et al. 2000, Cuppu and Jacob [2001], Briggs et al. [2002], Hur and Lin [2004], and Chapter 13, "*DRAM Memory Controller*").

3.5.2   Degree of Prediction

To what degree does the (on-line) algorithm predict requests before they are made? To what degree does the (off-line) algorithm know what requests will be made and when? Some examples are given below.

Reactive Scheme

A purely reactive algorithm can only respond to requests after they have been made, e.g., the demand-fetch on-line heuristic embodied in the typical processor cache and in simpler buffer caches. The scheme's effectiveness depends upon the temporal locality exhibited by the application. If one were to apply this characteristic to an off-line heuristic, it could describe an algorithm relatively conservative in

determining data use, e.g., the static partitioning of code and data shown in Figure 3.21.

Proactive Scheme

A proactive algorithm fetches an item into the cache before that item is actually requested, but it has a good idea that the item will be useful based upon the use of nearby items. This type of heuristic does not rely upon temporal locality for its effectiveness, but it does rely upon spatial and/or algorithmic locality. An on-line example would be lookahead prefetching. This would describe an off-line algorithm somewhat predictive in determining data use, but, nonetheless closely following the software application's tracks, e.g., Mowry's prefetching algorithm [Mowry 1994]. Jump pointers are another example [Luk & Mowry 1996, Roth & Sohi 1999]. A combined off-line/on-line mechanism would be vector machines.

Speculative Scheme

A speculative algorithm gambles on caching an item that has not been requested yet and is not adjacent to any requested item. This is a heuristic that relies upon neither temporal nor spatial locality for its effectiveness, but it does rely upon algorithmic locality to predict a pattern of behavior. In terms of an off-line heuristic, this would describe an algorithm making relatively risky predictions in determining data use (given that at design time one has access to the code), e.g., HPL-PD's code-management facility that enables the compiler to speculatively schedule load instructions.

3.5.3   Method of Classification

On what information do the various aspects of the management base their decisions? Some examples are the following:

- **Uniform Classification:** If the heuristic treats all addresses in the memory space equally, then its approach is *uniform*. An example is the transparent processor cache, which caches everything the processor fetches.

- **Programmer-Directed Classification:** An example is the programmer and compiler's use of aggressive code scheduling in the HPL-PD architecture [Abraham et al. 1993, Kathail et al. 2000].

- **Region-Based Classification:** A simple way to partition the memory space is into the fundamental process regions: code, data, heap, and stack, as in Lee and Tyson [2000]. Another example is the division into instructions and data in a typical split instruction/data cache.

- **PC-Based Classification:** It has been shown that certain load instructions are predictable and others unpredictable, even when loading the same address. This is exploited in both data-cache-management schemes [Tyson et al. 1995] and data-prefetching schemes [Baer & Chen 1991].

- **Time-Based Classification:** The heuristic maintains information about when an item is referenced; obvious examples include LRU replacement policy and buffer-management strategies such as CLOCK and other similar schemes [Carr & Hennessy 1981].

- **Frequency-Based Classification:** The heuristic maintains information about how often (per unit time) an item is referenced. Examples include the *LFU* replacement policy and similar dynamic management mechanisms [Johnson & Hwu 1997].

- **History-Based Classification:** The heuristic maintains information about the recent behavior of a particular object (program counter, data item, memory region, etc.). This is true of nearly every on-line mechanism, for example, branch predictors, data predictors, prefetching mechanisms, management schemes, etc. [Rechstschaffen 1983, Pomerene et al. 1989, Korner 1990, McFarling 1991 and 1992, Tait & Duchamp 1991, Griffioen et al. 1994, Rivers & Davidson 1996].

- **Context-Based Classification:** The heuristic considers context of use. For example, is it an instruction-fetch, a data-fetch, or a prefetch? If it is a prefetch, is it binding or non-binding? Is data being loaded through an array index (which lends itself well to off-line analysis) or through a general pointer (which typically does not)? This type of classification applies to nearly all mechanisms described in this chapter, as it is the foundation on which the divide-and-conquer approach works.

3.5.4 Method for Ensuring Availability

Does the scheme actively prefetch data to ensure that the instructions and data are at the right place at the right time? Does it actively manipulate, rearrange, or reorganize the data, the data's name/s, or even the memory system itself to increase data locality? In the simplest case, e.g., a transparent processor cache, the scheme provides no per-access assurances of behavior; the scheme demand-fetches into the cache anything it deems valuable, which is anything the application references. The scheme relies upon the degree of locality exhibited by the application to improve, in an average sense, the application's performance and energy consumption.

If the scheme is a bit more active in its attempts to guarantee the on-time availability of instructions and/or data, there are numerous means at its disposal.

Data- and Algorithm-Oriented Operations

Data-oriented schemes operate on the data itself. The most obvious is prefetching, which directly moves data from the backing store to higher levels in the hierarchy before the data is actually referenced.

One way to initiate prefetching is by inserting prefetch instructions into the program. This is called software prefetching and is typically performed statically by the compiler or programmer. Examples include prefetching array accesses [Mowry 1994] or jump pointers inserted into linked data structures [Luk & Mowry 1996, Roth & Sohi 1999]. Prefetching can also be initiated dynamically by observing the program's behavior—a technique that can be realized in any on-line agent (including the operating system, the microprocessor core, or the cache itself), as it requires no foreknowledge of the application's code or semantics. It is often called *hardware prefetching*, but that serves simply to distinguish it from prefetching mechanisms embedded within the application code by the programmer/compiler. "Hardware" prefetching could just as easily be a software implementation in the operating system's buffer cache, in an intelligent network router's DNS cache, or in a web proxy's file cache. Note that the hardware/software boundary is not firm. For example, prefetch instructions may be inserted dynamically by an on-line optimizer, whereas some hardware prefetching techniques may be implemented in software.

A data-oriented scheme can also pack data into smaller chunks, using less space to encode the same amount of information, which brings data in from the backing store faster and potentially increases a cache's effective capacity and thus its hit rate. Mechanisms such as compression of code and data [Cate & Gross 1991, Wolfe & Chanin 1992, Lefurgy et al. 1997, Brooks & Martonosi 1999] can reduce fetch time and increase a cache's effective capacity if the cache holds the compressed data. Static mechanisms to pack code and data include instruction-set support for encoding frequently used instructions in smaller formats (e.g., ARM's Thumb [Turley 1995]).

Another class of mechanisms, called *locality optimizations*, exploits knowledge of the cache organization and operation to enhance the locality of instruction and data memory references. These mechanisms either change the layout of data in memory or change the algorithm itself (and thus the order of accesses to the data), thereby improving the reuse of data in the cache. The type of optimization depends on the memory reference type. For affine array references, *tiling* (also called *blocking*) is used [McKellar & Coffman 1969, Lam et al. 1991]. Tiling combines strip-mining with loop permutation to form small tiles of loop iterations that are executed together. Alternatively, for indexed array references, run-time data-access reordering is used [Ding & Kennedy 1999, Mellor-Crummey et al. 1999, Mitchell et al. 1999]. This technique reorders loop iterations at run-time using an inspector-executor approach [Das et al. 1994] to bring accesses to the same data closer together in time. Some instruction-specific locality optimizations include *trace scheduling* [Fisher 1981]

and the various mechanisms described in conjunction with the trace cache in Chapter 2, Section 2.6.3: mechanisms that, among other things, increase the size of typically executed instruction paths.

Name-Oriented Operations

Name-oriented schemes can rearrange data within the memory system without actually moving the data. For instance, the impulse memory controller [Carter et al. 1999] allows an application to create an additional layer of indirection that remaps physical memory addresses to better exploit available memory-bus bandwidth. This supports the efficient movement and storage of both sparse regular and irregular access patterns (e.g., strided access as well as scatter/gather operations) by allowing the cache and memory controller to treat as contiguous those data items that are actually non-contiguous in the DRAM storage.

Note that the naming of instructions and data is closely tied to the cache's logical organization, as an object's name may prevent it from being cached simultaneously with another object that has a conflicting name. Another type of naming-based optimization that addresses this issue is a set of schemes that chooses object names by considering the cache's organization. *Cache-conscious heap* allocation [Calder et al. 1998, Chilimbi et al. 1999] names data within the system to reduce cache conflicts. The mechanism places logically linked heap elements physically close together in memory at memory allocation time to improve spatial locality. (This technique is related to data linearization, described in *Natural Pointer Techniques* in section 3.33.)

In general, the issue of naming and cache conflicts is very important. Choosing placement and thus a name for each item that will avoid cache conflicts is an NP-complete problem, though it is solvable in polynomial time with well-behaved applications and large memory spaces (see Section 3.4.5).

Request-Oriented Operations

One can increase locality by dynamically reordering memory requests to better exploit the current contents of the cache. McKee's memory scheduling unit and associated stream buffers [McKee & Wulf 1995, McKee et al. 1996] support software reordering of accesses to exploit locality and software partitioning of different reference streams into disjoint stream buffers. Cuppu shows that significant locality exists even in the stream of requests that miss all levels of cache and arrive at the DRAM system [Cuppu et al. 1999]. Active or open banks in a DRAM device act as a form of cache; a memory controller can access data held active in the sense amps much more quickly than if the bank must first be activated. Memory-controller designers thus spend significant effort to develop scheduling algorithms that exploit this phenomenon. For more discussion on this, see Chapter 13, *"DRAM Memory Controller."*

CHAPTER 4

Management of Cache Consistency

In any memory system of at least moderate complexity, maintaining cache consistency is a non-trivial matter. Cache consistency is loosely defined as follows:

> *In the presence of a cache, reads and writes behave (to a first order) no differently than if the cache were not there.*

The choice of the word *consistency* in this book is deliberate, despite the confusion that may result within the architecture community (a *memory-consistency model* is a contract between programmer and memory system, and a *cache-coherence* scheme is an implementation of a given memory-consistency model; by cache consistency we mean something different). The reasons for the choice include the following:

- We would rather not invent a new term unless it is unavoidable.
- The term "cache consistency" is no longer used in computer architecture. Rather, as mentioned, the terms "cache coherence" and "consistency model" are used.
- The web cache community already uses the term *cache consistency*, and their definition mirrors ours.

There are three things that lead to cache consistency, all of which are reflections of the fact that a datum must have one value and only one value. If two requests to the same datum at the same time return different values, then the correctness of the memory system is in question. Put another way, the presence of the cache must not alter the *correctness* of the memory system's handling of requests. The use of the term *correctness* is not an accident. There are many situations in which it is contractually *correct*, though perhaps not intuitively logical, for the memory system to provide different values for the same datum.

To return to the point, the three aspects of cache consistency are (i) that the cache remain consistent with the backing store, (ii) that the cache remain consistent with itself, and (iii) that the cache remain consistent in the presence of multiple requestors of the datum in question—other clients of the same backing store.

- **Consistency with Backing Store:** A cache's data must reflect wwhat is in the backing store, and the backing store must reflect what is in the cache to the extent that no request should get the "wrong" data if the two are out of sync.
- **Consistency with Self:** If a datum is allowed to exist in multiple locations within the cache, no request must be allowed to get the wrong value.
- **Consistency with Other Clients:** If multiple requestors are in the system (e.g., multiple processors, multiple caches), the presence of the cache must not enable incorrect data to be propagated to anyone.

The remaining sections discuss these three behaviors in more detail.

4.1   Consistency with Backing Store

Whenever a value is written into a cache, there is immediately a synchronization problem: the cache and its backing store have different values for the same datum. If the backing store serves no other caches, the problem is not particularly severe, as the only way that an incorrect value can be propagated is for the cache to lose the written value or forget that it has it. (Note that such a scenario *is* possible in virtually indexed caches; see Section 4.2.)

In a more general scenario, the backing store can serve multiple caches and requestors, and the synchronization problem must be solved. There are several obvious solutions to the problem:

- Write-through
- Delayed write, driven by the cache
- Delayed write, driven by the backing store or external client

4.1.1   Write-Through

In a write-through policy, every value written to the cache is written to the backing store immediately, thereby minimizing the window of vulnerability. Though it is far from a complete solution to the cache-consistency problem (it does not provide consistency between multiple clients), it provides a reasonable degree of consistency with the backing store. The scheme is simple and yields a system with, at least potentially, the fewest number of "gotchas."

However, the speed differential between the cache and its backing store is likely to be non-trivial; otherwise, why have the cache in the first place? If the differential is large, then the cost of sending every write to the backing store can overwhelm the system, bringing performance to a halt. The typical solution is to use the mechanisms of caching and pipelining to solve the problem, as shown in Figure 4.1. The speed differential is equalized by inserting a new memory structure into the system: one that is *physically* part of the cache (i.e., built of the same technology) and thus can handle frequent writes without slowing down the system, but one that is *logically* considered part of the backing store.

The new memory structure is called a *write buffer*[1] if it is a tagless FIFO organization or a *write cache* if it has tags and can be probed like a cache. Data in the write buffer or write cache is "newer" than the data in the backing store, and therefore it takes precedence over data in the backing store. Data is written to the write buffer/cache immediately, and it is written to the backing store from the write buffer/cache as a background task whenever the channel to the backing store is unused for demand data. Thus, the size of the write buffer/cache is an important consideration; it must be large enough to handle spikes in traffic without overfilling. Overfilling typically requires the structure to be emptied to the backing store, whether it is a convenient time or not.

When handling a request to the backing store, note that all associated write buffers/caches are logically part of the backing store, and therefore they must all be checked for the requested data. In the case of tagless structures (write buffers, as opposed to write caches), there is no way to probe the structure, and therefore its contents must be emptied to memory before the request is handled. Thus, any cache miss results in a write buffer dumping its entire contents to the backing store. Needless to say, this is expensive, and so many systems use tagged buffers, or write caches, which must be emptied to the backing store only when they become overfull.

However, back to the point: on any request to the backing store, all associated write caches must be considered logically part of the backing store, and thus all must be probed for the requested data. This can be avoided to some extent by the use of directories (see the cache-coherence protocols in Section 4.3.2). But, at the very least, the requesting processor usually checks its associated write cache for requested data before sending the request to the backing store.

---

[1]Much has been written on the development of write buffers and write caches (a good starting point is work by Jouppi [1993]). We will only discuss the minimum details of their operation.

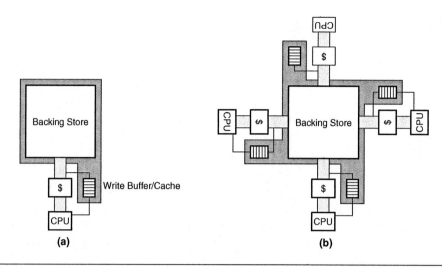

FIGURE 4.1: The use of write buffers and write caches in a write-through policy. (a) The write buffer or write cache is physically part of the cache, but logically part of the backing store. (b) Shows the implication as more caches become clients of the backing store.

4.1.2 Delayed Write, Driven By the Cache

This policy delays writing the data to the backing store until later, where "later" is determined by the cache. There are some obvious triggers.

Conflict-Driven Update

In this policy, the data written into the cache is written to the backing store when there is a cache conflict with that block, i.e., data from a written block (i.e., a "dirty" block) is written to the backing store when another block of data is brought into the cache, displacing the dirty block. This is called the *write-back* policy.

There are some obvious benefits to using a write-back policy. The main things are data coalescing and reduction of write traffic, meaning that oftentimes, an entire block of data will be overwritten, requiring multiple write operations (a cache block is usually much larger than the granularity of data that a load/store instruction handles). Coalescing the write data into a single transfer to the backing store is very beneficial. In addition, studies have found that application behavior is such that writes to one location are frequently followed by *more*

writes to the same location. So, if a location is going to be overwritten multiple times, one should not bother sending anything but the final version to the backing store.

Nonetheless, write-back causes problems in a multi-user scenario (e.g., multiprocessors). Sometimes you will *want* all of those little writes to the same location to be propagated to the rest of the system so that the other processors can see your activity. One can either return to a write-through policy, or one can create additional update scenarios driven by the backing store, i.e., in the case that the data is needed by someone else. This is discussed briefly in the next section and in more detail in Section 4.3.

Capacity-Driven Update

Note that there exist caches in which the concept of *cache conflicts* is hazy at best. Many software caches do not implement any organizational structure analogous to cache sets, and waiting to write data to the backing store until the cache is totally full (an event that would be analogous to a cache conflict) may be waiting too late. Such a cache might instead use a *capacity-driven* update. In this sort of scenario, for example, data could be written to the backing store after a certain threshold amount of data has passed through the cache.

Timer-Driven Update

It should be obvious that cache conflicts or capacity thresholds are not the only trigger events that one might want to have drive data from the cache into the backing store. Another event might be a countdown timer reaching zero: if the goal is to propagate the "final" version of a written datum, the cache could keep track of the time since its last update and write to the backing store once write activity has dropped below a threshold.

Power-Driven Update

An obvious policy is to write data to the backing store when the cost of keeping it in the cache exceeds some threshold. A popular cost metric is power dissipation: if an item is sitting in a solid-state cache, the very act of storing it dissipates power. The transistors dissipate leakage power, and the fact that the data is active means that its tag is checked when the cache is probed (something that applies equally well to software caches).

4.1.3 Delayed Write, Driven by Backing Store

The next obvious policy is for the backing store to decide when the data should be written back. This corresponds to software upcalls, hardware interrupts, coherence messages, etc. The cache holds onto the written data until it can no longer store the data (e.g., for capacity or power dissipation reasons or for other limitations of resources) or until the backing store asks for it.

This is an obvious extension of the write-buffer-write-cache-management policy described earlier, but it is more general than that. In this policy, the backing store serves as the synchronization point for multiple users of data, and it can demand that its client caches update it with the most recent versions of cached, written blocks. The most intuitive use for this is to implement coherence-driven updates (e.g., an incoming request triggers a broadcast or directory-driven request to client caches for the most recent copy of the requested data), but one can also envision other triggers, such as capacity (i.e., the backing store passes a threshold of available free space, particularly applicable to exclusive and non-inclusive caches), timers, or power dissipation.

4.2 Consistency with Self

A cache can run into problems if it allows a particular datum to reside at multiple locations within its structure. This is true of multiprocessor caches, wherein the "cache" can be thought of comprising all processor caches at the same level combined together. It is also true of monolithic caches. We will deal with the multiprocessor cache scenario in the next section; this section focuses on the problem in monolithic caches.

The primary enabler of monolithic caches containing multiple copies of a single datum is *naming*: to wit, if a datum can have more than one name, and the cache stores data within its extent according to their names, then it is certainly possible for a datum to reside at multiple places within the same cache. Moreover, the primary naming mechanism causing exactly these types of headaches is the virtual memory system and its implementation of shared memory. When these mix with virtual caches, headaches abound. Virtual cache organizations are discussed in "Virtual Addressing and Protection," Chapter 2, Section 2.4.

4.2.1 Virtual Cache Management

Shared memory causes many headaches for systems designers and developers porting operating systems across microarchitectures. It is beneficial in that it allows two otherwise independent address spaces to overlap at a well-defined intersection, thereby allowing two independent processes to communicate with little to no overhead. However, it also introduces the possibility for a single datum to be placed at multiple locations in a cache, requiring careful cache management to keep data inconsistencies from occurring.

It becomes clear that this feature—shared memory—breaks the cache model of virtual memory. If a single datum is allowed to have several equivalent names, then it is possible for the datum to reside in a cache at multiple locations. This can easily cause inconsistencies, for example, when one writes values to two different locations that map to the same datum. It is for this reason that virtual memory is described as a mapping between two namespaces; one must remember this when dealing with virtual caches. As long as there is a one-to-one mapping between data and names, no inconsistencies can occur, and the entire virtual memory mechanism behaves no differently than a traditional cache hierarchy. Thus, virtual caches can be used without fear of data inconsistencies. As soon as shared memory is introduced, the simple cache model becomes difficult to maintain, because it is very convenient for an operating system to allow one-to-many namespace mappings. However, as we will see in later chapters, there are many tricks one can play to keep the cache model and still support shared memory.

The Consistency Problem of Virtual Caches

A virtually indexed cache allows the processor to use the untranslated virtual address as an index. This removes the TLB from the critical path, allowing shorter cycle times and/or a reduced number of pipeline stages. However, it introduces the possibility of data-consistency problems occurring when two processes write to the same physical location through different virtual addresses; if the pages align differently in the cache, erroneous results can occur. This is called the virtual cache *synonym problem* [Goodman 1987]. The problem is illustrated in Figure 4.2; a shared physical page maps to different locations in two different process-address spaces. The virtual cache is larger than a page, so the pages map to different locations in the virtual cache. As far as the cache is concerned, these are two different pages, not two

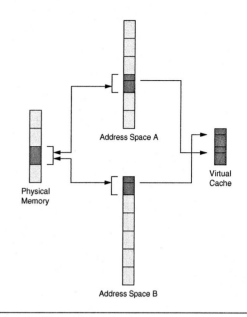

FIGURE 4.2: The synonym problem of virtual caches. If two processes are allowed to map physical pages at arbitrary locations in their virtual-address spaces, inconsistencies can occur in a virtually indexed cache.

different views of the same page. Thus, if the two processes write to the same page at the same time, using two different names, then two different values will be found in the cache.

Hardware Solutions The synonym problem has been solved in hardware using schemes such as dual tag sets [Goodman 1987] or back-pointers [Wang et al. 1989], but these require complex hardware and control logic that can impede high clock rates. One can also restrict the size of the cache to the page size or, in the case of set-associative caches, similarly restrict the size of each *cache bin* (the size of the cache divided by its associativity [Kessler & Hill 1992]) to the size of one page. This is illustrated in Figure 4.3; it is the solution used in many desktop processors such as various PowerPC and Pentium designs. The disadvantages are the limitation in cache size and the increased access time of a set-associative cache. For example, the Pentium and PowerPC architectures

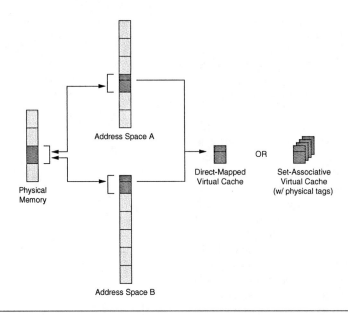

Address Space A

Physical Memory

Direct-Mapped Virtual Cache

OR

Set-Associative Virtual Cache (w/ physical tags)

Address Space B

FIGURE 4.3: Simple hardware solutions to page aliasing. If the cache is no larger than the page size and direct-mapped, then no aliasing can occur. Set-associative caches can be used, provided they have physical tags.

must increase associativity to increase the size of their on-chip caches, and both architectures have used 8-way set-associative cache designs. Physically tagged caches guarantee consistency within a single cache set, but this only applies when the virtual synonyms map to the same set.

Software Solutions Wheeler and Bershad describe a state-machine approach to reduce the number of cache flushes required to guarantee consistency [1992]. The mechanism allows a page to be mapped anywhere in an address space, and the operating system maintains correct behavior with respect to cache aliasing. The aliasing problem can also be solved through policy, as shown in Figure 4.4. For example, the SPUR project disallowed virtual aliases altogether [Hill et al. 1986]. Similarly, OS/2 locates all shared segments at the same address in all processes [Deitel 1990]. This reduces the amount of virtual memory available to each process, whether the process uses the shared segments or not. However, it eliminates the aliasing problem entirely and allows pointers to

be shared between address spaces. SunOS requires shared pages to be aligned on cache-size boundaries [Hennessy & Patterson 1990], allowing physical pages to be mapped into address spaces at almost any location, but ensuring that virtual aliases align in the cache. Note that the SunOS scheme only solves the problem for direct-mapped virtual caches or set-associative virtual caches with physical tags; shared data can still exist in two different blocks of the same set in an associative, virtually indexed, virtually tagged cache. Single address space operating systems such as Opal [Chase et al. 1992a, 1992b] or Psyche [Scott et al. 1988] solve the problem by eliminating the concept of individual per-process address spaces entirely. Like OS/2, they define a one-to-one correspondence of virtual to physical addresses and in doing so allow pointers to be freely shared across process boundaries.

Combined Solutions Note that it is possible, using a segmented hardware architecture and an appropriate software organization, to solve the aliasing problem.

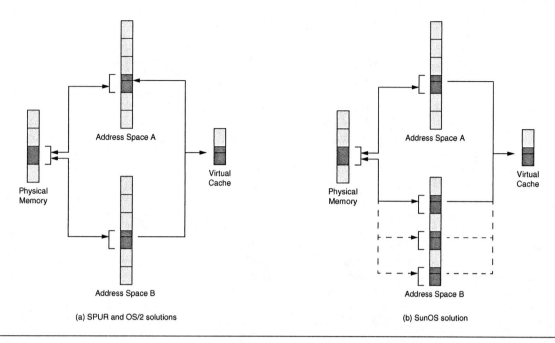

(a) SPUR and OS/2 solutions   (b) SunOS solution

FIGURE 4.4: Synonym problem solved by operating system policy. OS/2 and the operating system for the SPUR processor guarantee the consistency of shared data by mandating that shared segments map into every process at the same virtual location. SunOS guarantees data consistency by aligning shared pages on cache-size boundaries. The bottom few bits of all virtual page numbers mapped to any given physical page will be identical, and the pages will map to the same location in the cache. Note that this works best with a direct-mapped cache.

The discussion is relatively long, so we have placed it in Chapter 31, Section 31.1.7, "Perspective: Segmented Addressing Solves the Synonym Problem."

An important item to note regarding aliasing and set-associative caches is that set associativity is usually a transparent mechanism (the client is not usually aware of it), and the cache is expected to guarantee that the implementation of set associativity does not break any models. Thus, a set-associative cache cannot use virtual tags unless the set associativity is exposed to the client. If virtual tags are used by the cache, the cache has no way of identifying aliases to the same physical block, and so the cache cannot guarantee that a block will be unique within a set—two different references to the same block, using different virtual addresses, may result in the block being homed in two different blocks within the same set.

Perspective on Aliasing

Virtual-address aliasing is a necessary evil. It is useful, yet it breaks many simple models. Its usefulness outweighs its problems. Therefore, future memory-management systems must continue to support it.

Virtual-Address Aliasing Is Necessary Most of the software solutions for the virtual cache synonym problem address the consistency problem by limiting the choices where a process can map a physical page in its virtual space. In some cases, the number of choices is reduced to one; the page is mapped at one globally unique location or it is not mapped at all. While disallowing virtual aliases would seem to be a simple and elegant way to solve the virtual-cache-consistency problem, it creates another headache for operating systems—virtual fragmentation.

When a global shared region is garbage-collected, the region cannot help but become fragmented. This is a problem because whereas de-fragmentation (compaction) of disk space or physically addressed memory is as simple as relocating pages or blocks, virtually addressed regions cannot be easily relocated. They are location-dependent; all pointers referencing the locations must also be changed. This is not a trivial task, and it is not clear that it can be done at all. Thus, a system that forces all processes to use the same virtual address for the same physical data will have a fragmented shared region that cannot be de-fragmented without enormous effort. Depending on the amount of sharing, this could mean a monotonically increasing shared region, which would be inimical to a 24 × 7 environment, i.e., one that is intended to be operative 24 hours a day, 7 days a week. Large address SASOS implementations on 64-bit machines avoid this problem by using a global shared region that is so enormous it would take a very long time to become overrun by fragmentation. Other systems [Druschel & Peterson 1993, Garrett et al. 1993] avoid the problem by divid-ing a fixed-size shared region into uniform sections and/or turning down requests for more shared memory if all sections are in use.

Virtual-Address Aliasing Is Detrimental There are two issues associated with global addresses. One is that they eliminate virtual synonyms, and the other is that they allow shared pointers. If a system requires global addressing, then shared regions run the risk of fragmentation, but applications are allowed to place self-referential pointers in the shared regions without having to *swizzle* [Moss 1992] between address spaces. However, as suggested above, this requirement is too rigid; shared memory should be linked into address spaces at any (page-aligned) address, even though allowing virtual aliasing can reduce the ability to store pointers in the shared regions.

Figure 4.5 illustrates the problem: processes A and Z use different names for the shared data, and using each other's pointers leads to confusion. This problem arises because the operating system was allowed or

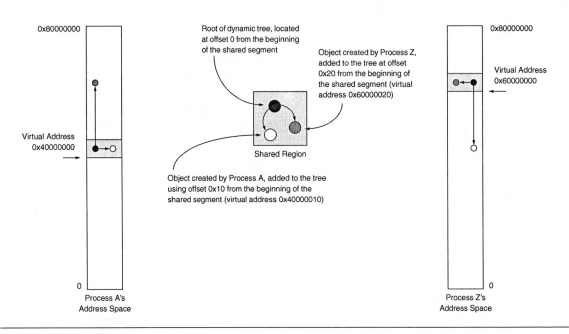

FIGURE 4.5: The problem with allowing processes to map shared data at different virtual addresses.

even instructed by the processes to place the shared region at different virtual addresses within each of the two address spaces. Using different addresses is not problematic until processes attempt to share pointers that reference data within the shared region. In this example, the shared region contains a binary tree that uses self-referential pointers that are not consistent because the shared region is located at different virtual addresses in each address space.

It is clear that unless processes use the same virtual address for the same data, there is little the operating system can do besides swizzle the pointers or force applications to use *base+offset* addressing schemes in shared regions. Nonetheless, we have come to expect support for virtual aliasing. Therefore, it is a requirement that a system support it.

Virtual Caches and the Protection Problem

A virtual cache allows the TLB to be probed in parallel with the cache access or to be probed only on a cache miss. The TLB traditionally contains page protection information. However, if the TLB probe occurs only on a cache miss, protection bits must be stored in the cache on a per-block basis, or else protection is effectively being ignored. When the protection bits for a page are replicated across several cache lines, changing the page's protection is non-trivial. Obvious mechanisms include flushing the entire cache on protection modification or sweeping through the cache and modifying the appropriate lines. The operating system changes page protections to implement such features as copy-on-write, to reduce copy overhead when a process forks, or simply to share memory safely between itself and user processes.

A similar problem happens when a process terminates. If the cache is write-back, it is possible for a stale portion of a process's address space to remain in the cache while the physical page is remapped into a new address space. When the stale portion is written back, it overwrites the data in the new address space. Obvious solutions include invalidating the entire cache or selected portions. These types of problems are often discovered when porting operating systems to architectures with virtual caches, such as putting Mach or Chorus on the PA-RISC.

4.2.2 ASID Management

Described earlier, ASIDs are a non-trivial hardware resource that the operating system must manage on several different levels. To begin with, an operating system can maintain hundreds or thousands of active processes simultaneously, and in the course of an afternoon, it can sweep through many times that amount. Each one of these processes will likely be given a unique identifier, because operating systems typically use 32-bit or 64-bit numbers to identify processes. In contrast, many hardware architectures only recognize tens to hundreds of different processes [Jacob & Mudge 1998b]—MIPS R2000/3000 has a 6-bit ASID; MIPS R10000 has an 8-bit ASID; and Alpha 21164 has a 7-bit ASID. The implication is that there cannot be a one-to-one mapping of process IDs to ASIDs, and therefore an operating system must manage a many-to-many environment. In other words, the operating system will be forced to perform frequent remapping of address-space IDs to process IDs, with TLB and cache flushes required on every remap (though, depending on implementation, these flushes could be specific to the ASID involved and not a whole-scale flush of the entire TLB and/or cache). Architectures that use IBM 801-style segmentation [Chang & Mergen 1988] and/or larger ASIDs tend to have an easier time of this.

ASIDs also complicate shared memory. The use of ASIDs for address space protection makes sharing difficult, requiring multiple page table and TLB entries for different aliases to the same physical page. Khalidi and Talluri describe the problem:

> *Each alias traditionally requires separate page table and translation lookaside buffer (TLB) entries that contain identical translation information. In systems with many aliases, this results in significant memory demand for storing page tables and unnecessary TLB misses on context switches. [Addressing these problems] reduces the number of user TLB misses by up to 50% in a 256-entry fully-associative TLB and a 4096-entry level-two TLB. The memory used to store hashed page tables is dramatically reduced by requiring a single page table entry instead of separate page table entries for hundreds of aliases to a physical page, [using] 97% less memory. [Khalidi & Talluri 1995]*

Since ASIDs identify virtual pages with the processes that own them, mapping information necessarily includes an ASID. However, this ensures that for every shared page there are multiple entries in the page tables, since each differs by at least the ASID. This redundant mapping information requires more space in the page tables, and it floods the TLB with superfluous entries. For instance, if the average number of mappings per page were two, the effective size of the TLB would be cut in half. In fact, Khalidi and Talluri [1995] report the average number of mappings per page on an idle system to be 2.3, and they report a decrease by 50% of TLB misses when the superfluous-PTE problem is eliminated. A scheme that addresses this problem can reduce TLB contention as well as physical memory requirements.

The problem can be solved by a global bit in the TLB entry, which identifies a virtual page as belonging to no ASID in particular; therefore, every ASID will successfully match. This is the MIPS solution to the problem; it reduces the number of TLB entries required to map a shared page to exactly one, but the scheme introduces additional problems. The use of a global bit essentially circumvents the protection mechanism and thus requires flushing the TLB of shared entries on context switch, as the shared regions are otherwise left unprotected. Moreover, it does not allow a shared page to be mapped at different virtual addresses or with different protections. Using a global-bit mechanism is clearly unsuitable for supporting sharing if shared memory is to be used often.

If we eliminate the TLB, then the ASID, or something equivalent to distinguish between different contexts, will be required in the cache line. The use of ASIDs for protection causes the same problem, but in a new setting. Now, if two processes share the same region of data, the data will be tagged by one ASID, and if the wrong process tries to access the data that is in the cache, it will see an apparent cache miss simply because the data is tagged by the ASID of the other process. Again, using a global bit to marked shared cache lines leaves them unprotected against other processes, and so the cache lines must be flushed on context switch. This is potentially much more expensive than flushing mappings from the TLB, because the granularity for flushing the cache is usually a cache line, requiring many operations to flush an entire page.

4.3 Consistency with Other Clients

When the concept of caching is introduced into a multi-client or multiprocessor system, the consistency of the memory system should not change—the mere existence of caches should not change the value returned by a client's request.

Or, at least, that is the way things started. However, while it is certainly possible to build mechanisms that ensure this happens (to wit, to ensure that a distributed system of caches and memories behaves like a monolithic memory system), and while systems are quite capable of doing it, the performance cost of doing so can be prohibitively expensive as compared to the performance one can get were one to relax the constraints a little. Consequently, different memory-consistency models have been proffered wherein the constraints are progressively relaxed—these are contracts with the memory system that provide looser guarantees on ordering but higher potential performance. In such scenarios, just as in a lossy data network, for example, the programmer can always ensure the desired behavior by using higher level synchronization protocols. For example, in a lossy network (i.e., any realistic network), one can implement a reliable transmission service by creating a handshaking protocol that notifies a sender of a packet's delivery and generates a retransmission in the event that no acknowledgment arrives within a given time period. Similar mechanisms can be used to make a relaxed consistency model behave like a tighter model for when the programmer needs such guarantees.

4.3.1 Motivation, Explanation, Intuition

To make the concepts more clear, we present the types of problems that can occur, give some intuition for the range of solutions, and then discuss specific implementation details.

Scenario One

Figure 4.6 illustrates an example scenario.

- Hardware device A transfers a block of data into memory (perhaps via a DMA [direct memory access] controller).
- Software process B is A's controller. It is a user-level process communicating with device A via a control link such as a serial port.
- Software process C is a consumer of the data and waits for B's signal that the data is ready.

Though the scenario is contrived to have a (potential) race condition buried within it, this general structure is representative of many embedded systems in which software processes interact with hardware devices. The specifics of the scenario are as follows:

1. B communicates to client processes via a synchronization variable called "ready" that indicates when a new block of data is valid in the memory system. At time 1, B sets this variable to the value 0 and initiates the transfer of data from hardware device A to the memory system.

2. When the data transfer is complete, the hardware device signals the controlling software process via some channel such as a device interrupt through the operating system, or perhaps the controlling software must continuously poll the hardware device. Whatever the implementation, process B is aware that the data transfer has finished at time 2.

3. At time 3, B updates the synchronization variable to reflect the state of the data buffer. It sets the variable to the value 1.

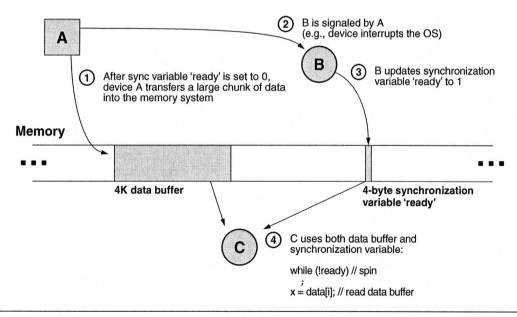

FIGURE 4.6: Race condition example. At time 1, the synchronization variable "ready" is initialized to 0. Meanwhile, hardware device A begins to transfer data into the memory system. When this transfer is complete, A sends B a message, whereupon B updates the synchronization variable. Meanwhile, another software process, C, has been spinning on the synchronization variable ready waiting for it to become non-zero. When it sees the update, it reads the data buffer.

4. Meanwhile, process C has been spinning on the synchronization variable, waiting for the data to become available. A simple code block for the client process C could be the following:

```
while (1) {

    // wait for data to become available
    while (!ready)
        ;

    // data is available; process buffer
    for (i=0; i<BUFSIZE; i++) {
        process( data[i] );
    }

    // reset synchronization variable
    ready = 0;

}
```

When the synchronization variable indicates that the data is in memory, the client process starts reading it. When it finishes, the process begins again. For example, the server process B could be responsible for initializing the variable ready at the outset, starting up C, and, from then on, B spins on ready to become 0, initiates a new data transfer, sets ready to 1, and spins again—in the steady state, B is responsible only for the 0 ->1 transition, and C is responsible only for the 1 ->0 transition.

The timing of events is shown in Figure 4.7. In a simple uniprocessor system, the example has very straightforward behavior; the memory system enforces sequentiality of memory references by definition; the single processor enforces sequentiality of task execution by definition; and the only thing that could cause a problem is if the software process that does the transferring of data from A into the memory system (e.g., perhaps a device driver within the operating system) takes too long to transfer the data from its own protected buffer space into the user-readable target buffer.

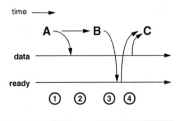

FIGURE 4.7: Event timing.

In a simple uniprocessor system, causality is preserved because the system can only do one thing at a time: execute one instruction, handle one memory request. However, once this no longer holds, e.g., if this example is run on a multiprocessor or networked multicomputer, then all bets are off. Say, for example, that the memory system is distributed across many subsystems and that each of the processes (B, C, and the data transfer for A) are each running on a different subsystem. The question arises in such a scenario: *does C get the correct data?* This is a perfectly reasonable question to ask. Which happens first, the data buffer being available or the synchronization variable being available? In a complex system, the answer is not clear.

An Analogy: Distributed Systems Design

Let's first explore why arbitrary ordering of memory requests might be a good thing. We have put forth a scenario in which arbitrary ordering in the memory system could create a race condition. This happens because our scenario exhibits a causal relationship between different, seemingly unrelated, memory locations, but note that not all applications do. Moreover, while consistency models exist that make a multiprocessor behave like a uniprocessor, their implementations usually come at the price of lower achievable performance. A better scheme may be to relax one's expectations of the memory system and instead enforce ordering between events explicitly, when and where one knows causal relationships to exist.

The same concepts apply in network-systems design, and the issues can be more intuitive when couched in network terms. In particular, the following analogy gives implementation details that apply not just to distributed systems, but also to cache-coherence implementations, both hardware and software. Those already familiar with the issues might want to skip ahead, as the analogy is long and intended for readers who have not really thought about the issues of timing and causality in a networked system.

Imagine the development of a *distributed system*, a set of software processes on a network that provide some function and that use the network for communication to coordinate their behavior. The details of the high-level algorithm (the function that the set of processes provides in their cooperative fashion) do not matter for this discussion. At the outset of the system design, the designer has a wide range of choices to make regarding his assumptions of the network. For instance,

- Is delivery of a message guaranteed? In particular, if a process places a message packet onto the network, does the network guarantee that the intended recipient will receive that packet? Can the recipient receive the packet more than once? Can the network lose the packet? If yes, is any process on the network alerted to the loss?

- Is the delivery time of a message bounded? A network, even if it does not guarantee delivery of a packet, may be able to guarantee that, if the packet is delivered, it will be delivered within a certain window of time; otherwise, the packet will not be delivered even if not lost.

- Is the ordering of messages on the network preserved? If a process places a series of packets on the network, will they be delivered in that same serial order?

Depending on the assumptions of how the network behaves, the developer will choose to code the program very differently.

- If delivery of a message is guaranteed to be 1 (not 0, not 2 or more times), the time is bounded, and the network is guaranteed to preserve the ordering of messages, then the code can look very much like that of a functional programming model written for a sequential processor. In such a scenario, processes can send messages as if they are executing functions, and, in many cases, this is exactly how distributed systems are built from originally monolithic software implementations: by dividing work between processes at the function-call boundary. This is the nature of the remote procedure call (RPC) paradigm. It makes for a very simple programming model, because neither the designer nor the programmer need concern himself with details of the underlying medium.

- What if it is possible for the network to deliver a given message multiple times? For example, what if a packet placed on the network can be delivered to the recipient twice? If such an event would make no difference whatsoever to the functional correctness of the program, then this is not a big deal. However, if it can cause problems (e.g., imagine banking software receiving a credit/debit message for a particular account more than once), then the software must *expect* such a situation to occur and provide a mechanism to handle it. For example, the software could add to every outgoing packet a message number that is unique[2] within the system, and a recipient discards any packet containing a message number that it has already seen.

---

[2]Unique within the system is not hard to guarantee: if the software has a unique ID, it need only generate a number that is unique locally, for example, a sequence number (incremented for every packet sent out) concatenated with a timestamp, all concatenated with the software ID.

- What if message ordering is not guaranteed? For example, what if a series of packets sent in a particular order arrive out of order at the destination? If such an event can cause problems, then the software must *expect* such a situation to occur and provide a mechanism to handle it. For example, the software could build into its message-handling facility a buffering/sequencing mechanism that examines incoming messages, delivering them up to the higher level if the sequence number is consecutive from the last packet received from that sender or buffering (and rearranging) the message until the packet/s with the intervening sequence number/s arrive. If the delivery time of a message is bounded, then the handler need only wait for that threshold of time. If the intervening sequence numbers are not seen by then, the handling software can assume that the sender sent packets with those sequence numbers to different recipients, and thus, there is no gap in the sequence as far as this recipient is concerned (the gap is not an indication of functional incorrectness).

- But what if delivery time is not bounded? Well, then things get a bit more interesting. Note that this is functionally (realistically) equivalent to the case that delivery is not guaranteed, i.e., a packet sent to a destination may or may not reach the destination. As before, if this poses any problem, the software must expect it and handle it. For instance, the recipient, upon detecting a gap in the sequence, could initiate a message to the recipient asking for clarification (i.e., *did I miss something?*), resulting in a retransmission of the intervening message/s if appropriate. However, the receiver in a distributed system is often a server, and, in general, it is a bad idea to allow servers to get into situations where they are blocking on something else, so this particular problem might best be handled by a sender-/client-side retry mechanism. To wit, build into the message-passing facility an explicit *send-acknowledge* protocol: every message sent expects a

simple acknowledgment message in return from the recipient. If a sender fails to receive an acknowledgment in a timely fashion, the sender assumes that the message failed to reach the destination, and the sender initiates a retry. Separate sequence numbers can be maintained per recipient so that gaps seen by a recipient are an indication of a problem.

- And so forth.

The bottom line is that

> *A designer always builds into a system explicit mechanisms to handle or counter any non-ideal characteristics of the medium.*

A designer that assumes the medium to be ideal needs no such mechanisms, and his code can look virtually identical to its form written for a single processor (no network). The less ideal a designer assumes the medium, the more workarounds his program must include.

In Particular, Cache Systems

How does the analogy apply here? It turns out that writing software to deal with a distributed cache system (e.g., a multiprocessor cache system, a web-document proxy cache, etc.) is very much like writing for a network. In particular, the memory-consistency model describes and codifies one's assumptions of the medium; it describes a designer's understanding of how the cache and memory systems behave, both independently of each other and interactively. The memory-consistency model represents an understanding of how the memory system will behave, on top of which a designer creates algorithms; it is a contract between programmer and memory system.

It is reasonable to ask why, in the network case, would anyone ever *choose* to write the complicated software that makes very few assumptions about the behavior of the network. The answer is that such systems always represent trade-offs. In general, there is no free lunch, and complexity will be found somewhere, either in the infrastructure (in the network), in the user of the infrastructure (the distributed-systems software), or somehow spread across the two. The level of guarantee that an infrastructure chooses to provide to its clientele is often a case of diminishing returns: an infrastructure stops providing guarantees once its implementation reaches a level of complexity where the next improvement in service would come at a prohibitive cost. Thus, as an example, the Internet Protocol (IP) provides message delivery, but not *reliable* message delivery, and in cases where a designer wants or needs reliable message delivery, the facility is built on top of the base infrastructure (e.g., TCP/IP, reliable datagrams, etc.).

The same is true in cache systems. It is very simple to write programs for a uniprocessor that has a single cache, and it is enticing to think that it should be no harder to write programs for multiprocessors that have many caches. In fact, many modern multiprocessor cache systems provide exactly that illusion: an extremely simple memory-consistency model and associated cache-coherence mechanism that support the illusion of simplicity by forcing a large number of distributed hardware caches to behave as one.

As one can imagine, such a system, lying as it does at one end of the complexity trade-off continuum, might not give the best performance. Thus, there are many different consistency models from which to choose, each representing a level of service guarantee less stringent than the preceding one, a hardware system that is less costly to build, and the potential for greater performance during those windows of time during which the software does *not* need the illusion of a single memory port.

The following are some example issues to note about the implementation, once the cache system becomes complex and/or distributed about a network:

- Suppose it is possible for writes to be buffered (not propagated directly to the backing store) and for reads to be satisfied from nearby caches. Such is the case with web proxies or multiprocessor caches. Such a system can have multiple cached copies of a given item, each with a different value, and if no effort is made to reconcile the various different versions with one another, problems can arise.

- Suppose that, in an implementation, the cache's backing store is not a monolithic entity, but rather a collection of storage structures, each with its own port. This is the case for NUMA multiprocessor organizations, a popular design choice today. If data migration is possible, i.e., if it is possible for a given datum to reside in two places in the distributed backing store, then one can envision scenarios in which two writes to the same datum occur in different orders, depending on which segment of the backing store handles the requests.

- Whatever mechanism is used to ensure consistency between different caches and different users/processors must also be aware of the I/O system, so that I/O requests behave just like "normal" memory requests. The reason for this will become clear in a moment.

Note that this is by no means a complete list of issues. It is just given to put the problem into perspective.

4.3.2 Coherence vs. Consistency

At this point we should formally discuss *memory coherence* and *memory consistency*, terms that speak to the ordering behavior of operations on the memory system. We illustrate their definitions within the scope of the race condition example and then discuss them from the perspective of their use in modern multiprocessor systems design.

Memory Coherence: The principle of memory coherence indicates that the memory system behaves rationally. For instance, a value written does not disappear (fail to be read at a later point) unless that value is explicitly overwritten. Write data cannot be buffered indefinitely; any write data must eventually become visible to subsequent reads unless overwritten. Finally, the system must pick an order. If it is decided that write X comes before write Y, then at a later point, the system may not act as if Y came before X.

So, in the race condition example, coherence means that when B updates the variable *ready*, C will eventually see it. Similarly, C will eventually see the data block written by A. When C updates the variable to 0 at the end of its outer loop, the spin loop immediately following that update [while(!ready)] will read the value 0 until and unless B updates the variable in the meantime.

Memory Consistency: Whereas coherence defines rational behavior, the consistency model indicates how long and in what way/s the system is allowed to behave irrationally with respect to a given set of references. A memory-consistency model indicates how the memory system interleaves read and write accesses, whether they are to the same memory location or not. If two references refer to the same address, their ordering is obviously important. On the other hand, if two references refer to two different addresses, there can be no data dependencies between the two, and it should, in theory, be possible to reorder them as one sees fit. This is how modern DRAM memory controllers operate, for instance. However, as the example in Figure 4.6 shows, though a data dependence may not exist between two variables, a causal dependence may nonetheless exist, and thus it may or may not be safe to reorder the accesses. Therefore, it makes sense to define allowable orderings of references to different addresses.

In the race condition example, depending on one's consistency model, the simple code fragment

```
if (ready)
    read data;
```

may or may not work as one expects. If the model allows arbitrary reordering, then the value of the variable *ready* may be seen by outside observers (i.e., by process C) before the values written to the data buffer become available, in which case C would get the wrong results.

To the newcomer, these terms have arguably unsatisfying definitions. Despite the clear distinction between the two, there is significant overlap when one goes a bit deeper. Many little items demonstrate a significant grey area at the intersection of the concepts of coherence and consistency. For instance,

- The popular definitions of consistency and coherence differentiate the two with the claim that one (coherence) defines the behavior of reads and writes to the *same* address, while the other (consistency) defines the behavior of reads and writes to *different* addresses. However, nearly every such discussion follows its definition of consistency with examples illustrating the behavior of reads and writes to the *same* memory location.
- Most memory-consistency models do not explicitly mention memory coherence. It is simply assumed to be part of the package. However, one cannot assume this to be the case generally, as several memory-consistency models violate[3] implicitly or explicitly the principle of memory coherence.
- The stated primary function of a cache-coherence scheme is to ensure memory coherence, but any caching mechanism also implicitly adheres to a particular consistency model.

As the editors at *Microprocessor Report* said long ago, and we paraphrase here, "*superpipelined* is a term that means, as far as we can tell, *pipelined*." Similarly, *memory consistency* is a term that means, as far as we can tell, *memory coherence, ... within a multi-client context*. In many ways, memory consistency behaves like a superset of memory coherence, subsuming the latter concept entirely, and, as far as

---

[3]For example, both *causal consistency* and *pipelined RAM consistency* allow multiple writes to a single memory address to take effect in different order to different clients [Tanenbaum 1995]. Thus, whereas client A would see the value "1" written to a memory location followed by the value "2," client B could see the value 2 written, followed by the value 1.

we can tell, the decision to give the two concepts different names[4] only serves to confuse newcomers to the field. Consequently, outside of this section of the book, we will avoid using both terms. We will use the term *memory consistency* to indicate the behavior of the memory system, including the degree to which the memory system ensures memory coherence.

That is the way the terms, arguably, *should* be used. In particular, in an ideal world, one could argue that the cache-coherence engine (or perhaps rename it to the "cache-consistency engine") should be responsible for implementing the given consistency model. However, the terms as used today within the computer-architecture community have very specific implementation-related connotations that differ from the ideal and must be explained to the uninitiated (as they were to us). In modern multiprocessor systems the cache-coherence mechanism is responsible for implementing memory coherence within a multi-client, multi-cache organization. Modern microprocessors execute their instructions out of order and can reorder memory requests internally to a significant degree [Jaleel & Jacob 2005]. This creates problems for the cache-coherence mechanism. In particular, when writes may be buffered and/or bypassed locally by other memory operations, the ability for the coherence engine to provide tight *consistency* guarantees becomes difficult to the point of impossibility (we will discuss this in more detail in Section 4.3.3). As a result, it would seem that all of the high-performance reordering and buffering mechanisms used in modern out-of-order cores—mechanisms that are necessary for good performance—must be thrown away to ensure correct operation.

To address this problem, researchers and developers propose relaxed consistency models that tolerate certain classes of irrational memory-system behavior for brief periods of time and thus define different programming models. Most significantly, these models *allow* the local reordering and buffering that modern processors implement by off-loading onto the shoulders of the programmer the responsibility of ensuring correct behavior when ordering is important. It is important to note that these models are implemented on top of the existing cache-coherence engines, an arrangement implying that the cache-coherence engines provide guarantees that are, perhaps, unnecessarily tight relative to the specific consistency model running on top. The relatively tight guarantees in the coherence engine are really only needed and used for synchronization variables so that fences and such[5] can be implemented through the memory system and not as message-passing primitives or explicit hooks into the coherence engine. Rather, the processors intentionally disable the reordering and buffering of memory operations in the neighborhood of synchronization activity (releases, acquires) so that memory requests are sent immediately and in process order to the coherence engine, which then provides tight consistency and coherence guarantees for those variables. Once the synchronization activity is over, the reordering and buffering are turned back on, and the processors return to high-performance operation.

4.3.3 Memory-Consistency Models

The memory-consistency model defines the ordering of externally visible events (i.e., reads and writes to the memory system: when a read is satisfied and when a write's data becomes visible to a subsequent request[6]), even if their corresponding requests are satisfied out of the local cache. Within the scope of a memory-consistency model, the cache is considered part of the memory system. In particular, read and write requests are allowed to be reordered to various degrees, as defined by the model in question. The

---

[4]A possible explanation of/justification for the existence of both terms is that *coherence* arose in the context of uniprocessor systems, and the term *consistency* was used to describe the behavior of multiprocessor systems rather than redefining or supplanting the original term.

[5]For a thorough discussion of synchronization primitives such as fences and barriers and release and acquire operations, see, for example, Hennessy and Patterson [1996].

[6]It is important to remember that, in discussions of memory-consistency models, the notion of *when a write happens* means *when its results are observed* and not *when the write is issued*.

Fails to satisfy strict consistency:

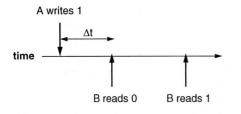

Satisfies strict consistency:

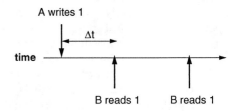

FIGURE 4.8: Strict consistency. Each timeline shows a sequence of read/write events to a particular location. For strict consistency to hold, B must read what A wrote to a given memory location, regardless of how little time passes between the events.

following are some of the most commonly used models for the behavior of the memory system (tenets stolen from Tanenbaum [1995]):

>   **Strict Consistency:** A read operation shall return the value written by the most recent store operation.
>
>   **Sequential Consistency:** The result of an execution is the same as a single interleaving of sequential, program-order accesses from different processors.
>
>   **Processor Consistency:** Writes from a process are observed by other clients to be in program order; all clients observe a single interleaving of writes from different processors.

The following sections describe these in more detail.

Strict Consistency

Strict consistency is the model traditionally provided by uniprocessors, and it is the model for which most programs are written. The basic tenet is

>   *A read operation shall return the value written by the most recent store operation.*

This is illustrated in Figure 4.8, which demonstrates the inherent problem with the model: it is not realistic in a multiprocessor sense. Nonetheless, the model is intuitively appealing. If any process has written a value to a variable, the next read to that variable will return the value written. The model is unrealistic for multiprocessors in that it fails to account for any communication latency: if A and B are on different processors and must communicate via a bus or network or some realistic channel with non-zero latency, then how does one support such a model? The "most recent store" definition causes non-trivial problems. Suppose B performs a read to the same location a fraction of a second ("Δt" in the figure) after A's write operation. If the time-of-flight between two processors is longer than the "fraction of a second" timing between the write and following read, then there is no means for B even to know of the write event at the moment its read request is issued. Such a system will not be strictly consistent unless it has hardware or software support[7] to prevent such race conditions, and such support will most likely degrade the performance of the common case.

As mentioned, a strictly consistent memory system behaves like a uniprocessor memory system, and note that it would, indeed, solve the problem demonstrated in Figure 4.6. Because C's read to the data buffer cannot happen before A has finished writing the

---

[7]For instance, numerous schemes exist that maintain time in a distributed system, including virtual clocks, causal clocks, broadcasts and revocations, timestamps, etc. So there are numerous ways to support such a scheme.

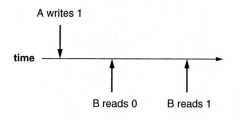

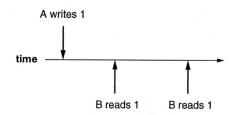

FIGURE 4.9: Sequential consistency. Unlike Figure 4.8, both scenarios are considered valid. Sequential consistency allows an arbitrary delay after which write data becomes available to subsequent reads.

data buffer, a cache-coherence scheme implementing a strict consistency model will ensure that C cannot get old data.

Sequential Consistency

Despite its appeal of simplicity, the strict consistency model is viewed by many as being far too expensive an implementation: one must give up *significant* performance to obtain the convenient synchronization benefits. The good news is that, with appropriate use of explicit synchronization techniques, one can write perfectly functional code on multiple processors without having to resort to using strict consistency. A slightly relaxed model that still provides much of the guarantees of the strict model is the sequential consistency model [Lamport 1979], which has the following basic tenet:

> The result of an execution is the same as a single interleaving of sequential, program-order accesses from different processors.

What this says is that accesses on different processors must be in program order (no reordering of memory requests is allowed); accesses from different processors can be interleaved freely, but all processors must see the same interleaving. Note that the interleaving may change from run to run of the program. The model is illustrated in Figure 4.9, which compares to Figure 4.8. Here, both sequences are considered valid by the model.

How does the model support the problem in Figure 4.6? At first glance, it would not handle the scenario correctly, which would be a little distressing, but there are more details to consider. In particular, the only realistic way for device A to propagate information to process B is through a device driver, whose invocation would involve a write to the memory system (see Figures 4.10 and 4.11). Figure 4.10 shows the previous example in more detail, including the device driver activity by which A propagates information to B. Figure 4.11 then compares the two scenarios in terms of timelines. Figure 4.11(a) shows the timeline of events as suggested by the original scenario, which would fail to behave as expected in a sequentially consistent memory system: a sequentially consistent model does not require that A's write to the variable *data* and B's write to the variable *ready* occur in any specific order. In particular, A's write to *data* may be seen by the system after B's write to *ready*.

However, as mentioned, the picture in Figure 4.6 and its corresponding timeline in Figure 4.11(a) are not realistic. The scenario implies that information propagates from A to B without going through the memory system. In contrast, Figure 4.11(b) paints a more realistic picture of what happens, including the movement of data through the device driver, in particular, through a variable in the driver's space called *done*. This scenario will behave as expected under a sequentially consistent memory system. In contrast with the simpler picture, in which the transmission of information from A to B is unobserved by the memory system (and thus a coherence mechanism would be hard pressed to deduce causality between the events), in this picture the memory system observes all of the relevant events. In particular, the following event orderings are seen in a sequentially consistent system:

1. A writes *data*, followed by A writing *done* (seen by A and thus seen by all)
2. A writes *done*, followed by B reading *done* or some other variable written by the device driver (seen by device driver and B and thus seen by all)

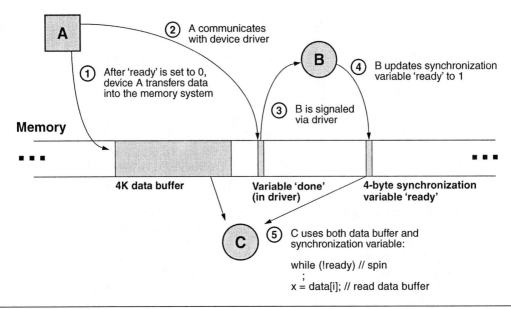

FIGURE 4.10: Race condition example, more detail. The previous model ignored (intentionally) the method by which device A communicates to process B: the device driver. Communication with the device driver is through the memory system—memory locations and/or memory-mapped I/O registers.

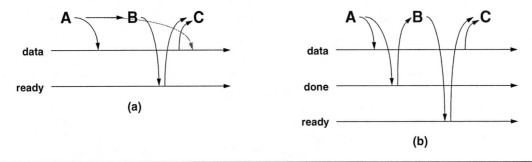

FIGURE 4.11: Realistic picture of data movement and causality. In (a), information propagates directly from A to B without going through the memory system. Because the memory system does not observe the information, it cannot deduce causality, and thus it is possible for A's write to *data* to be delayed until after C's read of *data*. In reality, A and B are most likely to communicate through a device driver. Assume that the driver has a variable called "done;" (b) shows the picture of data movement and causality that makes sequential consistency work for this scenario.

3. B reads *done* ... C reads *data* (seen by B and C and thus by all)

Because sequential consistency requires a global ordering of events that is seen by all clients of the memory system, any ordering seen by any process becomes *the* ordering that must be guaranteed by the memory system. Thus, C is guaranteed to read the correct version of the data buffer. Note again that the main reason this occurs is because the communication between A and B is actually through the memory system (either a memory location or memory-mapped I/O), and thus, the communication becomes part of the consistency model's view of causality.

Some example issues to note about the implementation of a sequentially consistent memory system are the following:

- All I/O must go through the coherence scheme. Otherwise, the coherence mechanism would miss A's write to the location *done*. Either I/O is memory-mapped, and the I/O locations are within the scope of the coherence mechanism, or, if I/O is not memory-mapped and instead uses special I/O primitives in the instruction set, the coherence scheme must be made aware of these special operations.

- The example assumes that A's write to the buffer *data* and A's write to the variable *done* are either handled by the same thread of control or at least handled on the same processor core. While this is a reasonable assumption given a uniprocessor implementation, it is not a reasonable assumption for a CMP (chip multiprocessor). If the assumption is not true, then event ordering #1 above (A writes *data*, followed by A writing *done*) does not hold true. As far as the system is concerned, if these operations are performed on different processor cores, then they are considered to be "simultaneous" and thus unrelated. In this event, they may be placed in arbitrary order by a sequentially consistent memory system.

- Another implication arises from the definition of sequential consistency: for all clients in the system to agree on an ordering, all clients will have to see external events in a timely manner, a fact that impacts the buffering of operations. In particular, write buffering, something long considered absolutely essential for good performance, is typically disallowed altogether in a sequentially consistent system. Modern processor cores have load/store queues into which write instructions deposit their store data. This store data is not propagated to the memory system (i.e., the local caches, which are visible to the coherence engine) until the write instruction *commits*, often long after the write is initiated. Thus, a write operation can be buffered for a relatively long period of time relative to local read operations, which are usually sent to the local caches as soon as their target addresses are known.

Sequential consistency requires that local interleavings of events be reflected globally. This is unlikely to happen if the rest of the system finds out about a local write operation much later, at which point all other clients will be forced to back out of operations that conflict with the local ordering of events. Consider the following operations on a given client: a write to location A, followed by reads that cause read misses to locations B, C, and D. If the reads to B, C, and D are seen by the rest of the system before the write to A is propagated out (i.e., the write is buffered until just after the read requests go out), an implementation will be very hard pressed to make all other clients in the system behave as if the write *preceded* the reads, as it did from the perspective of the initial client. One alternative is to make a node's write buffer visible to the coherence engine, as suggested in the write-through cache illustration (Figure 4.1). Note that this would require opening up a processor core's load/store queue to the coherence engine, a cost considered prohibitive if the cores are on separate chips. However, the current industry trend toward multi-cores on-chip may make this scheme viable, at least in providing a locally consistent (chip-wide consistent) cache system.

- A similar implication arises from studying Hennessy and Patterson's example, originally proposed by Goodman [1989], in which a symmetric race condition occurs between two simultaneously executing processes, P1 and P2:

P1:	(initially, A=0)	**P2:**	(initially, B=0)
	A=1;		B=1;
	if (B==0) {		if (A==0) {
	kill P2;		kill P1;
	}		}

A sequentially consistent memory system will allow 0 or 1 processes to be killed, but not both. For instance, P1 will only try to kill P2 if P1's read to B occurs before P2's write to B. By the definition of sequential consistency (which stipulates the in-order execution of memory events), this would imply that P1's write to A must come before P2's read of A. The symmetric argument holds equally well.

The implication for an implementation of this model is illustrated in Figure 4.12: not only must writes not be buffered (as mentioned in the previous bullet), but reads must be delayed long enough for write information to propagate to the rest of the system. To ensure that two processes synchronize their memory events in a way that ensures sequential consistency, an implementation must do one of two things: either (i) block all subsequent memory operations following a write until all processor cores have observed the write event or (ii) allow bypassing and/or early execution of memory instructions subsequent to the write operation, but hold their commitment until long enough after the write operation to ensure that all processor cores can observe the write. The implication of speculative bypassing is that if in the meantime a write is observed originating from another core that conflicts with an early executing memory operation, that instruction's commitment must be halted, its results must be discarded, and the instruction must be reexecuted in light of the new data.

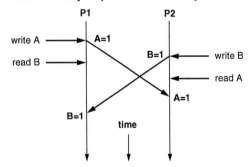

Fails to satisfy sequential consistency:

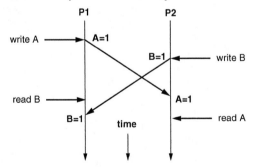

Satisfies sequential consistency:

FIGURE 4.12: Sequential consistency and racing threads. A memory system that satisfies sequential consistency must delay all memory operations following a write until the write is observed by all other clients. Otherwise, it would be possible to have both P1 and P2 try to kill each other (as in the scenario on the left), which is disallowed by the sequential model. For example, the earliest that a subsequent read can follow a write is the message-propagation time within the system. Alternatively, a processor can speculate, allowing reads to execute early and patching up if problems are later detected.

As the last two bullets attest, in a sequentially consistent memory system, write performance will be abysmal and read performance will suffer, or the implementation will embody significant complexity to avoid the performance limitations of the model.

Processor Consistency

So how does one avoid the limitations of a sequentially consistent memory system? A further relaxation of memory consistency is called processor consistency [Goodman 1989], also called *total store order*. Its basic tenet is

> *Writes from a process are observed by other clients to be in program order; all clients observe a single interleaving of writes from different processors.*

This simply removes the read-ordering restriction imposed by sequential consistency: a processor is free to reorder reads ahead of writes without waiting for write data to be propagated to other clients in the system. The racing threads example, if executed on an implementation of processor consistency, can result in both processes killing each other: reads need not block on preceding writes; they may even execute ahead of preceding writes (see Figure 4.13). Similarly, the example illustrated in Figures 4.10 and 4.11 could easily result in unexpected behavior: processor consistency allows reads to go as early as desired, which would allow C's read of the data buffer to proceed before C's read of the variable *ready* finishes (consider, for example, the scenario in which the conditional branch on the value of *ready* is predicted early and correctly):

```
if (ready) {
    read data buffer
}
```

Ensuring correct behavior in such a consistency model requires the use of explicit release/acquire mechanisms (e.g., see Hennessy and Patterson [1996] for example code) in the update of either the device driver variable *done* or the variable *ready*.

Other Consistency Models

This might seem all that is necessary, but there are many further relaxations. For instance,

- *Partial store order* allows a processor to freely reorder local writes with respect to other local writes.
- *Weak consistency* allows a processor to freely reorder local writes ahead of local reads.

Satisfies processor consistency:

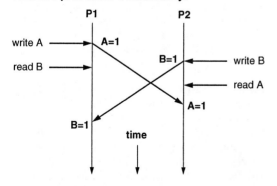

Satisfies processor consistency:

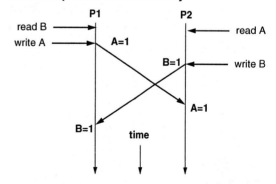

FIGURE 4.13: Processor consistency and racing threads. Processor consistency allows each processor or client within the system to reorder freely reads with respect to writes. As a result, the racing threads example can easily result in both processes trying to kill each other (both diagrams illustrate that outcome).

All of the consistency models up until this point preserve the ordering of synchronization accesses: to wit, locks, barriers, and the like may not be reordered and thus serve as synchronization points. Given this, there are further relaxations of consistency that exploit this.

- *Release consistency* distinguishes different classes of synchronization accesses (i.e., acquire of a lock versus release of the lock) and enforces synchronization only with respect to the acquire/release operations. When software does an *acquire*, the memory system updates all protected variables before continuing, and when software does a *release*, the memory system propagates any changes to the protected variables out to the rest of the system.

Other forms such as *entry consistency* and *lazy release consistency* are discussed in Section 4.3.5.

4.3.4 Hardware Cache-Coherence Mechanisms

So, given the various memory-consistency models to choose from, how does one go about supporting one? There are two general implementations:

- Software solutions that build cache coherence into the virtual memory system and add sharing information to the page tables, thereby providing shared memory across a general network
- Hardware solutions that run across dedicated processor busses and come in several flavors, including snoopy schemes and directory-based schemes.

This section will describe hardware solutions. Section 4.3.5 will describe software solutions.

Cache Block States

To begin with, a cache must track the state of its contents, and the states in which a block may find itself can be varied, especially when one considers the information required when multiple clients all

want access to the same data. Some of the requirements facing a cache include the following:

- The cache must be able to enforce exclusive updating of lines, to preserve the illusion that a single writer exists in the system at any given moment. This is perhaps the easiest way to enforce a global sequence of write events to a particular address. Caches typically track this with Modified and/or Exclusive states (M/E states).
- The cache must be able to tell if a cache block is out of sync with the rest of the system due to a local write event. Caches typically track this with Modified and/or Owned states (M/O states).
- An implementation can be more efficient if it knows when a client only needs a readable copy of a particular datum and does not intend to write to it. Caches typically track this with a Shared state (S).

(I)nvalid: Invalid means that the cache block is in an uninitialized state.

(M)odified: read-writable, forwardable, dirty: Modified means that the state of the cache block has been changed by the processor; the block is *dirty*. This usually happens when a processor overwrites (part of) the block via a store instruction. The client with a block in this state has the only cached copy of that block in the system and responds to snoops for this block by forwarding the block (returning the data in a response message) and also writing the block back to the backing store.

(S)hared: read-only (can be clean or dirty): Shared means that the cache line in question may have multiple copies in the caches of multiple clients. Being in a Shared state does not imply that the cache block is actively being shared among processes. Rather, it implies that another copy of the data is held in a remote processor's cache.

(E)xclusive: read-writable, clean: Exclusive means that a processor can modify a given cache block without informing any other clients. To write a cache block, the processor must first acquire the block in an exclusive state. Thus, even if the processor holds a copy of the data in the data cache, it first requires a transaction to the backing store (or wherever the coherence mechanism is homed) to request the data in Exclusive state. The client with a block in this state has the only cached copy of that block in the system, and it may forward that block in response to a snoop request. Once written by the client, the block is transitioned to the Modified state.

(O)wned: read-only, forwardable, dirty: Owned means that a cache can send other clients a copy of the (dirty) data without needing to write back, but the Owner is the only one who can write the block back to the backing store. The block is read-only: the client holding the block may forward it, but may not write it.

Note that this is just a sample of common states. Protocols exist that make use of many other states as well. This is enough to get an idea of what has been done.

Using Write-Through Caches (SI)

We start with a simple example: a system of write-through caches, as shown in Figure 4.14. In such a scheme, all writes are transmitted directly through

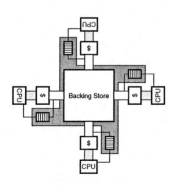

FIGURE 4.14: A system of write-through caches.

to memory, even if considering the existence of write buffers or write caches. Because the backing store is known to be consistent with each cache at all times, a cache may "silently" evict any cache block at any time, even if that block was recently written by the processor.

In such a scheme, cache blocks need only track SI states: a block is either present in a cache or not. Writes are propagated to the backing store immediately by definition of the scheme, and thus, in a sense, the problem of handling multiple writers to the same datum is transferred to the shoulders of the backing store.

Write-update: Typically, write events will cause one of two responses: *write-update* or *write-invalidate*. A write-update policy will transparently update the various cached copies of a block: if processor A writes to a block, the write data will find its way into all cached copies of that block. This clearly requires significant bandwidth: every local write immediately becomes a global broadcast of data. The mechanism, though expensive, is extremely beneficial in handling applications that make use of widely shared data. It is non-trivial to implement because it requires shoving unsolicited data into another client's data cache.

Write-invalidate: The alternative to write-update is a write-invalidate policy, in which all cached copies of the written block are set to the Invalid state. All clients actively sharing the block will suddenly find their cached copies unavailable, and each must re-request the block to continue using it. This can be less bandwidth-intensive than a write-update scheme, but the general implementation mechanism is similar: an address must be sent to remote caches, each of which must check in its tag store to see if the affected datum is present.

The primary difference between the two is that in a write-invalidate policy, there can be only one writable copy of a datum in the system at any given point in time. In contrast, a write-update policy can easily support multiple writers, and, in fact, this is precisely what software implementations of cache coherence do. In addition, note that, by its nature, a write-update scheme makes sequential consistency *extremely* hard to implement: to guarantee that all clients see all operations in the same order, an implementation must guarantee that all update messages are interleaved with all other system-wide coherence messages in the same order for all nodes. While systems exist that do this (e.g., ISIS [Birman & Joseph 1987]), they tend to be relatively slow.

Using Write-Back Caches (MSI)

To reduce bandwidth requirements, one can change the scheme slightly (use write-back caches instead of write-through caches) and not propagate write data immediately. The scheme exploits write-coalescing in the data caches: multiple writes to the same cache block will not necessarily generate multiple coherence broadcasts to the system; rather, coherence messages will only be sent out when the written block is removed from the cache. Unlike the write-through scenario, in this scheme, data in a particular cache may be out of sync with the backing store and the other clients in the system. The implementation must ensure that this allows no situations that would be deemed incorrect by the chosen consistency model. Figure 4.15 illustrates a possible state machine for the implementation.

Whereas a write-through cache is permitted to evict a block silently at any time (e.g., to make room for incoming data), a write-back cache must first update the backing store before evicting a block, if the evicted block contains newer data than the backing store. To handle this, the cache must add a new state, Modified, to keep track of which blocks are dirty and must be written back to the backing store. As with the write-through example, writes may be handled with either a write-update or write-invalidate policy.

MSI-protocol implementations typically require that reads to Invalid blocks (i.e., read misses) first ensure that no other client holds a Modified copy of the requested block and that a cache with a Modified block returns the written data to a requestor immediately. A write request to a Shared or Invalid block must first notify all other client caches so that they can change their local copies of the block to the Invalid state. These steps ensure that the most recently written data in the system is relayed to any client that wants to read the block. While this mirrors the read-modify-write nature of many data accesses, it forces the process to require two steps in all instances.

In particular, when an MSI client acquires a block on a read miss, the block is acquired in the Shared state, and to write it the client must then follow this with a write-invalidate broadcast so that it can place the block in the Modified state and overwrite the block with new data. In an alternative MSI implementation, all reads

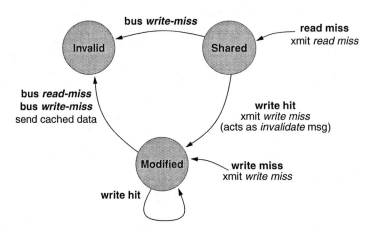

FIGURE 4.15: State machine for an MSI protocol [based on Archibald and Baer 1986]. Boldface font indicates observed action (e.g., local write miss to block in question, or a bus transaction from another cache on a block address matching in the local tags). Regular font indicates response action taken by local cache.

could use a write-invalidate broadcast to acquire *all* read blocks in a Modified state, just in case they might wish to write them later. This latter approach, while reducing the broadcast messages required for a write operation, would eliminate the possibility of real read-sharing (every block would be cached in, at most, one place). In addition, even if the block is not, in fact, modified by the requesting client, the fact that it is acquired in the Modified state implies that it must be written back to the backing store upon eviction, thereby turning all memory operations into *de facto* writes.

Alternatively, the addition of the Exclusive state solves the same problem: a MESI protocol provides another mechanism for acquiring read data that requires no global update or broadcast request when the client chooses to write the acquired block.

Reducing Write Broadcasts (MESI)

To provide a lower overhead write mechanism, the Exclusive state is added to the system's write-back caches. A client in the system may not write to a cache block unless it first acquires a copy of the block in the Exclusive state, and only one system-wide copy of that block may be marked Exclusive. Even if a client has a readable copy of the block in its data cache (e.g., in the Shared state), the client may not write the block unless it first acquires the block in an Exclusive

state. Figure 4.16 illustrates a possible state machine for the implementation.

Compared to the Modified and Shared states, the Exclusive state is somewhere in between—a state in which the client has the authority to write the block, but the block is not yet out of sync with the backing store. A block in this state can be written by the client without first issuing a write-invalidate, or it can be forwarded to another client without the need to update the backing store (in which case it can no longer be marked Exclusive). In a MESI implementation, the first step in a write operation is for a processor to perform a read-exclusive bus transaction. This informs all clients in the system of an upcoming write to the requested block, and it typically invalidates all extant copies of the block found in client caches. Once the block is acquired in an Exclusive state, the processor may freely overwrite the data at will. When the cache block is written, it changes to the Modified state, which indicates that the data is dirty—out of sync with the backing store and requiring a write-back at a later time.

The written data becomes visible to the rest of the system later when the block is evicted from the writer's cache, causing a write-back to the backing store. Alternatively, the cache-coherence mechanism could prompt the Exclusive owner to propagate changes back to the backing store early if, in the meantime,

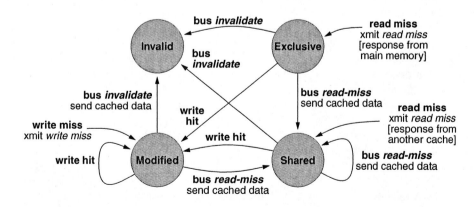

FIGURE 4.16: State machine for a MESI protocol [based on Archibald and Baer 1986]. Boldface font indicates observed action (e.g., local write miss to block in question, or a bus transaction from another cache on a block address matching in the local tags). Regular font indicates response action taken by local cache.

another client in the system experiences a read miss on the block, its cached copy having been invalidated (e.g., see Section 4.1.3). As with the MSI protocol, the chosen memory-consistency model defines whether a delayed write-back is considered correct behavior; most implementations require that a cache with a Modified block return the data immediately, but one can envision implementations of relaxed consistency models that allow the holder of the Modified block to delay writing the data back to the backing store until it is convenient for the owner of the block. Regardless of the implementation, the block is returned to the Exclusive state once the backing store is consistent with the cached copy.

One downside of the MESI protocol (as with MSI and SI protocols as well) is that, in a sense, all coherence activity passes through a centralized point (the backing store). While this may make sense for a typical symmetric multiprocessor organization with multiple clients and a central backing store, it may make less sense in a system where control is distributed across the clients rather than centralized in a single place. Alternatively, the protocol could be enhanced to support client-to-client transactions that need not pass through the backing store. This is one function of the Owned state that is added to MOESI protocols.

Distributing Control (MOESI)

To make it easier to distribute the task of maintaining cache coherence, the Owned state is added to the system. This state indicates transfer of ownership of a block from a writer to another client directly. Thus, the MOESI protocol is useful particularly in systems that have good client-to-client bandwidth, but not necessarily good bandwidth between the client and the backing store (e.g., CMPs or NUCA organizations).

In a MOESI system, just like a MESI system, a single client may hold a block in Exclusive state, enabling the client to write the block. When the block is written, the block becomes Modified. Unlike a MESI protocol, the MOESI protocol allows the holder of a Modified block to transfer the block directly to another client and to bypass the backing store completely, at which point the new client places the block into the

Owned state. Unlike the Exclusive state, the Owned state allows the block to be replicated to other clients (where it would be held in a Shared state). Only the holder of the Owned block may write the block back to the backing store, and an Owned block as well as any Shared copies derived from it may be out of sync (dirty) with respect to the backing store.

The primary mechanism that exploits the Owned state is "snarfing," illustrated in Figure 4.17. MOESI-based snarfing cache systems are found in AMD's Opteron and Athlon MP [Keltcher 2002, Huynh 2003] and Sun's UltraSPARC-I [Sun 1995]. In the process of snarfing, one processor's cache grabs an item off the bus that another processor's cache is writing back to main memory, with the expectation that the other processor may need that item in the near future. When a cache snarfs data off the shared bus, it tags the cache block locally as Owned. The idea behind this activity is that it would be far faster to retrieve the "snarfed" object from another cache than to retrieve it from main memory, and doing so would significantly reduce traffic to the DRAM system. This is the distributed processor cache realization of an observation made in the realm of distributed file caches [Nelson et al. 1988], namely that it can be faster to load a page of data over a 10-Mbps Ethernet link from the physical memory of a file server than it is to load the page from local disk. To wit, it can be faster to load a cache block from a neighboring microprocessor's cache than it is to load the cache block from main memory.

Cache Organization Issues

Several issues related to cache organization arise. The choice to maintain inclusion impacts the implementation significantly, and the choice of a private versus shared last-level cache can dramatically change application performance [Jaleel & Jacob 2006] as well as the coherence implementation.

Inclusive, Exclusive, or Non-Inclusive? First, the following are issues to consider in the choice of inclusive versus exclusive or non-inclusive caches:

- **Inclusive caches** simplify the coherence mechanism in many ways. For instance,

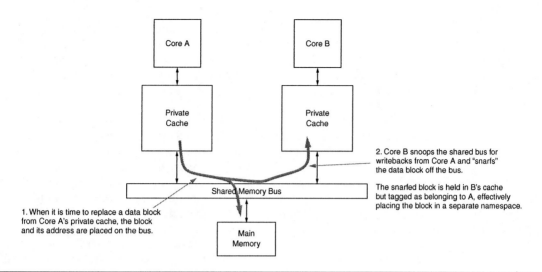

FIGURE 4.17: MOESI-based snarfing caches.

the coherence scheme need probe only the lowest level of a client's cache when performing invalidates or updates. If a block is not found in the lowest level of an inclusive cache hierarchy, the block cannot be found at a higher level. This allows a coherence probe to proceed without disturbing the core's interaction with the L1 cache. However, the duplication of data (and wastage of die area) in an inclusive cache hierarchy can become significant, especially if multiple processor cores and their associated L1/L2 caches feed off the same lower level shared cache.

- The advantage of **exclusive caches** is that they avoid the duplication of data and wastage of die area associated with inclusive caches. However, the costs are significant: a coherence probe must search the entire hierarchy, not just the lowest level cache (note that rather than probing all levels of the cache, potentially interrupting/stalling the core to probe the L1 cache, the higher level tag sets are typically replicated down at the last-level cache to centralize the tags needed for a coherence check). In addition,

managing the cascading evictions and allocations from/into the L1 cache is non-trivial.

- **Non-inclusive caches** attempt to achieve the best of both worlds. A non-inclusive cache tries neither to ensure exclusion nor to maintain inclusion. For instance, an inclusive cache will evict multiple blocks from an L1 cache in response to a single-block eviction from the L2 cache when the L1/L2 block sizes differ. In contrast, a non-inclusive cache makes no attempt to do so, and thus, the L1 cache may retain portions of a block recently evicted from the L2 cache. An exclusive cache will ensure that no data from a block promoted from the L2 cache to the L1 cache remains in the L2 cache, which will require data to be thrown away, either from the promoted block or from extra evicted L1 blocks. In contrast, a non-inclusive cache makes no attempt to ensure this. The disadvantage of the scheme is that, like the exclusive cache hierarchy, it must maintain copies of the higher level tag sets down with the last-level cache to avoid interrupting the processor cores in response to coherence traffic.

Shared or Private Last-Level Cache? Another cache-organization issue is the design choice of a shared versus private last-level cache [Jaleel & Jacob, 2006]. As multi-core processors become pervasive and the number of cores increases, a key design issue facing processor architects will be the hierarchy and policies for the last-level cache (LLC). The most important application characteristics that drive this cache hierarchy and design are the amount and type of sharing exhibited by important multi-threaded applications. For example, if the target multi-threaded applications exhibit little or no sharing, and the threads have similar working-set sizes, a simple "SMP on a chip" strategy may be the best approach. In such a case, each core has its own private cache hierarchy. Any memory block that is shared by more than one core is replicated in the hierarchies of the respective cores, thereby lowering the effective cache capacity. On a cache miss, the hierarchies of all the other cores' caches must be snooped (depending on the specifics of the inclusion policy).

On the other hand, if the target multi-threaded applications exhibit a significant amount of sharing, or if the threads have varying working-set sizes, a shared-cache CMP is more attractive. In this case, a single, large, last-level cache, which may be centralized or distributed, depending on bandwidth requirements, is shared by all the on-die cores. Cache blocks that are referenced by more than one core are not replicated in the shared cache. Furthermore, the shared cache naturally accommodates variations between the working-set sizes of the different threads. In essence (and at the risk of oversimplifying), the CMP design team, building a chip with C cores and room for N bytes of last-level cache, must decide between building C private caches of N/C bytes each or one large shared cache of N bytes. Of course, there is a large solution space between the two extremes, including replication of read-only blocks, migration of blocks, and selective exclusion, to name just a few. However, the key application characteristics concerning the amount of data sharing and type of sharing are important for the entire design space.

Note that the choice of LLC cache organization impacts how and where the cache coherence can be implemented, at least to maintain coherence between the caches on-chip. In a private cache organization, coherence must be maintained after the last-level cache. In a shared-cache organization, coherence can be part of the cache's existing interconnect infrastructure.

Interconnect Options and Their Ramifications

Figure 4.18 illustrates some of the choices facing a designer when organizing the backing store. The backing store is an abstraction, meaning *everything beyond this point*, but the realization of the abstraction in a physical system will significantly impact the design of the associated coherence scheme.

We will return to this later at the end of the section, but for now it is worthwhile to consider the ramifications of system organization on the design of a coherence protocol. Shared-bus organizations lend themselves to protocols that rely upon each cache observing all system-wide activity and responding to any requests that apply. Distributed organizations (called *links-based* systems, as opposed to bus-based systems) imply a less centralized approach, because, unless memory requests and/or coherence messages are explicitly relayed to achieve an effective broadcast within the system, not all clients will be aware of all system-wide activity. The distributed organization also suggests, at least potentially, a less serialized approach. It exhibits the obvious advantage that because different subnets can be operative simultaneously handling different requests, much more communication can be sustained throughout the system. The decentralization, while creating a potential controls problem, increases potential bandwidth and thus performance tremendously. Links-based organizations typically exhibit anywhere from a factor of two to an order of magnitude higher sustainable bandwidth than the fastest shared-bus organizations.

The two physical organizations translate to two different styles of coherence mechanism, though it is possible to implement either type of mechanism on either of the physical organizations. The two main types of cache-coherence implementations are *directory based* and *snoop based* (i.e., "snoopy"). A directory-based implementation maintains the state of

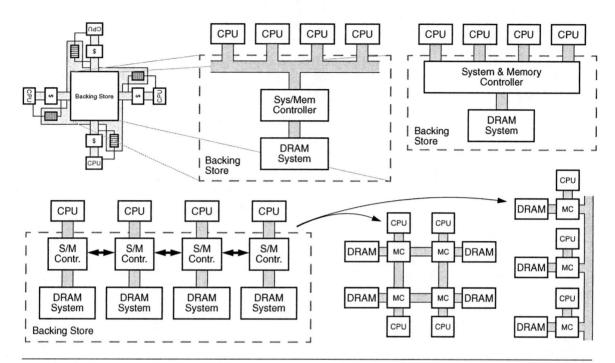

FIGURE 4.18: The many faces of backing store. The backing store in a multiprocessor system can take on many forms. In particular, a primary characteristic is whether the backing store is distributed or not. Moreover, the choices within a distributed organization are just as varied. The two organizations on the bottom right are different implementations of the design on the bottom left.

each cache block in a data structure associated with that cache block. The data structure contains such information as the block's ownership, its sharing status, etc. These data structures are all held together in a *directory*, which can be centralized or distributed; when a client makes a request for a cache block, its corresponding directory entry is first consulted to determine the appropriate course of action.

A snoop-based scheme uses no such per-block data structure. Instead, the appropriate course of action is determined by consulting every client in the system. On every request, each cache in the system is consulted and responds with information on the requested block; the collected information indicates the appropriate response. For instance, rather than looking up the owner of a block in the block's directory entry as would be the appropriate step in a directory-based scheme, in a snoopy scheme the owner of the block actively responds to a coherence broadcast,

indicating ownership and returning the requested data (if such is the appropriate response).

Snoopy Protocols

In a snoopy protocol, all coherence-related activity is broadcast to all processors. All processors analyze all activity, and each reacts to the information passing through the system based on the contents of its caches. For example, if one processor is writing to a given data cache line, and another processor has a copy of the data cache line, then the second processor must invalidate its own cache line. After writing the block, the first processor now has a dirty copy. If the second processor then makes a read request to that block, the first processor must provide it.

Snoopy protocols seem to imply the existence of a common bus for their implementation, but they need not use common busses if there is agreement between clients to propagate messages (e.g., thereby emulating bus-based broadcasts). The fundamental tenet of a snoopy protocol is that every cache watches the system, observes every request, checks its local state to determine if it should become involved, and does so if appropriate. Global state is maintained by a distributed state machine in the collected tags of the distributed cache; the caches all participate together in the state transitions. In a bus-based system, this means that every cache sits on the shared bus and watches every request go by ("snoops the bus"). To determine the correct location or state of a block in a links-based system, explicit messages must be sent to snoop the caches of other nodes.

Because the coherence communication is fundamentally between caches, which together manage the state of the system's cached blocks, memory bandwidth to the backing store is less of a concern. The primary issue is to supply enough inter-cache bandwidth to support the expected coherence traffic, which tends to grow linearly (as $O(n)$) with the number of clients in the system. Another issue is cache bandwidth. Because the caches manage the coherence state of the system's blocks, and because potentially every memory request may result in multiple coherence probes above and beyond the cache probes required by a

processor core to execute its software, caches must be designed to handle multiple simultaneous probes. As described earlier, inclusive caches make this relatively simple, as the lowest level cache can handle coherence probes at the same time that the highest level caches are handling processor-core data requests. Other cache organizations require multiple tag sets to handle the requisite probe bandwidth.

Source snoopy: One of the implementation choices in a snoopy protocol is a source-snoopy (2-hop) implementation versus a home-snoopy (3-hop) implementation. In a source-snoopy protocol, snoops are sent from a requestor to all peer clients. This tends to result in a relatively low average response time to requests, but an implementation must deal with issues such as many-to-many race conditions. Figure 4.19 illustrates the messages that are sent in a simple read-miss event in a source-snoopy protocol. Figure 4.20 illustrates the messages that are sent in a slightly more complex scenario (read miss to a Modified block). Since all coherence messages are broadcasts, the owner of a block will always be a recipient. When a client cache broadcasts a read request on a cache miss, the current owner of the block writes the data back

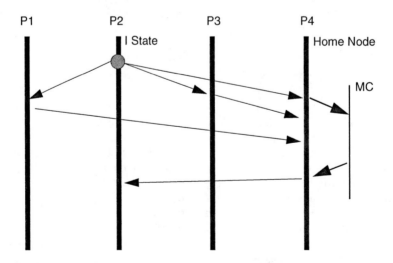

FIGURE 4.19: Read miss to uncached data, source snoopy. Time flows down the page.

to the backing store (e.g., assuming a MESI protocol) and sends a copy of the data to the requesting client. The requestor receives the data in two network hops.

Home snoopy: In a home-snoopy protocol, requests are sent to a datum's home node first, and then the home node sends snoops to other clients. The mechanism is much simpler than source-snoopy protocols because the serialization eliminates race conditions. However, the obvious cost is in a higher average latency. For example, Figure 4.21 illustrates the slightly more complex read-miss scenario in the context of a home-snoopy protocol. When a client experiences a read miss in its local cache, the initial coherence message is not a broadcast to the entire system, but a request directed at the block's home node, which then generates the appropriate snoop requests. Ultimately, the requested data is sent to the original client after three network hops.

Directory-Based Protocols

An alternative to snoopy implementations is to centralize the state information in a directory, as opposed to distributing the state information in the tags of the distributed cache. Thus, a directory-based protocol does not need the cooperation of all the caches in the system; a data request need only consult the directory to determine the correct course of action. The directory may be centralized or distributed, but the fact that it gathers all state information into one place simplifies the system-level state machine that implements the coherence scheme. A directory entry typically includes the following information:

- Current state of the block (cached or non-cached, readable and/or writable)
- What clients in the system have a copy of the block
- An identification of the client responsible for write-back, if such an owner exists (i.e., if the block is cached in a writable state)

On a local cache miss, a client first consults the directory entry for the requested block; the directory entry indicates where the block can be found and in what state, and the client makes a request directly to the client/s holding copies of the block. The mechanism has constant overhead in message passing (scales as O(1) with the number of clients in the system), but it tends to require more bandwidth

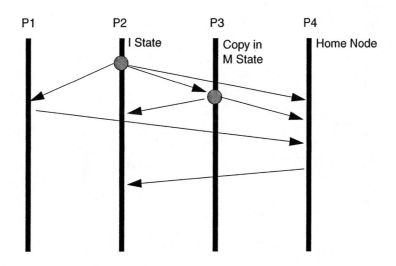

FIGURE 4.20: Read miss to remotely cached Modified data, source snoopy. Time flows down the page.

to the backing store than a snoopy protocol, because the directory structure, being large, is typically held in the backing store. In addition, the directory now becomes a point of serialization in the protocol and thus potentially limits performance (just as the shared bus in a bus-based snoopy protocol is a point of serialization and thus potentially limits performance). Directories are common for links-based organizations because, as a linked system scales in size, the latency to snoop the clusters of processors can quickly become greater than the latency to a node's local backing store (its DRAM system).

Full directory: There are several different options for implementation. First is the size and scope of the directory. As mentioned, the directory structure can be quite large, as a directory entry is on the same size scale of the cache block it manages. A *full directory* implementation maintains one directory entry for every cached block in the system, i.e., every block that is found within the distributed cache, not every cache-block-sized chunk of the backing store (though there have been proposals for such an implementation). A *miss* to the directory—a probe of the directory that fails to match the

requested block ID—thus indicates that the requested block is not cached within the system; the requested block will necessarily come from the backing store. A full directory is relatively large and held in the backing store; e.g., in a multiprocessor system, it is typically held in the DRAM system.

Partial and hybrid directories: A *partial directory* implementation reduces the size of the directory considerably by maintaining entries for only a subset of the cached blocks. A miss to the directory thus conveys no information as it does with a full directory implementation, and the partial directory system must then resort to a snoopy protocol to find the state of the requested block. In such a case, all caches in the system are probed. Because the partial directory is significantly smaller than a full directory, it is typically held in SRAM, thereby improving both the directory's access time and, at least potentially, any serialization issues in those cases when a directory probe hits. Similar to the partial directory is the *hybrid directory*: a multi-level, directory cache arrangement, where a smaller version of the directory, a cache of the full directory, is probed first. The directory

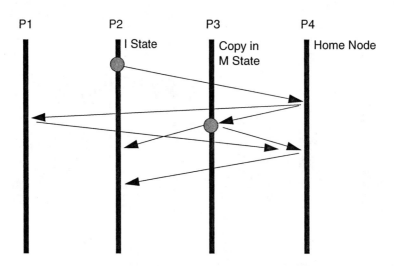

FIGURE 4.21: Read miss to remotely cached Modified data, home snoopy. Time flows down the page.

cache can be small enough to be stored in SRAM. It is similar to the partial directory, except that, in the case of an initial directory-probe miss, the full directory is probed instead of executing a system-wide snoop.

Explicit and coarse pointers: Another implementation option is the granularity with which the directory maintains information on clients holding cached copies of a shared block. Within each directory entry is a list of clients sharing that block, typically represented by a bit vector of Boolean values (e.g., "1" indicates the client has a copy of the block, and "0" indicates the client does not have a copy of the block). An implementation using *explicit pointers* maintains a bit in the vector for each client in the system. An implementation using coarse pointers overloads the bits to represent multiple clients. For example, each bit in the vector could represent a different, tightly coupled cluster of clients within the system. Setting the bit would indicate that one or more client caches within that cluster hold a copy of the block, but there would be no way to determine which cache/s within the cluster has the block.

Perspective on the Coherence Point

Figure 4.22 illustrates three different topologies for small-scale computer systems that are typically found with one to four processors: the classic small-system system topology, the point-to-point processor-controller system topology, and the integrated-controller system topology.

The classic small-system topology illustrates the topology of many different systems. For example, platforms based on Intel's Pentium, Pentium II, Pentium III, Pentium 4, and Itanium processors utilize the classic small-system topology. Also, platforms based on PowerPC 7xx and 74xx series of processors, as well as PA-RISC PA-7200 and PA-8000 processors that utilize the HP Runway bus, similarly utilize the classic small-system topology. In the classic small-system topology, one to four processors are connected to the system controller through a shared processor bus. The processors and the system controller dynamically negotiate for access to the shared processor bus. The owner of the processor bus then uses the shared processor bus to transmit transaction requests, memory addresses, snoop coherency results, transmission error signals, and data.

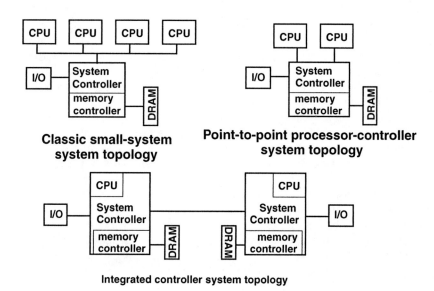

Classic small-system system topology

Point-to-point processor-controller system topology

Integrated controller system topology

FIGURE 4.22: Three different small-scale system topologies.

The point-to-point processor-controller system topology illustrates the topology of systems based on processors such as the Alpha 21264 (EV6), AMD K7, and IBM's PowerPC 970 processors. In the point-to-point processor-controller system topology, one to two processors are connected directly to dedicated ports on the system controller. The point-to-point system topology does not limit the number of processors connected to the system controller, but since the processor connects directly to the system controller, the system controller must have enough pins on the package of the controller and die area devoted to the interface of each processor in the system controller. As a result, systems such as Alpha 21264 processor-based multiprocessor systems that utilize more than two processors with point-to-point processor-controller system topology rely on multiple support chips rather than a single system controller. The point-to-point processor-controller system topology represents a gradual evolution from the classic small-system topology. The point-to-point processor-controller system topology provides an independent datapath between each processor and the system controller, and higher bandwidth is potentially available to the processor in the point-to-point processor-controller system topology as compared to the classic small-system topology.

The integrated system-controller system topology represents the topology of systems such as those based on the AMD Opteron or Alpha 21364 (EV7) processors. In these processors, the system controller and the DRAM memory controller are directly integrated into the processor. The integration of the DRAM memory controller greatly reduces the memory-access latency in a uniprocessor configuration. However, since each processor in a system has its own memory controller, the memory in the system is distributed throughout the system. In these systems, memory-access latency depends on the type of cache coherency protocol utilized, the number of processors in the system, and the location of the memory to be accessed.

In most modern computer systems, both uniprocessor and multiprocessor, the burden of cache coherence is placed in hardware, and cache coherence is enforced at the granularity of transactions.

In these systems, the system controller is typically the coherence point. That is, when a memory reference misses in the processor's private caches, that processor issues a transaction request to the system controller for the desired cache block. In response to the transaction request, the system controller is expected to return the most up-to-date copy data for the requested cache block. As described earlier, the requirement that the data must be the most up-to-date copy means that the system controller is responsible for checking the private caches of other processors in the system for copies of the requested cache line and invalidating the data in those cache lines if necessary. Figure 4.23 abstractly illustrates the concept of the coherence point. In Figure 4.23, the processor issues a transaction request, and coherence checks are issued to other processors in the system concurrently with the read command to the DRAM devices. The coherence status of the transaction and the data for the read transaction are collected at the coherence point, and the coherence point ensures that the data returned to the processor is the most up-to-date copy of the cache line in the system. Figure 4.24 illustrates the timing implication. Data is not returned to a requesting client until coherence is assured, and this remains true whether the coherence check takes longer than a DRAM access or not.

Figure 4.25 shows the respective coherence points in each system topology. These are points of synchronization at which the coherence information for each memory request is checked and processed. In the case of the classic system topology, the processors must dynamically arbitrate for the bus, which provides a form of serialization, and the client-level snooping of all bus transactions is what drives the distributed state machine implementing the consistency model. Thus, the coherence point is at the bus; coherence is assured before a request reaches the system controller. The coherence point is pushed a bit farther out for the point-to-point system topology, to the system controller, which is the first physical entity that sees all transactions (i.e., one microprocessor cannot see the bus transactions of another). Thus, the system controller is the coherence point. In the integrated-controller topology, coherence is assured by a distributed state machine that lies beyond the

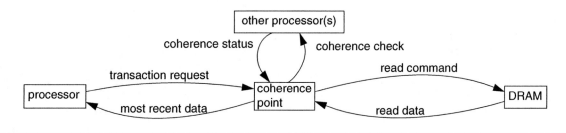

FIGURE 4.23: Abstract illustration of coherence point.

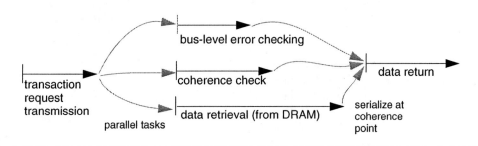

FIGURE 4.24: Abstract illustration of "transaction latency."

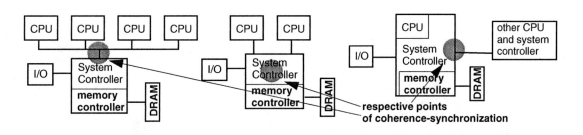

FIGURE 4.25: Coherence point in different system topologies.

system controller. Thus, the coherence point moves a bit farther out toward the rest of the system. Compare this with Figure 4.24; the implication is that, in an integrated-controller system in which each node has its own partition of the backing store, the cost of performing coherence can easily outweigh the cost of going to the local backing store. This implication can easily drive implementations. For instance,

a designer might want to proceed with a memory request speculatively before the coherence state of a block is known. This would require a client to back out of a set of operations if it is later determined that the data used (e.g., returned from the local DRAM system) was out of sync with another cached copy elsewhere in the system. However, such speculation would tend to reduce memory-request latency. Other implementations could include locally held partitions of the global directory that cover only blocks from the local memory system.

4.3.5 Software Cache-Coherence Mechanisms

At first glance, software-based cache-coherence implementations would simply mirror hardware-based implementations. However, as pioneers in the field point out [Li & Hudak 1986, 1989], there is at least one fundamental difference between the two: namely that the communication latency between clients in a software-based implementation is non-trivial compared to the cost of accessing a shared datum, and, consequently, the cost of coherence maintenance is extremely high relative to hardware-based implementations. In comparison, the cost of resolving coherence issues in a shared-bus implementation occurs at the bus level while making a request for a datum in physical memory. Coherence resolution is simply part of the cost of access. In a software implementation, communication may be between operating system kernels on different nodes or even between application-level processes on different nodes; the latency of communication may be many times that of accessing the backing store.

To illustrate some of the approaches used, we briefly discuss four of the earliest shared virtual memory systems:

- **Ivy** [Li & Hudak 1986, 1989], known for distinguishing the granularity of data transfer (large) from the granularity of coherence maintenance (small)
- **Munin** [Bennett et al. 1990a, b, c, Carter et al. 1991], known for its use of twinning and diffing to perform write merging, as well as its use of *release consistency* [Gharachorloo et al. 1990]
- **Midway** [Bershad & Zekauskas 1991, Bershad et al. 1993, Zekauskas et al. 1994], known for its introduction of *entry consistency*
- **TreadMarks** [Keleher et al. 1992, 1994], known for its introduction of *lazy release consistency*

These are admittedly focused on a narrow range of software implementations, namely those integrated with the virtual memory system. Many other software-based cache schemes exist, including those that distribute computational objects or web documents over a network (e.g., Emerald [Jul et al. 1988], Orca [Bal et al. 1992], and numerous web-proxy mechanisms), those that provide uniprocessor cache coherence in software (e.g., Wheeler and Bershad [1992]), and even those that provide multiprocessor cache coherence in software (recall from the mid-1990s the PowerPC-603-based BeBoxen, which implemented cache coherence between two microprocessors without the benefit of cache-coherence hardware [Gassée 1996]).

Ivy

As mentioned earlier, a disparity exists between the cost of access in a software-based cache-coherence implementation and the cost of access in a hardware-based implementation. In a hardware scheme, the coherence management is simply wrapped into the cost of accessing the backing store, while in a software scheme, the management costs are additive and can be extremely high. One of the fundamental results to come out of the shared virtual memory research, addressed in the Ivy system [Li & Hudak 1986, 1989], is a mechanism that addresses this disparity, namely the separation of data-access granularity from coherence-maintenance granularity.

In a shared virtual memory system, the granularity of data access is typically a page, as defined by the virtual memory system: when a node requests a readable copy of the backing store, an entire page of data is transferred to the requesting node. This amortizes the high cost of a network access over a relatively large amount of data transferred. However, the large granularity of data access gives rise to *false sharing*, a scenario in which two different clients try to write to different locations within the same page. Such a scenario is not true sharing; however, because the granularity of access is large, it appears to the coherence engine to be an instance of sharing, and the performance hit of ping-ponging the page back and forth between the two clients is predictably unacceptable.

Ivy's solution to the problem is to monitor coherence on a different scale. When the page is written, the coherence mechanism does not try to reconcile the entire page with clients that might be sharing the data. Rather, the coherence mechanism tracks write activity at the granularity of cache blocks, a choice that reduces the coherence-related communication tremendously.

Munin

Munin takes the concept of multiple writers a bit further [Bennett et al. 1990, Carter et al. 1991]. In the Munin system, write synchronization happens only at explicit boundaries, particularly at the release of a synchronization variable. The model is called *release consistency* [Gharachorloo et al. 1990]; earlier distributed shared memory systems implement sequential consistency. In Munin, clients can freely update shared variables between the acquisition and release of a synchronization variable without generating coherence traffic until the release point, at which point the shared variables are reconciled with the rest of the system.

The coherence engine supports multiple writers to the same data object, but the burden of correct behavior is placed on the shoulders of the programmer, for instance, to ensure that multiple concurrent writers to the same data array write to different parts of the array. In the case of multiple writers, a copy of the page, called a *twin*, is made, which is later used to determine which words within the page were modified. At the release point, the coherence engine merges write data from multiple clients transparently to application processes. Any object that has a twin is first *diffed* against its twin; the diffs represent the changes made by the client and are guaranteed by the programmer not to conflict/overlap with changes made by other clients to the same object. The coherence engine propagates the diffs out to all clients requiring updates, and the clients update their local copies with the changes. The use of release consistency allows many changes to be encapsulated via a diff into a single update message.

Midway

Midway introduces *entry consistency*, a consistency model that further reduces the cost of coherence management [Bershad & Zekauskas 1991, Bershad et al. 1993, Zekauskas et al. 1994]. Whereas *release consistency* in Munin proactively propagates changes to shared data to all sharing clients at the time of a *release* operation, Midway only propagates the changes to clients that explicitly request those changes by later performing an *acquire* operation on one of the changed variables. Thus, at an *acquire* operation, a client requests the latest copies of those variables protected within the critical section of code defined by the *acquire/release* pair. The *release* operation does not cause the coherence engine to propagate changes to the rest of the system. Rather, the *release* signals to the coherence engine that access to the encapsulated variable/s is now allowed.

For this to work, shared variables must be identified and associated with a particular synchronization variable, and clients must access shared variables only inside critical regions (acquire/release pairs on the appropriate synchronization variable). The result is that inter-process communication, rather than being a constant in the number of *release* operations, instead depends entirely on the degree of real sharing within the application.

TreadMarks

TreadMarks [Keleher et al. 1994], another widely cited implementation of distributed shared memory, is known for its introduction of *lazy release consistency* [Keleher et al. 1992], a consistency model that shares many features of *entry consistency* [Bershad & Zekauskas 1991]. Most importantly, both models propagate write information from producer to consumer only at the time of the consuming client's *acquire* operation, a detail that improves network communication tremendously over other mechanisms. The primary difference between the two is in the low-level implementation details of the two systems that implement these models (Midway and TreadMarks) and not necessarily in the consistency models themselves. In particular, Midway requires shared variables to be associated with specific synchronization variables; when an *acquire* operation is performed on a particular synchronization variable, diffs for only those variables associated with the synchronization variable are propagated to the acquiring client. TreadMarks requires shared variables to be protected within critical sections, but shared variables need not be associated with a particular synchronization variable. On an *acquire* operation, prior *release* operations become visible. In addition, Midway uses an update protocol, and TreadMarks uses an invalidate protocol. The two perform very similarly [Adve et al. 1996].

CHAPTER 5

Implementation Issues

This chapter presents the physical implementation (gate/transistor level) and architectural organization of modern-day caches, including a discussion of how this fits in a typical pipeline. One of the most important implementation issues today is that of dealing with the increasingly significant effects of technology scaling. In modern cache implementation, technology scaling exposes and/or exacerbates the following problems:

- The subthreshold leakage current caused by decreasing transistor threshold voltages becomes larger, increasing static power dissipation and requiring both evolutionary and revolutionary solutions to offset its effects.
- The decreasing amount of charge stored per bit makes it easier to corrupt a bit either by an external source (e.g., alpha emission, EMI) or by an internal source (e.g., crosstalk, ground bounce).
- Process variations increasingly cause mismatches of transistor characteristics in the implementation.
- The increasing contribution of wire propagation delay to the total delay must be taken into account in the pipeline's timing budget.

Some contemporary solutions are presented to counter some of the technology scaling problems present in deep and very deep submicron design.

5.1 Overview

To start things off, we discuss a sample cache operation, a cache read hit in moderate detail, exposing some of the implementation issues involved in its design.

Figure 5.1 shows an example cache organization: a two-way, set-associative cache with virtual addressing, along with a timing diagram showing the various events happening in the cache (to be discussed in much more detail in later sections).

Basically, the following steps involve:

1. Providing an address to the cache, along with an address strobe signal (ADS) confirming the validity of the address. A read/write signal (R/W#) is also sent to specify the operation.

2. The index part of the address chooses a word within the tag and data arrays of the two-way, set-associative cache (signified by the wordline signal, WL). This, in turn, causes the internal bitlines to develop a differential, which is amplified by sense amplifiers to produce a full-swing differential output voltage.

3. The translated address from the TLB is compared with the output of the tag array to decide if the cache access hit or miss. In case of a hit, the proper data is chosen among the two ways by controlling the output multiplexer and is forwarded. A cache miss requires the cache controller to perform

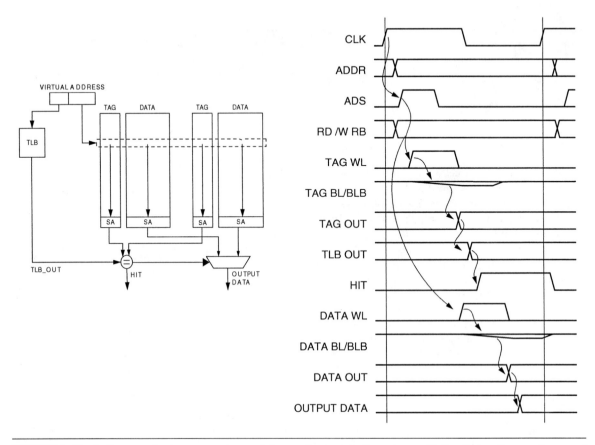

FIGURE 5.1: Block diagram of a two-way, set-associative cache organization, along with the timing diagram for a read operation.

a separate operation to retrieve data from external memory (or another level of cache) and to perform a write access to the cache.

We have now demonstrated the basic cache read operation and shown some of the blocks used in implementing a cache. We will proceed to more in-depth details, starting with the implementation of the basic storage structures comprising the tag and data array and moving on to how a cache is implemented and how these data arrays are used. Along the way, we also discuss advanced topics related to contemporary cache issues such as low-leakage operation.

5.2 SRAM Implementation

In this section, we discuss the implementation of a static random-access memory (SRAM). This is the type of memory used as the building block of most caches because of its superior performance over other memory structures, specifically DRAM. SRAM uses the same fabrication process as the microprocessor core, simplifying the integration of cache onto the processor die. By contrast, DRAM typically uses a different process that is sub-optimal for logic circuits, making the integration of logic and DRAM less attractive than the integration of logic and SRAM.

The discussion included here is complete enough to use as a basis for designing an SRAM from scratch.

5.2.1 Basic 1-Bit Memory Cell

This subsection describes how the most basic unit of an SRAM—a single data bit—is implemented. For SRAMs, the memory cell (MC) is implemented as two cross-coupled inverters accessed using two pass transistors, as shown in Figure 5.2.

This cross-coupled connection creates regenerative feedback that allows it to indefinitely store a single bit of data. This configuration shows a 1-bit memory cell with one R/W port that can be used for either a read or a write, but not both simultaneously. As shown in Figure 5.2, the bit is read by asserting a WL and detecting the voltage differential between the bitline pair, which is initially precharged to a logic high voltage.

The second phase, shown in Figure 5.1, is a write operation. The bitline is driven with a differential voltage from an external source to force the data onto the memory cell.

Physical Implementation of the 1-Bit Memory Cell

One of the assumptions of caches and memory, in general, is the ability to store digital data, and we have shown how a single bit can be stored by an SRAM using cross-coupled inverters.

This cross-coupled inverter has been implemented in different ways during its evolution, where the main difference has been how the inverter's pullup network is implemented. Figure 5.3 shows different circuit configurations that have been used to implement the memory cell.

Early SRAMs typically used either the full-CMOS or the polysilicon load memory cell configuration. The main advantage then of the poly-load configuration was its smaller area since only four transistors were required for one bit; the pullup was implemented using an additional highly resistive polysilicon layer such that the load was fabricated on top of the existing transistors, requiring less area.

With decrease in feature sizes, the amount of area occupied by the poly-load needed to produce a large enough resistance to overcome leakage currents that became too big. Along with its low soft error rate (SER) [List 1986], the poly-load implementation has now become impractical.

With the increase in space occupied by the poly-load, it started to be replaced by the poly-PMOS or thin-film-transistor (TFT) PMOS [Minato et al. 1987] load configurations, which could still be fabricated on top of the active NMOS, but with characteristics superior to the poly-load.

With the increasing on-chip integration of caches with microprocessor logic circuits, the additional process complexity required to implement the poly-PMOS/TFT-PMOS circuits on the same die as the digital circuits became too cumbersome.

An alternative to these circuits, the loadless four-transistor (LL4T) cell completely removes the pullup

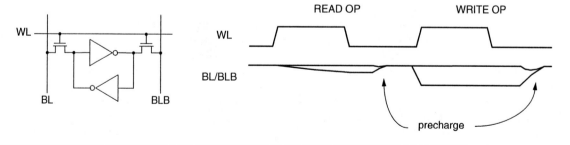

FIGURE 5.2: The basic SRAM cell showing cross-coupled inverters accessed through pass transistors. The state of important signals is also shown during a read and write access.

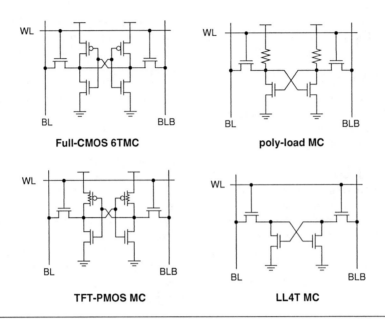

FIGURE 5.3: Different implementations of the SRAM cell.

load [Noda et al. 1998]. Although this scheme results in a smaller area compared to the full-CMOS implementation, because only four NMOS transistors are involved, the cell has to be very carefully designed to make sure that leakage currents do not interfere with the latching operation of the cell and its ability to retain data.

With continuous technology scaling, the charge stored within the cell decreases, while leakage current increases, making it more difficult to design reliable LL4T cells, especially if external radiation from alpha particles is taken into account.

Currently, most conventional designs use the full-CMOS six-transistor memory cell (6T MC), with different variations existing based on issues of sizing, physical layout, and transistor threshold voltages for low power (to be discussed later).

The rest of the discussion will be limited only to the 6T MC variant, and an example layout using MOSIS SCMOS rules for a 0.25-μm process

is shown in Figure 5.4, along with its transistor-level circuit defining the access, driver, and pullup transistors.

Transistor Sizing

The main initial considerations when sizing the transistors of the memory cell are the cell's area and its stability as measured by its static-noise margin (SNM). The SNM is defined as the amount of DC noise necessary to disturb the internal storage node of the cell and flip its stored data [Lohstroh et al. 1983]. The cell's stability affects the cell's SER and its sensitivity to PVT variations.

The cell's SNM can be calculated analytically by solving the cross-coupled inverter voltage transfer equations. Alternatively, it can be estimated using the graphical "maximum squares" method using the inverter's I/O voltage transfer function [Seevinck 1987], as shown in Figure 5.5.

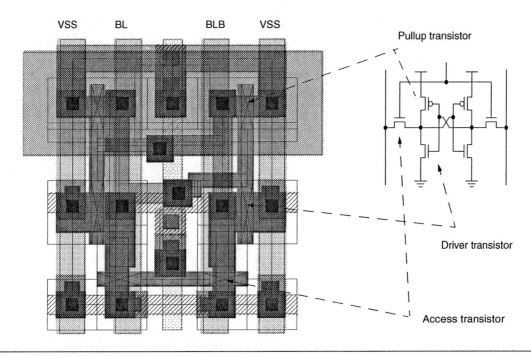

FIGURE 5.4: Layout of a six-transistor memory cell (6T MC) using MOSIS SCMOS rules (SCMOS_SUBM using TSMC 0.25 μm). Also shown is the definition of the access, driver, and pullup transistors.

When sizing, the main variables that can be varied are the widths and lengths of the driver, pullup, and access transistors.

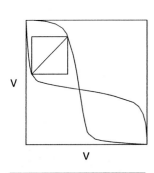

FIGURE 5.5: The inverter's voltage transfer function.

Using the terminology from Seevinck, sizing involves the parameters (r, β, q), where the beta figure β is the ratio of the widths and lengths of the individual FETs, r is the ratio between the beta figures of the driver and the access transistor, and q is the ratio of the beta figures of the pullup and the access transistors.

The main conclusions from Seevinck's analysis is as follows:

1. The SNM depends only on Vdd, transistor voltages, and beta ratios, not on the absolute values of the transistor betas.
2. Designing the cells for maximum SNM requires maximizing r and q/r by the appropriate choice of W/L ratios, constrained by area limitations and a proper cell-write operation (i.e., some choices of W/L ratios will be difficult to write to).
3. For fixed r and q, the SNM of 6T MC will be independent of Vdd variations.
4. Finally, the SNM increases with increasing threshold voltages.

All of these factors must be considered and balanced when designing the memory cell to achieve the desired cell area, stability, and performance.

Soft Error Rate (SER)

The SER is a measure of the rate at which the bits stored inside a memory's cells are corrupted. It is often discussed in the context of effects such as alpha particle radiation, where charged particles may induce enough voltage in a cell storage node that exceeds the cell's SNM, resulting in corruption of data.

The value Q_{crit} of a cell refers to the critical amount of charge that will result in exceeding the cell's SNM. It is directly related to the amount of charge inside the cell's storage nodes (the outputs of the cross-coupled inverters).

Various ways exist to increase Q_{crit} (hence improving the SER), among them increasing the diffusion area of the transistors, resulting in increased capacitance and, accordingly, the amount of stored charge

within the storage nodes. Other methods use more complex processing techniques to increase the node capacitance [Ishibashi 1990, Sato et al. 1999].

The SER and some accepted solutions will be discussed in more detail in the advanced sections.

5.2.2 Address Decoding

Address decoding is a conceptually simple process of receiving address information and providing signals to initiate and perform the desired operation on the addressed location.

At its simplest, it involves feeding an address value into a binary decoder (n to 2^n) and using the asserted output to activate the wordline of a subset of memory cells associated with this address. This involves a single AND operation on the input address, with the output connected to memory cell wordlines, as shown in Figure 5.6.

The main concern in address decoding is the large fan-in and fan-out requirements of typical memories

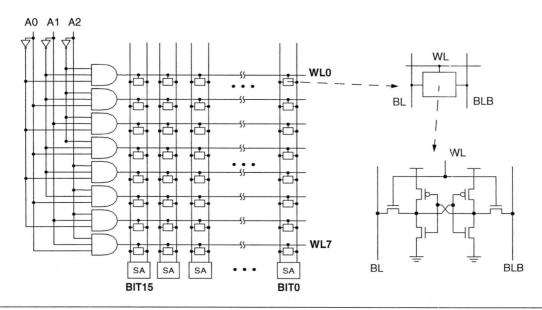

FIGURE 5.6: Address decoding shown for a simplistic 8 x 16 bit memory showing 8 3-input AND gates that enable the wordlines of a specific number of cells (16 for one wordline). Also shown are the sense amplifiers and the internals of a single cell.

because of the number of address bits being decoded and the large amount of cells that have to be driven. This makes the simple one-level AND structure inefficient, and virtually all SRAM designs implement a multi-level decode hierarchy to implement the logic AND function.

In typical designs, the address decoder contributes significantly to the critical path delay and total power dissipation, emphasizing the need to optimize the memory array's decode hierarchy implementation.

Predecoding

One of the main functions of a decode hierarchy is to minimize the fan-in of parts of the decode circuit, because higher fan-in gates have a large logical effort [Sutherland and Sproull 1991, Sutherland et al. 1999] making them less efficient. Simply put, logical effort expresses how hard it is to drive an arbitrary gate compared to an inverter of the same drive strength. High fan-in static gates typically have high logical efforts and are less efficient to use.

One of the techniques used in minimizing fan-in is a method called predecoding. Predecoding involves using one level of logic to AND subsets of the address. The outputs of these predecoders are then combined by low fan-in gates to produce the final decoder outputs, which are the wordline signals connected to the memory cells. In this way, predecoding simply involves performing the AND operation using multiple levels of logic.

Consider an example where an 8-bit address is to be decoded. A simplistic approach using 256 (2^8) 8-input AND gates is used (see Figure 5.7(a)). Although logically correct, these ANDs will have significantly higher gate capacitances compared to 2-input ANDs, resulting in larger delays, higher power dissipation, and larger area.

An alternative decoder implementation using predecoding is shown in Figure 5.7(b). The 8-bit address is divided into two subsets, each with 4 bits. For both subsets, 16 4-input ANDs are used to generate all possible combinations of the 4-bit address. The final wordlines are generated using 2-input AND gates to

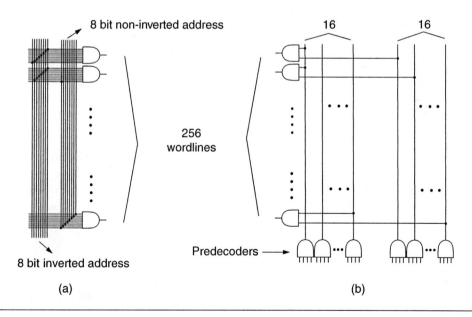

FIGURE 5.7: Sample wordline decoders for an 8-bit address: (a) a simplistic high fan-in AND approach and (b) a decoder with predecoding.

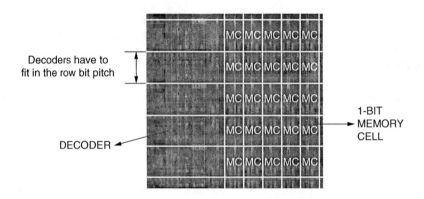

Decoders have to
fit in the row bit pitch

DECODER

1-BIT
MEMORY
CELL

FIGURE 5.8: Sample floor plan of the decoders beside the memory array showing the bit pitch limitation.

combine one output each from the two subsets. In this case, 256 2-input AND gates are used to generate all the 256 wordlines.

Although conceptually simple, predecoding has numerous advantages. Since the final AND gates only have two inputs, they will have significantly less gate capacitance compared to the first implementation. This results in a smaller, faster, lower power circuit that is also more scalable than the original. Although some of the area advantage is offset by requiring the initial high fan-in ANDs, this approach is overall still much better. One main reason that is not immediately obvious is that the possible implementation of the predecoders is more flexible since it can be separated from the memory arrays and will have less restrictions imposed by the memory array dimensions.

With this flexibility the predecoders can be implemented using sophisticated circuit designs that enable circuits with faster speed, lower power, and smaller area. Some of these techniques will be covered in more detail in a later subsection.

The application of these advanced circuit techniques to the first approach is not feasible because of the higher cost involved in applying it to a much larger number of gates (in the example, there are 256 gates for the simplistic approach and only 32 for the

predecoder approach). At the same time, the implementation possibilities for gates embedded within the regular structure of the memory array are much more limited since they are affected by other factors including the cell-to-cell spacing, or pitch, of the memory arrays, as shown in Figure 5.8.

The main disadvantage of predecoding is the need to distribute more wires to propagate all the intermediate predecoder outputs. This is a minor issue, and the advantages of predecoding make it almost necessary in most SRAM designs.

Row and Column Decoding

For added flexibility in operation, memory arrays like SRAMs (and in later chapters, DRAMs) typically employ two-dimensional decoding, where a subset of the address accesses a single row of the array (the row address), and a separate subset is used to select a fraction of all of the columns accessed within the row, as shown in Figure 5.9.

In the figure, predecoding for both the row and the column addresses is not shown for simplicity, and it is assumed that the row and/or column decoder utilize these predecoder outputs. The multiplexer allows multiple bitlines to share a single sense amplifier, saving both power and area. These

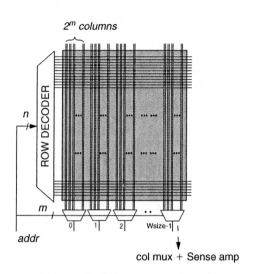

2^m columns

ROW DECODER

n

m

addr

0 | 1 | 2 | Wsize-1 |

col mux + Sense amp

FIGURE 5.9: Two-dimensional decoding.

multiplexers are almost always of the pass transistor variety, allowing them to multiplex small-swing voltages in the bitlines. To simplify the figure, only the data read path is shown since address decoding for read and write operations is essentially the same.

Non-Partitioned

A non-partitioned decode hierarchy refers to a memory organization where all cells in a given row are activated by a single wordline output from the row decoder; the organization of the sample memory system in the previous subsection and Figure 5.9 are examples of this.

For very small SRAMs (i.e., 1 kB and smaller), this simple non-partitioned approach is sufficient, but as the size of the SRAM increases, several problems start to become significant:

1. As the number of memory cells in an SRAM increases with increasing memory size, more and more transistors from each memory cell are connected to the row's wordlines and the column's bitlines,

increasing the total capacitance and resulting in an increase in delay and power dissipation.

2. Increasing the number of memory cells results in a physical lengthening of the SRAM array, increasing the wordline wire length and its parasitic wiring capacitance.

3. More power in the bitlines is wasted during each access because more and more columns are activated by a single wordline even though only a subset of these columns are actually accessed. In a non-partitioned scheme, every column will have an active memory cell, uselessly discharging the bitlines of the unaccessed columns and resulting in wasted power needed to precharge these bitlines back to their original value.

To a certain extent, this problem can be mitigated by minimizing the number of columns in an array. For a fixed memory size, this can be done by increasing the number of rows accordingly. This solution is obviously very shortsighted as it will eventually produce its own problems and doesn't solve the original one. Instead, the number of columns (and rows) is used as an additional parameter that can be changed to come up with an optimal memory partitioning and hierarchy.

Divided Wordline (DWL)

To solve the problems of the non-partitioned approach, the divided wordline (DWL) technique was introduced by Yoshimoto [Yoshimoto et al. 1983] and is now used in virtually all SRAMs because of its usefulness and minimal disadvantages.

DWL involves dividing the memory array along the top-level wordline (called the global wordline or GWL) into a fixed number of blocks. Instead of enabling all the cells within a row, the GWL is ANDed with a block-select signal (derived from another subset of the input address) and asserts a local wordline (LWL). Only cells connected to this asserted LWL are enabled.

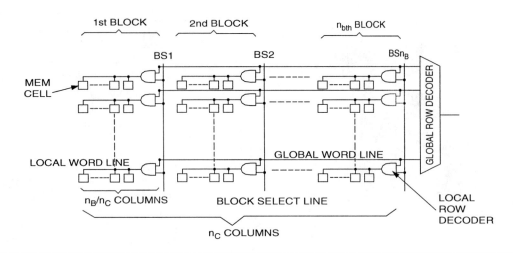

FIGURE 5.10: An SRAM using the DWL address decoding technique. (Figure used with permission from Yoshimoto et al. 1983.)

This DWL structure is shown in Figure 5.10, where the memory array is divided into n_B blocks. Assuming a total of n_C columns, each block contains n_C/n_B columns.

Since only a fraction of the total cells ($1/n_B$ to be exact) are connected to an asserted LWL and consequently activated during an access, the total power consumed in the bitlines is reduced significantly to roughly $1/n_B$ of the original. This value is exactly $1/n_B$ for reads since the nature of wasted power is similar to the power dissipated by the bitline read access, while the savings is less for a write access because of the higher power dissipated by accessed bitlines during a write.

Additionally, since fewer cells are connected to the LWLs, the power and delay will be significantly less. The GWL also only needs to drive the wire capacitance and the much smaller number of LWL decoders. The total wordline delay (the sum of the GWL and LWL delays), for the DWL compared to the non-partitioned implementation, will be much less for moderately sized SRAMs and above.

Figure 5.11 shows the effect in column power and wordline delay of changing the number of blocks for an 8k × 8 SRAM. Although this may seem like a small SRAM by today's standards, it is still useful as a basic

building block for wide caches. For example, a cache with a 128-bit block can employ 16 of these small SRAMs, resulting in a 128-kB cache, which is getting close to the typical size of an L2 cache. Figure 5.11 shows that even though column power can be continuously reduced by increasing the number of blocks, the benefit to the wordline delay lessens, and it reaches a point where it starts to adversely affect the delay.

The implementation of the DWL technique is simple, requiring only additional block-select circuits and LWL decoders that can be made simple since they drive less cells.

For the 8k × 8 SRAM here, dividing the array into 8 blocks (nB = 8) results in only a 4–6% increase in area, while resulting in very significant power and speed improvements, compared to a non-partitioned design.

Hierarchical Word Decoding (HWD)

A logical extension of the DWL scheme is a technique called hierarchical word decoding (HWD) [Hirose et al. 1990], shown in Figure 5.12.

As the memory size increases, maintaining a DWL structure requires an increase in the number of blocks, which results in an increase in the GWL capacitance since more wordline decoders tap into the GWL. HWD simply introduces additional levels of hierarchy into the decoding scheme to more efficiently distribute capacitances, with the number of levels determined by the total load capacitance of the word decoding path. At 256 KB, the difference between DWL and HWD is insignificant, but a 4-MB SRAM using the HWD architecture can reduce delay time by 20% and total load capacitance by 30%.

Pulsed Wordline

Early SRAM implementations asserted the wordlines for a significant fraction of the cycle time. The wordlines are typically asserted early (after the decode delay) and deasserted late in the access. This method, while functionally correct, is inefficient [Amrutur and Horowitz 1994]. For a read access, wordline assertion causes one of the bitline pair to be pulled down,

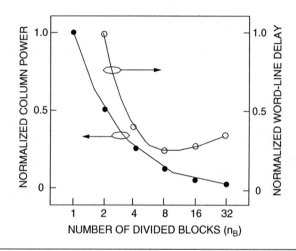

FIGURE 5.11: Graph showing the effect of the number of blocks, n_B, in the memory's column power and wordline delay. (Graph used with permission from Yoshimoto et al. 1993).

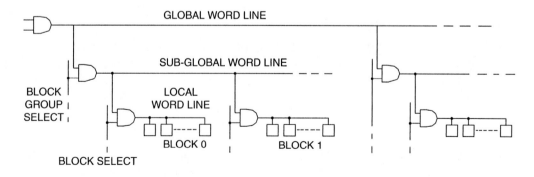

FIGURE 5.12: HWD architecture showing three levels of decoding. (Figure used with permission from Hirose et al. 1990).

creating a voltage differential across the bitlines. When a sufficient differential exists (the exact value will depend on the process technology and the off-set voltage of the sense amplifier), a sense amp can amplify this differential and speed up sensing. At this point, any additional differential developed across the bitlines, as a result of the continued assertion of the wordline, will not significantly speed up sensing and will require more power and precharge time.

Most SRAMs now use some kind of pulsed word-line, where the wordline is allowed to assert only for a small amount of time necessary to create a sufficient bitline differential voltage, after which it is turned off. This technique prevents the development of bitline voltage differential more than is necessary, reducing the power dissipated during the precharge process.

The width of the pulsed wordline is controlled either using static delays (where the wordline is turned off after a certain number of delays fixed at design time or fixed by special delay circuitry during a built-in self-test) or using some feedback taken from information extracted from the circuits (to be discussed in detail later).

Figure 5.13 shows timing diagrams for a system with and without the pulsed-wordline (PWL) scheme. As can be seen from the diagram, output data from both systems is produced almost at the same time, but continued assertion of the wordline for non-PWL

schemes results in larger differentials developed across the bitline, serving only to dissipate additional power during precharge.

5.2.3 Physical Decoder Implementation

With the division of the decoder into multiple levels of hierarchy (i.e., predecoders, GWL decoders, LWL decoders, column decoders, block decoders, etc.), different circuit styles and implementations can be used for each decode level depending on different factors including power, speed, area, complexity, and layout requirements.

The relative importance of these specifications varies within the decoder hierarchy because of the presence of different constraints. As a quick example, predecoders can use relatively power-hungry circuit styles, which is not true of the LWL decoders simply because of the much larger number of LWL decoders in the circuit compared to predecoders.

Much research has been done to optimize the decoders in the entire hierarchy from the initial pre-decoder to the final LWL decoder [Yoshimoto et al. 1983, Yamamoto 1985, Sasaki et al. 1988, Aizaki 1990, Nakamura 1997, Mai et al. 1998, Nambu et al. 1998, Osada et al. 2001]. Because of space limitations, only a small (but very relevant and proven valuable) subset of these circuits will be discussed here in detail.

Digital Logic Styles

Before proceeding, it is beneficial to discuss different logic circuit styles and where in the decode hierarchy each style is suited. CMOS logic circuits can be generalized by the circuit shown in Figure 5.14. The figure shows an output node connected to Vdd by a pullup network and connected to ground by a pulldown network, where both networks are controlled by inputs (e.g., data and/or a clock signal).

The pullup network consists of a combination of PMOS transistors that conditionally connect the output to Vdd, while the pulldown network consists of a combination of NMOS transistors that conditionally connect the output node to ground. Although the inputs and the clock signal are shown to be provided

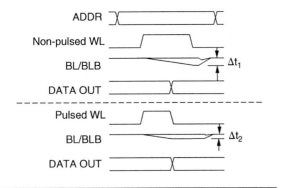

FIGURE 5.13: Timing diagrams showing pulsed and non-pulsed wordline schemes.

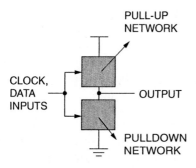

FIGURE 5.14: Generalized CMOS logic circuit.

to both the pullup and pulldown networks, they may or may not be utilized depending on the specific implementation.

Static CMOS The first logic style we review is *static* CMOS one in which there always exists a relatively low impedance path from output to either V_{dd} or ground depending on the logic inputs and desired output. This distinction will be clearer when *dynamic* CMOS is discussed, where we will see that some logic values depend on the charge stored within parasitic capacitances in the gates themselves.

Static CMOS is the easiest and most robust implementation, since there are fewer variations and problems associated with the design. The two variations

of the static CMOS style are the PMOS- or active-load and the full-CMOS styles. Figure 5.15 illustrates 3-input NAND and NOR gates for both styles. The main difference of the two styles is the implementation of the pullup net (notice that the pulldown networks are exactly the same). The full-CMOS implementation utilizes a pullup net that is the complement of the pulldown (i.e., parallel connections become series, and vice-versa), while the active-load uses an always-on PMOS transistor pulling up the output constantly to V_{dd}.

The main results of this difference are the following:

1. There is a typically smaller area for the active-load design because of fewer transistors.

2. The total active-load gate capacitance for each input is typically less than half of the full-CMOS implementation. This results in a smaller logical effort, making this gate easier to drive.

3. The always-on PMOS in the active-load design will result in significant static power dissipation whenever the pulldown net is enabled. In addition, the logic low voltage will not reach the full Vdd value because of the pulling up effect of the PMOS and how it fights the pulldown network. The exact output value will depend on the relative strengths of the transistors.

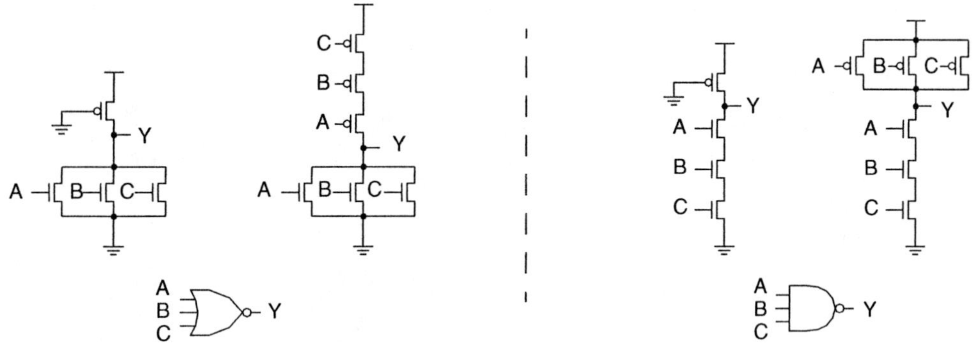

FIGURE 5.15: Active-load and full-CMOS circuit styles for 3-input NOR and NAND gates.

Speed and power comparisons of these circuits are interesting [Sasaki et al. 1988]. Given equal capacitance characteristics, the PMOS-load circuit will produce about 8% more delay than the full-CMOS decoder (because the PMOS-load will tend to fight the pulldown net, producing delay); however, the capacitance characteristics of these circuits, in practice, will usually be different and will tend to make the PMOS-load faster (about 15% faster). In addition, average currents in their decoder (which directly relates to power consumption) show that even though the PMOS-load consumes DC current, there exists a crossover point where cycle times become smaller and AC current becomes more dominant. It must be stressed, though, that these current numbers are greatly influenced by the sequencing and control of the gates.

Because of these factors, the speed comparison will be relevant regardless of how the memory is controlled, but the power comparison needs to be studied on a case-to-case basis to take into account the specific characteristics of a system. For example, a PMOS-load used with the PWL technique will be active for a smaller amount of time than if a non-PWL technique is used. This makes active-load circuits feasible for use in LWL decoders using PWL. Compared to a full-CMOS system, the speed is increased, and yet not too much power is wasted, since only a very small fraction of LWL decoders are active at the same time.

Dynamic CMOS One of the main objectives of dynamic CMOS is to minimize the capacitance of the logic gate inputs. At its simplest, this is done by implementing only either the pulldown or pullup network. Further discussions will involve only the dynamic CMOS circuits with the pulldown network, as, because of the better characteristics of NMOS transistors compared to PMOS transistors, pull up networks tend to be useful only in special applications.

Dynamic CMOS is similar to the circuit of the PMOS active-load gate. The main difference is that instead of having always-on loads, dynamic CMOS uses clocked elements that precharge (in this case, charge up to Vdd) the output node during the precharge phase. This output node is later conditionally discharged during the evaluate phase depending on the state of the inputs.

Figure 5.16 shows simple dynamic implementations of 3-input NAND and NOR gates, along with a timing diagram showing the precharge and evaluate phases of the dynamic gate operation.

Note the presence of the additional clocked NMOS in the pulldown net, called "foot" transistors. During

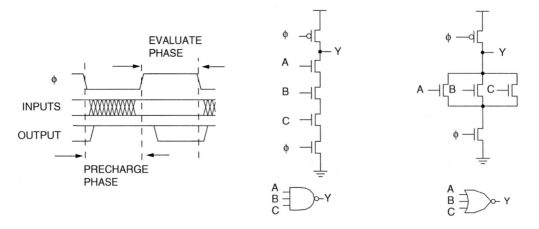

FIGURE 5.16: Simple dynamic NOR and NAND gates. Also shown is a generic timing diagram showing the precharge and evaluate phase.

the precharge phase, the PMOS precharge transistor precharges the output node Y to a logic high voltage. The precharge NMOS is not enabled, to prevent the possible inadvertent early discharge of the output and to prevent forming a low-impedance path from Vdd to ground. The evaluate phase is started when ϕ asserts, disabling the PMOS and enabling the NMOS input transistors. At this point, the output node dynamically stores charge that is conditionally discharged by the pulldown network if the right combination of input signals exists.

It is important to emphasize that inputs to dynamic gates must be carefully designed not to inadvertently discharge the output node. In general, we require the inputs to a dynamic gate to be valid before the evaluate phase or to change value monotonically to prevent an inadvertent discharge of the dynamic output node.

Domino Dynamic Logic

In general, individual dynamic logic gates are implemented with buffers at the output to provide more robust driving capability and to protect the dynamic node from being corrupted by noise. These buffers are usually implemented using full-CMOS inverters. This gives rise to a style called domino logic, and Figure 5.17 shows a circuit where domino gates are cascaded together.

During the precharge phase, all internal dynamic nodes are precharged high, causing Y1, Y2, and Y3 to go low (the inverted version of the dynamic nodes). At the start of the evaluate phase ($\phi = 1$, and for simplicity, assuming all other inputs required to form a pulldown path are already high), the dynamic node of gate 1 is discharged to ground, and consequently Y1 goes high. Y1 then discharges the dynamic node of gate 2, eventually causing Y2 to go high. This in turn enables the NMOS in gate 3 and causes Y3 to go high. This sequence of events gives rise to the name "Domino Logic," where the outputs of a gate cause downstream gates to be activated, even though all of the gates are put in the evaluate phase simultaneously. In domino logic, all outputs are initialized to a precharge value, and once the evaluate phase starts, the primary input causes a domino effect that eventually reaches the primary output.

An additional advantage in using cascaded domino gates is the possibility of removing all the NMOS foot transistors in all of the pulldown stages after the first one. When doing this, it must be ensured that no low-impedance path from Vdd to ground is created during the operation. If some inputs are supplied by non-domino logic, further analysis has to be done to ensure that the discharge path does not form. If all inputs are coming from other domino logic gates, it can be ensured that precharging the domino gates is enough to make sure that no pulldown path will be

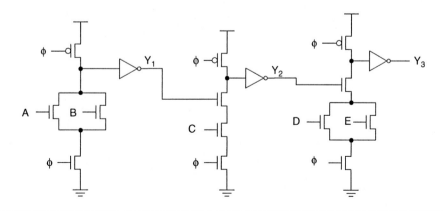

FIGURE 5.17: Cascaded domino gates. For simplicity, inputs not shown are assumed to also be driven by domino gates.

formed, making the clocked-NMOS unnecessary and making the gates both smaller (fewer transistors) and faster (less effective resistance and, hence, larger current drive).

Although domino logic has numerous advantages, it also introduces additional concerns, among them lower noise tolerance and the need of a clocking scheme to generate the precharge signal. As more and more dynamic gates are used in the system, the power dissipated by the precharge signal also increases. Because of this, more sophisticated dynamic circuits have been proposed and used for memory circuits in the form of self-resetting logic (discussed in a moment).

Source-Coupled Logic (SCL) One dynamic technique that has been used in memory decoders is the source-coupled logic (SCL) [Nambu et al. 1998 a,b]. (Note: It must be mentioned that the name source-coupled logic has been used for other completely unrelated techniques, and we chose to retain the original author's naming convention.)

A 3-input SCL NOR/OR gate is shown in Figure 5.18, along with a timing diagram showing its operation. This SCL circuit is similar to the basic dynamic 3-input NOR gate with an additional cascaded inverting branch and additional cross-coupled PMOS pullups to maintain stability.

This SCL circuit has three main advantages. First, increasing the gate fan-in causes only an insignificant increase in delay; unlike a full CMOS NOR, transistors added for fan-in are connected in parallel, and their associated diffusion capacities at the NOR output do not add as they would were they series-connected transistors in a PMOS NOR pull-up network. Note this is true for dynamic NOR gates in general. Second, the output delay of the NOR and OR signals are the same, which is not true of circuits deriving the complement signal using an additional inverter. This reduces the worst-case delay of the gate. Finally, a subtle, but very important advantage of this circuit is shown in Figure 5.19. Here, the gate output is considered active (i.e., selected) when the output is low. The timing diagram shows the activity of a domino OR and an SCL OR for two cycles, the first where both are unselected, and the second where both are selected. The important observation here is that the dynamic OR output undergoes a transition when it is unselected, it stays the same. Otherwise, When this dynamic OR is used as a predecoder gate that drives the GWL drivers of every row, all the unselected predecode lines will burn power because of the transitions of the unselected outputs. On the other hand, SCL eliminates this unnecessary power dissipation by ensuring that only the single selected predecode wire will burn power.

Here, the presence of the BUF-OR is only to emphasize that power is dissipated only for transitions of the OR output. The SCL still burns power in the internal

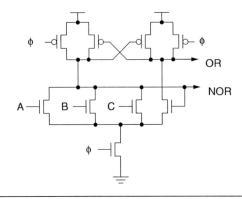
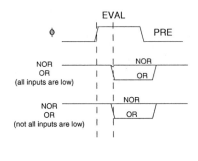

FIGURE 5.18: A 3-input SCL NOR/OR gate.

node transitions when it is unselected, but this is almost negligible compared to the power burned by the final gate output when driving its large load.

As mentioned earlier, the advantages of SCL become much clearer in the context of a decode hierarchy, where many NOR gates will exist (equivalent to many multiple-input ANDs) with only a very small minority of them being selected. It is therefore very desirable to have only this small minority burn significant power, as opposed to having most of the gates needlessly burn power.

Buffering and Skewing Before discussing the next two logic styles, we take some time to discuss the concept of buffering and device skewing in the context of memory decoders.

Figure 5.20 shows a typical SRAM floor plan showing where predecoders, GWL decoders, and LWL decoders are located. The figure shows an example amount wire length being driven by the various components of the decoder. The GWL decoder, for example, is driving 2×800 μm of wire. Given sample parameters of the TSMC 0.25-μm process taken from

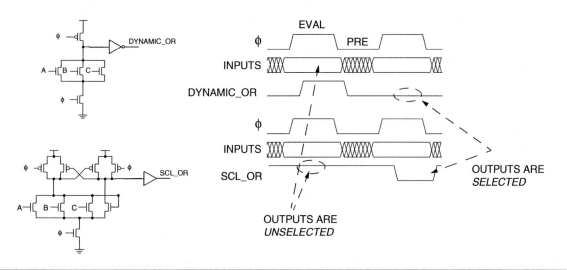

FIGURE 5.19: Comparison of domino and SCL 3-input OR gates.

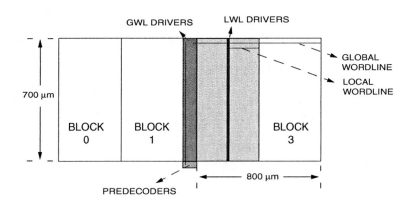

FIGURE 5.20: Example SRAM floor plan showing the memory arrays and the decoder hierarchy.

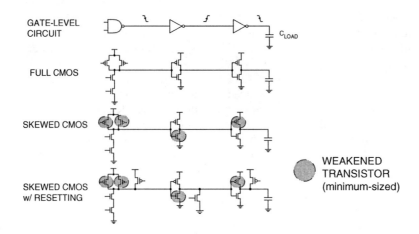

FIGURE 5.21: Different circuits demonstrating how to speed up an output edge.

MOSIS, a 1-µm thick metal 3 line of this length has roughly 200 fF effective capacitance.

This kind of load, in addition to the transistor capacitances connected to these lines, cannot be driven efficiently by any single-stage gate, and we will have to insert buffer chains to the outputs of our gates to drive the load properly while optimizing the delay, as shown in Figure 5.22. This is done by sizing each stage properly, which has been a very widely studied problem [Jaeger 1975, Cherkauer and Friedman 1995]. A rule of thumb [Jaeger 1975] is that delay optimization requires the delay of each stage to be the same and that the practical fan-out of each gate is set to be about 4. In addition, when it is important to speed up only one specific edge of the output, we can skew the devices inside the gates and buffers to speed up the important transition.

This device skewing is very useful in decoder design because it is important to speed up the assertion of the wordline to activate the memory cell access transistors, while the time to deassert the gates producing the wordline is less critical since it can be done in parallel with other operations within the SRAM. Figure 5.21 shows a gate-level circuit and three transistor-level circuits demonstrating these concepts.

The first circuit shows the gate-level representation that is equivalent to a 2-input NAND gate with the inverters assumed to be sized to drive the load optimally. In this example, we want to optimize the falling edge at the last output. Given this information, we can determine which edge has to be favored at every gate in the chain.

The second circuit simply shows the basic full-CMOS implementation of the 2-input NAND gate and the inverters where the drive strength of the pullup and pulldown network are the same to yield roughly the same speed for both the rising and the falling edge.

The third circuit is derived directly from the second circuit, where in all the transistors not participating in the favored edge are weakened and made minimum size. For example, the last stage has the PMOS weakened

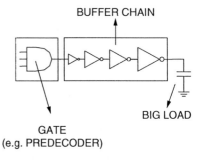

FIGURE 5.22: Gate sizing.

since it does not help in pulling down or discharging the output to get the desired fast falling edge.

The main advantage of this skewing technique is the reduction of the gate's logical effort because of the reduction of its input capacitances resulting from weakening some of the transistors significantly, making them easier to drive and resulting in significant speedup. The problem in weakening some of the transistors is that the reverse transition will proceed much more slowly than before, probably negating any speedup in the forward path by requiring a much longer reset period.

To offset this problem, additional reset transistors are inserted, as shown in the third circuit. These reset transistors are as strong as their full-CMOS counterpart, providing enough strength to perform the reset properly. A simple way to activate these reset transistors is to treat them as precharge logic for dynamic circuits and control them through an external precharge clock (being careful that no path from Vdd to ground is enabled during precharge). This is a simple method to use since no special circuits have to be designed other than distributing the existing precharge clock

(assuming the system already has one). But in the context of decoder design, this method will be very power inefficient because the precharge logic has to be fed to all gates using this technique even though most of these gates that are within the decoder tend to be inactive and will not require resetting. This results in an unnecessary increase in the power dissipation of the precharge clock.

One way to solve this power inefficiency is to generate localized reset signals such that only the few gates that are activated generate reset signals and burn power driving the reset transistors. Two different methods that accomplish this are discussed next.

SRCMOS   Self-resetting CMOS, or SRCMOS [Chappel et al. 1991, Park et al. 1998], uses its own output pulse to generate a local reset signal to precharge its transistors. As long as no output pulse is produced by the gate, the reset transistors are inactive and do not burn dynamic power.

Figure 5.23 shows two SRCMOS circuits, including the timing waveforms as a result of the pulse-mode inputs A and B. The first circuit is derived from the

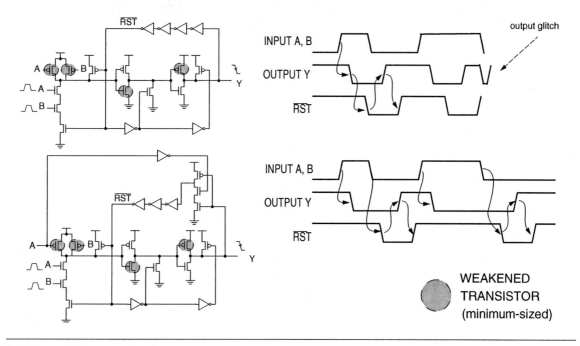

FIGURE 5.23: SRCMOS 2-input NAND circuits.

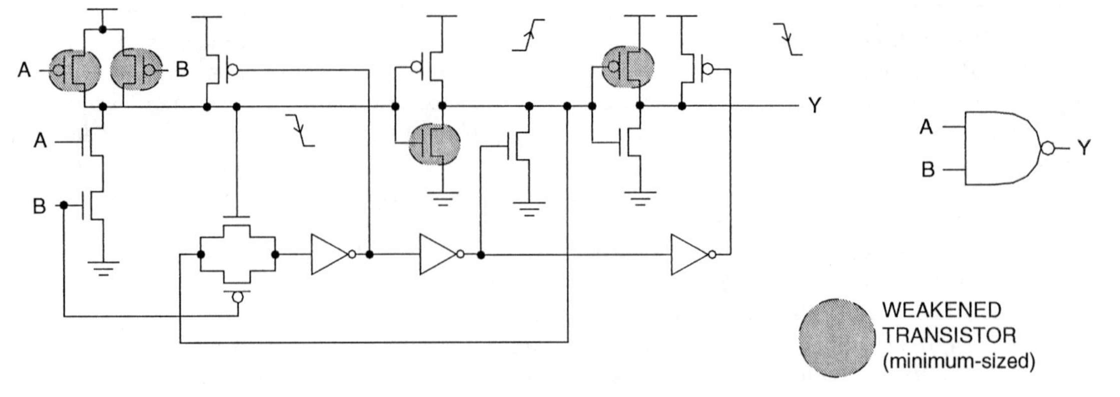

FIGURE 5.24: DRCMOS 2-input NAND circuit.

skewed CMOS with reset transistors in Figure 5.21. A delay chain has been inserted to derive the reset signals of all reset transistors from the output pulse. Without this pulse, all these circuits are quiet and burn no AC power. Once the reset signal has initialized the state of the gate, the new state travels back to deassert this reset. In addition, an extra series NMOS has been inserted in the initial NAND gate to disable the pulldown network in case the pulse-mode inputs are not guaranteed to turn off in time before the reset signal reenables the NAND PMOS for the next state of inputs, thereby creating a current path from Vdd to ground.

One problem with the first circuit exists if the pulse widths of the inputs are large enough that they are still active at the time when the reset signal reaches its original deasserted state after the entire reset process. When this occurs, an additional, undesired pulse will be produced at the output. In this case, one solution is to predicate the initial reset upon the falling edge of one of the inputs, as shown in the second circuit, where the first inverter in the delay chain requires one of the inputs to be low to be activated.

DRCMOS The extra series NMOS in SRCMOS will tend to increase the logical effort of the gate, which reduces the initial benefits of SRCMOS. Dynami-

cally Resettable CMOS, or DRCMOS [Nambu et al. 1998a,b, Amrutur and Horowitz 1998, Heald and Hoist 1993] solves this problem by predicating the reset signal activation with the falling input even for the initial propagation around the loop, as shown in Figure 5.24.

At its initial state, the transmission gate NMOS is enabled to initially provide no reset signals. Once the input and NAND output changes, the transmission gate is disabled and then enabled only when the input goes low again, allowing the reset signal to propagate through the gates and eventually return itself automatically back to its initial state.

With the removal of the extra series NMOS, the DRCMOS technique will have a lower logical effort and be faster than even SRCMOS logic. The main caveat is that the output pulse width is always longer than the input pulse width since the output is reset only after the inputs finish. This limits the number of levels in the decode path that DRCMOS can use without exceeding the cycle time.

The SRCMOS and DRCMOS techniques can be used for different kinds of logic, including full-CMOS logic used in the previous examples. Figure 5.25 shows how the SCL technique, discussed previously, can utilize DRCMOS logic in implementing a NOR-style decoder that is useful as a 4-to-16 predecoder [Amrutur and Horowitz 1998].

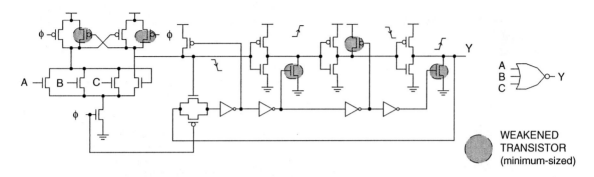

FIGURE 5.25: A 4-input SCL NOR circuit using the DRCMOS technique.

In this case, the delayed reset is predicated upon the precharge clock. It must be emphasized that although all gates of these types use the precharge clock, only the gates whose outputs actually undergo transitions will burn power to turn on the reset transistors.

SCL and DRCMOS complement each other in avoiding unnecessary power dissipation, since SCL logic only undergoes output transitions whenever they are activated and selected by the right combination of inputs. By not undergoing unnecessary transitions, DRCMOS further saves power in the reset circuitry and, at the same time, speeds up the favored transition due to its low logical effort and device-skewed implementation while keeping the reset period manageable.

Transfer-Word Driver (TWD)   As an alternative to full-CMOS NAND gates, the transfer-word driver (TWD) shown in Figure 5.26 can be used [Aizaki 1990]. By using a single, always-on PMOS as a pullup, and by using a single NMOS transistor to perform the ANDing operation, the circuit has a reduced input capacitance compared to a full-CMOS gate (less than half depending on PMOS sizing of the full-CMOS gate). This allows the TWD gate to operate faster than its full-CMOS counterpart. In addition, its simplicity results in a smaller decoder area (although this is not overly significant—20% according to Aizaki—

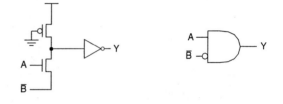

FIGURE 5.26: Transfer-word driver (TWD) circuit.

because the area of the decoder circuit will typically be dominated by the drivers, not the initial stage).

It should be noted from Figure 5.26 that the TWD configuration needs one of its inputs to be low asserted to perform the same functionality as a NAND gate. This is not typically a problem when used as part of a decode hierarchy, as the inversion can be done using an extra driver stage. This additional stage should not affect the critical path because it can be used on the non-critical part of the decode. For example, when used in the DWL/LDL decoder, the TWD ANDs together the GNL and block-select signal to drive the LDL; the block select usually arrives earlier than the GWL signal and can even absorb another stage if inversion if necessary.

The main potential disadvantage of the TWD circuit is the static current drawn because of the path from Vdd to ground whenever the gate is active (i.e., the NMOS is activated). Although this makes the TWD gate impractical for use in general circuits, it is only a minor concern when used in LWL decoders. The decreased gate capacitance lowers dynamic power and helps compensate for the static power. In addition, only a very, very small fraction of these gates within LWL decoders would actually be activated (and hence, dissipate static power) during any given access. Moreover, the use of PWL techniques serves to minimize the amount of time these gates are active, further decreasing the amount of static power dissipation.

5.2.4 Peripheral Bitline Circuits

To support the operation of the SRAM memory cells, the cells are accompanied by additional peripheral circuitry, as shown in Figure 5.27.

Referring again to part of Figure 5.1 (which is replicated in Figure 5.28), all bitlines are assumed to be precharged to a given voltage (currently, this is most often Vdd). When WL0 asserts, all the memory cells connected to this wordline have their access transistors enabled. For a read operation, the accessed memory cells are allowed to pull down the voltage of the bitline (the other bitline will be pulled up because of the complementary signals stored in the cell). Since the initial bitline voltage is already high, it is usually the pulldown operation that is important. The voltage of the bitline being pulled down will steadily drop, with the rate of change dependent on mainly the bitline capacitance (made up of the diffusion capacitances of each access transistor connected to the bitline and various wire parasitics) and

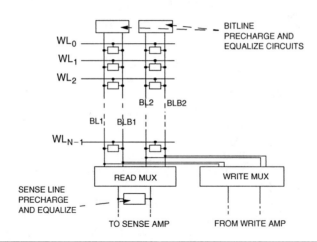

FIGURE 5.27: Memory cells showing peripheral bitline circuits, including precharge devices and read/write muxes.

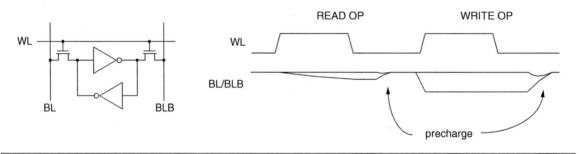

FIGURE 5.28: Read and write timing diagram for a memory cell, including the precharge operations.

the strength of the driver and access transistors. This process continues until WL0 is deactivated. Depending on the type of precharge circuit, the bitline voltage will either start to be precharged or stay constant (more on this later). In the timing diagram shown, it is assumed to stay constant.

During this process, the read mux selects the desired column based on the address input and relays its voltage difference to a sense amplifier that serves to speed up the sensing process. Before the next operation can occur, the bitlines (and the sense lines) again must be precharged to a fixed initial value. This is done by the precharge and equalization circuit in the bitlines and sense lines.

As WL0 is asserted for the second time for a write operation, the access transistors connected to WL0 are again enabled. But this time, external data from the write amplifier has imposed a full-swing differential voltage on the bitlines. Once the access transistors are enabled, the higher capacitance of the bitline and the stronger drive strength of the write amp forces the accessed memory cells to have the same logic value as the bitlines. As with the read operation, the bitlines are again precharged to an initial value after the operation.

We now discuss individual parts of the bitline peripheral circuits in more detail.

Precharge and Equalize Circuits

Various methods have been used for precharge and equalization, and some representative circuits are shown in Figure 5.29. The first circuit is one of the early implementations. It uses a diode-connected NMOS pair without equalization circuits. This configuration precharges the bitlines to Vdd–Vt, where Vt is the threshold voltage of the NMOS.

This configuration continuously tries to pull up the bitlines high, and this serves both as a strength and a weakness. Since there is no need for additional control to enable precharge, this circuit helps to control complexity. But at the same time, the constant current path provided by the transistor toward Vdd tends to slow down development of a bitline voltage differential during read operations (since it fights the memory cell pulling the bitline down) and burns more power during write operations where one of the bitlines is pulled low by the write amp, again fighting this constant pullup. In some cases, these pullups are implemented using always-on PMOS transistors.

The second circuit shows diode-connected NMOS transistors with a PMOS transistor bridging the two bitlines. This PMOS transistor serves to equalize the voltage between the two bitlines whenever it is enabled. This becomes especially important for active NMOS-load because of possible variations between the threshold voltage of the NMOS, causing a difference in the precharge level. As mentioned earlier, the active NMOS pullups can also be replaced by PMOS transistors if the inherent Vt level-shift due to the diode connection is unnecessary. (A typical use of this voltage shift is to adjust the bitline common-mode voltage to fit the sense amplifier's high-gain region.)

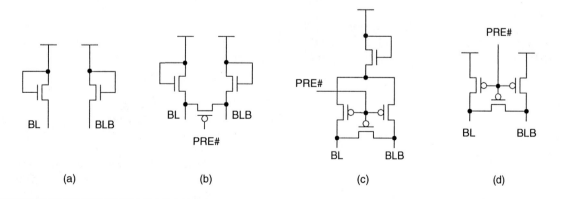

FIGURE 5.29: Different precharge and equalize circuitry.

The third circuit uses a combination of PMOS and NMOS transistors for the precharge and equalization circuits. It uses a single NMOS to establish a precharge level of Vdd–Vt, but it uses PMOS pass transistors to selectively connect the load to the bitlines only during precharge operations (more on this in the explanation of the next circuit). This kind of configuration was typical for moderate supply voltages (e.g., 3.3 V) or when the sense amplifiers used for amplification performed more optimally only at common-mode voltage levels below the supply voltage. But as supply voltages go down, and Vt differences due to process variations may significantly affect the performance, this configuration becomes impractical.

The last circuit shown is currently the most popular implementation. During precharge and equalize operations, all three PMOS transistors are enabled, providing low-impedance paths from both bitlines to Vdd and to each other. When the bitlines have been precharged, these transistors are turned off, resulting in very high impedances isolating Vdd from both bitlines. With this circuit, development of the bitline voltage differential is sped up because the pulldown only has to discharge the existing bitline capacitance. During write operations, no unnecessary power is wasted in the precharge circuit since it does not affect the operation of the write amp. The main disadvantage of this technique is the additional complexity and power needed to control the clocked precharge and equalization transistors. Although power dissipation during clocking of these precharge elements within the whole SRAM may be lessened by special circuits with conditional locally generated control signals, power will always be dissipated when switching the gates of these transistors on and off.

The sizing of these precharge transistors is dictated by how much time is allocated to the precharge operation. Larger transistors are able to precharge the bitlines faster, but they will dissipate more power. For example, using larger transistors for the hi-Z precharge implementation will dissipate more power in the precharge clock network (either global or local) because of the larger gate capacitances. The write operation often dictates how big these precharge

transistors have to be because bitlines during writes are discharged completely, unlike the partial discharge due to a typical read.

To take advantage of the difference between the read and write operation, the precharge circuits are often separated into read precharge and write precharge. The read precharge is usually enabled every time and is sized small enough to charge up the bitlines from the expected bitline voltage drop during a read. The write precharge is enabled only during writes and serves to help the read precharge to charge up the bitline. In clocked schemes, this avoids the power dissipated by in unnecessarily switching the gate inputs of big write precharge transistors during read operations.

Read and Write Multiplexers

Read and write multiplexers allow multiple bitlines to share common sense amps and write amps, as shown by the example in Figure 5.30, where a single sense amp and write amp are shared by multiple bitline pairs. The mux can easily be expanded to accomodate more bitline pairs, and these considerations are discussed later in the partitioning subsection.

The most efficient way of implementing these muxes is the use of simple pass transistors. For the read mux, PMOS transistors are used since the common-mode voltages that need to be passed through are near the logic high value, resulting in better device transconductance. For the write mux, the write amp will try to discharge one of the bitlines, requiring an NMOS pass transistor to pass a strong logic low value.

In both cases, only a single pass transistor and not a complementary transmission gate is needed since the complement transistor will not be used effectively. During reads, an NMOS will often go unused since it will not be able to pass voltages above Vdd–Vt, and modern SRAMs do not develop enough differential to dip below this value. During writes, only a logic low has to be transmitted to one side of the bitline pair, with the perfectly reasonable assumption that the bitlines being precharged high are enough to form a full-swing voltage differential to force a write to the memory cell.

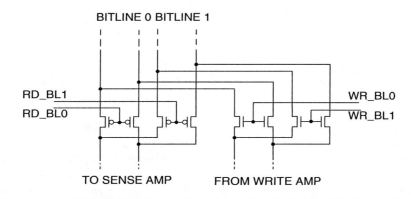

FIGURE 5.30: A circuit showing two bitline pairs sharing a single sense amp and write amp using read and write multiplexers.

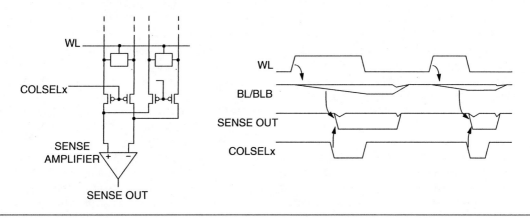

FIGURE 5.31: Use of a sense amplifier.

5.2.5 Sense Amplifiers

The development of a voltage differential in the bitline pairs during a read access is a slow process because the pulldown device of the memory cell is hard pressed to discharge the large capacitive load of the bitline.

A sense amplifier can be used to speed up the development of this bitline voltage differential. Figure 5.31 shows the operation of a sense amplifier along with a timing diagram showing some signal waveforms. When the wordline asserts, a differential slowly develops across the bitline pair. After some time, the PMOS pass gate is enabled (usually only after a minimum differential has been established as required by the particular sense amp). The sense amp then amplifies the bitline differential, quickly producing a full-swing differential output.

Note again that further development of the bitline differential is unnecessary and will actually be undesirable because more power will be dissipated to precharge the bitline. The second read access demonstrates how using a PWL serves to conserve power (by decreasing the final bitline differential) without any sacrifice in sense speed.

Although often advantageous, the use of sense amps is not absolutely necessary for sensing since it simply speeds up the development of the differential across the bitlines, which is continuously being discharged by the memory cell (as long as its wordline is enabled). This is unlike DRAM, where the differential voltage being sensed is due to a one-time contribution from the memory cell capacitor, which necessitates the use of sensing. In fact, most very small memories like register files often do not use sense amplifiers, as the bitline capacitances of these structures are often small enough to be discharged quickly by a memory cell; by doing so, they avoid the significant power consumed by typical sense amps.

Some contemporary caches that rely on single-ended sensing (like the Intel Itanium) also do away with the sense amplifiers in their cache hierarchy.

Physical Implementation

A large collection of different sense amp circuits can be found in the literature. These circuits range from simple cross-coupled inverters to very sophisticated amplifier circuits. Some of the more common sense amp circuits are shown in Figure 5.32.

The first circuit is the simple latch-type sense amplifier [Uchiyama et al. 1991] that forms cross-coupled inverters whenever the sense amp is enabled. Because of its simplicity, this sense amplifier occupies a very small area, and often satisfies the speed, area, and power trade-offs involved in designing wide memories that require a significant number of sense amps. One problem with the latch-type sense amp is the requirement to enable the amplifier only after a minimum voltage differential is present in the bitlines; otherwise, the latch could flip in the wrong direction and overpower the bitline differential.

The second and third circuits employ current mirror amplifiers. The first circuit uses a single current mirror amplifier, while the second circuit uses dual current mirror amplifiers and is named a paired current mirror amplifier (PCMA). These amplifiers offer fast sense speed, large voltage gain, and good output voltage stability. One problem with these circuits is their high power dissipation because of the existence of a static current path from Vdd to ground whenever the amplifier is enabled. In addition, this current becomes larger as the amplifier is designed to become faster. Moreover, its factor-of-two complexity wakes the PCMA circuit an impractical choice for wide-word applications that require large numbers of sense amplifiers.

The fourth circuit is the PMOS cross-coupled amplifier (PCCA) [Sasaki et al. 1989]. It offers fast sense speed at a much lower current than the PCMA because no static current path exists when the sense amp is enabled. The problem with the PCCA is its need for some preamplification to achieve its fast operation, and it is often better to pair it with a preamp like a PCMA or a latch-type sense amp to avoid spurious data output because of its high voltage gain. This is especially true when paired transistors in the amplifiers are mismatched [Sasaki et al. 1990].

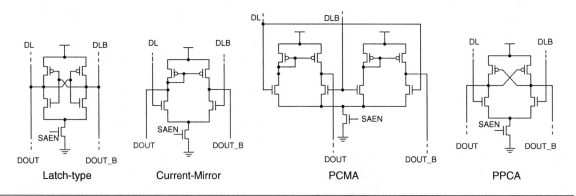

| Latch-type | Current-Mirror | PCMA | PPCA |

FIGURE 5.32: Sense amplifier circuits.

Sensing Hierarchy

Large megabit SRAMs typically use multi-level sense amp hierarchies such as the one shown in Figure 5.33. The figure shows a scheme with three levels of hierarchy and a single bit of output data. Oftentimes, amplifiers in different levels have differing topologies to optimize the entire hierarchy.

Although these types of sensing hierarchies are almost a given in discrete SRAMs, they are not widely used in typical on-core cache implementations, where a single level of sensing is most often adequate, and, in fact, some contemporary caches even dispense with the amplifier altogether (like the Intel Itanium). The main reason for this is the wide-word nature of caches, which is typically much greater than 32 bits in length, as opposed to most discrete SRAMs, which are typically from 1 to 9 or 18 bits wide.

The wide output of typical caches often necessitates the use of smaller, identical blocks of SRAM whose outputs are then used to form the required wide data bus. Consequently, the use of these similar SRAM blocks does not require the implementation of complex, multi-level sensing hierarchies.

5.2.6 Write Amplifier

Write amplifiers are used to generate the required voltages to flip the state of a memory cell when needed.

For the 1 R/W 6T MC shown in Figure 5.2 and repeated in Figure 5.34, the easiest way the cell can be written is by applying a full-swing differential voltage to the bitlines (BL and BLB) and enabling the cell's access transistors.

Typically, the performance of the write operation in any SRAM is not critical, so write amplifiers are much simpler than sense amps. In addition, if bitlines are assumed to be precharged to a high level, the write amp only needs to discharge one of the bitlines to ground, with the full differential voltage being applied with the help of the precharged high value of the remaining bitline. This concept is demonstrated by the fourth circuit shown in Figure 5.34, where the right NMOS transistor discharges BLB to ground, while the left NMOS is disabled, maintaining the precharged high state of BL.

A complete write amp circuit in shown in Figure 5.35, along with some of the other bitline peripheral circuits. In the figure, the NMOS write-mux transistors connect a single write amplifier to their corresponding

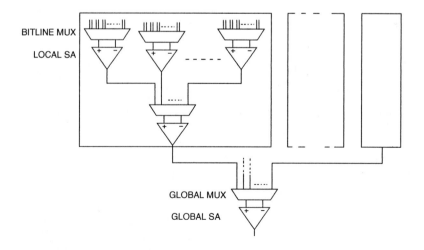

FIGURE 5.33: An example multi-level sensing hierarchy showing three levels of amplification.

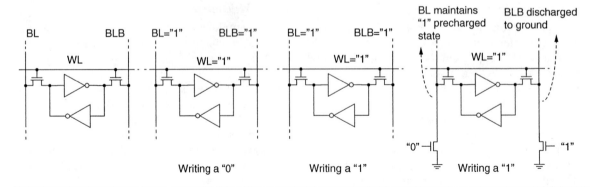

FIGURE 5.34: Writing to a memory cell.

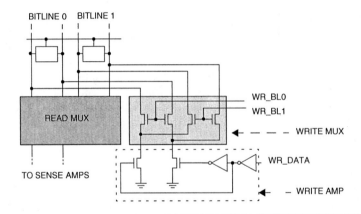

FIGURE 5.35: Bitline peripheral circuits showing a detailed write amplifier circuit.

bitline pairs. Each of these write muxes is enabled only if the column it is connected to is chosen during a write operation.

The write amplifier consists of two NMOS transistors and proper buffering and inversion logic to enable the proper discharging transistor. These transistors, along with the write mux, are sized to ensure that they can discharge the bitlines within the allotted time-window. Typically, this window is dictated by the bitline read time during read operations, so the write transistors need only moderate pulldown discharging capabilities.

Also, since write muxes employing differential writes only need to discharge one of the bitlines when

it is assumed that all bitlines are precharged high, only NMOS transistors are needed for the write amp.

Methods for current-mode writes have also been developed, aiming to avoid the significant power required to return fully discharged bitlines back to their precharged states. The main drawback of these methods is that they typically require the modification of the base memory cell to facilitate the current-mode write. For example, an equalizing transistor is often used to put the cell's cross-coupled inverters into a quasi-stable state and is eventually written to its final state by the relatively small current produced by the current-mode amplifier.

5.2.7 SRAM Partitioning

Having discussed many parameters involved in the organization of the SRAM in terms of its decode hierarchy and its peripheral circuits, we now discuss partitioning SRAMs to optimize performance in terms of speed, power, and area.

Among the SRAM parameters that have already been discussed (e.g., row height, number of blocks, number of columns per block, etc.), it is relatively easy to judge the isolated effect of varying a single parameter. Reducing the number of columns of an SRAM, for example, will serve to reduce the word-line capacitance, making the decode process faster. Another example is dividing the SRAM into as many blocks as possible to reduce the amount of unnecessary bitline power dissipation. When properly used, these techniques are effective, but improper application of these techniques without taking their consequences into account will result in a less-than-optimal implementation. In the first of the two previous examples, indiscriminately increasing the number of rows does reduce the wordline load (given constant memory size), but it also increases the bitline capacitance. In the second example, the increase in the number of blocks does lower bitline power dissipation, but it also increases both the decoder power dissipation and the delay.

The key to balancing these requirements is to partition the SRAM in such a way that the positive effects of changing a certain SRAM parameter are not counterbalanced by the negative effects caused by the same parameter.

Amrutur and Horowitz provide a very good discussion of speed and power paritioning for SRAMs [Amrutur and Horowitz 2000]. Amrutur and Horowitz model the speed, power, and area characteristics of an SRAM and solve for the optimal partitioning based on given priorities for speed, power, and area. Figure 5.36 shows the organizational parameters that are used for the optimization, a plot of optimal area versus delay (given no power constraints), and a plot of energy versus delay for a 4-MB, 0.25-μm SRAM. The figure shows a 1024×1024 array partitioned using three organizational parameters: the number of macros (nm), the block height (bh), and the block width (bw). Each macro supplies a subset of the output word (in this case, 16 bits of the 64-bit word), and each macro is divided into sub-blocks, with each sub-block being of size $bh \times bw$. The output of a macro is supplied by a single sub-block selected by the given address. As shown in the figure, the division of a macro into sub-blocks can be done both vertically or horizontally. When divided vertically, a multi-level sensing hierarchy can be used where sub-blocks in the same vertical axis can share a common global bitline and global sense amplfier.

The first graph in Figure 5.36 shows the optimal partitioning (given no power constraints), resulting in minimum area for a given delay, with the sweet spots labeled as points A and B. Amrutur and Horowitz find that the RAM delay is most sensitive to the block height, and small block heights result in the fastest access times.

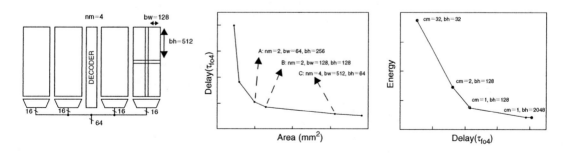

FIGURE 5.36: SRAM partitioning.

The second graph in Figure 5.36 shows the energy and delay relationship with no area constraints. An additional parameter, the amount of column multiplexing (*cm*, or the number of columns sharing a single sense amp), is shown. It shows that minimum delay is achieved first by having a *cm* of 1, where each bit has its own sense amp such that no columns are unnecessarily activated, and second, by having a large block height to allow the muxing to be performed in the bitlines.

5.2.8 SRAM Control and Timing

This subsection describes how the SRAM operation is controlled, both internally and externally. Figure 5.37 shows all of the components of an SRAM necessary to perform a complete read or write access to a specific memory cell. To simplify the figure, only one memory cell in a single column is shown.

It is important for an SRAM operation to have a distinct window of time within which it can perform

the desired operation and afterward reinitialize itself to perform the next access. Within this window of time, the SRAM must be allowed to finish the complete sequence of operations before the next access is started. Otherwise, both the present access and the next access will result in corruption of data. This characteristic is unlike combinational logic, whose inputs can be changed at any time while expecting the output to stabilize after a given propagation delay.

With this in mind, in general, there are two ways of starting the SRAM operation. The first is to detect transitions in the address or control inputs. An access is started when these inputs are sensed to have changed. This method is called the address transition detection (ATD) method, and a typical circuit implementation is shown in Figure 5.38.

The pulse generated by the ATD circuit propagates to control the SRAM sequencing of events, including precharging the SRAM to prepare for the next operation.

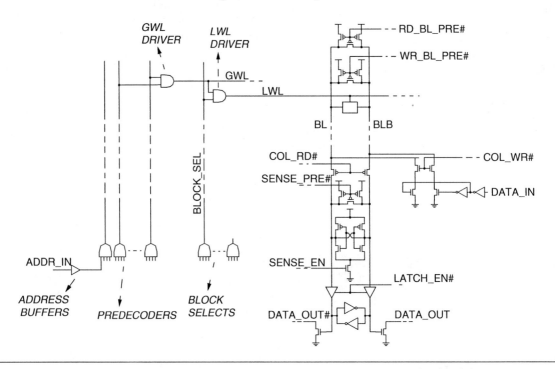

FIGURE 5.37: Important components of an SRAM. Also shown are data and control signals within the circuits.

ATD-controlled SRAMs are classified as asynchronous SRAMs because SRAM operations are started after its input change regardless of the presence of any synchronizing clock in the system.

A second way to start the SRAM operation is to use a synchronizing clock signal (or a signal directly related to the clock). It is important to note that, in this case, only the interface of the SRAM proceeds synchronously with the clock. Significant parts of the internal SRAM operation proceed asynchronously with the clock, triggered using various methods that we will discuss next. In this case, the clock is important only to define the start and/or end points of the SRAM operation, with the designer being careful that the clock period is long enough to allow the SRAM to perform all the required internal operations.

The start pulse that is either generated by the ATD circuit or derived from the system clock or any other external synchronizing signal then triggers parts of the SRAM in turn. This start pulse will serve a different purpose depending on whether the circuits are implemented using dynamic or static logic. For dynamic logic, the initial edge of the start pulse can be used to start the evaluate phase of the dynamic logic. It is important to emphasize that the address inputs of the decoder, especially the dynamic circuits, have to be stable to ensure the correctness of the SRAM operation. Otherwise, output nodes can be unwantedly discharged, with the circuit recovering only after a precharge operation, which will be too late for the present operation. In addition, we may want the start of a dynamic circuit's precharge to be dependent on a control signal different from the signal that triggered the evaluate phase.

Figure 5.39 shows five waveforms demonstrating this concept. The clock and address signals are

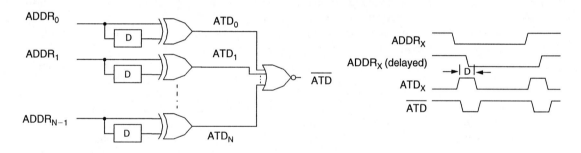

FIGURE 5.38: Address transition detection (ATD).

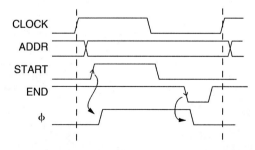

FIGURE 5.39: Generation of the dynamic circuit clock signal (ϕ). Although the START signal that is generated when the address signals are valid can be used to start the evaluate phase, its falling edge is not suitable to start the precharge phase. The END signal is generated internally when it is safe to start precharging, so it is used to trigger the falling edge of ϕ to start the precharge phase.

external inputs to the SRAM, where the address usually changes right after the clock edge (with the delay representing the clock to output delay of their respective storage elements). The third waveform is an internally generated signal that is a delayed version of the clock with enough delay to ensure the stability of the address. Alternatively, this could also be generated using an ATD circuit, with the falling edge occurring much earlier. In any case, only the first edge is of interest. The fourth waveform is an internally generated signal that is used to signify the start of the precharge phase to prepare the SRAM for the next access (later we will discuss how this is generated). To serve as a valid precharge/evaluate signal to our dynamic logic, we need something similar to the fifth waveform, whose rising edge follows the START signal's rise and its falling edge follows the END signal's fall. It is also important to note that even though the START signal by itself may be sufficient for the dynamic logic in the circuits, using the signal as is implies that equal time is allotted to the evaluate and precharge phases, which will be inefficient since the precharge phase is given more time than is necessary.

Figure 5.40 shows a circuit that can generate the clock signal of decoder dynamic circuits. Its main functionality is to produce a pulse whose rising edge is initiated by START's rising edge, while its falling edge is initiated by END's falling edge. It consists of level-to-pulse converters that convert the START and END signals to pulses that drive the inputs of a set-reset latch. A START rising edge generates a pulse that sets the latch, while an END falling edge generates a pulse that resets it. As with all RS latches, we need to insure that its inputs are not asserted simultaneously (causing indeterminate operation). We will see later that this is trivial for SRAM decoders as the START and END signals involved have very large separations relative to the width of the pulses being generated.

Amrutur and Horowitz [2001] state that an optimal decoder hierarchy will have high fan-in inputs only at the initial stage (the predecoder stage) and that all other succeeding blocks of the decoders (e.g., GWL and LWL decoders) should have minimal gate capacitances. The high fan-in requirement for predecoders necessitates the use of dynamic logic for their implementation. Although dynamic logic could also be used for the GWL and LWL decoders, the large number of these circuits will magnify the difficulty associated with dynamic logic.

For static decoders, the use of the START signal to trigger the decoder operation is not as critical as in the dynamic implementation. The reason is that the static logic will always be able to produce the correct output and assert the correct wordline after some delay once its inputs have stabilized. The same is not true with dynamic logic. The main consequence

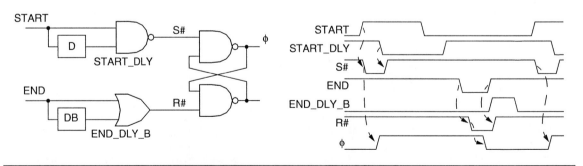

FIGURE 5.40: Generation of a signal triggered by two separate events. In this case, the rising edge of ϕ is triggered by the rising edge of START, while the ϕ falling edge is triggered by the falling edge of END.

of allowing the decoder to proceed without the start signal is the creation of glitches in some of the wordlines that are non-critical, but nevertheless will increase the power dissipation during bitline precharge.

As mentioned earlier, it is beneficial to use a PWL scheme, where the wordline is pulsed only for the minimum amount of time needed to develop a sufficient bitline voltage differential that can be used by the sense amp. Limiting the differential reduces the amount of power required to precharge the bitlines to their original state, and allows some of the precharge operations to proceed sooner and in parallel with the sensing operation, possibly resulting in a decrease to the total cycle time of the SRAM.

PWL schemes can be implemented using either open-loop or closed-loop schemes. In an open-loop scheme, the wordlines are turned off after a certain time delay determined at design time. This is often done with the use of gate delays that produce delayed outputs on parts of the decoder hierarchy which, when they catch up with the original signals, then serve to turn the signals off, producing a pulse whose width is determined by the gate delay, as shown in Figure 5.41. The total gate delay (and the corresponding pulse width) is designed to be long enough such that the memory cells have enough time to discharge the bitlines and develop sufficient differential.

Although this traditional way of implementing a PWL scheme performs sufficiently well, the effects of technology scaling has made it difficult to maintain the required correlation between the gate delays and the time required to discharge capacitive bitlines because of the varying extent to which scaling affects the memory cells and the decoder drivers. This is exacerbated by PVT variations, which affect the circuits' characteristics differently, worsening the correspondence. This problem is due to the bitline delay being dependent on the large bitline capacitance discharged by a memory cell's (often) minimum-sized pulldown transistor, which is affected more significantly by PVT variations compared to delay of non-minimum sized gates.

These effects discourage the use of open-loop techniques, necessitating the use of feedback from structures that more closely follow the run-time behavior of the circuit. Different structures have been proposed that use this kind of feedback [Amrutur and Horowitz 1998, Nambu et al. 1998, Osada et al. 2001]. A good example of this scheme

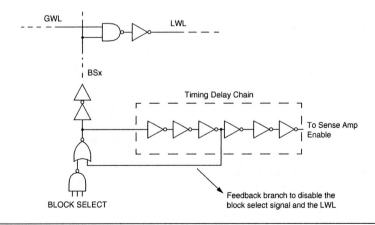

FIGURE 5.41: PWL using an open-loop gate delay.

is the replica technique by Amrutur and Horowitz [1998], as shown in Figure 5.42.

Figures 5.42(a–c) show a feedback scheme based on capacitance ratioing. Figure 5.42(a) shows the addition of a replica column to the standard memory array. The replica memory cell is hardwired to store a zero such that it will discharge the replica bitline once it is accessed. Because of its similarity with the actual memory cells (in terms of design and fabrication), the delay of the replica bitline tracks the delays of the real bitlines very well and can be made roughly equal by varying (at design time) the number of cells connected to the replica bitline. With this method of generating a delay that is equal to the bitline delay

even with significant PVT variations, the problem is shifted to equalizing the delays between two chains of gates, as shown in 5.42(c), which is a much easier problem.

Alternatively, feedback based on a current ratioing method can be used instead. The main advantage of this technique over the first method is the ability to generate local resets for each row, which can be used to directly turn off the LWL drivers. This makes the delay balancing easier to do and enables the use of skewed gates even for the LWL decoders, speeding up the decoder delay.

To accomplish this, a replica row and column are added to the regular memory block. In this method,

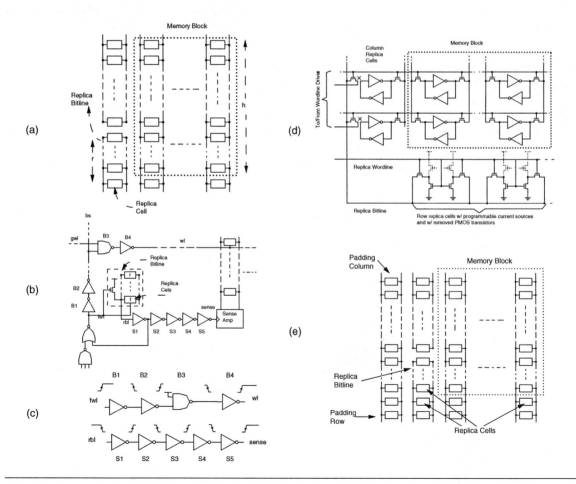

FIGURE 5.42: Replica technique.

it is the replica row that performs the bitline discharge instead of the replica column. The memory cells within the replica rows become programmable current sources and have their unnecessary PMOS transistors disabled or totally removed. They are configured such that they discharge the replica bitline whenever the replica LWL driver asserts (which is every cycle). Like the previous method, different numbers of current sources can be configured to activate to equalize the delays as desired. The signal at the replica bitline then propagates up the replica column (whose memory cells are used only as pass transistors) and propagates to the single LWL driver that is active. This signal can then be used to quickly deactivate the LWL driver and stop the memory cells from further discharging the bitlines.

Figure 5.42(d) shows how this scheme can be integrated within the entire scheme, while Figure 5.42(e) shows the addition of padding rows to minimize the PVT variations between the regular memory cells and the replica cells caused by the replica being in the outer edge of the array.

Whatever scheme is used (and, for that matter, whatever control circuitry), it is important to emphasize that the basic concept of these schemes is the generation of a control signal that can reliably track the development of the bitline voltage differential and, hence, can be used to control the proper activation of the sense amps for correct operation and the deactivation of the decoder to generate a PWL for lower power consumption.

The correct generation of its activation signal allows the sense amplifier to function correctly and speeds up the sensing of the voltage differential across the bitline. For a single-level sensing hierarchy, the output of the sense amp is typically a full-voltage swing output. It is typically desired to latch this output so that its value is retained until the end of the cycle (and some time after). Without a latch, the value is lost when the sense amp is precharged.

The data is gated on to the latch only after the sense output has stabilized to prevent a glitching in the output data (which may or may not be critical depending on the downstream circuits). Sophisticated feedback information like the replica technique used for bitline control is unnecessary to control this process since sense amp characterization is easier

and more tolerant of PVT variations compared to the minimum-sized pulldowns of the memory cells. Consequently, simple gate delays can be used to generate a delayed version of the sense-enable signals to gate the sense amp data to the output latches.

To prepare the SRAM for the next access, the dynamic nodes within the SRAM circuits have to be precharged back to their original values. Referring back to Figures 5.40 and 5.39, the END signal can be derived from the signal present at the replica bitline. This END signal then deasserts ϕ, starting the precharge phase. This ensures that the address decoder precharge is started only after it has performed its funtion and the selected bitlines have developed sufficient differential.

The END signal can also be used to directly derive the precharge signals of the bitline (including the replica) and the sense amplifier. Precharging of the bitlines (and the assumed early reset of the LWL drivers) also acts to precharge the replica bitline back to its high initial state. The complete process is summarized in a timing diagram shown in Figure 5.43.

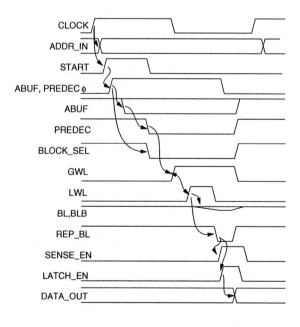

FIGURE 5.43: Timing diagram showing a complete sequence of an SRAM read operation.

The write operation shares much of the control sequence used for the read operation, especially the decoder and the replica technique. The main difference, aside from the obvious enabling of different sets of muxes and not enabling the sense amp and data latches, is that the data to be written has to be applied to the bitlines much earlier in the access, even before the LWL has asserted. This ensures that the moment the access transistors of selected cells are enabled, the full-swing differential is available to flip the cross-coupled inverter of the memory cell (if necessary). This requires the SRAM to receive write data early in the access. For most pipelines that buffer the write data, this requirement is not a problem because the data is easily available from the write buffer at the early part of the clock cycle. In situations where the data is not available early (like in cases where it is computed in the same cycle), care must be taken to delay the start of the SRAM write access until it is ensured that the data will be available at the right time.

It must also be ensured that memory cells are properly written during the short time that the wordlines are on. The width of the wordline pulse will be the same as in the read access, since the behavior of the replica bitline will be the same for both types of accesses.

Finally, the discharge of the replica bitline eventually triggers the precharge of the bitlines. In the case of systems with separate write precharge devices (as shown in Figure 5.43), both precharge devices are enabled to help the fully discharged bitline recover faster.

5.2.9 SRAM Interface

SRAMs can be used either synchronously or asynchronously. A typical discrete SRAM asynchronous interface is shown in Figure 5.44.

Aside from the address and bidirectional data bus, there are typically three other types of control signal: the chip enable (CE#), the write enable (WE#), and the output enable (OE#). The OE# signal serves to enable the 3-state output buffers of the data bus during read operations, while the WE# signal is used to signify write operations. The CE# signal is used for both operations to enable access to the SRAM. Typically, the entire address bus and the control signals are used by the internal ATD circuits to start an access. Figure 5.45 shows read and write timing diagrams for an SRAM with an asynchronous interface.

In a lot of instances, very fast cycle times for SRAMs are paramount (e.g., caches). In many cases, a further decrease in SRAM cycle times is difficult (i.e., no faster part exists for discrete applications, or techniques to reduce cycle time are currently in use and are too expensive to extend, in the case of embedded or integrated SRAM). In these cases, a straight forward technique to reduce the system cycle time is to use a technique called pipelined-burst access, and a typical interface is shown in Figure 5.46. The main concept behind this technique is the use of wrapper circuits that communicate with the external circuits at a fast frequency (small cycle time), but at the same time communicate with the SRAM at the memory's slower speed. This technique is shown in Figure 5.47.

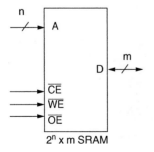

$\overline{CE}$	$\overline{WE}$	$\overline{OE}$	TYPE OF ACCESS
0	0	0	SRAM WRITE
0	1	0	SRAM READ
1	X	X	SRAM DISABLED

FIGURE 5.44: Discrete SRAM asynchronous interface.

Internally, the SRAM word width is made wider by an amount PB_{num} equal to the desired burst count (and corresponding decrease in cycle time). Figure 5.47 shows an SRAM with a burst count of four, so an SRAM communicating in a 32-bit-wide system has to be 128-bits wide internally. In effect, the serial-to-parallel interface (SPI) used for the writes collects PB_{num} words (at the faster system speed) before writing it out once to the SRAM (at the native SRAM speed). Likewise, the parallel-to-serial interface (PSI) reads a wide word at the native SRAM speed and then breaks it up into PB_{num} chunks before sending it out at the faster system speed.

Although this technique enables the use of an SRAM in a much faster environment, latency is sacrificed to obtain the speed gain. In the case of the previous example, the read data initiated on cycle N–1 only becomes avaiable at cycle $N+PB_{num}$.

5.3 Advanced SRAM Topics

5.3.1 Low-Leakage Operation

When CMOS circuits were first used, one of their main advantages was the negligible leakage current flowing when the gate was at DC or steady state. Practically all of the power dissipated by CMOS

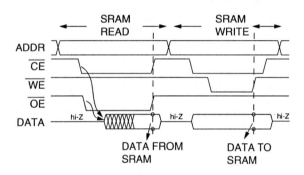

FIGURE 5.45: SRAM asynchronous read and write waveforms.

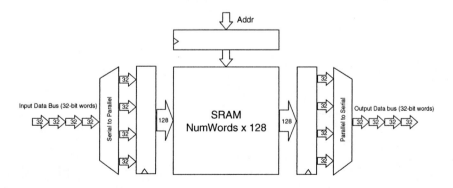

FIGURE 5.46: An example synchronous pipelined-burst SRAM interface showing a burst write and burst a read operation. In this example, the data I/O bus operates at 4x the speed of the internal SRAM core.

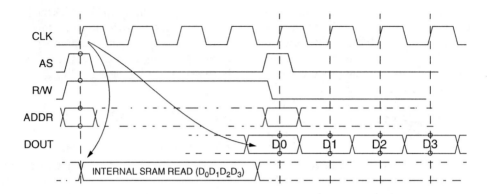

FIGURE 5.47: SRAM pipelined-burst read access.

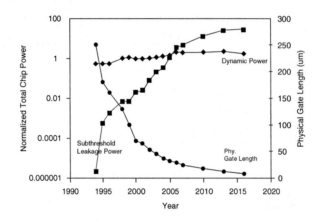

FIGURE 5.48: Projections for dynamic and leakage, along with gate length. (Used with permission from Kim [2004a]).

gates was due to dynamic power consumed during the transition of the gate. But as transistors become increasingly small, the CMOS leakage current starts to become significant and is actually projected to be larger than the dynamic power, as shown in Figure 5.48.

Aside from using techniques to reduce dynamic power (e.g., PWL, sub-blocking), SRAM designs targeted for low power also have to start accounting for the increasingly large amount of power dissipated by leakage currents. In this section, we present a collection of various solutions that have been

proposed to lessen the adverse effects of leakage current.

Multi-Vt Memory Cells

The main cause of leakage power is due to subthreshold leakage current (although leakage due to DIBL short-channel effects, as well as gate leakage, is also starting to become significant). This is due to the fact that when one scales transistors to increase performances one must also lower the transistor threshold voltage, and as Vt decreases, subthreshold

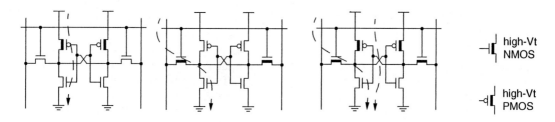

FIGURE 5.49: Different multi-Vt configurations for the 6T memory cell showing which leakage currents are reduced for each configuration.

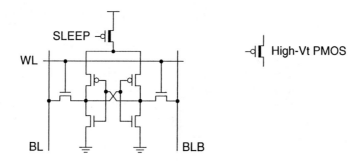

FIGURE 5.50: Gated-Vdd technique using a high-Vt transistor to gate Vdd.

leakage (which has an exponential dependence on the threshold) increases.

One of the conceptually simple solutions to the problem is the use of multi-threshold CMOS circuits. This solution involves using process-level techniques to increase the threshold voltage of transistors to reduce the leakage current. Increasing this threshold serves to reduce the gate overdrive and reduces the gate's drive strengths resulting in increased delay. Because of this, the technique is mostly used on the non-critical paths of the logic, and fast, low-Vt transistors are used for the critical paths. In this way, the delay penalty involved in using higher Vt transistors can be hidden in the non-critical paths while reducing the leakage currents drastically.

In this scheme, multi-Vt transistors are selectively used for the memory cells since they represent a majority of the circuit, reaping the most benefit in leakage power consumption with a minor penalty in the access time. Different multi-Vt configurations are shown in Figure 5.49, along with the leakage current path that each configuration is designed to minimize.

Gated-Vdd Technique

Another conceptually simple way to reduce the leakage current is to gate the power supply of the SRAM with a series transistor as shown in Figure 5.50. This is called the Gated-Vdd technique [Powell et al. 2000]. With the stacking effect introduced by this transistor, the leakage current is reduced drastically. This technique benefits from having both low-leakage current and a simpler fabrication process requirement since only a single threshold voltage is conceptually required (although the gating transistor can also have a high threshold to decrease the leakage even further at the expense of process complexity).

Without any special tricks, the parts of the memory that have their power supply gated will lose their state whenever the gating transistor is turned off. When applied to caches, this technique can be advantageous if the current working set is smaller than the cache size such that parts of the cache can be turned off without significantly adverse effects to performance. When the disabled part of the cache is accessed, the access misses, the addressed part of the cache is turned on, and the desired data can be retrieved from the lower level of the memory hierarchy.

Gated-Ground Technique

As an alternative to gating the power supply and corrupting the stored state in the memory, a technique called Data Retention Gated-ground (DRG) [Agarwal et al. 2003] can be used, where memory cells use a virtual ground that is connected to the actual ground through a gating transistor. This has the same effect on leakage current as power-supply gating. The main advantage of this technique is that, with proper sizing, the cells are able to retain their state even without being directly connected to ground. This technique is shown in Figure 5.51.

Aside from the reduced leakage current, this technique has the advantage that no other circuitry besides the gating transistor is required in the implementation. No extra control circuitry is necessary, as the gating transistor can be controlled with the wordline supplied to the row.

In cache applications, this technique has no impact on the cache hit rate since the data stored within the cache is retained even when the gating transistors are turned off. In addition, having the control use existing circuitry means that the cache controller isn't burdened with additional complexity to keep track of which parts of the cache are disabled.

The main disadvantage of the DRG technique is its reduced tolerance to noise, as evidenced by its smaller SNM margin compared to a conventional implementation, as shown in Figure 5.52. The technique also has a small negative effect on both the delay and the area of the circuit because of the introduction of the gating transistor. An additional minor disadvantage is the extra complexity in design required to carefully size the transistor within the memory cell to ensure that the data is actually retained even when the gating transistor is disabled.

Drowsy SRAMs

One last technique we present that reduces leakage power in SRAMs is the Drowsy technique [Kim et al. 2004]. This technique has similarities to both the gated-Vdd and the DRG techniques discussed previously in that it uses a transistor to conditionally enable the power supply to a given part of the

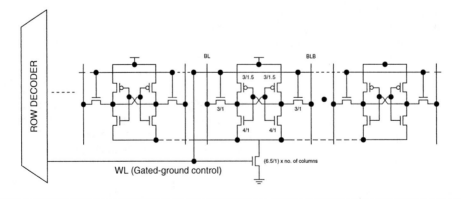

FIGURE 5.51: An SRAM row using the DRG technique.

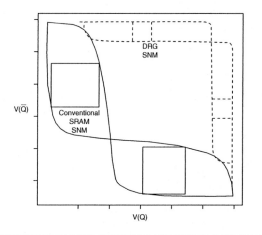

FIGURE 5.52: SNM of the DRG SRAM compared to a conventional SRAM.

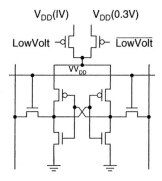

FIGURE 5.53: A drowsy SRAM cell containing the transistors that gate the desired power supply.

SRAM. This method reduces leakage power by putting infrequently accessed parts of the SRAM into a state-preserving, low-power drowsy mode.

This technique uses another power supply with a lower voltage than the regular supply to provide power to memory cells in the drowsy mode. Leakage power is effectively reduced because of its dependence on the value of the power supply. This technique is shown in Figure 5.53. The configuration is more tolerant to

noise compared to the DRG technique because the cross-coupled inverters within the memory cells are still active and driving their respective storage nodes, which is not exactly true for the DRG technique.

The control heuristic is straightforward: periodically, all blocks in the cache are made drowsy, and a block is only brought out of the drowsy mode if it is actually referenced

5.4 Cache Implementation

5.4.1 Simple Caches

After discussing the implementation of SRAM blocks, we could now use these memory primitives as building blocks for constructing caches. As shown in Figure 5.54, the tag and data part of the cache can be made up of appropriately sized memory arrays. Adding in the complete support circuitry to simple SRAM storage elements results in a complete, functional cache subsystem.

For an N-way associative cache, we use N tag data pairs (note that these are logical pairs and that they are not necessarily implemented in the same memory array), an N-way comparator, and an N-way multiplexer to determine the proper data and to select it appropriately. For systems that do not employ some form of virtual addressing, the TLB is optional, but otherwise it is needed, especially if physical addresses are stored in the tag area. Also, although the TLB access here is shown to be performed in parallel with the cache tag and data access, it can be performed at any time as long as the translation is available in time for use by the comparator.

In Figure 5.54, the cache controller has the responsibility of keeping track of cache operations and accesses to implement additional cache specifications like write-back/write-through behavior. It is also responsible for facilitating other functions like multiporting through banking to control each access and keep track of bank collisions. Finally, the cache controller is responsible for interfacing to the lower level of memory when the access misses in order to fill the cache. Although caches can be implemented

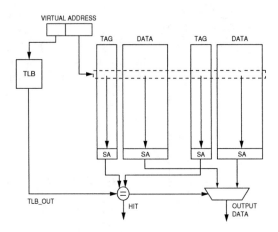

FIGURE 5.54: Cache block diagram.

in a myriad of different ways, this simple cache implementation serves as a usable, functional cache design.

5.4.2 Processor Interfacing

Figure 5.55 shows two typical ways of interfacing a microprocessor to a data cache. Figure 5.55(a) shows where the cache could connect to an in-order processor pipeline. It shows the address, control, and data being supplied to the cache stage by pipeline registers, and cache access is assumed to fit in one processor cycle, providing result signals (like HIT) and the data, in case of a load. The result signals are then used by the pipeline control circuitry to decide whether to stall the pipe depending on whether the access is a hit or a miss.

Alternatively, Figure 5.55(b) shows where and how the cache could fit in an out-of-order execution pipeline. The figure shows the internals of the load/store unit, and with the assumption that the proper structures exist outside this unit that allow for non-dependent instructions to execute out of order, this unit operates independently of the other functional units, and cache misses do not need to stall the processor core (unless during extreme

cases where internal data structures within the load/store unit have filled up and cannot accept new instructions).

The load/store unit typically includes a load/store queue used as a holding tank for memory instructions. When a load or store is cleared to access the cache (i.e., it has all its needed operands and performing the access will not cause any memory hazards or inconsistencies), information is retrieved from the load/store instruction and used to access the cache. Processor structures are updated with the results of the access. In the case of a miss, the load/store instruction is made to wait and retry the access, and in some implementations, the instruction is transferred to another structure inside the load/store unit that holds accesses that missed.

5.4.3 Multiporting

Caches can be multiported using different methods. True multiported caches employ multiported SRAMs that are specially designed to allow concurrent accesses to any location. Two examples of true multiported memory cells are shown in Figure 5.56.

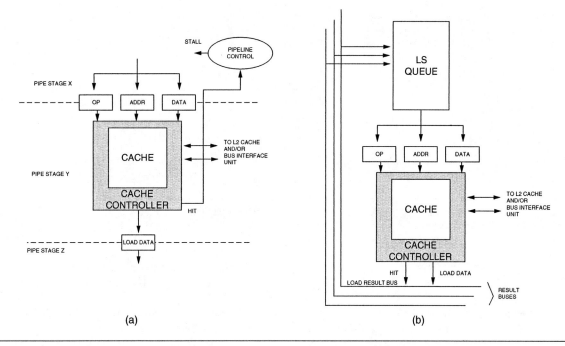

FIGURE 5.55: Cache-processor interface for an (a) in-order and (b) an out-of-order processor.

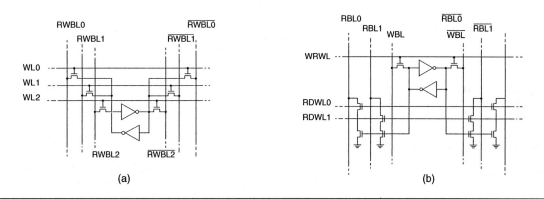

FIGURE 5.56: Multiported memory cells: (a) 3 R/W ports, (b) 2R 1 R/W port.

Although using true multiporting allows relatively simple control of the SRAM, the addition of multiple access transistors for each port results in a very significant increase in memory area. Aside from the area increase, this also adversely affects

the delay because of wire length increase within the memory.

An alternative to true multiporting is the use of multiple independent banks for the cache, where each bank is implemented as a simple single-ported

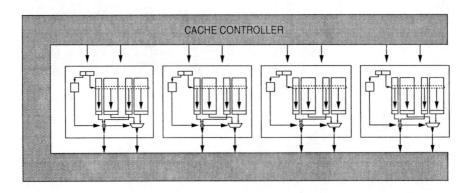

FIGURE 5.57: Multiported cache using banking. In this case, the cache is implemented as four banks of identical two-way associative, 1 R/W ported cache.

cache. This configuration can satisfy multiple cache accesses as long as the accesses are to different banks. This configuration is shown in Figure 5.57 for a two-way associative cache with four banks.

This configuration can perform a maximum of four R/W accesses concurrently. The main consequence of this configuration is the additional complexity and intelligence required in the cache controller to manage the control and I/O of each individual bank, along with keeping track of bank conflicts that may arise. Even with this complication, the benefits of true multiporting often do not justify the drastic increase in cache size, making the banking approach more popular.

CHAPTER 6

Cache Case Studies

This chapter presents details of cache organizations from three different contemporary microprocessors, mainly the Motorola MPC7450 (PowerPC ISA), the AMD Opteron (x86-64 ISA), and the Intel Itanium-2 (EPIC ISA) designs.

The logical organization of each cache architecture, including every level of the cache hierarchy, is first presented in brief detail (since these concepts have been explained thoroughly in the preceeding chapters), while notable features that are interesting in specific implementations are given more detailed explanations. This is followed by a presentation of the microprocessor block diagram, where each cache resides, to show how each cache interfaces to their respective processor pipeline. In addition, some in-depth circuit details will be shown to communicate important concepts (mainly from the Intel Itanium-2 with the help of published details regarding the internal circuitry). Finally, techniques used by each cache to maintain cache coherency are presented.

6.1 Logical Organization

6.1.1 Motorola MPC7450

The Motorola MPC7450 microprocessor supports three level of caches. The first two levels of the cache are implemented on-chip, while the data array for the third-level cache is designed to be implemented off-chip (the tags and status bits are implemented on-chip to enable fast miss detection to partly hide the slow off-chip access to the main data array).

The logical organization of the three cache levels showing their size, associativity, and other relevant information is shown in Table 6.1.

Some of the interesting features of the MPC7450 caches:

- The caches can either be disabled (i.e., no caches at all) or locked using software control. In this way, access times to data can be made predictable, which gives the system a better chance of performing well in a real-time environment.
- Each individual level of the cache can be configured to utilize either write-through or write-back write policies. The granularity of this configuration is chosen to be either a single page or a single cache block (with a cache block being, in PowerPC terminology, the smallest size defined by its own coherency status bits). In this way, programmers are given the flexibility to fine-tune the write policy depending on the application.
- The caches are well designed to provide 128-bit data to and from the load/store unit, which interfaces directly with the processor's vector units and register files. This allows it to efficiently support the strong SIMD capability of the PowerPC and its Altivec vector instructions.

6.1.2 AMD Opteron

The single-core, 64-bit AMD Opteron processor supports two levels of caches, both of which are implemented completely on-chip. The logical organization of the two caches is listed in Table 6.2.

TABLE 6.1   MPC7450 Cache Hierarchy Specifications

	L1 Cache	L2 Cache	L3 Cache
Size	32-KB Harvard	256-KB unified	1/2-MB unified
Associativity	8-way assoc.	8-way assoc.	8-way assoc.
Cache line size	32 bytes	64 bytes	64 bytes
Write policy	Write-through/write-back (programmable)	Write-through/write-back (programmable)	Write-through/write-back (programmable)
Replacement policy	Pseudo-LRU	Two different pseudo-random replacement algorithms	Two different pseudo-random replacement algorithms
Error correction	Parity generation (one parity bit/byte)	Parity generation for both tags and data	Parity generation for both tags and data
No. of ports	Dual-ported data tags (rest are single ported)		
Location	On-chip	On-chip	Data array is off-chip
Coherency	MESI (for data)	MESI	MESI

TABLE 6.2   AMD Opteron Cache Hierarchy Specifications

	L1 Cache	L2 Cache
Size	64-KB Harvard	
Associativity	2-way assoc.	16-way assoc.
Cache line size	64 bytes	
Write policy	Write-through/write-back	
Replacement policy	LRU	
Error correction	Data parity, ECC	
Number of ports	L1D is dual ported	
Location	On-chip	On-chip
Coherency	MOESI (L1D)	

An interesting feature of the Opteron cache:

- The Opteron L2 cache is an exclusive cache; it only contains victim or copy-back cache blocks (that are to be written back to the memory subsystem) as a result of conflict misses. By using this exclusive cache architecture, the effective size of the entire cache system is increased compared to an inclusive cache approach.

6.1.3 Intel Itanium-2

The Intel Itanium-2 microprocessor, like the MPC7450, has three levels of cache. Unlike the MPC7450, though, all three levels of this cache are implemented completely on-chip. The logical organization and other relevant information for the three cache levels are shown in Table 6.3.

The Intel Itanium-2 cache hierarchy has a number of important features and optimizations:

- All three cache levels employ single-ended sensing as opposed to double-ended or

differential sensing during bitline reads. Although differential sensing has been traditionally considered to be more tractable and easier to work with whenever working with low-swing voltage nodes is necessary, the designers believed that single-ended sensing scales well with technology and that it is much easier to treat the bitlines as full-swing logic instead of low swing.

- The L1 cache is optimized for latency and to keep up with the fast core clock. The L2 cache is optimized for bandwidth, as can be seen by the large number of read and write ports that are available to the L1 cache for fills so that access reordering can easily be accomplished. The L3 cache is optimized for area efficiency, as is evident by its huge size and the presence of only a single port. By ensuring a large L3 cache size, the amount of off-chip accesses caused by cache misses should be significantly reduced.

TABLE 6.3   Intel Itanium-2 Cache Hierarchy Specifications

	L1 cache	L2 cache	L3 cache
Size	16-KB Harvard	256-KB unified	3-MB unified
Associativity	4-way assoc.	8-way assoc.	24-way assoc.
Cache line size	64 bytes	128 bytes	128 bytes
Write policy	Write-through	Write-back	Write-back
Replacement policy	LRU	NRU	NRU
Error correction	ECC	ECC (SECDED)	ECC (SECDED)
No. of ports	2 read, 2 write	4 read, 4 write	1 R/W
Location	On-chip	On-chip	On-chip

6.2 Pipeline Interface

6.2.1 Motorola MPC7450

The entire block diagram of the Motorola MPC7450 microprocessor is shown in Figure 6.1. The figure shows the connection of the L1 caches (in the upper right corner of the diagram) to the fetch unit, the load/store unit, and the lower levels of the memory hierarchy (bottom part of the diagram).

Figure 6.2 shows how these logical blocks fit within the actual framework of the processor pipeline. The L1 instruction cache is accessed sometime during the fetch stages, while the L1 data cache is accessed in the load/store unit stages.

6.2.2 AMD Opteron

The block diagram of the AMD64 microprocessor is shown in Figure 6.3. Within the processor itself, the L1 instruction cache interfaces to the instruction-fetch (IF) unit, and the L1 data cache interfaces to the processor load/store unit. The load/store unit and data cache interface are shown in Figure 6.4.

6.2.3 Intel Itanium-2

A block diagram of the entire Intel Itanium-2 microprocessor is shown in Figure 6.5, showing the locations of the caches relative to the other units in the core. One of the most interesting things that can be seen

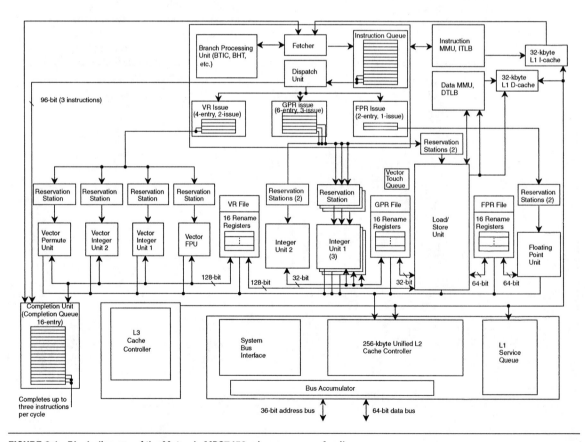

FIGURE 6.1: Block diagram of the Motorola MPC7450 microprocessor family.

in the diagram is the connection of the floating point unit directly to the L2 cache instead of the L1 cache.

6.3 Case Studies of Detailed Itanium-2 Circuits

In this section, we explore some of the interesting circuit techniques and topologies that were used in the design of the Itanium-2 caches.

6.3.1 L1 Cache RAM Cell Array

The L1 memory array of the Itanium is shown in Figure 6.6. This figure shows a dual-ported memory cell, with each side of the bitline pair being used for a different read port. During a read access, the proper single-ended bitline is then selected by one of four column selects and combined with another set of bitlines through the dynamic NAND in the center. This value is then latched and used to discharge the data output node.

It is important to note that by having only eight RAM cells connected to each bitline, the activated memory cell can easily and quickly discharge this bitline properly, allowing the use of single-ended sensing without any penalty in access latency.

6.3.2 L2 Array Bitline Structure

The bitline structure of the L2 cache is shown in Figure 6.7. This figure shows the single-ended read implementation of the L2 cache. One out of

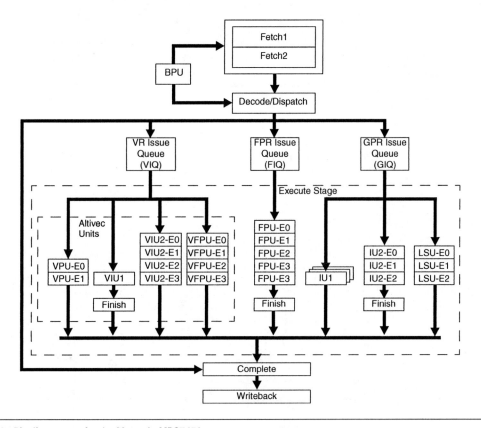

FIGURE 6.2: Pipeline stages for the Motorola MPC7450.

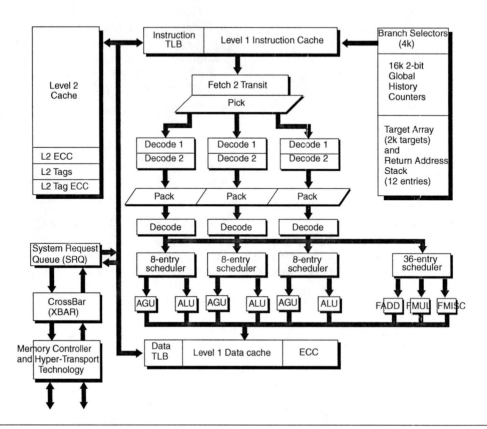

FIGURE 6.3: The AMD Opteron processor block diagram.

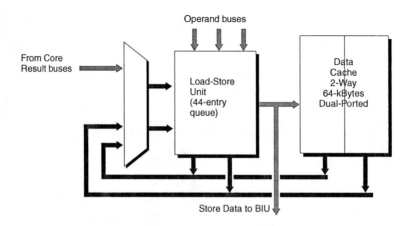

FIGURE 6.4: The AMD Opteron L1 data cache logical connection to the processor load/store unit.

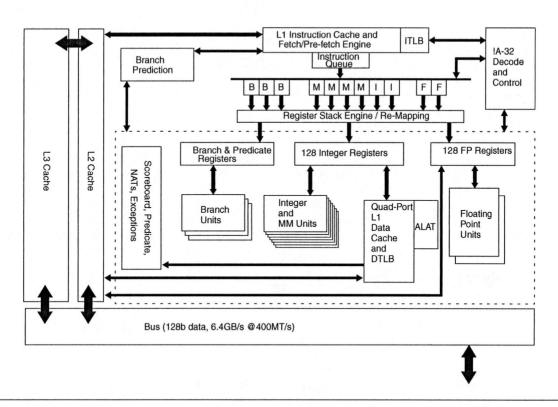

FIGURE 6.5: The Intel Itanium-2 processor block diagram.

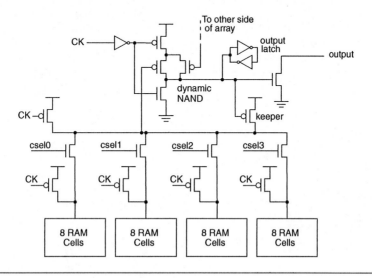

FIGURE 6.6: The Itanium-2 L1 cache array RAM structure.

32 memory cells is activated by its corresponding wordline. This activated memory cell discharges the precharged bitline, forcing the static NAND to go high. In combination with an 8:1 column-select signal, the output of the NAND then discharges a set of global bitlines. Finally, an activated bank-select signal gates these values on to the output latch.

For this cache, the high degree of banking used allows the creation of multiple read and write ports that can all potentially be active as long as different banks are accessed by each. This significantly increases the bandwidth between the L1 and L2 caches, allowing effective L1 fillups to proceed faster because of the added parallelism.

6.3.3   L3 Subarray Implementation

One of the techniques used in the implementation of the Itanium-2 L3 cache is the subarray technique. This method allows the cache to be built up of independent subarrays whose relative placements and operation are largely independent of one another. In this way, no exact and fixed floor plan for the L3 cache is necessary, and the subarrays can be arranged to maximize the usage of die area by optimizing the fit between core blocks, as shown in the sample floor plans in Figure 6.8 explored during the design of the cache. This is especially important for the L3 cache since it takes up the most space in the processor, and efficient use of this space is critical.

The internals of a subarray are shown in Figure 6.9. The figure shows each subarray divided into eight

groups and how decoding and sensing is accomplished within a single subarray and within individual groups.

Finally, although the subarray outputs can simply be used immediately, a faulty subarray would render the whole microprocessor inoperational. Instead, a level of redundancy and error corrections is added (5 ECC + 2 redundancy arrays for every 128 data subarrays) to maximize the yield, as shown in Figure 6.10.

Finally, the sensing unit of a single subarray is shown in Figure 6.11. The figure shows 16 different bitline pairs. The L3 cache also uses single-ended sensing, so in a read access, only the right parts of the bitline are actually utilized (the complementary bitlines to the left are used for writes, which are still accomplished differentially). On a read access, a falling bitline chosen by one of the eight column selects pulls down the lines DATA0 and DATA1 which are connected to a PMOS-based dynamic NAND gate whose value is then latched and serves to discharge the precharged output node.

6.3.4   Itanium-2 TLB and CAM Implementation

In this section, we present a method employed by the Intel Itanium-2 in optimizing the access of its virtual-memory-enabled L1 caches. Before proceeding, we provide a background on how this L1 cache access is conventionally performed before going into details of the Itanium-2 implementation.

The use of virtual memory has become an indispensable part of modern computing. In a typical

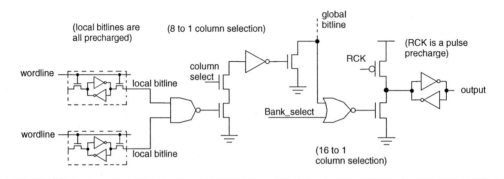

FIGURE 6.7: The Itanium-2 L2 cache array bitline structure.

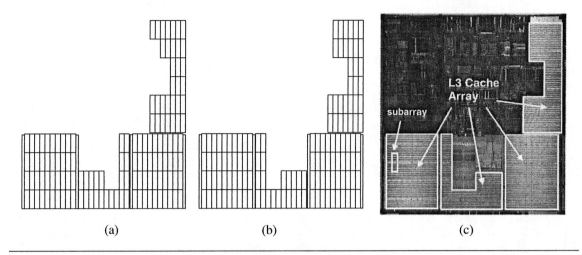

FIGURE 6.8: The Itanium-2 L3 cache subarray floor plan. (a) and (b) are candidate floor plans, and (c) shows the final die photo that implements (b). It is important to emphasize that when using this method, this kind of change can happen even during the later stages of the design cycle, something that would not be possible in most cache designs. (Pictures and diagrams used with permission from Weiss 2004).

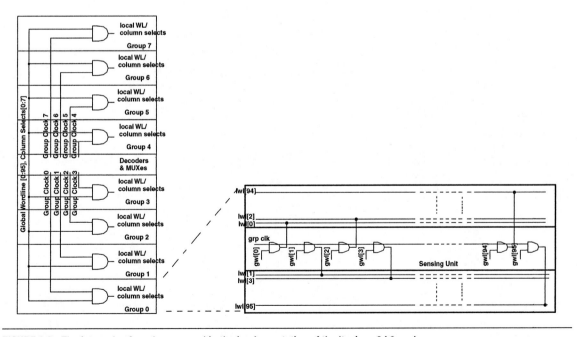

FIGURE 6.9: The internals of a subarray used in the implementation of the Itanium-2 L3 cache.

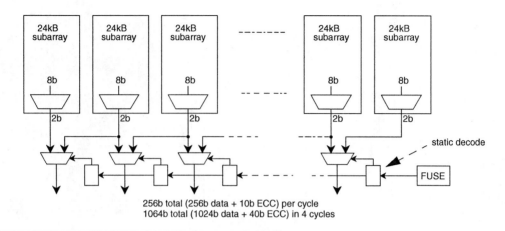

256b total (256b data + 10b ECC) per cycle
1064b total (1024b data + 40b ECC) in 4 cycles

FIGURE 6.10: The Itanium-2 L3 cache subarray interconnection for redundancy.

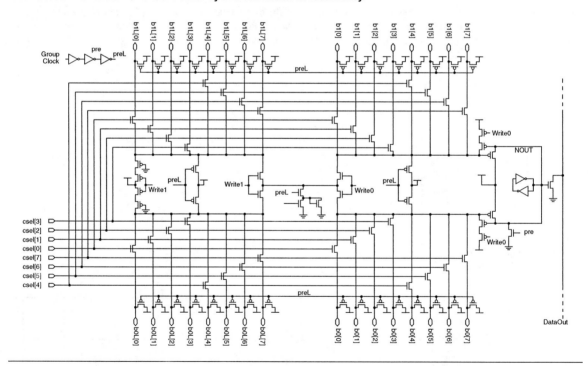

FIGURE 6.11: Itanium-2 L3 cache subarray structure and sensing.

microprocessor, the caches are physically indexed and either physically or virtually tagged such that access to the cache tags and data can be started at the same time as the translation (instead of having to wait for the full translation to be done before starting the actual cache access). This translation is conventionally performed by a structure called a translation lookaside buffer (TLB), which caches the most recent

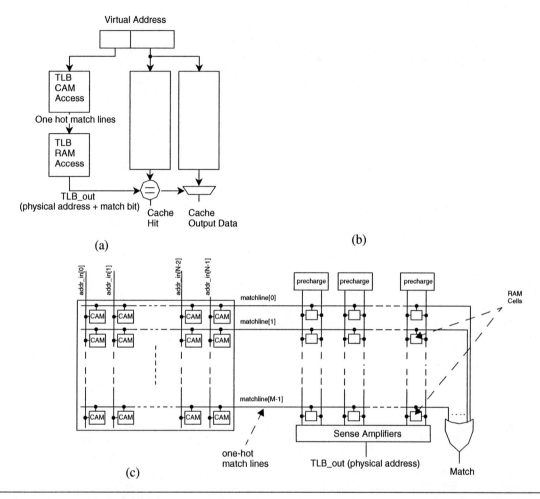

FIGURE 6.12: A conventional TLB and cache read access. (a) Shows a block diagram of the cache access, including the TLB access (both the CAM and RAM parts). (b) Shows internals of a CAM cell showing the inputs being compared to the internal state of the CAM cell and discharging a "match line" during a match. (c) Shows internals of the TLB CAM and RAM access. The left part shows the N-bit address input being matched to an M-entry CAM producing M-bit one-hot match signals which are then used as the wordlines of a conventional RAM array, which produces the actual data and a match signal signifying a TLB hit.

virtual-to-physical address translations that have been used by the microprocessor. TLBs, in turn, are best implemented as small, fully associated memories to maximize the hit rate to compensate for their small size. This full associativity is best implemented as a special content-addressable memory (CAM). Typically, the very basic CAM is capable only of indicating the presence of the desired data and which

line it is stored in. The multiple "match" signals (one per line) that are generated by this operation are then typically used as the wordline signals supplied to a conventional SRAM array that contains the actual data to be accessed. These concepts are shown and demonstrated in Figure 6.12, which shows the block diagram of the TLB access and the typical circuitry used to implement it.

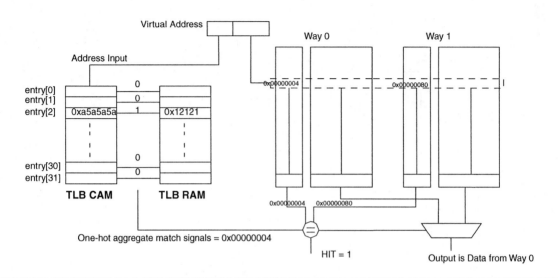

FIGURE 6.13: An Intel Itanium-2 prevalidated-tag microarchitecture (way-0 match). The cache tag arrays store a one-hot pointer to the TLB entry instead of the entire physical tag (here, Way 0 points to TLB entry 2, while Way 1 points to TLB entry 7). The tag comparison can be performed right after the access to the TLB CAM cells when the match lines are produced, instead of waiting for the actual address output from the TLB RAM. This example shows the prevalidated-tag microarchitecture for two ways, but the concept is readily applicable to caches with higher associativity.

The path described above typically lies on the critical path of most microprocessors. Speeding up a microprocessor requires that this path (among others that are also critical) be shortened. One way that this can be done on a microarchitectural level is by using a prevalidated tag microarchitecture, as implemented by the Intel Itanium-2.

The main concept behind the prevalidated-tag architecture is that instead of storing a physical address in the cache tag array and comparing this with the physical address output of the TLB, the cache tag array only contains a one-hot pointer to the TLB entry that contains the actual physical address. The main benefit behind this scheme is that the tag compare can be performed on the aggregate TLB match signals and the tag array output, removing the TLB RAM access from the critical path. Figure 6.13 shows an example demonstrating this prevalidated-tag microarchitecture.

It is important to note that although the prevalidated-tag microarchitecture speeds up the TLB cache critical path, it does introduce complexities into the system, with the main issue being the need to ensure that every pointer stored inside the tag array is properly defined as valid or not, even after changes are made to the TLB. Cache entries that point to a stale TLB entry (i.e., those that were pointing to a TLB entry that has been overwritten by a new one) must be invalidated to ensure that no false matches occur. Although this may sound like a significant problem, the fact that TLB misses occur infrequently and TLB fills themselves are expensive means that the additional cost of updating the cache to properly reflect the new TLB state can be easily absorbed during this operation—introducing additional delay to the infrequent case of TLB fills, while speeding up the common case of an access that hits the TLB.

PART II

DRAM

The first question I ask myself when something doesn't seem to be beautiful is why do I think it's not beautiful. And very shortly you discover that there is no reason.

— John Cage

CHAPTER 7

Overview of DRAMs

DRAM is the "computer memory" that you order through the mail or purchase at the store. It is what you put more of into your computer as an upgrade to improve the computer's performance. It appears in most computers in the form shown in Figure 7.1—the ubiquitous *memory module*, a small computer board (a *printed circuit board*, or *PCB*) that has a handful of chips attached to it. The eight black rectangles on the pictured module are the DRAM chips: plastic packages, each of which encloses a *DRAM die* (a very thin, fragile piece of silicon).

Figure 7.2 illustrates DRAM's place in a typical PC. An individual DRAM device typically connects indirectly to a CPU (i.e., a microprocessor) through a memory controller. In PC systems, the memory controller is part of the *north-bridge* chipset that handles potentially multiple microprocessors, the graphics co-processor, communication to the *south-bridge* chipset (which, in turn, handles all of the system's I/O functions), as well as the interface to the DRAM system. Though still often referred to as "chipsets" these days, the north- and south-bridge chipsets are no longer sets of chips; they are usually implemented as single chips, and in some systems the functions of both are merged into a single die.

Because DRAM is usually an external device by definition, its use, design, and analysis must consider effects of implementation that are often ignored in the use, design, and analysis of on-chip memories such as SRAM caches and scratch-pads. Issues that a designer must consider include the following:

- Pins (e.g., their capacitance and inductance)
- Signaling
- Signal integrity
- Packaging
- Clocking and synchronization
- Timing conventions

Failure to consider these issues when designing a DRAM system is guaranteed to result in a sub-optimal, and quite probably non-functional, design.

FIGURE 7.1: A memory module. A memory module, or DIMM (dual in-line memory module), is a circuit board with a handful of DRAM chips and associated circuitry attached to it.

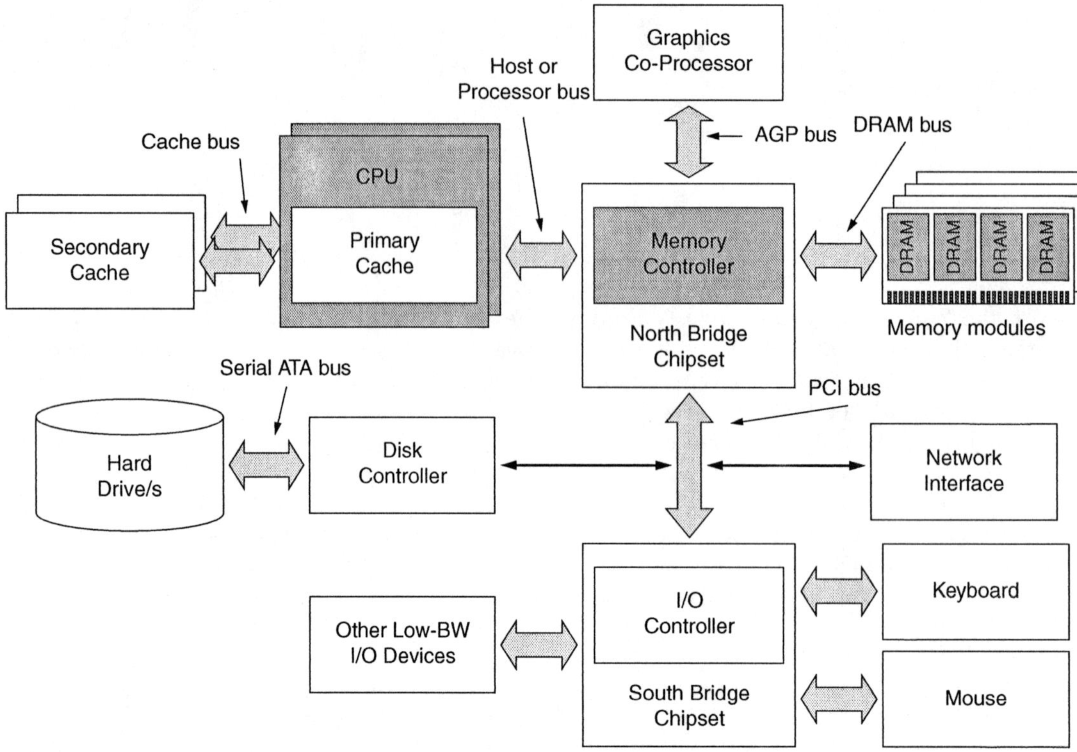

FIGURE 7.2: A typical PC organization. The DRAM subsystem is one part of a relatively complex whole. This figure illustrates a two-way multi-processor, with each processor having its own dedicated secondary cache. The parts most relevant to this report are shaded in darker grey: the CPU, the memory controller, and the individual DRAMs.

Thus, much of this section of the book deals with low-level implementation issues that were not covered in the previous section on caches.

7.1 DRAM Basics: Internals, Operation

A random-access memory (RAM) that uses a single transistor-capacitor pair for each bit is called a dynamic random-access memory or DRAM. Figure 7.3 shows, in the bottom right corner, the circuit for the storage cell in a DRAM. This circuit is *dynamic* because the capacitors storing electrons are not perfect devices, and their eventual leakage requires that, to retain information stored there, each

capacitor in the DRAM must be periodically *refreshed* (i.e., read and rewritten).

Each DRAM die contains one or more *memory arrays*, rectangular grids of storage cells with each cell holding one bit of data. Because the arrays are rectangular grids, it is useful to think of them in terms associated with typical grid-like structures. A good example is a Manhattan-like street layout with avenues running north–south and streets running east–west. When one wants to specify a rendezvous location in such a city, one simply designates the intersection of a street and an avenue, and the location is specified without ambiguity. Memory arrays are organized just like this, except where Manhattan is organized into *streets* and *avenues*, memory arrays are organized

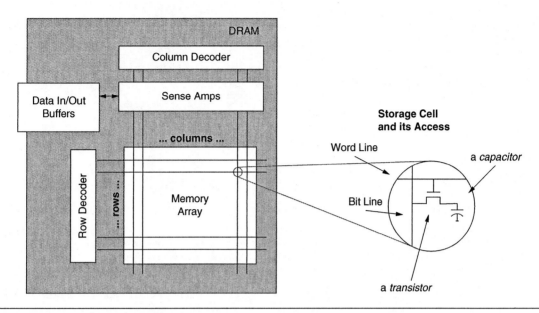

FIGURE 7.3: Basic organization of DRAM internals. The DRAM memory array is a grid of storage cells, where one bit of data is stored at each intersection of a *row* and a *column*.

into *rows* and *columns*. A DRAM chip's memory array with the rows and columns indicated is pictured in Figure 7.3. By identifying the intersection of a row and a column (by specifying a *row address* and a *column address* to the DRAM), a memory controller can access an individual storage cell inside a DRAM chip so as to read or write the data held there.

One way to characterize DRAMs is by the number of memory arrays inside them. Memory arrays within a memory chip can work in several different ways. They can act in unison, they can act completely independently, or they can act in a manner that is somewhere in between the other two. If the memory arrays are designed to act in unison, they operate as a unit, and the memory chip typically transmits or receives a number of bits equal to the number of arrays each time the memory controller accesses the DRAM. For example, in a simple organization, a x4 DRAM (pronounced "by four") indicates that the DRAM has at least four memory arrays and that a column width is 4 bits (each column read or write transmits 4 bits of data). In a x4 DRAM part, four arrays each read 1 data

bit in unison, and the part sends out 4 bits of data each time the memory controller makes a column read request. Likewise, a x8 DRAM indicates that the DRAM has at least eight memory arrays and that a column width is 8 bits. Figure 7.4 illustrates the internal organization of x2, x4, and x8 DRAMs. In the past two decades, wider output DRAMs have appeared, and x16 and x32 parts are now common, used primarily in high-performance applications.

Note that each of the DRAM illustrations in Figure 7.4 represents multiple arrays but a single *bank*. Each set of memory arrays that operates independently of other sets is referred to as a bank, not an array. Each bank is independent in that, with only a few restrictions, it can be activated, precharged, read out, etc. at the same time that other banks (on the same DRAM device or on other DRAM devices) are being activated, precharged, etc. The use of multiple independent banks of memory has been a common practice in computer design since DRAMs were invented. In particular, *interleaving* multiple memory banks has been a popular method used to achieve high-bandwidth memory busses using

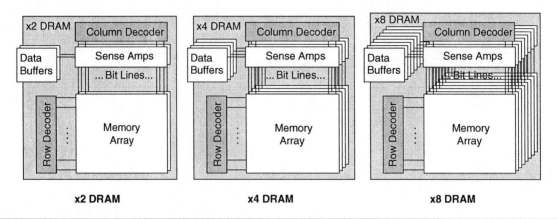

FIGURE 7.4: Logical organization of wide data-out DRAMs. If the DRAM outputs more than one bit at a time, the internal organization is that of multiple arrays, each of which provides one bit toward the aggregate data output.

low-bandwidth devices. In an interleaved memory system, the data bus uses a frequency that is faster than any one DRAM bank can support; the control circuitry toggles back and forth between multiple banks to achieve this data rate. For example, if a DRAM bank can produce a new chunk of data every 10 ns, one can toggle back and forth between two banks to produce a new chunk every 5 ns, or round-robin between four banks to produce a new chunk every 2.5 ns, thereby effectively doubling or quadrupling the data rate achievable by any one bank. This technique goes back at least to the mid-1960s, where it was used in two of the highest performance (and, as it turns out, best documented) computers of the day: the IBM System/360 Model 91 [Anderson et al. 1967] and Seymour Cray's Control Data 6600 [Thornton 1970].

Because a system can have multiple DIMMs, each of which can be thought of as an independent bank, and the DRAM devices on each DIMM can implement internally multiple independent banks, the word "rank" was introduced to distinguish DIMM-level independent operation versus internal-bank-level independent operation. Figure 7.5 illustrates the various levels of organization in a modern DRAM system. A system is composed of potentially many independent DIMMs. Each DIMM may contain one

or more independent ranks. Each rank is a set of DRAM devices that operate in unison, and internally each of these DRAM devices implements one or more independent banks. Finally, each bank is composed of slaved memory arrays, where the number of arrays is equal to the data width of the DRAM part (i.e., a x4 part has four slaved arrays per bank). Having concurrency at the rank and bank levels provides bandwidth through the ability to pipeline requests. Having multiple DRAMs acting in unison at the rank level and multiple arrays acting in unison at the bank level provides bandwidth in the form of parallel access.

The busses in a JEDEC-style organization are classified by their function and organization into *data*, *address*, *control*, and *chip-select* busses. An example arrangement is shown in Figure 7.6, which depicts a memory controller connected to two memory modules. The data bus that transmits data to and from the DRAMs is relatively wide. It is often 64 bits wide, and it can be much wider in high-performance systems. A dedicated address bus carries row and column addresses to the DRAMs, and its width grows with the physical storage on a DRAM device (typical widths today are about 15 bits). A control bus is composed of the row and column strobes,[1] output enable, clock, clock enable, and other related signals. These

---

[1]A "strobe" is a signal that indicates to the recipient that another signal, e.g., data or command, is present and valid.

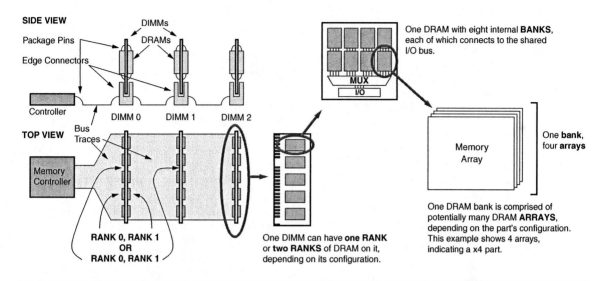

FIGURE 7.5: DIMMs, ranks, banks, and arrays. A system has potentially many DIMMs, each of which may contain one or more ranks. Each rank is a set of ganged DRAM devices, each of which has potentially many banks. Each bank has potentially many constituent arrays, depending on the part's data width.

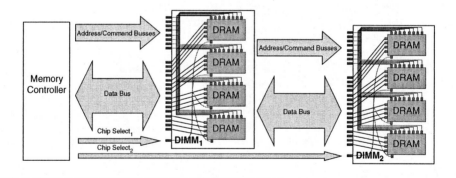

FIGURE 7.6: JEDEC-style memory bus organization. The figure shows a system of a memory controller and two memory modules with a 16-bit data bus and an 8-bit address and command bus.

signals are similar to the address-bus signals in that they all connect from the memory controller to every DRAM in the system. Finally, there is a chip-select network that connects from the memory controller to every DRAM in a *rank* (a separately addressable set of DRAMs). For example, a memory module can contain two ranks of DRAM devices; for every DIMM in the system, there can be two separate chip-select

networks, and thus, the size of the chip-select "bus" scales with the maximum amount of physical memory in the system.

This last bus, the chip-select bus, is essential in a JEDEC-style memory system, as it enables the intended recipient of a memory request. A value is asserted on the chip-select bus at the time of a request (e.g., read or write). The chip-select bus

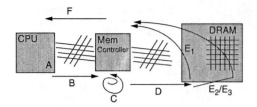

A: Transaction request may be delayed in Queue
B: Transaction request sent to Memory Controller
C: Transaction converted to Command Sequences
                  (may be queued)
D: Command/s Sent to DRAM
E_1: Requires only a **CAS** or
E_2: Requires **RAS + CAS** or
E_3: Requires **PRE + RAS + CAS**
F: Transaction sent back to CPU

DRAM Latency = A + B + C + D + E + F

FIGURE 7.7: System organization and the steps of a DRAM read. Reading data from a DRAM is not as simple as an SRAM, and at several of the stages the request can be stalled.

contains a separate wire for every rank of DRAM in the system. The chip-select signal passes over a wire unique to each small set of DRAMs and enables or disables the DRAMs in that rank so that they, respectively, either handle the request currently on the bus or ignore the request currently on the bus. Thus, only the DRAMs to which the request is directed handle the request. Even though all DRAMs in the system are connected to the same address and control busses and could, in theory, all respond to the same request at the same time, the chip-select bus prevents this from happening.

Figure 7.7 focuses attention on the microprocessor, memory controller, and DRAM device and illustrates the steps involved in a DRAM request. As mentioned previously, a DRAM device connects indirectly to a microprocessor through a memory controller; the microprocessor connects to the memory controller through some form of network (bus, point-to-point, crossbar, etc.); and the memory controller connects to the DRAM through another network (bus, point-to-point, etc.). The memory controller acts as a liaison between the microprocessor and DRAM so that the microprocessor does not need to know the details of the

DRAM's operation. The microprocessor presents requests to the memory controller that the memory controller satisfies. The microprocessor connects to potentially many memory controllers at once; alternatively, many microprocessors could be connected to the same memory controller. The simplest case (a *uniprocessor* system) is illustrated in the figure. The memory controller connects to potentially many DRAM devices at once. In particular, DIMMs are the most common physical form in which consumers purchase DRAM, and these are small PCBs with a handful of DRAM devices on each. A memory controller usually connects to at least one DIMM and, therefore, multiple DRAM devices at once.

Figure 7.7 also illustrates the steps of a typical DRAM read operation. After ordering and queueing requests, the microprocessor sends a given request to the memory controller. Once the request arrives at the memory controller, it is queued until the DRAM is ready and all previous and/or higher priority requests have been handled. The memory controller's interface to the DRAM is relatively complex (compared to that of an SRAM, for instance); the row-address strobe (RAS) and column-address strobe (CAS) components are shown in detail in Figure 7.8. Recall from Figure 7.3 that the capacitor lies at the intersection of a wordline and a bitline; it is connected to the bitline through a transistor controlled by the wordline. A transistor is, among other things, a switch, and when the voltage on a wordline goes high, all of the transistors attached to that wordline become closed switches (turned on), connecting their respective capacitors to the associated bitlines. The capacitors at each intersection of wordline and bitline are extremely small and hold a number of electrons that are miniuscule relative to the physical characteristics of those bitlines. Therefore, special circuits called *sense amplifiers* are used to detect the values stored on the capacitors when those capacitors become connected to their associated bitlines. The sense amplifiers first *precharge* the bitlines to a voltage level that is halfway between logic level 0 and logic level 1. When the capacitors are later connected to the bitlines through the transistors, the capacitors change the voltage levels on those bitlines very slightly. The sense amplifiers detect the minute changes and pull

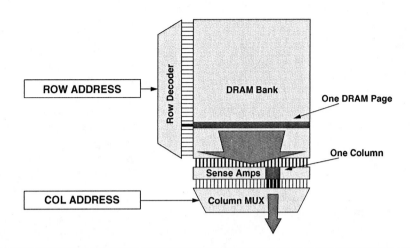

FIGURE 7.8: The multi-phase DRAM-access protocol. The row access drives a DRAM page onto the bitlines to be sensed by the sense amps. The column address drives a subset of the DRAM page onto the bus (e.g., 4 bits).

the bitline voltages all the way to logic level 0 or 1. Bringing the voltage on the bitlines to fully high or fully low, as opposed to the precharged state between high and low, actually recharges the capacitors as long as the transistors remain on.

Returning to the steps in handling the read request. The memory controller must decompose the provided data address into components that identify the appropriate rank within the memory system, the bank within that rank, and the row and column inside the identified bank. The components identifying the row and column are called the *row address* and the *column address*. The bank identifier is typically one or more address bits. The rank number ends up causing a chip-select signal to be sent out over a single one of the separate chip-select lines.

Once the rank, bank, and row are identified, the bitlines in the appropriate bank must be *precharged* (set to a logic level halfway between 0 and 1). Once the appropriate bank has been precharged, the second step is to *activate* the appropriate row inside the identified rank and bank by setting the chip-select signal to activate the set of DRAMs comprising the

desired bank, sending the row address and bank identifier over the address bus, and signaling the DRAM's $\overline{\text{RAS}}$ pin (*row-address strobe*—the bar indicates that the signal is active when it is low). This tells the DRAM to send an entire row of data (thousands of bits) into the DRAM's sense amplifiers (circuits that detect and amplify the tiny logic signals represented by the electric charges in the row's storage cells). This typically takes a few tens of nanoseconds, and the step may have already been done (the row or page could already be open or activated, meaning that the sense amps might already have valid data in them).

Once the sense amps have recovered the values, and the bitlines are pulled to the appropriate logic levels, the memory controller performs the last step, which is to *read* the column (*column* being the name given to the data subset of the row that is desired), by setting the chip-select signal to activate the set of DRAMs comprising the desired bank,[2] sending the column address and bank identifier over the address bus, and signaling the DRAM's $\overline{\text{CAS}}$ pin (*column-address strobe*—like $\overline{\text{RAS}}$, the bar indicates that it is

---

[2]This step is necessary for SDRAMs; it is not performed for older, asynchronous DRAMs (it is subsumed by the earlier chip-select accompanying the RAS).

active when low). This causes only a few select bits[3] in the sense amplifiers to be connected to the output drivers, where they will be driven onto the data bus. Reading the column data takes on the order of tens of nanoseconds. When the memory controller receives the data, it forwards the data to the microprocessor.

The process of transmitting the address in two different steps (i.e., separately transmitted row and column addresses) is unlike that of SRAMs. Initially, DRAMs had minimal I/O pin counts because the manufacturing cost was dominated by the number of I/O pins in the package. This desire to limit I/O pins has had a long-term effect on DRAM architecture; the address pins for most DRAMs are still multiplexed, meaning that two different portions of a data address are sent over the same pins at different times, as opposed to using more address pins and sending the entire address at once.

Most computer systems have a special signal that acts much like a heartbeat and is called the *clock*. A clock transmits a continuous signal with regular intervals of "high" and "low" values. It is usually illustrated as a square wave or semi-square wave with each period identical to the next, as shown in Figure 7.9. The upward portion of the square wave is called the *positive* or *rising edge* of the clock, and the downward portion of the square wave is called the *negative* or *falling edge* of the clock. The primary clock in a computer system is called the system clock or global clock, and it typically resides on the motherboard (the PCB that contains the microprocessor and memory bus). The system clock drives the microprocessor and memory controller and many of the associated peripheral devices directly. If the clock drives the DRAMs directly, the DRAMs are called *synchronous DRAMs*. If the clock does not drive the DRAMs directly, the DRAMs are called *asynchronous DRAMs*. In a synchronous DRAM, steps internal to the DRAM happen in time with one or more edges of this clock. In an asynchronous DRAM, operative steps internal to the DRAM happen when the memory controller commands the DRAM to act, and those commands typically happen in time with one or more edges of the system clock.

7.2 Evolution of the DRAM Architecture

In the 1980s and 1990s, the conventional DRAM interface started to become a performance bottleneck in high-performance as well as desktop systems. The improvement in the speed and performance of microprocessors was significantly outpacing the improvement in speed and performance of DRAM chips. As a consequence, the DRAM interface began to evolve, and a number of revolutionary proposals [Przybylski 1996] were made as well. In most cases, what was considered evolutionary or revolutionary was the proposed *interface* (the mechanism by which the microprocessor accesses the DRAM). The DRAM core (i.e., what is pictured in Figure 7.3) remains essentially unchanged.

Figure 7.10 shows the evolution of the basic DRAM architecture from *clocked* to the conventional *asynchronous* to *fast page mode* (FPM) to *extended data-out* (EDO) to *burst-mode EDO* (BEDO) to *synchronous* (SDRAM). The figure shows each as a stylized DRAM in terms of the memory array, the sense amplifiers, and the column multiplexer (as well as additional components if appropriate).

As far as the first evolutionary path is concerned (asynchronous through SDRAM), the changes have largely been structural in nature, have been relatively minor in terms of cost and physical implementation, and have targeted increased throughput. Since SDRAM, there has been a profusion of designs proffered by the DRAM industry, and we lump these new DRAMs into two categories: those targeting reduced latency and those targeting increased throughput.

7.2.1 Structural Modifications Targeting Throughput

Compared to the conventional DRAM, FPM simply allows the row to remain open across multiple $\overline{CAS}$ commands, requiring very little additional circuitry. To this, EDO changes the output drivers to become output latches so that they hold the data valid on the

---

[3]One bit in a "x1" DRAM, two bits in a "x2" DRAM, four bits in a "x4" DRAM, etc.

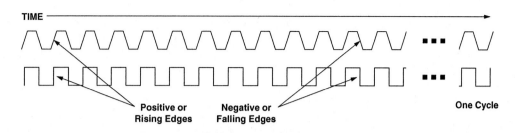

FIGURE 7.9: Example clock signals. Clocks are typically shown as square waves (bottom) or sort of square waves (top). They repeat *ad infinitum*, and the repeating shape is called a clock cycle. The two clocks pictured above have the same frequency—the number of cycles in a given time period.

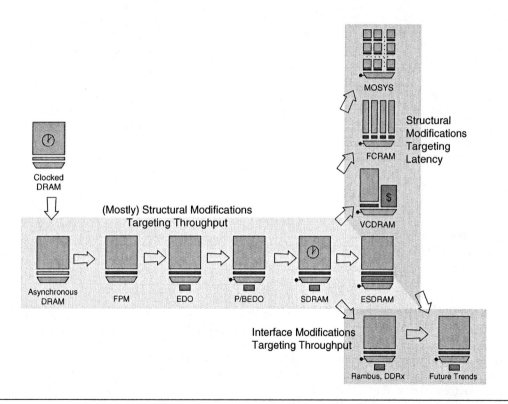

FIGURE 7.10: Evolution of the DRAM architecture. To the original DRAM design, composed of an array, a block of sense amps, and a column multiplexor, the fast page mode (FPM) design adds the ability to hold the contents of the sense amps valid over multiple column accesses. To the FPM design, extended data-out (EDO) design adds an output latch after the column multiplexor. To the EDO design, the burst EDO (BEDO) design adds a counter that optionally drives the column-select address latch. To the BEDO design, the synchronous DRAM (SDRAM) design adds a clock signal that drives both row-select and column-select circuitry (not just the column-select address latch).

bus for a longer period of time. To this, BEDO adds an internal counter that drives the address latch so that the memory controller does not need to supply a new address to the DRAM on every $\overline{\text{CAS}}$ command if the desired address is simply one off from the previous $\overline{\text{CAS}}$ command. Thus, in BEDO, the DRAM's column-select circuitry is driven from an internally generated signal, not an externally generated signal; the source of the control signal is close to the circuitry that it controls in space and therefore time, and this makes the timing of the circuit's activation more precise. Finally, SDRAM takes this perspective one step further and drives all internal circuitry (row select, column select, data read-out) by a clock, as opposed to the $\overline{\text{RAS}}$ and $\overline{\text{CAS}}$ strobes. The following paragraphs describe this evolution in more detail.

Clocked DRAM

The earliest DRAMs (1960s to mid-1970s, before de facto standardization) were often clocked [Rhoden 2002, Sussman 2002, Padgett and Newman 1974]; DRAM commands were driven by a periodic clock signal. Figure 7.10 shows a stylized DRAM in terms of the memory array, the sense amplifiers, and the column multiplexer.

The Conventional Asynchronous DRAM

In the mid-1970s, DRAMs moved to the asynchronous design with which most people are familiar. These DRAMs, like the clocked versions before them, require that every single access go through all of the steps described previously: for every access, the bitlines need to be precharged, the row needs to be activated, and the column is read out after row activation. Even if the microprocessor wants to request the same data row that it previously requested, the entire process (row activation followed by column read/write) must be repeated. Once the column is read, the row is deactivated or closed, and the bitlines are precharged. For the next request, the entire process is repeated, even if the same datum is requested twice in succession. By convention and

circuit design, both $\overline{\text{RAS}}$ and $\overline{\text{CAS}}$ must rise in unison. For example, one cannot hold $\overline{\text{RAS}}$ low while toggling $\overline{\text{CAS}}$. Figure 7.11 illustrates the timing for the conventional asynchronous DRAM.

Fast Page Mode DRAM (FPM DRAM)

FPM DRAM implements page mode, an improvement on conventional DRAM in which the row address is held constant and data from multiple columns is read from the sense amplifiers. This simply lifts the restriction described in the previous paragraph: the memory controller may hold $\overline{\text{RAS}}$ low while toggling $\overline{\text{CAS}}$, thereby creating a de facto cache out of the data held active in the sense amplifiers. The data held in the sense amps form an "open page" that can be accessed relatively quickly. This speeds up successive accesses to the same row of the DRAM core, as is very common in computer systems (the term is locality of reference and indicates that oftentimes memory requests that are nearby in time are also nearby in the memory-address space and would therefore likely lie within the same DRAM row). Figure 7.12 gives the timing for FPM reads.

Extended Data-Out DRAM (EDO DRAM)

EDO DRAM, sometimes referred to as hyper-page mode DRAM, adds a few transistors to the output drivers of an FPM DRAM to create a latch between the sense amps and the output pins of the DRAM. This latch holds the output pin state and permits the $\overline{\text{CAS}}$ to rapidly deassert, allowing the memory array to begin precharging sooner. In addition, the latch in the output path also implies that the data on the outputs of the DRAM circuit remain valid longer into the next clock phase, relative to previous DRAM architectures (thus the name "extended data-out"). By permitting the memory array to begin precharging sooner, the addition of a latch allows EDO DRAM to operate faster than FPM DRAM. EDO enables the microprocessor to access memory at least 10 to 15% faster than with FPM [Kingston 2000, Cuppu et al. 1999, 2001]. Figure 7.13 gives the timing for an EDO read.

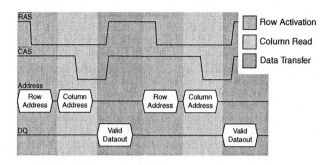

FIGURE 7.11: Read timing for the asynchronous DRAM.

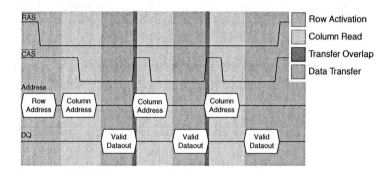

FIGURE 7.12: FPM read timing. The FPM allows the DRAM controller to hold a row constant and receive multiple columns in rapid succession.

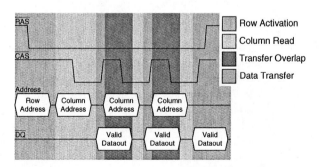

FIGURE 7.13: EDO read timing. The output latch in EDO DRAM allows more overlap between column access and data transfer than in FPM.

Burst-Mode EDO DRAM (BEDO DRAM)

Although BEDO DRAM never reached the volume of production that EDO and SDRAM did, it was positioned to be the next-generation DRAM after EDO [Micron 1995]. BEDO builds on EDO DRAM by adding the concept of "bursting" contiguous blocks of data from an activated row each time a new column address is sent to the DRAM chip. An internal counter was added that first accepts the incoming address and then increments that value on every successive toggling of $\overline{\text{CAS}}$, driving the incremented value into the column-address latch. With each toggle of the $\overline{\text{CAS}}$, the DRAM chip sends the next sequential column of data onto the bus. In previous DRAMs, the column-address latch was driven by an externally generated address signal. By eliminating the need to send successive column addresses over the bus to drive a burst of data in response to each microprocessor request, BEDO eliminates a significant amount of timing uncertainty between successive addresses, thereby increasing the rate at which data can be read from the DRAM. In practice, the minimum cycle time for driving the output bus was reduced by roughly 30% compared to EDO DRAM [Prince 2000], thereby increasing bandwidth proportionally. Figure 7.14 gives the timing for a BEDO read.

IBM's High-Speed Toggle Mode DRAM

IBM's High-Speed Toggle Mode ("toggle mode") is a high-speed DRAM interface designed and fabricated in the late 1980s and presented at the International Solid-State Circuits Conference in February 1990 [Kalter et al. 1990a]. In September 1990, IBM presented toggle mode to JEDEC as an option for the next-generation DRAM architecture (minutes of JC-42.3 meeting 55). Toggle mode transmits data to and from a DRAM on both edges of a high-speed data strobe rather than transferring data on a single edge of the strobe. The strobe was very high speed for its day; Kalter reports a 10-ns data cycle time—an effective 100 MHz data rate—in 1990 [Kalter

et al. 1990b]. The term "toggle" is probably derived from its implementation: to obtain twice the normal data rate,[4] one would toggle a signal pin which would cause the DRAM to toggle back and forth between two different (interleaved) output buffers, each of which would be pumping data out at half the speed of the strobe [Kalter et al. 1990b]. As proposed to JEDEC, it offered burst lengths of 4 or 8 bits of data per memory access.

Synchronous DRAM (SDRAM)

Conventional, FPM, and EDO DRAM are controlled asynchronously by the memory controller. Therefore, in theory, the memory latency and data toggle rate can be some fractional number of microprocessor clock cycles.[5] More importantly, what makes the DRAM asynchronous is that the memory controller's RAS and $\overline{\text{CAS}}$ signals directly control latches internal to the DRAM, and those signals can arrive at the DRAM's pins at any time. An alternative is to make the DRAM interface synchronous such that requests can only arrive at regular intervals. This allows the latches internal to the DRAM to be controlled by an internal clock signal. The primary benefit is similar to that seen in BEDO: by associating all data and control transfer with a clock signal, the timing of events is made more predictable. Such a scheme, by definition, has less skew. Reduction in skew means that the system can potentially achieve faster turnaround on requests, thereby yielding higher throughput. A timing diagram for synchronous DRAM is shown in Figure 7.15. Like BEDO DRAMs, SDRAMs support the concept of a burst mode; SDRAM devices have a programmable register that holds a burst length. The DRAM uses this to determine how many columns to output over successive cycles; SDRAM may therefore return many bytes over several cycles per request. One advantage of this is the elimination of the timing signals (i.e., toggling $\overline{\text{CAS}}$) for each successive burst, which

---

[4]The term "normal" implies the data cycling at half the data-strobe rate.
[5]In practice, this is not the case, as the memory controller and DRAM subsystem are driven by the system clock, which typically has a period that is an integral multiple of the microprocessor's clock.

reduces the command bandwidth used. The underlying architecture of the SDRAM core is the same as in a conventional DRAM.

The evolutionary changes made to the DRAM interface up to and including BEDO have been relatively inexpensive, especially when considering the pay-off: FPM was essentially free compared to the conventional design, EDO simply added a latch, and BEDO added a counter and mux. Each of these evolutionary changes added only a small amount of logic, yet each improved upon its predecessor by as much as 30% in terms of system performance [Cuppu et al. 1999, 2001]. Though SDRAM represented a more significant cost in implementation and offered no performance improvement over BEDO at the same clock speeds,[6] the presence of a source-synchronous data strobe in its interface (in this case, the global clock signal) would allow SDRAM to scale to much

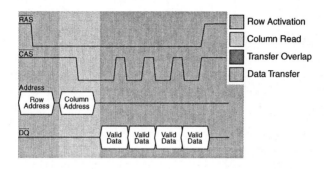

FIGURE 7.14: BEDO read timing. By driving the column-address latch from an internal counter rather than an external signal, the minimum cycle time for driving the output bus was reduced by roughly 30% over EDO.

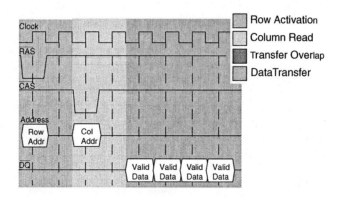

FIGURE 7.15: SDR SDRAM read operation clock diagram (CAS-2).

---

[6]By some estimates, BEDO actually had higher performance than SDRAM [Williams 2001].

higher switching speeds more easily than the earlier asynchronous DRAM interfaces such as FPM and EDO.[7] Note that this benefit applies to any interface with a source-synchronous data strobe signal, whether the interface is synchronous or asynchronous, and therefore, an asynchronous burst-mode DRAM with source-synchronous data strobe could have scaled to higher switching speeds just as easily—witness the February 1990 presentation of a working 100-MHz asynchronous burst-mode part from IBM, which used a dedicated pin to transfer the source-synchronous data strobe [Kalter 1990a, b].

7.2.2 Interface Modifications Targeting Throughput

Since the appearance of SDRAM in the mid-1990s, there has been a large profusion of novel DRAM architectures proposed in an apparent attempt by DRAM manufacturers to make DRAM less of a commodity [Dipert 2000]. One reason for the profusion of competing designs is that we have apparently run out of the same sort of "free" ideas that drove the earlier DRAM evolution. Since BEDO, there has been no architecture proposed that provides a 30% performance advantage at near-zero cost; all proposals have been relatively expensive. As Dipert suggests, there is no clear heads-above-the-rest winner yet because many schemes seem to lie along a linear relationship between additional cost of implementation and realized performance gain. Over time, the market will most likely decide the winner;

those DRAM proposals that provide sub-linear performance gains relative to their implementation cost will be relegated to zero or near-zero market share.

Rambus DRAM (RDRAM, Concurrent RDRAM, and Direct RDRAM)

Rambus DRAM (RDRAM) is very different from traditional main memory. It uses a bus that is significantly narrower than the traditional bus, and, at least in its initial incarnation, it does not use dedicated address, control, data, and chip-select portions of the bus. Instead, the bus is fully multiplexed: the address, control, data, and chip-select information all travel over the same set of electrical wires but at different times. The bus is 1 byte wide, runs at 250 Mhz, and transfers data on both clock edges to achieve a theoretical peak bandwidth of 500 MB/s. Transactions occur on the bus using a split request/response protocol. The packet transactions resemble network request/response pairs: first an address/control packet is driven, which contains the entire address (row address and column address), and then the data is driven. Different transactions can require different numbers of cycles, depending on the transaction type, location of the data within the device, number of devices on the channel, etc. Figure 7.16 shows a typical read transaction with an arbitrary latency.

Because of the bus's design—being a single bus and not composed of separate segments dedicated to separate functions—only one transaction can use

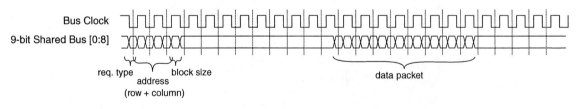

req. type   block size
address
(row + column)

data packet

FIGURE 7.16: Rambus read clock diagram for block size 16. The original Rambus design (from the 1990 patent application) had but a single bus multiplexed between data and address/control. The request packet is six "cycles," where a cycle is one beat of a cycle, not one full period of a cycle.

---

[7]Making an interface synchronous is a well-known technique to simplify the interface and to ease scaling to higher switching speeds [Stone 1982].

the bus during any given cycle. This limits the bus's potential *concurrency* (its ability to do multiple things simultaneously). Due to this limitation, the original RDRAM design was not considered well suited to the PC main memory market [Przybylski 1996], and the interface was redesigned in the mid-1990s to support more concurrency.

Specifically, with the introduction of "Concurrent RDRAM," the bus was divided into separate address, command, and data segments reminiscent of a JEDEC-style DRAM organization. The data segment of the bus remained 1 byte wide, and to this was added a 1-bit address segment and a 1-bit control segment. By having three separate, dedicated segments of the bus, one could perform potentially three separate, simultaneous actions on the bus. This divided and dedicated arrangement simplified transaction scheduling and increased performance over RDRAM accordingly. Note that at this point, Rambus also moved to a four clock cycle period, referred to as an octcycle. Figure 7.17 gives a timing diagram for a read transaction.

One of the few limitations to the "Concurrent" design was that the data bus sometimes carried a brief packet of address information, because the 1-bit address bit was too narrow. This limitation has been removed in Rambus' latest DRAMs. The divided arrangement introduced in Concurrent RDRAM has been carried over into the most recent incarnation of RDRAM, called "Direct RDRAM," which increases the width of the data segment to 2 bytes, the width of the address segment to 5 bits, and the width of the control segment to 3 bits. These segments remain separate and dedicated—similar to a JEDEC-style organization—and the control and address segments are wide enough that the data segment of the bus never needs to carry anything but data, thereby increasing data throughput on the channel. Bus operating speeds have also changed over the years, and the latest designs are more than double the original speeds (500 MHz bus frequency). Each half-row buffer in Direct RDRAM is shared between adjacent banks, which implies that adjacent banks cannot be active simultaneously. This organization has the result of increasing the row buffer miss rate as compared to having one open row per bank, but it reduces the cost by reducing the die area occupied by the row buffers, compared to 16 full row buffers. Figure 7.18 gives a timing diagram for a read operation.

Double Data Rate DRAM (DDR SDRAM)

Double data rate (DDR) SDRAM is the modern equivalent of IBM's High-Speed Toggle Mode. DDR doubles the data bandwidth available from single data rate SDRAM by transferring data at both edges of the clock (i.e., both the rising edge and the falling

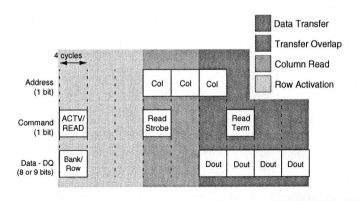

FIGURE 7.17: Concurrent RDRAM read operation. Concurrent RDRAMs transfer on both edges of a fast clock and use a 1-byte data bus multiplexed between data and addresses.

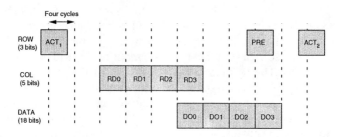

FIGURE 7.18: Direct Rambus read clock diagram. Direct RDRAMs transfer on both edges of a fast clock and use a 2-byte data bus dedicated to handling data only.

edge), much like the toggle mode's dual-edged clocking scheme. DDR SDRAM is very similar to single data rate SDRAM in all other characteristics. They use the same signaling technology, the same interface specification, and the same pin-outs on the DIMM carriers. However, DDR SDRAM's internal transfers from and to the SDRAM array, respectively, read and write twice the number of bits as SDRAM. Figure 7.19 gives a timing diagram for a CAS-2 read operation.

7.2.3 Structural Modifications Targeting Latency

The following DRAM offshoots represent attempts to lower the latency of the DRAM part, either by increasing the circuit's speed or by improving the average latency through caching.

Virtual Channel Memory (VCDRAM)

Virtual channel adds a substantial SRAM cache to the DRAM that is used to buffer large blocks of data (called segments) that might be needed in the future. The SRAM segment cache is managed explicitly by the memory controller. The design adds a new step in the DRAM-access protocol: a row activate operation moves a page of data into the sense amps; "prefetch" and "restore" operations (data read and data write, respectively) move data between the sense amps and the SRAM segment cache one segment at a time; and column read or write operations move a column of data between the segment cache and the output

buffers. The extra step adds latency to read and write operations, unless all of the data required by the application fits in the SRAM segment cache.

Enhanced SDRAM (ESDRAM)

Like EDO DRAM, ESDRAM adds an SRAM latch to the DRAM core, but whereas EDO adds the latch after the column mux, ESDRAM adds it *before* the column mux. Therefore, the latch is as wide as a DRAM page. Though expensive, the scheme allows for better overlap of activity. For instance, it allows row precharge to begin immediately without having to close out the row (it is still active in the SRAM latch). In addition, the scheme allows a write-around mechanism whereby an incoming write can proceed without the need to close out the currently active row. Such a feature is useful for write-back caches, where the data being written at any given time is not likely to be in the same row as data that is currently being read from the DRAM. Therefore, handling such a write delays future reads to the same row. In ESDRAM, future reads to the same row are not delayed.

MoSys 1T-SRAM

MoSys, i.e., Monolithic System Technology, has created a "1-transistor SRAM" (which is not really possible, but it makes for a catchy name). Their design wraps an SRAM interface around an extremely fast DRAM core to create an SRAM-compatible part that approaches the storage and power consumption

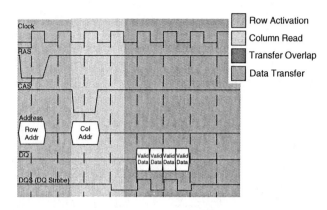

FIGURE 7.19: DDR SDRAM read timing (CAS-2). DDR SDRAMs use both a clock and a source-synchronous data strobe (DQS) to achieve high data rates. DQS is used by the DRAM to sample incoming write data; it is typically ignored by the memory controller on DRAM reads.

characteristics of a DRAM, while simultaneously approaching the access-time characteristics of an SRAM. The fast DRAM core is made up of a very large number of independent banks; decreasing the size of a bank makes its access time faster, but increasing the number of banks complicates the control circuitry (and therefore cost) and decreases the part's effective density. No other DRAM manufacturer has gone to the same extremes as MoSys to create a fast core, and thus, the MoSys DRAM is the lowest latency DRAM in existence. However, its density is low enough that OEMs have not yet used it in desktop systems in any significant volume. Its niche is high-speed embedded systems and game systems (e.g., Nintendo GameCube).

Reduced Latency DRAM (RLDRAM)

Reduced latency DRAM (RLDRAM) is a fast DRAM core that has no DIMM specification: it must be used in a direct-to-memory-controller environment (e.g., inhabiting a dedicated space on the motherboard). Its manufacturers suggest its use as an extremely large off-chip cache, probably at a lower spot in the memory hierarchy than any SRAM cache. Interfacing directly to the chip, as opposed to through a DIMM,

decreases the potential for clock skew, thus the part's high-speed interface.

Fast Cycle DRAM (FCRAM)

Fujitsu's fast cycle RAM (FCRAM) achieves a low-latency data access by segmenting the data array into subarrays, only one of which is driven during a row activate. This is similar to decreasing the size of an array, thus its effect on access time. The subset of the data array is specified by adding more bits to the row address, and therefore the mechanism is essentially putting part of the column address into the row activation (e.g., moving part of the column-select function into row activation). As opposed to RLDRAM, the part does have a DIMM specification, and it has the highest DIMM bandwidth available, in the DRAM parts surveyed.

7.2.4 Rough Comparison of Recent DRAMs

Latter-day advanced DRAM designs have abounded, largely because of the opportunity to appeal to markets asking for high performance [Dipert 2000] and because engineers have evidently run out of design ideas that echo those of the early-on evolution; that is, design ideas that are relatively inexpensive to implement and yet yield tremendous performance advantages. The DRAM industry tends to favor building the simplest design that achieves the desired benefits [Lee 2002, DuPreez 2002, Rhoden 2002]. Currently, the dominant DRAM in the high-performance design arena is DDR.

7.3 Modern-Day DRAM Standards

DRAM is a commodity; in theory, any DRAM chip or DIMM is equivalent to any other that has similar specifications (width, capacity, speed grade, interface, etc.). The standard-setting body that governs this compatibility is JEDEC, an organization formerly known as the *Joint Electron Device Engineering Council*. Following a recent marketing decision reminiscent of Kentucky Fried Chicken's move to be known as simply "KFC," the organization is now known as the "JEDEC" Solid-State Technology Association. Working within the Electronic Industries Alliance (EIA), JEDEC covers the standardization of discrete semiconductor devices and integrated circuits. The work is done through 48 committees and their constituent subcommittees; anyone can become a member of any committee, and so any individual or corporate representative can help to influence future standards. In particular, DRAM device standardization is done by the 42.3 subcommittee (JC-42.3).

7.3.1 Salient Features of JEDEC's SDRAM Technology

JEDEC SDRAMs use the traditional DRAM-system organization, described earlier and illustrated in Figure 7.6. There are four different busses, with each classified by its function—a "memory bus" in this organization is actually composed of separate (1) data, (2) address, (3) control, and (4) chip-select busses. Each of these busses is dedicated to handle only its designated function, except in a few instances, for example, when control information is sent over an otherwise unused address bus wire. (1) The data bus is relatively wide: in modern PC systems, it is 64 bits wide, and it can be much wider in high-performance systems. (2) The width of the address bus grows with the number of bits stored in an individual DRAM device; typical address busses today are about 15 bits wide. (3) A control bus is composed of the row and column strobes, output enable, clock, clock enable, and other similar signals that connect from the memory controller to every DRAM in the system. (4) Finally, there is a chip-select network that uses one unique wire per DRAM rank in the system and thus scales with the maximum amount of physical memory in the system. Chip select is used to enable ranks of DRAMs and thereby allow them to read commands off the bus and read/write data off/onto the bus.

The primary difference between SDRAMs and earlier asynchronous DRAMs is the presence in the system of a clock signal against which all actions (command and data transmissions) are timed. Whereas asynchronous DRAMs use the RAS and CAS signals as strobes—that is, the strobes directly cause the DRAM to sample addresses and/or data off the bus—SDRAMs instead use the clock as a strobe, and the RAS and CAS signals are simply commands that are themselves sampled off the bus in time with the clock strobe. The reason for timing transmissions with a regular (i.e., periodic) free-running clock instead of the less regular RAS and CAS strobes was to achieve higher dates more easily; when a regular strobe is used to time transmissions, timing uncertainties can be reduced, and therefore data rates can be increased.

Note that any regular timing signal could be used to achieve higher data rates in this way; a free-running clock is not necessary [Lee 2002, Rhoden 2002, Karabotsos 2002, Baker 2002, Macri 2002]. In DDR SDRAMs, the clock is all but ignored in the data transfer portion of write requests: the DRAM samples the incoming data with respect not to the clock, but instead to a separate, regular signal known as DQS [Lee 2002, Rhoden 2002, Macri 2002, Karabotsos 2002, Baker 2002]. The implication is that a free-running clock could be dispensed with entirely, and the result would be something very close to IBM's toggle mode.

Single Data Rate SDRAM

Single data rate SDRAM use a *single-edged clock* to synchronize all information; that is, all transmissions on the various busses (control, address, data) begin in time with one edge of the system clock (as so happens, the rising edge). Because the transmissions on the various busses are ideally valid from one clock edge to the next, those signals are very likely to be valid during the other edge of the clock (the falling edge). Consequently, that edge of the clock can be used to sample those signals.

SDRAMs have several features that were not present in earlier DRAM architectures: a burst length that is programmable and a CAS latency that is programmable.

Programmable Burst Length   Like BEDO DRAMs, SDRAMs use the concept of *bursting* data to improve bandwidth. Instead of using successive toggling of the CAS signal to burst out data, however, SDRAM chips only require CAS to be signaled once and, in response, transmit or receive in time with the toggling of the clock the number of bits indicated by a value held in a programmable mode register. Once an SDRAM receives a row address and a column address, it will burst the number of columns that correspond to the burst length value stored in the register. If the mode register is programmed for a burst length of four, for example, then the DRAM will automatically burst four columns of contiguous data onto the bus. This eliminates the need to toggle the CAS to derive a burst of data in response to a microprocessor request. Consequently, the potential parallelism in the memory system increases (i.e., it improves) due to the reduced use of the command bus—the memory controller can issue other requests to other banks during those cycles that it otherwise would have been toggling CAS.

Programmable CAS Latency   The mode register also stores the CAS latency of an SDRAM chip. Latency is a measure of delay. CAS latency, as the name implies, refers to the number of clock cycles it takes for the SDRAM to return the data once it receives a CAS command. The ability to set the CAS latency to a desired value allows parts of different generations fabricated in different process technologies (which would all otherwise have different performance characteristics) to behave identically. Thus, mixed-performance parts can easily be used in the same system and can even be integrated onto the same memory module.

Double Data Rate SDRAM

DDR SDRAMs have several features that were not present in single data rate SDRAM architectures: dual-edged clocking and an on-chip delay-locked loop (DLL).

Dual-Edged Clocking   DDR SDRAMs, like regular SDRAMs, use a single-edged clock to synchronize control and address transmissions, but for data transmissions DDR DRAMs use a *dual-edged clock*; that is, some data bits are transmitted on the data bus in time with the rising edge of the system clock, and other bits are transmitted on the data bus in time with the falling edge of the system clock.

Figure 7.20 illustrates the difference, showing timing for two different clock arrangements. The top design is a more traditional arrangement wherein data is transferred only on the rising edge of the clock; the bottom design uses a data rate that is twice the speed of the top design, and data is transferred on both the rising and falling edges of the clock. IBM had built DRAMs using this feature in the late 1980s and presented their results in the International Solid-State Circuits Convention in February of 1990 [Kalter 1990a]. Reportedly, Digital Equipment Corp. had been experimenting with similar schemes in the late 1980s and early 1990s [Lee 2002, minutes of JC-42.3 meeting 58].

In a system that uses a single-edged clock to transfer data, there are two clock edges for every data "eye;" the data eye is framed on both ends by a clock edge, and a third clock edge is found somewhere in the middle of the data transmission (cf. Figure 7.20(a)). Thus, the clock signal can be used directly to perform two actions: to drive data onto the bus and to read data off the bus. Note that in a single-edged clocking scheme, data is transmitted once per clock cycle.

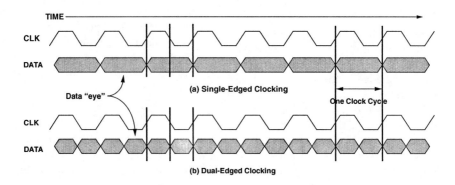

FIGURE 7.20: Running the bus clock at the data rate. The top diagram (a) illustrates a single-edged clocking scheme wherein the clock is twice the frequency of the data transmission. The bottom diagram (b) illustrates a dual-edged clocking scheme in which the data transmission rate is equal to the clock frequency.

By contrast, in a dual-edged clocking scheme, data is transmitted twice per clock cycle. This halves the number of clock edges available to drive data onto the bus and/or read data off the bus (cf. Figure 7.20(b)). The bottom diagram shows a clock running at the same rate as the data transmission. Note that there is only one clock edge for every data eye. The clock edges in a dual-edged scheme are either "edge-aligned" with the data or "center-aligned" with the data. This means that the clock can either drive the data onto the bus or read the data off the bus, but it cannot do both, as it can in a single-edged scheme. In the figure, the clock is edge-aligned with the data.

The dual-edged clocking scheme by definition has fewer clock edges per data transmission that can be used to synchronize or perform functions. This means that some other mechanism must be introduced to get accurate timing for both driving data and sampling data, i.e., to compensate for the fact that there are fewer clock edges, a dual-edged signaling scheme needs an additional mechanism beyond the clock. For example, DDR SDRAM specifies along with the system clock a center-aligned data strobe that is provided by the memory controller on DRAM writes that the DRAM uses directly to sample incoming data. On DRAM reads, the data strobe is edge-aligned with the data and system clock; the memory controller is responsible for providing its own mecha-nism for generating a center-aligned edge. The strobe is called DQS.

On-Chip Delay-Locked Loop In DDR SDRAM, the on-chip DLL synchronizes the DRAM's outgoing data and DQS (data strobe) signals with the memory controller's global clock [JEDEC Standard 21-C, Section 3.11.6.6]. The DLL synchronizes those signals involved in DRAM reads, not those involved in DRAM writes; in the latter case, the DQS signal accompanying data sent from the memory controller on DRAM writes is synchronized with that data by the memory controller and is used by the DRAM directly to sample the data [Lee 2002, Rhoden 2002, Karabotsos 2002, Baker 2002, Macri 2002]. The DLL circuit in a DDR DRAM thus ensures that data is transmitted by the DRAM in synchronization with the memory controller's clock signal so that the data arrives at the memory controller at expected times. The mem-ory controller typically has two internal clocks: one in synch with the global clock, and another that is delayed 90° and used to sample data incoming from the DRAM. Because the DQS is in-phase with the data for read operations (unlike write operations), DQS cannot be used by the memory controller to sample the data directly. Instead, it is only used to ensure that the DRAM's outgoing DQS signal (and therefore data signals as well) is correctly aligned with the mem-ory controller's clocks. The memory controller's 90°

delayed clock is used to sample the incoming data, which is possible because the DRAM's DLL guarantees minimal skew between the global clock and outgoing read data. The following paragraphs provide a bit of background to explain the presence of this circuit in DDR SDRAMs.

Because DRAMs are usually external to the microprocessor, DRAM designers must be aware of the issues involved in propagating signals between chips. In chip-to-chip communications, the main limiting factor in building high-speed interfaces is the variability in the amount of time it takes a signal to propagate to its destination (usually referred to as the *uncertainty* of the signal's timing). The total uncertainty in a system is often the sum of the uncertainty in its constituent parts, e.g., each driver, each delay line, each logic block in a critical path adds uncertainty to the total. This additive effect makes it very difficult to build high-speed interfaces for even small systems, because even very small fixed uncertainties that seem insignificant at low clock speeds become significant as the clock speed increases.

There exist numerous methods to decrease the uncertainty in a system, including sending a strobe signal along with the data (e.g., the DQS signal in DDR SDRAM or the clock signal in a source-synchronous interface), adding a phase-locked loop (PLL) or DLL to the system, or matching the path lengths of signal traces so that the signals all arrive at the destination at (about) the same time. Many of the methods are complementary; that is, their effect upon reducing uncertainty is cumulative. Building systems that communicate at high frequencies is all about engineering methods to reduce uncertainty in the system.

The function of a PLL or DLL, in general, is to synchronize two periodic signals so that a certain fixed amount of phase-shift or apparent delay exists between them. The two are similar, and the terms are often used interchangeably. A DLL uses variable delay circuitry to delay an existing periodic signal so that it is in synch with another signal; a PLL uses an oscillator to create a new periodic signal that is in synch with another signal. When a PLL/DLL is added to a communication interface, the result is a "closed-loop" system, which can, for example, measure and cancel the bulk of the uncertainty in both the transmitter and the receiver circuits and align the incoming data strobe with the incoming data (see, for example, Dally and Poulton [1998]).

Figure 7.21 shows how the DLL is used in DDR SDRAM, and it shows the effect that the DLL has upon the timing of the part. The net effect is to delay the output of the part (note that the output burst of the bottom configuration is shifted to the right, compared to the output burst of the top configuration). This delay is chosen to be sufficient to bring into alignment the output of the part with the system clock.

7.3.2 Other Technologies, Rambus in Particular

This section discusses Rambus' technology as described in their 1990 patent application number 07/510,898 (the '898 application) and describes how some of the technologies mentioned would be used in a Rambus-style memory organization as compared to a JEDEC-style memory organization.

Rambus' '898 Patent Application

The most novel aspect of the Rambus memory organization, the aspect most likely to attract the reader's attention and the aspect to which Rambus draws the most attention in the document, is the physical bus organization and operation. The bus' organization and protocol are more reminiscent of a computer network than a traditional memory bus. When the word *revolutionary* is used to describe the Rambus architecture, this is the aspect to which it applies.[8]

---

[8]There is also significant discussion (and illustration) in the patent application describing Rambus' unorthodox/revolutionary proposed packaging technology, in which a DRAM's pins are all on one edge of the chip and in which the chips are inserted directly into a backplane-type arrangement individually, as opposed to being integrated onto a memory module.

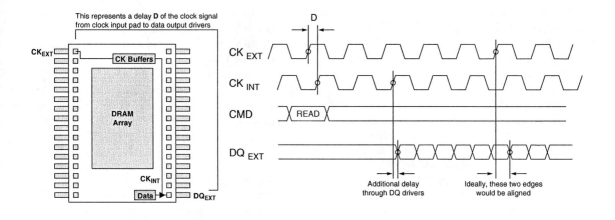

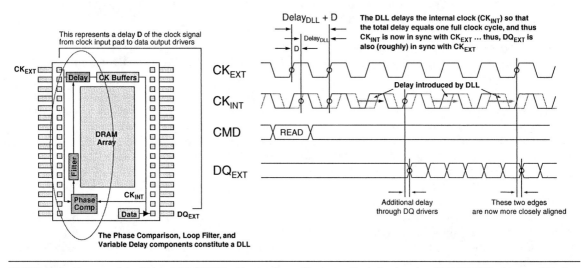

FIGURE 7.21: The use of the DLL in DDR SDRAMs. The top figure illustrates the behavior of an DDR SDRAM without a DLL. Due to the inherent delays through the clock receiver, multi-stage amplifiers, on-chip wires, output pads and bonding wires, output drivers, and other effects, the data output (as it appears from the perspective of the bus) occurs slightly delayed with respect to the system clock. The bottom figure illustrates the effect of adding the DLL. The DLL delays the incoming clock signal so that the output of the part is more closely aligned with the system clock. Note that this introduces extra latency into the behavior of the part.

Figure 7.22 illustrates the "new bus" that Rambus describes in the 898 application. It juxtaposes Rambus' bus with a more traditional DRAM bus and thereby illustrates that these bus architectures are substantially different. As described earlier, the traditional memory bus is organized into four dedicated busses: (1) the data bus, (2) the address bus, (3) the command bus, and (4) the chip-select bus. In contrast, all of the information

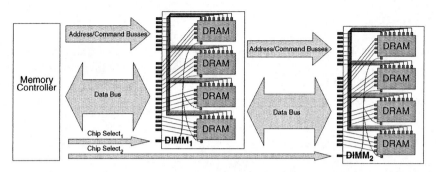

(a) Traditional Memory-Bus Organization: A "Wide-Bus" Architecture

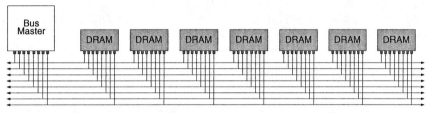

(b) Rambus Memory-Bus Organization: A "Narrow-Bus" Architecture

FIGURE 7.22: Memory bus organizations. The figure compares the organizations of a traditional memory bus and a Rambus-style organization. (a) shows a system of a memory controller and two memory modules, with a 16-bit data bus and an 8-bit address and command bus. (b) shows the Rambus organization with a bus master and seven DRAM slave devices.

for the operation of the DRAM is carried over a single bus in Rambus' architecture. Moreover, there is no separate chip-select network. In the specification, Rambus describes a narrow bus architecture over which command, address, and data information travels using a proprietary packetized protocol. There are no dedicated busses in the Rambus architecture described in the '898 application. In the Rambus bus organization, all addresses, commands, data, and chip-select information are sent on the same bus lines. This is why the organization is often called "multiplexed." At different points in time, the same physical lines carry dissimilar classes of information.

Another novel aspect of the Rambus organization is its width. In Rambus' architecture, all of the infor-

mation for the operation of the DRAM is carried over a very narrow bus. Whereas the bus in a traditional system can use more than 90 bus lines,[9] the Rambus organization uses "substantially fewer bus lines than the number of bits in a single address." Given that a single physical address in the early 1990s was 20–30 bits wide, this indicates a very narrow bus, indeed. In the Rambus specification, the example system uses a total of nine (9) lines to carry all necessary information, including addresses, commands, chip-select information, and data. Because the bus is narrower than a single data address, it takes many bus cycles to transmit a single command from a bus master (i.e., memory controller) to a DRAM device. The information is transmitted over an uninterrupted sequence of

---

[9]In a PC system, the data bus is 64 bits; the address bus can be 16 bits; and there can be 10 or more control lines, as the number of chip-select lines scales with the number of memory modules in the system.

bus cycles and must obey a specified format in terms of both time and wire assignments. This is why the Rambus protocol is called "packetized," and it stands in contrast to a JEDEC-style organization in which the command and address busses are wide enough to transmit all address and command information in a single bus cycle.[10]

As mentioned, the bus' protocol is also unusual and resembles a computer network more than a traditional memory bus. In an Internet-style computer network, for example, every packet contains the address of the recipient; a packet placed on the network is seen by every machine on the subnet, and every machine must look at the packet, decode the packet, and decide if the packet is destined for the machine itself or for some other machine. This requires every machine to have such decoding logic on board. In the Rambus memory organization, there is no chip-select network, and so there must be some other means to identify the recipient of a request packet. As in the computer network, a Rambus request packet contains (either explicitly or implicitly) the identity of the intended recipient, and every DRAM in the system has a unique identification number (each DRAM knows its own identity). As in the computer network, every DRAM must initially assume that a packet placed on the bus may be destined for it; every DRAM must receive and decode every packet placed on the bus so that each DRAM can decide whether the packet is for the DRAM itself or for some other device on the bus. Not only does each DRAM require this level of intelligence to decode packets and decide if a particular packet is intended for it, but ultimately the implication is that each DRAM is in some sense an autonomous device—the DRAM is not *controlled*; rather, *requests* are made of it.

This last point illustrates another sense in which Rambus is a revolutionary architecture. Traditional DRAMs were simply marionettes. The Rambus architecture casts the DRAM as a semi-intelligent device capable of making decisions (e.g., determining whether a requested address is within range), which represented an unorthodox way of thinking in the early 1990s.

Low-Skew Clock Using Variable Delay Circuits
The clocking scheme of the Rambus system is designed to synchronize the internal clocks of the DRAM devices with a non-existent, ideal clock source, achieving low skew. Figure 7.23 illustrates the scheme. The memory controller sends out a global clock signal that is either turned around or reflected back, and each DRAM as well as the memory controller has two clock inputs,

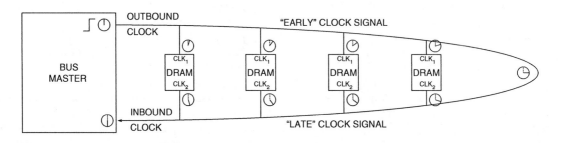

FIGURE 7.23: Rambus clock synchronization. The clock design in Rambus' 1990 patent application routes two clock signals into each DRAM device, and the path lengths of the clock signals are matched so that the delay average of the two signals represents the time as seen by the midpoint or clock turnaround point.

---

[10] A "bus cycle" is the period during which a bus transaction takes place, which may correspond to one clock cycle, more than one clock cycle, or less than one clock cycle.

CLK_1 and CLK_2, with the first being the "early" clock signal and the second being the "late" clock signal.

Because the signal paths between each DRAM have non-zero length, the global clock signal arrives at a slightly different time to each DRAM. Figure 7.23 shows this with small clock figures at each point representing the absolute time (as would be measured by the memory controller) that the clock pulse arrives at each point. This is one component contributing to clock skew, and clock skew traditionally causes problems for high-speed interfaces. However, if the clock path is symmetric, i.e., if each side of the clock's trace is path-length matched so that the distance to the turnaround point is equal from both CLK_1 and CLK_2 inputs, then the combination of the two clocks (CLK_1 and CLK_2) can be used to synthesize, at each device, a local clock edge that is in synch with an imaginary clock at the turnaround point. In Figure 7.23, the memory controller sends a clock edge at 12:00 noon. That edge arrives at the first DRAM at 12:03, the next DRAM at 12:06, the next at 12:09, and so on. It arrives at the turnaround point at 12:15 and begins to work its way back to the DRAM devices' CLK_2 inputs, finally arriving at the memory controller at 12:30. If at each point the device is able to find the average of the two clock arrival times (e.g., at the DRAM closest to the memory controller, find the average between 12:03 and 12:27), then each device is able to synthesize a clock that is synchronized with an ideal clock at the turnaround point; each device, including the memory controller, can synthesize a clock edge at 12:15, and so all devices can be "in synch" with an ideal clock generating an edge at 12:15. Note that even though Figure 7.23 shows the DRAMs evenly spaced with respect to one another, this is not necessary. All that is required is for the path length from CLK_1 to the turnaround point to be equal to the path length from CLK_2 to the turnaround point for each device.

Rambus' specification includes on-chip variable delay circuits (very similar to traditional DLLs) to perform this clock signal averaging. In other words, Rambus' on-chip "DLL" takes an early version and a late version of the same clock signal and finds the midpoint of the two signals. Provided that the wires making up the U-shaped clock on the motherboard (or wherever the wires are placed) are symmetric, this allows every DRAM in the system to have a clock signal that is synchronized with those of all other DRAMs.

Variable Request Latency Rambus' 1990 patent application defines a mechanism that allows the memory controller to specify how long the DRAM should wait before handling a request. There are two parts to the description found in the specification. First, on each DRAM there is a set of registers, called *access-time registers*, that hold delay values. The DRAM uses these delay values to wait the indicated number of cycles before placing the requested data onto (or reading the associated data from) the system bus. The second part of the description is that the DRAM request packet specifies which of these registers to use for a delay value in responding to that particular request.

The patent application does not delve into the uses of this feature at all; the mechanism is presented simply, without justification or application. Our (educated) guess is that the mechanism is absolutely essential to the successful operation of the design—having a variable request latency is not an afterthought or flight of whimsy. Without variable request latencies, the support of variable burst lengths, and indeed the support of any burst length other than one equal to the length of a request packet or one smaller than the request latency, cannot function even tolerably well. This is illustrated in Figure 7.24. The figure shows what happens when a multiplexed, split transaction bus has back-to-back requests: if the request shapes are symmetric (e.g., the request and response packets are the same length, and the latency is slightly longer) or if the latency is long relative to the request and response packet lengths, then it is possible to pipeline requests and achieve good throughput, though neither scenario is optimal in bus efficiency. If the request packet and transaction latency are both short relative to the data transfer (a more optimal arrangement for a given request), later requests must be delayed until earlier requests finish, negating the value of having a split transaction bus in the first place (cf. Figure 7.24(a)). This is the most likely arrangement. Long data bursts are desirable, particularly if the target application is video processing or something similar. The potential problem is that these long data bursts necessarily generate asymmetric

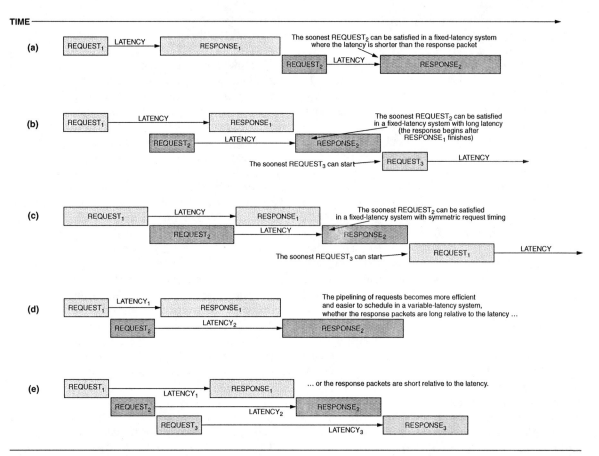

FIGURE 7.24: The importance of variable request latencies in the Rambus organization. Scheduling odd-sized request-response pairs on a multiplexed bus can be difficult to the point of yielding unacceptable performance.

request-response shapes because the request packet should be as short as possible, dictated by the information in a request. If the DRAM supports variable request latencies, then the memory controller can pipeline requests, even those that have asymmetric shapes, and thus achieve good throughput despite the shape of the request.

Variable Block Size Rambus' 1990 patent application defines a mechanism that allows the memory controller to specify how much data should be transferred for a read or write request. The request packet that the memory controller sends to the

DRAM device specifies the data length in the request packet's *BlockSize* field. Possible data length values range from 0 bytes to 1024 bytes (1 KB). The amount of data that the DRAM sends out on the bus, therefore, is programmed at every transaction.

Like variable request latency, the variable block size feature is necessitated by the design of the bus. To dynamically change the transaction length from request to request would likely have seemed novel to an engineer in the early 1990s. The unique features of Rambus' bus—its narrow width, multiplexed nature, and packet request protocol—place unique scheduling demands on the bus. Variable block size is used to cope with the unique scheduling demands; it enables the use of Rambus' memory in many different engineering settings, and it helps to ensure that Rambus' bus is fully utilized.

Running the Clock at the Data Rate The design specifies a clock rate that can be half what one would normally expect in a simple, non-interleaved memory system. Figure 7.25 illustrates this, showing timing for two different clock arrangements. The top design is a more traditional arrangement; the bottom design uses a clock that is half the speed of the top design. Rambus' 1990 application describes the clock design and its benefits as follows:

> *Clock distribution problems can be further reduced by using a bus clock and device clock rate equal to the bus cycle data rate divided by two, that is, the bus clock period is twice the bus cycle period. Thus a 500 MHz bus preferably uses a 250 MHz clock rate. This reduction in frequency provides two benefits. First it makes all signals on the bus have the same worst case data rates—data on a 500 MHz bus can only change every 2 ns. Second, clocking at half the bus cycle data rate makes the labeling of the odd and even bus cycles trivial, for example, by defining even cycles to be those when the internal device clock is 0 and odd cycles when the internal device clock is 1.*

As the inventors claim, the primary reason for doing so is to reduce the number of clock transitions per second to be equal to the maximum number of data transitions per second. This becomes important as clock speeds increase, which is presumably why IBM's toggle mode uses the same technique. The second reason given is to simplify the decision of which edge to use to activate which receiver or driver (the labelling of "even/odd" cycles). Figure 10 in the specification illustrates the interleaved physical arrangement required to implement the clock-halving scheme: the two edges of the clock activate different input receivers at different times and cause different output data to be multiplexed to the output drivers at different times.

Note that halving the clock complicates receiving data at the DRAM end, because no clock edge exists during the eye of the data (this is noted in the figure), and therefore, the DRAM does not know when to sample the incoming data—that is, assuming no additional help. This additional help would most likely be in the form of a PLL or DLL circuit to accurately delay the clock edge so that it would be 90° out of phase with the data and thus could be used to sample the data. Such a circuit would add complexity to the DRAM and would consequently add cost in terms of manufacturing, testing, and power dissipation.

7.3.3 Comparison of Technologies in Rambus and JEDEC DRAM

The following paragraphs compare briefly, for each of four technologies, how the technology is used in a JEDEC-style DRAM system and how it is used in a Rambus-style memory system as described in the '898 application.

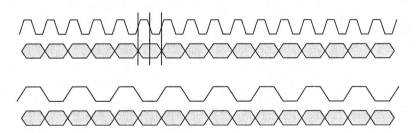

FIGURE 7.25: Running the bus clock at the data rate. Slowing down the clock so that it runs at the same speed as the data makes the clock easier to handle, but it reduces the number of clock edges available to do work. Clock edges exist to drive the output circuitry, but no clock edge exists during the eye of the data to sample the data.

Programmable CAS Latency

JEDEC's *programmable CAS latency* is used to allow each system vendor to optimize the performance of its systems. It is programmed at system initialization, and, according to industry designers, it is never set again while the machine is running [Lee 2002, Baker 2002, Kellogg 2002, Macri 2002, Ryan 2002, Rhoden 2002, Sussman 2002]. By contrast, with Rambus' *variable request latency*, the latency is programmed every time the microprocessor sends a new request to the DRAM, but the specification also leaves open the possibility that each access register could store two or more values held for each transaction type. Rambus' system has the potential (and we would argue the *need*) to change the latency at a request granularity, i.e., each request could specify a different latency than the previous request, and the specification has room for many different latency values to be programmed. Whereas the feature is a convenience in the JEDEC organization, it is a necessity in a Rambus organization.

Programmable Burst Length

JEDEC's *programmable burst length* is used to allow each system vendor to optimize the performance of its systems. It is programmed at system initialization, and, according to industry designers, it is never set again while the machine is running [Lee 2002, Baker 2002, Kellogg 2002, Rhoden 2002, Sussman 2002]. By contrast, with Rambus' *variable block size*, the block size is programmed every time the microprocessor sends a new request to the DRAM. Whereas a JEDEC-style memory system can function efficiently if every column of data that is read out of or written into the DRAM is accompanied by a CAS signal, a Rambus-style memory system could not (as the command would occupy the same bus as the data, limiting data to less than half of the available bus cycles). Whereas the feature is a convenience in the JEDEC organization, it is a necessity in a Rambus organization.

Dual-Edged Clocking

Both JEDEC- and Rambus-style DRAMs use a clocking scheme that goes back at least to IBM's high-speed toggle-mode DRAMs, in which on-chip interleaving allows one to toggle back and forth between two buffers (e.g., on the rising and falling edges of a strobe signal) to achieve a data rate that is twice that possible by a single buffer alone. Both JEDEC- and Rambus-style DRAMs transfer data on both edges of a timing signal. In JEDEC-style DRAMs, the timing signal is an internal clock generated from the system clock and the DQS data strobe—a source-synchronous strobe that accompanies the data sent and is quiescent when there is no data on the bus. The data is edge-aligned with the system clock. In Rambus-style DRAMs, the timing signal is a synthesized internal clock signal in synch with no other clock source in the system and generated from two different phases of the U-shaped global clock (described previously). The U-shaped clock is not source synchronous and remains free running whether there is data on the bus or not. As opposed to the DDR clocking scheme, in the Rambus scheme the data is *not* aligned with either phase of the system clock at all; it is neither edge-aligned nor center-aligned. Furthermore, a different phase relationship exists between each Rambus DRAM's output data and the global clock's early and late signals, whereas DDR DRAMs strive to maintain the same phase relationship between each DRAM's output data and the system clock.

On-Chip PLL/DLL

JEDEC uses an *on-chip DLL* in their DDR SDRAMs to ensure that data being driven onto the data bus is aligned with the global clock signal. The DLL does this by delaying the DRAM's response to a read request just long enough that the data is driven at the same time the DRAM sees the next clock edge. Rambus uses an *on-chip variable delay* circuit to ensure that every DRAM in the system as well as the memory controller has a synchronized clock (i.e., they all believe that it is precisely 12:00 at the same time). The delay circuit does this by finding the midpoint in time between an early version and a late version (i.e., two different phases) of the same clock signal and thereby creates a synthesized internal clock signal in synch with no other physical clock in the system. This is a process that is significantly more complicated than a simple DLL, and thus Rambus' variable delay circuit is more complex than a simple DLL.

7.3.4 Alternative Technologies

Numerous alternative technologies could achieve the same result as the technologies described. Many of these alternatives are simply applications of long-understood techniques to solving particular problems. This section discusses a sample of those mechanisms; it is not intended to be exhaustive, but rather to be illustrative. This should give insight into issues that DRAM designers consider.

Programmable CAS Latency

The primary benefit of programmable CAS latency is flexibility. Its presence in a DRAM allows a fast part to emulate the behavior of a slow part, which would enable an OEM or end consumer to intermingle parts from different generations (with different speeds) in the same system or intermingle same-generation parts from different manufacturers (which might have slightly different performance capabilities due to slight variations in process technologies) in the same DIMM. To illustrate, if a DRAM manufacturer has a part with a minimum 20-ns CAS read-out, the part could conceivably work as a CAS-2, 100-MHz part (20 ns requires 2 cycles at 100 MHz); a CAS-3, 150-MHz part (20 ns requires 3 cycles at 150 MHz); or a CAS-4, 200-MHz part (20 ns requires 4 cycles at 200 MHz). Note that the part would never be able to make CAS-2 latencies at the higher bus speeds or CAS-3 at the highest bus speed (CAS-2 requires 13.33 ns at 150 MHz and 10 ns at 200 MHz; CAS-3 requires 15 ns at 200 MHz). Alternative technologies include the following:

- Use fixed CAS latency parts.
- Explicitly identify the CAS latency in the read or write command.
- Program CAS latency by blowing fuses on the DRAM.
- Scale CAS latency with clock frequency.

Use Fixed CAS Latency Fixing the CAS latency would simply mean that each individual SDRAM would operate with a single, predetermined latency. Although using fixed latency would reduce flexibility, it would simplify testing considerably [Lee 2002], as only one mode of operation would need to be tested

instead of two or more, and it would simplify design slightly. In a JEDEC-style bus organization, where the command, address, and data busses are all separate, the scheduling of requests is simplified if all requests have the same latency. Thus, memory controllers typically set the CAS latency at initialization and never change it again while the machine is powered on; i.e., current systems use a *de facto* fixed CAS latency while the machine is running [Lee 2002, Baker 2002, Kellogg 2002, Macri 2002, Ryan 2002, Rhoden 2002, Sussman 2002].

Explicitly Identify CAS Latency in the Command One option would be to design the DRAM command set so that each *column read* command explicitly encodes the desired CAS latency. Instead of initializing the DRAM to use a latency of 2 or 3 cycles, and then presenting generic CAS commands, each of which would implicitly use a latency of 2 or 3 cycles, respectively, a memory controller could present commands to the SDRAM that would explicitly specify a desired latency. For example, the memory controller would use "CAS-2" read commands if it desired a latency of two and "CAS-3" read commands if it desired a latency of three.

Program CAS Latency Using Fuses The CAS latency value could also be determined by the use of on-chip fuses. Modern DRAMs have numerous fuses on them that, when blown, enable redundant circuits, so at test time a DRAM manufacturer can, for example, disable memory arrays that contain fabrication errors and in their place enable redundant arrays that are error free. A typical DRAM has thousands of such fuses. One could add one or more similar fuses that set different CAS latencies. This would enable a DRAM manufacturer to sell what are essentially fixed-latency parts, but because they could be programmed at the last possible moment, the DRAM manufacturer would not need separate stocks for parts with different latencies; one part would satisfy for multiple latencies, as the DRAM manufacturer could set the fuses appropriately right before shipping the parts. The manufacturer could also sell the parts with fuses intact to OEMs and embedded-systems manufacturers, who would likely have the technical savvy necessary to set the fuses properly, and who might want the ability to program the latency according to their own needs. This level of flexibility would be almost on par with the current level of flexibility, since in most systems the CAS latency is set once at system initialization and never set again.

Scale CAS Latency with Clock Frequency One option is for the DRAM to know the bus speed and deliver the fastest CAS latency available for that bus speed. The programming of the DRAM could be either explicit, in which case the memory controller tells the DRAM the bus speed using a command at system initialization, or implicit, in which case the DRAM senses the timing of the clock on the bus and "learns" the bus speed on its own. To return to the earlier example, if a DRAM part had an internal CAS read-out latency of 20 ns, it could deliver CAS-2 in a 100-MHz/10-ns bus environment, CAS-3 in a 133-MHz/7.5-ns bus environment, and CAS-4 in a 200-MHz/5-ns bus environment. This would satisfy most DRAM consumers, because OEMs and end-users usually want the fastest latency possible. However, without an additional mechanism in either the DRAM or the memory controller, the scheme would not allow parts with different internal CAS read-out latencies to be mixed within the same system. Disallowing mixed-latency systems would not cause undue confusion in the marketplace, because asynchronous parts in the 1980s and 1990s were sold as "70ns DRAMs" or "60ns DRAMs," etc.; the speed rating was explicit, so both OEMs and end-users were already accustomed to matching speed ratings in their systems. However, if support for mixed-latency systems was desired, one could always design the memory controller so that it determines at initialization the latency of each DIMM in its system[11] and accounts for any latency differences between DIMMs in its scheduling decisions.

Programmable Burst Length

In JEDEC-style DRAM systems, the ability to set the burst length to different values is a convenience for system designers that can also system performance. Numerous subtle interactions between the chosen parameters of a DRAM system (such as request latency, burst length, bus organization, bus speed, and bus width) can cause the resulting performance of that system to vary significantly, even for small changes in those parameters [Cuppu & Jacob 2001]. The ability to fine-tune the burst length of the DRAMs enables a designer to find better combinations of parameters for his system, given the expected workload. In most systems, the burst length is set once at system initialization and never set again [Lee 2002, Baker 2002, Kellogg 2002, Rhoden 2002, Sussman 2002]. Alternative technologies include the following:

- Use a short, fixed burst length.
- Explicitly identify the burst length in the read or write command.
- Program the burst length by blowing fuses on the DRAM.
- Use a long, fixed burst length coupled with the *burst-terminate* command.
- Use a BEDO-style protocol where each CAS pulse toggles out a single column of data.

The first three are analogous to the alternative solutions for programmable CAS latency, described above.

Use Burst-Terminate Command One can use a fixed burst length, where the length is some number large enough to satisfy developers of systems that prefer large chunks of data, and use the *burst-terminate* command, also called *burst stop*, to halt data read-out of the DRAM or to signal the end of data written to the DRAM. The advantage of the scheme is that the *burst stop* command is already part of the specification, and bursts must also be interruptible by additional commands such as reads and writes. Therefore, an efficient pipeline of multiple column reads is already possible by simply sending multiple read commands spaced as closely as the desired burst length dictates (e.g., every four cycles to achieve a burst length of

---

[11]One would probably not want to create a DIMM out of DRAM parts with different fixed CAS latencies.

four, even if the nominal burst length is longer). Each successive request would implicitly terminate the request immediately preceding it, and only the last burst in the pipeline would need to be terminated explicitly. The disadvantage of the scheme is that it would increase pressure slightly on the command bus: during a *burst-terminate* command the memory controller would not be able to control any other bank on the same command bus. If the increase was determined to be significant, it could be alleviated by redesigning the memory controller to support multiple control busses (which is already supported by memory controllers).

Toggle Data-Out Using CAS   JEDEC could have adopted the BEDO style of bursting data, with each successive column read-out driven by toggling the CAS pin or holding it at a low voltage until the desired number of columns has been read out (e.g., holding it low for four cycles to read out four columns of data). This would require some modification to the specification, enabling the DRAM to distinguish between a CAS accompanied by a new column address and a CAS signifying a serial read-out based on the most recent column address received. There are numerous possibilities for solving this, including the following:

- Redefine the command set to have two different CAS commands: one for a new address, and one signifying a sequential read-out based on the most recent column address received.
- Add a pin to the command bus (which is usually thought of as comprising signals such as RAS, CAS, WE, and CKE) that is dedicated for the sequential read-out version of CAS. This would be similar to IBM's implementation of the high-speed toggle mode, where the data strobe signal uses a different pin than the CAS signal [Kalter 1990a, b].

The advantage of the second scheme, as compared to the first, is that it allows the memory controller to control other DRAM banks simultaneously while the first bank is involved in data transfer.

Dual-Edged Clocking

The advantage of using dual-edged clocking in a JEDEC-style DRAM bus organization is that it increases DRAM bandwidth without having to drive the clock any faster and without a commensurate increase in the clock signal's energy consumption. Alternative technologies include the following:

- Use two or more interleaved memory banks on-chip and assign a different clock signal to each bank (e.g., use two or more out-of-phase clocks).
- Keep each DRAM single data rate, and interleave banks on the module (DIMM).
- Increase the number of pins per DRAM.
- Increase the number of pins per module.
- Double the clock frequency.
- Use simultaneous bidirectional I/O drivers.

Interleave On-Chip Banks   As mentioned earlier, interleaving multiple memory banks has been a popular method used to achieve high-bandwidth memory busses using low-bandwidth devices. The technique goes back at least to the mid-1960s, where it was used in the IBM System/360 Model 91 [Anderson et al. 1967] and Seymour Cray's Control Data 6600 [Thornton 1970]. In an interleaved memory system, the data bus uses a frequency that is faster than any one DRAM bank can support; the control circuitry toggles back and forth between multiple banks to achieve this data rate. An alternative to using dual-edged clocking (e.g., to double or triple or even quadruple the memory bandwidth of SDRAM without using both edges of the clock to send/receive data) is to specify two, three, or four independent banks per DRAM (respectively) and assign each bank its own clock signal. The memory controller would send one request to the DRAM, and that request would be handed off to each bank in synch with the clock assigned to that bank. Thus, each bank would receive its request slightly advanced or delayed with respect to the other banks. There are two ways to create the different clock signals:

- The different clock signals driving each of the different banks could be generated by the memory controller (or any entity outside the DRAM). Thus, if there were two interleaved banks, the memory controller would send two clock signals; if there were four interleaved banks, the memory controller would send four clock signals; and so on.

- The DRAM could receive one clock signal and delay and distribute it internally to the various banks on its own. Thus, if there were two interleaved banks, the DRAM would split the incoming clock signal two ways, delaying the second a half-phase; if there were four interleaved banks, the DRAM would split the incoming clock signal four ways, delaying the second clock one-quarter of a phase, delaying the third clock one-half of a phase, and delaying the last clock three-quarters of a phase; and so on.

The first implementation would require extra DRAM pins (one CK pin for each bank); the latter would require on-DRAM clock generation and synchronization logic.

Interleave Banks on the Module Instead of increasing the bandwidth of individual DRAMs, an argument could be made that the only place it matters is at the DIMM level. Therefore, one could take SDRAM parts and create a DDR DIMM specification where on-module circuitry takes a single incoming clock and interleaves two or more banks of DRAM (transparently, as far as the memory controller is concerned). Kentron [2002] shows that this is certainly within our limits, even at very high data rates; they currently take DDR parts and interleave them transparently at the module level to achieve quadruple data rate DIMMs.

Increase DRAM Data Width To achieve higher bandwidth per DRAM, the trend in recent years has been not only to increase DRAM speed, but also to increase the number of data-out pins; x32 parts are now common. Every increase from x4 to x8 to x16 and so on doubles the DRAM's data rate. Doubling the data rate by doubling the data width of existing parts requires very little engineering know-how. It only requires the addition of more pins and doubling the

width of the data bus to each individual DRAM. Note that the number of data pins has increased from x1 parts in the late 1980s to x32 parts today [Przybylski 1996], while over the same time period the data rate has increased from 16 MHz to the 400-MHz clocks found in DDR SDRAM today. JEDEC, therefore, could have simply put their weight more firmly behind this trend and increased bandwidth by increasing pin-out. The advantage of this approach is that it combines very well with the previous alternative—interleaving multiple banks at the module level—because doubling the data width of a DRAM decreases the number of DRAM parts needed to achieve the DIMM data width, effectively doubling the number of independent banks one can put on the DIMM. If the DRAM pin-out increases, then fewer DRAMs would be needed per DIMM to create the 64-bit data bus standard in PC-compatible systems. This would leave extra room on the DIMM for more DRAMs that could make up extra banks to implement an interleaved system.

Increase Module Data Width As mentioned earlier, one could argue that the DIMM bandwidth is more important than the bandwidth of an individual DRAM. Therefore, one could simply increase the data width of the memory bus (the number of wires between the DIMMs and the memory controller) to increase bandwidth, without having to increase the clock speed of the individual DRAMs at all. The disadvantage is the increased cost of the de-skewing circuitry.

Double the Clock Frequency An alternative to using a dual-edged clock is to use a single-edged clock and simply speed up the clock. There are several advantages of a single-edged clocking scheme over a dual-edged clocking scheme (cf. Figure 7.20). One advantage illustrated in Figure 7.20 is the existence of more clock edges to be used to drive data onto the bus and sample data off the bus. Another advantage is that the clock does not need to be as symmetric as it is in a dual-edged clocking scheme. A single-edged clock's duty cycle does not need to be 50%, as it needs to be for a dual-edged clock, and the rise and fall times (i.e., slew rates) do not need to match, as they need to for a dual-edged clock. Consequently, one can achieve the same speed clock in a single-edged clocking scheme with much less effort than in a dual-edged clocking scheme. The disadvantage of this alternative is that it requires more engineering effort than simply widening the memory bus or increasing the number of data pins on a DRAM.

Use Simultaneous Bidirectional I/O Running the data at the same rate as the clock doubles a DRAM's bandwidth over previous, single-edged clock designs without an increase in the number of data pins. An alternative is to use simultaneous bidirectional I/O, in which it is possible to conduct a read from the DRAM and a write to the DRAM at exactly the same time; that is, both data values (the read data and the write data) are on the bus simultaneously, which is an effective doubling of the available bandwidth. Using the simultaneous bidirectional I/O does not require additional data pins. Such a scheme would require structural changes at the DRAM side to accommodate reading and writing simultaneously, and those changes would most likely resemble the ESDRAM design by Enhanced Memory Systems [ESDRAM 1998], which was proposed for DDR2 [Davis et al. 2000b]. ESDRAM places a buffer after the sense amps that holds an entire DRAM row for reading and allows concurrent writes to the DRAM array; once the read data is in the buffer, the sense amplifiers are no longer needed.

On-Chip PLL/DLL

DDR SDRAMs use an on-chip DLL circuit to ensure that the DRAM transmits its data and DQS signal to the memory controller as closely as possible to the next appropriate edge of the system clock. Its use is specified because the clock rates in DDR are high enough to warrant relatively strong methods for reducing the effects of dynamic changes in timing skew. Alternative technologies include the following:

- Achieve high bandwidth using more DRAM pins or module pins, not clock frequency.
- Use a Vernier method to measure and account for dynamic changes in skew.
- Put the DLL on the memory controller.

- Use off-chip (on-module) DLLs.
- Use asynchronous DRAM, for example, toggle mode or BEDO.

Go Wider, Not Faster As the previous section indicates, there are numerous ways to achieve higher bandwidth at the DRAM, DIMM, or memory-system level, and many of the methods that achieve higher bandwidth are easier to implement than increasing clock speed. The use of a DLL is dictated only by the desired increase in clock speed. Therefore, one can forgo the use of an on-chip DLL by increasing DRAM or DIMM data width.

Vernier Mechanism There are two main components to the uncertainty of signal propagation time. The first is a static component that is due to differences in process technologies, process variations, electrical loading of an unknown number of memory modules, etc. The second is a dynamic component that is typically due to temperature or voltage fluctuations. Some fluctuations change too fast to be handled effectively, but most of the fluctuations in voltage and temperature change over a relatively long time period. Most voltage fluctuations are associated with the 60-Hz AC power cycle, which is a relatively long time-span, and most temperature fluctuations occur on the order of milliseconds or longer [Lee 2002, Macri 2002]. In many DDR systems, the static component is corrected by using a Vernier mechanism in the memory controller at system initialization. It is essentially a trial-and-error method in which the upper and lower limits of timing failure are found and the midpoint is used for signal transmission (analogous to setting the tracking on one's VCR by going forward and backward to the points of noise and then leaving the tracking set somewhere in between) [Lee 2002]. The dynamic component is then corrected by the on-chip DLL.

An alternative to the on-chip DLL is to perform recalibration of the Vernier correction often enough to account for the slower changes in voltage and temperature, as opposed to performing the timing correction only once at system initialization. Assuming that the most significant voltage fluctuations are associated with the 60-Hz AC power supply and that most of the temperature fluctuations occur on the order of milliseconds or longer [Lee 2002, Macri 2002], recalibration would be needed roughly once or twice every millisecond.

Move the DLL onto the Memory Controller Because the DLL is only used on the DRAM to synchronize outgoing data and DQS signals with the global clock for the benefit of the memory controller [Lee 2002, Rhoden 2002, Karabotsos 2002, Baker 2002, Macri 2002], it is possible to move that functionality onto the memory controller itself. The memory controller could maintain two clocks: the first, for example, could be synchronized with the global clock, and the second could be delayed 90°. The incoming DQS and data signals could be given a variable delay, with the amount of delay controlled by a DLL/PLL on the memory controller so that the DQS signal would be in-phase with the delayed clock. This arrangement could align the incoming data so that the eye would be centered on the global clock signal, which could be used to sample the data. The weakness of this scheme is that, as clock speeds increase to very high rates, the timing differences between different DIMMs would become significant. Therefore, each DIMM in the system would require a different phase shift between the memory controller's two clocks, which would imply that the memory controller would need to maintain a separate timing structure for each DIMM.[12]

Move the DLL onto the DIMM One alternative is to place the DLL on the DDR module instead of the DDR device itself. Sun has used this alternative for many years [Becker 2002, O'Donnell 2002, Prein 2002, Walker 2002]. Moreover, it is similar in nature to the off-chip driver mechanism used by IBM in their high-speed toggle-mode DRAM [Kalter 1990a, b]. As mentioned previously, the only function of the DLL on the DDR SDRAM is to synchronize the outgoing DQS and data signals with the global clock. This can be

accomplished just as easily on the module, especially if the module is *buffered* or *registered* (which simply means that the module has local storage to hold the commands and addresses that are destined for the module's DRAMs). Note that it is presently common practice for engineers to disable DDR's on-chip DLL to achieve higher performance—the on-chip DLL is a convenience, not a necessity [Rhoden 2002, Kellogg 2002, Macri 2002]. A module-level DLL is perfectly workable; even if the data exiting the DRAM is completely out of synch with the global clock, the module can use its DLL to delay the clock/s, commands, and addresses so that the output of the DRAMs is in synch with the global clock. However, this might come at the expense of an extra CAS latency cycle.

7.4 Fully Buffered DIMM: A Compromise of Sorts

An interesting development in the DRAM industry is the recent introduction of the fully buffered DIMM (FB-DIMM). This is a system-level DRAM organization developed by Intel that, at first glance, looks a bit like a compromise between a traditional JEDEC wide-bus design and a Rambus-like narrow-bus design. Chapter 14 explores the FB-DIMM in more detail. Here, we will simply introduce it and present a motivation for its development.

An important trend facing system designers ultimately argues for FB-DIMM or something like it. As DRAM technology has advanced, the channel speed has improved at the expense of channel capacity. SDR SDRAMs could populate a channel with eight DIMMs. DDR SDRAMs operate at a higher data rate and limit the number of DIMMs to four per channel. DDR2 SDRAMs operate at an even higher data rate and limit the number of DIMMs to two per channel. DDR3 is expected to limit the number of DIMMs per channel to one. This is a significant limitation;

---

[12]Most DLLs/PLLs require many cycles to lock onto a signal and create the correct phase shift. Forcing the memory controller to wait many cycles before switching from reading from one DIMM to reading from another DIMM would be an unsatisfactory situation.

for a server designer, it is critical, as servers typically depend on memory capacity for their performance.

The trend is clear: to improve data rates, one must reduce the number of drops on the bus. The designers of graphics subsystems have known this for a long time—for every DRAM generation, graphics cards use the same DRAM technology as is found in commodity DIMMs, but the graphics cards operate their DRAMs at significantly higher data rates because they use point-to-point connections. Note that this is possible in a marketing sense because graphics cards are *de facto* embedded systems. Users do not expect to upgrade their graphics cards by adding more memory to them; they instead replace the entire card.

So there is an obvious dilemma: future designers would like both increased channel capacity and increased data rates. How can one provide both?

The relationship between a modular organization and the graphics-card organization is shown in Figure 7.26, which depicts a multi-drop DRAM bus next to a DRAM bus organization typical of graphics cards. The graphics-card organization uses the same DRAM technology as in the multi-drop organization, but it also uses point-to-point soldered connections between the DRAM and memory controller and can therefore reach higher rates of speed. How can one exploit this to increase data rates without sacrificing channel capacity? One solution is to redefine

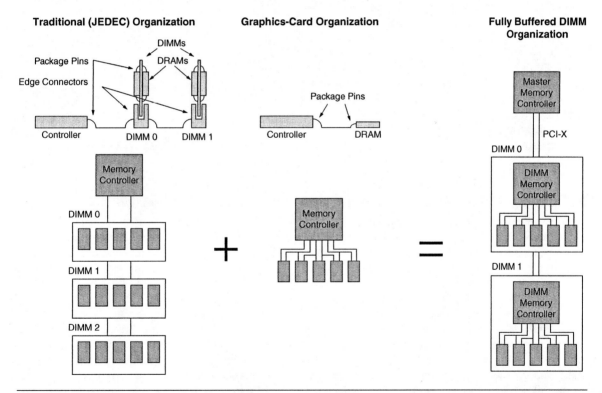

FIGURE 7.26: Motivation for the design of FB-DIMM. The first two organizations compare a modular wide-bus and a high-performance embedded system such as a graphics card. Above each design is its side profile, indicating potential impedance mismatches (sources of relections). The organization on the far right shows how FB-DIMM takes the graphics-card organization as its *de facto* DIMM. In the FB-DIMM organization, there are no multi-drop busses; DIMM-to-DIMM connections are point-to-point.

one's terms—to call the graphic-card arrangement a "DIMM" in one's future system. This is shown on the right-hand side of the figure and is precisely what is happening in FB-DIMM: the memory controller has been moved onto the DIMM, and all connections in the system are point-to-point. The channel connecting the master memory controller to the DIMM-level memory controllers (called *Advanced Memory Buffers*, or *AMBs*) is very narrow and very fast, based on the PCI-X standard. Moreover, each DIMM-to-DIMM connection is a point-to-point connection, making an entire channel a *de facto* multi-hop store and forward network. The FB-DIMM architecture limits the channel length to eight DIMMs, and the width of the inter-module bus is narrow enough to require roughly one-third the number of pins as a traditional organization. The result is that an FB-DIMM organization can handle roughly 24 times the storage capacity as a traditional DDR3-based system (assuming DDR3 systems will indeed be limited to one DIMM per channel), without sacrificing any bandwidth and even leaving room for increased intra-module bandwidth (note that the FB-DIMM module should be capable of reaching the same performance as a graphics-card organization).

7.5 Issues in DRAM Systems, Briefly

The previous section already touched on an important issue facing the system designers of tomorrow: bandwidth increases are not free and require some form of trade-off. The traditional approach has been to reduce the number of drops on the shared bus, but this approach cleary fails to scale. The *Overview* section described other issues, namely that protocol-level details interact with system-level organization parameters in non-intuitive ways that can reduce performance by factors of two or more. There are many other issues facing future DRAM systems, and these will be treated in more detail in the upcoming chapters. The following is a brief introduction to several of the issues.

7.5.1 Architecture and Scaling

The bandwidth improvements in each DRAM generation have come at a cost in channel capacity, but they have also come at a cost in the granularity of access. Through a trick of trading off space for time, DRAM designers have increased the data rate at the DRAM's I/O pins without having also to increase the speed of the DRAM's core. DDR improves speed relative to single data rate (SDR) by moving to a *2n prefetch* architecture—one in which twice the number of bits are fetched from the DRAM core. The bandwidth increase on one side of the interface is matched by a bandwidth increase on the other side; the I/O side is twice as fast, and the core side is twice as wide (on the I/O side of the DRAM, bits are transmitted twice as fast as before; on the core side, twice as many bits are fetched in a single cycle). DDR2 improves speed again by moving to *4n prefetch*; DDR3 is expected to implement *8n prefetch*. In each instance, the minimum number of bits that the DRAM can read or write increases by a factor of two. The implication is that processors need to double the amount of data that they read and write in each operation, but the question remains as to how far a cache block will scale before SRAM designers say *enough*: 128 B per block? 256 B? 1 KB?

7.5.2 Topology and Timing

As previously discussed, there is a direct connection between signal integrity and system organization; changes to the system organization can significantly improve or degrade signal integrity. The same is true of bus topologies. For example, designers of unidirectional busses do not need to concern themselves with turnaround time, a limitation on throughput when the masters of bi-directional buses change. A related issue is that of the timing convention used. When the topology changes, the timing convention may need to be changed to follow suit. Unidirectional busses would tend to work better with source-synchronous clocking, for example, but source-synchronous clocking is not as simple as a global clocking scheme.

7.5.3 **Pin and Protocol Efficiency**

Pin cost is becoming a major concern; the cost of a transistor or a capacitor on-die is reducing at a tremendous rate, and packaging costs are not decreasing as rapidly. The obvious conclusion is that in the future, DRAM design will be far more concerned about pin count than transistor count. The only way to reduce significantly the number of pins needed in a part, without also significantly reducing the part's data bandwidth (e.g., by simply reducing the number of data pins on the package), is to rethink the protocol and allow a trade-off between pins used for data and control (address, command, etc.).

7.5.4 **Power and Heat Dissipation**

DRAMs have traditionally not accounted for much of a design's power or heat dissipation. For instance, DRAMs typically do not come with heat sinks, nor do DIMMs. However, with modern inter-chip signaling rates exceeding 1 Gbps per pin (as in present-day FB-DIMMs), both power dissipation and heat dissipation become serious issues. Previous-era DIMMs exhibited power dissipation on the order of 1 W. Current FB-DIMMs dissipate nearly ten times that. Couple this with the ability to put 25 times the number of FB-DIMMs into a system (three times as many channels, eight times as many DIMMs per channel), and

you now have a significant heating problem. Modern blade servers are a popular design choice and work because only a handful of components in the system dissipate significant heat, and DRAM was never one of these. Now, the DRAM subsystem threatens to complicate blade-server design, among other things.

7.5.5 **Future Directions**

Currently, much of the focus in future DRAM design has been placed on increasing bandwidth via increased pin rates. This only scales well for a limited design window. In particular, it places too much emphasis on optimizing the device and not enough on optimizing the system. This is precisely the type of narrow-scope thinking that has led to the systemic problems described in the *Overview* chapter: designers thinking only at the device level can create system-level problems, just as designers thinking only at the system level can create device-level problems.

The solution is non-trivial, because it requires facing economic arguments. DRAM is a device that tries to suit many different needs. A design solution must work just as well in a DIMM organization as being soldered directly to a motherboard, talking one-on-one with the microprocessor. In other words, in many cases the device *is* the system. How to marry these two perspectives will be an ongoing concern.

CHAPTER 8

DRAM Device Organization: Basic Circuits and Architecture

In this chapter, basic circuits and architecture of DRAM devices are described. Modern DRAM devices exist as the result of more than three decades of devolutionary development, and it is impossible to provide a complete overview as well as an in-depth coverage of circuits and architecture of various DRAM devices in a single chapter. The limited goal in this chapter is to provide a broad overview of circuits and functional blocks commonly found in modern DRAM devices, and then proceed in subsequent chapters to describe larger memory systems consisting of DRAM devices composed of the commonly found circuits and functional blocks described herein.

This chapter proceeds through an examination of the basic building blocks of modern DRAM devices by first providing a superficial overview of a *Fast Page Mode* (FPM) DRAM device. Basic building blocks such as DRAM storage cells, DRAM array structure, voltage sense amplifiers, decoders, control logic blocks, data I/O structures, and packaging considerations are examined in this chapter. Specific DRAM devices, such as SDRAM, DDR SDRAM and D-RDRAM devices,

and the evolution of DRAM devices, in general, are examined in Chapter 12.

8.1 DRAM Device Organization

Figure 8.1 illustrates the organization and structure of an FPM DRAM device that was widely used in the 1980s and early 1990s. Internally, the DRAM storage cells in the FPM DRAM device in Figure 8.1 are organized as 4096 rows, 1024 columns per row, and 16 bits of data per column. In this device, each time a row access occurs, a 12-bit address is placed on the address bus and the *row-address strobe* (RAS)[1] is asserted by an external memory controller. Inside the DRAM device, the address on the address bus is buffered by the row address buffer and then sent to the row decoder. The row address decoder then accepts the 12-bit address and selects 1 of 4096 rows of storage cells. The data values contained in the selected row of storage cells are then sensed and kept active by the array of sense amplifiers. Each row of

---

[1] RAS is known as both row-address strobe (more common) or as row-access strobe. The author prefers "access" because of the way the DRAM access protocol has morphed from more of a signal-based interface to a command-based interface. Both "address" and "access" are commonly accepted usage for "A" in both RAS and CAS.

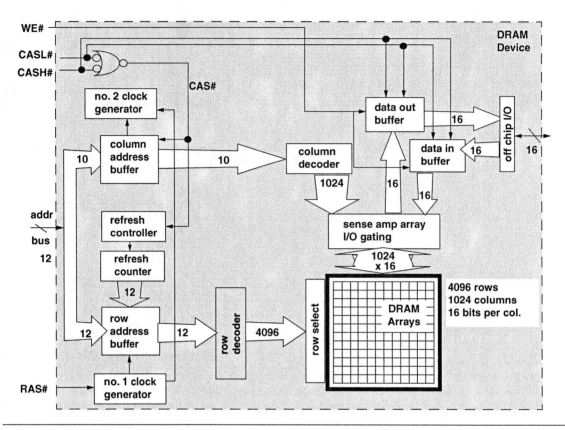

FIGURE 8.1: A 64-Mbit Fast Page Mode DRAM device (4096 x 1024 x 16).

DRAM cells in the DRAM device illustrated in Figure 8.1 consists of 1024 columns, and each column is 16 bits wide. That is, the 16-bit-wide column is the basic addressable unit of memory in this device, and each column access that follows the row access would read or write 16 bits of data from the same row of DRAM.[2]

In the FPM DRAM device illustrated in Figure 8.1, column access commands are handled in a similar manner as the row access commands. For a column access command, the memory controller places a 10-bit address on the address bus and then asserts the appropriate *column-access strobe* (CAS#) signals. Internally, the DRAM chip takes the 10-bit column

---

[2]The FPM DRAM device illustrated in Figure 8.1 does allow each 8-bit half of the 16-bit column to be accessed independently through the use of separate *column-access strobe high* (CASH) and *column-access strobe low* (CASL) signals. However, since the data bus is 16 bits wide, a column of data in this device is 16 bits rather than 8 bits. Equivalently, modern DRAM devices make use of data mask signals to enable partial data write operations within a single column. Some other DRAM devices such as XDR devices make use of sophisticated command encoding to control sub-column read and write operations.

address, decodes it, and selects 1 column out of 1024 columns. The data for that column is then placed onto the data bus by the DRAM device in the case of an ordinary column read command or is overwritten with data from the memory controller depending on the *write enable* (WE) signal.

All DRAM devices, from the venerable FPM DRAM device to modern DDRx SDRAM devices, to high data rate XDR DRAM devices to low-latency RLDRAM devices, to low-power MobileRAM devices, share some basic circuits and functional blocks. In many cases, different types of DRAM devices from the same DRAM device manufacturer share the exact same cells and same array structures. For example, the DRAM cells in all DRAM devices are organized into one or more arrays, and each array is arranged into a number of rows and columns. All DRAM devices also have some logic circuits that control the timing and sequence of how the device operates. The FPM DRAM device shown in Figure 8.1 has internal clock generators as well as a built-in refresh controller. The FPM DRAM device keeps the address of the next row that needs to be refreshed so that when a refresh command is issued, the row address to be refreshed can be loaded from the internal refresh counter instead of having to be loaded from the off-chip address bus. The inclusion of the fresh counter in the DRAM device frees the memory controller from having to keep track of the row addresses in the refresh cycles.

Advanced DRAM devices such as ESDRAM, Direct RDRAM, and RLDRAM have evolved to include more logic circuitry and functionality on-chip than the basic DRAM device examined in this chapter. For example, instead of a single DRAM array in an FPM DRAM device, modern DRAM devices have multiple banks of DRAM arrays, and some DRAM devices have additional row caches or write buffers that allow for read-around-write functionality. The discussion in this chapter is limited to basic circuitry and architecture, and advanced performance-enhancing logic circuits not typically found on standard DRAM devices are described separately in discussions of specific DRAM devices and memory systems.

8.2 DRAM Storage Cells

Figure 8.2 shows the circuit diagram of a basic one-transistor, one-capacitor (1T1C) cell structure used in modern DRAM devices to store a single bit of data. In this structure, when the access transistor is turned on by applying a voltage on the gate of the access transistor, a voltage representing the data value is placed onto the bitline and charges the storage capacitor. The storage capacitor then retains the stored charge after the access transistor is turned off and the voltage on the wordline is removed. However, the electrical charge stored in the storage capacitor will gradually leak away with the passage of time. To ensure data integrity, the stored data value in the DRAM cell

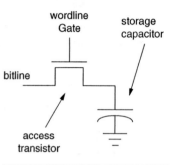

FIGURE 8.2: Basic 1T1C DRAM cell structure.

must be periodically read out and written back by the DRAM device in a process known as *refresh*. In the following section, the relationships between cell capacitance, leakage, and the need for refresh operations are briefly examined.

Different cell structures, such as a three-transistor, one-capacitor (3T1C) cell structure in Figure 8.3 with separate read access, write access, and storage transistors, were used in early DRAM designs.[3] The 3T1C cell structure has an interesting characteristic in that reading data from the storage cell does not require the content of the cell to be discharged onto a shared bitline. That is, data reads to DRAM cells are not destructive in 3T1C cells, and a simple read cycle does not require data to be restored into the storage cell as they are in 1T1C cells. Consequently, random read cycles are faster for 3T1C cells than 1T1C cells. However, the size advantage of the 1T1C cell has ensured

---

[3]The first commercial DRAM device, Intel's 1103 DRAM device, utilized a 3T1C cell structure.

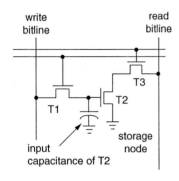

write bitline

read bitline

T3

T2

T1

storage node

input capacitance of T2

FIGURE 8.3: 3T1C DRAM cell.

that this basic cell structure is used in all modern DRAM devices.

Aside from the basic 1T1C cell structure, research is ongoing to utilize alternative cell structures such as the use of a single transistor on a Silicon-on-Insulator (SOI) process as the basic cell. In one proposed structure, the isolated substrate is used as the charge storage element, and a separate storage capacitor is not needed. Similar to data read-out of the 3T1C cell, data read-out is not destructive, and data retrieval is done via current sensing rather than charge sensing. However, despite the existence of alternative cell structures, the 1T1C cell structure is used as the basic charge storage cell structure in all modern DRAM devices, and the focus in this chapter is devoted to this dominant 1T1C DRAM cell structure.

8.2.1 Cell Capacitance, Leakage, and Refresh

In a 90-nm DRAM-optimized process technology, the capacitance of a DRAM storage cell is on the order of 30 fF, and the leakage current of the DRAM access transistor is on the order of 1 fA. With a cell capacitance of 30 fF and a leakage current of 1 fA, a typical DRAM cell can retain sufficient electrical charge that will continue to resolve to the proper digital value for an extended period of time—from hundreds of milliseconds to tens of seconds. However, transistor leakage characteristics are temperature-dependent, and DRAM cell data retention times can vary dramatically not only from cell to cell at the same time and temperature, but also at different times for the same DRAM cell.[4] However, memory systems must be designed so that not a single bit of data is

lost due to charge leakage. Consequently, every single DRAM cell in a given device must be refreshed at least once before any single bit in the entire device loses its stored charge due to leakage. In most modern DRAM devices, the DRAM cells are typically refreshed once every 32 or 64 ms. In cases where DRAM cells have storage capacitors with low capacitance values or high leakage currents, the time period between refresh intervals is further reduced to ensure reliable data retention for all cells in the DRAM device.

8.2.2 Conflicting Requirements Drive Cell Structure

Since the invention of the 1T1C DRAM cell, the physical structure of the basic DRAM cell has undergone continuous evolution. DRAM cell structure evolution occurred as a response to the conflicting requirements of smaller cell sizes, lower voltages, and noise tolerances needed in each new process generation. Figure 8.4 shows an abstract implementation of the 1T1C DRAM cell structure. A storage capacitor is formed from a *stacked* (or folded plate) capacitor structure that sits in between the polysilicon layers above active silicon. Alternatively, some DRAM device manufacturers instead use cells with *trench* capacitors that dive deeply into the active silicon area. Modern DRAM devices typically utilize one of these two different forms of the capacitor structure as the basic charge storage element.

In recent years, two competing camps have been formed between manufacturers that use a trench capacitor and manufacturers that use a stacked capacitor as the basic charge storage element. Debates are ongoing as to the relative costs and long-term scalability of each design. For manufacturers that seek to integrate DRAM cells with logic circuits on the same process technology, the trench capacitor structure allows for better integration of embedded DRAM cells with logic-optimized semiconductor process technologies. However, manufacturers that focused on stand-alone DRAM devices appear to

---

[4]The variable leakage problem is a well-known and troublesome phenomenon for DRAM manufacturers that leads to variable retention times (VRTs) in DRAM cells.

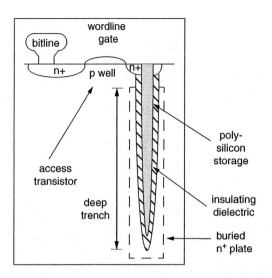

FIGURE 8.4: Cross-section view of a 1T1C DRAM cell with a trench capacitor. The storage capacitor is formed from a trench capacitor structure that dives deeply into the active silicon area. Alternatively, some DRAM device manufacturers instead use cells with a **stacked** capacitor structure that sits in between the polysilicon layers above the active silicon.

favor stacked capacitor cell structures as opposed to the trench capacitor structures. Currently, DRAM device manufacturers such as Micron, Samsung, Elpida, Hynix, and the majority of the DRAM manufacturing industry use the stacked capacitor structure, while Qimonda, Nanya, and several other smaller DRAM manufacturers use the trench capacitor structure.

8.2.3 Trench Capacitor Structure

Currently, the overriding consideration for DRAM devices, in general, and commodity DRAM devices, in particular, is that of cost-minimization; This over-riding consideration leads directly to the

pressure to reduce the cell size—either to increase selling price by putting more DRAM cells onto the same piece of silicon real estate or to reduce cost for the same number of storage cells. The pressure to minimize cell area, in turn, means that the storage cell either has to grow into a three-dimensional stacked capacitor above the surface of the silicon or has to grow deeper into and trench below the surface of the active silicon. Figure 8.4 shows a diagram of the 1T1C DRAM cell with a deep trench capacitor as the storage element. The abstract illustration in Figure 8.4 shows the top cross section of the trench capacitor.[5] The depth of the trench capacitor allows a DRAM cell to decrease the use of the silicon surface area without decreasing storage cell capacitance. Trench capacitor structures and stacked capacitor structures have respective advantages and disadvantages. One advantage of the trench capacitor design is that the three-dimensional capacitor structure is under the interconnection layers so that the higher level metallic layers can be more easily made planar. The planar characteristic of the metal layers means that the process could be more easily integrated into a logic-optimized process technology, where there are more metal layers above the active silicon. The buried structure also means that the trench capacitor could be constructed before logic transistors are constructed. The importance of this subtle distinction means that processing steps to create the capacitive layer could be activated before logic transistors are fabricated, and the performance characteristics of logic transistors would not be degraded by formation of the (high-temperature) capacitive layer.[6]

8.2.4 Stacked Capacitor Structure

The stacked capacitor structure uses multiple layers of metal or conductive polysilicon above the surface of the silicon substrate to form the plates of the capacitor to form the plates of the capacitor that holds the stored electrical charge. Figure 8.5 shows an abstract

---

[5]In some modern DRAM devices that use trench capacitors, the depth-to-width aspect ratio of the trench cell exceeds 50:1.
[6]The integration of DRAM cells with the logic circuit on the same process technology is non-trivial. Please see the continuing discussion in Section 8.10.

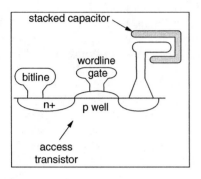

FIGURE 8.5: Abstract view of a 1T1C DRAM cell with stacked capacitor.

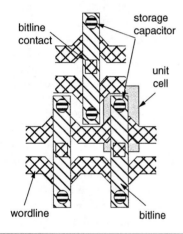

FIGURE 8.6: Top-down view of a DRAM array.

illustration of the stacked capacitor structures. The capacitor structure in Figure 8.5 is formed between two layers of polysilicon, and the capacitor lies underneath the bitline. It is referred to as the *Capacitor-under-Bitline* (CUB) structure. The stacked capacitive storage cell can also be formed above the bitline in the *Capacitor-over-Bitline* (COB) structure. Regardless of the location of the storage cell relative to the bitline, both the CUB and COB structures are variants of the stacked capacitor structure, and the capacitor resides in the polysilicon layers above the active silicon. The

relentless pressure to reduce DRAM cell size while retaining cell capacitance has forced the capacitor structure to grow in the vertical dimension, and the evolution of the stacked capacitor structure is a natural migration from two-dimensional plate capacitor structures to three-dimensional capacitor structures.

8.3 RAM Array Structures

Figure 8.6 illustrates an abstract DRAM array in a top-down view. The figure shows a total of six cells, with every two cells sharing the same bitline contact. The figure also abstractly illustrates the size of a cell in the array. The size of a unit cell is 8 F^2. In the current context, "F" is a process-independent metric that denotes the smallest feature size in a given process technology. In a 90-nm process, F is literally 90 nm, and an area of 8 F^2 translates to 64,800 nm^2 in the 90-nm process. The cross-sectional area of a DRAM storage cell is expected to scale linearly with respect to the process generation and maintains the cell size of 6~8 F^2 in each successive generation.

In DRAM devices, the process of data read out from a cell begins with the activation of the access transistor to that cell. Once the access transistor is turned on, the small charge in the storage capacitor is placed on the bitline to be resolved into a digital value.[7] Figure 8.7 illustrates a single bank of DRAM storage cells where the row address is sent to a row decoder, and the row decoder selects one row of cells. A row of cells is formed from one or more wordlines that are driven concurrently to activate one cell on each one of thousands of bitlines. There may be hundreds of cells connected to the same bitline, but only one cell per bitline will share its stored charge with the bitline at any given instance in time. The charge sharing process by the storage capacitor minutely changes the voltage level on the bitline, and the resulting voltage on the bitline is then resolved into a digital value by a differential sense amplifier. The differential sense amplifier is examined in the following section.

In modern DRAM devices, the capacitance of a storage capacitor is far smaller than the capacitance of the bitline. Typically, the capacitance of a storage

---

[7]Bitlines are also known as digitlines.

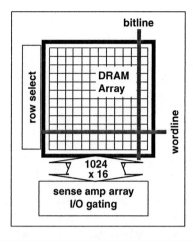

FIGURE 8.7: One DRAM bank illustrated: consisting of one DRAM array, one array of sense amplifiers, and one row decoder—note that the row decoder may be shared across multiple banks.

capacitor is one-tenth of the capacitance of the long bitline that is connected to hundreds or thousands of other cells. The relative capacitance values create the scenario that when the small charge contained in a storage capacitor is placed on the bitline, the resulting voltage on the bitline is small and difficult to measure in an absolute sense. In DRAM devices, the voltage sensing problem is resolved through the use of a differential sense amplifier that compares the voltage of the bitline to a reference voltage.

The use of the differential sense amplifier, in turn, places certain requirements on the array structure of the DRAM device. In particular, the use of a differential sense amplifier means that instead of a single bitline, a pair of bitlines is used to sense the voltage value contained in any DRAM cell. Furthermore, in order to ensure that bitlines are closely matched in terms of voltage and capacitance values, they must be closely matched in terms of path lengths and the number of cells attached. These requirements lead to

two distinctly different array structures: open bitline structures and folded bitline structures. The structural difference between an array with an open bitline structure and an array with a folded bitline structure is that in the open bitline structure, bitline pairs used for each sense amplifier come from separate array segments, while bitline pairs in a folded bitline structure come from the same array segment. The different structure types have different advantages and disadvantages in terms of cell size and noise tolerance. Some of the important advantages and disadvantages are selected for discussion in the following sections.

8.3.1 Open Bitline Array Structure

Figure 8.8 shows an abstract layout of an *open bitline* DRAM array structure. In the open bitline structure, bitline pairs used for each sense amplifier come from separate array segments. Figure 8.8 shows that the open bitline structure leads to a high degree of regularity in the array structure, and the result is that cells in an open bitline structure can be packed closely together. Typically, DRAM cells in an open bitline structure can occupy an area as small as 6 F^2. In contrast, DRAM cells in a *folded bitline* structure typically occupy a minimum area of 8 F^2.[8] The larger area used by cells in a folded bitline structure is due to the fact that two bitlines are routed through the array for each DRAM cell in the folded bitline structure, while only one bitline is routed through the array for each cell in an open bitline structure.

Open bitline array structures were used in 64-Kbit and earlier DRAM generations. Some 256-Kbit DRAM devices also used open bitline structures. However, despite the advantage of smaller cell sizes, open bitline structures also have some disadvantages. One disadvantage of the open bitline structure is that it requires the use of dummy array segments at the edges of the DRAM array in order to ensure that the lengths and capacitance characteristics of the bitline pairs are closely matched. Another disadvantage of the classic

[8]Currently, most manufacturers utilize DRAM cells that occupy an area of 8 F^2, and the International Technology Roadmap for Semiconductors (ITRS) predicts that DRAM manufacturers will begin transition to new DRAM cell structures that are only 6 F^2 in 2008. However, Micron announced in 2004 that it had succeeded in the development of a Metal-Insulator-Metal (MIM) capacitor that occupies an area of 6 F^2 and began shipping products based on this structure in 2004 and 2005.

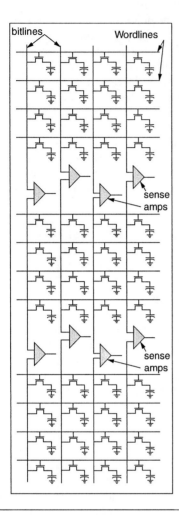

FIGURE 8.8: Open bitline DRAM array structure.

currently used in modern DRAM devices. However, as process technology advances, open bitline structures promise potentially better scalability for the DRAM cell size in the long run. Research in the area of basic DRAM array structure is thus ongoing. Open bitline array structures or more advanced twisting or folding of the bitline structure with the cell size advantage of the open bitline architecture can well make a comeback as the mainstream DRAM array structure in the future.

8.3.2 Folded Bitline Array Structure

Figure 8.9 shows a DRAM array with a folded bitline structure. In the folded bitline configuration, bitlines are routed in pairs through the DRAM array structure, fulfilling several critical requirements of the sensitive differential sense amplifier. The close proximity of the bitline pairs in the folded bitline structure means that the differential sense amplifier circuit, when paired with this array structure, exhibits superior common-mode noise rejection characteristics. That is, in the case of a charge spike induced by a single event upset (SEU) neutron or alpha particle striking the DRAM device, the voltage spike would have a good chance of appearing as common-mode noise at the input of the differential sense amplifier. In the case of the open bitline array structure, the charge spike induced by the SEU would likely appear as noise on only one bitline of a bitline pair that connects to a sense amplifier.

Figure 8.9 shows a logical layout of the folded bitline structure where alternate pairs of DRAM cells are removed from an open bitline array. The array of DRAM cells is then compressed, resulting in the folded bitline structure illustrated in Figure 8.9. The folded bitline structure shown in Figure 8.9 is a simple twisting scheme where the bitline pairs cross over each other for every two transistors on the bitline. More advanced bitline folding schemes are being study to reduce the area impact while retaining the noise immunity aspect of the folded bitline structure.

open bitline structure is that bitline pairs in the open bitline array structure come from different array segments, and each bitline would be more susceptible to electronic noises as compared to bitlines in the folded bitline structure.

The larger area for routing and dummy array segments in open bitline structure minutely dilutes the cell size advantage of the open bitline structures. The various trade-offs, in particular, the noise tolerance issue, have led to the predominance of folded bitline structures in modern DRAM devices. Consequently, open bitline array structures are not

8.4 Differential Sense Amplifier

In DRAM devices, the functionality of resolving small electrical charges stored in storage capacitors into digital values is performed by a differential

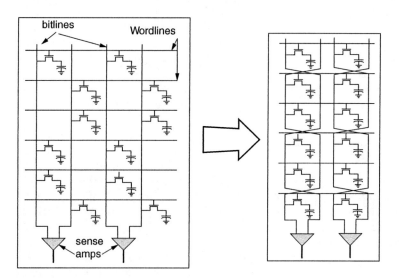

FIGURE 8.9: One type of folded bitline array structure.

sense amplifier. In essence, the differential sense amplifier takes the voltages from a pair of bitlines as input, senses the difference in voltage levels between the bitline pairs, and amplifies the difference to one extreme or the other.

8.4.1 Functionality of Sense Amplifiers in DRAM Devices

Sense amplifiers in modern DRAM devices perform three generalized functions. The first function is to sense the minute change in voltage that occurs when an access transistor is turned on and a storage capacitor places its charge on the bitline. The sense amplifier compares the voltage on that bitline against a reference voltage provided on a separate bitline and amplifies the voltage differential to the extreme so that the storage value can be resolved as a digital 1 or 0. This is the sense amplifier's primary role in DRAM devices, as it senses minute voltage differentials and amplifies them to represent digital values.

The second function is that it also restores the value of a cell after the voltage on the bitline is sensed and amplified. The act of turning on the access transistor allows a storage capacitor to share its stored charge with the bitline. However, the process of sharing

the electrical charge from a storage cell discharges that storage cell. After the process of charge sharing occurs, the voltage within the storage cell is roughly equal to the voltage on the bitline, and this voltage level cannot be used for another read operation. Consequently, after the sensing and amplification operations, the sense amplifier must also restore the amplified voltage value to the storage cell.

The third function is that the sense amplifiers also act as a temporary data storage element. That is, after data values contained in storage cells are sensed and amplified, the sense amplifiers will continue to drive the sensed data values until the DRAM array is precharged and readied for another access. In this manner, data in the same row of cells can be accessed from the sense amplifier without repeated row accesses to the cells themselves. In this role, the array of sense amplifiers effectively acts as a row buffer that caches an entire row of data. As a result, an array of sense amplifiers is also referred to as a row buffer, and management policies are devised to control operations of the sense amplifiers. Different row buffer management policies dictate whether an array of sense amplifiers will retain the data for an indefinite period of time (until the next refresh), or will discharge it immediately after data has been restored to the storage cells. Active sense amplifiers consume additional current above quiescent power levels, and effective management of the sense amplifier operation is an important task for systems seeking optimal trade-off points between performance and power consumption.

8.4.2 Circuit Diagram of a Basic Sense Amplifier

Figure 8.10 shows the circuit diagram of a basic sense amplifier. More complex sense amplifiers in modern DRAM devices contain the basic elements shown in Figure 8.10, as well as additional circuit elements for array isolation, careful balance of the sense amplifier structure, and faster sensing capability. In the basic sense amplifier circuit diagram shown in Figure 8.10, the equalization (*EQ*) signal line controls the voltage equalization circuit. The functionality of this circuit is to ensure that the voltages on the bitline pairs are as closely matched as possible. Since the differential sense amplifier is designed to amplify the voltage differential between the bitline pairs, any voltage imbalance that exists on the bitline pairs prior to the activation of the access transistors would degrade the effectiveness of the sense amplifier.

The heart of the sense amplifier is the set of four cross-connected transistors, labelled as the sensing circuit in Figure 8.10. The sensing circuit is essentially a bi-stable circuit designed to drive the bitline pairs to complementary voltage extremes, depending on the respective voltages on the bitlines at the time the *SAN* (Sense-Amplifier N-Fet Control) and *SAP* (Sense-Amplifier P-Fet Control) sensing signals are activated. The *SAN* signal controls activation of the NFets in the sensing circuit, and the *SAP* signal controls the activation of the PFets in the sensing circuit. After the assertion of the *SAN* and *SAP*, the bitlines are driven to the full voltage levels. The column-select line (*CSL*) then turns on the output transistors and allows the fully driven voltage to reach the output and be read out of the DRAM device. At the same time, the access transistor for the accessed cell remains open, and the fully driven voltage on the bitline now recharges the storage capacitor. Finally, in case of a write operation, the column-select line and the write enable (WE) signals collectively allow the input write drivers to provide a large current to overdrive the sense amplifier and the bitline voltage. Once the sense amplifier is overdriven to the new data value, it will then hold that value and drive it into the DRAM cell through the still open access transistor.

8.4.3 Basic Sense Amplifier Operation

The maximum voltage that can be placed across the access transistor is $V_{gs} - V_t$. (V_t is the threshold

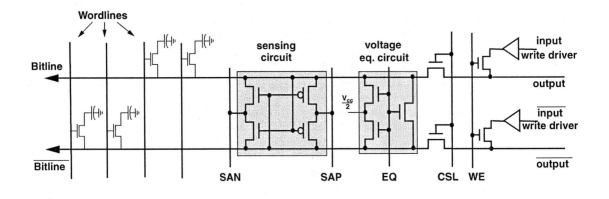

FIGURE 8.10: Basic sense amplifier circuit diagram.

voltage of the access transistor, and V_{gs} is the gate-source voltage on the access transistor.) By overdriving the wordline voltage to $V_{cc} + V_t$, the storage capacitor can be charged to full voltage (maximum of V_{cc}) by the sense amplifier in the restore phase of the sensing operation. In modern DRAM devices, the higher-than-V_{cc} wordline voltage is generated by additional level-shifting voltage pumping circuitry not examined in this text.

Figure 8.11 shows four different phases in the sensing operations of a differential sense amplifier. The precharge, access, sense, and restore operations of a sense amplifier are labelled as phases zero, one, two, and three, respectively. The reason that the precharge phase is labelled as phase zero is because the precharge phase is typically considered as a separate operation from the phases of a row-access operation. That is, while the *Precharge* phase is a prerequisite for a row-access operation, it is typically performed separately from the row-access operation itself. In contrast, *Access, Sense,* and *Restore* are three different phases that are performed in sequence for the row-access operation.

Phase zero in Figure 8.11 is labelled as *Precharge,* and it illustrates that before the process of reading data from a DRAM array can begin, the bitlines in a DRAM array are precharged to a reference voltage, V_{ref}. In many modern DRAM devices, $V_{cc}/2$, the voltage halfway between the power supply voltage and ground, is used as the reference voltage. In Figure 8.11, the equalization circuit is activated to place the reference voltage for the bitlines, and the bitlines are precharged to V_{ref}.

Phase one in Figure 8.11 is labelled as (cell) *Access,* and it illustrates that as a voltage is applied to a wordline, that wordline is overdriven to a voltage that is at least V_t above V_{cc}. The voltage on the wordline activates the access transistors, and the selected storage cells discharge their contents onto the respective bitlines. In this case, since the voltage in the storage cell represents a digital value of "1," the charge sharing process minutely increases the voltage on the bitline from V_{ref}

to V_{ref}^+. Then, as the voltage on the bitline changes, the voltage on the bitline begins to affect operations of the cross-connected sensing circuit. In the case illustrated in Figure 8.11, the slightly higher voltage on the bitline begins to drive the lower NFet to be more conductive than the upper NFet. Conversely, the minute voltage difference also drives the lower PFet to be less conductive than the upper PFet. The bitline voltage thus biases the sensing circuit for the sensing phase.

Phase two in Figure 8.11 is labelled *Sense,* and it illustrates that as the minute voltage differential drives a bias into the cross-connected sensing circuit, SAN, the DRAM device's NFet sense amplifier control signal, turns on and drives the voltage on the lower bitline down.[9] The figure shows that as SAN turns on, the more conductive lower NFet allows SAN to drive the lower bitline down in voltage from V_{ref} to ground. Similarly, SAP, the PFet sense amplifier control signal, drives the bitline to a fully restored voltage value that represents the digital value of "1." The SAN and SAP control signals thus collectively force the bi-stable sense amplifier circuit to be driven to the respective maximum or minimum voltage rails.

Finally, phase three of Figure 8.11 is labelled as *Restore,* and it illustrates that after the bitlines are driven to the respective maximum or minimum voltage values, the overdriven wordline remains active, and the fully driven bitline voltage now restores the charge in the storage capacitor through the access transistor. At the same time, the voltage value on the bitline can be driven out of the sense amplifier circuit to provide the requested data. In this manner, the contents of a DRAM row can be accessed concurrently with the row restoration process.

8.4.4 Voltage Waveform of Basic Sense Amplifier Operation

Figure 8.12 shows the voltage waveforms for the bitline and selected control signals illustrated in Figure 8.11. The four phases labelled in Figure 8.12 correspond

---

[9]In modern DRAM devices, the timing and shape of the SAN and SAP control signals are of great importance in defining the accuracy and latency of the sensing operation. However, for the sake of simplicity, the timing and shape of these important signals are assumed to be optimally generated by the control logic herein.

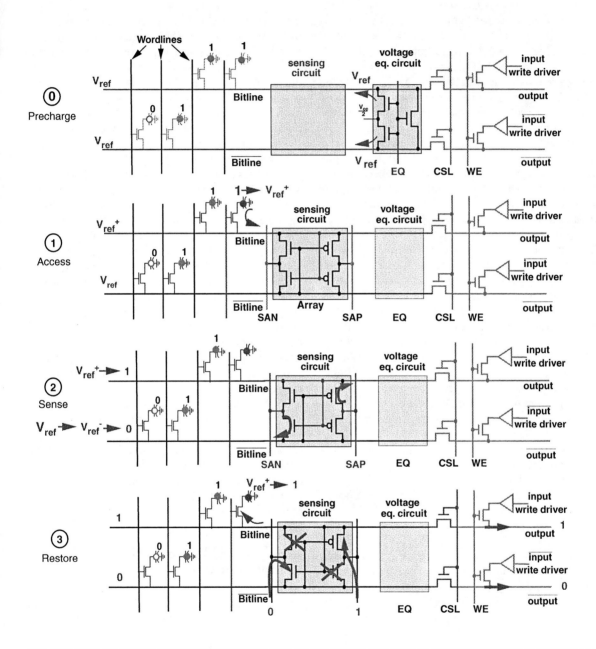

FIGURE 8.11: Illustrated diagrams of the sense amplifier operation. Read(1) example.

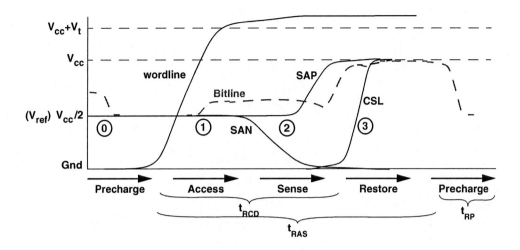

FIGURE 8.12: Simplified sense amplifier voltage waveform. Read(1) example.

to the four phases illustrated in Figure 8.11. Figure 8.12 shows that before a row-access operation, the bitline is precharged, and the voltage on the bitline is set to the reference voltage, V_{ref}. In phase one, the wordline voltage is overdriven to at least V_t above V_{cc}, and the DRAM cell discharges the content of the cell onto the bitline and raises the voltage from V_{ref} to V_{ref}^+. In phase two, the sense control signals SAN and SAP are activated in quick succession and drive the voltage on the bitline to the full voltage. The voltage on the bitline then restores the charge in the DRAM cells in phase three.

Figure 8.12 illustrates the relationship between two important timing parameters: t_{RCD} and t_{RAS}. Although the relative durations of t_{RCD} and t_{RAS} are not drawn to scale, Figure 8.12 shows that after time t_{RCD}, the sensing operation is complete, and the data can be read out through the DRAM device's data I/O. However, after a time period of t_{RCD} from the beginning of the activation process, data is yet to

be restored to the DRAM cells. Figure 8.12 shows that the data restore operation is completed after a time period of t_{RAS} from the beginning of the activation process, and the DRAM device is then ready to accept a precharge command that will complete the entire row cycle process after a time period of t_{RP}.

8.4.5 Writing into DRAM Array

Figure 8.13 shows a simplified timing characteristic for the case of a write command. As part of the row activation command, data is automatically restored from the sense amplifiers to DRAM cells. However, in the case of a write command in commodity DRAM devices, data written by the memory controller is buffered by the I/O buffer of the DRAM device and used to overwrite the sense amplifiers and DRAM cells.[10] Consequently, in the case of a write command that follows a row activation command, the restore phase may be extended by the write recovery phase.[11]

---

[10]Some DRAM devices, such as Direct RDRAM devices, have write buffers. Data is not driven directly into the DRAM array by the data I/O circuitry in that case, but the write mechanism into the DRAM array remains the same when the write buffer commits the data into the DRAM array prior to a precharge operation that closes the page.

[11]The row cycle times of most DRAM devices are write-cycle limited. That is, the row cycle times of these DRAM devices are defined so that a single, minimal burst length column write command can be issued to a given row, between an activation command and a precharge command to the same row.

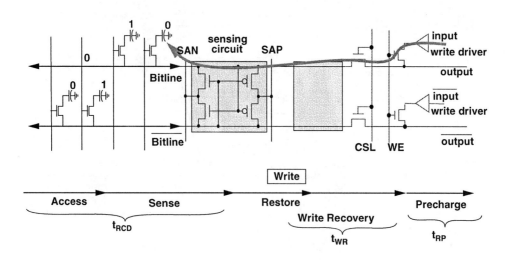

FIGURE 8.13: Row activation followed by column write into a DRAM array.

Figure 8.13 shows that the timing of a column write command means that a precharge command cannot be issued until after the correct data values have been restored to the DRAM cells. The time period required for write data to overdrive the sense amplifiers and written through into the DRAM cells is referred to as the write recovery time, denoted as t_{WR} in Figure 8.13.

8.5 Decoders and Redundancy

Modern DRAM devices rely on complex semiconductor processes for manufacturing. Defects on the silicon wafer or subtle process variations lead directly to defective cells, defective wordlines, or defective bitlines. The technique adopted by DRAM designers to tolerate some amount of defects and increase yield is through the use of redundant rows and columns. Figure 8.14 shows an array with redundant wordlines and redundant bitlines. The figure shows a DRAM array with 2^n rows and m redundant rows. The row decoder must select one out of $2^n + m$ rows with an n-bit-wide row address. The constraint placed on the decoder is that the spare replacement mechanism should not introduce unacceptable area overhead or additional delays into the address decode path.

In modern DRAM devices, each row of a DRAM array is connected to a decoder that can be selectively disconnected via a laser (or fuse) programmable link. In cases where a cell or an entire wordline is found to be defective, the laser or electrical programmable link for the standard decoder for that row disconnects the wordline attached to that standard decoder, and a spare row is engaged by connecting the address lines to match the address of the disconnected row. In this manner, the spare decoder can seamlessly engage the spare row when the address of the faulty row is asserted. The programmable links in the decoders may be laser programmable fuses or electrically programmable fuses, depending on the process technology and the mechanism selected by the DRAM design engineers as optimal for the specific manufacturing process technology.

Figure 8.15 shows a set of standard and spare decoder designs that are used to drive rows of DRAM cells in some DRAM devices. In such a DRAM device, a standard decoder is attached to each of the 2^n row of cells, and a spare decoder is attached to each of the spare rows. The figure shows that the standard decoder illustrated is functionally equivalent to an n-input NOR gate. In the standard decoder, each input of the functionally equivalent n-input NOR gate is

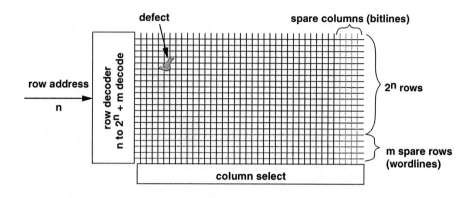

FIGURE 8.14: Redundant rows and columns in a DRAM array.

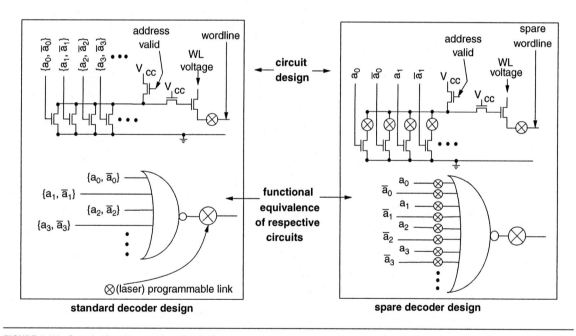

FIGURE 8.15: Standard and spare decoder design.

connected to one bit in the n-bit address—either the inverted or the non-inverted signal line. Figure 8.15 shows that the spare decoder illustrated is functionally equivalent to a $2n$-input NOR gate, and each bit in the n-bit address as well as the complement of

each bit of the n-bit address is connected to the $2n$ inputs. In cases where a spare decoder is used, the input of the NOR gate is selectively disabled so that the remaining address signals match the address of the disabled standard decoder.

8.5.1 Row Decoder Replacement Example

Figure 8.16 illustrates the replacement of a standard decoder circuit with a spare decoder for a DRAM array with 16 standard rows and 2 spare rows. In Figure 8.16, the topmost decoder becomes active with the address of 0b1111, and each of the 16 standard decoders is connected to one of 16 standard rows. In the example illustrated in Figure 8.16, row 0b1010 is discovered to be defective, and the standard decoder for row 0b1010 is disconnected. Then, the inputs of a spare decoder are selectively disconnected, so the remaining inputs match the address of 0b1010. In this manner, the spare decoder and the row associated with it take over the storage responsibility for row 0b1010.

A second capability of the decoders shown in Figure 8.15, but not specifically illustrated in Figure 8.16, is the ability to replace a spare decoder with another spare decoder. In cases where the spare row connected to the spare decoder selected to replace row 0b1010 is itself defective, the DRAM device can still be salvaged by disconnecting the spare decoder at its output and programming yet another spare decoder for row 0b1010.

8.6 DRAM Device Control Logic

All DRAM devices contain some basic logic control circuitry to direct the movement of data onto, within, and off of the DRAM device. Essentially, some control logic must exist on DRAM devices that accepts externally asserted signal and control and then orchestrates appropriately timed sequences of internal control signals to direct the movement of data. As an example, the previous discussion on sense amplifier operations hinted to the complexity of the intricate timing sequence in the assertion of the wordline voltage followed by assertion of the SAN and SAP sense amplifier control signals followed yet again by the column-select signal. The sequence of timed control signals is generated by the control logic on DRAM devices.

Figure 8.17 shows the control logic that generates and controls the timing and sequence of signals for the sensing and movement of data on the FPM DRAM device illustrated in Figure 8.1. The control logic on the FPM DRAM device asynchronously accepts external signal control and generates the sequence of internal control signals for the FPM DRAM device.

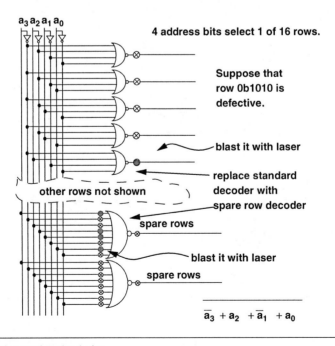

FIGURE 8.16: Standard and spare decoder design.

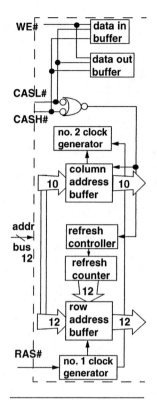

FIGURE 8.17: Control logic for a 32-Mbit, x16-wide FPM DRAM device.

The external interface to the control logic on the FPM DRAM device is simple and straightforward, consisting of essentially three signals: the *row-address strobe* (RAS), the *column-address strobe* (CAS), and the *write enable* (WE). The FPM DRAM device described in Figure 8.1 is a device with a 16-bit-wide data bus, and the use of separate CASL and CASH signals allows the DRAM device to control each half of the 16-bit-wide data bus separately.

In the FPM DRAM device, the control logic and external memory controller directly control the movement of data. Moreover, the controller to the FPM DRAM device interface is an asynchronous interface. In early generations of DRAM devices such as the FPM DRAM described here, the direct control of the internal circuitry of the DRAM device by the external memory controller meant that the DRAM device could not be well pipelined and new commands to the DRAM device could not be initiated until the previous command completed the movement of data. The movement of data was measured and reported by DRAM manufacturers in terms of nanoseconds. The asynchronous nature of the interface meant that system design engineers could implement a different memory controller that operated at different frequencies, and designers of the memory controller were solely responsible to ensure that the controller could correctly control different DRAM devices with subtle variations in timings from different DRAM manufacturers.

8.6.1 Synchronous vs. Non-Synchronous

Modern DRAM devices such as *synchronous DRAM* (SDRAM), *Direct Rambus DRAM* (D-RDRAM), and *dual data rate synchronous DRAM* (DDR SDRAM) contain control logic that is more complex than the control logic contained in an FPM DRAM device. The inclusion of the clock signal into the device interface enables the design of programmable synchronous state machines as the control logic in modern DRAM devices. Figure 8.18 shows the control logic for an SDRAM device.

DRAM circuits are fundamentally analog circuits whose timing is asynchronous in nature. The steps that DRAM circuits take to store and retrieve data in capacitors through the sense amplifier have relatively long latency, and these latencies are naturally specified in terms of nanoseconds rather than numbers of cycles. Moreover, different DRAM designs and process variations from different DRAM manufacturers lead to different sets of timing parameters for each type and design of DRAM devices. The asynchronous nature and the variations of DRAM devices introduce

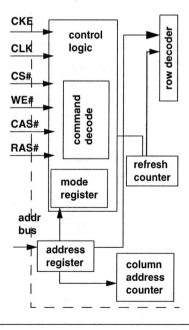

FIGURE 8.18: Control logic for a synchronous DRAM device.

design complexity to computing platforms that use DRAM devices as temporary memory storage. The solution deployed by the DRAM industry as a whole was the migration of DRAM devices to the synchronous interface.

The control logic for synchronous DRAM devices such as SDRAM and D-RDRAM differs from non-synchronous interface DRAM devices such as FPM and EDO in some significant ways. Aside from the trivial inclusion of the clock signal, one difference between control logic for synchronous and previous non-synchronous DRAM devices is that the synchronous DRAM devices can exhibit slight variations in behavior to a given command. The programmable variability for synchronous DRAM devices can be controlled by mode registers embedded as part of the control logic. For example, an SDRAM device can be programmed to return different lengths of data bursts and different data ordering for the column read command. A second difference between the control logic for synchronous DRAM devices and non-synchronous DRAM devices is that the synchronous control logic circuits have been designed to support pipelining naturally, and the ability to support pipelining greatly increases the sustainable bandwidth of the DRAM memory system. Non-synchronous DRAM devices such as EDO and BEDO DRAM can also support pipelining to some degree, but built-in assumptions that enable the limited degree of pipelining in non-synchronous DRAM devices, in turn, limit the frequency scalability of these devices.

8.6.2 Mode Register-Based Programmability

Modern DRAM devices are controlled by state machines whose behavior depends on the input values of the command signals as well as the values contained in the programmable mode register in the control logic. Figure 8.19 shows that in an SDRAM device, the mode register contains three fields: CAS latency, burst type, and burst length. Depending on the value of the CAS latency field in the mode register, the DRAM device returns data two or three cycles after the assertion of the column read command. The value of the burst type determines the ordering of how the SDRAM device returns data, and the burst

length field determines the number of columns that an SDRAM device will return to the memory controller with a single column read command. SDRAM devices can be programmed to return 1, 2, 4, or 8 columns or an entire row. D-RDRAM devices and DDRx SDRAM devices contain more mode registers that control an ever larger set of programmable operations, including, but not limited to, different operating modes for power conservation, electrical termination calibration modes, self-test modes, and write recovery duration.

8.7 DRAM Device Configuration

DRAM devices are classified by the number of data bits in each device, and that number typically quadruples from generation to generation. For example, 64-Kbit DRAM devices were followed by 256-Kbit DRAM devices, and 256-Kbit devices were, in turn, followed by 1-Mbit DRAM devices. Recently, half- generation devices that simply double the number of data bits of previous-generation devices have been used to facilitate smoother transitions between different generations. As a result, 512-Mbit devices now exist alongside 256-Mbit and 1 Gbit devices.

In a given generation, a DRAM device may be configured with different data bus widths for use in different applications. Table 8.1 shows three different configurations of a 256-Mbit device. The table shows that a 256-Mbit SDRAM device may be configured with a 4-bit-wide data bus, an 8-bit-wide data bus, or a 16-bit-wide data bus. In the configuration with a 4-bit-wide data bus, an address provided to the SDRAM device to fetch a single column of data will receive 4 bits of data, and there are 64 million separately addressable locations in the device with the 4-bit data bus. The 256-Mbit SDRAM device with the 4-bit-wide data bus is thus referred to as the 64 Meg x4 device. Internally, the 64 Meg x4 device consists of 4 bits of data per column, 2048 columns of data per row, and 8192 rows per bank, and there are 4 banks in the device. Alternatively, a 256-Mbit SDRAM device with a 16-bit-wide data bus will have 16 bits of data per column, 512 columns per row, and

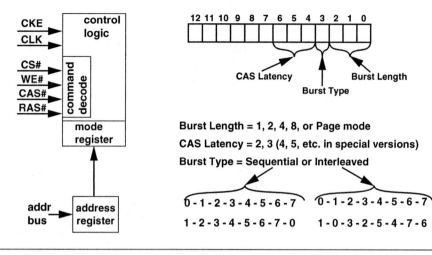

FIGURE 8.19: Programmable mode register in an SDRAM device.

TABLE **8.1** 256-Mbit SDRAM device configurations

Device Configuration	64 Meg x 4	32 Meg x 8	16 Meg x 16
Number of banks	4	4	4
Number of rows	8192	8192	8192
Number of columns	2048	1024	512
Data bus width	4	8	16

8192 rows per bank; there are 4 banks in the 16 Mbit, x16 device.

In a typical application, 4 16 Mbit, x16 devices can be connected in parallel to form a single rank of memory with a 64-bit-wide data bus and 128 MB of storage. Alternatively, 16 64 Mbit, x4 devices can be connected in parallel to form a single rank of memory with a 64-bit-wide data bus and 512 MB of storage.

8.7.1 Device Configuration Trade-offs

In the 256-Mbit SDRAM device, the size of the row does not change in different configurations, and the number of columns per row simply decreases with wider data busses specifying a larger number of bits per column. However, the constant row size between different configurations of DRAM devices within the

same DRAM device generation is not a generalized trend that can be extended to different device generations. For example, Table 8.2 shows different configurations of a 1-Gbit DDR2 SDRAM device, where the number of bits per row differs between the x8 configuration and the x16 configuration.

In 1-Gbit DDR2 SDRAM devices, there are eight banks of DRAM arrays per device. In the x4 and x8 configuration of the 1-Gbit DDR2 SDRAM device, there are 16,384 rows per bank, and each row consists of 8192 bits. In the x16 configuration, there are 8192 rows, and each row consists of 16,384 bits. These different configurations lead to different numbers of bits per bitline, different numbers of bits per row activation, and different number of bits per column access. In turn, differences in the number of bits moved per command lead to different power consumption

TABLE 8.2   1-Gbit DDR2 SDRAM device configurations

Device Configuration	256 Meg x 4	128 Meg x 8	64 Meg x 16
Number of banks	8	8	8
Number of rows	16,384	16,384	8192
Number of columns	2048	1024	1024
Data bus width	4	8	16

and performance characteristics for different configurations of the same device generation. For example, the 1-Gbit, x16 DDR2 SDRAM device is configured with 16,384 bits per row, and each time a row is activated, 16,384 DRAM cells are simultaneously discharged onto respective bitlines, sensed, amplified, and then restored. The larger row size means that a 1-Gbit, x16 DDR2 SDRAM device with 16,384 bits per row consumes significantly more current per row activation than the x4 and x8 configurations for the 1-Gbit DDR2 SDRAM device with 8192 bits per row. The differences in current consumption characteristics, in turn, lead to different values for t_{RRD} and t_{FAW}, timing parameters designed to limit peak power dissipation characteristics of DRAM devices.

8.8   Data I/O

8.8.1   Burst Lengths and Burst Ordering

In SDRAM and DDRx SDRAM devices, a column read command moves a variable number of columns. As illustrated in Section 8.6.2 on the programmable mode register, an SDRAM device can be programmed to return 1, 2, 4, or 8 columns of data as a single burst that takes 1, 2, 4, or 8 cycles to complete. In contrast, a D-RDRAM device returns a single column of data with an 8 beat[12] burst. Figure 8.20 shows an 8 beat, 8 column read data burst from an SDRAM device and an 8 beat, single column read data burst from a D-RDRAM device. The distinction between the 8 column burst of an SDRAM device and the single column data burst

of the D-RDRAM device is that each column of the SDRAM device is individually addressable, and given a column address in the middle of an 8 column burst, the SDRAM device will reorder the burst to provide the data of the requested address first. This capability is known as critical-word forwarding. For example, in an SDRAM device programmed to provide a burst of 8 columns, a column read command with a column address of 17 will result in the data burst of 8 columns of data with the address sequence of 17-18-19-20-21-22-23-16 or 17-16-19-18-21-20-23-22, depending on the burst type as defined in the programmable register. In contrast, each column of a D-RDRAM device consists of 128 bits of data, and each column access command moves 128 bits of data in a burst of 8 contiguous beats in strict burst ordering. An D-RDRAM device supports neither programmable burst lengths nor different burst ordering.

8.8.2   N-Bit Prefetch

In SDRAM devices, each time a column read command is issued, the control logic determines the duration and ordering of the data burst, and each column is moved separately from the sense amplifiers through the I/O latches to the external data bus. However, the separate control of each column limits the operating data rate of the DRAM device. As a result, in DDRx SDRAM devices, successively larger numbers of bits are moved in parallel from the sense amplifiers to the read latch, and the data is then pipelined through a multiplexor to the external data bus.

---

[12]In DDRx and D-RDRAM devices, 2 beats of data are transferred per clock cycle.

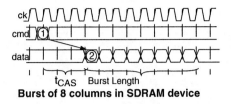

Burst of 8 columns in SDRAM device

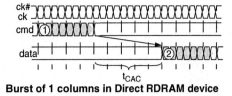

Burst of 1 columns in Direct RDRAM device

FIGURE 8.20: Burst lengths in DRAM devices.

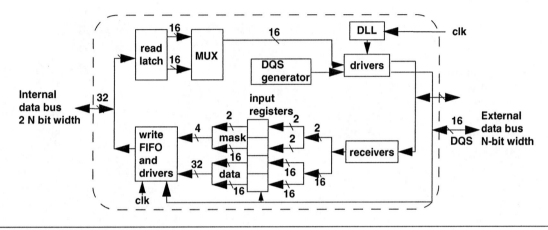

FIGURE 8.21: Data I/O in a DDR SDRAM device illustrating 2-bit prefetch.

Figure 8.21 illustrates the data I/O structure of a DDR SDRAM device. The figure shows that given the width of the external data bus as N, 2N bits are moved from the sense amplifiers to the read latch, and the 2N bits are then pipelined through the multiplexors to the external data bus. In DDR2 SDRAM devices, the number of bits prefetched by the internal data bus is 4N. The N-bit prefetch strategy in DDRx SDRAM devices means that internal DRAM circuits can remain essentially unchanged between transitions from SDRAM to DDRx SDRAM, but the operating data rate of DDRx SDRAM devices can be increased to levels not possible with SDRAM devices. However, the downside of the N-bit prefetch architecture means that short column bursts are no longer possible. In DDR2 SDRAM devices, a minimum burst

length of 4 columns of data is accessed per column read command. This trend is likely to continue in DDR3 and DDR4 SDRAM devices, dictating longer data bursts for each successive generations of higher data rate DRAM devices.

8.9 DRAM Device Packaging

One difference between DRAM and logic devices is that most DRAM devices are commodity items, whereas logic devices such as processors and *application-specific integrated circuits* (ASICs) are typically specialized devices that are not commodity items. The result of the commodity status is that, even more so than logic devices, DRAM devices are extraordinarily sensitive to cost. One area that

TABLE 8.3 Package cost and pin count of high-performance logic chips and DRAM chips (ITRS 2002)

	2004	2007	2010	2013	2016
Semi generation (nm)	90	65	45	32	22
High perf. device pin count	2263	3012	4009	5335	7100
High perf. device cost (cents/pin)	1.88	1.61	1.68	1.44	1.22
Memory device pin count	**48–160**	**48–160**	**62–208**	**81–270**	**105–351**
DRAM device pin cost (cents/pin)	0.34–1.39	0.27–0.84	0.22–0.34	0.19–0.39	0.19–0.33

reflects the cost sensitivity is the packaging technology utilized by DRAM devices. Table 8.3 shows the expected pin count and relative costs from the 2002 *International Technology Roadmap for Semiconductors* (ITRS) for high-performance logic devices as compared to memory devices. The table shows the trend that memory chips such as DRAM will continue to be manufactured with relatively lower cost packaging with lower pin count and lower cost per pin.

Figure 8.22 shows four different packages used in DRAM devices. DRAM devices were typically packaged in low pin count and low cost *Dual In-line Packages* (DIP) well into the late 1980s. Increases in DRAM device density and wider data paths have required the use of the larger and higher pin count *Small Outline J-lead* (SOJ) packages. DRAM devices then moved to the *Thin, Small Outline Package* (TSOP) in the late 1990s. As DRAM device data rates increase to multiple hundreds of megabits per second, *Ball Grid Array* (BGA) packages are needed to better control signal interconnects at the package level.

8.10 DRAM Process Technology and Process Scaling Considerations

The 1T1C cell structure places specialized demands on the access transistor and the storage capacitor. Specifically, the area occupied by the 1T1C DRAM cell structure must be small, leakage through the access transistor must be low, and the capacitance of the storages capacitor must be large. The data retention time and data integrity requirements provide the bounds for the design of a DRAM cell. Different DRAM devices can be designed to meet the demand of different markets. DRAM devices can be designed for high performance or low cost. DRAM-optimized process technologies can also be used to fabricate logic circuits, and logic-optimized process technologies can also be used to fabricate DRAM circuits. However, DRAM-optimized process technologies have diverged substantially from logic-optimized process technologies in recent years. Consequently, it has become less economically feasible to fabricate DRAM circuits in logic-optimized process technology, and logic circuits fabricated in DRAM-optimized

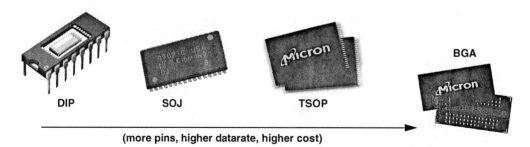

(more pins, higher datarate, higher cost)

FIGURE 8.22: DRAM package evolution.

process technology are much slower than similar circuits in a logic-optimized process technology. These trends have conspired to keep logic and DRAM circuits in separate devices manufactured in process technologies optimized for the respective device.

8.10.1 Cost Considerations

Historically, manufacturing cost considerations have dominated the design of standard, commodity DRAM devices. In the spring of 2003, a single 256-Mbit DRAM device, using roughly 45 mm^2 of silicon die area on a 0.11-μm DRAM process, had a selling price of approximately $4 per chip. In contrast, a desktop Pentium 4 processor from Intel, using roughly 130 mm^2 of die area on a 0.13-μm logic process, had a selling price that ranged from $80 to $600 in the comparable time-frame. Although the respective selling prices were due to the limited sources, the non-commodity nature of processors, and the pure commodity economics of DRAM devices, the disparity does illustrate the level of price competition

in the commodity DRAM market. The result is that DRAM manufacturers are singularly focused on the low-cost aspect of DRAM devices. Any proposal to add additional functionalities must then be weighed against the increase in die cost and possible increases in the selling price.

8.10.2 DRAM- vs. Logic-Optimized Process Technology

One trend in semiconductor manufacturing is the inevitable march toward integration. As the semiconductor manufacturing industry dutifully fulfills Moore's Law, each doubling of transistors allows design engineers to pack more logic circuitry or more DRAM storage cells onto a single piece of silicon. However, the semiconductor industry, in general, has thus far resisted the integration of DRAM and logic onto the same silicon device for various technical and economic reasons.

Figure 8.23 illustrates some technical issues that have prevented large-scale integration of logic circuitry

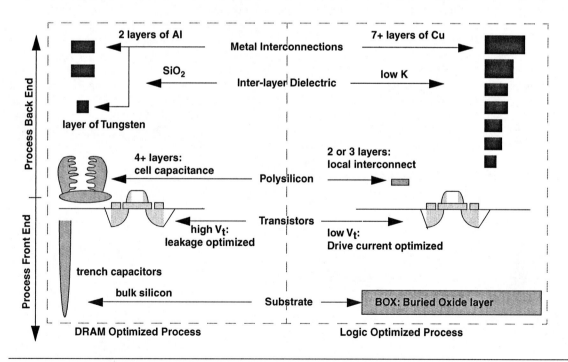

FIGURE 8.23: Comparison of a DRAM-optimized process versus a logic-optimized process.

with DRAM storage cells. Basically, logic-optimized process technologies have been designed for transistor performance, while DRAM-optimized process technologies have been designed for low cost, error tolerance, and leakage resistance. Figure 8.23 shows a typical logic-based process with seven or more layers of copper interconnects, while a typical DRAM-optimized process has only two layers of aluminum interconnects along with perhaps an additional layer of tungsten for local interconnects. Moreover, a logic-optimized process typically uses low K material for the inter-layer dielectric, while the DRAM-optimized process uses the venerable SiO_2. Figure 8.23 also shows that a DRAM-optimized process would use four or more layers of polysilicon to form the structures of a stacked capacitor (for those DRAM devices that use the stacked capacitor structure), while the logic-optimized process merely uses two or three layers of polysilicon for local interconnects. Also, transistors in a logic-optimized process are typically tuned for high performance, while transistors in a DRAM-optimized process are tuned singularly for low-leakage characteristics. Finally, even the substrates of the respectively optimized process technologies are diverging as logic-optimized process technologies move to depleted substrates and DRAM-optimized process technologies largely stays with bulk silicon.

The respective specializations of the differently optimized process technologies have largely succeeded in preventing widespread integration of logic circuitry with DRAM storage cells. The use of a DRAM-optimized process as the basis of integrating logic circuits and DRAM storage cells leads to slow transistors with low-drive currents connected to a few layers of metal interconnects and a relatively high K SiO_2 inter-layer dielectric. That is, logic circuits implemented on a DRAM-optimized process would be substantially larger as well as slower than comparable circuits on a similar generation logic-optimized process. Conversely, the use of a higher cost logic-optimized process as the basis of integrating logic circuits and DRAM storage cells leads to high-performance but leaky transistors coupled with DRAM cells with relatively lower capacitance, necessitating large DRAM cell structures and high refresh rates.

In recent years, new hybrid process technologies have emerged to solve various technical issues involving the integration of logic circuits and DRAM storage cells. Typically, the hybrid process starts with the foundation of a logic-optimized process and then additional layers are added to the process to create high-capacitance DRAM storage cells. Also, different types of transistors are made available for use as low-leakage access transistors as well as high-drive current high-performance logic transistors. However, hybrid process technology then becomes more complex than a logic-optimized process. As a result, hybrid process technologies that enable seamless integration of logic and DRAM devices are typically more expensive, and their use has thus far been limited to specialty niches that require high-performance processors and high-performance and yet small DRAM memory systems that are limited by the die size of a single logic device. Typically, the application has been limited to high-performance System-on-Chip (SOC) devices.

CHAPTER 9

DRAM System Signaling and Timing

In any electronic system, multiple devices are connected together, and signals are sent from one point in the system to another point in the system for the devices to communicate with each other. The signals adhere to predefined signaling and timing protocols to ensure correctness in the transmission of commands and data. In the grand scale of things, the topics of signaling and timing require volumes of dedicated texts for proper coverage. This chapter cannot hope to, nor is it designed to, provide a comprehensive coverage on these important topics. Rather, the purpose of this chapter is to provide basic terminologies and understanding of the fundamentals of signaling and timing—subjects of utmost importance that drive design decisions in modern DRAM memory systems. This chapter provides the basic understanding of signaling and timing in modern electronic systems and acts as a primer for further understanding of the topology, electrical signaling, and protocols of modern DRAM memory systems in subsequent chapters. The text in this chapter is written for those interested in the DRAM memory system but do not have a background as an electrical engineer, and it is designed to provide a basic survey of the topic sufficient only to understand the system-level issues that impact the design and implementation of DRAM memory systems, without having to pick up another text to reference the basic concepts.

9.1 Signaling System

In the decades since the emergence of electronic computers, the demand for ever-increasing memory capacity has constantly risen. This insatiable demand for memory capacity means that the number of DRAM devices attached to the memory system for a given class of computers has remained relatively constant despite the increase in per-device capacity made possible with advancements in semiconductor technology. The need to connect multiple DRAM devices together to form a larger memory system for a wide variety of computing platforms has remained unchanged for many years. In the cases where multiple, discrete DRAM devices are connected together to form larger memory systems, complex signaling systems are needed to transmit information to and from the DRAM devices in the memory system.

Figure 9.1 illustrates the timing diagram for two consecutive column read commands to different DDR SDRAM devices. The timing diagram shows idealized timing waveforms, where data is moved from the DRAM devices in response to commands sent by the DRAM memory controller. However, as Figure 9.1 illustrates, signals in real-world systems are far from ideal, and signal integrity issues such as ringing, attenuation, and non-monotonic signals can and do negatively impact the setup and hold time requirements of signal timing constraints. Specifically, Figure 9.1 illustrates that a given signal may be considered high-quality if it transitions rapidly and settles rapidly from one signal level to another. Figure 9.1 further illustrates that a poorly designed signaling system can result in a poor quality signal that overshoots, undershoots, and does not settle rapidly into its new signal value, possibly resulting in the violation of the setup time or the hold time requirements in a high-speed system.

Figure 9.2 illustrates the fundamental problem of frequency-dependent signal transmission in a

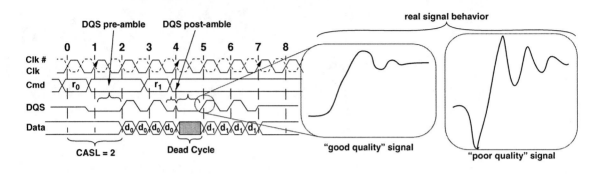

FIGURE 9.1: Real-world behavior of electrical signals.

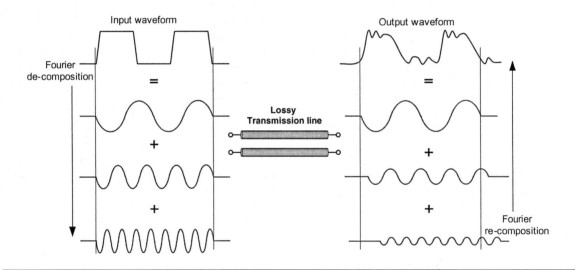

FIGURE 9.2: Frequency-dependent signal transmission in lossy, real-world transmission lines.

lossy, real-world transmission line. That is, an input waveform, even an idealized, perfect square wave signal, can be decomposed into a Fourier series—a sum of sinusoidal and cosinusoidal oscillations of various amplitudes and frequencies. The real-world, lossy transmission line can then be modelled as a non-linear low-pass filter where the low-frequency components of the Fourier decomposition of the input waveform pass through the transmission line without substantial impact to their respective amplitudes or phases. In contrast, the non-linear, low-pass transmission line will significantly attenuate and phase shift the high-frequency components of the input waveform. Then, recomposition of the various frequency components of the input waveform at the output of the lossy transmission line will result in an output waveform that is significantly different from that of the input waveform.

Collectively, constraints of the signaling system will limit the signaling rate and the delivery of symbols between discrete semiconductor devices such as DRAM devices and the memory controller. Consequently, the

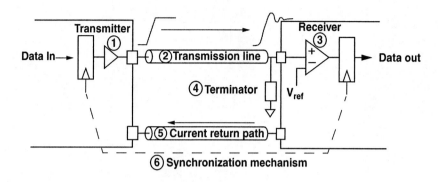

FIGURE 9.3: A basic signaling system.

construction and assumptions inherent in the signaling system can and do directly impact the access protocol of a given memory system, which in turn determines the bandwidth, latency, and efficiency characteristics of the memory system. As a result, a basic comprehension of issues relating to signaling and timing is needed as a foundation to understand the architectural and engineering design trade-offs of modern, multi-device memory systems.

Figure 9.3 shows a basic signaling system where a symbol, encoded as a signal, is sent by a transmitter along a transmission line and delivered to a receiver. The receiver must then resolve the value of the signal transmitted within valid timing windows determined by the synchronization mechanism. The signal should then be removed from the transmission line by a resistive element, labelled as the terminator in Figure 9.3, so that it does not interfere with the transmission and reception of subsequent signals. The termination scheme should be carefully designed to improve signal integrity depending on the specific interconnect scheme. Typically, serial termination is used at the receiver and parallel termination is used at the transmitter in modern high-speed memory systems. As a general summary, serial termination reduces signal ringing at the cost of reduced signal swing at the receiver, and parallel termination improves signal quality, but consumes additional active power to remove the signal from the transmission line.

Figure 9.3 illustrates a basic signaling system where signals are delivered unidirectionally from a transmitter

to a single receiver. In contemporary DRAM memory systems, signals are often delivered to multiple DRAM devices connected on the same transmission line. Specifically, in SDRAM and SDRAM-like DRAM memory systems, multiple DRAM devices are often connected to a given address and command bus, and multiple DRAM devices are often connected to the same data bus where the same transmission line is used to move data from the DRAM memory controller to the DRAM devices, as well as from the DRAM devices back to the DRAM memory controller.

The examination of the signaling system in this chapter begins with an examination of basic transmission line theory with the treatment of wires as ideal transmission lines, and it proceeds to an examination of the termination mechanism utilized in the DRAM memory system. However, due to their relative complexity and the limited coverage envisioned in this chapter, specific circuits utilized by DRAM devices for signal transmission and reception are not examined herein.

9.2 Transmission Lines on PCBs

Modern DRAM memory systems are typically formed from multiple devices mounted on *printed circuit boards* (PCBs). The interconnects on PCBs are mostly wires and vias that allow an electrical signal to deliver a symbol from one point in the system to another point in the system. The symbol may be

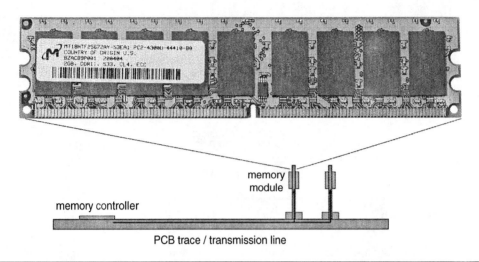

FIGURE 9.4: Signal traces in a system board and a DRAM memory module.

binary (1 or 0) as in all modern DRAM memory systems or may, in fact, be multi-valued, where each symbol can represent two or more bits of information. The limitation on the speed and reliability of the data transport mechanism in moving a symbol from one point in the system to another point in the system depends on the quality and characteristics of the traces used in the system board. Figure 9.4 illustrates a commodity DRAM memory module, where multiple DRAM devices are connected to a PCB, and multiple memory modules are connected to the memory controller through more PCB traces on the system board. In contemporary DRAM memory systems, multiple memory modules are then typically connected to a system board where electrical signals that represent different symbols are delivered to the devices in the system through traces on the different PCB segments.

In this section, the electrical properties of signal traces are examined by first characterizing the electrical characteristics of idealized transmission lines. Once the characteristics of idealized transmission lines have been established, the discussion then proceeds to examine the non-idealities of signal transmission on a system board such as *attenuation,*

reflection, skin effect, crosstalk, inter-symbol interference (ISI), and *simultaneous switching outputs* (SSO). The coverage of these basic topics will then enable the reader to proceed to understand system-level design issues in modern, high-speed DRAM memory systems.

9.2.1 Brief Tutorial on the Telegrapher's Equations

To begin the examination of the electrical characteristics of signal interconnects, an understanding of transmission line characteristics is a basic requirement. This section provides the derivation of the telegrapher's equations that will be used as the basis of understanding the signal interconnect in this chapter.

Figure 9.5 illustrates that an infinitesimally small piece of transmission line can be modelled as a resistive element R that is in series with an inductive element L, and these elements are parallel to a capacitive element C and a conductive element G. To understand the electrical characteristics of the basic transmission line, Kirchhoff's voltage law can be applied to the transmission line segment in

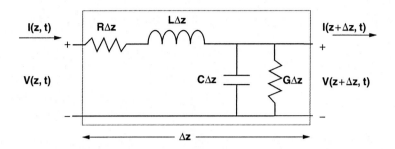

FIGURE 9.5: Mathematical model of a basic transmission line. Top wire (+) is signal; bottom wire (−) is signal return.

Figure 9.5 to obtain Equation 9.1,

$$v(z, t) - (R \cdot \Delta z \cdot i(z, t)) - \left(L \cdot \Delta z \cdot \frac{\partial i(z, t)}{\partial t} \right)$$
$$- v(z + \Delta z, t) = 0 \qquad \text{(EQ 9.1)}$$

and Kirchhoff's current law can be applied to the same transmission line segment in Figure 9.5 to obtain Equation 9.2.

$$i(z, t) - (G \cdot \Delta z \cdot v(z, + \Delta z, t)) - \left(C \cdot \Delta z \cdot \frac{\partial v(z + \Delta z, t)}{\partial t} \right)$$
$$- i(z + \Delta z, t) = 0 \qquad \text{(EQ 9.2)}$$

Then, dividing Equations 9.1 and 9.2 through by Δz, and taking the limit as Δz approaches zero, Equation 9.3 can be derived from Equation 9.1, and Equation 9.4 can be derived from Equation 9.2.

$$\frac{\partial v(z, t)}{\partial t} = -Ri(z, t) - L \frac{\delta i(z, t)}{\delta t} \qquad \text{(EQ 9.3)}$$

$$\frac{\partial i(z, t)}{\partial t} = -Gv(z, t) - C \frac{\delta v(z, t)}{\delta t} \qquad \text{(EQ 9.4)}$$

Equations 9.3 and 9.4 are time-domain equations that describe the electrical characteristics of the transmission line. Equations 9.3 and 9.4 are also known as the Telegrapher's Equations.[1]

Furthermore, Equations 9.3 and 9.4 can be solved simultaneously to obtain steady-state sinusoidal wave equations. Equations 9.5 and 9.6 are derived from Equations 9.3 and 9.4, respectively,

$$\frac{\partial^2 V(z)}{\partial z^2} - \gamma^2 V(z) = 0 \qquad \text{(EQ 9.5)}$$

$$\frac{\partial^2 I(z)}{\partial z^2} - \gamma^2 V(z) = 0 \qquad \text{(EQ 9.6)}$$

where γ is represented by Equation 9.7.

$$\gamma = \sqrt{(R + j\omega L)(G + j\omega C)} \qquad \text{(EQ 9.7)}$$

Furthermore, solving for voltage and current equations, Equations 9.8 and 9.9 are derived

$$V(z) = V_0^+ e^{-\gamma z} + V_0^- e^{-\gamma z} \qquad \text{(EQ 9.8)}$$

$$I(z) = I_0^+ e^{-\gamma z} + I_0^- e^{-\gamma z} \qquad \text{(EQ 9.9)}$$

where V_0^+ and V_0^- are the respective voltages, and I_0^+ and I_0^- are the respective currents that exist at locations Z^+ and Z^-, locations infinitesimally close to reference location Z. That is, Equations 9.8 and 9.9 are the standing wave equations the describe transmission line characteristics.

Finally, rearranging Equations 9.8 and 9.9, Equations 9.10 and 9.11 can be derived

$$I(z) = \frac{\gamma}{R + j\omega L} \cdot (V_0^+ e^{-\gamma z} + V_0^- e^{-\gamma z}) \qquad \text{(EQ 9.10)}$$

$$Z_0 = \frac{R + j\omega L}{\gamma} = \sqrt{\frac{R + j\omega L}{G + j\omega C}} \qquad \text{(EQ 9.11)}$$

where Z_0 is the characteristic impedance, and α and β are the attenuation constant and the phase constant of

---

[1]The Telegrapher's Equations were first derived by William Thomson in the 1850s in his efforts to analyze the electrical characteristics of the underwater telegraph cable. Their final form, shown here, was later derived by Oliver Heaviside.

the transmission line, respectively. Although the characteristic impedance of the transmission line has the unit of ohms, it is conceptually different from simple resistance. Rather, the characteristic impedance is the resistance seen by propagating waveforms at a specific point of the transmission line.

9.2.2 RC and LC Transmission Line Models

Equations 9.1–9.11 illustrate a mathematical derivation of basic transmission line characteristics. However, system designer engineers are often interested in transmission line behavior within relatively narrow frequency bands rather than the full frequency spectrum. Consequently, simpler high-frequency LC (Inductor-Capacitor) or low-frequency RC (Resistor-Capacitor) models are often used in place of the generalized model. Figure 9.6 shows the same model for an infinitesimally small piece of transmission line as in Figure 9.5, but a closer examination of the characteristic impedance equation reveals that the equation can be simplified if the magnitude of the resistive component R is much smaller than or much greater than the magnitude of the frequency-dependent inductive component $j\omega L$. That is, in the case where the magnitude of R greatly exceeds $j\omega L$, the characteristic

impedance of the transmission line can be simplified as $Z_0 = \text{SQRT}(R/j\omega C)$,[2] hereafter referred to as the RC model. Conversely, in the case where the magnitude of the frequency-dependent inductive component $j\omega L$ greatly exceeds the magnitude of the resistive component R, the characteristic impedance of the transmission line can be simplified as $Z_0 = \text{SQRT}(L/C)$, hereafter referred to as the LC model. Given that the general transmission line model can be simplified into the LC model or the RC model, the key to choosing the correct model is to compute the characteristic frequency f_0 for the transmission line where the resistance R equals $j\omega L$. The characteristic frequency f_0 can be computed with the equation $f_0 = R / 2\pi L$. The simple rule of thumb that can be used is that for operating frequencies much above f_0, system designer engineers can assume a simplified LC transmission line model, and for operating frequencies much below f_0, system designer engineers can assume a simplified RC transmission line model. Due to the fact that signal paths on silicon are highly resistive, the characteristic frequency f_0 is much lower for silicon interconnects than system interconnects. As a result, the RC model is typically used for silicon interconnects on silicon, and the LC model is typically used for package-level and system-level interconnects.

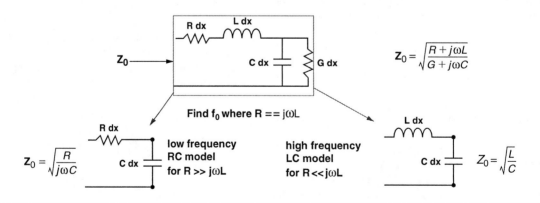

FIGURE 9.6: Simplified transmission line models.

---

[2]The conductive element G is assumed to be much smaller than $j\omega C$.

9.2.3   LC Transmission Line Model for PCB Traces

Figure 9.7 shows the cross section of a six-layer PCB. The six-layer PCB consists of signaling layers on the top and bottom layers with two more signaling layers sandwiched between two metal planes devoted to power and ground. Typically, inexpensive PC systems use only four-layer PCBs due to cost considerations, while more expensive server systems and memory modules typically use PCBs with six, eight, or more layers (on some systems, upwards of twenty-plus layers) for better signal shielding, signal routing, and power supplies.

Figure 9.7 also shows a close-up section of a trace on the uppermost signaling layer and the respective electrical characteristics of that signal trace. Given the resistive component of the signal trace as 0.003 Ω/mm and the inductance component of the signal trace as 0.25 nH/mm, the characteristic frequency of the signal trace can be computed as 1.9 MHz. That is, the signal traces on the illustrated PCB can be modelled effectively—to the first order—by relying only on the LC characteristics of the transmission line, since the edge transition frequencies of

signals in contemporary DRAM memory systems are considerably higher than 1.9 MHz.[3]

9.2.4   Signal Velocity on the LC Transmission Line

The electrical characteristics of the transmission line derived in Equations 9.1–9.11 and discussed in the previous section assert that typical PCB traces in modern DRAM memory systems can be typically modelled as LC transmission lines. In this and the following sections, properties of typical PCB traces are further examined to qualify signal traces found on contemporary PCBs from idealized LC transmission lines.

Figure 9.8 illustrates two important characteristics of the ideal LC transmission line: the wave velocity and the superposition property of signals that travel on the transmission line. In an ideal LC transmission line, the resistive element is assumed to be negligible, and signals can theoretically propagate down an ideal LC transmission line without attenuation. Figure 9.8 also shows that the signal propagation speed on an ideal lossless LC transmission line is a function of the

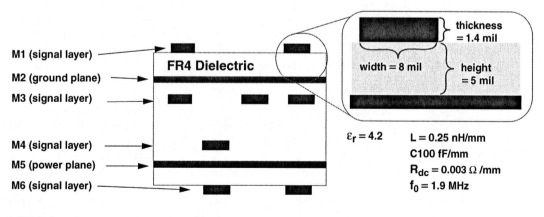

1 mil = 0.001 inch

FIGURE 9.7: Derivation of characteristic frequency for PCB traces.

---

[3]The frequency of interest here is not the operating frequency of the signals transmitted in DRAM memory systems, but the high-frequency components of the signals as they transition from one state to another.

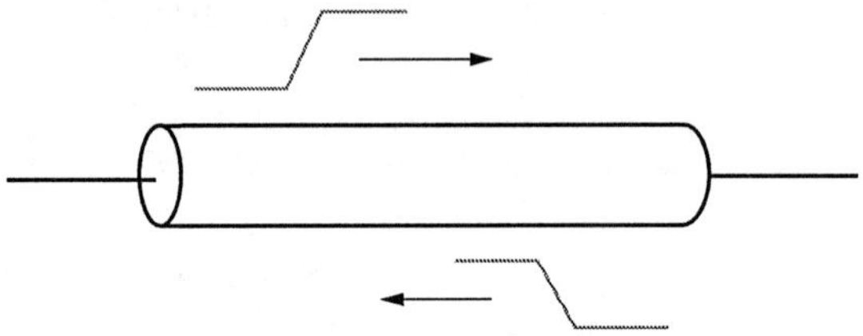

wave velocity

$$v = \frac{1}{\sqrt{LC}}$$

$$v = \frac{1}{\sqrt{(.25nH/mm * 100fF/mm)}}$$

$$v = 2 * 10^8 \ M/s$$

FIGURE 9.8: Idealized LC transmission line.

impedance characteristics of the LC transmission line, and signal velocity can be computed with the equation 1/SQRT(LC). Substituting in the capacitance and inductance values from Figure 9.7, the wave velocity of an electrical signal as it propagates on the specific transmission line is computed to be 200,000,000 M/s. That is, on the transmission line with the specific impedance characteristics, signal wave-fronts propagate at two-thirds the speed of light in vacuum, and signal wave-fronts travel a distance of 20 cm/ns.

Finally, in the lossless LC transmission line, signals can propagate down the transmission line without interference from signals propagating in the opposite direction. In this manner, the transmission line can support bidirectional signaling, and the voltage at a given point on the transmission line can be computed by the instantaneous superposition of the signals propagating on the transmission line.

9.2.5 Skin Effect of Conductors

The skin depth effect is a critical component of signal attenuation. That is, the resistance of a conductor is typically a function of the cross-sectional area of the conductor, and the resistance of a signal trace is typically held as a constant in the computation of transmission line characteristics. However, one interesting characteristic of conductors is that electrical current does not flow uniformly throughout the cross section of the conductor at high frequencies. Instead, current flow is limited to a certain depth of the conductor cross section when the signal is switching rapidly at high frequencies. The frequency-dependent current penetration depth is illustrated as the skin depth in

Figure 9.9. The net effect of the limited current flow in conductors at high frequencies is that resistance of a conductor increases as a function of frequency. The skin effect of conductors further illustrates that a lossless ideal LC transmission line cannot completely model a real-world PCB trace.

9.2.6 Dielectric Loss

The LC transmission line is often used as a first-order model that approximates the characteristics of traces on a system board. However, real-world signal traces are certainly not ideal lossless LC transmission lines, and signals do attenuate as a function of trace length and frequency. Figure 9.10 illustrates signal attenuation through a PCB trace as a function of trace length and data rate. The figure shows that signal attenuation increases at higher data rates and longer trace lengths. In the context of a DRAM memory system, a trace that runs for 10 inches and operates at 500 Mbps will lose less than 5% of the peak-to-peak signal strength. Moreover, Figure 9.10 shows that signal attenuation remains below 10% for the 10" trace that operates at data rates upward to 2.5 Gbps. In this sense, the issue of signal attenuation is a manageable issue for DRAM memory systems that operate at relatively modest data rates and relatively short trace lengths. However, the issue of signal attenuation is only one of several issues that system design engineers must account for in the design of high-speed DRAM memory systems and one of several issues that ensures the lossless LC transmission line model remains only as an approximate first-order model for PCB traces.

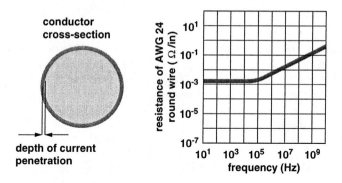

FIGURE 9.9: Illustration of skin depth in cross section of a circular conductor.

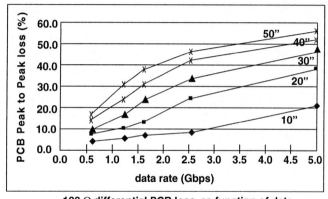

100 Ω differential PCB loss, as function of data
rate, PCB lengths from 10" to 50" (8 mil line width)

FIGURE 9.10: Attenuation factor of a signal on a PCB trace. Graph taken from North East Systems Associates Inc. Copyright 2002, North East Systems Associates Inc. with permission.

One common way to model dielectric loss is to place a distributed shunt conductance across the line whose conductivity is proportional to frequency. Most transmission lines exhibit quite a large metallic loss from the skin effect at frequencies well below those where dielectric loss becomes important. In most modern memory systems, signal reflection is typically a far more serious problem for the relatively short trace length, multi-drop signaling system. For these reasons, dielectric loss is often ignored, but its onset is very fast when it does happen. For DDR2

SDRAM and other lower speed memory systems (<1 Gbps), dielectric loss is not a dominant effect and can be generally ignored in the signaling analysis. However, in higher data rate memory systems such as the Fully Buffered DIMM and DDR3 memory systems, dielectric loss should be considered for complete signaling analysis.

The physics of the dielectric loss can be described with basic electron theory. The dielectric material between the conductors is an insulator, and electrons that orbit the atoms in the dielectric material are locked in place in the insulating material. When there is a difference in potential between two conductors, the excessive negative charge on one conductor repels electrons on the dielectric toward the positive conductor and disturbs the orbits of the electrons in the dielectric material. A change in the path of electrons requires more energy, resulting in the loss of energy in the form of attenuating voltage signals.

9.2.7 Electromagnetic Interference and Crosstalk

In an electrical signaling system, the movement of a voltage signal delivered through a transmission line involves the displacement of electrons in the direction of, or opposite to the direction of, the voltage signal delivery. The conservation of charge, in turn, means that as current flows in one direction, there must exist a current that flows in the opposite direction. Figure 9.11 shows that current flow on a transmission line must be balanced with current flow through a current return path back to the originating device. Collectively, the signal current and the return current form a closed-circuit loop. Typically, the return current flow occurs through the ground plane or an adjacent signal trace. In effect, a given signal and its current return path form a basic current loop where the magnitude of the current flow in the loop and the area of the loop determine the magnitude of the *Electromagnetic Interference* (EMI). In general, EMI generated by the delivery of a signal in a system creates inductive coupling between signal traces in a given system. Additionally, signal traces in a closely packed system board will also be susceptible to capacitive coupling with adjacent signal traces.

In this section, electronic noises injected into a given trace by signaling activity from adjacent traces are collectively referred to as *crosstalk*. Crosstalk may be induced as the result of a given signal trace's capacitive or inductive coupling to adjacent traces. For example, in the case where a signal and its presumed current return path (signal ground) are not routed closely to each other, and a different trace is instead routed closer to the signal trace than the current return path of the signal trace, this adjacent (victim) trace will be susceptible to EMI that emanates from the poorly designed current loop, resulting in crosstalk between the signal traces. The issue of crosstalk further deviates the modelling of real-world system board traces from the idealities of the lossless LC transmission line, where closely routed signal traces can become attackers on their neighboring signal traces and significantly impact the timing and signal integrity of these neighboring traces. The magnitude of the crosstalk injected by capacitively or inductively coupled signal traces depends on the peak-to-peak voltage swings of the attacking signals, the slew rate of the signals, the distance of the traces, and the travel direction of the signals.

To minimize crosstalk in high-speed signaling systems, signal traces are often routed closely with a dedicated current return path and are then routed with the dedicated current return path shielding active signal traces from each other. In this manner, the minimization of the current loop reduces EMI, and the spacing of active traces and the respective

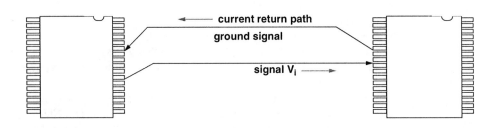

FIGURE 9.11: Voltage signal delivery and the return current, forming a current loop.

current return paths also reduces capacitive coupling. Unfortunately, the use of dedicated current return paths increases the number of traces required in the signaling system. As a result, dedicated shielding traces are typically found only in high-speed digital systems. For example, high-speed memory systems such as Rambus Corp's XDR memory system rely on differential traces over closely routed signaling pairs to ensure high signaling quality in the system, while lower cost, commodity-market-focused memory systems such as DDR2 SDRAM reserve differential signaling to clock signal and high-speed data strobe signals.

9.2.8 Near-End and Far-End Crosstalk

In general, two types of crosstalk effects exist in signal systems: near-end crosstalk and far-end crosstalk. These two types of crosstalk effects are, respectively, illustrated in Figures 9.12 and 9.13. Although Figures 9.12 and 9.13 illustrate crosstalk for capacitively coupled signal traces, near-end and far-end crosstalk effects are similar for inductively coupled signal traces. Figures 9.12 and 9.13 show that as a voltage signal travels from the source to the destination, it generates eletronic noises in an adjacent trace.

At each point on the transmission line, the attacking signal generates a victim signal on the victim trace. The victim signal will then travel in two directions: in the same direction as the attacker signal and in the opposite direction of the attacker signal. Figure 9.12 shows that the victim signal traveling in the opposite direction of the attacker signal will result in a relatively long duration, low-amplitude noise at the near (source) end of the victim trace.

In contrast, Figure 9.13 shows that the electronic noise traveling in the same direction as the attacker signal will result in a victim signal that is relatively short in duration, but high in amplitude at the far (destination) end of the victim signal trace. In essence, the near-end and far-end crosstalk effects can be analogized to the Doppler effect. That is, as the attacker signal wave front moves from the source to the destination on a given transmission line, it creates sympathetic signals in closely coupled victim traces that are routed in close proximity. The sympathetic signals that travel backward toward the source of the attacking signal will appear as longer wavelengths and lower amplitude noise, and sympathetic signals that travel in the same direction as the attacking signal will add up to appear as a short wavelength, high-amplitude noise.

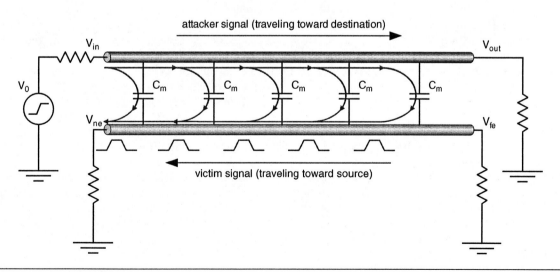

FIGURE 9.12: Near-end crosstalk.

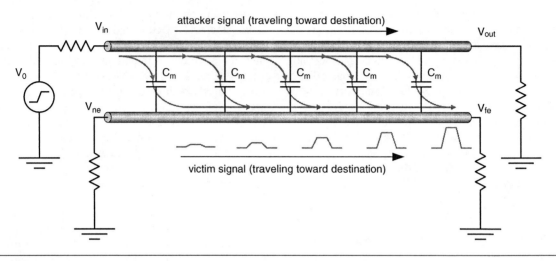

FIGURE 9.13: Far-end crosstalk.

Finally, an interesting general observation is that since the magnitude of the crosstalk depends on the magnitude of the attacking signals, an increase in the signal strength of one signal in the system would, in turn, increase the magnitude of the crosstalk experienced by other traces in the system, and the increase in signal strength of all signals in the system, in turn, exacerbates the crosstalk problem on the system level. Consequently, the issue of crosstalk must be solved by careful system design rather than a simple increase in the strength of signals in the system.

9.2.9 Transmission Line Discontinuities

In an ideal LC transmission line with uniform characteristic impedance throughout the length of the transmission line, a signal can, in theory, propagate down the transmission line without reflection or attenuation at any point in the transmission line. However, in the case where the transmission line consists of multiple segments with different characteristic impedances for each segment, signals propagating on the transmission line will be altered at the interface of each discontinuous segment.

Figure 9.14 illustrates that at the interface of any two mismatched transmission line segments, part of the incident signal will be transmitted and part of the incident signal will be reflected toward the source. Figure 9.14 also shows that the characteristics of the mismatched interface can be described in terms of the reflection coefficient ρ, and ρ can be computed from the formula $\rho = (Z_L - Z_S)/(Z_L + Z_S)$. With the formula for the reflection coefficient, the reflected signal at the interface of two transmission line segments can be computed by multiplying the voltage of the incident signal and the reflection coefficient. The voltage of the transmitted signal can be computed in a similar fashion since the sum of the voltage of the transmitted signal and the voltage of the reflected signal must equal the voltage of the incident signal.

In any classroom discussion about the reflection coefficient of transmission line discontinuities, there are three special cases that are typically examined in detail: the well-matched transmission line segments, the open-circuit transmission line, and the short-circuit transmission line. In the case where the characteristic impedances of two transmission line segments are matched, the reflection coefficient of that interface ρ is 0 and all of the signals are

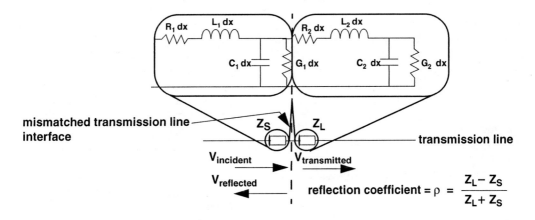

FIGURE 9.14: Signal reflection at an unmatched transmission line interface.

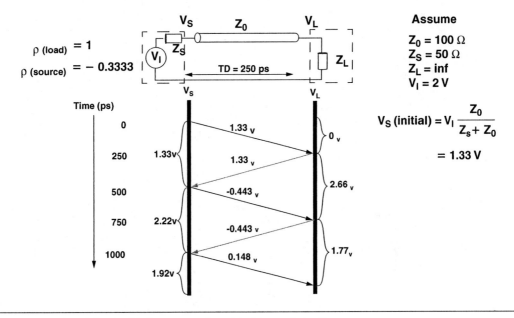

FIGURE 9.15: Illustration of signal reflection on a poorly matched transmission line.

transmitted from one segment to another segment. In the case that the load segment is an open circuit, the reflection coefficient is 1, the incident signal will be entirely reflected toward the source, and no part of the incident signal will be transmitted across the open circuit. Finally, in the case where the load segment is a short circuit, the reflection coefficient is −1, and the

incident signal will be reflected toward the source with equal magnitude but opposite sign.

Figure 9.15 illustrates a circuit where the output impedance of the voltage source is different from the impedance of the transmission line. The transmission line also drives a load whose impedance is comparable to that of an open circuit. In the circuit illustrated to the figure, there are three different segments, each with a different characteristic impedance. In this transmission line, there are two different impedance discontinuities. Figure 9.15 shows that the reflection coefficients of the two different interfaces are represented by ρ(source) and ρ(load), respectively. Finally, the figure also shows that the transmission line segment that connects the source to the load has finite length, and the signal flight time is 250 ps on the transmission line between the mismatched interfaces.

Figure 9.15 shows the voltage ladder diagram where the signal transmission begins with the voltage source driving a 0-V signal prior to time zero and switching instantaneously to 2 V at time zero. The figure also shows that the initial voltage V_S can be computed from the basic voltage divider formula, and the initial voltage is computed and illustrated as 1.33 V. The ladder diagram further shows that due to the signal flight time, the voltage at the interface of the load, V_L, remains at 0 V until 250 ps after the incident signal appears at V_S. The 1.33-V signal is then reflected with full magnitude by the load with the reflection coefficient of 1 back toward the voltage source. Then, after another 250 ps of signal flight time, the reflected signal reaches the interface between the transmission

line and the voltage source. The reflected signal with the magnitude of 1.33 V is then itself reflected by the transmission line discontinuity at the voltage source, and the re-reflected signal of −0.443 V once again propagates toward the load.

Figure 9.16 illustrates that the instantaneous voltage on a given point of the transmission line can be computed by the sum of all of the incident and reflected signals. The figure also illustrates that the superposition of the incident and reflected signals shows that the output signal at V_L appears as a severe ringing problem that eventually converges around the value driven by the voltage source, 2 V. However, as the example in Figure 9.16 illustrates, the convergence only occurs after several round-trip signal flight times on the transmission line.

9.2.10 Multi-Drop Bus

In commodity DRAM memory systems such as SDRAM, DDR SDRAM, and similar DDRx SDRAM, multi-drop busses are used to carry command, address, and data signals from the memory controller to multiple DRAM devices. Figure 9.17 shows that from the perspective of the PCB traces that carry

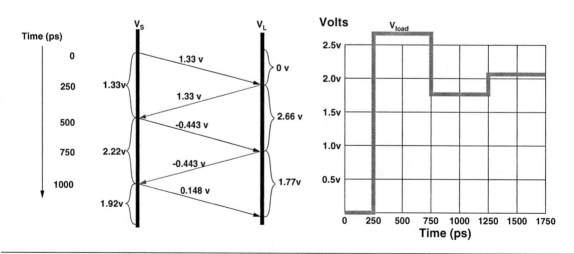

FIGURE 9.16: Signal waveform construction from multiple reflections.

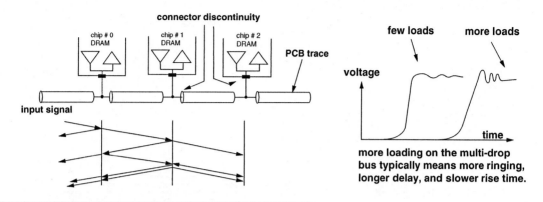

FIGURE 9.17: Multi-drop bus in a commodity DRAM memory system.

signals on the system board, each DRAM device on the multi-drop bus appears as an impedance discontinuity. The figure shows an abstract ladder diagram where a signal propagating on the PCB trace will be partly reflected and transmitted across each impedance discontinuity. Typical effects of signal propagation across multiple impedance discontinuities are more ringing, a longer delay, and a slower rise time.

The loading characteristics of a multi-drop bus, as illustrated in Figure 9.17, means that the effects of impedance discontinuities must be carefully controlled to enable a signaling system to operate at high data rates. As part of the effort to enable higher data rates in successive generations of DRAM memory systems, specifications that define tolerances of signal trace lengths, impedance characteristics, and the number of loads on the multi-drop bus have become ever more stringent. For example, in SDRAM memory systems that operate with the data rate of 100 Mbps, as many as eight SDRAM devices can be connected to the data bus, but in DDR3 SDRAM memory systems that operate with the data rate of 800 Mbps and above, the initial specification requires that no more than two devices can be connected to the same data bus in a connection scheme referred to as point-to-two-point (P22P), where the controller is specified to be limited to the connection of two DRAM devices located adjacent to each other.

9.2.11 Socket Interfaces

One feature that is demanded by end-users in commodity DRAM memory systems is the feature that allows the end-user to configure the capacity of the DRAM memory system by adding or removing memory modules as needed. However, the use of memory modules means that socket interfaces are needed to connect PCB traces on the system board to PCB traces on the memory modules that then connect to the DRAM devices. Socket interfaces are highly problematic for a transmission line in the sense that a socket interface represents a capacitive discontinuity for the transmission line, even in the case where the system only has a single memory module and the characteristic impedances of the traces on the system board and the memory module are well matched to each other.

To ensure that DRAM memory systems can operate at high data rates, memory system design engineers must carefully model each component of the memory system as well as the overall behavior of the system in response to a signal injected into the system. Figure 9.18 illustrates an abstract model of the data bus of a DDR SDRAM memory system, and it shows that a signal transmitted by the controller will first propagate on PCB traces in the system board. As the propagated signal encounters a socket interface, part of the signal will be reflected back toward the controller and part of the signal will continue

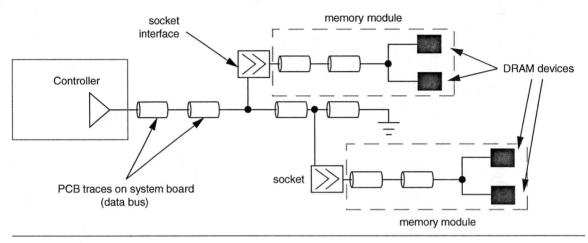

FIGURE 9.18: Transmission line representation of data bus in a DDR SDRAM memory system.

to propagate down the PCB trace, while most of the signal will be transmitted through the socket interface onto the memory module where the signal continues propagation toward the DRAM devices.

9.2.12 Skew

Figure 9.8 shows that wave velocity on a transmission line can be computed with the formula 1/SQRT(LC). For the transmission line with the specific impedance characteristics given in Figure 9.8, a signal would travel through the distance of 20 cm/ns. As a result, any signal path lengths that are not well matched to each other in terms of distances would introduce some amounts of timing skew between signals that travel on those paths.

Figure 9.19 illustrates the concept of signal skew in a poorly designed signaling system. In Figure 9.19, two signal traces carry signals on a parallel bus from the controller to modules labelled as module *A* and module *B*. Figure 9.19 shows that due to the poor design, path 1 which carries bus signal #1 is shorter than path 2 which carries bus signal #2. In this system, the different path lengths introduce static skew between bus signal #1 and bus signal #2.

In this chapter, *skew* is defined as the timing differential between two signals in a system. Skew can exist between data signals of a wide parallel data bus or between data signals and the clock signal. Moreover, signal skew can be introduced into a signaling system by differences in path lengths or the electrical loading characteristics of the respective signal paths. As a result, skew minimization is an absolute requirement in the implementation of high-speed, wide, and parallel data busses. Fortunately, the skew component of the timing budget is typically static, and with careful design, the impact of the data-to-data and data-to-clock skew can be minimized. For example, the PCB image in Figure 9.19 shows the trace routing on the system board of a commodity personal computer, and it illustrates that system design engineers often purposefully add extra twists and turns to signal paths to minimize signal skew between signal traces of a parallel bus.

9.2.13 Jitter

In the broad context of analog signaling, jitter can be defined as unwanted variations in amplitude or timing between successive pulses on a given signal line. In this chapter, the discussion on jitter is limited to the context of DRAM memory systems with digital voltage levels, and only the short-term phase variations that exist between successive cycles of a given signal are considered. For example, electronic

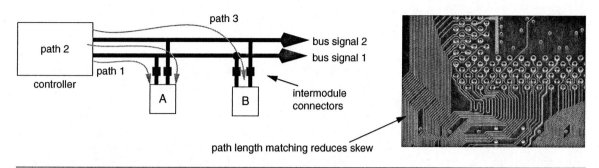

FIGURE 9.19: Mismatched path lengths introduces signal-to-signal skew, and PCB with path-length-matched signal traces.

components are sensitive to short-term variations in supply voltage and temperature, and effects such as crosstalk depend on transitional states of adjacent signals. Collectively, the impact of short-term variations in supply voltage, temperature, and crosstalk can vary dramatically between successive cycles of a given signal. As a result, the propagation time of a signal on a given signal path can exhibit subtle fluctuations on a cycle-by-cycle basis. These subtle variations in timing are defined as *jitter* on a given signal line.

To ensure correctness of operation, signaling systems account for timing variations introduced into the system by both skew and jitter. However, due to the unpredictable nature of the effects that cause jitter, it is often difficult to fully characterize jitter on a given signal line. As a result, jitter is also often more difficult than skew to deal with in terms of timing margins that must be devoted to account for the timing uncertainty.

9.2.14 Inter-Symbol Interference (ISI)

In this chapter, crosstalk, signal reflections, and other effects that impact signal integrity and timing are examined separately. However, the result of these effects can be summarized in the sense that they all degrade the performance of the signaling system. Additionally, multiple, consecutive signals on the same transmission line can have collective, residual effects that can interfere with the transmission of subsequent signals on the same transmission line. The intra-trace inference is commonly referred to as *inter-symbol interference* (ISI).

Inter-symbol interference is intrinsically a band-pass filter issue. The interconnect is a non-linear low-pass filter. The energy of the driver signal resides mostly within the third harmonic frequency. But the interconnect low-pass filter is non-linear, which causes the dispersion of the signal. In other words, a given signal that is not promptly removed from the transmission medium by the signal termination mechanism may disperse slowly and affect later signals that make use of the same transmission medium. For example, a single pulse has a long tail beyond its "ideal" pulse range. If there are consecutive "1"s, the accumulated tails may add up to overwrite the following "0." The net effect of ISI is that the interference degrades performance and limits the signaling rate of the system.

9.3 Termination

Previous sections illustrate that signal propagation on a transmission line with points of impedance discontinuity will result in multiple signal reflections, with one set of reflections at each point of impedance discontinuity. Specifically, the example in Figure 9.15 shows that in a system where the input impedance of the load[4] differs significantly from the characteristic impedance of the transmission line, the impedance discontinuity at the interface between the transmission line and the load results in multiple, significant signal reflections that delay the settle time of the transmitted signal. To limit the impact of signal reflection at the end of a transmission line, high-speed system design engineers typically place termination elements whose resistive value matches the characteristic impedance of the transmission line. The function of the termination element is to remove the signal from the transmission line and eliminate the signal reflection caused by the impedance discontinuity at the load interface. Figure 9.20 shows the placement of the termination element Z_T at the end of the transmission line. Ideally, in a well-designed system, the resistive value of the termination element, Z_T, matches exactly the characteristic impedance of the transmission line, Z_0. The signal is then removed from the transmission line by the termination element, and no signal is reflected toward the source of the signal.

9.3.1 Series Stub (Serial) Termination

The overriding consideration in the design and standardization process of modern DRAM memory systems designed for the commodity market is the cost of the DRAM devices. To minimize the manufacturing cost of the DRAM devices, relatively low-cost packaging types such as SOJ and TSOP are used in

SDRAM memory systems, and the TSOP is used in DDR SDRAM memory systems.[5]

Unfortunately, the input pin of the low-cost SOJ and TSOP packages contains relatively large inductance and capacitance characteristics and typically represents a poorly matched load for any transmission line. The poorly matched impedance between the system board trace and device packages is not a problem for DRAM memory systems with relatively low operating frequencies (below 200 MHz). However, the mismatched impedance issue gains more urgency with each attempt to increase the data rate of the DRAM memory system.

Figure 9.21 shows the series stub termination scheme used in DDR SDRAM memory systems. Unlike the ideal termination element, the series stub terminator is not designed to remove the signal from the transmission line once the signal has been delivered to the receiver. Rather, the series resistor is designed to increase the damping ratio and to provide an artificial impedance discontinuity that isolates the complex impedances within the DRAM package, resulting in the reduction of signal reflections back onto the PCB trace from within the DRAM device package.

9.3.2 On-Die (Parallel) Termination

The use of series termination resistors in SDRAM and DDR SDRAM memory systems to isolate the complex impedances within the DRAM

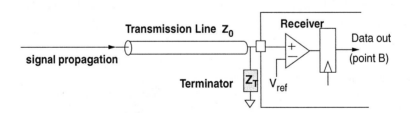

FIGURE 9.20: A well-matched termination element removes the signal at the end of the transmission line.

---

[4]In this case, the load is the receiver of the signal.

[5]SOJ stands for Small Outline J-lead, and TSOP stands for Thin Small Outline Package. Due to their proliferation, these packages currently enjoy cost advantages when compared to Ball Grid Array (BGA) type packages.

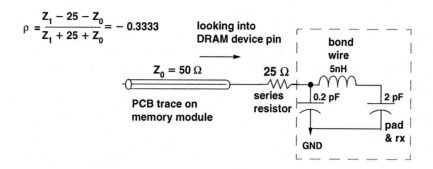

$$\rho = \frac{Z_1 - 25 - Z_0}{Z_1 + 25 + Z_0} = -0.3333$$

FIGURE 9.21: Series stub termination in DDRx SDRAM devices.

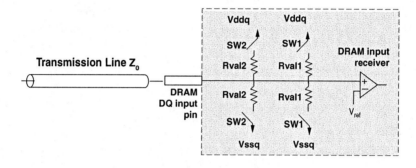

FIGURE 9.22: On-die termination scheme of a DDR2 SDRAM device.

device package means that the burden is placed on system design engineers to add termination resistors to the DRAM memory system. In DDR2 and DDR3 SDRAM devices, the use of the higher cost Fine Ball Grid Array (FBGA) package enables DRAM device manufacturers to remove part of the inductance that exists in the input pins of SOJ and TSOP packages. As a result, DDR2 and DDR3 SDRAM devices could then adopt an on-die termination scheme that more closely represents the ideal termination scheme illustrated in Figure 9.20.

Figure 9.22 shows that in DDR2 devices, depending on the programmed state of the control register and the value of the on-die termination (ODT) signal line, switches SW1 and SW2 can be controlled independently to provide different termination values as needed. The programmability of the on-die termination of DDR2 devices, in turn, enables the respective DRAM devices to adjust to different

system configurations without having to assume worst-case system configurations.

9.4 Signaling

In DRAM memory systems, the signaling protocol defines the electrical voltage or current levels and the timing specifications used to transmit and receive commands and data in a given system. Figure 9.23 shows the eye diagram for a basic binary signaling system commonly used in DRAM memory systems, where the voltage values V_0 and V_1 represent the two states in the binary signaling system. In the figure, t_{cycle} represents the cycle time of one signal transfer in the signaling system. The cycle time can be broken down into different components: the signal transition time t_{tran}, the skew and jitter timing budget t_{skew}, and the valid bit time t_{eye}.

To achieve high operating data rates, the cycle time, t_{cycle}, must be as short as possible. The goal in the design and implementation of a high-speed signaling system is then to minimize the time spent by signals on state transition, account for possible skew and jitter, and respect signal setup and hold time requirements. The voltage and timing requirements of the signaling protocol must be respected in all cases regardless of the existence of transient voltage noises such as those caused by crosstalk or transient timing noises such as those caused by temperature-dependent signal jitter. In the design and verification process of high-speed signaling systems, eye diagrams such as the one illustrated in Figure 9.23 are often used to describe the signal quality of a signaling system. A high-quality signaling system with properly matched and terminated transmission lines will minimize skew and jitter, resulting in eye diagrams with well-defined eye openings and minimum timing and voltage uncertainties.

9.4.1 Eye Diagrams

Figure 9.24 is an example that shows the practical use of eye diagrams. The eye diagram of a signal in a system designed without termination is shown on the left, and the eye diagram of a signal in a system designed with termination is shown on the right. Figure 9.24 illustrates that in a high-quality signaling system, the eye openings are large, with clearly defined voltage and timing margins. As long as the eye opening of the signal remains intact, buffers can

effectively eliminate voltage noises and boost binary voltage levels to their respective maximum and minimum values. Unfortunately, timing noises cannot be recovered by a simple buffer, and once jitter is introduced into the signaling system, the timing uncertainty will require a larger timing budget to account for the jitter. Consequently, a longer cycle time and lower data rate may be needed to ensure the correctness of signal transmission in the system—for a poorly designed signaling system.

9.4.2 Low-Voltage TTL (Transistor-Transistor Logic)

Figure 9.25 illustrates the input and output voltage response for a low-voltage TTL (LVTTL) device. The LVTTL signaling protocol is used in SDRAM memory systems and other DRAM memory of its generation, such as Extended Data-Out DRAM (EDO DRAM), Virtual Channel DRAM (VCDRAM), and Enhanced SDRAM (ESDRAM) memory systems. The LVTTL signaling specification is simply a reduced voltage specification of the venerable TTL signaling specification that operates with a 3.3-V voltage supply rather than the standard 5-V voltage supply.

Similar to the TTL devices, LVTTL devices do not supply voltage references to the receivers of the signals. Rather, the receivers are expected to provide internal references so that input voltages lower than 0.8 V are resolved as one state of the binary signal and input voltages higher than 2.0 V are resolved as the alternate state of the binary signal. LVTTL devices are expected

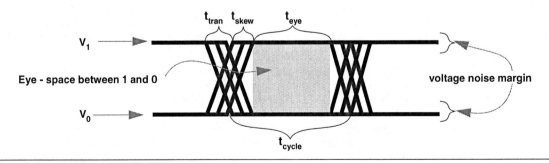

FIGURE 9.23: Eye diagram for binary signaling.

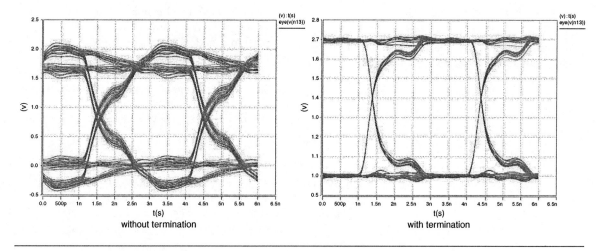

FIGURE 9.24: Eye diagrams of a signaling system with and without termination.

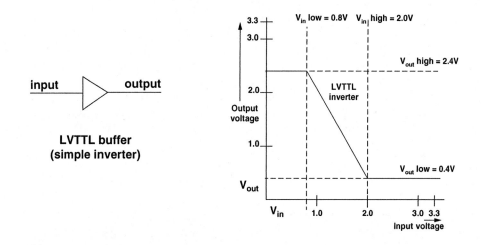

FIGURE 9.25: Inverter buffer and comparator input.

to drive voltage-high output signals above 2.4 V and low output signals below 0.4 V. For a LVTTL signal to switch state, the signal must traverse a large voltage swing. The large voltage swing and the large voltage range of undefined state between 0.8 and 2.0 V effectively limits the use of TTL and LVTTL signaling protocols to relatively low-frequency systems. For example, SDRAM memory systems are typically limited to operating frequencies below 167 MHz. Subsequent generations of DRAM memory systems have since migrated to more advanced signaling protocols such as Series Stub Terminated Logic (SSTL).

9.4.3 Voltage References

In modern DRAM memory systems, voltage-level-based signaling mechanisms are used to transport command, control, address, and data from the controller to and from the DRAM devices. However, for the delivered signals to be properly resolved by the receiver, the voltage level of the delivered signals must be compared to a reference voltage. While the use of implicit voltage references in TTL and LVTTL devices is sufficient for the relatively low operating frequency ranges and generous voltage range of the TTL and LVTTL signaling protocols, implicit voltage references are inadequate in modern DRAM memory systems that operate at dramatically higher data rates and with far smaller voltage ranges. As a result, voltage references are used in modern DRAM memory systems just as they are typically used in high-speed ASIC signaling systems.

Figure 9.26 illustrates two common schemes for reference voltage comparison. The diagram on the left illustrates the scheme where multiple input signal pins share a common voltage reference that is delivered by the transmitter along with the data signals. The diagram on the right shows differential signaling where each signal is delivered with its complement. The common voltage scheme is used in DRAM memory systems where low cost predominates over the requirement of high data rate, and differential signaling is used to achieve a higher data rate at the cost of higher pin count in high-speed DRAM memory systems. Aside from the advantage of being able to make use of the full voltage swing to resolve signals to one state or another, complementary pinpairs are always routed closely together, and the minimal distance allows differential pin pairs to exhibit superior common-mode noise rejection characteristics.

9.4.4 Series Stub Termination Logic

Figure 9.27 illustrates the voltage levels used in 2.5-V Series Stub Termination Logic signaling (SSTL_2). SSTL_2 is used in DDR SDRAM memory systems, and DDR2 SDRAM memory systems use SSTL_18 as the signaling protocol. SSTL_18 is simply a reduced voltage version of SSTL_2, and SSTL_18 is specified to operate with a supply voltage of 1.8 V.

Figure 9.27 shows that, unlike LVTTL, SSTL_2 signaling makes use of a common voltage reference to accurately resolve the value of the input signal. The figure further shows that where V_{ref} is set to 1.25 V, signals in the range of 0 to 1.1 V at the input of the SSTL_2 buffer are resolved as voltage low and signals in the range of 1.4 to 2.5 V are resolved as voltage high. In this manner, SSTL_2 exhibits better noise margins for the low-voltage range and nearly comparable noise margins for the high-voltage range when

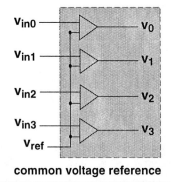

common voltage reference

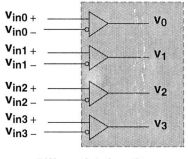

Differential signaling

FIGURE 9.26: Local and remote voltage references.

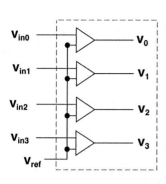

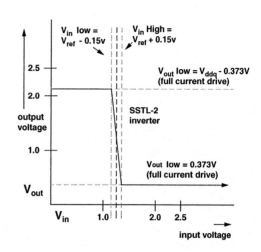

FIGURE 9.27: SSTL_2 voltage level illustration.

compared to LVTTL despite the fact that the supply voltage used in SSTL_2 is far lower than the supply voltage used in LVTTL.[6]

9.4.5 RSL and DRSL

In recent years, Rambus Corp. introduced two different signaling systems that are used in two different high-speed DRAM memory systems. The Rambus signaling level (RSL) signaling protocol was used in the Direct RDRAM memory system, and the differential Rambus signaling level (DRSL) signaling protocol was used in the XDR memory system. RSL and DRSL are interesting due to the fact that they are different from LVTTL and SSTL-x signaling protocols.

Figure 9.28 illustrates that both RSL and DRSL utilize low-voltage swings compared to SSTL and LVTTL. In SSTL and LVTTL signaling systems, signals swing the full voltage range from 0 V to V_{ddq}, enabling a common voltage supply level for the DRAM core as well as the signaling interface at the cost of longer signal switch times. In the RSL

signaling system, signals swing from 1.0 to 1.8 V; in the DRSL signaling system, signals swing from 1.0 to 1.2 V. While the low voltage swing enables fast signal switch time, the different voltage levels mean that the signaling interface must be carefully isolated from the DRAM core, thus requiring more circuitry on the DRAM device.

Finally, Figure 9.28 shows that similar to SSTL, RSL uses a voltage reference to resolve signal states, but DRSL does not use shared voltage references. Rather, DRSL is a bidirectional point-to-point differential signaling protocol that uses current mirrors to deliver signals between the memory controller and XDR DRAM devices.

9.5 Timing Synchronization

Modern digital systems, in general, and modern DRAM memory systems, specifically, are often designed as synchronous state machines. However, the address, command, control, data, and clock

---

[6]DDR SDRAM was originally only specified with speed bins up to 166 MHz at a supply voltage level, V_{ddq}, of 2.5 V. However, market trends and industry pressure led to the addition of the 200-MHz (400-Mbps) speed bin in DDR SDRAM memory systems. The 200-MHz DDR SDRAM memory system is specified to operate with a supply voltage, V_{ddq}, of 2.6 V.

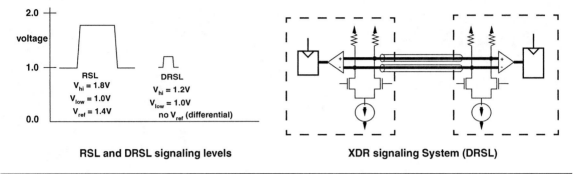

RSL and DRSL signaling levels   XDR signaling System (DRSL)

FIGURE 9.28: Rambus signaling levels (RSL and DRSL), and the DRSL signaling system.

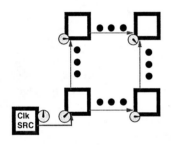

FIGURE 9.29: System-level synchronization with distributed clock signals.

signals in a modern high-speed DRAM memory system must all propagate on the same type of signal traces in PCBs. As a result, the clock signal is subject to the same issues of signal integrity and propagation delay that impact other signals in the system. Figure 9.29 abstractly illustrates the problem in high-speed digital systems, where the propagation delay of the clock signal may be greater than a non-negligible fraction of a clock period. In such a case, the notion of synchronization must be reexamined to account for the phase differences in the distribution of the clock signal.

In general, there are three types of clocking systems used in synchronous DRAM memory systems: a global clocking system, a source-synchronous clock forwarding system, and a phase or delay compensated clocking system. The global clocking system assumes that the propagation delay of the clock signal between different devices in the system is relatively minor compared to the length of the clock period. In such a case, the timing variance due to the propagation delay of the clock signal is simply factored into the timing margin of the signaling protocol. As a result, the use of global clocking systems is limited to relatively lower frequency DRAM memory systems such as SDRAM memory systems. In higher data rate DRAM memory systems such as Direct RDRAM and DDR SDRAM memory systems, the global clocking scheme is replaced with source-synchronous clock signals to ensure proper synchronization for data transport between the memory controller and the DRAM devices. Finally, as signaling data rates continue to climb, ever more sophisticated circuits are deployed to ensure proper synchronization for data transport between the memory controller and the DRAM devices. Specifically, *Phase-Locked Loop* (PLL) or *Delay-Locked Loop* (DLL) circuits are used in DRAM memory controllers to actively compensate for signal skew. In the following sections, the clocking schemes used in modern DRAM memory systems to enable system synchronization are examined.

9.5.1 Clock Forwarding

Figure 9.30 illustrates the trivial case where a reference clock signal is sent along with the data signal from the transmitter to the receiver. The clock forwarding technique is used in DRAM memory systems such as DDR SDRAM and Direct DRAM, where subsets of signals that must be transported in parallel from the transmitter to the receiver are routed with clock or strobe signals that provide the synchronization reference. For example, the 16-bit-wide data bus in Direct RDRAM memory systems is divided into two sets of signals with separate reference clock signals for each set, and DDR SDRAM memory systems provide separate DQ strobe signals to ensure that each 8-bit subset of the wide data bus has an independent clocking reference.

The basic assumption here is that by routing the synchronization reference signal along with a small groups of signals, system design engineers can more easily minimize variances in the electrical and mechanical characteristics between a given signal and its synchronization reference signal, and the signal-to-clock skew is minimized by design.

Figure 9.30 also shows that the concept of clock forwarding can be combined with more advanced circuitry that further minimizes signal-to-clock skew.

9.5.2 Phase-Locked Loop (PLL)

Two types of circuits are used in modern digital systems to actively manage the distribution and synchronization of the clock signal: a PLL and a DLL. PLLs and DLLs are used in modern high-speed DRAM devices to adjust and compensate for the skew and buffering delays of the clock signal. Figure 9.31 illustrates a basic block diagram of a PLL that uses an input clock signal and a *voltage-controlled oscillator* (VCO) in a closed-loop configuration to generate an output clock signal. With the use of the VCO, a PLL is capable of adjusting the phase of the output clock signal relative to the input clock signal, and it is also capable of frequency multiplication. For example, in an XDR memory system where the data bus interface

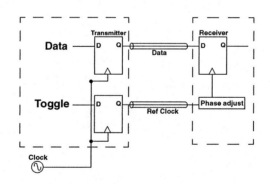

FIGURE 9.30: Clock forwarding.

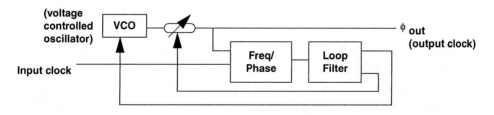

FIGURE 9.31: Basic PLL block diagram.

operates at a data rate of 3.2 Gbps, a relatively low-frequency clock signal that operates at 400 MHz is used to synchronize data transfer between the memory controller and the DRAM devices. In the XDR DRAM memory system, PLL circuits are used to multiply the 400-MHz clock frequency and generate a 1.6-GHz output clock signal from the slower input clock frequency. The devices in the XDR memory system then make use of the phase-compensated 1.6-GHz clock signal as the clock reference signal for data movement. In this manner, two silicon devices can operate synchronously at relatively high frequencies without the transport of a high-frequency clock signal on the system board.

PLLs can be implemented as a discrete semiconductor device, but they are typically integrated into modern high-speed digital semiconductor devices such as microprocessors and FPGAs. Depending on the circuit implementation, PLLs can be designed to lock in a range of input clock frequencies and provide the phase compensation and frequency multiplication needed in modern high-speed digital systems.

9.5.3 Delay-Locked Loop (DLL)

Figure 9.32 illustrates the basic block diagram of a DLL. The difference between the DLL and the PLL is that a DLL simply inserts a voltage-controlled phase delay between the input and output clock signals. In a PLL, a voltage-controlled oscillator synthesizes a new clock signal whose frequency may be a multiple of the frequency of the input clock signal, and the phase delay of the newly synthesized clock signal is also adjustable for active skew compensation. In this manner, while DLLs only delay the incoming clock signals, the PLLs actually synthesize a new clock signal as the output.

The lack of a VCO means that DLLs are simpler to implement and more immune to jitter induced by voltage supply or substrate noise. However, since DLLs merely add a controllable phase delay to the input clock signal and produce an output clock signal, jitter that is present in the input clock signal is passed directly to the output clock signal. In contrast, the jitter of the input clock signal can be better filtered out by a PLL.

The relatively lower cost of implementation compared to PLLs makes DLLs attractive for use in commodity DRAM devices designed to minimize manufacturing costs and in any application where clock synthesis is not required. Specifically, DLLs are found in DRAM devices such as DDRx SDRAM and GDDRx (Graphics DDRx) devices.[7]

9.6 Selected DRAM Signaling and Timing Issues

Signaling in DRAM memory systems is alike in many ways to signaling in logic-based[8] digital systems and different in other ways. In particular,

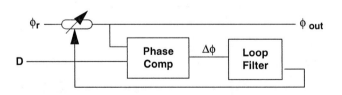

FIGURE 9.32: Basic DLL block diagram.

---

[7]DDRx denotes different generations of SDRAM devices such as DDR SDRAM, DDR2 SDRAM, and DDR3 SDRAM. Similarly, GDDRx denotes different generations of GDDR devices such as GDDR2 and GDDR3.

[8]Logic based, as opposed to memory based.

the challenges of designing high data rate signaling systems such as proper impedance matching, skew, jitter, and crosstalk minimization, as well as a system synchronization mechanism, are the same for all digital systems. However, commodity DRAM memory systems such as SDRAM, DDR SDRAM, and DDR2 SDRAM have some unique characteristics that are unlike high-speed signaling systems in non-DRAM-based digital systems. For example, in commodity DRAM memory systems, the burdens of timing control and synchronization are largely placed in the sophisticated memory controllers, and commodity DRAM devices are designed to be as simple and as inexpensive to manufacture as possible. The asymmetric master-slave relationship between the memory controller and the multiple DRAM devices also constrains system signaling and timing characteristics of commodity DRAM memory systems in ways not commonly seen in more symmetric logic-based digital systems.

Figure 9.18 illustrates the data bus structure of a commodity DRAM memory system. Figure 9.33 illustrates the command and address bus structure of the same DRAM memory system. Despite the superficial resemblance to the data bus structure illustrated in Figure 9.18, Figure 9.33 shows that in a commodity DRAM memory system, all of the DRAM devices within a DRAM memory system are typically connected to a given trace on the command and address bus. Figure 9.34 illustrates the topology of a typical

commodity DRAM memory system where the address and command busses are connected to every device in the system.

The difference in the loading characteristics means that signals propagate far slower on the command and address bus than on the data bus in a typical commodity DRAM memory system. To alleviate the constraints placed on timing by the large number of loads on the command and address busses, numerous strategies have been deployed in modern DRAM memory systems. One strategy to alleviate timing and signaling constraints on

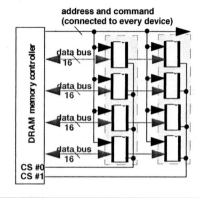

FIGURE 9.33: Typical topology of commodity DRAM memory systems such as DDRx SDRAM. Address and command busses are connected to every device.

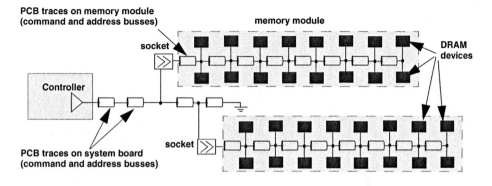

FIGURE 9.34: Transmission line model of DDR SDRAM memory system command and address busses.

the command and address buses is to make use of buffered or registered memory modules. For example, *registered dual in-line memory modules* (RDIMM) use separate buffer chips on the memory module to buffer command and address signals from the memory controller to the DRAM devices. Figure 9.35 illustrates that, from the perspective of the DRAM memory controller, the signal delivery path is limited to the system board through the socket interface and up to the input of the buffer chips on the memory modules. The buffer chips then drive the signal to the DRAM devices in a separate transmission line. The benefits of the buffer devices in the registered memory modules are shorter transmission lines, fewer electrical loads per transmission line, and fewer transmission line segments. The drawbacks of the buffer devices in the registered memory modules are higher cost associated with the buffer devices and the additional latency required for the address and command signal buffering and forwarding.

9.6.1 Data Read and Write Timing in DDRx SDRAM Memory Systems

Figure 9.33 illustrates that the command and address busses in a commodity DRAM memory system are typically more heavily loaded than the data bus, and timing margins are tighter on the command and address busses when compared to the data bus. Modern DDRx SDRAM memory systems capitalize on the lighter loading characteristics of the data bus by operating the data bus at twice the data rate as the command and address busses. The difference in operating the various busses at different data rates as well as the difference between the role of the DRAM memory controller and the commodity DRAM devices introduces several interesting aspects in the timing and synchronization of DDRx SDRAM devices. Figure 9.36 illustrates several interesting aspects of data read and write timing in commodity DDRx SDRAM devices: the use of a *Data Strobe Signal* (DQS) in DDRx SDRAM memory systems as the source-synchronous timing reference signal on the data bus, the

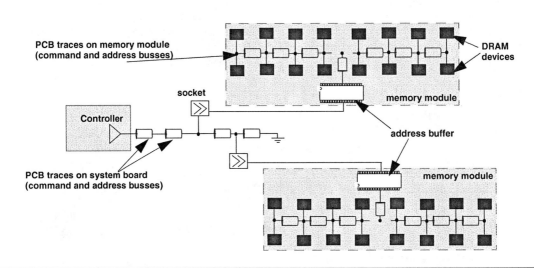

FIGURE 9.35: Register chips buffer command, control, and address signals in a Registered memory system.

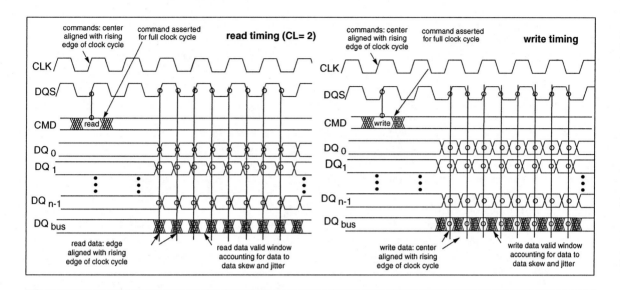

FIGURE 9.36: Column read, column write command and data timing in DDRx SDRAM memory systems.

transmission of symbols on half clock cycle boundaries on the data bus as opposed to full clock cycle boundaries on the command and address busses, and the difference in phase relationships between read and write data relative to the DQS signal.

First, Figure 9.36 illustrates that in DDRx SDRAM memory systems, address and command signals are asserted by the memory controller for a full clock cycle, while symbols on the data bus are only transmitted for half cycle durations. The doubling of the data rate on the data bus is an effective strategy that significantly increases bandwidth of the memory system from previous generation SDRAM memory systems without wholesale changes in the topology or structure of the DRAM memory system. However, the doubling of the data rate, in turn, significantly increases the burden on timing margins on the data bus. Figure 9.36 illustrates that valid data windows on the command, address, and data busses are constrained by the worst-case data skew and data jitter that exist in wide, parallel busses. Typically, in a DDRx SDRAM memory system with a 64-bit-wide data bus, the data bus is divided into smaller groupings of

8 signals per group, and a separate DQS signal is used to provide timing reference for each group of data bus signals. In this manner, the amount of timing budget allocated to account for skew and jitter is minimized on a group-by-group basis. Otherwise, much larger timing budgets would have to be allocated to account for skew and jitter across the entire width of the 64-bit-wide data bus. Figure 9.23 illustrates that where the timing budget devoted to t_{skew} increases, t_{cycle} must be increased proportionally, resulting in lower operation frequency.

Figure 9.36 also shows that read and write data are sent and received on different phases of the DQS signal in DDRx SDRAM memory systems. That is, DRAM devices return data bursts for read commands on each edge of the DQS signal. The DRAM memory controller then determines the centers of the valid data windows and latches in data at the appropriate time. In contrast, the DRAM memory controller delays the DQS signal by 90° relative to write data. The DRAM devices then latch in data relative to each edge of the DQS signal without shifting or delaying the data. One reason that the phase relationship between the read data and the DQS signal differs from the phase relationship between write data and the DQS signal is that the difference in the phase relationships shifts the burden of timing synchronization from the DRAM devices and places it in the DRAM memory controller. That is, the commodity DDRx SDRAM devices are designed to be inexpensive to manufacture, and the DRAM controller is responsible for providing the correct phase relationship between write data and the DQS signal. Moreover, the DRAM memory controller must also adjust the phase relationship between read data and the DQS signal so that valid data can be latched in the center of the valid data window despite the fact that the DRAM devices place read data onto the data bus with the same phase relative to the DQS signal.

9.6.2 The Use of DLL in DDRx SDRAM Devices

In DDRx SDRAM memory systems, data symbols are, in theory, sent and received on the data bus relative to the timing of the DQS signal as illustrated in Figure 9.30, rather than a global clock signal used by the DRAM memory controller. Theoretically, the DQS signal, in its function as the source-synchronous clocking reference signal, operates independently from the global clock signal. However, where the DQS signal does operate independently from the global clock signal, the DRAM memory controller must either operate asynchronously or devote additional stages to buffer read data returning from the DRAM devices. A complete decoupling of the DQS signal from the global clock signal is thus undesirable. To mitigate the effect of having two separate and independent clocking systems, on-chip DLLs have been implemented in DDR SDRAM devices to synchronize the read data returned by the DRAM devices, the DQS signals, and the memory controller's global clock signal. The DLL circuit in a DDR DRAM thus ensures that data returned by DRAM devices in response to a read command is actually returned in synchronization with the memory controller's clock signal.

Figure 9.37 illustrates the use of an on-chip DLL in a DDR SDRAM device, and the effect that the DLL has upon the timing of the DQS and data signals. The upper diagram illustrates the operation of a DRAM device without the use of an on-chip DLL, and the lower diagram illustrates the operation of a DRAM device with the use of an on-chip DLL. Where the DRAM device operates without an on-chip DLL, the DRAM device internally buffers the global clock signal and uses it to generate the source-synchronous DQS signal and return data to the DRAM memory controller relative to the timing of the buffered clock signal. However, the buffering of the clock signal introduces phase delay into the DQS signal relative to the global clock signal. The result of the phase delay is that data on the DQ signal lines is aligned closely with the DQS signal, but can be significantly out of phase alignment with respect to the global clock signal.

The lower diagram in Figure 9.37 illustrates that where the DRAM device operates with an on-chip DLL, the DRAM device also internally buffers the global clock signal, but the DLL then introduces more delay into the DQS signal. The net effect is to delay the output of the DRAM device by a full clock cycle so that the DQS signal along with the DQ data signals becomes effectively phase aligned to the global clock signal.

9.6.3 The Use of PLL in XDR DRAM Devices

In an effort devoted to the pursuit of high bandwidth in DRAM memory systems, the Rambus Corp. has designed several different clocking and timing synchronization schemes for its line of DRAM memory systems. One scheme utilized in the XDR memory system involves the use of PLLs in both the DRAM devices and the DRAM memory controller. Figure 9.38 abstractly illustrates an XDR DRAM device with two data pin pairs on the data bus along with a differential clock pin pair. The figure shows that the signals in the XDR DRAM memory system are transported via differential pin pairs. Figure 9.38 further illustrates that a relatively low system clock signal that operates at 400 MHz is used as a global clock reference between the XDR DRAM controller and the XDR DRAM device. The XDR DRAM device then makes use of a PLL to synchronize data latch operations at a higher data rate relative to the global clock signal. Figure 9.38 shows that the use of the PLL enables the XDR DRAM device to synchronize the transportation of eight data symbols per clock cycle. Moreover, the XDR DRAM controller contains a set of adjustable delay elements labelled as FlexPhase. The XDR DRAM

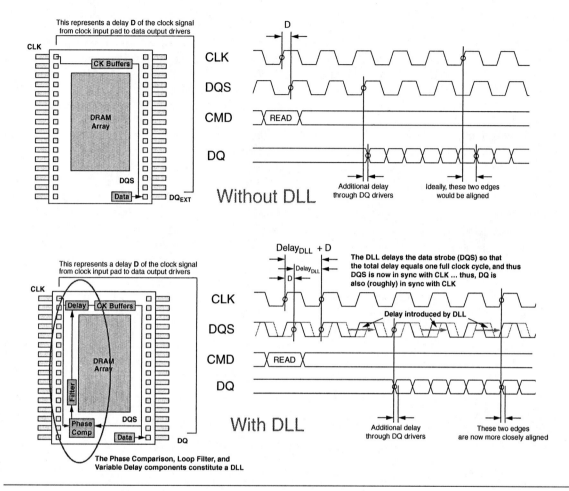

FIGURE 9.37: The use of DLL in DDRx SDRAM devices.

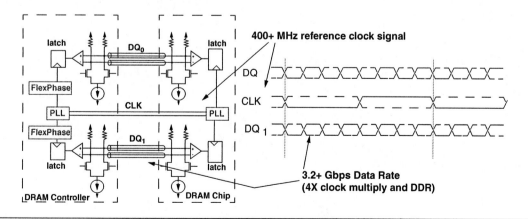

FIGURE 9.38: Use of PLL in XDR DRAM devices.

memory controller can set the adjustable delay in the FlexPhase circuitry to effectively remove timing uncertainties due to signal path length differentials. To some extent, the FlexPhase mechanism can also account for drift in skew characteristics as the system environment changes. The XDR memory controller can adjust the delay specified by the FlexPhase circuitry by occasionally suspending data movement operations and reinitializing the FlexPhase adjustable delay setting based on the transportation of predetermined test patterns.

9.7 Summary

This chapter covers the basic concepts of a signaling system that form the essential foundation for data transport between discrete devices. Specifically, the physical requirements of high data rate signaling in modern multi-device DRAM memory systems directly impact the design space of system topology and memory-access protocol. Essentially, this chapter illustrates that the task of transporting command, address, and data between the DRAM memory controller and DRAM devices becomes more difficult with each generation of DRAM memory systems that operate at higher data rates. Increasingly, sophisticated circuitry such as DLLs and PLLs is being deployed in DRAM devices, and the desire to continue to increase DRAM memory system bandwidth has led to restrictions to the topology and configuration of modern DRAM memory systems.

CHAPTER 10

DRAM Memory System Organization

Previous chapters examine the basic building blocks of DRAM devices and signaling issues that constrain the transmission and subsequent storage of data into the DRAM devices. In this chapter, basic terminologies and building blocks of DRAM memory systems are described. Using the building blocks described in the previous chapters, the text in this chapter examines the construction, organization, and operation of multiple DRAM devices in a larger memory system. This chapter covers the terminologies and topology, as well as the organization of various types of memory modules.

10.1 Conventional Memory System

The number of storage bits contained in a given DRAM device is constrained by the manufacturing process technology, the cell size, the array efficiency, and the effectiveness of the defect-cell remapping mechanism for yield enhancement. As the manufacturing process technology advances in line with Moore's Law, the number of storage bits contained in a given DRAM device doubles every few years. However, the unspoken corollary to Moore's Law states that software written by software companies in the Pacific Northwest and elsewhere will automatically expand to fill available memory in a given system. Consequently, the number of storage bits contained in a single DRAM device at any given instance in time has been and will continue to be inadequate to serve as the main memory for most computing platforms with the exception of specialty embedded systems.

In the past few decades, the growth rate of DRAM device storage capacity has roughly paralleled the growth rate of the size of memory systems for desktop computers, workstations, and servers. The parallel growth rates have dictated system designs in that multiple DRAM devices must be connected together to form memory systems in most computing platforms. In this chapter, the organization of different multi-chip DRAM memory systems and different interconnection strategies deployed for cost and performance concerns are explored.

In Figure 10.1, multiple DRAM devices are interconnected together to form a single memory system that is managed by a single memory controller. In modern computer systems, one or more *DRAM memory controllers* (DMCs) may be contained in the processor package or integrated into a system controller that resides outside of the processor package. Regardless of the location of the DRAM memory controller, its functionality is to accept read and write requests to a given address in memory, translate the request to one or more commands to the memory system, issue those commands to the DRAM devices in the proper sequence and proper timing, and retrieve or store data on behalf of the processor or I/O devices in the system. The internal structures of a system controller are examined in a separate chapter. This chapter focuses on the organization of DRAM devices in the context of multi-device memory systems.

10.2 Basic Nomenclature

The organization of multiple DRAM devices into a memory system can impact the performance of the

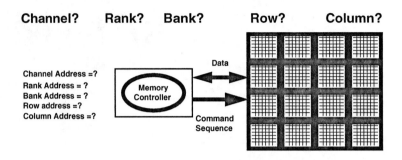

Channel? Rank? Bank? Row? Column?

Channel Address =?
Rank Address = ?
Bank Address = ?
Row address =?
Column Address =?

Memory Controller

Data

Command Sequence

FIGURE 10.1: Multiple DRAM devices connected to a processor through a DRAM memory controller.

memory system in terms of system storage capacity, operating data rates, access latency, and sustainable bandwidth characteristics. It is therefore of great importance that the organization of multiple DRAM devices into larger memory systems be examined in detail. However, the absence of commonly accepted nomenclature has hindered the examination of DRAM memory-system organizations. Without a common basis of well-defined nomenclature, technical articles and data sheets sometimes succeed in introducing confusion rather than clarity into discussions on DRAM memory systems. In one example, a technical data sheet for a system controller used the word *bank* in two bulleted items on the same page to mean two different things. In this data sheet, one bulleted item proclaimed that the system controller could support 6 *banks* (of DRAM devices). Then, several bulleted items later, the same data sheet stated that the same system controller could support SDRAM devices with 4 *banks*. In a second example, an article in a well-respected technical journal examined the then-new i875P system controller from Intel and proceeded to discuss the performance advantage of the system controller due to the fact that the i875P system controller could control 2 *banks* of DRAM devices (it can control two entire channels).

In these two examples, the word *bank* was used to mean three different things. While the meaning

of the word *bank* can be inferred from the context in each case, the overloading and repeated use of the word introduces unnecessary confusion into discussions about DRAM memory systems. In this section, the usage of channel, rank, bank, row, and column is defined, and discussions in this and subsequent chapters will conform to the usage in this chapter.

10.2.1 Channel

Figure 10.2 shows three different system controllers with slightly different configurations of the DRAM memory system. In Figure 10.2, each system controller has a single *DRAM memory controller* (DMC), and each DRAM memory controller controls a single channel of memory. In the example labelled as the *typical system controller*, the system controller controls a single 64-bit-wide channel. In modern DRAM memory systems, commodity DRAM memory modules are standardized with 64-bit-wide data busses, and the 64-bit data bus width of the memory module matches the data bus width of the typical personal computer system controller.[1] In the example labelled as *Intel i875P system controller*, the system controller connects to a single channel of DRAM with a 128-bit-wide data bus. However, since commodity DRAM modules have 64-bit-wide data busses,

---

[1]Commodity memory modules designed for error correcting memory systems are standardized with a 72-bit-wide data bus.

the i875P system controller requires matching pairs of 64-bit wide memory modules to operate with the 128-bit-wide data bus. The paired-memory module configuration of the i875P is often referred to as a *dual channel* configuration. However, since there is only one memory controller, and since both memory modules operate in lockstep to store and retrieve data through the 128-bit-wide data bus, the paired-memory module configuration is, logically, a 128-bit-wide single channel memory system. Also, similar to SDRAM and DDR SDRAM memory systems, standard

Direct RDRAM memory modules are designed with 16-bit-wide data busses, and high-performance system controllers that use Direct RDRAM, such as the Intel i850 system controller, use matched pairs of Direct RDRAM memory modules to form a 32-bit-wide channel that operates in lockstep across the two physical channels of memory.

In contrast to system controllers that use a single DRAM memory controller to control the entire memory system, Figure 10.3 shows that the Alpha EV7 processor and the Intel i925x system controller each have

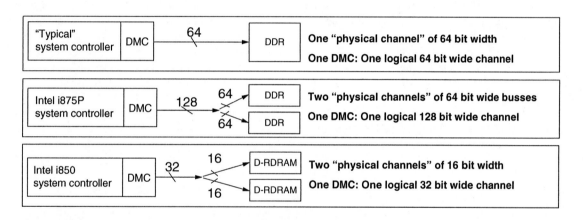

FIGURE 10.2: Systems with a single memory controller and different data bus widths.

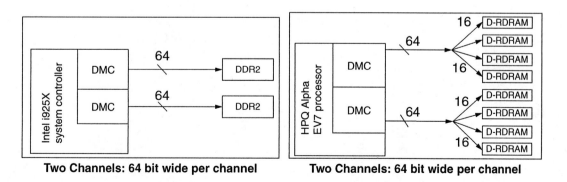

FIGURE 10.3: Systems with two independent memory controllers and two logical channels of memory.

two DRAM controllers that independently control 64-bit-wide data busses.[2] The use of independent DRAM memory controllers can lead to higher sustainable bandwidth characteristics, since the narrower channels lead to longer data bursts per cacheline request, and the various inefficiencies dictated by DRAM-access protocols can be better amortized. As a result, newer system controllers are often designed with multiple memory controllers despite the additional die cost.

Modern memory systems with one DRAM memory controller and multiple physical channels of DRAM devices such as those illustrated in Figure 10.2 are typically designed with the physical channels operating in lockstep with respect to each other. However, there are two variations to the single-controller-multiple-physical-channel configuration. One variation of the single-controller-multiple-physical-channel configuration is that some system controllers, such as the Intel i875P system controller, allow the use of mismatched pairs of memory modules in the different physical channels. In such a case, the i875P system controller operates

in an *asymmetric* mode and independently controls the physical channels of DRAM modules. However, since there is only one DRAM memory controller, the multiple physical channels of mismatched memory modules cannot be accessed concurrently, and only one channel of memory can be accessed at any given instance in time. In the asymmetric configuration, the maximum system bandwidth is the maximum bandwidth of a single physical channel.

A second variation of the single-controller-multiple-physical-channel configuration can be found in high-performance FPM DRAM memory systems that were designed prior to the emergence of SDRAM-type DRAM devices that can burst out multiple columns of data with a given column access command. Figure 10.4 illustrates a sample timing diagram of a column access in an SDRAM memory system. Figure 10.4 shows that an SDRAM device is able to return a burst of multiple columns of data for a single column access command. However, an FPM DRAM device supported neither single-access-multiple-burst capability nor the ability to pipeline multiple column access commands. As a result, FPM DRAM

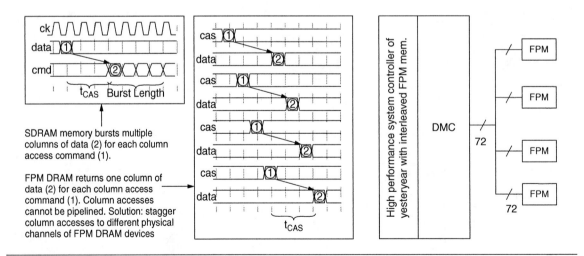

FIGURE 10.4: High-performance memory controllers with four channels of interleaved FPM DRAM devices.

---

[2]Ignoring additional bitwidths used for error correction and cache directory.

devices need multiple column accesses to retrieve the multiple columns of data for a given cacheline access, column accesses that cannot be pipelined to a single FPM DRAM device.

One solution deployed to overcome the shortcomings of FPM DRAM devices is the use of multiple FPM DRAM channels operating in an interleaved fashion. Figure 10.4 also shows how a sophisticated FPM DRAM controller can send multiple column accesses to different physical channels of memory so that the data for the respective column accesses appears on the data bus in consecutive cycles. In this configuration, the multiple FPM DRAM channels can provide the sustained throughput required in high-performance workstations and servers before the appearance of modern synchronous DRAM devices that can burst through multiple columns of data in consecutive cycles.

10.2.2 Rank

Figure 10.5 shows a memory system populated with 2 ranks of DRAM devices. Essentially, a *rank* of memory is a *"bank"* of one or more DRAM devices that operate in lockstep in response to a given command. However, the word *bank* has already been used to describe the number of independent DRAM arrays within a DRAM device. To lessen the confusion associated with overloading the nomenclature, the word *rank* is now used to denote a set of DRAM devices that operate in lockstep to respond to a given command in a memory system.

Figure 10.5 illustrates a configuration of 2 ranks of DRAM devices in a classical DRAM memory system topology. In the classical DRAM memory system topology, address and command busses are connected to every DRAM device in the memory system,

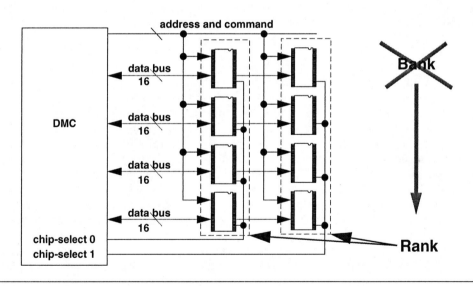

FIGURE 10.5: Memory system with 2 ranks of DRAM devices.

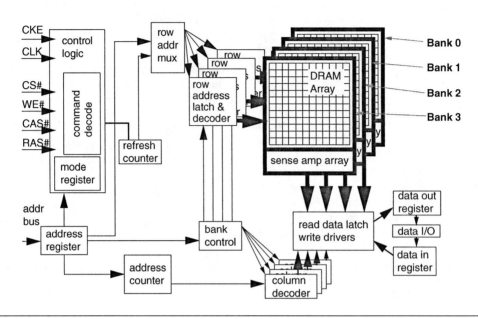

FIGURE 10.6: SDRAM device with 4 banks of DRAM arrays internally.

but the wide data bus is partitioned and connected to different DRAM devices. The memory controller in this classical system topology then uses chip-select signals to select the appropriate rank of DRAM devices to respond to a given command.

In modern memory systems, multiple DRAM devices are commonly grouped together to provide the data bus width and capacity required by a given memory system. For example, 18 DRAM devices, each with a 4-bit-wide data bus, are needed in a given rank of memory to form a 72-bit-wide data bus. In contrast, embedded systems that do not require as much capacity or data bus width typically use fewer devices in each rank of memory—sometimes as few as one device per rank.

10.2.3 Bank

As described previously, the word *bank* had been used to describe a set of independent memory arrays inside of a DRAM device, a set of DRAM devices that collectively act in response to commands,

and different physical channels of memory. In this chapter, the word *bank* is only used to denote a set of independent memory arrays inside a DRAM device.

Figure 10.6 shows an SDRAM device with 4 banks of DRAM arrays. Modern DRAM devices contain multiple banks so that multiple, independent accesses to different DRAM arrays can occur in parallel. In this design, each bank of memory is an independent array that can be in different phases of a row access cycle. Some common resources, such as I/O gating that allows access to the data pins, must be shared between different banks. However, the multi-bank architecture allows commands such as read requests to different banks to be pipelined. Certain commands, such as refresh commands, can also be engaged in multiple banks in parallel. In this manner, multiple banks can operate independently or concurrently depending on the command. For example, multiple banks within a given DRAM device can be activated independently from each other—subject to the power constraints of the DRAM device that may specify how closely such activations can occur in a given period of time. Multiple banks in a given DRAM device can also be precharged or refreshed in parallel, depending on the design of the DRAM device.

10.2.4 Row

In DRAM devices, a *row* is simply a group of storage cells that are activated in parallel in response to a row activation command. In DRAM memory systems that utilize the conventional system topology such as SDRAM, DDR SDRAM, and DDR2 SDRAM memory systems, multiple DRAM devices are typically connected in parallel in a given rank of memory. Figure 10.7 shows how DRAM devices can be connected in parallel to form a rank of memory. The effect of DRAM devices connected as ranks of DRAM devices that operate in lockstep is that a row activation command will activate the same addressed row in all DRAM devices in a given rank of memory. This arrangement means that the size of a row—from the perspective of the memory controller—is simply the size of a row in a given DRAM device multiplied by

the number of DRAM devices in a given rank, and a DRAM row spans across the multiple DRAM devices of a given rank of memory.

A *row* is also referred to as a DRAM page, since a row activation command in essence caches a page of memory at the sense amplifiers until a subsequent precharge command is issued by the DRAM memory controller. Various schemes have been proposed to take advantage of locality at the DRAM page level. However, one problem with the exploitation of locality at the DRAM page level is that the size of the DRAM page depends on the configuration of the DRAM device and memory modules, rather than the architectural page size of the processor.

10.2.5 Column

In DRAM memory systems, a column of data is the smallest addressable unit of memory. Figure 10.8 illustrates that, in memory systems such as SDRAM and DDRx[3] SDRAM with topology similar to the memory system illustrated in Figure 10.5, the size of

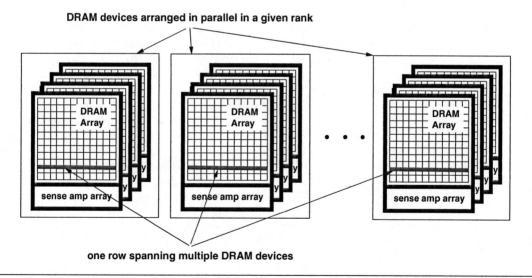

DRAM devices arranged in parallel in a given rank

DRAM Array

sense amp array

DRAM Array

sense amp array

DRAM Array

sense amp array

one row spanning multiple DRAM devices

FIGURE 10.7: Generic DRAM devices with 4 banks, 8196 rows, 512 columns per row, and 16 data bits per column.

[3]DDRx denotes DDR SDRAM and evolutionary DDR memory systems such as DDR2 and DDR3 SDRAM memory systems, inclusively.

DRAM devices arranged in parallel in a given rank

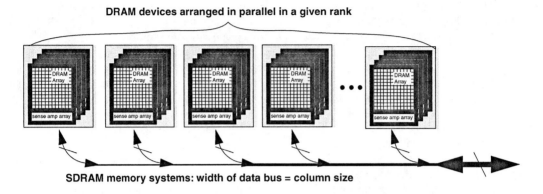

SDRAM memory systems: width of data bus = column size

FIGURE 10.8: Classical DRAM system topology; width of data bus equals column size.

a column of data is the same as the width of the data bus. In a Direct RDRAM device, a column is defined as 16 bytes of data, and each read command fetches a single column of data 16 bytes in length from each physical channel of Direct RDRAM devices.

A *beat* is simply a data transition on the data bus. In SDRAM memory systems, there is one data transition per clock cycle, so one beat of data is transferred per clock cycle. In DDRx SDRAM memory systems, two data transfers can occur in each clock cycle, so two beats of data are transferred in a single clock cycle. The use of the beat terminology avoids overloading the word *cycle* in DDRx SDRAM devices.

In DDRx SDRAM memory systems, each column access command fetches multiple columns of data depending on the programmed burst length. For example, in a DDR2 DRAM device, each memory read command returns a minimum of 4 columns of data. The distinction between a DDR2 device returning a minimum burst length of 4 *beats* of data and a Direct RDRAM device returning a single column of data over 8 beats is that the DDR2 device accepts the address of a specific column and returns the requested columns in different orders depending on the programmed behavior of the DRAM device. In this manner, each column is separately addressable. In contrast, Direct RDRAM devices do not reorder data within a given burst, and a 16-byte burst from a single channel of

Direct RDRAM devices is transmitted in order and treated as a single column of data.

10.2.6 Memory System Organization: An Example

Figure 10.9 illustrates a DRAM memory system with 4 ranks of memory, where each rank of memory consists of 4 devices connected in parallel, each device contains 4 banks of DRAM arrays internally, each bank contains 8192 rows, and each row consists of 512 columns of data. To access data in a DRAM-based memory system, the DRAM memory controller accepts a physical address and breaks down the address into respective address fields that point to the specific channel, rank, bank, row, and column where the data is located.

Although Figure 10.9 illustrates a uniformly organized memory system, memory system organizations of many computer systems, particularly end-user configurable systems, may be typically non-uniformly organized. The reason that the DRAM memory systems organizations in many computer systems are typically non-uniform is because most computer systems are designed to allow end-users to upgrade the capacity of the memory system by inserting and removing commodity memory modules. To support memory capacity upgrades by the end-user, DRAM controllers have to be designed to

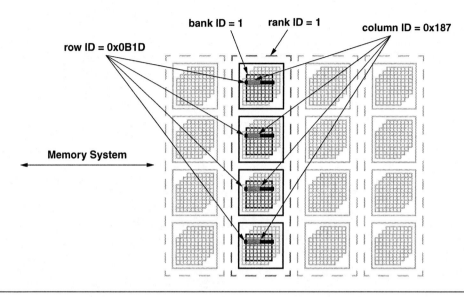

bank ID = 1   rank ID = 1   column ID = 0x187

row ID = 0x0B1D

Memory System

FIGURE 10.9: Location of data in a **DRAM** memory system.

flexibly adapt to different configurations of DRAM devices and modules that the end-user could place into the computer system. This support is provided for through the use of address range registers whose functionality is examined separately in the chapter on memory controllers.

10.3 Memory Modules

The first generations of computer systems allowed end-users to increase memory capacity by providing sockets on the system board where additional DRAM devices could be inserted. The use of sockets on the system board made sense in the era where the price of DRAM devices was quite expensive relative to the cost of the sockets on the system board. In these early computer systems, system boards were typically designed with sockets that allowed end-users to remove and insert individual DRAM devices, usually contained in dual in-line packages (DIPs). The process of memory upgrade was cumbersome and

difficult, as DRAM devices had to be individually removed and inserted into each socket. Pins on the DRAM devices may have been bent and not visually detected as such. Defective DRAM chips were difficult to locate, and routing of sockets for a large memory system required large surface areas on the system board. Moreover, it was physically possible to place DRAM devices in the wrong orientation in the socket—180° from the intended placement. Correct placement with proper orientation depended on clearly labelled sockets, clearly labelled devices, and an end-user that paid careful attention while inserting the devices into the sockets.[4] The solution to the problems associated with memory upgradability was the creation and use of memory modules.

Memory modules are essentially miniature system boards that hold a number of DRAM devices. Memory modules provide an abstraction at the module interface so that different manufacturers can manufacture memory upgrades for a given computer system with different DRAM devices. DRAM memory

---

[4]The author of this text can personally attest to the consequences of inserting chips into sockets with incorrect orientation.

modules also reduce the complexity of the memory upgrade process. Instead of the removal and insertion of individual DRAM chips, memory upgrades with modules containing multiple DRAM chips can be quickly and easily inserted into and removed from a module socket. The first generations of memory modules typically consisted of specially created, system-specific memory modules that a given computer manufacturer used in a given computer system. Over the years, memory modules have obtained a level of sophistication, and they are now specified as a part of the memory-system definition process.

10.3.1 Single In-line Memory Module (SIMM)

In the late 1980s and early 1990s, the personal computer industry first standardized on the use of 30-pin SIMMs and then later moved to 72-pin SIMMs. SIMMs, or *Single In-line Memory Modules,* are referred to as such due to the fact that the contacts on either side of the bottom of the module are electrically identical.

A 30-pin SIMM provides interconnects to 8 or 9 signals on the data bus, as well as power, ground, address, command, and chip-select signal lines between the system board and the DRAM devices. A 72-pin SIMM provides interconnects to 32 to 36 signals on the data bus in addition to the power, ground, address, command, and chip-select signal lines. Typically, DRAM devices on a 30 pin, 1 Megabyte SIMM collectively provide a 9-bit, parity protected data bus interface to the memory system. Personal computer systems in the late 1980s typically used sets of four matching 30-pin SIMMs to provide a 36-bit-wide memory interface to support parity checking by the memory controller. Then, as the personal computer system moved to support memory systems with wider data busses, the 30-pin SIMM was replaced by 72-pin SIMMs in the early 1990s.

10.3.2 Dual In-line Memory Module (DIMM)

In the late 1990s, as the personal computer industry transitioned from FPM/EDO DRAM to SDRAM, 72-pin SIMMs were, in turn, phased out in favor of *Dual In-line Memory Modules* (DIMMs). DIMMs are physically larger than SIMMs and provide a 64- or 72-bit-wide data bus interface to the memory system. The difference between a SIMM and a DIMM is that contacts on either side of a DIMM are electrically different. The electrically different contacts allow a denser routing of electrical signals from the system board through the connector interface to the memory module.

Typically, a DIMM designed for the commodity desktop market contains little more than the DRAM devices and passive resistor and capacitors. These DIMMs are not buffered on either the address path from the memory controller to the DRAM devices or the datapath between the DRAM devices and the memory controller. Consequently, these DIMMs are also referred to as *Unbuffered DIMMs* (UDIMMs).

10.3.3 Registered Memory Module (RDIMM)

To meet the widely varying requirements of systems with end-user configurable memory systems, memory modules of varying capacity and timing characteristics are needed in addition to the typical UDIMM. For example, workstations and servers typically require larger memory capacity than those seen for the desktop computer systems. The problem associated with large memory capacity memory modules is that the large number of DRAM devices in a memory system tends to overload the various multi-drop busses. The large number of DRAM devices, in turn, creates the loading problem on the various address, command, and data busses.

Registered Dual In-line Memory Modules (RDIMMs) alleviate the issue of electrical loading of large numbers of DRAM devices in a large memory system through the use of registers that buffer the address and control signals at the interface of the memory module. Figure 10.10 illustrates that registered memory modules use registers at the interface of the memory module to buffer the address and control signals. In this manner, the registers greatly reduce the number of electrical loads that a memory controller must drive directly, and the signal interconnects in the memory system are divided into two separate segments: between the memory controller and the register and between the register and DRAM devices. The segmentation allows timing characteristics of the memory system to be optimized by limiting the number of electrical loads, as well as by reducing the path lengths of the critical control signals in individual segments of the memory system. However, the drawback to the use of the registered latches on a memory module is that the buffering of the address and control signals introduces delays into the memory-access latency, and the cost of ensuring signal

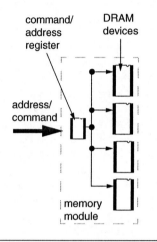

FIGURE 10.10: Registered latches buffer the address and command and also introduce additional latency into the DRAM access.

integrity in a large memory system is paid in terms of additional latency for all memory transactions.

10.3.4 Small Outline DIMM (SO-DIMM)

Over the years, memory module design has become ever more sophisticated with each new generation of DRAM devices. Currently, different module specifications exist as standardized, multi-source components that an end-user can purchase and reasonably expect trouble-free compatibility between memory modules manufactured by different module manufacturers at different times. To ensure system-level compatibility, memory modules are specified as part of the memory system standards definition process. More specifically, different types of memory modules are specified, with each targeting different markets. Typically, UDIMMs are used in desktop computers, RDIMMs are used in workstation and server systems, and the *Small Outline Dual In-line Memory Module* (SO-DIMM) has been designed to fit into the limited space found in mobile notebook computers.

Figure 10.11 shows the standardized placement of eight DDR2 SDRAM devices in *Fine Ball Grid Array* (FBGA) packages along with the required serial termination resistors and decoupling capacitors on

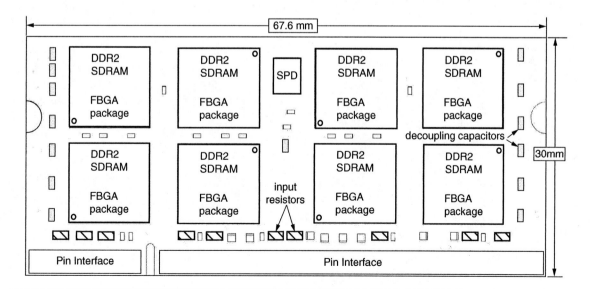

FIGURE 10.11: Component placement specification for a DDR2 SO-DIMM.

a 200-pin SO-DIMM. Figure 10.11 shows that the outline of the SO-DIMM is standardized with specific dimensions: 30 mm × 67.6 mm. The specification of the SO-DIMM dimension illustrates the point that as part of the effort to ensure system-level compatibility between different memory modules and system boards, mechanical and electrical characteristics of SO-DIMMs, UDIMMs, and RDIMMs have been carefully defined. Currently, commodity DRAM devices and memory modules are defined through long and arduous standards-setting processes by DRAM device manufacturers and computer-system design houses.

The standards-setting process enables DRAM manufacturers to produce DRAM devices that are functionally compatible. The standards-setting process further enables memory-module manufacturers to take the functionally compatible DRAM devices and construct memory modules that are functionally compatible with each other. Ultimately, the multi-level standardization enables end-users to freely purchase memory modules from different module manufacturers, using DRAM devices from different DRAM manufacturers, and to enjoy reasonably trouble-free interoperability. Currently, standard commodity DRAM devices and memory modules are specified through the industry organization known as the JEDEC Solid-State Technology Association.[5]

Finally, to further minimize problems in achieving trouble-free compatibility between different DRAM devices and memory module manufacturers, JEDEC provides reference designs to memory module manufacturers, complete with memory module raw card specification, signal trace routings, and a bill of materials. The reference designs further enable memory module manufacturers to minimize their expenditure of engineering resources in the process to create and validate memory module designs, thus lowering the barrier of entry to the manufacturing of high-quality memory modules and enhancing competition in the memory module manufacturing business.

10.3.5 Memory Module Organization

Modern DRAM memory systems often support large varieties of memory modules to give end-users the flexibility of selecting and configuring the desired memory capacity. Since the price of DRAM devices fluctuates depending on the unpredictable commodity market, one memory module organization may be less expensive to manufacture than another organization at a given instance in time, while the reverse may be true at a different instance in time. As a result, a memory system that supports different configurations of memory modules allows end-users the flexibility to purchase and use the most economically organized memory module. However, one issue that memory-system design engineers must account for in providing the flexibility of memory system configuration to the end-user is that the flexibility translates into large combinations of memory modules that may be placed into the memory system at one time. Moreover, multiple organizations often exist for a given memory module capacity, and memory system design engineers must often account for not only different combinations of memory modules of different capacities, but also different modules of different organizations for a given capacity.

Table 10.1 shows that a 128-MB memory module can be constructed from a combination of 16 64-Mbit DRAM devices, 8 128-Mbit DRAM devices, or 4 256-Mbit DRAM devices. Table 10.1 shows that the different memory-module organizations not only use different numbers of DRAM devices, but also present different numbers of rows and columns to the memory controller. To access the memory on the memory module, the DRAM controller must recognize and support the organization of the memory module inserted by the end-user into the memory system. In some cases, new generations of DRAM devices can enable memory module organizations that a memory controller was not designed to support, and incompatibility follows naturally.

---

[5]JEDEC was once known as the **J**oint **E**lectron **D**evice Engineering Council.

10.3.6 Serial Presence Detect (SPD)

Memory modules have gradually evolved as each generation of new memory modules gains additional levels of sophistication and complexity. Table 10.1 shows that a DRAM memory module can be organized as multiple ranks of DRAM devices on the same memory module, with each rank consisting of multiple DRAM devices, and the memory module can have differing numbers of rows and columns. What is not shown in Table 10.1 is that each DRAM memory module may, in fact, have different minimum timing characteristics in terms of minimum t_{CAS}, t_{RAS}, t_{RCD}, and t_{RP} latencies. The variability of the DRAM modules, in turn, increases the complexity that a memory-system design engineer must deal with.

To reduce the complexity and eliminate the confusion involved in the memory upgrading process, the solution adopted by the computer industry is to store the configuration information of the memory module on a read-only memory device whose content can be retrieved by the memory controller as part of the system initialization process. In this manner, the memory controller can obtain the configuration and timing parameters required to optimally access data from DRAM devices on the memory module. Figure 10.12 shows the image of a small flash memory device on a DIMM. The small read-only memory device is known as a *Serial Presence Detect* (SPD) device, and it stores a wide range of variations that can exist between different memory modules. Table 10.2 shows some parameters and values that are stored in the SPD of the DDR SDRAM memory module.

TABLE **10.1** Four different configurations for a 128-MB SDRAM memory module

Capacity	Device Density	Number of Ranks	Devices per Rank	Device Width	Number of Banks	Number of Rows	Number of Columns
128 MB	64 Mbit	1	16	x4	4	4096	1024
128 MB	64 Mbit	2	8	x8	4	4096	512
128 MB	128 Mbit	1	8	x8	4	4096	1024
128 MB	256 Mbit	1	4	x16	4	8192	512

serial presence detect (SPD)

FIGURE 10.12: The SPD device stores memory module configuration information.

TABLE **10.2** Sample parameter values stored in SPD

Configuration	Value (interpreted)
DRAM type	DDR SDRAM
No. of row addresses	16384
No. of column addresses	1024
No. of banks	4
Data rate	400
Module type	ECC
CAS latency	3

10.4 Memory System Topology

In Figure 10.13, a memory system where 16 DRAM devices are connected to a single DRAM controller is shown. In Figure 10.13, the 16 DRAM devices are organized into 4 separate *ranks* of memory. Although all 16 DRAM devices are connected to the same DRAM controller, different numbers of DRAM devices are connected to different networks for the unidirectional address and command bus, the bidirectional data bus, and the unidirectional chip-select lines. In this topology, when a command is issued, electrical signals on the address and command busses are sent to all 16 DRAM devices in the memory system, but the separate chip-select signal selects a set of 4 DRAM devices in a single rank to provide the data for a read command or receive the data for a write command. In this topology, each DRAM device in a given rank of memory is also connected to a subset of the width of the data bus along with three other DRAM devices in different ranks of memory.

Memory system topology determines the signal path lengths and electrical loading characteristics in the memory system. As a result, designers of modern high-performance DRAM memory systems must pay close attention to the topology and organizations of the DRAM memory system. However, due to the evolutionary nature of the memory system, the classic system topology described above has remained essentially unchanged for Fast Page Mode DRAM (FPM), Synchronous DRAM (SDRAM), and Dual Data Rate SDRAM (DDR) memory systems. Furthermore, variants of the classical topology with fewer ranks are expected to be used for DDR2 and DDR3 memory systems.

10.4.1 Direct RDRAM System Topology

One memory system with a topology dramatically different from the classical topology is the Direct RDRAM memory system. In Figure 10.14, four Direct RDRAM devices are shown connected to a single Direct RDRAM memory controller. Figure 10.14 shows that in a Direct RDRAM memory system, the DRAM devices are connected to a well-matched network of interconnects where the clocking network, the data bus, and the command busses are all path-length matched by design. The benefit of the well-matched interconnection network is that signal skew is minimal by design, and electrical signaling rates in the Direct RDRAM memory system can be increased to higher frequencies than a memory system with the classic memory system topology. Modern DRAM systems with conventional multi-rank topology can also match the raw signaling rates of a Direct RDRAM memory system. However, the drawback is that idle cycles must be designed into the access protocol and devoted to system-level synchronization. As a result,

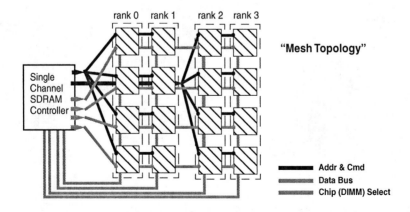

FIGURE 10.13: Topology of a generic DRAM memory system.

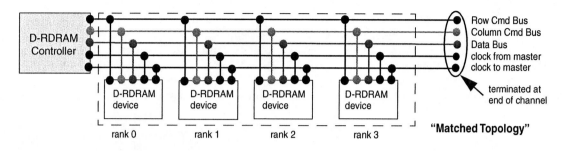

FIGURE 10.14: Topology of a generic Direct RDRAM memory system.

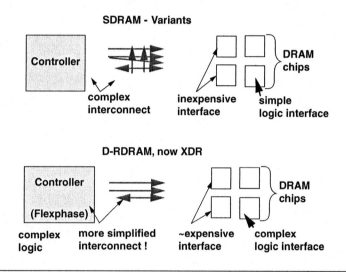

FIGURE 10.15: Philosophy differences.

even when pushed to comparable data rates, multi-rank DRAM memory systems with classical system topologies are somewhat less efficient in terms of data transported per cycle per pin.

The Direct RDRAM memory system achieves higher efficiency in terms of data transport per cycle per pin through the use of a novel system topology. However, in order to take advantage of the system topology and enjoy the benefits of higher pin data rates as well as higher data transport efficiency, Direct RDRAM memory devices are by design more complex than comparable DRAM memory devices that use the classic memory system topology. In DRAM devices, complexity translates directly to increased costs. As a result, the higher data transport efficiency of Direct RDRAM memory systems has to be traded off against relatively higher DRAM device costs.

10.5   Summary

Figure 10.15 shows the difference in philosophy of commodity SDRAM variant devices such as DDR SDRAM and high data rate DRAM memory devices such as Direct RDRAM and XDR DRAM. Similar to SDRAM variant memory systems, Direct RDRAM and XDR DRAM memory systems are engineered to allow tens of DRAM devices to be connected to a single DRAM controller. However, to achieve high signaling data rates, Direct RDRAM and XDR DRAM memory systems rely on the re-engineering of the interconnection interface between the memory controller and the DRAM devices. In these high data rate DRAM devices, far more circuitry is placed on the DRAM devices in terms of pin interface impedance control and signal drive current strength.

CHAPTER 11

Basic DRAM Memory-Access Protocol

The basic structures of modern DRAM devices and memory system organizations have been described in previous chapters. This chapter continues the examination of the DRAM memory system with a discussion on a basic DRAM memory-access protocol. A DRAM memory-access protocol defines commands and timing constraints that a DRAM memory controller uses to manage the movement of data between itself and DRAM devices. The basic DRAM memory-access protocol described in this chapter is generic in nature, and it can be broadly applied to modern memory systems such as SDRAM, DDR SDRAM, DDR2 SDRAM, and DDR3 SDRAM memory systems. The examination of the generic DRAM memory-access protocol begins by focusing on basic DRAM commands and the sequence of events that occurs in a DRAM device in the execution of the basic DRAM commands. Different DRAM memory systems, in particular, high-performance-oriented and low-power-oriented DRAM memory systems, have slightly differing access protocols. Specialized or high-performance DRAM memory systems such as Direct RDRAM, GDDRx, and FCRAM have slightly varying sets of DRAM commands and different command timings and interactions as those

described in this chapter. However, the fundamental command interactions in all DRAM memory systems are substantially similar to each other, and understanding of the basic DRAM memory-access protocol can aid in the understanding of more complex memory-access protocols in more specialized DRAM memory systems.

11.1 Basic DRAM Commands

A detailed examination of any DRAM memory-access protocol is a difficult and complex task. The complexity of the task arises from the number of combinations of commands in modern DRAM memory systems. Fortunately, a basic memory-access protocol can be modelled by accounting for a limited number of basic DRAM commands.[1] In this section, five basic DRAM commands are described. The descriptions of the basic commands form the foundation of the DRAM memory-access protocol examined in this chapter. The interactions of the basic DRAM commands are then used to determine the latency response and sustainable bandwidth characteristics of DRAM memory systems in this book.

---

[1]Modern DRAM devices such as Direct RDRAM and DDR2 SDRAM devices support larger sets of commands. However, most are used to manage the electrical characteristics of the DRAM devices, and only indirectly impacts access latency and sustainable bandwidth characteristics of a DRAM memory system at a given operating frequency. Commands such as those used to manage power-down states and self-refresh modes are not examined in this chapter for the sake of simplification.

Throughout this chapter, the SDRAM device illustrated in Figure 11.1 is used as the generic DRAM device for the purpose of defining the basic memory-access protocol. The generic DRAM memory-access protocol described in this chapter is based on a resource usage model. That is, the generic DRAM memory-access protocol assumes that two different commands can be fully pipelined on a given DRAM device as long as they do not require the use of a shared resource at a given time.[2] Figure 11.1 illustrates that in the movement of data in modern DRAM devices,

a given command would progress through different phases of operation to facilitate the movement of data, and in each phase, a given command would require the use of certain resources that often cannot be shared with a different command. Figure 11.1 illustrates four overlapped phases of operation for an abstract DRAM command. In phase 1, the command is transported through the address and command busses and decoded by the DRAM device. In phase 2, data is moved within a bank, either from the cells to the sense amplifiers or from the sense amplifiers

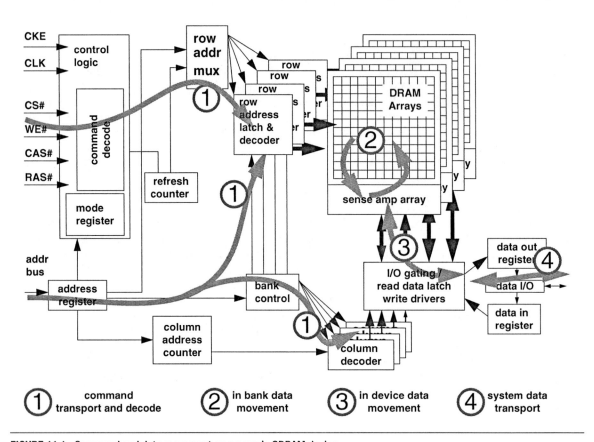

FIGURE 11.1: Command and data movement on a generic SDRAM device.

[2]Additional timing parameter constraints on the scheduling of DRAM commands such as t_{RRD} and t_{FAW} exist in addition to the resource-sharing based timing parameter constraints. These timing parameters are used to limit the maximum current draw of DRAM devices, so while the resource on the DRAM device is not used, these timing parameters limit the rate of resource utilization to limit peak power consumption characteristics on a given DRAM device.

back into the DRAM arrays. In phase 3, the data is moved through the shared I/O gating circuit and then through the read latches or write drivers, as appropriate in each case. In phase 4, read data is placed onto the data bus by the DRAM device in the case of a column-read command or by the memory controller in the case of a column-write command. Since the data bus may be connected to multiple ranks of memory, no two commands to different ranks of memory can use the shared data bus at the same instance in time.

A DRAM-access protocol also defines the timing constraints between combinations of consecutive DRAM commands. In this chapter, the description of the DRAM memory-access protocol begins with the examination of individual DRAM commands and progresses with the examination of combinations of DRAM commands. The impact of power-limitation-based constraints such as the row-to-row activation delay and the four-bank activation window are then described in detail in Sections 11.3.2 and 11.3.3, respectively.

11.1.1 Generic DRAM Command Format

Figure 11.2 illustrates the progression of a generic DRAM command. In Figure 11.2, the time period that it takes to transport the command from the DRAM controller to the DRAM device is illustrated and labelled as t_{CMD}. Figure 11.2 also illustrates $t_{parameter1}$, a generic timing parameter that measures the duration of "phase 2." In Figure 11.2, $t_{parameter1}$ defines the amount of time that the described command spends in the use of the selected bank, and $t_{parameter2}$ defines the amount of time that the described command spends in the use of resources common to multiple

banks of DRAM arrays in the same DRAM device. In this manner, $t_{parameter1}$ also denotes the minimum amount of time that must pass between the scheduling of two commands whose relative timing is limited by the sharing of resources within a given bank of DRAM arrays, and $t_{parameter2}$ also denotes the minimum amount of time that must pass between the start of two commands whose relative timing is limited by the sharing of resources by multiple banks of DRAM arrays within the same DRAM device.

DRAM commands are abstractly defined in this chapter, and the abstraction separates the actions of each command from the timing-specific nature of each action in specific DRAM-access protocols. That is, the abstraction enables the same set of DRAM command interactions to be applied to different DRAM memory systems with different timing parameter values. By abstracting out protocol-specific timing characteristics, DRAM commands can be described in abstract terms. The generic DRAM memory-access protocol, in turn, enables abstract performance analysis of DRAM memory systems that can then be broadly applied to different memory systems and retain relevance in the cross comparison.

11.1.2 Summary of Timing Parameters

The basic timing parameters used in the examination of the basic DRAM-access protocol are summarized in Table 11.1. The timing parameters summarized in Table 11.1 are far from a complete set of timing parameters used in the description of every modern DRAM memory-access protocol. Nevertheless, the limited set of timing parameters described in Table 11.1 is sufficient to characterize and illustrate

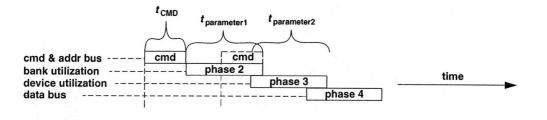

FIGURE 11.2: Different phase of an abstract DRAM command in a generic DRAM device.

the operations of a basic DRAM memory-access protocol of a modern DRAM memory system.

11.1.3 Row Access Command

Figure 11.3 abstractly illustrates the progression of a row access command. The row access command is also known as the row activation command. The purpose of a row access command is to move data from the cells in the DRAM arrays to the sense amplifiers and then restore the data back into the cells in the DRAM arrays as part of the same command. Two timing parameters are associated with a row access command: t_{RCD} and t_{RAS}. The time it takes for the row access command to move data from the DRAM cell arrays to the sense amplifiers is known as the *Row-Column (Command) Delay*, t_{RCD}. After t_{RCD} time from the assertion of the row access command, the entire row of activated data is held in the sense amplifiers, and subsequent column read or column-write commands can then move data between the sense amplifiers and the memory controller through the data bus.

TABLE **11.1** Summary of timing parameters used in a generic DRAM-access protocol

Parameter	Description	Illustration
t_{AL}	Added Latency to column accesses, used in DDRx SDRAM devices for posted CAS commands.	Figure 11.11
t_{BURST}	Data burst duration. The time period that data burst occupies on the data bus. Typically 4 or 8 beats of data. In DDR SDRAM, 4 beats of data occupy 2 full clock cycles.	Figure 11.4
t_{CAS}	Column Access Strobe latency. The time interval between column access command and the start of data return by the DRAM device(s). Also known as t_{CL}.	Figure 11.4
t_{CCD}	Column-to-Column Delay. The minimum column command timing, determined by internal burst (prefetch) length. Multiple internal bursts are used to form longer burst for column reads. t_{CCD} is 2 beats (1 cycle) for DDR SDRAM, and 4 beats (2 cycles) for DDR2 SDRAM.	Figure 11.4
t_{CMD}	Command transport duration. The time period that a command occupies on the command bus as it is transported from the DRAM controller to the DRAM devices.	Figure 11.2
t_{CWD}	Column Write Delay. The time interval between issuance of the column-write command and placement of data on the data bus by the DRAM controller.	Figure 11.5
t_{FAW}	Four (row) bank Activation Window. A rolling time-frame in which a maximum of four-bank activation can be engaged. Limits peak current profile in DDR2 and DDR3 devices with more than 4 banks.	Figure 11.32
t_{OST}	ODT Switching Time. The time interval to switching ODT control from rank to rank.	Figure 11.19
t_{RAS}	Row Access Strobe. The time interval between row access command and data restoration in a DRAM array. A DRAM bank cannot be precharged until at least t_{RAS} time after the previous bank activation.	Figure 11.3
t_{RC}	Row Cycle. The time interval between accesses to different rows in a bank. $t_{RC} = t_{RAS} + t_{RP}$.	Figure 11.6
t_{RCD}	Row to Column command Delay. The time interval between row access and data ready at sense amplifiers.	Figure 11.3
t_{RFC}	Refresh Cycle time. The time interval between Refresh and Activation commands.	Figure 11.7
t_{RP}	Row Precharge. The time interval that it takes for a DRAM array to be precharged for another row access.	Figure 11.6

(continued)

TABLE **11.1**   (*continued*)

Parameter	Description	Illustration
t_{RRD}	Row activation to Row activation Delay. The minimum time interval between two row activation commands to the same DRAM device. Limits peak current profile.	Figure 11.32
t_{RTP}	Read to Precharge. The time interval between a read and a precharge command.	Figure 11.13
t_{RTRS}	Rank-to-rank switching time. Used in DDR and DDR2 SDRAM memory systems; not used in SDRAM or Direct RDRAM memory systems. One full cycle in DDR SDRAM.	Figure 11.18
t_{WR}	Write Recovery time. The minimum time interval between the end of a write data burst and the start of a precharge command. Allows sense amplifiers to restore data to cells.	Figure 11.5
t_{WTR}	Write To Read delay time. The minimum time interval between the end of a write data burst and the start of a column-read command. Allows I/O gating to overdrive sense amplifiers before read command starts.	Figure 11.5

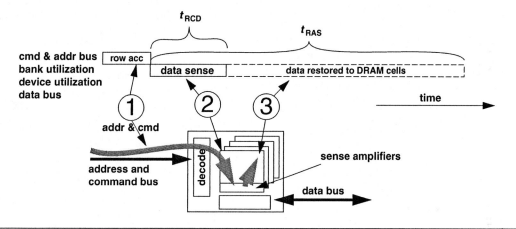

FIGURE 11.3: Row access command and timing.

After t_{RCD} time from the assertion of the row access command, data is available at the sense amplifiers, but not yet fully restored to the DRAM cells. The time it takes for a row access command to discharge and restore data from the row of DRAM cells is known as the *Row Access Strobe latency* or t_{RAS}. After t_{RAS} time from the assertion of the row access command, the sense amplifiers are assumed to have completed data restoration to the DRAM arrays, and the sense amplifiers can then be precharged for another row access to a different row in the same bank of DRAM arrays.

11.1.4 Column-Read Command

Figure 11.4 illustrates the progression of a column-read command. A column-read command moves data from the array of sense amplifiers of a given bank of DRAM arrays through the data bus back to the memory controller. Three basic timing parameters are associated with a column-read command: t_{CAS}, t_{CCD}, and t_{BURST}. The *Column Access Strobe Latency* (t_{CAS}, or t_{CL}) is the time it takes for the DRAM device to place the requested data onto the data bus after issuance of the column-read command. Modern DRAM devices move data internally in short and continuous bursts. Figure 11.4 illustrates the case where the DRAM device internally moves the data in two short burst durations, but data is placed onto the data bus in a longer, continuous burst. The internal burst length of the DRAM device is labelled as t_{CCD} in Figure 11.4, and the duration of the data burst on the data bus for a single column-read command is labelled as t_{BURST}. The timing parameter t_{CCD} represents the timing of minimum burst duration, or minimum column-to-column command timing. The minimum burst duration is determined by the prefetch length of the DRAM device. For example, the prefetch length of the DDR SDRAM device is 2 beats of data, so t_{CCD} is one full clock cycle in DDR SDRAM devices; the prefetch length of the DDR2 SDRAM device is 4 beats of data, so t_{CCD} is two full clock cycles in DDR2 SDRAM devices; and so on.

The difference in the prefetch length of column access commands has limited impact on the generic memory-access protocol as long as t_{CCD} is shorter than t_{BURST}. In the case where t_{CCD} is longer than t_{BURST}, the intra-rank column access commands are limited by t_{CCD} rather than t_{BURST}. Otherwise, the only case where the differences in the prefetch lengths impact the memory-access protocol occurs when the column-read command is followed immediately by a precharge command. The read-to-precharge timing is examined separately in Section 11.2.2.

11.1.5 Column-Write Command

Figure 11.5 illustrates the progression of a column-write command. A column-write command moves data from the memory controller to the sense amplifiers of the targeted bank. The column-write command goes through a similar set of overlapped phases as the column-read command, but the direction of data movement differs between a column-read command and a column-write command. As a result, the ordering of the phases is reversed between the column-read and the column-write commands.

One timing parameter associated with a column-write command is t_{CWD}, *column write delay*. The column-write delay specifies the timing between assertion of the column-write command on the command bus and the placement of the write data onto the data bus by the memory controller. Different memory-access protocols have different settings for t_{CWD}. Figure 11.5 shows that in SDRAM devices, write data is placed onto the data bus at the same time as the column-write command, and t_{CWD} is zero. In DDR SDRAM devices, t_{CWD} is specified as one clock cycle in the memory system. In DDR2 SDRAM memory-access protocol, t_{CWD} is specified as one cycle less than t_{CAS}, and t_{CWD} has a range of programmability in the DDR3 SDRAM memory-access protocol between five and eight cycles. Finally, Figure 11.5 also illustrates t_{WR}, the write recovery time, and

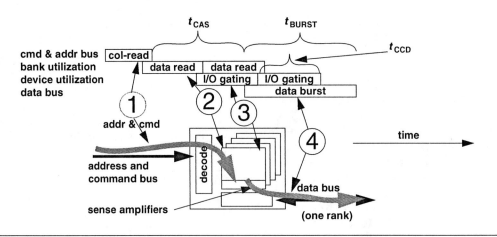

FIGURE 11.4: Column-read command and timing.

t_{WTR}, the write-to-read turnaround time. The write recovery time, t_{WR}, is the time it takes for the write data to propagate into the DRAM arrays, and it must be respected in the case of a precharge command that follows the write command. The write-to-read time, t_{WTR}, accounts for the time that the I/O gating resources are released by the write command, and it must be respected in the case of a read command that follows the write command.

11.1.6 Precharge Command

Data access in a typical DRAM device is composed of a two-step process. First, a row access command moves data from the array of DRAM cells to the array of sense amplifiers. Then, after an entire row of data is moved into the sense amplifiers by the row access command, that data is cached by the sense amplifiers for subsequent column access commands to move data between the DRAM device and the DRAM controller. The precharge command completes the row access sequence as it resets the sense amplifiers and the bitlines and prepares them for another row access command to the same array of DRAM cells. Figure 11.6 illustrates the progression of a precharge command. The timing parameter associated with the (row) precharge command is t_{RP}. That is, t_{RP} time after the assertion of the precharge command, the

bitlines and sense amplifiers of the selected bank are properly precharged, and a subsequent row access command can be sent to the just-precharged bank of DRAM cells.

The two row-access-related timing parameters, t_{RP} and t_{RAS}, can be combined to form t_{RC}, the row cycle time. The row cycle time of a given DRAM device denotes the minimum amount of time that a DRAM device needs to bring data from the DRAM cell arrays into the sense amplifiers, restore the data to the DRAM cells, and precharge the bitlines to the reference voltage level for another row access command. The row cycle time is the fundamental limitation to the speed at which data can be retrieved from different rows within the same DRAM bank. As a result, t_{RC} is also commonly referred to as the random row-cycle time of a DRAM device.

11.1.7 Refresh Command

The word "DRAM" is an acronym for Dynamic Random-Access Memory. The nature of the non-persistent charge storage in the DRAM cells means that the electrical charge stored in the storage capacitors will gradually leak out through the access transistors. Consequently, to maintain data integrity, data values stored in DRAM cells must be periodically read out and restored to their respective, full voltage level before the

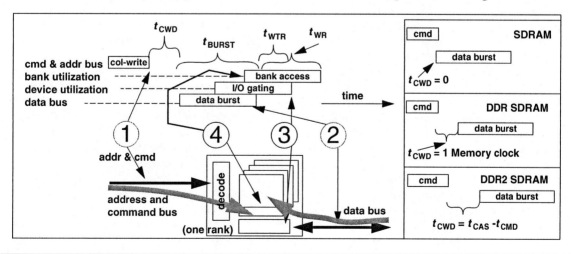

FIGURE 11.5: Column-write command and timing for DDR SDRAM and DDR2 SDRAM devices.

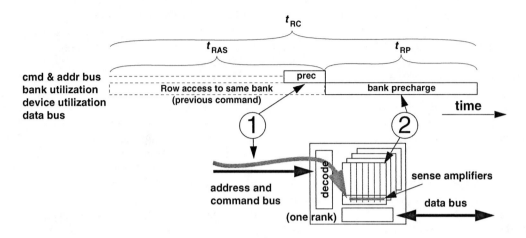

FIGURE 11.6: Row precharge command and timing.

stored electrical charges decay to indistinguishable levels. The refresh command accomplishes the task of data read-out and restoration in DRAM devices, and as long as the time interval between refresh commands made to a given row of a DRAM array is shorter than the worst-case data decay time, DRAM refresh commands can be used to ensure data integrity. The drawback to the refresh mechanism is that the refresh action consumes available bandwidth and power. Consequently, different refresh mechanisms are used in different systems; some are designed to minimize controller complexity, and some are designed to minimize bandwidth impact, while still others are designed to minimize power consumption.

To simplify the control complexity associated with the refresh command, most DRAM devices use a refresh row address register to keep track of the address of the last refreshed row. Typically, the memory controller sends a single refresh command to the DRAM device, and the DRAM device increments the address in the refresh row address register and goes through a row cycle for all rows with that row address in all of the banks in the DRAM device. Figure 11.7 illustrates a basic all-banks-concurrent refresh command that modern DRAM memory controllers use to send a single refresh command to refresh one row of DRAM cells in all banks. When this all-banks-concurrent basic refresh command is issued, the DRAM device takes the row address from the refresh address register and then sends the same row address to all banks to be refreshed concurrently. As illustrated in Figure 11.7, the single refresh command to all banks takes one refresh cycle time t_{RFC} to complete.

Table 11.2 shows the general trend of refresh cycle times in DDR and DDR2 SDRAM devices. With increasing DRAM device density, an increasing number of DRAM cells must be refreshed. The choice that DRAM manufacturers have apparently made, for larger DDR2 devices, is to keep the number of refresh commands per 64-ms period constant despite the doubling of the number of rows in successive generations of higher capacity DRAM devices. Consequently, regardless of the capacity of the DRAM device in the system, the memory controller will send 8192 refresh commands to the DRAM device every 64 ms. However, in high-capacity DRAM devices, there are more than 8192 rows, and each refresh command must refresh 2, 4, or 8 rows in these DRAM devices. In the case of the 4-Gbit DDR2 SDRAM device, there are eight times the number of rows than the number of refresh commands. Consequently, a given 4-Gbit DDR2 SDRAM device will cycle through and refresh 8 rows with each refresh command—a sequence of events that takes a long time to complete. Table 11.2 shows that each refresh command in the 4-Gbit DDR2 SDRAM device takes 327.5 ns to complete.

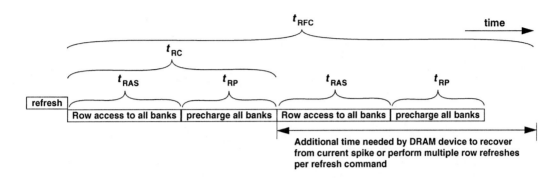

FIGURE 11.7: All-banks-concurrent row refresh timing.

TABLE **11.2**   Refresh cycle times for DDR and DDR2 SDRAM devices

DRAM Device Family	Voltage	DRAM Device Capacity	Number of Banks	Number of Rows	Row Size	Refresh Count	t_{RC}	t_{RFC}
DDR	2.5 V	256 Mb	4	8192	1 kB	8192	60 ns	67 ns
		512 Mb	4	8192	2 kB	8192	55 ns	70 ns
DDR2	1.8 V	256 Mb	4	8192	1 kB	8192	55 ns	75 ns
		512 Mb	4	16384	1 kB	8192	55 ns	105 ns
		1024 Mb	8	16384	1 kB	8192	54 ns	127.5 ns
		2048 Mb	8	32768	1 kB	8192	~	197.5 ns
		4096 Mb	8	65536	1 kB	8192	~	327.5 ns

DRAM device design engineers and DRAM memory system design engineers are actively exploring alternatives to the bank-concurrent refresh command. Some advanced memory systems are designed in such a manner that the controller manually injects row cycle reads to individual banks. The per-bank refresh scheme can decrease the bandwidth impact of refresh commands at the cost of increased complexity in the memory controller.

11.1.8   A Read Cycle

Figure 11.8 illustrates a read cycle in generic DRAM memory systems such as SDRAM and DDRx SDRAM memory systems. In a typical, modern DRAM device, each row access command brings thousands of bits of data to the array of sense amplifiers in a given bank.

A subsequent column-read command then brings tens or hundreds of those bits of data through the data bus into the memory controller. For applications that access data by streaming through memory, keeping thousands of bits of a given row of data active at the sense amplifiers ensures that subsequent memory reads from the same row do not incur the latency or energy cost of another row access. In contrast, applications that are not likely to access data in adjacent locations favor memory systems that immediately precharge the DRAM arrays after each row access to prepare the DRAM bank for a subsequent access to a different row within the same bank. Figure 11.8 illustrates a sequence of commands issued in rapid succession to access one bank of DRAM cells. Data is brought in from the DRAM cells to the sense amplifiers by the row access command. After t_{RCD} time,

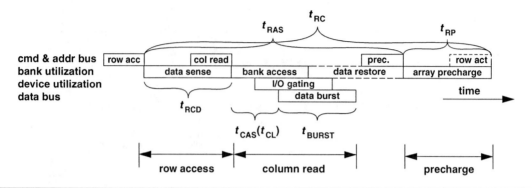

FIGURE 11.8: A read cycle.

data from the requested row is resolved by the sense amplifiers, and the memory controller can then issue column read or write commands to the DRAM device. Concurrent with the issuance of column access commands, the memory device actively restores data from the sense amplifiers to the DRAM cells. Then, after t_{RAS} time from the initial issuance of the row access command, the DRAM cells are ready for a precharge command to reset the bitlines and the sense amplifiers. Collectively, memory systems that immediately precharge a bank to prepare it for another access to a different row are known as *close-page* memory systems. Memory systems that keep rows active at the sense amplifiers are known as *open-page* memory systems.

11.1.9 A Write Cycle

Similar to the illustration of a read cycle in Figure 11.8, Figure 11.9 illustrates a write cycle in a generic DRAM memory system. In modern DRAM devices, the row cycle time is limited by the duration of the write cycle. That is, a row cycle time is defined as the minimum time period that a DRAM device needs to provide access to any data to any row in a given bank of DRAM cells. Implicitly, the access in the definition of a row access can be a read access or a write access.

In the case of a write access, data must be provided by the memory controller, driven through the data bus, passed through the I/O gating multiplexors, over-drive the sense amplifiers, and finally stored into the DRAM cells. This complex series of actions must be completed before the precharge command that completes the sequence can proceed. As a result, the row cycle time must be defined so that it can account for the row access time, the column write delay, the data transport time, the write data restore time, as well as the precharge time. That is, to account for the timing of the more complex write access time, t_{RAS} must be long enough to account for t_{RCD}, t_{CWD}, t_{CCD},[3] and t_{WR}. As a result, the timing parameter t_{RAS} must be set so that it is at least equal to $t_{RCD} + t_{CWD} + t_{CCD} + t_{WR}$ in SDRAM, DDR SDRAM, and DDR2 SDRAM devices, subject to the clock cycle granularity of the respective latency values, thus demonstrating the write cycle time constraint of the row cycle time in these commodity DRAM devices.

11.1.10 Compound Commands

In the previous discussion about the read cycle, Figure 11.8 illustrates a read cycle in a generic DRAM memory system by issuing a sequence of three separate commands. As part of the evolution of DRAM

---

[3]DRAM devices such as DDR SDRAM and DDR2 SDRAM use multiple internal data bursts to form longer burst durations. The t_{RAS} definition needs only account for the shortest t_{BURST} duration possible, t_{CCD}.

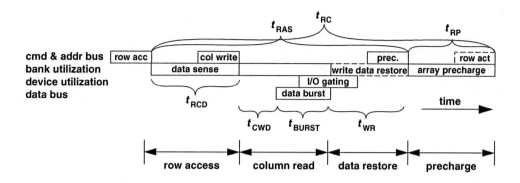

FIGURE 11.9: A write cycle.

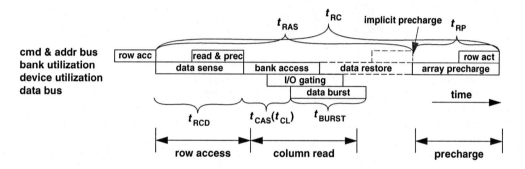

FIGURE 11.10: A read cycle with a row access command and a column-read-and-precharge command.

devices and architecture, some DRAM devices have been designed to support compound commands that perform more complex series of actions. Figure 11.10 shows the same sequence of DRAM commands as presented in Figure 11.8. However, the simple column-read command in Figure 11.8 is replaced with a compound *column-read-and-precharge* command in Figure 11.10. As the name implies, the column-read-and-precharge command combines a column-read command and a precharge command into a single command. The advantage of a column-read-and-precharge command is that for close-page memory systems that precharge the DRAM bank immediately after a read command, the column-read-and-precharge command reduces the bandwidth requirement on the command and address bus. The implicit precharge command means that the DRAM memory controller can now place a

different command on the address and command bus that a separate precharge command would have otherwise occupied.

Figure 11.10 shows a column-read-and-precharge command as issued by the memory controller to the DRAM device in the earliest time slot possible after the row access command while still respecting the t_{RCD} timing requirement, but the implicit precharge command is delayed so that it does not violate the t_{RAS} timing requirement. Modern DRAM devices such as DDR2 SDRAM devices have implemented a feature that is referred to as t_{RAS} lockout to ensure that the auto-precharge component of the column read-and-precharge command will not violate the t_{RAS} timing requirement. That is, in the case where a column-read-and-precharge command is issued into the DRAM device before the DRAM device has

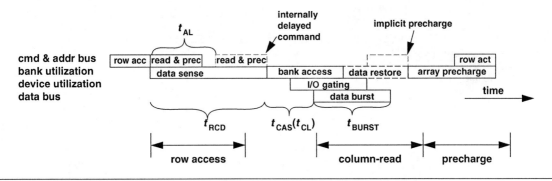

FIGURE 11.11: Posted CAS defers CAS commands in DRAM devices by a preset delay value, t_{AL}.

completed the data restoration phase of the row access command, as illustrated in Figure 11.10, the DRAM device will delay the implicit precharge command until the t_{RAS} timing requirement for the row access has been met. In this manner, close-page memory systems can issue the column-read-and-precharge command with best possible timing to retrieve data from the DRAM device without worrying about the precharge aspect of the random row access.

A second type of complex commands supported by some memory systems such as the DDR2 SDRAM memory system is the posted column access (posted CAS) command. The posted CAS command is simply a column access command whose action is delayed (or posted) by a fixed number of cycles in the DRAM device. In DRAM devices that support the posted CAS command, the device internally delays the actions of the CAS command by a preset value, labelled as t_{AL} in Figure 11.11. The number of delay cycles for the posted CAS command is preprogrammed into the DDR2 DRAM device, and the DRAM device cannot dynamically or intelligently defer the column access command. Some DRAM devices, such as the XDR DRAM device, allow the command to be optionally encoded with a delay value so that the controller can flexibly schedule a DRAM command that the DRAM device will then execute or act upon after the number of specified delay cycles.

Figure 11.11 illustrates a posted column-read-and-precharge command in a read cycle. The column-read-and-precharge command is also commonly referred to as the column-read command with auto-precharge. The sequence of commands illustrated in Figure 11.11 is the same as the sequence of DRAM commands illustrated in Figure 11.10. The difference between the command sequences illustrated in Figures 11.10 and 11.11 is that the column-read-and-precharge command is a posted CAS command, and the posted column-read command is issued immediately after the row access command in Figure 11.11. In Figure 11.11, the preset value of t_{AL} defers the action of the column-read-and-precharge command to ensure that the column read aspect of the command does not violate the t_{RCD} timing requirement.

The advantage of the posted CAS command is that it allows a memory controller to issue the column access command immediately after the row access command and greatly simplifies controller design for close-page memory systems. However, the posted CAS command is not a panacea that reduces controller complexity for all types of memory controllers, since the posted command must still respect the timing of the column access commands and normal protocol timing requirements.

11.2 DRAM Command Interactions

In the previous section, basic DRAM commands are described in some detail. In this section, the interactions between the basic DRAM commands are examined in further detail. In this chapter, a resource usage model is used as the primary model to describe DRAM command interactions and the need for specification of the various timing parameters. In the resource usage model, DRAM commands can be scheduled consecutively subject to availability of shared on-chip resources such as sense amplifiers, I/O gating multiplexors, and the availability of off-chip resources such as the command, address, and data busses. However, even with the availability of shared resources, considerations such as device current limitations can prohibit commands from being scheduled consecutively.[4]

This section examines read and write commands in a memory system with simplistic open- and close-page row-buffer-management policies. In a memory system that implements the open-page row-buffer-management policy, once a row is opened for access, the array of sense amplifiers continues to hold the data for subsequent read and write accesses to the same row until another access to a different row within the same bank forces the controller to precharge the sense amplifiers and prepare for access to the different row. Open-page memory systems rely on workloads that access memory with some amount of spatial locality so that multiple column accesses can be issued to the same row without the need for multiple DRAM row cycles. In an open-page memory system, the DRAM command sequence for a given request depends on the state of the memory system, and the dynamic nature of DRAM command sequences in open-page memory systems means that there are larger numbers of possible DRAM command interactions and memory system state combinations in an open-page memory system. The large number of command interactions leads to a higher degree of difficulty in scheduling command sequences. In the following sections, a large number of possible DRAM command interactions for open-page memory systems are examined in detail. The detailed examination of DRAM command combinations enables the creation of a table that summarizes the minimum scheduling distances between DRAM commands. The summary of minimum scheduling distances, in turn, enables performance analysis of DRAM memory systems in this chapter.

11.2.1 Consecutive Reads and Writes to Same Rank

In modern DRAM memory systems such as SDRAM, DDR SDRAM, and Direct RDRAM memory systems, read commands to the same open row of memory in the same bank, rank, and channel can be pipelined and scheduled consecutively subject to the burst durations of data on the data bus and the internal prefetch length of the DRAM device. Figure 11.12 shows two column-read commands, labelled as read 0 and read 1, pipelined consecutively. As illustrated in Figure 11.4, t_{CAS} time after a column-read command is placed onto the command and address busses, the DRAM device begins to return data on the data bus. Since column-read commands to any open banks of the same rank can be pipelined consecutively, consecutive column-read commands to the same open row of the same bank of memory can be ideally scheduled every t_{BURST} time period. One caveat to the scheduling of consecutive column-read commands to an open row of a bank is that t_{BURST} has to be greater than or equal to t_{CCD}. Trivially, t_{BURST} is greater than t_{CCD} in all RDRAM, SDRAM, DDR SDRAM, and DDR2 SDRAM memory systems. The one exception to the rule is that t_{CCD} is 4 cycles in DDR3 SDRAM devices, since the prefetch length of DDR3 SDRAM devices is 8 data beats. Consequently, the best-case timing for consecutive column-read commands to the same or different banks of the same rank of DRAM devices is $MAX(t_{BURST}, t_{CCD})$.

Finally, similar to the case of consecutive column-read commands to the same bank of a given rank of memory, consecutive column-write commands can be scheduled to different open banks within the same rank of memory once every $MAX(t_{BURST}, t_{CCD})$ time period.

---

[4]That is t_{RRD} and t_{FAW}.

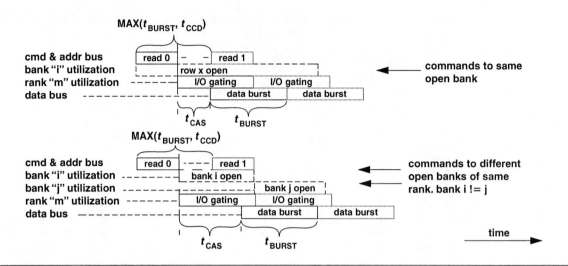

FIGURE 11.12: Consecutive column-read commands to the same bank, rank, and channel.

11.2.2 Read to Precharge Timing

Figure 11.13 illustrates the minimum command timing for a precharge command that immediately follows a column-read command. Figure 11.13 illustrates the formula for minimum command timing as $t_{BURST} + t_{RTP} - t_{CCD}$.[5] In the case where the internal burst length of the DRAM device t_{CCD} is equivalent to the column burst duration t_{BURST}, the minimum command timing between a column-read command and a precharge command is simply t_{RTP}. However, in some DRAM devices, the burst duration can be composed of multiple internal data bursts. For example, as previously illustrated in Figure 11.4, in a DDR2 SDRAM memory system where column access commands are programmed to move data in burst durations of 8 beats, the internal burst duration of a DDR2 SDRAM device is only 4 beats. As a result, the column read to precharge timing in the aforementioned DDR2 SDRAM memory system can be simply rewritten as $t_{RTP} + t_{CCD}$.

Essentially, the timing parameter t_{RTP} itself specifies the minimum amount of time that is needed between a column-read command and a precharge command. However, in DRAM devices such as the DDR2 SDRAM device, multiple shorter bursts are used to construct one continuous burst for a column-read command. In such a case, the DRAM device must keep the sense amplifiers open to drive multiple short bursts through the I/O gating multiplexors, and the timing parameter t_{RTP} must be modified to account to the extended time that the sense amplifiers are kept open. More generally, the formula for column read to precharge timing can be written as $t_{RTP} + (N - 1) * t_{CCD}$, where N is the number of internal bursts required to form one extended burst for a single column-read command.

11.2.3 Consecutive Reads to Different Rows of Same Bank

In most modern DRAM devices, multiple column-read commands to the same row of the same open bank can be issued and pipelined consecutively as illustrated in Figure 11.12. However, column-read

---

[5]Implicit in this formula is that the column-read command does not use posted CAS timing. Otherwise, t_{AL} must be added, and the formula rewritten as $t_{AL} + t_{BURST} + t_{RTP} - t_{CCD}$.

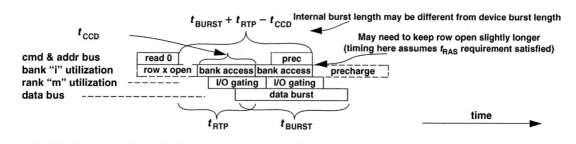

FIGURE 11.13: Read to precharge command timing.

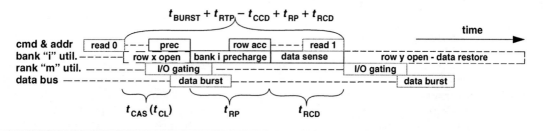

FIGURE 11.14: Consecutive column-read commands to different rows of the same bank: best-case scenario.

commands to different rows within the same bank would incur the cost of an entire row cycle time as the current DRAM array must be precharged and a different row activated by the array of sense amplifiers.

Best-Case Scenario

Figure 11.14 illustrates the timing and command sequence of two consecutive read requests to different rows within the same bank of memory array. In this sequence, as the first read command, labelled as read 0, is issued, the array of sense amplifiers must be precharged before a different row to the same bank can be opened for access. After time period t_{RP} from the assertion of the precharge command, a different row access command can then be

issued, and time period t_{RCD} after the row access command, the second read command labelled as read 1 can then proceed. Figure 11.14 illustrates that consecutive column read accesses to different rows within the same bank can be scheduled with the best-case timing of $t_{BURST} + t_{RTP} - t_{CCD} + t_{RP} + t_{RCD}$ as long as the row restoration time t_{RAS} had been satisfied.

Worst-Case Scenario

Figure 11.14 illustrates the best-case timing of two consecutive read commands to different rows of the same bank. However, the timing illustrated in Figure 11.14 assumes that at least t_{RAS} time has passed since the previous row access, and data had been restored to the DRAM cells. In the case where data from the current row has not yet been restored to the DRAM cells, a precharge command cannot be issued until t_{RAS} time period after the previous row access command to the same bank. In contrast to the best-case timing shown in Figure 11.14, Figure 11.15 shows the worst-case timing for two consecutive read commands to different rows of the same bank where the first column command was issued immediately after a row access command. In this case, the precharge command cannot be issued immediately after the first column-read command, but must wait until t_{RAS} time period after the previous row access command has elapsed. Then, t_{RP} time period after the precharge command, the second row access command can be issued, and t_{RCD} time period after that row access command, the second column-read command completes this sequence of commands.

Figure 11.14 illustrates the best-case timing of two consecutive read commands to different rows of the same bank, and Figure 11.15 illustrates the worst-case timing between two column-read commands to different rows of the same bank. The difference between the two different scenarios means that a DRAM memory controller must keep track of the timing of a row access command and delay any row precharge command until the row restoration requirement has been satisfied.

11.2.4 Consecutive Reads to Different Banks: Bank Conflict

The case of consecutive read commands to different rows of the same bank has been examined in the previous section. This section examines the case of consecutive read requests to different banks with the second request hitting a bank conflict against an active row in that bank. The consecutive read request scenario with the second read request hitting a bank conflict to a different bank has several different combinations of possible minimum scheduling distances that depend on the state of the bank as well as the capability of the DRAM controller to reorder commands between different transaction requests.

Without Command Reordering

Figure 11.16 illustrates the timing and command sequence of two consecutive read requests to different banks of the same rank, and the second read request is made to a row that is different than the active row in the array of sense amplifiers of that bank. Figure 11.16 makes three implicit assumptions. The first assumption made is that both banks i and j are open, where bank i is different from bank j. The second read request is made to bank j, but to a different row than the row of data presently held in the array of sense amplifiers of bank j. In this case, the precharge command to bank j can proceed concurrently with the column read access to a bank i. The second assumption made is that the t_{RAS} requirement has been satisfied in bank j, and bank j can be immediately precharged. The third and final assumption made is that the DRAM controller does not support command or transaction reordering between different transaction requests. That is, all of the DRAM commands associated with the first request must be scheduled before any DRAM commands associated with the second request can be scheduled.

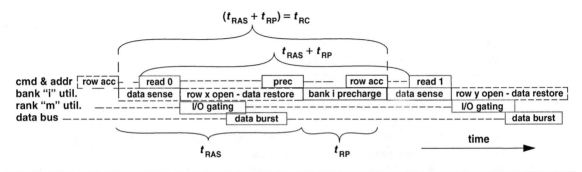

FIGURE 11.15: Consecutive column-read commands to different rows of same bank: worst-case scenario.

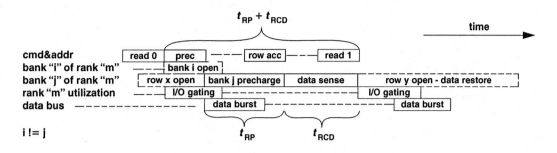

FIGURE 11.16: Consecutive DRAM read commands to different banks; bank conflict; no command reordering.

Figure 11.16 shows that due to the bank conflict, the read request to bank j is translated into a sequence of three DRAM commands. The first command in the sequence precharges the sense amplifiers to bank j, the second command brings the selected row to the sense amplifiers, and the last command in the sequence performs the actual read request and returns data from the DRAM devices to the DRAM controller. Figure 11.16 illustrates a case where consecutive read requests are made to different rows, with the second read request made to a different row of the same bank. In the case where the DRAM command sequence is not dynamically reordered by the memory controller, then the two requests can, at best, be scheduled with minimum timing distance of $t_{RP} + t_{RCD}$.

With Command Reordering

Figure 11.16 illustrates the timing of two requests to different banks with the second request hitting a bank conflict and the DRAM controller not supporting command or transaction reordering. In contrast, Figure 11.17 shows that the DRAM memory system can obtain bandwidth utilization if the DRAM controller can interleave or reorder DRAM commands from

different transactions requests. Figure 11.17 shows the case where the DRAM controller allows the precharge command for bank j to proceed ahead of the column-read command for the transaction request to bank i. In this case, the column-read command to bank i can proceed in parallel with the precharge command to bank j, since these two commands utilize different resources in different banks. To obtain better utilization of the DRAM memory system, the DRAM controller must be designed with the capability to reorder and interleave commands from different transaction requests. Figure 11.17 shows that in the case where the DRAM memory system can interleave and reorder DRAM commands from different transaction requests, the two column-read commands can be scheduled with the timing of $t_{RP} + t_{RCD} - t_{CMD}$. Figure 11.17 thus illustrates one way that a DRAM memory system can obtain better bandwidth utilization with advanced DRAM controller designs.

11.2.5 Consecutive Read Requests to Different Ranks

Figure 11.12 illustrates that consecutive read commands to open banks of the same rank of DRAM device can be issued and pipelined consecutively.[6] However, consecutive read commands to different

---

[6]That is, assuming that the burst duration is equal to or longer than the minimum column-to-column delay time, t_{CCD}. This assumption is inherently true for SDRAM, DDR SDRAM, and DDR2 SDRAM devices, but may not be true for DDR3 and future generation devices where t_{BURST} may be shorter than t_{CCD}.

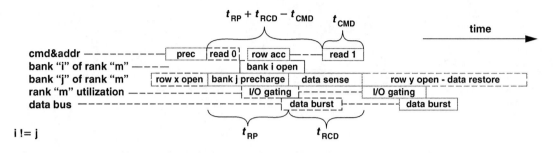

FIGURE 11.17: Consecutive DRAM read commands to different banks, bank conflict, with command reordering.

ranks of memory may not be issued and pipelined back to back depending on the system-level synchronization mechanism and the operating data rate of the memory system. In some memory systems, consecutive read commands to different ranks of memory rely on system-level synchronization mechanisms that are non-trivial for multi-rank, high data rate memory systems. In these systems, the data bus must idle for some period of time between data bursts from different ranks on the shared data bus. Figure 11.18 illustrates the timing and command sequence of two consecutive read commands to different ranks. In Figure 11.18, the read-write (DQS) data strobe resynchronization time is labelled as t_{RTRS}. For relatively low-frequency SDRAM memory systems, data synchronization strobes are not used, and t_{RTRS} is zero. For Direct RDRAM memory systems, the use of the topology-matched source-synchronous clocking scheme obviates the need for a separate strobe signal, and t_{RTRS} is also zero. However, for DDR SDRAM and DDR2 SDRAM memory systems, the use of a system-level data strobe signal shared by all of the ranks means that the t_{RTRS} data strobe resynchronization penalty is non-zero.

11.2.6 Consecutive Write Requests: Open Banks

Differing from the case of consecutive column-read commands to different ranks of DRAM devices, consecutive column-write commands to different ranks of DRAM devices may be pipelined consecutively in

modern DRAM memory systems, depending on the bus termination strategy deployed. The difference between consecutive column-write commands to different ranks of DRAM devices and consecutive column-read commands to different ranks of DRAM devices is that in case of consecutive column-read commands to different ranks of DRAM devices, one rank of DRAM devices must first send data on the shared data bus and give up control of the shared data bus, then the other rank of DRAM devices must gain control of the shared data bus and send its data to the DRAM controller. In the case of the consecutive column-write commands to different ranks of memory, the DRAM memory controller can send data to different ranks of DRAM devices without needing to give up control of the shared data bus to another bus master. Consequently, write bursts to different ranks of DRAM devices can be pipelined consecutively in SDRAM and DDR SDRAM memory systems. However, as signaling on a multi-drop bus becomes more challenging with increasing data rates, DRAM device manufacturers and system design engineers have been forced to deploy more sophisticated mechanisms to improve system-level signal integrity. One mechanism deployed in DDR2 SDRAM memory systems to improve signal integrity is the use of active, *On-Die Termination* (ODT) on DDR2 SDRAM devices. However, one unfortunate side effect of ODT as designed in the DDR2 SDRAM memory system is that it takes 2 cycles to turn on ODT in a DDR2 SDRAM device and 2 1/2 cycles to turn off ODT, and the difference in

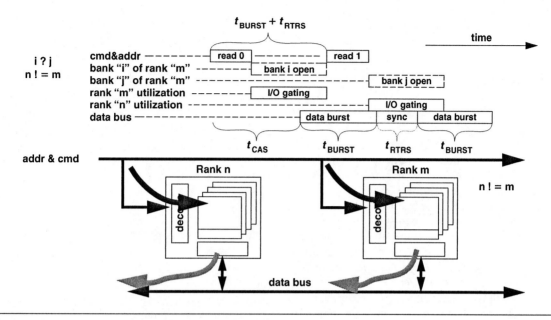

FIGURE 11.18: Consecutive column-read commands to different ranks.

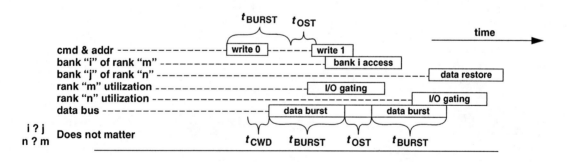

FIGURE 11.19: Consecutive column-write commands to different ranks.

turn-on and turn-off times necessitates an additional bubble between write bursts.[7] Figure 11.19 shows two write commands to different ranks, labelled as write 0 and write 1, pipelined consecutively, but with an ODT switching time penalty, labelled as t_{OST}, between different ranks. Figure 11.19 shows that consecutive column-write commands to open banks of memory can occur every $t_{BURST} + t_{OST}$ cycle. In the case of SDRAM and DDR SDRAM memory systems, write data bursts to different ranks can occur without needing any idle time on the data bus. In the case of DDR2 and DDR3 memory systems, the need to accurately control data bus signaling characteristics means that an additional cycle is needed to switch the location of the termination element in the memory channel. In reality, t_{OST} is needed in the case of a rank-to-rank read as well.

---

[7]The difference is needed to ensure a properly terminated system topology for the duration of data transfers.

However, since t_{RTRS} is typically greater than or equal to t_{OST}, MAX(t_{RTRS}, t_{OST}) may be simplified as t_{RTRS}.

11.2.7 Consecutive Write Requests: Bank Conflicts

Similar to the case of the consecutive read requests to different rows of the same bank, consecutive write requests to different rows of the same bank must also respect the timing requirements of t_{RAS} and t_{RP}. Additionally, column-write commands must also respect the timing requirements of the write recovery time t_{WR}. In the case of write commands to different rows of the same bank, the write recovery time means that the precharge cannot begin until the write recovery time has allowed data to move from the interface of the DRAM devices through the sense amplifiers into the DRAM cells. Figure 11.20 shows two of the best-case timing of two consecutive write requests made to different rows in the same bank. The minimum scheduling distance between two write commands to different rows of the same bank is $t_{CWD} + t_{BURST} + t_{WR} + t_{RP} + t_{RCD}$.

Figure 11.20 also shows the case where consecutive write requests are issued to different ranks of DRAM devices, with the second write request resulting in a bank conflict. In this case, the first write command proceeds, and assuming that bank j for rank n has previously satisfied the t_{RAS} timing requirement, the precharge command for a different bank or different rank can be issued immediately. Similar to the case of the consecutive read requests with bank conflicts to different banks, bank conflicts to different banks and different ranks for consecutive write requests can also benefit from command reordering.

11.2.8 Write Request Following Read Request: Open Banks

Similar to consecutive read commands and consecutive write commands, the combination of a column-write command that immediately follows a column-read command can be scheduled consecutively subject to the timing of the respective data bursts on the shared data bus. Figure 11.21 illustrates a column-write command that follows a column-read

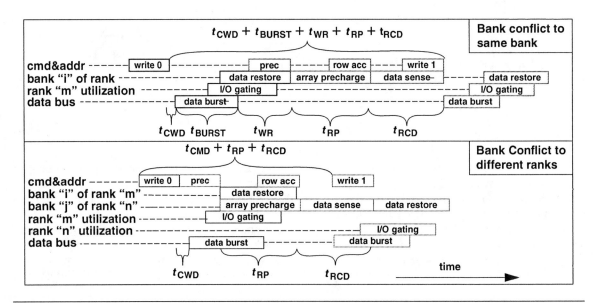

FIGURE 11.20: Consecutive write commands, bank conflict, best cases.

command and shows that the internal data movement of the column-write command does not conflict with the internal data movement of the column-read command. As a result, a column-write command can be issued into the DRAM memory system immediately after a column-read command as long as the timing of data burst returned by the DRAM device for the column-read command does not conflict with the timing of the data burst sent by the DRAM controller to the DRAM device for the column-write command. Figure 11.21 shows that the minimum scheduling distance between a column-write command that follows a column-read command is simply $t_{CAS} + t_{BURST} + t_{RTRS} - t_{CWD}$.

The minimum timing distance between a column-write command that follows a column-read command is different for different memory-access protocols. However, the minimum timing expression of $t_{CAS} + t_{BURST} + t_{RTRS} - t_{CWD}$ is valid for an SDRAM memory system as well as various DDRx SDRAM memory

systems. For example, in an SDRAM memory system, t_{CWD} and t_{RTRS} are both zero, so the minimum timing distance between a write request that follows a read request in an SDRAM memory system is simply $t_{CAS} + t_{BURST}$. Comparatively, in a DDR SDRAM memory system, t_{CWD} and t_{RTRS} both require 2 beats (1 full memory clock cycle), and the minimum timing distance between a write request that follows a read request in a DDR SDRAM memory system is also $t_{CAS} + t_{BURST}$. In both cases, the timing is the same, but arrives at the same equation through different means.

11.2.9 Write Request Following Read Request to Different Banks, Bank Conflict, Best Case, No Reordering

Figure 11.22 illustrates the case where a write request follows a read request to different banks. In the figure, the column-read command is issued

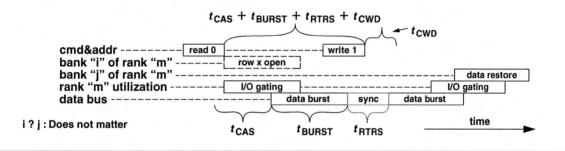

FIGURE 11.21: Write command following read command to open banks.

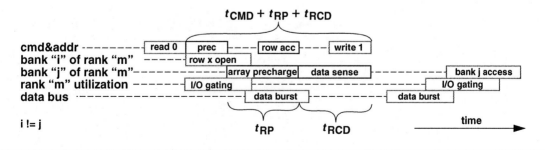

FIGURE 11.22: Write command following read command to different banks: bank conflict, best case.

to bank i, the column-write command is issued to bank j, and i is different from j. In the common case, the two commands can be pipelined consecutively with the minimum scheduling distance shown in Figure 11.21. However, the assumption given in Figure 11.22 is that the write command is a write command to a different row than the row currently held in bank j. As a result, the DRAM controller must first precharge bank j and issue a new row access command to bank j before the column-write command can be issued. In the best-case scenario presented, the row accessed by the write command in bank j had already been restored to the DRAM cells, and more than t_{RAS} time period had elapsed since the row was initially accessed. Figure 11.22 shows that under this condition, the read command and the write command that follows it to a different bank can be scheduled with the minimum scheduling distance of $t_{CMD} + t_{RP} + t_{RCD}$.

Figure 11.22 shows the case where the ordering between DRAM commands from different requests is strictly observed. In this case, the precharge command sent to bank j is not constrained by the column-read command to bank i. In a memory system with DRAM controllers that support command reordering and interleaving DRAM commands from different transaction requests, the efficiency of the DRAM memory system in scheduling a write request with a bank conflict that follows a read request can be increased in the same manner as illustrated for consecutive read requests in Figures 11.16 and 11.17.

11.2.10 Read Following Write to Same Rank, Open Banks

Figure 11.23 shows the case for a column-read command that follows a column-write command to open banks in the same rank of DRAM devices. The difference between a read command and a write command is that the direction of data flow within the selected DRAM devices is reversed with respect to each other. The importance in the direction of data flow can be observed when a read command is scheduled after a write command to the same rank of DRAM devices. Figure 11.23 shows that the difference in the direction of data flow limits the minimum scheduling distance between the column-write command and the column-read command that follows to the same rank of devices. Figure 11.23 shows that after the DRAM controller places the data onto the data bus, the DRAM device must make use of the shared I/O gating resource in the DRAM device to move the write data through the buffers into the proper columns of the selected bank. Since the I/O gating resource is shared between all banks within a rank of DRAM devices, the sharing of the I/O gating device means that a read command that follows a write command to the same rank of DRAM devices must wait until the write command has been completed before the read command can make use of the shared I/O gating resources regardless of the target or destination bank IDs of the respective column access commands. Figure 11.23 shows that the minimum scheduling distance between a write command and

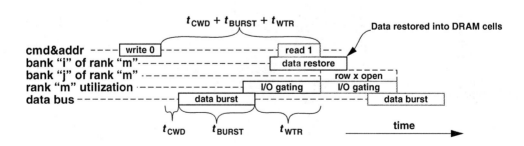

FIGURE 11.23: Read following write to the same rank of DRAM devices.

a subsequent read command to the same rank of memory is $t_{CWD} + t_{BURST} + t_{WTR}$.

In order to alleviate the write-to-read turnaround time illustrated in Figure 11.23, some high-performance DRAM devices such as Rambus Direct RDRAM have been designed with write buffers so that as soon as data has been written into the write buffers, the I/O gating resource can be used by another command such as a column-read command.

11.2.11 Write to Precharge Timing

Figure 11.24 shows the subtle difference between a column write to column read timing and a column write to precharge timing. Essentially, t_{WTR} is used to denote the time that is needed for the multiplexors in the interface of DRAM devices—the I/O gating phase illustrated in Figure 11.24—to drive the data into the array of sense amplifiers. After t_{WTR} time from the assertion of the column-write command, a column-read command is able to use the I/O gating resource to

move data from an array of active sense amplifiers out of the DRAM device. The column write to precharge command combination differs from the column write to read combination in that the precharge command releases data stored in the sense amplifiers and precharges the sense amplifiers, while, as a result, a precharge command that follows a write command cannot be initiated until the write command has moved the data through the I/O gating resources to the sense amplifiers and driven the new data values directly into the DRAM cells. Figures 11.23 and 11.24 illustrate that in DRAM devices where t_{WTR} is separately specified from t_{WR}, t_{WTR} is typically shorter in duration than t_{WR}.

11.2.12 Read Following Write to Different Ranks, Open Banks

Figure 11.25 shows a slightly different case for a column-read command that follows a column-write command than the case illustrated in Figure 11.23. The combination of a column-read command

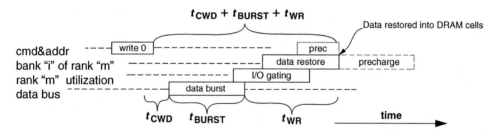

FIGURE 11.24: Write to precharge command timing.

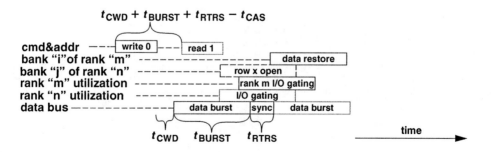

FIGURE 11.25: Read following write to different ranks of DRAM devices.

issued after a column-write command illustrated in Figure 11.25 differs from the combination of a column-read command issued after a column-write command illustrated in Figure 11.23 in that the column-write command and the column-read command are issued to different ranks of memory. Since the data movements occur in different ranks of memory, the conflict in the directions of data movement inside of each rank of memory is irrelevant. The timing constraint between the issuance of a read command after a write command to different ranks is then reduced to the data bus synchronization overhead of t_{RTRS}, the burst duration t_{BURST}, and the relative timing differences between read and write command latencies. The minimum time period between a write command and a read command to different ranks of memory is thus $t_{CWD} + t_{BURST} + t_{RTRS} - t_{CAS}$.

In a DDR SDRAM memory system, t_{CWD} is one cycle, t_{RTRS} is on clock cycle, and the minimum scheduling distance between a column-write command and a column-read command that follows it to a different rank of memory is MAX (t_{CMD}, $t_{BURST} - t_{CAS} -2$). In contrast, in a DDR2 SDRAM memory system, t_{CWD} is one full cycle less than t_{CAS}, and if t_{RTRS} can be minimized to one full cycle, $t_{CWD} + t_{RTRS} - t_{CAS}$ would cancel to zero, and the minimum scheduling distance between a read command that follows a write command to a different rank in the DDR2 SDRAM memory system is simply t_{BURST}.

11.2.13 Read Following Write to Same Bank, Bank Conflict

Figure 11.26 illustrates the case where a read request follows a write request to different rows of the same bank. In the best-case scenario, the row accessed by the write request had already been restored to the DRAM cells, and more than t_{RAS} time period had elapsed since the previous row was initially accessed. Figure 11.26 shows that under this condition, the precharge command cannot be issued until the data from the column-write command has been written into the DRAM cells. That is, the write recovery time t_{WR} must be respected before the precharge command can proceed to precharge the DRAM array. Figure 11.26 shows that the best-case minimum scheduling distance between a read request that follows a write request to different rows of the same bank is $t_{CWD} + t_{BURST} + t_{WR} + t_{RP} + t_{RCD}$.

Figure 11.26 shows the command interaction of a read request that follows a write request to different rows of the same bank on a DRAM device that does not have a write buffer. In DRAM devices with write buffers, the data for the column-write command is temporarily stored in the write buffer. In case a read request arrives after a write request to retrieve data from a different row of the same bank, a separate commit data command may have to be issued by the DRAM controller to the DRAM devices to force the write buffer to commit the data stored in the write buffer into the DRAM cells before the array can be precharged for another row access.

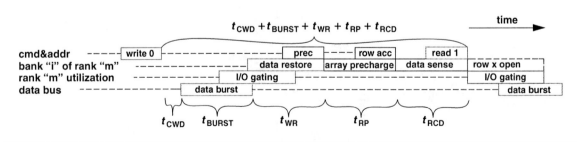

FIGURE 11.26: Read following write to different rows of the same bank.

11.2.14 Read Following Write to Different Banks of Same Rank, Bank Conflict, Best Case, No Reordering

Finally, Figure 11.27 illustrates the case where a read request follows a write request to different banks of the same rank of DRAM devices. However, the read request is sent to bank j, and a different row is active in bank j than the row needed by the read request. Figure 11.27 assumes that the t_{RAS} timing requirement has already been satisfied for bank j, and the DRAM memory system does not support DRAM command reordering between different memory transactions. Figure 11.27 shows that in this case, the precharge command for the read request command can be issued as soon as the write command is issued. Figure 11.27 thus shows that the minimum scheduling distance in this case is $t_{CMD} + t_{RP} + t_{RCD}$.

Figure 11.27 also reveals several points of note. One obvious point is that the DRAM command sequence illustrated in Figure 11.27 likely benefits from command reordering between different memory transactions. A second, less obvious point illustrated in Figure 11.27 is that the computed minimum scheduling distance depends on the relative duration of the various timing parameters. That is, Figure 11.27 assumes that the precharge command can be issued immediately after the write command and that $t_{CMD} + t_{RP} + t_{RCD}$ is greater than $t_{CWD} + t_{BURST} + t_{WR}$. In case $t_{CMD} + t_{RP} + t_{RCD}$ is, in fact, less than $t_{CWD} + t_{BURST} + t_{WR}$, the use of the shared I/O gating resource becomes the bottleneck, and the column-read command must wait until the write recovery phase of the column-write command has completed before the column-read command can proceed. That is, the minimum scheduling distance between a write request and a read request to a different bank with a bank conflict is in fact the larger of $t_{CMD} + t_{RP} + t_{RCD}$ and $t_{CWD} + t_{BURST} + t_{WR}$.

11.2.15 Column-Read-and-Precharge Command Timing

Figure 11.13 illustrates the minimum command timing for a precharge command that immediately follows a column-read command, and the minimum command timing was computed as $t_{BURST} + t_{RTP} - t_{CCD}$. Additionally, in the case where the column-read command is a posted column-read command, the additive latency parameter t_{AL} must be added to the overall command timing, resulting in the minimum command timing for a precharge command that follows a column-read command as $t_{AL} + t_{BURST} + t_{RTP} - t_{CCD}$. The column-read-and-precharge command would, in essence adopt the same timing specification and atomically perform an implicit precharge command $t_{AL} + t_{BURST} + t_{RTP} - t_{CCD}$ time after the column-read command is issued. However, the precharge component of the must still respect the row data restoration time t_{RAS} from the previous row activation command. Consequently, modern DRAM devices such as DDR2 SDRAMs have additional hardware that internally delays the precharge component of the unified column-read-and-precharge command to ensure that t_{RAS} timing to the row access is

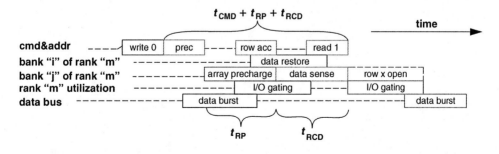

FIGURE 11.27: Read following write to different banks, bank conflict, best case.

respected before the integrated precharge component of the command is engaged. Figure 11.28 illustrates that the minimum timing of a column-read-and-precharge command that follows a row access command is simply $t_{RCD} - t_{AL}$.

11.2.16 Column-Write-and-Precharge Timing

The timing for a column-write-and-precharge command that immediately follows a row access command must ensure that both the column write component and the precharge component of the integrated column-write-and-precharge command respects the timing constraints imposed by the row access command. Fortunately, the timing parameter t_{RAS} has been defined to include a column-write command, and a column-write-and-precharge command can be freely issued after a row access command without violating precharge timing for the integrated precharge component of the command. Figure 11.29 shows the minimum timing required between a column-write command and a precharge command that follows it. Similar to the column-read-and-precharge command, the column-write-and-precharge command adopts the same timing specification and atomically performs an implicit precharge command.

Finally, DRAM devices are typically write-cycle limited, and t_{RAS} is often defined with enough timing margin for a single column-write command in SDRAM, and DDRx SDRAM memory systems. However, other memory systems and future memory systems may define t_{RAS} differently, and the timing of a column-write-and-precharge command may have additional constraints in such memory systems.

11.3 Additional Constraints

In previous sections, the resource contention model is used to justify various specified minimum timing constraints between different DRAM command combinations. However, additional constraints exist in modern DRAM memory systems and limit bandwidth utilization of modern DRAM memory systems. One such constraint is related to the power consumption of DRAM devices, and a second constraint is related to the distribution of commands and addresses to DRAM devices in the memory system. In the following sections, these additional constraints in the operations of the memory system are respectively examined.

11.3.1 Device Power Limit

With continuing emphasis placed on memory system performance, DRAM manufacturers are pushing for ever-higher data transfer rates in each successive generation of DRAM devices. However, just as increasing operating frequencies leads to higher activity rates and higher power consumption in modern processors, increasing data rates for DRAM devices also increases the potential for higher activity rates and higher power consumption on

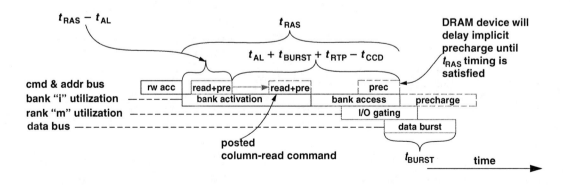

FIGURE 11.28: Row access to column-read-and-precharge command timing.

DRAM devices. One solution used by DRAM device design engineers to limit the power consumption of DRAM devices is to constrain the activity rate of DRAM devices. Constraints on the activity rate of DRAM devices, in turn, limit the capability of DRAM devices to move data and limit the performance of DRAM memory systems.

In modern DRAM devices, each time a row is activated, thousands of data bits are discharged, sensed, and then restored in parallel. As a result, the row activation command is a relatively energy intensive operation. Figure 11.30 shows the abstract current profile of a DRAM read cycle. In the figure, an active DRAM device draws a relatively low and constant quiescent current level as a result of active I/O buffers and DLLs. The DRAM device then draws additional current for each activity on the DRAM device. The total current

draw of the DRAM device is simply the summation of the quiescent current draw and the current draw of each activity on the DRAM device. The current profiles shown in Figures 11.30 and 11.31 are described in terms of abstract units rather than concrete values. The reason that the current profiles are shown in abstract units in Figures 11.30 and 11.31 is that the magnitude of the current draw for the row activation command depends on the number of bits in a row that are activated in parallel, and the magnitude of the current draw for the data burst on the data bus depends on the data bus width of the DRAM device. As a result, the current profile of each command on each respective device depends not only on the type of the command, but also on the configuration of the DRAM device.

Modern DRAM devices contain multiple banks of DRAM arrays that can be pipelined to achieve high

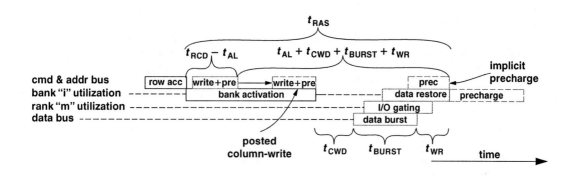

FIGURE 11.29: Row access to column-write-and-precharge command timing.

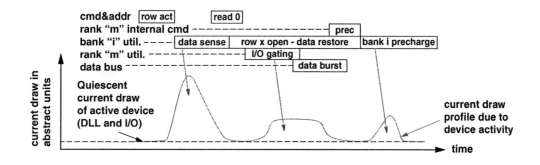

FIGURE 11.30: Current profile of a DRAM read cycle.

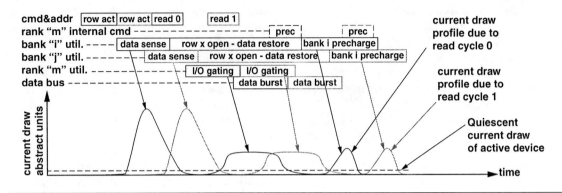

FIGURE 11.31: Current profile of two pipelined DRAM read cycles.

performance. Unfortunately, since the current profile of a DRAM device is proportional to its activity rate, a high-performance, highly pipelined DRAM device can also draw a large amount of active current. Figure 11.31 shows the individual contributions to the current profile of two pipelined DRAM read cycles on the same device. The total current profile of the pipelined DRAM device is not shown in Figure 11.31, but can be computed by the summation of the quiescent current profile and the current profiles of the two respective read cycles. The problem of power consumption for a high-performance DRAM device is that instead of only two pipelined read or write cycles, multiple read or write cycles can be pipelined, and as many as t_{RC}/t_{BURST} number of read or write cycles can be theoretically pipelined and in different phases in a single DRAM device. To limit the maximum current draw of a given DRAM device and avoid the addition of heat removal mechanisms such as head spreaders and heat sinks, new timing parameters have been defined in DDR2 and DDR3 devices to limit the activity rate and power consumption of DRAM devices.

11.3.2 t_{RRD}: Row-to-Row (Activation) Delay

In DDR2 SDRAM devices, the timing parameter t_{RRD} has been defined to specify the minimum time period between row activations on the same DRAM device. In the present context, the acronym RRD stands for row-to-row activation delay. The timing parameter t_{RRD} is specified in terms of nanoseconds, and Table 11.3 shows that by specifying t_{RDD} in terms of nanoseconds instead of number of cycles, a minimum spacing between row activation is maintained regardless of operating data rates. For memory systems that implement the close-page row-buffer-management policy, t_{RRD} effectively limits the maximum sustainable bandwidth of a memory system with a single rank of memory. In memory systems with two or more ranks of memory, consecutive row activation commands can be directed to different ranks to avoid the t_{RRD} constraint.

Table 11.3 shows t_{RRD} for different configurations of a 1-Gbit DDR2 SDRAM device from Micron. The 1-Gbit DDR2 SDRAM device with the 16-bit-wide data bus is internally arranged as 8 banks of 8192 rows per bank and 16384 bits per row. Comparatively, the 512-Mbit ×4 and 256-Mbit ×8 configurations of the 1-Gbit DDR2 SDRAM device are arranged internally as 8 banks of 16384 rows per bank and 8192 bits per row. Table 11.3 thus demonstrates that with larger row size, each row activation on the 128-Mbit ×16, 1-Gbit DDR2 SDRAM device draws more current than a row activation on the 256-Mbit ×8 or 512-Mbit ×4, 1-Gbit DDR2 SDRAM devices. As a result, row activations in the 128-Mbit ×16, 1-Gbit DDR2

TABLE 11.3 t_{RRD} and t_{FAW} for a 1-Gbit DDR2 SDRAM device

Device Configuration	512 Mbit x 4	256 Mbit x 8	128 Mbit x 16
Data bus width	4	8	16
Number of banks	8	8	8
Number of rows	16384	16384	8192
Number of columns	2048	1024	1024
Row size (bits)	8192	8192	16384
t_{RRD} (ns)	7.5	7.5	10
t_{FAW} (ns)	37.5	37.5	50

SDRAM device must be spaced farther apart in time, as specified in Table 11.3.

11.3.3 t_{FAW}: Four-Bank Activation Window

The topic of DRAM device configuration was covered in some detail in a previous chapter. The coverage provided was lacking discussions in regard to the reasoning behind the trade-offs of bank count, row count, and row size. That is, the difficulties of determining the optimal bank count, row count, and column count (row size) were not discussed. However, with the description of t_{RRD} and t_{FAW}, the discussion can now proceed with some context. Basically, as DRAM devices grow in density, DRAM device configuration becomes a tug of war between some rather unpalatable choices. DRAM device manufacturers are reluctant to increase the number of banks, since bank control logic overhead increases die size. However, larger rows increase the current draw of the row activation command, necessitating longer t_{RRD} and t_{FAW} parameter specifications. Increasing the number of rows per bank means that there are more cells on a given bitline, contributing possibly to longer t_{RCD} and t_{RAS} parameters, not to mention that with more rows, more row refresh requests are needed per unit time.

To manage the ever-increasing capacity of DRAM devices, 1-Gbit and larger DDR2 SDRAM devices have been designed with 8 banks of DRAM arrays. However, the larger number of banks means that a 1-Gbit DDR2 SDRAM device can have more than 4 banks of DRAM arrays that are activated in rapid succession, and the current draw of the 8-bank device can exceed the current draw of a comparable device with only 4 banks of DRAM arrays. To limit the increase in current draw in the larger DDR2 SDRAM devices, the timing parameter t_{FAW} has been defined to specify a rolling time-frame in which a maximum of four row activations on the same DRAM device can be engaged concurrently. The acronym FAW stands for *Four-bank Activation Window*. Figure 11.32 shows a sequence of row activation requests to different banks on the same DDR2 SDRAM device that respects both t_{RRD} as well as t_{FAW}. Figure 11.32 shows that the row activation requests are spaced at least t_{RRD} apart from each other and that the fifth row activation to a different bank is deferred until at least t_{FAW} time period has passed since the first row activation was initiated. For memory systems that implement the close-page row-buffer-management policy, t_{FAW} places great constraints on the maximum sustainable bandwidth of a memory system with a single rank of memory regardless of operating data rates. Finally, the timing parameters t_{RRD} and t_{FAW} have been defined for DDR2 SDRAM devices, and these timing parameters will carry over to DDR3 and future DDRx devices. Furthermore, these timing parameters are expected to increase in importance as future DRAM devices are introduced with even larger row sizes.

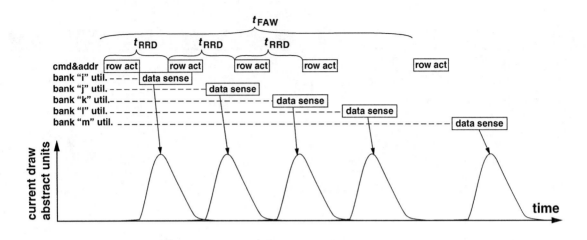

FIGURE 11.32: Maximum of four row activations in any t_{FAW} time frame.

11.3.4 2T Command Timing in Unbuffered Memory Systems

In high data rate, unbuffered memory systems, the address and command must be distributed to a large number of DRAM devices with the constraint of limited cycle times. To ensure functional correctness in the delivery of addresses and commands to the large number of DRAM devices in the memory system, the memory controller may be designed to hold the address and command for two full clock cycles. In this mode of operation, the memory controller is described as having 2T command timing. The net effect is that the command and address bandwidth of the memory system is reduced by one-half in these memory systems.

Figure 11.33 shows two memory systems populated with 4 ranks of DRAM devices. The memory system on the left has a single set of address and command busses connected to all four ranks of memory in the system. In contrast, the memory system on the right has two sets of address and command busses, with one set of busses devoted to each half of the memory system. Figure 11.33 shows that as a consequence of the number of loads on the address and command busses on the single set of address and command busses, the memory system on the left may be forced

to use 2T command timing, while the memory system on the right may be able to retain the use of 1T command timing.

11.4 Command Timing Summary

In previous sections, the minimum timing between different combinations of DRAM commands was examined in detail. Table 11.4 summarizes the minimum timing equations for basic DRAM command interactions between the row access, column read, column write, column-read-and-precharge, column-write-and-precharge, precharge, and refresh commands. Table 11.4 is organized by each DRAM command, the possible commands that can precede each command, and the respective minimum timing constraints that must be met in between each command combination before the second command can be issued.

11.5 Summary

In this chapter, a basic DRAM-access protocol is described in detail. The basic DRAM-access protocol

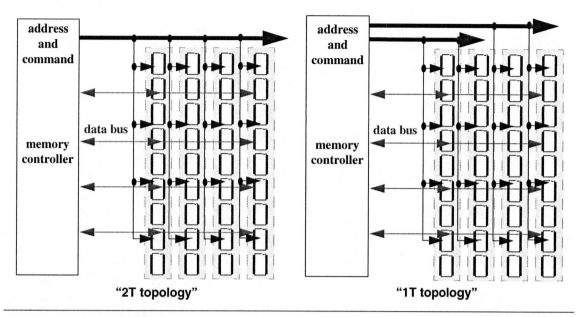

"2T topology"   "1T topology"

FIGURE 11.33: Unbuffered memory systems with 4 ranks of DRAM devices with one set of address and command busses and two sets of address and command busses.

is illustrated through the use of a resource utilization model. That is, two DRAM commands can be pipelined consecutively if they do not require the use of a shared resource at the same instance in time. The basic resource usage model is then qualified by stating that additional constraints such as power consumption limitation can further limit the issue rate of DRAM commands.

One popular question that is often asked, but not addressed by the description of the generic DRAM-access protocol, is in regard to what happens if the timing parameters are not fully respected. For example, what happens when a precharge command is issued before the t_{RAS} data restoration timing parameter has been fully satisfied? Does the DRAM device contain enough intelligence to delay the precharge command until t_{RAS} has been satisfied?

The answer to questions such as these is that, in general, DRAM devices contain very little intelligence in terms of logic circuitry to ensure functional correctness. The DRAM device manufacturers provide data sheets to specify the minimum timing constraints for individual DRAM commands. To ensure that the DRAM devices operate correctly, the DRAM controller must respect the minimum and maximum timing parameters as defined in the data sheet. In the specific case of a precharge command issued to a DRAM device before t_{RAS} has been satisfied, the DRAM device may still operate correctly, since the DRAM cell *may* have already been largely restored by the time the precharge command was engaged. The issue of early command issuance is thus analogous to that of the practice of processor overclocking. That is, a processor manufacturer can

TABLE 11.4 Summary of minimum DRAM command timing equations

Prev	Next	Rank	Bank	Minimum Timing	Illustration	Notes
A	A	s	s	t_{RC}	Figure 11.8	
A	A	s	d	t_{RRD}	Figure 11.32	Plus t_{FAW} for 5th RAS to same rank
P	A	s	d	t_{RP}	Figure 11.6	
F	A	s	s	t_{RFC}	Figure 11.7	
A	R	s	s	$t_{RCD} - t_{AL}$	Figure 11.11	$t_{AL} = 0$ without posted-CAS command
R	R	s	a	$MAX(t_{BURST}, t_{CCD})$	Figure 11.12	t_{BURST} is burst of prev. CAS to same rank
R	R	d	a	$t_{BURST} + t_{RTRS}$	Figure 11.18	t_{BURST} is burst of prev. CAS to diff rank
W	R	s	a	$t_{CWD} + t_{BURST} + t_{WTR}$	Figure 11.23	t_{BURST} is burst of prev. CASW to same rank
W	R	d	a	$t_{CWD} + t_{BURST} + t_{RTRS} - t_{CAS}$	Figure 11.25	t_{BURST} is burst of prev. CASW to diff rank
A	W	s	s	$t_{RCD} - t_{AL}$	Figure 11.11	
R	W	a	a	$t_{CAS} + t_{BURST} + t_{RTRS} - t_{CWD}$	Figure 11.21	t_{BURST} is burst of prev. CAS to any rank
W	W	s	a	$MAX(t_{BURST}, t_{CCD})$	Figure 11.19	t_{BURST} is burst of prev. CASW to same rank
W	W	d	a	$t_{BURST} + t_{OST}$	Figure 11.21	t_{BURST} is burst of prev. CASW to diff. rank
A	P	s	s	t_{RAS}	Figure 11.8	
R	P	s	s	$t_{AL} + t_{BURST} + t_{RTP} - t_{CCD}$	Figure 11.13	t_{BURST} is burst of prev. CAS to same rank
W	P	s	s	$t_{AL} + t_{CWD} + t_{BURST} + t_{WR}$	Figure 11.24	t_{BURST} is burst of prev. CASW to same rank
F	F	s	a	t_{RFC}	Figure 11.7	
P	F	s	a	t_{RP}	Figure 11.6	

A = row Access; R = column Read; W = column Write; P = Precharge; F = reFresh; s = same; d = different; a = any.

specify that a processor will operate correctly within a given frequency and supply voltage range. An end-user may increase the supply voltage and operating frequency of the processor in hopes of obtaining better performance from the processor. In such a case, the processor may well operate correctly. However, the parameters of operation are then outside of the bounds specified by the processor manufacturer, and the correctness of operation is no longer guaranteed by the processor manufacturer. Similarly, in the case where a DRAM command is issued at a timing that is more aggressive than that specified by the DRAM device data sheet, the DRAM device may still operate correctly, but the correctness of operation is no longer guaranteed by the DRAM device or module manufacturer.

CHAPTER 12

Evolutionary Developments of DRAM Device Architecture

The first Dynamic Random-Access Memory (DRAM) device, based on the operation of Field Effect Transistors (FET), was invented by Robert Dennard of IBM in 1966. Then in 1970, Intel Corp. produced the first commercial DRAM device, the 1103. In the decades since the introduction of Intel's 1103 DRAM device, DRAM device architecture has undergone continuous and gradual evolution. However, up until the mid-1990s, the evolutionary path of DRAM device architecture had been dominated by a single path devoted to high-capacity, low-cost commodity devices.

In recent years, the differing requirements placed on modern DRAM memory systems have strained the evolutionary development of modern DRAM devices. Consequently, the largely monolithic path of DRAM device architecture evolution has fractured into multiple evolutionary paths in recent years to respectively satisfy the varying system requirements of low cost, high bandwidth, low latency, and low power.

In previous chapters, basic structures of DRAM devices, common system configurations, abstract timing parameters, and abstract access protocols were described in detail. These chapters provide the foundation that enables the discussion in the rationale and capability of different DRAM devices. This chapter is devoted to the description and architectural evolution of different families of stand-alone DRAM devices.

12.1 DRAM Device Families

In the decades since the invention of the basic charge-storage DRAM circuit and the introduction of the first DRAM device, a myriad of DRAM devices, each with slightly different device architectures, has been developed to meet specific system requirements of low cost, low latency, high bandwidth, low power, or a reasonable combination thereof. In this chapter, the role of different DRAM devices is examined in context by classifying the different paths of the DRAM family tree illustrated in Figure 12.1.

12.1.1 Cost (Capacity), Latency, Bandwidth, and Power

The utility and cost effectiveness of commodity DRAM devices have allowed them to proliferate and become critical design components in large varieties of computer systems and computing devices. However, the specific requirements of different computer systems and computing devices have, in turn, forced DRAM device architectures to evolve and meet the wide spectrum of system requirements. Consequently, large numbers of DRAM devices that vary widely in their respective architecture, feature set, and performance characteristics now exist and occupy different market niches. To begin the difficult task of describing and comparing different DRAM

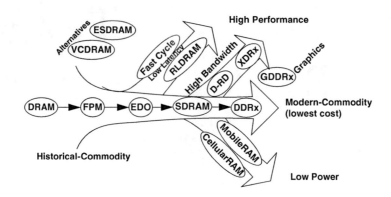

FIGURE 12.1: A broad classification of the DRAM family tree.

devices and different device architectures, four simple metrics are used in this chapter to broadly evaluate all DRAM devices and classify them into one of the four general paths of the family of DRAM devices described in this section. The four metrics are cost (capacity), latency, bandwidth, and power.

As described previously, different DRAM devices have been designed and manufactured to target low cost, low latency, high bandwidth, low power, or a reasonable compromise thereof. However, the single overriding consideration that has greatly impacted and constrained the evolutionary developments of DRAM device architectures is the issue of cost. In the general sense, cost-focused DRAM devices strive for the lowest cost per bit, and in this chapter, the focus on the lowest cost per bit is equated to the focus on capacity. In the decades since the invention of the DRAM circuit, the vast majority of DRAM devices manufactured and sold are commodity DRAM devices focused on cost, and these DRAM devices are classified in this chapter as belonging in the *Commodity* path of the DRAM device family tree. The classification of the DRAM family tree in this chapter follows the evolutionary family tree illustrated in Figure 12.1. Figure 12.1 separates and classifies the myriad of DRAM devices into four evolutionary paths in the DRAM family tree: the *Commodity* path, the *Low-Latency* path, the *High-Bandwidth* path, and the *Low-Power* path. To facilitate the examination of the numerous DRAM devices in the *Commodity*

path, the *Commodity* path is further separated into *Historical-Commodity* and *Modern-Commodity* subpaths. Alternatively, DRAM devices that focus on providing fast random accesses are classified as belonging to the *Low-Latency* path of the DRAM device family tree. DRAM devices that focus on delivering the highest bandwidth are classified as belonging to the *High-Bandwidth* path. Finally, the near-commodity *Graphics-Oriented* GDDR devices and *Alternative* DRAM devices that had appeared along the way in the evolution of the DRAM family tree—yet do not readily belong in the primary paths of the DRAM family tree—are also examined in Sections 12.5 and 12.6.

12.2 Historical-Commodity DRAM Devices

As stated previously, the overriding factor that has driven and continues to drive the development of DRAM devices is the cost per storage bit. As a consequence of the singular focus on cost, nearly all legacy DRAM devices that existed prior to the emergence of *Synchronous* DRAM (SDRAM) devices are classified in this chapter as belonging in the *Historical-Commodity* path of the DRAM family tree. Specifically, the commodity DRAM device evolved from *asynchronous* to *fast page mode* (FPM) to *extended data-out* (EDO) to *burst-mode EDO* (BEDO) and then finally into *synchronous* (SDRAM). In this chapter, SDRAM and its direct descendants such as DDR SDRAM, DDR2 SDRAM, and DDR3 SDRAM devices are classified as belonging in the *Modern-Commodity* path of the DRAM family tree, and these devices are examined in Section 12.3.

In this section, DRAM devices that belong to the *Historical-Commodity* path of the DRAM family tree are selectively examined, and the selected devices are the Intel 1103 DRAM device, the asynchronous DRAM device, the FPM DRAM device, the EDO DRAM device, and the BEDO DRAM device. These selectively examined devices represent important milestones in the evolutionary path of historical-commodity DRAM devices. However, a large number of different DRAM devices were produced by various DRAM manufacturers in the time period between the appearance of Intel's 1103 DRAM device and the BEDO DRAM device. Consequently, it is important to note that while the DRAM devices selectively examined in this section illustrate well the gradual evolution of commodity DRAM devices from the early 1970s to the late 1990s, the few illustrated devices do not represent all of the DRAM devices and evolutionary attempts in that time period.

In the evolution of DRAM device architecture from Intel's 1103 DRAM device to the BEDO DRAM device, the changes to the DRAM device have largely been structural in nature and relatively minor in terms of implementation cost; yet device functionality and throughput have increased significantly in each successive generation of DRAM devices. In the following section, the general description of the *Historical-Commodity* path of the DRAM family tree begins with a cursory examination of Intel's 1103 DRAM device.

12.2.1 The Intel 1103

The first commercially successful DRAM device, the 1103, was introduced by Intel in 1971. Due to its relatively low cost, the 1103 gained wide acceptance and rapidly replaced magnetic core memory in many different applications. Figure 12.3 shows the package pin configuration of the 1103, and it shows that this device was packaged in a low-cost, 18-pin, plastic dual in-line package. The 1103 had a row cycle time of 580 ns and a random access time of 300 ns. The 1103

also had a data retention time that was guaranteed to be longer than 2 ms; as long as each cell was refreshed at least once every 2 ms, data integrity was guaranteed. Differing from DRAM devices that followed it in subsequent years, the 1103 also had some interesting features such as unidirectional data input and output. The unidirectional input and output gave the early DRAM devices such as the 1103 (up to FPM devices) an interesting capability—an atomic read-modify-write cycle. That is, as the DRAM device drives data out of the output, the memory controller can hold the address on the address bus. Then, the controller can read, process, and immediately write data back through the input to the same address—something not practical in later DRAM devices with bidirectional data busses. Also, the 1103 used dedicated pins for row and column addresses, while later devices typically multiplexed row and column addresses over a single set of address pins. Moreover, the 1103 was a rudimentary device in terms of power supply requirements. Unlike the more modern DRAM devices, the 1103 required separate power supplies to properly bias the transistors. Finally, one feature that differentiated the 1103 from later DRAM devices was that it utilized the 3 transistor, 1 capacitor (3T1C) structure as the basic storage cell. Due to the 3T1C cell structure in the 1103 illustrated in Figure 12.2, data readout from the 1103 is nondestructive. Consequently, data does not need to be restored into the DRAM cell immediately after it is read out.

In comparison to the myriad of DRAM devices that followed it, Intel's 1103 DRAM device was a

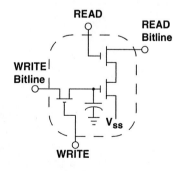

FIGURE 12.2: One (3T1C) bit cell of Intel's 1103 DRAM device.

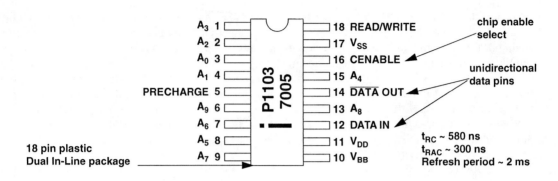

FIGURE 12.3: Pin configuration of Intel's 1103 DRAM device.

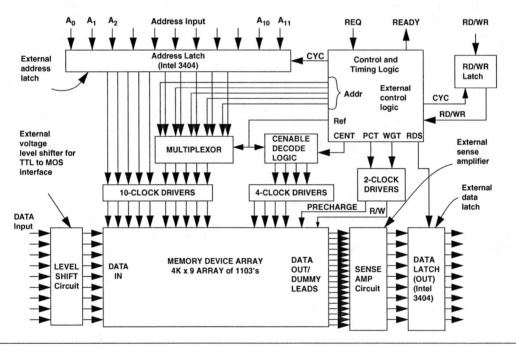

FIGURE 12.4: Structural block diagram of an 1103 memory system, consisting of 9 1103 devices.

rudimentary device that contained little more than address decoders and an array of 1024 DRAM cells. Common structures that were found in later devices, such as integrated address latches and sense amplifiers, were not present in the 1103. Consequently, a memory system that utilized the 1103 required more external circuitry than later devices. Figure 12.4 illustrates the structural block diagram of a memory system that utilizes the 1103.[1] The figure shows that several important external circuits are needed to

---

[1]Memory system block diagram taken from 1103 data sheet.

create a memory system based on the 1103. First, external voltage level shifters were needed to interface TTL devices to the MOS signal levels of the 1103. Second, the 1103 memory system required a significant amount of external logic to perform a simple read or write. Finally, the memory system used external sense amplifiers to resolve the stored data value from an 1103 DRAM device.

12.2.2 Asynchronous DRAM Devices

In the 1970s, subsequent to the introduction of Intel's 1103 DRAM device, many other DRAM devices were produced by Intel and other DRAM manufacturers. These DRAM devices were not standardized, and each DRAM device was unique in some way, containing subtle improvements from the previous generation of DRAM devices. For example, subsequent to the 1103, Intel introduced the 2104 DRAM device that multiplexed the row address and the column address over the same address bus, the 2116 DRAM device that was Intel's first 16-kbit DRAM device, and the 2118 DRAM device that was the first DRAM device to use a single 5-V power supply.

Other early DRAMs were sometimes clocked, where the DRAM commands were driven by a periodic clock signal. However, by the mid-1970s, DRAM device interfaces moved away from the clock-driven interface and moved to an *Asynchronous* command–data timing interface. These *Asynchronous* DRAM devices, like the clocked versions before them, require that every single access go through separate row activation and column access steps. Even if the microprocessor wants to request data contained in the same row that it previously requested, the entire row activation and column access process must be repeated. Figure 12.5 illustrates the timing for an asynchronous DRAM device. The figure shows that in the early asynchronous DRAM device, a row-activation command and a column-access command are needed to read data from the DRAM device, and two entire row cycles are needed to move data to or from any two addresses.

12.2.3 Page Mode and Fast Page Mode DRAM (FPM DRAM)

Since the introduction of Intel's 1103 DRAM device, each successive DRAM device has introduced new features to improve upon previous DRAM devices. One important feature that greatly improved DRAM device performance and was found in all later DRAM devices is *page mode* operation. In page mode operation, an entire row (page) of data is held by an array of sense amplifiers integrated into the DRAM device, and multiple column accesses to data in the same row can occur without having to suffer the latency of another row access. Page mode operation in DRAM devices improves system performance by taking advantage of the spatial locality present in the memory-access patterns of typical application

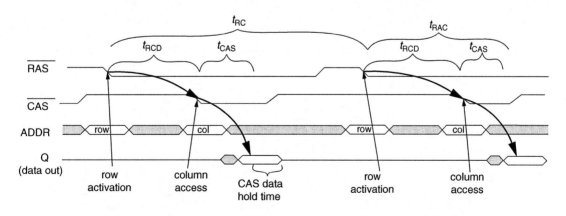

FIGURE 12.5: Read timing for a conventional asynchronous DRAM device.

programs. Page mode operation was not possible in the earliest DRAM devices due to the fact that the sense amplifiers were located off-chip. However, this mode of operation was enabled by the integration of sense amplifiers into the DRAM device, and data for an entire row could be sensed and buffered by the array of integrated sense amplifiers in parallel. Page mode permitted fast column accesses, and FPM improved the timing of the column access by allowing the column address buffers to remain open and active for as long as the row address strobe signal was held low. In this manner, the column addresses could be sent through the column address buffer and decoded before the column address strobe signal was asserted by the memory controller. Consequently, FPM was introduced into many 64-kbit DRAM devices in the early 1980s. FPM DRAM remained as the mainstream commodity memory well into the 1990s until it was replaced, in part, by EDO DRAM and finally entirely by *Synchronous DRAM* (SDRAM) in the late 1990s.

Figure 12.6 illustrates the organization and structure of a 64-Mbit FPM DRAM device with a 16-bit-wide bidirectional data bus. The FPM DRAM device illustrated in Figure 12.6 is a relatively modern DRAM device with a bidirectional data bus, while early generations of FPM DRAM devices typically had separate and unidirectional data input and output pins. Internally, the DRAM storage cells in the FPM DRAM device in Figure 12.6 are organized as 4096 rows, 1024 columns per row, and 16 bits of data per column. In this device, each time a row access occurs, the row address is placed on the address bus, and the *row address strobe* (RAS) is asserted by an external memory controller. Inside the DRAM device, the address on the address bus is buffered by the row address buffer and then sent to the row decoder. The row address decoder then accepts the row address and selects 1 of 4096 rows of storage cells. The data values contained in the selected row of storage cells are then sensed and kept active by the array of sense amplifiers. Each row of DRAM cells in the illustrated FPM DRAM device consists of 1024 columns, and each column is 16 bits wide. That is, a 16-bit-wide column is the basic addressable unit of memory in this device, and each column access that follows the row access would read or write 16 bits of data from the same

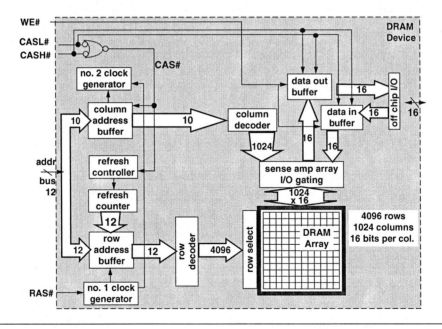

FIGURE 12.6: Internal organization of a 64-Mbit past page mode DRAM device (4096 x 1024 x 16).

row of DRAM. The FPM DRAM device illustrated in Figure 12.6 does allow each 8-bit half of the 16-bit column to be accessed independently through the use of separate *column access strobe high* (CASH) and *column access strobe low* (CASL) signals. In FPM DRAM devices, column access commands are handled in a similar manner as the row access commands. For a column access command, the memory controller places the column address on the address bus and then asserts the appropriate CAS signals. Internally, the DRAM chip takes the column address, decodes it, and selects 1 column out of 1024 columns. The data for that column is then placed onto the data bus by the DRAM device in the case of an ordinary column read command or overwritten with data from the memory controller depending on the write enable (WE) signal.

Figure 12.7 illustrates the timing for page mode read commands in an FPM device. The figure shows that once a row is activated by holding the $\overline{\text{RAS}}$ signal low, multiple column accesses can be used to retrieve spatially adjacent data from the same DRAM row with the timing of t_{PC}, the page mode cycle time. Figure 12.7 also shows that the output data valid time period is implicitly controlled by the timing of the $\overline{\text{CAS}}$ signal. That is, the DRAM device will hold the value of the read data out for some period of time after $\overline{\text{CAS}}$ goes high. The DRAM device then prepares for a subsequent column-access command without an intervening precharge command or row-access command.

In FPM DRAM devices, the page mode cycle time can be as short as one-third of the row cycle time. Consequently, (fast) page mode operation increased DRAM device bandwidth for spatially adjacent data by as much as three times that of a comparable generation asynchronous DRAM device without page mode operation.

12.2.4   Extended Data-Out (EDO) and Burst Extended Data-Out (BEDO) Devices

FPM DRAM devices were highly popular and proliferated into many different applications in the 1980s and the first half of the 1990s. Then, in the mid-1990s, EDO, a new type of DRAM device, was introduced into the market and achieved some degree of success in replacing FPM DRAM devices in mainstream personal computers. The EDO DRAM device added a new output enable ($\overline{\text{OE}}$) signal and allowed the DRAM device to hand over control of the output buffer from the $\overline{\text{CAS}}$ signal to the $\overline{\text{OE}}$ signal. Consequently, read data on the output of the DRAM device can remain valid for a longer time after the $\overline{\text{CAS}}$ signal is driven high, thus the name "extended data-out."

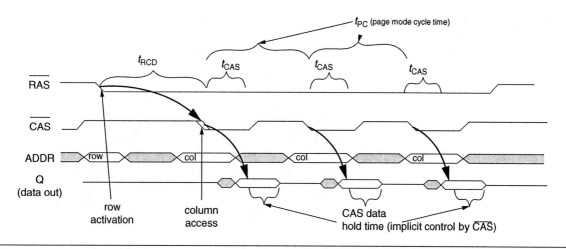

FIGURE 12.7: Multiple column read command timing for an FPM DRAM device.

Figure 12.8 gives the timing for three column read commands in an EDO DRAM device. The figure shows that the explicit control of the output data means that the $\overline{CAS}$ signal can be cycled around faster in an EDO DRAM device as compared to a FPM DRAM device, without impacting CAS data hold time. Consequently, EDO devices can achieve better (shorter) page mode cycle time, leading to higher device bandwidth when compared to FPM DRAM devices of the same process generation.

The EDO DRAM device achieved some success in replacing FPM DRAM devices in some markets, particularly the personal computer market. The higher bandwidth offered by the EDO DRAM device was welcomed by system design engineers and architects, as faster processors drove the need for higher memory bandwidth. However, the EDO DRAM device was unable to fully satisfy the demand for higher memory bandwidth, and DRAM engineers began to seek an evolutionary path beyond the EDO DRAM device.

The BEDO DRAM device builds on EDO DRAM by adding the concept of "bursting" contiguous blocks of data from an activated row each time a new column address is sent to the DRAM device. Figure 12.9 illustrates the timing of several column access commands

for a BEDO DRAM device. The figure shows that the row activation command is given to the BEDO device by driving the $\overline{RAS}$ signal low. The column access command in the BEDO device is then initiated by driving the $\overline{CAS}$ signal low, and the address of the column access command is latched in at that time. Figure 12.9 shows that unlike the DRAM devices that preceded it, the BEDO DRAM device then internally generates four consecutive column addresses and places the data for those columns onto the data bus with each falling edge on the $\overline{CAS}$ signal. By eliminating the need to send successive column addresses over the bus to drive a burst of data in response to each microprocessor request, the BEDO device eliminates a significant amount of timing uncertainty between successive addresses, thereby further decreasing the page mode cycle time that correlates to increasing DRAM device bandwidth.

12.3 Modern-Commodity DRAM Devices

The nature of the commodity DRAM business means that any proposed change to the DRAM device must incur relatively low circuit overhead

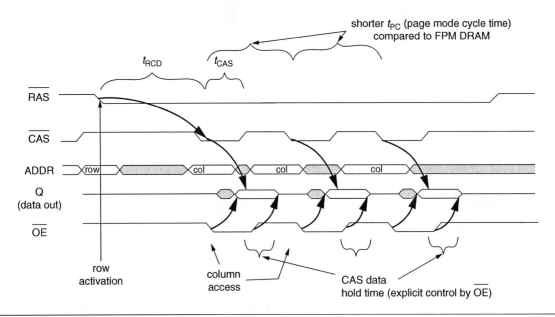

FIGURE 12.8: Multiple read command timing for an EDO DRAM device.

for the change to be acceptable to DRAM device manufacturers. Consequently, changes to DRAM devices are often evolutionary (low die cost) rather than revolutionary (high die cost). For example, the circuit overhead for an EDO DRAM device over that of an FPM DRAM device was minimal, and the evolutionary step required only a subtle change in protocol. However, owing to the convergence of factors such as the push to attain higher device bandwidth and more functionality from the DRAM device, DRAM manufacturers and systems manufacturers gathered through the *Joint Electron Device Engineering Council* (JEDEC) and collectively defined a new DRAM device, the SDRAM device. Compared to the EDO DRAM device that preceded it, the SDRAM device contained many new features that separated it distinctly from DRAM devices that preceded it. In this manner, the SDRAM device represents a break in the commodity path of the DRAM family tree and separates the *Modern-Commodity DRAM* devices from the *Historical-Commodity DRAM* devices.

The SDRAM device proved to be a highly successful DRAM device that proliferated into many different applications. The SDRAM device also became the basis for many different DRAM devices that followed it. The device architecture of commodity DRAM devices such as the Dual Data Rate (DDR) SDRAM, the Dual Data Rate II (DDR2) SDRAM, and Dual Data Rate III (DDR3) SDRAM is the direct descendant of the

SDRAM device architecture. The venerable SDRAM device can also claim as its descendant, directly or indirectly, DRAM devices such as the *Graphics DDR (GDDR) SDRAM*, *Graphics DDR2 (GDDR2) SDRAM*, *Graphics DDR3 (GDDR3) SDRAM*, *Enhanced SDRAM (ESDRAM)*, and *Virtual Channel SDRAM (VCDRAM)*, as well as *Mobile SDRAM* and *Mobile DDR SDRAM*. In this section, the evolutionary development for modern-commodity DRAM devices from SDRAM to DDR3 SDRAM devices are described and examined in detail.

12.3.1 Synchronous DRAM (SDRAM)

The SDRAM device is the first device in a line of modern-commodity DRAM devices. The SDRAM device represented a significant departure from the DRAM devices that preceded it. In particular, SDRAM devices differ from previous generations of FPM and EDO DRAM devices in three significant ways: the SDRAM device has a synchronous device interface, all SDRAM devices contain multiple internal banks, and the SDRAM device is programmable.

DRAM devices are controlled by memory controllers optimized for specific systems. In the case of FPM and EDO DRAM devices used in modern computer systems, the memory controller typically operated at specific, fixed frequencies to interface with other components of the system. The asynchronous nature

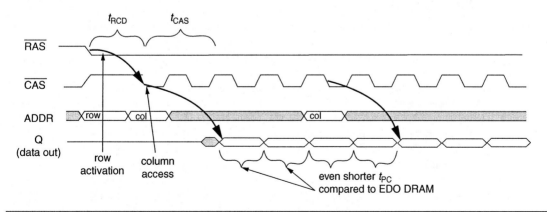

FIGURE 12.9: Multiple column read command timing for a BEDO DRAM device.

of FPM and EDO devices—that can, in theory, enable different controller and system designs to aggressively extract performance from different DRAM devices with different timing parameters—was more of a hindrance than an asset in the design of high volume and relatively high-performance memory systems. Consequently, computer manufacturers pushed to place a synchronous interface on the DRAM device that also operated at frequencies commonly found in the computer systems of that era, resulting in the SDRAM device.

In FPM and EDO DRAM devices, the $\overline{\text{RAS}}$ and $\overline{\text{CAS}}$ signals from the memory controller directly control latches internal to the DRAM device, and these signals can arrive at the DRAM device's pins at any time. The DRAM devices then respond to the $\overline{\text{RAS}}$ and $\overline{\text{CAS}}$ signals at the best possible speed that they are inherently capable of. In SDRAM devices, the $\overline{\text{RAS}}$ and $\overline{\text{CAS}}$ signal names were retained for signals on the command bus that transmits commands, but these specific signals no longer control latches that are internal to the DRAM device. Rather, the signals deliver commands on the command bus of the SDRAM device, and the commands are only acted upon by the control logic of the SDRAM device at the falling edge of the clock signal. In this manner, the operation of the state machine in the DRAM device moved from the memory controller into the DRAM device, enabling features such as programmability and multi-bank operation.

The second feature that significantly differentiated the SDRAM device from FPM and EDO devices that preceded it was that the SDRAM device contained multiple banks internally. The presence of multiple, independent banks in each SDRAM device means that while one bank is busy with a row activation command or a precharge command, the memory controller can send a row access command to initiate row activation in a different bank or can send a column access command to a different open bank. The multi-bank architecture of the SDRAM device means that multiple memory requests can be pipelined to different banks of a single SDRAM device. The first-generation 16-Mbit SDRAM device contained only 2 banks of independent DRAM arrays, but higher capacity SDRAM devices contained 4 independent banks in each device.

The SDRAM device also contains additional functionalities such as a column-access-and-precharge command. These functionalities along with the programmable state machine and multiple banks of sense amplifiers mean that the SDRAM device contains significant circuit overhead compared to FPM and EDO DRAM devices of the same capacity and process generation. However, since the circuit overhead was relatively constant and independent of device capacity, the die size overhead of the additional circuitry became less of an issue with larger device capacities. Consequently, the relatively low delta in manufacturing costs in combination with demonstrable performance benefits enabled 100-MHz, 64-Mbit SDRAM devices to take over from FPM and EDO devices as the mainstream commodity DRAM device.

Figure 12.10 shows a block diagram of an SDRAM device. The figure shows that the SDRAM device, unlike the FPM DRAM device in Figure 12.6, has 4 banks of DRAM arrays internally, each with its own array of sense amplifiers. Similar to the FPM device, the SDRAM device contains separate address registers that are used to control dataflow on the SDRAM device. In case of a row access command, the address from the address register is forwarded to the row address latch and decoder, and that address is used to activate the selected wordline. Data is then discharged onto the bitlines, and the sense amplifiers array senses, amplifies, and holds the data for subsequent column accesses. In the case of a column read command, the data is sent through multiple levels of multiplexors, then through the I/O gating structure out to the data bus, and eventually driven into the memory controller. In the case of a column write command, the memory controller places data on the data bus, and the SDRAM device then latches the data in the data in register, drives the data through the I/O gating structure, and overwrites data in the sense amplifier arrays; the sense amplifiers, in turn, drive the new data values into the DRAM cells through the open access transistors.

In an SDRAM device, commands are decoded on the rising edge of the clock signal (CLK) if the chip-select line (CS#) is active. The command is asserted by the DRAM controller on the command bus, which consists of the write enable (WE#), column access (CAS#), and row access (RAS#) signal lines. Although the signal lines have function-specific names, they essentially form a command bus, allowing the SDRAM device to recognize more commands without the use of

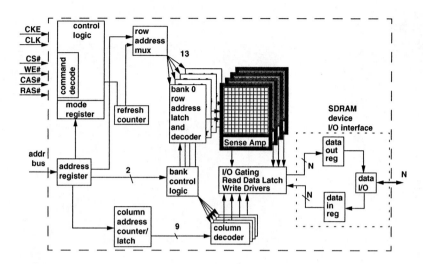

FIGURE 12.10: SDRAM device architecture with 4 banks.

additional signal lines. Table 12.1 shows the command set of the SDRAM device and the signal combinations on the command bus. The table shows that as long as CS# is not selected, the SDRAM device ignores the signals on the command bus. In the case where CS# is active on the rising edge of the clock, the SDRAM device then decodes the combination of control signals on the command bus. For example, the SDRAM device recognizes that the combination of an active low voltage value on RAS#, an interactive high voltage value on CAS#, and an inactive high voltage value on WE# as a row activation command and begins the row activation process on the selected bank, using the row address as provided on the address bus.

A different combination of signal values on the command bus allows the SDRAM device to load in new values for the mode register. That is, in the case where CS#, RAS#, CAS#, and WE# are all active on the rising edge of the clock signal, the SDRAM device decodes the load mode register command and loads the mode register from values presented on the address bus.

The third feature in an SDRAM device that differentiates it from previous DRAM devices is that the SDRAM device contains a programmable mode register, and the behavior of the DRAM device depends on the values contained in the various fields of the mode register. The presence of the mode register means that the SDRAM device can exhibit different behaviors in response to a given command. Specifically, the mode register in an SDRAM device allows it to have programmable CAS latency, programmable burst length, and programmable burst order.

Figure 12.11 shows that in an SDRAM device, the mode register contains three fields: CAS latency, burst type, and burst length. Depending on the value of the CAS latency field in the mode register, the DRAM device returns data two or three cycles after the assertion of the column read command. The value of the burst type determines the ordering of how the SDRAM device returns data, and the burst length field determines the number of columns that an SDRAM device will return to the memory controller with a single column read command. SDRAM devices can be programmed to return 1, 2, 4, or 8 columns or an entire row. Direct RDRAM devices and DDRx SDRAM devices contain more mode registers that control an ever-larger set of programmable operations, including, but not limited to, different operating modes for power conservation, electrical termination calibration modes, self-test modes, and write recovery duration.

To execute a given command, the control logic block on the SDRAM device accepts commands sent on the command bus from the memory controller. Then, depending on the type of command

Table 12.1   Command definition on the SDRAM device

Command	CS#	RAS#	CAS#	WE#	addr
command inhibit (nop)	H	X	X	X	X
no operation (nop)	L	H	H	H	X
active (activate row - RAS)	L	L	H	H	addr
read (start read - CAS)	L	H	L	H	addr
write (start write - CAS W)	L	H	L	L	addr
burst terminate	L	H	H	L	X
precharge	L	L	H	L	**
auto refresh	L	L	L	H	X
load mode register	L	L	L	L	code

**Bank address, or all banks with a_10 assertion.

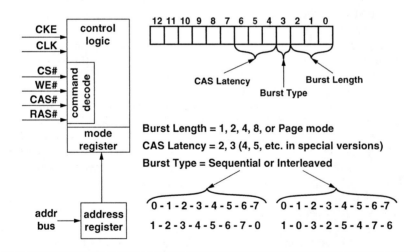

FIGURE 12.11: Programmable mode register in an SDRAM device.

and values contained in the respective fields of the mode register, the SDRAM device performs specific sequences of operations on successive clock cycles without requiring clock-by-clock control from the memory controller. For example, in the case of the column-read-and-precharge command, the SDRAM device accepts the command, and then, depending on the value programmed into the mode register, the SDRAM device begins to return data two or three clock cycles after the command was asserted on the command bus. The burst length and burst order of the single column access command also depends on the value programmed in the mode register. Then, the SDRAM device automatically precharges the DRAM bank after the column read command completes.

SDRAM-Access Protocol

Figure 12.12 illustrates some basic concepts of data access to an SDRAM memory system. The figure shows a total of three commands: a row activation command to bank i of rank n, followed by a column read access command to the same bank, followed by another column read access command to an open bank in a different rank. Figure 12.12 shows that the interface of the SDRAM memory system presents the memory system as a synchronous state machine that responds to commands issued from the memory controller. Specifically, Figure 12.12 shows that a row activation is started in an SDRAM device by the device latch-ing the command and addresses on the rising edge of the clock signal. The SDRAM device then decodes the command and transitions the state machine on the DRAM device that is appropriate to the specific command received. In Figure 12.12, two cycles after the row activation command, the row-column delay time is satisfied, and the row is then assumed by the memory controller to be open. The memory controller then places the column read access command on the command bus, and t_{CAS} time later, the SDRAM device begins to return data from the just-opened row to the memory controller. In Figure 12.12, the SDRAM devices are programmed to return four consecutive columns of data for each column access command, so four consecutive columns of data are placed onto the data bus by the DRAM device without further interaction from the memory controller. Finally, Figure 12.12 subtly illustrates that the synchronous interface of the SDRAM memory system is only a convenient illusion. For the case of two column read commands to different ranks, the change in the bus master of the data bus on back-to-back clock cycles leads to some minor uncertainty on the timing.

Die Photo and a TSOP Package

Figure 12.13 shows the die photograph of a 256-Mbit SDRAM device from Micron. In the figure, much of the surface area of the silicon die is dominated by the regular structures of the DRAM arrays.

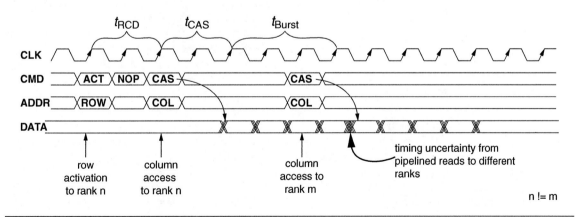

FIGURE 12.12: A row activation, followed by a column access to rank n, followed by a column access to rank m.

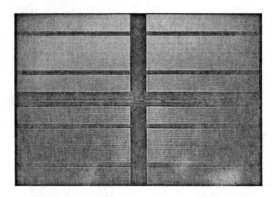

FIGURE 12.13: 256-Mbit SDRAM device from Micron. (Photo courtesy of Micron.)

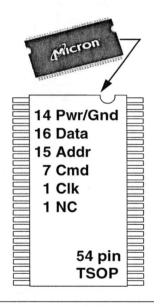

FIGURE 12.14: TSOP for an SDRAM device.

In this case, roughly 70% of the silicon surface is used by the DRAM arrays, and the rest of the area is taken up by I/O pads, sense amplifiers, decoders, and the minimal control logic. The SDRAM device shown in Figure 12.13 is manufactured on a DRAM-optimized, 0.11-μm process with three layers of metal interconnects and six layers of polysilicon. The die size of the SDRAM device is approximately 45 mm^2.

SDRAM devices are packaged in a low-cost *Thin, Small Outline Package* (TSOP). Figure 12.14 shows a 54-pin TSOP for an SDRAM device with a 16-bit-wide data bus. In a x16 SDRAM device, 14 pins on the 54-pin TSOP are used for power and ground, 16 pins are used for the data bus, 15 pins are used for the address bus, 7 pins are used for the command bus, and 1 pin is used for the clock signal.

PC100—The Proliferation of Extended, Rigorous DRAM Standardization and Qualification Processes

In April 1998, Intel Corp. introduced a new system controller that was the first controller to operate the SDRAM memory system at 100 MHz. Prior to the rollout of the 440BX AGPset, engineers at Intel discovered that memory modules manufactured by different module manufacturers, possibly utilizing different DRAM devices from different manufacturers, may not inter-operate in a seamless manner when placed into the same SDRAM memory system despite the fact that each module individually meets technical requirements for 100-MHz operation according to JEDEC standards specification. To ensure the success of the 440BX system controller chipset and the associated Pentium II processor platform, Intel Corp., in conjunction with DRAM device, DRAM module, and system manufacturers, adopted a more stringent set of standards for 100-MHz SDRAM memory. This set of stringent requirements for SDRAM memory to operate at 100 MHz was referred to as the PC100 standard.

The PC100 SDRAM standard ensured module inter-operability by further decreasing the allowable timing margins on the chip and module interface. The decreased timing margins placed more stringent requirements on SDRAM device and SDRAM memory module manufacturers. In an effort to alleviate the demand placed on these manufacturers, Intel began to provide reference designs of SDRAM memory modules complete with bills of materials that specified prequalified SDRAM parts, schematics that illustrated connection points on a memory module, and Gerber files that specified the connections within the PCB layers of a memory module, as well as the values and placement of resistors and capacitors on a memory module. The reference design approach reduced the burden placed on memory module manufacturers and allowed the PC100 standard to proliferate. Consequently, PC100 SDRAM memory modules quickly gained popularity as end-users were assured of high performance and trouble-free memory system configuration, regardless of configuration and manufacturer of the DRAM device or modules.

Subsequent to the PC100 standardization effort, Intel attempted to shift industry memory system architecture to Direct RDRAM. Consequently, Intel

did not drive the 133-MHz PC133 standardization effort. Nevertheless, the qualification path set down by Intel to ensure compatibility between different manufacturers was used to drive subsequent standard qualification efforts for faster SDRAM and DDRx memory systems. Currently, the module standardization effort to ensure trouble-free inter-operability resides in a subcomittee within JEDEC.

12.3.2 Double Data Rate SDRAM (DDR SDRAM)

The *Double Data Rate* (DDR) Synchronous DRAM device evolved from, and subsequently replaced, the SDRAM device as the mainstream commodity DRAM device. Consequently, DDR SDRAM device architecture closely resembles SDRAM device architecture. The primary difference between DDR SDRAM device architecture and the SDRAM device architecture is that the SDRAM device operates the data bus at the same data rate as the address and command busses, while the DDR SDRAM device operates the data bus at twice the data rate of the address and command busses. The reason that the data bus of the DDR SDRAM device operates at twice the data rate of the address and command busses is that signal lines on the data bus of the traditional SDRAM memory system topology are more lightly loaded than signal lines on the address and command busses. Figure 12.15 shows

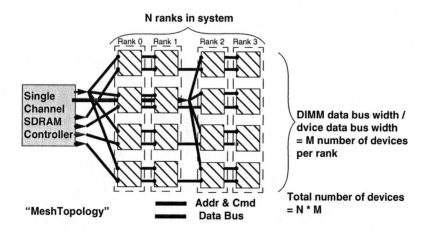

FIGURE 12.15: SDRAM memory system topology shows uneven loading on the different busses. Electrical loading on the address bus is much heavier than on the data bus.

the general topology of the SDRAM memory system where there are N ranks of DRAM devices in the memory system with M ranks of DRAM devices per rank. In the topology shown in Figure 12.15, each pin on the address and command bus may drive as many as N * M loads, whereas the pins on the data bus are limited to the maximum of N loads. Consequently, the data bus can switch states at a much higher rate as compared to the address and command busses. DDR SDRAM devices are architected to take advantage of the imbalance in loading characteristics and operate the data bus at twice the data rate as the command and address busses.

DDR SDRAM-Access Protocol

Figure 12.16 illustrates basic concepts of data access to a DDR SDRAM memory system. A total of three commands are shown: a row activation command to bank i of rank n, followed by a column read access command to the same bank, followed by another column read access command to an open bank in a different rank. Figure 12.16 shows that data transfer occurs at twice the rate on the data bus as compared to the address and command bus. Figure 12.16 also shows that the DDR SDRAM memory system uses the data strobe signal (DQS), a signal not found in previous-generation SDRAM devices, to provide a source-synchronous timing reference signal between the source and the destination. In DDR SDRAM devices, the DQS signal is controlled by the device that sends the data on the data bus. In the case of a read command, the DQS signal is used by the DRAM device to indicate the timing of read data delivery to the memory controller. In the case of a write command, the DQS signal is used by the memory controller to indicate the timing of write data delivery from the memory controller to the DRAM device.

The timing diagram in Figure 12.16 shows a one-cycle bubble between data bursts from different ranks of DRAM devices. The one-cycle bubble exists because the DQS signal is a shared signal used by all data sources in the memory system. Consequently, one idle cycle is needed for one bus master to hand off control of the DQS signal line to another bus master, and the one-cycle bubble appears on the data bus as a natural result.

DDR SDRAM I/O Interface

Figure 12.17 presents a block diagram view of the DDR SDRAM device I/O interface. As Figure 12.16

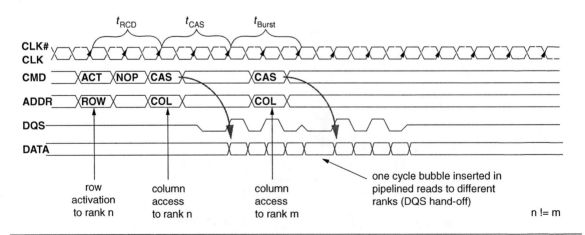

FIGURE 12.16: Accessing data in a DDR SDRAM memory system.

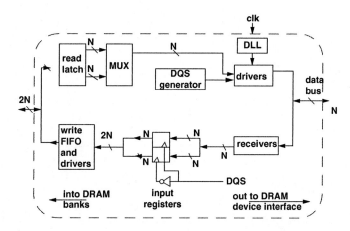

FIGURE 12.17: DDR SDRAM device I/O.

illustrates, DDR SDRAM memory systems transfer data on both edges of the DQS strobe signal. However, despite the increase in the rate of data transfer on the device interface, the rate of internal data transfer in the DDR SDRAM device is not similarly increased. Instead, in DDR SDRAM devices, the rate of data transfer is internally halved so that data movement occurs internally at twice the width, but half the rate of the device interface. DRAM device manufacturers have adopted the terminology of *M-bit prefetch* to describe the data rate multiplication architecture, where M represents the multiplication factor between the DRAM device's internal width of data movement and the width of the data bus on the device interface. In this nomenclature, DDR SDRAM devices are said to have a 2-bit prefetch architecture where $2 * N$ bits are moved internally at rate Y, but the DDR SDRAM device provides an N-bit-wide interface to the memory system that moves data at rate $2 * Y$.

Aside from the difference in the I/O interface of the DRAM device, DDR SDRAM device architecture is otherwise identical to SDRAM device architecture. Consequently, some DRAM manufacturers created unified designs that can be bonded out as a DDR SDRAM device of data width X or an SDRAM device of data width 2 * X. These unified designs allowed these manufacturers to quickly shift wafer allocations to meet shifting market demands. However, these unified designs typically cost several percentage points of die overhead, so their use was limited to the transitional period between SDRAM and DDR SDRAM devices.

Series Stub Terminated Signaling Protocol

Aside from the changes to the I/O architecture of the DRAM device, the signaling protocol used by the DDR SDRAM device also differed from the signaling protocol used by the SDRAM device. The signaling protocol used in DDR SDRAM devices had to meet two conditions: better signal integrity to achieve the higher data rate and a signaling protocol that would still permit the DRAM device core and the DRAM device interface to share a common, yet lower voltage level. The *2.5-V Series Stub Terminated Logic* (SSTL-2) signaling protocol met the requirement for DRAM manufacturers to simultaneously achieve the higher signaling rates found in DDR SDRAM memory systems and to lower the device voltage from the 3.3 V used by SDRAM devices to 2.5 V. Consequently, SSTL-2 is used in all DDR SDRAM devices.

Figure 12.18 illustrates the idealized signal input and output characteristics for an SSTL-2 inverter. The figure shows that SSTL-2 differs from *Low-Voltage Transistor-Transistor Logic* (LVTTL) in that SSTL-2 uses a common reference voltage V_{ref} to differentiate between a logically high voltage state and a logically low voltage state. The use of the common voltage reference enables SSTL-2 devices to enjoy better voltage margins than LVTTL, despite the decrease in the overall voltage range from 3.3 to 2.5 V.

12.3.3 DDR2 SDRAM

In the search for an evolutionary replacement to the DDR SDRAM device as the commodity DRAM device of choice, DRAM device manufacturers sought to achieve higher device data rates and lower power dissipation characteristics without substantially increasing the complexity, which translates to higher manufacturing cost, of the DRAM device. The DDR2 SDRAM device architecture was developed by a consortium of DRAM device and system manufacturers at JEDEC to meet these stringent requirements. The DDR2 SDRAM device was able to meet the requirement of a higher data transfer rate without substantially increasing the manufacturing cost of the DRAM device by further increasing the prefetch length, from 2 bits in DDR SDRAM device architecture to 4 bits. In the *M*-bit prefetch nomenclature, DDR2 SDRAM devices move 4 * *N* bits internally at rate *Y*, but provide an *N*-bit-wide interface to the memory system that moves data at a rate of 4 * *Y*. Figure 12.19 presents a block diagram view of the DDR2 SDRAM device I/O interface. The figure shows that DDR2 SDRAM devices further double the internal datapath of the DRAM device compared to that of a comparable DDR SDRAM device.

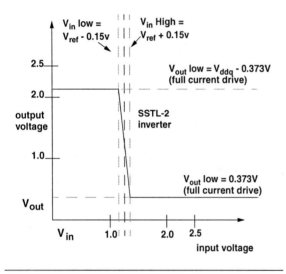

FIGURE 12.18: SSTL-2 signaling in DDR SDRAM devices.

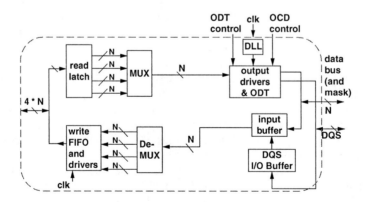

FIGURE 12.19: DDR2 SDRAM device I/O interface.

Figure 12.19 also shows another subtle difference between DDR and DDR2 SDRAM devices. The I/O interface of the DDR2 SDRAM device has an additional signal to control the termination characteristic of the input pin. The *On-Die Termination* (ODT) signal can be controlled by a DDR2 SDRAM memory controller to dynamically adjust the electrical characteristics of the memory system, depending on the configuration of the specific memory system.

12.3.4 Protocol and Architectural Differences

The evolutionary relationship between DDR SDRAM and DDR2 SDRAM device architectures means that the two devices architectures are substantially similar to each other. However, there are subtle architectural and protocol differences that separate the DDR2 SDRAM device from the DDR SDRAM device. For example, DDR2 SDRAM devices can support posted CAS commands, and DDR2 devices now mandate a delay between the column write command and data from the memory controller.

Figure 12.20 illustrates two pipelined transactions to different banks in a DDR2 SDRAM device. The figure shows that the DDR2 SDRAM device is programmable to the extent that it can hold a column access command for a certain number of cycles before it executes the command. The posted CAS command feature allows a DDR2 SDRAM memory controller to treat a row activation command and a column access command as a unitary command pair to be issued in consecutive cycles rather than two separate commands that must be controlled and timed separately. In Figure 12.20, the additional hold time for the CAS command is three cycles, and it is labelled as t_{AL}, for Additional Latency. Figure 12.20 also shows that the DDR2 SDRAM device now requires a write delay that is equivalent to $t_{CAS} - 1$ number of cycles. With the addition of t_{AL}, column read command timing can be simply referred to as Read Latency, or t_{RL}, and column write command timing can be simply referred to as Write Latency, or t_{WL}.

Differential Strobes and FBGA Packages

In addition to dynamic termination control, DDR2 SDRAM device architecture also contains other features that differentiate it from DDR SDRAM device architecture. For example, DDR2 SDRAM devices can optionally support a differential DQS signal, while DDR SDRAM devices only support a single ended DQS signal. The differential DQS signal enables the DDR2 SDRAM device to bolster the signal integrity

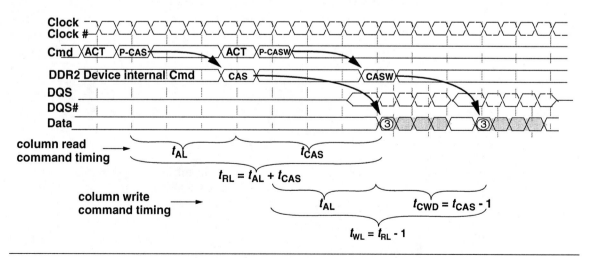

FIGURE 12.20: A posted column read command and a posted column write command in a DDR2 SDRAM system.

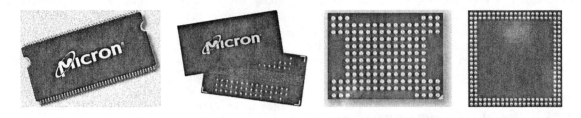

FIGURE 12.21: A DDR SDRAM device in a TSOP and a DDR2 SDRAM device in an FBGA package. (Photos courtesy of Micron.)

of the reference strobe, thus enabling it to operate at higher data rates. In addition to illustrating the progression of the posted column read and posted column write commands, Figure 12.20 also shows that data for column read commands, sent by the DRAM devices, is edge-aligned to the data strobe signal, while data for column write commands, sent by the DRAM controller, is center-aligned to the DQS and DQS# data strobe signals.[2]

Finally, Figure 12.21 shows a DDR SDRAM device in a TSOP and a DDR2 SDRAM device in a *Fine Ball Grid Array* (FGBA) package. FBGA packaging is more expensive than TSOP, but the ball grid contacts present less electrical parasitics for the signal transmission line. Consequently, FBGA packaging is required for the higher data rate DDR2 devices, while it remains optional for DDR SDRAM devices.

12.3.5 DDR3 SDRAM

Having learned many lessons in the evolutionary development of DDR and DDR2 SDRAM devices, DRAM device and systems manufacturers have continued on the path of further increasing DRAM device prefetch lengths to enable higher device data rates in the next-generation commodity DRAM device—DDR3 SDRAM. The DDR3 SDRAM device continues the technique of increasing prefetch lengths and employs a prefetch length of 8. Consequently, DDR3 SDRAM devices are expected to attain data rates that range between 800 Mbps per pin to 1.6 Gbps per pin, doubling the range of 400 to 800 Mbps per pin for DDR2 SDRAM devices.[3]

DDR3 SDRAM devices also contain additional enhancements not found in DDR2 SDRAM devices. For example, DDR3 SDRAM devices of all capacities have at least 8 banks of independent DRAM arrays, while the 8-bank architecture is limited to DDR2 devices with capacities of 1 Gbit or larger. DDR3 SDRAM devices will also have two features that may enable them to reduce refresh power consumption. One optional feature that will enable DDR3 SDRAM devices to reduce refresh power consumption is a temperature-dependent self-refresh mode. In this self-refresh mode, the rate of refresh and current of the self-refresh circuitry will be adjusted automatically by the DDR3 device, depending

---

[2]Read data in SDRAM devices is edge-aligned to the clock signal, while write data is center-aligned to the clock signal. The data timing described herein for DDR2 is similar for DDR, DDR2, and DDR3 SDRAM devices.
[3]At the time of the writing of this text, discussions are underway to extend the range of DDR3 data rate past 2 Gbps.

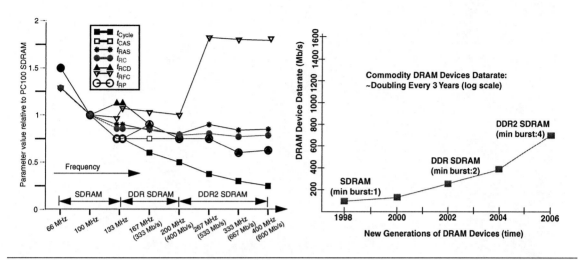

FIGURE 12.22: Commodity DRAM device timing and data rate scaling trends.

on the temperature of the device. The second feature that will enable DDR3 devices to reduce refresh power is that a DDR3 device can be programmed to refresh only a subset of the rows that contain data, rather than all of the rows once per fresh loop.[4] These features, in combination with the lower 1.5 V supply voltage, enable DDR3 devices to consume less power per unit of storage or unit of bandwidth.

Unfortunately, the high data transfer rate of DDR3 SDRAM devices requires significant trade-off in memory system configuration flexibility, a trade-off that will limit the utility of the device in unbuffered memory systems. To reach the high data rate of DDR3 SDRAM devices, DRAM device and system manufacturers have imposed the limit of two ranks of DRAM devices in a memory system, and the two ranks of DRAM devices are assumed to be located close to each other. Consequently, computer system manufacturers will not be able to design and market computers with traditional, unbuffered memory systems that still allow end-users to flexibly configure the capacity of the memory system as could be done with DDR and DDR2 SDRAM memory systems.

12.3.6 Scaling Trends of Modern-Commodity DRAM Devices

In the decade since the definition of the SDRAM standard, SDRAM devices and their descendants have continued on a general scaling trend of exponentially higher data rates and slowly decreasing timing parameter values for each generation of DRAM devices. Table 12.2 contains a summary of timing parameter values for selected SDRAM, DDR SDRAM, and DDR2 SDRAM devices. Table 12.2 shows that fundamental device operation latencies in terms of wall clock time have gradually decreased with successive generations of DRAM devices, while DRAM device data rates have increased at a much higher rate. Consequently, DRAM device operation latencies have, in general, increased in terms of cycles, despite the fact that the latency values in nanoseconds have decreased in general.

Figure 12.22 shows the scaling trends of commodity DRAM devices from 1998 to 2006. In the time period illustrated in Figure 12.22, random row cycle times in commodity DRAM devices decreased on the order of 7% per year. In contrast, the data rate of

---

[4]Partial array refresh is also present in DDR2 SDRAM devices.

TABLE 12.2 Timing parameter values of various x4 SDRAM, DDR, and DDR2 devices

	SDRAM						DDR SDRAM						DDR2 SDRAM					
Capacity	16 Mbit		256 Mbit				512 Mbit						1 Gbit					
Manf.	Siemens		Micron		Micron		Micron		Micron		Micron		Micron		Micron		Micron	
Part No.	64V16220GU		48LC64M4A2		48LC64M4A2		46V128M4		46V128M4		46V128M4		47H256M4		47H256M4		47H256M4	
Bin	−10		−75		−7E		−6		−5B		−5		−3		−3E		−25	
Freq.	66 MHz		100 MHz		133 MHz		133 MHz		167 MHz		200 MHz		267 MHz		333 MHz		400 MHz	
Data rate	66 Mbps		100 Mbps		133 Mbps		266 Mbps		333 Mbps		400 Mbps		533 Mbps		667 Mbps		800 Mbps	
	clks	ns	clks	ns	clks	ns	clks	ns	clks	ns	clks	ns	clks	ns	clks	ns	clks	ns
t_{Cycle}	1	15	1	10	1	7.5	1	7.5	1	6	1	5	1	3.75	1	3	1	2.5
t_{CAS}	2	30	2	20	2	15	2	15	2.5	15	3	15	4	15	4	12	5	12.5
t_{FAW}	—		—		—								10	37.5	13	39	15	37.5
t_{RAS}	5	75	5	50	6	45	6	45	7	42	8	40	11	41.25	14	42	17	42.5
t_{RC}	6	90	7	70	8	60	8	60	10	60	11	55	15	56.25	18	54	22	55
t_{RCD}	2	30	2	20	3	22.5	3	22.5	3	18	3	15	4	15	4	12	5	12.5
t_{RFC}	6	90	7	70	9	67.5	10	75	12	72	14	70	34	127.5	42	129	51	127.5
t_{RP}	2	30	2	20	2	15	2	15	3	18	3	15	4	15	4	12	5	12.5
t_{RRD}	2	30	2	20	2	15	2	15	2	12	2	10	3	11.25	3	9	4	10
t_{RTP}	1	15	1	10	1	7.5	1	7.5	1	6	1	5	2	7.5	3	9	3	7.5
t_{WR}	2	30	2	20	2	15	2	15	3	18	3	15	4	15	5	15	6	15
t_{WTR}	—		—		—		1	7.5	2	12	2	10	2	7.5	3	9	3	7.5

TABLE **12.3**   Quick summary of SDRAM and DDRx SDRAM devices

		SDRAM	DDR SDRAM	DDR2 SDRAM	DDR3 SDRAM
Supply voltage		3.3 V	2.5[a] V	1.8 V	1.5 V
Signaling		LVTTL	SSTL-2	SSTL-18	SSTL-15
Bank count		4[b]	4	4[c]	8
Data rate range		66~133	200~400	400~800	800~1600
Prefetch length		1	2	4	8
Internal datapath width	×4	4	8	16	32
	×8	8	16	32	64
	×16	16	32	64	128

[a]400-Mbps DDR SDRAM standard voltage set at 2.6 V.
[b]16-Mbit density SDRAM devices only have 2 banks in each device.
[c]256- and 512-Mbit devices have 4 banks; 1-, 2-, and 4-Gbit DDR2 SDRAM devices have 8 banks in each device.

commodity DRAM devices doubled every three years. Consequently, the relatively constant row cycle times and rapidly increasing data rates mean that longer requests or a larger number of requests must be kept in flight by the DRAM memory controller to sustain high bandwidth utilization.

Figure 12.22 also shows an anomaly in that the refresh cycle time t_{RFC} has increased rather than decreased in successive generations of DRAM devices, unlike the scaling trends for other timing parameters. Although the t_{RFC} values reported in Table 12.2 are technically correct, the illustrated trend is somewhat misleading. That is, t_{RFC} increased for the DDR2 devices examined over that for the DDR SDRAM devices due to the fact that the DDR SDRAM devices examined in Table 12.2 are 512-Mbit devices, whereas the DDR2 SDRAM devices examined in Table 12.2 are 1-Gbit devices. In this case, the larger capacity means that a larger number of cells must be refreshed, and the 1-Gbit DDR2 DRAM device must take longer to perform a refresh command or draw more current to refresh twice the number of DRAM storage bits in the same amount of time as the 512-Mbit DDR SDRAM device. Table 12.2 shows that DRAM manufacturers have, in general, chosen to increase the refresh cycle time t_{RFC}, rather than significantly increase the current draw needed to perform a refresh command. Consequently, the refresh cycle time t_{RFC} has not decreased in successive generations of DRAM devices when the general trend of increasing capacity in each generation is taken into account.

Table 12.3 contains a summary of modern-commodity SDRAM devices, showing the general trends of lower supply voltages to the devices and higher operating data rates. Table 12.3 also summarizes the effect of the increasing prefetch length in SDRAM, DDR SDRAM, DDR2 SDRAM, and DDR3 SDRAM devices. Table 12.3 shows the worrying trend that the increasing data rate of commodity DRAM devices has been achieved at the expense of increasing granularity of data movement. That is, in a ×4 SDRAM device, the smallest unit of data movement is a single column of 4 bits. With increasing prefetch length, the smallest unit of data movement has also increased proportionally. The increasing granularity of data movement means that the commodity DRAM system is losing randomness of data access, and the higher device bandwidth is achieved only by streaming data from spatially adjacent address locations. The situation is being compounded with the fact that ×8 DRAM devices are far outselling ×4 DRAM devices, and ×4 DRAM devices are only being used in memory systems that require maximum capacity. Consequently, ×4 DRAM devices are now selling at a price premium over ×8 and ×16 DRAM devices.

The larger granularity of data movement has serious implications in terms of random access performance as well as memory system reliability. For example, in a DDR2 SDRAM memory system, the loss of a single device will take out 16 bits of data in a ×4 device and 32 bits of data in a ×8 device. Consequently, a minimum data bus width of 144 bits is needed, in combination with sophisticated error correction hardware circuitry to cover for the loss of 16 bits of data in a ×4 device and 32 bits of data in a ×8 device.

12.4 High Bandwidth Path

In 1990, the 80386 processor was the dominant desktop processor, and memory bandwidth was not a limiting issue as it is in more modern memory systems. However, in that same year, Rambus Corp. was founded with a focus to design high-speed chip interfaces, specifically memory system interfaces. Rambus Corp.'s focus on high-speed signaling technology led it to design high bandwidth memory interfaces and systems that differ radically from commodity DRAM memory systems in terms of signaling protocol, system topology, device architecture, and access protocol. As a result of its singular focus on high device and system bandwidth, the high bandwidth path of DRAM device architecture evolution is dominated by memory systems developed by Rambus Corp.

In the years since its founding, Rambus Corp. has had various levels of contribution and involvement in different memory systems. However, two high bandwidth memory systems are often cited when Rambus technology is brought up for discussion: the *Direct Rambus Dynamic Random-Access Memory* (Direct RDRAM) memory system and the *Extreme Data Rate* (XDR) memory system. In this section, the unique features of these two memory systems are singled out for examination.

12.4.1 Direct RDRAM

The Direct RDRAM device and system architectures are radically different from the conventional, commodity DRAM device and system architectures. In this section, we begin with the fundamental difference between the Direct RDRAM memory system and the commodity, cost-focused DRAM memory systems by starting with an examination of the high-speed signaling technology developed by Rambus, the *Rambus Signaling Level* (RSL) signaling protocol. RSL enabled Rambus Corp. to design high-speed DRAM device interfaces. However, the relatively slow DRAM circuits designed for use in low-cost commodity DRAM devices mean that the high-speed RSL signaling protocol must be coupled with suitable device and system architectures to attain high values of practical, sustainable bandwidth. In the following sections, the signaling technology, system architecture, device architecture, and access protocol of the Direct RDRAM memory system are systematically examined. The systematic examination of the Direct RDRAM memory system architecture begins with an examination of RSL.

The Rambus Signaling Level (RSL)

The RSL was Rambus' first signaling technology. RSL was designed as a high-speed, singled-ended, multi-drop, bidirectional bus signaling technology. RSL is designed as a signaling technology that can support a variable number of loads on the same bus—between 1 and 32 DRAM devices can be connected to the same bus. RSL debuted with data rates of 500 Mbps and reached over 1.2 Gbps in various configurations.

Figure 12.23 shows that the RSL is defined to swing between 1.0 and 1.8 V. RSL is designed to operate as a high-speed signaling system that makes use of current mode output drivers with carefully controlled slew rates to deliver low-voltage signals across transmissions lines with carefully controlled impedance characteristics.

Memory System Architecture

The system architecture of the Direct RDRAM memory system differs dramatically from system architectures of SDRAM and DDRx SDRAM memory systems. The key elements of the Direct RDRAM memory system architecture that differentiate it from SDRAM and DDRx SDRAM memory system architectures are path-matched address, command and data bus topology, separate row and column address

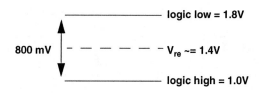

FIGURE 12.23: Direct RDRAM signaling: Rambus signaling levels.

channels with encoded command packets, separate data channel, multiple cycle, packet-based command and address assertion from memory controller to memory device, and the absence of a critical word forwarding data burst.

The system architecture of the Direct RDRAM memory system was designed to sustain high pin-bandwidth regardless of the number of DRAM devices in the memory system. The motivation for this design decision is that it allows for a high degree of performance scalability with multiple channels of memory, regardless of the number of DRAM devices per channel. In theory, an embedded system with a single channel memory system with a single DRAM device in the memory system can enjoy as much pin-bandwidth as a server system with multiple channels of memory and fully populated with 32 devices per channel. Unlike high data rate DDR2 and DDR3 memory systems that rely on multiple ranks of DRAM devices to collectively provide sufficient bandwidth to saturate the channel, a single-rank Direct RDRAM memory system can provide as much bandwidth as a multi-rank Direct RDRAM memory system.

Device Architecture

Figure 12.24 illustrates the device organization of a 288-Mbit Direct RDRAM device with 32 interleaved and dependent (32d) banks internally. The Direct RDRAM device can be architected to contain different numbers of banks. The organization illustrated in Figure 12.24 contains 32 dependent banks.[5] In the 32d Direct RDRAM device architecture, each bank is split into two halves, an upper half bank and a lower half bank, and adjacent banks share common sets of sense amplifiers. That is, the lower half of bank i shares the same set of sense amplifiers with the upper half of bank $i + 1$. Consequently, adjacent banks i and $i + 1$ cannot both be open at the same time.

One difference between Direct RDRAM memory systems versus SDRAM and DDRx SDRAM memory systems is that SDRAM and DDRx SDRAM memory systems rely on wide data busses with a non-power-of-two number of devices in parallel to provide the requisite number of data and check bits for error detection and correction. In contrast, a single Direct RDRAM device may form the entire data bus width of a Direct RDRAM memory system. Consequently, different versions of Direct RDRAM devices are used in different Direct RDRAM memory systems. Direct RDRAM memory systems that do not require error correction use Direct RDRAM devices with a 16-bit-wide data bus, and Direct RDRAM memory systems that require error correction use Direct RDRAM devices with an 18-bit-wide data bus. Figure 12.24 illustrates a Direct RDRAM device with an 18-bit-wide data bus. The figure shows that the 18-bit-wide data bus is organized as two separate 9-bit-wide data busses.

Unlike SDRAM and DDRx SDRAM devices where a given command and the associated address are sent in a single clock cycle, Direct RDRAM devices encode

---

[5] A 4 independent (4i) banks per device architecture was promoted as a cost reduction initiative for desktop systems that are typically configured with multiple DRAM systems on a given RIMM. However the initiative did not gain traction, and the 32d device architecture was the primary device architecture at the 256-/288-Mbit device node.

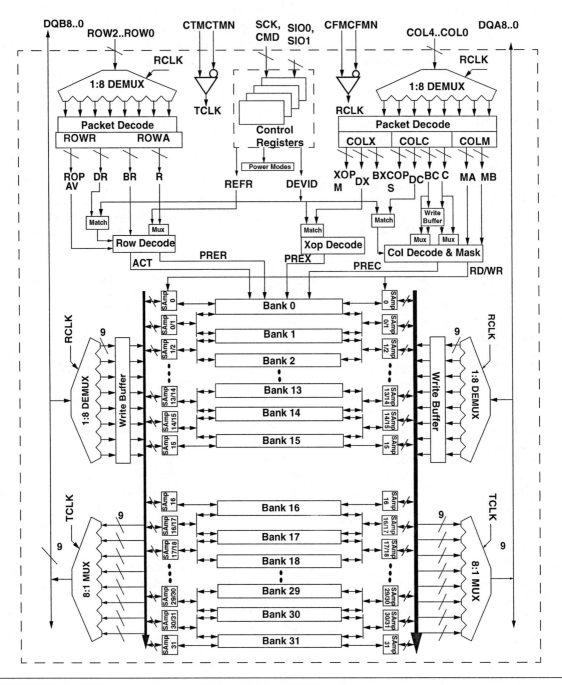

FIGURE 12.24: Split (32 interleaved) bank architecture of a Direct RDRAM device.

the command and address into a multi-cycle packet that must be buffered, de-multiplexed, and decoded by the Direct RDRAM device. In the case of a column read command, a read command packet (40 bits in size) is sent over the 5-bit-wide COL[4:0] column command bus on both the rising edge and the falling edge of the clock-from-master (CFM) clock signal. The 40-bit-wide packet is received and decoded by the Direct RDRAM device into COLX, COLC, and COLM command and address fields. The Direct RDRAM device then moves the requested data from the array of sense amplifiers through the 8:1 multiplexor onto the data bus. In this manner, the data prefetch architecture of Direct RDRAM devices is very similar to the internal device architecture of DDR3 SDRAM devices. However, unlike DDR3 SDRAM devices, Direct RDRAM devices do not support burst reordering to send the critical word first.

Topology

To take advantage of the high-speed signaling system, Rambus designed a new system topology for Direct RDRAM. Figure 12.25 shows that each Direct RDRAM device appears on a Direct DRAM channel as a single load. Figure 12.25 presents a topological view of the Direct RDRAM memory system with the memory controller connected to two memory modules, and each module contains four memory devices. The memory module for the Direct RDRAM memory system is referred to as a *Rambus In-line Memory Module* (RIMM) by Rambus. Each memory device illustrated in the Direct RDRAM memory system in Figure 12.25

presents a 16-bit-wide data interface to the data bus. In Figure 12.25, all of the Direct RDRAM devices are connected on the same channel with a 16-bit-wide data bus. In essence, each Direct RDRAM device is a single rank of memory in a Direct RDRAM memory system.

In a Direct RDRAM memory system, the clock-from-master signal, the clock-to-master signal, the column address and command bus, the row address and command bus, and the two 8-bit-wide data busses are routed in parallel. Unlike the mesh topology of the SDRAM and the DDRx SDRAM memory systems, the topology of the Direct RDRAM memory system allows all of the signal interfaces of the DRAM device to operate with minimal skew relative to the system clock signals. The Direct RDRAM memory system uses a scheme where the clock signals propagate alongside data signals to minimize timing skew between clock and data. The minimal clock-data timing skew means that the Direct RDRAM memory system can avoid the insertion of idles in the protocol to account for timing uncertainties and achieve high bandwidth efficiency. The arrangement of the memory device in the Direct RDRAM memory system also means that with more devices, the bus turnaround time increases and results in longer memory latency.

Access Protocol

The memory-access protocol of the Direct RDRAM memory system is quite different from access protocols of traditional memory systems such as SDRAM,

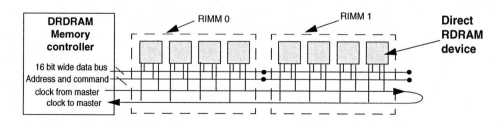

FIGURE 12.25: Direct RDRAM system topology.

DDR SDRAM, and DDR2 SDRAM memory systems. As a consequence of the matched topology of the clock, data, and command and address busses, the Direct RDRAM memory controller encodes all commands and addresses into packets[6] and transmits them in 8 half cycles,[7] a period of time called an *octcycle*, from the controller to the DRAM device. In the case of row commands, the Direct RDRAM controller encodes the row address and access commands into row access command packets that are 24 bits in length and transports the 24-bit-long packets from the controller to a Direct RDRAM device over 3 signal wires in 8 half cycles. In the case of column access commands, the Direct RDRAM controller encodes the column addresses and column access commands into packets that are 40 bits in length for transport to a Direct RDRAM device over 5 signal wires in 8 half cycles.

The Direct RDRAM memory system transports data in a manner that is similar to the command transport mechanism. In the case of a column read command, 128 bits of data are transported from a single Direct RDRAM device over 16 signal wires in 8 half cycles to the memory controller. The timing of a memory read command in a Direct RDRAM memory system is illustrated in three separate steps in Figure 12.26. The figure shows that the Direct RDRAM memory controller first packs and encodes a row activation command and then transmits the packed row activation command over the span of four clock cycles in step 1. The packed column access command is then transmitted to the Direct RDRAM device in step 2. Finally, in step 3, data is returned to the controller by a given Direct RDRAM device (device 0 in Figure 12.26) in over 8 half cycles. The 128 bits, or 16 bytes, of data are also referred to as a *dualoct* by Rambus.

One interesting detail about the Direct RDRAM memory-access protocol illustrated in Figure 12.26 is that the Direct RDRAM controller began to transmit the column read command almost immediately after the row access command, before t_{RCD} timing had been satisfied. The reason that the transmission of the column read command can begin almost immediately after the transmission of the row access command is that each command packet must be buffered, decoded, and then executed by the addressed Direct RDRAM device. Consequently, the column access command shown as step 2 in Figure 12.26 is not decoded until the transmission of the command has been completed and the entire packet has been received by the Direct RDRAM device. The optimal timing to minimize delay is then to coincide the row-activation-to-column-access delay with the end of the column access packet as shown in Figure 12.26.

The Direct RDRAM memory system is designed to sustain high bandwidth throughput, and the Direct RDRAM memory-access protocol allows a large combination of different memory-access commands to be

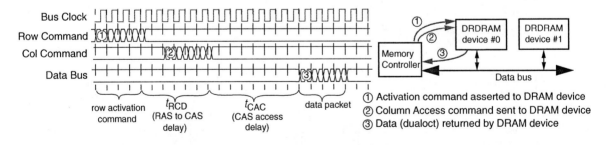

FIGURE 12.26: A row activation command followed by a column read command in a Direct RDRAM system.

---

[6]The command and address packets are not network packets with a header and payload. Rather, these packets are simply multi-cycle, fixed-duration, predefined format, command and address data sent by the controller to the DRAM device.
[7]The Direct RDRAM memory system sends and receives data, commands, and addresses on each edge of a clock signal. Consequently, in the Direct RDRAM memory system, the time period of 8 half cycles is equal to 4 full clock cycles.

issued by the memory controller consecutively without the need for idle cycles. Figure 12.27 illustrates the full utilization of the data bus by showing three consecutive column read commands that return data to the memory controller without the presence of any idle cycles between data packets on the data bus. Figure 12.27 shows two consecutive column read commands to device #0, followed by a third command sent to device #1. The figure then shows the return of data by the memory devices after the appropriate CAS delay. In theory, no idle cycles are needed in between

column read commands, since the data transmission on the data bus is synchronized by the common *clock-to-master* signal, even in the case where the column read commands are sent to different Direct RDRAM devices in the Direct RDRAM channel.[8]

The Write-to-Read Turnaround Issue

Figure 12.28 illustrates the problematic case of a column read command that follows a column write command in commodity DRAM devices such as a

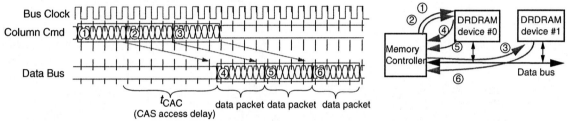

t_{CAC} (CAS access delay)

① Column Access command sent to DRAM device #0
② Column Access command sent to DRAM device #0
③ Column Access command sent to DRAM device #1
④ Data packet returned by DRAM device #0
⑤ Data packet returned by DRAM device #0
⑥ Data packet returned by DRAM device #1

FIGURE 12.27: A row activation command followed by a column read command in a Direct RDRAM system.

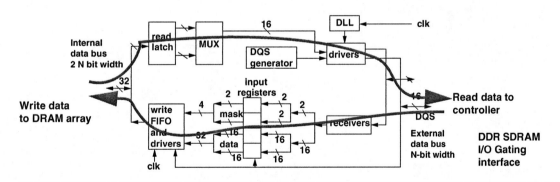

FIGURE 12.28: I/O gating sharing problem for read following write to same rank of DRAM devices—commodity DDRx SDRAM.

---

[8]In theory, although no idle cycles are needed in between any two column read commands to open pages in a Direct RDRAM memory system, idle cycles are sometimes inserted into Direct RDRAM memory systems between column access commands to reduce the activity rate of the Direct RDRAM device and to reduce the peak power dissipation of Direct RDRAM memory systems and Direct RDRAM devices.

DDR SDRAM device. The figure illustrates that despite the existence of separate read and write FIF buffers and drivers, both read data and write data must share the use of internal and external data busses through the I/O gating structure. The sharing of the data busses means that write data must be driven into and through the internal data busses to the selected bank of sense amplifiers before data for a subsequent read command to the same device can be placed onto the internal data bus. The bottleneck of the internal data bus leads directly to long write-to-read turnaround times in high data rate DRAM devices.

Write Buffer in Direct RDRAM Devices

To reduce the long write-read turnaround time in high data rate DRAM devices, Rambus designed Direct RDRAM devices and XDR DRAM devices with specialized structures to alleviate the write-to-read turnaround problem. The solution to the write-to-read turnaround problem implemented in the Direct RDRAM device is through the use of a write buffer. The existence of the write buffer in the Direct RDRAM device means that as soon as data is written into the write buffers, the I/O gating resource can be used by a subsequent column read command. Figure 12.29 illustrates the sequence of three column access commands to a Direct RDRAM device: a column write command followed by a column read command that is, in turn, followed by a retire command. Figure 12.29 illustrates that the write-to-read turnaround time is significantly reduced through the use of the write buffer. Essentially, actions typically performed by column write commands are separated into a write-into-write-buffer command and a retire-from-write-buffer-into-sense-amplifier command. The separation of the column write command enables a subsequent read command to be issued

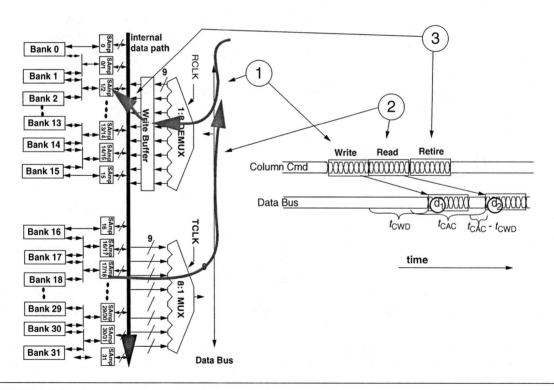

FIGURE 12.29: A write-to-read-to-retire command sequence in a Direct RDRAM device.

immediately after a column write command since the column write command does not have to immediately drive the data through the internal datapath and into the sense amplifiers.

The use of the write buffer by the Direct RDRAM device has several implications from the perspective of the memory-access protocol. First, a column write command places write data temporarily in the write buffer, but addresses of subsequent column read commands are not checked against addresses of pending data in the write buffer by the Direct RDRAM device. The interesting result is that a column read command that immediately follows a column write command to the exact same location in a Direct RDRAM device will read stale data from the sense amplifiers while the most recent data is held in the write buffers. The use of the write buffer by the Direct RDRAM device thus requires the memory controller to keep track of the addresses of column write commands that have not yet been retired from the write buffer to enforce memory consistency.

The use of write buffers to alleviate the write-to-read turnaround time directly increases the complexity of the DRAM device as well as the complexity of the DRAM memory controller. In the case of the DRAM device, die area devoted to the write buffer increases the die cost of the DRAM device. From the perspective of the memory-access protocol, the memory controller has to manage a new retire-write-data command, further increasing its complexity.

12.4.2 Technical and Pseudo-Technical Issues of Direct RDRAM

In the late 1990s, the Direct RDRAM memory system was chosen by Intel Corp. as the next-generation memory system that would replace the 100-MHz SDRAM memory system. However, due to a number of issues, Direct RDRAM memory systems failed to gain market acceptance and did not replace SDRAM as the mainstream memory system. Instead, a more moderate evolutionary path of DDRx SDRAM memory systems replaced the SDRAM memory system. The issues that prevented Direct RDRAM memory systems from gaining market acceptance consisted of a number of technical issues that were primarily

engineering trade-offs and a number of non-technical issues that were related to the licensing of the Direct RDRAM memory system by Rambus Corp. to DRAM device manufacturers and system design houses. In this chapter, the focus is placed on the technical issues rather than the business decisions that impacted the failure of the Direct RDRAM memory system to achieve commodity status. Moreover, the challenges faced by Direct RDRAM memory systems in attempting a revolutionary break from the commodity SDRAM memory system are quite interesting from the perspective that future memory systems that attempt similar revolutionary breaks will have to overcome similar challenges faced by the Direct RDRAM memory system. Consequently, the engineering trade-offs that increased the cost of implementation or reduced the performance advantage of the Direct RDRAM memory systems are examined in detail.

Die Size Overhead

In practical terms, the Direct RDRAM memory system increased memory device complexity to obtain higher pin-bandwidth and increased data transport efficiency. For example, the baseline Direct RDRAM device contained 16 or 32 dependent banks, requiring separate bank control circuitry and arrays of sense amplifiers. Each Direct DRAM device also contained circuitry to carefully manage the electrical characteristics of the Direct RDRAM device. The high-speed RSL signaling interface further required separate I/O voltage rings for the Direct RDRAM device. Collectively, the sophisticated architectural features and electrical control circuitry added significantly to the die cost. Consequently, Direct RDRAM devices were approximately 20~30% larger than SDRAM devices at the 64-Mbit node. This die size overhead resulted from a combination of the required circuit overhead and the fact that these first-generation devices were designed for speed rather than die size. Fortunately, the circuit overhead of Direct RDRAM devices was relatively constant in terms of the number of transistors. Consequently, the die size overhead of Direct RDRAM devices, as a percentage of die area, decreases with increasing DRAM device capacity. At the 128-Mbit density node, Toshiba produced an SDRAM device with a die size of

91.7 mm², while its Direct RDRAM device on the same process had a die size of 103 mm², making the die size overhead 12% for Toshiba at the 128-Mbit node. The die size overhead for Direct RDRAM devices was expected to drop below 10% for the 256-Mbit density node and decrease further at higher density nodes.

Sophisticated System Engineering Requirement

The high system-level signaling rates of the Direct RDRAM memory system required careful control and understanding of the electrical characteristics of the memory controller I/O interface, the system board, the memory modules, and the DRAM device package and I/O interface. Analogously, the issues in implementing Direct RDRAM memory systems were similar to the issues that necessitated the PC100 standard, and the solutions were similar: significant amounts of engineering resources had to be devoted to design a high data rate memory system. Consequently, system manufacturers were reluctant to devote the engineering resources required to implement Direct RDRAM memory systems. In particular, some low-cost-focused system manufacturers lacked the engineering resources required to design low-cost Direct RDRAM memory systems.

One issue that illustrated the importance of engineering resources in the deployment of cost-effective Direct RDRAM memory systems is the issue of multi-layer system boards. The Direct RDRAM memory system architecture required matching signal flight times for parallel signals on various command and data busses. To minimize crosstalk and ensure signal integrity, first-generation proof-of-concept system boards that implemented Direct RDRAM memory systems were designed on 8-layer PCBs, and many second-generation system boards that shipped commercially with Direct RDRAM memory systems were designed on 6-layer PCBs. Compared to commodity systems that used 4-layer PCBs, the 6-layer system board further increased cost to the early implementation of Direct RDRAM memory systems. Finally, with the passage of time and the devotion of engineering resources by Rambus and various system manufacturers, the system-level cost issue of Direct RDRAM memory systems was eventually brought to parity with commodity systems as Direct RDRAM memory systems on 4-layer PCBs were proven to be practical.

Advanced Packaging and Testing Equipment Requirement

The high signaling rate Direct RDRAM device required careful control of the electrical characteristics of the DRAM device package and I/O interface. Consequently, Direct RDRAM devices could not use similar low-cost TSOPs and SOJ packages that were used for SDRAM devices. Instead, Direct RDRAM devices were shipped with BGA packages that minimized the impedance contributions of the pin interface of the package. Figure 12.30 illustrates one type of BGA packaging used for Direct RDRAM devices. Unfortunately, the use of the BGA package further added cost to DRAM device and memory module manufacturers that were not accustomed to the new packaging. For example, memory module manufacturers could

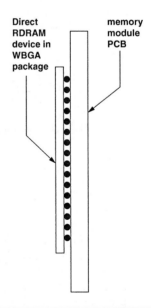

Direct RDRAM device in WBGA package

memory module PCB

FIGURE 12.30: Edge view of a Wirebond Ball Grid Array (WBGA) Direct RDRAM device mounted on a memory module.

not visually inspect the solder connections between the BGA package and the memory module as they could with SOJ and TSOPs. Consequently, new equipment had to be purchased to handle the new packaging, further increasing the cost delta between Direct RDRAM memory systems and the then-commodity SDRAM and DDR SDRAM memory systems.

Heat Density—Heat Spreader—Enforced Idle Cycles

In the classical mesh topology of SDRAM and DDRx SDRAM memory systems, multiple DRAM devices are connected in parallel to form a given rank of memory. Moreover, high data rate DDR2 and DDR3 SDRAM devices do not contain enough banks in parallel in a single rank configuration to fully saturate the memory channel. Consequently, the on-chip and in-system data movements associated with any given command issued by the memory controller are always distributed across multiple DRAM devices in a single rank and also typically across different ranks in standard 64- or 72-bit-wide SDRAM and DDRx SDRAM memory systems. In contrast, the Direct RDRAM memory system is architected for high bandwidth throughput, and a single Direct RDRAM device provides full bandwidth for a given channel of Direct RDRAM devices. However, the ability of the single Direct RDAM device to provide full bandwidth to the memory channel means that the on-chip and in-system data movements associated with a given command issued by the memory controller are always limited to a single DRAM device. Moreover, Figure 12.31 illustrates that in the worst-case memory-access pattern, a sustainable stream of row activation and column access commands can be pipelined to a single device in a given channel of the Direct RDRAM memory system. Consequently, localized hot spots associated with high access rates to a given device can appear and disappear on different sections of the Direct RDRAM channel. The localized hot spots can, in turn, change the electrical characteristics of the transmission lines that Direct RDRAM memory systems rely on to deliver command and data packets, thus threatening the functional correctness of the memory system itself. To counter the problem of localized hot spots in Direct RDRAM memory systems, Rambus Corp. deployed two solutions: heat spreaders and new command issue rules designed to limit access rates to a given Direct RDRAM device. Unfortunately, the use of heat spreaders on the RIMMs further increased the cost of the Direct RDRAM memory system, and the new command issue rules further increased controller complexity and decreased available memory bandwidth in the Direct RDRAM memory system.

Low Request Rate Systems

The Direct RDRAM memory system provided a revolutionary approach to memory system architecture that required significant cost adders in many different components of the memory system. Consequently, first-generation Direct RDRAM memory systems were significantly more expensive than SDRAM memory systems. However, these first-generation Direct RDRAM memory systems were used in Pentium III-based computer systems, and these Direct

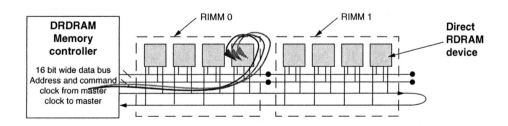

FIGURE 12.31: Worst-case memory-access pattern can create localized hot spots in DRDRAM system topology.

RDRAM memory systems did not illustrate significant performance benefits over SDRAM-based memory systems to justify their cost premium.

Figure 12.32 shows that in the memory-access sequence of a Direct RDRAM memory system, the controller first sends a packet command to the Direct RDRAM device, and then the DRAM device buffers the command, decodes it, moves the data to the I/O interface, and then bursts that data over 8 half cycles back to the controller. Memory access in the Direct RDRAM memory system thus suffers from the additional latency components of command transmission to the DRAM device and data burst time back to the controller. Consequently, the SDRAM memory system has lower idle system latency as compared to the Direct RDRAM memory system. Figure 12.32 illustrates that the advantage of the Direct RDRAM memory system is that its higher bandwidth and higher efficiency allows it to return data with lower average latency when it is coupled with a processor that has a high rate of memory access. Unfortunately, first-generation Direct RDRAM memory systems were primarily coupled to uniprocessor Pentium III-based systems that did not and could not sustain a high rate of memory access. Potentially, Direct RDRAM memory systems coupled to advanced high-frequency, multi-threaded, and multi-core processors would have provided the tangible performance benefit that could justify the cost premium. Unfortunately, the average consumer could not envision the advanced processors that were yet to come, but could readily observe that the Direct RDRAM memory system did not present significant performance advantage over SDRAM memory systems when attached to Pentium III-based systems.

Different Devices for Different Systems

In a Direct RDRAM memory system, a single Direct RDRAM device returns a dualoct for a given column access command. However, memory systems designed for reliability require additional data storage locations to store check bits. In traditional commodity memory systems, the check bits are stored in additional DRAM devices as the width of the data bus is increased from 64 to 72 bits. Consequently, the same DRAM devices can be used in desktop computers that do not require error correction and in high-end servers that do. In contrast, the 16-bit data bus width of the Direct RDRAM memory system means that it was not practical to create an analogous memory system where a single logical channel of memory consists of 9 physical channels of Direct RDRAM devices in parallel. Aside from the extraordinary cost of 9 physical channels of Direct RDRAM memory, a single column access command to such a memory system would move 144 bytes of data, a granularity that is too large

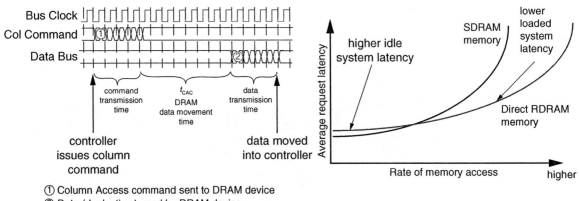

① Column Access command sent to DRAM device
② Data (dualoct) returned by DRAM device

FIGURE 12.32: Longer idle system latency and lower loaded system latency for a Direct RDRAM system.

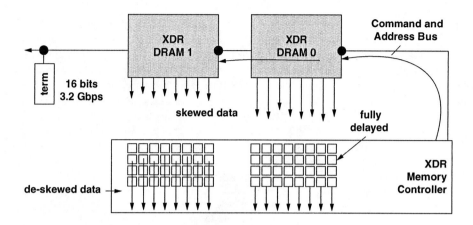

FIGURE 12.33: Basic topology of the XDR memory system.

for the cacheline sizes of all mainstream processors.[9] Consequently, different versions of Direct RDRAM devices had to be designed for error correcting memory systems and systems that did not require error correction. At the 64-Mbit density node, 64-Mbit Direct RDRAM devices with 16-bit-wide data busses were available alongside 72-Mbit Direct RDRAM devices with 18-bit-wide data busses. Similarly, 144-, 288-, and 576-Mbit Direct RDRAM devices were available alongside 128-, 256-, and 512-Mbit devices in each density node, respectively. The different versions of Direct RDRAM devices split the volume demand for Direct RDRAM devices, providing yet another obstacle that hindered cost-reduction efforts in Direct RDRAM memory systems.

Lessons for Future Memory Systems

The Direct RDRAM memory system introduced a high level of complexity and new cost adders into the memory system, but the fact that it was coupled to a relatively low-frequency Pentium III-based system meant that it did not demonstrate its best-case performance advantage over lower cost SDRAM and DDR SDRAM memory systems. Consequently, it met a great deal of resistance and encountered numerous obstacles in its way of reaching high volume production

status, approaching price parity with SDRAM memory systems and demonstrating a tangible performance advantage in production systems. Ultimately, the Direct RDRAM memory system failed to reach commodity status. However, the technical challenges faced by Direct RDRAM memory systems were important lessons that Rambus Corp. heeded in the design of its next-generation high bandwidth memory system, the XDR memory system.

12.4.3 XDR Memory System

Rambus Corp., having learned valuable lessons from the drawbacks of the Direct RDRAM memory system, proceeded to design its next-generation high bandwidth memory system that avoided many of the technical pitfalls that hindered acceptance of the Direct RDRAM memory system. The *Extreme Data Rate* (XDR) memory system has been designed to further increase DRAM device and memory system signaling rate, yet at the same time to reduce system design complexity and DRAM device overhead.

Topology

Figure 12.33 illustrates the basic system topology of the XDR memory system. The figure shows

---

[9]Intel's Itanium and IBM's server-oriented POWER processors do have 128-byte cachelines, but neither system seriously contemplated such a memory system.

that in the XDR memory system, as in DDRx SDRAM systems, the command-and-address busses operates at a relatively lower data rate as compared to the data bus. In the XDR memory system, the command and address datapath is a path-length-matched, unidirectional datapath that the XDR memory controller uses to broadcast command and address information to DRAM devices. Figure 12.33 also shows that the XDR controller uses FlexPhase to do skew compensation on the datapath—removes skew on read data coming into the controller and adds skew to ensure that write data reaches DRAM device interface in sync.

Device Architecture

Figure 12.34 illustrates the device organization of an XDR device. The XDR DRAM device is characterized by numerous features that distinguish it from the Direct RDRAM device. For example, the XDR DRAM device has a prefetch length of 16, so the minimum burst length is 16. However, the XDR device architecture has been designed with variable device data bus width control so that a device may be configured with a data bus width as low as 1 bit. Consequently, the minimum granularity of data movement in such a device may be as small as 16 bits. Figure 12.34 also shows that the XDR device is internally organized into two different, odd and even, bank sets.

Finally, Figure 12.34 shows that the XDR device differs from the Direct RDRAM device in that unlike the Direct RDRAM device, the XDR DRAM device has a common command bus that is used by row access commands as well as column access commands. Moreover, unlike the Direct RDRAM device, the XDR DRAM device does not have a write buffer. Instead, it relies on the differing bank sets and an intelligent controller to alleviate the write-to-read data bus turnaround issue.

Signaling

Figure 12.35 shows the octal data rate signaling system that Rambus Corp. introduced with the XDR memory system. In this signaling system, a relatively slow master clock signal (400~800 MHz) is shared by both the memory controller and the DRAM device. The DRAM device and the memory controller use current mirrors to transmit differential signals that are locked in-phase with the system clock signal, but operate at four times the frequency of the system clock signal. Data is transmitted on both edges of the signal, so 8 1-bit symbols per pin pair are transmitted in every clock cycle. The low voltage swing, point-to-point, differential signaling enables high bandwidth in commodity ASIC and DRAM processor technologies at the cost of higher power consumption.

FlexPhase

In the XDR memory system, Rambus Corp. uses a system of bit-adjustable DLL circuitry to remove bit-to-bit signal skew from the high-speed parallel data bus. This system of bit-adjustable DLL circuitry is referred to as FlexPhase. Figure 12.35 shows how Rambus uses the FlexPhase circuit to account for differences in signal flight time. FlexPhase takes care of data-to-data skew, and it can be recalibrated to lock in new phase differentials to account for thermal drifts between cold and warm systems. Figure 12.35 shows that the FlexPhase circuitry is placed in the controller interface. In this manner, the FlexPhase technology removes the path-length matching requirement from the XDR memory system without increasing the cost of the DRAM device. In this case, the additional cost is paid for in terms of increased controller sophistication.

XDR Early Read After Write

To counter the various drawbacks of a write buffer in Direct RDRAM devices, Rambus did not include write buffers in the design of its next-generation, high-performance XDR DRAM device. Instead, XDR DRAM devices are architected to support a feature that Rambus refers to as the Early Read After Write (ERAW) feature. Essentially, XDR devices avoid the large write-to-read command overhead by using separate internal paths for banks separated into odd and even sets. In this organization, a read command can proceed in parallel with a write command, as long as the read and write commands are directed to banks in

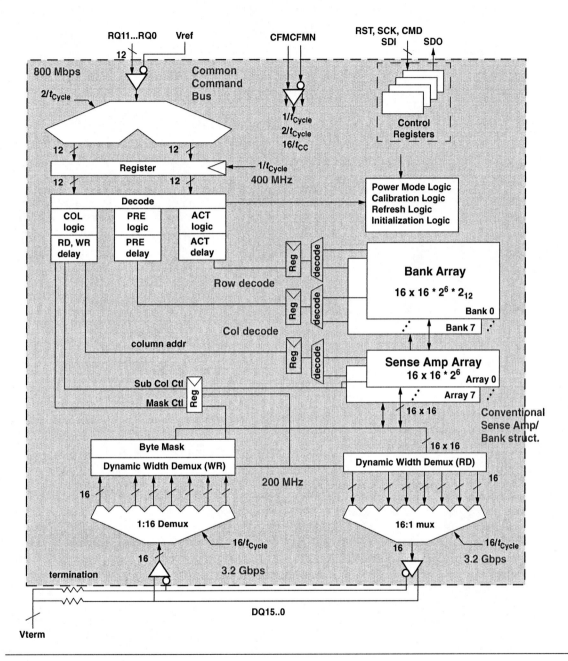

FIGURE 12.34: Architecture of an XDR device.

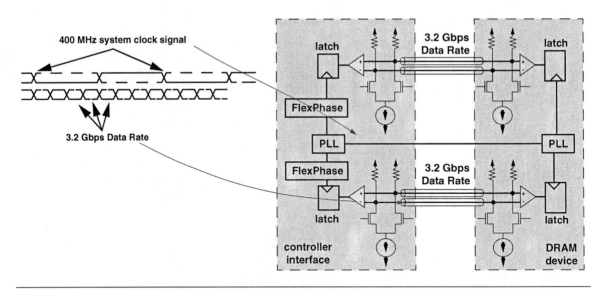

FIGURE 12.35: Octal data rate signaling using per-bit FlexPhase de-skewing and PLL in an XDR memory system.

different bank sets. Figure 12.36 shows that although the write-to-read turnaround overhead still occupies several cycles, the overhead is much smaller than if the write and read commands are issued to the same set of banks.

12.5 Low Latency

The proliferation of low-cost commodity DRAM devices means that high-speed, low-latency SRAM devices have been pushed into increasingly small niches as design engineers seek to use DRAM devices wherever they can to reduce system cost. However, even as DRAM devices replace SRAM in more and more applications, the desire for lower-than-commodity-DRAM latency characteristics remains. Consequently, DRAM device manufacturers have been developing specialty low-latency DRAM devices as semi-commodity, moderately low-latency replacements for SRAM replacement application. Two families of DRAM devices, the Reduced Latency DRAM (RLDRAM) and Fast Cycle DRAM (FCRAM), have been designed specifically to target the low-latency SRAM replacement market.

12.5.1 Reduced Latency DRAM (RLDRAM)

RLDRAM is a low-latency DRAM device with random access latency as low as 10–12 ns and row cycle times as low as 20 ns. The first-generation RLDRAM device was designed by Infineon to meet the demands of the market for networking equipment. Subsequently, Micron was brought in as a partner to co-develop RLDRAM and provide a second source. However, Infineon has since abandoned RLDRAM development, and Micron proceeded ahead to develop the second-generation RLDRAM II. RLDRAM and RLDRAM II were designed for use in embedded applications. Primarily, RLDRAM is designed for the network market. However, it may also be used for other applications where cost is less of a concern, low latency is a highly desirable feature, and smaller-than-commodity-DRAM capacity is not an issue. For example, RLDRAM may be used as a large lookup table or a large off-chip cache. RLDRAM has been designed with an SRAM-like mentality in that it is designed for SRAM-like random access to any part of the DRAM device; row address and column addresses are combined together and sent as a single access command.

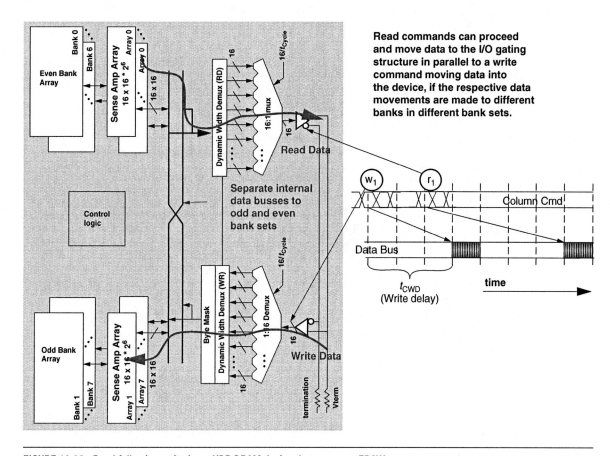

FIGURE 12.36: Read following write in an XDR DRAM device that supports ERAW.

12.5.2 Fast Cycle DRAM (FCRAM)

In contrast to RLDRAM, Fujitsu and Toshiba's FCRAM achieves low-latency data access by segmenting the data array into multiple subarrays, only one of which is driven during a row-activation command. The sub-row activation process effectively decreases the size of an array and improves access time. Unlike RLDRAM, FCRAM was designed with a DDRx SDRAM-like mentality, where row access commands and column access commands are sent separately, and the FCRAM command set was designed specifically to mimic the DDRx SDRAM command set. The purpose of the commonality is to enable controller designs that can use either FCRAM or commodity DDRx SDRAM devices. Finally, differing

from RLDRAM devices, FCRAM was designed with a DIMM specification.

12.6 Interesting Alternatives

12.6.1 Virtual Channel Memory (VCDRAM)

Virtual channel adds a substantial SRAM cache to the DRAM that is used to buffer large blocks of data (called *segments*) that might be needed in the future. The SRAM segment cache is managed explicitly by the memory controller. The design adds a new step in the DRAM-access protocol: a row activate operation moves a page of data into the sense amplifiers; "prefetch" and "restore" operations (data-read and data-write, respectively) move data between the sense amps and the SRAM segment cache one segment at a time; and column read or write operations move a column of data between the segment cache and the output buffers. The extra step adds latency to read and write operations, unless all of the data required by the application fits in the SRAM segment cache.

12.6.2   Enhanced SDRAM (ESDRAM)

Like EDO DRAM, ESDRAM adds an SRAM latch to the DRAM core, but whereas EDO added the latch after the column multiplexor, ESDRAM adds it *before* the column multiplexor. Therefore, the latch is as wide as a DRAM page. Though expensive, the scheme allows for better overlap of activity. For instance, it allows row precharge to begin immediately without having to close out the row (it is still active in the SRAM latch). In addition, the scheme allows a write-around mechanism whereby an incoming write can proceed without the need to close out the currently active row. Such a feature is useful for write-back caches, where the data being written at any given time is not likely to be in the same row as data that is currently being read from the DRAM. Therefore, handling such a write delays future reads to the same row. In ESDRAM, future reads to the same row are not delayed.

CHAPTER 13

DRAM Memory Controller

In modern computer systems, processors and I/O devices access data in the memory system through the use of one or more memory controllers. Memory controllers manage the movement of data into and out of DRAM devices while ensuring protocol compliance, accounting for DRAM-device-specific electrical characteristics, timing characteristics, and, depending on the specific system, even error detection and correction. DRAM memory controllers are often contained as part of the system controller, and the design of an optimal memory controller must consist of system-level considerations that ensure fairness in arbitration for access between different agents that read and store data in the same memory system.

The design and implementation of the DRAM memory controllers determine the access latency and bandwidth efficiency characteristics of the DRAM memory system. The previous chapters provide a bottom-up approach to the design and implementation of a DRAM memory system. With the understanding of DRAM device operations and system level provided by the previous chapters, this chapter proceeds to examine DRAM controller design and implementation considerations.

13.1 DRAM Controller Architecture

The function of a DRAM memory controller is to manage the flow of data into and out of DRAM devices connected to that DRAM controller in the memory system. However, due to the complexity of DRAM memory-access protocols, the large numbers of timing parameters, the innumerable combinations of memory system organizations, different

workload characteristics, and different design goals, the design space of a DRAM memory controller for a given DRAM device has nearly as much freedom in the design space as the design space of a processor that implements a specific instruction-set architecture. In that sense, just as an instruction-set architecture defines the programming model of a processor, a DRAM-access protocol defines the interface protocol between a DRAM memory controller and the system of DRAM devices. In both cases, actual performance characteristics depend on the specific microarchitectural implementations rather than the superficial description of a programming model or interface protocol. That is, just as two processors that support the same instruction-set architecture can have dramatically different performance characteristics depending on the respective microarchitectural implementations, two DRAM memory controllers that support the same DRAM-access protocol can have dramatically different latency and sustainable bandwidth characteristics depending on the respective microarchitectural implementations. DRAM memory controllers can be designed to minimize die size, minimize power consumption, maximize system performance, or simply reach a reasonably optimal compromise of the conflicting design goals. Specifically, the *Row-Buffer-Management Policy*, the *Address Mapping Scheme*, and the *Memory Transaction and DRAM Command Ordering Scheme* are particularly important to the design and implementation of DRAM memory controllers.

Due to the increasing disparity in the operating frequency of modern processors and the access latency to main memory, there is a large body of active and ongoing research in the architectural community devoted to the performance optimization of the DRAM memory controller. Specifically, the *Address Mapping Scheme*, designed to minimize bank address conflicts, has been studied by Lin et al. [2001] and Zhang et al. [2002a]. *DRAM Command and Memory Transaction Ordering Schemes* have been studied by Briggs et al. [2002], Cuppu et al. [1999], Hur and Lin [2004], McKee et al. [1996a], and Rixner et al. [2000]. Due to the sheer volume of research into optimal DRAM controller designs for different types of DRAM memory systems and workload characteristics, this chapter is not intended as a comprehensive summary of all prior work. Rather, the text in this chapter describes the basic concepts of DRAM memory controller design in abstraction, and relevant research on specific topics is referenced as needed.

Figure 13.1 illustrates some basic components of an abstract DRAM memory controller. The memory controller accepts requests from one or more microprocessors and one or more I/O devices and provides the arbitration interface to determine which request agent will be able to place its request into the memory controller. From a certain perspective, the request arbitration logic may be considered as part of the system controller rather than the memory controller. However, as the cost of memory access continues to increase relative to the cost of data computation in modern processors, efforts in performance optimizations are combining

transaction scheduling and command scheduling policies and examining them in a collective context rather than separate optimizations. For example, a low-priority request from an I/O device to an already open bank may be scheduled ahead of a high-priority request from a microprocessor to a different row of the same open bank, depending on the access history, respective priority, and state of the memory system. Consequently, a discussion on transaction arbitration is included in this chapter.

Figure 13.1 also illustrates that once a transaction wins arbitration and enters into the memory controller, it is mapped to a memory address location and converted to a sequence of DRAM commands. The sequence of commands is placed in queues that exist in the memory controller. The queues may be arranged as a generic queue pool, where the controller will select from pending commands to execute, or the queues may be arranged so that there is one queue per bank or per rank of memory. Then, depending on the DRAM command scheduling policy, commands are scheduled to the DRAM devices through the electrical signaling interface.

In the following sections, the various components of the memory controller illustrated in Figure 13.1 are separately examined, with the exception of the electrical signaling interface. Although the electrical signaling interface may be one of the most critical

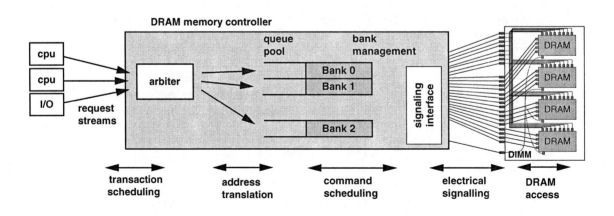

FIGURE 13.1: Illustration of an abstract DRAM memory controller.

components in modern, high data rate memory systems, the challenges of signaling are examined separately in Chapter 9. Consequently, the focus in this chapter is limited to the digital logic components of the DRAM memory controller.

13.2 Row-Buffer-Management Policy

In modern DRAM devices, the arrays of sense amplifiers can also act as buffers that provide temporary data storage. In this chapter, policies that manage the operation of sense amplifiers are referred to as *row-buffer-management policies*. The two primary row-buffer-management policies are the *open-page* policy and the *close-page* policy, and depending on the system, different row-buffer-management policies can be used to optimize performance or minimize power consumption of the DRAM memory system.

13.2.1 Open-Page Row-Buffer-Management Policy

In commodity DRAM devices, data access to and from the DRAM storage cells is a two-step process that requires separate row activation commands and column access commands.[1] In cases where the memory-access sequence possesses a high degree of temporal and spatial locality, memory system architects and design engineers can take advantage of the locality by directing temporally and spatially adjacent memory accesses to the same row of memory. The *open-page* row-buffer-management policy is designed to favor memory accesses to the same row of memory by keeping sense amplifiers open and holding a row of data for ready access. In a DRAM controller that implements the *open-page* policy, once a row of data is brought to the array of sense amplifiers in a bank of DRAM cells, different columns of the same row can

be accessed again with the minimal latency of t_{CAS}. In the case where another memory read access is made to the same row, that memory access can occur with minimal latency since the row is already active in the sense amplifier and only a column access command is needed to move the data from the sense amplifiers to the memory controller. However, in the case where the access is to a different row of the same bank, the memory controller must first precharge the DRAM array, engage another row activation, and then perform the column access.

13.2.2 Close-Page Row-Buffer-Management Policy

In contrast to the open-page row-buffer-management policy, the *close-page* row-buffer-management policy is designed to favor accesses to random locations in memory and optimally supports memory request patterns with low degrees of access locality. The open-page policy and closely related variant policies are typically deployed in memory systems designed for low processor count, general-purpose computers. In contrast, the close-page policy is typically deployed in memory systems designed for large processor count, multiprocessor systems or specialty embedded systems. The reason that an open-page policy is typically deployed in memory systems of low processor count platforms while a close-page policy is typically deployed in memory systems of larger processor count platforms is that in large systems, the intermixing of memory request sequences from multiple, concurrent, threaded contexts reduces the locality of the resulting memory-access sequence. Consequently, the probability of row hit decreases and the probability of bank conflict increases in these systems, reaching a tipping point of sorts where a close-page policy provides better performance for the computer system. However, not all large processor

---

[1]In some DRAM devices that strive to be SRAM-like, the row-activation command and the column-access command are coupled into a single read or write command. These devices do not support the open-page row-buffer-management policies. Typically, these DRAM devices are designed as low-latency, random-access memory and used in speciality embedded systems.

count systems use close-page memory systems. For example, Alpha EV7's Direct RDRAM memory system uses open-page policy to manage the sense amplifiers in the DRAM devices. The reason for this choice is that a fully loaded Direct RDRAM memory system has 32 ranks of DRAM devices per channel and 32 split banks per rank. The large number of banks in the Direct RDRAM memory system means that even in the case where a large number of concurrent processes are accessing memory from the same memory system, the probability of bank conflicts remains low. Consequently, Alpha EV7's memory system demonstrates that the optimality in the choice of row-buffer-management policies depends on both the type and the number of the processor, as well as the parallelism available in the memory system.

13.2.3 Hybrid (Dynamic) Row-Buffer-Management Policies

In modern DRAM memory controllers, the row-buffer-management policy is often neither a strictly open-page policy nor a strictly close-page policy, but a dynamic combination of the two policies. That is, the respective analyses of the performance and power consumption impact of row-buffer-management policies illustrate that the optimality of the row-buffer-management policy depends on the request rate and access locality of the memory request sequences. To support memory request sequences whose request rate and access locality can change dramatically depending on the dynamic, run-time behavior of the workload, DRAM memory controllers designed for general-purpose computing can utilize a combination of access history and timers to dynamically control the row-buffer-management policy for performance optimization or power consumption minimization.

Previously, the minimum ratio of memory read requests that must be row buffer hits for an open-page memory system to have lower read latency than a comparable close-page memory system was computed as $t_{RP} / (t_{RCD} + t_{RP})$. The minimum ratio of row buffer hits means that if a sequence of bank conflicts occurs in rapid succession and the ratio of memory read requests that are row buffer hits falls below a precomputed threshold, the DRAM controller can

switch to a close-page policy for better performance. Similarly, if a rapid succession of memory requests to a given bank is made to the same row, the DRAM controller can switch to an open-page policy to improve performance. One simple mechanism used in modern DRAM controllers to improve performance and reduce power consumption is the use of a timer to control the sense amplifiers. That is, a timer is set to a predetermined value when a row is activated. The timer counts down with every clock tick, and when it reaches zero, a precharge command is issued to precharge the bank. In case of a row buffer hit to an open bank, the counter is reset to a higher value and the countdown repeats. In this manner, temporal and spatial locality present in a given memory-access sequence can be utilized without keeping rows open indefinitely.

Finally, row-buffer-management policies can be controlled on a channel-by-channel basis or on a bank-by-bank basis. However, the potential gains in performance and power savings must be traded off against the increase in hardware sophistication and design complexity of the memory controller. In cases where high performance or minimum power consumption is not required, a basic controller can be implemented to minimize die size impact of the DRAM memory controller.

The definition of the row-buffer-management policy forms the foundation in the design of a DRAM memory controller. The choice of the row-buffer-management policy directly impacts the design of the address mapping scheme, the memory command reordering mechanism, and the transaction reordering mechanism in DRAM memory controllers. In the following sections, the address mapping scheme, the memory command reordering mechanism, and the transaction reordering mechanism are explored in the context of the row-buffer-management policy used.

13.2.4 Performance Impact of Row-Buffer-Management Policies

A formal analysis that compares the performance of row-buffer-management policies requires an in-depth analysis of system-level queuing delays, the locality

TABLE **13.1** Current specification for 16 256-Mbit Direct RDRAM devices in 32-bit RIMM modules

Condition Specification	Current
One RDRAM device per channel in Read, balance in NAP mode	1195 mA
One RDRAM device per channel in Read, balance in standby mode	2548 mA
One RDRAM device per channel in Read, balance in active mode	3206 mA

and rate of request arrival in the memory-access sequences. However, a first-order approximation of the performance benefits and trade-offs of different policies can be made through the analysis of memory read access latencies. Assuming nominally idle systems, the read latency in a close-page memory system is simply $t_{RCD} + t_{CAS}$. Comparably, the read latency in an open-page memory system is as little as t_{CAS} or as much as $t_{RP} + t_{RCD} + t_{CAS}$.[2] In this context, t_{CAS} is the row buffer hit latency, and $t_{RP} + t_{RCD} + t_{CAS}$ is the row buffer miss (bank conflict) latency. If x represents the percentage of memory accesses that hit in an open row buffer, and $1 - x$ represents the percentage of memory accesses that miss the row buffer, the average DRAM-access latency in an open-page memory system is x * (t_{CAS}) + $(1 - x)$ * $(t_{RP} + t_{RCD} + t_{CAS})$. Taking the formula and equating to the memory read latency of $t_{RCD} + t_{CAS}$ in a close-page memory system, the minimum percentage of memory accesses that must be row buffer hits for an open-page memory system to have lower average memory-access latency than a close-page memory system can be solved for.

Solving for x, the minimum ratio of memory read requests that must be row buffer hits for an open-page memory system to have lower read latency is simply $t_{RP}/(t_{RCD} + t_{RP})$. That is, as t_{RP} approaches infinity,[3] the percentage of row buffer hits in an open-page memory system must be nearly 100% for the

open-page memory system to have lower (idle system) memory read latency than a comparable close-page memory system. Alternatively, as the t_{RP} approaches zero,[4] an open-page system will have lower DRAM memory-access latency for any non-zero percentage of row buffer hits. Given specific values for t_{RCD} and t_{RP} specific requirements of row buffer hit versus row buffer miss ratio can be computed, and the resulting ratio can be used to aid in design decisions of a row-buffer-management policy for a DRAM memory system.

13.2.5 Power Impact of Row-Buffer-Management Policies

The previous section presents a simple mathematical exercise that compares idle system read latencies of an abstract open-page memory system to a comparable close-page memory system. In reality, the choice of the row-buffer-management policy in the design of a DRAM memory controller is a complex and multifaceted issue. A second factor that can influence the selection of the row-buffer-management policy may be the power consumption of DRAM devices.[5] Table 13.1 illustrates the operating current ratings for a Direct RDRAM memory system that contains a total of 16 256-Mbit Direct RDRAM devices. The act of keeping the DRAM banks active and the DRAM device

---

[2]That is, assuming that the probability of having to wait for t_{RAS} of the previous row activation is equal in open-page and close-page memory systems. If the probability of occurrence is the same, then the latency overheads are the same and can be ignored.

[3]Or increase to a significantly higher multiple of t_{RCD}.

[4]Or decrease to a small fraction of t_{RCD}.

[5]Commodity DRAM devices such as DDR2 SDRAM devices consume approximately the same amount of power in active standby mode as it does in precharge standby mode, so power optimality of the paging policy is device-dependent.

in active standby mode requires a moderate amount of current draw in Direct RDRAM devices. Table 13.1 illustrates that a lower level of power consumption in Direct RDRAM devices can be achieved by keeping all the banks inactive and the DRAM device in a power-down NAP mode.

The power consumption characteristics of different DRAM device operating modes dictate that in cases where power consumption minimization is important, the optimality of the row-buffer-management policy can also depend on the memory request rate. That is, the close-page row-buffer-management policy is unambiguously better for memory request sequences with low access locality, but it is also better for power-sensitive memory systems designed for request sequences with relatively low request rates. In the power-sensitive memory systems, Table 13.1 shows that for Direct RDRAM devices, it may be better to pay the cost of the row activation and precharge current for each column access than it is to keep the rows active for an indefinite amount of time waiting for more column accesses to the same open row.

13.3 Address Mapping (Translation)

Many factors can impact the latency and sustainable bandwidth characteristics of a DRAM memory system. Aside from the row-buffer-management policy, one factor that can directly impact DRAM memory system performance is the address mapping scheme. In this text, the address mapping scheme is used to denote the scheme whereby a given physical address is resolved into indices in a DRAM memory system in terms of channel ID, rank ID, bank ID, row ID, and column ID. The task of address mapping is also sometimes referred to as address translation.

In a case where the run-time behavior of the application is poorly matched with the address mapping scheme of the DRAM memory system, consecutive memory requests in the memory request sequence may be mapped to different rows of the same bank of DRAM array, resulting in bank conflicts that degrade performance. On the other hand, an address mapping scheme that is better suited to the locality property of the same series of consecutive memory

requests can map them to different rows of different banks, where accesses to different banks can occur with some degree of parallelism. Fundamentally, the task of an address mapping scheme is to minimize the probability of bank conflicts in temporally adjacent requests and maximize the parallelism in the memory system. To obtain the best performance, the choice of the address mapping scheme is often coupled to the row-buffer-management policy of the memory controller. However, unlike hybrid row-buffer-management policies that can be dynamically adjusted to support different types of memory request sequences with different request rates and access locality, address mapping schemes cannot be dynamically adjusted in conventional DRAM memory controllers.

Figure 13.2 illustrates and compares the conventional system architecture against a novel system architecture proposed by the Impulse memory controller research project. The figure shows that in the conventional system architecture, the processor operates in the virtual address space, and the TLB maps application addresses in the virtual address space to the physical address space without knowledge or regard to the mapping scheme in the DRAM memory address. The Impulse memory controller from the University of Utah proposes a technique that allows a system to utilize part of the address space as *shadow addresses*. The shadow addressing scheme utilizes a novel virtual-to-physical address translation scheme and, in cooperation with the intelligent memory controller, eliminates bank conflicts between sequences of streaming requests by dynamically remapping address locations in the address space.

Essentially, the Impulse memory controller assumes the system architecture where the memory controller is tightly integrated with the TLB. With full understanding of the organization of the DRAM memory system, the Impulse memory controller is better able to minimize bank conflicts in mapping application request sequences from the virtual address space to the DRAM address space.

However, Impulse memory controller research is based on a novel system architecture, and the technique is not currently utilized in contemporary DRAM memory controllers within the context of

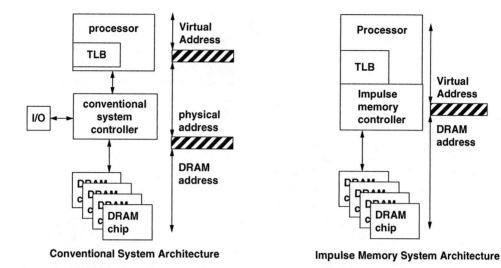

Conventional System Architecture　　　　**Impulse Memory System Architecture**

FIGURE 13.2: Comparison of conventional system architecture and the Impulse memory controller architecture.

conventional system architectures.[6] As a result, the discussion in the remaining sections of this chapter is focused on the examination of a DRAM controller in the context of conventional system architectures, and the address mapping schemes described herein are focused on the mapping from the physical address space into DRAM memory system organization indices.

13.3.1 Available Parallelism in Memory System Organization

In this section, available parallelism of channels, ranks, banks, rows, and columns is examined. The examination of available parallelism in DRAM memory system organization is then used as the basis of discussion of the various address mapping schemes.

Channel

Independent channels of memory possess the highest degree of parallelism in the organization of DRAM memory systems. There are no restrictions from the perspective of the DRAM memory system on requests issued to different logical channels controlled by independent memory controllers. For performance-optimized designs, consecutive cacheline accesses are mapped to different channels.[7]

Rank

DRAM accesses can proceed in parallel in different ranks of a given channel subject to the availability of the shared address, command, and data busses. However, rank-to-rank switching penalties in high-frequency, globally synchronous DRAM memory

---

[6]Fully Buffered DIMM memory systems present an interesting path to an unconventional system architecture that the Impulse memory controller or an Impulse-like memory controller may be able to take advantage of. That is, with multiple memory controllers controlling multiple, independent channels of Fully Buffered DIMMs, some channels may be designated for general-purpose access as in a conventional system architecture, while other channels may be used as high bandwidth, application-controlled, direct-access memory systems.

[7]The exploration of parallelism in the memory system is an attempt to extract maximum performance. For low-power targeted systems, different criteria may be needed to optimize the address mapping scheme.

systems such as DDRx SDRAM memory systems limit the desirability of sending consecutive DRAM requests to different ranks.

Bank

Similar to the case of consecutive memory accesses to multiple ranks, consecutive memory accesses can proceed in parallel to different banks of a given rank subject to the availability of the shared address, command, and data busses. In contemporary DRAM devices, scheduling consecutive DRAM read accesses to different banks within a given rank is, in general, more efficient than scheduling consecutive read accesses to different ranks since idle cycles are not needed to switch between different bus masters on the data bus. However, in most DRAM devices without a write buffer or separate internal datapaths for separate read and write data flow, a column read command that follows a column-write command is more efficiently performed to different ranks of memory as compared to a column-read command that follows a column-write command to different banks of the same rank. In modern computer systems, read requests tend to have higher spatial locality than write requests due to the existence of write-back caches. Moreover, the number of column-read commands that immediately follow column-write commands can be minimized in advanced memory controllers by deferring individual write requests and instead group schedule them as a sequence of consecutive write commands. Consequently, bank addresses are typically mapped lower than rank addresses in most controllers to favor the extraction of spatial locality from consecutive memory read accesses over the reduction of write-to-read turnaround times to open rows.[8]

Row

In conventional DRAM memory systems, only one row per bank can be active at any given instance

in time provided that additional ESDRAM-like or VCDRAM-like row buffers are not present in the DRAM device. The result of the forced serialization of accesses to different rows of the same bank means that row addresses are typically mapped to the highest memory address ranges to minimize the likelihood that spatially adjacent consecutive accesses are made to different rows of the same bank.

Column

In open-page memory systems, cachelines with sequentially consecutive addresses are optimally mapped to the same row of memory to support streaming accesses. As a result, column addresses are typically mapped to the lower address bits of a given physical address in open-page memory systems. In contrast, cachelines with sequentially consecutive addresses are optimally mapped to different rows and different banks of memory to support streaming accesses in close-page memory systems. The mapping of sequentially consecutive cachelines to different banks, different ranks, and different channels scatters requests in streaming accesses to different rows and favors parallelism in lieu of spatial locality. The result is that in close-page memory systems, the low address bits of the column address that denote the column offset within a cacheline are optimally mapped to the lowest address bits of the physical address, but the remainder of the column address is optimally mapped to the high address ranges comparable to the row addresses.

13.3.2 Parameter of Address Mapping Schemes

To facilitate the examination of address mapping schemes, parametric variables are defined in this section to denote the organization of memory systems. For the sake of simplicity, a uniform memory system is assumed throughout this chapter. Specifically, the memory system under examination is assumed to

---

[8]Overhead-free scheduling of consecutive column accesses to different banks of a given rank of DRAM devices has long been the most efficient way to schedule memory commands. However, constraints such as burst chop in DDR3 SDRAM devices and t_{FAW} constraints in 8-bank DDRx SDRAM devices is now shifting the overhead distribution. Consequently, rank parallelism may be more favorable than bank parallelism in future DDRx SDRAM memory systems.

Table **13.2** Summary of system configuration variables

Symbol	Variable Dependence	Description
K	Independent	Number of channels in system
L	Independent	Number of ranks per channel
B	Independent	Number of banks per rank
R	Independent	Number of rows per bank
C	Independent	Number of columns per row
V	Independent	Number of bytes per column
Z	Independent	Number of bytes per cacheline
N	Dependent	Number of cachelines per row

have K independent channels of memory, and each channel consists of L ranks per channel, B banks per rank, R rows per bank, C columns per row, and V bytes per column. The total size of physical memory in the system is simply $K * L * B * R * C * V$. Furthermore, it is assumed that each memory request moves data with the granularity of a cacheline. The length of a cacheline is defined as Z bytes, and the number of cachelines per row is denoted as N. The number of cachelines per row is a dependent variable that can be computed by multiplying the number of columns per row by the number of bytes per column and divided through by the number of bytes per cacheline. That is, $N = C * V / Z$. The organization variables are summarized in Table 13.2.

In general, the value of system configuration parameters can be any positive integer. For example, a memory system can have six ranks of memory per channel and three channels of memory in the memory system. However, for the sake of simplicity, system parameters defined in this chapter are assumed to be integer powers of two, and the lowercase letters of the respective parameters are used to denote that power of two. For example, there are $2^b = B$ banks in each rank, and $2^l = L$ ranks in each channel of memory. A memory system that has the capacity of $K * L * B * R * C * V$ bytes can then be indexed with $k + l + b + r + c + v$ number of address bits.

13.3.3 Baseline Address Mapping Schemes

In the previous section, the available parallelism of memory channels, ranks, banks, rows, and columns was examined in abstraction. In this section, two baseline address mapping schemes are established. In an abstract memory system, the total size of memory is simply $K * L * B * R * C * V$. The convention adopted in this chapter is that the colon (:) is used to denote separation in the address ranges. As a result, k:l:b:r:c:v not only denotes the size of the memory, but also the order of the respective address ranges in the address mapping scheme. Finally, for the sake of simplicity, $C * V$ is replaced with $N * Z$. That is, instead of the number of bytes per column multiplied by the number of columns per row, the number of bytes per cacheline multiplied by the number of cachelines per row can be used equivalently. The size of the memory system is thus $K * L * B * R * N * Z$, and an address mapping scheme for this memory system can be denoted as k:l:b:r:n:z.

Open-Page Baseline Address Mapping Scheme

In performance-optimized, open-page memory systems, adjacent cacheline addresses are striped across different channels so that streaming bandwidth can be sustained across multiple channels and then mapped into the same row, same bank, and same rank.[9]

---

[9]Again, assume a uniform memory system where all channels have identical configurations in terms of banks, ranks, rows, and columns.

The baseline open-page address mapping scheme is denoted as r:l:b:n:k:z.

Close-Page Baseline Address Mapping Scheme

Similar to the baseline address mapping scheme for open-page memory systems, consecutive cacheline addresses are mapped to different channels in a close-page memory system. However, unlike open-page memory systems, mapping cachelines with sequentially consecutive addresses to the same bank, same rank, and same channel of memory will result in sequences of bank conflicts and greatly reduce available memory bandwidth. To minimize the chances of bank conflict, adjacent lines are mapped to different channels, then to different banks, and then to different ranks in close-page memory systems. The baseline close-page address mapping scheme is denoted as r:n:l:b:k:z.

13.3.4 Parallelism vs. Expansion Capability

In modern computing systems, one capability that system designers often provide to end-users is the ability to configure the capacity of the memory system by adding or removing memory modules. In the context of address mapping schemes, the memory expansion capability means that respective channel, row, column, rank, and bank address ranges must be flexibly adjustable in the address mapping scheme depending on the configuration of the DRAM modules inserted into the memory system. As an example, in contemporary desktop computer systems, system memory capacity can be adjusted by adding or removing memory modules with one or two ranks of DRAM devices per module. In these systems, rank indices are mapped to the highest address range in the DRAM memory system. The result of such a mapping scheme means that an application that utilizes only a subset of the memory address space would typically make use of fewer ranks of memory than are available in the system. The address mapping scheme that allows for expansion capability thus presents less rank parallelism to memory accesses. Similarly, in cases where multiple channels can be configured independently and the memory system

supports asymmetrical channel configurations, channel indices are also mapped to the high address ranges, and parallelism presented by multiple channels may not be available to individual applications. As a result, some high-performance systems enforce configuration rules that dictate symmetrical channel configurations.

In the respective baseline address mapping schemes described previously, channel and rank indices are mapped to the low-order address bits. However, in a flexible, user-configurable memory system, the channel and rank indices are moved to the high-order address bits. The result is that an expandable open-page memory system would utilize an address mapping scheme that is comparable to the ordering of k:l:r:b:n:z, and the k:l:r:n:b:z address mapping scheme would be used in an expandable, close-page memory system. In these address mapping schemes geared toward memory system expandability, some degrees of channel and rank parallelism are lost to single threaded workloads that use only a subset of the contiguous physical address space. The loss of parallelism for single threaded workloads in memory systems designed for configuration flexibility is less of a concern for memory systems designed for large multi-processor systems. In such systems, concurrent memory accesses from different memory-access streams to different regions of the physical address space would make better use of the parallelism offered by multiple channel and multiple ranks than the single threaded workload.

13.3.5 Address Mapping in the Intel 82955X MCH

In this section, Intel's 82955X Memory Controller Hub (MCH) is used as an example to illustrate address mapping schemes in a high-performance, multi-channel, multi-rank memory system. The 82955X MCH contains two memory controllers that can independently control two channels of DDR2 SDRAM devices. Each channel in the 82955X MCH supports up to four ranks of DRAM devices, and Table 13.3 summarizes six possible rank configurations supported by the 82955X MCH. In practical terms, system boards that utilize the 82955X MCH can support one or two memory modules in each channel, and each memory module is composed of one or two identically configured ranks listed in Table 13.3.

The 82955X MCH supports address mapping schemes that are optimized for an open-page memory system. The interesting aspect of the 82955X MCH is that it supports different mapping schemes that are respectively targeted to obtain higher performance or configuration flexibility, and the 82955X MCH can deploy different mapping schemes depending on the organization of the memory modules inserted into the system. Specifically, the 82955X MCH can support the two channels configured with symmetric or asymmetric organizations of memory modules. Moreover, the 82955X MCH uses rank configuration registers to perform address mapping on a rank-by-rank basis. The topics of channel symmetry and per-rank address mapping in the 82955X MCH are examined in detail in the following sections.

Symmetric and Asymmetric Dual Channel Modes

In the case that the two channels are populated with memory modules with symmetrically matched capacities, the 82955X MCH can operate in *symmetric dual channel mode*. In the symmetric dual channel mode, sequentially consecutive cacheline addresses are mapped to alternating channels so that requests from a streaming request sequence are mapped to both channels concurrently. In the case where the

82955X MCH is configured with different capacities of memory modules in the two channels, the 82955X MCH operates in *asymmetric dual channel mode*. In the asymmetric dual channel mode, the physical address is mapped from 0 MB to the capacity of channel 0 and then to the full capacity of channel 1. In this manner, requests from a streaming request sequence are mapped to one channel at a time unless the array address space spans both channels.

Figure 13.3 illustrates a symmetric configuration and an asymmetric configuration for the 82955X MCH. The figure shows that in the symmetric configuration, both channel 0 and channel 1 are populated with a single-rank, 512-MB memory module that occupies rank 0 and a single-rank, 256-MB memory module that occupies rank 1. Although the 256-MB memory modules in rank 1 of both channels are not identical in organization, the fact that they are identical in capacity is sufficient for the 82955X MCH to utilize the symmetric dual channel mode. In contrast, the asymmetric configuration example shows that the two channels are populated with memory modules with different capacities and different numbers of ranks. In the asymmetric configuration, the physical address space extends from 0 to 512 MB in channel 0 and then from 512 to 1536 MB in channel 1.

Address Mapping Configuration Registers

The 82955X MCH uses configuration registers to support different address mapping schemes for performance optimization or configuration flexibility.

TABLE **13.3** DDR2 SDRAM rank configurations

Rank Capacity	Device Configuration: bank count x row count x col count x col size (col size in bytes)	Rank Composition: device density x device count	Rank Configuration: bank count x row count x col count x col size (B x R x C x V)	Bank Address Bits (b)	Row Address Bits (r)	Column Address Bits (c)	Column Address Offset (v)
128 MB	4 x 8192 x 512 x 2	256 Mbit x 4	4 x 8192 x 512 x 8	2	13	9	3
256 MB	4 x 8192 x 1024 x 2	512 Mbit x 4	4 x 8192 x 1024 x 8	2	13	10	3
256 MB	4 x 8192 x 1024 x 1	256 Mbit x 8	4 x 8192 x 1024 x 8	2	13	10	3
512 MB	8 x 8192 x 1024 x 2	1 Gbit x 4	8 x 8192 x 1024 x 8	3	13	10	3
512 MB	4 x 16384 x 1024 x 1	512 Mbit x 8	4 x 16384 x 1024 x 8	2	14	10	3

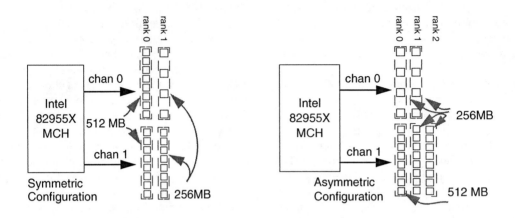

FIGURE 13.3: Symmetric and asymmetric channel configurations in the 82955X MCH.

Two types of configuration registers are used in the 82955X MCH to aid it in the task of address mapping: rank address boundary registers and rank architectural registers.

The function of the rank address boundary register is to define the upper address boundaries for a given rank of DRAM devices. There are four rank address boundary registers per channel. In asymmetrical channel model, each register contains the highest addressable location of a single channel of memory. In symmetrical channel mode, cacheline addresses are interleaved between the two channels, and the rank address boundary registers contain the upper address boundaries for a given rank of DRAM devices for both channels of memory. The rank architectural registers identify the size of the row for the DRAM devices inserted into the system. In the 82955X MCH, there are four rank architectural registers per channel, with one register per rank.

Per-Rank Address Mapping Schemes

The address mapping configuration registers are set at system initialization time by the 82955X MCH, and they contain values that reflect the capacity and organization of the DRAM devices in the memory system. With the aid of the rank address boundary configuration registers, the 82955X MCH can unam-

biguously resolve a physical address location to a given rank of memory. Then, with the aid of the rank architectural registers, the organization of the DRAM devices to the given rank of memory is also known, and the physical address can be further separated into row, bank, and column addresses. That is, the address mapping scheme in the 82955X MCH is generated on a rank-by-rank basis.

Figure 13.4 illustrates the address mapping scheme of 82955X MCH. The figure shows that in single channel or asymmetric dual channel mode, the 82955X MCH maps the three least significant bits of the physical address as the byte offset of the 8-byte-wide memory module. Then, depending on the number of columns on the memory module, the next 9 or 10 bits of the physical address are used to denote the column address field. The bank address then follows the column address, and the most significant address bits are used for the row address.

In the 82955X MCH, the channel address is mapped to different address bit fields, depending on the operating mode of the memory controller. Figure 13.4 does not show the channel address field for the single channel or asymmetric channel mode, since each channel is a contiguous block of memory, and the channel address is mapped to the highest available physical address bit field. However,

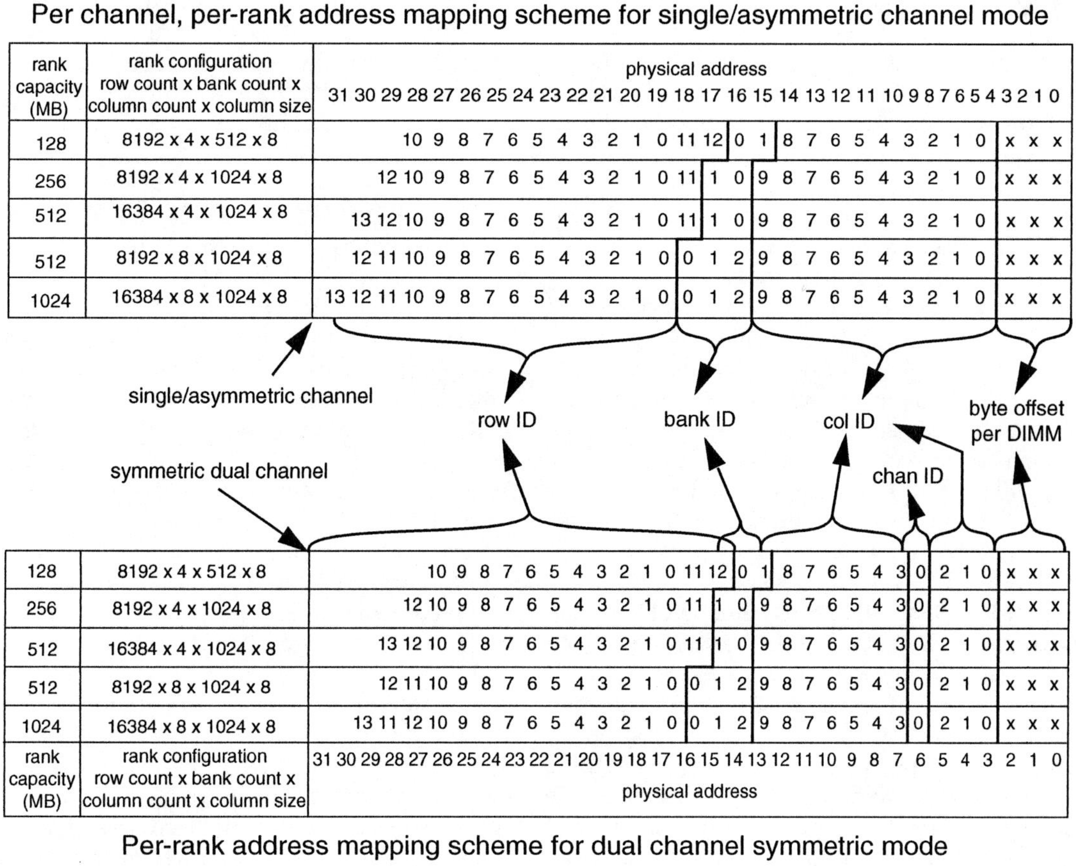

Per channel, per-rank address mapping scheme for single/asymmetric channel mode

rank capacity (MB)	rank configuration row count x bank count x column count x column size	physical address 31 30 29 28 27 26 25 24 23 22 21 20 19 18 17 16 15 14 13 12 11 10 9 8 7 6 5 4 3 2 1 0
128	8192 x 4 x 512 x 8	10 9 8 7 6 5 4 3 2 1 0 11 12 0 1 8 7 6 5 4 3 2 1 0 x x x
256	8192 x 4 x 1024 x 8	12 10 9 8 7 6 5 4 3 2 1 0 11 1 0 9 8 7 6 5 4 3 2 1 0 x x x
512	16384 x 4 x 1024 x 8	13 12 10 9 8 7 6 5 4 3 2 1 0 11 1 0 9 8 7 6 5 4 3 2 1 0 x x x
512	8192 x 8 x 1024 x 8	12 11 10 9 8 7 6 5 4 3 2 1 0 0 1 2 9 8 7 6 5 4 3 2 1 0 x x x
1024	16384 x 8 x 1024 x 8	13 12 11 10 9 8 7 6 5 4 3 2 1 0 0 1 2 9 8 7 6 5 4 3 2 1 0 x x x

single/asymmetric channel

row ID   bank ID   col ID   byte offset per DIMM

symmetric dual channel   chan ID

128	8192 x 4 x 512 x 8	10 9 8 7 6 5 4 3 2 1 0 11 12 0 1 8 7 6 5 4 3 0 2 1 0 x x x
256	8192 x 4 x 1024 x 8	12 10 9 8 7 6 5 4 3 2 1 0 11 1 0 9 8 7 6 5 4 3 0 2 1 0 x x x
512	16384 x 4 x 1024 x 8	13 12 10 9 8 7 6 5 4 3 2 1 0 11 1 0 9 8 7 6 5 4 3 0 2 1 0 x x x
512	8192 x 8 x 1024 x 8	12 11 10 9 8 7 6 5 4 3 2 1 0 0 1 2 9 8 7 6 5 4 3 0 2 1 0 x x x
1024	16384 x 8 x 1024 x 8	13 11 12 10 9 8 7 6 5 4 3 2 1 0 0 1 2 9 8 7 6 5 4 3 0 2 1 0 x x x
rank capacity (MB)	rank configuration row count x bank count x column count x column size	31 30 29 28 27 26 25 24 23 22 21 20 19 18 17 16 15 14 13 12 11 10 9 8 7 6 5 4 3 2 1 0 physical address

Per-rank address mapping scheme for dual channel symmetric mode

FIGURE 13.4: Per-rank address mapping schemes in the 82955X MCH.

in symmetric dual channel mode, the cacheline addresses are interleaved between the two channels, and the channel address is mapped to the low range of the address bit fields. Specifically, Figure 13.4 shows that the address mapping schemes shown for the single/asymmetric channel mode and the dual channel symmetric mode are essentially the same, and the only difference between the two sets of address mapping schemes is that the 6th bit in the physical address is used to denote the channel address, and the respective addresses in the dual channel mode are shifted over by 1 bit position to the left.

Quick Summary of Address Mapping in the 82955X MCH

Figure 13.4 serves as a concrete example that illustrates some interesting aspects of address mapping schemes used in contemporary memory controllers. In particular, the address mapping schemes illustrated in Figure 13.4 for the 82955X MCH are classical open-page-optimal address mapping schemes. For example, Figure 13.4 shows that in the single/asymmetric channel mode, the address mapping scheme in the 82955X MCH can be represented as k:l:r:b:n:z, and in the symmetric dual channel mode, the address mapping scheme can be represented as l:r:b:n:k:z. In both cases, the column address fields are mapped to the low address ranges so that spatially adjacent memory address locations can be directed to the same open page. Similarly, in the various address mapping schemes illustrated in Figure 13.4, the 82955X MCH shows that the side effect of granting the end-users the ability to configure the memory system with differently organized memory modules is that rank parallelism to spatially adjacent memory accesses is lost. Although the rank address field is not explicitly illustrated in Figure 13.4, the use of the address boundary registers and per-rank address mapping schemes means that the rank address field is mapped to the high address ranges above the row address field.

Figure 13.4 shows that the 82955X MCH has been cleverly designed so that most of the bit positions are directed to the same address fields regardless of the organization of the memory modules in the memory system. For example, Figure 13.4 shows that physical address bits 16 through 26 are used to denote row addresses 0 through 10 in the single/asymmetric channel mode, regardless of the number and type of memory modules placed in the memory system. In this manner, only a few bit positions will have to be dynamically adjusted depending on the organization of the memory system, and bit positions shown with the grey background in Figure 13.4 are always directed to the same address fields.

Finally, the address mapping scheme in the 82955X MCH means that single threaded streaming applications often cannot take advantage of the parallelism afforded by multiple ranks and the two channels in asymmetric channel mode. Fortunately, multiprocessor and multi-threaded processor systems with concurrently executing contexts can access different regions of memory and may be able to take advantage of the parallelism afforded by the multiple

ranks and multiple channels in asymmetric channel mode. However, the amount of achievable parallelism depends on the specific access request sequences and the locations of the data structures accessed by the concurrently executing process contexts.

13.3.6 Bank Address Aliasing (Stride Collision)

One additional issue in the consideration of an address mapping scheme is the problem of bank address aliasing. The problem of bank address aliasing occurs when arrays whose respective sizes are relatively large powers-of-two are accessed concurrently with strided accesses to the same bank. Figure 13.4 shows that in a system that uses 1-GB DDR2 SDRAM memory modules with the 82955X MCH in dual channel mode, the bank address for each access is obtained from physical address bit positions 14 through 16. That is, in this system configuration, all contiguously allocated arrays that are aligned on address boundaries that are integer multiples of 2^{17} bytes from each other would have array elements that map to identical banks for all corresponding array elements.

For example, the task of array summation, where the array elements of arrays A and B are added together and then stored into array C, requires that the corresponding elements of A, B, and C be accessed concurrently. In the case where arrays A, B, and C are contiguously allocated by the system and mapped to integer multiples of 128-kB address boundaries from each other, then array elements A[i], B[i], and C[i], would be mapped to different rows within the same bank for all valid array indices i, resulting in multiple bank conflicts for each step of the array summation process in the system described above.

In general, the bank address aliasing problem can be alleviated by several different methods. One method that can alleviate the bank address aliasing problem is the conscientious application of padding or offsets to large arrays so that bank conflicts are not generated throughout concurrent array accesses to those large arrays.[10] A second method that can alleviate the bank address aliasing problem is the conscientious design

---

[10]A simple offset insertion increased STREAM Triad bandwidth by 25% in a test system with an Intel i875P system controller.

of a memory management unit that can purposefully allocate large arrays to non-contiguous pages in the physical address space. In this manner, the chance of a bank conflict changes from a guaranteed event that occurs for every single access to the array to a probabilistic event that depends on the number of banks and ranks in the memory system. Finally, improved address mapping schemes have been proposed to alleviate the bank address aliasing problem, and they are described in the following section.

Hardware Solution to the Address Aliasing Problem

The bank address aliasing problem has been investigated by Lin et al. [2001] and Zhang et al. [2000]. The schemes proposed by Lin and Zhang are similar to schemes applied to different memory systems. The basic idea of taking the row address and bitwise XOR'ed with the bank address to generate new bank addresses that are not aligned for concurrent accesses to large arrays is common to both designs. However, the generous rank and bank parallelism in the fully configured Direct RDRAM memory system allowed Lin to create a 1:1 mapping that permutes the available number of banks through the entire address space in the system configuration examined. In contrast, Zhang illustrated a more modest memory system where the page index was larger than the bank index. The mapping scheme described by Zhang is shown in Figure 13.5. Figure 13.5 shows that the problem for the scheme described by Zhang is that there are relatively few banks in contemporary SDRAM and DDRx SDRAM memory systems, and

for a DRAM memory system with 2^b banks, there are only 2^b possible permutations in a 1:1 mapping that maps a physical address to the memory address. In the bank address permutation scheme for the conventional SDRAM-type memory system proposed by Zhang, the address aliasing problem is simply shifted to a larger granularity. That is, without the bank permutation scheme illustrated in Figure 13.5, arrays aligned on address boundaries of $2^{(b+p)}$ bytes would suffer a bank conflict on every pair of concurrent array accesses. The implementation of the bank permutation scheme means that arrays aligned on address boundaries of $2^{(b+p)}$ bytes no longer suffer from the same address aliasing problem, but arrays that are aligned on address boundaries of $2^{(b+p+b)}$ bytes continue to suffer a bank conflict on every pair of concurrent array accesses. Essentially, there are not enough banks to rotate through the entire address space in a contemporary memory system to completely avoid the memory address aliasing problem.

13.4 Performance Optimization

The performance characteristic of a modern DRAM memory controller depends on implementation-specific DRAM command and memory transaction ordering policies. A DRAM controller can be designed to minimize complexity without regard to performance or designed to extract the maximum performance from the memory system by implementing aggressive DRAM command and memory transaction ordering policies. DRAM command and transaction

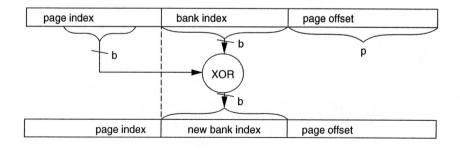

FIGURE 13.5: Address mapping scheme proposed by Zhang et al. [2000].

ordering policies have been studied by Briggs et al. [2002], Cuppu et al. [1999], Hur and Lin [2004], McKee et al. [1996], Lin et al. [2001], and Rixner et al. [2000]. In studies performed by Briggs et al., Cuppu et al., McKee et al., Lin et al., and Rixner et al., various DRAM-centric scheduling schemes are examined. In the study performed by Hur et al., the observation is noted that the ideal DRAM scheduling algorithm depends not only on the optimality of scheduling to the DRAM memory system, but also on the requirement of the application. In particular, the integration of DRAM memory controllers with the processor core onto the same silicon die means that the processor core can interact directly with the memory controller and provide direct feedback to select the optimal DRAM command scheduling algorithm.

The design of a high-performance DRAM memory controller is further complicated by the emergence of modern, high-performance, multi-threaded processors and multi-core processors. While the use of multi-threading has been promoted as a way to hide the effects of memory-access latency in modern computer systems, the net effect of multi-threaded and multi-core processors on a DRAM memory system is that the intermixed memory request stream from the multiple threaded contexts to the DRAM memory system disrupts the row locality of the request pattern and increases bank conflicts [Lin et al. 2001]. As a result, an optimal DRAM controller design not only has to account for the idiosyncrasies of specific DRAM memory systems, application-specific requirements, but also the type and number of processing elements in the system.

The large number of design factors that a design engineer must consider underlines the complexity of a high-performance DRAM memory controller. Fortunately, some basic strategies exist in common for the design of high-performance DRAM memory controllers. Specifically, the strategies of bank-centric organization, write caching, and seniors first are common to many high-performance DRAM controllers, while specific adaptive arbitration algorithms are unique to specific DRAM controllers and systems.

13.4.1 Write Caching

One strategy deployed in many modern DRAM controllers is the strategy of write caching. The basic idea for write caching is that write requests are typically non-critical in terms of latency, but read requests are typically critical in terms of latency. As a result, it is typically desirable to defer write requests and allow read requests to proceed ahead of write requests, as long as the memory ordering model of the system supports this optimization and the functional correctness of programs is not violated. Furthermore, DRAM devices are typically poorly designed to support back-to-back read and write requests. In particular, a column read command that occurs immediately after a column write command typically incurs a large penalty in the data bus turnaround time in conventional DDRx SDRAM devices due to the fact that the column read command must await the availability of the internal datapath of the DRAM device that is shared between read and write commands.

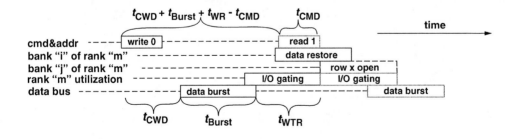

FIGURE 13.6: Write command following read command to open banks.

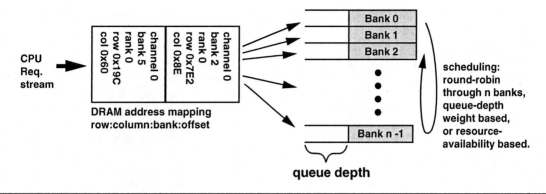

FIGURE 13.7: Per-bank organization of DRAM request queues.

Figure 13.6 repeats the illustration of a column read command that follows a write command and shows that, due to the differences in the direction of data flow between read and write commands, significant overheads exist when column read and write commands are pipelined back to back. The strategy of write caching allows read requests that may be critical to application performance to proceed ahead of write requests, and the write caching strategy can also reduce read-write overheads when combined with a strategy to burst multiple write requests to the memory system consecutively. One memory controller that utilizes the write caching strategy is Intel's i8870 system controller which can buffer upwards of 8 kB of write data to prioritize read requests over write requests. However, in systems that implement write caching, significant overhead in terms of latency or hardware complexity may exist due to the fact that the address of all pending read requests must be checked against the address of cached writes, and the memory controller must provide the consistency guarantee to ensure the correctness of memory-access ordering.

13.4.2 Request Queue Organizations

To control the flow of data between the DRAM memory controller and DRAM devices, memory transactions are translated into sequences of DRAM commands in modern DRAM memory controllers. To facilitate the pipelined execution of these DRAM commands, the DRAM commands may be placed into a single queue or multiple queues. With the DRAM commands organized in the request queuing structure, the DRAM memory controller can then prioritize DRAM commands based on many different factors, including, but not limited to, the priority of the request, the availability of resources to a given request, the bank address of the request, the age of the request, or the access history of the agent that made the request.

One organization that can facilitate the pipelined execution of DRAM commands in a high-performance DRAM memory controller is the per-bank queuing organization.[11] In the per-bank queuing structure, memory transaction requests, assumed to be of equal priority, are sorted and directed to different queues on a bank-by-bank basis. Figure 13.7 shows one organization of a set of request queues organized on a

---

[11]The per-bank request queuing construct is an abstract construct. Memory controllers can utilize a unified queue with sophisticated hardware to perform the transaction reordering and bank rotation described herein, albeit with greater difficulty.

per-bank basis. In the organization illustrated in Figure 13.7, memory transaction requests are translated into memory addresses and directed into different request queues based on their respective bank addresses. In an open-page memory controller with request queues organized comparably to Figure 13.7, multiple column commands can be issued from a given request queue to a given bank if the column access commands are directed to the same open row. In the case where a given request queue has exhausted all pending requests to the same open row and all other pending requests in the queue are addressed to different rows, the request queue can then issue a precharge command and allow the next bank to issue commands into the memory system.[12]

Figure 13.7 shows that one way to schedule requests from the per-bank queuing structure is to rotate the scheduling priority in a round-robin fashion from bank to bank. The round-robin, bank-rotation command scheduling scheme can effectively hide DRAM bank conflict overhead to a given bank if there are sufficient numbers of pending requests to other banks that can be processed before the scheduling priority rotates back to the same bank. In a close-page memory controller, the round-robin bank-rotation scheme maximizes the temporal distance between requests to any given bank without sophisticated logic circuits to resolve against starvation. However, the round-robin scheme may not always produce optimal scheduling, particularly, for open-page memory controllers. In open-page memory controllers, the address mapping scheme maps spatially adjacent cachelines to open rows, and multiple requests to an open row may be pending in a given queue. As a result, a weight-based priority scheduling scheme, where the queue with the largest number of pending requests, is prioritized ahead of other queues with fewer pending requests,

may be more optimal than a strictly round-robin priority scheduling scheme.[13]

The per-bank queue organization may be favored in large memory systems where high request rates are directed to relatively few banks. In memory systems where there are relatively lower access rates to a large number of banks in the system, dedicated per-banks queues are less efficient in organizing requests. In these memory systems, the queue structure may be more optimally organized as a pool of general-purpose queue entries where each queue entry can be directed to different banks as needed.

13.4.3 Refresh Management

One issue that all modern DRAM controllers must deal with to ensure the integrity of data stored in DRAM devices is the refresh function. In the case where a modern memory system is inactive for a short period of time, all DRAM devices can make use of a DRAM device controlled self-refresh mode, where the DRAM memory controller can be temporarily powered down and placed into a sleep state while the DRAM device controls its own refresh function. However, the entry into and exit out of the self-refresh mode is typically performed under the explicit control of the DRAM memory controller, and the self-refresh action is not engaged in during normal operations in most modern DRAM devices.

One exception to the explicit management of the refresh function by the memory controller can be found in some pseudo-static DRAM devices such as MobileRAM, where temperature-compensated self-refresh is used as part of the normal operating mode to minimize refresh power consumption. Moreover, the hidden self-refresh removes the complexity of refresh control from the memory controller

---

[12]The bank-centric organization assumes that all requests from different agents are of equal priority and access rates from different agents are comparable. In practical terms, additional safeguards must be put in place to prevent the scenario where a constant stream of requests to an open row starves other requests to different rows. In some controllers, a limit is placed on the maximum number of consecutive column commands that can be scheduled to an open row before the open row is closed to prevent starvation and to ensure some degree of fairness to requests made to different rows of the same bank.

[13]Weight-based schemes must also be constrained by age considerations to prevent starvation.

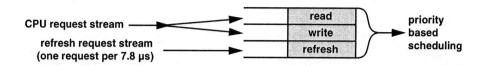

FIGURE 13.8: Priority-based scheduling for refresh requests.

and contributes to the illusion of the MobileRAM DRAM device as a pseudo-static memory device. The timing and interval of the DRAM refresh action in these devices are hidden from the memory controller. Therefore, in the case where a memory request from the memory controller collides with the hidden refresh action, the pseudo-static DRAM device asserts a wait signal to inform the memory controller that the data return from the pseudo-static DRAM device will be delayed until after the self-refresh action within the pseudo-static DRAM device is completed and the wait signal is deasserted by the pseudo-static DRAM device. However, a wait signal from the pseudo-static DRAM device that can delay state transition in the memory controller effectively introduces a slow signal path into the memory controller and effectively limits the operating frequency of the memory controller. Consequently, the explicit wait state signal that enables the hidden self-refresh function in normal operating mode is only used in relatively low-frequency, pseudo-static DRAM-based memory systems designed for battery-operated mobile platforms, and the refresh function in DRAM devices targeted for high-frequency DRAM memory systems remains under the purview of the DRAM memory controller.

To ensure the integrity of data stored in DRAM devices, each DRAM row that contains valid data must be refreshed at least once per refresh period, typically 32 or 64 ms in duration.[14] In terms of a DRAM device that requires 8192 refresh commands

every refresh period, mathematics dictate that an all-banks-concurrent refresh command must be issued to the DRAM device once every 7.8 μs for the device with a 64-ms period requirement. Fortunately, DRAM refresh commands can be deferred for short periods of time to allow latency-critical memory read requests to proceed ahead. Consequently, the DRAM controller need not adhere to a strict requirement of having to send an all-banks-concurrent refresh command to the DRAM device every 7.8 μs. To take advantage of the fact that refresh commands can be deferred within a reasonable timing window, Figure 13.8 shows an organization of the queuing structure where the microprocessor request stream is separated into read and write request queues and the request commands are placed into the refresh queue at a constant rate of one refresh command every 7.8 μs. In the structure illustrated in Figure 13.8, each refresh request is attributed with a count that denotes the number of cycles that the request has been deferred. In this manner, in the case that the refresh request is below a preset deferral threshold, all read and write requests will have priority over the refresh request.[15] In the case where the system is idle with no other pending read or write requests, the refresh request can then be sent to the DRAM devices. In the case where the system is filled with pending read and write requests but a DRAM refresh request has nearly exceeded the maximum deferral time, that DRAM refresh request will then receive the highest scheduling priority to ensure that

---

[14]Some DRAM devices contain additional registers to define the ranges of rows that need to be refreshed. In these devices, the refresh action can be ignored for certain rows that do not contain valid data.

[15]The maximum refresh request deferral time is defined in the device data sheet for DRAM devices. In modern DRAM devices such as DDR2 SDRAM devices, the period DRAM refresh command can be deferred for as long a 97.8-μs refresh command intervals.

TABLE 13.4   Refresh cycle times of DDR2 SDRAM devices

Density	Bank Count	Row Count	Row Size (bits)	t_{RC}: Row Cycle Time (ns)	t_{RFC}: Refresh Cycle Time (ns)
256 Mbit	4	8192	8192	55	75
512 Mbit	4	16384	8192	55	105
1 Gbit	8	16384	8192	54	127.5
2 Gbit	8	32768	8192	54	197.5
4 Gbit	8	65536	8192	54	327.5

the refresh request occurs within the required time period to ensure data integrity in the memory system.

One feature under consideration that could further increase the complexity of future DRAM memory controllers is the functionality of per-bank refresh. Table 13.4 illustrates that t_{RFC}, the refresh cycle time, is increasing with each generation of higher density DRAM devices, and the bandwidth overhead of the refresh functionality grows proportionally.[16] One proposal to minimize the bandwidth impact of DRAM refresh is to replace or supplement the all-banks-concurrent refresh command with separate refresh commands that refresh one row in one bank at a time as opposed to refreshing one row in all banks within a rank of DRAM devices concurrently.[17]

The performance benefit of the separate per-bank refresh command can be easily computed since each per-bank refresh command need only respect the t_{RC} row cycle time constraint rather than the t_{RFC} refresh cycle time constraint. However, one caveat of the per-bank refresh command proposal is that the fine-grained control of the refresh function on a per-bank basis means that the complexity of the DRAM memory controller must increase proportionally to deal with separate refresh requests to each bank,

and the queueing structure required may be far more complex than the sample queuing structure illustrated in Figure 13.7. Finally, the all-banks-concurrent refresh command also serves as a time period where the DRAM device can perform housekeeping duties such as signal recalibration between DRAM devices and the memory controller. Without the all-banks-concurrent refresh command, DRAM devices would lose the guaranteed time period where circuits within the DRAM devices are active, but the interface of the DRAM devices are idle to perform these types of housekeeping duties.

13.4.4   Agent-Centric Request Queuing Organization

In previous sections, techniques to maximize bandwidth utilization and decrease effective read latency were examined. However, one issue that was left out of previous discussions is that regardless of the performance techniques deployed, an overriding consideration in the design of a modern DRAM memory controller is one of fairness. That is, in any transaction request reordering mechanism, anti-starvation safeguards must exist to ensure that no

---

[16]There are more than 8192 rows in higher density DDR2 SDRAM devices, but the number of refresh commands per 64-ms time period remains constant. For example, the 4-Gbit DDR2 device must refresh 8 rows of data with each refresh command.

[17]The refresh command is a relatively energy-intensive operation. The instantaneous power draw of large, multi-rank memory systems, where all ranks are refreshed concurrently with a single refresh command, could significantly increase the peak power consumption profile of the memory system. To limit the peak power consumption profile, some DRAM memory controllers are designed to refresh each rank of DRAM devices separately and scheduled some time apart from each other.

request can be deferred for an indefinite period of time. The anti-starvation safeguards are particularly important in the context of multiple agents that share use of the same memory system. In particular, the issues of fairness and performance optimization for multiple agents with drastically different request rates and address sequences must be carefully traded off against each other. For example, a microprocessor running a typical application may require relatively low bandwidth, but read requests from the processor must be considered as latency critical. In contrast, a graphics processor that is connected to the same memory system may require a large amount of guaranteed bandwidth, but individual memory transaction requests from the graphics processor may be deferred in favor of requests from the microprocessor. Finally, memory transaction requests from relatively low-bandwidth and low-priority I/O devices may be deferred, but these requests cannot be deferred for an indefinite period of time so as to cause starvation for the I/O devices. That is, in the context of multiple agents that share a common memory system, better performance may be measured in terms of achieving an equitable balance in the usage of the memory system rather than obtaining the absolute maximum bandwidth from the DRAM devices.

The conflicting requirements of fairness and performance are important considerations that must be accounted for by the DRAM memory controller's scheduling mechanism. Fortunately, the scheduling mechanism used to deal with the DRAM device refresh requirement can be broadly extended to deal with a broad range of agents that require low latency or guaranteed bandwidth. That is, DRAM refresh commands can be considered as a sequence of requests from an agent that requires some amount of guaranteed bandwidth from the DRAM memory system. This agent, along with a number of other agents that require differing amounts of guaranteed bandwidth, must share the memory system with other agents that have no fixed requirements in terms of bandwidth, but must have low average access latency.

Figure 13.9 shows an organization of the queuing structure where the memory controller selects between requests from low-latency agents and guaranteed bandwidth agents. Figure 13.9 shows that requests from low-bandwidth and guaranteed bandwidth agents are directed to a two-level queuing structure, where requests are first sent to a pending queue and then moved to a scheduling queue under respective rate-controlled conditions. The rate controls ensure that the non-latency critical request agents

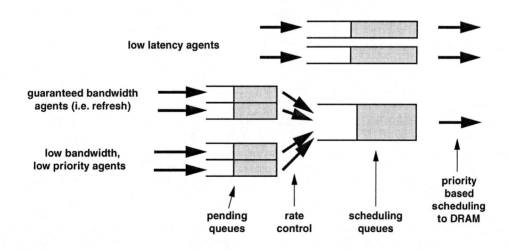

FIGURE 13.9: Sample system-level arbiter design.

cannot saturate the memory system with requests at the expense of other agents. In the queuing structure illustrated in Figure 13.9, requests from the low-latency agents are typically scheduled with the highest priority, except when the scheduling queue for the guaranteed bandwidth agents are full. To ensure that the bandwidth guarantees are met, the scheduling priority must favor the guaranteed bandwidth agents in the case where the shared scheduling queue for the guaranteed bandwidth agents is full.

In the previous section, DRAM-centric request scheduling algorithms are examined in the context of obtaining the highest performance from the DRAM memory system, given that all requests are equal in importance and that requests can be freely reordered for better performance. However, in a system where multiple agents must share the use of the memory system, not all requests from different agents are equal in importance. As a result, to obtain better performance in the system as a whole, both DRAM-centric and agent-centric algorithms must be considered. Figure 13.9 thus illustrates a two-level scheduling algorithm to ensure fairness and system throughput.

13.4.5 Feedback-Directed Scheduling

In modern computer systems, memory access is performed by the memory controller on behalf of processors or intelligent I/O devices. Memory-access requests are typically encapsulated in the form of transaction requests that contain the type, address, and data for the request in the case of write requests. However, in the majority of systems, transaction requests typically do not contain information to allow a memory controller to prioritize the transactions based on the specific requirements of the workload. Rather, memory controllers typically rely on the type, the access history, the requesting agent, and the state of the memory system to prioritize and schedule the memory transactions. In one recent study performed by Hur and Lin [2004], the use of a history-based arbiter that selects among different scheduling policies is examined in detail. In this study, the memory-access request history is used to select from different prioritization policies dynamically, and speedups between 5 and 60% are observed on some benchmarks.

The exploration of a history-based DRAM transaction and command scheduling algorithm by Hur and Lin is enabled by the use of a processor with an integrated DRAM controller, the IBM POWER5. The trend in the integration of memory controllers and processors means that the memory controllers will gain access to transaction scheduling information that they could not access as stand alone controllers.

As more processors are designed with integrated DRAM memory controllers, these processors can communicate directly with the DRAM memory controllers and schedule DRAM commands based not only on the availability of resources within the DRAM memory system, but also on the DRAM command-access history. In particular, as multi-threaded and multi-core processors are integrated with DRAM memory controllers, these DRAM memory controllers not only have to be aware of the availability of resources within the DRAM memory system, but they must also be aware of the state and access history of the respective threaded contexts on the processor in order to achieve the highest performance possible.

13.5 Summary

An analogy that may be made for the transaction queuing mechanism of a modern, high-performance DRAM memory controller is one that compares the transaction queuing mechanism of a high-performance DRAM controller to the instruction Reorder Buffer (ROB) of high-performance microprocessors that dynamically convert assembly instructions into internal microoperations that the processor executes out of order. In the ROB, the microprocessor accepts as input a sequence of assembly instructions that it converts to microoperations. In the transaction queue of the memory controller, the transaction queue accepts read and write requests that it must convert to DRAM commands that the memory controller then attempts to execute. Similar to the microoperations in the ROB, DRAM commands can be scheduled subject to the ordering constraints of the transaction requests and availability of the resources.

CHAPTER 14

The Fully Buffered DIMM Memory System

Owing to advancements in semiconductor process technology, processing power in modern computer systems is growing at extraordinary rates. The growth in processing power, in turn, places additional demands on the memory system in terms of larger capacity and higher speed to increase the overall processing and storage capability of the system. Unfortunately, existing multi-drop, bus-based memory system architecture has proven to be difficult to scale in terms of capacity and speed. That is, the traditional memory system architecture can be scaled in capacity or speed, but not in both attributes simultaneously. Additionally, economic forces of the DRAM memory market dictate that any memory system targeted for high-volume computer systems application must use commodity components and be comparable in cost as compared to previous-generation memory systems, regardless of the additional capacity and higher speeds that such a new memory system provides. Consequently, very little additional cost can be expended in the design and implementation of such larger capacity and higher speed memory systems.

To meet the stringent demands imposed on the memory system, a new memory system architecture, the Fully Buffered DIMM, has been designed so that it can meet simultaneously the requirements of larger capacity and higher speed without needing new or expensive DRAM devices. The Fully Buffered DIMM replaces the conventional memory system bus topology with a narrow, point-to-point interface between the memory controller and the memory modules,

enabling the use of a high data rate signaling system. The Fully Buffered DIMM memory system represents an intriguing attempt to meet the simultaneous demands placed on the memory system. In this chapter, the rationale used to justify the implementation and technical details of the Fully Buffered DIMM memory system is examined.

14.1 Introduction

Table 14.1 summarizes the generalized trend in the development of modern electronic devices as projected by the International Technology Roadmap for Semiconductors (ITRS). Table 14.1 shows that if semiconductor process technology continues to advance as projected, the number and speed of logic transistors are expected to continue to increase exponentially. In comparison, the numbers of pins per package are also expected to increase, and the costs per pin are expected to decrease, albeit at much lower rates than advancements in transistor technology. From this perspective, Table 14.1 demonstrates that the cost of logic computation on a given piece of semiconductor device is decreasing at a much higher rate relative to the cost of data transport between semiconductor devices. Consequently, systems architects are seeking solutions that will dramatically increase the pin-bandwidth at the interface of the high-performance processors. Unfortunately, the traditional multi-drop, bus-based memory system organization

TABLE 14.1   Projected scaning trends of modern electronic devices (ITRS 2001)

	Year				
	2004	2007	2010	2013	2016
Semi-generation (nm)	90	65	45	32	22
CPU MHz	3990	6740	12000	19000	29000
MLogicTransistors/cm^2	77.2	154.3	309	617	1235
High-performance chip pin count	2263	3012	4009	5335	7100
High-performance chip cost (cents/pin)	1.88	1.61	1.68	1.44	1.22
Memory pin cost (cents/pin)	0.34–1.39	0.27–0.84	0.22–0.34	0.19–0.39	0.19–0.33
Memory pin count	**48–160**	**48–160**	**62–208**	**81–270**	**105–351**

has reached a point where it cannot scale well into the future—the electrical characteristics and topology of the high-speed parallel busses collectively constrain the traditional memory system's scaling characteristics in terms of capacity and speed.

Figure 14.1 illustrates the profile view and topology of the traditional, module-based, end-user-configurable memory system typically found in personal computers and server systems. As a consequence of the system topology and the number of loads on the different busses in the system, the traditional, module-based, end-user-configurable, multi-drop memory system is difficult to scale in terms of operating data rate. In order to meet the requirement of higher operating data rates, DRAM device manufacturers have resorted to specifying reduced loads at higher data rates. For example, a DDR2 SDRAM memory system operating at 400 MT/s can be configured with upwards of 4 memory modules with 2 ranks of DRAM devices per module on the same address, command, and data busses. In contrast, a DDR3 SDRAM memory system operating at 800 MT/s and above is limited to a single memory module with 2 ranks of DRAM devices per module on the same address, command, and data busses.

To address the capacity and pin data rate scalability issues, the *Fully Buffered DIMM* (FB-DIMM, or FBD) memory system is introduced as an alternate DRAM memory system technology that addresses these

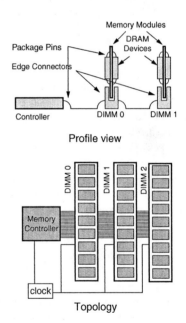

FIGURE 14.1: Profile view and topology of the traditional module-based memory system.

specific issues. The FB-DIMM memory system retains the use of commodity DRAM devices, but replaces the multiple multi-drop busses between the memory controller and memory modules with a point-to-point

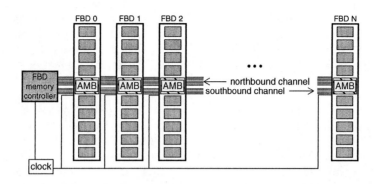

FIGURE 14.2: In the FB-DIMM organization, multi-drop busses are removed from the system board and confined to the DIMMs; DIMM-to-DIMM connections are point to point. The memory controller is connected to the nearest FB-DIMM via uni-directional links.

interconnect between the memory controller and a buffer chip, the *Advanced Memory Buffer* (AMB). The memory controller sends commands and receives data and status from the AMBs in the high-speed FB-DIMM channel with a packetized frame-relay protocol. The AMB receives and decodes frames to extract DRAM commands and then controls the DRAM devices on behalf of the memory controller. Furthermore, the same point-to-point interconnect is also used to relay commands and data between neighboring AMBs.

To retain the use of commodity DDR2 and DDR3 DRAM devices, the traditional, unbalanced multi-drop memory system topology is retained for use as the on-DIMM interface between the AMB and the DRAM devices. The FB-DIMM memory system architecture was designed as a scalable memory system architecture to accomplish a specific set of goals. The memory system must retain the use of commodity DRAM devices. It must retain the flexibility of a user-configurable memory system. The memory system must be able to scale and support a large memory capacity. It must also significantly increase the pin data rate of the memory system from the perspective of the memory controller. The FB-DIMM memory system accomplishes the set of goals stated above as a standards-based memory system.[1] However, the

FB-DIMM memory system architecture and the use of the AMB significantly increases idle system latency as well as power consumption of the memory system. Moreover, the use of the ASIC-based AMB in the memory system introduces a cost component that does not scale with the well-known market economics of the commodity DRAM device market. Consequently, the FB-DIMM memory system is meeting some resistance from system manufacturers in attaining its anointed role as the ubiquitous memory system of the future for all workstation and server computers.

In this chapter, the system architecture, protocol, and engineering trade-offs of the FB-DIMM memory system are examined in detail. Moreover, possible evolutionary paths of the FB-DIMM memory system are also discussed.

14.2 Architecture

Figure 14.2 depicts the FB-DIMM memory system topology. The figure shows that the FB-DIMM memory controller sends commands and writes data to the AMB nearest to it through a point-to-point interconnect (bit lanes) labelled as the southbound channel. The FB-DIMM memory controller sends commands and

---

[1]Memory hubs have been designed and used to significantly increase the pin data rate of the interconnect to high-performance memory systems. However, these memory hubs are system specific and non-standard. The FB-DIMM memory system is a standards-based memory system designed initially by Intel, but examined and adopted as a standard through JEDEC, an industry consortium of electronic device and equipment manufacturers.

writes data encapsulated in frames that are then relayed by each AMB to the next AMB down the southbound channel of the FB-DIMM memory system. The contents of the frames are examined by each AMB in the FB-DIMM memory system, and if a command encapsulated in a given frame specifically addresses the DRAM devices in a given FB-DIMM, the AMB on that DIMM decodes the command and controls the DRAM devices on behalf of the memory controller. In the case where the encapsulated command is a column read command, the AMB accepts the data returned by the DRAM devices, encapsulates the data burst into one or more frames, and then sends the data frames back to the memory controller on the northbound channel. Each AMB in the FB-DIMM memory channel then relays the data frames on the northbound channel until the frames are received by the memory controller.

Since each DIMM-to-DIMM connection is a point-to-point connection, the FB-DIMM channel is a *de facto* multi-hop store and forward network where each AMB represents a node in the network. However, one characteristic that separates the FB-DIMM memory system from the classical multi-hop store and forward network is that the AMBs in the FB-DIMM memory system will forward frames

before the frames are decoded. That is, in a classical multi-hop store and forward network, the frames may be analyzed by a receiving node, and that node can then decide whether or not to redrive the frame to the next node. However, in the case where the frames are decoded before they are relayed in the FB-DIMM memory system, significant latency would be added to the memory system. Consequently, the AMB in the FB-DIMM memory system is designed to quickly relay frames to the next AMB before the content of the frame is decoded. The AMB then deskews and examines frames separately from its relay functionality.

Figure 14.3 illustrates the interconnection scheme between the memory controller and a single FB-DIMM. The figure shows that the interconnects used to transport frames between the FB-DIMM memory controller and the AMBs are all point-to-point connections, meaning that the electrical characteristics of the data transport interconnects can be more easily controlled as compared to the electrical characteristics of the various multi-drop busses in the DDR2 SDRAM memory system. Consequently, the signaling rate of the point-to-point interconnects between the memory controller and the AMBs can be increased to a rate that is much

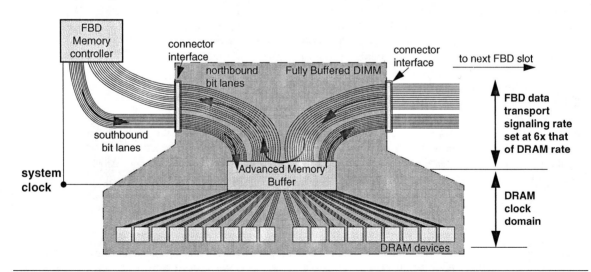

FIGURE 14.3: Illustration of the AMB on an FB-DIMM.

higher than the signaling rate of the DDR2 SDRAM memory system. Figure 14.3 illustrates that the signaling rate of the data transport interconnects between the memory controller and the FB-DIMMs is set at six times that of the DRAM devices. That is, the data transport channels in the FB-DIMM memory system operate at a fixed multiple relative to the data rate of the DRAM devices. For example, in an FB-DIMM memory system populated with 667 MT/s DDR2 SDRAM devices, the interconnects between the AMBs and the FB-DIMM memory controller operate at 4 GT/s.

Figure 14.3 shows that the FB-DIMM memory system is designed so that the slower, multi-drop busses in the DDR2 SDRAM memory subsystems are confined on each DIMM. The figure also shows that the same reference clock signal is used to generate higher speed clock signals used locally by the FB-DIMM memory controller and the AMB to control the slower DDR2 SDRAM memory subsystems. That is, the FB-DIMM memory controller and the AMBs operate in a mesochronous manner where the multiple clock domains are synchronous with respect to each other, but the phase relationships between them are not strictly defined. Moreover, as the point-to-point interconnects in the FB-DIMM channel operate at multi-gigabit data rates, any skew or jitter that exists between the signal paths can easily exceed the bit cycle time. Consequently, the bit lanes in the northbound and southbound

channels are designed to be timing-independent, and the transported frames must be de-skewed in silicon before they can be decoded and acted upon.

The architecture of the FB-DIMM memory system allows for high signaling rates between the memory controller and the AMBs without the need for closely matched signal path lengths. Consequently, the FB-DIMM system architecture removes the burden of system-level design—of having to carefully match signal path lengths in synchronous parallel busses—from the DRAM memory system. Figure 14.4 shows that the channel routing comparison between a DDR2 SDRAM memory system and an FB-DIMM memory system. The figure shows that a DDR2 SDRAM memory system requires many signal traces to be routed in parallel and path-length matched to each other. In contrast, Figure 14.4 shows that the FB-DIMM memory system uses far fewer signal traces between the memory controller and the DIMM's than the DDR2 SDRAM memory system—signal traces that do not have to be path-length matched to each other, greatly simplifying the task of system interconnect design.

Figure 14.4 graphically illustrates the stated advantage of the FB-DIMM memory system in that the memory system is able to attain a high pin data rate from the perspective of the memory controller and yet still retain the use of commodity DDR2 SDRAM devices. Consequently, if the scaling trends outlined in Table 14.1

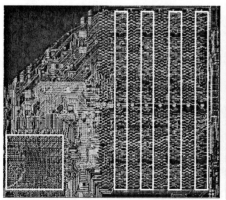

DDR2 SDRAM channel routing

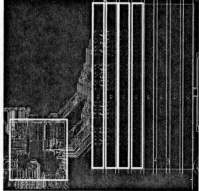

FB-DIMM channel routing

FIGURE 14.4: DDR2 and FB-DIMM channel routing comparison. (Illustrations courtesy of Intel Corp.)

become the predominant trends in computer systems architecture, the design of the FB-DIMM memory system will permit a high-performance processor to integrate multiple FB-DIMM memory controllers and attain the highest pin data rate without using non-standard, specialized DRAM devices.

14.3 Signaling and Timing

In modern, high-performance computer systems, wide parallel busses in I/O subsystems have been replaced with high-speed serial interfaces to attain significantly higher pin data rates. For example, the venerable parallel port was replaced by the Universal Serial Bus (USB), and the Peripheral Connect Interface (PCI) and the Advanced Graphics Port (AGP) is being replaced with PCI Express (PCIe). Interestingly, the high-speed PCIe interface possesses characteristics that are needed in the FB-DIMM memory system. For example, PCIe signaling operates at multi-gigabit data rates on the same PCB as the FB-DIMM memory system. Also, the same system controller would likely contain the PCIe controller as well as the memory controller. Consequently, the FB-DIMM memory system uses signaling technology similar to that already used for PCIe signaling to leverage the design and development work that had already been invested for PCIe. In this manner, the FB-DIMM memory system did not have to impose a new set of system design requirements on system design engineers, but could simply make use of an interconnect technology that is well understood.

The high-speed interconnect of the FB-DIMM memory system operates at six times that of the data rate of the DRAM devices. For DDR2 SDRAM devices that operate at 667 MT/s, the high-speed interconnects operate at 4 Gbps per pin pair. To operate at multi-gigabit data rates, Figure 14.5 shows that the FB-DIMM memory system uses high-speed, 1.5-V differential signaling technology, similar to the phyiscal signaling layer of PCIe and optimized for operation in commodity FR4 PCB[2] boards.

14.3.1 Clock Data Recovery

One issue that exists in high-speed signaling systems is the issue of data recovery from serialized input data streams without the use of a clock signal that has a guaranteed phase relationship relative to the input data signal. One common way to recover data from the input data stream is to use circuits that can recover a clock signal from the input data stream and use the self-aligned clock signal to recover data from the input data stream. However, the clock recovery scheme requires a guaranteed number of signal transitions in the input data stream, and generic data streams cannot be relied upon to provide the required number of signal transitions. One scheme used by high-speed signaling protocols such as Ethernet is to make use of 8b/10b data encoding schemes to guarantee the minimum number of signal transitions in the data stream. In 8b/10b code, every 8 bits of data in the data stream are mapped into 10 binary bits for transmission, and redundancy is built into the code to ensure a minimum

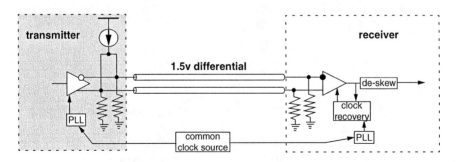

FIGURE 14.5: FB-DIMM physical layer signaling system—one single bit lane.

---

[2]FR4 PCB (laminate) is the most commonly used base material for printed circuit boards. "FR" stands for Flame Retardant, and "4" is the type that indicates woven glass reinforced epoxy resin.

number of transitions in each 10-bit sequence. The input receivers can then make use of the guaranteed number of transitions to recover a reference clock signal and use the reference clock signal to recover the transmitted data in the data stream.

To simplify system-level design, the physical signaling protocol of the FB-DIMM memory system does not specify phase relationships between the different bit lanes. Instead, the signaling layer of the FB-DIMM memory system makes use of clock recovery circuits to generate self-aligning reference clock signals and then uses these clock signals to de-skew and synchronize the independent bit lanes in the FB-DIMM memory system. However, in an effort to minimize overhead, the FB-DIMM memory system does not use data encoding schemes such as the 8B/10B scheme used in Ethernet. Instead, the physical layer of the FB-DIMM signaling protocol specifies a minimum transition density in the transmitted data streams. Currently, the minimum transition density is specified for the FB-DIMM memory system as 6 transitions from 0 to 1 or from 1 to 0 per 512 bits.

14.3.2 Unit Interval

Figure 14.6 illustrates the concept of a Unit Interval (UI), a basic unit of timing in the FB-DIMM memory system. In the mesochronous FB-DIMM memory system, multiple, high-speed signals are switching states at multi-gigabit data rates, and the concept of the UI provides a convenient unit of time measurement to describe the various delays in the FB-DIMM

memory system that are independent of the specific operating data rate. Figure 14.6 illustrates that there are 12 UIs in each DRAM clock cycle. For example, in an FB-DIMM memory system that uses DDR2-667 devices, the base operating frequency of the DRAM devices is 333 MHz, the duration of a single clock cycle is 3 ns, and 1 UI has the duration of 250 ps. In the FB-DIMM memory system, a given latency value may be adjustable in UI increments, and such latency values in terms of wall clock time would scale inversely relative to the increasing data rate.

14.3.3 Resample and Resync

The timing independence of the bit lanes in the FB-DIMM memory system means that data on each bit lane can be out of phase and skewed by several UIs relative to other bit lanes. Consequently, the FB-DIMM memory controller and the AMBs must have the necessary logic to de-skew data across the independent bit lanes. Figure 14.7 shows that a given frame can be out of alignment to the tune of several UIs, and a given AMB can realign the timing of the data streams on the independent bitlanes, redriving

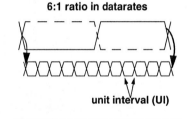

FIGURE 14.6: Unit Interval (UI) illustrated.

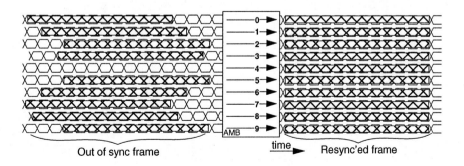

Out of sync frame   time ➤ Resync'ed frame

FIGURE 14.7: An out-of-sync frame resync'ed by an AMB.

them out of the AMB in alignment to the next AMB. However, the realignment of data across the independent bit lanes means that the redriven frame must be delayed until the slowest data stream of a given frame arrives at the receiver interface of the AMB. Since access latency is a critical access component of memory system performance, the AMB has two different modes of frame relay: resample mode and resync mode.

Figure 14.8 shows the southbound pass-through logic interface of the AMB. The figure shows that as data is received across the multiple bit lanes by the AMB, it is directed internally to three different datapaths. In the resample datapath, the data on each bit lane is repeated to the downstream AMB as soon as it is resolved by the AMB, although bit-to-bit jitter is still removed by the AMB using the derived data clock

signal. In the resample mode, skew that exists between the bit lanes is not removed at each node. Consequently, as each frame is repeated down the channel to successive AMBs, the worst-case skew between the different bit lanes may add up to a worst-case situation where data between bit lanes is out of alignment by tens of UIs. Currently, the FB-DIMM memory system is designed to tolerate as much as 46 UIs of accumulated skew, and each AMB must be designed to de-skew data to this depth. In the resync datapath, the pass-through logic delays and realigns the data on each bit lane before redriving the data downstream. Figure 14.8 also shows that concurrently with the resync or resample datapath, data on the bit lanes is de-skewed, demultiplexed, and decoded by the AMB to extract the command in the frame.

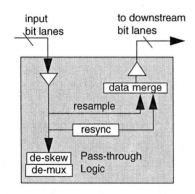

FIGURE 14.8: The pass-through logic interface of the AMB.

14.4 Access Protocol

The FB-DIMM system uses a frame-based protocol to communicate between the memory controller and the AMBs. Each AMB is responsible for accepting frames that are transmitted to it and retransmitting the frames downstream in the respective northbound and southbound channels. In the FB-DIMM protocol, each frame may contain commands, read data, write data, or status information. Figure 14.9 illustrates three types of frames commonly used by the FB-DIMM memory system: a command-only frame, a command-plus-write-data (W-D) frame, and a read data (R-D) frame. Figure 14.9 shows

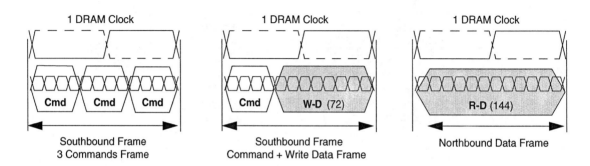

FIGURE 14.9: General FB-DIMM frame formats.

that a southbound frame may contain up to three commands or one command and a single burst of 72 bits of write data. In contrast, a northbound data frame may contain status information or 144 bits of read data. In terms of data transport times on the respective southbound and northbound channels, a command sub-frame occupies 4 UIs of data transport time, a write data sub-frame occupies 8 UIs of data transport time, and a read data frame occupies 12 UIs of data transport time.

One intriguing point illustrated by Figure 14.9 is that the FB-DIMM memory system is designed to be asymmetric in terms of read and write bandwidth. That is, in the saturation case where the FB-DIMM channel is completely filled with read and write data frames in flight, the southbound channel is filled with command-plus-write-data frames and the northbound channel is filled with read data frames. In such a case, the southbound channel is able to deliver a single command and a single burst of 72 bits of data per DRAM clock cycle, whereas the northbound channel is able to deliver 144 bits of data per DRAM clock cycle. In this manner, the FB-DIMM channel is able to transport the full peak read bandwidth from a given rank of DRAM devices in addition to transporting half peak write bandwidth to a different rank of DRAM devices. Consequently, the FB-DIMM channel is commonly attributed as being capable of providing one and a half times the bandwidth of a single DRAM channel using DRAM devices operating at the same data rates.

14.4.1 Frame Definitions

Figure 14.9 illustrates that both northbound and southbound frames are designed to occupy a fixed duration of 12 UIs on the respective channels. Since the southbound channel is composed of 10 bit lanes and the northbound channel is composed of 14 bit lanes, each southbound frame delivers 120 bits of information, and each northbound frame delivers 168 bits of information. In addition to the data and command information, the 120-bit and 168-bit frames also carry Cyclic Redundancy Checksums (CRCs) used by the receiving agent to check for transmission errors. The three generalized types of frames illustrated in Figure 14.9 are described in more detail below.

Southbound Command-Only Frame

A command-only frame comprises up to three independent commands. Each command in the frame is typically sent to a separate DIMM on the southbound channel and directs them to operate in parallel. In some cases, different commands can be addressed to different ranks on the same DIMM. Also, certain commands can be directed to affect operations in multiple DIMMs in parallel. For example, a CKE command can be used to put the DRAM devices in multiple DIMMs down to a power-down state. In the case where a command-only frame contains fewer than three commands, no-ops or platform-specific debug patterns are used to pad the frame.

Southbound Command Plus (Write) Data Frame

A southbound frame can carry up to three commands or one command plus 72 bits of write data. Typically, the 72 bits of write data consist of 64 bits of application data and 8 check bits used for error correction. Alternatively, the 8 bits can be used for data masking on a byte-by-byte basis in memory modules that do not support error correction. The command-plus-data frames are used to deliver write data from the memory controller to the FB-DIMMs, and multiple frames are needed to construct a contiguous burst to write into a given rank of DRAM devices. However, the multiple command-plus-data frames needed to form a single write burst need not be contiguous on the FB-DIMM channel. In fact, the command-plus-data frames may be interleaved with command-only frames. Finally, one quirk of the FB-DIMM protocol is that each write data sub-frame only contains one bit of the destination AMB address, and three write data sub-frames are needed to identify the AMB address. Consequently, all AMBs are required to buffer write data sub-frames in their respective write FIFOs until the address of the destination AMB is known.

Northbound Data Frame

Each northbound data frame is composed of 128 bits of data and 16 bits of check bits for use by the error correction mechanism in the memory controller. Each northbound data frame is filled by the data transferred from the DRAM in two beats or a single DIMM clock cycle.

14.4.2 Command Definitions

In general, the FB-DIMM memory controller delivers one of two types of commands to the AMBs: DRAM commands and channel commands. DRAM commands are commands that the AMBs use to control the DRAM devices on behalf of the FB-DIMM memory controller, and channel commands are commands that the FB-DIMM memory controller uses to manage the AMBs. DRAM commands that the FB-DIMM memory controller sends to the DRAM devices are simply commands in the DDR2 SDRAM command set.[3] In contrast, a new set of channel commands are needed by the FB-DIMM memory controller to manage operating conditions in the FB-DIMM channel.

The FB-DIMM channel command set includes several debug commands, the write configuration register command, the read configuration register command, the soft channel-reset command, DRAM CKE (clock enable) management commands, and the channel sync command.

The soft channel-reset command is a command that the FB-DIMM controller uses to recover from a detected transmission error. For example, in the case where the FB-DIMM memory controller detects an incorrect CRC checksum signature in a given frame, denoting a transmission error, or in the case where the FB-DIMM memory controller receives an alert frame from an AMB, informing it of a CRC error on a frame received by the AMB, the FB-DIMM memory controller can issue a soft channel-reset to the AMBs to reset the state of the AMBs in the channel. In the case where a soft channel-reset command is issued by the FB-DIMM memory controller, the FB-DIMM memory controller will retry to send the failed frames and all previous write data that had not been committed into the DRAM devices.

The channel-sync command is a command that the FB-DIMM controller uses to ensure that the clock recovery circuits in the AMB have a minimum number of state transitions that they can use to retain phase lock on every bit lane. In response to a sync command, a status frame with the same timing as the read data return frame is sent by the last AMB back toward the FB-DIMM memory controller on the northbound channel. In this manner, the sync frame guarantees that a minimum number of transitions are seen by the clock recovery circuits of the AMB on both the southbound and the northbound channels. Finally, the requirement of the sync frame means that the FB-DIMM channel cannot be easily and indefinitely powered down, since a sync frame must be inserted once every 42~46 frames.[4]

14.4.3 Frame and Command Scheduling

Currently, the FB-DIMM-access protocol is designed as a master-to-multiple-slave control protocol. DRAM command and frame scheduling are performed exclusively by the FB-DIMM memory controller. The AMB contains very little logic to act independently from the FB-DIMM memory controller. The AMB responds to channel commands with predictable, predefined timing, and it converts the packetized frame commands to DRAM commands without implementing any scheduling functionality. The AMB does not check for DRAM protocol compliance, and it does not protect against frame collision on the northbound channel in the case where multiple AMBs are asked to return read data or status concurrently. Consequently, the FB-DIMM is required to schedule commands in such a way as to ensure that DRAM commands observe DRAM command-access protocol constraints and that multiple frames do not collide on the northbound frames.

Figure 14.10 shows the processing of a read transaction in an FB-DIMM channel. In the figure the single southbound command-only frame contains both a row activation command as well as a posted column-access-and-precharge command. The row access command is contained in command slot A, and the posted column-access-and-precharge

---

[3]DDR3 is expected to be used for FB-DIMM2.
[4]The sync frame interval requirement depends on the specific AMB implementation and its adherence to the JEDEC AMB specification.

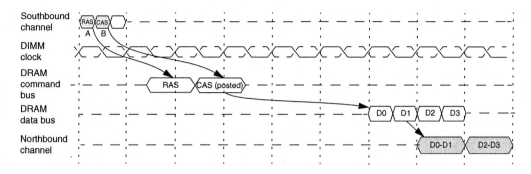

FIGURE 14.10: Illustration of a read transaction in the FB-DIMM channel (not drawn to accurate timescale).

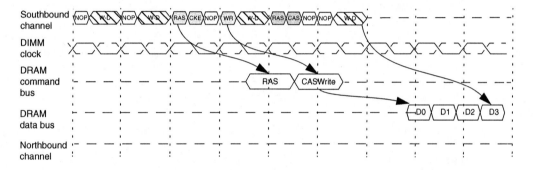

FIGURE 14.11: Illustration of a write transaction in the FB-DIMM channel (not drawn to accurate timescale).

command is contained in command slot B. Figure 14.10 thus illustrates a peculiarity of the FB-DIMM-access protocol in that command A in a given frame is actually scheduled to a different DRAM clock cycle from commands B and C. That is, command A of frame n will be forwarded by the AMB to the DRAM devices in DRAM clock i, and DRAM commands B and C of frame n will be forwarded by the AMB to the DRAM devices in DRAM clock i + 1. Alternatively, command B and command C of frame n will be scheduled to the same clock cycle as command A of frame n + 1. The split-cycle scheduling of a command-only frame means that both the row activation command and the posted column read command can be placed in a single frame, as illustrated in Figure 14.10. The split-cycle scheduling also means that for best performance,

latency-critical DRAM commands should be placed in command slot A whenever possible.

In Figure 14.10, the AMB sends the row access command and the posted column-access-and-precharge command to the DRAM devices, and the DRAM devices return data to the AMB three cycles later.[5] The AMB then encapsulates the read data into two frames and returns them to the FB-DIMM memory controller via the northbound channel. Figure 14.10 illustrates a DRAM device programmed to return a 4-beat data burst. In the case where the DRAM device is programmed to return an 8-beat data burst, the AMB would then return the data to the FB-DIMM controller via four contiguous northbound frames.

Figure 14.11 shows the processing of a memory write transaction in an FB-DIMM system. The write

---

[5]Not drawn to proper timescale, AMBs latencies are far longer than illustrated, and no DDR2 SDRAM device is fast enough to return data a mere four cycles after a row access command.

data requires twice the number of frames to carry it through the southbound channel as compared to the read data through the northbound channel. Figure 14.11 illustrates several important aspects of the write transaction in the FB-DIMM memory system. One important aspect of the write transaction illustrated in Figure 14.11 is that the southbound frames that carry write data for a single write burst into the DRAM devices need not be scheduled contiguously on the southbound channel. Rather, as Figure 14.11 illustrates, frames that contain write data may be scheduled separately, allowing for the insertion of command-only frames that schedule DRAM read commands to return data on the northbound channel. A second important aspect illustrated in Figure 14.11 is that the column write command need not wait until all of the data needed for the write command has been delivered into the AMB. Rather, as Figure 14.11 illustrates, the write command may be initiated before all of the write data has been delivered to the AMB. Instead, Figure 14.11 shows that as long as the frame carrying the last beat of needed write data is sent to the AMB before the minimum required write data pass-through time, write data may be decoupled from the write command timing. Finally, the encoding of the AMB address in the separate write data frames means that different write data frames for different burst-length-of-four write bursts cannot be interleaved with each other.

14.5 The Advanced Memory Buffer

The current, first-generation AMB is designed as a largely non-intelligent interface for the FB-DIMM memory controller to control the DRAM devices. All DRAM commands, with the exception of the self-refresh command sequence that the AMB uses to preserve DRAM data in the case of a channel-reset event, must come from the host memory controller. Figure 14.12 illustrates a block diagram of the AMB. The figure shows that the AMB can be roughly divided into three sub-blocks: the southbound pass-through logic block, the core block, and the northbound pass-through logic block.

Figure 14.12 further illustrates that the three sub-blocks operate semi-independently in their respective clock domains. However, the local clocks in the different clock domains are derived from the same clock input, and each operates at an integer multiple of the base frequency. Moreover, Figure 14.12 should not be taken as the only possible implementation for an AMB. Instead, depending on the specific implementation, the AMB may be designed with more sub-blocks that all operate mesochronously relative to each other.

The pass-through logic blocks of the AMB allow command and command-plus-data frames on the southbound channel to flow through the AMB and northbound read data frames to flow through the AMB toward the FB-DIMM memory controller. On the southbound pass-through logic, all commands are partially decoded to see if the command targets the DIMM, and all write data sub-frames are speculatively placed into the write FIFO. Since each write data sub-frame only contains 1 bit of the destination AMB address, and 3 write data sub-frames are needed to identify the 3-bit AMB address, the AMB buffers write data in the write FIFOs until the address of the destination AMB is known. Then, once the AMB address of the write data is known, the speculatively buffered write data is discarded by the write FIFOs of the non-matching AMBs, while the AMB with the matching address continues to buffer the write data until a column write command arrives from the memory controller to move the data into the selected rank of DRAM devices. However, since write commands may be deferred in favor of read commands that are latency critical, the write FIFO must buffer multiple write bursts. Currently, the AMBs have been designed to buffer up to 32 frames of 72 bits of write data in addition to the 3 frames of write data that must be speculatively buffered before the target AMB address can be decoded.

The core sub-block of the AMB examines each frame that passes through and acts upon the commands in the frame as required. In the case of a column read command addressed to the DRAM devices on the DIMM controlled by the AMB, the AMB sends the command to the addressed DRAM devices and accepts the read data burst from the DRAM devices. Then, the AMB prepares the read data for transport

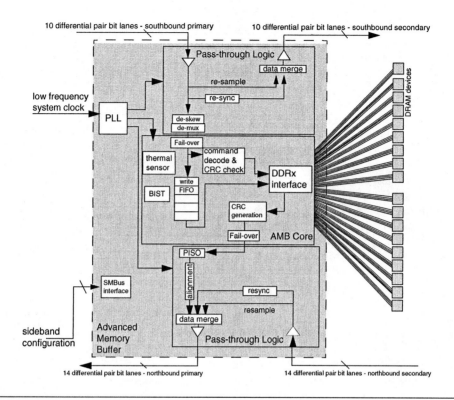

FIGURE 14.12: Important sub-blocks of an advanced memory buffer.

by computing the required CRC checksum and encapsulates the data into a frame format. The data is then forwarded to the northbound pass-through logic sub-block so that it can be sent back toward the FB-DIMM memory controller. In the northbound logic sub-block, the data is first serialized through a *Parallel In Serial Out* (PISO) logic circuit. Finally, the read data frame is placed onto the northbound bit lanes after the bit lanes are individually time aligned to match the bit lane to bit lane skew that exists in the free-flowing northbound bit lanes. In this manner, the read data frame may be seamlessly merged onto the northbound bit lanes without requiring rank-to-rank data bus turnaround times to switch between different bus masters as is required in the classical multi-drop bus topology in DDRx SDRAM memory systems. The seamless burst merging capability of the AMB allows the FB-DIMM memory system to sustain

high data read bandwidth across different ranks in a given channel of the memory system.

In addition to the illustration of the internal structure of the AMB, Figure 14.12 also illustrates the various interfaces that the AMB provides to the system. Figure 14.12 shows that the channel connections toward the FB-DIMM memory controller are referred to as the southbound primary and northbound primary connections, respectively. The channel connections from the AMB away from the FB-DIMM memory controller are then referred to as the secondary channel connections.

14.5.1 SMBus Interface

Figure 14.12 also shows an additional interface into the AMB, labelled as the SMBus interface. The *System-Management Bus* (SMBus) is an industry standard, low-speed bus interface that the FB-DIMM memory controller uses to write to and read from the AMB's internal configuration registers. The SMBus interface gives the FB-DIMM memory controller a sideband interface to access the AMB's internal configuration registers, independent of the high-speed, in-band, point-to-point northbound and southbound channel connections. The use of the SMBus interface is narrowly limited to the defined role of configuration and status register access and is not used as a sideband access connection to allow the memory controller to off-load data from the DRAM devices in the case of catastrophic failure of multiple northbound bit lanes. The reason that the role of the SMBus interface is limited to register read and write functions is that the SMBus is a low pin count, multi-drop bus interface that operates with the frequency of tens of kilo-hertz, and moving gigabytes of memory through such a low data rate interface would take weeks or months.

14.5.2 Built-In Self-Test (BIST)

One issue that exists in large memory systems is the memory test time. In a fully configured FB-DIMM memory system, the total memory test time could be significant, since the test time is essentially proportional to the memory capacity divided by the available memory bandwidth. Consequently, the AMB provides a convenient control interface to allow memory testing in multiple FB-DIMMs to proceed in parallel. To support parallel testing of memory, the AMBs include several autonomous *Built-In Self-Test* (BIST) state machines that can be configured and initiated by the memory controller.

14.5.3 Thermal Sensor

In a DDR2 SDRAM-based FB-DIMM, the AMB and 2 ranks of DDR2 SDRAM devices can collectively consume up to 20 W. The high power consumption in the FB-DIMM means that temperature-sensitive electrical characteristics can change in relatively short periods of time. The AMB contains an integrated thermal sensor interface that the FB-DIMM memory controller can use to read the temperature of the AMB and initiate throttle actions if required.

14.6 Reliability, Availability, and Serviceability

The FB-DIMM memory system is designed as the next-generation memory system for servers and workstations. In these computer systems, the reliability of the memory system is of great importance. To meet the reliability requirements of these systems, the FB-DIMM memory system was designed with a range of reliability features that, when fully implemented, protect the memory system to the extent that no single point of failure can take down the system. One example of the reliability feature is the inclusion of the CRC into the data transport layer of the FB-DIMM memory system. The FB-DIMM memory system also requires mechanisms for write data retry, to protect against bit lane failures, and to allow for the removal of faulting FB-DIMMs from a system and insertion of new FB-DIMMs into a system without powering down the entire system. In the following sections, these *Reliability, Availability, and Serviceability* (RAS) features are respectively summarized.

14.6.1 Checksum Protection in the Transport Layer

In the FB-DIMM memory system, a basic CRC mechanism is used to provide a baseline protection against transmission errors. Since the FB-DIMM memory system encapsulates commands and data into frames for transmission between the memory controller and the AMBs, the FB-DIMM memory system adds a new layer of interconnects into the traditional memory system where errors can be introduced. More specifically, reliance of the FB-DIMM memory system on clock recovery from the independent bit lanes without the use of an encoded data stream to ensure a high density of bit transitions means that the density of state transitions on the bit lanes may be relatively low, and the clock recovery circuit may be slow to adjust to voltage noises or temperature-induced jitter. Even more egregiously, in the case where the clock recovery circuit in a given bit lane loses phase tracking due to higher-than-expected jitter, multiple, successive bits in a given frame transmitted on a given bit lane may be lost, resulting in an uncorrectable multi-bit error. As a result, the FB-DIMM memory system was designed with features and mechanisms that protect against such failures. In the FB-DIMM channel protocol, each transmitted frame is protected by a CRC designed specifically to protect against multi-bit failures in a given bit lane. In the case where a CRC error in a southbound command or write data frame is detected by an AMB, the AMB returns an alert frame via its northbound channel, enters into a command error standby state, and stops responding to further DRAM commands. Subsequently, the FB-DIMM memory controller may reset the channel with a soft channel-reset command. As a consequence of the CRC protection mechanism, an FB-DIMM memory controller designed to be highly reliable has to retain copies of commands and write data that are in flight in the FB-DIMM channel so that they can be resent after the channel is reset and retrained to map out the failed bit lane in the case of a bit lane failure.

14.6.2 Bit Lane Steering

One common and yet unavoidable failure that occurs on a DRAM module is interconnect failure. In particular, as memory modules are inserted and removed from sockets by the end-user, unevenly applied pressure exerted at different points on the memory module can and does stress interconnects on the memory module and system connector interface. The stress on the memory modules can, in turn, introduce micro-fractures into solder connections and lead to connector failures after a number of thermal cycles that apply repeated thermal stresses to the micro-fractures. Consequently, memory modules can and do fail after months of apparently reliable operation. Typically, the error correction capability of the memory system in high-end servers and workstations can protect against interconnection failure between the memory controller and the DRAM devices. However, the FB-DIMM memory system introduces a new level of interconnects between the AMBs and the memory controller. As described previously, the FB-DIMM memory system uses CRC to protect against transmission errors. However, neither the chipkill protection mechanism in the memory

controller nor the CRC can protect against the failure of an interconnect between the memory controller and an AMB and between the AMBs. To protect against a single point failure of the interconnect fabric between the AMBs, the FB-DIMM memory system relies on bit lane steering and predefined fail-over modes in case of a single point interconnect failure.

In the case of a failed bit lane in the southbound channel, the AMBs would detect a CRC error in each transmitted frame and send an alert frame back toward the FB-DIMM memory controller through the northbound channel. The FB-DIMM memory controller would then attempt to recover the channel with a soft channel-reset command and retrain the AMBs in the channel to lock in on the data bit timings in the point-to-point northbound and southbound channels. The faulty bit lane would then fail the channel timing training in the allotted time. In such a case, the FB-DIMM memory system is designed so that the remaining bit lanes can be relied upon to continue to operate and transport commands, status, and data between the FB-DIMM memory controller and the AMBs. Figure 14.13 shows block diagrams that illustrate the bit lane steering logic circuit where the top diagram illustrates the data flow in the case of normal functionality, and the bottom

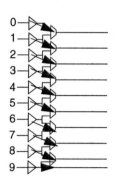

Bit steering logic passes through in functional case

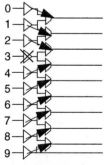

Bit steering logic merges around failed bit lane

FIGURE 14.13: Bit lane steering logic.

diagram illustrates the data flow around a failed bit lane in the case of a bit lane failure. Figure 14.13 shows that the vector input of the bit lanes was designed so that with the exception of the topmost bit lane, each external input can be directed to one of two internal bit lanes. In the point of a bit lane failure that may be attributed to interconnect failure or output driver of the previous AMB stuck-at-value fault, the bit lane steering circuit can merge the remaining bit lanes to map out the faulting bit lane and continue to operate with reduced transmission capacity. In such a mode, the basic frame format and the payload of the frame are unaffected, but the CRC of the payload is reduced to a weaker form that uses fewer bits. In essence, the frame transport layer has enough payload transmission capability so that it can sustain the failure of a bit lane and continue to operate.

14.6.3 Fail-over Modes

The FB-DIMM channel is nominally configured with 10 bit lanes in the southbound channel and 14 bit lanes in the northbound channel. Normal southbound frames consist of 12 transfers delivering 120 bits of data over the 10 bit lanes, and normal northbound frames consist of 12 transfers delivering 168 bits of data over the bit lanes. In the design of the FB-DIMM memory system, the northbound and southbound channels are designed with sufficient over capacity so that each channel can tolerate the failure of a given bit lane.

In a southbound command-plus-write-data frame, each frame contains 2 bits of frame type, 24 bits of command, 64 bits of data, 8 check bits or data mask bits, and 22 bits of CRC data. In the case of a failed bit lane in the southbound channel, the bit steering logic can be used to ensure that the southbound channel continues to function with 9 bit lanes. In this case, the 10-bit-lane southbound channel is described as having failed-over to a 9-bit-lane channel and continues to operate with weaker CRC protection. In the 9-bit-lane fail-over mode, the command frame transmitted by the FB-DIMM memory controller remains the same, with the exception that the 22-bit CRC is reduced to 10 bits of CRC. Despite the reduced strength in CRC protection, the 10-bit CRC

will continue to detect all random 1-bit, 2-bit, and 3-bit faults, as well as continuous faults in the case of a second bit lane failure. However, the FB-DIMM channel does not have sufficient capacity to continue to operate with only 8 bit lanes in the southbound channel.

In the northbound channel, a data frame consists of 128 data bits, 16 check bits, and 24 CRC bits. The 24 CRC bits are separated into two groups of 12 CRC bits that separately protect the transmission of the two groups of 64 data bits and 8 check bits. In the case of a bit lane failure, the northbound channel can be placed into a 13-bit-lane fail-over mode where the CRC protection is reduced in strength to 6 CRC bits per group in each frame. Finally, the FB-DIMM-access protocol defines an optional fail-over mode that allows for a 13-bit-lane northbound channel to fail-over to a 12-bit-lane northbound channel. In this mode, the northbound framing protocol is defined to be able to continue to operate without transmitting check bits, but with 6 CRC bits per group in each frame. However, the FB-DIMM memory system is designed to tolerate the failure of a single bit lane, and the bit lane merging logic circuit has been designed with that assumption in mind. Consequently, the current-generation AMBs are not designed to continue to operate with the failure of 2 bit lanes in the northbound channel. In essence, the fail-over modes are defined to provide the memory controller with a mechanism to safely move data from an FB-DIMM channel in the case of a bit lane failure. Presumably, the bit lane failure occurred in a given FB-DIMM as a result of an interconnect failure to the AMB or a failure of the AMB's I/O interface. Then, once the data is safely transported off of the partly failed FB-DIMM, the end-user or system administrator can then proceed to remove the failed FB-DIMM and replace it with a functional FB-DIMM.

14.6.4 Hot Add and Replace

The FB-DIMM memory system is designed as the next-generation memory system for a variety of high-end computer systems. One class of high-end system that the FB-DIMM is designed for is the high-availability, mission critical class of compute servers. Although the probability of failure for any given memory module is relatively low, the probability of system-level failure increases with the number of components. Consequently, in mission critical systems that make use of large numbers of memory modules, the mechanism has to exist to isolate a failing component in a given memory module from the system, replace the failing memory module, and then restore system operation to the memory channel. The point-to-point system architecture of the FB-DIMM memory system is naturally suited to fault isolation. Moreover, the FB-DIMM memory system access protocol has been designed to facilitate the removal and replacement of faulting FB-DIMMs from a running system and reinitialization of the FB-DIMM channel to take the newly added FB-DIMM on-line.

In the case of a failed DRAM device causing ECC errors, or a failed bit lane causing CRC errors, the FB-DIMM memory system can continue to operate with the built-in error correction capabilities. However, additional errors in an FB-DIMM memory system that is already actively recovering from a single error may not be covered. Consequently, the system controller may generate an error log that informs the end-user or system administrator that a memory module has failed or is in the process of failing. The end-user or system administrator can then direct the memory controller to move active data out of the failing channel into a secure storage location and to power-down the portion of the FB-DIMM channel that contains the failure. Since the AMB itself performs the frame relay function on both the northbound and the southbound channels, it can be instructed to stop driving the secondary southbound channels and stop receiving frames from the secondary northbound channels. The system can then remove power from the active sockets. The end-user can then insert new FB-DIMM into the channel and then instruct the FB-DIMM memory controller to retrain the channels, allowing the AMBs in the FB-DIMM channel to lock-in on the timing of the individual bit lanes, and to reconfigure the latency characteristics of the FB-DIMM channel, given the addition of the new FB-DIMM or FB-DIMMs.

14.7 FB-DIMM Performance Characteristics

The FB-DIMM memory system significantly increased the pin-bandwidth of the memory system from hundreds of mega-transfers per pin to giga-transfers per pin. However, the frame-based access protocol added significant latency into the memory-access protocol due to the 4-point serial-to-parallel and parallel-to-serial conversion, as well as the frame relay times on the northbound and southbound channels. A performance evaluation of the FB-DIMM memory system thus requires an in-depth understanding of the bandwidth and latency characteristics of the FB-DIMM memory system, and that evaluation is initiated in this section with an examination of the various latency components in an FB-DIMM memory system.

Figure 14.14 illustrates the southbound to northbound, pin-to-pin, closed-page DRAM-access latency for a two-AMB FB-DIMM memory channel from the perspective of the FB-DIMM memory controller. The latency diagram illustrated in Figure 14.14 does not include the serialization and deserialization overheads that the FB-DIMM memory controller needs to generate and decode the frames, nor does it include the various address decoding, queuing, and scheduling overheads needed by the memory controller.

The latency components illustrated in Figure 14.14 are labelled from A to L, and their respective values are summarized in Table 14.2. Table 14.2 summarizes the sample latency values for a memory system with 1, 2, 3, and 4 FB-DIMMs populated with DDR2 SDRAM devices that operate at 667 MT/s at the DRAM device timing of 4-4-4.

Table 14.2 shows that for latency component A, the bit flight time between the FB-DIMM memory controller and the first AMB in the system is dependent on the distance between the FB-DIMM memory controller and the AMB. Typically, the FB-DIMMs are located at a small distance away from the microprocessor and the system controller, resulting in bit flight times between 800 and 1200 ps. In contrast, the value of the pin-to-pin frame relay pass-through latency illustrated as component B depends not on the distance of the bit flight times, but on the speed

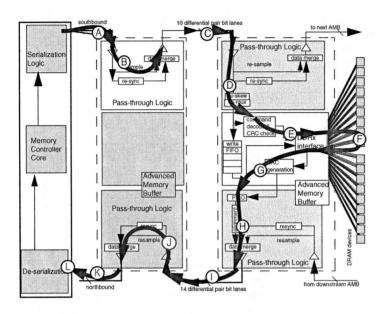

FIGURE 14.14: Latency component breakdown in a two-AMB FB-DIMM channel.

TABLE **14.2** Sample FB-DIMM channel latency breakdown (667 MT/s DDR2 DRAM)

Latency component	MIN	MAX	Unit	Notes
A Controller-to-DIMM flight	800	1200	ps	Depends on controller-to-DIMM routing distance
B SB frame resample	900	1600	ps	Depends on silicon resample speed of AMB
C SB DIMM-to-DIMM flight	600	900	ps	Depends on DIMM-to-DIMM routing distance
D Frame de-skew and parallelize	5000	5900	ps	Realign independent bit lanes
E Command check and decode	3000	3000	ps	AMB specific
F DRAM access	25200	25200	ps	$t_{RCD} + t_{CAS} + t_{DQSCK} +$ CLK delay
G Data serialization	4500	4500	ps	Includes time for CRC generation
H Data merge onto NB traffic	1800	2800	ps	Time to wait for correct frame alignment
I NB DIMM-to-DIMM flight	600	900	ps	
J NB frame resync	2000	3200	ps	May need to remerge data onto NB frame
K DIMM-to-controller flight	800	1200	ps	
L Frame-into-controller	3000	3000	ps	

Note: SB = southbound; NB = northbound.

of the signals traversing through the AMB silicon. The latency value illustrated in Table 14.2 is for the resample datapath. In the case where the resync datapath is selected to redrive the frame to the next AMB, the pin-to-pin latency may be greater than 2 ns, as illustrated for the resync time of latency component J.

In the FB-DIMM channel, the AMB redrives the southbound command frame out of the secondary southbound channel toward the next AMB, and the latency of the frame relay depends on the signal traversal speed from the output of one AMB to the input of the next AMB. The DIMM-to-DIMM flight time is labelled as latency component C in Figure 14.14, and that latency value is typically in the range of 600–900 ps.

Once the command frame reaches the targeted AMB, the frame is de-skewed, parallelized, and commands are extracted from the frame and checked againt the checksum for transmission errors.[6] Although the de-skewing and decoding process is shown as two separate components that collectively range between 8000 and 8900 ps in Table 14.2, that latency value is implementation specific and depends separately on the amount of bit-to-bit skew in the southbound channel and the speed of the AMB in checking the CRC and moving the command to the interface of the DRAM devices. The separation of latency components D and E provides the delineation of the frame command decoding latency into a component D that does not scale with respect to faster AMB silicon and a component E that does.

Component F of the latency diagram illustrates the contribution of DRAM-access latency to the FB-DIMM memory-access latency. In the case of a 667-MT/s DDR2 SDRAM device operating with the DRAM device timing of 4-4-4, it takes 12 ns to open a row and 12 ns to access a critical column of data. Component F further adds the clock-to-command and clock-to-data skew of the DDR2 SDRAM-access protocol, and data is expected to be returned into the AMB after 25.2 ns for the 667 MT/s, 4-4-4 DDR2 SDRAM devices.

Then, the AMB accepts the return data, serializes the data word, computes the CRC for data transport, and seamlessly merges the data frame onto the independent northbound bit lanes. Similar to latency components D and E, latency components G and H are not wholly independent latency components, but depend on specific implementation of the AMB as well as the bit-to-bit skew that exists on the northbound bit lanes at the time of the frame insertion.

Thereafter, the latency components of I, J, and K depend on the latency of signal traversal from the AMB back toward the controller. In particular, latency component J is illustrated with the resync datapath and the resync latency contribution. Typically, the memory controller would not operate the AMB with the northbound and the southbound pass-through logic in different resync and resample modes. However, the latency component breakdown in Figure 14.14 and Table 14.2 is designed to be illustrative in nature, and the differences in latency serve to reinforce the difference in resample and resync modes.

Finally, after the data first appears on the northbound pin-interface of the controller, it takes an entire frame duration time to move the frame into the memory controller, and the controller can begin the serial-to-parallel conversion after that time. The contribution frame duration time is labelled as component L in Figure 14.14 .

One unfortunate consequence of the daisy-chained FB-DIMM channel topology is that channel latency increases with the insertion of more AMBs into the channel. Figure 14.14 and Table 14.2 collectively illustrate the contributions of various components to the overall channel latency, and Table 14.3 summarizes the channel latency values for 1, 2, 3, and 4 FB-DIMMs in the FB-DIMM channel, respectively.

The channel latency values summarized in Table 14.3 are based on the latency component values listed in Table 14.2, and there are two caveats worthy of note in the examination of the FB-DIMM channel latency. The first caveat worthy of note is the previously noted caveat that the northbound and southbound lanes are in different frame relay modes, and the actual channel latency of a multi-FB-DIMM channel depends on the specific channel configuration. Typically, the

---

[6]The same frame de-skewing and decoding occurs in all AMBs. The AMB stops processing a given frame when it determines that the commands in the frame do not impact the state of the AMB or the DRAM devices controlled by the AMB.

TABLE **14.3** FB-DIMM multi-DIMM channel latency (667 MT/s DDR2 DRAM)

Latency of	MIN	MAX	Unit	Notes
1 FB-DIMM	44.1	46.8	ns	SB resample, NB resync
2 FB-DIMM	48.2	53.2	ns	SB resample, NB resync
3 FB-DIMM	52.3	59.6	ns	SB resample, NB resync
4 FB-DIMM	56.4	66	ns	SB re sample, NB resync

AMBs are configured so that the first AMB in the channel operates in resync mode, and subsequent AMBs operate in resample mode.

The second caveat of the latency values summarized in Table 14.3 is that the actual net increase in the FB-DIMM channel latency depends not just on the additive latencies of the intervening components, but also on the frame arrival time into the AMB relative to the rising clock edge of the local DDR2 SDRAM command clock. That is, the frame arrival time at the interface of an AMB may be as low as 1 UI too late to move the command in command slot A into the DRAM device at the earliest possible time. That command would then have to wait 11 UIs for the next DDR2 SDRAM command clock. Then, the addition of an AMB into the channel may add another 4 ns of signal flight time into the FB-DIMM channel, but the net latency contribution may be as little as 3 ns. Conversely, the addition of an AMB and 4 ns of signal flight time may increase the overall latency by 6 ns. Consequently, the actual latency of the FB-DIMM channel as a function of the number of FB-DIMMs in the channel may appear partly with the effect of a staircase function. Nevertheless, the latency values summarized in Table 14.3 are adequate as first-order estimates in the subsequent sections to compare the performance of different FB-DIMM channel configurations.

14.7.1 Fixed vs. Variable Latency Scheduling

In the previous section, FB-DIMM channel latency values are summarized in Tables 14.2 and 14.3, and

Figure 14.15 graphically illustrates the peculiarity of the FB-DIMM channel latency characteristics in that FB-DIMMs closer to the memory controller have lower access latency than FBDIMMs farther away from the memory controller. Moreover, since the FB-DIMM memory controller is responsible for all command and frame scheduling in the FB-DIMM channel, the FB-DIMM memory controller has the difficult task of having to flexibly adjust to different channel configurations that may be composed of different FB-DIMMs from different module manufacturers, using different AMBs from different AMB manufacturers.

To deal with the issue of variable access latency, the AMB is designed with two different access modes to facilitate frame scheduling by the FB-DIMM memory controller: fixed latency mode and variable latency mode. The fixed latency mode is the baseline frame scheduling mechanism, and all AMBs must support the fixed latency channel scheduling mode. The AMB may also optionally support a variable channel scheduling latency mode to enhance performance.

In the fixed latency mode, the round-trip latency of all read data frames is set to that of the slowest responding FB-DIMM. Typically, the slowest responding FB-DIMM is the last FB-DIMM in the FB-DIMM channel. However, in the case where the next-to-last FB-DIMM has slower DRAM devices than the last FB-DIMM in the channel and where the FB-DIMM is the slowest FB-DIMM, then the frame latency of all FB-DIMMs in the FB-DIMM channel is set to equal the latency of that slowest DIMM.[7] In the fixed latency mode, the memory controller individually determines

---

[7]An FB-DIMM with DDR2 SDRAM devices operating at 667 MT/s with DRAM device latency of 5-5-5 in the next-to-last FB-DIMM socket may be slower than the last FB-DIMM with DDR2 SDRAM devices operating at 667 MT/s with DRAM device latency of 4-4-4.

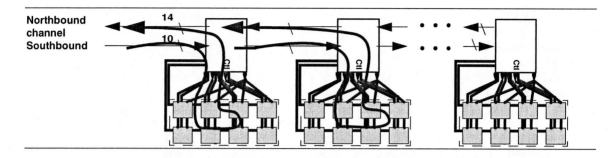

FIGURE 14.15: Variable access latency for different FB-DIMMs in the FB-DIMM channel.

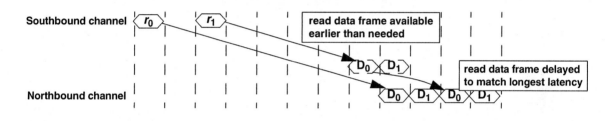

FIGURE 14.16: Latency equalization enables fixed latency scheduling.

the latency value of each FB-DIMM, and then programs in additional delays to each AMB so that all FB-DIMMs appear to the memory controller as having the same latency from the perspective of the memory controller.

In the fixed latency mode, the AMB delays read data frames until the data return time equals the latency of the slowest FB-DIMM in the channel. Figure 14.16 illustrates the case where request r_0 is sent to the slowest FB-DIMM in the memory system, and request r_1 is sent to a faster FB-DIMM located closer to the FB-DIMM controller. Figure 14.16 shows that although request r_1 is issued two frame times after request r_0, data from request r_1 is available earlier than data from request r_0. However, if request r_1 places the read data frame immediately onto the northbound channel, the second read data frame of request r_1 would collide with the return data frame of request r_0. Instead, the faster FB-DIMM delays

the data return for request r_1 until the read latency of request r_1 matches that of request r_0. The matched delay scheme ensures that read data frames would return to the memory controller with the same spacing and ordering as the command frames leaving the controller via the southbound channels.

In the variable latency mode, the AMB simply returns read data as soon as the data is made available by the DRAM devices. However, due to the complexity of scheduling, the variable delay latency is currently limited to scheduling frames in short channel configurations. In such configurations, the limited parallelism from the DRAM devices and the relatively long latencies mean that few requests can be kept in flight in the channel. Moreover, the memory controller can more easily keep track of the different latency characteristics of the different FB-DIMMs in a short channel configuration.

Finally, studies are underway to examine possible extensions to the FB-DIMM-access protocol to allow for dynamic additive latency scheduling. That is, in the current framework, read data frames are returned to the memory controller either with a static additive latency to match the worst-case channel latency or with no additive latency, resulting possibly in sub-optimal channel utilization characteristics. In a dynamic additive latency scheduling channel, the memory controller dynamically specifies the additive latency value to be added to the return of each read data frame. In the case where the channel traffic is sparse, each request can be scheduled to return with no additive latency, and in the case where the channel is fully saturated with traffic, the requests to each FB-DIMM can be specified to optimize for channel bandwidth throughput.

14.8 Perspective

Conceptually, the AMB is designed to operate as a piece of wire that allows the memory controller to directly control the DRAM devices, and it is currently not much more than that. However, the FB-DIMM memory system decouples the direct control of the DRAM devices from the processor, and it could potentially evolve into a highly advanced, highly intelligent memory system. That is, if Intel doesn't end up cutting and running.

CHAPTER 15

Memory System Design Analysis

In recent years, the importance of memory system performance as a limiter of computer system performance has been widely recognized. However, the commodity nature of mainstream DRAM devices means that DRAM design engineers are reluctant to add functionalities or to restructure DRAM devices that would increase the manufacturing cost of those devices. The direct consequence of the constraints on available features of commodity DRAM devices is that system architects and design engineers must carefully examine the system-level, multi-variable equations that trade off cost against performance, power consumption, reliability, user configuration flexibility, and a myriad of other design considerations. Consequently, the topic of memory system performance analysis is important not only to system architects, but also to DRAM system and device design engineers to evaluate design trade-off points between the cost and benefits of various features.

This chapter examines performance issues and proceeds along a generalized framework to examine memory system performance characteristics. The goal of the illustrative examples contained in this chapter is not to answer every and all design questions that a memory system architect may have in the evaluation of his or her memory system architecture. Rather, the goal of this chapter is to provide illustrative examples that a potential system architect can follow and gain potential insight into how his or her memory system should or could be analyzed.

15.1 Overview

Figure 15.1 shows the scaling trends of commodity DRAM devices. The figure shows that in the time period shown, from 1998 to 2006, random row cycle times in commodity DRAM devices decreased on the order of 7% per year, and the data rate of commodity DRAM devices doubled every three years. The general trend illustrated in Figure 15.1 means that it is more difficult to sustain peak bandwidth from successive generations of commodity DRAM devices, and the topic of memory system performance analysis becomes more important with each passing year. Consequently, the topic of memory system design and performance analysis is similarly gaining more interest from industry and academia with each passing year. However, the topic of memory system design and performance analysis is an extremely complex topic; a system-specific, optimal memory system design depends on system-specfic workload characteristics, cost constraints, bandwidth versus latency performance requirements, and power design envelope, as well as reliability considerations. That is, there is no single memory system that is near-optimal for all workloads. The topic is of sufficient complexity that a single chapter designed to outline the basic issues cannot provide complete coverage in terms of width and depth. Rather, the limited scope of this chapter is to provide an overview and some illustrative examples of how memory system performance analysis can be performed.

The logical first step in the design process of a memory system is to define the constraints that are important to the system architect and design engineers. Typically, a given memory system may be cost constrained, power constrained, performance constrained, or a reasonable combination thereof. In the case where one constraint predominates the design consideration process, the system architect and engineer may have

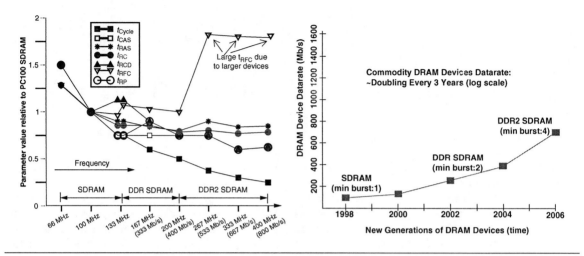

FIGURE 15.1: Commodity DRAM device timing and data rate scaling trends.

little choice but to pursue design points that optimize for the singular, overriding constraint. However, in the cases where the design process has multi-dimensional flexibility in trading off cost against performance, the second step that should be taken in the design process of the memory system is to explore the workload characteristics that the memory system is designed to handle. That is, without an understanding of the workload characteristics that the memory system should be optimized for, the mismatch in respective points of optimality can lead to a situation where the system may be overdesigned for workload characteristics that seldom occur and at the same time poorly designed to handle more common workload characteristics.

This chapter on the performance and design analysis of memory system performance characteristics begins with a section that examines several single threaded workloads commonly used for benchmarking purposes. The section on workload characteristics examines the various single threaded workloads in terms of their respective request inter-arrival rate, locality characteristics, and read-versus-write traffic ratio. The rationale for the examination of the workload characteristics is to provide a basis for understanding different types of workload characteristics. However, one caveat that should be observed is that the workloads examined in Section 15.2 are somewhat

typical workloads for uniprocessor desktop and workstation class computer systems. More modern memory systems designed for multi-threaded and multi-core processors must be designed to handle complex multi-threaded and multiple concurrent process workloads. Consequently, the workloads examined in Section 15.2 are not broadly applicable to this class of systems. In particular, systems designed for highly threaded, on-line transaction processing (OLTP) types of applications will have drastically different memory system requirements than systems designed for bandwidth-intensive scientific workloads. Nevertheless, Section 15.2 can provide the reader with a baseline understanding of issues that are important in the design and analysis of a memory system.

The remainder of the chapter following the workload description section can be broadly divided into two sections that use slightly varying techniques to analyze a similar set of issues. In Section 15.3 the *Request Access Distance* (RAD) analytical framework provides a set of mathematical equations to analyze sustainable bandwidth characteristics, given specific memory-access patterns and scheduling policies from the memory controller. The RAD analytical framework is then used to examine a variety of issues relating to system-level parallelism and bandwidth characteristics. Finally, to complement the equation-based RAD analytical framework for DRAM memory system bandwidth analysis, Sections 15.4 and 15.5 use the more traditional approach of a memory system simulator to separately examine the issue of controller scheduling policy, controller queue depth, burst length, memory device improvements, and latency distribution characteristics.

15.2 Workload Characteristics

The performance characteristics of any given DRAM memory system depend on workload-specific characteristics of access rates and access patterns. In essence, one of the first steps in the design process of a memory system should be an examination of workloads that the memory system is to be optimized for. To facilitate a general understanding of workload

behavior, and to examine a range of workload-specific variances, a large set of memory address traces from different applications is examined in this section and is summarized in Table 15.1. From the SPEC CPU 2000 benchmark suite, address traces from 164.gzip, 176.gcc, 197.parser, 255.vortex, 172.mgrid, 178.galgel, 179.art, 183.equake, and 188.ammp are used. The address traces from the SPEC CPU 2000 benchmark suite were captured with the MASE simulation framework through the simulated execution of 2 to 4 billion instructions, and the number of requests in each address trace is reported as trace length in Table 15.1 [Larson 2001]. In addition to the address traces captured with MASE, processor bus traces captured with a digital logic analyzer from a personal computer system running various benchmarks and applications such as JMark 2.0, 3DWinbench, SETI@HOME, and Quake 3 are added to the mix. Collectively, the SPEC

TABLE 15.1   Workload summary

Workload Name	Type	Trace Length	Description
164.gzip	MASE	2.87 M	Popular data compression program written by Jean-Loup Gailly. CPU 2000 INT
176.gcc	MASE	4.62 M	Compiler benchmark. CPU 2000 INT
197.parser	MASE	31.2 M	Syntactic parsing of English, based on link grammar. CPU 2000 INT
255.vortex	MASE	7.17 M	Single user, object-oriented database transaction benchmark. CPU 2000 INT
172.mgrid	MASE	47.5 M	Multi-grid solver of 3D potential field. CPU 2000 FP
178.galgel	MASE	3.1 M	Computational Fluid Dynamics. CPU 2000 FP
179.art	MASE	90 M	Neural networks-object recognition. CPU 2000 FP
183.equake	MASE	7.9 M	Seismic wave propagation simulations. CPU 2000 FP
188.ammp	MASE	60 M	Computational Chemistry. CPU 2000 FP
JMark 2.0	CPU BUS	3 * 1M	Java benchmarks (CPU, AWT, Complex Arithmetic)
3DWinbench	CPU BUS	1 * 1M	Synthetic test of 3D graphics system
SETI@HOME	CPU BUS	3 * 1M	Popular search for alien signal distributed computing
Quake 3	CPU BUS	6 * 1M	Popular desktop game with 3D graphics

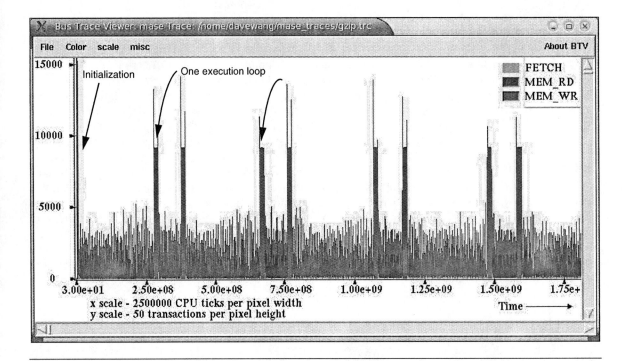

FIGURE 15.2: 164.gzip trace overview.

CPU 2000 workload traces and desktop computer application traces form a diverse set of workloads that are described herein. In the following subsections, the characteristics for a small subsection of each workload are represented graphically. The various diagrams graphically illustrate the request inter-arrival rates and the respective read-versus-write ratios within short periods of time. The diagrams are captured from a bus trace viewer written specifically for the purpose of demonstrating the bursty nature of memory-access patterns.

15.2.1 164.gzip: C Compression

164.gzip is a popular data compression program written by Jean-Loup Gailly for the GNU project, and it is included as part of the SPEC CPU 2000 integer

benchmark suite. 164.gzip uses Lempel-Ziv coding (LZ77) as its compression algorithm. In the captured trace for 164.gzip, 4 billion simulated instructions were executed by the simulator over 2 billion simulated processor cycles, and 2.87 million memory requests were captured in the trace. Figure 15.2 shows the memory traffic of 164.gzip for the first 4 billion simulated instructions in terms of the number of memory transactions per unit time. Each pixel on the x-axis in Figure 15.2 represents 2.5 million simulated processor cycles, and Figure 15.2 shows that 164 gzip typically averages less than 5000 transactions per 2.5 million microprocessor cycles, but for short periods of time, write bursts can average nearly 10,000 cacheline transaction requests per 2.5 million simulated processor cycles.[1] Figure 15.2 shows that in the first 1.75 billion processor cycles, 164.gzip undergoes a short duration

---

[1]The cacheline size is 64 bytes.

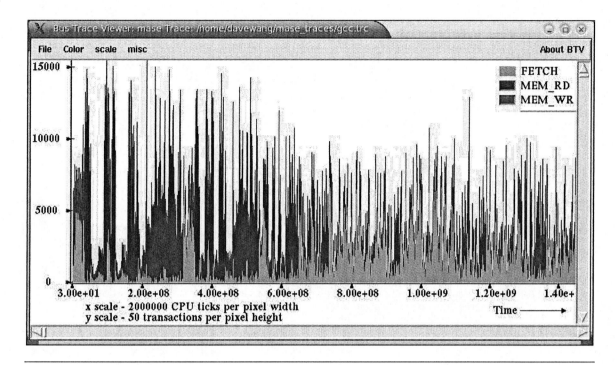

FIGURE 15.3: 176.gcc trace overview.

of program initialization and then quickly enters into a series of repetitive loops. Figure 15.2 also shows that 164.gzip is typically not memory intensive, and the trace averages less than 1 memory reference per 1000 instructions for the time period shown.

15.2.2   176.gcc: C Programming Language Compiler

176.gcc is a benchmark in the SPEC CPU 2000 integer benchmark suite that tests compiler performance. In the captured trace for 176.gcc, 1.5 billion instructions were executed by the simulator over 1.63 billion simulated processor cycles, and 4.62 million memory requests were captured in the trace during this simulated execution of the 176.gcc benchmark. Unlike 164.gzip, 176.gcc does not enter into a discernible and repetitive loop behavior within the first 1.5 billion instructions. Figure 15.3 shows the memory system activity of 176.gcc through the first 1.4 billion

processor cycles, and it shows that 176.gcc, like 164.gzip, is typically not memory intensive, although it does averages more than 3 memory references per 1000 instructions. Moreover, in the time-frame illustrated in Figure 15.3, 176.gcc shows a heavy component of memory access due to instruction-fetch requests and relatively fewer memory write requests. The reason that the trace in Figure 15.3 shows a high percentage of instruction-fetch requests may be due to the fact that the trace was captured with the L2 cache of the simulated processor set to 256 kB in size. Presumably, a processor with a larger cache may be able to reduce its bandwidth demand on the memory system, depending on the locality characteristics of the specific workload.

15.2.3   197.parser: C Word Processing

197.parser is a benchmark in the SPEC CPU 2000 integer suite that performs syntactic parsing of

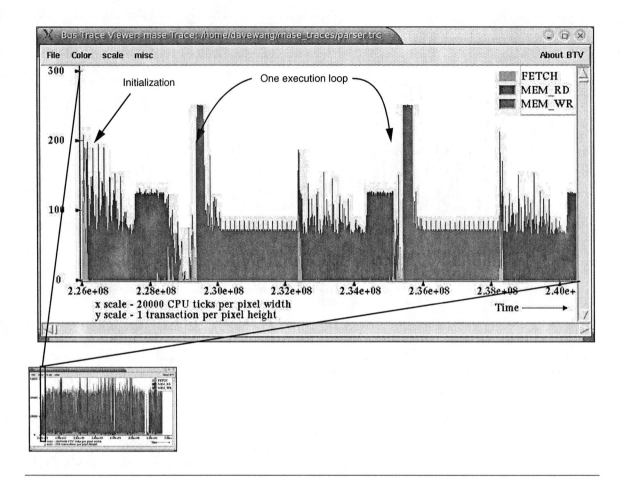

FIGURE 15.4: 197.parser trace overview.

English based on link grammar. In the captured trace for 197.parser, 4 billion instructions were executed by the simulator over 6.7 billion simulated processor cycles, and 31.2 million cacheline requests to memory were captured in the memory-access trace. Similar to 164 gzip, 197.gzip undergoes a short duration of program initialization and then quickly enters into a repetitive loop. However, 197.gzip enters into loops that are relatively short in duration and are difficult to observe in an overview. The close-up view provided in Figure 15.4 shows that each loop lasts for approximately 6 million microprocessor cycles, and the number of reads and write requests is roughly equal.

Overall, Figure 15.4 shows the memory system activity of 197.parser through the first 6.7 billion processor cycles, and it shows that 197.parser is moderately memory intensive, averaging approximately 8 cacheline transaction requests per 1000 instructions.

15.2.4 255.vortex: C Object-Oriented Database

255.vortex is a benchmark in the SPEC CPU 2000 integer suite. In the captured trace for 255.vortex, 4 billion simulated instructions were executed by the simulator over 3.3 billion simulated processor cycles, and 7.2 million cacheline transaction requests

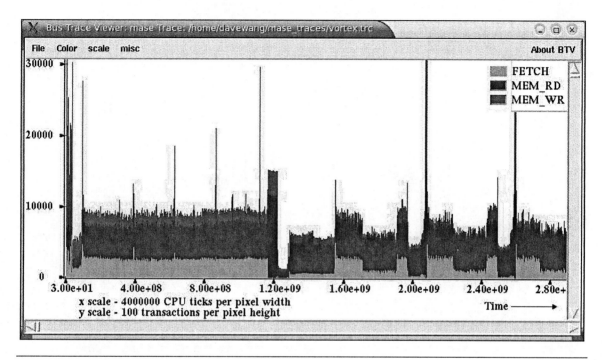

FIGURE 15.5: 255.vortex overview.

to memory were captured in the trace. In the first 3.3 billion processor cycles, 255.vortex goes through several distinct patterns of behavior. However, after a 1.5-billion-cycle initialization phase, 255.vortext appears to settle into execution loops that last for 700 million processor cycles each, and each loop appears to be dominated by instruction-fetch and memory read requests with relatively fewer memory write requests. Figure 15.5 shows the memory system activity of 255.vortex through the first 3.3 billion processor cycles. Figure 15.5 also shows that 255.vortex is typically not memory intensive, since it averages less than 2 memory transaction requests per 1000 instructions.

15.2.5   172.mgrid: Fortran 77 Multi-Grid Solver: 3D Potential Field

172.mgrid is a benchmark that demonstrates the capabilities of a very simple multi-grid solver in computing a three-dimensional (3D) potential

field. It was adapted by SPEC from the NAS Parallel Benchmarks with modifications for portability and a different workload. In the captured trace for 172. mgrid, 4 billion simulated instructions were executed by the simulator over 9 billion simulated processor cycles, and 47.5 million requests were captured in the trace. 172.mgrid is moderately memory intensive, as it generates nearly 12 memory requests per 1000 instructions. Figure 15.6 shows that after a short initialization period, 172.mgrid settles into a repetitive and predictable loop behavior. The loops are dominated by memory read transaction requests, and memory write transaction requests are relatively fewer.

15.2.6   SETI@HOME

Distinctly separate from the SPEC CPU benchmark traces captured through the use of a simulator, a different set of application traces was captured through the use of a logic analyzer. The SETI@HOME application

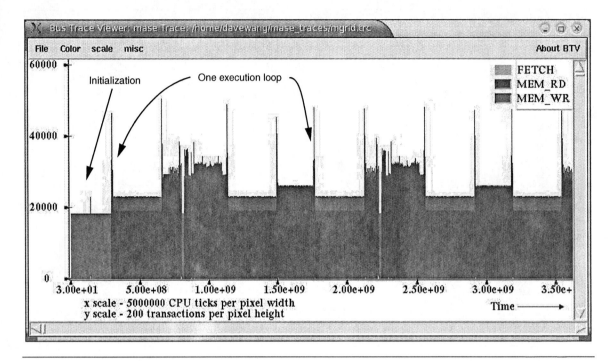

FIGURE 15.6: 172.mgrid trace overview.

trace is one of four processor bus activity traces in Table 15.1 that was captured through the use of a logic analyzer. SETI@HOME is a popular program that allows the *SETI* (Search for Extra Terrestrial Intelligence) Institute to make use of spare processing power on idle personal computers to search for signs of extraterrestrial intelligence. The SETI@HOME application performs a series of fast Fourier transforms (FFTs) on captured electronic signals to look for the existence of signal patterns that may be indicative of an attempt by extraterrestrial intelligence to communicate. The series of FFTs are performed on successively larger portions of the signal file. As a result, the size of the working set for the program changes as it proceeds through execution. Figure 15.7 shows a portion of the SETI@HOME workload. In this segment, the memory request rate is approximately 12~14 transactions per microsecond, and the workload alternates between read-to-write transaction ratios of 1:1 and 2:1. Finally, the effects of the disruption caused by the system context switch can be seen once every 10 ms in Figure 15.7.

15.2.7 Quake 3

Quake 3 is a popular game for the personal computer, and Figure 15.8 shows a short segment of the Quake 3 processor bus trace, randomly captured as the Quake 3 game runs in a demonstration mode on a personal computer system. Figure 15.8 shows that the processor bus activity of the game is very bursty. However, a cyclic behavior appears in the trace with a frequency of approximately once every 70 ms. Interestingly, the frequency of the cyclic behavior coincides with frame rate of the Quake 3 game on the host system.

15.2.8 178.galgel, 179.art, 183.equake, 188. ammp, JMark 2.0, and 3DWinbench

In the following sections, memory-access characteristics for several workloads are described, but not separately illustrated. The workloads listed in Table 15.1, but not separately illustrated, are 178.galgel, 179.art, 183.equake,188.ammp, JMark 2.0, and 3DWinbench.

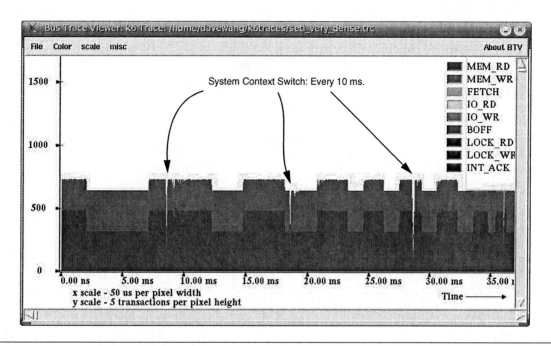

FIGURE 15.7: Portions of SETI@HOME workload.

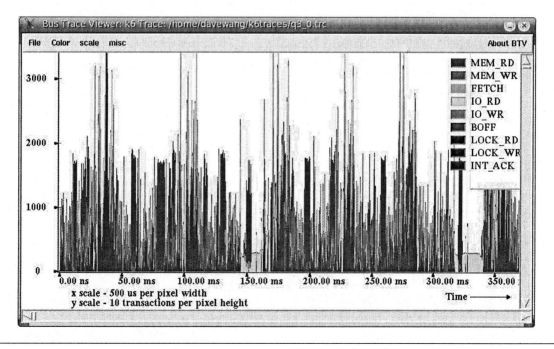

FIGURE 15.8: Quake 3: random trace segment.

In the captured trace for 178.galgel, 4 billion simulated instructions were executed by the simulator over 2.2 billion simulated processor cycles, and 3.1 million requests were captured in the trace. Relative to the other workloads listed in Table 15.1, 178 galgel is not memory intensive, and it generates less than 1 memory request per 1000 instructions. In the captured trace, 178.galgel settles into a repetitive and predictable loop behavior after a short initialization period.

179.art is a benchmark derived from an application that emulates a neural network and attempts to recognize objects in a thermal image. In the captured trace for 179.art, 450 million simulated instructions were executed by the simulator over 14.2 billion simulated processor cycles, and 90 million requests were captured in the trace. 179.art is extremely memory intensive, and it generates nearly 200 memory transaction requests per 1000 instructions. In the captured trace for 179.art, more than 95% of the memory traffic are memory read transactions.

In the captured trace for 183.quake, 1.4 billion simulated instructions were executed by the simulator over 1.8 billion simulated processor cycles, and 7.9 million requests were captured in the trace. In the captured trace, after an initialization period, 183.equake settles into a repetitive and predictable loop behavior. The loops are dominated by memory read requests, and memory write requests are relatively fewer outside of the initialization phase. 183.equake is moderately memory intensive, and it generates almost 6 memory references per 1000 instructions.

For the 188.ammp benchmark, 4 billion simulated instructions were executed by the simulator over 10.5 billion simulated processor cycles, and 60 million requests were captured in the trace. Table 15.1 shows that 188.ammp is moderately memory intensive. It generates approximately 15 memory references per 1000 instructions.

Differing from the SPEC CPU workloads, 3DWinbench is a suite of benchmarks that is designed to test the 3D graphics capability of a system, and the trace for this workload was captured by using a logic analyzer that monitors activity on the processor bus of the system under test. The CPU component of the 3DWinbench benchmark suite tests the processor capability, and the trace shows a moderate amount of memory traffic. 3DWinbench achieves a sustained peak rate of approximately 5 transactions per microsecond during short bursts, and it sustains at least 1 transaction per microsecond throughout the trace.

Finally, for the JMark 2.0 CPU, AWT and Complex Mathematics benchmarks from the JMark 2.0 suite are independent benchmarks in this suite of benchmarks. Compared to other workloads examined in this work, the benchmarks in JMark 2.0 access memory only very infrequently. Ordinarily, the relatively low access rate of these benchmarks would exclude them as workloads of importance in a study of memory system performance characteristics. However, the benchmarks in JMark 2.0 exhibit an interesting behavior in access memory in that they repeatedly access memory with locked reads and locked write requests at the exact same location. As a result, these application traces are included for completeness to illustrate a type of workload that performs poorly in DRAM memory systems regardless of system configuration.

15.2.9 Summary of Workload Characteristics

Figures 15.2–15.8 graphically illustrate workload characteristics of selected benchmarks listed in Table 15.1. Collectively, Figures 15.2–15.8 show that while the memory-access traces for some workloads exhibited regular, cyclic behavior as the workloads proceeded through execution, other workloads exhibited memory-access patterns that are non-cyclic and non-predictive in nature. Consequently, Figures 15.2–15.8 show that it is difficult to design a memory system that can provide optimal performance for all applications irrespective of their memory-access characteristics, but it is easier to design optimal memory systems in the case where the workload and the predominant memory-access patterns are known *a priori*. For example, low-latency memory systems designed for network packet switching applications and high-bandwidth memory systems designed for graphics processors can respectively focus on and optimize for the predominant access patterns in each case, whereas the memory controller for a multi-core processor may have to separately support single threaded, latency-critical applications as well as multi-threaded, bandwidth-critical applications.

Aside from illustrating the bursty and possibly non-predictive nature of memory-access patterns in general, Figures 15.2–15.8 also illustrate that for most workloads, the ratio of read and instruction-fetch requests versus write requests far exceeds 1:1. In combination with the observation that write requests are typically not performance critical, Figures 15.2–15.8 serve as graphical justification. For memory systems that design in asymmetrical bandwidth capabilities as part of the architectural specification. For example, the FB-DIMM memory system and IBM's POWER4 and POWER5 memory systems all respectively design in a 2:1 ratio in read-to-write bandwidth.

15.3 The RAD Analytical Framework

The RAD analytical framework computes the maximum sustainable bandwidth of a DRAM memory system by meticulously accounting for the various overheads in the DRAM memory-access protocol. In the RAD analytical framework, DRAM refresh is considered as a fixed overhead, and its effects are not accounted for in the framework, but must be accounted for separately. Aside from the effects of DRAM refresh, the methodology to account for the primary causes of bandwidth inefficiency in DRAM memory systems is described in detail in the following sections.

The RAD analytical framework formalizes the methodology for the computation of maximum sustainable DRAM memory system bandwidth, subjected to different configurations, timing parameters, and memory-access patterns. However, the use of the RAD analytical framework does not reduce the complexity of analysis nor does it reduce the number of independent variables that collectively impact the

performance of a DRAM memory system. The RAD analytical framework simply identifies the factors that limit DRAM bandwidth efficiency and formalizes the methodology that computes their interrelated contributions that collectively limit DRAM memory system bandwidth.

The basic idea of the RAD analytical framework is simply to compute the number of cycles that a given DRAM memory system spends in actively transporting data, as compared to the number of cycles that must be wasted due to various overheads. The maximum efficiency of the DRAM memory system can then be simply computed as in Equation 15.1.

$$Efficiency = \frac{\text{data transport times}}{\text{data transport times} + \text{overhead}} \quad \text{(EQ 15.1)}$$

15.3.1 DRAM-Access Protocol

The basic DRAM memory-access protocol and the respective inter-command constraints are examined in a separate chapter and will not be repeated here. Rather, the analysis in this chapter simply assumes that the interrelated constraints between DRAM commands in terms of timing parameters are understood by the reader. Nevertheless, the basic timing parameters used in the basic DRAM-access protocol are summarized in Table 15.2. These timing parameters are used throughout the remainder of this chapter to facilitate in the analysis of the memory system.

15.3.2 Computing DRAM Protocol Overheads

In the RAD analytical framework, the limiters of DRAM memory system bandwidth are separated into three general catagories: inter-command constraints, row cycle constraints, and per-rank, row activation constraints. These respective categories are examined separately, but ultimately are combined into a single set of equations that form the foundation of the RAD analytical framework.

The first category of constraints that limit DRAM memory system bandwidth consists of inter-command constraints. Inter-command constraints

TABLE 15.2 Summary of timing parameters used in the generic DRAM-access protocol

Parameter	Description
t_{AL}	Added Latency to column accesses, used in DDRx SDRAM devices for posted CAS commands.
t_{BURST}	Data **burst** duration. The number of cycles that data burst occupies on the data bus. In DDR SDRAM, 4 beats occupy 2 clock cycles.
t_{CAS}	Column Access Strobe latency. The time interval between column access command and the start of data return by the DRAM device(s).
t_{CCD}	Column-to-Column Delay. Minimum intra-device column-to-column command timing, determined by internal burst (prefetch) length.
t_{CMD}	Command transport duration. The time period that a command occupies on the command bus.
t_{CWD}	Column Write Delay. The time interval between issuance of a column write command and placement of data on data bus by the controller.
t_{FAW}	Four (row) bank Activation Window. A rolling time-frame in which a maximum of four bank activations can be initiated.
t_{OST}	ODT Switching Time. The time interval to switching ODT control from rank to rank.
t_{RAS}	Row Access Strobe. The time interval between row access command and data restoration in a DRAM array.
t_{RC}	Row Cycle. The time interval between accesses to different rows in a bank. $t_{RC} = t_{RAS} + t_{RP}$.
t_{RCD}	Row to Column command Delay. The time interval between row access and data ready at sense amplifiers.
t_{RFC}	Refresh Cycle Time. The time interval between refresh and activation commands.
t_{RP}	Row Precharge. The time interval that it takes for a DRAM array to be precharged for another row access.
t_{RRD}	Row activation to Row activation Delay. The minimum time interval between two row activation commands to the same DRAM device.
t_{RTP}	Read to Precharge. The time interval between a read and a precharge command. Can be approximated by $t_{CAS} - t_{CMD}$.
t_{RTRS}	Rank-to-rank switching time. Used in DDR and DDR2 SDRAM memory systems.
t_{WR}	Write Recovery time. The minimum time interval between the end of write data burst and the start of a precharge command.
t_{WTR}	Write To Read delay time. The minimum time interval between the end of write data burst and the start of a column read command.

are simply the inability to issue consecutive column access commands to move data in the DRAM memory system. For example, read-write turnaround overhead on the data bus or rank-to-rank switching times are both examples of inter-command constraints. Collectively, these inter-command constraints are referred to as DRAM protocol overheads in the RAD analytical framework. Table 15.3 summarizes the DRAM protocol overheads for consecutive column access commands. Table 15.3 lists the DRAM protocol overheads in terms of gaps between data bursts on the data bus, and that gap is reported in units of t_{BURST}. In the RAD analytical framework, the DRAM protocol overhead between a request (column access command) j and the request that immediately precedes it, request j – 1, is denoted by $D_o(j)$, and $D_o(j)$

can be computed by using request j and request j – 1 as indices into Table 15.3.

15.3.3 Computing Row Cycle Time Constraints

The second category of command constraints that limit DRAM memory system bandwidth consists of DRAM bank row cycle time constraints. In the RAD analytical framework, the minimum access distance D_m is defined as the number of requests (column access commands) that must be made to an open row of a given bank or to different banks, between two requests to the same bank that require a row cycle for that bank. In the RAD analytical framework, the basic unit for the minimum access distance statistic is the data bus utilization time for a single transaction

TABLE 15.3 DRAM protocol overheads for DDR and DDR2 SDRAM memory systems

prev	next	rank	bank	Minimum scheduling distance between column access commands No command reordering	DRAM protocol overhead between column access command pairs (unit: t_{BURST})
R	R	s	s	t_{BURST}	0
R	R	s	d	t_{BURST}	0
R	R	d	—	$t_{RTRS} + t_{BURST}$	t_{RTRS} / t_{BURST}
R	W	s	s	$t_{CAS} + t_{BURST} + t_{RTRS} - t_{CWD}$	$(t_{CAS} + t_{RTRS} - t_{CWD}) / t_{BURST}$
R	W	s	d	$t_{CAS} + t_{BURST} + t_{RTRS} - t_{CWD}$	$(t_{CAS} + t_{RTRS} - t_{CWD}) / t_{BURST}$
R	W	d	—	$t_{CAS} + t_{BURST} + t_{RTRS} - t_{CWD}$	$(t_{CAS} + t_{RTRS} - t_{CWD}) / t_{BURST}$
W	R	s	s	$t_{CWD} + t_{BURST} - t_{WTR}$	$(t_{CWD} + t_{WTR}) / t_{BURST}$
W	R	s	d	$t_{CWD} + t_{BURST} - t_{WTR}$	$(t_{CWD} + t_{WTR}) / t_{BURST}$
W	R	d	—	$t_{CWD} + t_{BURST} - t_{RTRS} - t_{CAS}$	$(t_{CWD} + t_{WTR}) / t_{BURST}$
W	W	s	s	t_{BURST}	0
W	W	s	d	t_{BURST}	0
W	W	s	—	$t_{OST} + t_{BURST}$	t_{OST}

Note: R = read; W = write; s = same; d = different.

request, t_{BURST} time period, and each request has a distance value of 1 by definition. In a close-page memory system with row cycle time of t_{RC} and access burst duration of t_{BURST}, D_m is simply $(t_{\text{RC}} - t_{\text{BURST}})$ / t_{BURST}.

In the RAD analytical framework, a request j is defined to have a request access distance $D_r(j)$ to a prior request made to a different row of the same bank as request j. The request access distance $D_r(j)$ denotes the timing distance between it and the previous request to a different row of the same bank. In the case where two requests are made to different rows of the same bank and where there are fewer than D_m requests made to the same open bank or different banks, some idle time must be inserted into the command and data busses of the DRAM memory system. Conseqeuntly, if $D_r(j)$ is less than D_m, some amount of idle time, $D_i(j)$, must be added so that the total access distance for request j, $D_r(j) + D_i(j)$, is greater than or equal to D_m. The definition for the various distances, D_m, $D_r(j)$, and $D_i(j)$, holds true for close-page memory systems as defined.

The key element in the RAD analytical framework for the computation of DRAM memory system bandwidth efficiency is the set of formulas used to compute the necessary idling distances for each request in a request stream. The fundamental insight that enables the creation of the request access distance statistic is that idling distances added for $D_r(j)$ requests immediately preceding request j must be counted toward the total access distance needed by request j since these idling distances increase the effective access distance of request j. The formula for computing the additional idling distances needed by request j for close-page memory systems is illustrated as Equation 15.2.

$$\substack{\text{Close-page} \\ \text{system}} \quad \left\{ D_i(j) = \left(MAX\, D_0(j), \left(D_m - D_r(j) + \sum_{n=j-D_r(j)}^{j-1} D_i(n) \right) \right) \right.$$

(EQ 15.2)

However, due to the differences in row buffer management, different request distances and equations are needed for open-page memory systems separate from close-page memory systems. In an open-page memory system, a row is kept active at the sense amplifiers once it is activated so that subsequent column accesses to the same row can be issued without additional row cycles. In the case of a bank conflict in an open-page memory system between two requests to different rows of the same bank, the second request may not need to wait the entire row cycle time before it can be issued. Figure 15.9 shows that in the best case, bank conflicts between two different column access requests can be scheduled with the timing of $t_{\text{BURST}} + t_{\text{RP}} + t_{\text{RCD}}$ if the row restoration time t_{RAS} has already been satisfied for the previous row access. In the best-case scenario, the minimum scheduling distance between two column commands in an open-page system to different rows of the same bank is $(t_{\text{RP}} + t_{\text{RCD})}$ / t_{BURST}. The best-case scenario illustrated

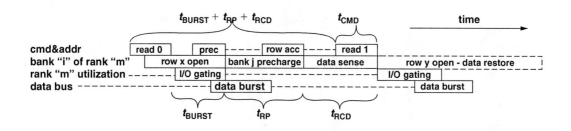

FIGURE 15.9: Consecutive read commands to the same bank: bank conflict.

in Figure 15.9 shows that D_m is by itself insufficient to describe the required minimum access distance in an open-page system. Consequently, two different minimum request access distances, $D_{m\text{-ff}}$ and $D_{m\text{-lf}}$, are separately defined for open-page memory systems to represent the worst-case and best-case timing between column accesses to different rows of the same bank in the RAD framework, respectively. The variable $D_{m\text{-ff}}$ denotes the minimum request access distance between the first column access of a row access and the first column access to the previously accessed row of the same bank. The variable $D_{m\text{-lf}}$ denotes the first column access of a row access and the last column access to the previously accessed row of the same bank. In the same manner that request access distance for request j, $D_r(j)$, is defined to compute the number of additional idle distances that is needed to satisfy D_m for close-page memory systems, two different request distances, $D_{r\text{-ff}}(j)$ and $D_{r\text{-lf}}(j)$, are defined in open-page memory systems to compute the additional idling distances needed to satisfy $D_{m\text{-ff}}$ and $D_{m\text{-lf}}$, respectively.

In the computation for additional idling distances, $D_{r\text{-ff}}(j)$ and $D_{r\text{-lf}}(j)$ are needed for request j if and only if request j is the first column access of a given row access. If request j is not the first column access of a row access to a given bank, then the respective row activation and precharge time constraints do not apply, and $D_{r\text{-ff}}(j)$ and $D_{r\text{-lf}}(j)$ are not needed.

In cases where either $D_{r\text{-ff}}(j)$ is less than $D_{m\text{-ff}}$ or $D_{r\text{-lf}}(j)$ is less than $D_{m\text{-lf}}$, additional idling distances

must be added. In an open-page memory system, $D_i(j)$ is equal to the larger value of $D_{i\text{-ff}}(j)$ and $D_{i\text{-lf}}(j)$ for request j that is the first column access of a given row. In the case that a given request j is not the first column access of a given row, $D_i(j)$ is zero. The equations for the computation of idling distances $D_{i\text{-ff}}(j)$ and $D_{i\text{-lf}}(j)$ are illustrated as Equations 15.3 and 15.4, respectively. Finally, the various request access distance definitions for both open-page and close-page memory systems are summarized in Table 15.4.

15.3.4 Computing Row-to-Row Activation Constraints

The third category of command constraints that limit DRAM memory system bandwidth consists of DRAM intra-rank row-to-row activation time constraints. Collectively, the row-to-row activation time constraints consist of t_{RRD} and t_{FAW}. The RAD analytical framework accounts for the row-to-row activation time constraints of t_{RRD} and t_{FAW} by computing the number of row activations in any rolling t_{RC} time period that is equivalent to the four-row activation limit in any t_{FAW} time period. The equivalent number of row activations in a rolling t_{RC} window is denoted as A_{max} in the RAD analytical framework, and it can be obtained by taking the four row activations in a rolling t_{FAW} window, multiplying them by t_{RC}, and then dividing through by t_{FAW}. The formula for computing A_{max} is shown in Equation 15.5.

$$\text{open-page system} \quad \left\{ D_{i-ff}(j) = MAX\left(D_0(j), \left(D_{m-ff} - \left(D_{r-ff}(j) + \sum_{n=j-(D_{r-ff}(j))}^{j-1} D_i(n) \right) \right) \right) \right. \qquad \text{(EQ 15.3)}$$

$$\text{open-page system} \quad \left\{ D_{i-lf}(j) = MAX\left(D_0(j), \left(D_{m-lf} - \left(D_{r-lf}(j) + \sum_{n=j-D_{r-lf}(j)}^{j-1} D_i(n) \right) \right) \right) \right. \qquad \text{(EQ 15.4)}$$

TABLE 15.4 Summary of Request Access Distance definitions and formulas

System	Notation	Description	Formula
close-page system	$D_o(j)$	DRAM protocol overhead for request j	Table 15.3
	D_m	Minimum access distance required for each request j	$(t_{RC} - t_{BURST}) / t_{BURST}$
	$D_r(j)$	Access distance for request j	—
	$D_i(j)$	Idling distance needed for request j to satisfy t_{RC}	Equation 15.2
open-page system	$D_{m\text{-}ff}$	Minimum distance needed between first column commands of different row accesses	$(t_{RC} - t_{BURST}) / t_{BURST}$
	$D_{m\text{-}lf}$	Between last column and first column of different rows	$(t_{RP} + t_{RCD}) / t_{BURST}$
	$D_{r\text{-}ff}(j)$	Access distance for request j to first column of last row	—
	$D_{r\text{-}lf}(j)$	Access distance for request j to last column of last row	—
	$D_{i\text{-}ff}(j)$	Idling distance needed by request j to satisfy t_{RC}	Equation 15.3
	$D_{i\text{-}lf}(j)$	Idling distance needed by request j to satisfy $t_{RP} + t_{RCD}$	Equation 15.4
	$D_i(j)$	Idling distance needed by request j that is the first column access of a row access	$D_i(j) = \max(D_{i\text{-}ff}(j), D_{i\text{-}lf}(j))$
	$D_i(j)$	Idling distance needed by request j that is not the first column access of a row access	0

Maximum Row Activation (per rank, per t_{RC}):

$$A_{max} = 4 \times \frac{t_{RC}}{t_{FAW}} \quad \text{(EQ 15.5)}$$

The maximum number of row activations per rolling t_{RC} window can be implemented as A_{max} number of column accesses that are the first column accesses of a given row access in any rolling t_{RC} time-frame, and additional idling distances, denoted as $D_{i\text{-}xtra}(j)$, are needed in the RAD framework to ensure that the t_{FAW} timing constraint is respected. The computation of $D_{i\text{-}xtra}(j)$ requires the definition of a new variable, $D_{iv}(j,m)$, where m is the rank ID of request j, and $D_{iv}(j,m)$ represents the idling value of request j. The basic idea of the idling value of a given request is that in a multi-rank memory system, requests made to different ranks mean that a given rank is idle for that period of time. As a result, a request j that incurs the cost of a row activation made to rank m means that request j has an idling value of 1 to all ranks other than rank m, and it has an idling value of 0 to rank m. Equation 15.6 illustrates the formula for the computation of additional idling distances required to satisfy the t_{FAW} constraint. Finally, Equation 15.7 shows the formula for $D_{i\text{-}total}(j)$, the total number of idling distance for request j that is the first column accesses of a row activation. The process of computing bandwidth

$$D_{i-xtra}(j) = MAX\left[0, D_{m-ff} - \left(A_{max} - 1 + \sum_{n = j - (A_{max} - 1)}^{j} D_i(n) + D_{iv}(n, m)\right)\right]$$ (EQ 15.6)

$D_{iv}(j, m) = 0$ For request n that is the first column access of a row activation to a bank in the same rank as request j.

$D_{iv}(j, m) = 1$ For request n that is not the first column access of a row activation or if request n is not made to the same rank as request j.

$$D_{i-total}(j) = D_i(j) + D_{i-xtra}(j)$$ (EQ 15.7)

efficiency in a DRAM memory system constrained by t_{FAW} is then as simple as replacing $D_i(j)$ with $D_{i\text{-total}}(j)$ in the formulas for computation of additional idling distances.

15.3.5 Request Access Distance Efficiency Computation

The RAD analytical framework accounts for three categories of constraints that limit DRAM memory system bandwidth: inter-command protocol constraints, bank row cycle time constraints, and intra-rank row-to-row activation time constraints. Collectively, Equations 15.2–15.7 summarize the means of computing the various required overheads. Then, substituting the computed overheads into Equation 15.1, the maximum bandwidth efficiency of the DRAM memory system can be obtained from Equation 15.8. Equation 15.8 illustrates that the maximum sustainable bandwidth efficiency of a DRAM memory system can be obtained by dividing the number of requests in the request stream by the sum of the number of requests in the request stream and the total number of idling distances needed by the stream to satisfy the DRAM inter-command protocol overheads, the row cycle time, constraints, and the intra-rank row-to-row activation constraints needed by the requests in the request stream.

$$Efficiency = \frac{r}{r + \sum_{n=1}^{r} D_{i-total}(n)}$$ (EQ 15.8)

r = number of
    requests in
    request stream

The RAD analytical framework, as summarized by Table 15.4 and Equations 15.1–15.8, accounts for inter-command protocol constraints, bank row cycle time constraints, and intra-rank row-to-row activation time constraints. However, there are several caveats that must be noted in the use of the RAD analytical framework to compute the maximum sustainable bandwidth of a DRAM memory system. One caveat that must be noted is in the way the RAD framework accounts for intra-rank row-to-row activation time constraints. In the RAD framework, the impact of t_{FAW} and t_{RRD} are collectively modeled as a more restrictive form of t_{RRD}. Consequently, the RAD framework, as presently designed, cannot differentiate between bandwidth characteristics of t_{FAW}-aware DRAM command scheduling algorithms and non-intelligent rank-alternating DRAM command scheduling algorithms. Finally, DRAM refresh overhead is not accounted for in the RAD framework since the RAD framework as currently constructed is based on the deterministic computation of idle times needed for rolling row cycle time-windows, and the impact of DRAM refresh cannot be easily incorporated into the same timing basis. Since the impact of refresh can be computed separately and its effects factored out in the system-to-system comparisons, it is believed that the omission of DRAM refresh from the RAD framework does not substantively alter the results of the analyses performed herein. However, as DRAM device densities continue to climb, and more DRAM cells need to be refreshed, the impact of DRAM refresh overhead is expected to grow, and the RAD framework should be modified to account for the impact of DRAM refresh in the higher density devices.

15.3.6 An Applied Example for a Close-Page System

The request access distance statistic can be used to compute maximum bandwidth efficiency for a workload subjected to different DRAM row cycle times and device data rates. Figure 15.10 shows how maximum bandwidth efficiency can be computed for a request stream in a close-page memory system. In Figure 15.10, the request stream has been simplified down to the sequence of bank IDs. The access distances for each request are then computed from the sequence of bank IDs. The example illustrated as Figure 15.10 specifies that a minimum of eight requests needs to be active at any given instance in time in order to achieve full bandwidth utilization. In terms of access distances, each pair of accesses to the same bank needs to have seven other accesses in between them. At the beginning of the sequence in Figure 15.10, a pair of requests needs to access bank 0 with only four other requests to different banks in between them. As a result, an idling distance of 3 must be added to the access sequence before the second request to bank 0 can be processed. Two requests later, the request to bank 2 has an access distance of 5. However, idling distances added to requests in between accesses to bank 2 also count toward its effective total access distance. The result is that the total access distance for the second access to bank 2 is 8, and no additional idling distances ahead of the access to bank 2 are needed. Finally, after all idling distances have been

computed, the maximum bandwidth efficiency of the access sequence may be computed by dividing the total number of requests by the sum of the total number of requests and all of the idling distances. In the example shown in Figure 15.10, the maximum sustained bandwidth efficiency is 54.2%.

15.3.7 An Applied Example for an Open-Page System

In this section, an example is used to illustrate the process for obtaining maximum sustainable bandwidth in an open-page memory system. Figure 15.11 shows a request stream that has been simplified down to a sequence of bank IDs and row IDs of the individual requests, and the access distances are then computed from the sequence of bank IDs and row IDs. The example illustrated in Figure 15.10 specifies that a minimum of nine requests need to be active at any given instance in time in order to achieve full bandwidth utilization, and there must be eight requests between row activations as well as four requests between bank conflicts. Figure 15.11 shows that $D_{i\text{-ff}}(j)$ and $D_{i\text{-lf}}(j)$ are separately computed, but the idling distance $D_i(j)$ is simply the maximum of $D_{i\text{-ff}}(j)$ and $D_{i\text{-lf}}(j)$. After all idling distances have been computed, the maximum bandwidth efficiency of the request sequence can be computed by dividing the total number of requests by the sum of the total

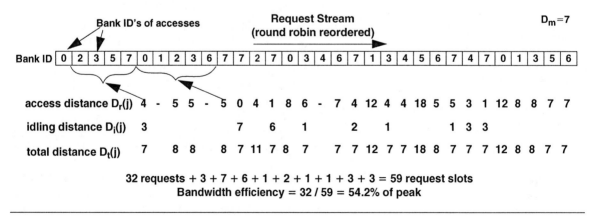

FIGURE 15.10: Efficiency computation example: close-page, $D_m = 7$.

number of requests and all of the idling distances. In the example shown in Figure 15.11, the maximum sustained bandwidth efficiency is 56.1%.

Finally, one caveat that must be noted in the examples shown in Figures 15.10 and 15.11 is that the request access distances and idling distances illustrated are integer values. However, data transport times and row cycle times seldom divide evenly as integer values, and the respective values are often real numbers rather than simple integer values.

15.3.8 System Configuration for RAD-Based Analysis

The RAD analytical framework is used in this section to compute the maximum bandwidth efficiency of DRAM memory systems. However, the bandwidth efficiency of any DRAM memory system is workload specific and sensitive to the organization of the DRAM memory system and the scheduling policy of the memory controller. Figure 15.12 shows the

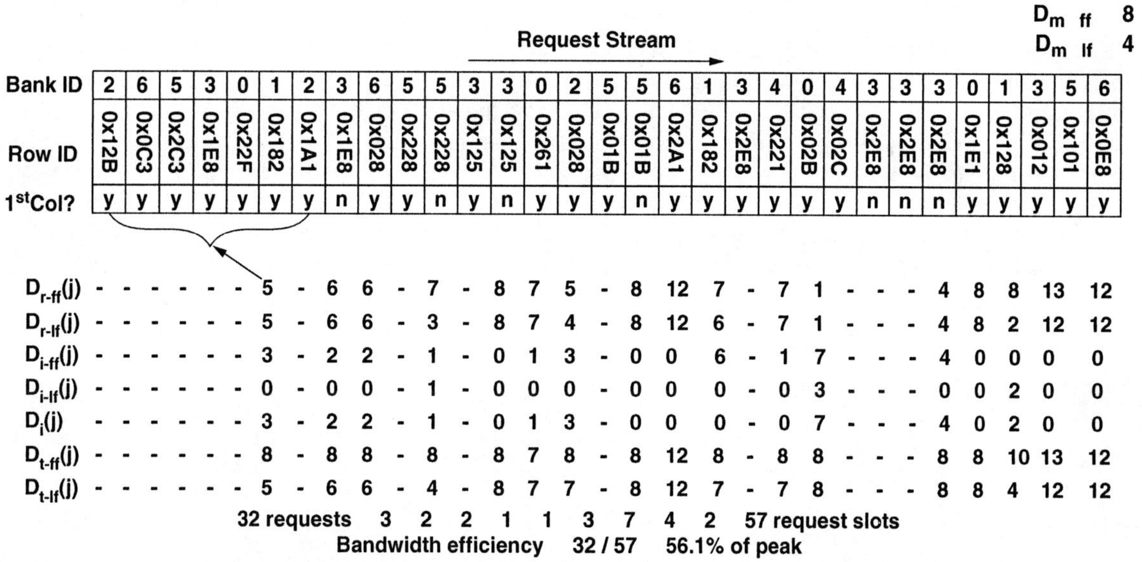

Dm ff 8
Dm lf 4
Request Stream
Bank ID 2 6 5 3 0 1 2 3 6 5 5 3 3 0 2 5 5 6 1 3 4 0 4 3 3 3 0 1 3 5 6
Row ID 0x12B 0x0C3 0x2C3 0x1E8 0x22F 0x182 0x1A1 0x1E8 0x028 0x228 0x228 0x125 0x125 0x261 0x028 0x01B 0x01B 0x2A1 0x182 0x2E8 0x221 0x02B 0x02C 0x2E8 0x2E8 0x2E8 0x1E1 0x128 0x012 0x101 0x0E8
1stCol? y y y y y y y n y y n y n y y y n y y y y y y n n n y y y y y
Dr-ff(j) - - - - - - - 5 - 6 6 - 7 - 8 7 5 - 8 12 7 - 7 1 - - - 4 8 8 13 12
Dr-lf(j) - - - - - - - 5 - 6 6 - 3 - 8 7 4 - 8 12 6 - 7 1 - - - 4 8 2 12 12
Di-ff(j) - - - - - - - 3 - 2 2 - 1 - 0 1 3 - 0 0 6 - 1 7 - - - 4 0 0 0 0
Di-lf(j) - - - - - - - 0 - 0 0 - 1 - 0 0 0 - 0 0 0 - 0 3 - - - 0 0 2 0 0
Di(j) - - - - - - - 3 - 2 2 - 1 - 0 1 3 - 0 0 0 - 0 7 - - - 4 0 2 0 0
Dt-ff(j) - - - - - - - 8 - 8 8 - 8 - 8 7 8 - 8 12 8 - 8 8 - - - 8 8 10 13 12
Dt-lf(j) - - - - - - - 5 - 6 6 - 4 - 8 7 7 - 8 12 7 - 7 8 - - - 8 8 4 12 12
32 requests 3 2 2 1 1 3 7 4 2 57 request slots
Bandwidth efficiency 32 / 57 56.1% of peak

FIGURE 15.11: Efficiency computation example: open page, $D_{m\text{-}ff} = 8$, $D_{m\text{-}lf} = 4$.

0x1C27FE2C
0x04EEF16C
0x1C27FE30
0x1900EF10
0x249B1154
0x1C27FE34
request stream
channel 0
bank 2
rank 0
row 0x7E2
col 0x8E
channel 0
bank 5
rank 0
row 0x19C
col 0-x60
DRAM address mapping scheme
saturation request rate
Bank 0
Bank 1
Bank 2
Bank n −1
Q depth
request reordering
compute idling distances
request access distance recorded

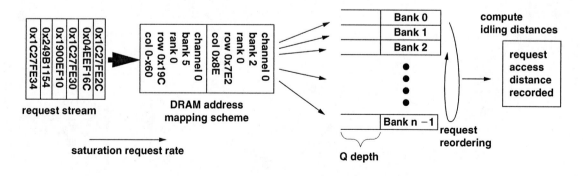

FIGURE 15.12: Generic system configuration in the RAD analytical framework.

general system configuration used in the RAD analytical framework, where requests within a request stream are subjected to an address mapping scheme and mapped to a specific DRAM channel, rank, bank, row, and column address. The requests can then be reordered to a limited degree, just as they may be reordered in a high-performance memory controller to minimize the amount of idling times that must be inserted into the request stream to satisfy the constraints imposed by DRAM protocol overheads, DRAM bank row cycle times, and t_{FAW} row activation limitations.

In this study, the DRAM memory bandwidth characteristics of eight different DRAM memory system configurations are subjected to varying data rate scaling trends and t_{FAW} row activation constraints. Table 15.5 summarizes the different system configurations used in this study. The eight different system configurations consist of four open-page memory systems and four close-page memory systems. In the open-page

memory systems, consecutive cacheline addresses are mapped to the same row in the same bank to optimize hits to open row buffers. In the close-page memory systems, consecutive cacheline addresses are mapped to different banks to optimize for bank access parallelism. Aside from the difference in row-buffer-management policies and address mapping schemes, two of the four close-page memory systems also support transaction reordering. In these memory systems, transaction requests are placed into queues that can enqueue as many as four requests per bank. Transaction requests are then selected out of the reordering queues in a round-robin fashion through the banks to maximize the temporal scheduling distance between requests to a given bank. In this study, the memory systems are configured with 1 or 2 ranks of DRAM devices, and each rank of DRAM devices has either 8 or 16 banks internally. The eight respective system configurations in Table 15.1 are described in terms of the paging policy, reordering depth,

TABLE 15.5 Summary of system configurations

System Con-figuration	Row-Buffer-Management Policy	Address Mapping Scheme	Transaction Re-ordering	Rank Count	Bank Count	Row Count	Column Count
open-F-1-8	Open-page	Row/bank/column	FIFO	1	8	16384	1024
open-F-2-8	Open-page	Row/rank/bank/column	FIFO	2	8	16384	1024
open-F-1-16	Open-page	Row/bank/column	FIFO	1	16	16384	1024
open-F-2-16	Open-page	Row/rank/bank/column	FIFO	2	16	16384	1024
close-F-1-8	Close-page	Row/column/bank	FIFO	1	8	16384	1024
close-F-1-16	Close-page	Row/column/bank	FIFO	1	16	16384	1024
close-4-1-8	Close-page	Row/column/bank	Q Depth 4	1	8	16384	1024
close-4-1-16	Close-page	Row/column/bank	Q Depth 4	1	16	16384	1024

rank count, and bank count per rank. For example, open-F-1-8 represents an open-page system with no transaction reordering, 1 single rank in the system, and 8 banks per rank. Finally, all of the systems have 16384 rows per bank and 1024 columns per row.

This study examines the maximum sustainable bandwidth characteristics of modern DRAM memory systems with data rates that range from 533 to 1333 Mbps. Furthermore, one assumption made in the studies in this section is that the device data rate of the DRAM devices is twice that of the operating frequency of the DRAM device. Therefore, the operating frequency of the memory system examined in this study ranges from 266 to 667 MHz, and the notion of a clock cycle corresponds to the operating frequency of the DRAM device. Throughout this study, the row cycle time of the DRAM devices is assumed to be 60 ns. The rank-to-rank turnaround time, t_{RTRS}, is set to either 0 or 3 clock cycles. Furthermore, t_{CWD} is set to 3 clock cycles, t_{CMD} is set

to 1 clock cycle, t_{WR} is set to 4 clock cycles, t_{BURST} is set to 4 clock cycles, and t_{CAS} is set to 4 clock cycles. Finally, the t_{FAW} row activation constraint is set to the extreme values of either 30 or 60 ns. That is, t_{FAW} is set to equal t_{RC} or $t_{RC}/2$, where t_{FAW} equal to t_{RC} is assumed to be a worst-case value for t_{FAW}, and t_{FAW} equal to $t_{RC}/2$ is assumed to an optimistic best-case value for t_{FAW} constraints.

15.3.9 Open-Page Systems: 164.gzip

Figure 15.13 shows the computed maximum bandwidth efficiency of four different open-page memory systems for the 164.gzip address trace. Figure 15.13 shows that with a constant row cycle time of 60 ns, the maximum bandwidth efficiency of the DRAM memory system gradually decreases as a function of increasing data rate. For the address trace from 164.gzip, factors such as a restrictive t_{FAW} value and the rank-to-rank turnaround time have only minimum

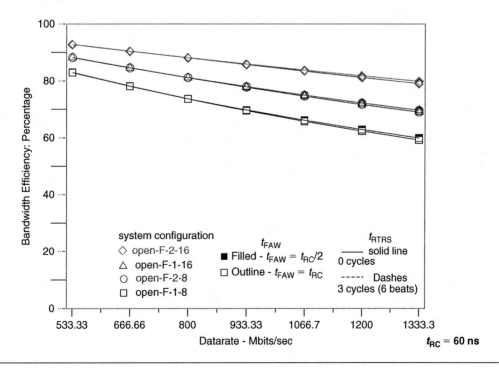

FIGURE 15.13: Maximum bandwidth efficiency of the 164.gzip address trace: open-page systems.

impact on available DRAM bandwidth, illustrating a fair degree of access locality and resulting in open-page hits and fewer row accesses. Finally, Figure 15.13 shows that the additional parallelism afforded by the 2 rank, 16 bank (2R16B) memory system greatly improves bandwidth efficiency over that of a 1 rank, 8 bank (1R8B) memory system.

Figure 15.13 shows the maximum bandwidth available to the address trace of 164.gzip in terms of maximum bandwidth efficiency. Figure 15.14 shows the same data as Figure 15.13, but represents the data in terms of sustainable bandwidth by assuming a specific system configuration with an 8-byte-wide data bus. With the 8-byte-wide data bus operating at different data rates, the theoretical peak bandwidth available to the DRAM memory system is shown as a solid line labelled as peak bandwidth in Figure 15.14. Figures 15.13 and 15.14 show that 164.gzip is an outlier in the sense that the workload has a high degree of access locality, and a large majority of the requests are kept within the same rank of memory systems. In the case where DRAM accesses are made to a different rank, a bank conflict also follows. As a result, the impact of t_{RTRS} is not readily observable in any system configuration, and a 2 rank, 8 bank (2R8B) system performs identically to a 1 rank, 16 bank (1R16B) memory system. Also, the number bank conflicts are relatively few, and the impact of t_{FAW} is minimal and not observable until data rates reach significantly above 1 Gbps. Finally, the maximum sustainable bandwidth for 164.gzip scales nicely with the total number of banks in the memory system, and the bandwidth advantage of a 2R16B memory system over that of a 1R16 memory system is nearly as great as the bandwidth advantage of the 1R16B memory system over that of a 1R8B memory system.

15.3.10 Open-Page Systems: 255.vortex

Figure 15.15 shows the maximum sustainable bandwidth characteristic of 255.vortex in open-page memory systems. Figure 15.15 shows that in contrast to the maximum sustainable bandwidth characteristics shown by the address trace of 164.gzip in Figure 15.14, 255.vortex is an outlier that is not only sensitive to the system configuration in terms of the

number of ranks and banks, but it is also extremely sensitive to the impacts of t_{FAW} and t_{RTRS}. Figure 15.15 also shows that the address trace of 255.vortex has relatively lower degrees of access locality, and fewer column accesses are made to the same row than other workloads, resulting in a relatively higher rate of bank conflicts. The bank conflicts also tend to be clustered to the same rank of DRAM devices, even in 2-rank system configurations. The result is that the t_{FAW} greatly limits the maximum sustainable bandwidth of the DRAM memory system in all system configurations.

Figure 15.15 shows that 255.vortex is greatly impacted by the rank-to-rank switching overhead, t_{RTRS}, in system configurations with 2 ranks of memory. The overhead attributable to t_{RTRS} is somewhat alleviated at higher data rates, as other limitations on available memory system bandwidth become more significant. At higher data rates, the bandwidth impact of t_{RTRS} remains, but the effects become less discernible as a separate source of hindrance to data transport in a DRAM memory system. Furthermore, Figure 15.15 shows an interesting effect in that the rank-to-rank switching overhead, t_{RTRS}, can also impact the performance of a single rank memory system due to the fact that t_{RTRS} contributes to the read-write turnaround time, and the contribution of t_{RTRS} to the read-write turnaround time can be observed in Table 15.3. Finally, Figure 15.15 shows the impact of t_{FAW} on 255.vortex, where the simulation assumption of $t_{FAW} = t_{RC}$ completely limits sustainable bandwidth for all system configurations beyond 800 Mbps. At data rates higher than 800 Mbps, no further improvements in maximum sustainable bandwidth can be observed for the address trace of 255.vortex in all t_{FAW} limited memory systems.

15.3.11 Open-Page Systems: Average of All Workloads

Figures 15.14 and 15.15 show the maximum sustainable bandwidth characteristics of 164.gzip and 255.vortex, two extreme outliers in the set of workloads listed in Table 15.1 in terms of sensitivity to system configuration and timing parameters. That is, while the address trace of 164.gzip was relatively

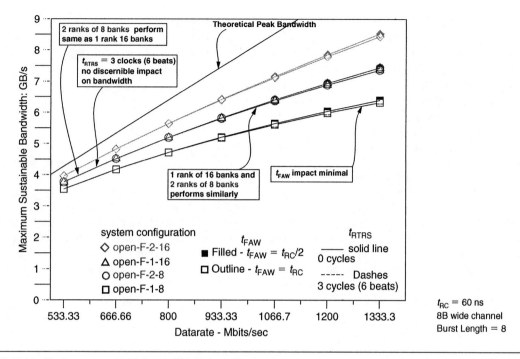

FIGURE 15.14: Maximum sustainable bandwidth of the 164.gzip address trace: open-page systems.

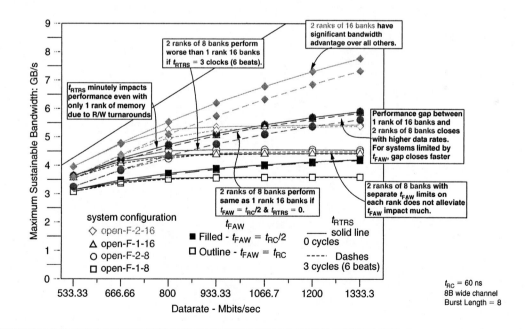

FIGURE 15.15: Maximum sustainable bandwidth of the 255.vortex address trace: open-page systems.

insensitive to the limitations presented by t_{RTRS} and t_{FAW}, the address trace for 255.vortex was extremely sensitive to both t_{RTRS} and t_{FAW}. Figure 15.16 shows the maximum sustainable bandwidth averaged across all workloads used in the study. Figure 15.16 shows that for the open-page memory system, the high degree of access locality provided by the address traces of the various single threaded workloads enables the open-page systems to achieve relatively high bandwidth efficiency without the benefit of sophisticated transaction request reordering mechanisms. Figure 15.16 also shows that the open-page address mapping scheme, where consecutive cacheline addresses are mapped to the same row address, effectively utilizes parallelism afforded by the multiple ranks, and the performance of a 2R8B memory system is nearly equal to that of a 1R16B memory system. The bandwidth degradation suffered by the 2R8B memory system compared to the 1R16B memory system is

relatively small, even when the rank-to-rank switching overhead of t_{RTRS} equals 3 clock cycles. The reason for this minimal impact is that the access locality of the single threaded workloads tend to keep accesses to within a given rank, and rank-to-rank switching time penalties are relatively minor or largely hidden by row cycle time impacts.

One surprising result shown in Figure 15.16 is that the four-bank activation window constraint, t_{FAW}, negatively impacts the sustainable bandwidth characteristic of a two-rank memory system just as it does for a one-rank memory system. This surprising result can be explained with the observation that the address mapping scheme, optimized to obtain bank parallelism for the open-page row-buffer-management policy, tends to direct accesses to the same bank and the same rank. In this scheme, bank conflicts are also often directed onto the same rank in any given time period. The result is that multiple row cycles tend to

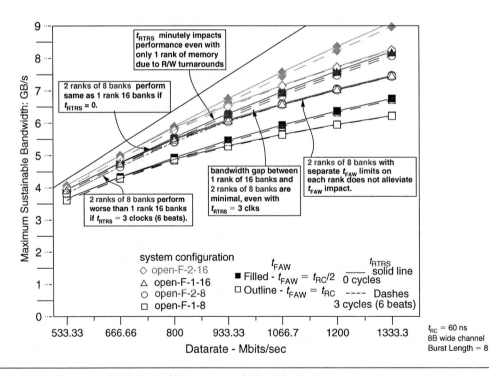

FIGURE 15.16: Maximum sustainable bandwidth—average of all workloads: open-page systems.

congregate in a given rank of memory, rather than become evenly distributed across two different ranks of memory, and t_{FAW} remains a relevant issue of concern for higher performance DRAM memory systems, even for a dual rank memory system that implements the open-page row-buffer-management policy.

Finally, Figure 15.16 shows that the impact of t_{RTRS} is relatively constant across different data rates for systems that are not impacted by t_{FAW}. A close examination of the bandwidth curves for the 2R16B system reveals that in systems impacted by t_{FAW} limitations, the impact of t_{RTRS} is mitigated to some extent. That is, idle cycles inserted into the memory system due to rank-to-rank switching times can be used to reduce the addition of more idle times as needed by DRAM devices to recover between consecutive row accesses. In that sense, the same idle cycles can be used to satisfy multiple constraints, and the impact of these respective constraints are not strictly additive.

15.3.12 Close-Page Systems: 164.gzip

Figure 15.17 shows the maximum bandwidth available to the address trace of 164.gzip for the four different close-page memory systems listed in Table 15.5. Figure 15.17 shows that for the address trace of 164.gzip in close-page memory systems without transaction reordering, the maximum sustainable bandwidth increases very slowly with respect to increasing data rate of the memory system, and neither the number of banks available in the system nor the t_{FAW} parameter has much impact. However, Figure 15.17 also shows that in close-page memory systems with a reorder queue depth of 4, representing memory systems with relatively sophisticated transaction reordering mechanisms, the memory system can effectively extract available DRAM bandwidth for the address trace of 164.gzip. In the case where t_{FAW} equals $t_{RC}/2$, the sustained bandwidth for the address trace of 164.gzip continues to increase until the data rate of the DRAM memory system reaches

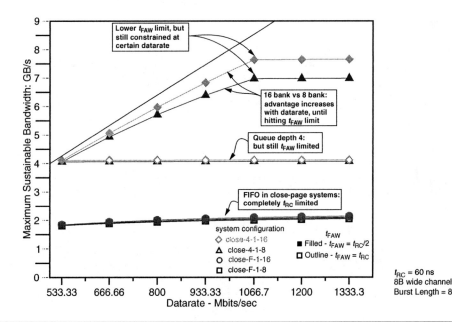

FIGURE 15.17: Maximum sustainable bandwidth of the 164.gzip address trace: close-page systems.

1.07 Gbps. At the data rate of 1.07 Gbps, the ratio of t_{RC} to t_{BURST} equals the maximum number of concurrently open banks as specified by the ratio of t_{FAW} to t_{RC}, and the maximum sustained bandwidth reaches a plateau for all system configurations. However, Figure 15.17 also shows that in the case where t_{FAW} equals t_{RC}, the DRAM memory system can only sustain 4 GB/s of bandwidth for the 164.gzip address trace regardless of data rate since t_{FAW} severely constrains the maximum number of concurrently open banks in close-page memory systems. Finally, Figure 15.17 shows the performance benefit from having 16 banks compared to 8 banks in the DRAM memory system. Figure 15.17 shows that at low data rates, the performance benefit of having 16 banks is relatively small. However, the performance benefit of 16 banks increases with increasing data rate until the t_{FAW} constraint effectively limits the available DRAM bandwidth in the close-page memory system.

15.3.13 Close-Page Systems: SETI@HOME Processor Bus Trace

Figure 15.18 shows the maximum sustainable bandwidth graph for a short trace captured on the processor bus with a digital logic analyzer while the host processor was running the SETI@HOME application. Similar to the bandwidth characteristics of the 164.gzip address trace shown in Figure 15.17, Figure 15.18 shows that the SETI@HOME address trace is completely bandwidth bound in cases where no transaction reordering is performed. However, differing from the bandwidth characteristics of the 164.gzip address trace shown in Figure 15.17, Figure 15.18 shows that in close-page memory systems that perform transaction reordering, the SETI@HOME address trace benefits greatly from a memory system with a 16-bank device. Figure 15.18 shows that a highly sophisticated close-page 1R16B memory system can provide nearly twice the bandwidth compared to the same memory system with a 1R8B

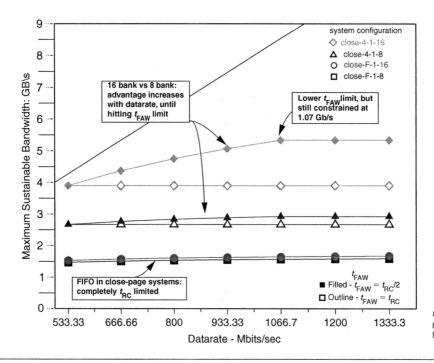

FIGURE 15.18: Maximum sustainable bandwidth of the SETI@HOME address trace: close-page systems.

configuration. In this respect, the SETI@HOME address trace is an outlier that benefits greatly from the larger number of banks.

15.3.14 Close-Page Systems: Average of All Workloads

Figure 15.19 shows the maximum sustainable bandwidth that is the average of all workloads listed in Table 15.1. Figure 15.19 shows that the all workloads average graph is similar to the maximum sustainable bandwidth graph shown for the address trace of 164.gzip in Figure 15.17 with some minor differences. Similar to Figure 15.17, Figure 15.19 shows that in close-page memory systems without transaction reordering, the maximum sustainable bandwidth of the DRAM memory system increases very slowly with respect to increasing data rate of the memory system, and neither the number of banks available in the system nor

the t_{FAW} parameter shows much impact. However, Figure 15.19 also shows that in close-page memory systems with a reorder queue depth of 4, the memory system can effectively extract available DRAM bandwidth across different workloads. Figure 15.19 further shows that similar to the maximum sustainable bandwidth characteristics for the address traces of 164.gzip and SETI@HOME, the maximum sustained bandwidth for the average workload continues to increase until the data rate of the DRAM memory system reaches 1.07 Gbps in the case that t_{FAW} equals $t_{RC}/2$. Finally, Figure 15.19 shows that the bandwidth advantage seen by the average workload is closer to that shown by the 164.gzip address trace in Figure 15.17 than the SETI@HOME address trace in Figure 15.18, and the bandwidth advantage of the 1R16B configuration increases with increasing data rate until the t_{FAW} constraint effectively limits the available DRAM bandwidth in the close-page memory system.

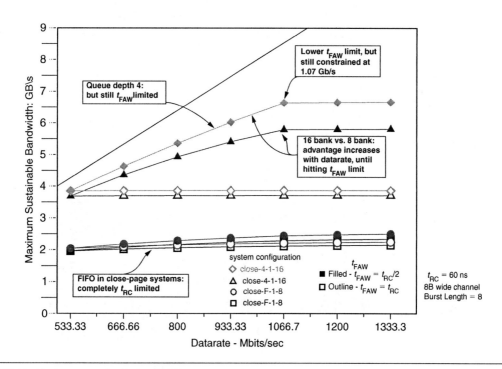

FIGURE 15.19: Maximum sustainable bandwidth—average of all workloads: close-page system.

15.3.15 t_{FAW} Limitations in Open-Page System: All Workloads

Figures 15.17, 15.18, and 15.19 collectively illustrate the point that close-page memory systems are very sensitive to the row activation limitations presented by t_{FAW}. The simple explanation is that in a single rank, close-page memory system, t_{FAW} defines the maximum number of banks that can be open concurrently for access, and once that limit is reached, no further scaling in utilizable bandwidth is possible regardless of the data rate of the memory system. However, in open-page memory systems, there are likely multiple column accesses for each row access, and the limitation on the number of row activations per unit time presented by t_{FAW} is more difficult to quantify. Figure 15.20 shows the impact of t_{FAW} in a 1R16B memory system in terms of the percentage of bandwidth differential between the case where $t_{FAW} = t_{RC} = 60$ ns and the case where $t_{FAW} = t_{RC}/2 = 30$ ns. The bandwidth differential curves for different workloads used in the simulation are drawn as separate lines in Figure 15.20, illustrating the wide variance in workload sensitivity

to the limitation presented by a restrictive t_{FAW} parameter. One workload worthy of note is 255.vortex, where bandwidth impact for the case of $t_{FAW} = 60$ ns reduces available bandwidth by upwards of 30% at data rates above 1.2 Gbps. However, on average, a workload running on a memory system where $t_{FAW} = 60$ ns suffers a bandwidth loss on the order of 0~12% compared to the same system with a less restrictive t_{FAW} value where $t_{FAW} = 30$ ns.

15.3.16 Bandwidth Improvements: 8-Banks vs. 16-Banks

Figure 15.21 examines the bandwidth advantage of a 16-bank device over that of an 8-bank device. Figure 15.21 shows mean bandwidth improvement curves for the 1R16B versus 1R8B comparison for the open-page memory system and the close-page memory system with a per-bank reordering queue depth of 4. Figure 15.21 also shows the mean bandwidth improvement curves for the 2R8B versus 1R8B and 2R16B versus 2R8B comparisons for open-page memory systems. Figure 15.21 shows that despite

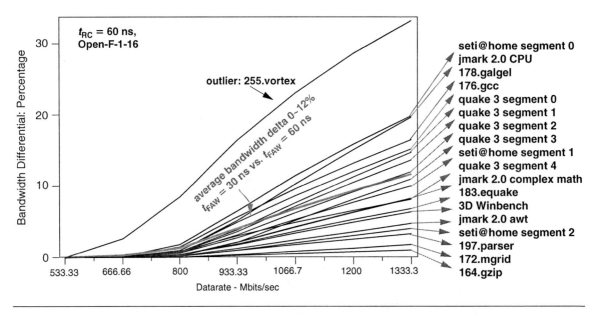

FIGURE 15.20: Comparing $t_{FAW} = 30$ ns versus $t_{FAW} = 60$ ns in a 1R16B open-page system.

the differences in the row-buffer-management policy and the differences in the reordering mechanism, the bandwidth advantage of a 1R16B memory system over that of a 1R8B memory system correlates nicely between the open-page memory system and the close-page memory system. In both cases, the bandwidth advantage of having more banks in the DRAM device scales at roughly the same rate with respect to increasing data rate and constant row cycle time. In both open-page and close-page memory systems, the bandwidth advantage of the 1R16B memory system over that of the 1R8B memory system reaches approximately 18% at 1.07 Gbps. However, Figure 15.21 also shows that at 1.07 Gbps, close-page memory systems become bandwidth limited by the restrictive t_{FAW} value, while the bandwidth advantage of the 1R16B memory system continues to increase with respect to increasing data rate, reaching 22% at 1.33 Gbps. Finally, Figure 15.21 shows that with a 2-rank configuration,

the bandwidth advantage afforded by a 16-bank DRAM device over that of an 8-bank device is nearly halved, and the bandwidth advantage of a 2R16B system configuration over that of a 2R8B system configuration reaches 12% at 1.33 Gbps.

A study of DRAM memory system bandwidth characteristics based on the RAD analytical framework is performed in this section. As reaffirmed in this section, the performance of DRAM memory systems depends on workload-specific characteristics, and those workload-specific characteristics exhibit large variances from each other. However, some observations about the maximum sustainable bandwidth characteristics of DRAM memory systems can be made in general.

- The benefit of having a 16-bank device over an 8-bank device in a 1-rank memory system configuration increases with data rate. The performance benefit increases to

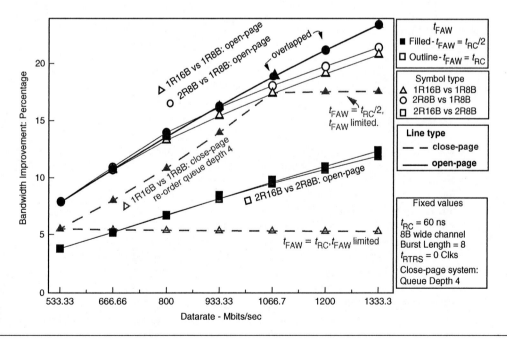

FIGURE 15.21: Bandwidth improvements: 16 banks versus 8 banks.

approximately 18% at 1 Gbps for both open-page and close-page memory systems. While some workloads may only see minimal benefits, others will benefit greatly. Embedded systems with a single rank of DRAM devices and limited in the variance of workload characteristics should examine the bank count issue carefully.

- Single threaded workloads have high degrees of access locality, and sustainable bandwidth characteristics of an open-page memory system for a single threaded workload are similar to that of a close-page memory system that performs relatively sophisticated transaction reordering.

- The t_{FAW} activation window constraint greatly limits the performance of close-page memory systems without sophisticated reordering mechanisms. The impact of t_{FAW} is relatively less in open-page memory systems, but some workloads, such as 255. vortex, apparently contain minimal spatial locality in the access sequences, and their performance characteristics are similar to that of workloads in close-page memory systems. In this study, even a two-rank memory system did not alleviate the impact of t_{FAW} on the memory system. Consequently, a DRAM scheduling algorithm that accounts for the impact of t_{FAW} is needed in DRAM memory controllers that may need to handle workloads similar to 255.vortex.

The RAD analytical framework is used in this section to examine the effect of system configurations, command scheduling algorithms, controller queue depths, and timing parameter values on the sustainable bandwidth characteristics of different types of DRAM memory systems. However, the analytical framework-based analysis is limiting in some ways, and a new simulation framework, DRAMSim, was developed at the University of Maryland to accurately simulate the interrelated effects of memory system configuration, scheduling algorithms, and timing parameter values. The remainder of the chapter is devoted to the study of memory system performance characteristics using the DRAMSim simulation framework.

15.4 Simulation-Based Analysis

In the previous section, the equation-based RAD analytical framework was used to examine the respective maximum sustainable bandwidth characteristics of various DRAM memory system configurations. The strength of the RAD analytical framework is that it can be used as a mathematical basis to construct a first-order estimate of memory system performance characteristics. Moreover, the accuracy of the RAD analytical framework does not depend on the accuracy of the simulation model, since the basis of the framework relies on the set of equations that can be separately examined to ensure correctness. However, the weakness of the RAD analytical framework is that it is limited to specific controller scheduling algorithms and saturation request rates to examine the sustainable bandwidth characteristics of a given memory system, and it cannot be used to analyze a wide range of controller scheduling policies, memory-access latency distribution characteristics, and controller queue depth examinations. To remedy this shortcoming, the more traditional approach of a simulator-based analytical framework is used in this section to examine memory system performance characteristics.

15.4.1 System Configurations

The basis of the simulation work performed in this section is a highly accurate DRAM memory simulator, DRAMSim. In this section, the impact of varying system configurations, DRAM device organizations, read-versus-write traffic ratios, and protocol-constraining timing parameters that affect memory system performance characteristics in DDR2 SDRAM and DDR3 SDRAM memory systems are examined with the DRAMSim memory system simulator. The studies performed in this section are more generally based on random address workloads—the study on latency distribution characteristics excepted—so parameters such as the read-versus-write traffic ratio can be independently adjusted. Table 15.6 summarizes the four different system configuration parameters and two workload characteristics varied in this section for the study on the sustainable bandwidth characteristics of high-speed memory systems. The hardware

TABLE **15.6** Parameters varied in the study of DDR3 memory system performance characteristics.

	Parameter	Choices
System configuration	Rank count per section	1, 2
	Bank count per rank	8, 16
	Command scheduling algorithm	Rank Round-Robin, Bank Round-Robin, Wang Rank Hop, Greedy
	Command queue depth	4, 6, 8, 10, 12, 14, 16
Workload characteristics	Read-write ratio	0% ~ 100%
	Short burst duration ratio	0% ~ 100%

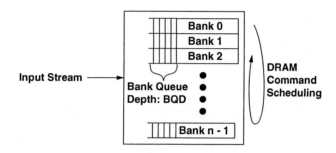

FIGURE **15.22:** Assumed DRAM memory controller structure.

architecture and various parameters of the simulated DRAM memory system and workload characteristics in terms of read-write ratios and differing burst lengths are described in the following sections.

15.4.2 Memory Controller Structure

In contrast to the basic controller structure assumed in the studies performed in the previous sections using the RAD analytical framework, the DRAMSim simulator uses a more generic memory controller model to schedule DRAM commands rather than memory transactions. The ability to schedule DRAM commands separately ensures that the controller can obtain the highest performance from the DRAM memory system. Figure 15.22 illustrates the basic hardware architecture of a single channel memory controller assumed in this section. In the controller structure illustrated in Figure 15.22, transactions are translated into DRAM commands and placed into separate queues that hold DRAM commands destined for each bank.[2] The depth of the per-bank queues is a parameter that can be adjusted to test the effect of queue depth on maximum sustainable bandwidth of the memory system. The basic assumption for the memory controller described in Figure 15.22 is that each per-bank queue holds all of the DRAM commands destined

---

[2]At least 8 queues are needed in the controller for a 1 rank, 8 bank memory system, and 32 queues are needed in the controller for a 2 rank, 16 banks per rank memory system.

for a given bank, and DRAM commands are executed in FIFO order within each queue. In the architecture illustrated in Figure 15.22, a DRAM command scheduling algorithm selects a command from the head of the per-bank queues and sends that command to the array of DRAM devices for execution. In this manner, the controller structure described in Figure 15.22 enables the implementation of aggressive memory controller designs without having to worry about write-to-read ordering issues. That is, since read and write transactions destined for any given bank are executed in order, a read command that semantically follows a write command to the same address location cannot be erroneously reordered and scheduled ahead of the write command. On the other hand, the controller structure allows an advanced memory controller to aggressively reorder DRAM commands to different banks to optimize DRAM memory system bandwidth. Finally, the queue depth in the simulated controller structure describes the depth of the queue in terms of DRAM commands. In a close-page memory system, each transaction request converts directly to two DRAM commands: a row access command and a column-access-with-auto-precharge command.

15.4.3 DRAM Command Scheduling Algorithms

In the studies performed in this section, sustainable bandwidth characteristics of four DRAM command scheduling algorithms for close-page memory systems are compared. The four DRAM command scheduling algorithms are *Bank Round-Robin* (BRR), *Rank Round-Robin* (RRR), *Wang Rank Hop* (Wang), and *Greedy*. The role of a DRAM command scheduling algorithm is to select a DRAM command at the top of a per-bank queue and send that command to the DRAM devices for execution. In a general sense, the DRAM command scheduling algorithm should also account for transaction ordering and prioritization requirements. However, the study on the DRAM command scheduling algorithm is narrowly focused on the sustainable bandwidth characteristics of the DRAM memory system. Consequently, all transactions are assumed to have equal scheduling priority in the following studies.

Bank Round-Robin (BRR)

The *Bank Round-Robin* (BRR) command scheduling algorithm is a simple algorithm that rotates through the per-bank queues in a given rank sequentially and then moves to the next rank. The BRR algorithm is described as follows:

- The row access command and the column-access-with-precharge command are treated as a command pair. The row access and column-access-with-precharge command pair are always scheduled consecutively.
- Due to the cost of write-to-read turnaround time in DDR3 devices, implicit write sweeping is performed by scheduling only read transactions or write transactions in each loop iteration through all banks in the system.
- The BRR algorithm goes through the per-bank queues of rank i and looks for transactions of a given type (read or write). If a given queue is empty or has a different transaction type at the head of the queue, BRR skips over that queue and goes to bank (j + 1) to look for the next candidate.
- When the end of rank i is reached, switch to rank ((i + 1) % rank_count) and go through the banks in that rank.
- If the rank and bank IDs are both 0, switch over the read/write transaction type. Consequently, BRR searches for read and write transactions in alternating iterations through all banks and ranks in the memory system.

Rank Round-Robin

The *Rank Round-Robin* (RRR) command scheduling algorithm is a simple algorithm that rotates through per-bank queues by going through all of the rank IDs for a given bank and then moves to the next bank. In a single-rank memory system, RRR and BRR are identical to each other. The RRR algorithm is described as follows:

- The RRR algorithm is identical to the BRR algorithm except that the order of traversal through the ranks and banks is reversed. That is, after the RRR algorithm looks at bank j of rank i for a candidate to schedule, it then moves to bank j of rank (i + 1) instead of bank (j + 1) of bank i. In the case where rank i is the highest rank ID available in the system, the bank ID is incremented and the process continues.

- DRAM command pairs for a given transaction are always scheduled consecutively, just as in BRR.

- Just as in BRR, if the rank ID and bank ID are both 0, RRR switches over the read/write transaction type. In this manner, RRR searches for read transactions and write transactions in alternating iterations through all banks and ranks in the memory system.

Wang Rank Hop (Wang)

The *Wang Rank Hop* (Wang) command scheduling algorithm is a scheduling algorithm that requires the presence of at least two ranks of DRAM devices that share the data bus in the DRAM memory system, and it alleviates timing constraints imposed by t_{FAW}, t_{RRD}, and t_{RTRS} by distributing row activation commands to alternate ranks of DRAM devices while group scheduling column access commands to a given rank of DRAM devices. In contrast to the BRR and RRR scheduling algorithms, the Wang algorithm requires

that the row access command and the column -access-with-precharge command be separated and scheduled at different times.

Figure 15.23 illustrates an idealized, best-case timing diagram for the Wang algorithm. Figure 15.23 shows that the row access (row activation) commands are sent to alternate ranks to avoid incurring the timing penalties associated with t_{FAW} and t_{RRD}, and column access commands are group scheduled to a given rank of DRAM devices. Ideally, rank switching only occurs once per N column access commands, where N is the number of banks in the DDR3 DRAM device.

One simple way to implement the Wang algorithm is to predefine a command sequence so that the row access commands are sent to alternating ranks and the column access commands are group scheduled. Figure 15.24 illustrates two simple command scheduling sequences for dual rank systems with 8 banks per rank and 16 banks per rank, respectively. Although the sequences illustrated in Figure 15.24 are not the only sequences that accomplish the scheduling needs of the Wang algorithm, they are the simplest, and other subtle variations of the sequences do not substantially improve the performance of the algorithm. The Wang command schedule algorithm is described as follows:

- Follow the command sequence as defined in Figure 15.24. Select a row access command

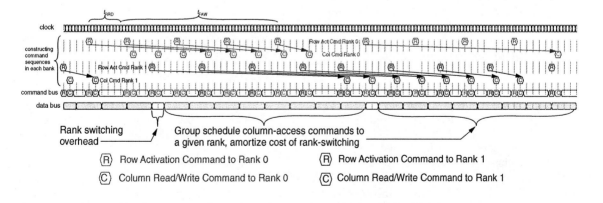

FIGURE 15.23: Idealized timing diagram for the Wang Rank Hop algorithm in a dual rank, 8 banks per rank system.

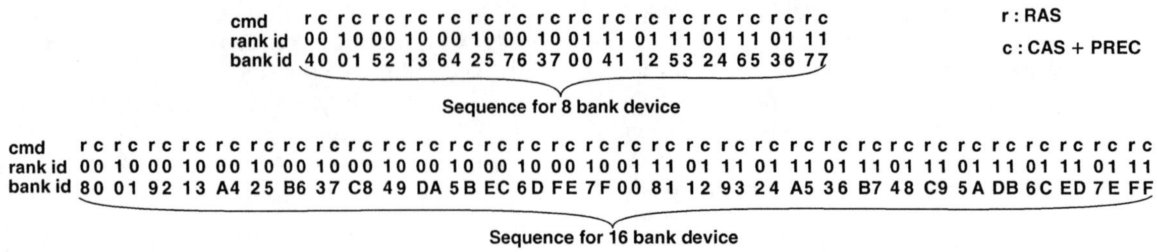

```
cmd      r c r c r c r c r c r c r c r c r c r c r c r c r c r c r c r c      r : RAS
rank id  00 10 00 10 00 10 00 10 01 11 01 11 01 11 01 11
bank id  40 01 52 13 64 25 76 37 00 41 12 53 24 65 36 77      c : CAS + PREC
```

Sequence for 8 bank device

```
cmd      r c r c r c r c r c r c r c r c r c r c r c r c r c r c r c r c r c r c r c r c r c r c r c r c r c r c r c r c
rank id  00 10 00 10 00 10 00 10 00 10 00 10 00 10 00 10 01 11 01 11 01 11 01 11 01 11 01 11 01 11 01 11
bank id  80 01 92 13 A4 25 B6 37 C8 49 DA 5B EC 6D FE 7F 00 81 12 93 24 A5 36 B7 48 C9 5A DB 6C ED 7E FF
```

Sequence for 16 bank device

FIGURE 15.24: Command scheduling sequence for the Wang Rank Hop algorithm for devices with 8 and 16 banks.

for issue if and only if the column access command that follows is the correct type for the current sequence iteration. If the column access command for that queue is the wrong type, or if the queue is empty, skip that queue and go to next command in the sequence.

- If rank ID and bank ID are both 0, switch over the read/write type and continue the sequence.

Greedy

The *Greedy* command scheduling algorithm differs from the BRR, RRR, and Wang command scheduling algorithms in that these other algorithms are based on the notion that commands are selected for scheduling based on a logical sequence of progression through the various banks and ranks in the memory system, while the Greedy algorithm does not depend on a logical sequence to select commands for scheduling. Instead, the Greedy algorithm examines pending commands at the top of each per-bank queue and selects the command that has the smallest wait-to-issue time. That is, after commands are selected in the BRR, RRR, and Wang command scheduling algorithms, the memory controller must still ensure that the selected command meets all timing constraints of the DRAM memory system. In contrast, the Greedy algorithm computes the wait-to-issue time for the command at the head of each per-bank queue and then selects the command with the smallest wait-to-issue time regardless of the other attributes of that command. In the case where two or more commands have the same wait-to-issue time, a secondary factor is used to select the command that will be issued next.

In the current implementation of the Greedy algorithm, the age of the competing commands is used as the secondary factor, and the Greedy algorithm gives preference to the older command. Alternatively, the Greedy command scheduling algorithm can use other attributes as the secondary factor in the selection mechanism. For example, in the case where two column access commands are ready to issue at the same time, a variant of the Greedy algorithm can allow the column read commands to proceed ahead of column write commands. Alternatively, the concept of queue pressure can be used to allow the command in the queue with more pending commands to proceed ahead of commands from queues with fewer pending commands. These subtle modifications can minutely improve upon the sustainable bandwidth characteristics of the Greedy algorithm. However, these other variants may introduce problems of their own, such as starvation. These issues must be addressed in a Greedy scheduling controller. Consequently, the Greedy algorithm must be complemented with specific anti-starvation mechanisms.

The Greedy algorithm as simulated in DRAMSim2 is described as follows:

- Compute the wait-to-issue time for the command at the head of each per-bank queue.
- Select the command with the smallest wait-to-issue time regardless of all command attributes—type, age, or address IDs.
- In the case where two or more commands have the same, shortest wait-to-issue time, select the oldest command from the set.

15.4.4 Workload Characteristics

In this work, a random number generator is used to create transaction request sequences that drive the simulated DRAM memory systems. A study is performed in this section to compare the bandwidth efficiency of memory systems as a function of burst length and queue depth, culminating in figure 15.25. The simulation conditions are described in this section. For this study, a random number generator is used to create transaction request sequences, that drive the simulated DRAM memory systems. In general, transaction request sequences possess three attributes that can greatly impact the sustainable bandwidth characteristics of the closed-page DRAM memory systems examined in this section. The three attributes are the address locality and distribution characteristics of the transaction request sequence, the read-to-write ratio of the transaction request sequence, and the ratio of short burst requests in the transaction request sequence. These attributes are described in detail here.

Address Distribution

In this study, requests within the input stream are equally distributed to all banks in the memory system. So the probability of a transaction request hitting a given bank is inversely proportional to the total number of banks in the DRAM memory system. Moreover, the address generation process is memoryless so that the address of each transaction is not dependent on the addresses of previous transactions. Although the capability to specify locality characteristics exists in the simulator, it is not used in this study.

Read Transaction Percentage

In this study, the random number generator is also used to select the read or write type of transaction in the input stream. In this study, the ratio of read transactions to write transactions is used as a variable parameter, and it can be adjusted by specifying the percentage of read requests in the transaction request sequence. In the request sequence used in this study, all transactions that are not read transactions are write transactions. Consequently, a transaction request sequence that has 0% read transactions consists of 100% write transactions.

Short Burst Request Percentage

The prefetch length of DDR3 SDRAM devices is 8. In the case where fewer than 8 beats of data are needed, an 8-beat burst can be chopped so that only 4 beats of data are transmitted by the DDR3 SDRAM device. In this study, the percentage of short, burst-length-of-4 (Bo4) requests can be specified as a variable parameter. The basic assumption used in this study is that the percentage of read transactions is the same for burst-length-of-4 (bo4) and burst-of-8 (bo8) transaction requests.

15.4.5 Timing Parameters

The timing parameters used in DRAMSim for the study of high-speed DRAM memory systems are summarized in Table 15.7. The parameters have been chosen to generally model a high-speed, high-performance DDR3 SDRAM memory system operating at 1.33 Gbps with t_{CAS}, t_{RCD}, and t_{RP} timing of 6-6-6. In the studies performed in this section, the maximum sustainable bandwidths of different system configurations are compared at the data rate of 1.33 Gbps. The preliminary timing parameter values assumed in this study for the 1.33 Gbps DDR3 SDRAM memory system are listed in Table 15.7 in terms of number of cycles. Since the base frequency of the 1.33-Gbps DDR3 SDRAM memory system is 667 MHz, 1 cycle in the 1.33 Gbps memory system is exactly 1.5 ns in duration.

15.4.6 Protocol Table

DRAMSim2 uses a protocol table to simulate timing constraints between pairs of DRAM commands in a DRAM memory system, and the protocol table is shown in Table 15.8. Table 15.8 is organized by each DRAM command and the possible commands that can precede each respective command. The table specifies the respective minimum timing constraints between each command pair in terms of an equation of timing parameters. The timing equations used in Table 15.8 can be independently verified against timing specifications given in various DRAM device data sheets, and the literal implementation of the protocol table in DRAMSim2 ensures that the timing relationships specified in DRAM device data sheets are observed with absolute accuracy. Table 15.8 summarizes the minimum timing equations for basic DRAM

TABLE 15.7 Summary of timing parameters used in a generic DRAM-access protocol

Parameter	Description	Cycles @ 1.33 Gbps
t_{AL}	Added Latency to column accesses, used in DDRx SDRAM devices for posted CAS commands.	5
t_{BURST}	Data **burst** duration. The number of cycles that data burst occupies on the data bus. In DDRx SDRAM, 4 beats = 2 cycles.	2 or 4
t_{CAS}	Column Access Strobe latency. The time interval between column access command and the start of data return by the DRAM device(s).	8
t_{CCD}	Column-to-Column Delay. The minimum intra-device column-to-column command timing, determined by internal prefetch length.	4
t_{CMD}	Command transport duration. The time period that a command occupies on the command bus.	1
t_{CWD}	Column Write Delay. The time interval between issuance of a column write command and data placement on a data bus by the controller.	5
t_{FAW}	Four (row) bank Activation Window. A rolling time-frame in which a maximum of four bank activation can be initiated.	20
t_{OST}	ODT Switching Time. The time interval to switching ODT control from rank to rank. (Assume termination scheme for 0 cycle ODT switching.)	0
t_{RAS}	Row Access Strobe. The time interval between a row access command and data restoration in a DRAM array.	18
t_{RC}	Row Cycle. The time interval between accesses to different rows in a bank. $t_{RC} = t_{RAS} + t_{RP}$.	24
t_{RCD}	Row to Column command Delay. The time interval between row access and data ready at sense amplifiers.	6
t_{RFC}	Refresh Cycle Time. The time interval between Refresh and Activation commands.	-
t_{RP}	Row Precharge. The time interval that it takes for a DRAM array to be precharged for another row access.	6
t_{RRD}	Row activation to Row activation Delay. The minimum time interval between two row activation commands to the same DRAM device.	4
t_{RTP}	Read to Precharge. The time interval between a read and a precharge command. Can be approximated by $t_{CAS} - t_{CMD}$.	5
t_{RTRS}	Rank-to-rank switching time. Used in DDR and DDR2 SDRAM memory systems.	1 ~ 3
t_{WR}	Write Recovery time. The minimum time interval between the end of write data burst and the start of a precharge command.	6
t_{WTR}	Write To Read delay time. The minimum time interval between the end of write data burst and the start of a column read command.	5

TABLE **15.8** Summary of minimum DRAM command timing equations

prev	next	rank	bank	Minimum Timing	Notes
A	A	s	s	t_{RC}	
A	A	s	d	t_{RRD}	
P	A	s	d	t_{RP}	Plus t_{FAW} for 5th RAS to same rank
F	A	s	s	t_{RFC}	
A	R	s	s	$t_{RCD} - t_{AL}$	$t_{AL} = 0$ without posted-CAS command
R	R	s	a	$MAX(t_{BURST}, t_{CCD})$	t_{BURST} is burst of prev. CAS to same rank
R	R	d	a	$t_{BURST} + t_{RTRS}$	t_{BURST} is burst of prev. CAS to diff. rank
W	R	s	a	$t_{CWD} + t_{BURST} + t_{WTR}$	t_{BURST} is burst of prev. CASW to same rank
W	R	d	a	$t_{CWD} + t_{BURST} + t_{RTRS} - t_{CAS}$	t_{BURST} is burst of prev. CASW to diff. rank
A	W	s	s	$t_{RCD} - t_{AL}$	
R	W	a	a	$t_{CAS} + t_{BURST} + t_{RTRS} - t_{CWD}$	t_{BURST} is burst of prev. CAS to any rank
W	W	s	a	$MAX(t_{BURST}, t_{CCD})$	t_{BURST} is burst of prev. CASW to same rank
W	W	d	a	$t_{BURST} + t_{OST}$	t_{BURST} is burst of prev. CASW to diff. rank
A	P	s	s	t_{RAS}	
R	P	s	s	$t_{AL} + t_{BURST} + t_{RTP} - t_{CCD}$	t_{BURST} is burst of prev. CAS to same rank
W	P	s	s	$t_{AL} + t_{CWD} + t_{BURST} + t_{WR}$	t_{BURST} is burst of prev. CASW to same rank
F	F	s	a	t_{RFC}	
P	F	s	a	t_{RP}	

Note: A = row **A**ccess; R= column-**R**ead; W = column-**W**rite; P = **P**recharge; F = re**F**resh; s = **s**ame; d = **d**ifferent a = **a**ny.

command interactions between row access, column read, column write, precharge, and refresh commands.

15.4.7 Queue Depth, Scheduling Algorithms, and Burst Length

Figure 15.25 shows simulation results for various scheduling algorithms with different system configurations. In Figure 15.25, the bandwidth efficiency and the associated bandwidth of an 8-byte-wide, 1.33 Gbps DDR3 memory system are respectively characterized at different queue depths, with different system configurations and different scheduling algorithms. Figure 15.25 shows that the Greedy DRAM command scheduling algorithm achieves the highest bandwidth efficiency over all other scheduling algorithms and system configurations. Figure 15.25 also shows that sustainable bandwidth increases with deeper queue

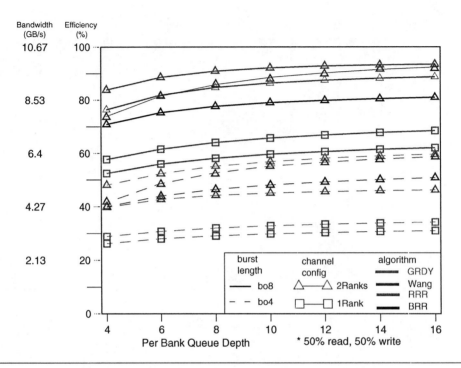

FIGURE 15.25: Bandwidth efficiency and sustainable bandwidth as a function of burst length and queue depth.

depths for nearly all algorithms and all system configurations, but the bandwidth typically plateaus at a queue depth of 10.

Figure 15.25 shows that the available bandwidth of a high-speed DDR3 memory system drops dramatically when the traffic consists of short, bo4 requests. Due to the fact that t_{CCD} is 4 cycles and t_{RRD} is also 4 cycles, short bo4 requests cannot be pipelined from a single rank of DRAM devices, and the highest available bandwidth can be obtained from a system with multiple ranks of DRAM devices. However, even in the case where two ranks of DRAM devices exist in the memory system, the rank-to-rank switching time effectively limits the peak bandwidth efficiency of the memory system to 66.7%. However, due to the existence of other bandwidth-constraining timing parameters, Figure 15.25 also shows that the highest performance, two-rank, 1.33 Gbps DDR3 SDRAM memory system merely approaches 60% bandwidth efficiency.

Finally, one issue not specifically illustrated in Figure 15.25 is that the Greedy algorithm is not itself an algorithm that guarantees fairness. Whereas BRR, RRR, and Wang algorithms all guarantee that a request will be serviced within a predictable number of cycles upon entering a queue of a given depth, a request can, in theory, be deferred for an indefinitely long period of time. Consequently, the Wang algorithm may be preferred in certain high-performance applications where an anti-starvation requirement must be guaranteed by the scheduling algorithm.

15.4.8 Effect of Burst Length on Sustainable Bandwidth

Figure 15.25 shows that the sustainable bandwidth of the high-speed DDR3 SDRAM memory system is very sensitive to the burst length of the request stream. Figure 15.26 reveals the extent of the bandwidth sensitivity to different short burst ratios and read percentages. Figure 15.26 shows the maximum sustainable bandwidth characteristics of a system with two ranks of DRAM devices. The Greedy command scheduling algorithms and the queue depth of 8 is used for all simulations in Figure 15.26, and the maximum sustainable bandwidth of the memory system is characterized against varying percentages of bo4 requests and read requests. Figure 15.26 shows that with 0% bo4 requests and 0% read transactions, meaning 100% write transactions, the dual rank DDR3 memory system achieves 100% bandwidth efficiency and sustains 10.67 GB/s of maximum bandwidth. Figure 15.26 also shows that as the percentage of read requests increases, the maximum sustainable bandwidth decreases, reaching a local minimum between 50 and 70%, depending on the percentage of bo4 requests in the input stream. Figure 15.26 also shows that the maximum sustainable bandwidth of the memory system is a non-linear function of the percentage of short burst requests in the input stream. That is, Figure 15.26 shows that the bandwidth loss between an input stream with 40% bo4 requests compared with an input stream with 20% bo4 requests is typically larger than the bandwidth loss between an input stream with 20% bo4 requests compared with an input stream with 0% bo4 requests. Finally, Figure 15.26 provides an identically configured, 800-Mbps DDR2 memory system as reference and shows that the DDR2 system is much less sensitive to the short burst ratio.

15.4.9 Burst Chop in DDR3 SDRAM Devices

One consequence of the 8-bit prefetch length of the DDR3 device is that the natural burst length in DDR3 SDRAM memory systems is 8 beats. In the case where only 4 beats of data are needed, DDR3 devices implement a burst chop mechanism where an 8-beat burst can be chopped so that only 4 beats of data are transmitted to or from the DRAM device. However, the burst chop mechanism does not allow the

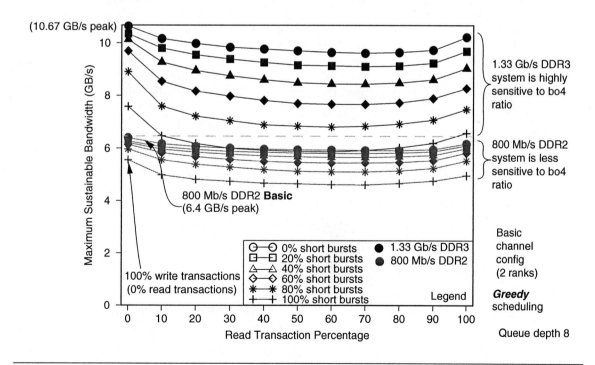

FIGURE 15.26: Bandwidth of an 8-byte channel @ 1.33 Gbps—varying short burst and read percentages.

DRAM device to pipeline data from the same bank or another bank on the same device after a burst is chopped. The reason that the burst chop mechanism does not allow 4 beat bursts to be pipelined is that the I/O gating structure on the DDR3 device is designed to transport 8 consecutive beats in a single data burst, and the data bus simply idles after a read burst is chopped. Figure 15.27 illustrates that in a DDR3 memory system, a DDR3 device cannot be pipelined consecutively from different banks for the 4-beat (short) burst. Consequently, the only real benefit to the burst chop mechanism is that it allows better data bus utilization in dual rank memory systems, where the rank switching overhead may be shorter than the (same rank) burst chop idle time.

Currently, the DDR3 device architecture as defined by JEDEC does not allow seamless burst merging on the data bus between 4-beat-long bursts from different banks. Rather, the I/O interface of the DDR3 device remains idle for the second half of the 8-beat burst when the standard burst chop mechanism is used to reduce the burst length of the access request. The study in this section examines the gain in sustainable bandwidth when the I/O interface of the DDR3 device is modified to allow the quasi-4-bit prefetch bursts to and from different banks within the same rank of DDR3 SDRAM devices to be seamlessly merged. In this section, three different short burst merging mechanisms are described and compared: the standard (STD) burst chop burst merging mechanism, the short write burst bank switching (WBS) burst merging mechanism, and the short read burst and short write burst bank switching (RWBS) burst merging mechanism. These mechanisms and their respective impact on the DDR3 SDRAM-access protocol are described in the following sections.

Standard (STD) Burst Chop

The *standard* **(STD)** *burst chop* mechanism is the standard mechanism that exists in the DDR3 SDRAM protocol. The STD burst chop mechanism simply terminates the transmission of the second half of the 8-beat burst in the case where a burst chop and the DRAM device I/O interface cannot handle another data burst until two clock cycles later. Figure 15.28 shows the timing of six short column access commands—three short column read access commands and three short column write access commands—for a DDR3 memory system that implements the STD burst chop mechanism. Figure 15.28 shows that in the STD burst chop mechanism, a read burst chop forces the data bus to remain idle for two clock cycles in between two short column read commands to different banks of the same rank, while the timing of two short column read commands to different ranks depends on the rank-to-rank switching time, assumed to be one clock cycle in Figure 15.28.

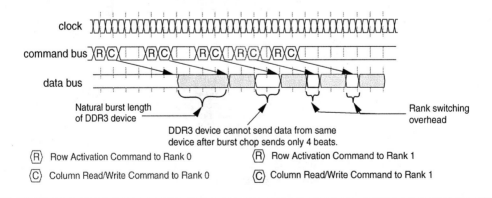

FIGURE 15.27: Benefits of burst chop in multi-rank DDR3 SDRAM memory systems.

The figure also shows the timing of the short write bursts in the STD burst chop mechanism, and the data bus idles for two clock cycles between two short column write access commands to different banks of the same rank. In contrast, the DRAM controller can direct two short column write access commands to different ranks without having to insert idle cycles between the short bursts on the data bus. That is, Figure 15.28 assumes a data bus termination scheme that allows the memory controller to direct consecutive, bo4 write requests to different ranks without incurring a bubble in the command scheduling timing. In general, the study of the STD burst chop mechanism follows the protocol table as defined in Table 15.8. The timing parameter values for all studies are as defined in Table 15.7.

Short Write Burst Bank Switching (WBS)

The *short write burst bank switching* (WBS) burst merging mechanism is a mechanism designed to improve the short burst bandwidth characteristics of DDR3 devices. The proposal is based on the premise that it would be simple for the I/O interface of the DDR3 device to be redesigned to support consecutive short write bursts to different banks within the same rank of DDR3 SDRAM devices, but more difficult to merge consecutive short read bursts from different banks within the same rank. Figure 15.29 shows the timing on the data bus of a DDR3 SDRAM memory system that implements the WBS burst chop merging mechanism for the same six short column access commands as illustrated in Figure 15.28. Figure 15.29 shows that in the WBS mechanism, the timing between consecutive, short column read commands is not changed from the STD burst chop mechanism. However, Figure 15.29 shows that with the ability to write short bursts to different banks consecutively, WBS allows DDR3 SDRAM devices to seamlessly merge short write bursts to different banks of a given rank, as well as to different ranks of DRAM devices.

Table 15.9 shows the minimum timing constraints for column write commands to column write commands in a DDR3 SDRAM memory system that implements the WBS short burst merging mechanism. Table 15.9 shows that the only change that the WBS short burst merging mechanism makes to the protocol table is in the case of consecutive column write commands to different banks of a given rank. Unlike the case where consecutive column write commands are made to the same bank, the timing of two consecutive column write commands to different banks of the same rank in Table 15.9 depends on the length of the request itself.

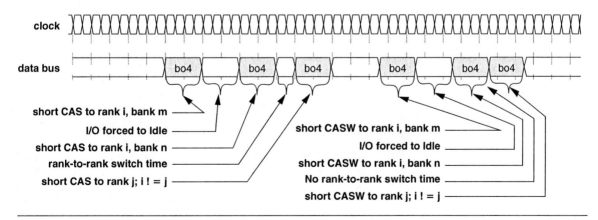

FIGURE 15.28: Data bus timing of short read and write column access commands—STD chop.

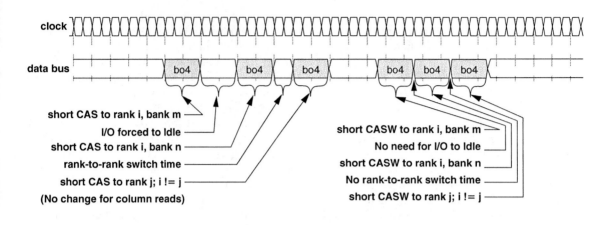

FIGURE 15.29: Data bus timing of short read and write column access commands—WBS chop merge.

TABLE 15.9   Protocol table modification for a DDR3 device with WBS chop merge

prev	next	rank	bank	Minimum Timing	Notes
W	W	s	d	MAX(t_{BURST}, 2)	Depends on actual request length of prev CASW (minimum length of 4 beats - 2 cycles)

Short Read Burst and Short Write Burst Bank Switching (RWBS)

The *short read burst and write burst bank switching* (RWBS) burst merging mechanism is the more aggressive mechanism proposed to improve the bo4 bandwidth characteristics of DDR3 devices. The RWBS proposal requires the I/O interface of the DDR3 device to be redesigned to support consecutive, short read bursts and short write bursts to and from different banks within the same rank of DDR3 SDRAM devices. Figure 15.30 shows the timing on the data bus of a DDR3 SDRAM memory system with devices that implement the RWBS burst chop merging mechanism for the same six short column access commands as illustrated in Figures 15.28 and 15.29. Figure 15.30 shows that with the redesign of the I/O interface to implement the RWBS mechanism, consecutive, short read data bursts from different banks of the same rank can be pipelined consecutively without any idle time on the data bus.

Table 15.10 shows column read-to-read and write-to-write timing constraints for the DDR3 SDRAM protocol that accounts for the RWBS short burst merging mechanism. Table 15.10 shows that the RWBS short burst merging mechanism changes the minimum timing constraints for consecutive column read commands and consecutive column write commands to different banks of the same rank. In both cases, implementation of the RWBS short burst merging mechanism means that the minimum timing between consecutive column accesses to different banks of the same rank depends on the requested burst transfer length rather than the 8-bit prefetch length of the DDR3 SDRAM device.

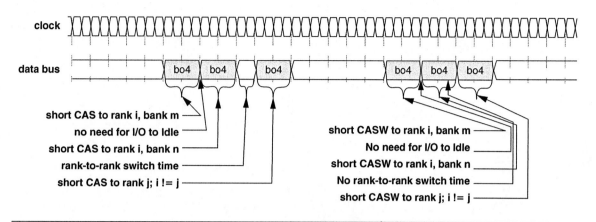

FIGURE 15.30: Data bus timing of short read and write column access commands—RWBS chop merge.

TABLE 15.10   Protocol table modification for a DDR3 device with RWBS chop merge

prev	next	rank	bank	Minimum Timing	Notes
R	R	s	d	MAX(t_{BURST}, 2)	Depends on actual request length of prev CAS (minimum length of 4)

Simulation Results

The simulations in this section assume the ***basic*** channel configuration with a single 64-bit-wide channel and 2 ranks of DDR3 SDRAM devices in the single channel memory system. The timing parameter values of the DRAM memory system are as described in Table 15.7. For each simulation, the percentage of read transactions in the input stream is set at a specific value, and the percentage of transactions with a request bo4 rather than bo8 is also set at a specific value. In this work, the percentage of read transactions and the percentage of short bursts are the two independent variables used to characterize the performance benefit of the two different short burst merging mechanisms.

Figure 15.31 shows the maximum sustainable bandwidth of a single channel, dual rank, closed-page, no refresh, 1.33 Gbps DDR3 memory system with a memory controller that uses Greedy command scheduling to achieve maximum sustainable bandwidth.

Figure 15.31 shows the bandwidth characteristics of the DRAM memory system subjected to different percentages of read transactions and different percentages of short bursts. In Figure 15.31, the x-axis shows the different read percentages, and different curves show the bandwidth characteristics of the memory system for a given percentage of short burst requests in the input stream. Comparatively, the y-axis of Figure 15.31 shows the bandwidth efficiency and the maximum sustained bandwidth

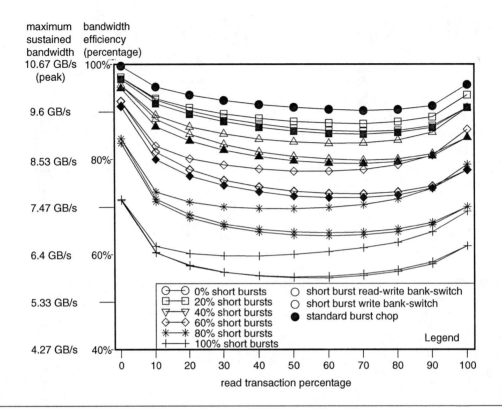

FIGURE 15.31: Bandwidth comparison of an 8-byte channel @ 1.33 Gbps—STD, WBS, and RWBS merge.

of the memory system. Figure 15.31 shows that the memory system achieves the highest bandwidth with 100% write requests with 0% short bursts. Figure 15.31 also shows that the WBS burst merging scheme gains minimal bandwidth, and the RWBS burst merging mechanism achieves significant gains in bandwidth with higher read request and higher short burst request percentages.

Finally, Figure 15.32 shows the improvement in bandwidth of the RWBS burst chop merging mechanism over the STD burst chop merging mechanism in a 3D graph. Figure 15.32 presents the same data as Figure 15.31, but focuses specifically on the bandwidth improvement of the RWBS burst chop merging mechanism over the STD burst chop merging mechanism, with better grid resolutions for the short burst percentage. Figure 15.32 confirms the intuitive notion

that the benefits of the RWBS burst chop merging mechanism over the STD burst chop merging mechanism increases with higher percentages of read requests and higher percentages of short requests.

15.4.10 Revisiting the 8-Bank and 16-Bank Issue with DRAMSim

In DDR3 SDRAM devices, the 8-bit prefetch architecture enables DRAM design engineers to significantly increase the data rate of DRAM device interface while maintaining a relatively low activity rate for the DRAM cell arrays. However, the high interface data rate and relatively constant row cycle times require higher degrees of bank parallelism to maintain a given level of bandwidth efficiency. In this section, the bandwidth characteristics of the

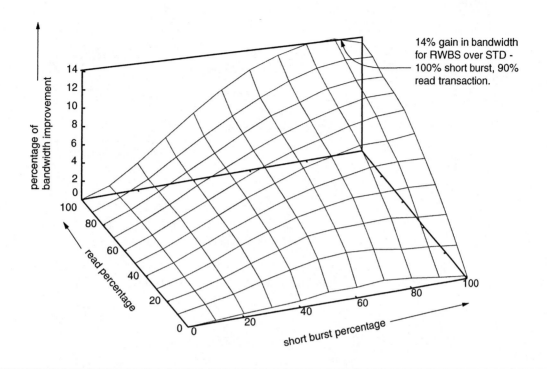

FIGURE 15.32: Sustainable bandwidth improvement of RWBS burst merge over STD chop.

8-bank DDR3 device are compared to the bandwidth characteristics of a hypothetical 16-bank DDR3 device. The basis of the comparison is a 64-bit-wide, 1.33 Gbps DDR3 SDRAM memory system configured in the *Basic* channel configuration. The Greedy scheduling algorithm is used throughout, and the input stream consists of 0% bo4 requests and 50% read transactions.

Figure 15.33 compares the sustainable bandwidth characteristics of four different system configurations: a 1 rank, 8 banks per rank (1R8B) system; a 1 rank, 16 banks per rank (1R16) system; a 1 rank, 8 banks per rank (2R8B) system; and a 2 rank, 16 banks per rank (2R16) system. In the 8-bank versus 16-bank comparison, all timing parameters are held as constants across all configurations. The difference in each respective configuration is limited to the number of ranks and the number of banks. Figure 15.33 shows that while the 1R16B system configuration achieves significantly higher bandwidth than the

1R8B configuration, the 2R8B system also outperforms the 1R16B memory system by nearly the same margin of sustainable bandwidth; the exact differential in sustainable bandwidth depends on the value of the rank-to-rank switching penalty. Finally, Figure 15.33 also shows that the 2R16B memory system can provide substantial benefit in sustainable bandwidth over the 2R8B memory system, although the benefit of having more banks decreases with increasing queue depth.

Figure 15.34 shows the same data as Figure 15.33, but cross compares the various system configurations in terms of percentage improvements of sustainable bandwidth. In each case, the system configuration with the lower sustainable bandwidth characteristic is used as the baseline, and the graph illustrates the percentage of bandwidth improvement of having a 16-bank, 1.33 Gbps DDR3 SDRAM device over that of an 8-bank, 1.33 Gbps DDR3 device in different system configurations with different queue depths and rank-to-rank switching penalties. Figure 15.34 shows that upwards

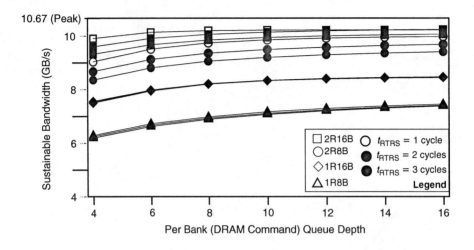

FIGURE 15.33: Sustainable bandwidth—16-bank versus 8-bank DDR3 devices—8-byte channel @ 1.33 Gbps.

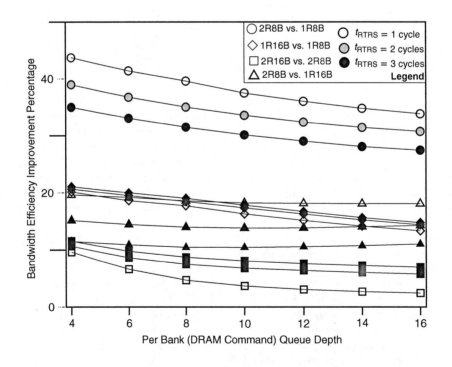

FIGURE 15.34: Bandwidth improvement—16-bank versus 8-bank DDR3 devices—8-byte channel @ 1.33 Gbps.

of 40% improvement in sustainable bandwidth can be obtained by the 2R8B configuration over the 1R8B configuration. Figure 15.34 also shows that the 1R16B configuration improves sustainable bandwidth over that of the 1R8B configuration between 15 and 21%. Finally, Figure 15.34 shows that the 2R16B configuration improves sustainable bandwidth over that of the 2R8B configuration between 4 and 12%.

The immediate conclusion that can be drawn from Figure 15.34 is that dual rank memory systems have the greatest benefit in terms of increased bandwidth over single rank memory systems, and the contributing bandwidth benefit of the 16-bank DDR3 device over that of the 8-bank DDR3 device is roughly half of the bandwidth benefit of dual rank memory systems over single rank memory systems. Also, the respective bandwidth benefits of dual rank and 16-bank memory systems over single rank and 8-bank memory systems generally decrease with increasing queue depths.

15.4.11 8 Bank vs. 16 Banks — Relaxed t_{FAW} and t_{WTR}

Figures 15.33 and 15.34 show that a substantial increase in sustainable bandwidth can be obtained with a 16-bank DRAM device over that of an 8-bank device. However, the dual constraints of t_{FAW} and t_{WTR} greatly limit the maximum sustainable bandwidth of single rank memory systems. In this section, we explore the effects of t_{FAW} and t_{WTR} on the sustainable bandwidth characteristics of different memory system configurations.

In Figures 15.33 and 15.34, the simulations are performed with the assumed timing parameters from Table 15.7, and the parameter values listed in Table 15.7 for t_{FAW} and t_{WTR} are 20 cycles and 5 cycles, respectively. To relax the constraints imposed on the DRAM memory system, we repeat the simulations used to obtain Figures 15.33 and 15.34, but with redefined t_{FAW} and t_{WTR} parameter values of 16 cycles and 3 cycles, respectively. All other parameter values remain unchanged from those listed in Table 15.7.

Figure 15.35 shows the maximum sustainable bandwidth of a single channel, 1.33 Gbps DDR3 SDRAM memory system with both sets of t_{FAW} and t_{WTR} parameter values. Figure 15.35 shows that with the relaxed t_{FAW} and t_{WTR} parameter values, the largest gain in sustainable bandwidth over that of the more restrictive t_{FAW} and t_{WTR} values can be found in the 1R16B system configuration, and a smaller gain in sustainable bandwidth can be found in the 1R8B system configuration. In contrast, relaxing t_{FAW} and t_{WTR} impacts the dual rank system configurations to a far lesser degree.

Figure 15.36 shows the cross comparison of the various system configurations with the relaxed t_{FAW} and t_{WTR} values. Figure 15.36 shows that with the elimination of t_{FAW} in combination with the reduced write-to-read turnaround time, the increase in sustainable bandwidth in a 1R16B system over that of a 1R8B system is now a relatively constant 25%. Figure 15.36 also shows that with the elimination of t_{FAW} in combination with the reduced t_{WTR}, the differential in sustainable bandwidth between 1R16B and 2R8B systems drops to single digit percentages. In the extreme case of t_{RTRS} equal to 3 cycles and a queue depth of 16, the 1R16B configuration can, in fact, sustain higher bandwidth throughput than the 2R8B configuration.

15.4.12 Effect of Transaction Ordering on Latency Distribution

In modern uniprocessor and multi-processor systems, multiple memory transactions may be sent to the memory system concurrently. In case the memory system is not immediately available to service a memory transaction, or if a memory transaction is deferred to allow a later transaction to proceed ahead of it, the latency of the later transaction will decrease at the expense of the increased latency of the prior memory transaction. However, if the transaction or DRAM command reordering algorithm results in a more efficient utilization of the memory system, then the average memory-access latency for all memory transactions will decrease. Figure 15.37 shows the impact of a Command Pair Rank Hopping (CPRH) scheduling algorithm on the memory-access latency distribution for the 179.art through 2 billion instructions as compared to the First Come First

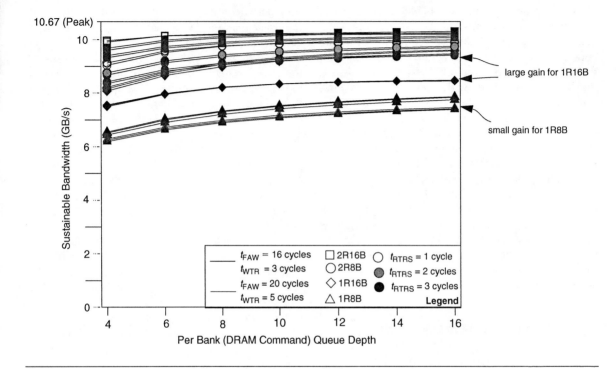

FIGURE 15.35: Sustainable bandwidth—16 bank versus 8-bank DDR3 devices; relaxed t_{FAW} and t_{WTR}.

Served (FCFS) scheduling algorithm.[3] The memory-access latency distribution illustrated in Figure 15.37 is obtained by a mechanism that records the access latency for each memory transaction in the bus interface unit (BIU) between the processor simulator and DRAMSim. In the simulation framework, each time a memory transaction is sent to the BIU, the start time of the transaction is recorded by the BIU. Upon completion of the memory transaction, the BIU simply computes the latency and keeps track of the number of transactions for each specific latency value.

In the simulated memory system, the minimum latency of a memory transaction is simply the delay through the BIU added to the delay of the memory controller and the minimum DRAM latencies of t_{RCD} + t_{CAS}. In the simulated memory system, the delays

through the BIU and memory controller are set to 10 ns, and the minimum access latency is approximately 30 ns for the set of timing values used in this study and illustrated in Figure 15.37. Figure 15.37 shows that the CPRH scheduling algorithm greatly decreases the queueing delay for many pending memory transactions in 179.art, and the number of transactions with memory-access latency greater than 400 ns is significantly less than the same workload operating with the FCFS scheduling algorithm.

In Figure 15.37, the memory-access latency distribution curve graphically illustrates the benefits of the CPRH algorithm for 179.art. However, just as the memory-access latency distribution curve can be used to illustrate the benefit of the CPRH scheduling algorithm, it can also be used to illustrate possible

---

[3]The Command Pair Rank Hopping (CPRH) scheduling algorithm is a patent-pending scheduling algorithm, and the algorithm is not specifically described herein. The simulation results are provided for illustrative purposes only.

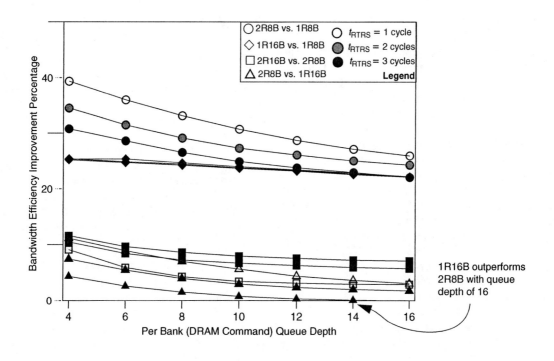

FIGURE 15.36: Bandwidth improvement—16-bank versus 8-bank DDR3 devices; relaxed t_{FAW} and t_{WTR}.

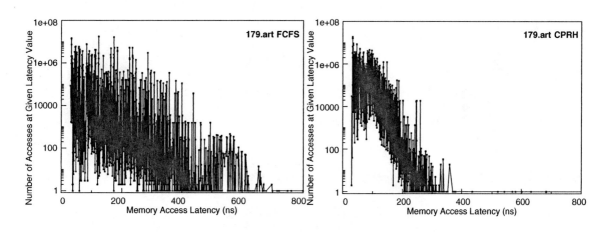

FIGURE 15.37: Impact of scheduling policy on memory-access latency distribution: 179.art.

problems with the CPRH scheduling algorithm for other workloads. Figure 15.38 shows the latency distribution curve for 188.ammp, and 188.ammp was one workload that points to possible issues with the CPRH algorithm. Figure 15.38 shows that the CPRH scheduling algorithm resulted in longer latencies for a number of transactions, and the number of transactions with memory-access latency greater than 400 ns actually increased. Figure 15.38 also shows that the increase of a small number of transactions with memory-access latency greater than 400 ns is offset by the reduction of the number of transactions with memory transaction latency around 200 ns and the increase of the number of transactions with memory-access latency less than 100 ns. In other words, the CPRH scheduling algorithm redistributed the memory-access latency curve so that most memory transactions received a modest reduction in access latency, but a few memory transactions suffered a substantial increase in access latency. The net result is that the changes in access latency cancelled each other out, resulting in limited speedup for the CPRH algorithm over the FCFS algorithm for 188.ammp.

15.5 A Latency-Oriented Study

In the previous section, we examined the impact of transaction ordering on the memory-access latency distribution for various applications. Memory controller schedulers typically attempt to maximize performance by taking advantage of memory application access patterns to hide DRAM-access penalties. In this section, we provide insight into the impact that DRAM architectural choices make on the average read latency or memory-access latency. We briefly examine how the choice of DRAM protocol impacts memory system performance and then discuss in detail how aspects of the memory system protocol and configuration contribute to the observed access latency.[4]

15.5.1 Experimental Framework

This study uses DRAMSim, a stand-alone memory subsystem simulator. DRAMSim provides a detailed execution-driven model of a Fully Buffered (FB) DIMM memory system. The simulator also supports the variation of memory system parameters of interest, including scheduling policies and memory

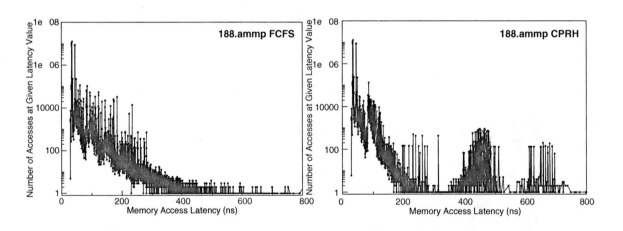

FIGURE 15.38: Impact of scheduling policy on memory-access latency distribution: 188.ammp.

---

[4]Some of this section's material appears in "Fully-Buffered DIMM memory architectures: Understanding mechanisms, overheads and scaling," by B. Ganesh, A. Jaleel, D. Wang, and B. Jacob. In Proc. 13th International Symposium on High Performance Computer Architecture (HPCA 2007). Phoenix, AZ, February 2007. Copyright IEEE. Used with permission.

configuration, i.e., number of ranks and channels, address mapping policy, etc.

The architecture modelled is shown in Figure 15.39. The memory controller comprises read and write transaction queues for each channel, from which commands and command frames are scheduled to the channel. The memory trace inputs are all placed in the BIU. The BIU is set to be infinite in size for the limit studies. For the trace-driven studies, we use a BIU which can hold as many outstanding transactions as the combined transaction queue capacity. The read and write transaction queues, which are equal in size, can hold 32 transactions—16 active reads and writes. Transactions are moved to a response queue (not shown in the figure)

after they are scheduled to the memory modules. Read transactions remain in the response queue till the read data returns, while write transactions are retained till completion.

The memory controller scheduler builds a schedule using an algorithm that prioritizes read transactions over write transactions. Natarajan et al. [2004] and Ganesh et al. [2007] have demonstrated in their papers that a memory controller that prioritizes read over write transactions achieves significant performance improvement over one that does not. This scheduling rule is maintained except when the read and write transactions are to the same location in memory. In general, older transactions of a given type are given priority over transactions of the same type that arrived

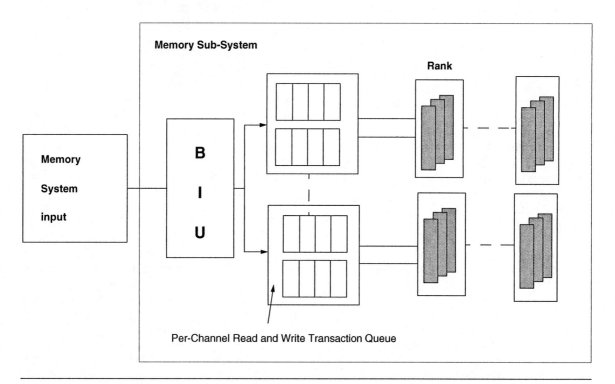

FIGURE 15.39: Memory controller architecture. The figure shows the basic architecture of the memory controller modelled in DRAMsim and used for these experiments. The figure also shows the memory system inputs used to drive the simulator. Memory requests are issued into the BIU either froma file created by a random address generator or from a memory request trace file obtained from microprocessor simulation infrastructures. Note that for the limit studies using a random address generator, we assume that the BIU is infinite in size. For the microprocessor trace-based studies, we use a fixed-size BIU.

later. An older read transaction can be scheduled later than a newer read transaction if the required resources are available later.

We studied two different DRAM types: a conventional DDR2 system with a data-rate of 667 Mbps, and its corresponding FB DIMM systems: an FB DIMM organization with DDR2 on the DIMM. FB DIMMSare modelled using the parameters available for a 4-GB module [Micron 2005]; DDR2 devices are modelled as 1-Gb it parts with 8 banks of memory [Micron 2006]. The microprocessor driver is assumed to be running at 4 GHz. In this particular study, we focus on closed-page systems which are commonly used in the server space. It is common in such a case to use posted CAS, i.e., the RAS and CAS are transmitted to the memory controller in the same cycle. For FB DIMM systems using posted CAS, the RAS and CAS are placed in the same frame. We also assume that each DIMM has only a single rank of memory.

15.5.2 Simulation Input

There are two types of inputs used to drive the simulations:

Random Address Traces These input traces are generated using a random number generator. The input address stream is modelled as a poisson arrival process where each request is independent of the previous request. Each random address stream is identified using the following parameters:

- Average issue bandwidth is the average arrival rate for the Poisson process used to model the trace.
- Number of ranks in the system.

Since the commonly observed ratio read to write traffic is 2:1, the input traces are set to have a 2:1 ratio of read to write traffic. The traffic is distributed equally to all the ranks in the system.

Application Traces Input traces from the SPEC workloads in combination to generate 2, 4, and 8 way multi-programming traces. The application traces used in this study were generated using sim-

alpha [Desikan et al. 2001] using a processor configuration with a 1MB 8-way set associative L2 cache with a 64-byte cacheline. All traces were collected after fast-forwarding the application by 2 billion instructions and executing for 200 million instructions. The applications are grouped together to form workload mixes which are memory intensive. Note that the classification is based on the behavior of the workload in the region when the traces are grabbed.

TABLE 15.11   Application traces used

Mem-2	art,mcf
Mem-4	art,mcf,swim,lucas
Mem-8	art,mcf,swim,lucas,mgrid,art,mcf,applu

15.5.3   Limit Study : Latency Bandwidth Characteristics

One of the commonly used approaches to gauge the performance of a memory system protocol is to conduct a limit study using random-address traces as input. The latency and bandwidth values are measured for a random address trace whose input arrival rate is varied. The latency typically gradually increases till a particular bandwidth value after which it dramatically increases. This point on the latency-bandwidth curve represents the maximum sustainable bandwidth of the system prior to its getting overloaded. Memory controller design is focussed on moving this latency-bandwidth curve to the right, i.e., improving the read latency values at higher bandwidth values. Figure 15.40 shows the latency bandwidth characteristic of a DDR2 and FB-DIMM DDR2 system. The graphs are shown for the FB-DIMM DDR2 system in fixed latency mode.

We observe that the maximum sustainable bandwidth of a multi-rank FB-DIMM system is approximately 25% times greater than that achieved by a multi-rank DDR2 system. The increased sustainable bandwidth is due to the increased DIMM-level parallelism in an FB-DIMM system and the additional available data-bandwidth. The separation of the read and write data buses from the memory controller to the DIMMs enables the memory controller to keep simultaneously scheduled read and write transactions to two ranks on two different DIMMs. This factor contributes to being significantly higher than that seen in a DDRx system.

The single rank configuration has the lowest maximum sustainable bandwidth for both systems. In a single rank channel, the DIMM emerges as a significant bottleneck due to the constraints imposed by the various DRAM timing parameters. Increasing the number of ranks from 1 to 2 significantly improves the maximum sustainable bandwidth by reducing the contention for the DRAM banks. Further increases in the number of ranks in the channel have no impact in DDRx systems because of the increasing competition for the bus. In the case of FB-DIMM systems, doubling the number of ranks from 2 to 4 has marginal impact while going from 4 to 8 ranks has almost no impact. We observed that typically the reduction in the queueing delay due to the DRAM availability is replaced with that of the channel being unavailable.

15.5.4 Latency

In this section, we look at the trends in latency, and the factors impacting them, in further detail.

Figure 15.41 shows the average read latency divided into queueing delay overhead and the transaction processing overhead. The queueing delay component refers to the duration the transaction waiting in the queue for one or more resources to become available. The causes for queueing delay include memory controller request queue availability, south link availability, DIMM availability (including on-DIMM command and data buses and bank conflicts), and north link availability. Note that the overlap of queueing delay is monitored for all components except the memory controller request queue factor. The default latency cost is the cost associated with making a read request in an unloaded channel.

The queueing delay experienced by a read transaction is rarely due to any single factor, but usually due to a combination of factors. Changing the system configuration, by adding more ranks in the channel or increasing the number of channels in the system, results in a change in the availability of all the resources to a different degree. Thus, we see that the latency trends due to changes in a configuration are affected by how exactly these individual queueing delays change.

Single-rank configurations experience higher latencies due to an insufficient number of memory

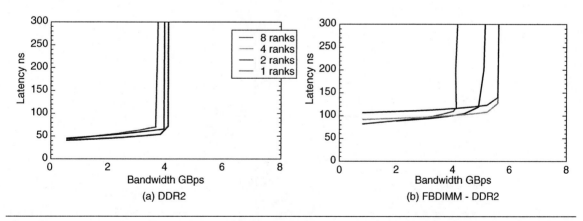

FIGURE 15.40: DDR2 and FB-DIMM-DDR2 latency bandwidth characteristics. The figure shows the latency bandwidth characteristics of a DDR2 and FB-DIMM DDR2 system. The graphs are generated using a random-input address trace with 66% read traffic and varying input arrival rate. A transaction is equally likely to be addressed at any of the given banks in the system.

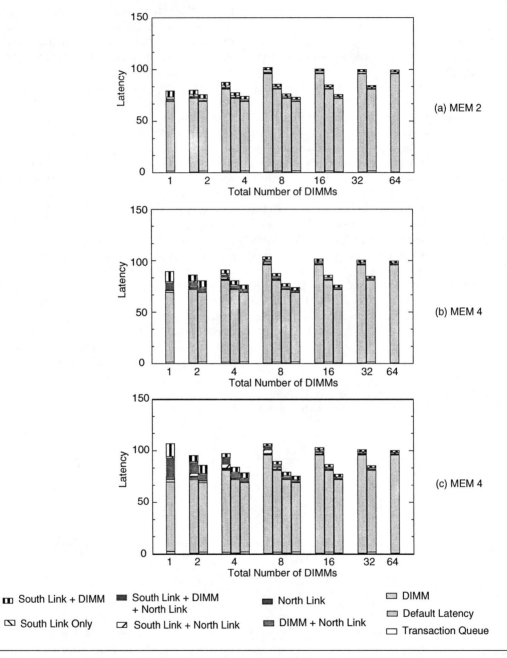

(a) MEM 2

(b) MEM 4

(c) MEM 4

Legend:

- ▥ South Link + DIMM
- ▨ South Link Only
- ■ South Link + DIMM + North Link
- ▧ South Link + North Link
- ■ North Link
- ▨ DIMM + North Link
- ▥ DIMM
- ▥ Default Latency
- ▢ Transaction Queue

FIGURE 15.41: Read latency for various configurations systems with identical numbers of DIMMS are grouped together. Within a group, the bars on the left represent topologies with fewer numbers of channels. The DRAM configuration was FBD-DDR2 using fixed latency mode. The *y*-axis shows latency in nano-seconds.

banks to distribute requests to and the inability to schedule take advantage of any parallelism the FB-DIMM channel offers. In such systems the DIMM is a dominant system bottleneck and can contribute as much as 50% of the overall transaction queueing delay. Adding more ranks in these systems helps reduce the DIMM-based queueing delays. The reductions are 20–60%, when going from a one rank to a two-rank channel. For 4–8 rank channel, the DIMM-based queueing delay is typically only 10% of that in the single-rank channel.

The sharing of the southbound bus by command and write data results in a significant queueing delay associated with southbound channel unavailability. Since all three memory workload mixes have nearly 33% write traffic we find that the southbound channel is a significant bottleneck. The southbound channel queueing delay is reduced by increasing the number of channels in the system. Some reductions in southbound channel unavailability are also achieved by adding more ranks in the system. In a multi-rank channel, the memory controller is more likely to be able to pack multiple commands in the same frame. Though the opportunities to do so are limited, this can result in a decrease in southbound channel unavailability by 10–20% when increasing the number of ranks in a channel from 1 to 2.

Increasing the channel depth raises the transmission costs for frames on the channel. This results in an increase in the read latency with increasing channel depth for MEM-2 (Figure 15.41(a)) and for the other workloads for larger number of channels, when the utilization is low. Interestingly, the additional DRAM-level parallelism available in a deeper channel can counter the rise in frame transmission costs sufficiently to reduce overall latency (Figure 15.41(b) and (c)). The gains in parallelism are especially apparent when going from a single-rank to a two-rank channel. These gains gradually taper off with further increases in channel depth.

With deeper channels, the increased number of in-flight transactions results in an increase in the queueing delay due to the link-unavailability. This is attributable to the heightened competition for the bus due to the additional number of in-flight transactions. This increase can combine with the increase in processing cost to offset the gains due to increased DIMM-level parallelism. Thus, we see that for MEM-4 and MEM-8, Figures 15.41(b) and 15.41(c) respectively, that the latency increases in a single channel system when the channel depth is increased from 4 to 8.

The interaction of the increase in processing overhead, the number of in-flight transactions using the channel, the type of these transactions and the lowering of DIMM-level conflicts result in the different latency trends observed. Depending on which trend dominates, the latency can increase linearly with the number of ranks in the channel (Figure 15.41 (a)) or decrease initially and then increase as more ranks are added to the channel (Figures 15.41(b) and (c)). In general, the former occurs in a relatively lightly loaded system while the latter occurs in a system with higher bandwidth demand.

Figure 15.42 shows the variation in read latency contributors in a DDR2 system for the MEM-2 and MEM-4 workloads. The latency in a DDRx system unlike an FB-DIMM system changes marginally with the number of ranks in the channel. This is because unlike in an FB-DIMM system, the default latency of an operation does not vary with the number of ranks in the channel for a DDRx system as seen from Figures 15.41 and 15.42. Further, the queueing delay due to DRAM unavailability is replaced by that due to the link being unavailable as the number of ranks in the channel is increased.

A single channel configuration for MEM-4 experiences fairly significant queueing delay due to the transaction queues being full. Although the BIU has as many entries as the transaction queue, these entries can hold a read or a write transaction. The distinction between the read and write transaction queues in the memory controller queues results in a write transaction waiting for the transaction queue to become available when the write transaction queue fill up. This in turn delays later read transactions. By enforcing starvation awareness this problem is alleviated marginally but not completely in a busy system.

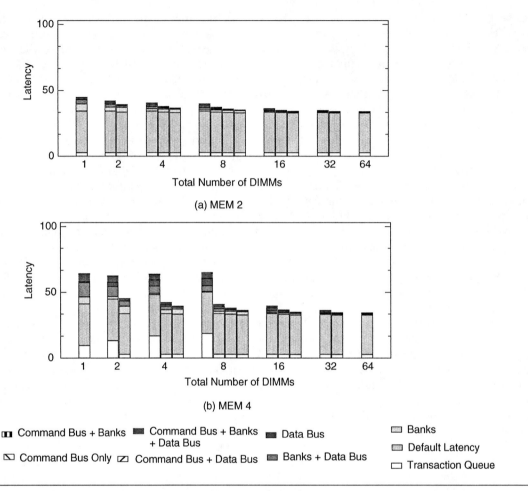

FIGURE 15.42: Read latency for various configurations for DDR2 systems with identical numbers of DIMMS are grouped together. Within a group, the bars on the left represent topologies with fewer numbers of channels. The DRAM configuration was DDR2 using fixed latency mode. The y-axis shows latency in nano-seconds. The y-axis scales are different for graphs.

15.6 Concluding Remarks

The difficulty of sustaining high bandwidth utilization has increased in each successive generation of commodity DRAM memory systems due to the combination of relatively constant row cycle times and increasing data rates—increasing data rates that translate directly to shorter data transport times per bit. The growing disparity between the relatively constant row cycle times and shorter data transport times means that longer requests or larger numbers of requests must be kept in flight by the DRAM memory controller to sustain high bandwidth utilization. For DDR3 SDRAM memory systems, the task of sustaining high bandwidth utilization is made even more complex by timing constraints such as t_{FAW} and t_{RRD}, timing constraints designed to limit the rate of row activation commands in DDR3 SDRAM devices and provide a relatively constant power envelope with increasing DRAM device data rates.

The complexity of the various inter-related constraints in DRAM memory system performance characteristics means that sustaining high bandwidth utilization in a high speed DRAM memory system is a multi-dimensional optimization problem, where sustainable bandwidth depends on factors such as DRAM memory system configuration, DRAM timing parameter values, workload-specific request access sequences, and memory controller sophistication. Fortunately, the increasing sophistication will serve to keep memory system architects gainfully employed for a long time to come.

PART III

Disk

I love bass guitar, because it has so little to do, yet it's so important.

— Brian Eno

CHAPTER 16

Overview of Disks

Disk technology has advanced tremendously in the past few years. Providing virtually unlimited on-line storage at extremely low cost, it enables highly complex software to be created without worry about size limitation, as well as frees users from having to be conscientious about what and how much data to retain. While disk storage may not be the central engine of a computer, its dynamic growth and development certainly played a pivotal role in fostering the tremendous advancement of computer systems from their early days to where they are today. Imagine what the personal computer would be like if its secondary storage had a capacity of only tens of megabytes instead of the tens of gigabytes that we now take for granted.

From its original inception as a double-freezer-size storage device for accounting application, the impact of disk-based storage has now gone beyond computer systems. It is moving into our everyday lives as pervasive embedded devices in consumer products such as digital video recorders, cameras, music players, automotive navigation systems, cell phones, etc. While the basic principles of disk drives remain the same, such applications call for a different set of requirements and performance characteristics.

Despite today's disk drives becoming commodity products, the fact remains that a disk drive is a highly complex electro-mechanical system encompassing decades of finely honed research on a vast multitude of diverse disciplines. They run the gamut of physics, chemistry, material science, tribology, electrical and electronics engineering, mechanical engineering, coding theory, computer science, and manufacturing science. Part III of this book presents a high-level discussion of disk drive technologies involving these topics, just sufficient for the reader to understand how a disk drive works. This provides the background knowledge to study some of the design issues and trade-offs that can affect the performance of a disk drive and disk-based storage subsystems. Emphasis on performance discussion is the major attribute that distinguishes this book from other previous books on disk drives.

While the disk section of this book is focused on the physical disk drive itself, there are two supporting software constituents that reside in the host system, namely the file system and the disk driver. Unlike the DRAM main memory which a user's program makes direct access to, an operating system typically provides the service for storing and retrieving data to and from a disk-based storage on behalf of the application program. The file system and the disk driver are the two operating system components providing this service. The reader is assumed to have some general knowledge about file systems and disk drivers.

16.1 History of Disk Drives

Before the invention of the magnetic disk drive, magnetic tapes, introduced by IBM in 1953, were the dominant mode for secondary storage. The performance disadvantages of tapes are obvious. To locate a piece of data, the tape must be sequentially searched, which can easily take many seconds and even minutes. A different kind of device having random-access capability would provide much better performance and therefore be more desirable. In 1950, Engineering Research Associates of Minneapolis built the first commercial magnetic drum storage unit for the U.S. Navy, the ERA 110. It could store 1 million bits of

FIGURE 16.1: The first disk drive, the IBM RAMAC 305.

data. Magnetic drums, announced in 1953 by IBM but not shipped until December of 1954, allowed for fast random access of data, but were not able to achieve as high a recording density as tapes. The higher cost of magnetic drums limited their use to serving only as main memory for the IBM 650, the first commercial general-purpose computer from IBM.

In 1952, Reynold Johnson of IBM, a prolific inventor of electro-mechanical devices, was asked to start a new research team in San Jose, CA. One of his mandates was to create a better technology for fast access to large volumes of data. It was decided early on to use inductive magnetic recording as the base technology, as it was a proven technology with the magnetic tapes and drums. The open question was what configuration the new device should be for achieving fast random access at low cost. In the end, a new, flat platter design, as first reported in 1952 by Jacob Rabinow of the National Bureau of Standards, was chosen over a simpler cylinder concept. Johnson accurately foresaw its better potential for future improvements.

RAMAC (Random-Access Method of Accounting Control), as the first disk drive[1] system was designated, was successfully demonstrated in 1955 [Stevens 1981, 1998]. The 1-ton, double-freezer-size disk drive (see Figure 16.1) consisted of fifty 24″ diameter aluminum disks mounted on a common shaft. The shaft was driven by an AC motor spinning at 1200 rpm. The disks were coated on both sides with a magnetic iron oxide material, a variation of the paint primer used for the Golden Gate Bridge, so there were 100 recording surfaces. The whole disk stack was served by two read/write heads shuttling up and down the disk stack to access the selected platter (see Figure 16.2). Data is stored on 100 concentric recording tracks per surface. The original RAMAC had a total capacity of 5 million characters (7 bits each), achieved with an areal density of about 2000 bits per square inch. The linear bit

---

[1]Up until the 1990s, disk drive was also called DASD (pronounced "des-dee") for direct-access-storage-device, a term coined by IBM.

FIGURE 16.2: Close-up of IBM RAMAC 305.

density varied from 100 bits per inch at the innermost track to 55 bits per inch at the outermost track.[2] The average access time for any record was around 1 s, a remarkable achievement at the time. The prototype was so successful that in 1956 it was marketed as RAMAC 305, the first commercial magnetic disk drive.

16.1.1 Evolution of Drives

Since the beginning, and continuing to today, four major forces drive the continual developments and evolutions in disk drive technologies, namely capacity, cost, performance, and reliability. Computer users are always hungry for more storage space. In the early days, only the biggest systems of Fortune 500 companies could afford to add a disk drive to their machines. Lowering the cost would help to expand the number and the variety of applications. While faster than tapes, disk drives were, are, and always will be orders of magnitude slower than the host system's main memory. There is always the pressure for drives to narrow this gap, especially with the ever-improving main memory

speed a moving target. Finally, with more and more critical information being placed on-line, the reliability of disk drives where such data is stored becomes more and more critical. Data integrity and data availability are both not only desirable, but absolutely essential in many cases.

Over the past half century, disk drives have undergone many improvements over the original RAMAC [Harker et al. 1981]; yet the underlying principles of operation remain essentially the same. While evolutions in the disk drive came in many forms and occurred in different components, they all have a common theme: miniaturization. It is the key to increasing the recording density, lowering cost, and improving performance. Oftentimes, miniaturization was achieved by coming up with more integrated, and sometimes simpler, designs. As a result, reliability and manufacturing efficiency were also improved. The relentless pursuit of better performance and higher reliability created many intriguing problems and challenges and fostered the inventions of some interesting approaches.

One key invention in the realization of the disk drive was to "fly" the read/write head over the recording surface with a constant, but close spacing. In the original RAMAC, this was achieved with a hydrostatic (pressurized) air bearing, wherein compressed air was forced out of tiny holes on the head's surface. One early and very important evolution was the introduction of the hydrodynamic (self-acting) air bearing utilizing a contoured structure called a *slider* to carry the head. This important simplification, introduced in 1962 in the IBM 1301, eliminated the need for compressed air. This made it feasible for each recording surface to have its own dedicated head, something that was not practical if compressed air was required. Any disk surface can now be selected by electronically activating its associated head. As a result, the average access time was drastically improved, to 165 ms in the IBM 1301. Most of the subsequent improvements in slider design were mainly in reducing its dimensions. The latest femto slider has a dimension of less than 1 mm × 1 mm.

---

[2]Recording density varied because each track held the same number of bits.

In 1963, the concept of a removable disk pack was introduced. The IBM 1311 operated on swappable disk packs, each consisting of six 14-in. diameter disks. As the cost of a total disk subsystem was still very high at the time, this technique, borrowed from tapes, allowed the cost to be amortized over many times the capacity of a single disk stack. However, off-line storage would not have the access performance of on-line storage. Removable disk packs became the dominant form of disk drives for the next 13 years until fixed spindle drives returned in the IBM 3350. While fixed spindle remains the dominant disk drive configuration today, the removable disk pack concept continued to appear in various products, such as the once popular Iomega ZIP drive and, of course, the ubiquitous 5 1/4" floppy disks and 3 1/2" diskettes. Removable disk format is also the mainstay of all optical disk drives.

The concept of integrating the disks and the head arm assembly as a sealed unit was introduced by IBM in 1973 in the IBM 3340. Nicknamed the Winchester drive (it had two spindles with 30 MB each, thus "30/30 Winchester"), its concept of an integrated heads and disks assembly can be considered to be the predecessor of all of today's hard drives (see head disk assembly, HDA discussion in Chapter 17, Section 17.2.9).

Up until the 1970s, disk drives remained big and expensive and were used exclusively in the realm of large computer systems. In 1980, Seagate revolutionized the disk drive industry by introducing the ST506, a 5 1/4" form factor disk drive for the nascent personal computer market. Eventually, the PC disk drive market far exceeded the enterprise storage market in terms of volume shipment. Undoubtedly, the personal computer would not have reached its success today if it was not for the availability of rapidly increasing capacity on-line storage at an ever-decreasing price.

Perhaps the most noticeable feature in the evolution of disk drives is its external dimension, dictated by the size of the disk platter being used. The RAMAC's 24" disk platters gave way to 14" disks in 1963 when the IBM 1311 was introduced. This became the *de facto* standard for the next 16 years, not to be changed until the first 8" diameter disk was introduced in 1979. Seagate introduced the 5 1/4" form factor in 1980. The first 3 1/2" form factor drive was introduced by Rodime

in 1983. Prairie Tek shipped the first 2 1/2" disk drive in 1988. As people started to realize the feasibility of the disk drive being used as a mass storage device outside the confines of computing, different sub-2" form factors were explored for various mobile applications. The 1.8" form factor was first pioneered by Integral Peripherals and MiniStor around 1991. In 1993, HP introduced the 21-MB Kitty Hawk, a 1.3" disk drive, but that form factor failed to take off. In 1999, IBM introduced the 1-in. microdrive, with a capacity of 340 MB at the time of introduction. Reaching a capacity of 8 GB in 2006, today it is successfully being used in digital cameras and MP3 players. The evolution history of disk diameter is plotted in Figure 16.3.

Control of early disk drive operations was handled entirely by an external controller often residing in the host computer. IPI (Intelligent Peripheral Interface) and, later, SMD (Storage Module Device) were some of the early standard interfaces used in disk drives for mainframes and minicomputers in the 1970s. The interface used in the first 5.25" disk drive ST-506, introduced in 1980, became a *de facto* standard for microcomputers until it was supplanted by ESDI (Enhanced Small Device Interface) and then eventually replaced by SCSI (Small Computer Standard Interface).

As disk drives acquired more functionality and intelligence, control gradually migrated into the drive to be handled internally and autonomously. SCSI was introduced in 1983 and officially became an ANSI standard in 1986 as X3.131-1986. The IDE (Integrated Device Electronics)/ATA (Advanced Technology Architecture)

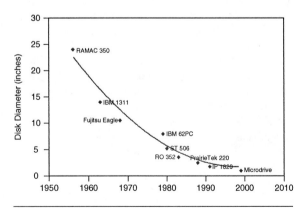

FIGURE 16.3: Evolution of disk diameter.

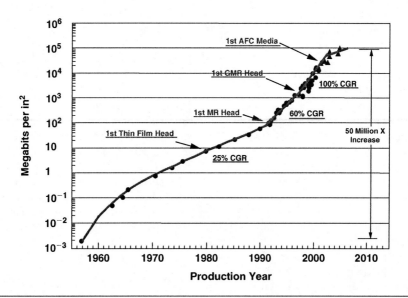

FIGURE 16.4: Evolution of areal density. Actual products of IBM/Hitachi-GST. Courtesy of Ed Grochowski of Hitachi Global Storage Technologies. CGR = compound growth rate.

interface,[3] a simpler and lower cost alternative to SCSI, was first introduced in products around 1987, though it did not become an ANSI standard until 1994 as X3.221-1994. The first high-performance Fiber Channel (FC) interface disk drives were shipped in 1997. Both SCSI and ATA are parallel interfaces, while FC is serial. Parallel interface suffers the disadvantage of bulky cables and short cable length. As a result, serial ATA (SATA) and serial attached SCSI (SAS) have recently been developed and standardized and will completely replace their parallel counterparts within a few years. Details on interface are covered in Chapter 20.

Evolutions of many of the less visible technologies within a disk drive, such as the recording head, media, codes, etc., are equally important, but not covered here and will be discussed in Chapter 17.

16.1.2 Areal Density Growth Trend

One of the most important parameters for a disk drive is its areal density, which is the number of bits that can be recorded per square inch. For a given disk diameter, this parameter determines the amount of data that can be stored on each platter. This, in turn, dictates the total storage capacity of a disk drive given the number of platters it contains. Even though there are many other contributing factors, ultimately, this is the single most important parameter that governs the cost per megabyte of a disk drive. It is the incredible and consistent rapid growth rate of areal density over the past 30 years that has driven the storage cost of disk drives down to the level that makes it still the technology of choice for on-line data storage. Areal density has reached the point where it is economically feasible to miniaturize disk drives, pushing them to fast becoming ubiquitous in our daily lives as tiny embedded components in many mobile products. As will be explained in Chapter 19, areal density also has a profound influence on performance.

The original RAMAC 305 had a lowly areal density of only 2000 bits per square inch. In late 2005, with the introduction of perpendicular recording, areal density had grown to an astounding 200 Gbits per square inch. This represents a growth of 100 million folds. The evolutionary history of areal density growth is summarized in Figure 16.4.

---

[3]It is nowadays commonly called simply ATA.

Some of the technology improvements that have enabled areal density growth are the following:

- Thinner magnetic coating; improved magnetic properties
- Head design
- Fabrication for smaller heads/sliders
- Flying height; reduced spacing between head and magnetic material, resulting in higher linear recording density
- Accuracy of head positioning servo, enabling tracks to be closer

Areal density, being a two-dimensional entity, consists of two components. The recording density in the radial direction of a disk is measured in terms of numbers of recording tracks per inch, or *tpi* (recording tracks are discussed in Chapter 18, Section 18.2). The recording density along a track is measured in terms of bits per inch, or *bpi*. For a rotating storage device spinning at a constant angular speed, the highest bpi is at the innermost diameter, or *ID*, of the recording area (a more detailed discussion can be found in Chapter 18). The product of tpi and bpi at the ID defines the areal

density of a disk drive. The evolution history of bpi and tpi growth is plotted in Figure 16.5.

To increase the areal density by a factor of 2, it might seem reasonable that bpi and tpi each be increased by a factor of $\sqrt{2}$. However, even though bpi and tpi are both components of recording density, they are, in part, affected by different technologies and mechanisms. Since 1990, tpi has been growing at a faster rate than bpi. As can be observed in Figure 16.5, bpi has roughly been increasing at an annual compound growth rate of 30% in recent years. On the other hand, the compound growth rate of tpi has been roughly 40% during the same period. Chapter 19 will discuss the impact of tpi and bpi on drive performance.

16.2 Principles of Hard Disk Drives

While the first airplane flown by the Wright brothers at Kitty Hawk in 1903 may look quite different from today's Boeing 777, many of the fundamental principles for powered flight have not changed. Both have wings to provide lift, engines to propel the plane forward, a movable rudder to control the yaw,

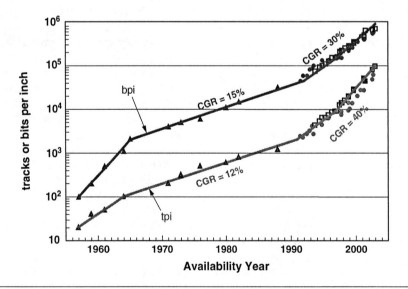

FIGURE 16.5: Evolution of linear recording density bpi and track density tpi. Actual products of IBM/Hitachi Global Storage Technologies. From multiple sources. CGR = compound growth rate.

FIGURE 16.6: Internals of a Hitachi Global Storage Technologies Microdrive™ device.

and elevators to control the pitch. A similar parallel can be drawn between the first RAMAC machine and today's disk drives, such as the microdrive (Figure 16.6). The physical appearances and dimensions of the two storage devices may seem very different, but their working principles and main components are quite similar, as explained below.

16.2.1 Principles of Rotating Storage Devices

The hard disk drive is not the only type of rotating platter storage device. The very first such device of this type is, of course, the phonograph, which stored audio information in analog form. Different types of rotating storage devices use different recording media for storage. Mechanical storage devices, such as the phonograph and the still-experimental atomic force microscopy (AFM) technology, store data as indentations on a recording surface. Optical storage devices, including CDs and DVDs, use variations in reflectivity for recording data. Magnetic storage devices record data with the magnetic polarization of ferromagnetic material.

Regardless of the recording method and the recording media, all rotating storage devices share some common features and operate on the same principles. They all use a platter to hold the recording material on one or both surfaces. They all have "heads," which are transducers for converting the signal extracted from the recorded media (magnetic field, reflected light, or mechanical motion) into electrical signals, or vice-versa. A read element in the head is used to detect and retrieve the recorded data. For the read-only type of storage devices, such as DVD-ROM, this is the only type of head needed. For recordable devices, such as magnetic disks and DVD-RW, the head also contains a write element to write (record) the data onto the recording material. The functioning of the head and its elements depends on the type of storage mechanism.

The location of a data bit on a storage disk can be specified with two parameters or, more precisely, two coordinates. The first parameter is the radial distance from the center of the disk. This parameter defines a circle. The second parameter is the angular position of the location from a fixed reference axis. This is as shown in Figure 16.7. To access a bit of data, the head must be at the location where it is recorded or to be recorded. This can be accomplished in one of two ways: either the head moves to the bit location, or the bit location can be brought to where the head is. In all rotating storage devices, a combination of both methods i s used. The head is mounted on some movable mechanism which can place the head at any desired radial position. Again, the structure of the movable mechanism depends on the type of storage, thus the mechanism for carrying the laser and mirror used in optical recording is completely different than the structure for holding the magnetic recording head. The radial positioning of the head is commonly referred to as "seek." Once it is at the target radial position, it essentially becomes stationary, making only minute adjustments to stay on track.

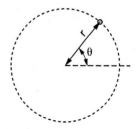

FIGURE 16.7: The angular and radial coordinates of a location on a disk surface.

Next, the disk is rotated to bring the desired bit location to where the head is located. Unlike the head, the disk is constantly rotating. This is for performance reasons. First, the disk is much heavier than the head, and so it takes much more time and power to move it to a new angular orientation from a standstill. Second, data is accessed in quantities much larger than just a single bit. By constantly rotating the disk, many data bits are continuously brought under the head. An electric motor spins the disk platter, some at a constant rotational speed and some at a variable speed depending on the head location so as to maintain a constant linear speed of the recorded material under the head. More about these two methods will be discussed in Chapter 18.

All rotating storage devices have electronics for controlling the rotation of the disks and electronics for controlling the servo mechanism of the head positioning. The servo affects the seek time, which is an important factor in performance, and it will be discussed in Chapters 17 and 18 for hard disk drives. There are circuitries for converting between users' data and the actual recorded signal. Details of this will be covered in Chapter 17, Section 17.3.3, for magnetic recording. Finally, there are electronics to handle the interface between the storage device and the host to which the device is attached, which will be discussed in Chapter 20.

More than one platter can be mounted in the same motor spindle for increased capacity. This adds a third dimension to the storage device, as illustrated in Figure 16.8. Since moving a shared head in this z-dimension,

as was done with the original RAMAC, is a very slow mechanical process, it is desirable to have a dedicated head for each recording surface, as Figure 16.8 illustrates. Selection of storage location in this dimension then becomes simply electronically activating the right head. However, some recording technology, such as optical recording, may not be possible to implement such configuration in a cost effective manner.

16.2.2 Magnetic Rotating Storage Device— Hard Disk Drive

Magnetic recording technology is used in magnetic tapes as well as both fixed and removable media disk drives. Whether analog or digital, it consists of some type of magnetic storage medium, read and write heads to detect and induce a magnetic field, and recording channel electronics. The digital form of magnetic recording technology additionally requires data encoding and clocking logic for conversion between digital data and analog waveforms. It also must have some mechanism for controlling the designed spacing between the heads and the storage medium.

The rotating magnetic storage device is the result of combining magnetic recording technology with rotating recording technology. The resulting components of a magnetic hard disk drive are discussed in greater detail in Chapter 17. Refer to Chapter 17, Figure 17.8, for a view of some of these components. Briefly, a disk drive consists of one or more platters of magnetic media spun by an electric motor. When a biaxially oriented, polyethylene terephthalate material is used as the substrate of the disk platter, the storage device is a flexible media disk. When an aluminum-magnesium alloy or glass is used as the substrate material, the storage device is a hard disk drive. The recording media for magnetic hard disks is discussed in Chapter 17, Section 17.2.1. A magnetic field sensing read head and a magnetic field inducing write head are used for accessing data on each recording surface. Magnetic recording heads are covered in Chapter 17, Section 17.2.3. The mechanical structure that holds the heads is called the arm, and the mechanism for positioning the heads is called the actuator. They are described in Chapter 17, Section 17.2.4.

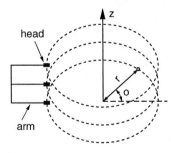

FIGURE 16.8: Multiple platters add a third dimension to a disk drive. Each ring represents a track on a different recording surface.

16.3 Classifications of Disk Drives

In the early days of data storage, there was only one class of disk drives—large disk drives attached to big computers. That picture began to change with the introduction of ST506 for the personal computer. Today, there are several ways disk drives can be classified.

16.3.1 Form Factor

One way to classify disk drives would be according to the dimensions of its external enclosure, or *form factor*. For reason of interchangeability, today drives usually come in one of four main standard sizes, namely 3.5", 2.5", 1.8", and 1". This dimension refers to the width of the sealed disk drive unit. The depth of the unit is longer than its width and is more or less also standard. The height is shorter and may come in one of two or three standard sizes for a given form factor. Around the 1980s, the 5 1/4" form factor, as pioneered by the ST506, was dominant, but had essentially disappeared by mid-1990s. Form factor alone is not always a good way to classify drives because two different drives with very different technologies inside and with very different functionality, performance, and reliability can have the same external form factor.

16.3.2 Application

Another way to classify a disk drive would be according to the platform in which it is being used. In the information technology (IT) world, traditionally there are server class drives for use in higher end or enterprise systems, desktop class drives for use in personal computers and low-end workstations, and mobile class drives for use in laptop or notebook computers. Each class of drives has different characteristics and requirements because of the application environment it is being used in. Server drives need to have high reliability and performance. Desktop drives must have low cost due to the highly price-competitive personal computer market. Low power consumption is an obvious yet important criterion for mobile drives. Today, the boundaries for this way of classification are starting to blur. As tremendous progress has been made in the reliability of all disk drives, some higher end system builders are beginning to use desktop drives in certain applications to take advantage of their low cost.

Almost coincidental with the start of the new millennium, disk drives have begun to move outside of the IT world and into consumer electronics (CE) applications. Such applications include digital video recorders, MP3 music players, game boxes, still and video digital cameras, cell phones, PDAs, and automotive applications such as GPS guidance systems. The list will continue to expand as the price of disk storage continues to fall. So far, most of these diverse applications have rather similar performance characteristics, and low cost is an important attribute for the disk drives being used. While highest possible capacity is always desirable, the size and power limitations of these consumer devices naturally dictate the form factor of the drives to be used. Thus, 1" microdrives are used in cameras and music players. On the other hand, home video recorders, which do not have any size or power limitation, are built with 3.5" disk drives to provide the most hours of recording.

16.3.3 Interface

Yet another way to classify disk drives is by the type of interface the drive provides. Current choices of interface are Fiber Channel (FC), parallel SCSI (Small Computer System Interface), parallel ATA (Advanced Technology Attachment), and the emerging serial ATA (SATA) and serial attached SCSI (SAS). A more detailed discussion of interface can be found in Chapter 20. Server class drives are available in either FC or SCSI interface. Desktop, mobile, and CE drives invariably come with an ATA interface, either the original parallel version or the newer serial flavor. Server class drives are more than twice as expensive as desktop drives. This association with interface leads some people to mistakenly think that SCSI drives are expensive because of the SCSI interface, when it is mostly the more costly technologies that go into a server class drive for achieving higher reliability and performance that makes it more expensive. As mentioned before, some storage systems are starting

TABLE 16.1   Classifications of disk drives by form factors, by applications, and by interfaces

	3.5"	2.5"	1.8"	1.0"
Server	FC, SCSI	FC, SCSI		
Desktop	ATA			
Mobile		ATA		
Video recorder	ATA			
Game Box		ATA		
Music, automotive			ATA	
Camera, music, cell phone				ATA

to use ATA desktop drives in certain applications to achieve a lower system cost.

The above various ways of classifying disk drives are summarized in Table 16.1. This is only a snapshot of 2007. A few years from now, the composition of this table may look different. Note that both SCSI and ATA can be either parallel or serial.

16.4   Disk Performance Overview

This section is a brief introduction to disk performance. It will define a few terms and set the background for the in-depth performance discussions that are to follow in some of the coming chapters. In particular, Chapter 19 discusses how a drive's physical design parameters can affect the user performance. Chapter 21 presents various methods of operation within a disk drive to improve its performance. Testing of drive performance is discussed in Chapter 23.

16.4.1   Disk Performance Metrics

There is no single standard for defining disk performance. Depending on the requirements of the application or user, disk performance can be evaluated in a variety of ways. The most commonly used metrics of drive performance are discussed here.

Response Time and Service Time

A common measure of disk performance is the *response time*. This measures the elapsed time from when a command[4] is issued to the disk drive to when data transfer is completed and the disk drive signals completion of the command. When a command is issued to the disk drive one at a time (this is called *synchronous I/O*), response time is the same as the drive's *service time*. Response time is basically a measure of how fast a drive is in servicing a request. Hence, it is a measurement of speed. Chapter 19 discusses many of the factors influencing response time.

The response time of one single particular I/O is usually not very interesting. The result of a sample of one is also often misleading. Thus, it is more common to quantify a drive's performance by the *average response time* for a large number of requests. Sometimes, much information about the performance of a drive is lost by quantifying it with just a single number. A more illuminating method is to report the distribution of response times, i.e., by the use of a histogram. Finally, for better understanding of the performance behavior of a disk drive, it may be desirable to report response time by I/O type, such as reads and writes, random and sequential, etc. This is discussed further in Chapter 23, Section 23.2.

---

[4]A request or command to a drive is oftentimes referred to as an I/O (input/output) operation or request. In this book, the terms request, command, I/O, and I/O request are used interchangeably.

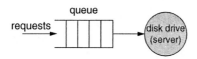

FIGURE 16.9: A traditional single queue, single server model.

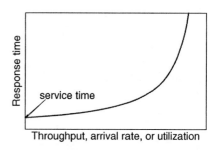

FIGURE 16.10: General shape of response time versus throughput curve for a queueing system.

Throughput

Another measurement of drive performance is the *throughput,* or its capacity to handle work. Throughput is commonly measured in one of two ways: (i) the number of I/Os per second (*IOPS*) or (ii) the amount of data transferred per second, or *transfer rate,* often stated in megabytes per second (MB/s). Some people refer to transfer rate as *bandwidth.* These two throughput measurements are related by how much data is transferred for each I/O request (*block size*),

$$\text{IOPS} \times \text{average block size} = \text{transfer rate} \quad \textbf{(EQ 16.1)}$$

and, hence, are equ0ivalent ways of describing performance.

Throughput, by its very nature, is measured by the aggregate of many I/Os. Thus, "average" is implied here. As with response time, it may also be desirable to report throughput according to I/O type. IOPS is commonly used for reporting random I/O performance, while transfer rate is used for reporting sequential I/O performance.

Response Time vs. Throughput

When multiple commands are allowed to be queued up inside a disk drive, as shown in Figure 16.9, then the response time will also include the time that a command sits in the queue waiting for its turn to be serviced plus its actual service time. Response time and throughput are somewhat related and are generally inversely proportional to each other. Also, a drive with fast service time will yield high throughput. Their relationship is governed by queueing theory [Kleinrock 1975, Breuer and Baum 2006]. In general, it looks something like the graph in Figure 16.10. Throughput (IOPS), as seen by the user, is the rate at which the user's requests arrive at the disk drive. A server's *utilization* is defined as

$$\text{utilization} = \text{arrival rate} \times \text{service time}^5 \quad \textbf{(EQ 16.2)}$$

Assuming that the disk drive has a constant average service time, then utilization is directly proportional to arrival rate. Therefore, Figure 16.10 has the same general shape whether throughput, arrival rate, or utilization is plotted on the *x*-axis; only the scale will be different. The precise shape of the curve is determined by what the distributions of the I/O arrival time and the service time are. For example, when both times are exponentially distributed,[6] the curve is given by

$$\text{response time} = \text{service time} / (1 - \text{utilization}) \quad \textbf{(EQ 16.3)}$$

The service time is, of course, determined by the performance characteristics of the disk drive.

For detailed discussions on queueing, refer to Kleinrock [1975] and Brewer and Baum [2006]. Section 4 of Chapter 6 in the computer architecture book of Hennesy and Patterson [1996] also has a nice introductory discussion of this subject.

---

[5]Equivalent forms of this equation are *utilization = service time/inter-arrival time* and *utilization = arrival rate/service rate.*

[6]In queueing theory, such a single server queue is called an M/M/1 queue.

16.4.2 Workload Factors Affecting Performance

For a given disk drive, the response time and throughput that it can produce and be measured are dependent on the workload that it is given. The characteristics of a workload that can influence performance are the following:

- Block size: The sizes of the I/O requests clearly affect the response time and the throughput, since, when everything else is equal, a large block size takes longer to transfer than a small block size.
- Access pattern: Sequential, random, and other in between types of accesses will be discussed in greater detail in Chapters 21 and 23.
- Footprint: How much of the total available space in a disk drive is accessed affects the performance. A small fraction of the disk being accessed means the seek distances between I/Os would be small, while a large fraction of the disk being accessed means longer seeks.
- Command type: Read performance can be different from write performance, especially if write caching is enabled in the disk drive. Reads afford the opportunity for read hits in the drive's cache which give much faster response time. Writing to the disk media may also take longer than reading from the media.
- Command queue depth: If both the disk drive and the host that it is attached to support queueing of multiple commands in the drive, throughput is affected by how deep a queue depth is being used. The deeper the queue is, the more choices are available for optimization and hence the higher the throughput. Command queueing will be discussed in Chapter 21.
- Command arrival rate: If command queueing is supported by the drive, response time is affected by the rate at which I/Os are being issued to the drive. If commands are issued at a higher rate, then more commands will be queued up in the drive,

and a newly arrived command will, on average, have to wait longer before it gets serviced. Hence, response time will be higher. This is discussed previously in Section 16.4.1.

16.4.3 Video Application Performance

Video recording is a relatively new application for disk drives, and it has a different performance requirement than computer applications. Video needs to have the data ready to display every frame of a picture without miss. As long as data is guaranteed to be ready, there is no advantage to having the data ready quickly way ahead of time. Thus, the metric of performance for video application is how many streams of video that a disk drive can support and still guarantee on-time data delivery for all the streams. A home entertainment center in the near future will be required to record multiple programs and, at the same time, send different video streams to different rooms with support for fast-forward, pause, and other VCR-like functions. This type of throughput quantification has less to do with the speed of the disk drive rather than by how data is laid out on a drive, how the drive manages its buffer, and how a drive does its scheduling.

16.5 Future Directions in Disks

The demise of the disk drive as the most cost-effective way of providing cheap secondary storage at an acceptable level of performance has every now and then been predicted by some over the years. Such predictions have always turned out to be premature or "grossly exaggerated" as Mark Twain would put it. Magnetic hard disk drives will continue to be the dominant form of secondary storage for the foreseeable future. The transition of magnetic recording from that where magnetization is in the plane of the disk (*horizontal magnetic recording*) to one where magnetization is normal to the plane of the disk (*perpendicular magnetic recording*) is starting to take place and will help sustain the current pace of areal density growth. This continual growth in recording density will help to maintain the trend toward smaller and smaller form factors for disk drives.

As the cost of disk storage continues to drop, its application will expand beyond on-line data storage to near-line and even off-line data storage. These are applications traditionally served by tapes. To handle the large number of disk drives required for such applications in an enterprise system, the architecture of massive array of idle disks (MAID) has been created. In this architecture, at any point in time only a small fraction of the disks in the storage system are powered up and active to receive data, with the remaining vast majority of drives powered down. The drives being powered up are rotated among all the drives to even out their usage. This will significantly reduce the amount of power being consumed and, at the same time, extend the life of the disk drives.

Disk drives will also find more and more applications outside of the computing world. Already, disk drive-based personal video recorders (PVR) replacing VHS machines seem to be almost a foregone conclusion at this point. Other examples of applications in consumer electronics have already been mentioned earlier in Section 16.3. The penetration of disk drives into those markets can be expected to grow.

Just as disk drives today have become a commodity product, so too will small RAID (Redundant Array of Independent Disks) systems. In a few years it may become commonplace for us to have in our personal computer not a disk drive, but a storage "brick" inside of which are multiple disk drives, arrayed in some sort of RAID configuration. Such bricks will be the field replaceable units, rather than the individual drives themselves.

CHAPTER 17

The Physical Layer

This chapter presents a high-level overview of magnetic recording and the major physical components of a disk drive. Continual research and development have been widely conducted for the past 50 years in the many disciplines involved, driven by intense competition not only among disk drive makers, but also from other competing technologies eager to supplant disk drives as the low-cost storage technology of choice. The goal of this chapter is to provide enough general background knowledge of how a disk drive is created so as to facilitate the understanding of other chapters to follow.

The chapter is divided into three main sections. Section 17.1 is a brief review of the physics behind magnetic recording. Section 17.2 describes the electromechanical and magnetic components of a disk drive. The electronics integrated into today's disk drives are discussed in Section 17.3.

17.1 Magnetic Recording

An essentially non-mathematical overview of magnetic recording principles is discussed here, introducing some of the more frequently used terms along the way [Bertram 1994, Mee & Daniel 1996]. The ingredients of magnetic recording are materials that can be permanently magnetized, magnetic fields, and the interaction between the two. Permanently magnetizable materials are called *ferromagnetic* materials, and they provide the storage media for recording due to the non-volatility of its magnetization. Externally applied magnetic fields are used to induce magnetism in ferromagnetic materials and, hence, are the means for recording when such fields can be

controlled. Finally, by sensing the magnetic fields of magnetized ferrormagnetic material, what has been recorded can be detected and retrieved. That, in a nut shell, is how data is stored, written, and read in magnetic recording.

Permanent magnets occur in nature, and their existence, as well as their magnetic properties, was discovered many hundreds of years ago. A magnet always comes with two poles of opposite polarity. Hence, a magnet is one form of a *magnetic dipole*. A dipole is simply a pair of magnetic poles of opposite polarity. While these two polarities are commonly referred to as north (N) and south (S), in scientific literature they are oftentimes labelled as positive (+) and negative (−) poles instead. By convention, lines drawn in diagrams to represent magnetic fields are shown as flowing from the +ve (N) pole to the −ve (S) pole, as illustrated in Figure 17.1. A magnet can be simply represented by a thick arrow pointing from the −ve pole to the +ve pole; the $+/-$ or N/S labelling is superfluous.

17.1.1 Ferromagnetism

Ferromagnetic materials are substances that can be permanently magnetized, which means that once they have been magnetized they stay magnetized, even after the mechanism or driving force for magnetizing them has been removed. Iron, nickel, cobalt, and some of the rare earth elements such as gadolinium and dysprosium are ferromagnetic materials. One can also make amorphous (non-crystalline) ferromagnetic metallic alloys by rapid quenching of certain liquid alloys.

The spin of an electron has a magnetic dipole moment and creates a magnetic field. In many

615

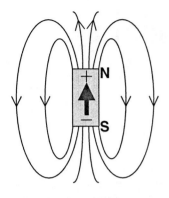

FIGURE 17.1: Representation of a magnet and its magnetic field.

materials the electrons come in pairs of opposite spin, cancelling one another's dipole moments. However, atoms with unpaired electrons will have a net magnetic moment from spin. Ferromagnetic materials have such electrons, and they exhibit a long-range ordering phenomenon at the atomic level in which the unpaired electron spins line up parallel with each other in a region called a *domain*. This long-range order is remarkable in that the magnetic moments of neighboring atoms are locked into a rigid parallel order over a large number of atoms in spite of the thermal agitation which tends to randomize any atomic-level order. Within the domain, the magnetic field is strong. In a bulk sample, however, the material will usually be unmagnetized because the many domains will themselves be randomly oriented with respect to one another. This is illustrated in Figure 17.2(a).

Ferromagnetism manifests itself in the fact that when a small external magnetic field is applied, the magnetic domains will line up with each other (as shown in Figure 17.2(b)), and the material is said to be magnetized. The driving magnetic field, now reinforced with the magnetic field generated by the magnetized material, will then be increased by a large factor which is expressed as the *relative permeability* of the material. Thus, a piece of

ferromagnetic material initially has little or no net magnetic moment. However, if it is placed in a strong enough external magnetic field, the domains will reorient in parallel with that field. Furthermore, and importantly, the domains of ferromagnetic materials will retain much of this new parallel orientation when the field is turned off, thus creating a permanent magnet.

Although this state of aligned domains is not a minimal-energy configuration, it is extremely stable. However, all ferromagnets have a maximum temperature where the ferromagnetic property disappears. This temperature is called the *Curie temperature*. As temperature increases, thermal oscillation, or entropy, competes with the ferromagnetic tendency for spins to align. When the temperature rises beyond the material's Curie temperature, the material can no longer maintain its state of magnetization without the aid of an external field.

17.1.2 Magnetic Fields

A *magnetic field* is a region of space where magnetic forces are present. Magnetic forces are produced by the movement of electrically charged particles. A wire carrying electrical current is really a stream of flowing electrons (moving in the opposite direction of the current, as defined by convention), and hence, it generates a magnetic field around it, as shown in Figure 17.3(a). The magnetic field created by one small current is weak. However, when the wire is wrapped around many times to form a coil, all the magnetic fields generated from each turn reinforce each other and result in a strong and nearly uniform magnetic field in the center of the coil. Such a coil is called a *solenoid*, as shown in Figure 17.3(b).

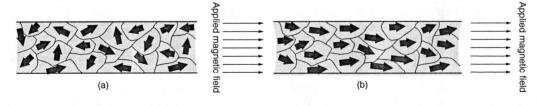

(a)   (b)

FIGURE 17.2: Domains of ferromagnetic materials: (a) before subject to external magnetic field and (b) with external magnetic field applied.

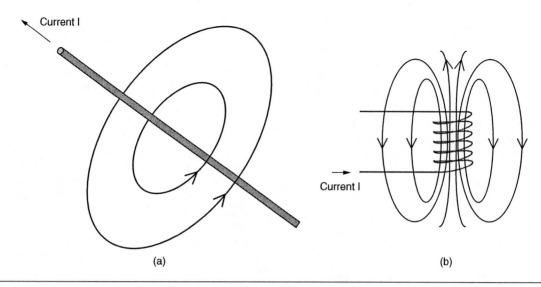

FIGURE 17.3: Current-induced magnetic fields: (a) a straight wire and (b) a solenoid.

The magnetic field of a solenoid is similar to that of a permanent magnet (shown earlier in Figure 17.1). This is not a coincidence. An electron orbiting around the nucleus of an atom is a form of charged particle in motion and, hence, creates a magnetic field. Additionally, electrons that rotate about their own axis (spin) also create a magnetic field from that motion. When that atom does not have another electron spinning in an opposite direction to cancel that magnetic field, the atom will have a net magnetic field. When a large assembly of such atoms is lined up in the same direction, as in ferromagnetic materials, their individual magnetic fields reinforce each other, and a strong net magnetic field becomes detectable externally.

The strength of a magnetic field is a measure of its magnetic force at a given location of the field. By convention, it is represented by the symbol H. Unfortunately, H and the other magnetic measurements to be defined here can be given in several different units. In an MKS (meter-kilogram-second) system, H is given in amperes per meter (A/m). In a CGS (centimeter-gram-second) system, it is given in oersted (1 oe = $(\frac{1}{4\pi}) \times 10^3$).

The *magnetization* of a magnetized material is defined as the density of its magnetic strength, called

dipole moment, i.e., dipole moment per unit volume. By convention, it is represented using the symbol M. In an MKS system, M is also given in amperes per meter (A/m). In a CGS system, it is given in electromagnetic units (emu) per cubic centimeter (1 emu/cc = 10^3 A/m).

The lines of force surrounding a permanent magnet are called its *magnetic flux*, denoted by the symbol F. The amount of flux per unit area perpendicular to the magnetic flow is called the *magnetic flux density*, also known as *magnetic induction*. It is usually represented with B. In an MKS system, it is given in webers per square meter (W/m^2), while in a CGS system, its unit is gauss (1 G = 10^{-4} W/m^2). In magnetism, B is oftentimes used in formulas instead of H. In free space, the relationship between H and B is given by

$$B = \mu_0 \times H \qquad \text{(EQ 17.1)}$$

where l_0 is called the *permeability* of free space, and it is assigned the value

$$\mu_0 = 4\pi \times 10^{-7} \qquad \text{(EQ 17.2)}$$

17.1.3 Hysteresis Loop

The capability of ferromagnets to stay magnetized after being subjected to an external magnetic field, i.e., to remember their magnetic history, is the very basis of magnetic recording. The magnetization M of a ferromagnetic material as a function of the externally applied magnetic field H is described by a *hysteresis loop* plot. Figure 17.4 shows a typical hysteresis loop. It can be seen from Figure 17.4 that the magnetization is not a unique function of the applied field, but depends on the state of the ferromagnetic material when the field is applied. This state is governed by the magnitude and the direction of previous applied fields.

Starting in the non-magnetized state of the ferromagnetic material, as the magnetic fields increases from 0 in the positive H direction, the magnetization of the material increases following the path of the dashed line, which is called the material's *magnetization curve*. Eventually, a maximum value of magnetization is reached, where increasing H further will not result in any additional increase in M. This is called the *saturation magnetization*, M_s. When the applied field H is now reduced toward 0, the magnetization M is also

reduced, but it no longer follows the magnetization curve; it follows the top curve of the hysteresis loop. At the point where no external magnetic field is applied, i.e., H = 0, the ferromagnetic material still exhibits a certain amount of magnetization. The value of this magnetization is called the *remanent magnetization*, M_r. A magnetic field must be applied in the negative H direction before the ferromagnetic material finally becomes demagnetized, i.e., M = 0. The value of H required to achieve demagnetization of the ferromagnet is called the *coercivity*, H_c. Thus, coercivity is a measure of how resistant the material is to demagnetization. Note that the hysteresis loop is completely symmetrical with respect to both the H and the M axes. Hence, the absolute values of M_s, M_r, and H_c are all independent of magnetic direction. The product $M_r \times H_c$ is a measure of the strength of the magnetic material.

Ferromagnetic materials can be broadly classified according to their magnetic behavior, which is manifested in their hysteresis loops. Figure 17.5(a) shows the hysteresis loop of a hard magnetic material. It is characterized by high coercivity and high remanence. Such materials are suitable for magnetic recording media. Figure 17.5(b) shows the hysteresis loop of a soft magnetic material. It is characterized by low coercivity and low remanence. Such materials are suitable for magnetic recording head applications.

Finally, a magnetic material has an *easy axis*, which is the direction that its magnetization prefers to point to. For the discussion in this chapter, we will assume magnetic recording materials that have easy axes parallel to the plane of recording. For such materials, longitudinal recording results, which is the type of magnetic recording used since the early days.

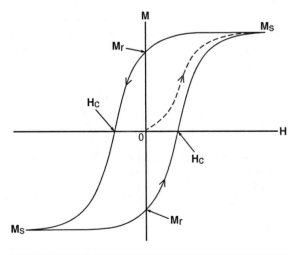

FIGURE 17.4: Hysteresis loop. The resulting amount of magnetization M when a magnetic field H is applied is dependent on the state of the ferromagnetic material.

17.1.4 Writing

Writing is the process of recording a pattern of magnetization on the recording medium. Ideally, saturated recording, in which magnetic fields of sufficient strength to induce saturation magnetization are applied to the recording material, should be used in magnetic recording for the storage of digital data. This is as opposed to analog recording, such as cassette tape music and VHS video, where magnetic fields

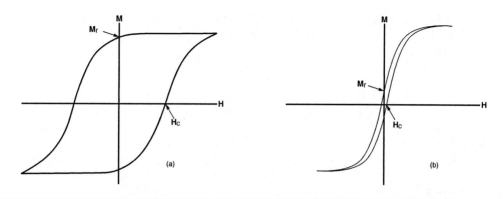

FIGURE 17.5: Hysteresis loops of magnetic materials: (a) hard magnetic material and (b) soft magnetic material.

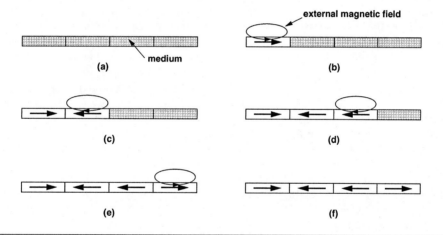

FIGURE 17.6: Write process example. (a) Medium before writing. Write magnetic field applied to (b) first compartment, (c) second compartment, (d) third compartment, and (e) fourth compartment, and (f) magnetic pattern in medium after writing.

corresponding to recording signals of continuously varying magnitude and less than what is required for saturation magnetization are applied to the recording media. Since only the polarity, or direction, of magnetization needs to be distinguished in digital storage, magnetizing the recording medium to saturation will produce the strongest possible signal the material can provide, thus maximizing the signal-to-noise ratio.

To illustrate the basic process of writing, consider a small, thin sample of magnetic medium and visualize

that this sample consists of four recording compartments, as shown in Figure 17.6(a). Note that these compartments are only conceptual; they do not actually exist predefined in a real disk. A tiny external magnetic field is locally applied to the first compartment, which results in a left-to-right magnetization being induced in that compartment. This is as shown in Figure 17.6(b). Since ferromagnetic material is used, a remanent magnetization will remain in that compartment even after the external field is removed. Next, an external magnetic field is applied to the second compartment.

This field is in the opposite direction of the previous field, and hence, a right-to-left magnetization is induced in the second compartment, as Figure 17.6(c) indicates. An external magnetic field, in the same direction as the previous field, is next applied to the third compartment, resulting in the third compartment being magnetized in the same polarity as the second compartment. Finally, a magnetic field in the opposite direction as that of the second and third compartments is applied to the fourth compartment, resulting in its left-to-right magnetization. When no more external fields are applied, the magnetic pattern of Figure 17.6(f) is left on the magnetic medium.

We have just described the basic principle of writing the magnetic recording media. The mechanism with which electrical signals representing user's data are converted to magnetic fields for writing is the function of the *write head* and the write channel electronics, which will be discussed later.

17.1.5 Reading

Reading is the process of determining the magnetic pattern that has been recorded in a medium. This is done by sensing the very weak magnetic field that emanates from the surface of each of the tiny magnetized compartments. Continuing with the above example, the magnetic fields just above the medium would look something like Figure 17.7.

Thus far, we have not defined how the magnetized compartments or their externally observable magnetic field can be used to represent binary data. Intuitively, one would think that the polarity of the recorded magnetization can be used directly to represent a 0 or a 1. For instance, we might define

left-to-right magnetization to represent 0 and right-to-left magnetization to represent 1. Then, in the above example 0110 would have been recorded in the four compartments of the medium. However, finding a transducer that can detect the magnetic orientation of such very weak fields reliably posed a challenge during the formative years of magnetic recording. Instead, a different technique was used in the very early days of magnetic recording which is still universally used today. This technique operates on the *change* in orientation of magnetization rather than the orientation itself. This change in orientation is referred to as a *transition*. In our example, there is a reversal of magnetic orientation at the boundary between the first compartment and the second compartment, and another reversal is between the third compartment and the fourth compartment. There is no reversal of magnetic orientation at the boundary between the second and third compartments. By convention, a magnetic field reversal represents a 1, and the absence of a field reversal is used to present a 0. Note that which way a field is reversed is immaterial. In our example, therefore, the recorded magnetic pattern represents the binary sequence 101. Due to this method of data representation, writing needs to be done one complete block (called a *sector*) at a time; it is not possible to only write singly an individual bit. By sensing the presence or absence of field orientation reversals, or transitions, recorded data is read.

The *read head* is the transducer that detects magnetic field reversals and outputs electrical signals that can be processed and interpreted. The mechanism of how it does the detection and conversion is dependent on what type of read head is used. Various kinds of read heads will be discussed later.

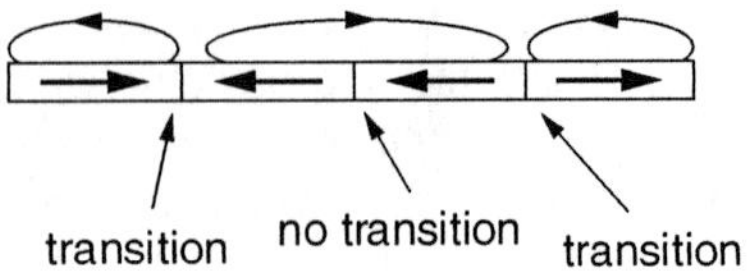

FIGURE 17.7: Magnetic field emanating from recorded medium.

17.2 Mechanical and Magnetic Components

While a disk drive's working components have not changed much over the years, its size and construction has evolved greatly [Harker et al. 1981]. The packaging of all these components into a disk drive has also undergone dramatic changes, thanks to continual miniaturization, from the double-freezer-size

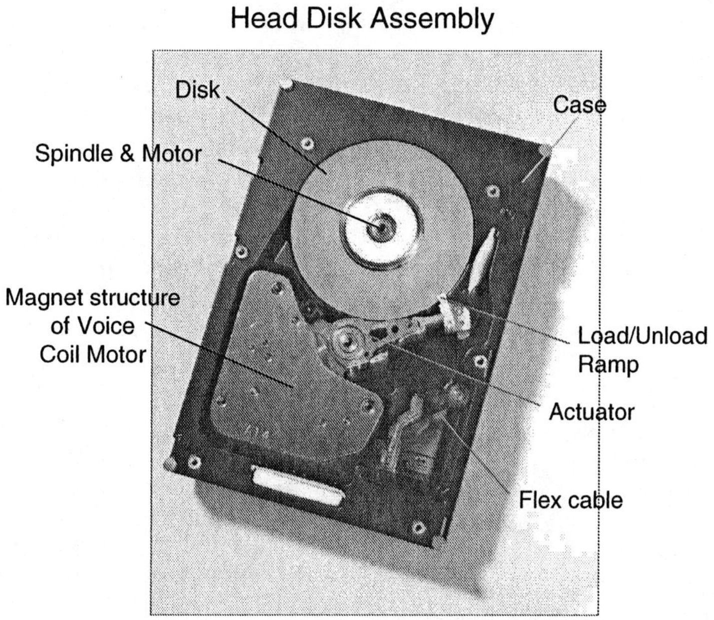

Head Disk Assembly

FIGURE 17.8: Major components of today's typical disk drive. The cover of a Hitachi Global Storage Technologies UltraStar™ 15K147 is removed to show the inside of a head-disk assembly. The actuator is parked in the load/unload ramp.

RAMAC to the washing machine-size disk drives of the 1970s and 1980s and, finally, to the palm-size disk drives of the 1990s and today. Today's disk drives all have their working components sealed inside an aluminum case, with an electronics card attached to one side. The components must be sealed because, with the very low flying height of the head over the disk surface, just a tiny amount of contaminant can spell disaster for the drive.

This section very briefly describes the various mechanical and magnetic components of a hard disk drive [Sierra 1990, Wang & Taratorin 1999, Ashar 1997, Mee & Daniel 1996, Mamun et al. 2006, Schwaderer & Wilson 1996]. The desirable characteristics of each of these components are discussed. The major physical components are illustrated in Figure 17.8, which shows an exposed view of a disk drive with the cover removed. The principles of operation for most components can be fully explained within this chapter. For the servo system, additional information will be required, and it will be described in Chapter 18.

17.2.1 Disks

The recording medium for hard disk drives is basically a very thin layer of magnetically hard material on a rigid circular substrate [Mee & Daniel 1996]. A flexible substrate is used for a flexible, or floppy, disk. Some of the desirable characteristics of recording media are the following:

- Thin substrate so that it takes up less space
- Light substrate so that it requires less power to spin
- High rigidity for low mechanical resonance and distortion under high rotational speed; needed for servo to accurately follow very narrow tracks
- Flat and smooth surface to allow the head to fly very low without ever making contact with the disk surface
- High coercivity (H_c) so that the magnetic recording is stable, even as areal density is increased

- High remanence (M_r) for good signal-to-noise ratio
- A square hysteresis loop for sharp transitions (to be discussed in Section 17.2.3)

Magnetic material is composed of *grains* of magnetic domains, as previously illustrated in Figure 17.2. The grain size of a material strongly affects its magnetic properties and the media transition noise. More grains at a transition boundary produce less noise and are therefore desirable. Yet, if grains size is decreased too much to accommodate higher tpi, the grains may become magnetically unstable.

Substrates

Up until the 1990s, aluminum was exclusively the material of choice for the hard disk substrate. More recently, electroless nickel-phosphorus plated aluminum has been used, which provides a surface capable of being polished to a high degree of smoothness. It is still the most common type of substrate in use today, mainly because of its low cost. However, there is a limit to how flat its surface can be polished, and the softness of aluminum makes it susceptible to accidental head slaps.

Glass and ceramics have been considered for many years as substrate materials, but only in recent years has glass been adopted in real products. The brittleness of glass has become less of a concern as disk diameter shrinks. Though costing more than aluminum, its ability to be polished to a very fine surface finish makes it an attractive alternative. Additionally, its hardness makes it less susceptible to head slap, and it is therefore a better choice for mobile applications. Its higher tensile strength also allows disks to be thinner.

Magnetic Layer

For the first 25 years of disk drives, what is known as *particulate media* was used exclusively in disk drives. With this type of magnetic coating, dispersions of magnetic particles in organic binders of polymer resins and solvents are essentially spray-painted onto a rotating substrate. Any excess "paint" is spun off by the rapid spinning of the disk, resulting in a thin film of polymer-magnetic particles. Before the film is dried, a magnetic field is applied to align the particles circumferentially to enhance their magnetic properties. Baking in an oven bonds the film onto the substrate. Finally, buffing and applying a coat of lubricant finish off the steps in creating a particulate media disk.

The most commonly used magnetic material in particulate media is particles of gamma ferric oxide, which are acicular in shape. Later developed particles include cobalt-modified gamma ferric oxide, chromium dioxide, metal particles, and barium ferrite. However, such newer particulate developments are applied more to flexible substrates, as thin film media made particulate media obsolete for hard disks.

With thin film media, a thin layer of magnetic metallic thin is deposited and bound directly onto the substrate without the use of polymer. The clear advantage of thin film media over particulate media is that more magnetic material is available as it is not being diluted by a non-magnetic binder. This enables a thinner layer of magnetic material to be used, which is a good thing because that allows narrower transitions to be written. Narrower transitions mean higher areal density.

Early methods of making thin film media include electroplating, chemically plating, and depositing onto the substrate by heating the desired material in a vacuum. The current method of production uses sputtering. Sputtering is performed by applying a high voltage across a low-pressure gas (argon is universally used), resulting in a plasma of electrons and argon ions in a high-energy state. The target magnetic material is bombarded by the energized argon ions accelerating toward it, displacing its surface atoms. The atoms are ejected with enough velocity to travel to the substrate and bond with it, resulting in the film of magnetic material on the substrate.

Disk Structure

A magnetic disk actually consists of more than just a substrate and a magnetic coating. Figure 17.9 shows a cross-section view of a typical thin film disk using an aluminum substrate. Starting from the bottom, above the substrate is a sublayer of nickel-phosphorus,

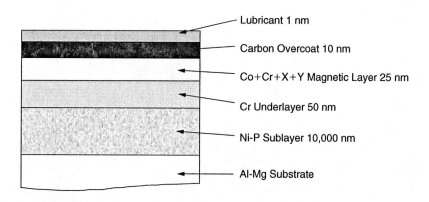

FIGURE 17.9: Cross-section view of a typical disk structure: aluminum substrate. Not drawn to scale.

which provides a much harder surface than aluminum, allowing it to be polished to a higher degree of smoothness and at the same time presenting a more damage-resistant surface. Next is an underlayer of chromium. Its purpose is to set up a desirable microstructure that the magnetic layer material is to replicate when deposited on this underlayer. The magnetic layer invariably uses some cobalt alloy, as cobalt alone does not have sufficient coercivity. Chromium is quite commonly used as one of the alloy metals. The thickness of this layer and grain size have a strong effect on coercivity and squareness. Grain size is influenced by rate of deposition, temperature of substrate, and other factors.

A layer of exposed magnetic material would leave it unprotected from potential scratches and corrosion. Therefore, a layer of wear-resistant overcoat is needed. The material for this layer should, naturally, be hard but not brittle, and it should be chemically inert but bond well to the magnetic layer. Today, the most common overcoat material is hard carbon, sputtered onto the disk. Finally, a very thin layer of lubricant is applied for reducing any wear and friction between the head and the disk.

17.2.2 Spindle Motor

For the disk media platter to rotate, it is rigidly attached to a spindle, and the spindle is driven by a motor [Shirle & Lieu 1996]. In the earliest days,

synchronous AC motors were used, which phase locked to the 60 Hz of power lines to provide speeds such as 1200, 2400, and 3600 rpm. The spindles were belt driven by such AC motors, though direct drive was later introduced also. The resulting rotational speed was not very precise, but was acceptable for the relatively low bits per inch (bpi) in those times.

As the size of disk drives shrank, and the technology for low-cost switching control of DC motors became available, the AC disk drive motor became obsolete. Today, compact and efficient DC motors with the spindles directly integrated are universally used in all disk drives. Three-phase, eight-pole motors are typical. The motor with its stationary stator is attached to the base casing of the disk drive. The rotor is part of the outer sleeve of the motor which forms the spindle onto which the disk platters are mounted. Hence, the spindle is driven directly by the motor. Speed is electronically governed using servo control (see Section 17.3.4). Figure 17.10 is a photo of a cutaway spindle motor.

Ideally, the spindle drive motor should have the following characteristics:

- High reliability. If the motor does not spin properly, the disk drive is dead. Therefore, the motor must be able to run for many years and be able to go through tens of thousands or even hundreds of thousands of start/stop cycles.

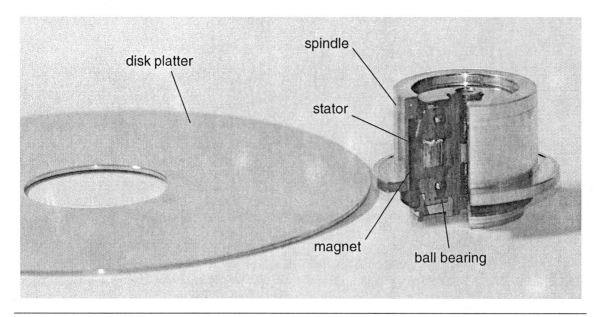

FIGURE 17.10: Photo of a cutaway spindle motor and a disk platter.

- Low vibration. Vibration affects the ability of the head to stay in a stable position relative to the platter, thus impacting performance. This can also affect areal recording density.
- Minimal wobble. Wobble in the disk drive is known as *Non-Repeatable Runout* (NRRO). NRRO is a main contributor to *track misregistration* (TMR).[1] Besides impacting performance, it is also an inhibitor to increasing tracks per inch (tpi), as it prevents tracks written to the disk from being perfectly circular.
- Low power consumption. Power causes heat, which must be dissipated or else it will shorten the life of the disk drive. For mobile applications, low power consumption is also important for making a battery last longer.
- Low acoustic noise. This is especially important for disk drives used in consumer electronics.

- High shock tolerance. This is true of every component in the disk drive, especially one used in mobile applications.

Bearings

Bearings are needed to both support and separate the spindle hub from the stator shaft so that the spindle can rotate smoothly and quietly. For many years, time-tested metal ball bearings confined to raceways inside the spindle were used in spindle drive motors. However, there is limit as to how perfectly round these tiny balls can be manufactured. The raceway in which these ball bearings run is not 100% perfect either. As mentioned, NRRO is a significant contributor to TMR. Spindle motors with ball bearings have an NRRO in the 0.1-microinch range. Additionally, materials in high-speed contact are subject to invariable wear and tear and are dependent on the

---

[1]TMR is the amount of offset between the center of the head and the center of the written track.

age and durability of the lubricant protecting them. As the rpm of spindle drive motor increases over the years, heat and noise issues plus these limitations of ball bearing motors become more and more apparent. Figure 17.11(a) is a cross-section drawing of a ball bearing motor.

In recent years, disk drives have started to transition to spindle motors using *fluid dynamic bearing* (FDB). With FDB, the ball bearings are eliminated and replaced by a very thin layer of high-viscosity lubrication oil trapped in a carefully machined housing. Without the ball bearings and with the damping effect of a lubricant film, the FDB spindle motors run more quietly, showing roughly a 4-dBA decrease in acoustic noise. Furthermore, wobble is also greatly minimized, with NRRO in the 0.01-microinch range, which is an order of magnitude improvement over ball bearing spindle motors. Non-operational shock resistance is also improved due to increased area of surface-to-surface contact, while the lubricant film provides additional damping also. Initially, FDB motors will cost more. However, as production volume increases and manufacturing techniques mature, they will become cheaper to build than ball bearing motors as fewer parts are required. Figure 17.11(b) is a cross-section drawing of an FDB motor.

17.2.3 Heads

Heads are really the heart of a disk drive. In Section 17.1.4, the principle of recording information by applying an external magnetic field to magnetize and manipulate the orientation of magnetization of the magnetic media is qualitatively described. It is the write head that provides the source of the externally applied magnetic field. The detection of the magnetic recording, as described in Section 17.1.5 on the principle of retrieving magnetically recorded information, is performed by the read head.

Write Heads

The principle governing the operation of today's write heads is exactly the same as that for the earliest recording heads [Robertson et al. 1997]. Nonetheless, the dimension, the geometry, the materials used, and the fabrication process have all evolved substantially over the years. While it is hard to tell by looking at the size and shape of today's write heads and those of the RAMAC 350, all write heads are basically inductive ring heads.

The inductive write head basically consists of a ring core of magnetically soft material, such as ferrite, and a coil of wire wrapped around the core. There is a break in the core, forming a very short gap. The head "flies" very closely over the magnetic recording media, with the gap adjacent to the media. When an applied current passes through the coil, it induces a magnetic field inside the core, just like electromagnets, and hence the name inductive head. The direction of the magnetic field is dependent on the direction of the current in the coil. The two ends of the core at the gap form two magnetic poles of opposite

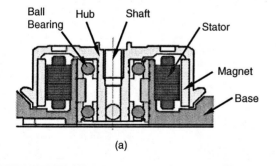
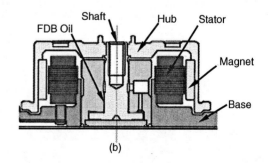

(a)

(b)

FIGURE 17.11: Cross-section drawing of spindle motors: (a) a ball bearing motor, and (b) a fluid dynamic bearing motor. (Drawing by Michael Xu of Hitachi GST.)

polarities. At this gap, the magnetic flux leaks outside the core and fringes away from the gap. The leaked magnetic flux passes through the media, magnetizing the magnetically hard material of the media in accordance to its hysteresis loop characteristics and the amount of magnetic flux applied. This is illustrated in Figure 17.12. The space within which the magnetic field of the write head is strong enough for magnetic record to occur is sometimes called the *write bubble*. The magnetically hard media retains most of the magnetization after the magnetic field of the head is removed. This basic write head structure is used for both analog and digital recording.

In digital magnetic recording, the head/media/ channel are designed such that when current is applied to the head, the resulting magnetic flux going through the media is of sufficient strength as to align the magnetic domains immediately adjacent to the head completely in the same direction as the applied magnetic field, regardless of the previous orientation. This is saturation magnetization. Since the magnetic media is moving under the write head due to the rotation of the disk platter, saturated magnetization occurs along the path (called *track* in recording terminology) that passes directly underneath the head, as long as the current is applied to the coil. When the current is switched off and then a current in the opposite direction is applied, the magnetic flux in the core reverses direction, and saturated magnetization in the opposite orientation as the previous magnetization now occurs in the magnetic media. This creates a transition in the media where magnetization changes from one orientation to the opposite orientation. This

is shown in Figure 17.13. The transition is, of course, not a sharp line as drawn, but has a finite length to it, as the dipoles within it gradually change from predominantly pointing in one direction to predominantly pointing in the opposite direction. Media with a more square hysteresis loop will create sharper transitions. This transition length determines how closely the transitions can be spaced, which, in turn, determines the linear recording density. The sequence of pictorials illustrating the write process in Figure 17.6 can now be depicted with a write head as the source of the recording magnetic field, as shown in Figure 17.14. The size of the recorded bits relative to the head and its gap is not properly drawn to scale; in reality, the bit size is much smaller and closer to the dimension of the head's gap. Writing, i.e., the creation of transitions, actually takes place at the trailing (left-hand side in Figure 17.14) side of the write bubble, as that is where the medium sees the final orientation of the magnetization field applied to it.

The desirable characteristics of the write head are the following:

- A narrow write width as it determines the tpi. This means that not only the width of the poles needs to be narrow, but also the gap between the pole needs to be short, or else there will be too much undesirable side writing.
- Core material must have high enough saturation flux density in order to produce enough magnetization to write media with ever-increasing coercivities.

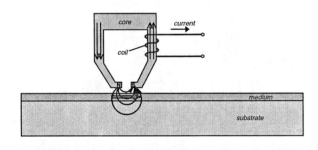

FIGURE 17.12: An illustration of an inductive ring head.

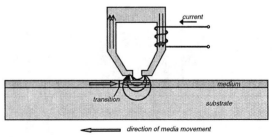

FIGURE 17.13: Writing a transition.

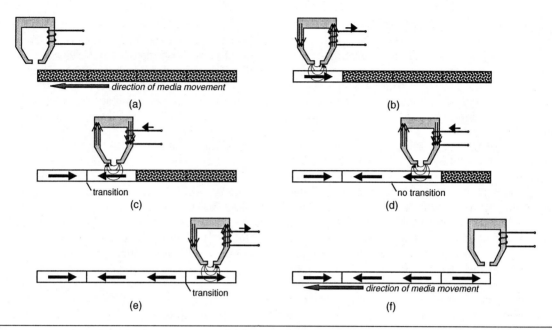

direction of media movement

(a)

(b)

transition

(c)

no transition

(d)

transition

(e)

direction of media movement

(f)

FIGURE 17.14: Write process example revisited, showing the write head.

- The inductance of the electric circuitry needs to be low enough to handle signals that are several tens of megahertz frequencies.
- Core material must be mechanically strong so that the poles are not easily damaged by contacts with the disk.
- It must be light weight.

The first heads for the RAMAC 350 used permalloy (an alloy of nickel and iron) as the core material, and the coils were hand wound and assembled by former watchmakers. Needless to say, they share little of the above list of desirable characteristics. The shape and dimension of write heads have greatly evolved since then. Ferrites, which are ceramic-like compounds of iron oxides and other metallic oxides, replaced permalloy as the core material during the mid-1960s. While having other desirable characteristics, ferrites suffer from having a much lower saturation flux density than permalloy. By the mid-1980s, they simply did not have enough magnetic flux to work on the high coercivity of thin film disks. The solution was to add (sputter on) a thin layer of metallic material, commonly sendust which is an alloy of iron, aluminum, and silicon, to the poles near the gap. Hence, this type of head was called a *metal-in-gap* (MIG) head. The result is a head that has the high saturation flux density of sendust and the other desirable characteristics of ferrites.

MIG heads were gainfully used from the late 1980s to the early 1990s. However, the way they were manufactured, which involved mechanically grinding and polishing the ferrite material and actual winding of the copper coil, placed a limit on how small the dimensions of the head could be reduced to. Miniaturization of the head was the key to increasing areal density. With research starting in the 1960s, by the early 1980s, a completely new technique for manufacturing the heads was perfected. This new fabrication method leveraged on the tools and thin film technology of semiconductor manufacturing. By using lithography to define the features of the head and thin film deposition to construct all its components, including the core, the gap, and the copper windings, a miniature head with well-controlled dimension could be easily manufactured. Thin film heads, as these heads came to be called, were introduced in the IBM enterprise class of disk drives in 1980 and eventually became economical for all disk drives by the mid-1990s.

While the fabrication process of thin film heads differs from that for the ferrite and MIG heads, not to mention their miniaturized dimensions, functionally, they are really just like ferrite heads. Structurally, they are essentially three-dimensional inductive heads collapsed front to back to become almost just two-dimensional. Even the core material has gone back to permalloy, the original material used in the RAMAC 350 heads. Figure 17.15 illustrates conceptually the typical construction of a thin film head, fabricated using semiconductor technology. While the front-to-back spacing is much more compressed, and the coil takes on a flattened arrangement, functionally, it is exactly an inductive head.

Read Heads

For reading in digital magnetic recording, the read head detects the transitions that are recorded in the media. Transitions detected in the sync field (to be described in more detail in Chapter 18, Section 18.1.3) are used to establish the clock (self-clocking) for data reading. In the data field, each transition is used to represent a binary "1," while the absence of a transition in a clocked period represents a binary "0," as discussed earlier in this chapter. The read channel samples at each clock interval the signal coming out of the read head to check for the presence or absence of transition.

Up until the introduction of the magnetoresistive head in 1991, the inductive head was used also for reading, in addition to its function as the write head. It operates on the well-known magnetic phenomenon that a change in magnetic flux inside a coil of wire would induce a voltage in that coil. In fact, Faraday's Law provides that the induced voltage is

$$V = -N \cdot \frac{d\Phi}{dt} \qquad \text{(EQ 17.3)}$$

where N is the number of turns in the coil. While used as a read head, no current is applied to the coil by the drive's electronics. As the media moves next to the head, its core collects the magnetic flux emanating from the recorded magnetization on the media. When it comes across a transition, a magnetic flux change occurs as the magnetic field reverses polarity, and this flux change induces a voltage in the coil which

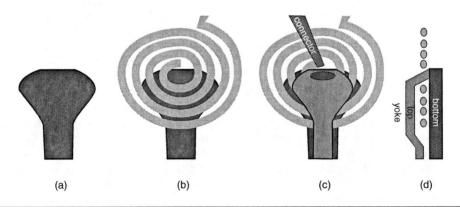

(a)   (b)   (c)   (d)

FIGURE 17.15: Conceptual drawing of a fabrication of a thin film inductive head. (a) Deposit permalloy film to form bottom yoke. (b) Add coil. (c) Add top yoke/pole and coil connector. Top yoke is connected to bottom yoke under the oval at the top. (d) Side view. (Artwork by Michael Xu of Hitachi GST.)

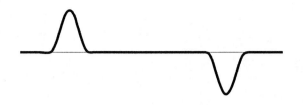

FIGURE 17.16: Read voltage waveform for "101."

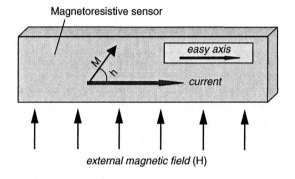

FIGURE 17.17: MR sensor.

can then be detected by the read channel circuitry. Figure 17.16 shows the read voltage signal for the sample sequence of "101" of Figure 17.14. Equation 17.3 suggests that having more turns in the coil would increase the read signal; however, making N too large would increase the inductance of the head, limiting its high frequency, and hence high data rate, handling. Also, because the inductive head operates by detecting the rate of flux change, the higher the velocity is, the stronger the read signal. Thus, higher rpm and larger disk diameter are both favorable for inductive read heads.

While inductive read heads operate by detecting flux change, *magnetoresistive* (MR) *heads* operate by sensing the flux directly [Tsang et al. 1997, 1994]. There is a class of materials, of which permalloy happens to be one, which exhibits the phenomenon of *magnetoresistance*. Basically, when a magnetic field H is applied to such a material, its electrical resistance

changes as a function of the angle θ between the resultant magnetization M and the direction of flow of an applied electric current, as shown in Figure 17.17, in accordance to

$$\Delta R = C_{MR} \cdot R \cdot \cos^2 \theta \qquad \text{(EQ 17.4)}$$

where ΔR is the change in resistance, R is the sensor's nominal resistance, and C_{MR} is the *magnetoresistance coefficient* of the material. For permalloy, C_{MR} is about 2–3%.

By applying a constant current I to the MR sensor, the presence of a magnetic field is detected by a change in the voltage across this sensor in accordance with Ohm's Law,

$$\Delta V = I \cdot \Delta R \qquad \text{(EQ 17.5)}$$

as a result of the change in the direction of magnetization due to the applied field H. Because a magnetic field is applied during fabrication of the sensor to give it an easy axis parallel to the current direction (θ = 0°), the biggest change in resistance will be when the external magnetic field H is in a vertical direction, either up or down, perpendicular to the current direction (θ = 90°), as shown in Figure 17.17. The biggest resistance change generates the biggest signal. Such vertical magnetic fields occur on the media's recorded surface only at the transitions, where magnetic fields emanating from both sides of the transition are both either going up or going down, as can be seen in Figure 17.7. Common practice is to bias[2] the MR sensor so that θ = 45° when no external magnetic field is present. As a result, the MR sensor generates up or down peak ΔV signals at transitions, with a waveform similar to the one shown in Figure 17.16 for inductive read heads. In order to prevent the MR sensor from detecting stray magnetic fields from adjacent transitions, the sensor is shielded front and back so that it can only "see" the magnetic field right underneath it.

The signal that can be created by an MR head is several times larger than that of an inductive read head. This is what drove the rapid increase in areal density after the introduction of the MR head in 1991.

---

[2]Biasing is a long topic beyond the scope of this book. The choice of biasing scheme needs to trade off between maximizing signal amplitude and minimizing signal asymmetry.

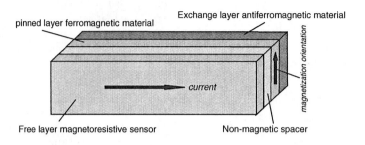

FIGURE 17.18: Example of a GMR sensor.

In fact, by increasing the sense current I, a bigger signal can be obtained, as Equation 17.5 indicates. However, heat and other heat-related issues limit the amount of current that can be practically applied. With no coil involved, the inductance of the MR head is so low that there is practically no limit to its high-frequency performance. Finally, since the MR head detects magnetic flux rather than the rate of change of flux, its signal is independent of the velocity of the media going by, unlike an inductive read head. This attribute is what makes small diameter drives with low rpm possible.

The MR sensor is constructed of a homogeneous ferromagnetic material such as permalloy. Around the early 1990s, researchers discovered that by constructing a composite sensor with multiple thin layers of different ferromagnetic and anti-ferromagnetic materials, made possible by the molecular beam epitaxy process, a sensor with *giant magnetoresistance* (GMR) results. An example of such a structure, as illustrated in Figure 17.18, consists of a "free" ferromagnetic layer and a "pinned" ferromagnetic layer separated by some non-magnetic material. The magnetization orientation of the pinned layer is fixed (pinned) by an adjacent layer[3] of *anti-ferromagnetic material* (AFM). The GMR head was first introduced in a product in 1997.

Read/Write Heads

The transducers for reading and writing are oftentimes referred to collectively as the read/write head, or just simply the head. This is probably carried over from the earlier days when the inductive head was used for both reading and writing. Therefore, there is truly only one head. Requiring the same head to perform the read and the write functions means that compromise in design and performance would be necessary, as the optimum design for writing differs from that for reading.

Since the introduction of MR heads, the "head" is now really composed of an inductive write transducer and the MR (or GMR) read transducer. Having a separate read head and write head allows each design to be independently optimized for the function it needs to perform. The inductive head and the MR head are placed in tandem, with the write head going behind the read head, as illustrated in Figure 17.19. Standard practice today is for the write head to write a wider path (track) than the width of the read head, a technique called "*write wide, read narrow*," by constructing the MR read sensor to be narrower than the width of the write pole tip, as shown in Figure 17.20. The advantage of such an approach is that the read head does not have to be perfectly centered over a track in order to have good read-back and not pick up noise from adjacent tracks. This also permits tracks to be placed closer together, thus increasing tpi.

In Figure 17.19, the width of a track W is determined by the width of the tip of the trailing pole of the thin film head. The distance between the center of two adjacent tracks is called the *track pitch*. It is different from the width of a track because standard recording technique places a *guard band* between two tracks.

---

[3]Called the "exchange layer."

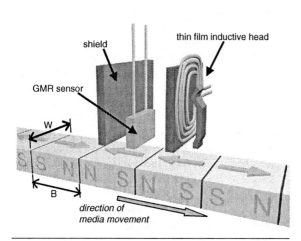

FIGURE 17.19: Conceptual drawing of a GMR read head with inductive write head. (Artwork by Michael Xu of Hitachi GST.)

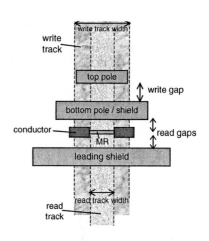

FIGURE 17.20: Bottom view of read/write heads. The MR sensor is narrower than the write pole tip.

The guard band provides protection against stray magnetic fields fringing from the sides of the write head which can partially erase adjacent tracks. It is this track pitch, rather than the track width W, that determines the tpi:

$$\text{tpi} = 1/\text{track pitch} = 1/(W + \text{guard band width}) \quad \textbf{(EQ 17.6)}$$

but track pitch is pretty much dominated by track width. The distance B between two back-to-back transitions defines the flux change density, fcpi:

$$\text{fcpi} = 1/B \quad \textbf{(EQ 17.7)}$$

The actual linear bit density depends on the *density ratio* (DR) of data bits per flux change of the modulation code being used to encode the data bits (see Section 17.3.3):

$$\text{bpi} = \text{DR} \times \text{fcpi} = \text{DR}/B \quad \textbf{(EQ 17.8)}$$

However, many of the newer codes have a value quite close to 1 for DR, so it is not too far off to refer to B as the bit length. Historically, W has always been much larger than B. However, as areal density has increased over the years, tpi has been going up faster than bpi. As a result, the ratio of W to B has been dropping. Today, this ratio is close to 4:1.

The location of the outermost track that the write head can write is commonly referred to as the *OD* (outer diameter), while the innermost location is referred to as the *ID* (inner diameter).

17.2.4 Slider and Head-Gimbal Assembly

Contrary to what Figure 17.19 seems to portray, the heads don't just magically float freely in space over the media. Rather, they are integrated as part of a mechanical structure whose function is to support the heads and to position them at the right location in order to access a specific bit of data.

The read/write transducers are bonded to a small piece of material called the *slider*. While the heads of the very earliest disk drives may actually slide on the media surface, hence the name, having the head in contact with the disk moving at high speed simply creates too much wear and tear for both the head and the media.[4] For decades now the slider has been designed to ride hydrodynamically on a cushion of

---

[4]Actually, with improving protective overcoats for both the head and the media, better lubricants, and the constant pressure to reduce flying height in order to increase areal density, contact recording is now again a subject of discussion and investigation. To achieve practical contact recording, a tougher disk overcoat needs to be engineered, and lubricants that can be used as liquid bearings will have to be developed.

air, commonly called an *air bearing*, so as to maintain the proper spacing between the head and the media. This spacing is referred to as the *flying height*. There are many different designs for the *air bearing surface* (ABS): taper-flat, bi-rail, tri-rail, and tri-pad (Figure 17.21), just to name a few.

Maintaining the proper flying height is important, as it is one of the key factors that determines magnetic recording signals and linear bit density, as will be discussed in a later section. Yet, it is not a simple task as the linear velocity of the disk surface under the head, and hence the speed of air flow, varies with the radial position of the head. Flying height can also be affected by the skew angle of the head for rotary actuators (to be described later). Additionally, flying height must not be unduly affected by the atmospheric pressure of the environment that the disk drive operates in.

The slider is itself attached to the end of a load beam, also called a suspension or a disk arm (term probably comes from the similarity to the arm of a phonograph), by means of a flexure, as illustrated in Figure 17.22. Today's suspension beam is typically triangular in shape with holes in the middle to reduce its weight. The flexure, acting as a gimbal, allows some limited rolling and pitching motion of the slider. The suspension is spring-loaded

such that when the drive is not rotating it will press the slider against the disk surface to hold it in place, and when the disk is rotating at operating speed the head will be flying at the designed flying height. This structure of suspension, slider, and head is called the *head-gimbal assembly* (HGA).

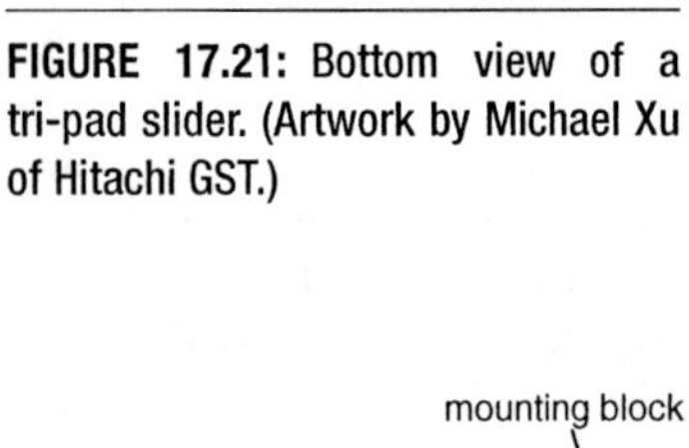

As the size of the read/write element has been decreasing in size over the years, so has the slider. The generation of sliders introduced in 1980 was designated by the industry as the 100% mini slider (4.0 × 3.2 × 0.86 mm, 55 mg). In 1986 the 70% micro slider (2.8 × 2.24 × 0.6 mm, 16.2 mg) was introduced, followed in 1990 by the 50% nano slider (2.0 × 1.6 × 0.43 mm, 5.9 mg), and followed in 1997 by the 30% pico slider (1.25 × 1.0 × 0.3 mm, 1.6 mg). Finally, in 2003 the 20% femto slider (0.85 × 0.7 × 0.23 mm, 0.6 mg) was introduced. The percentage refers only to the length; the volume and mass actually shrink by a much higher percentage, e.g., the femto slider is only about 1% of the volume and mass of a mini slider. Also, the prefixes do not reflect their scientific meanings—they were more likely chosen just for marketing hype. There are several clear advantages of a smaller slider.

- A smaller slider means the suspension can also be made lighter. This combined reduction in mass reduces the power required for positioning of the heads and improves seek time.
- Reduction in mass also improves shock resistance and head-disk reliability.
- Smaller slider size makes it easier to respond to unevenness of a disk's surface, hence reducing the variation in flying height.

FIGURE 17.21: Bottom view of a tri-pad slider. (Artwork by Michael Xu of Hitachi GST.)

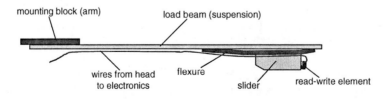

FIGURE 17.22: Side view of a head-gimbal assembly.

- Because a slider cannot fly outside of the disk's surface, having a smaller slider means more of a disk's surface area is usable, and thus, storage capacity is increased. This is especially important for smaller diameter disks since a larger percentage of the disk becomes available.
- Smaller size means more sliders can be produced from a same size wafer, and thus, production cost is reduced.

17.2.5 Head-Stack Assembly and Actuator

All the head-gimbal assemblies of a drive, one per recording surface, are stacked together, lining up vertically, by attaching to a structure called the *E-block*. The wires from each head element are connected to a flex cable which also contains a tiny electronic circuitry called the *arm electronics module* (AEM). This complete structure of E-block, HGAs, and flex cable is called a *head-stack assembly* (HSA). The HSA is installed in a disk drive during final assembly as a single unit. To assemble a disk drive, the HSA is integrated with a *voice coil motor* (VCM) to form the *actuator*. These components are illustrated in Figure 17.23. The function of the actuator is to move the set of arms of the HSA so as to transport the heads from one radial position to a new target radial position in order to access the desired data. Because the arms are rigidly ganged together as a unit, all the heads move in unison. This movement of the heads is referred to as a *seek* operation.

The earliest disk drives made use of actuators that were driven with hydraulics! Mechanical detents were utilized to establish the cylinder positions, achieving a track density of less than 100 tpi. That was more or less the upper limit of what an open-loop control system could achieve. Mechanical tolerance of mechanical parts, variations in operating temperature together with materials having different coefficients of expansion, and vibrations all conspire to place such an upper limit. In order to further increase track density, an electronic servo system using closed-loop control logic was necessary. The IBM 3330, introduced in 1971, was the first drive to incorporate such a servo system. Since a special servo data pattern needs to be placed on the disk surface as part of the servo system, a more detailed discussion will be deferred to Chapter 18, which deals with all aspects of placing data on a disk surface.

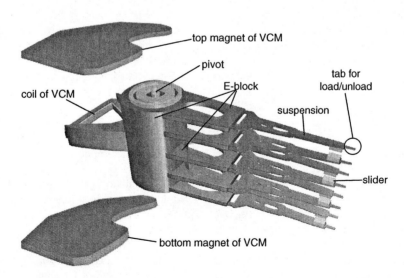

FIGURE 17.23: Illustrative example of an HSA and the components of a VCM for a rotary actuator. The flex cable and AEM are not shown. Drawing by Michael Xu of Hitachi GST.

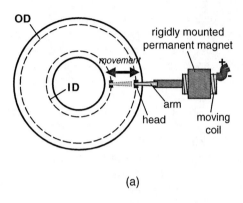

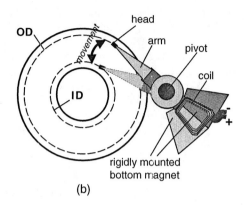

(a) (b)

FIGURE 17.24: Top views of actuators. (a) Linear actuator. (b) Rotary actuator, with the top magnets removed to expose the voice coil.

The earlier actuators had the arms perpendicular to the tracks and moved them straight in and out across the surfaces of the disks, as shown in Figure 17.24(a). The first such *linear actuator* motors were made from loudspeakers with the cones removed, hence the name VCM. By passing current through the voice coil in one direction, the magnetic force due to the magnetic field of the rigidly mounted permanent magnet propels the HSA forward, and the heads would be seeking toward the ID of the disks. The amount of current applied determines the size of the electro-magnetic force generated, which, in turn, determines the motion of the HSA. By passing current in the opposite direction, the HSA is retracted, and the heads would be seeking toward the OD. Hence, by controlling the direction and the amount of current to the coil, the positioning of the actuator can be controlled.

As disk diameter decreased, disk drive designs switched to a rotary type of actuator. In a *rotary actuator* the arms are held roughly tangential to the tracks, and the HSA swivels at a fixed pivot point in the actuator assembly, as shown in Figure 17.24(b). A coil is wrapped around a protruding metal piece at the back side of the E-block. Two strong magnets, each vertically magnetized with opposite polarities on each half, are placed above and below this coil such that the top magnet faces opposing polarities in the bot-

tom magnet. Figure 17.25 shows a cross-section view of this arrangement.[5] When current flows in the coil in one direction, electromagnetic force moves the coil to the right (in reference to the top view shown in Figure 17.24(b)), causing the actuator to rotate in a counter-clockwise direction. This results in the heads seeking towards the ID of the disks. When a current is applied to the coil in the opposite direction, the HSA rotates in a clockwise direction resulting in the heads seeking towards the OD. Once again, as with the linear actuator, by controlling the direction and amplitude of the current applied to the coil, the positioning of the rotary actuator can be controlled.

Today, the rotary actuator is used in all disk drives. Its advantages over a linear actuator are the following:

- Simpler design, and, hence, lower cost
- Smaller and lighter, which means faster seek performance and lower power consumption

The disadvantage of a rotary actuator is that there is only one radial position on the disk surface at which the head is exactly tangential to the track. Move away from that point and there is a small skew angle of the head with respect to the track underneath it. This would not be much of a problem if read and write used the same transducer. However, with MR/GMR heads,

---

[5]Even though the configuration of the coil and magnets here is completely different from that of a cone speaker, the term "voice coil motor" sticks.

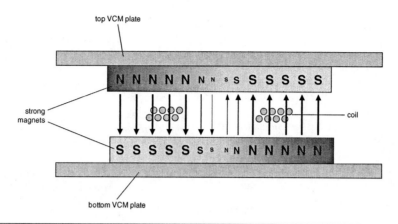

top VCM plate

strong magnets

coil

bottom VCM plate

FIGURE 17.25: Cross-section view of a VCM for a rotary actuator.

the read element is separate from the write element, as described previously. This means that when there is a skew angle, the two elements cannot be both dead center over the track at the same time. Hence, to switch between reads and writes, the servo actuator must do a slight position adjustment, called a *micro-jog*. Since the amount of micro-jog is dependent on the radial position and varies from head to head, the disk drive needs to go through a self-calibration during manufacturing to establish a micro-jog table for each of its heads.

It is by controlling the current in the coil of the (linear or rotary) actuator that its position is governed. However, if power to the drive is lost during a seek operation, no current can be applied to slow down and stop the actuator which is already in motion. To prevent a crash from happening, crashstops are installed at both ends of the actuator's intended range of movement. This is not unlike the crashstops found at train station terminals.

Servo control of the actuator and seek performance will be covered in Chapter 18 and Chapter 20.

17.2.6 Multiple Platters

For a long time, when recording density was relatively low and the cost of a hard disk drive was relatively expensive, economics called for designing disk drives to hold as much data as possible. One way

to do that is to use disks of large diameters. The disadvantages of larger diameter disks are the following:

- The seek stroke is longer, resulting in higher average seek time.
- The arms are longer, which, in turn, requires it to be thicker to provide the necessary stiffness. The result is an actuator with more mass, which means either the actuator will move slower (longer seek times) or more power will be needed to achieve the same performance as for a smaller diameter disk.
- A larger surface area means there is more air friction (windage). This translates to a greater power requirement to spin the disk at a given rotational speed.
- To attain the necessary stiffness so the disk does not sag, the thickness of the disk platter must increase proportionally to the increase in diameter. The total increase in weight from both a bigger diameter and more thickness means that even more power is needed to attain a given rotational speed.

For all of the above reasons, increasing the disk diameter in order to increase its capacity is not a good approach. Instead, the alternative is to grow in the z-dimension, namely increasing the number of disk platters per drive. This is a better approach for the same reasons as why increasing the diameter is a less desirable approach:

- The seek stroke is not increased, and the added weight to an actuator for having additional HGAs is minimal. Thus, seek performance is not affected.
- While the added platters do increase the total weight that the spindle motor must spin, it is less than the increase from a larger diameter disk, as the smaller diameter platters are thinner while providing the same rigidity.

An obvious disadvantage of having more platters is that more heads are required, and the head is one of the most expensive components of a disk drive. In recent years, due to the exponential growth in areal density, it has been possible to satisfy the per-drive capacity requirement of disk drive applications with fewer and fewer platters.

17.2.7 Start/Stop

When a disk drive is powered off or stops rotating, as when it is placed in an idle mode, something needs to be done to safeguard the heads from damage. There are two differing technologies for handling this, namely *contact start/stop* (CSS) and *load/unload*.

Contact Start/Stop

In this method, the head comes to rest on the disk surface as there is no longer an air bearing to support it [Bhushan et al. 1992]. When the disk starts spinning again, the head slides in contact over the disk surface until gradually an air bearing is formed under the slider and the head is lifted off the disk surface. With today's high areal density, it is not a good idea to park the head on the portion of the disk where data is recorded, as the data with its tiny bit size can easily be damaged. Therefore, a designated landing zone is reserved on the disk surface for the head to park. While the landing zone can be placed outside either the OD or the ID, there are couple of reasons why placing it outside the OD is a bad design choice.

- The space reserved for a landing zone is lost for data storage. For a landing zone of a given width, the space lost is much bigger if it is at the outside of the disk.
- When the head slider is stopped in contact with the disk surface, there is an adhesive force, called *stiction* (short for static friction), that works against the disk spinning up, against which the drive must provide enough torque to overcome. A bigger torque is required if the stiction occurs at the OD than if it is at the ID. This means more power is used, and also perhaps a more powerful spindle motor would be needed to provide this larger torque.

For the above reasons, the landing zone is placed at the inside of the disk. To further reduce the effect of stiction, the landing zone is textured so that the total surface area in actual contact is reduced. During a normal shutdown, the disk drive controller firmware would instruct the actuator to position itself over the landing zone before spinning down the disk. To guarantee that in the event of an unexpected power loss the head still gets properly stowed away in the landing zone, some sort of auto-park feature is needed. Some older drives use a weak spring to pull the actuator to the landing zone. Newer drives use the kinetic energy of the spinning platters to generate back-EMF (electro-magnetic force) power from the spindle motor to move the actuator to the landing zone.

Load/Unload

This technology was previously used in large diameter disk drives and is now being re-introduced into small form factor drives. Prior to spinning down, the actuator moves off the disk platters. A lift tab at the front of the suspension of each HGA slides up a ramp structure and comes to a rest at a detent, as shown in Figure 17.26. The heads are now safely off the disk surfaces, and only then are the disks spun down. To start up the disk drive, the disks are first spun up until a sufficient rotational speed is reached, and then the actuator is moved off the ramp; the heads will have enough air cushion for them to fly as soon as they reach the disk surfaces. With this

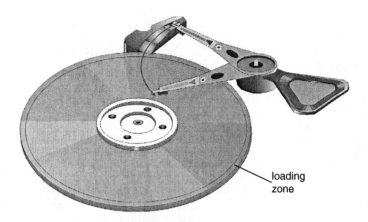

loading
zone

FIGURE 17.26: Ramp load/unload dynamics. (Drawing by Michael Xu of Hitachi GST.)

technique, intentional contact between the head and disk surface is eliminated.

Just as in CSS, a self-parking mechanism is needed to ensure that the heads are safely unloaded up the ramp in the event of a power loss. Again, this can be accomplished by extracting energy from the spinning disks by using a circuit to apply current from the spindle motor back-EMF to the actuator.

Since there is no intentional contact of the head with the disk, reliability of the disk drive is improved as there is less likelihood of head or media damage. It also means the drive can handle more stop/start cycles in its lifetime than CSS. Additionally, because the heads are completely moved off the surfaces of the disks, the whole disk drive is more shock tolerant than drives using CSS. This makes load/unload especially attractive for mobile applications. The downside of load/unload is that it requires a loading zone on each disk surface outside the OD for the head to load onto the disk surface, and no data is stored in this loading zone. This loading zone takes up a lot more space than the landing zone of CSS, which is at the outside of the ID.

17.2.8 Magnetic Disk Recording Integration

One of the most important parameters of a disk drive is its areal recording density. Not only does a high areal density lower the cost per byte of storage, it also has profound impact on performance (discussed in Chapter 19, "Performance Issues and Design Trade-Offs"). All the components of a disk drive described in the previous sections and the way they interact with each other affect the areal density realized in the final integrated product. Of these, the head and the media carry the most weight.

Areal density is the product of two disk drive parameters, namely tpi and bpi. We will examine these two parameters separately and take a high-level overview of how the drive components affect them. As we shall see, miniaturization of the drive components is the key for increasing areal density. Most fortunately, miniaturization to gain higher areal density also results in better performance: smaller heads and lighter actuators enable faster seek, and smaller diameter and thinner disk platters enable higher rotational speed.

Tracks per Inch

As discussed in Section 17.2.3 and stated in Equation 17.6, tpi is the reciprocal of the track pitch, which is the distance between the center of two adjacent tracks. The track width accounts for much of the track pitch, and the track width is basically dictated by the width of the pole tip of the inductive write head.

Hence, the width of the write head is a key factor in determining tpi.

While the head may be able to write very narrow tracks, other components of the disk drive must also be able to support a high tpi. The actuator and the servo system controlling it need to be able to both position the head accurately on the center of a track and maintain this centered position while the head is accessing the data on the track. In addition, while the guard bands on both sides of a track allow for a small amount of deviation, such deviation must be kept small. If a normal distribution is assumed for the position of the head with respect to the track center, a value of 3 sigma (representing a range with 99.7% probability) is designated as the TMR of the drive. Clearly, as track pitch decreases, TMR must decrease proportionally if the head is to write and read data properly. NRRO of the spindle motor (discussed previously), mechanical vibrations coming from sources both inside the disk drive and external to the disk drive (e.g., another neighboring disk drive), disk flutter, and even electronic noise in the servo control circuits all contribute to TMR.

Bits per Inch

The linear recording density bpi is predominantly determined by the head and the media. As given by Equation 17.8, bpi is inversely proportional to the distance B between two back-to-back transitions. Thus, bpi depends on how closely transitions can be placed one after the other. The ability to place two transitions closely without the detected pulse signals from them (Figure 17.16) overly interfering with each other[6] depends on the width of each pulse—the narrower the pulse width the better. The standard measure of pulse width in magnetic recording is the half width, called PW50, which is measured at the 50% amplitude (see Figure 17.27).

Without derivation here, a number of analytical studies have shown that PW50 can be approximately represented by

$$PW50 = \sqrt{g^2 + 4 \cdot (d + a) \cdot (d + a + t)} \quad \text{(EQ 17.9)}$$

where a is the transition parameter (transition length), d is the magnetic separation, g is the half gap in MR head (or pole gap in inductive head), and t is the thickness of media (as shown

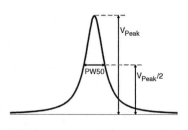

FIGURE 17.27: Pulse width.

in Figure 17.28). It should be noted that the magnetic separation d is not the same as the flying height of the slider. Magnetic separation is the spacing between the tip of the sensor and the top of the recording media; so it includes the flying height, and the thickness of the lubricant, and the thickness of the carbon overcoat (on both the media and the sensor).

The transition parameter a can be approximately modelled with the following equation:

$$a = K \times \sqrt{\frac{M_r \cdot t \cdot (d + t/2)}{H_c}} \quad \text{(EQ 17.10)}$$

where M_r and H_c are the remanent magnetization and coercivity of the medium, respectively, and K is some constant. From Equation 17.9, it can be seen that PW50 can be decreased (which means bpi can be increased) by reducing the MR sensor gap g (miniaturizing the head), the magnetic separation d (lowering the flying height which is the major component), the thickness of the media t, and the transition parameter a. Furthermore, according to Equation 17.10, the transition length a itself can also be shortened by reducing d and t. Selecting a medium material with high coercivity will also help to reduce a, but it requires more current in the inductive head for writing. While a medium with low remanence will also help to make the transition parameter small, it must produce a sufficient magnetic field for the read sensor to detect.

Because reducing the magnetic separation is one of the most significant factors in increasing areal density, flying height has continuously been decreasing over the years. When the RAMAC 350 was first introduced in 1956, the head-disk separation was 800 microinches. Today,

---

[6]Current channel technology can handle a small degree of inter-symbol interference.

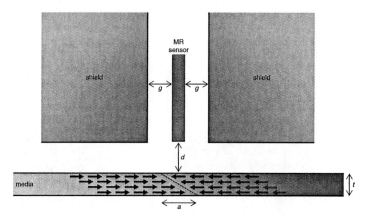

FIGURE 17.28: Key parameters of MR sensor model for PW50.

the flying height of a typical disk drive is well below 1 microinch. To put things in perspective, the thickness of human hair is about 3000 microinches, and the size of a typical dust particle is about 1500 microinches.

Tribology

Tribology[7] is the study of interaction of surfaces in relative motion, in this case between the head slider and the disk. While tribology is of great importance for CSS, even during the normal flying of the head, interactions between the slider and the disk surface can still occur. This is because asperities on a disk surface are inevitable and can result in contact with the head. Hence, tribology is an important aspect of disk drive design, even for drives using the load/unload technology which theoretically eliminates all intentional contact between the head and the disk. In addition to potentially causing wear due to physical abrasion (which, in turn, can also create contaminants), contact of the head with asperities on a disk surface raises the temperature of the MR head, resulting in temporarily changing its resistance. This phenomenon, known as thermal asperity, manifests itself as severe noise in the read signal. Thus, a high enough flying height is needed to avoid the surface asperities. Unfortunately,

a higher flying height is not good for areal density, as discussed previously. This is why tribology is so important in disk drive design, as it holds the key to how low the head can fly over the media and hence dictates what areal density can be achieved. Surface texture, overcoat material, and lubricant material are all part of the tribology domain.

17.2.9 Head-Disk Assembly

All the foregoing physical components described in this section are assembled together to form a *head-disk assembly* (HDA). It basically includes all the major components of a disk drive except for most of the electronics. The only electronics that is part of the HDA is the small AEM which is integrated with the flex cable. As discussed previously, the size of a dust particle is thousands of times greater than the head's flying height. With the surface of the disk traveling at over 100 mph past the head, a collision of the head with any contaminant can result in damage to either the head or the recording media. Therefore, assembling the HDA is done inside a clean room. The HDA is mounted inside a housing which is then sealed to keep contaminants out. However, the compartment is not airtight. Rather, air exchange with the outside is allowed through a breather filter so that the drive

---

[7]"Tribo" comes from Greek meaning "friction."
[8]Special disk drives for high altitude and space applications are exceptions. They have to be truly sealed to keep the air from leaking out since the heads must have air to fly.

can adjust to the outside air pressure.[8] To capture any contaminants that may come off the HDA after the drive leaves the assembly line, a recirculation filter can also be found inside the HDA compartment.

17.3 Electronics

The remaining physical components of a disk drive are the electronics that control its operation. Except for the AEM, they are located outside the sealed HDA compartment. Due to a high degree of integration, today's disk drive electronics are reduced to basically a handful of *Integrated Circuit* (IC) chips which all fit on a small printed circuit board. Figure 17.29 shows the major functional electronic components. The chip boundaries are deliberately not drawn as they may evolve as drive electronics technology changes. In this section, a high-level description of the functions of these components and their sub-components will be described. ICs performing some of these functions are available from several companies and are constantly being refreshed.

17.3.1 Controller

The controller is the brain of the disk drive. It either performs a disk drive function itself directly, or it makes sure that the function gets performed correctly by one of the other components. Figure 17.30 is a high-level block diagram of a controller's major sub-components. Some of the major functions handled by the controller are the following:

- Receive commands (I/O requests) from the user, schedule the execution of the commands, and report to the user when a command is completed
- Manage the cache
- Interface with the HDA, including telling it where to seek to and which sectors to read or write
- Error recovery and fault management
- Power management
- Starting up and shutting down the disk drive

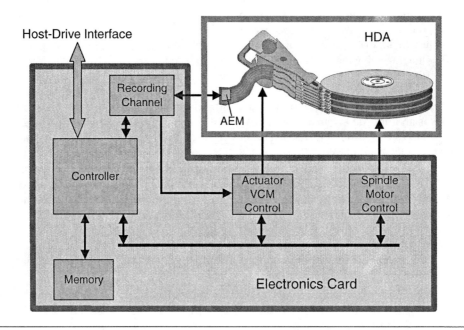

FIGURE 17.29: High-level electronic components of a disk drive.

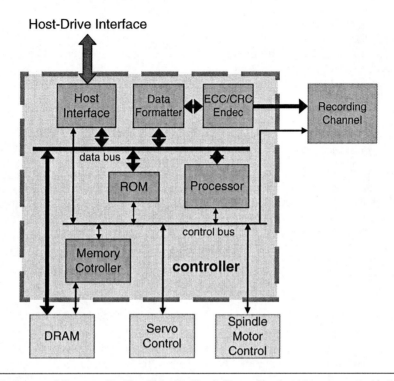

FIGURE 17.30: Block diagram of the controller. The dashed outline indicates functional boundary, not chip boundary.

Processor—A microprocessor is commonly used to execute the above list of functions and to carry out any related computations. The speed with which those functions can be performed not only depends on the speed and power of the microprocessor, but also on how much of a particular function is automated with hardware by one of the other sub-components. For instance, cache function can be completely handled by the processor firmware, or it can be fully or partially automated as part of the memory controller.

ROM—The executable code of the microprocessor resides here. Optionally, only the boot code for the processor is stored here, with the remainder of the controller code read in from a reserved area in the disk. During development of the disk drive, E^2PROM can be used instead. Executable code may be copied to SRAM for faster access by the processor.

Memory Controller—This can be as simple as just an interface to some DRAM, or it can include a cache manager performing cache space allocation and cache lookup. Cache is an important subject and will be covered in Chapter 22, "The Cache Layer."

Host Interface—This is the physical link of the disk drive to the host system it is attached to. It provides the necessary interface hardware (such as specific registers), performs the handshakes of the interface's protocol, and exchanges data with the user over this link. The host-disk interface will be discussed in greater detail in Chapter 20, "Drive Interface."

Data Formatter—Its function is to move the data from the memory, partition it into sector size chunks, and route it to the ECC and CRC logic.

ECC and CRC Encoder/Decoder—Error correcting code (ECC) and cyclic redundancy checksum (CRC) are added to each sector of data to be stored together in the media. They are used to provide data integrity and fault tolerance. More detail will be covered in Chapter 18, "The Data Layer."

17.3.2 Memory

The memory in the disk drive is used mainly to serve three distinct purposes:

1. Part of the memory is used as a scratch-pad for the controller. Each time the drive is powered up, it loads from protected areas in the disk operational tables and parameters onto the memory. Examples include the zoning table (discussed in Chapter 18) which is generally the same for all the drives of a given model, defect maps and no-ID tables (both discussed in Chapter 18) which are drive specific, and various parameters (many of them related to the operation of each individual head) that were self-calibrated during final manufacture testing. Memory is also used for run-time applications, such as for storing the queue of commands received from the host system.

2. The media data transfer rate is different from the data rate of the interface of the disk drive. Part of the memory is used for the purpose of speed-matching between these two different data rates. For instance, during a write operation, data from the host must be buffered in the memory and streamed out to the write channel at the media data rate. For a read operation, data from the media can be temporarily stored in the buffer memory even if the host or the drive interface happens to be busy. Without a buffer, write data may not be available, and read data may have no place to go right at the particular moment the head is ready to write or read that piece of data. The drive will then have to wait for one full disk revolution before it can attempt the same data access again, a condition commonly referred to as "*missed rev.*" The buffer is therefore essential in eliminating, or at least greatly reducing the number of, such performance-robbing missed revs.

3. Today's disk drives all have some memory for cache. Caching is an important aspect of disk drive performance and will be treated separately in Chapter 22.

While buffering and caching are two distinct functions, the address space of cache is usually also used for buffering. Today, DRAM is typically used for cache/buffer memory. Non-time-critical data or tables are also stored in DRAM. Tables needed for time-critical functions, such as address translation, are stored in SRAM for faster access by the processor which has dedicated access, unlike DRAM in which the processor has to share access with other hardware. In the future, if newer and better semiconductor memory technology comes along, it may be adopted in the disk drive to replace DRAM or SRAM.

17.3.3 Recording Channel

The read/write recording channel is a critical component of the disk drive which works hand in glove with the head and media to deliver the ultimate linear bit density of the drive. While improvements in heads and media oftentimes get credited for the high growth rate in recording density, advancements in channel technology have actually also contributed substantially. The recording channel controls the placing of user data onto the media (as described earlier in Section 17.2.3) by applying the right polarity of voltage to the inductive write head (hence controlling the direction of current flow in the coil) at the right time and retrieves previously recorded data by interpreting the voltage signal presented by the read sensor. Control signals received from the controller include whether to enable the write circuitry or the read circuitry and a selection of which head to turn on.

The AEM is actually part of the read/write channel. Because the signals to and from (especially from) the heads are small, the write drivers and read preamplifiers are placed in the AEM and located as close to the heads as possible so as to minimize resistance and inductance in the circuit. Hence, sub-components of the AEM are described here as part of the recording channel, even though physically AEM is separated and placed inside the HDA.

Write Channel

The write channel is the set of circuits that transforms the user data from its binary logic format into actual currents being sent to the write head. When writing data, the write channel supplies current to the write head, reversing the direction of current flow whenever a magnetic transition is to be created in the media. However, the 1's and 0's of user's data are not directly recorded as is. Rather, some modulation code is employed to ensure that the sequence of bits recorded and later retrieved satisfies certain desirable properties. Such properties include the following:

- Because the clocking for the reading of data is extracted from the recorded data bits, a very long string of 0's would mean there is no transition and hence no clocking information. This can lead to read errors as the clock can drift if it is not resynchronized for an extended period. Thus, it is necessary to limit the maximum length of run of 0's.
- If an error occurs in reading one bit, propagation of its effect must be well contained so that it does not turn into a long burst of errors.
- Have a high density ratio (DR) of data bits per flux change. This directly affects bpi, as indicated in Equation 17.8.

The coding method of using a transition to represent a 1, as discussed in Section 17.1.5, is known as *non-return to zero inverted* (NRZI) *encoding*. NRZI encoding places no limit on the number of consecutive 0's that can appear. One of the earliest methods introduced to prevent long runs of 0's in recorded signal is the *FM* (frequency modulation) encoding. In this scheme, a 1 is simply inserted after every data bit. For example, the data sequence 10001 would be encoded as 1101010111. FM is a rather poor encoding technique as the coding efficiency is only 50%. A slightly improved modified frequency modulation (MFM) scheme is to encode 1 into 01, while a 0 is encoded into 10 if the preceding bit is 0 and into 00 if the preceding bit is 1. Hence, the sample sequence of 10001 would be encoded as 0100101001. While the code rate for MFM is still only 50%, because two 1's are separated by at least one 0, higher recording density can

be achieved (assuming recording density is limited by the minimum distance between two transitions).

Modulation coding has gone through several major changes and many evolutionary changes over the years. FM and MFM are actually special cases of *run-length-limited* (RLL) codes. RLL code is specified as m/n(d,k), where m is the number of data bits encoded into n code bits, d is the minimum number of 0's required between two 1's, and k is the maximum number of 0's allowed. Thus, FM is a 1/2(0,1) RLL code, and MFM is a 1/2(1,2) RLL code. The DR is given by

$$DR = (d + 1) \times \frac{m}{n} \qquad \text{(EQ 17.11)}$$

For example, the 8/9(0,4) RLL code has a DR of 8/9, which makes the achievable bpi with that code 0.89 that of the fcpi of what the head-disk technology can deliver. Newer and more efficient codes have been developed in recent years, and multiple choices are oftentimes offered by suppliers of channel chips for disk drive designers to select the one that meets their needs.

The k parameter of RLL code is determined by how long the clocking can go without resync. The d parameter is a function of how well the channel can handle inter-symbol interference. *Inter-symbol interference* (ISI) occurs when the transitions are packed so close together that the detectable signal from a transition is distorted by those of its neighboring transitions. The pattern of ISI depends on the particular recorded bit sequence.

The simplest example would be of two 1's in the midst of a string of 0's. Figure 17.31(a) shows that when the two transitions are placed far enough apart, there is no interference of one pulse with the other. When the two transitions are packed closer together to increase bpi, the two pulses start to cancel each other. As a result, the amplitudes of the two pulses are reduced, and, more importantly, their peaks are shifted, as shown in Figure 17.31(b). The first peak arrives early, while the second peak arrives late. As the read process of today's disk drives is done synchronously based on a fixed clock rate, a shift causes the peak to be out of step with the clock signal and can potentially lead to read error. Since ISI is the unavoidable result of packing transitions more densely in order to increase bpi, multiple techniques have been developed to deal with ISI. One such technique is to precompensate the write signal delivered to the write driver. For the

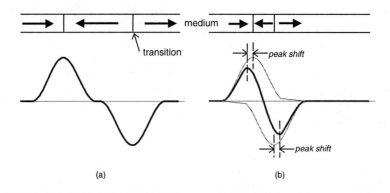

(a)   (b)

FIGURE 17.31: An example of ISI: (a) two transitions spaced far apart—no ISI; (b) two transitions placed close together—peak shift results.

simple peak shift example of the double transitions, precompensation would delay the first transition and move up the second transition. *Write precompensation* is sometimes referred to as *write equalization.*

Figure 17.32 is a functional block diagram of the sub-components of a write channel. The write driver, by means of a simple flip-flop circuit, uses a current source to apply a voltage of the right polarity, in accordance to the write signal provided by the write precompensation circuit, to the inductive write head.

However, before it can do that, the write driver must be enabled by three control signals:

1. The controller must first signal that it wants to do a write to the read/write gate.

2. The controller needs to determine which of the heads is to do the write and tells the decoder to enable that head.

3. There is a circuit which detects any condition which makes it unsafe to write, such as the head is not over the right track. This circuit must signal that it is okay to write.

All three conditions must be met all the time during the write for the write driver to apply current to the head.

Read Channel

The read channel is a series of circuits that converts the analog signals sensed by the read head back into the original user data in their binary logic format. Figure 17.33 shows a block diagram of the major

components of a typical read channel. With today's microscopic bit size, the signal picked up by the GMR head is very small, well below 1 mV. The first order of business is to greatly amplify this signal as soon as possible before it picks up more noise. This is handled by the preamp which is a differential amplifier located in the AEM. For the preamp of a read head to go active, the controller must first signal that it wants to do a read to the read/write selector, and the head must also be selected by the decoder based on the controller's selection of which head to use. When enabled, the selected head's AEM module applies a sensing current to its MR sensor.

The amplified signal from the AEM is passed on to an automatic gain control (AGC) circuit to adjust the peak voltages of the signal to within the range required by subsequent circuitries. A low-pass filter following the AGC reduces high-frequency noise. The equalizer is a circuit which slims the pulses, that is, makes the shape of the pulses narrower. This is another technique employed to combat ISI, in addition to write precompensation described previously.

The conditioned signal is now ready for the detection circuit. The detector extracts servo information (see Section 17.3.4 and Chapter 18), as well as the original recorded binary information. Servo information is fed to the actuator servo control circuit. Encoded user data is written to the disk synchronously using a clocking signal. Hence, to extract data accurately from the readback signal, the detector must also extract the clocking

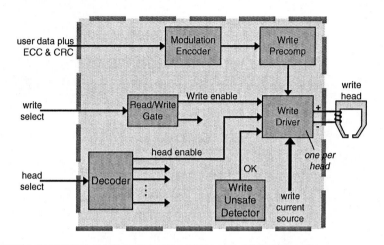

FIGURE 17.32: Block diagram of a write channel.

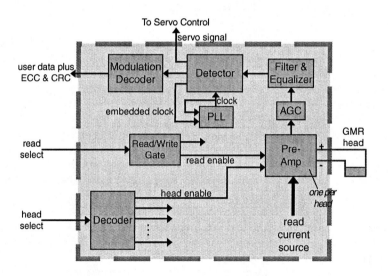

FIGURE 17.33: Block diagram of a read channel.

information embedded with the data. The extracted clock signal is fed to a phase-locked loop (PLL) circuit to regulate the clock that the detector uses to recover data. While the frequency of the clock is adjusted gradually based on the average of several bits, adjustment for individual data pulse timing is immediate and based only on the current detected clock pulse.

Earlier disk drives used peak detection to directly look for pulses created by transitions in the media. With this technique, the pulse signal is differentiated, and the detection logic looks for zero-crossing of the differentiated output as where a peak has occurred. In 1990, the IBM 0681 disk drive introduced *PRML* (partial response maximum likelihood) as a new method

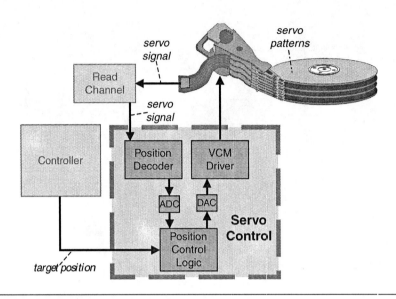

FIGURE 17.34: Schematic and logic flow of the servo control circuit.

for data recovery. While known to the data communication field for a long time, PRML was a breakthrough technology for magnetic recording. It is a very effective technique for dealing with ISI and permits denser packing of transitions than peak detection. There are two key aspects to PRML. First, the signal is sampled, which is called a partial response signal. Second, instead of decoding each pulse individually as in peak detection, it decodes a short sequence of bits in a sliding window. For each sequence of sampled signal, it looks for the bit sequence which is most likely (hence, maximum likelihood) to generate that sampled sequence.

Regardless of the data detection method used, the last stage of a read channel is to run the data output of the detector through a modulation code decoder to recover the original user data and ECC/CRC information.

17.3.4 Motor Controls

The spindle motor and the actuator VCM are two different types of electric motors with two distinct forms of motion to perform two very different mechanical functions. One is to spin the disk platters at a constant rotational speed. The other is to move

the actuator so as to place the active head at a radial position very precisely. Yet, the desired motion of both can be controlled by governing the current (amplitude and direction) being applied to the motor. Both use a feedback loop for control by constantly monitoring the status of the motor and sending the information to the control logic. The control logic then computes the amount of correction that is needed and adjusts the current output to the motor accordingly.

Figure 17.34 shows a high-level schematic of the actuator servo control system and how the logic flows [Chen et al. 2006, Oswald 1974]. The key of the servo system is that special servo patterns are written on the disks at manufacturing time. These servo patterns provide precise information of their location. Detailed descriptions of the servo patterns are covered in Chapter 18. The read channel detects these servo patterns and forwards the signals from these patterns to a decoding circuit which decodes the signals into positional information. The positional information is fed to the servo control logic which compares it with the target track position requested by the disk drive's controller. The difference is used to generate a corrective action signal, which is fed to the VCM driver for adjusting the current that is being applied to the VCM. This closed-loop logic flow takes place continuously as long as the drive is active, whether it is seeking a new location or following a track to keep the head centered over it. Earlier drives used analog circuits to perform the servo control functions. Today, the job is being handled by a digital signal processor (DSP), which means the servo control includes an analog to digital converter (ADC) for converting the analog servo signals to digital form and a digital to analog converter (DAC) for converting the digital correction signal into analog input for the power amplifier of the VCM driver.

The spindle motor is also controlled using a feedback loop. Here, the motor status information being fed back to its control circuit is simply its rotational speed. Some earlier disk drives used Hall sensors to measure the motor speed. Today's disk drives determine the motor's rotational speed by measuring the back-EMF voltage from the motor coil generated by the spinning motor.

CHAPTER 18

The Data Layer

The previous chapter discusses the physical components of a disk drive for recording/retrieving data bits onto/from the magnetic media. But how should these data bits be placed and organized on the disks? In this chapter, we explore some of the data placement alternatives and evaluate some design trade-offs.

It is intuitively obvious that the bits of a given piece of data should be stored together for best storage efficiency and access performance. The piece of data can be a transaction record, a text file, a spreadsheet, a compressed music file, or some other type of file. The reasons are obvious. First, since every piece of data needs to have some sort of identification, storing a piece of data in a single place instead of splitting it up into multiple pieces means that this overhead is paid only once. Second, when all the bits of a piece of data are located together, it is necessary to go to only one place to access that piece of data instead of having to go to multiple locations to do the retrieval. This is the ideal, and certainly should be adhered to for small files or records. For very large files, this may not be practical, and there is no choice but to split the data up into smaller pieces. The number of errors or defects encountered may become too many in a large single record for the implemented error correcting code to handle. It may also be undesirable to store a very large file as a single record, since only a small portion of the file may be needed at a time by its application. Still, the split up smaller pieces should be stored close to each other so that efficiency of access is not lost. The retrieving of related data which is in close physical proximity is commonly referred to in the disk community as *locality of access*.

18.1 Disk Blocks and Sectors

When a user's data is saved in a disk drive, it is written by the recording head as a string of bits. The first question to ask on data organization is: How should space be allocated on a disk drive for such strings of bits? There are two clear alternatives, namely *fixed-size allocation* and *variable length allocation*.

18.1.1 Fixed-Size Blocks

In fixed-size allocation, the storage space in a disk drive is partitioned into blocks of one single size. The host system to which the disk drive is attached allocates disk space by such fixed-size blocks. As many blocks as necessary are allocated to store a user file or record. Ideally, as mentioned above, all the blocks of the same file should be physically contiguous, or *sequential*, so as to gain the performance benefit of locality of access. However, a strict policy of physically contiguous allocation has some drawbacks:

- It is more difficult to look for enough contiguous blocks, especially for large files and when the drive has already been highly utilized.
- After many allocations and deallocations, holes (short run of free blocks) will invariably materialize in the storage space. Such holes are one form of *external fragmentation* of memory space.
- Garbage collection becomes necessary to consolidate these holes.

For these reasons, it is more practical for the host system to map logically contiguous data blocks to possibly physically non-contiguous disk blocks. Naturally, even with such flexibility, physically contiguous blocks should still be allocated to a single file as much as possible to improve locality of access.

With fixed-size blocks, the last block of a user file will generally be only partially filled, with the remaining space wasted. This is *internal fragmentation* of memory space. The design trade-offs of the size of a fixed-size block architecture are the following:

- If the block size is too small, then it is hard to keep all the data of a large user file in sequential blocks. If the block size is 200 bytes and a user file is 1 MB, then 5000 blocks are required to hold this file; it would be difficult to maintain this file as a single string of sequential blocks.
- If the block size is too large, then for users with many small files internal fragmentation would cause a lot of wasted space. Imagine a 200-GB disk with fixed-size blocks of 4 KB each. If a user is using it to store exclusively data records that are only 100 bytes each, then that disk drive effectively becomes just a 5-GB disk.

What block size is too small or too large is dependent on the intended usage of the disk drive—it is all relative. Selecting the correct size is an important design parameter.

18.1.2 Variable Size Blocks

In the first disk drive, the RAMAC 350, data was stored as 100-character, fixed-length records (one character is 7 bits, not quite a byte). If a user's record is less than 100 characters, that means the remaining space is wasted. Since storage was expensive in the early days of disk drives, variable record size was introduced as a means to improve storage efficiency. One such format that IBM used was known as the "Count-Key-Data" (CKD) format, which was used in mainframe computers up to the 1990s. In this format, the data field holding the user's record is preceded by a count field which specifies the size of the data field and by an optional key field which the user can use to store identification information of the ensuing

record. The key is used by the application program to facilitate searching for a desired record. Main frame I/O programming can be a long discussion in itself and will not be discussed here. All count, key, and data fields are separated by physical gaps.

With variable size data blocks, the size of a disk block is exactly the same size as the user's data record. The host tells the disk drive how big the data record is, and the drive writes a string with that number of bytes onto the media. Now the drive does not waste any space when storing a small record, i.e., there is no internal fragmentation. However, variable size blocks have the following issues:

- Similar to large contiguous allocations using fixed-size blocks, it has to deal with the issue of external fragmentation. Thus, space allocation for large records may become difficult, and garbage collection may become necessary.
- When used to store many small records, the space taken by the gaps between fields and the need for some sort of "count" field can become a substantial storage overhead. For example, let's say the gaps are 10 bytes each and the count field is 30 bytes, then the overhead for storing a 100-byte record is 50 bytes. This represents a storage efficiency of only 67%. A more efficient storage method would perhaps be for the host to pack multiple small records into larger blocks and store them into fixed-size disk blocks.

18.1.3 Sectors

Today, all disk drives use a fixed-size block formatting. The blocks are referred to as *sectors*. The huge price advantage accorded to drives with standard interface from economy of scale has rendered proprietary disk drives no longer economically competitive. Disk drives with ATA interface for the low-end market and drives with SCSI or FC interface for the high-end market account for essentially all drives being manufactured today. All these standards specify fixed block size architecture. ATA specifies a sector size of 512 data bytes. SCSI allows for different sector sizes to be declared by a disk drive; however, a 512-data-byte sector is also by far the most common. Some RAID systems and other higher end storage subsystems, such as IBM's AS/400, choose to use disk drives with a bigger sector size, such as 520, to store some metadata information together with the user's 512 data bytes. The sector size of a SCSI drive is specified as a mode page parameter.

Anatomy of a Sector

Figure 18.1 shows the various parts of a typical sector; there may be some slight variation from manufacturer to manufacturer and from product family to product family. Each sector is separated from a preceding recorded field and a succeeding field by physical gaps which have no recording of any sort. The preceding and succeeding fields can be, but are not necessarily, another sector, as will become clear in later sections. The physical gap is mainly there to allow time and buffering for the read and write heads to access any sector individually. It is especially important for writes, because without the gap if the write head is turned on just a little early or late, the preceding or succeeding field would be overwritten and hence corrupted. The buffering is also needed to allow for some drifting of the clock with which the data is written.

The first field of a sector is a field of about 10 bytes called the *preamble*. Some practitioners call this the *sync field*. Its recorded signals establish the frequency and amplitude with which the remainder of the sector is written so that a read channel can later use these signals to adjust its phase-locked loop (PLL) and automatic gain control (AGC) circuits. The preamble is followed by a special recording pattern of

a few bytes called the *data sync* or *data address mark*. It demarcates the end of the preamble and signals the beginning of data. Next comes the actual user data— 512 user bytes encoded by run-length-limited (RLL) code into some 544 (depending what code is used) physical bytes.

The data field is protected with an *error correcting code* (ECC). A systematic code for error correction is invariably used. With systematic codes the user data is not altered, and the ECC redundancy information is a distinguishable field appended to the end of the original user data. The size of this ECC field, while typically around 40 or so bytes, is dependent on the correction power of the ECC being used. Burst error correction codes are always used as any sort of defect is likely to affect multiple bits in magnetic disks.

To further enhance data integrity, a cyclic redundancy checksum (CRC) is also included as part of a sector, the size of which is product-dependent. The CRC is simply the remainder of dividing a binary string by some polynomial and is used for detecting transmission errors. Reading of previously recorded data is, of course, one kind of transmission—temporal transmission or transmission over time.

Finally, even though the ECC is the last field with useful information, a few more bytes of signal need to be padded at the end to keep the clock running while the last of the data is flushed through the read channel, the RLL decoder and ECC decoder.

Sector Size

With standardized sector size, design trade-off considerations of block size discussed earlier become moot for the general user and even for the disk drive

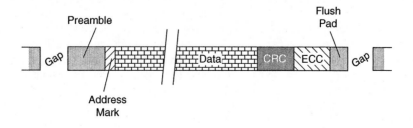

FIGURE 18.1: Components of a sector.

designer. System software, particularly file systems and device drivers, is written with the sector size hard-coded. The BIOS (Basic I/O System, bootup instructions stored in a computer's ROM) also assumes standard 512-byte sectors. Thus, to change the size of user-addressable sectors in disk drives will require coordinated changes in system software.

One alternative is for the disk drive to internally adopt a block size that is desirable, such as 2 KB, as its physical sector size, but emulate a 512-byte sector device so that externally it retains a 512-byte sector interface to the host system that it talks to. That means it would receive logical addresses for 512-byte sectors from the host, but internally map them to the actual physical sectors. With a 2-KB sector as an example, four 512-byte logical sectors would map to a single 2-KB physical sector. Emulation will work fine, allowing disk drives to have internally larger sector sizes without depending on changes in the host software. Reads will essentially have the same performance as before. Writes, however, may suffer; this happens when the host asks to update data that is not aligned in 2-KB boundaries and in multiples of 2 KB. To handle such update writes, the drive needs to first read into buffer memory the to-be partially updated 2-KB blocks, insert the new data, and then write out the modified sectors. Such read-modify-writes for updates can cause substantial performance degradation, as they will add one full revolution to the access time.

A simple change in system software to guarantee aligned 2-KB accesses, or whatever the new sector size is, together with 512-byte sector emulation by the disk drive, is a reasonable evolution path for the disk drive to migrate to bigger sector sizes. This approach assures that those who care about performance can update to this new software to avoid any performance penalty, while legacy systems will still be compatible with new disk drives, albeit at the cost of performance degradation.

As described previously, every sector carries its own ECC for error protection. ECC is a necessary overhead. As areal density increases, the accompanying decrease in signal-to-noise ratio means the raw error rate (commonly called the soft error rate or SER) will keep going higher and higher. Additionally,

as the bit size gets smaller, a same size physical defect will affect more bits. This means the burst length of errors also becomes longer. Yet, the uncorrectable error rate (commonly called the hard error rate or HER) acceptable to users does not get higher with time; if anything, users are demanding more and more reliability. These two factors, viz., more and longer errors, dictate that more and more powerful ECC needs to be used in order to provide to the user an acceptable level of data reliability and integrity. However, more powerful ECC requires more redundancy bits. The ECC bits constitute an overhead for a sector. Therefore, when the size of a data sector is held constant at 512 bytes while more and more ECC bits are added, an increasing fraction of the available storage bits on a disk will become lost to ECC overhead. For this very reason, the disk drive industry is under pressure to increase the sector size. In 2005, the industry agreed to adopt 4 KB as another standard sector size, in addition to the old 512-byte sector. Windows' new OS Vista will provide support for large block size.

18.2 Tracks and Cylinders

When a string of data bits is recorded by the write head onto a disk surface, an arc is naturally formed due to the rotation of the disk surface under the head. If the head is stationary, the arc is part of a circle. If the head is moving while the disk is rotating, the arc is part of a spiral. Hence, there are two possible choices for laying out data bits. The data blocks, or sectors, can either be arranged as concentric circles or be arranged as a long spiral, as shown in Figure 18.2.

The standard track formatting chosen by magnetic hard disk drives since the beginning is that of a series of concentric circles. Each circle is commonly referred to as a *track*. One spot on each track is designated as the beginning of the track. The beginning of a track is also the end of a track. An integer number of sectors, evenly spaced, are placed on each track. The number of sectors to be placed on a track will be discussed later in this chapter. The sectors on a track are numbered from 1 to N, where N is the number of sectors on that track. The *de facto* standard is to number the

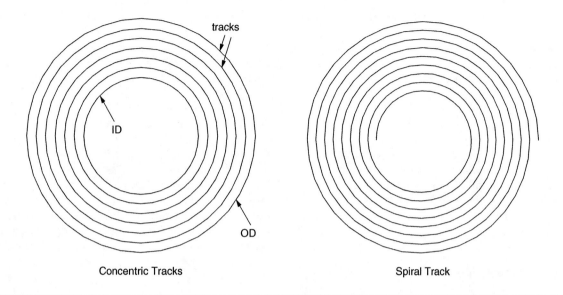

tracks

ID

OD

Concentric Tracks

Spiral Track

FIGURE 18.2: Two kinds of tracks: concentric tracks versus spiral track.

tracks starting at the outermost diameter or OD and incrementing toward the innermost diameter or ID; convention is to label the first track as track 0.

Some optical disks, such as CD and DVD, have opted to adopt a spiral track format. In this format, recording is done along a single contiguous track that spirals from the ID of the disk surface all the way to the OD.

There is interplay among the relationship of the choice of track formatting (i.e., concentric or spiral), linear recording density (bpi), and rotational speed. These relationships are discussed in Section 18.4. Hence, discussion on the design trade-offs between concentric and spiral tracks is deferred until some other needed topics have been discussed first. It will be covered in Chapter 19, "Performance Issues and Design Trade-offs."

Cylinders

A conventional disk drive with concentric tracks and multiple recording surfaces has the same number of tracks on each surface. Tracks are numbered, by convention starting with track 0 at the OD and

incrementing toward the ID. All the tracks with the same track number, one from each surface, collectively are called a *cylinder*. Cylinders are similarly numbered as tracks, with cylinder 0 being the first user data cylinder. In practice, the disk drive oftentimes reserves several outermost cylinders to store internal information. This internal information is for the operation of the disk drive and is not accessible by the general users. User data cylinder 0 starts after the reserved cylinders; for this reason, the reserved cylinders are sometimes referred to as the *negative cylinders*.

Conceptually and ideally, tracks of a cylinder are aligned vertically, one atop of the other, hence its name. In the past when track density (tpi) was relatively low, this was more or less true, and all the heads of the actuator were over their respective tracks of the same cylinder. So every track in a cylinder could be accessed by simply electronically enabling its head without having to move the actuator. Hence, previously a cylinder was commonly defined as the tracks addressable by all the heads when the actuator is at a given position. Nowadays, however, with track pitch being smaller than 20 microinches, it is difficult to achieve the tight mechanical tolerance necessary for that to happen. It is more than likely that switching from one head to another now also entails some tiny movement by the actuator in order to properly position the newly selected head.

18.3 Address Mapping

Every sector in a disk drive needs to be uniquely identifiable in order for it to be unambiguously accessed. Externally, a user needs to tell the disk drive which sector block he wants. Internally, the disk drive has to be able to go to the right location to access the requested sector.

18.3.1 Internal Addressing

Internally, every sector in the drive is given a physical block address (PBA); sometimes it is also called an absolute block address (ABA). The PBA or ABA is simply a number between 0 and N – 1, where N is the total number of sectors in the disk drive. Additionally, each sector's physical location is given in terms of its cylinder number, its head or recording surface number, and its sector number on the track. This is commonly referred to as CHS addressing. For example, a sector's physical location may be Cylinder 23,609, Head 5, Sector 723. The cylinder number represents the radial position, the head number represents the z-axis position, and the sector number represents the angular position of the sector. Thus, the CHS address gives the coordinates of a sector in a three-dimensional space.

18.3.2 External Addressing

Originally, host systems also used CHS physical addressing to specify to a disk drive what data block was wanted. This was appropriate in the early days when disk drives were simple and the host systems did all the housekeeping functions of a disk drive, such as defect management. As disk drives became more sophisticated and complex (see Sections 18.4

and 18.9), it became impractical for the drive to relate all the necessary internal structure information to the host for it to be able to interface with the drive using absolute addressing. A simpler and also more flexible alternative is for the host to interface with a disk drive using some sort of logical addressing.

One possible logical addressing scheme is to retain the CHS addressing structure, except the cylinder, head, and sector numbers are not real physical numbers but are actually some artificially defined logical numbers. Internally, the drive translates the logical CHS to a PBA. As an example, for many generations now, ATA[1] drives have been reporting to the host during initialization that it has 63 sectors per track and 16 heads, even though the number of sectors per track is really much larger than 63 and the number of heads is fewer than 16. This is because the original ATA specifications only allowed for 6 addressing bits for the sector number and 4 bits for the head number. Drive makers made use of the larger logical head number to compensate for the small maximum sector number limit so that the total drive capacity could be accounted for. An advantage of logical CHS addressing is that old software that deals with physical CHS would not have to be changed. Drives using logical CHS can transparently replace physical CHS drives since there is no difference in the host-disk interface.

A second logical addressing scheme alternative is to change the host-disk interface so that the host simply uses a logical block number, called an LBA (for Logical Block Address), for specifying a sector. LBA is the most common form of external addressing in use today. One reason is that the maximum number of cylinders that can be specified using ATA interface's old CHS format is 16,383. Together with the maximum number of heads of 16 and the maximum number of sectors per track of 63, a drive with a maximum capacity of only 8.4 GB can be specified. This capacity is far below that of most of the disk drives manufactured today. LBA is the only alternative that allows ATA drives with capacity of more than 8.4 GB to be addressed.

---

[1]ATA and other interface standards are discussed in Chapter 20, "Drive Interface."

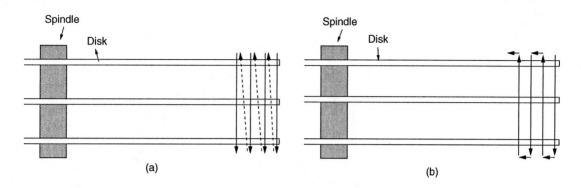

FIGURE 18.3: Cylinder mode formatting.

18.3.3 Logical Address to Physical Location Mapping

An LBA presented to the disk drive needs to be first converted to PBA. This step is necessary, due to the presence of defective sectors, and will be discussed in Section 18.9. Internally, the disk drive has a fixed mapping of PBAs to their CHS physical locations. Logically sequential blocks are naturally laid out physically sequential on a track.[2] The design decision that needs to be made when laying the logical blocks in a drive is after the end of a track is reached, where to go for the next logical block. There are two main choices: move in the radial direction or move in the z-axis direction.

Cylinder Mode

When it is possible to access the next track in a cylinder without actuator repositioning, as discussed previously, the choice seems clear: go to the next track in the cylinder. This is often referred to as operating the drive in *cylinder mode*. When the end of a cylinder is reached, go to the next cylinder. Even here there are two choices. Assuming we start from the top in cylinder 0, one can go back to the top of the next cylinder each time the bottom track has been reached, as

illustrated in Figure 18.3(a). Alternatively, one can go to the adjacent track in the next cylinder on the same surface, i.e., no head change, as shown in Figure 18.3b. Which scheme performs better depends on the servo. With today's high tpi going even higher, it is likely that the actuator can reposition itself to the next track on the same surface more easily; it knows exactly where it is currently, and it knows exactly where it needs to go. On the other hand, there is more uncertainty involved when a different head is involved. In fact, it is not inconceivable that moving the actuator inward to seek the next cylinder of a different head may actually be going in the wrong direction, as illustrated in Figure 18.4. Therefore, the address formatting scheme of Figure 18.3(b) may have a performance advantage over that of Figure 18.3(a).

Serpentine Format

To carry the above argument one step further, it may be even easier and faster to seek to the adjacent track on the same surface than switching head to access the next track of the same cylinder. As far as the actuator is concerned, a different track of the same cylinder may actually be physically farther away than an adjacent track, thus requiring a longer seek. Worse, the direction of the seek may not even

---

[2]Historically, this is called 1:1 interleave, because some old drives and floppy disks used 3:1 interleave; e.g., 1-7-13-2-8-14-3-9-15-4-10-16-5-11-17-6-12 for a 17-sector-per-track layout.

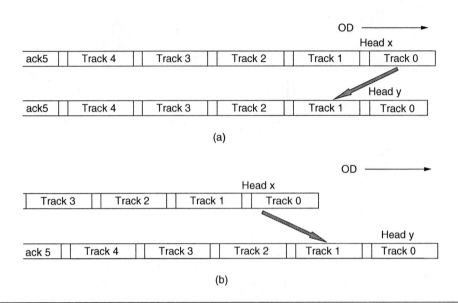

FIGURE 18.4: Tracks of two different heads. (a) The two tracks are perfectly aligned vertically. The actuator moves away from the OD when going from track 0 of head x to track 1 of head y. (b) The two tracks are not perfectly aligned vertically. The actuator needs to move toward the OD in order to go from track 0 of head x to track 1 of head y, opposite to the direction for perfectly aligned tracks.

be known until after it has switched head and read the servo information (discussed in Section 18.5) of the new surface. To handle this type of situation, the sensible thing to do would then be to increment in the radial direction, as shown in Figure 18.5(a). This addressing pattern is referred to as *serpentine* formatting.

All of a user's data requests are usually logically near each other; that is, their logical addresses are close together. This is what contributes to locality of access in the I/O pattern as seen by the disk drive. The problem with the serpentine formatting of Figure 18.5(a) is that for such accesses the average seek distance is increased compared to that of the cylinder mode formatting. This is especially true for drives with a larger number of heads. Assuming a user's data access footprint can all fit on less than a disk surface, a very reasonable assumption with today's high-capacity drive, the average seek distance is increased by a factor equal to the number of heads in the drive. This increase in

seek distance offsets the benefit of a shorter next track access time. As a compromise, one can partition the disk drive into bands of tracks and limit the serpentine formatting to each band, as illustrated in Figure 18.5(b). When the end of a band is reached, the first track of the next band comes next. We call this *banded serpentine* formatting.

Skewing

Long sequential accesses, where a user reads or writes a large amount of data, is a common I/O pattern. For such type of accesses, crossing a track boundary in the middle of a command frequently happens. When reaching the end of a track and advancing to the next logical track, a small time delay is required. It does not matter whether the next logical track is another track in the same cylinder or the next track on the same surface. The servo needs the time delay to make sure that the head is correctly positioned over

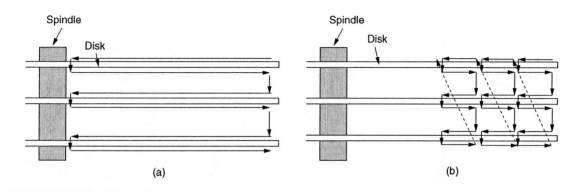

FIGURE 18.5: Serpentine formatting: (a) full serpentine and (b) banded serpentine.

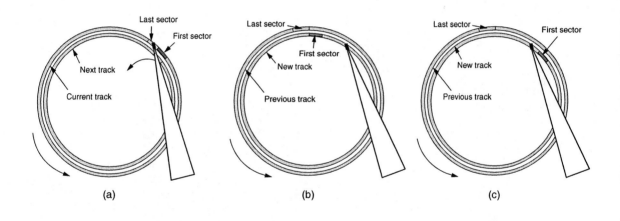

FIGURE 18.6: Skewing. (a) End of current track reached; (b) after track switch—with no skew, first sector is missed; (c) after track switch—with skewing; first sector coming up.

the new track, regardless of whether cylinder mode or serpentine formatting is used.

If the first logical sector of each track starts at the same angular position, then by the time the head is ready to read or write the next logical sector after finishing accessing the last sector of a track, that next sector would have already rotated past the head, as shown in Figure 18.6. The drive must then wait for basically one full rotation of the disk before it can access that sector. This would incur a big performance penalty for sequential accesses.

To compensate for this track switching delay, the standard technique is to skew the first logical sector of every track from the end of the previous track. The skew amount is selected to allow for the switching time or head positioning time, as shown in Figure 18.6(c). A sufficient margin must be included since the penalty for missing is so large.

This skew is referred to as the *track skew*. When the skew is introduced for going to the first track of the next cylinder when operating in cylinder mode, it is commonly called the *cylinder skew*.

18.4 Zoned-Bit Recording

All magnetic hard disk drives rotate at a constant speed. This is called *constant angular velocity* (CAV) recording. In the early days, a disk drive had the same number of sectors per track for every track, as conceptually illustrated in Figure 18.7, where every track is shown to have 16 sectors. Since the same number of sectors passes under the head for each revolution of the drive regardless of which track the head is over, and every rotation of the drive takes the same amount of time, this means the data rate stays constant, as represented by the following equation where all the terms are fixed for this type of drive:

$$\text{data rate} = \text{sectors per track} \times \text{bytes}$$
$$\text{per sector} \times \text{rpm} \qquad \textbf{(EQ 18.1)}$$

Implementation is simple and straightforward, since the drive has to deal with one single constant data rate.

It is clear from Figure 18.7 that the physical length of a sector at the OD is much longer than at the ID. If the OD is twice the ID, then the sector at the OD is physically twice as long as that at the ID. Since the number of bytes is the same for all sectors, that means the recording density (bpi) is lower as one

moves from the ID toward the OD. This relationship is as shown in Figure 18.8(a) for an example where ID is three-tenths of the OD.

Since the recording density anywhere on the disk cannot exceed the bpi that the technology of the disk drive is capable of supporting, that bpi must be applied at the ID. The recording density everywhere else on the disk is lower. This means that the total recording capacity of the disk is less than the theoretical maximum. This is as shown in Figure 18.8(b), where the area under each curve represents the total disk capacity. The theoretical capacity of one disk surface is

$$\text{capacity} = \text{tpi} \times \text{bpi} \times \pi \times (\text{OD}^2 - \text{ID}^2)/4 \qquad \textbf{(EQ 18.2)}$$

In reality, the capacity that can be achieved with a fixed number of sectors per track is

$$\text{capacity} = \text{tpi} \times \text{bpi} \times \pi \times \text{ID} \times (\text{OD} - \text{ID})/2 \qquad \textbf{(EQ 18.3)}$$

If one hopes to gain more recording area by continuing to do recording until a very small ID is reached, a small number of sectors per track are established for all the other tracks. If one tries to come up with a greater number of sectors per track for all the tracks on the disk, one needs to stop recording early so as to have a large ID, but this strategy results in a small total recording area. To determine the optimal ID to use in a constant number of sectors per track recording, we can treat ID in Equation 18.3 as a variable, take the derivative with respect to ID, and equate it to zero. The result is that the maximum capacity is achieved when

$$\text{ID} = \text{OD}/2 \qquad \textbf{(EQ 18.4)}$$

This is illustrated in Figure 18.9. Substituting Equation 18.4 into Equations 18.2 and 18.3, it can be seen that recording with the same number of sectors per track has an efficiency of two-thirds if recording stops at an ID equal to OD/2. When compared to using the entire disk surface for recording (which is not possible because of the mounting hole for the spindle motor) with constant bpi, then the efficiency drops to only one-half.

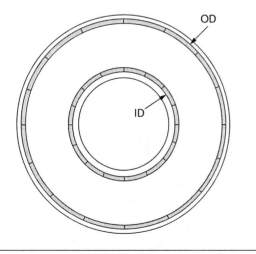

FIGURE 18.7: Same number of sectors per track. An example of 16 sectors per track.

Because a sector, including its overhead and gap, has a fixed number of bytes, and there can only be whole integer number of sectors on a track, there may be some leftover bits at the ID if it is set to exactly half of the OD. For this reason, in practice one can continue the recording area inwards until an ID is reached where exactly the number of bits for the number of sectors at OD/2 can be recorded.

The small gain from the just-described adjustment is minute compared to the unrealized capacity illustrated in Figure 18.8(b) stemming from most of the disk surface being utilized at a bpi much lower than what the drive can handle. To attain the maximum capacity, it will be necessary for every track to be recorded at the maximum bpi. Then, not only is the unrealized capacity of Figure 18.8(b) now becoming realized, but also there no longer is a penalty for extending the recording area deeper than the OD/2 boundary, since the linear recording density anywhere on the disk is no longer dictated by what is established at the ID. As a matter of fact, the deeper one goes, the more total storage is achieved. This is illustrated in Figure 18.10, as contrasted to Figure 18.9. Of course, because of the need for a center mounting hole, allowance for crash

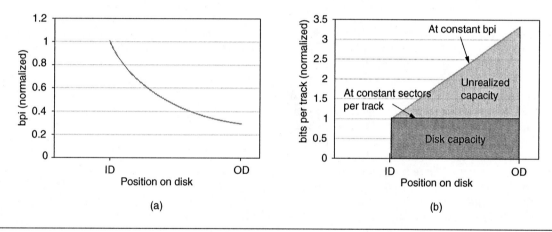

(a)   (b)

FIGURE 18.8: Same number of sectors per track: (a) bpi as a function of position on disk and (b) track capacity as a function of position on disk.

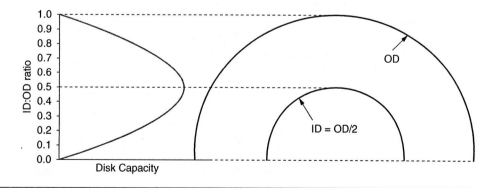

FIGURE 18.9: Capacity of disk as a function of ID for an equal number of sectors per track. The maximum is when ID = OD/2.

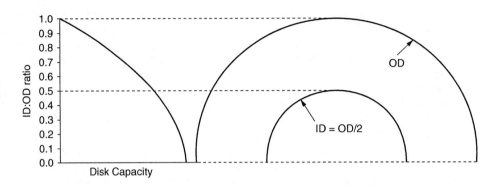

FIGURE 18.10: Capacity of disk as a function of ID for equal bpi in all tracks. Maximum is when ID = 0.

stop, and perhaps a landing zone, it is not possible to have a recording ID of 0, but there no longer is any limitation on where recording optimally should stop.

While capacity is maximized, implementation is complex when there are hundreds of thousands of tracks all having different data rates which the electronics have to contend with. To simplify things, a compromise is to partition the recording areas into a handful of concentric zones, where all the tracks within a zone have the same number of sectors. This is conceptually illustrated in Figure 18.11. This data formatting is called *zoned-bit recording* (ZBR).

Assuming that the width (outer radius minus inner radius) of each zone is the same for all the zones, namely $(OD - ID)/2N$, where N is the number of zones, the same arguments given earlier which explain why there is an optimum (capacity-wise) ID for same number of sectors per track formatting also apply for ZBR. The total bit capacity of a ZBR disk surface with N zones is

$$tpi \cdot bpi \cdot \pi \cdot \sum_{i=0}^{N-1} \left(ID + i \cdot \frac{OD - ID)}{N} \right) \cdot \left(\frac{OD - ID}{2N} \right) \quad \text{(EQ 18.5)}$$

which sums to

$$\frac{tpi \cdot bpi \cdot \pi}{4N} \cdot [(N-1) \cdot OD^2 - (N+1) \cdot ID^2 + 2 \cdot OD \cdot ID] \quad \text{(EQ 18.6)}$$

To determine the optimal ID, again we can take the derivative of Equation 18.6 with respect to the ID and

set it equal to zero. The capacity for a ZBR disk with N zones is maximized when

$$ID = \frac{OD}{N+1} \quad \text{(EQ 18.7)}$$

Substituting Equation 18.7 into Equation 18.6 gives

$$capacity_{Max} = \frac{tpi \cdot bpi \cdot \pi \cdot N \cdot OD^2}{4 \cdot (N+1)} \quad \text{(EQ 18.8)}$$

When compared to the maximum capacity with no zoning, which is tpi × bpi × π × OD^2/8, the fraction of improvement is

$$improvement = \frac{N-1}{N+1} \quad \text{(EQ 18.9)}$$

As N becomes very large, the improvement approaches 100%, which is the case for when the entire disk surface, with no mounting hole, is recorded at the maximum bpi.

It should be emphasized that while Equation 18.7 gives the optimal ID for a given number of zones, it is not to be used for the reverse, i.e., determining the number of zones when given an ID. For example, if the ID is 1/5 of the OD, one must not use Equation 18.7 to come up with the conclusion that N = 4 is the best number of zones to use. When it comes to the number of zones, more is always better, regardless of the ID, subject to implementation constraints, of course. In practice, today's disk platters have a mounting hole that is at least 25% of the disk diameter. While

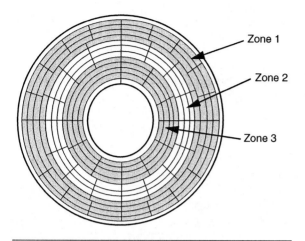

FIGURE 18.11: Conceptual example of a disk with zoned-bit recording. There are three zones with four tracks in each zone. Zone 1 has 20 sectors per track. Zone 2 has 16 sectors per track. Zone 3 has 12 sectors per track.

N = 3 yields ID = OD/4 from Equation 18.7, all drives being manufactured today have many more zones than three.

18.4.1 Handling ZBR

Referring to Equation 18.1, it is clear that, because the number of bytes per sector is fixed, when the number of sectors per track is changed, as is the case in going from one zone to another, one of three things can happen:

1. The data rate changes while the speed of rotation stays constant.
2. The rotational speed changes while the data rate remains constant.
3. Both data rate and rotational speed change.

These are exactly the alternatives for handling ZBR. An implementation that involves both varying data rate and rotational speed does not make practical sense and so will not be considered here. The remaining practical ways to handle ZBR are to deal with either varying data rate or varying rotational speed.

Variable Rotational Speed

With this method, the speed of rotation of the drive is varied from zone to zone. This is accomplished by electro-mechanically driving the spindle motor faster or slower. The advantage of this method is that the data rate stays constant, making the design of the read/write channel simpler than for the variable data rate. However, it suffers from two major drawbacks:

1. Even though motor speed is electronically controlled, the result depends on the whole disk stack mechanically spinning faster or slower. Speed change cannot occur instantaneously. The hundreds of milliseconds it takes for the drive to spin faster or slow down to reach the correct speed is like an eternity when compared to the milliseconds of typical disk accesses.
2. The rotational speed would be inversely proportional to the diameter of the zone. Hence, the rotational speed at the OD would be more than twice as slow as that at the ID. This means the rotational delay (to be more fully discussed in Chapter 19) would be more than doubled. Thus, performance is degraded for those data stored toward the OD as compared to those stored near the ID. For example, a disk with an OD:ID ratio of 3 and a rotational speed of 10,000 rpm at the ID would have an average rotational delay of 3 ms at the ID and 9 ms at the OD. Worse, since the OD holds more data than the ID, a greater percentage of the data will have this slower performance.

For these two performance-affecting reasons, variable rotational speed is not implemented in magnetic disk drives. Variable rotational speed is used in optical CDs and DVDs, however, where a much lower performance requirement is acceptable.

Variable Data Rate

With this method, rotational speed stays constant, and the data rate of the disk varies from zone to zone. This is called CAV recording. The variable data rate is handled by changing the clocking of the read/write electronics. This method has a couple of advantages:

1. Because data rate change is done electronically, it happens at electronic speed. Thus, there is almost no delay when switching from zone to zone.

2. The data rate is directly proportional to the diameter of the zone. Hence, the data rate at the OD would be more than twice the data rate at the ID. So, performance is higher for those data stored toward the OD as compared to those stored near the ID. This is the opposite of variable rotational speed. Again, since more data is stored at the OD than at the ID, having better performance at the OD is a good thing.

18.5 Servo

The servo system in the disk drive is the control mechanism by which the actuator is manipulated to accurately position the read/write head [Chen et al. 2006, Oswald 1974]. It has two major functions:

1. To move the actuator from its current track position to a new track location on the disk, possibly for a different head. This movement is called the *seek*. The number of tracks or cylinders from the original track to the new track is referred to as the *seek distance*.

2. While accessing data on a particular track, or after arrival at the destination track as a result of a seek operation, ensure that the read/write head stays on that track by continually making corrective adjustments to prevent it from drifting off the center of the track. This process is known as *track following*.

For today's high tpi disk drives, where tracks are a mere 10 microinches (10×10^{-6} inch) apart or closer, closed-loop servo system designs are a must to accomplish the above two tasks. Information needs to be present to tell the servo system what its current position is. Such servo information is written on the disk surface which can be read by a read head. There

are two different methods for placing the servo data, namely dedicated servo and embedded servo.

18.5.1 Dedicated Servo

In dedicated servo, one of the surfaces of the stack of platters is totally dedicated to storing servo information. A surface in the middle of the stack is usually chosen. Figure 18.12 shows a simple drive with three disks. The bottom surface of disk two is dedicated for storing servo patterns exclusively, and its corresponding head, which is constructed like the other read heads, becomes a dedicated servo head. From the servo patterns, the precise location of the track center can be determined for every track. As all the heads, including the servo head, are mounted on head-gimbal assemblies (HGAs) which are, in turn, rigidly attached to a common actuator, the servo head establishes a master position for all other heads.

Figure 18.12 shows a very high level diagram of the components of a dedicated servo control system. A continuous servo pattern on the servo surface generates a signal to the read head which can be demodulated by a position transducer circuit to indicate the degree to which the head is off-center and in which direction. This information is processed by some control logic to generate a *position error signal* (PES). The size of the PES is proportional to how much the head is off track-center. This signal is used to drive the control circuits of the *voice coil motor* (VCM), which moves the actuator toward the desired position. When the servo head is centered over the reference track of the desired cylinder, all the other heads in the actuator should, in theory, also be centered over their respective data tracks.

There are several problems with the dedicated servo architecture, which was used in disk drive designs for more than two decades from 1971 to the mid-1990s.

1. In earlier days of disk drives, a disk stack commonly had 10 or more disk platters or over 20 recording surfaces. Dedicating one surface for servo information represented an acceptable 5% or less loss in usable capacity. Today, like all other disk drive

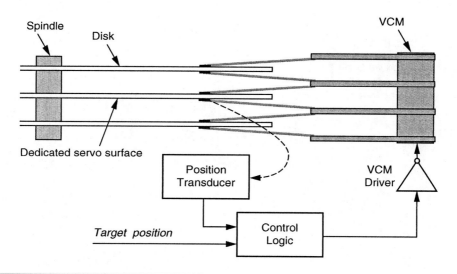

FIGURE 18.12: Dedicated servo components.

dimensions, the number of disk platters has shrunk considerably, averaging about two per drive, with many low-cost drives having only one disk. Losing one entire disk surface to servo is clearly no longer an economically viable architecture.

2. The servo head establishes the radial position for all the other data heads. Ideally, if the servo head is centered over a track, all the other data heads should be similarly centered over their respective tracks in the same cylinder. However, as operating temperature changes inside the disk drive, due to uneven temperature distribution of the platters plus the difference in coefficients of expansion of arms and disks, there can be some relative displacement of the data heads with respect to the servo head. To handle this, a drive with a dedicated servo needs to periodically perform a *thermal recalibration* so that it knows how to compensate for this shift in relative position. During thermal recalibration, the heads are moved, and the distance between tracks is measured and recorded. This can take hundreds of milliseconds or even seconds.

Thus, if a user request arrives during this time, the request is delayed for a long time. In the best case, this represents a decrease in throughput of the drive. In the worst case, where the drive is used for real-time applications such as audio or video playback/record, which depend on on-time delivery of data, this long pause in data access is not acceptable.

3. Today, with track density reaching 100K TPI and beyond, it will be very difficult to deliver the mechanical precision where one single servo head can accurately position the other data heads in its stack over the center of their respective tracks. Even if it is achievable, it undoubtedly will increase the manufacturing cost.

For these reasons, dedicated servo has been abandoned since the mid-1990s.

18.5.2 Embedded Servo

In embedded servo, every disk surface contains its own servo information intermingled with user's data, which can be read by its respective head. Thus, each

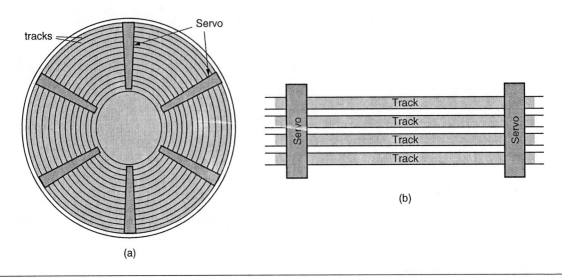

FIGURE 18.13: Embedded sector servo: (a) conceptual example showing six servo wedges per disk surface and (b) illustration showing servo pattern crossing track boundaries.

head is responsible for its own servo positioning in order to access the data on its respective disk surface. There no longer is a separate servo head, and every head pulls double duty time-multiplexing to read both user data and servo information. Clearly, servo information can no longer be recorded on the entire surface. Instead, wedges on a disk's surface, evenly spaced around the disk,[3] are reserved and allocated for servo information, as illustrated in Figure 18.13(a).

Embedded servo is also referred to by some as *sectored servo*. The implication is that each wedge is composed of a small section of a track from all the tracks on the disk surface, and each one of these small sections of servo data can be called a *servo sector*. Such a description, which is perhaps conceptually helpful and sometimes makes discussion easier, is not entirely correct. Servo patterns actually cross track boundaries, as shown in Figure 18.13(b) and described in Sections 18.5.3 to 18.5.5. Servo information used for track following purpose is often referred

to as *servo bursts*, while servo information used for seek operation is called the *track id*. The details of this information and how it works are explained in Sections 18.5.3 and 18.5.4.

Just as in the case of dedicated servo, the servo wedges are written on each disk surface at the time of manufacturing. Since user data and servo data are intermingled and accessible by the same read/write head, care must be taken by the drive controller to never accidentally overwrite the servo areas. Even though a disk drive is quite a resilient device and has schemes to tolerate some amount of corruption of servo areas, this is still not a good thing to happen. Because dedicated servo does not have a write head for the servo surface, such accidents can never happen. This is one disadvantage of embedded servo compared to dedicated servo,

The components of an embedded servo are quite similar to those of a dedicated servo, shown in Figure 18.12. The only differences are that instead of

---

[3]Some older drives use a highly simplified form of embedded servo in which there is only one single servo wedge on each disk surface. Hence, this type of servo was referred to as *wedge servo*. The disadvantages of getting the servo signal only once per revolution are obvious, and performance is rather poor. One might think of embedded servo as an extension of the wedge servo concept.

the servo signal coming from a single dedicated servo surface and servo head, it comes from the active head and surface, and instead of the servo signal being time-continuous, only a time-sampled servo signal is available from embedded servo.

Embedded servo nicely addresses the problems of dedicated servo mentioned in the previous section:

1. The overhead imposed by servo on a drive's capacity is fixed, regardless of the number of disks in the drive. A drive with a single disk or even a single head has the same formatting efficiency as a drive with 20 disks.

2. Because each head is responsible for its own servo positioning in order to access the data on its respective disk, it is no longer affected by thermal expansions of a drive's various components as operating temperature changes. Thermal calibration becomes a thing of the past. Even today's lowest cost consumer disk drives can handle very nicely the on-time delivery requirement of real-time audio and video applications.

3. Again, because each head is responsible for its own servo positioning and not dependent on another servo head in its stack to establish correct positioning, not only does very high tpi become possible, but manufacturing cost is also reduced as ultra-high mechanical precision is not needed.

There is a design trade-off on how many servo wedges to put on a disk. The servo data is an overhead which is a tax on the overall storage capacity available on a disk. Therefore, it is desirable to keep the number of servo sectors low to maximize usable storage capacity. On the other hand, the fact that embedded servo is being time-sampled creates a couple of disadvantages:

1. For track following, since no servo information is available in between servo bursts, the head is flying blind and can drift off center. This would be especially bad when the head is writing, as it can potentially corrupt the recorded signal on adjacent tracks. To decrease this period of vulnerability, it is

desirable to have the servo sectors closely spaced so that the head gets its guidance frequently.

2. For seek, the head must encounter a servo wedge to determine which track it is currently on so that it knows how much further to go and whether it has arrived at its destination. If there are fewer servo wedges around the disk, that means a longer wait before seek can be completed. For example, if a disk rotates at 6000 rpm, one revolution time is 10 ms. If there are 10 servo sectors per track, then the average waiting time to see the first servo after arriving on track is 0.5 ms, the worst case being 1 ms. This adds to the actuator move time. In practice, it is actually worse than that. To ensure that a head has really arrived on a track *and* settled on it, it is common practice to require the head to read several good servo sectors before read or write of user data is allowed to proceed. So, for this example, seek time is actually increased by 3 or 4 ms. On the other hand, if there are 100 servo sectors per track instead of 10, then the seek time is only increased by 0.3 or 0.4 ms. Thus, again, from a seek performance standpoint, the more servo wedges there are, the better.

From this it would seem that from a performance perspective, more servo sectors are better. Yet, this is not necessarily the case. There is a performance trade-off on how many servo sectors to use. Since the spaces taken up by servos reduce the amount of data that can be placed on a track, the effective user data rate is proportionally reduced. Hence, if servo occupies 10% of a track's space, the user's data rate is reduced by roughly 10%. In fact, it gets worse than that. This is because fewer data on each track means track switches will also occur more often for sequential accesses. A track switch takes time to complete and therefore imposes an additional performance penalty. (A more complete treatment of user data rate will be covered in Section 18.8.)

Hence, having more servo wedges is good for random-access performance, but bad for sequential

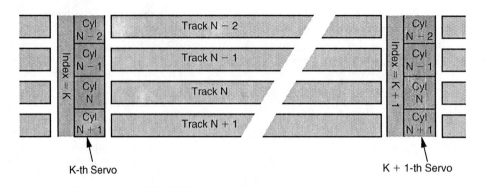

FIGURE 18.14: Servo ID information recorded in portions of two adjacent servos.

performance. A right balance needs to be reached in selecting the number of servos per track when designing a disk drive. Today's disk drives typically have around 100–200 servos per track. Capacity consumed by servo sectors runs around 8–12%.

18.5.3 Servo ID (Identification) and Seek

The servo ID information of each servo sector gives its radial and circumferential, or angular, positions. Only the radial information is needed by the closed-loop servo system to move the actuator so as to position the head to the desired track. Usage of the circumferential position information will be explained later.

Figure 18.14 illustrates the servo ID information portion of two adjacent servos. The circumferential position is simply the servo number. For example, if the disk drive has 100 servo wedges, the first servo wedge has an index = 0, the next servo wedge has an index = 1, and the last servo wedge

	Codeword
0	0 0 0 0
1	0 0 0 1
2	0 0 1 1
3	0 0 1 0
4	0 1 1 0
5	0 1 1 1
6	0 1 0 1
7	0 1 0 0
8	1 1 0 0
9	1 1 0 1
10	1 1 1 1
11	1 1 1 0
12	1 0 1 0
13	1 0 1 1
14	1 0 0 1
15	1 0 0 0

FIGURE 18.15: Example of a Gray code.

has an index = 99. Servo index 50 is diagonally opposite from servo index 0. The index number information is constant for each servo wedge, but is incremented when going from one servo wedge to the next.

The radial position is recorded as the cylinder number of the track that a servo sector is on. Since all the servo sectors on a given track have the same cylinder number, this same number is repeated on all the servo sectors at the same radial position. It is incremented as the radial position decreases toward the ID (remember cylinder 0 is at the OD by convention) and decremented as the radial position increases toward the OD.

Some form of Gray code is used for representing the cylinder numbers. A Gray code is one in which two adjacent codewords always differ by exactly one bit position. An example of a 4-bit Gray code representing the numbers 0–15 is shown in Figure 18.15. As the head is being moved across the disk surface during a seek operation, it tries to read the cylinder ID information whenever a servo wedge rotates under it in an attempt to determine its current position. This is a necessary part of closed-loop servo, both during transit so as to determine progress and make necessary adjustments in speed and during arrival at destination so as to ensure it has indeed arrived on the right track. Since the head is moving in a radial direction while the disk is rotating, the resultant trajectory is such that it may be passing over portions of two adjacent servo sectors, as shown in Figure 18.16. This means the head can be getting part of the cylinder information from one track and another part from another track.

However, because Gray code is used to represent the cylinder numbers, any two adjacent cylinder numbers will differ by only one bit, so the value read by the head is guaranteed to be one of the two valid adjacent values rather than some third invalid combination. For example, referring to the table of example Gray code, if the head reads the first 2 bits of cylinder 8 (1 1) and the last 2 bits of cylinder 7 (0 0), it will get (1 1 0 0) and think it is over cylinder 8. Similarly, if it passes over cylinder 7 and then cylinder 6, it would get at least the first bit from cylinder 7 and at least the

last bit from cylinder 6, ending up with (0 1 0 1), indicating that it is over cylinder 6.

18.5.4 Servo Burst and Track Following

The second piece of servo information present in a servo wedge is what is known as the servo bursts, which are used by the closed-loop servo to accurately place a head over the middle of a track. Centering the head has to be done at the end of a seek operation after the head has already determined from the servo ID that it has arrived at the destination track. This fine adjustment of the head's position to the center of a track at the end of a seek is called *settle*, and the time that it takes to do so is referred to as the *settling time*. Maintaining a centered position for the head after settle has already been completed is also critical for the proper reading and writing of data. This process is known as *track following*. Servo bursts are used for both settling and track following.

Imagine there is a center line down the middle of every track. Wherever a servo wedge occurs, there is one of two alternating special magnetic patterns, called simply the *A burst* and the *B burst*, between every pair of adjacent center lines, as shown in Figure 18.17a. The signal processor associated with the read channel recognizes the servo bursts, and the read channel measures the amplitude or strength of

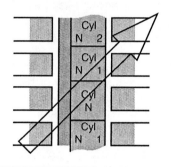

FIGURE 18.16: Trajectory of the head during seek.

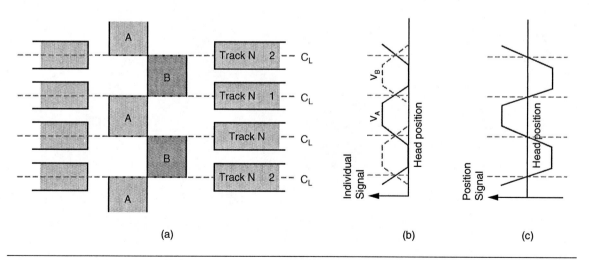

FIGURE 18.17: Embedded servo—servo bursts for track following: (a) duo bursts A and B; (b) signal amplitudes for A and B bursts as a function of head position; and (c) position signal as a function of head position.

the signal detected by the read head. Call the signal detected from the A burst V_A and the signal detected from the B burst V_B. The amplitudes of V_A and V_B detected depend on where the head is located with respect to the center line when it encounters these bursts. This is plotted in Figure 18.17(b). The signal strengths recorded in A and B are equal. Hence, when the head is directly over the center line, it should detect equal amplitudes for V_A and V_B. As the head moves away from the center line, the amplitude of either V_A or V_B would increase while the other one would decrease, depending on which direction the head has moved. Thus, a difference signal, as computed by (V_A-V_B), can be used as a position signal for the servo to use as the PES for making corrections. This signal is plotted in Figure 18.17(c). When this signal is 0, the head is perfectly over the track center, and no adjustment is needed. When the signal is positive, the head has drifted toward the A direction. Likewise, when the signal is negative, the head has drifted in the B direction. Hence, based on the polarity of this signal, the servo knows the *direction of correction* that is needed. The *amount of correction* needed is proportional to the magnitude of this signal—a larger signal means the head has drifted more off course and needs a bigger correction.

The duo servo bursts arrangements work fine, except for the flat parts of the positional signal curve. The plateaus and valleys of Figure 18.17(c) exist because, as discussed in the previous chapter, the read head is designed to be narrower than the written data track. Looking at Figure 18.17(a), it can be seen that the servo bursts span from track center line to center line, thus occupying the same width as the track pitch, which is also wider than the data track due to the guard bands separating the data tracks. Therefore, there is a range of positions within each servo burst where the read head is entirely over the servo burst. It is within this range that the head would be getting maximum, and equal, signal, accounting for the plateaus of Figure 18.17(b). The problem is that when the head is in that range, the position signal can no longer indicate exactly how far off the head is from the center line, unlike when the head is on the slope of the curve, and so the servo does not know how much correction to make.

To remedy this situation, today's drives add two more servo bursts, C and D, for a total of four servo bursts. C and D bursts follow A and B bursts and are offset from A and B by the width of half a servo burst, as shown in Figure 18.18(a). A difference signal, as computed by (V_C-V_D), can be used as a second position signal to augment (V_A-V_B) for the servo to use to compute

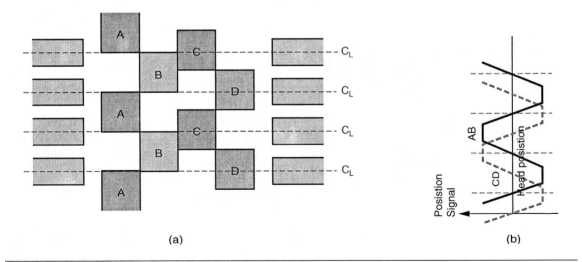

(a)   (b)

FIGURE 18.18: Embedded servo—4 servo bursts: (a) quad bursts A, B, C, and D; and (b) position signals for AB and CD as a function of head position.

a complete PES for making a correction. Hence, if the $(V_A–V_B)$ signal is at the flat part of the curve, the slope of $(V_C–V_D)$ can now be used to determine the amount of correction that needs to be made.

18.5.5 Anatomy of a Servo

Putting it all together, Figure 18.19 shows the complete set of components making up a wedge of servo. There is a gap before and after each servo to separate it from user data. The preamble serves the same purpose as the data sector's preamble, for the read channel to synchronize its PLL with the servo's clock frequency. The *servo address mark,* also called by some the *servo sync mark,* is a unique recorded

pattern indicating that this group of signals is servo information which follows immediately. The index field, the track number field, and the servo bursts have all been explained earlier.

18.5.6 ZBR and Embedded Servo

If embedded servo is implemented in a disk drive that does not use ZBR, the servo wedges can simply be located in between sectors. However, with ZBR it is very difficult to do so for all the wedges. One solution would be to leave larger gaps between servo and data sectors just to avoid conflict. However such a solution is too costly since too much capacity would be lost.

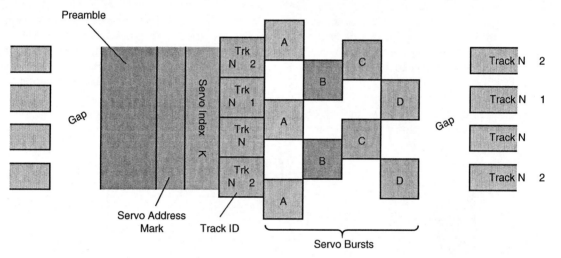

FIGURE 18.19: Components of the K-th servo.

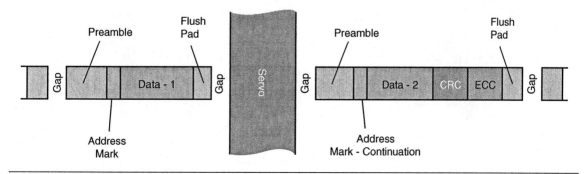

FIGURE 18.20: Split sector. Components of a data sector being split by servo.

A more palatable solution is to allow a servo wedge to split a sector if the two happen to cross paths. Figure 18.20 shows the implementation result of bisecting a data sector into two parts. Gaps need to be added to allow time for switching from write mode (if write is going on) to read mode when exiting the first part of the data sector and entering the servo area and switching from read mode back to write mode when exiting the servo area and entering the second part of the data sector. The second half of the split data sector needs its own preamble of data sync field to reestablish bit sync and address mark field to spot the start of data. These extra gaps and preamble represent additional overhead cost for embedded servo. For a disk with 200 servo wedges and 1001 sectors per track at the OD, about 20% of the sectors are split. At the ID, where the number of sectors per track will likely be around 500 for this drive, 40% of the sectors are split and have to incur this additional overhead.

Information must be stored someplace in the disk drive to inform the disk controller which sectors are split so that it knows to deal with them properly.

Where this information is stored is discussed in the next section.

18.6 Sector ID and No-ID Formatting

In older drives, every sector is preceded by a stand-alone *ID field*, also known as a *header*, which explicitly contains the ID information related to the immediately following data sector. Such information includes the sector's physical address (cylinder, head, and sector number); a flag to indicate the sector is split by servo; whether the sector is defective; and, if defective, where the data is relocated to. The ID is just like a mini sector, with its own sync field, ECC or CRC, and gaps. Unlike user's data sectors, its contents have a fixed format, and it is not accessible by the user.

The presence of sector IDs, with their associated gaps, as shown in Figure 18.21(a), represents a significant consumption of storage space on a drive's surface. The ID fields can occupy up to 10% of a track, while the gaps can take up another 5%. Hence, a track's capacity can increase by about 18% if the ID field can be dispensed with.

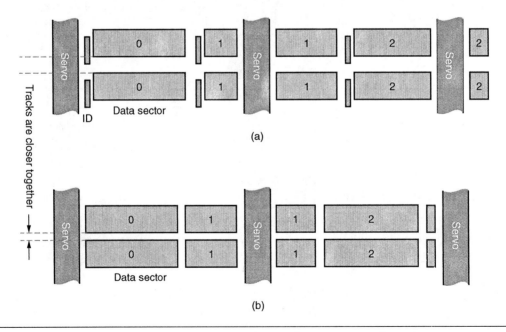

FIGURE 18.21: Two alternatives for formatting: (a) formatting with an ID field, and (b) no-ID formatting.

With today's MR or GMR heads and rotary actuators, there is a secondary capacity benefit if the ID field can be gotten rid of. As described in the previous chapter, the MR read head is staggered in front of the inductive write head. With a rotary actuator, there can only be one track on a disk surface which the arm is precisely tangential to, where both read and write heads can be placed over the track center line simultaneously. As the actuator moves away from this track, the heads become somewhat skewed, as shown in Figure 18.22. The result is a lateral offset between the read and write head center lines, with the center of the read head and the center of the write head over different spots on the track. One solution to compensate for this offset is to write the ID field slightly off-track, as shown in Figure 18.21(a). Such an approach requires increasing the track pitch in order to accommodate the off-track ID field, thus decreasing tpi.

An alternative solution, one that does not require writing the ID field off-track, is to make a small repositioning adjustment of the actuator. After reading the ID field with the read head centered over the track and confirming that it is the correct sector, the servo repositions the head to center the write head over the track. This is a fine adjustment and is known as a *micro-jog*. This is a blind adjustment with no feedback loop. The amount of micro-jog changes with radius and varies from head to head due to manufacturing tolerances. Self-calibration needs to be performed at manufacturing time to determine the amount. While using micro-jog can avoid writing the ID field off-track, it may require a larger gap between the ID field and the data sector in order to allow enough time for this mechanical function to complete.

The *no-ID format*, also called *headerless format*, allows the ID field to be removed from a disk's formatting. There are two major components to this technique. First, it makes use of the servo's information to provide a track's ID, making the cylinder and head information contained in an ID field superfluous. Second, the composition of the tracks within each zone can be predetermined and stored in a *no-ID table*. This table is stored on the disk's protected area and loaded into the disk controller's DRAM at startup time for fast access. While the exact format of the entries of this table varies from product to product, it basically contains the following information:

- Zone number
- Servo number
- Sector number of the first sector after this servo

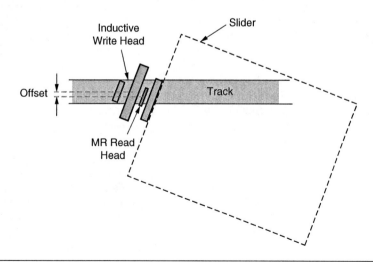

FIGURE 18.22: Offset introduced by read and write heads skew.

- Number of sectors between this servo and the next servo
- Is the first sector split (a continuation)
- Is the last sector split

Given an LBA, the disk controller determines the zone, track, head, and sector number of this sector from the zoning table. It can then look up in this no-ID table the servo number of the servo preceding this sector and the location of the sector relative to this servo.

For example, suppose an LBA is translated into Track 8326, Head 2, and Sector 533. Track 8326 is in Zone 5 according to the zone table. Looking up the no-ID table, it is determined that for Zone 5, Sector 533 is the third sector after Servo 37. Hence, for the drive to access this sector, it enables Head 2 and seeks to Cylinder 8326. After confirming with the track ID information contained in the embedded servo that it has arrived at Track 8326, it looks for the servo wedge with servo index = 37. When this servo is encountered, it starts counting the sectors that come by. Finally, when the third sector arrives, it knows this is the target sector that the host request wants to access.

To summarize, the no-ID format has several important advantages:

- Track capacity's increased due to the spaces freed up by eliminating the ID fields and their associated gaps.
- tpi is increased because there are no more offset ID fields whose presence would demand wider track-to-track separation.
- Reliability is improved because there are no more ID fields which may get corrupted by defects or scratches—one less thing to go wrong.
- Increasing both track capacity and tpi will improve performance, as will be discussed in a Chapter 19.
- Eliminating the need to do a micro-jog after reading an ID field will improve write performance.

Because of all these advantages and the lack of any drawbacks, the no-ID format is universally adopted by all drive makers today.

18.7 Capacity

Starting from a blank disk, after discounting for the surface areas required for various mechanical needs, the capacity for user data that can be placed on the net available surface area is reduced from the theoretical value afforded by the areal density

$$theoretical\ capacity = tpi \times bpi \times area \qquad \text{(EQ 18.10)}$$

due to the various formatting items discussed in this chapter. To summarize,

- The wedges taken up by embedded servo, including the necessary gaps before and after each wedge, account for 8–12% of the capacity space, depending on how many servo wedges are used.
- The servo wedges split the sectors that they cross, necessitating adding gaps inside those sectors and another preamble for the continuation part of a sector. This overhead takes away about 1% of the usable capacity, again depending on how many servo wedges are used.
- Each track is divided into sectors, with physical gaps in between the sectors.
- Each sector incurs overheads in the form of the preamble, address mark, ECC, CRC, and pad, as shown in Figure 18.1. The total of these overheads is about 12%, depending what ECC and CRC are used.
- RLL coding, which is applied to the data, ECC, and CRC, adds another 3–8% of overhead cost, depending on which code is used.
- Even with ZBR, most tracks are not recorded at the maximum bpi, as explained earlier.
- Spare sectors are reserved for defect management.
- Tracks are reserved for disk drive internal use, such as tables and parameters and space for saving various logs.

All of these overheads and factors conspire to reduce the net capacity available to the user from the theoretical capacity of Equation 18.10.

18.8 Data Rate

Similar to user capacity being less than the theoretical maximum capacity, and for many of the same reasons, the actual user data rate that is obtainable from a disk is also less than the theoretical maximum. Theoretically, the data rate available is a function of the radius r of where on the disk measurement is taken:

theoretical data rate = bpi × 2 × π × r × rpm/60

(EQ 18.11)

However, for many of the reasons and factors given in the previous section on capacity, the actual data rate is substantially less.

A more accurate, and simpler, way to determine the user data rate is to use the sector per track (SPT) number for the zone where data transfer is taking place:

track data rate = SPT × 512 × rpm/60   **(EQ 18.12)**

This is accurate while data transfer is entirely for the data of a track only. For continuously transferring a large amount of data which spans many tracks, the sustained data rate that the user will actually observe is

$$sustained\ data\ rate = \frac{SPTw \times 512}{60/rpm + T_{CS}}$$ **(EQ 18.13)**

for a disk drive using the serpentine formatting, where T_{CS} is the cylinder switch time as represented by the cylinder skew. For a drive with N heads and using the cylinder mode formatting, the user observable sustained data rate is

$$sustained\ data\ rate = \frac{N \times SPT \times 512}{(N \times 60)/rpm + (N-1) \times T_{HS} + T_{CS}}$$

(EQ 18.14)

where T_{HS} is the head switch time as represented by the track skew.

For example, a 10,000 RPM drive with 1000 SPT at the OD has a track data rate of about 85.3 MB/s for the first zone. Assume this drive has four heads and it uses the cylinder mode formatting. If the head switch time is 1 ms and the cylinder switch time is 2 ms, its first zone only has a sustained data transfer rate of

$$\frac{4 \times 1000 \times 512}{(4 \times 60)/10000 + 3 \times 0.001 + 0.002} = 70.6\ MB/s$$

(EQ 18.15)

which is about 83% of the track data rate. This ratio will go down even lower as one moves toward the ID, since the skews are constant in time regardless of zone, but the number of sectors per track will be smaller.

18.9 Defect Management

No disk drive is perfect in the sense that every disk drive contains some sectors that are defective. The SER, which is basically the raw error rate of a disk and the read channel, has been gradually rising over the years. This is partly due to the incessant push to increase bpi and tpi, resulting in lowering the signal-to-noise ratio (SNR) of magnetic recording. Reduced bit size also means that the effect of media defects becomes more prominent, as a same-sized defect will affect more bits. More powerful ECCs have been continually introduced as the means to counter this ever-rising SER. As a result, disk drives' HER, which is the error rate after ECC has been applied to do error correction, has been fairly stable over the years.

Despite the ECC's best effort, some errors remain too large to be successfully corrected. Such errors within a sector render the sector defective. A sector is defective if data written to it cannot be properly or reliably read back, even with the help of ECC. A sector with a few bad bits that are within the error correction handling capability of the ECC employed is usable for data storage and not considered to be defective. Without any ECC, the soft bit error rate of today's disk drive runs typically on the order of 1 in 10^5, or roughly on the order of 1 out of every 20 sectors. This is clearly unacceptable and the reason why ECC is needed. With the aid of ECC, the HER drops to 1 in 10^{14} for typical desktop drives and 1 in 10^{15} for typical server class drives. This is equivalent to about 1 in 20 billion or 200 billion sectors, respectively. A 100-GB disk drive has 200 million sectors.

There are multiple causes of defect. Weak spots on the media due to insufficient magnetic coating material will not be able to reliably retain recorded information. Too much lubrication over one spot can cause the head-to-media gap to increase and thus produce insufficient signal strength for the underlying magnetic material to properly record it. Deterioration of the magnetic media over time can also create weak spots. Scratches, causing magnetic material to be removed, can be caused either by contaminants being caught between the flying head and the disk surface or by the head accidentally hitting the disk surface due to vibration.

18.9.1 Relocation Schemes

The are two possible solutions to dealing with a defective sector. The drive can tell the host system the address of the bad sector, and the host will then not assign any data to it so that the address will never be used. In this way, the disk drive will only receive access requests for good sectors. This is not a very convenient thing to do, as the drive needs to communicate all defect information to the host, and it is burdensome to the host system for having to work around such defects. This was the old way of doing things, when physical addressing was used and the host system was responsible for defect management. A second alternative is to use logical addressing and have the disk drive controller allocate a different physical sector to replace the defective one. This is much more convenient, because as far as the host is concerned, all of a disk drive's LBAs are good and usable for data storage, and hence, it does not need to pay any attention to stepping around bad LBAs.

There are two main reallocation methods. Both methods require that the disk drive internally has some extra number of sectors above and beyond its stated capacity to be used as spares.

Sector Slipping

Assuming the sector immediately following a defective sector is good, the LBA of the defective sector is assigned to that next sector. All the LBAs from that point on will be slipped one place over to the

next sector. This is shown in Figure 18.23(a). If there are n consecutive defective sectors, then the LBAs are slipped n places over, as illustrated in Figure 18.23(b). When another defect is encountered further down, sector slipping is applied again at that location, as shown in Figure 18.23(c).

Sector slipping has essentially no negative impact on performance. The flow in accessing a range of LBAs that include a defective sector is not interrupted, requiring only very minimal additional time to access one more sector sequentially. Hence, this is a preferred method for relocating defective sectors. However, if data has already been stored on a disk, to apply sector slipping would then mean that all the sectors to be slipped must be read and rewritten to their new locations. This is the downside of the sector slipping method.

Sector Sparing

An alternative scheme is to only map a defective sector to one of the spare sectors. While one can put all the spare sectors together in one place, such as at the end of the disk, from a performance standpoint it is more preferable to sprinkle them throughout the disk drive. In this way, a defective sector can be relocated to the closest spare. Almost every conceivable sparing scheme has been used by various products and manufacturers at one time or another—one or two spare sectors at the end of every track, a few spare sectors at the end of every cylinder, many spare sectors or even spare tracks at the end of a group of cylinders, etc.

The pros and cons of sector sparing are the opposite of those of sector slipping. It is very simple and easy to relocate a defective sector to a spare, and it does not require disturbing other sectors. However, the flow of accessing a range of LBAs which includes the relocated sector will be interrupted. The drive must go to a different location to pick up the remapped sector, incurring a mechanical delay. The smart way to do this is to skip over the defective sector first and continue to read or write the remaining sectors of the command before going off to the relocated sector to finish off the command. Some drives access the sectors in a straight, logical sequence and would go off to the relocated sector and then return to

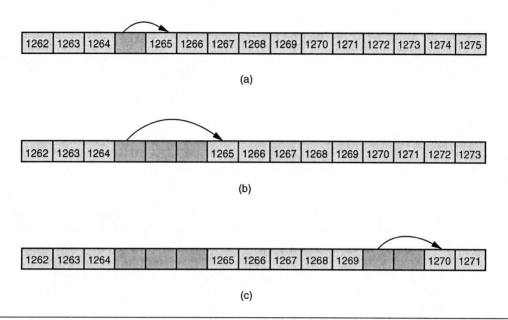

FIGURE 18.23: **Sector slipping:** (a) slipping over a single defective sector; (b) slipping over three contiguous defective sectors; and (c) slipping over another group of defects of two sectors.

resume accessing the remaining sectors, thus incurring a double penalty.

Many variations and combinations of these two basic schemes have been used in different disk drives over the years. For example, sector slipping can be applied to a track with spares sectors reserved at the end of the track. In this way, only affected sectors on that track need to be moved, greatly reducing the amount of work required to do sector slipping upon discovering a new defect.

18.9.2 Types of Defects

Defects can be categorized into two types: those present at the time the disk drive is manufactured and those that develop later after leaving the factory. These two types of defects are handled differently.

Primary Defects

As one of the final steps of manufacturing, a disk drive will write and read every sector to scan for defective sectors. Defects thus found are called primary defects. Because of the transparent impact on performance of sector slipping, and because there is no user data on the drive yet and hence no need to move them, sector slipping is the method used for handling primary defects. These defects are recorded in a list called the P-List (Primary List). While different drives may have a slightly different format for the P-List, essentially they all contain the same information. In its simplest form, the P-List is simply a list of the defective ABAs.

Grown Defects

Defects that develop after a disk drive has left the factory are known as grown defects. These defects are usually discovered when the drive fails to read a previously written sector, even after various error recovery methods have been tried, as discussed below. These are called non-recoverable errors. Since user data has already been populated in the disk drive, to perform sector slipping may involve moving too much user data around. Therefore, sector sparing is commonly used to handle grown defects. Such relocated grown defects are recorded in a table called the

G-List (Grown List). Basically, the G-List is a list of all the defective sectors uncovered during the usage of the drive and the associated spare sector locations to which these defective sectors have been assigned.

18.9.3   Error Recovery Procedure

When an error is encountered while reading a sector, every attempt will be made by the disk drive to try to recover the data. Error is detected by either the sector's ECC or CRC. There are two kinds of errors. One kind of error is due to the data not being written perfectly, such as slightly off-center. The second kind of error is due to everything else, including permanent defects on the disk. Correspondingly, there are two methods for recovering from read errors. One method is to try reading again with the head positioned at various degrees of offset from center and/or with different settings of the various read channel parameters. A second method is to do error correction using a sector's ECC. Today's drive ECC can correct both some small number of random errors and also long bursts of errors.

Re-reading a sector requires waiting one disk revolution for the sector to come around again, and it may take many such trials, using different read channel parameters as well as offsets. Hence, re-reading has a significant performance impact. Correcting small random errors with ECC can be done on-the-fly and incurs no performance penalty. Therefore, it is the preferred method to try first. However, if deep ECC correction is required to try to recover more serious errors, the probability of miscorrection (ECC incorrectly reconstructs what it thought was the original data) increases. Since miscorrection is a very bad thing, deep ECC correction is used only after all attempts to re-read fail, even though re-reading carries a high performance penalty.

Performance Issues and Design Trade-Offs

In this chapter, we will examine certain aspects of disk drive performance in more detail. Some of the topics covered earlier are revisited here again, with the purpose of discussing some of their performance issues and analyzing their related design trade-offs. Chapter 16, Section 16.4, "Disk Performance Overview" has some introductory discussion of disk performance. This is a good time to review that section before continuing with this chapter.

19.1 Anatomy of an I/O

The one underlying thing that determines both response time and throughput of a disk drive is the I/O completion time [Schwaderer & Wilson, 1996, Ng 1998, Ruemmler & Wilkes 1994]. The time required by a disk drive to execute and complete a user request consists of four major components: *command overhead, seek time, rotational latency,* and *data transfer time,* as diagrammed in Figure 19.1.

1. **Command overhead** This is the time it takes for the disk drive's microprocessor

and electronics to process and handle an I/O request. This is usually not a simple fixed number, but rather depends on the type of drive interface (ATA, SCSI, or FC), whether the command is a read or a write, whether the command can be satisfied from the drive's cache if it is a read, and whether write cache can be used if it is a write. Most of the overhead occurs at the beginning of an I/O, when the drive controller needs to interpret the command and allocate the necessary resources to service the command, and then again at the end of the I/O to signal completion back to the host and also to clean up. Certain processing by the disk drive controller may be overlapped with other disk activities, such as doing command sorting while the drive is seeking. As such, they are not counted as overhead here; only non-overlapped overhead is counted. Like all other disk drive parameters, command overhead has been steadily declining over the years due to faster embedded controller chips and more

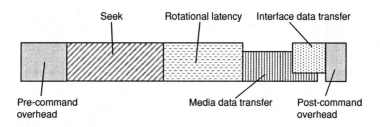

FIGURE 19.1: Time components of an I/O. Shown for a read command.

functions, such as cache lookup, being handled by hardware.

2. **Seek time** This is the time to move the read/write head from its current cylinder to the target cylinder of the next command. Because it is mechanical time, it is one of the largest components of an I/O and naturally has been receiving a lot of attention. Seek time has been decreasing ever since the early IBM RAMAC days. Much of the improvement comes from smaller and lighter drive components, especially shrinking disk diameter, as shown in Chapter 16, Figure 16.3, since it means the arm has less distance to travel. Smaller disk diameter also means the actuator and arm can be lighter and therefore easier to move. Seek time is composed of two sub-components, viz., the travel, or move, time and the settle time—the time after arriving at the target track to when correct track identification is confirmed and the head is ready to do data transfer. As seek distance decreases, settle time becomes a relatively more important component. Typical average seek time for today's server drives is about 4 ms, while for desktop drives it is about 8 ms. Mobile drives for power conservation reasons are typically slower.

Seek time will be discussed further in Section 19.2.3.

3. **Rotational latency** Once the head has arrived at the target cylinder and settled, rotational latency is the time it takes for the disk rotation to bring the start of the target sector to the head. Since magnetic disk drive's rotational speed is constant, the average rotational latency is simply one-half the time it takes the disk to do one complete revolution. Therefore, it is inversely proportional to rotational speed. Here again, because it is also mechanical time, it is another one of the largest components of an I/O. The drive's rpm, for some reason, does not make gradual evolutionary improvements like most other disk drive parameters, but goes up in several discrete steps. This step-wise progress of rpm and its associated average latency are plotted in Figure 19.2. Just because a new higher rpm is being introduced does not mean all disk drives being manufactured will immediately be using the higher rpm. Usually, higher rpm is first introduced in the high-end server drives. It takes a few years for the majority of server drives to adopt the new speed, then it takes another few more years before it becomes commonplace

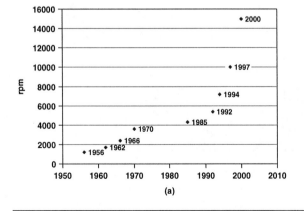

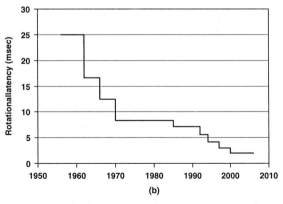

FIGURE 19.2: Year of first introduction of (a) rpm and (b) associated rotational latency. Note that just because a higher rpm is introduced in one drive model, it does not mean all other drive models will also use that new rpm.

among desktop drives, and then it takes yet another few more years for it to be introduced in mobile drives. Take 7200 rpm, for example. It was first introduced in server drives back in 1994, but it was not until the late 1990s before it appeared in desktop drives. The first 7200 rpm mobile drive was not available until 2003, almost ten years after the first 7200 rpm drive was introduced. Today's high-end server drives run at 15K rpm, with 10K rpm being the most common, while desktop drives are mostly 7200 rpm.

4. **Data transfer time** Data transfer time depends on data rate and transfer size. The average transfer size depends on the host operating system and the application. While there may be some gradual increase in average transfer size over time, with some video applications transferring 256 KB or more per I/O, a more modest 4-KB transfer size is still fairly common today.

There are two different data rates associated with a disk drive: the *media data rate* and the *interface data rate*. The media data rate is how fast data can be transferred to and from the magnetic recording media. It has been increasing continuously over the years simply as a consequence of increasing recording bit density and rotational speed. For instance, today a typical server drive rotating at 10K rpm with 900 sectors (512 data bytes each) per track will have a user media data rate of 75 MB/s. Sustained media data rate was discussed in Chapter 18, Section 18.8. Interface data rate, on the other hand, is how fast data can be transferred between the disk drive and the host over the interface. The latest ATA-7 standard supports interface speeds up to 133 MB/s. For SCSI, the data rate for the latest Ultra 320 standard is 320 MB/s for a 16-bit-wide bus. SATA (serial ATA) and SAS (Serial Attached SCSI), both of which share compatible cabling and connectors, support interface speeds up to 300 MB/s, with future plans for 600 MB/s. FC is currently at 200 MB/s and working on 400 MB/s. All these interfaces are substantially faster than the media data rate.

For reads, most of the interface data transfer can be overlapped with the media data transfer, except for the very last block, since every sector of data must be all in the drive buffer for error checking and possible ECC correction before it can be sent to the host. For interfaces where the drive disconnects from the bus during seeks, ideally it should time the reconnection of the bus such that interface data transfer of the next to last sector will be finished just in time when the media transfer of the last sector is completed and is ready to be sent back to the host. For writes, all of the interface data transfer from the host can be overlapped with the seek and latency time, spilling over to overlap with the media transfer if necessary.

19.1.1 Adding It All Up

These I/O time components are put into perspective for the two major types of I/O requests.

Random Access

Consider a hypothetical 10K rpm disk drive with an average media transfer rate of 50 MB/s and an interface of 100 MB/s. Assume an average seek time of 4.5 ms and overhead of 0.3 ms. The time for one revolution is 6 ms, so the average rotational latency is 3 ms. The media transfer time for 4 KB is 0.08 ms, and the interface transfer time for the last sector is 0.005 ms. Therefore, the average time to do a random read of a 4-KB block with this disk drive is

$$0.3 + 4.5 + 3 + 0.085 = 7.885 \text{ ms} \qquad \textbf{(EQ 19.1)}$$

For many applications and systems, I/Os are not completely random. Rather, they are often confined to some small address range of the disk drive during any given short window of time. This phenomenon or behavioral pattern is called *locality of access*. The net effect is that the actual seek time is much smaller than the random average, often roughly one-third of the average. Hence, in this local access environment, the average time to read the same 4-KB block becomes

$$0.3 + 1.5 + 3 + 0.085 = 4.885 \text{ ms} \qquad \textbf{(EQ 19.2)}$$

Figure 19.3 graphically illustrates the relative contributions of the four major time components of an I/O to the overall disk I/O time, for both random access and local access. It shows that for local access, which is likely to be the dominant environment for single user machines or small systems, rotational latency accounts for the greatest share of I/O time. For disk drives used in very large servers receiving I/O requests from many different users, a more or less random request pattern is probably more likely. For such random I/Os, seek time is the biggest component. Note that for 4-KB accesses, which is a typical average in many operating systems and applications, the data transfer time is rather insignificant compared to the mechanical times.

Sequential Access

Understanding the performance of a drive in servicing a random access is important because this type of I/O exacts the greatest demand on a drive's available resources and is also most noticeable to the user due to its long service time. The overall performance of a drive for most classes of workloads is generally gated by how fast it can handle random accesses. Yet, on the flip side, sequential access is an important class of I/O for exactly the opposite reasons. It can potentially be serviced by the drive using only the least amount of resources and be completed with a very fast response time.

A sequential access is a command in which the starting address is contiguous with the ending address of the previous command, and the access types (read or write) of both commands are the same. If handled properly, such a command can be serviced without requiring any seek or rotational latency. Using the parameters of the hypothetical drive above, the service time for a sequential 4-KB read is only

$$0.3 + 0.085 = 0.835 \text{ ms} \qquad \textbf{(EQ 19.3)}$$

Compared to 7.885 ms for a random access, it is an order of magnitude of difference. Thus, a good strategy, both at a system level and at the drive level, is to make the I/O requests as seen by the drive to have as high a fraction of sequential accesses as possible. Naturally, it is important that a disk drive handles sequential I/Os properly so that it does not miss out on the good performance opportunity afforded by this type of access.

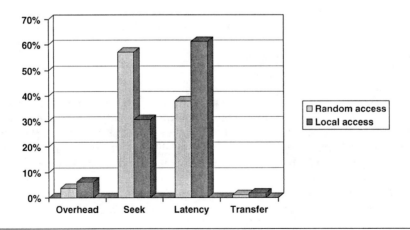

FIGURE 19.3: Percent contribution of various components to total I/O time: 4-KB read—random access and local access.

In addition to strictly sequential I/O, there are some other types of commonplace accesses that also have the potential of being serviced by the drive with very short service times if handled properly,

- **Near sequential.** Two commands that are otherwise sequential separated by a *few* (no precise definition) other commands in terms of arrival time at the drive.
- **Skip sequential.** Two back-to-back commands where the starting address of the second command is a *small* (no precise definition) number of sectors away (in the positive direction) from the ending address of the previous command, and the access types (read or write) of both commands are the same. Note that this is similar, but not identical, to *stride* access, a behavior observed and exploited in processor design wherein the application walks sequentially through data with a non-unit offset between accesses (e.g., addresses 1, 4, 7, 10, 13, …).
- **Near and skip sequential.** Combination of both near sequential and skip sequential.

The ability of a drive to take advantage of the close spatial and temporal proximity of these types of I/Os to reduce service time is an important facet in creating a drive with good performance.

19.2 Some Basic Principles

Disk drive performance is improved when I/O completion time is reduced. Hence, anything that directly shortens one or more of the four major components of an I/O will obviously improve performance. Disk drive makers are always on a quest to shorten the seek time by designing faster actuators to cut down the move time and adding more servo wedges per revolution to decrease the settle time. As discussed earlier, rotational speed has been increasing over the years mainly to cut down rotational latency time, but as a side benefit it also results in increasing the media data transfer rate and, hence, reducing data transfer time. The

performance impact of such direct performance improvement design actions is self-evident and needs no additional discussion in this chapter. Other more elaborate techniques and schemes for reducing seek time and rotational latency time are discussed in Chapter 21.

In this section, several fundamental guiding principles governing disk drive performance which go somewhat beyond the obvious are laid down. The performance impact of any design trade-off can then be interpreted using one or more of these principles [Ng 1998].

19.2.1 Effect of User Track Capacity

The capacity for user data on a track is completely specified by the number of sectors on that track, SPT as previously defined. Some of the things that affect this number are:

- The linear recording density, or bpi
- The radius of the track
- Formatting efficiency

Many factors affect the formatting efficiency. Refer back to Chapter 18 for a detailed discussion.

Increasing the user track capacity has several effects on a drive's performance, which are discussed in the following.

Media Data Rate

As indicated in Chapter 18, Equations 18.13 and 18.14, user data rates are directly proportional to the SPT number. As a higher data rate reduces data transfer time, this effect is obviously good for performance. While for a 4-KB random access this effect is negligible, as discussed above, faster media data rate is important for applications that do large sequential accesses. Unlike random access, an I/O in a properly handled stream of sequential accesses does not require any seek or rotational latency. Furthermore, because the interface data rate is typically faster than the media data transfer rate, the media data rate is the gating factor in determining the performance of large sequential accesses. Proper handling of the drive's cache should allow most, if not all, of the overheads to be overlapped with the media data transfer, as discussed in Chapter 22 on caching.

Number of Track/Cylinder Switches

Whenever the end of a track is reached, some amount of finite time is required to either switch to the next head in a cylinder (head switch) or move the actuator to the next track or cylinder (cylinder switch), as discussed in Chapter 18. The time to do the switch is hard-coded in the disk drive geometry in the form of track skew or cylinder skew and is typically of the order of 1 or 2 ms. This switch time adds to the total I/O time, as part of the data transfer time, if the requested piece of data spans multiple tracks or happens to cross a track boundary.

For example, consider the same drive parameters as in Section 19.1.1, and assume a track switch time of 1.5 ms. The same 4-KB local access that normally takes 4.885 ms to complete will now take 6.385 ms, an increase of 30%, if that data block happens to cross a track boundary.

For a request size of K sectors, the probability that this request will cross a track boundary is

$$p_{cross} = (K - 1) \ / \ SPT \qquad \text{(EQ 19.4)}$$

For a drive using the serpentine formatting, in addition to the actual media transfer time, the average data transfer time for a request of K sectors needs to be increased by an average switch time T_S,

$$T_S = p_{cross} \times T_{CS} \qquad \text{(EQ 19.5)}$$

where T_{CS} is the cylinder switch time. A drive with N heads and using the cylinder mode formatting will have an average switch time of

$$T_S = p_{cross} \times \frac{T_{CS} + (N - 1) \times T_{HS}}{N} \qquad \text{(EQ 19.6)}$$

where T_{HS} is the head switch time. Since p_{cross} is inversely proportional to SPT, increasing the track capacity will reduce the probability of a block crossing a track boundary and, hence, the average added switch time. This is, of course, good for performance.

Constraint on rpm

While increasing the media data rate and reducing the average add-on switch time are good for improving performance, increasing the track capacity too much may run into the possibility of pushing the data rate beyond what the drive's data channel can handle. This limitation can be due to either technology or cost consideration. While today's disk drive read/write channel electronics can comfortably handle the media data rate encountered in any drive, things can look different if there is a new technology breakthrough that suddenly sends linear density and data rate soaring. For a given radius, bpi and rpm are the two main factors that determine data rate. Hence, when bumped up against this limit, the disk drive designer is faced with a dilemma: forfeit some of the increase in bpi and thus the drive would not gain as much capacity as it otherwise would, or reduce the rotational speed. Neither is desirable. Even if channel technology can keep up with the bpi increase, putting a limitation on increasing rpm is an impediment to improving performance.

This brings up a third design choice, and that is to decrease the diameter of the disk. Going with a smaller disk diameter has the additional advantage of making it mechanically easier to spin the disk faster. Indeed, these are some of the reasons for the downward trend in disk diameter, as shown in Chapter 16, Figure 16.3. The trade-off here is, of course, reduced drive capacity when disk diameter is smaller. As a matter of fact, 3.5" form factor, 15K rpm server drives typically use 70-mm diameter disks internally, even though 95-mm disks are used in 7200 rpm desktop drives with the same form factor.

19.2.2 Effect of Cylinder Capacity

An increase in the capacity of a cylinder can be brought about in one of two ways:

- Increase in track capacity—this, in turn, can be due to several different factors, as discussed in the previous section
- Increase in the number of heads and recording surfaces in a cylinder

In many systems, especially single-user personal computers, only one or a few applications are active at a time. In such an environment, typically just a small fraction of the disk drive's data is being accessed during any window of time. When operating within a narrow range of data, having more data sectors in a cylinder has two effects:

1. **The seek distance is reduced** For example, assume bpi is increased by 33%, resulting in the size of each cylinder increasing by the same percentage. Then, a fixed amount of data would now occupy only 100/133 = 75% as many cylinders as before. As a result, seek distance within this range of data would, on average, be reduced by 25%. Shorter seek distance means shorter seek time.

2. **The number of seeks is reduced** When dealing only with a small amount of data, having a cylinder with larger capacity increases the likelihood that the next piece of data required by the user will be found in the current cylinder, thus avoiding a seek completely. For instance, assume a user is working on a file which is 64 MB in size. For a hypothetical drive with 4 tracks per cylinder and 300 KB per track, the probability that two different

sectors from that file are located in the same cylinder is

$$\frac{4 \times 300}{64000} = 0.01875 \qquad \textbf{(EQ 19.7)}$$

Switch to another hypothetical drive with 8 tracks per cylinder and 500 KB per track, the probability increases to

$$\frac{8 \times 500}{64000} = 0.0625 \qquad \textbf{(EQ 19.8)}$$

These two effects of having a more capacious cylinder result in either shortening or eliminating seek time, thereby improving performance. This is illustrated by using an event-driven simulator which tracks the total number of seeks and total seek time. A hypothetical disk drive with 900 sectors per track is simulated, first with 1 track per cylinder as the base and then with 2, 4, and 8 tracks per cylinder. This is one way to compare the effect of cylinders whose capacities are 2×, 4×, and 8× that of the base case. A trace of over 10 PC applications with about 15K reads and about twice as many writes is used as the input. Figure 19.4 shows (a) the total number of seeks and (b) the total seek times for all the reads; the effect on writes is very similar and not shown here. The beneficial effect of having a larger cylinder is clearly illustrated by this simulation result.

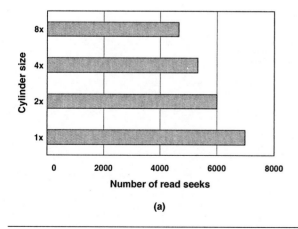

(a)

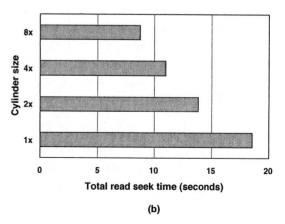

(b)

FIGURE 19.4: Simulation showing the effect of cylinder size on seek: (a) total number of seeks and (b) total seek time.

Keep in mind that the concept of a cylinder applies only if the disk drive uses the cylinder mode formatting. While the above discussion has no meaning for a drive using the straight serpentine formatting, however, the reduced seek distance effect does apply to some extent to drives using the banded serpentine formatting. In fact, the narrower the band is, the more the above applies—one can think of cylinder mode as banded serpentine where the width of a band is one track.

19.2.3 Effect of Track Density

Unlike the previous two disk drive characteristics which can be affected by other characteristics, track density can only be influenced by one thing, namely tpi (tracks per inch). The main impact that tpi has on performance is in its seek time. Seek time consists of two components: (1) a *travel time* for the actuator to move from its current radial position to the new target radial position and (2) a *settle time* for centering the head over the target track and staying centered so that it is ready to do data access:

$$seek\ time = travel\ time + settle\ time \qquad \text{(EQ 19.9)}$$

Travel Time

The travel time is a function of how far the head needs to move. This distance, in turn, is a function of how many cylinders the head needs to traverse and the disk's tpi, as given by this relationship:

$$seek\ distance = number\ of\ cylinders\ of\ seek\ /\ tpi$$
$$\text{(EQ 19.10)}$$

In a simplistic case, to complete the travel in the shortest time, the actuator would accelerate at its maximum acceleration until half the seek distance is covered and then decelerate at an equal rate (by reversing the current in the VCM so that a torque in the opposite direction is applied). This *bang-bang seek* model is illustrated in Figure 19.5(a), which plots both the acceleration and the velocity as a function of time. For such a model, the seek time is given by

$$travel\ time = 2 \times \sqrt{(seek\ distance\ /\ acceleration)} \qquad \text{(EQ 19.11)}$$

from elementary physics. This model is only approximate because today all drives use rotary actuators, and so the seek "distance" should really be measured by the angle that the actuator needs to rotate. Such an angle for any given number of tracks

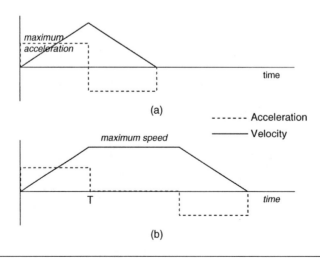

(a)

- - - - - - Acceleration
———— Velocity

(b)

FIGURE 19.5: Travel time: (a) short seek and (b) long seek.

is dependent on the radial positions of those tracks on the disk. However, the above linear approximation model is adequate for our discussion here.

The bang-bang seek is applicable up to a certain seek distance. Beyond that, it may be necessary to limit the actuator speed not to exceed some maximum limit. For one reason, if the head is travelling too fast, then it could be crossing too many tracks in between servo wedges, meaning it would be flying blind for too long without getting feedback on its current location and progress. Another consideration may be that the head stack must not hit the crashstop at excessive speed should power be lost in the middle of a seek. Power consumption may be yet another limiting consideration, especially for portable computers or devices. Hence, for longer seeks, acceleration may be turned off once the maximum speed has been reached, and the actuator coasts until it is time to decelerate. This is illustrated in Figure 19.5(b). For this model, the travel time is given by

travel time = T + seek distance / (acceleration × T)

(EQ 19.12)

where T is the time required to reach maximum speed, which is maximum speed divided by acceleration. The difference in the travel time profile between

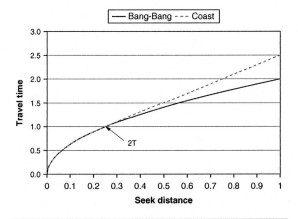

FIGURE 19.6: Example of travel time profiles for two strategies. Normalized to acceleration of 1 unit. Example is for T = 0.5 unit.

a bang-bang seek (no speed limit) and one which coasts after reaching a maximum speed limit is illustrated in the example shown in Figure 19.6. In this example, the seek distance is expressed as a fraction of the maximum (full stroke) seek, and the travel time is normalized to an acceleration unit of 1. Thus, from Equation 19.11, the full stroke or maximum seek time is 2 units. T is set to 0.5 in this example, which occurs at a seek distance of 12.5% of full stroke. Any seek distance greater than 25% of full stroke will require part of its travel limited to coasting at the maximum allowed speed. In this case, the coasting method is 25% slower than the aggressive bang-bang method in the worse case, as illustrated in Figure 19.6.

Because seek distance is inversely proportional to tpi, as stated in Equation 19.10, regardless of whether the seek is for a short distance or for a longer distance, both Equations 19.11 and 19.12 show that travel time will be reduced if tpi is increased. Hence, the travel time component of seek time is improved with higher track density. This statement is true only for seeking between two given logical blocks. The tpi would not have any effect on the travel time of a totally random seek.

Today, many drives that are used for consumer electronics have a "quiet seek" mode. When used in this mode, the drive does not try to achieve fastest seek performance, but rather accelerates and decelerates the actuator at a lower rate so as to cut down on the acoustic noise generated. Since slower acceleration is achieved by applying less current to the VCM, power consumption is also reduced as an added side benefit, and less heat is also generated. However, performance is traded off in return for such benefits.

Settle Time

While travel time is relatively simple, settle time is more complex and depends on many factors. To achieve a faster total seek time, the servo system is designed to be slightly underdamped. Thus, the actuator will overshoot the destination track by a small amount and wobble back and forth a few times before the ringing dies out. The alternative to overshooting is to gracefully approach the destination track more slowly and carefully, but that would increase the travel time, resulting in a longer total seek time.

Settle time is often defined as the time from when the head is within half a track from the destination track's center line to when the head is ready to do data transfer. Some drives define it as ready to read if it is within about 10% of the track center line (relative to the track width) and can successfully read several correct SIDs in a row. Because it is a much bigger problem if a write is mishandled (off-center or, worse, wrong track) than a read, the write settling condition is more stringent than that for read settling. Hence, it is quite typical for write settling time to be about 0.5 ms longer than read settling time. This is the reason for write seek time being spec'ed higher than read seek time.

When every other factor is the same, it is intuitive that tracks that are narrower and closer together would require a longer settle time. Indeed, a simplistic first-order approximation model of the settling time is

$$settle\ time = C \times ln(D \times tpi) \qquad \text{(EQ 19.13)}$$

where C and D are some constants specific to the disk drive. This equation indicates that settle time goes up with tpi logarithmically.

Disk drive designers have been combatting this undesirable effect of tpi increase with different techniques. A standard technique is to increase the bandwidth of the servo system. Newer techniques include more clever algorithms for determining that the drive is ready to do data transfer earlier. Such methods have been able to keep the settle time more or less constant despite rising tpi. However, it is becoming harder and harder to maintain this status quo.

To summarize, tpi has two opposing effects on the seek time of an I/O. Higher tpi shortens the physical seek distance and hence can shorten the travel time. On the other hand, higher tpi may increase the settle time. Thus, whether increasing tpi is good for performance depends on which of these two opposing effects is more dominant. In many applications, the user accesses only a small portion of the disk during any window of time. In such cases, seek distance

is short, and the settle time dominates, making increasing tpi bad for performance.

19.2.4 Effect of Number of Heads

It is common practice for drive manufacturers to take advantage of an increase in recording density to reduce the cost of a disk drive by achieving a given capacity using fewer disk platters and heads. This approach has been applied for many years to deliver a lower cost, but equal capacity version of an existing product. For instance, say, an older recording technology allows 80 GB of data to be stored on one disk platter. A 400-GB drive would require five platters. If the next generation of recording density is increased by 67%, then only three platters would be required to provide the same 400-GB capacity. Saving two platters and four heads represents a very substantial reduction in cost.

The effect that the number of heads in a disk drive has on performance depends on whether the drive is using the cylinder mode formatting or the serpentine formatting. In cylinder mode formatting there are two effects:

Data Rate

This effect is a little subtle and kind of minor. Here, we consider the effect of the number of heads in a drive when everything else is equal. This would be the case of comparing the performances of two drives having different capacities within the same family. Referring back to Chapter 18, Equation 18.14, on sustained data rate, let's assume the head switch time T_{HS} to be 10% of the time of one disk revolution, and let K be the ratio of the cylinder switch time T_{CS} to the head switch time T_{HS}. Then, Chapter 18, Equation 18.14, can be restated as

$$sustained\ data\ rate = \frac{N \times SPT \times 512 \times (rpm)/60}{N + (N-1) \times 0.1 + K \times 0.1} \qquad \text{(EQ 19.14)}$$

If the sustained data rate for N heads is normalized to that of a drive with a single head, the ratio is

$$\frac{N \times (1 + K \times 0.1)}{N + (N-1) \times 0.1 + K \times 0.1} \qquad \text{(EQ 19.15)}$$

Since cylinder switch time is typically higher than head switch time, i.e., K > 1, it can be seen from Equation 19.15 that the sustained data rate is higher with a greater number of heads. This simple relationship is illustrated in Figure 19.7, which shows the sustained data rate, normalized to that for N = 1, for N from 1 to 10, and for values of K = 1, 2, and 3. It can be seen that when K = 1, i.e., cylinder switch time is the same as the head switch time, the number of heads has no effect on the sustained data rate. When K > 1, the sustained data rate goes up with the number of heads, and the effect is greater with a larger difference between cylinder switch and head switch times. Again, this comparison is for when everything else is equal. If the number of heads is reduced as a result of increased bpi, then the increase in data rate due to a greater number of sectors per track will more than offset the minor effect of head and cylinder switches.

Cylinder Size

An increase in areal density is a result of increases in both bpi and tpi. Hence, if the number of heads is reduced as a result of taking advantage of a higher recording density to achieve constant drive capacity, then the total number of sectors in a cylinder actually decreases. In fact, the capacity of a cylinder needs to be decreased by the same factor that tpi is increased in order for the drive net capacity to stay constant. Since bpi also goes up, a decrease in the number of sectors in a cylinder would have to come from having fewer heads.

One of the benefits of a bigger cylinder is that the number of seeks is reduced, as discussed earlier in Section 19.2.2. A smaller cylinder, then, would have just the opposite effect, increasing the number of seeks and therefore hurting performance.

However, there is no change in the average physical seek distance in this case. This is because even though the seek distance in the number of cylinders is increased, the track density is also increased by the same factor. Consider an example where the original drive has 2400 sectors per cylinder—3 heads with 800 sectors per track. If tpi is increased by 33% and bpi is increased by 12.5%, then a new drive with the same capacity would only have 1800 sectors per cylinder—2 heads with 900 sectors per track. In the space of 3 cylinders of the original drive, there are 3% 2400 = 72,000 sectors. In that same amount of space, due to a 33% increase in tpi, the new drive can hold 4 cylinders, for a total capacity of 4%1800 = 72,000 sectors, the same as before. Hence, seeking from one sector to another sector will require crossing 33% more cylinders in the new drive, but the physical distance remains the same. While the physical seek distance may remain the same, the effect of higher tpi on the settle time was discussed earlier in Section 19.2.3.

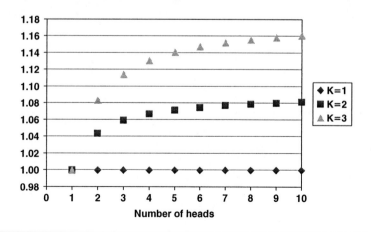

FIGURE 19.7: Sustained data rate, normalized to that of one head.

Serpentine Formatting

For drives using the serpentine formatting, since a track switch taking T_{CS} is always involved at the end of a track, the number of heads in the drive has no effect on its sustained data rate. Instead, the number of heads affects performance through different dynamics involving whether the number of heads is even or odd.

When the number of heads is even, as was illustrated in Figure 18.4(b) in Chapter 18, the head stack ends up at the end of a band in the same radial position as when it started. Hence, a long seek is required to position the head stack to the next band. This is a break in the physical sequential nature of things. While this would not affect performance of a workload that is random in nature, it would most certainly affect the performance of sequential accesses around band boundaries.

On the other hand, when the number of heads is odd, the head stack ends up at the end of each band in the opposite radial position as when it started. Thus, it can move to the beginning of the next band without incurring any long seek. Figure 19.8 shows two ways of laying out the data for an odd number of heads, one requires switching heads while the other does not require switching heads. Not having to switch heads will perform a little faster since one track seek with the same head can be carried out without the uncertainty associated with head switch.

19.3 BPI vs. TPI

An increase in areal density, which is happening at an amazing rate for so many years as discussed in Chapter 16, comes from increases in both bpi and tpi. With the understandings gained in the previous sections, we can now discuss, if given a choice, whether it is more desirable to increase bpi more or tpi more.

An increase in bpi leads directly to increasing track capacity, which is good for performance. An increase in track capacity can, in turn, lead to increasing cylinder capacity, which is also good for performance. Hence, an increase in bpi, as long as it is done within the capability of what the state-of-the-art read/write channel can handle, is a good thing.

An increase in tpi, on the other hand, can eventually lead to a higher settle time. Couple that with the possibility that cylinder capacity may be decreased to take advantage of an increase in tpi as a means to lower cost, then increasing tpi is not likely to be beneficial to performance.

Therefore, if there is a choice, it is more desirable to grow areal density by increasing bpi rather than tpi. Unfortunately, the industry trend seems to be doing the opposite. Figure 19.9 shows the historical trend of the ratio of bpi to tpi (sometimes called the bit aspect ratio). In the early 1990s, this ratio hovered around 20. Today, this ratio is less than 10. This means that tpi is increasing at a faster rate than bpi. Indeed, in recent years the annual compound growth rate (CGR) for bpi has been about 30%, while the CGR for tpi has been about 50%.

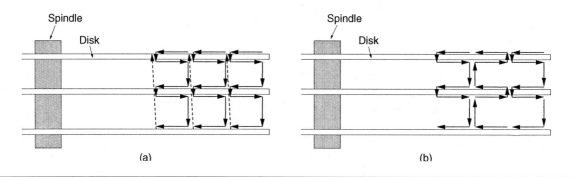

FIGURE 19.8: Odd number of heads for serpentine formatting: (a) head switch and (b) no head switch.

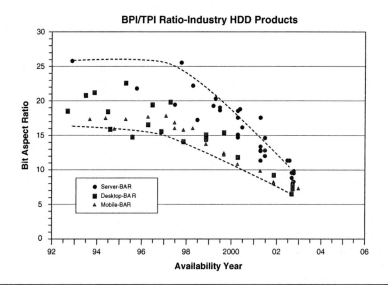

FIGURE 19.9: Historical trend of the bit aspect ratio. (Chart courtesy of Ed Grochowski of Hitachi Global Storage Technologies.)

19.4 Effect of Drive Capacity

For a random I/O, the capacity of a drive has no direct effect on its performance. However, because of the way some file systems manage and use the space of a disk drive, a drive's capacity can itself have an effect on users' or applications' performance. File systems assign disk space to a user's file in allocation units, basically fixed-size chunks of sectors. These allocation units must be kept track of in tables—which units are free and which units are assigned to what files.

There is a great variety of file systems, and they have different architectures and data structures. Some use more elaborate schemes and table structures for faster searches of free space and file locations. Some file systems keep track of the allocation status of units using a bit map—one bit for each allocation unit. Windows NTFS file system and the file systems for various flavors of Unix/Linux are examples of this type of file system. Invariably, pointers are needed to point to the allocation units that have been assigned to each file. One of the simplest forms of allocation structure is a table in which each entry in the table corresponds to one allocation unit. With such an architecture, the table size can get unwieldy if small allocation unit size is used for a disk drive with large capacity, as there will be a huge number of allocation units. An example of this type of file system is Windows FAT (File Allocation Table) file system.[1] Since Windows operating systems and FAT file systems are so ubiquitous, it is worth spending some time here to discuss this particular type of file system.

For the allocation table type of file systems, in order to keep the table for managing allocation units reasonably small, one approach is to limit the number of such units for a given disk drive by increasing the size of an allocation unit as disk capacity increases. Thus, when the capacity of a disk is doubled, one could either keep the allocation unit size the same and double the size and number of entries of the file system's table, or one could double the size of each allocation unit and retain the original size of the file table.

As an example, the FAT32 file system for Windows uses a 4-byte file allocation table entry for each

---

[1] Actually, it is a family of file systems, including FAT12, FAT16, and FAT32.

allocation unit, which is called a cluster. Hence, each 512-byte sector of the file allocation table can hold the entries for 128 clusters. If the cluster size is 1 KB, then for a 256-GB drive[2] a FAT table with 256M entries would be needed, taking up 1 GB of storage space or 2 million sectors. If the cluster size is increased to 64 KB each, then the FAT table size can be reduced by a factor of 64, down to only 16 MB.

The choice of the allocation unit size affects both how efficiently the disk drive's storage space is used and the performance of user's application I/Os.

19.4.1 Space Usage Efficiency

The previous discussion indicates that a larger allocation unit size results in a smaller file system allocation table and, therefore, saves space for this overhead. However, this does not necessarily mean that a larger allocation unit size translates to better space usage efficiency. This is because file space allotted to a file is allocated in multiples of allocation units. Space not used in the last allocation unit of each file is wasted, as it can not be used by anyone else. This is the internal fragmentation issue, previously discussed in Chapter 18. This wastage is sometimes referred to as *slack* by some.

If file sizes are completely random and equally distributed, then on average each file would waste the space of half an allocation unit. So, for example, if there are 20,000 files on the disk drive and the allocation unit size is 64 KB, 20,000 × 32 KB = 640 MB of storage space is wasted due to internal fragmentation. On the other hand, if 1-KB allocation units are used instead, then the amount of wasted space is reduced to only 10 MB. Going back to the FAT32 example above for a 256-GB drive, a 1-KB cluster size requires 1 GB of file allocation table space, but wastes only 10 MB of storage space with 20,000 user files, while a 64-KB cluster size requires only 16 MB of table space, but wastes 640 MB of storage space for the same number of files.

In reality, things can be even worse for a larger allocation unit size, such as 64 KB. This is because many files are small, and hence, more than half of

an allocation unit's space is going to be wasted. For instance, if 80% of the user's 20,000 files have an average size of 4 KB, then those 16,000 files alone would be wasting 16,000 × (64 − 4) KB = 960 MB of storage space, plus the remaining 20% would be wasting 4000 × 32 KB = 128 MB of storage space, for a total of 1.088 GB.

Naturally, the correct choice of allocation unit size, from a space efficiency point of view, depends on the dominant file size of the user or application. If the typical file size is large, such as files for videos or pictures, a larger allocation unit size is appropriate. If the typical files are small, then allocation units with a smaller granularity are better. The correct choice for a drive (or a volume) with storage capacity C is an allocation unit size U that minimizes:

$$FS\ overhead = allocation\ table\ size + expected$$
$$wasted\ space \qquad \text{(EQ 19.16)}$$

where

$$allocation\ table\ size = allocation\ table$$
$$entry\ size \times C / U \qquad \text{(EQ 19.17)}$$

and

$$expected\ wasted\ space = expected\ number$$
$$of\ files \times U / 2 \qquad \text{(EQ 19.18)}$$

19.4.2 Performance Implication

One clear advantage of a larger allocation unit size, and, therefore, a smaller allocation table, is that with a smaller allocation table there is a higher probability that the needed allocation table entry to process a user's access request will be found in cache, either the disk drive's internal cache or the cache in the host system, and an entry that can be looked up in a cache is much faster than one requiring a disk access. This comes about in two different ways:

- A very large table would not all fit in the cache. On the other hand, the smaller the table is, the higher percentage of its content

---

[2]Windows XP can only format a volume up to 32 GB. However, it can mount FAT32 volumes larger than 32 GB that were created by other systems.

would be in the cache. For example, say, 32 MB of cache space happens to be used for a file system's allocation table in the host system. If the allocation table is 320 MB in size, then there is only a 10% chance that an allocation lookup will be a cache hit. However, if the allocation table is 40 MB in size, by increasing the allocation unit size by a factor of 8, then the probability of an allocation lookup being a cache hit is 80%.

- The allocation table of a disk drive is stored in the disk itself. When one sector of an allocation table covers more data sectors, as would be the case for a larger allocation unit size, there will be more read and write accesses to that sector. That means it will make that sector both more recently used and more frequently used. Hence, regardless of whether the cache uses an LRU or LFU replacement strategy, that sector is more likely to stay in the cache, meaning the next time that sector is accessed for the purpose of an allocation lookup it will more likely be a cache hit.

In addition to the above effect on cache hits for file table lookups, how the choice of allocation unit size affects a user's performance also depends on the size of the user's files.

Large Files

For the file allocation table type of file systems, an entire file system allocation table is large and requires many disk sectors to store, as each sector can only store the entries for a relatively small number of allocation units. When the allocation unit size is large, a sector of the file system table will cover many more user's data sectors, so it takes fewer such sectors of the file system table to completely describe a large file, say, one with hundreds or thousands of data sectors. For a user, this means fewer file system accesses are needed to look up the allocation table to find the locations for all the data associated with the file. Fewer file system table accesses means fewer disk accesses and, therefore, faster performance. This effect is in addition to the greater number of cache

hits associated with a larger allocation unit size while doing file table lookups. Finally, when the size of a file is much larger than the allocation unit size, the file will take up many allocation units. This increases the chance that the file's physical storage space on the disk is fragmented into multiple pieces, especially for a system that has been running for a long time and has gone through numerous file allocations and deallocations. The more fragmented a file's space is, the worse its performance is compared to if the file space is all contiguous. This is because it takes more file table lookups to find all the pieces of a fragmented file, and also, the sequentiality of data access is interrupted.

Small File

While applications using large files are helped by a larger allocation unit size, as would be the case out of necessity for drives with a greater capacity, those using small files (relative to the cluster size) may see worse performance. Here, a different set of dynamics is at work, and it applies to all file systems, not just those using file allocation tables. Because an allocation unit is the smallest number of sectors that can be allocated to a file, a small file of a few kilobytes will occupy only a small fraction of a large allocation unit, such as one with 32 or 64 KB. This has two negative effects on performance:

- As illustrated in Figure 19.10, the user's data is more spread out with larger cluster sizes due to the unused sectors. This means all of a user's files will occupy a wider portion of the disk drive. Thus, to access another file after accessing one file will require a longer seek distance. For example, a user with many 2-KB files will see an 8-fold increase in seek distance as he changes from an allocation unit size of 4 KB to one of 32 KB.
- Most disk drives today do lookahead prefetch (this will be discussed in detail in Chapter 22) into a buffer whenever possible, allowing quick servicing of sequential or nearly sequential data requests in the near

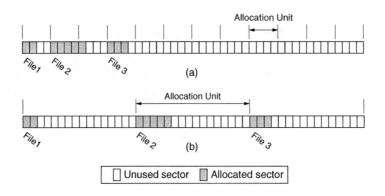

FIGURE 19.10: Effect of allocation unit size on small files: (a) 4-sector allocation unit size and (b) 16-sector allocation unit size.

future. When a file occupies only a small portion of an allocation unit, prefetch is filling the lookahead buffer with mostly useless data from unused sectors, rendering prefetching less effective.

19.5 Concentric Tracks vs. Spiral Track

We will now revisit the issue of concentric tracks versus spiral track formatting first described in Chapter on data organization Chapter 18, Section 18.2. With the understandings that we have gained so far up to this point, we can now examine some of the design issues facing this choice of formatting.

As mentioned earlier, concentric tracks have always been the formatting used by magnetic disk drives, including removable media types such as floppy disks and the 3.5" diskettes. The major reasons for this are partly historical and partly ease of implementation. In the early days of disk drives, when open-loop mechanical systems were used to position the head, using discrete concentric tracks seemed the natural choice. Today, the closed-loop embedded servo system provides on track head positioning guidance, making spiral track formatting feasible. Nonetheless, concentric tracks are a well-understood and well-used technology and seems easier to implement than spiral track. Servo writing (placing of servo information on a disk at the time of manufacturing) for spiral track seems more complicated and will require new

study and perhaps new invention ideas to make it practical. Therefore, unless there is some compelling advantages that spiral track offers, it will not likely be adopted by magnetic disk drives.

Spiral track does have a couple of advantages:

Formatting efficiency Concentric tracks have discrete track boundaries. The capacity of each track is fixed, dictated by the BPI and the radial position of the track, in accordance to

$$\text{track capacity} = 2 \times \pi \times \text{radius} \times \text{bpi} \quad \textbf{(EQ 19.19)}$$

However, since each track must hold an integer number of fixed-size sectors, there is a quantization effect, rendering some of the capacity of a track to be unavoidably wasted. Take a simple example where the capacity of some track, after discounting for servo wedges, is 420,000 bytes. Assume a sector, including all the overheads, is 602 bytes in length; then this track can hold 697 such sectors for a total of 419,594 bytes, effectively losing 406 bytes in capacity. Granted, this seems like a small number compared to the capacity of a track; nonetheless, if there are, say, 100,000 such tracks in the drive, 40 MB are lost.

Things get worse for concentric tracks when zoned-bit recording (ZBR) is applied. The track at the OD of a zone is recorded at a lower bpi than at the ID of that same zone, resulting in a loss in capacity equal to the difference between the track capacities of this zone and of the next outer zone.

If each concentric track is allowed to record at the maximum bpi, subject to the limitation of the quantization effect, then on average each track would lose half a sector of capacity. However, because magnetic disk drives rotate at a fixed speed, known as *constant angular velocity* (CAV) recording, this would require the drive to be able to handle an almost continuous spectrum of data rates. This is not yet practical.

Spiral track clearly does not have to deal with the quantization effect afflicting concentric tracks

Sustained data rate As discussed in the section on data rate, in the chapter on data organization, the drive must incur a head switch time or a cylinder switch time when going from the end of one concentric track to the beginning of the next logical track. The switch time is basically to position either the same head or a different head onto a new track. This causes a hiccup in the continuous flow of data. When transferring a large amount of sequential data, the sustained data is reduced from the number of user bytes per track × revolutions per second to

$$data\ rate_{sustained} =$$
$$\frac{N \times SPT \times 512}{(N \times 60)/rpm + (N-1) \times T_{HS} + T_{CS}} \quad \textbf{(EQ 19.20)}$$

where T_{HS} is the head switch time, T_{CS} is the cylinder switch time, and N is the number of heads.

If spiral track formatting is used, there is no end of one track and start of another track. Data just flows continuously from one sector to the next. Hence, when accessing sequential data, there is no head switching to speak of, and there is no reduction in sustained data rate, which is simply

$$data\ rate_{sustained} = SPT \times 512 \times rpm\ /\ 60 \quad \textbf{(EQ 19.21)}$$

Here, "SPT" is really the number of sectors encountered by the head in one full revolution, and it can be a fractional number since spiral track does not have the quantization restriction of concentric tracks, as we just discussed. Therefore, for the sequential type of data access, spiral track formatting has a data rate advantage over concentric tracks.

19.5.1 Optical Disks

Unlike magnetic disk drives, certain optical recordings such as CDs and DVDs have adopted the spiral track formatting. The playback of audio CDs and move DVDs operates in a *constant linear velocity* (CLV) mode in which a constant data transfer rate is maintained across the entire disk by moving the spiral track under the optical head at a fixed speed. This means the rotational speed varies depending on the radial position of the head, slower toward the OD and faster toward the ID. For example, a DVD rotates at roughly 1400 rpm at the ID, decreasing to 580 rpm at the OD.

While CLV recording is fine for long sequential reads and writes, it gives poor performance for random accesses because of the need to change the rotational speed which is a comparatively slow mechanical process. This is one of the reasons why the CLV recording method has never been adopted by magnetic disk drives. The constant data rate delivery of CLV recording fits well for audio/video applications, and those applications have little demand for high random-access performance. A fixed data rate also makes the read channel electronics simple, which matches well with the low-cost objective of mass market consumer electronics.

As various forms of recordable CDs and DVDs have been added for computer data storage applications, higher performance becomes a requirement. The 1× CLV speed of a DVD only delivers a paltry data transfer rate of 1.32 MB/s, a far cry from the 40+ MB/s of today's magnetic disks. To deliver a higher data transfer rate, drives for these recordable optical disks rotate at speeds many times faster than their consumer electronics brethren. For example, a 16× DVD operates at a competitive speed of 21.13 MB/s. In addition to rotating faster, DVD recorders employ a variety of operating modes to deliver higher performance.

In addition to the CLV mode, they also use the CAV mode and the *Zoned Constant Linear Velocity* (ZCLV) mode. In ZCLV, the spiral track formatted disk is divided into zones. One method, as employed by DVD+R or DVD+RW, uses a different CLV speed for each zone. This only approximates the behavior of CAV, as the rotational speed still varies within each zone in order to maintain a constant linear speed. For instance, an 8× ZCLV DVD recorder might write the first 800 MB at 6× CLV and the remainder at 8× CLV. Another ZCLV method, as employed by DVD-RAM, uses a constant rotational speed within each zone, but varies that speed from zone to zone, faster toward the ID and slower toward the OD. This provides a roughly constant data rate throughout the whole disc, thus approximating the behavior of CLV.

19.6 Average Seek

As mentioned in the beginning of this chapter, seek time and rotational latency time are the biggest components of an I/O request that require a disk access. Since all magnetic disk drives rotate at a constant rpm, the average rotational delay is simply one-half the time of one disk revolution. The average seek time, however, is more complex and will be revisited and examined in greater detail here. The analysis given here is for purely random accesses, where every single sector in the drive is accessed with equal probability.

19.6.1 Disks without ZBR

We begin by making the simplifying assumption that the next I/O request resides in any cylinder with equal probability. This assumption is true only for disks with a constant number of sectors per track and not true for disks with ZBR. Consider a drive with C cylinders. The maximum seek distance, or full stroke seek, is then C − 1 cylinders. The probability of a 0 cylinder seek, i.e., the next request is for the current cylinder that the actuator is at, is simply $1/C$. There are C^2 possible combinations of a start cylinder and an end cylinder, of which $2(C - s)$ combinations will yield a seek distance of exactly s cylinders. Thus, the probability mass function for the discrete random variable s is $2(C - s)/C^2$. The average seek distance can be calculated by

$$\bar{s} = \left(0 \cdot \frac{1}{C}\right) + \sum_{s=1}^{C-1} \left(s \cdot \frac{2 \cdot (C - s)}{C^2}\right) = \frac{C^2 - 1}{3C} \quad \textbf{(EQ 19.22)}$$

which is approximately equal to $(C - 1)/3$ for a large value of C. So, if all cylinders have equal probability of access, the average seek distance is 1/3 the maximum seek, which has been used in the literature for many decades.

Some people use the average seek distance to determine the average seek time, i.e., they assume the average seek time to be the time to seek the average distance. However, this is not correct because, as discussed in Section 19.2.3, the relationship between the seek time and seek distance is not linear. To simplify the mathematics for determining the true average seek time, we will resolve the average seek distance in Equation 19.22, this time using s as a continuous random variable. This method is accurate because the number of cylinders in a drive is a very large number, typically in the tens of thousands. Furthermore, for the remainder of this section, the full stroke seek distance is normalized so that s is expressed as a fraction of the maximum seek distance and has a value between 0 and 1.

The position of a cylinder can also be expressed as a fraction of the maximum seek distance. Let x and y be two random variables representing a starting cylinder position and an ending cylinder position. The seek distance s when seeking from x to y is simply $|x - y|$. By symmetry, the seek distance when seeking from y to x is also $|x - y|$. Hence, without loss of generality, it can be assumed that $x \leq y$.

To determine the mean value of s, it is necessary to have its density function f(s). To do that, we first determine its distribution function F[s] = Prob[seek distance [s] = 1 − Prob[s [seek distance]. With the assumption of $x [y$, to produce a seek distance that is greater than or equal to s, x must be less than or equal to 1 − s, and y must be at least $x + s$. Hence,

$$F[s] = 1 - 2 \int_0^{(1 - s)} f(x) \int_{(x+s)}^{1} f(y) \, dy \, dx \quad \textbf{(EQ 19.23)}$$

where $f(x)$ and $f(y)$ are the density functions for x and y. With the assumption that every cylinder has an equal probability of being accessed, the density function for both x and y is simply 1, giving

$$F[s] = 1 - 2 \int_0^{(1-s)} 1\left(\int_{(x+s)}^1 1 dy \right) dx = 2s - s^2 \qquad \text{(EQ 19.24)}$$

The density function for s is simply

$$f(s) = \frac{dF[s]}{ds} = 2 - 2s \qquad \text{(EQ 19.25)}$$

The mean seek distance can now be determined to be

$$\bar{s} = \int_0^1 s \cdot f(s) ds = \int_0^1 s \cdot (2 - 2s) ds = 1/3 \qquad \text{(EQ 19.26)}$$

which is the same result as that obtained before using s as a discrete random variable.

For disk drives employing the bang-bang method of seek, the seek profile can be expressed as

$$t_{seek} = t_{settle} + t_{travel} = A + B \cdot \sqrt{s} \qquad \text{(EQ 19.27)}$$

where A is the settle time component of the seek, B is some constant related to acceleration as indicated in Equation 19.11, and s is the normalized seek distance. Since the settle time is a constant in this simple model, we can study only the effect of seek distance on the travel time. For the case where every cylinder has an equal probability of being accessed, the average travel time can be computed using the seek distance density function $f(s)$ of Equation 19.25:

$$\overline{t_{travel}} = \int_0^1 (B \cdot \sqrt{s}) f(s) ds =$$

$$\int_0^1 (B \cdot \sqrt{s})(2 - 2s) ds = \frac{8}{15} B \qquad \text{(EQ 19.28)}$$

Compare with $B\sqrt{1/3}$, which is the travel time for the mean 1/3 seek distance that some mistakenly use as the mean travel time; the incorrect method overestimates the real mean travel time by 8.25%.

Next, consider the case for seek with a maximum speed limit. Let a be acceleration and T, as previously defined in Section 19.2.3, be the time required to reach maximum speed. Then, from Equations 19.11 and 19.12, the travel time for a seek distance of s is

$$t_{travel} = \begin{cases} 2\sqrt{s/a} & 0 \le s \le aT^2 \\ T + s/aT & aT^2 \le s \le 1 \end{cases} \qquad \text{(EQ 19.29)}$$

The average travel time can now be calculated, again using the density function f(s) of Equation 19.25, as

$$\overline{t_{travel}} = \int_0^{aT^2} 2\sqrt{s/a} \cdot (2 - 2s) ds +$$

$$\int_{aT^2}^1 \left(T + \frac{s}{aT} \right)(2 - 2s) ds \qquad \text{(EQ 19.30)}$$

which, with a little bit of work, can be solved to be

$$\overline{t_{travel}} = T + \frac{1}{3aT} - \frac{aT^3}{3} + \frac{a^2T^5}{15} \qquad \text{(EQ 19.31)}$$

Continuing with the example of Section 19.2.3, which normalizes the acceleration a to a unit of 1 and selects T = 0.5 with such a unit, the weighted average travel time is 1.127 units. In comparison, the travel time for covering the average seek distance of 1/3 is, from Equation 19.29, 1.167 units, which is a 3.5% overestimation. It can be concluded that with either the bang-bang seek or the speed limited seek, the approximate method of using the seek time for 1/3 the maximum seek distance as the average seek time gives a reasonably accurate estimate, with an error of less than 10% of the true weighted average.

19.6.2 Disks with ZBR

So far, the assumption has been used that all cylinders are accessed with equal probability, which is the case for disks not using ZBR. The results and equations thus derived are not accurate for today's drives, since all disks today use ZBR. With ZBR, tracks or cylinders nearer the OD have more sectors than those closer to the ID and, therefore, have higher probability of being accessed if all sectors in the drive are accessed equally.

To simplify the analysis, we will assume that the entire recording surface is recorded at the same areal density, as in the ideal case. Then the distribution function for a cylinder's position is simply proportional to the recording area:

$$F[x] = \frac{\pi(x + ID/2)^2 - \pi(ID/2)^2}{\pi(OD/2)^2 - \pi(ID/2)^2} \qquad \text{(EQ 19.32)}$$

The maximum seek distance is (OD − ID)/2. Let k be the ratio of OD to ID. Furthermore, if the full stroke seek distance is normalized to 1, then

$$ID = \frac{2}{k - 1}$$ (EQ 19.33)

Substituting OD = k × ID and Equation 19.33 into Equation 19.32 results in

$$F[x] = \frac{(k - 1)x^2 + 2x}{k + 1}$$ (EQ 19.34)

The density function for cylinder position x is simply

$$f(x) = \frac{dF[x]}{dx} = \frac{2(k - 1)x + 2}{k + 1}$$ (EQ 19.35)

Next, the distribution function for the seek distance s of a ZBR disk can now be calculated by substituting the density function of Equation 19.35 for starting and ending cylinder positions x and y of Equation 19.23. With some work, the solution turns out to be

$$F[s] = \frac{8(1 + k + k^2)s - (6 - k + 7k^2)s^2 + 2k(k - 1)s^3 - (k - 1)s^4}{3(k + 1)^2}$$
(EQ 19.36)

Figure 19.11 is a plot of this distribution function for a value of k = 3.5 and that of Equation 19.24 which is for no ZBR. Even for a ratio as large as 3.5, the two distribution functions are surprisingly close. This means that treating ZBR disks as non-ZBR disks in most performance analysis is, in general, an acceptably close approximation.

Taking the derivative of F[s] produces the density function

$$f(s) = \frac{8(1 + k + k^2) - 2(6 - k + 7k^2)s + 6k(k - 1)s^2 - 4(k - 1)s^3}{3(k + 1)^2}$$
(EQ 19.37)

Finally, the average seek distance for a ZBR disk can be computed by substituting Equation 19.37 into

$$\bar{s} = \int_0^1 s \cdot f(s)\,ds$$ (EQ 19.38)

to yield

$$\bar{s} = \frac{50k^2 + 142k + 48}{180(k + 1)^2}$$ (EQ 19.39)

Figure 19.12 plots this average seek distance as a function of k. Note that this average for ZBR disks is lower than the average of 1/3 of full stroke seek for non-ZBR drives. This is as expected since it is less likely to access the tracks toward the ID.

To determine the average travel time for ZBR disks, again consider the case for bang-bang seek. Substituting Equation 19.37 for f(s) into

$$\overline{t_{travel}} = \int_0^1 (B \cdot \sqrt{s}) f(s)\,ds$$ (EQ 19.40)

produces

$$\overline{t_{travel}} = \frac{456k^2 + 1112k + 448}{945(k + 1)^2} \cdot B$$ (EQ 19.41)

This is plotted in Figure 19.13 as a function of the OD to ID ratio k, with the full stroke seek time normalized to 1. Also plotted are the normalized travel time of for traversing the average normalized seek distance of $\sqrt{1/3}$ and the normalized average travel time of 8/15 for non-ZBR disks. For k = 3, the travel time for 1/3 the maximum seek is off by more than 10% from the ZBR weighted average travel time.

Computing the average travel time of ZBR disks for speed limited seek is left as an exercise for motivated readers.

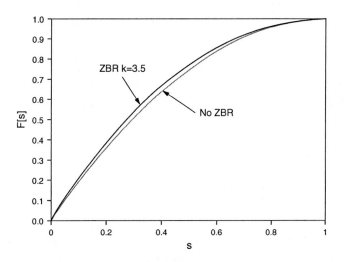

FIGURE 19.11: Distribution functions for the seek distance of disks with ZBR and without ZBR.

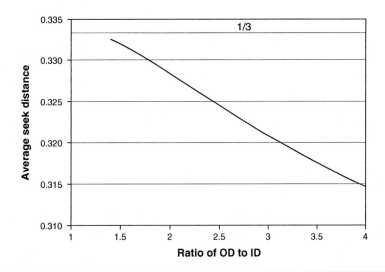

FIGURE 19.12: Average seek distance as a function of k.

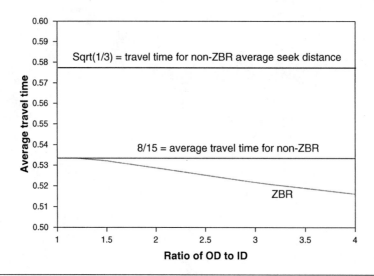

FIGURE 19.13: Normalized average travel time for bang-bang seek.

CHAPTER 20

Drive Interface

The disk drive is not a stand-alone device. To fulfill its function as a device for storing user data, the disk drive needs to be attached to the user's system, traditionally called the host. It operates by receiving requests, or I/O commands, from the host to either store the data that the host is sending to it or retrieve and return to the host some piece of data that the host had previously stored in the drive.

For the disk drive to provide its data storage service to a host, it needs to have a protocol established to receive I/O commands from the host and to signal back to the host their completions. The protocol also has to define the mechanisms for receiving the user data when asked to store them and returning the stored user data when requested. This interface between the disk drive and its host will be discussed in this chapter.

A disk drive has a predefined set of commands which is standard for the interface that the disk drive is designed for. While many of the commands in the command set have to do with housekeeping and other miscellaneous things, the vast majority of the time, the commands being sent to the disk drive by its user are I/O requests, i.e., requests to either read or write a piece of data. Since such requests are the primary function and purpose of a disk drive, they are the commands of the greatest interest in this book. Common to all standard interfaces, when an I/O request is issued to a disk drive, three basic parameters are needed before the drive knows what to do: (i) whether the command is for a read or a write operation, (ii) the starting address for the command, and (iii) the number of sectors of data to be read or written. When the drive has finished performing an I/O request, regardless of which standard interface is being used, the drive needs to inform the host of this completion.

In this chapter, the most common standard interfaces in use today for disk drives are discussed. It starts off with a general overview of interfaces, followed by high-level descriptions of the major characteristics and features of five different interface standards. It concludes with a discussion of a disk drive's cost, performance, and reliability with respect to its interface.

20.1 Overview of Interfaces

The interface is the communication channel over which I/O requests are sent from the host to the disk drive and through which all data transfers for reading and writing take place. For it to function, both ends of the interface, namely the host system and the disk drive, must conform to some predefined protocol specific to that interface.

A basic logical model for directly attaching a disk drive to a system is shown in Figure 20.1. This model is applicable whether the host system is a server, a personal computer (PC), or some consumer electronics such as a digital video recorder (DVR). For large enterprise computing systems, directly attached drives are usually only for things such as booting and program loading, with data drives indirectly attached via some storage servers. Various flavors of storage servers and configurations will be discussed in Chapter 24. For PCs, the system I/O bus would be the PCI bus. For DVRs, the processor would be responsible for the MPEG-2 coder/decoder function, as well as scheduling on-time delivery of video stream data to/from the disk. The host side controller may have different names. Host bus adapter (HBA) is a commonly used term. In mainframes it is called a Storage Controller,

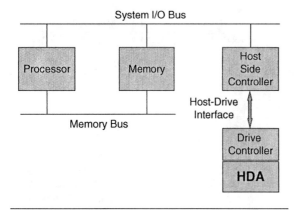

System I/O Bus

Processor

Memory

Host Side Controller

Memory Bus

Host-Drive Interface

Drive Controller

HDA

FIGURE 20.1: Model of a disk drive attached to a host system via an interface.

such as the IBM 3880. In PCs, it may be integrated on the motherboard with no special name, or it may be a PCI card and called simply the controller card or sometimes referred to as the disk drive adapter. Multiple host side controllers may be attached to the system I/O bus, and multiple drives may be attached to each host side controller. The main point is that the host processor issues I/O requests to the drive via the host side controller, and the disk drive exchanges data with the system's memory through the interface and the host side controller. By using a specific host side controller to bridge between a standard interface and a specific system's I/O bus, a disk drive with a standard interface can be connected to different systems with distinct processors and architectures. For example, SCSI drives and ATA drives can be connected to a PC with an Intel processor, an Apple computer with a PowerPC processor, or a Sun workstation with a SPARC processor by using the right controller.

In the early days, before *Large Scale Integration* (LSI) made adequate computational power economical to be put in a disk drive, the disk drives were "dumb" peripheral devices. The host system had to micromanage every low-level action of the disk drive. Hence, most of the intelligence resided in the host side of the interface, with the drive side controller doing not much more than controlling the rotation of the drive and the servo. The host system had to know the detailed physical geometry of the disk drive, e.g.,

number of cylinders, number of heads, number of sectors per track, etc. It even had to handle the defect management of the drive. Upgrading to a new disk drive meant having to upgrade the software on the host system. The interfaces were proprietary and not standardized, although IBM, having the dominant market share at the time, was the *de facto* standard for the mainframe.

Two things changed this picture. First, with the emergence of PCs, which eventually became ubiquitous, and the low-cost disk drives that went into them, interfaces became standardized. Second, large-scale integration technology in electronics made it economical to put a lot of intelligence in the drive side controller. Volume production of disk drives driven by the fast-expanding PC market reinforced the trend. The end result is that today's disk drive handles all the nitty-gritty details of its internal housekeeping and management. The host side controller becomes much simpler and standardized. Logical addressing allows the host system to do all its disk accesses using simple high-level I/O commands, freeing it from having to know anything about the geometry of the disk drive. New disk drives can be added to a system without having to change its software. Furthermore, instead of proprietary, the computer industry has adopted a handful of standard interfaces. While mainly used by hard disk drives, these standard interfaces can also be used by other storage devices such as tape drives and optical drives.

There are several common standard interfaces for disk drives today. They are the parallel and serial versions of ATA, parallel and serial versions of SCSI, and the serial Fiber Channel. They will be discussed in the remainder of this section. A few others, such as *Serial Storage Architecture* (SSA) and various flavors of *Intelligent Peripheral Interface* (IPI), have come and gone and will not be covered in this book. Since these interfaces are standardized by standards committees, their details are fully described in their respective official standard documents which are generally thousands of pages long. Hence, it is not necessary, nor possible, for this book to present all the fine details. Rather, the purpose here is to give a very high level overview of each so that the reader can more readily reference the standard documents for precise specifications.

20.1.1 Components of an Interface

An interface logically consists of two protocol levels. The lower level deals with transmission (physical, link, and transport layers), which includes the cables and the connectors for carrying the data, the voltages and electrical signals that are to be applied to the cables, coding schemes, and transmission procedures. It is necessary to define what form each signal takes. Is it level-triggered or edge-triggered? If it is level-triggered, is it active high or active low? If it is edge-triggered, is it triggered on the rising edge, the falling edge, or both? At the higher level is the logical layer, which defines the protocol and the set of commands that can be issued by the host to the drive. The protocol specifies the precise sequence of handshakes that needs to be observed by both the host and the drive. The command set defines what each command code represents and what actions the drive must take in response.

Because of the dual layering of the interface, two standard interfaces may share the same lower or higher level. For instance, parallel ATA and serial ATA share the same higher level protocol, but have different transmission layers. Ditto for parallel SCSI, serial SCSI, and Fibre Channel, which all use the SCSI command set. On the other hand, serial ATA and serial SCSI, while using different logical protocols, have similar and compatible, though not identical, transmission layers. This is because serial SCSI borrowed much of the physical layer technology from serial ATA.

All the standard interfaces are not static. Instead, they have all gone through multiple generations of evolutions. New versions are defined usually to add features and to increase speed. Fortunately, each new version is backward compatible with earlier versions, most of the time. This means a newer disk drive can be attached to an older version of host side controller, and vice-versa, and things will still function properly, albeit only at the functional and performance level of the older version of the two. Data rate generally increases from one version to the next. This is usually accomplished by increasing the clock rate of the interface.

20.1.2 Desirable Characteristics of Interface

Ideally, from a performance point of view, an interface should have the following desirable characteristics:

- Simple protocol. The fewer handshakes that need to be exchanged between the host and the drive to complete a command, the lower the overhead.
- High autonomy. The less the host processor needs to be involved in completing a command, the more it is freed up to handle other tasks.
- High data rate, up to a point. It is essential for good performance that the interface data rate be higher than the media data rate of the drive. Otherwise, data-overrun for reads and data-underrun for writes[1] will occur, causing the disk drive to suspend media data transfer, thus requiring one or more extra revolutions to complete the command. However, there is not much performance benefit for the interface data rate to be much faster than the media data rate. The only time this benefit is observable is when a command with a large block size is being satisfied with the cache. This is because, as discussed in Chapter 19, the data transfer time is an insignificant portion of an I/O's total time for random access. For a long sequential transfer, data must come from the media, and hence, the throughput is gated by the media data rate.
- Overlapping I/Os. If multiple disk drives can be placed on a shared interface, the interface should support concurrent commands to be issued to those disk drives by the host so that all drives on the interface can be kept busy.
- Command queueing. A disk drive's throughput can be greatly improved by allowing multiple requests to be queued up at the drive so that the drive can have the flexibility

---

[1]Data-overrun is when the read buffer is being emptied at a slower rate than the disk drive is filling it, causing it to become full. Data-underrun is when the write buffer is being emptied by the disk drive at a faster rate than the host is filling it, causing it to become empty.

of choosing which command to service next. Hence, an interface should support this feature for better performance. Command queueing will be discussed in Chapter 21.

20.2 ATA

The ATA interface [see www.T13.org] is the most common interface in use in PCs and consumer electronics today, mainly due to its low cost. It is a parallel interface,[2] and is starting to be explicitly referred to as PATA to distinguish it from the emerging serial ATA. The first hard disk drive to be attached to a PC was Seagate's ST506, a 5 $\frac{1}{4}$" form factor 5-MB drive introduced in 1980. The drive itself had little on-board control electronics; most of the drive logic resided in the host side controller. Around the second half of the 1980s, drive manufacturers started to move the control logic from the host side to the drive side and integrate it with the drive.[3] The interface for such drives was referred to as *AT Attachment* (ATA) interface because those drives were designed to be attached to the IBM PC-AT.[4]

ATA has had six revisions since ATA-1 was standardized in 1994 as ANSI standard X3.221-1994, four years after the standard was first submitted for approval. Currently, the seventh revision, ATA-8, is being worked on by the T13 Technical Committee, which was also responsible for all previous versions of ATA. Each revision usually increased the data rate over its predecessor, sometimes resolved problems with the interface definition (twice to address the maximum disk drive capacity imposed by the standard), and sometimes added new features.

To accommodate devices such as CD-ROMs and tape drives which use SCSI commands, a feature was added to ATA to allow packets to be sent over the transport and physical layers. This is called *ATAPI* (pronounced "a-tap-pee), for *ATA Packet Interface.*" With this feature, SCSI commands can be placed in packets and sent over the ATA link. This enables such devices to be added to a system without requiring a SCSI controller card. ATA interface is often referred to as ATA/ATAPI.

Cabling For many years ATA used a 40-wire ribbon cable with commensurate connectors.[5] A separate 4-wire cable and connector is used for power. Because the cables are unshielded, crosstalk became a problem as the clock rate increased. Today, 80-conductor cables are used, but the original 40-pin connectors are retained. The extra 40 new wires are simply ground wires added between every pair of original conductors. The maximum cable length officially approved is only 18 in. This limit makes it difficult to build a large storage system with many PATA drives. Of the original 40 pins, 6 of them are ground, 16 are for data (2 bytes of parallel transfer), and the remainder are for various signals.

Topology Each ATA channel can have two drives attached to it. A typical host adapter would have two ATA channels, as shown in Figure 20.2. Only one drive on each channel can be active at a time, so I/O overlapping is not allowed and the other drive must be kept idle.

Device Address A drive on an ATA channel is either Drive 0 ("Master") or Drive 1 ("Slave"). A jumper or a dip switch on a drive is usually used to set the drive's address.

Data Transfer Modes PATA supports three different types of data transfer modes:

- PIO Mode: Program I/O mode is the original and oldest method of doing data transfer in ATA. It requires the host processor to be actively involved in transferring every 2 bytes of data. Hence, the host's CPU utilization is high for handling transfer, reducing its ability

---

[2]Parallel in the sense that multiple signals are sent in parallel over multiple wires.
[3]Such drives became known as "Integrated Drive Electronics," or *IDE* drives, and the name IDE was also used to refer to the interface. Hence, IDE and ATA are oftentimes synonymous. Later, when an industry committee was formed to standardize this interface, ATA became the chosen name of the standard.
[4]AT stands for Advanced Technology.
[5]Cables are used by 3.5" form factor drives. Most 2.5" and smaller form factor drives are plugged directly into system connectors.

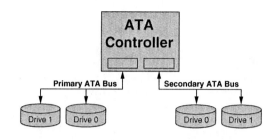

FIGURE 20.2: Configuration of a dual channel ATA control.

to do multi-tasking and negatively impacting performance. The fastest PIO data rate is PIO Mode-4, which has a cycle time of 120 ns and a data rate of 16.7 MB/s. Because of its high CPU utilization, PIO is no longer used except for some lower end consumer electronics.

- DMA mode: First party, or bus mastering, DMA (*direct memory access*) is the standard DMA mode for ATA. First party means the data sender can initiate data transfer without the use of an external, or third party, DMA controller. DMA is more efficient than PIO because the host processor is not needed to babysit the mundane process of transferring data. The fastest DMA data rate is DMA Mode-2, which has a cycle time of 120 ns and a data rate of 16.7 MB/s.

- Ultra DMA Mode: The double transition clocking technique was introduced with the Ultra DMA Mode as a means of further increasing data rate. Instead of doing one data transfer on the rising edge of each clock cycle, as is done in DMA mode, data is transferred on both the rising and the falling edges, thus doubling the data rate for a given clock rate. Adding CRC to data transferring using Ultra DMA greatly improves data integrity. Today, Ultra DMA is the dominant mode of data transfer of ATA, with 133 MB/s (30 ns cycle time) being the current fastest Ultra DMA mode, commonly referred to as Ultra/133.

Different command codes indicate which data transfer mode is to be used.

Error Checking ATA initially had no error checking, but CRC was added in Ultra DMA to check for errors in transmission.

Command Delivery The host sends an I/O request to an ATA drive via a set of registers. Command parameters (address[6] and block size) are first written into the appropriate registers by the host, and then, by writing a command code into the command register, the disk drive is triggered into action to service the command. Status registers are used by the drive to communicate back to the host, such as to indicate that it is busy or that a requested command has been completed.

Command Queueing A simple form of tagged command queueing was defined in ATA-5, but was not widely used. Only IBM/Hitachi-GST implemented this ATA command queueing in their 3.5" drives.

20.3 Serial ATA

Several factors drove the development of *serial ATA* (SATA) [see www.serialata.org]. As discussed previously, the ribbon cable of PATA is unshielded, and its susceptibility to crosstalk makes increasing data rate difficult. Furthermore, as the clock rate goes up, the window for all the parallel signals to arrive without skew becomes narrower and difficult to achieve. The wide ribbon cable, which takes up a lot of room, and its short distance place a great deal of limitations on what storage subsystem can be constructed out of PATA drives. The answer is to use a simple serial link that transmits one bit at a time, but at a much faster clock rate.

SATA was created so that the lower transport and link level of PATA could be replaced with a much faster serial link, while at the same time keeping the upper logical layer of ATA. In this way, a new SATA controller and a new SATA drive can be transparently introduced to an existing system to improve performance.

---

[6]Address can be given in either the older Cylinder-Head-Sector format or the newer and more commonly used Logical Block Address format.

Any host that already can deal with standard ATA devices will not have to change any of its software. Similarly, for drive manufacturers, only the physical layer of ATA drives needs to be replaced; the logical layer remains intact. In fact, the first generation of SATA drives was typically built by using PATA drives and adding a bridge circuit to convert between the SATA and PATA physical layers.

A new private consortium, called SATA-IO, was formed to develop the standards for SATA, and is currently working on the second generation SATA-2 standard. SATA-1 was adopted by the T13 standards committee as part of the ATA-7 standard.

Cabling SATA uses a 7-wire cable for signals and a separate 5-wire cable for power. Three of the wires of the signal cable are for ground, while the other four wires are two pairs of differential signals—one pair for transmitting in each direction. The maximum cable length is 1 m from controller to drive, but can be as long as 6 m between external boxes, which is one of the reasons why using SATA drives is becoming an attractive option for building large storage systems.

Topology SATA is a point-to-point interface, meaning that each SATA port in the host system can have only one SATA drive connected to it. Thus, each SATA drive has its own cable. Of course, a SATA controller card can have multiple ports on it. Four ports is a typical number; Figure 20.3 illustrates such a configuration. Additionally, a SATA port can be expanded by a *port multiplier* which enables

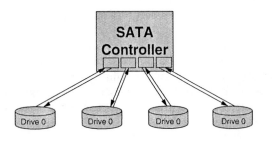

system builders to attach up to 15 SATA devices to a single port.

Device Address Since only one drive can be attached to a SATA cable, there is no need to give an identification to the drive.

Data Transfer Modes The raw speed of the first-generation SATA link is 1.5 Gbps; 8b/10b encoding is used over the link. Hence, this translates to a user data rate of 150 MB/s. SATA controllers and disk drives with 3 Gbps are starting to appear, with 6 Gbps on SATA's roadmap. Since SATA is emulating the ATA logical interface on top of a serial physical interface, all the original ATA commands are supported. This means commands that explicitly call for one of the ATA transfer modes, such as PIO, will still work and at close to the much higher speed of the underlying SATA link.

Error Checking SATA uses CRC to check for errors in transmission.

Command Delivery Since SATA's upper level interface is still the standard ATA logical layer (called the application layer), software communicates by using exactly the same protocol as ATA. However, at the lower level interface, that same information is delivered using a different mechanism. Packets, called *Frame Information Structures* (FIS), are used to send command and status information serially over the link. Unique FIS codes are used to specify the format and content of an FIS, as well as its purpose. For example, a command FIS will contain the ATA command code along with the parameters of the command such as address and block size.

Command Queueing SATA-1 uses the same tagged command queueing that has been defined for ATA. In SATA-2, a newer standard for command queueing, called *Native Command Queueing* (NCQ), is added. A maximum queue depth of 32 is supported in NCQ, which is adequate.

FIGURE 20.3: Configuration of a four-port SATA controller.

20.4 SCSI

The *Small Computer Systems Interface* (SCSI) [see www.T10.org] is a more advanced interface with some functionalities and features not available in ATA. Consequentially, it is a more costly interface to implement and, hence, is not as widely used in lower end systems where those added functionalities and features are not needed. Because it is a more costly interface, it tends to be used by more expensive devices, such as disk drives with higher performance and reliability than those used in PCs. Thus, SCSI is more likely to be used in higher end workstations and servers, due to both its functionalities and the availability of disk drives with higher performance and reliability.

SCSI consists of an upper logical protocol level and a lower transmission level. It originated from a simple interface called the *Shugart Associates Systems Interface* (SASI) back in 1979 and has since evolved into a much more complex and advanced interface. Today, it is an ANSI standard under the control of the T10 technical standards committee. The term SCSI, unless otherwise noted, usually implies the original parallel transmission interface (officially referred to as *SCSI Parallel Interface* or *SPI*). In a sense, SCSI can be considered to be a collection of several related interface standards grouped under its umbrella label, and they are all governed by an *SCSI Architecture Model* (SAM)—a common ground for all the sub-standards. SCSI logical protocol using a serial transmission link will be discussed in Section 20.5, and Section 20.6 talks about SCSI logical protocol running on top of Fibre Channel link.

Cabling There are a multitude of options for cables and connectors in SCSI. First, SCSI cable can be "narrow" (for 8-bit parallel data transfer) or "wide." For a given transmission speed, a wide cable has twice the data rate of a narrow cable. There are 50 conductors in a narrow cable and 68 conductors in a wide cable. SCSI cables need to be properly terminated to eliminate reflec-

tion of signals. Next, three different signaling methods can be used in SCSI, viz., single ended (SE), high voltage differential (HVD), and low voltage differential (LVD). The maximum cable length depends on the number of devices on the cable and the signaling method. Higher speed transfer modes require LVD signaling and are not supported for narrow cable. Therefore, today's SCSI cable is typically wide and uses LVD, with a maximum length of up to 12 m. Finally, cables can be used internally inside a box or externally outside a box. External cables are shielded and better constructed than internal cables as they have to work in an unprotected environment. To add to all of these choices, there are at least eight different types of SCSI connectors, four each for external and internal connections. SCSI devices use the same four conductor power cables and connectors as ATA.

Topology SCSI is really a bus, allowing multiple devices[7] to be connected to the same cable. Every device on the bus has a unique ID which is assigned a priority. Since each data line in a cable is also used by one device to signal its ID, up to 8 devices can be attached to a narrow bus and 16 devices to a wide bus. The host controller[8] is one of the devices and is usually assigned the highest priority. Figure 20.4 illustrates a simple SCSI configuration with four disk drives. Because multiple devices share the same bus, they must arbitrate for the bus before the winning device (the one with the highest priority arbitrating) can put data on the bus. Each device on the SCSI bus can have up to eight *logical units*, called LUNs, associated with it—LUN 0 is required and is the default if the device itself is the only LUN. With this feature, it is possible to attach a new type of controller onto the SCSI bus as a device on that bus and connect multiple drives to that controller.

---

[7]In SCSI speak, a device is anything that can be attached to the SCSI bus, including the host bus adapter and, of course, disk drive.

[8]In SCSI speak, a host or host controller is called the "initiator," and a storage device is called the "target."

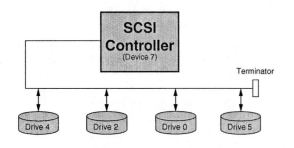

FIGURE 20.4: Configuration of an SCSI controller with four disk drives. Note the drive numbers can be in any order.

Device Address A device on an SCSI bus must have a unique device address between 0 and 7/15 (narrow/wide). A jumper or a dip switch on a drive is usually used to set the drive's address.

Data Transfer Modes The data speed of SCSI has been doubled five times since its beginning. Naming convention has also evolved: Original SCSI (5 MB/s) and Wide SCSI (10 MB/s); Fast SCSI (10 MB/s) and Fast Wide SCSI (20 MB/s); Ultra or Fast-20 SCSI (20 MB/s) and Fast-20 Wide SCSI (40 MB/s); Ultra2 or Fast-40 SCSI (40 MB/s) and Fast-40 Wide SCSI (80 MB/s); Ultra3 or Ultra160 SCSI (160 MB/s, wide only); and Ultra4 or Ultra320 SCSI (320 MB/s, wide only).

Error Checking SCSI uses parity across 8 parallel bits of data for checking errors in transmission. CRC was also added in Ultra3.

Command Delivery The SCSI logical layer protocol uses a data structure called *command descriptor block* (CDB) to communicate to the device or disk drive an I/O request. The CDB contains the command code and the parameters such as address and sector count. SCSI uses LBA only to specify addresses; the CHS format was never used. A CDB can be 6, 10, 12, or 16 bytes long, depending on how much accompanying information needs to be transferred along with the command. CDBs, status information from

the drive, and other messages are transmitted asynchronously between the host controller and the disk drive.

Command Queueing Tagged command queueing is supported since SCSI-2 and has been in use for quite some time, especially in servers which typically support many users and, hence, can benefit the most from command queueing. SCSI devices are free to implement a maximum queue depth of any size up to 256, though there is not much benefit for greater than 64 or even just 32.

20.5 Serial SCSI

Serial Attached SCSI (SAS) came about for the same reason that SATA was created, viz., use serial link technology to overcome the drawbacks of a parallel interface while retaining the logical layer of the interface so that existing software does not have to be changed to take advantage of new hardware that incorporates this better performing technology. In fact, SAS development people smartly took advantage of the technical work already carried out by the SATA developers and leveraged off of the technical solutions SATA came up with. As a result, SAS quickly got off the ground, using cables and connectors and other link layer designs that are essentially borrowed from SATA. In 2002, about a year after an initial brainstorming meeting to create SAS, it gained rapid approval from the ANSI INCITS T10 technical committee to be a part of the SCSI family of standards.

In a nutshell, one can consider SAS to be an interface using the SCSI upper level command set on a lower level serial transmission. By adopting similar cables and connectors as SATA, it is possible to mix both SAS and SATA disk drives in the same SAS domain, as the transmission layers of the SAS lower level interface are designed to be compatible with those of the SATA interface. Thus, a host system with an SAS domain can use the *SATA Tunneling Protocol*[9] (STP) to talk to a SATA disk drive that is attached using a STP/SATA bridge.

---

[9]One of three possible protocols in SAS. The other two are Serial SCSI Protocol (SSP) for talking to SAS devices and SAS Management Protocol (SMP) for talking to expanders.

Cabling SAS uses a similar type of cable and connector as SATA, except, as discussed next, SAS devices are dual ported. For each port, two pairs of wires carry differential signals—one pair for transmitting in each direction. The maximum cable length is 1 m from controller to drive. External cables can be as long as 8 m between boxes, which is quite adequate for storage systems with racks of disk drives.

Topology Like SATA, SAS is a point-to-point interface, meaning that each SAS port can have only one SAS device connected to it. However, an SAS device is dual ported, with each port connected with a separate physical link so that the device can be accessed by two different hosts or devices independently. This feature provides fail-over capability for improved reliability/availability as is required by high-end systems.

The SAS standard also provides for optional *expander* devices which enable a very large SAS domain to be constructed—up to 16,256 devices. Two types of expanders are defined: *fan-out expanders* (maximum of one per SAS domain) and *edge expanders*. Both types of expanders have 128 ports each. Any combination of edge expanders, host adapters, and storage devices can be attached to a fan-out expander, but an edge expander can have no more than one other expander attached to it. Figure 20.5 shows a very simple SAS domain with just one edge expander and four disk drives.

Device Address Each SAS port has a worldwide unique identifier, and each SAS device has a worldwide unique name, both of which are used as SAS addresses. The SAS address conforms to the NAA (Name Address Authority) IEEE Registered format identification descriptor, with 4 bits of NAA ID, 24 bits for IEEE company ID, and 36 bits for vendor-specific ID. Since an SATA drive does not have a worldwide name, it is provided by the expander to which it is attached.

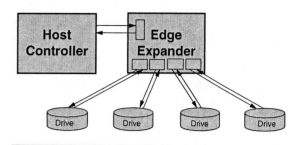

FIGURE 20.5: Configuration of an SAS domain with one edge expander and four disk drives.

Data Transfer Modes SAS leapfrogged SATA and provided for a transmission speed of 3.0 Gbps for the first-generation SAS. With 8b/10b encoding, this translates to a user data rate of 300 MB/s. However, the SAS physical link is full-duplex (data transmission can take place simultaneously in each direction over the two differential signal pairs), unlike SATA which is defined to be half-duplex. Therefore, the first-generation SAS has a theoretical bandwidth of 600 MB/s per physical link. A transmission speed of 600 MB/s (theoretical bandwidth of 1.2 GB/s per link) is being planned for the second-generation SAS.

Command Delivery Since SAS's upper level interface is the standard SCSI logical layer, software communicates by using exactly the same protocol as SCSI. Packets, called "frames," are used to send command and status information serially over the link. The payload of the packets consists of CDBs and other SCSI constructs.

Command Queueing SAS uses the same command queueing as parallel SCSI.

20.6 Fibre Channel

Fibre[10] *Channel* (FC) [see www.fibrechannel.org] is a high-end, feature-rich, serial interface. It is a transmission-level protocol which carries a higher cost than the interfaces discussed previously. Although

---

[10]Spelling reflects the European origins of the standard.

presented last in this chapter, it actual predates SATA an SAS. It was designed originally to operate over fiber optic physical links and hence its name. Later, it evolved to add support for using the same transport and link protocols over copper wiring physical links, but the name Fibre Channel remains. Different logical level protocols can run on top of FC,[11] but SCSI is, by far, dominant. In fact, FC is part of the SCSI-3 family of standards.

Cabling Different types of copper cables can be used, including coaxial wires and shielded twisted pair. For fiber, 62.5 μm multi-mode, 50 μm multi-mode, and single mode are the choices. Both short-wave and long-wave lasers can be used. With copper cabling, FC can have a range of 30 m, enough to locate storage devices in a different room or even on a different floor from the host system. With optical cabling, the range can be as long as 50 km, easily covering a campus or even a city.

Topology Each FC device, called a node, has two serial paths, one for receiving and one for transmitting. The most basic configuration is that of a point-to-point connection between two nodes, as shown in Figure 20.6(a). However, such a configuration is seldom used in storage applications. Instead, a much more common topology is one in which all the devices are connected in a loop as shown in Figure 20.6(b). Up to 127 nodes can be connected in a loop configuration. Any device on the loop that wishes to transmit data must first arbitrate and gain control of the loop. Hence, this topology is known as the *Fibre Channel Arbitrated Loop*, or FC-AL, topology. A third topology, one which gives FC its power and flexibility as a high-end storage interface, is the switched fabric topology. With a fabric, any port in the fabric can communicate with any other port in the fabric by means of a cross-point switch. A single FC node can be connected to a port in a fabric in a point-to-point connection. Alternatively, a port in the

fabric can be part of an arbitrated loop. Furthermore, two switches can be connected together, essentially forming a bigger fabric. All of these are as illustrated in Figure 20.7.

FC drives are used exclusively in high-performance systems, which also demand high reliability and availability where higher drive cost can be justified. To improve overall system reliability, FC drives are typically dual ported, meaning that a drive can be connected to two different links. Thus, if one link is down, the drive can still be accessed using the second link. With FC-AL, it is customary to have data flow in opposite directions in a dual loop setup.

Device Address Standard FC addressing uses a 3-byte address identifier. For FC-AL, the low byte is used as an Arbitrated Loop Physical Address (AL_PA). Only 127 of the 256 addresses are valid, and the remainder are reserved for special FC-AL functions. AL_PA is dynamically assigned to each FC node in an FC-AL loop at initialization. Numerically lower AL_PA has higher priority. AL_PA 0 has the highest priority and is used for the fabric connection to the loop, which will win initialization select to become the loop master. The upper 2 bytes of an FC port's address are assigned by the fabric; they are set to "0000" if no fabric exists on the loop.

Data Transfer Modes The original definition of FC was for a 1 Gbps (100 MB/s) link.[12] Since then, the data rate has been doubled to 200 MB/s, with 400 MB/s in the works. As in other serial links used for storage devices, the IBM 8b/10b encoding scheme is used for transmission.

Command Delivery Packets, or frames, are used to deliver command and status information of the upper level protocol serially over the link. As mentioned earlier, SCSI command protocol is typically used today, although initially other interface standards such as HIPPI

---

[11]One of the original goals of FC was to allow HIPPI (High-Performance Parallel Interface) to map to it.
[12]Half speed, quarter speed, and eighth speed were also defined.

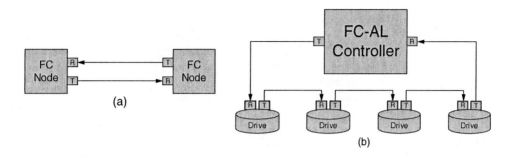

FIGURE 20.6: FC topology: (a) point-to-point topology, and (b) loop topology showing a host controller and four FC disk drives in the loop.

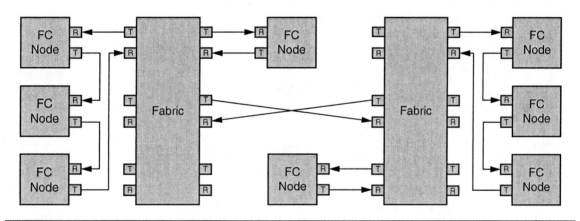

FIGURE 20.7: Example of FC Fabric Topology. Two switches are connected in this example. Each fabric has a point-to-point connection and an FC-AL loop connection.

and IPI-3 were also used. Frames are variable lengths, consisting of 36 bytes of overhead and from 128 up to 2112 bytes (2048 bytes of data plus 64 bytes of optional header), in increments of 4, of payload for a total maximum size of 2148 bytes. For improved data reliability, a 4-byte CRC is used. Each port is required to have a frame buffer, so the maximum frame size is dictated by the smallest of the frame buffer sizes at all the ports involved.

20.7 Cost, Performance, and Reliability

It is generally true today that SCSI and FC disk drives[13] cost significantly more, have higher performance, and are more reliable than ATA drives. It is a common misconception that these are all inherently due to the interface difference. While it is true that SCSI and FC interface electronics are more costly to implement on a disk drive than the simple ATA, it is nowhere near the two to three times cost difference

---

[13]SCSI drives and FC drives from the same manufacturer generally share the same HDA and have similar electronics except for the interface.

between those two classes of drives. The main reason for the large difference in cost is that, because it also costs more to implement SCSI or FC in a system than ATA, SCSI and FC are used only in systems that really need their more advanced features and flexibility. These are the systems that require higher performance and reliability, and these are the more expensive higher end systems which can afford to pay more for such capabilities in a disk drive. It is to deliver higher performance and reliability in SCSI/FC drives that makes them more expensive—the design and engineering are more difficult, components used are more expensive, and manufacturing and testing also take longer and cost more [Anderson et al. 2003].

SCSI and FC disk drives generally have higher raw performance, while ATA drives have lower performance. SCSI drives are either 10K or 15K rpm and have sub-4 ms average seek times, while ATA drives are usually 7200 rpm or lower and have average seek times of around 8 ms. The media data rate tends to be not that much different because 3.5" ATA drives use 95-mm diameter disks, while SCSI drives with the same form factor actually use smaller diameter disks (75 mm for 10K rpm and 65 mm for 15K rpm) internally.

Whether the difference in interface in itself makes a difference to user's I/O performance depends on the application environment and workload.

- A difference in interface speed does not matter for random I/O accesses, as

discussed in Chapter 19, since the data transfer time is an insignificant component of the total I/O time for such accesses. Even for long sequential accesses, there is little benefit in having a faster interface speed as long as it is faster than the disk's media data rate, as the sustained data rate is then gated by how fast data can be transferred to/from the disk.

- For a simple single user and low level of multi-tasking, when most I/O requests show up at the disk drive one at a time synchronously, ATA will outperform SCSI because it has less overhead.

- In the parallel interface world, SCSI will have a definite advantage over ATA in terms of throughput for a multi-user environment, in that it can support concurrent I/Os in multiple drives on the same channel, and commands can also be queued up in each drive.

As serial interfaces are starting to replace parallel interfaces, the difference in performance between SATA and SAS will likely become insignificant. This is especially true as SATA drives implement NCQ. Not only does having command queueing in SATA level the playing field between ATA and SCSI interfaces, command queueing in itself can also reduce the performance advantage of a higher rpm of SCSI drives, as we will discuss in Chapter 21.

Operational Performance Improvement

In many systems the access speed to data is the limiting factor for the performance of the entire system. While a disk drive with a given electro-mechanical design comes with certain raw performance characteristics that cannot be changed, such as its revolution time and seek profile, operation of the drive by its controller can bring about some differences in user-observable performance. Some of these techniques may also be implemented at the operating system level, in the form of data placement and scheduling algorithms. However, the drive controller, having detailed information about all the drive's parameters (e.g., formatting) and its current states (e.g., position of the head), usually has an advantage in applying such techniques.

Once a user request has been received by a disk drive, it has some latitude in how to handle the request. A disk drive can take advantage of this limited degree of freedom to determine how best to perform the command, as long as it is transparent to the user and the command is satisfied correctly. In fact, the drive can even change the size, shape, and location of a user's stored data as long as the drive is able to guarantee that the original data can be returned to the user. This chapter will explore some of the strategies available for handling a user's data and commands to improve a disk drive's overall performance. Not all strategies are good for all environments and situations. Some of the strategies make sense only for certain types of workload or under certain circumstances.

21.1 Latency Reduction Techniques

As discussed in Chapter 19, rotational latency is a major time component of any I/O which is not part of a sequential access. Besides the obvious approach of increasing rpm, which is fixed for a given design and not for the drive controller to change freely, there are several other methods for reducing rotational latency [Ng 1991]. Unfortunately, all of these methods are costly to implement.

21.1.1 Dual Actuator

One method for a drive to reduce rotational latency is to add a second set of read/write heads and actuator [Ng 1994b]. The actuator would be placed such that the second set of heads operate 180° from the original set of heads, as illustrated in Figure 21.1. When a read or a write request is to be serviced, the controller sends both actuators to the target track. Both actuators should arrive at the destination at roughly the same time. Based on the servo ID of the first servo wedge encountered (from either head), the drive controller can determine which head is rotationally closer to the target sector and use that head to service the read or write request. The rotational delay is between zero and one-half of a disk revolution with a constant distribution. Hence, the average rotational latency is reduced from the one-half revolution standard case to one-fourth of a revolution.

This is a clean solution for latency reduction, but it is also an expensive solution. The addition of a

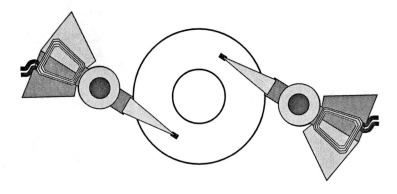

FIGURE 21.1: Disk drive with dual actuators.

second set of heads and actuator increases the cost of the drive by about 30–40%. The highly price competitive nature of the disk drive business makes this solution economically not very viable. Conner Peripherals introduced such a product called Chinook in 1994, but it failed to take off, and no other drive makers have attempted to produce such a design since.

21.1.2 Multiple Copies

A second approach to reducing rotational latency of I/O accesses is to maintain two or more complete copies of data on the drive.[1] For ease of discussion, dual copy is discussed here—extension to multiple copies is straightforward. Every sector of data is arranged such that it and its duplicate copy are located 180° out of phase with respect to each other. In other words, if a copy is currently under the head, its second copy is half a revolution away from the head. There are multiple ways with which this can be implemented. One method is to divide each track into two halves. The data recorded on the first half of a track is repeated in the second half. This means that each track should have an even number of sectors. With this approach, the number of logical tracks in a cylinder is not changed, but the capacity of each track is reduced by a factor of

two. An alternative method is to pair up the heads in the actuator of the drive, assuming that there are an even number of heads. Data on the tracks of the odd-numbered heads are duplicated on the tracks of the corresponding even-numbered heads, with the start (first sector) of the odd tracks offset by 180° from the start of the even tracks. With this approach, the number of logical tracks in a cylinder is halved, but the capacity of each track is not changed.

With either method of data layout, any requested data always has one copy that is within half a revolution from the head. For reading, this cuts the average rotational latency to one-fourth of a revolution. Unfortunately, for writing, two copies of the same data must be written. Although the average rotational latency for reaching the closest copy is one-fourth of a revolution, the write is not completed until the second copy is written. Since the second copy is half a revolution away, the average rotational latency for writes effectively becomes three-fourths of a revolution. The resulting net average rotational latency for all I/O accesses is

$$f_R \cdot \tfrac{1}{4} + (1 - f_R) \cdot \tfrac{3}{4} \qquad \text{(EQ 21.1)}$$

revolution, where f_R is the fraction of I/Os being reads. Thus, whether rotational latency is reduced or

---

[1]Using multiple copies of data on multiple drives, such as mirroring or RAID-1, also works and is discussed in Section 24.2 of Chapter 24.

increased depends on the read-to-write ratio of the users' access pattern.

While no additional hardware is required with the dual copy approach, the capacity of the drive is reduced by one-half. This essentially doubles the dollar per gigabyte of the drive. In some high-end server applications, where the storage capacity per drive is deliberately kept low for performance reasons (drives are added to a system for the arms rather than capacity), a drive's capacity is not fully used anyway. For such environments, there is less or even no real increase in cost to the user. The only cost is then that of having to pay a higher performance penalty for writes.

21.1.3 Zero Latency Access

While there is some increased cost associated with the previous two methods for rotational latency reduction, a third approach carries no added cost and, hence, is implemented in many of today's disk drives. However, this method only benefits large I/O requests, providing little or no improvement for those I/O requests with small block sizes. This approach, called *zero latency read/write* (also sometimes referred to as roll-mode read/write), employs the technique of reading or writing the sectors of a block on the disk out of order. Since this method works in the same way for reads and for writes, reads will be used for discussion here.

Traditionally, after a head has settled on the target track, the drive waits for the first sector of the requested block to come around under the head before data access is started. This is true regardless of whether the head first lands outside the block or inside the block. With zero latency read (ZLR), the head will start reading the next sector it encounters if it lands inside the requested block. Consider an example where the requested block is half a track's worth of data, all of which resides on the same track. Assume that the head lands right in the middle of this block. A traditional access method would require the drive to wait for 3/4 of a revolution for the beginning of the block to arrive under the head and then take another 1/2 revolution to retrieve the block, for a total of 1¼ revolutions to complete the request. With ZLR, the drive will first read the second half of the block,[2] wait for one-half of a revolution for the beginning of the block to come around, and then take another one-fourth of a revolution to retrieve the remainder (first half) of the requested block. This entire process takes only one full revolution, saving one-fourth of a revolution compared to the traditional method. In essence, the effective rotational latency is reduced. If the head lands outside the requested block, ZLR works in the same way as the traditional method.

In general, let B be the block size in number of sectors. For the case where the block resides all on one track, the probability of landing inside the block is $p = B/SPT$, which is also the fraction of a track being requested. The total rotational time to access the block is one disk revolution. Since the data transfer time is B/SPT of a revolution, this means an effective rotational latency of (1 – B/SPT) of a revolution. The probability of landing outside the block is (1 – p), and the average rotational latency for this case is (1 – B/SPT)/2 revolutions. Therefore, the average rotational latency is

$$p \cdot \left(1 - \frac{B}{SPT}\right) + (1 - p) \cdot \frac{1}{2} \cdot \left(1 - \frac{B}{SPT}\right) = \frac{1 - p^2}{2} \quad \textbf{(EQ 21.2)}$$

of a revolution. This is plotted in Figure 21.2. When p is very small, the average rotational latency is about 1/2, as expected. When p approaches 1, the latency is effectively reduced to 0 with this technique.

Next, consider the case where the requested block crosses a track boundary and resides in two consecutive tracks. Let D be the track switch time (either head switch or cylinder switch) expressed in number of sectors. If B is the number of sectors of the requested block that resides on the first track, and C is the number of remainder sectors of the requested block that resides on the second track, then the

---

[2]In this discussion, the average one-half sector delay for reading the first available sector is ignored, since it is only a very small fraction of a revolution.

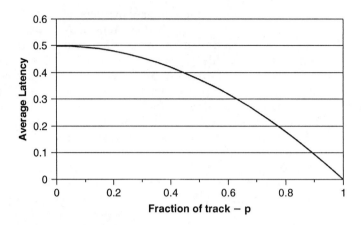

FIGURE 21.2: Average rotational latency with zero latency access; requested block all on one track.

requested block size is equal to B + C. There are two cases to consider:

1. Requested block size is less than (SPT − 2D). ZLR can be made to work to produce the same result as when the entire block is on a single track. As shown in Figure 21.3(a), when the head lands inside the requested block of the first track, it can start reading to retrieve the middle portion of the block, switch to the second track to read the last portion of the block, and then switch back to the first track to complete reading the initial portion of the block. Because there is sufficient time and spacing for track switches, the whole process can be completed in one disk revolution. Hence, for this case, Equation 21.2 and Figure 21.2 can be applied.

2. Requested block size is greater than (SPT − 2D), but less than (2 × SPT − 2D). Let the fraction of the first track being requested be $p = B/SPT$, the fraction of the second track being requested be $q = C/SPT$, and $\Delta = D/SPT$. When the head lands inside the requested block on the first track, with probability p, it can be seen in Figure 21.3(b) that it takes two revolutions of disk rotation time to complete the data

access if ZLR is employed. The data transfer time is $(B + D + C)/SPT = p + q + \Delta$ revolutions, which means the effective rotational latency is $(2 − (p + q + \Delta))$ revolutions. The probability of landing outside the block is $(1 − p)$, and the average rotational latency in this case is $(1 − B/SPT)/2 = (1 − p)/2$ revolutions. Therefore, the average rotational latency is

$$p \cdot (2 − (p + q + \Delta)) + (1 − p) \cdot \frac{1 − p^2}{2}$$

$$= \frac{1 − p^2 + 2(1 − q − \Delta)}{2} \qquad \text{(EQ 21.3)}$$

of a revolution. This is plotted in Figure 21.4 for $q = 0.2, 0.4, 0.6,$ and 0.8. A value of 0.1 is chosen for D, which is typical. It can be observed from Figure 21.4 that except for large values of $p + q$, ZLR in this case actually performs worse than not doing ZLR. A simple strategy for the disk drive controller to implement can be to turn on ZLR in this case only when q exceeds a certain threshold, say, 0.7.

When the requested block spans more than two tracks, all the tracks in the middle require one full revolution plus track switch to access, so it does not make

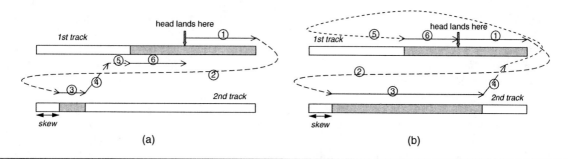

FIGURE 21.3: Zero latency access procedure for requested block spanning two tracks. Step 1: Read middle portion of block from first track. Step 2: Switch to second track. Step 3: Read last portion of block from second track. Step 4: Switch back to first track. Step 5: Wait for start of block to come around. Step 6: Read first portion of block from first track. (a) Requested block < SPT − 2D. (b) SPT − 2D < requested block < 2 x SPT − 2D.

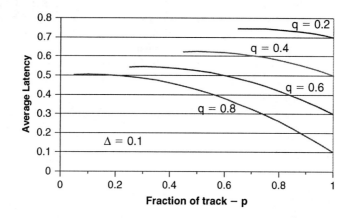

FIGURE 21.4: Average rotational latency for zero latency access: requested block spans two tracks and is greater than (SPT − 2D). Example with $\Delta = 0.1$.

any difference whether ZLR is used or not. Only the first track and last track need to be examined. Therefore, the preceding analysis can be applied—just substitute the last track for the second track in the above.

21.2 Command Queueing and Scheduling

For a long time, it was common for the host to issue a single I/O command to a disk drive and wait for that request to be completed before giving the disk drive the next I/O command. Even today, ATA drives, which

are the predominant type of disk drives sold in 2005, operate in this mode. The host CPU makes use of the long waiting time for an I/O request to be completed by switching tasks to perform some other activities for another program or application. The widening of the gap between the speed of CPU and that of disk drive over the years has been dealt with by increasing the level of multi-programming so as to keep the overall throughput of the system up.

It would be a more efficient use of a disk drive's capability if the host presented to the drive a list of I/O requests that need to be serviced and let the disk drive decide the most efficient order of servicing those commands. This is indeed the rationale behind command queueing and reordering. In command queueing, a unique tag ID is assigned to each I/O request issued by the host and sent to the drive as part of the command structure. When the drive has completed a command, the host is notified using this tag so that the host knows which of the many outstanding I/O requests is done. The host is free to reuse this tag ID for a new command.

The number of commands outstanding in a disk drive is called the *queue depth*. Clearly, the longer the queue depth is, the more choices are available for the drive to optimize, and the more efficient command reordering will be. Host-disk interface standards define an upper limit for the allowable queue depth. For SATA, this limit is 32. For SCSI, it is 256; however, the host and disk drive usually negotiate for some smaller value at the disk drive's initialization time. Even though performance improves with queue depth, the percentage of improvement decreases with queue depth so that beyond a certain point there is little benefit in increasing the queue depth. Sorting the queue to select the next command requires computation, and this is done while the drive is servicing the current command. Ideally, this computation should be overlapped with the drive's seek and rotational times so that it does not add any visible overhead. This may not be achievable if a very long queue needs to be sorted. For these two reasons, limited gain and excessive computation, queue depth should be kept to some reasonable number. What is reasonable depends on the computational complexity of the sorting algorithm chosen and the processing power of the drive's microprocessor.

With command queueing, the drive has the flexibility to schedule the ordering of execution of the commands for better performance. The benefit of command reordering is that the average service time of an I/O is reduced, which means the net throughput of the disk drive is increased. As discussed in Chapter 20, seek time and rotational latency time are the two major components of a random I/O's time. Thus, command reordering that can result in reducing one or both of these components will be able to improve the overall throughput of the disk drive.

The response time of an I/O request is the time from when the command is sent to the disk drive to when the disk drive has completed servicing the command and signals back to the host of the completion. This time includes the time for the actual servicing of the command and the time of the command sitting in the command queue waiting for its turn to be serviced. For a *First-Come-First-Serve* (FCFS) scheduling policy, commands are serviced in the order of their arrival, i.e., there is no reordering, and the waiting time of an I/O is simply the total service times of all the other I/O requests in front of it in the queue. While command reordering will reduce the *average* response time since the average service time of I/Os is reduced, there will be a greater variance in response time. Some I/Os that just arrive may get selected for servicing quickly, while others may sit in the queue for a long time before they get picked.

Typically, with command reordering, some kind of aging algorithm needs to be put in place so that no I/O will wait for an unduly long time. In fact, most host-disk interfaces require an I/O to be completed within some time limit or else the host will consider an error condition has occurred. An aging policy increases the selection priority of a request as it ages in the queue so that after some time it gains the highest selection priority for execution.

In the following, several of the most common scheduling algorithms will be described [Geist & Daniel 1987, Seltzer et al. 1990, Worthington et al. 1994, Thomasian & Liu 2002, Zarandioon & Thomasian 2006]. Typical implementations are usually some variations or enhancements of one of these algorithms. Normal operation is to redo or update the command sorting each time a new command arrives at the queue. This has the overall best performance, but can lead to a long delay for some I/Os. One compromise variation is to sort on only the first N commands in the queue until all of them are executed, and then the next group of N commands are sorted and executed. This trades off efficiency for guaranteeing that no command will be delayed for more than N – 1 I/Os.

21.2.1 Seek-Time-Based Scheduling

Earlier scheduling policies are a class of algorithms which are based on reducing seek time. Since seek time monotonically increases with seek distance, the algorithms simply operate on seek distance reduction techniques. Furthermore, because in early systems the host was cognizant of the geometry of an attached disk drive, it was possible to perform this type of scheduling at the host level instead of inside the disk drive. Later, even when logical addressing was introduced to replace physical addressing on the host-disk interface, due to the fact that with traditional (meaning, not serpentine) data layout there is a linear relationship between the logical address and physical location, host scheduling was still feasible. Today, with the disk drive's internal data layout scheme unknown to the host, such as the serpentine formatting described in Chapter 18, Section 18.3.3, it makes more sense to do the scheduling inside the drive.

SSTF One seek time based scheduling algorithm is called the *Shortest-Seek-Time-First*. As its name implies, it searches the command queue and selects the command that requires the least amount of seek time (or equivalently, seek distance) from the current active command's position. SSTF is a greedy policy, and the bad effect is that it tends to favor those requests that are near the middle of the disk, especially when the queue depth is high. Those requests near the OD and ID will be prone to starvation. An aging policy definitely needs to be added to SSTF.

LOOK Also called *Elevator Seek*. In this algorithm, the scheduling starts from one end of the disk, say, from the outside, and executes the next command in front of (radially) the actuator's current position as it works its way toward the inside. So, it is doing SSTF in one direction—the direction that the actuator is moving. New commands that arrive in front of the current actuator position will get picked up during the current sweep, while those that arrive behind the actuator position will not be selected. As the drive finishes the radially innermost command in the queue, the actuator will reverse direction and move toward the OD, and scheduling will now be done in the outward direction. Since all commands in the queue are guaranteed to be visited by the actuator in one complete cycle, no aging policy is required.

C-LOOK Even though LOOK is a more fair scheduling algorithm than SSTF, it still favors those requests that are near the middle of the disk. The middle of the disk is visited twice in each cycle, whereas the outside and inside areas are visited only once. To address this, the Circular-LOOK algorithm schedules only in one direction. Thus, when the actuator has finished servicing the last command in one direction, it is moved all the way back to the farthest command in the opposite direction without stopping. This trades off some efficiency for improved fairness.

21.2.2 Total-Access-Time-Based Scheduling

The previous group of scheduling policies is based on reducing seek time only. Although, on average, that is better than no reordering, it is not the most effective way to reduce total the I/O time since it ignores the rotational latency component of an I/O. A command with a short seek may have a long rotational delay and, hence, a longer total access time than another command which requires a longer seek but a shorter rotational delay. This is clearly illustrated in Figure 21.5. A scheduling policy based on minimizing the total *access time*, defined as the sum of seek time and rotational latency time, is called *Shortest-Access-Time-First* (*SATF*) or *Shortest-Positioning-Time-First* (*SPTF*) [Jacobson & Wilkes 1991, Worthington et al. 1994, Ng 1999]. Some people also use the term *Rotational Position Optimization* (*RPO*). All disk drives today that support command queueing use SATF reordering because of its superior performance over policies that are based on seek time only. Just like SSTF, SATF is a greedy algorithm; it simply selects from among the commands in the queue the one that can be accessed the quickest as the next command to be serviced.

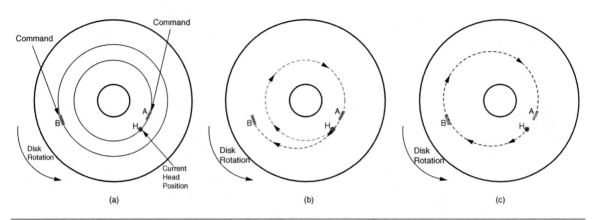

FIGURE 21.5: Scheduling policies. (a) Two commands in queue. Command A is on the same track as the current head position, but has just rotated pass it. Command B is on a different track. (b) Seek time based policy. Command A is selected next, ahead of command B. It takes almost one-and-a-half revolutions to service both A and B. (c) Access time-based policy. Command B is selected ahead of command A. It takes less than one revolution to service both A and B.

As a new I/O arrives at the drive's command queue, its starting LBA is translated into a CHS physical address. The cylinder number represents its radial position, and the sector number represents its angular position. This translation is done only once, and the physical address information, which is needed for estimating the command's access time each time the queue is sorted, is stored with the command.

Estimating Access Time

To sort the command queue for SATF selection, a direct approach would be to estimate for each command its seek time and the ensuing rotational latency, and then sum them up. The reference position for such calculations is from the current active command's expected ending position. A reasonably accurate seek profile would be needed, unlike seek time-based policies which can sort by seek distance in place of seek time. The seek profile is generally stored as a piece-wise linear table of seek times for a number of seek distances. The number of seek table entries is relatively small compared to the number of cylinders in the drive so as to keep the table size compact. Because the seek time tends to be fairly linear for large seek distances, as discussed

in Chapter 19 and illustrated in Figure 19.6, the seek table entries typically are focused on shorter seek distances and become sparse as the seek distance increases. Seek time for any seek distance can be calculated using linear interpolation. Rotational latency is straightforward to estimate as the drive rotates at a constant rpm.

The constant rotation of the disk has a quantization effect in the sense that a given sector comes directly under the head at a regular interval, which is once every revolution. This fact can be taken advantage of to simplify the access time calculation. The expected ending position of the currently active command can be computed based on its starting LBA and the block size. The difference in radial position between this ending position and the starting position of a command in the queue can be used to estimate the seek time, t_{seek}, for that command by using the seek table. Similarly, a rotation time, $t_{rotation}$, can be calculated from the difference in angular positions (this total rotation time is not to be confused with rotational latency, which is the rotation time *after* the seek has been completed). If t_{seek} is less than $t_{rotation}$, then $t_{access} = t_{rotation}$; otherwise, the time of one or more disk revolution, $t_{revolution}$, has to be added until $t_{seek} < t_{rotation} + n \cdot t_{revolution}$. This is a smarter way than the direct method of computing how much rotation has occurred during t_{seek}, figuring out how much more rotation needs to take place, and then computing the rotational latency.

Simplified Sorting Methods

The preceding procedure for estimating access time needs to be carried out for each command to be sorted in order to determine which command has the shortest access time. While this is the most accurate method, it is also somewhat computationally intensive, and if there are many commands in the queue, there may not be enough time to sort through all of them before the currently active command is completed. There are various methods to simplify the sorting by trading off some degree of preciseness.

One method is to divide angular positions evenly into N buckets. If N = 10, then each bucket accounts for 36° of a disk's angular positions, and if there are 1000 sectors in a track, the first 100 sectors belong to the first bucket, the next 100 sectors belong to the next bucket, etc. The larger N is, the more precise this method; the trade-off is between access time estimation accuracy and table space. In practice, the number of servo wedges in a drive is a sensible and practical choice for N, since the no-ID table can be used to identify which servo ID. (SID) a sector belongs to. In this case, a bucket would correspond to a SID. However, such a choice is optional and not required for this scheme to work. Each command in the queue is placed in one of these buckets according to its starting angular position. A table with N entries is created for the drive at manufacturing time. Each entry corresponds to an angular distance in terms of the buckets. For example, the sixth entry is for angular positions that are five buckets away; the first entry is for zero distance. The first column of this table is for the maximum seek distances that can be reached within the rotational times of the corresponding angular distances. Thus, the sixth entry in this first column is the maximum seek distance reachable within the time for rotating to an angular position that is five buckets away. The second column of the table is for the maximum seek distances that can be reached within the rotational times of the

corresponding angular distances plus the time of one complete disk revolution. This continues until the full stroke seek distance is reached in the table.

Figure 21.6 shows an example of such a table with N = 10 for a hypothetical disk with 10,000 cylinders. To use this table, after the current command has started, the drive controller determines the expected ending position of the current command. Say, its angular position belongs in the i-th bucket. The controller looks in the (i + 1) bucket, modulo N, to see if it contains any queued command. If the bucket is empty, it goes to the next bucket, then the bucket after that, etc., until a non-empty bucket is found. Let's say this is the (i + k) bucket. It then checks each command in that bucket to see if its seek distance relative to the ending position of the current command is less than the k-th entry of the first column of the RPO table. If an entry that satisfies this criteria can be found, then the sorting is done. This is rotationally the closest command that can also be seeked to within the rotational time. All previously examined commands are rotationally closer than this one, but none of them can have their seeks completed within their rotational times. Hence, this is going to be the command with the shortest access time. All other remaining commands will require longer rotational time and do not need to be examined. If no entry in the bucket can satisfy the seek criteria, then move on to the next bucket and continue searching. When k has reached N − 1 and still no selectable command is found, the process is repeated, this time using the second column of the table, and so on.

Performance Comparison

The effectiveness of command queueing for disk drives that support it is often measured in terms of the maximum achievable throughput at various

X	1,600	6,500
X	2,025	7,000
2	2,500	7,500
25	3,000	8,000
100	3,500	8,500
225	4,000	9,000
400	4,500	9,500
625	5,000	9,999
900	5,500	9,999
1,225	6,000	9,999

FIGURE 21.6: Example of an RPO table based on angular distance. X means the rotational time is inadequate to start any data access.

queue depths. The command queue is kept at a given queue depth for the measurement of each data point. Thus, when an I/O is completed, a new one is immediately added back to the queue. The typical workload chosen for doing comparisons is pure random I/Os of small block sizes over the entire address range of the disk drive. This is the most demanding workload, and it is representative of one that would be observed for drives used in a multi-user server environment, such as on-line transaction processing (OLTP) which demands high performance from disk drives. Sequential accesses, while also an important class of workload, are less demanding and exercise other aspects of a drive's capability such as caching.

It is intuitive that SATF policy should outperform policies that are based only on seek time. Command reordering is not amenable to analytical solutions. Determining the effectiveness of a particular policy requires either simulation or actual measurement on a working disk drive which has that policy implemented. In this section, some simulation results based on random number generation are discussed.

A hypothetical disk drive with an OD to ID ratio of 2.5 and 1000 SPT at the OD is assumed. It uses a simple bang-bang seek with A = 0.5 and B = 10 for normalized seek distances. Hence, according to Chapter 19, Equations 19.27 and 19.41, the average seek time is 5.75 ms. The workload is pure random reads of 1 KB blocks. Non-overlapped controller overhead is negligible and ignored here. Initially, a rotation speed of 10K rpm is chosen; later it will be varied to study the effect of rpm. It can be easily computed that without reordering the average I/O time is 5.75 ms + 3 ms (average latency) + 0.016 ms (average data transfer time) = 8.766 ms. Thus, with FCFS scheduling, this drive is capable of handling 114 IOPS (I/Os per second).

Figure 21.7 shows the simulated throughput of SSTF, C-LOOK, and SATF for various queue depths. One million I/Os are simulated for each data point. The superiority of SATF is clearly demonstrated. One point of interest is that at low queue depth SSTF outperforms C-LOOK, while at high queue depth the two have essentially identical throughput.

As the queue depth is increased, it can be expected that eventually a point of diminishing return would be reached as the throughput approaches the theoretical maximum. For seek time based scheduling, the minimum I/O time would be 0.5 ms for settling + 3 ms average latency + 0.016 ms data transfer time, yielding an upper bound throughput of 284 IOPS. Indeed, the gain for SSTF and C-LOOK in going from a queue depth of 128 to 256 has slowed down to 4.5% compared to the gain in throughput of 6.6% of going from 64 to 128. On the other hand, the upper bound for SATF is much higher as it can also eliminate rotational latency when there is an infinite number of commands in the queue. The theoretical maximum throughput for SATF is 1938 IOPS. The 478 IOPS at a queue depth of 256 is still far below this upper bound, and, hence, the point of diminishing return is nowhere in sight yet.

Practical Issues of SATF

So far, the discussion has been on the theoretical aspect of SATF with simple idealized conditions. Here, some real-world practical issues facing the actual implementation of SATF in a disk drive are discussed.

Seek Time Variability This is the practical issue that has the biggest impact on SATF scheduling. Since SATF is based on minimizing the sum of seek time and latency time, a selected command may have a very short latency component. For such a command, there is little room for error in performing the seek. If the seek actually takes longer than estimated to complete, it may consume all the projected latency time, and the target sector may just have passed by. In this case, the drive must wait a full disk revolution before it can access the data. This situation, called a *miss revolution*, is a very costly error. This will not happen if the actuator servo can produce seek times that are precisely repeatable all the time so that the controller can make accurate seek time projection in scheduling for SATF. Unfortunately, due to a number of factors, some of which may not even be in the control of the servo, there will always be some degree of variation in the seek time. These factors include vibration, operating temperature, transient errors while reading a servo ID, etc.

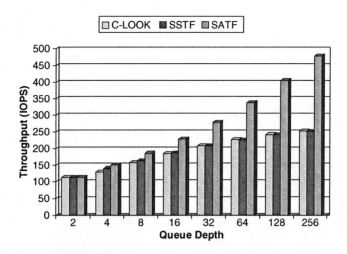

FIGURE 21.7: Comparison of performance for three different scheduling algorithms.

To deal with this seek time variance by being conservative and allowing a good margin for the seek time may not be the most optimum solution. Even though this would avoid the mis-revolution penalty completely, it also leads to missing out on some better selections which have a good chance of completing on time. Being overly aggressive in scheduling based on an optimistic seek profile, one that does not have a high percentage of making the seek in time, would also be bad, obviously, due to paying the miss revolution penalty too frequently. Thus, a good compromise strategy should be adopted. Simulation seems to suggest that a scheduling that results in roughly 3–4% miss revolutions yields the best overall throughput.

One method for handling seek time variance in SATF scheduling is to modify the estimated access time according to the probability of its seek being successfully on time. Thus, if a seek has a probability p of not completing in t_{seek}, then its contribution to access time is computed to be

$$t_{seek} + p \times t_{revolution} \qquad \text{(EQ 21.4)}$$

An example of how this enhancement in assessing the cost of an I/O can be added to the earlier discussed simplified sorting method

is as follows. Instead of just one seek distance number in each entry in the RPO table, as illustrated in Figure 21.6, there are M distances, $d_1, d_2,..., d_M$ per table entry. d_1 represents the distance below which a seek is 100% likely to complete within the rotational time associated with the corresponding bucket, d_M represents the distance above which a seek has 0% chance of completing. A distance between d_i and d_{i+1} has a $(M - i)/M$ probability of completing in the available time. When searching through the command queue as described before, if a command is found k-th bucket away from the current I/Os bucket, and this command has a distance d which is between d_i and d_{i+1} of the k-th table entry, then the access cost function (in terms of buckets) of this command is

$$k + i/M \times N \qquad \text{(EQ 21.5)}$$

where N is the number of buckets. The minimum estimated cost of all the commands examined so far is remembered. When a first command is encountered such that its seek distance is less than the d_1 of its corresponding table entry (100% seek completion probability), its cost function is compared with the minimum cost computed so far. The command with the lower estimated cost is selected to be the next command. All remaining commands do not need to be examined.

To illustrate this algorithm, the previous example, in which N = 10, is expanded using M = 4, and the new RPO table is shown in Figure 21.8; only the first column is shown for brevity. Assume the ending position of the currently active command is in bucket 35. Search the command queue, which is presorted by bucket, starting at bucket 37. The first non-empty bucket is, say, bucket 40, and it has one command with a seek distance of 196 cylinders from the current active command. Looking at the sixth entry in the table, 196 is between d_1 (180) and d_2 (212). Hence, it has a 3/4 probability of completing the seek, and its access cost (in terms of buckets) is

$$(40 - 35) + 1/4 \times 10 = 7.5 \qquad \textbf{(EQ 21.6)}$$

X			
X			
0,	1,	2,	3
19,	23,	26,	30
75,	96,	104,	125
180,	212,	238,	270
340,	385,	415,	460
565,	610,	640,	685
840,	885,	915,	960
1165,	1210,	1240,	1285

FIGURE 21.8: Example of an expanded RPO table based on angular distance. M = 4, and only the first column is shown.

Since this is the first command examined, it is remembered as the lowest cost command so far. Assume the next non-empty bucket is bucket 42, and it has one command with a seek distance of 513. Since 513 is smaller than d_1 (565) of the eighth entry in the table, it has 100% of completing in time. The estimated access cost of this command is therefore simply 42 – 35 = 7. Since this is the first command with a seek distance less than d_1, its cost is compared to the minimum cost computed so far, which is 7.5. This newly examined command in bucket 42 has a smaller cost and is thus selected to be the next command. Other commands in the queue do not need to be checked. In contrast, if the simple table of Figure 21.6 is used, the command in bucket 40 would have been selected.

Environmental Change A change in the operating environment of the disk drive, such as temperature, can cause the seek characteristics of the drive to change. Therefore, it is important to continually monitor the drive's seek behavior and adjust its seek profile or the RPO table accordingly.

Workload While the previous discussion on performance comparison assumed a pure random workload, many real-world workloads are a mix of random and sequential accesses. While doing scheduling, care must be taken to ensure that two sequential commands that are in a command queue get scheduled and executed back to back without missing a revolution. This is discussed in more detail in Section 21.2.3.

Priority The discussions on scheduling so far have been assuming that all I/O requests are of the same priority. If supported by the interface, some commands may arrive at the queue at a higher priority. Such commands need to be serviced first even though they may not be optimal selections from a performance viewpoint. Furthermore, for drives operating in certain environments, such as attached to a storage controller which has non-volatile write caching, write commands received by the drive are only for destaging from the controller's write cache and have no effect on the host system's performance, whereas read requests, on the other hand, are needed by host's applications and therefore their response times can affect such applications' performance. For such environments, it makes sense to give read commands higher priority than writes, even if such priority is not explicitly specified by the host, provided the read is not for a sector of one of the outstanding write commands. This can be accomplished by multiplying the estimated access time of writes with a weighing factor greater than 1 or adding to it some fixed additional time. For example, multiplying with a factor of 2 means that a write command will not be selected unless its estimated access time is less than half of that of the fastest read.

Aging As mentioned earlier, some sort of aging algorithm needs to be added on top of SATF to ensure that no command waits in the command queue for an unduly long time. One simple way is to have a counter for each command which is initialized to zero on its arrival at the queue. Each time a selection is made from the queue, the counters of all other commands in the queue are incremented. The estimated access time for a command is then adjusted by subtracting this counter multiplied by some fixed number. The result of adding aging is that the variance in response time is reduced, but overall throughput will also be slightly decreased.

N-Step Lookahead SATF is a Greedy algorithm as it always selects the pending request with the shortest estimated access time as the next command for servicing. Some simulation studies have shown that an alternative approach of looking ahead so that the sum of the estimated access times for the next N commands is the shortest can produce somewhat better performance. The event that can invalidate the tenet of this approach is when a new arrival results in a whole different sequence of optimal commands. For example, command sequence ABCD has been selected, and after A has been completed, command G arrives. If it was known that G was going to arrive, a better sequence would have been ECGF, and so selecting A to be executed next was not the best choice after all. The probability of this happening increases with N and when the workload is heavy. The computational complexity of this approach also goes up exponentially with N. For these two reasons, N should probably be kept small.

21.2.3 Sequential Access Scheduling

In Chapter 19, Section 19.1.1, the importance of the sequential type of accesses in increasing the effective performance of a disk drive was explained, since such an access could be completed faster than one that involved a seek and a rotational latency by an order of magnitude. Thus, for a drive to deliver good performance, it is imperative that it be able to handle properly various kinds of sequential accesses, as defined in Chapter 19, Section 19.1.1, so as not to miss out on the opportunity of short service time accorded by such I/O requests.

Regardless of which scheduling policy is used, the drive controller must ensure that if there are two commands in the queue and their addresses are sequential, then they get scheduled and executed back to back without missing any revolutions. This means the controller should coalesce all sequential or near-sequential commands before execution of the first command in the sequence is started. The commands need to be coalesced because starting a new command involves a certain amount of overhead which is substantially longer than the rotation time of the gap between two sectors. Thus, if the two sequential commands are not coalesced and executed as one, the second command will suffer a misrevolution. Ideally, the drive also should have the capability to extend a currently executing command to access more data. This is so that if a new command arrives and it is sequential to the currently active command, it can be handled immediately and efficiently.

A good drive controller should also be able to handle skip sequential commands in a similar manner. Since the command overhead can be the rotation time of multiple sectors, it is also necessary to coalesce such commands. While this is not a problem for reads, as the controller can simply read the not requested sectors along with the requested sectors into the drive's buffer, it is a problem for writes since the write buffer does not contain the data for the skipped sectors. This can be handled by using a skip mask. By setting the appropriate bits in a special register, the drive controller can signal to the write channel electronics which sectors to write and which sectors to skip. For instance, a mask of 111000011111 would signal to write three sectors starting at the command's LBA, then skip four sectors, and then write the next five sectors after that.

21.3 Reorganizing Data on the Disk

It is a fact that related data are generally accessed together, either all at once or within a very small window of time. Examples of related data are the blocks of a file, the source code of a program and its header files, or all the boot-time startup modules. This spatial and temporal locality of access is the basis of many strategies for improving disk drive performance. As pointed out previously, sequential accesses can be completed much more quickly than accesses that require a seek and rotational latency. Therefore, one class of strategies is to locate related data physically together so that it can be accessed more efficiently. Any such data layout reorganization activity should be done in the background and, preferably, during lull periods in the disk drive or storage system so that the performance of regular user requests is not affected.

Since the content of data blocks is known to the file system, e.g., "this file consists of these eight blocks" or "these twelve files are all in the same sub-directory and therefore are likely to be related," this class of strategies is best handled at wherever the file manager is located, which today is in the host system. The drive, lacking such higher level information, is less suitable. Nonetheless, there are still a few things that the drive controller may be able to do, especially since it knows the internal geometry of the drive which the host does not know. Also, there are classes of files, such as databases, large files, memory-mapped files, etc., where not all blocks are necessarily accessed together, and, hence, the lack of file system knowledge is not a big drawback.

21.3.1 Defragmentation

The first obvious thing to do with regard to related data is to locate all the blocks of a file in contiguous address space. Generally, this is the case when starting out with a fresh system or when creating a new file in a drive that has lots of not-yet used space. Depending on the file system, each time a file grows, its growth blocks may be located somewhere else if the original blocks are not to be moved. This leads to the file being fragmented. Also, after the system has gone through many file allocations and de-allocations, the disk address space may be left with many small holes, and it may be difficult to find contiguous space to fit a new large file. The result is, again, a fragmented file. Over time, the performance of a disk drive will degrade if the percentage of fragmented files goes up. The solution to this

problem is to perform *defragmentation*. During this process, all the blocks of each fragmented file are gathered together and relocated to a new contiguous address space. At the same time, the files are repacked together so as to squeeze out all the holes so that the drive ends up with one large free space available for future new file allocations. This may involve moving some of the files more than once. Defragmentation is one form of data reorganization.

21.3.2 Frequently Accessed Files

Another form of data reorganization is to relocate those files that are most frequently accessed close together. While this does not help to increase the fraction of sequential accesses, it helps reduce the overall average seek distance as the head moves only short distances from one frequently accessed file to another, which should occur more often on average. Additionally, by locating these files in the middle of all the cylinders, roughly halfway between OD and ID (skewed toward the OD for ZBR), it also reduces the average seek from any random location on the disk to one of these files, from roughly one-third of full stroke to one-fourth. For this method, the file access frequencies need to be monitored and the collected data used periodically to dynamically reorganize the file locations. A classical algorithm for placing these files is to locate the most frequently accessed file in the logical center of the drive, where the LBA is one-half the drive's total number of sectors. The other frequently accessed files, in descending order of frequencies, are next placed on either side of it, alternating from one side to the other, as shown in Figure 21.9. This is known as the *organ pipe arrangement*, for obvious reasons [Knuth 1973].

Data reorganization imposes a great deal of extra work on the disk drive. The previous set of frequently accessed files first needs to be moved out from their central locations, then the new set of frequently accessed files is moved into those vacated locations. To reduce the amount of work, one strategy is to not migrate newly identified frequently accessed files out of their present location. Instead, they are duplicated in the central location of the

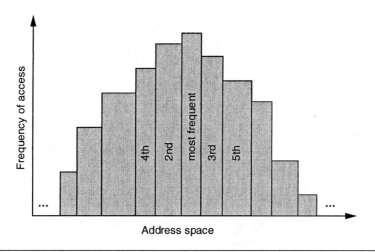

FIGURE 21.9: Illustration of the organ pipe organization.

disk. The advantage is that since the original copy of each file is always in its permanent location, there is no need to move out data from the central location. It can simply be overwritten; only the file system table needs to be updated. However, now there are two copies of those files. There are two options for handling a write to one of these files. One choice is to write to both copies of the file, which doubles the amount of work to be done. A second choice is to write only to the permanent copy of the file and invalidate the second copy in the file system table, making the second and more conveniently located copy no longer available for access. Neither solution is ideal, and which one is better depends on the ratio of writes to reads for that file. If write is more dominant, then it is better to forfeit the second copy. If read is more dominant, then it is better to update both copies so that the more frequent reads can benefit from faster access.

While disk drives do not yet have file system awareness,[3] they can adopt the data reorganization technique of relocating frequently accessed data close together on a block basis rather than on a file basis. However, it may not be practical, as the overhead of monitoring access frequency on a block basis may be too great for the resource-constrained drive controller to handle.

21.3.3 Co-Locating Access Clusters

Certain files tend to be accessed together. Furthermore, they are accessed in exactly, or almost exactly, the same sequence each time. For such files, it makes sense to relocate them permanently so that they are stored together in the disk drive as a cluster and in the order with which they are likely to be accessed. In this way, each time they are accessed, they can be accessed efficiently as some form of sequential access. One good example and candidate of this class of data reorganization is the boot sequence of a system. Various *boot optimizers* have been developed which learn how a system is configured to boot up. After the system has been booted a few times, the optimizer is able to determine the likely sequence with which various files and applications are loaded from the disk drive into the system memory. It then sees to it that these files get co-located accordingly. Application loadings are another class of candidates for this strategy, with programs called *application launch accelerators* as the counterpart to boot optimizers.

---

[3]This is a concept that has been discussed for many years, but has not materialized yet.

21.3.4 ALIS

The *Automatic Locality-Improving Storage* (ALIS) methodology [Hsu and Smith 2004, Hsu et al. 2005] combines both the strategy of relocating frequently accessed data together and the strategy of co-locating an observed common sequence of data accesses. It calls the first strategy *heat clustering* (data that is frequently accessed is said to be hot) and the second strategy *run clustering* (run as in "a continuous sequence of things"). Data monitoring and reorganization are performed at a block level, not on a file basis. Hence, it can be implemented either in the host or in the disk drive if the drive has enough resources such as computational power and temporary storage to do so. Fixed-size blocks are the reorganization units, with the block size being a design parameter.

Heat Clustering

ALIS recognizes that the organ pipe organization of data, whose goal is to reduce the average seek distance, has these shortcomings:

- A small amount of seek is not that much saving over a slightly longer seek.
- It has the tendency to move the head back and forth across the central most frequently accessed file as it accesses hot files on both sides of it.
- Rotational latency is not reduced.
- The concept was born of an era when disk I/Os were basically first come first serve. With today's command queueing and reordering, this approach provides little, if any, benefit.
- It was not designed to take advantage of the prefetching that is commonly performed today both in the host cache and in the drive cache.

Instead of organ pipe data placement, ALIS recommends a heat clustering strategy of simple sequential layout, whereby the hot data blocks identified for duplication are arranged in a reserved reorganization area in the order of their original block addresses. The underlying theory of this strategy is to retain the sequentiality of the original data, but with those data that are inactive filtered out. In a typical real workload, only a small fraction (empirical measurements indicate about 15%) of a disk's total data is normally in active use.

Run Clustering

ALIS also takes advantage of the fact that in most real workloads there are long read sequences that are often repeated due to certain tasks being asked to be performed repeatedly. Launching a common application is one such example. To identify such runs, ALIS constructs an *access graph* to continuously keep track of I/O request sequencing. Each vertex of the graph represents a block, and the edge from vertex i to vertex j represents the desirability for locating block j after block i. Each time block j is accessed within k commands of accessing block i, the value of the edge from vertex i to vertex j is incremented by $t - k + 1$ if $k \leq t$, where t is a design parameter called the *context size*. A context size greater than 1 is needed to make allowance for a user's request stream being intermixed with other users' request streams, as in a multi-programming or a server environment. Figure 21.10 illustrates a simple example of such an access graph for the block sequence ABCAXBC with t = 2. Since the number of blocks in a drive is likely to be huge for any sensible block size, the size of the access graph needs to be kept to some reasonable maximum size by pruning. Edges with low weights and vertices whose edges are all with low weights are dropped. To enable old patterns to exit the graph gracefully and not become stagnant, an aging algorithm is added to the edge weights.

To identify a run for clustering from an access graph, first select the edge with the highest weight; its two vertices form the seed of the run. Next, find

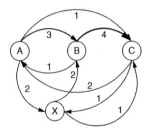

FIGURE 21.10: An access graph for the block sequence ABCAXBC with t = 2.

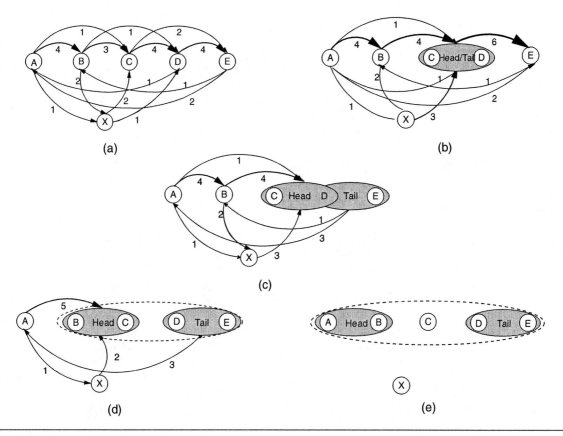

FIGURE 21.11: Example of the heat cluster discovery procedure: (a) reference stream = ABCDEABXCDE; (b) discovered run CD; (c) discovered run CDE; (d) discovered run BCDE; and (e) discovered run ABCDE.

and add to the run the vertex whose edges to all the vertices in the run have the highest weight sum. This can be a vertex that gets added to the beginning or to the end of the run. This continues until the length of the run exceeds t, the context size. From this point on, the *head* of the run is defined to be the first t vertices of the run, and the *tail* of the run is defined to be the last t vertices. Continue to grow by iteratively finding and adding to the run the vertex whose edges to either the head or the tail have the highest weight sum. Finally, this growth process terminates when the head weight and the tail weight fall below some threshold. This threshold is another ALIS design parameter. Figure 21.11 shows a highly

simplified example of this process in identifying the run ABCDE from an original reference stream of ABCDEABXCDE.

Cluster Selection During Service Time

Heat clustering and run clustering co-exist in the reorganization space. A block may appear multiple times in different clusters. Hence, when an I/O request arrives, there may be choices as to which cluster to use for servicing the request. Because runs are specific patterns of access that are likely to be repeated, they are selected first. If a matching run cannot be found, then heat clusters are searched. When still no match can be found, then it is necessary to use the original copy of the data as no duplicate of the data exists.

21.4 Handling Writes

In some environments, write commands arrive at the disk drive in bursts. One such example is when there is write caching at the host or storage controller, which periodically destages all the writes that have been cached to the disk drive. Furthermore, the writes are random writes that update data scattered throughout the drive, with each write requiring a seek and a rotational latency. To service all the writes of a burst can tie up the drive for some time, even if a command reordering technique is used to minimize the mechanical times, thus affecting the response time of any read command that comes during this period.

The class of strategies designed to handle this situation is, again, based on the observation that sequential accesses are a lot faster than random accesses. The general idea is that, instead of updating the individual write data in its original locations, all the new data is written together in a sequential string to some new location. A directory or relocation table must be maintained to point to the location of every piece of data in the drive. Sections 21.4.1 and 21.4.2 discuss two strategies for batching the writes as one sequential access.

21.4.1 Log-Structured Write

When this method is implemented at the host level, it is known as the *log-structured file system* (LFS). A similar technique can also be applied at the disk level by the drive controller, transparently and unbeknown to the host. In this method, the disk address space is partitioned into fixed-size segments, with each segment containing many sectors. This segment size is a design parameter. A certain number of free segments must be available at all times, one of which is being used as the active write segment. When a sufficient number of writes requests (e.g., enough data to fill a segment) have accumulated at the level where this log-structured write is implemented, the new data are all written out together sequentially to the

active write segment, starting at the next available sector. A log of these individual writes is appended to the end of this new sequence of data. Each log entry contains the original LBA of each write and the LBA of its new location.

An in-memory directory is updated with the same information as the log. Once the directory is updated, references to the old copies of data are gone, basically invalidating the old data and freeing up its space. It may be desirable to keep a list of such free spaces or how much free space each segment has so that future cleanup can be expedited. The directory is periodically, and also during normal shut down, saved to the disk at a fixed known location. When the drive and the system are next started up, the directory can be read back in to memory. The purpose of the logs is for reconstructing the directory since its last known good state should the drive or system be shut down abnormally, such as during a power interruption. The disk drive maintains a flag which indicates whether it was powered down properly or unexpectedly. All systems also have a similar status indicator.

The main advantage of this log-structured write strategy is that many random small writes are turned into a long sequential write which can be completed very quickly. However, it comes with the following disadvantages:

- An originally contiguous piece of data will be broken up when part of it gets an update write. The more writes it goes through, the more fragmented it becomes. Thus, if the user reads the data, what was once data that could be accessed with a single sequential read now becomes many random reads. Thus, this strategy makes sense only for workloads that are dominated by small writes.

- Because of the holes created in segments by writes invalidating data in previous locations, they need to be consolidated so as to create new empty segments for new writes, in a process known as *garbage collection*. This is extra work that the drive needs to take care of, and in a heavily used system, there may not be sufficient idle times for this function to be performed non-intrusively.

- The disk drive needs to have a sizable amount of excess capacity, as much as 20%, over the total amount of actual data stored so that it does not run out of free segments too frequently. In this way, it can have more leeway in scheduling when to do garbage collection.

- Address translation for an I/O request must now go through one more level of indirection, adding extra overhead to each command.

- All data in a log-structured storage would be lost if its directory is lost or corrupted. The system must be carefully designed so that the directory can be recovered or reconstructed if needed. Reconstruction of the directory will be a time-consuming process.

Because of these shortcomings, log-structured writes should not be, and have not been, implemented in a general-purpose disk drive. Even for heavy write environments where this strategy may make sense, either at the system or at the drive level, careful design considerations and trade-offs should be evaluated before deciding on adopting this strategy.

Finally, if ALIS or some other usage-based clustering technique is used in conjunction with a log-structured write, data reorganization can be opportunistically performed during the garbage collection process. As valid data needs to be consolidated to create full segments, those data that are discovered to belong to the same heat cluster or run cluster can be placed in the same segment.

21.4.2 Disk Buffering of Writes

This method can be considered to be doing a partial log-structured write and only on a temporary basis. While it may be possible to implement this strategy at the host level, it is more practical to implement it inside the disk drive. In this technique, the drive has a small amount of reserved space dedicated to this function, preferably divided into a few areas scattered throughout the drive. Similar to a log-structured write, when a sufficient number of write commands have been accumulated, all these random writes are gathered and written out to one of these areas, preferentially the one that is closest to the current head position, as one long sequential write. Again, a log of these writes is appended to the end. This is where similarity with the log-structured write ends.

Here, relocation of data is only temporary. The home location of each piece of data is not changed—just its content is temporarily out of date. In other words, the disk has been used to buffer the writes. During idle periods in the disk drive, the drive controller reads back the buffered data and writes each of them to its home location. In essence, the drive delays all the random writes from a time when the drive is busy with other concurrent read requests requiring fast response time to a time when no user requests are waiting to be serviced and so the long completion time of random writes does not matter. While the amount of work that the drive ends up doing is increased, the apparent performance of the drive to the user is improved. Furthermore, since the update data is eventually written back to its home location, the long-term sequentiality of a user's data does not get damaged over time—an important advantage over the log-structured write strategy. A small directory or relocation table is needed to properly point to where the temporarily buffered data is located. LBAs not listed in the relocation table can be found in their home locations.

21.5 Data Compression

When data is first compressed before storing to the disk, more data can be stored. Compressing the data can be performed either at the host level, at the storage subsystem controller level, or inside the disk drive. If data can be compressed at an average compression ratio of C to 1, then, in essence, the storage capacity of the disk drive is increased C times. In addition to this seemingly marvelous attribute, data compression can also potentially improve performance. First, the media transfer rate is effectively increased C folds. Second, the track capacity is increased C times, reducing or even eliminating seek distances between a user's data. (Refer back to Chapter 19, Section 19.2.1, for a more in-depth discussion of performance impact of a larger track capacity.)

However, data compression has a few major issues.

- Data compression is computationally intensive, although using a dedicated compression chip or hardware can alleviate the problem.
- The compression ratio is highly data content sensitive. Some data compresses well, while other data cannot be compressed at all. Furthermore, a piece of data will likely be compressed to a different size each time its content is changed. Thus, when data is modified, its new compressed output may no longer fit in the space previously allocated to that data. One solution is to use compression in conjunction with the log-structured write, since the log-structured write does not write back to the original location and, hence, the size of the data does not matter. Another solution is to allocate some slack space for each piece of compressed data so as to minimize the probability of not being able to fit a modification back into the allocated space. For those rare occasions when the modification does not fit, then the data is relocated to some new space.
- If multiple pieces of compressed data are packed into a sector, then modifying any one of them and writing it back will require a read-modify-write of the sector. This degrades performance very substantially as the process requires a read, waiting basically one revolution, and then a write. Again, the log-structured write can be a solution to this problem.

CHAPTER 22

The Cache Layer

The disk drive's cache is a great equalizer of performance. It can reduce the net performance gap between two drives with a vast difference in raw performance capability such as seek time and rotational speed. Cases exist in which a mechanically slow desktop or even mobile drive whose caching strategy is better tuned for certain applications outperforms a much faster server drive whose cache is not designed to handle those applications. Caching is, therefore, a key factor in a disk drive's performance, whose importance is equal to other basic drive attributes such as seek time, rotational speed, and data rate.

Because of its importance, this chapter is devoted to disk cache exclusively. There are two aspects to the design of a disk cache. One aspect is its *logical organization,* which deals with how the memory space for caching is structured and allocated and how data is placed and identified within the cache memory. A second aspect is the cache's content- and consistency-management *algorithms,* which define the behavior of the cache and include deciding which piece of old data to throw out (deallocate) to make room for new data, what and how much data to prefetch, etc. Hence, the organizational aspect of cache design deals with *where* to put data, and the algorithmic aspect deals with *what* data to put in the cache. These two aspects are orthogonal, in the sense that one does not depend on the other, although certain algorithms may be easier to implement with a particular type of organization. Both aspects will be discussed in this chapter, following an overview of caching at the disk drive level.

22.1 Disk Cache

Today's disk drives all come with a built-in cache as part of the drive controller electronics, ranging in size from 512 KB for the microdrive to 16 MB for the largest server drives. The earliest drives did not have any cache memory, as they did not have much in the way of control electronics. As the data transfer control function migrated down from the host side control logic to the drive's own controller, a small amount of memory was used to act as a speed-matching buffer, needed because the disk's media data rate is different from that of the interface. Buffering is also needed because when the head is at a position ready to do data transfer, the host or the interface may be busy and not ready to receive read data or send write data. DRAM is usually used as this buffer memory.

As data from the previous transfer was left in the buffer, it became obvious that on those rare occasions when the next request was for the same data, the drive could return the data from the buffer instead of retrieving it from the media. In other words, the buffer can double as a data reuse cache. As the cell size and cost of DRAM go down, the size of this buffer gradually grows over time, and it becomes a full-fledged cache. The buffering function now can actually be satisfied with just a small fraction of the total buffer/cache memory, with the majority of the data occupying the memory being there as a result of some explicit caching function or activity.

22.1.1 Why Disk Cache Works

In a system, the host typically has some memory dedicated for caching disk data, and if a drive is attached to the host via some external controller, that controller also typically has a cache. Both the system cache and the external cache are much larger than the disk drive's internal cache. Hence, for most workloads, the drive's cache is not likely to see too many reuse cache hits. This, however, does not mean that the drive's cache is not very useful. Quite the contrary: it is very effective in opportunistically prefetching data, as only the controller inside the drive knows the state the drive is in and when and how it can prefetch without adding any cost in time. To *prefetch* is to read data in before it is requested by the host, and there is no assurance that it will actually be needed or requested in the near future. Because of this speculative nature, ideally, prefetch should be done unobtrusively and with no added cost so that if the speculation does not pan out there is no penalty. For this reason, the drive's cache is a good match for prefetch caching. Finally, the drive needs cache memory if it is to support write caching.

An I/O request that can be satisfied with the disk cache improves performance over a request that requires accessing the disk media by avoiding the mechanical times of seek and rotational latency, which are the dominant components of a disk I/O time, as discussed in Chapter 19, Section 19.1. Furthermore, the controller overhead time for a cache hit is typically smaller than for a cache miss, which needs to look for cache space and set up the hardware to do media data access. Continuing with the example of Chapter 19, Section 19.1.1, data transfer between the host and the cache runs at the interface data rate[1] of 100 MB/s. Assuming a cache hit overhead of 0.15 ms, then the I/O service time for a 4-KB cache hit takes $0.15 + 0.04 = 0.19$ ms. This is better than an order of magnitude faster than the 7.885 ms for a random read and the 4.885 ms for a local access cache miss. This clearly illustrates the importance of a disk cache.

22.1.2 Cache Automation

In some disk drives, hardware is used to automate the entire process of cache lookup and handling those I/O requests that can be satisfied from the cache. The result is that the cache hit overhead is very small. This sounds good, since the previous 4-KB cache hit can now be completed in 0.05 ms if an overhead time of 0.01 msec is assumed. However, the overall effect to the disk drive's performance for this hardware automation is somewhat less dramatic. This is because, for most workloads and applications, the cache miss ratio is relatively high, and so the overall performance of the drive is dominated by the cache miss service time. The miss ratio (hit ratio) is the percentage of I/Os that cannot (can) be serviced completely with the cache. The overall average I/O time is given by

hit ratio × avg. hit time + miss ratio × avg. miss time

$$\text{(EQ 22.1)}$$

Using the above numbers from our example and assuming local access, Figure 22.1(a) plots the average I/O time with and without hardware automation for varying hit ratios, and Figure 22.1(b) shows their ratio. It is clear from Figure 22.1(a) that improving the hit ratio is much more important than having hardware automation to speed up the response time of I/Os that are cache hits in reducing the overall average I/O time. Not until the hit ratio is well above 80% does the effect of automation become observable, according to Figure 22.1(b). At 100% hit ratio, the difference is significant. This is the territory of sequential reads and cache writes, as will be discussed later.

22.1.3 Read Cache, Write Cache

Caching can be applied to both read access and write access. While the caching actions for reads and writes are different, their effects on the I/O time are the same when the transaction can be completed using the cache memory and not any disk media access.

Read Caching

All disk drives today perform read caching. A very small fraction of a disk drive's data is replicated and stored in its cache memory. When a read command

---

[1]Ideally, though, in general, the net data rate is slightly below the interface speed due to various low-level interface overheads.

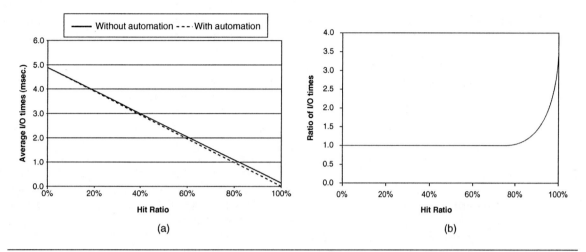

FIGURE 22.1: The effect of hardware automation to do a cache search and transfer cache hit data: (a) average I/O time, assuming local access; and (b) ratio of average I/O times for without automation to with automation.

arrives at the disk drive, its cache memory is checked to see if it contains the data requested. If all the requested data can be found in the cache, then it is a *full hit*, and the command can be quickly serviced without involving any of the drive's mechanical components. If only part of the requested data is found in the cache (this is called a *partial hit* or a *partial miss*), or if none is found in the cache, then it is necessary to go to the disk media to retrieve the missing data.

To have any measurable impact on a drive's performance, the read cache must provide full hits a fairly good percentage of the time. That means its content should be holding data that the user has a good likelihood of requesting. Hence, one of the key elements in designing the disk cache is figuring out what data to place in the read cache so as to maximize this likelihood. Since the size of the disk cache is typically about 0.01% of the storage capacity of a drive, clearly, it will have no effect for completely random I/O requests. This would be the environment a drive operates in when used in a storage subsystem serving many users and applications. Fortunately, in many other environments the I/O request stream seen by the disk drive *does* exhibit locality of reference. Such an environment provides an opportunity for the cache to produce the maximum beneficial effect. Temporal locality means a recently used piece of data will likely be accessed

again in the near future. Spatial locality means neighboring data of a recently used piece of data will likely be accessed soon. Thus, caching algorithms, to be discussed later, are all about identifying the cache data with locality of access and retaining them.

Write Caching

Write caching operates on a completely different mechanism than read caching. With write caching, the drive controller services a write request by transferring the write data from the host to the drive's cache memory and then reports back to the host that the write is "done," even though the data has not yet been written to the disk media. (Data not yet written out to disk is referred to as "*dirty*"). Thus, the service time for a cached write is about the same as that for a read cache hit, involving only some drive controller overhead and electronic data transfer time but no mechanical time. Clearly, unlike read caching, write caching does not depend on having the right data content in the cache memory; write caching will always work, i.e., a write command will always be a cache hit, as long as there is available space in the cache memory. When the cache becomes full, some or all of the dirty data is written out to the disk media to free up space. This process is commonly referred to as *destage*.

Ideally, destage should be done while the drive is idle so that it does not affect the servicing of users' requests. However, this may not always be possible. The drive may be operating in a high-usage system with little idle time ever, or the writes oftentimes arrive in bursts that quickly fill up the limited memory space of the cache. When destage must take place while the drive is busy, such activity adds to the load of the drive at that time, and a user will notice a longer response time for his requests. Instead of providing the full benefit of cache hits, write caching in this case merely delays the disk writes. However, even in this scenario, write caching still provides some performance benefits:

Scheduling of Queued Writes Because disks can often have multiple writes outstanding in the cache, these writes can be destaged using one of the scheduling algorithms discussed in Chapter 21. This reduces the total amount of time the drive gets tied up doing these writes compared to executing the writes as they arrive and in the order of their arrival. Even if the drive's interface does not support command queueing, write caching is a *de facto* form of command queueing for writes. If the drive's interface does support command queueing, write caching effectively increases the queue depth available for sorting by the number of writes that have been cached, making more choices available and thus enhancing performance. For example, if a disk drive can support up to 32 cached writes, it allows a non-queueing drive to behave like a queueing drive with a queue depth of 32 for write commands, and it increases the queue depth of a queueing drive by up to 32.

Write Avoidance In many environments, the same data may get updated multiple times within a relatively short period of time. One common example is someone working on a document and saving it periodically. If a new write arrives before the previous one has a chance to be destaged, that previous write no longer needs to be destaged. Therefore, with write caching, the total number of actual writes to the disk may be fewer than the total number of write commands received by the drive. This means less total work needs to be done by the drive.

Because cached write data is not written out to disk immediately, and because, so far, all disk drives use as cache memory DRAM, which is volatile, there is a chance that cached write data may be lost. This happens when the drive loses power before it is able to destage all the write data, such as an improper powering down of the drive or some sudden interruption in the system's power supply. Thus, write caching should only be used for those applications that find such occasional loss of data tolerable. For those applications requiring high data integrity from disk storage, the drive must run with its write cache disabled, forfeiting the performance benefit of write caching. For those applications that are in between, with some data that need integrity guarantee while loss of other data is acceptable, two options permit them to run with write caching enabled, both of which are available in the SCSI and the ATA standard interfaces. These two options are the following:

- **Flush** A *Flush* command can be issued by the host, instructing the drive to immediately destage all outstanding cached writes. This method is used by various journaling and logging systems to guarantee data consistency while taking advantage of write caching.
- **FUA** An individual write command can have the *Force Unit Access* (FUA) option selected which informs the drive that this write must not be cached, but written to the disk directly. This permits the host application to control what critical data to bypass the write cache.

Read Caching in the Presence of a Write Cache

There are several things that can be done to improve the performance of reads when the disk cache does both read caching and write caching.

Read hits in write cache If a drive does write caching, the write cache should also be checked for possible read hits. While the probability of getting a hit there is usually small and is highly workload dependent, the cost for checking is basically free.

Read priority over destage Obviously, a read miss should be serviced first over any write cache destage. A delay in handling a read request that is a cache miss is directly observable by the user. The effect of delay in destaging is less directly observable.

One cache memory space The cache memory spaces should not be divided to have one part permanently dedicated for reading only and a second part for writing only. Having such a fixed partitioning of read cache and write cache is inefficient use of the cache space. It prevents the cache from dynamically adjusting itself to handle workload bursts dominated by either reads or writes. A good cache architecture should allow more space to be used for reads when there are more read commands in the workload that the drive is handling, and vice-versa.

Use same allocation space Taking the above concept one step further, a good cache architecture should allow cached write data and cached read data of the same LBA to use the same cache memory space. More specifically, if an LBA already exists in the cache from some prior disk read, a new write command using that same LBA should have its data stored into the same cache location. An organization that requires separate read and write cache spaces would have to allocate new write space to hold this new write data and invalidate the read cache space holding the old read data. This is inefficient use of cache space and creates unnecessary work for the drive controller.

22.2 Cache Organizations

The disk drive's cache evolved from a humble beginning. Understandably, its data structures were fairly simple when initially developed, as the typical cache size was quite small. Some of those early simple designs have been carried over from generation to generation and are still used by today's disk drives. One of these simple structures is actually assumed in the SCSI standard.

When some piece of disk data is to be stored in the disk cache, the cache space allocated to it is commonly called a *cache segment*, notionally equivalent to a solid-state *cache block*. Cache segments can be either fixed size or variable size. All the data stored within a segment is logically contiguous. When an I/O request arrives at the disk drive, the cache is checked to see if a segment has already been allocated for the LBAs of the request. If such a segment exists, then that segment will be used for the request. If no such segment exists, then a new segment will be assigned. If a segment contains some but not all of the requested LBAs, there are two choices: expand that segment if it is possible to do so or assign a new and different segment. After the cache's initial startup period, to assign, or allocate, a new segment means that one or more existing segments must first be *deallocated*. When a segment is deallocated, association with its previously assigned LBAs is removed, and the data of those LBAs will be overwritten in the cache by new data.

22.2.1 Desirable Features of Cache Organization

The disk cache memory space is relatively small, so it is important to use it efficiently. The more user data that can be stored in the cache, the more likely a read request can get a cache hit out of it. A good cache organization should have the following features:

High space utilization Cache space allocation should not result in lots of wasted space. This may seem obvious, but if a relatively large-size cache allows for only a limited number of segments, then each segment may be much bigger than what is required to hold the data.

Single copy of data There should not be more than one copy of data for any LBA in the cache. This is a generalization of the shared memory space between the reads and writes concept discussed in the previous section. Again, this may seem obvious, but in practice it does happen with a number of cache organizations that the same LBA can appear in multiple segments. A cache organization allowing such duplication must ensure correctness of behavior, and the wasted space should be the cost of increased performance (e.g., similar duplication is possible in *trace caches*—see "Another Dynamic Cache Block: Trace Caches" was dicussed in Chapter 2, Section 2.6.3).

One cache memory space The cache space should not be partitioned into a read cache and a write cache, as discussed in the previous section.

Ease of allocation Finding space for a new segment should be a simple task, as it is part of the overhead for handling a command and affects the command's response time.

In this section, the basic structures of three main classes of organization will be discussed. They are the segmentation, circular buffer, and virtual memory schemes.

22.2.2 Fixed Segmentation

The most common disk cache architecture is the *fixed-segmentation* scheme. With this organization, the cache memory space is divided equally into fixed-size segments, as illustrated in Figure 22.2. For example, an 8-MB cache with 16 segments will have 500 KB (one thousand 512 byte sectors) per segment. The number of segments may be fixed in a disk drive. Alternatively, since SCSI assumes drives to have such a cache organization, a host system can specify to an SCSI drive the number of segments that it wishes the drive to have.

Associated with the segments is a *segment table*, with each table entry corresponding to one seg-

ment. A segment table entry contains the starting LBA of the data block allocated to that segment and the number of sectors of that block currently stored in the segment. The entry also contains a flag indicating whether the segment's data is dirty. Cache lookup is performed by searching through the segment table.

Because the segments are of fixed and equal size, a segment's number can be used as the index for calculating the memory address of the segment:

$$\text{seg. address} = \text{start address of cache} + \text{seg. no.} \times \text{seg. size} \qquad \textbf{(EQ 22.2)}$$

With respect to the list of desirable features listed in Section 22.2.1, the fixed-segmentation scheme has the following properties:

- Because the fixed-size segments are usually quite large, with space typically for hundreds of sectors, they are not very efficient for caching small blocks of data.
- Depending on the implementation, it is possible to have multiple copies of the same data in the cache. As a simple example, a command causes a segment to be created for LBAs 1000–1300. Later, another request for LBAs 900–1100 arrives. Since LBAs 900–999 are not in the cache, it is a partial miss. Because LBA 1000 starts at the beginning of the segment, there is no room in the segment to put LBAs 900–999, and so a new segment is allocated for the new command. For simplicity, the implementation chooses to load LBAs 900–1100 all in from the disk to the new segment. Now, two different segments contain LBAs 1000–1100.
- Generally, with the segmentation organization, segments created to handle

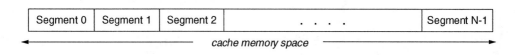

FIGURE 22.2: Address space organization of N fixed-size segments.

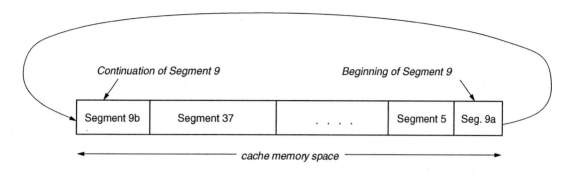

FIGURE 22.3: Cache memory space organization of the circular buffer scheme. Variable size segments are allocated from the buffer.

write commands are distinct from segments created for read commands. However, any segment can be allocated for either read or write. Thus, there is no requirement for permanent partitioning of read cache space and write cache space, unless the designer chooses to for some other reasons.

- Typically, the segments are arranged in an LRU (Least Recently Used) list. When a segment is first assigned, or when there is a cache hit on an existing segment, that segment becomes MRU (Most Recently Used) and gets moved to the bottom of the LRU list.[2] If a new segment is required for a new command, the segment at the top of the LRU list is deallocated and assigned to be the new segment. Hence, space allocation is a very simple procedure.

22.2.3   Circular Buffer

Another cache organization that dates back to the early days of disk cache is the *circular buffer*. In this architecture, the cache memory space is managed circularly. This means that when the last physical address of the cache memory space is reached, the hardware wraps the address around back to the beginning, as illustrated in Figure 22.3.

Thus, the cache, or buffer, space becomes a ring with no beginning or end. The operation of the circular buffer, also called *ring*, organization is described here in the context of the desirable features listed in Section 22.2.1.

- In the circular buffer organization, variable size segments are allocated. As a new command arrives and a new segment is needed (cache miss), contiguous cache memory space, just enough to service the command (including any prefetching), is allocated. Since only the required amount of data is allocated each time, space utilization can be quite efficient.
- Other than the segment size being variable, a circular buffer segment does not look that different from a segment of a fixed-size segmentation scheme. A segment of both schemes consists of physically contiguous memory space, and there are no rules or restrictions on the placement of LBAs within a segment (the virtual memory scheme is different in this respect). Thus, it is also possible here for an LBA to appear more than once in the cache.
- It is also not necessary for a circular buffer organization to have dedicated read cache and write cache partitioning. A newly

---

[2]Variations to this simple strategy can be made, but the discussion is beyond the scope of this book.

created segment at any memory location can be used for either reading or writing.

- Looking for the necessary amount of contiguous memory space to create a segment is a more complex job here than the segmentation scheme. It is further complicated by the fact that write segments are intermixed with read segments, and a write segment cannot be deallocated without first destaging its data. Thus, ideally, one would prefer to look for read segments to deallocate first, using write segments as a last resort. Two main selection options are the classical best fit or first fit strategies. Best fit has better space utilization, but requires more search overhead.

A circular buffer organization also requires a segment table. In addition to information about what LBAs have been assigned to each segment, the segment's starting cache memory address and its length must also be part of each segment entry, since that information can no longer be computed. Cache lookup is performed by searching through the segment table.

22.2.4 Virtual Memory Organization

The fixed-segmentation scheme is easy to manage, but not very space efficient. The circular buffer scheme is space efficient, but harder to manage. A scheme that combines the best of those two worlds is the virtual memory organization, which borrows from the general-purpose world and adapts the base mechanism to the disk drive—just as with virtual memory within the operating system, the virtual memory disk cache organization is a software implementation of a fully associative cache. Different variations of caching schemes based on the virtual memory concept are possible; the following discussion is but one example.

In the virtual memory scheme, the cache memory space is partitioned into N *pages*, which are the allocation units. The size of a page is 2^M disk sectors, where M is a design parameter that governs the efficiency of space utilization. A smaller value of M allows more

precise space allocation, but it incurs greater management overhead, so it is a design trade-off. For an 8-MB cache, if M = 5, then each page will hold thirty-two 512-B sectors or 16 KB of data, and there will be N = 512 pages. By choosing a reasonably small value of M, the virtual memory scheme can have equal or better space utilization as the circular buffer with variable segment size. In the following, M = 5 is used as the example for all discussions.

Logical Segment

Each segment can consist of one or more pages. Therefore, there can be up to N segments in the cache. While the contents of the pages within a segment are logically contiguous, the pages themselves do not have to be physically contiguous in memory. In other words, physically non-contiguous pages are mapped to form a logically contiguous segment. The physically non-contiguous pages of a segment form a logical chain. For example, pages 35, 101, and 8 can be the pages of a segment allocated to LBAs 19200–19295, with page 35 holding LBAs 19200–19231, page 101 holding LBAs 19232–19263, and page 8 holding LBAs 19264–19295. Since the contents of pages 35, 101, and 8 are logically contiguous, they form a logical chain. This flexibility of being able to dynamically create logical chains using non-contiguous pages simplifies the search for space to form a new segment of any length.

All the pages can be arranged in some replacement list, such as LRU, similar to the segmentation scheme, for the purpose of allocation. A page can be used for either read data or write data or both. Associated with each page is a Dirty Flag; this flag is set if the page contains one or more dirty sectors, i.e., sectors with cached write data that needs to be written out to disk. When the drive decides that K pages need to be allocated for a new segment, it simply takes the first K units that do not have the Dirty Flag set from the top of the LRU list.

LBA Mapping

An LBA of the disk drive is divided into L upper bits and M lower bits, as shown in Figure 22.4. The

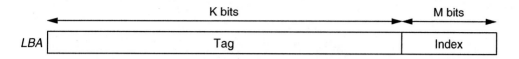

FIGURE 22.4: Partitioning of an LBA. The LBA consists of a tag and an index.

L upper bits together form the *tag* of the LBA. All the 2^M LBAs having the same tag form an allocation group. Sectors belonging to the same allocation group are stored together in the same page. When a sector of an allocation group is stored in a page, the M lower bits of its LBA are used as the index into the page to determine its location within that page. Thus, the LBA with the lower bits 00000 will be stored in the first sector location of a page, 00001 will be stored in the second sector location, 00010 will be stored in the third sector location, ..., and 11111 will be stored in the last sector location.

If an LBA already exists in some page, that page will be used for that LBA, and no new page will be assigned. Furthermore, new write data will be placed right over previous read/write data of the same LBA if it exists in the cache. Hence, no more than one page will ever be assigned to the same LBA, and an LBA will never have more than one occurrence in the cache. This is one of the desirable features of a cache organization.

Hashing

While it is certainly possible to do cache lookup by sequentially examining the content of each page, this can be a slow process, and it is much faster to use a hashing technique instead. A simple hash function is applied on the K upper bits, or tag, of an LBA to generate a hash number with H bits. Any hashing function can be used; it can be as simple as taking the lower H bits of the tag. All 2^M LBAs in the same allocation group will generate the same hash since they all have the same M upper bits (tag). Additionally, K is usually greater than H, thus many allocation groups,

in fact 2^{K-H} of them, will also have the same hash; the hash is a many-to-one mapping. When two pages are allocated to tags which have the same hash, the condition is known as *collision*. Handling of collision is discussed below.

There is a *hash table* with 2^H entries. Each hash table entry contains a pointer to a page containing an allocation group whose hash is the offset (entry number) of this entry in the hash table. See Figure 22.5. This pointer is the head pointer for a *hash chain* (see later). If no allocation unit is associated with this hash table entry, then the entry contains a NULL pointer.

Page Table

In addition to a segment table, there is a page table,[3] with each entry corresponding to one page. Each entry contains:

1. The tag of the LBAs of the allocation group assigned to this page.
2. A valid data bit map of 2^M bits corresponding to the sectors in the page. A bit is set if valid data is present for the corresponding sector.
3. A dirty data bit map of 2^M bits. A bit is set if the data for the corresponding sector is dirty. This bit map constitutes the Dirty Flag mentioned earlier.
4. A hash chain pointer. As pointed out earlier, multiple allocation groups have the same hash. This pointer points to the next page whose allocation group has the same hash number as this page. The last page

---

[3] Actually, the segment table can be dispensed with by incorporating the segment information into the page table.

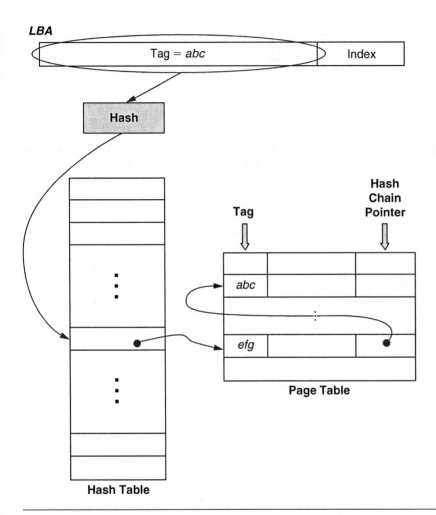

FIGURE 22.5: Relationship of LBA, hash table, and page table. Tags abc and efg have the same hash, which is the offset into the hash table.

in the chain has a NULL for this pointer to indicate the end of chain.

Cache Lookup Procedure

To determine if an LBA exists in the cache, the tag field of that LBA is used to generate a hash. This hash number is used to index into the hash table, as illustrated in Figure 22.5. If that entry in the hash table is NULL, then the LBA does not exist in the cache. If the hash entry points to a page table entry, the tag field of

that entry is compared with the tag of this LBA. If they match, then the page containing this LBA is found. If they do not match, then the hash chain pointer of the page table entry is used to locate the next entry, and the comparison is repeated for the next entry. The hash chain is thus followed until either a match is found and the page containing this LBA is located or the end of chain is reached in which case the LBA is not in the cache.

If a section containing the LBA being searched is located in the cache, its valid bit map can be examined to see if the bit corresponding to this LBA is set. If it is set, then valid data for this LBA is in the cache, and it is a cache hit. The page number and the lower M bits of the LBA completely determine the physical address of the sector in the cache memory space.

Attributes of Architecture

It should be clear from the foregoing discussions that a cache architecture based on the virtual memory concept can possess all the desirable features of a cache organization listed in Section 22.2.1. Because the pages, which are the allocation units, are typically of relatively small granularity, space utilization is very efficient. As explained in the LBA mapping, read and write data share the same space, further enhancing space utilization efficiency. Finally, because non-contiguous pages can easily be stitched together to form a logical chain of any length, space management is a simple task.

22.3 Caching Algorithms

While the cache organization defines how the address space of cache memory is to be structured and managed, another equally important aspect of cache design has to do with how the cache is to be utilized to provide good performance.

As mentioned earlier, write commands can always be cached as long as there is available space in the cache. Thus, good handling of write caching is mainly issues of using the write cache space efficiently and timely destaging of cached writes to make room for new write requests. Segmentation is a poor utilization of cache space, especially for small random writes where write caching provides the biggest benefit. Therefore, it is not a good cache design choice if the disk cache supports write caching. Schemes such as the circular buffer, which allows segment size to match exactly the write request size, or the virtual memory organization, which allows a fine granularity of allocation unit size, are much more suitable for supporting write caching.

Unlike writes, a read command is a full cache hit if, and only if, all the data it requests is already in

the cache. So the focus of this chapter is on cache handling for reads. In Section 22.1.1, it was explained that the benefit provided by a disk cache mainly comes from data prefetch, as the much larger cache in the host and/or storage subsystem controller generally filters out the majority of requests that are for data reuse. Thus, the emphasis of disk cache algorithms is mainly on data prefetching.

22.3.1 Perspective of Prefetch

The ultimate goal for a disk cache is to maximize the percentage of cache hits for any workload to which it is applied. When the hit ratio is maximized, disk media accesses and, hence, mechanical times will be minimized, leading to shorter average I/O time and higher throughput. With respect to prefetch, there are a couple of principles for achieving the ultimate goal:

1. Bring as much useful data into the cache as possible at as little cost as possible.
2. Retain as much data brought in as possible and for as long as possible.

Prefetch is an exercise in speculation. There is no guarantee that prefetched data will ever get used. Yet, prefetch is not free; it requires the disk drive's resources (disk arm, read/write electronics, etc.) to bring the prefetch data into the cache, thus tying up the drive and preventing it from doing other work. So, if there is a user request waiting while prefetch is ongoing, the user request gets delayed, and the user sees an increased response time. Therefore, a common strategy is not to start any prefetch if there are I/O requests waiting to be serviced. Along the same line of reasoning, another common strategy is to preempt, or terminate, any ongoing prefetch as soon as a new I/O request arrives. One exception to this rule is when the new request happens to be a cache hit and therefore can be fully serviced from the cache alone without requiring the other disk resources that are being used in prefetching.

Another cost of data prefetching is that prefetched data takes up space in the cache. In order to provide space for the prefetched data, some other data already in the cache will have to be displaced, which is against the second principle cited previously. If data that is not to be used in the near future is brought into the cache and results in throwing out some useful data from the cache, the situation is referred to as *cache pollution*. The net effect is negative for future performance.

The host system can, and oftentimes does, initiate data prefetching. The argument for the drive to initiate its own prefetch is that the drive knows when it can do prefetch without interfering with normal requests. On the other hand, one of the reasons why data prefetched by the drive does not always get used is that today's drive has no file system knowledge of the data that it stores. Thus, the data that the drive prefetches is usually only based on the principle of locality of access, which is a probabilistic rather than a deterministic thing. One possible remedy to this situation is for the host to provide hints to the drive on what it should and should not prefetch. Also, there are proposals to turn the drive into an *object-based storage device* (OSD) by migrating part of the file system from the host down to the disk drive, but these are only just proposals at this time.

22.3.2 Lookahead Prefetch

The most common type of prefetch is known as *look-ahead*. This is prefetching for data that immediately follows the data requested by a user. For example, if a user requests LBAs 1000–1100, lookahead prefetch would be for data from LBA 1101 to 1100 + M, where M is some maximum prefetch limit set by the drive controller. There are two reasons why lookahead prefetch is a good strategy and is adopted by all disk drives:

1. Due to spatial locality of access, there is generally a good probability that lookahead data may be requested soon. For example, the initial request may be for the first sheet of a spreadsheet. When the user goes to the second sheet, which presumably is stored on disk right after the first sheet, then its I/O request will be for the lookahead data of the first request. Therefore, in many cases, lookahead data

satisfies the "usefulness" criterion of the first principle of Section 22.3.1.

2. For the drive to do lookahead prefetch, it only needs to continue reading from the disk after retrieving the block requested by the user. There is no seek or latency involved. Thus, it satisfies the "low cost" criterion of the first principle of Section 22.3.1.

Determining the amount of data to prefetch is a difficult design choice. As pointed out earlier, one of the costs of prefetching is the cache space that prefetched data takes up. As a general rule, the farther away a piece of data is from the current data, the less likely it is that that data would have any correlation with the current data and, hence, the lower the probability that it will be used in the near future. Therefore, bringing too much data in during prefetch, even when the drive is otherwise idle, can pollute the cache and hurt performance. There is no single correct choice, since the correct choice is really workload dependent and varies from application to application.

22.3.3 Look-behind Prefetch

Another type of prefetch, which is becoming almost as common as lookahead, is known as *look-behind*. As its name implies, this is prefetching for data that immediately precedes the data requested by a user. Using the previous example where a user requests LBAs 1000–1100, look-behind prefetch would be for data from LBA 1000 – N to 999, where N is some maximum prefetch limit set by the drive controller.

The backward referencing of preceding data occurs less commonly than forward referencing, but it does occur in real-life applications. Therefore, look-behind prefetching is not as useful as lookahead prefetching, but it is still useful.

To keep the cost of look-behind prefetching low, it is common practice to do such prefetching only during the rotational latency time of a read. It prefetches only as much data as it can read, or less, during this latency period, as illustrated in Figure 22.6. If it happens to be just a few bytes, then so be it. A policy that imposes the drive to always prefetch a fixed amount or some minimum amount of look-behind data is

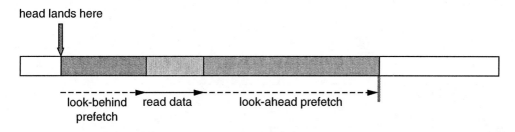

FIGURE 22.6: Common practice for look-behind prefetch. Look-behind prefetch takes place immediately if the head lands on the portion of track preceding requested data.

counterproductive. To do so would force the drive to wait extra time for the missed data if the head happens to land closer to the requested data than the desired look-behind prefetch amount. This significantly increases the cost of prefetch for data that only has a moderate-to-low probability of use.

22.3.4 Zero Latency Prefetch

In Chapter 21, Section 21.1.3, the technique of zero latency access was introduced, which improves the performance of accessing requested data by reducing the net effective rotational latency. This same technique can be extended in an obvious manner to cover the case of data prefetching. Consider the case where the head lands on the track *after* the requested data, somewhere in the middle of the lookahead prefetch area. Figure 22.7(a) shows the common practice where the drive will stay on the track and wait for the beginning of the requested data to come around, doing look-behind prefetch before that as just described above. After the requested data has been read, then the drive continues to do lookahead prefetch as described in Section 22.3.2, taking more than one disk revolution to finish the data read, lookahead prefetch, and look-behind prefetch processes. On the other hand, Figure 22.7b shows the operation of zero latency access in the prefetch area. The drive starts reading immediately the very next sector encountered on arrival in the middle of the lookahead prefetch area. It reads until the end of the maximum prefetch limit and then waits for the beginning of the requested data to come around, prefetching look-behind data in the process.

After the requested data has been read, then the drive continues to complete the lookahead prefetch, stopping just before the first sector where reading started. Thus, the data read, lookahead prefetch, and look-behind prefetch processes together take roughly one disk revolution.

22.3.5 ERP During Prefetch

Chapter 18, Section 18.9.3, describes recovering a non-correctable read error by retrying to read the sector multiple times, perhaps with different head offsets and read channel parameters. Each retry takes one full revolution of the disk, and hence the ERP *(error-recovery procedure)* can take a very long time to complete. Furthermore, error recovery is not always successful. Since prefetched data may not actually get used, it does not make sense to spend a lot of time doing ERP when a non-correctable error is encountered during prefetch. The drive controller should either terminate the prefetch completely or skip over the defective sector if it is possible to mark the data for that sector invalid in the cache.

22.3.6 Handling of Sequential Access

The importance of sequential accesses was pointed out in Chapter 19, Section 19.1.1: if handled properly, sequential access can be completed faster than non-sequential accesses by more than an order of magnitude. Proper prefetching for such data is extremely important; if sequential or skip-sequential data is not ready and waiting in the cache when a request

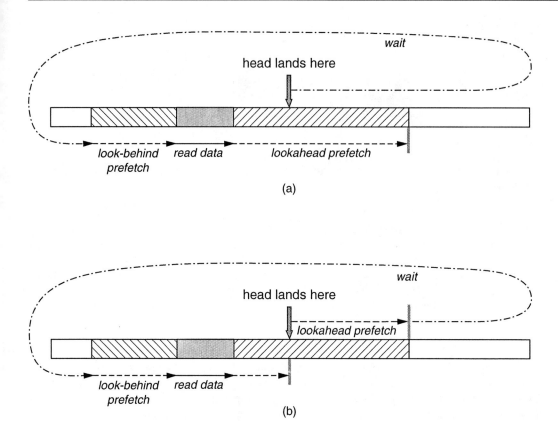

FIGURE 22.7: Zero latency prefetch: (a) Common operation and (b) operation with zero latency access.

for those data come, then the drive will have to wait (usually the better part of one disk revolution) to read the data off the disk.

There are four aspects of handling prefetch for sequential accesses that need to be pointed out.

Sequential detect The drive controller should monitor the I/O requests arriving to detect those I/Os that are part of a sequential pattern. It should be able to identify not only straightly sequential requests that are back to back, but also near-sequential and skip-sequential accesses (see Chapter 19, Section 19.1.1, for definitions).

Prefetch extension When a prefetch is first initiated, the drive controller usually establishes an upper bound of how much data to prefetch. If,

while prefetch is still ongoing, new I/O requests arrive that are hits in this prefetch segment, i.e., some type of sequential hits, then it makes sense to extend the amount of data to be prefetched. At a minimum, one should reset the upper bound LBA using the same maximum amount starting from the current hit location. For example, if the maximum prefetch amount is 200 sectors, and the current prefetch is for LBAs 1001–1200, then a hit in LBA 1050 will cause the prefetch range to be extended to LBA 1250.

Minimum prefetch In Section 22.3.1, it was discussed that a common strategy is to immediately terminate an ongoing prefetch if a new command that requires accessing the disk media is received. While, in general, that is a policy that makes good sense, if the prefetch happens to be initiated by an I/O which is detected to be part of a series of sequential accesses, then the probability that the prefetched data will get used becomes very high. In this case, it makes sense to prefetch some minimum amount of data before allowing the prefetch to be preempted. The size of the minimum prefetch is a design parameter. Ideally, it should be adaptively determined by the drive controller, based on the number of I/Os in the sequential series that the drive has seen so far and the requested block size, with the minimum amount proportional to both of these two measurements.

Space allocation Data accessed in a long sequential series is generally not likely to be re-read again in the near future. In other words, such data, once consumed, is no longer useful. Therefore, when allocating space for prefetch extension, it is best to reallocate the space for the sequential data that has just been consumed. A common technique is to use the current segment circularly. If attention is not paid to this aspect of sequential access, the entire content of a cache can be completely wiped out by a long sequential series.

22.3.7 Replacement Policies

When a new segment needs to be allocated for the servicing of a new command, one or more existing segments must first be deallocated so that their spaces can be used. Determining which segment to discard is an important part of caching, since removing data that will soon be used instead of data that will not be used any time soon is obviously detrimental to the performance of the drive. The rules that the drive controller follows in choosing what data to discard is called the *replacement policy*.

The most common cache replacement policies include first-in-first-out (FIFO), least-recently-used (LRU),[4] and least-frequently-used (LFU). None of these policies in their purest form are ideally suited for disk cache application. FIFO is probably no better than random selection in choosing the least likely to be used data for replacement. LRU is appropriate for most applications, as it is basically based on the principle of temporal locality of access which does occur in those applications. One very major exception is with sequential accesses, as discussed previously in Section 22.3.5. If LRU is followed strictly, then recently consumed sequential data, while no longer useful, will stay in the cache for a long time before it finally becomes least-recently-used. Thus, if LRU is to be used, at the minimum, modification needs to be made to recognize that sequential data should be detected and not be promoted to be most-recently-used. LFU is good for keeping certain regularly used data, such as the root directory of a file system, in the cache. However, without some modification, it would not be very effective in handling data references due to locality of access. For these reasons, a good cache replacement policy usually involves some combinations of common strategies for achieving better cache performance.

---

[4]Also called Most-recently-used (MRU).

CHAPTER 23

Performance Testing

Performance testing is an important part of the design and development of a new disk drive. This chapter is devoted to the discussion of testing and measuring the performance of a disk drive. Because of the complexity of the entire disk drive and the sensitivity of its behavior to different environments and access sequences, precise performance information can only be obtained by running tests on the actual drive. Simulation may be able to predict the mechanical timing quite accurately. Exact prediction of the cache's effect is harder, as the amount of data that gets prefetched is sensitive to how accurately the time available for prefetching is simulated. This available time for prefetching depends not only on the drive's own overhead, but also on activities that go on in the host in between I/Os.

Benchmarks are standard test programs which allow a user to test different devices in an identical manner such that the devices' performance can be compared on an equal footing. They play an important role in the world of disk drives as buyers, large and small, do pay attention to benchmark results when making their purchase decisions. This chapter will discuss some of the ins and outs of benchmark programs.

Not only can testing the timing of execution of a particular I/O command reveal the performance characteristics of a drive, it can also be used to determine many of the implementation details of a disk drive. By applying specially designed I/O test patterns to a drive and measuring the response times of those commands, it is possible to derive certain drive parameters such as its geometry (data layout scheme) and seek profile [Worthington et al. 1995]. This technique and some of these test patterns will be discussed in this chapter.

23.1 Test and Measurement

As discussed in Chapter 16, Section 16.3, the performance of a drive is measured in terms of either throughput or response time. Throughput can either be expressed as the number of I/Os per second (IOPS) completed, or as number of megabytes per second (MB/s) transferred. The two are related by the block sizes of the I/Os. For example, 200 IOPS with a single block size of 4 KB translates to 0.8 MB/s. If half of the blocks are of size 4 KB and the other half are of size 64 KB, then the 200 IOPS translates to 6.8 MB/s. Throughput implies measuring the total elapsed time for completing a large number of I/Os and then dividing either the number of I/Os or the number of bytes by that total time. Response time, on the other hand, is measured for an individual I/O. However, it is much more typical to discuss performance in terms of average response time, in which case the response times of many I/Os over a period of time are added up and divided by the number of I/Os.

Three components are needed for testing the performance of a disk drive. The first component is some mechanism, call it a test initiator, for generating and issuing the I/O commands for the drive to execute as the test sequence for performance measurement. The second component is some means for monitoring and measuring. The third component is, of course, the disk drive itself.

23.1.1 Test Initiator

A dedicated piece of hardware, one which provides a standard interface to which a disk drive can be attached, is certainly one option for a test initiator.

A simpler, and perhaps more flexible, option is to use a general-purpose personal computer or workstation. One or more types of standard interfaces are usually available in such a machine. Add-on interface cards for any interface are also available. One can write software that issues test I/O commands to the drive directly. Alternatively, one can issue high-level read and write commands to the system's device driver. A *device driver* is a piece of operating software that provides the service of performing high-level read and write commands by handling all the necessary standard interface handshakes. By using the service of the device driver, the test initiator creator does not need to know the intricate details of talking to a disk drive directly, though, of course, knowledge of the device driver interface is required.

Test Sequence Characteristics

The sequence of I/O commands issued by a test initiator to a disk drive is characterized by the following elements:

Command type Read and write are the most commonly used commands, but other commands such as flush and reset may also be issued by the test initiator. A sequence may be composed of a certain percentage of reads and a certain percentage of writes, or it may be composed of all reads or all writes.

LBA distribution The addresses may be sequential from one command to the next, localized to a small section of the disk's address space, composed of multiple sequential streams interleaved, or perhaps completely random.

Block size The request size can be a fixed number of sectors, all small blocks, all large blocks, a mixture with some predefined distribution (e.g., 70% 4 KB and 30% 64 KB), or some random mixture of block sizes.

Command arrival time The test initiator has control of the inter-arrival time between issuing commands. Thus, it can determine both the average command arrival rate and the distribution.

Queue depth The test initiator can also control how many I/Os to queue up in the disk drive at any point in time. For example, it can keep the queue at its maximum at all times, or it can throttle the number of commands sent to the drive in order to achieve a certain response time (maximum or average).

Methods of Test Generation

There are three main ways of generating the test I/Os that are to be sent to the disk drive:

Internally created The I/Os are created by the test initiator according to certain characteristics. The characteristics are usually specifiable by the user. For instance, a user may ask for testing how a disk drive performs doing random reads of 4 KB blocks with a queue depth of 16 within an address range of 100 MB between LBAs 600,000 and 800,000. More commonly, the user would ask for a battery of such tests with a range for each characteristic, e.g., block sizes of 1, 2, 4, 8, 16, 32, 64, and 128 KB; queue depths of 1, 2, 4, 8, 16, and 32; for read and for write commands; etc. The test initiator uses a random number generator to create I/O requests in accordance with the specified characteristics.

Predefined sequence The test initiator reads an input file which contains a predefined I/O sequence, and issues those I/Os to the disk drive in exactly the same order and with the same inter-arrival time between commands as recorded in the file. The I/O sequence can be manually created by the user to very specifically probe for how a disk drive performs or behaves with that particular sequence. This is how some drive parameters can be extracted, as will be discussed later. Alternatively, the sequence can be a recorded trace obtained by monitoring the I/Os sent to a disk drive while performing certain activities. In this case, the test initiator is simply playing back the previously recorded trace. Because exactly the same I/O sequence is sent to the drive every time, analysis of the results from this method of testing can be very precise. For instance, the change in performance due to an alteration in the disk drive can be accurately measured. One can also use this method to compare the performances of two different drives fairly, since the drives will be seeing exactly the same sequence of I/O requests. Some benchmark programs use this method of testing.

Application based A third way of generating the I/O test sequence is for the test initiator to invoke application programs to perform certain tasks. The objective is to see how well a disk drive performs in the execution of such applications. A predefined test script of what application functions to call and what commands to issue is used. Unlike the playback of predefined I/O commands, real files need to be set up first for the application programs to work on. This method of testing at a higher level is also used by some benchmark programs. The sequence of I/O commands that actually gets sent to the disk drive depends on the operating systems, where the test files are created, how much system memory there is in the host system, and a host of other factors. Therefore, it is likely that there is variation in the I/O sequence from system to system and even from run to run.

23.1.2 Monitoring and Measuring

Whether determining throughput or response time, testing the performance of a drive requires timing the elapse time between one event and another event. The first event is usually the start of an I/O request, and the second event is the end of the same or some other I/O request. There are three points in the system where monitoring and clocking of the events can be done, as shown in Figure 23.1.

Inside the disk drive By instrumenting the firmware of the drive controller, the beginning and the end of almost any drive activity can be very precisely monitored and timed. Clearly, only the drive maker will have this capability. Some drive activities may also be measured by probing

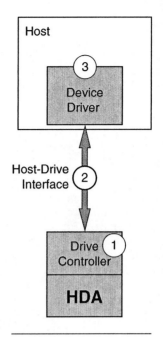

FIGURE 23.1: Monitor points: 1. inside the disk drive; 2. at the interface; 3. at the device driver level.

with an oscilloscope. However, very good knowledge of the drive's circuit will be needed to know what points to probe. When making measurements at this low level, it is possible to measure just the execution time of an I/O and exclude the overhead of the drive controller. Thus, one can measure precisely the time to fetch data out of the cache if it is a cache hit or the seek, latency, and media transfer time if disk access is required. Of course, controller overhead can be measured here also. Instrumentation of the firmware adds code to perform the monitoring function while executing an I/O request. Thus, this method necessarily perturbs the actual execution timing of running a sequence of I/Os.

At the interface Bus monitors are available for all standard interfaces. Such hardware usually consists of a pod containing the monitoring circuits and either a dedicated system or a general-purpose computer which runs the control software. The pod intercepts and passes on all the signals that go between the drive and the host. The cable coming out of the drive plugs into one end of the pod, while the cable coming out of the host plugs into another end. No internal knowledge or access of the drive is required for doing measurements at this level. A bus monitor will work with any drive from any manufacturer. However, it does require understanding of the interface standard to use and interpret the results of this tool. Quite accurate timing, with sub-microsecond accuracy, can be measured. Writing the command register by the host in ATA or sending the CDB in SCSI marks the start of an I/O request. The drive responding with completion status marks the end of a command. The elapsed time between those two events measures the sum of the I/O execution time of the drive and the overhead incurred by the drive controller. Because this method is non-invasive, the actual timing of running a sequence of I/Os is not perturbed.

At or above the device driver By instrumenting the device driver or adding a monitor layer just above the device driver, the execution time of an I/O as seen by the device driver or the user of the device driver can be measured. This method is simple because knowledge of the internal disk drive or the interface is not required. The timing accuracy is dependent on the resolution of the system clock readable by the software. Also, the timing of an I/O will necessarily include the overhead of the device driver, obscuring the actual execution time of the disk drive. Finally, the addition of monitor code adds extra overhead which will perturb the actual execution timing of running a sequence of I/Os.

23.1.3 The Test Drive

There are a few things that one should be aware of regarding the drive whose performance is to be measured.

Drive-to-drive variation Even for drives of the same model and capacity, it is likely that there will be some degree of variation from drive to drive. Part of this is simply due to the nature of electro-mechanical devices, where some variation is to be expected. Other factors may also contribute. For example, the data layouts and address mappings of two same model drives may be different because of adaptive formatting (discussed in Chapter 25, Section 25.5). Therefore, ideally, several drives should be tested in order to get the average performance for a particular model of disk drive.

Run-to-run variation For a given test drive, there is also some variation likely from one test run to the next. Again, this is simply the nature of the electro-mechanical device. Certain things such as media data rate will be quite stable and show no variation. Other things such as I/O times that require seeking will exhibit some variation. Therefore, depending on the nature of the test being conducted, some tests may need to be repeated a number of times to get an average measurement.

Mounting Seek time is susceptible to vibration in the disk drive, and vibration is dependent on how the drive is mounted. There are two acceptable ways to mount a drive for testing its performance. One method is to mount the test drive to a heavy metal block resting on a solid surface so as to minimize the amount of vibration. This measures the performance of the drive under an ideal condition. A second method is to test the drive mounted in the actual system where it is intended to be used. This measures the real-life performance that the drive can be expected to produce in its target system.

Write tests For test sequences that are generated below the operating system's file system, such as randomly generated I/Os or a replay of some predefined sequence, writes can go to any location in the disk drive. This means that previously recorded data on the test drive can be overwritten without any warning. One should be aware of this consequence before doing any testing on a disk drive.

23.2 Basic Tests

The raw performance of a disk drive can be measured using a number of basic tests. The performance characteristics that can be measured include data rate (bandwidth), IOPS (throughput), and response time, for reads as well as for writes. The basic tests are therefore quite simple and straightforward.

A user can fairly easily create his own test initiator for performing basic tests. However, there are a number of such test programs available for free that can be downloaded from the Internet, and so, unless one

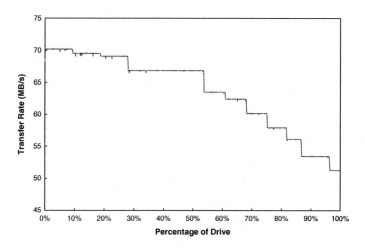

FIGURE 23.2: An example of the media data rate read test result.

has a need to very precisely control the testing in a particular way, there is little reason to build one from scratch. Most of these tools perform similar tests, differing only in the user interface.

There is no standard definition of what a set of basic tests should consist of. A few common ones are selected to be discussed here.

23.2.1 Media Data Rate

Most programs test the data rate of a drive by issuing a long sequence of sequential reads of a large block size. Since this results in reading many tracks of data, what gets measured is the drive's sustained data rate, as discussed in Chapter 18, Section 18.8. When measurement is taken at the host level, the results may be somewhat affected by the overhead for handling each command. However, by using a large block size to reduce the frequency of such overheads, the combined effect of a faster interface data rate and the action of lookahead prefetch will be able to hide these overheads so that the measured results are truly the drive's sustained data rate.

Because of zoned-bit recording, the measured data rate of a drive depends on where on the disk the test is run. If the entire disk is tested, then a picture of the test drive's zones is revealed. Figure 23.2 shows

an example of such a read test result for an actual disk drive. Here, the average data rates measured for each 0.1% of the drive's total capacity are plotted. For this drive, 11 distinct data rates and zones are clearly visible. A similar write test can be performed for measuring the media data rate. Write results typically exhibit more noise due to some occasional write-inhibits, as writes require more stringent conditions to proceed than reads. A write-inhibit would cause the drive to take one or more revolutions to retry the write. Thus, the test result for the write data rate usually shows up slightly lower than the read data rate for the same drive, even though in reality the raw media data rate is the same for both reads and writes.

23.2.2 Disk Buffer Data Rate

Though the speed of the drive's DRAM buffer is high, its actual realizable data rate as observed by the host is limited by both the speed of the drive-host interface and the overhead of the drive in doing data transfer. To test this data rate, the test pattern would simply be reading the same block of data repeatedly many times. Since the same block of data is read, only the cache memory is involved. If a large block size is chosen, then the effect of command overhead is minimized, just as in the media data rate test discussed previously. Smaller block sizes can be chosen to observe the impact of command overhead.

23.2.3 Sequential Performance

The media data rate test is one special case of sequential performance measurement. In many actual applications, smaller block sizes are used for data requests. With small block sizes, the effect of command overhead in lowering the achievable data rate becomes visible. Therefore, a standard sequential performance test would measure the throughput at various block sizes. Figure 23.3 shows an example of sequential read measurement results of another actual drive. The throughput expressed as IOPS is also plotted. Note that as the block size increases, the data rate attained also increases as the amount of command overhead per byte becomes less. By the time a block size of 16 KB is reached, all overheads can be overlapped with the media data transfer time, and the sustained data rate is being measured.

Because lookahead prefetch, if properly implemented, can take care of streaming sequential read data from the media to the buffer without interruption, command queueing has almost no effect for sequential reads. Usually, only a very slight increase

in throughput can be observed for small block sizes when going from no queueing to a queue depth of 2.

A similar situation occurs for sequential writes if write caching is enabled. The interface data rate is fast enough to fill the buffer with data for streaming to the media without any hiccup. However, if write caching is not enabled, each write command will take one disk revolution to complete, resulting in very low throughput, as shown in Figure 23.4. Using command queueing with a sizable queue depth is needed to avoid having to take one revolution to do each write command when write caching is not enabled.

23.2.4 Random Performance

Sequential performance tests measure the media data rate of the drive, its command handling overhead, and the effectiveness of its cache in lookahead prefetch. As such, the performance of the mechanical components does not get exercised. On the other hand, random accesses require seeks and rotational latencies. Thus, the purpose of random performance tests is to measure the mechanical speed of the drive. It is conducted by generating random addresses within a specified test range, oftentimes the whole drive, to do reads and writes. While it certainly is possible to measure and report random performance in a fashion

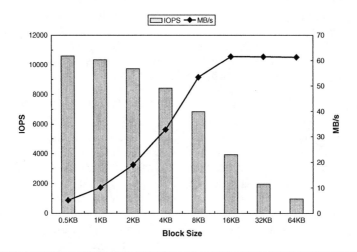

FIGURE 23.3: An example of a sequential read throughput test.

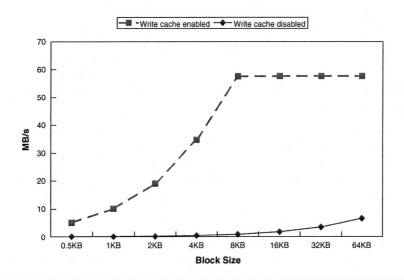

FIGURE 23.4: An example of a sequential write performance.

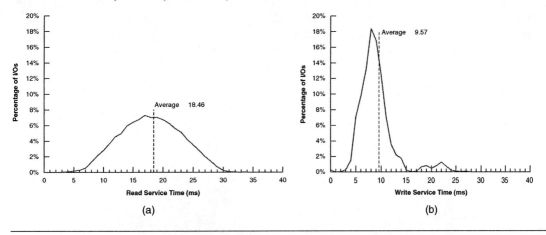

FIGURE 23.5: Histogram of the I/O completion time for single sector random accesses. The drive is 4500 rpm with write cache enabled: (a) random reads and (b) random writes.

similar to that shown in Figure 23.3 for sequential performance, the use of larger block sizes is a distraction as the longer data transfer time only serves to dilute any differences in mechanical times. It is more informative to measure random performance using the smallest possible block size.

An alternative way to report random performance is to tabulate and plot a histogram of the fraction of I/Os that is completed for each incremental unit of

time. Figure 23.5 illustrates such a result for an actual 4200 rpm drive, with a bucket size of 1 ms increments. The test result for single sector reads is shown in Figure 23.5(a). The average response time is calculated to be 18.46 ms, which should be the sum of average seek time, average latency time (one-half revolution time), all command overheads, and a negligible data transfer time. Since the average latency for a 4200-rpm drive is 7.1 ms, it can be deduced that the average read seek time for this drive is in the neighborhood of 10 ms. There is a bell-shaped distribution around this average read I/O time. The near tail at around 2 ms represents approximately no seek and very little latency and so is essentially the sum of all the overheads.

The far tail, at around 31 ms, represents approximately full stroke seek and maximum latency (one revolution). The test result for single sector writes of the same drive is shown in Figure 23.4(b). It looks very different from the curve for reads because of write caching. While for most drives the shapes of the read curves will be similar to the one shown here, the write curves will likely have different shapes since they depend on the write caching algorithm implemented, and different drives are likely to have somewhat different algorithms. For instance, the number of cached writes allowed to be outstanding and the timing of when to do destaging are design parameters that vary from drive to drive. If write caching is disabled, then the write curve will look similar to the read curve, with the average I/O time and the curve shifted slightly to the right due to the higher settling time for write seeks compared to read seeks.

Another informative way to display the result of a random access test is to plot the I/O completion time for each command against the seek distance for that command. To simplify things, the seek distance can be expressed in number of LBAs, i.e., take the LBA of the previous command and subtract that from the LBA of the current command. An example of such a plot for 32,000 random reads is shown in Figure 23.6, which is for an actual 40-GB, 4200-rpm mobile drive. Some refer to such a plot as a "whale tail," while others call it a "moustache," for obvious reasons. The bottom outline of the "tail" approximately represents the seek curve of the drive, since those are the I/Os that can be completed immediately after arrival on the target track without any latency. For this drive, the forward seek (toward the ID) time is slightly longer than the backward seek (toward the OD) time. The vertical thickness of the tail represents the revolution time of the drive, which is 14.3 ms for a 4200-rpm drive. There are a few sprinkles of points above the top outline of the tail. These are reads that need to take an extra revolution or two for retries (see Chapter 18, Section 18.9).

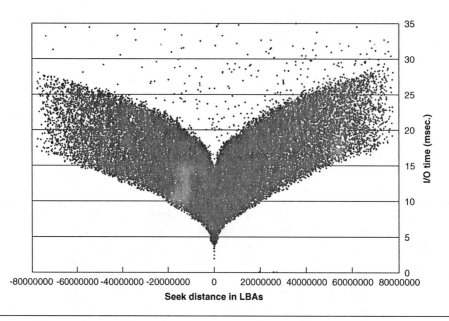

FIGURE 23.6: A whale tail plot of random reads. The drive is 4200 rpm and 40 GB in capacity.

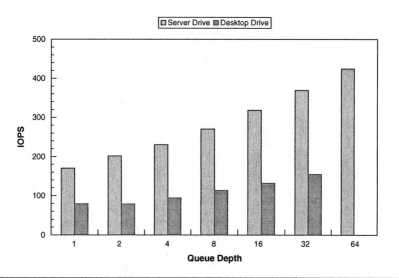

FIGURE 23.7: Throughputs for single sector random reads at various queue depths.

23.2.5 Command Reordering Performance

Command reordering, as discussed in Chapter 21, Section 21.2, can significantly boost the performance of a disk drive. Since the name of the game is to reduce the mechanical portion of an I/O's execution time, especially in handling random accesses, it would make sense to test for a drive's command reordering effectiveness using the smallest block size, just as in the case for random access performance measurement. The most straightforward way to conduct a performance measurement test of command reordering is to issue random single sector accesses to a drive over a reasonable period of time at various queue depths.

The average throughput for each queue depth can then be recorded and plotted. The access type can be all reads, all writes, or a certain percentage of each that is of interest to the tester. Throughput is a better metric than response time in this case because response time (lower is better) will go up with queue depth (a command needs to wait longer when there are more other commands in the queue), even though command reordering effectiveness usually improves with higher queue depths. Figure 23.7 plots the test results of two different drives: a 15000-rpm SCSI server drive with an average seek time of around 3.3 ms and a 7200-rpm SATA desktop drive with an average seek time of about 8.2 ms. While the throughputs for these two drives both improve as command queue depth is increased, the far superior mechanical properties of the high-end server drive are quite evident.

23.3 Benchmark Tests

The purpose of benchmarks is for users and developers to have a means to measure and make meaningful apple-to-apple performance comparison, whether between two products from two different manufacturers, from generation to generation of a product by the same manufacturer, or from one design/implementation revision to the next during product development. A benchmark is a test, or a set of tests, which measures performance, and it must be generally available to the public. Benchmark tests for storage have been around for many years; some have come and gone, while others evolve. Some storage benchmarks are targeted for storage systems with multiple drives, and some are designed for individual disk drives. Most disk drive benchmarks can also be tested on a logical volume of a storage system.

Some drive benchmarks are application based, constructed to determine how well a drive does in running the applications of interest. The Disk WinMark tests of WinBench™99,[1] which has been one of the popular disk benchmarks in the past few years, is one such example. It was created by surveying the user community to gather a collection of the most commonly used application programs in a PC. Other benchmark programs are replays of predefined sequences, although such sequences can be from tracing the execution of application programs and so, in a sense, are application based rather than artificially created. PCMark™05,[2] which is now popular as a disk benchmark, is one such example.

There is another group of special tests that are also designed to measure drive performances. These are the proprietary tests that large original equipment manufacturers (OEMs) have created for their own internal use in evaluating disk drives that would go into their products. While these tests serve the same purpose as benchmarks, technically they cannot be called benchmarks because they are not available to the general public. Nonetheless, for all intents and purposes, these proprietary tests can be treated the same as benchmarks, and the discussion in the following section applies to them equally.

23.3.1 Guidelines for Benchmarking

There are a few points that one should be aware of when benchmarking disk drives. Understanding and following these guidelines are necessary for obtaining correct benchmark measurements. Otherwise, misleading results might be obtained, leading to incorrect conclusions.

Test System

It matters what system is being used to measure the benchmark performance score of a disk drive. Because a benchmark does its test monitoring and timing high up in the system level, it is unavoidable

that measurements include at least some amount of system time. Thus, a benchmark, in reality, measures the combined performance of the host system, the interface, and the disk drive. The percentage of a benchmark's score that is actually attributed to the disk drive's performance depends on which benchmark is used. A good disk benchmark should have a high percentage, minimizing, though not eliminating, the influence of the host system and interface.

Various components of the system all contribute to affecting a benchmark's result. The speed of the CPU has the obvious effect on the timing on the system side. The data rate of the interface affects the data transfer time. Additionally, for application-based benchmarks, the amount of memory in the system determines how much data would be cached in the host, thus affecting the number of I/Os that actually get sent down to the disk drive. The operating system also plays a visible role. The file system determines the size of allocation units and where to place the test data. A journaling file system issues additional I/Os for logging the journal compared to a non-journaling file system. Finally, how I/Os are being sent to the drive can be influenced by the device driver used.

If a report says that drive A has a benchmark score of 1000, and somebody measures drive B in his system to have a score of 900 using the same benchmark, what conclusion can be drawn? Nothing. The two systems may be very different, and so it is possible that drive B is actually a faster drive despite the lower score. Therefore, to obtain meaningful comparison, benchmarking should be performed using the same system or two identically configured systems.

Ideal Setup

An ideal way to set up for benchmarking is to have a disk drive in the system already loaded with the operating system and all the benchmark programs of interest, and the drive to be tested is simply attached to this system as another disk. One obvious advantage is avoiding having to spend the time to install the operation

---

[1]WinBench™99 was created by Ziff Davis Media which publishes *PCMagazine*.
[2]PCMark™05 was created by Futuremark Corporation.

system and load the benchmark programs onto the test drive. Thus, once the system is set up, many different drives can quickly be tested this way since there is no preparation work required for the disk drive.

A second advantage is that such a setup allows a completely blank disk to be tested. This allows all disks to be tested in exactly the same condition. It also enables the same disk to be tested repeatedly in exactly the same condition. If, on the other hand, the test disk must have an operating system and other software loaded into it first, then the test result can potentially be affected by how things are loaded into the drive.

Multiple Runs

As discussed earlier, a disk drive is an electro-mechanical device, and so most performance measurements will likely vary somewhat from run to run. Hence, a benchmark test should be repeated a few times to obtain an average score.

Between one run to the next, the drive should be either reformatted to restore it to a blank disk if the drive is tested as a separate drive in an ideal setup or defragged to remove any fragmentation if it also holds the operating system and other software. Certain application-based benchmarks may generate temporary files, thus creating some fragmentation at the conclusion of the tests. Such fragmentations will accumulate if not cleaned up after each run and degrade user performance over time. Finally, the drive should then be power-cycled to set it back to its initial state, such as an empty cache.

23.4   Drive Parameters Tests

When specially designed test patterns are applied to a disk drive and the response times of each command are monitored and measured, some of the parameters of a disk drive can be deduced. The media data rate test, as illustrated in Figure 23.2, can be considered to be one such test which measures the number of recording zones in a drive. The whale tail plot for random accesses, as illustrated by Figure 23.6, may also be considered as another example in which a drive's seek

profile and rotational time can be measured, albeit not very accurately. In this section, a couple of examples of special test patterns for precisely determining several important parameters of a drive are discussed.

23.4.1   Geometry and More

The geometry of a drive is described by such things as the number of sectors per track, how the tracks are laid out (number of tracks per cylinder if cylinder mode is used, or serpentine formatting), and the number of recording zones. More than one method involving distinctly different test patterns can be used to extract such drive parameters [Ng 2001a,b]. One such method will be discussed in this section. The overall approach is the same for all methods. The first step is to identify the track boundaries. Then, the number of LBAs between two identified track boundaries is used to establish the number of sectors per track. The skew at each track boundary is next derived from the measured data. For most drives the cylinder skew is bigger than a track skew. By comparing the sizes of the skews for a large enough group of track boundaries, the cylinder boundaries can be identified and the number of heads per cylinder deduced. This would be the scenario for cylinder mode formatting. For a drive with serpentine formatting, there will be many (tens or even hundreds) same size skews followed by a different size skew. Finally, if the process is applied to the whole drive, then details of every zone can be exposed.

The following describes one test method by way of an example of a highly simplified hypothetical disk drive using the traditional cylinder formatting. Read commands will be used in the discussion. Either reads or writes can be used with the test pattern, but reads would be preferable since the content of the drive would then not be destroyed in the testing process. Caching will need to be turned off for the test to force the drive to access the media for each command.

A Test Method

The test pattern for this method is very simple. A single sector read command is issued for a range of sequential addresses. The address range is for the area

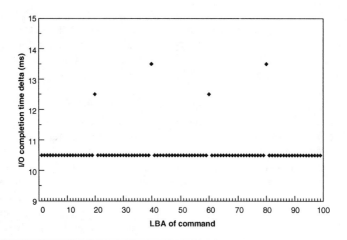

FIGURE 23.8: The result of the geometry test for a portion of a hypothetical drive.

of the disk drive that is to be tested. The size of the range should be at least two or three times the estimated size of a cylinder of the drive and can be as large as the complete address range of the whole drive. The commands are issued one at a time synchronously, with the next command issued by the host as soon as the previous command is completed. The time of completion of each command, which can be monitored at any of the levels described in Section 23.1.2, is recorded. The elapsed time between the completion times of every pair of consecutive commands is calculated and plotted. This elapsed time, while consisting of the drive overhead, seek time (if any), rotational latency time, data transfer time, as well as the host system's processing time, is actually dictated by the physical relationship between the two addresses. For example, if the two addresses are physically contiguous on the disk, then the delta time is one revolution plus the rotation time of one sector. If one address is the last logical sector of a track and the other address is the first logical sector of the next track, then the delta time is most likely one revolution plus the track/cylinder skew plus the rotation time of one sector.

Figure 23.8 shows the results for reading LBAs 0–99 of the hypothetical example disk drive. It can be seen here that most of the delta times are 10.5 ms. These are the times for reading the next physical sector on

the same track, which is naturally the most frequent. Hence, each represents one revolution plus a sector time. It can be observed that the delta times to read LBAs 20, 40, 60, and 80 are longer than the typical 10.5 ms. It can be assumed that these sectors are the first logical sectors after a track boundary, and hence, the delta time includes a skew time in addition to the revolution and one sector time. Since there are 20 sectors between each of these LBAs, it can be deduced that there are 20 sectors per track for this disk drive. Furthermore, the 13.5-ms delta times at LBAs 40 and 80 are larger than the 12.5-ms delta times at LBAs 20 and 60. It can be concluded that this drive exhibits the typical characteristics of a traditional cylinder mode format. Whereas LBAs 20 and 60 are after a head switch, with a track skew of 12.5–10.5 = 2.0 ms, LBAs 40 and 80 are after a cylinder switch, with a cylinder skew of 13.5–10.5 = 3.0 ms. Since there is only one head switch between cylinder switches, it can be deduced that there are only two tracks per cylinder. Hence, this must be a single platter disk with two heads.

This example illustrates a simple idealized drive. It shows a drive with the same number of sectors per track. In real drives, some tracks may have fewer sectors than the majority of tracks. The missing sectors are either reserved for sparing or defective sectors that have been mapped out. If a drive uses a cylinder

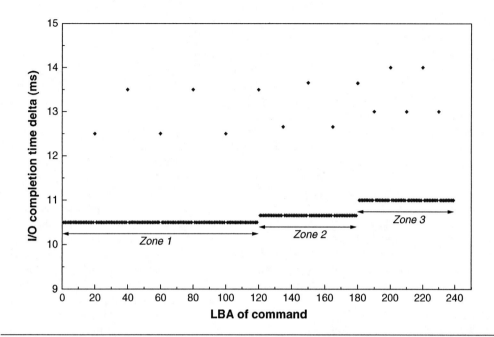

FIGURE 23.9: The result of the geometry test for the entire hypothetical drive. Three zones are clearly visible.

skew which is equal to the track skew, then this test method will not be able to determine the number of tracks per cylinder. However, the number of heads in a drive is usually given in the drive's spec sheet.

If a track has N sectors, then the rotation time of one sector is simply 1/N of a revolution. In other words,

$$\frac{N+1}{N} \times \text{Revolution time} = \text{Revolution time} + \text{sector time.}$$
(EQ 23.1)

For this example, N = 20, and the revolution time plus sector time is 10.5 ms. Using these numbers Equation 23.1 can be solved to give a revolution time of 10 ms. This translates to a rotational speed of 6000 rpm for the hypothetical drive of this example.

Finally, by running the test pattern of this method from LBA 0 all the way to the last LBA of the drive, the precise zoning information of the entire drive can be revealed. Continuing with the example, Figure 23.9 illustrates the results of doing so for the hypothetical drive. Three zones are clearly visible. The first zone,

whose sectors per track, tracks per cylinder, and skews have already been analyzed, contains three cylinders with the address range of LBAs 0–119. The second zone, from LBAs 120–179, has 15 sectors per track and 2 cylinders. The third zone, with the address range LBAs 180–239, has 3 cylinders and 10 sectors per track.

Roughly one revolution is needed to read one sector; hence, for a 400-GB disk with 7200 rpm, it would take over 1800 hours to complete. This is clearly not practical. The alternative is to apply this test method to various portions of the disk to sample the geometry at those locations. If the precise zone boundaries need to be determined, a binary hunt method can be applied to zero in on those boundaries.

23.4.2 Seek Time

While the random access test result presented in a whale tail plot format gives a rough profile of a drive's seek characteristics, a specialized test procedure tailored to measure seek time will provide more precise information. One such method is described here.

The first step is to apply the test method discussed in the previous section to extract the geometry information of the drive. To test for the seek time between two cylinders of interest, select any sector in the starting cylinder. This will be the anchor sector for the test. Next, select a track in the ending cylinder to be the target track. The test pattern is to alternate reading the anchor sector and a sector from the target track. For example, if the target track has LBAs 10000–10999, and the anchor sector is selected to be LBA 0, then the test pattern is to read LBA 0, 10000, 0, 10001, 0, 10002, ..., 0, 10998, 0, and 10999. The purpose of reading the anchor sector is to reorient the head of the disk to a fixed starting position. As in the geometry test, the delta times between the completion of commands are recorded and plotted, except that here only the delta times going from the anchor sector to the target track are plotted. Each of these delta times represents the sum of the seek time, the rotational latency time, all command overheads, and the data transfer time of one sector.

Analysis of the test result is explained by way of another highly simplified hypothetical drive. Figure 23.10(a) shows the piece-wise linear approximation of the seek profile of the hypothetical drive. At a seek distance of 3000 cylinders, the seek time is 10 ms. Let's assume that we want to measure the seek time from cylinder 0 to cylinder 3000. LBA 0 is as good as any to be selected as the anchor sector. For this hypothetical drive, there are 100 sectors per track at cylinder 3000. Figure 23.10(b) plots the test result, showing the delta times between completion of an anchor read and read completion for each of the sectors in the target track. The maximum delta time, as marked with B, is for the sector which just misses the head when the head arrives on the target track and has to wait for basically one full revolution. The minimum delta time, as marked with A, is for the first sector that the head is able to read after it has arrived on track and settled. Thus, its rotational latency, which is half a sector's time on average, is negligible. Therefore, the minimum delta time is essentially the sum of the seek time, all command overheads, and one sector rotation time (0.1 ms in this hypothetical example, but typically much smaller for a real disk

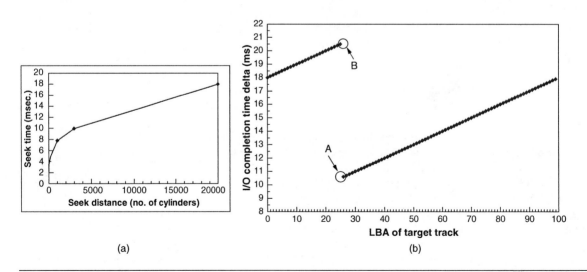

(a)

(b)

FIGURE 23.10: Seek test example: (a) the seek profile of a hypothetical drive, and (b) the result of the seek test for going from cylinder 0 to cylinder 3000.

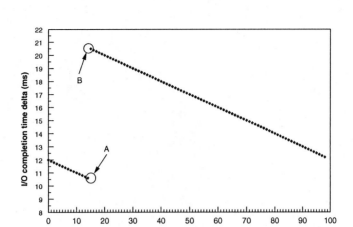

FIGURE 23.11: The seek test result for the reverse direction.

with many times more sectors per track). So, this test method yields a result of 10.5 ms for a 3000-cylinder seek, including overheads. If command overheads can somehow be measured and subtracted from the result of this test, then a pure seek time close to the actual 10 ms can be determined.

While the above measures the seek time going from cylinder 0 to cylinder 3000, the seek time for the reverse direction can also be derived from the same test. Rather than plotting the delta times going from the anchor sector to the target track, plot the delta times going from each sector of the target track to the anchor sector instead. This is illustrated in Figure 23.11. Again, by noting the minimum delta time, the seek time in the reverse direction plus command overheads are measured. In this highly simplified and idealized example, the reverse seek time is identical to the forward seek time. This is not necessarily always true for all disk drives.

Finally, due to mechanical variability, the test pattern should be repeated multiple times to get an average. Also, the test should be repeated using different tracks in the starting and ending cylinders.

CHAPTER 24

Storage Subsystems

Up to this point, the discussions in Part III of this book have been on the disk drive as an individual storage device and how it is directly connected to a host system. This *direct attach storage* (DAS) paradigm dates back to the early days of mainframe computing, when disk drives were located close to the CPU and cabled directly to the computer system via some control circuits. This simple model of disk drive usage and configuration remained unchanged through the introduction of, first, the mini computers and then the personal computers. Indeed, even today the majority of disk drives shipped in the industry are targeted for systems having such a configuration.

However, this simplistic view of the relationship between the disk drive and the host system does not tell the whole story for today's higher end computing environment. Sometime around the 1990s, computing evolved from being computation-centric to storage-centric. The motto is: "He who holds the data holds the answer." Global commerce, fueled by explosive growth in the use of the Internet, demands 24/7 access to an ever-increasing amount of data. The decentralization of departmental computing into networked individual workstations requires efficient sharing of data. Storage subsystems, basically a collection of disk drives, and perhaps some other backup storage devices such as tape and optical disks, that can be managed together, evolved out of necessity. The management software can either be run in the host computer itself or may reside in a dedicated processing unit serving as the storage controller. In this chapter, welcome to the alphabet soup world of storage subsystems, with acronyms like DAS, NAS, SAN, iSCSI, JBOD, RAID, MAID, etc.

There are two orthogonal aspects of storage subsystems to be discussed here. One aspect has to do with how multiple drives within a subsystem can be organized together, cooperatively, for better reliability and performance. This is discussed in Sections 24.1–24.3. A second aspect deals with how a storage subsystem is connected to its clients and accessed. Some form of networking is usually involved. This is discussed in Sections 24.4–24.6. A storage subsystem can be designed to have any organization and use any of the connection methods discussed in this chapter. Organization details are usually made transparent to user applications by the storage subsystem presenting one or more virtual disk images, which logically look like disk drives to the users. This is easy to do because logically a disk is no more than a drive ID and a logical address space associated with it. The storage subsystem software understands what organization is being used and knows how to map the logical addresses of the virtual disk to the addresses of the underlying physical devices. This concept is described as *virtualization* in the storage community.

24.1 Data Striping

When a set of disk drives are co-located, such as all being mounted in the same rack, solely for the purpose of sharing physical resources such as power and cooling, there is no logical relationship between the drives. Each drive retains its own identity, and to the user it exhibits the same behavioral characteristics as those discussed in previous chapters. A term has been coined to describe this type of storage subsystems—*JBOD*, for just-a-bunch of disks. There is nothing more to be said about JBOD in the remainder of this chapter.

The simplest organizational relationship that can be established for a set of drives is that of *data striping.* With data striping, a set of K drives are ganged together to form a *data striping group* or *data striping array*, and K is referred to as the *stripe width*. The data striping group is a logical entity whose logical address space is sectioned into fixed-sized blocks called *stripe units*. The size of a stripe unit is called the *stripe size* and is usually specifiable in most storage subsystems by the administrator setting up the stripe array. These stripe units are assigned to the drives in the striping array in a round-robin fashion. This way, if a user's file is larger than the stripe size, it will be broken up and stored in multiple drives. Figure 24.1 illustrates how four user files of different sizes are stored in a striping array of width 3. File e takes up four stripe units and spans all three disks of the array, with Disk 1 holding two units, while Disks 2 and 3 hold one unit each. File f continues with seven stripe units and also spans all three disks with multiple stripe units in each disk. File g is a small file requiring only one stripe unit and is all contained in one disk. File h is a medium size file and spans two of the three disks in the array.

The purpose of data striping is to improve performance. The initial intent for introducing striping was so that data could be transferred in parallel to/from multiple drives, thus cutting down data transfer time. Clearly, this makes sense only if the amount of data transfer is large. To access the drives in parallel, all drives involved must perform a seek operation and take a rotational latency overhead. Assuming the cylinder positions of all the arms are roughly in sync, the seek times for all drives are about the same. However, since most arrays do not synchronize the rotation of their disks,[1] the average rotational latency for the last drive out of K drives to be ready is $R \times K/(K + 1)$, where R is the time for one disk revolution. This is higher than the latency of R/2 for a single drive. Let FS be the number of sectors of a file. The I/O completion time without data striping is[2]

$$\text{seek time} + R/2 + FS \times R/SPT \qquad \text{(EQ 24.1)}$$

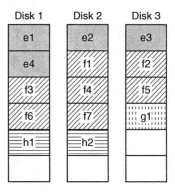

FIGURE 24.1: An example of a data striping array with a stripe width = 3. Four user files e, f, g, and h of different sizes are shown.

where SPT is the number of sectors per track. When data striping is used, the I/O time is

$$\text{seek time} + R \times K/(K + 1) + FS \times R/K \times SPT$$
$$\text{(EQ 24.2)}$$

Assuming the seek times are the same in both cases, data striping is faster than non-striping when

$$R/2 + f \times R/SPT > R \times K/(K + 1) + f \times R/K \times SPT$$
$$\text{(EQ 24.3)}$$

which happens when

$$f > K \times SPT/2(K + 1) \qquad \text{(EQ 24.4)}$$

Thus, the stripe size should be chosen to be at least $SPT/2(K + 1)$ sectors in size[3] so that smaller files do not end up being striped.

That, however, is only part of the story. With striping, all the drives are tied up servicing a single command. Furthermore, the seek and rotational latency overhead of one command must be paid by every one of the

---

[1]Actually, synchronizing the rotation of the disks would not necessarily help either, since the first stripe unit of a file in each of the drives may not be the same stripe unit in all the drives. As File f in Figure 24.1 illustrates, f1 and f2 are the second stripe unit in Disks 2 and 3, but f3 is the third stripe unit in Disk 1.
[2]Track skew is ignored in this simple analysis.
[3]Later, in Section 24.3.2, there is an opposing argument for using a smaller stripe size.

drives involved. In other words, the overhead is paid for K times. On the other hand, if striping is not used, then each drive can be servicing a different command. The seek and latency overhead of each command are paid for by only one disk, i.e., one time only. Thus, no matter what the stripe size and the request size are, data striping will never have a better total throughput for the storage subsystem as a whole when compared to non-striping. In the simplest case where all commands are of the same size f, the throughput for data striping is inversely proportional to Equation 24.1, while that for non-striping is inversely proportional to Equation 24.2 times K. Only when both seek time and rotational latency are zero, as in sequential access, can the two be equal. Thus, as long as there are multiple I/Os that can keep individual disks busy, parallel transfer offers no throughput advantage. If the host system has only a single stream of long sequential accesses as its workload, then data striping would be a good solution for providing a faster response time.

This brings up another point. As just discussed, parallel data transfer, which was the original intent of data striping, is not as effective as it sounds for improving performance in the general case. However, data striping is effective in improving performance in general because of a completely different dynamic: its tendency to evenly distribute I/O requests to all the drives in a subsystem. Without data striping, a logical volume will be mapped to a physical drive. The files for each user of a storage subsystem would then likely end up being all placed in one disk drive. Since not all users are active all the time, this results in what is known as the 80/20 access rule of storage, where at any moment in time 80% of all I/Os are for 20% of the disk drives, which means the remaining 80% of the disk drives receive only 20% of the I/Os. In other words, a small fraction of the drives in the subsystem is heavily utilized, while most other drives are lightly used. Users of the heavily utilized drives, who are the majority of active users at the time, would experience slow response times due to long queueing delays,[4] even though many other drives are sitting idle. With data striping, due to the way logical address space is spread among the drives, each user's files are likely to be more or less evenly distributed to all the drives instead of all concentrated in one drive. As a result, the workload to a subsystem at any moment in time is likely to be roughly divided evenly among all the drives. It is this elimination of hot drives in a storage subsystem that makes data striping a useful strategy for performance improvement when supporting multiple users.

24.2 Data Mirroring

The technique of using data striping as an organization is purely for improving performance. It does not do anything to help a storage subsystem's reliability. Yet, in many applications and computing environments, high data availability and integrity are very important. The oldest method for providing data reliability is by means of replication. Bell Laboratories was one of the first, if not the first, to use this technique in the electronic switching systems (ESS) that they developed for telephony. Data about customers' equipment and routing information for phone lines must be available 24/7 for the telephone network to operate. "Dual copy" was the initial terminology used, but later the term "data mirroring" became popularized in the open literature. This is unfortunate because mirroring implies left-to-right reversal, but there definitely is no reversal of bit ordering when a second copy of data is made. Nevertheless, the term is now universally adopted.

Data mirroring provides reliability by maintaining two copies[5] of data [Ng 1986, 1987]. To protect against disk drive failures, the two copies are kept on different disk drives.[6] The two drives appear as one logical drive with one logical address space to the user. When one drive in a mirrored subsystem fails,

---

[4]The queueing delay is inversely proportional to (1 − utilization). Thus, a drive with 90% utilization will have 5× the queueing delay of a drive with 50% utilization.
[5]For very critical data, more than two copies may be used.
[6]A duplicate copy of certain critical data, such as boot record and file system tables, may also be maintained in the same drive to guard against non-recoverable errors. This is independent of mirroring.

its data is available from another drive. At this point the subsystem is vulnerable to data loss should the second drive fail. To restore the subsystem back to a fault-tolerant state, the remaining copy of data needs to be copied to a replacement disk.

In addition to providing much improved data reliability, data mirroring can potentially also improve performance. When a read command requests a piece of data that is mirrored, there is a choice of two places from which this data can be retrieved. This presents an opportunity for some performance improvement. Several different strategies can be applied:

- Send the command to the drive that has the shorter seek distance. For random access, the average seek distance drops from 1/3 of full stroke to 5/24 (for no zone bit recording). This assumes that both drives are available for handling a command. Thus, its disadvantage is that it ties up both drives in servicing a single command, which is not good for throughput.
- Send the read command to both drives and take the data from the first one to complete. This is more effective than the previous approach in cutting the response time for the command, as it minimizes the sum of seek time and rotational latency. It also has the same disadvantage of tying up both drives in servicing a single command.
- Assign read commands to the two drives in a ping-pong fashion so that each drive services half of the commands. Load sharing by two drives improves throughput.
- Let one drive handle commands for the first half of the address space, and the other drive handle commands for the second half of the address space. This permits load sharing, while at the same time reduces the average seek distance to one-sixth of full stroke. However, if the workload is such that address distribution is not even, one drive may become more heavily utilized than the other. Also, a drive may become idle while there is still a queue of commands for the other drive.
- A good strategy is to maintain a single queue of commands for both mirrored disks. Each

drive that becomes available fetches another command from the shared queue. In this way, both drives get fully utilized. If RPO could be applied in selecting the next command to fetch, that would be the best strategy.

Mirrored disks have a write penalty in the sense that both drives containing the mirrored data need to be updated. One might argue that this is not really a penalty since there is no increase in workload on a per physical drive basis. If write caching is not on, a write is not complete until both drives have done the write. If both drives start the write command at the same time, the mechanical delay time is the larger of the sum of seek and latency of the two drives. If the drives do not start at the same time, then the delay for the write completion is even longer.

There are different ways that data can be mirrored in a storage subsystem [Thomasian & Blaum 2006]. Three of them are described in the following, followed by discussions on their performance and reliability.

24.2.1 Basic Mirroring

The simplest and most common form of mirroring is that of pairing off two disks so that they both contain exactly the same data image. If M is the number of disk drives in a storage subsystem, then there would be M/2 pairs of mirrored disks; M must be an even number. Figure 24.2 illustrates a storage subsystem with six drives organized into three sets of such mirrored disks. In this and in Figures 24.3 and 24.4 each letter represents logically one-half the content, or logical address space, of a physical drive.

24.2.2 Chained Decluster Mirroring

In this organization, for any one of the M drives in the subsystem, half of its content is replicated on a second disk, while the other half is replicated on a third disk [Hsiao & DeWitt 1993]. This is illustrated in Figure 24.3 for M = 6. In this illustration, half of the replication resides in a drive's immediate neighbors on both sides. Note that for this configuration, M does not have to be an even number, which makes this approach more flexible than the basic mirroring method.

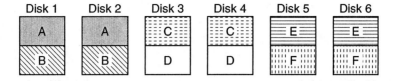

FIGURE 24.2: Basic mirroring with M = 6 drives.

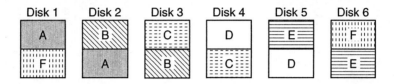

FIGURE 24.3: Chained decluster mirroring with N = 6 drives.

24.2.3 Interleaved Decluster Mirroring

In this third organization, for any one of the M drives in the subsystem, half of its content is divided evenly into (M − 1) partitions. Each partition is replicated on a different drive. The other half of the content of a drive consists of one partition from each of the other (M − 1) drives. Figure 24.4 illustrates such a subsystem with M = 6 drives. M also does not have to be an even number for this mirroring organization.

24.2.4 Mirroring Performance Comparison

When looking into the performance of a fault-tolerant storage subsystem, there are three operation modes to be considered. When all the drives are working, it is called the normal mode. Degraded mode is when a drive has failed and the subsystem has to make do with the remaining drives to continue servicing user requests. During the time when a replacement disk is being repopulated with data, it is called the rebuild mode.

Normal Mode

One factor that affects the performance of a subsystem is whether data striping is being used. Data striping can be applied on top of mirroring in the obvious way. Figure 24.5 illustrates applying the striping example of Figure 24.1 to basic mirroring. As discussed earlier, one benefit of data striping is that it tends to distribute the workload for a subsystem evenly among the drives. So, if data striping is used, then during normal mode all mirroring organizations have similar performance, as there is no difference in the I/O load among the drives. Any write request must go to two drives, and any read request can be handled by one of two drives.

When data striping is not used, hot data can make a small percentage of mirrored pairs very busy in the basic mirroring organization. For the example illustrated in Figure 24.2, high I/O activities for data in A and B will result in more requests going to Disks 1 and 2. Users of this pair of mirrored drives will experience a longer delay. With chained decluster mirroring, it can be seen in Figure 24.3 that activities for A and B can be handled by three drives instead of two, namely Disks 1, 2, and 3. This is an improvement over basic mirroring. Finally, with interleaved decluster mirroring, things are even better still as all drives may be involved for handling read requests for A and B, even though Disks 1 and 2 must handle more writes than the other drives.

Degraded Mode

During normal mode, a read request for any piece of data can be serviced by one of two possible disks,

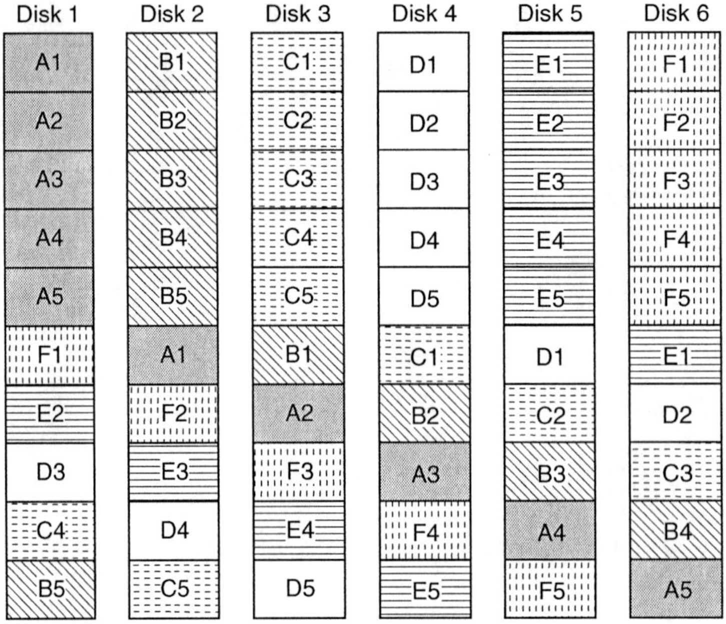

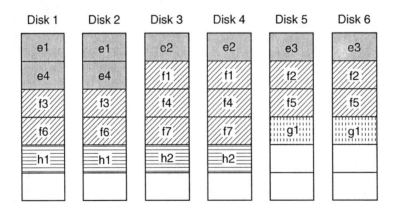

FIGURE 24.4: Interleaved decluster mirroring with M = 6 drives.

FIGURE 24.5: An example of applying data striping to basic mirroring. Using the example of Figure 24.1, four user files e, f, g, and h are shown.

regardless of which mirroring organization is used. When one drive fails, in basic mirroring all read requests to the failed drive must now be handled by its mate, doubling its load for read. For chained decluster mirroring, the read workload of the failed drive is borne by two drives. For the example of Figure 24.3,

if Disk 3 fails, then read requests for data B and C will have to be handled by Disks 2 and 4, respectively. On the surface, the workload for these two drives would seem to be increased by 50%. However, the subsystem controller can divert much of the read workload for D to Disk 5 and much of the workload for

A to Disk 1. This action can ripple out to all the remaining good drives in the chained decluster array until every drive receives an equal workload. This can happen only if the array is subject to a balanced workload distribution to begin with, as in data striping. Finally, with interleaved decluster mirroring, reads for the failed drive are naturally shared by all remaining (M – 1) good drives, giving it the best degraded mode performance.

Rebuild Mode

A similar situation exists in degraded mode. In addition to handling normal user commands, the mirrored data must be read in order for it to be rewritten onto the replacement drive. In basic mirroring, all data must come from the failed drive's mate, adding even more workload to its already doubled read workload. With chained decluster mirroring, half of the mirrored data comes from one drive, while the other half comes from another drive. For interleaved decluster mirroring, each of the (M – 1) remaining good drives is responsible for doing the rebuild read of $1/(M - 1)^{th}$ of the mirrored data.

In summary, of the three different organizations, basic mirroring provides the worst performance, especially during degraded and rebuild modes. Interleaved decluster mirroring has the most balanced and graceful degradation in performance when a drive has failed, with chained decluster mirroring performing between the other two organizations.

24.2.5 Mirroring Reliability Comparison

For a user, a storage subsystem has failed if it loses any of his data. Any mirroring organization can tolerate a single drive failure, since another copy of the failed drive's data is available elsewhere. Repair entails replacing the failed drive with a good drive and copying the mirrored data from the other good drive, or drives, to the replacement drive. When a subsystem has M drives, there are M ways to have the first disk failure. This is where the similarity ends. Whether a second drive failure before the repair is completed will cause data loss depends on the organization and which drive is the second one to fail out of the remaining (M – 1) drives [Thomasian & Blaum 2006].

Basic Mirroring

With this organization, the data of a drive is replicated all on a second drive. Thus, only if this second drive fails will the subsystem suffer a data loss. In other words, there is only one failure out of (M – 1) possible second failures that will cause data loss. The mean time to data loss (MTTDL) for an M disk basic mirroring subsystem is approximately

$$MTTDL = \frac{MTTF^2}{M \cdot MTTR} \qquad \text{(EQ 24.5)}$$

where MTTF is the mean time to failure for a disk, and MTTR is the mean time to repair (replace failed drive and copy data). This is assuming that both failure and repair are exponentially distributed.

Chained Decluster Mirroring

With this organization, the data of a drive is replicated onto two other drives. Thus, if either of these two drives also fails, the subsystem will suffer data loss, even though half and not all of the data of a drive is going to be lost. In other words, there are two possible second failures out of (M – 1) possible failures that will cause data loss. The MTTDL for an M disk chained decluster mirroring subsystem is approximately

$$MTTDL = \frac{MTTF^2}{2M \cdot MTTR} \qquad \text{(EQ 24.6)}$$

which is one-half shorter than that for basic mirroring.

Interleaved Decluster Mirroring

With this organization, the data of a drive is replicated onto all the other drives in the subsystem. Thus, if any one of these (M – 1) drives fails, the subsystem will suffer data loss, even though $1/(M - 1)^{th}$ and not all of the data of a drive is going to be lost. The MTTDL for an M disk interleaved decluster mirroring subsystem is approximately

$$MTTDL = \frac{MTTF^2}{M \cdot (M - 1) \cdot MTTR} \qquad \text{(EQ 24.7)}$$

which is (M – 1) times worse than that for basic mirroring.

In summary, interleave decluster mirroring has the lowest reliability of the three organizations, while basic mirroring has the highest; chained decluster in between these two. This ordering is exactly the reverse of that for performance. Thus, which mirroring organization to use in a subsystem is a performance versus reliability trade-off.

24.3 RAID

While data replication is an effective and simple means for providing high reliability, it is also an expensive solution because the number of disks required is doubled. A different approach that applies the technique of error correcting coding (ECC), where a small addition in redundancy provides fault protection for a larger amount of information, would be less costly. When one drive in a set of drives fails, which drive has failed is readily known. In ECC theory parlance, an error whose location is known is called an erasure. Erasure codes are simpler than ECCs for errors whose locations are not known. The simplest erasure code is that of adding a single parity bit. The parity P for information bits or data bits, say, A, B, C, D, and E, is simply the binary exclusive-OR of those bits:

$$P = A \oplus B \oplus C \oplus D \oplus E \qquad \textbf{(EQ 24.8)}$$

A missing information bit, say, B, can be recovered by XORing the parity bit with the remaining good information bits, since Equation 24.8 can be rearranged to

$$B = P \oplus A \oplus C \oplus D \oplus E \qquad \textbf{(EQ 24.9)}$$

The application of this simple approach to a set of disk drives was first introduced by Ken Ouchi of IBM with a U.S. patent issued in 1978 [Ouchi 1978].

A group of UC Berkeley researchers in 1988 coined the term *redundant array of inexpensive drives*[7]

(RAID) [Patterson et al. 1988] and created an organized taxonomy to different schemes for providing fault tolerance in a collection of disk drives. This was quickly adopted universally as standard, much to the benefit of the storage industry. In fact, a RAID Advisory Board was created within the storage industry to promote and standardize the concept.

24.3.1 RAID Levels

The original Berkeley paper, now a classic, enumerated five classes of RAID, named Levels[8] 1 to 5. Others have since tacked on additional levels. These different levels of RAID are briefly reviewed here [Chen et al. 1988] .

RAID-0

This is simply data striping, as discussed in Section 4.1. Since data striping by itself involves no redundancy, calling this RAID-0 is actually a misnomer. However, marketing hype by storage subsystem vendors, eager to use the "RAID" label in their product brochures, has succeeded in making this terminology generally accepted, even by the RAID Advisory Board.

RAID-1

This is the same as basic mirroring. While this is the most costly solution to achieve higher reliability in terms of percentage of redundancy drives required, it is also the simplest to implement. In the early 1990s, EMC was able to get to the nascent market for high-reliability storage subsystem first with products based on this simple approach and had much success with it.

When data striping, or RAID-0, is applied on top of RAID-1, as illustrated in Figure 24.5, the resulting array is oftentimes referred to as RAID-10.

---

[7]The word "inexpensive" was later replaced by "independent" by most practitioners and the industry.
[8]The choice of using the word "level" is somewhat unfortunate, as it seems to imply some sort of ranking, when there actually is none.

RAID-2

In RAID-2, fault tolerance is achieved by applying ECC across a set of drives. As an example, if a $(7,4)$[9] Hamming code is used, three redundant drives are added to every four data drives. A user's data is striped across the four data drives at the bit level, i.e., striping size is one bit. Corresponding bits from the data drives are used to calculate three ECC bits, with each bit going into one of the redundant drives. Reads and writes, even for a single sector's worth of data, must be done in parallel to all the drives due to the bit-level striping. The RAID-2 concept was first disclosed by Michelle Kim in a 1986 paper. She also suggested synchronizing the rotation of all the striped disks.

RAID-2 is also a rather costly solution for achieving higher reliability. It is more complex than mirroring and yet does not have the flexibility of mirroring. It never was adopted by the storage industry since RAID-3 is a similar but simpler and less costly solution.

RAID-3

This organization concept is similar to RAID-2 in that bit-level striping[10] is used. However, instead of using Hamming ECC code to provide error correction capability, it uses the simple parity scheme discussed previously to provide single drive failure (erasure) fault tolerance. Thus, only one redundant drive, called the *parity drive*, needs to be added, regardless of the number of data drives. Its low overhead and simplicity makes RAID-3 an attractive solution for designing a high-reliability storage subsystem. Because its data access is inherently parallel due to byte-level striping, this architecture is suitable for applications that mostly transfer a large volume of data. Hence, it is quite popular with supercomputers. Since the drives cannot be individually accessed to provide high IOPS for small block data accesses, it is not a good storage subsystem solution for on-line transaction processing (OLTP) and other database-type applications.

RAID-4

This architecture recognizes the shortcoming of the lack of individual disk access in RAID-3. While retaining the use of single parity to provide for fault tolerance, it disassociates the concept of data striping from parity striping. While each parity byte is still the parity of all the corresponding bytes of the data drives, the user's data is free to be striped with any striping size. By choosing a striping width that is some multiple of sectors, accessibility of user's data to individual disks is now possible. In fact, a user's data does not even have to be striped at all, i.e., striping size can be equal to one disk drive.

RAID-4 is a more flexible architecture than RAID-3. Because of its freedom to choose its data striping size, data for any workload environment can be organized in the best possible optimization allowable under data striping, and yet it enjoys the same reliability as RAID-3. However, this flexibility does come at a price.

In RAID-3, writes are always done in full stripes so that the parity can always be calculated from the new data. With RAID-4, as drives are individually accessible, a write request may only be for one of the drives. Take Equation 24.8, and generalize it so that each letter represents a block in one drive. Suppose a write command wants to change block C to C'. Because blocks A, B, D, and E are not changed and therefore not sent by the host as part of the write command, the new parity P',

$$P' = A \oplus B \oplus C' \oplus D \oplus E \qquad \textbf{(EQ 24.10)}$$

cannot be computed from the command itself. One way to generate this new parity is to read the data blocks A, B, D, and E from their respective drives and then XOR them with the new data C'. This means that the write command in this example triggers four read commands before P' can be calculated and C' and P' can be finally written. In general, if the total number of data and parity drives is N, then a single small write command to a RAID-4 array becomes $(N-2)$ read commands and two write commands for the underlying drives.

---

[9]A (n,k) code means the code word is n bits wide and contains k information bits.
[10]In practice, byte-level striping is more likely to be used as it is more convenient to deal with, but the concept and the net effect are still the same.

It can be observed that when Equations 24.8 and 24.10 are combined, the following equation results:

$$P \oplus P' = C \oplus C' \qquad \text{(EQ 24.11)}$$

or

$$P' = P \oplus C \oplus C' \qquad \text{(EQ 24.12)}$$

Therefore, an alternative method is to read the original data block C and the original parity block P, compute the new parity P' in accordance with Equation 24.12, and then write the new C' and P' back to those two drives. Thus, a single, small write command becomes two read-modify-write (RMW) commands, one to the target data drive and one to the parity drive. The I/O completion time for a RMW command is the I/O time for a read plus one disk revolution time.

Either method adds a lot of extra disk activities for a single, small write command. This is often referred to as the small write penalty. For N > 3, which is usually the case, the second method involving RMW is more preferable since it affects two drives instead of all N drives, even though RMW commands take longer than regular commands.

RAID-5

With RAID-4, parity information is stored in one dedicated parity drive. Because of the small write penalty, the parity drive will become a bottleneck for any workload that has some amount of small writes, as it is involved in such writes for any of the data drives. Also, for a heavily read workload, the parity drive is underutilized. The Berkeley team recognized this unbalanced distribution of workload and devised the RAID-5 scheme as a solution.

RAID-5 uses an organization which is very similar to that of data striping. The address space of each disk drive in the group is partitioned into fixed-size blocks referred to as *parity stripe blocks*, and the size is called the *parity stripe block size*. The corresponding blocks from each disk together form a *parity group*. The number of disks in a parity group is referred to as the *parity group width*. Each parity group includes N data blocks and one parity block.[11] Finally, the parity blocks from different parity groups are distributed evenly among all the drives in the array. Figure 24.6 illustrates an example of a 6-disk RAID-5 with the placement of the parity blocks P_i rotated among all the drives. Note that Figure 24.6 is only a template for data placement, and the pattern can be repeated as many times as necessary depending of the parity stripe block size. For example, if drives with 60 GB are used here, and the block size is chosen to be 1 MB, then the pattern will be repeated 10,000 times.

As it is possible to access individual disk drives, RAID-5 has the same small block write penalty of RAID-4. However, since parity blocks are evenly distributed among all the drives in an array, the bottleneck problem associated with the dedicated parity drive of RAID-4 is eliminated. Because of this advantage of RAID-5, and everything else being equal, RAID-4 is not used in any storage subsystems.

The parity stripe block size does not have to be the same as the data stripe size. In fact, there is no requirement that data striping needs to be used in RAID-5 at all. Figure 24.7 illustrates how the example of data striping of Figure 24.1 can be organized in a 4-disk RAID-5 with the parity stripe block size 2x the data stripe size. While there is no requirement that parity stripe size and data stripe size must be equal, doing so will certainly make things a little easier to manage for the array control software, which needs to map user's address space to drives' address spaces while keeping track of where the parity blocks are.

RAID-6

RAID-5 offers a single drive failure protection for the array. If even higher reliability of protection against double drive failures is desired, one more redundancy drive will be needed. The simple bitwise parity across all data blocks schemes is retained for the first redundancy block, but cannot be used for the

---

[11]RAID-5 is oftentimes described as an N + P disk array, with N being the equivalent number of data disks and P being the equivalent of one parity disk. Thus, a 6-disk RAID-5 is a 5 + P array.

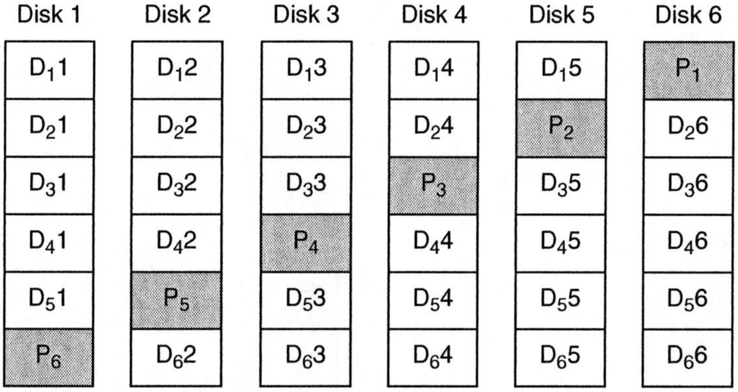

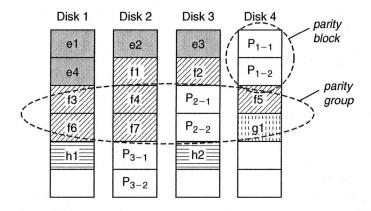

FIGURE 24.6: An example of RAID-5 with 6 disks (5 + P). Parity block P_i is the parity of the corresponding D_i data blocks from the other disks.

FIGURE 24.7: An example of RAID-5 where parity stripe size and data stripe size are different. P_{2-2} is the parity for f6, f7, and g1.

second redundancy. A more complex coding scheme is required. Furthermore, because updating this second redundancy also requires RMW for small writes, the new redundancy blocks are also distributed among all the drives in the array à la RAID-5. The resulting organization is RAID-6, as illustrated in Figure 24.8 for a 6-disk array.[12] P_i is parity of the corresponding D_i data blocks in the ith parity group, and Q_i is the second redundancy block computed from D_is and P_i.

When one drive in a RAID-6 fails, requests for its content can be reconstructed from the remaining good drives using the simple parity P in exactly the same way as RAID-5. Repair consists of replacing the failed drive and rebuilding its content from the other good drives. If another drive fails before the first failure can be repaired, then both P and the more complicated redundancy Q will be needed for data reconstruction. Some form of Reed-Solomon

---

[12]RAID-6 is oftentimes described as an N + P + Q array, with N being the equivalent number of data disks, P being the equivalent of one parity disk, and Q being the equivalent of a second redundant disk. Thus, a 6-disk RAID-6 is a 4 + P + Q array.

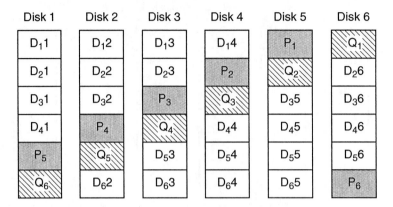

FIGURE 24.8: An example of RAID-6 with 6 disks (4 + P + Q).

code was suggested for the second redundancy in the original RAID-6 description. However, Reed-Solomon decoding logic is somewhat complex, and so later on others came up with alternative types of code, such as Even-Odd [Blaum et al. 1995] that uses simple XOR logic for the decoder. Regardless of what code is used, any array with two redundant drives to provide double failure protection can be referred to as RAID-6.

24.3.2 RAID Performance

Mirroring and RAID-4/5/6 have some performance similarity and dissimilarity [Ng 1989, Schwarz & Burkhard 1995]. RAID-3 has different performance characteristics because its component drives cannot be accessed individually. In the following, for ease of discussion, it will be assumed that the workload to an array is normally evenly distributed among all the disks, as in the case with data striping.

Normal Mode Performance

Mirroring has the best normal mode read performance because read requests can be serviced by one of two different drives. RAID-5/6 have the same read performance as that of JBOD, with RAID-4 slightly worse since it has one fewer data drive. RAID-3 has good read performance with large block requests, but the component drives are underutilized when servicing small block requests.

For write requests, RAID-3 performs the same as reads. Both mirroring and RAID-4/5/6 have write penalties. In the case of mirroring, the penalty is that the write must be done to both disks. For RAID-4/5, a small block write request becomes two RMW requests. In the case of RAID-6, a small block write request becomes three RMW requests. For RAID-4/5/6, if a full data stripe is written, there is no penalty since it is not necessary to read the old data. This argues for using a smaller data stripe size to increase the likelihood of writes being full stripe, which is contrary to the discussion on data striping in general in Section 24.1.

This is summarized in Table 24.1 for different arrays with N data disks, or N equivalent data disks. Each array is given a total workload of R reads and W small writes. The table shows the workload as seen by each drive in the array for various organizations. The total number of disks in an array is an indication of its relative cost in providing the equivalent of N disks of storage space. Mirroring has the lightest workload per drive and, therefore, should have the best performance, but it is also the most expensive solution. Not surprisingly, the double-fault-tolerant RAID-6 has a high workload per drive and thus low performance. RAID-3 also has low small block performance.

TABLE **24.1** Normal workload per disk; array is given R reads and W writes

	JBOD	Mirroring	RAID-3	RAID-5	RAID-6
Total number of disks	N	2N	N + 1	N + 1	N + 2
Workload per disk	(R + W)/N	(R + 2W)/2N	R + W	(R + 2RMW)/(N + 1)	(R + 3RMW)/(N + 2)

Degraded Mode and Rebuild Mode Performance

The impact on performance of a disk failure in mirroring depends on which one of the mirroring schemes is used and has been discussed in Section 24.2.4. For RAID-3, performance is not affected by a drive failure since it is always reading in parallel anyway, so the missing data can be reconstructed on the fly. For RAID-4/5, read requests to the failing drive translates to reads of the corresponding sectors from every surviving drive in order to do data reconstruction. This means the read workload for the surviving drives is doubled.

As for writes to the failed drive, instead of doing RMW, it must read from the other data drives in the parity group to generate a new parity for the new write data. Therefore, the read workload of the surviving drives is further increased due to writes. The new parity can simply be written to the parity drive of the parity group—no RMW required. If a write to one of the surviving disks causes a parity block in the failed drive to be updated, this parity operation will have to be ignored; in fact, the data write itself will just be a simple write and not an RMW since there is no point in generating a new parity that cannot be written.

The motivated reader can develop the degraded mode scenarios for RAID-6, for single and for double drive failures, in a similar fashion.

The rebuild process of RAID-4/5/6 is somewhat different from that of mirroring. In mirroring, the replacement drive can be repopulated by simply copying the duplicated data, either all from one disk or parts from multiple disks, depending on the mirroring scheme. With RAID-4/5/6, the entire content of every surviving disk must be read in order to reconstruct the complete content of the failed drive. The rebuild process is broken up into reconstructing one small chunk at a time so that the array can continue servicing user requests. Still, rebuild adds even more workload to the entire array during the rebuild mode period.

24.3.3 RAID Reliability

The reliability of mirroring has already been discussed in Section 24.2.4. RAID-3/4/5 are all single-fault-tolerant architectures. Data of a failed drive can be reconstructed from the remaining drives in the event of a single drive failing, albeit with degraded performance. If a second drive, any one of the drives in the array, fails before the first failed drive can be replaced and its content rebuilt, then there is no way to recover the lost data in those two failed drives from the remaining drives. This data loss condition is identical to that of interleaved decluster mirroring, although in that situation part of the data of one drive is lost, whereas here the entire contents of two disks are lost. Without distinguishing the amount of data loss, then for RAID-3/4/5, the MTTDL is approximately

$$MTTDL = \frac{MTTF^2}{(N + 1) \cdot N \cdot MTTR} \qquad \text{(EQ 24.13)}$$

While the MTTF of the disk drives here is the same as that of Equation 24.7 (assuming the same model of disks are used), the MTTR is likely to be different. Repair includes repopulating the content of the replacement drive, and this process for RAID-/4/5 requires more work and hence will likely take longer to complete.

In the case of RAID-6, reliability is tremendously improved since it is fault tolerant to two simultaneous disk failures. Thus, it takes a third disk drive in the array to fail before data will be lost. Its MTTDL is approximately given by

$$MTTDL = \frac{MTTF^3}{(N + 2) \cdot (N + 1) \cdot N \cdot MTTR^2} \quad \text{(EQ 24.14)}$$

Table 24.2 shows a comparison of the reliability of various mirroring schemes and RAID-5 and RAID-6. A MTTF of 1 million hours is assumed for the disk drives being used. MTTR is assumed to be 1 hour for mirroring and 4 hours for RAID-5/6. These short repair times are based on the assumption that a spare drive is available in the subsystem, so it is not necessary to wait for a replacement drive. The first row is a comparison based on equal total number of disks, with the net number of data disks for each case given in parentheses. The second row is a comparison based on equal number of data disks, with the total number of disks in the array given in parentheses. In both cases, expectedly the double-fault-tolerant RAID-6 has the highest reliability of all array configurations. Among the single-fault-tolerant configurations, basic mirroring has the highest reliability, while RAID-4/5 has the lowest reliability.

No single storage subsystem organization has the best reliability, performance, and cost at the same time. This fact is reflected in the marketplace as subsystems based on mirroring, RAID-5, and RAID-6 are all available with no clear-cut winner. What is the right design choice depends on which one or two of the three characteristics are more important to the user or application.

A quick note about a drive's MTTF and a subsystem's MTTDL. An MTTF of 1 million hours may seem like a very long time. Some people may even have the misconception that it means most of the drives will last that long. This is far from the truth. Assuming an exponential failure distribution, i.e., the probability that a drive has already failed at time t is $(1 - e^{-kt})$, where k is the failure rate, MTTF = 1/k. Then a 1-million-hour MTTF means the drive is failing at a rate of $k = 10^{-6}$ per hour. By the time MTTF is reached, there is $1 - e^{-1} = 0.63$

probability that the drive would have already failed. For a pool of 1000 drives, statistically 1 drive will have failed in 1000 hours, which is only a little over a month's time. In five years' time, about 44 of the drives will have failed. Without fault tolerance to improve reliability, this represents a lot of data loss. The MTTDL numbers listed in Table 24.2 are definitely orders of magnitude better than that of a raw disk. Still, for a subsystem maker that has sold 100,000 eight-disk RAID-5s[13] each with an MTTDL of 4.46×10^3 million hours, in ten years' time two of those RAIDs will have suffered data loss, even though the owners thought they had purchased a fault-tolerant storage subsystem to provide reliable data storage. This is why subsystems with RAID-6, triplicated or even quadruplicated mirroring, and other more complex schemes for higher fault tolerance are sought after by those businesses for whom data is their lifeline.

The discussion on MTTDL so far is only based on drive failures alone. When other components of a storage subsystem are factored in, such as the electronics, cooling, power supply, cabling, etc., the MTTDL of the entire subsystem will actually be lower. Finally, the MTTDL equations given in this chapter are from highly simplified models and assume disk drive failures are independent, which is an optimistic assumption.

24.3.4 Sparing

It can be seen that in all the above MTTDL equations for various configurations, MTTDL is always inversely proportional to MTTR. This is intuitively obvious, since the longer it takes the subsystem to return to a fault-tolerant state, the bigger the window in which the subsystem is vulnerable to another drive failure. Thus, a key to improving the reliability is to make the repair time as short as possible.

As discussed earlier, repair of a fault-tolerant storage subsystem includes replacing the failed drive and rebuilding its content. Waiting for a repairman to come and swap out the bad drive usually takes hours, if not days. A commonly used strategy for avoiding

---

[13]A medium-size installation typically has hundreds of disk drives.

TABLE 24.2   Reliability comparison—MTTDL (in million hours)

	Basic Mirroring (RAID-1)	Chained Decluster Mirroring	Interleave Decluster Mirroring	RAID-4/5	RAID-6
Equal total number of disks = 8	1.25×10^5 (4 data disks)	6.25×10^4 (4 data disks)	1.79×10^4 (4 data disks)	4.46×10^3 (7 data disks)	1.86×10^8 (6 data disks)
Equal number of data disks = 4	1.25×10^5 (8 total disks)	6.25×10^4 (8 total disks)	1.79×10^4 (8 total disks)	1.25×10^4 (5 total disks)	5.21×10^8 (6 total disks)

this long delay is to have one or more spare drives built in the subsystem. As soon as a drive fails, the subsystem can immediately start the repair process by rebuilding onto the spare drive. This essentially makes the drive replacement time zero.

There are two concepts regarding sparing that will be discussed here [Ng 1994c].

Global Sparing

A storage subsystem usually contains multiple RAIDs. While it is probably a simpler design to have a spare drive dedicated to each RAID, a better reliability design and more cost-effective solution is to place all the spare drives together into a common pool that can be shared by all the RAIDs. Without sharing, if one RAID has a failure and consumes its spare drive, it no longer has a spare until a serviceman comes and swaps out the bad drive and puts in a new spare. During this window, that RAID will have a longer repair time should another failure occur. On the other hand, if all spares are shared, then any RAID in the subsystem can go through multiple drive-failure/fast-repair cycles as long as there are still spares available in the pool. Global sparing is more cost-effective because fewer total number of spares will be needed, and the serviceman can defer his visit until a multiple number of spares have been used up instead of every time a spare is consumed.

Distributed Sparing

Traditionally, a spare drive would sit idly in the subsystem until called upon to fulfill its function as a spare. This is a waste of a potential resource. Furthermore, there is always the possibility that the spare will not actually work when it is finally needed, unless the subsystem periodically checks its pulse, i.e., sees if it can do reads and writes.

A better strategy is to turn the "spare" disk into another active disk. This is achieved by off-loading some of the data from the other drives onto this additional drive [Menon et al. 1993]. The spare space is now distributed among all the drives in the array. This is illustrated in Figure 24.9 for a 4 data disk RAID-5. Each parity group has its own spare block, S_i, which can be used to hold any of the blocks in its parity group. For example, if Disk 2 fails, then $D_1 2$ is rebuilt onto S_1 in Disk 6, $D_2 2$ is rebuilt onto S_2 in Disk 5, etc., and P_4 is rebuilt onto S_4 in Disk 3. Note that there is no rebuild for S_5. Again, the advantage of distributed sparing is that the total workload to the array is now shared by N + 2 drives instead of N + 1, so total throughput should increase. Reliability should stay about the same. On the one hand, there is now one additional data carrying disk drive whose failure can lead to data loss, so Equation 24.13 for RAID-5 becomes

$$MTTDL = \frac{MTTF^2}{(N + 2) \cdot (N + 1) \cdot MTTR} \qquad \textbf{(EQ 24.15)}$$

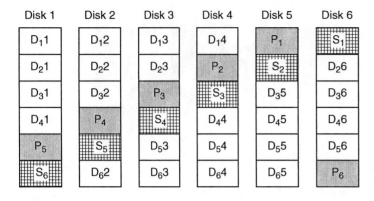

FIGURE 24.9: An example of distributed sparing for a 4 + P + S RAID-5.

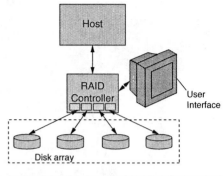

FIGURE 24.10: A simple example of a hardware RAID with an outboard RAID controller.

On the other hand, this is mitigated by the fact that rebuild will be faster because each drive is only $(N + 1)/(N + 2)$ full, thus the MTTR here is reduced from that of Equation 24.13 by this factor.

24.3.5 RAID Controller

For a group of disks to perform together as a RAID, they must be managed as such. The management function can be performed by software in a host to which the drives of the array are connected directly. This is called a *software RAID* and is usually found in low-end systems such as personal workstations. More commonly, the RAID functions are handled by a dedicated controller which typically includes some specialized hardware, such as an XOR engine for parity calculations. This type of subsystem is called a *hardware RAID*. For smaller systems, the controller can be an adapter card that goes on the system bus inside the host. For larger systems, the RAID controller is likely to be an outboard unit. Adapter card RAID solutions are generally fairly basic, support only one or two RAIDs, and are not sharable between different machines. RAID systems with outboard controllers can be shared by multiple clients, so they usually provide more functions, such as zoning/fencing to protect an individual client's data. They are generally more complex and can support a larger number of RAIDs. Even though a controller failure would not cause data loss, it does make data unavailable, which is not acceptable for 24/7 applications. Therefore, the highest end storage subsystems have dual controllers to provide fail-over capability.

Figure 24.10 shows a simple system configuration for an outboard RAID. The connections between drives and the RAID controller are standard disk interfaces, depending on what types of drives are used. The RAID controller also uses a standard disk interface to connect to the host; however, this does not have to be of the same type as the interface to the drives. For example, the connection between the RAID controller and host may be FC-AL, while drives with an SCSI interface or SATA interface may be used in the array. One of the many functions performed by the RAID controller is to bridge between these two interfaces. The controller provides a user interface that allows the user to configure the drives. Most controllers allow the user to create any combinations of RAID-0, 1, 3, and 5 from the available drives in the array. Many even allow multiple RAIDs to be constructed out of each drive by using different portions of its address space. For example, half of Disk 1 and Disk 2 may form a mirrored pair, and half of Disk 3 and Disk 4 may form a second mirrored pair, with the remaining spaces of Disks 1, 2, 3, and 4 forming a 3 + P RAID-5. Stripe size is usually also selectable by the user; most use the same block size for both parity stripe and data stripe, for simplicity.

Another function performed by the RAID controller is that of caching. The read cache in the controller is typically orders of magnitude larger than the disk drive's internal cache. This allows full stripes of data to be prefetched from the drives even though only a few sectors may be requested in the current user command. As discussed earlier, the main performance disadvantage of RAID-5/6 is the small block write. Hence, write caching would be very beneficial here. However, traditional caching of writes in DRAM is not acceptable since it is susceptible to power loss. Hence, higher end storage subsystems that provide both reliability and performance use non-volatile storage (NVS), typically by means of battery backup, to implement write caching. Until data is written out to the target drive and the corresponding parity is updated, it is still vulnerable to single fault failure in the NVS. To address this issue, a common solution is to maintain two cached copies of data, one copy in NVS and another copy in regular DRAM. Since different hardware is used for the two copies, a single failure can only wipe out one copy of data.

24.3.6 Advanced RAIDs

Since the introduction of the RAID concept in 1988, others have expanded on this field with additional ideas such as declustered RAID [Mattson & Ng 1992, 1993; Ng & Mattson 1994], cross-hatched disk array [Ng 1994a, 1945], hierarchical RAID [Thomasian 2006], Massive Arrays of Idle Disks (MAID) [Colarelli et al. 2002], etc. In this section, two of these more advanced architectures are discussed.

Declustered RAID

It was pointed out in Section 24.3.2 that in RAID-5 degraded mode, the workload for each surviving drive in the array is roughly doubled (depending on the read-to-write ratio). The situation gets even worse during rebuild mode, when all the drives in the RAID-5 have to participate in the data reconstruction of every read request to the failed drive and at the same time contribute to the rebuild effort of the entire drive. If there are multiple RAID-5s in the subsystem, this

means only one is heavily impacted while the other RAIDs are not affected. Using the same logic behind interleaved decluster mirroring (where mirrored data of a drive is evenly spread out to all other drives in the subsystem, instead of being placed all in a single mate drive as in basic mirroring), one can similarly architect a RAID so that its parity groups are evenly distributed among all the drives in the array instead of always using the same set of drives. The resulting array is called *declustered RAID*.

In a traditional N + P RAID-5, the parity group width is N + 1, and if there are k such RAIDs, the total number of drives T in the subsystem is equal to k × (N + 1). With declustering, there is only one declustered RAID in T drives. There is no fixed relationship between T and N other than (N + 1) < T. Figure 24.11 illustrates a simple example of a declustered RAID-5 with T = 4 total drives and a parity group width of 3. W, X, Y, and Z represent four different parity groups, with each group being 2 + P. Again, Figure 24.11 is only a template for data placement which can be repeated many times. The parity blocks can also be rotated in a similar fashion to RAID-5. The declustering concept can equally be applied to RAID-6.

To generate a declustered array with parity groupings that are uniformly distributed among all the drives, partition each disk into B logical blocks to be used for forming parity groups. In the example of Figure 24.11, B = 3. When forming a parity group, no two logical blocks can be from the same disk, for failure protection reason. Finally, every pair of disks must have exactly L parity groups in common. L = 2 for the example of Figure 24.11. For the reader familiar with the statistical

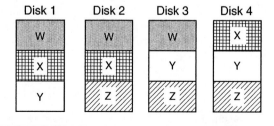

FIGURE 24.11: A simple example of declustered RAID. There are four total drives. W, X, Y, and Z represent parity groups of width 3.

field of design of experiments, it can be seen that the balanced incomplete block design (BIBD) construct can be used to create such declustered arrays.

Hierarchical RAID

While RAID-6 provides fault tolerance beyond a single disk failure, the error coding scheme for the second redundancy can look a little bit complicated. Some have chosen to implement a higher level of fault protection using a different approach, which is to construct a hierarchical RAID using basic levels of RAID such as RAID-1, 3, and 5.

An example is RAID-15 which, in its simplest form, is to construct a RAID-1 on top of two RAID-5s, as shown in Figure 24.12. To the RAID-1 controller on top, each RAID-5 below it appears as a logical disk. The two logical disks are simply mirrored using basic mirroring. For disaster protection, the two RAID-5s can even be located in two different sites, perhaps linked to the RAID-1 controller using optical fiber. Other configurations such as RAID-11, RAID-13, and RAID-51 can be constructed in a similar fashion.

In the simple configuration of Figure 24.12, the subsystem is fault tolerant to one single logical disk failure, that is, double or more failures in one of the RAID-5s and concurrently a single failure in the other RAID-5. Using exactly the same total number of disks, a more sophisticated RAID-15 would integrate all the RAID-1 and RAID-5 controllers into one supercontroller. This supercontroller will be cognizant of the configuration of all the disk drives in the subsystem. With this intelligent supercontroller, the subsystem can be fault tolerant to more combinations of disk failures. As long as there is only one mirrored pair failure, the subsystem is still working. This is illustrated in Figure 24.13 for a 14-disk RAID-15. Data for all disks except Disk 1 are available. Data for Disk 1 can be reconstructed using RAID-5 parity.

24.4 SAN

As the enterprise computing paradigm evolved during the 1990s from stand-alone mainframes to that of distributed computing with networked servers, the long time I/O architecture of dedicated storage connected directly to a single host machine became inadequate. A new architecture in which storage could be more readily shared among multiple computers was needed. A natural evolution at the time was to have the distributed application servers, each with its own *Direct Access Storage* (DAS), share data with each other and with clients by sending data over the local area network (LAN) or the wide area network (WAN) that they were attached to. This is illustrated in Figure 24.14. Management of data storage is distributed since it must be handled by the individual servers. This architecture has a few drawbacks. First, in the 1990s, the speed of Ethernet, with which networks were built, was slow in comparison to that of disk drives. Thus, accessing data in a different machine on the LAN suffered from poor performance. Second, sending a large volume of data over the LAN or WAN clogged up the network, slowing other communications between the servers and clients. Third, if a server was down, then the data in its DAS became unavailable to the rest of the system.

At about the same time, prodded by customer interest, there was movement afoot for high-end computing to evolve from systems using captive proprietary components of a single manufacturer to an open architecture in which the customer could pick and choose products from multiple vendors based on price, performance, functionality, and reliability instead of on brand name. Furthermore, as demand for data storage space grew exponentially, driven by such new applications as data warehousing and mining, e-mail, and digitization of all information from books to movies, scalability of storage subsystem also became a very important feature for a storage subsystem. Finally, with the cost of storage management becoming a very significant portion of an IT department's budget, IT professionals were rediscovering the efficiency of centralized data management over distributed management.

In the late 1990s, the concept of *storage area network* (SAN) was conceived to be the solution that could satisfy all the above requirements. In this architecture, a vast array of open standard storage devices are attached to a dedicated, high-speed, and easily growable backend network. All the data of these devices is accessible to any number of servers that are similarly connected to this network. This is illustrated in Figure 24.15. The resulting decoupling of storage from direct attachment to servers has some important benefits:

- Placing all data traffic in a separate backend network frees up the LAN/WAN for application traffic only.
- Data availability is improved over that of DAS.

- Maintenance activities can be performed on storage subsystems without having to shut down the servers, as is the case with DAS.
- Non-disk types of storage devices such as tape and optical disks can easily be added and shared.

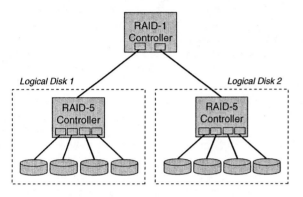

FIGURE 24.12: A Simple RAID-15 configuration. Each RAID-5 appears as a logical disk to the RAID-1 controller.

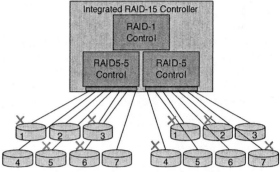

FIGURE 24.13: An integrated RAID-15 controller. Example shows the subsystem is good as long as there is only one mirrored pair failure.

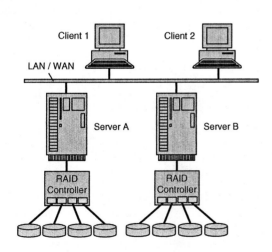

FIGURE 24.14: System configuration using DAS. Server A must access the data of Server B over the network.

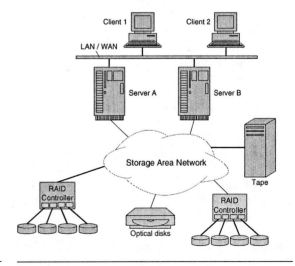

FIGURE 24.15: System configuration of SAN. The SAN is an FC switched fabric.

- Storage management can more readily be centralized.

High-speed Fibre Channel (FC) technology became mature at just about the time that SAN was being proposed. FC switched fabric, discussed earlier in Chapter 20, Section 20.6, seemed to be the perfect instrument for implementing SAN. In fact, one could argue, and perhaps rightfully so, that the idea of SAN was really the product of the availability of FC technology. By leveraging the topological flexibility afforded by FC switched fabric's connectivity, SAN can be configured in many shapes and forms. SAN also inherits the multi-gigabit speed of FC, which additionally allows remote placement of storage subsystems a long distance away from servers when optical cables are used.

With SAN technology, all the storage space of a subsystem appears to the user as logical volumes. Thus, data is accessed at the block level, with file systems in the servers managing such blocks.

24.5 NAS

The flexibility of SAN comes at a cost. For smaller systems the price of acquiring an FC switched fabric may be too high an entry fee to pay. Vendors in the storage industry offer an alternative approach for off-loading data traffic and file service from an application server with captive DAS, while at the same time providing an easier path to scalability with a subsystem that is relatively simple to deploy. Such products are called *network attached storage* (NAS).

NAS is a specialized device, composed of storage, a processor, and an operating system, dedicated to function solely as a file server. While it can certainly be implemented using a general-purpose machine with a general-purpose, full-function operating system such as Unix or Windows, it is cheaper and simpler to use stripped down hardware and software to perform its one specific function. Such a slimmed down system is sometimes referred to as a *thin server*. The major pieces of software required by NAS are a file system manager, storage management software, network interface software, and device drivers for talking to the disk drives.

As its name implies, NAS is connected to a working group's LAN or WAN, and its data is accessed by clients and application servers over the network. This is illustrated in Figure 24.16. TCP/IP is typically the networking protocol used for communication. Some NAS products support Dynamic Host Configuration Protocol (DHCP) to provide a plug-and-play capability. When connected to the network, they discover their own IP addresses and broadcast their availability without requiring any user intervention.

Unlike SAN, where storage data is accessed in blocks, in NAS the user does file accesses. Two main network file access protocols are most commonly used. They are the Network File System (NFS) and the Common Internet File System (CIFS). NFS was introduced by Sun Microsystems in 1985 and is the *de facto* standard for Unix types of systems. CIFS is based on the Server Message Block (SMB) protocol developed by Microsoft, also around mid-1980s, and is the standard for Windows-based systems. Due to the fundamental differences between these two protocols, most NAS subsystems are used exclusively by either all Unix or all Windows machines in a network, but not both at the same time.

Since NAS uses the working group's network for data transfer, it is not an ideal solution for regularly transferring a large volume of data, as that would create too much traffic on that network. SAN is more suitable for that purpose. On the other hand, low

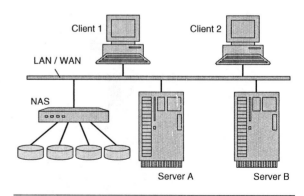

FIGURE 24.16: System configuration of NAS. The NAS is a dedicated file server.

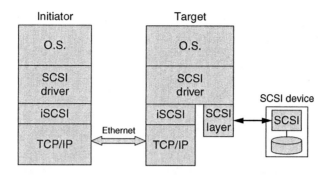

FIGURE 24.17: High-level view of iSCSI.

entry cost and ease of deployment make NAS an attractive solution for file sharing purposes within a small working group. In fact, some IT system builders may find SAN and NAS technologies complementary and able co-exist within the same system.

24.6 iSCSI

SAN allows users to maintain their own files and do block access to the storage of SAN, but requires the addition of an FC switched fabric. NAS does not require any additional networking equipment, but users have to access data at the file level (not implying that it is good or bad here). The storage industry came up with a third choice for users which is a combination of these two options. In this third option, the storage subsystem is attached to the work group's network, as in NAS, but data access by the user is at the block level, as in SAN. This technology is called *iSCSI*, for *Internet SCSI*. It was developed by the Internet Engineering Task Force (IETF) and was ratified as an official standard in February 2003.

In iSCSI, SCSI command-level protocols are encapsulated at the SCSI source into IP packets. These packets are sent as regular TCP/IP communication over the network to the SCSI target. At the target end, which is a dedicated special iSCSI storage server, the packets are unwrapped to retrieve the original SCSI message, which can be either command or data. The iSCSI controller then forwards the SCSI information to a standard SCSI device in the normal fashion. This is illustrated in Figure 24.17.

With the availability of Gigabit and 10-Gbit Ethernets, the raw data rate of iSCSI becomes competitive to that of FC. Efficient network driver code can keep the overhead of using TCP/IP to an acceptable level. Hardware assist such as the TCP Offload Engine (TOE) can also reduce overhead.

CHAPTER 25

Advanced Topics

The preceding chapters on disks cover the fundamentals of today's disk drives. In this chapter, some more advanced topics will be discussed. These are new concepts and approaches that are significantly different from current methods of doing things. As such, they are above and beyond simply making evolutionary improvements over current technologies. While no attempt is made to create an exhaustive list of all such topics, the topics selected here are deemed to be important for the reader to be aware of. The topics run the gamut from fundamental magnetic recording physics (perpendicular recording), to recording media (patterned media), to heads (thermally assisted recording), to servo (dual stage actuator), to data format (adaptive formatting), to caching (hybrid HDD), and all the way up to drive interface and storage subsystems (object-based storage). Some of these technologies are already starting to be incorporated into disk drives that are being shipped today. Some will be in products in the near future. Others may not be in any product plans yet, but look promising to be worth some discussion here.

25.1 Perpendicular Recording

In 2005 a couple of disk drive manufacturers had announced their intentions to deliver products using perpendicular recording. Currently, in 2007, all major disk drive manufacturers are shipping some drives in perpendicular recording. Longitudinal recording is expected to be phased out within the next few years.

In Chapter 17, where the fundamentals of magnetic recording were discussed, the discussions assumed longitudinal recording which have been exclusively in use for the past 50 years. In longitudinal recording, the magnetization for representing data bits is in the plane of the recording medium. Thus, the magnetic domains are lying down along the path of each track, as illustrated in Figure 25.1(a). These domains can remain stable in such a configuration because the magnetic medium is fabricated to have an easy axis parallel to the disk surface so that it is natural to assume a horizontal position. However, as the bit size decreases due to increasing areal density, the amount of energy required to reverse the polarity of a recorded bit becomes less and less. Eventually, the point will be reached when mere excitations from ambient thermal energy would be sufficient to cause the magnetic grains making up a recorded bit to spontaneously "flip," i.e., reverse magnetic orientation. When enough numbers of the grains within a bit have flipped, the state of the bit's polarity becomes ambiguous and therefore unreadable. Data storage is no longer feasible without thermal stability. This point is known as the *superparamagnetic* limit.

There is no simple physical law that precisely dictates at what recording areal density the

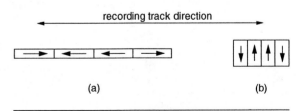

recording track direction

(a)   (b)

FIGURE 25.1: Two magnetic recording methods: (a) longitudinal recording and (b) perpendicular recording.

superparamagnetic limit would occur. It is governed by many complex interacting factors, including the materials used for the recording medium and the write head; the design of the write head; the parameters used during the write process, such as flying height and write current; etc. Back in the 1970s, it was conjectured that the limit would be reached at around 25 Mbits/in^2. Research and innovations over the years have been able to continually push this predicted limit out by orders of magnitude. The use of higher coercivity recording material has been one of the key factors. Today's disk drives are operating close to 100 Gbits/in^2. However, there seems to be a consensus that longitudinal recording will be hitting its limit in the near foreseeable future.

A different recording technology holds promise to pack magnetic recording bits much closer without encountering thermal instability, thus extending the superparamagnetic limit further out. This technology is *perpendicular recording*[1] [Hoagland 2003; Iwasaki 1980, 1984, 2002; Suzuki & Iwasaki 1982, Honda et al. 2002]. As the name implies, in perpendicular recording, magnetization is normal to the plane of the recording medium. The magnetic domains are standing up along the path of the track, as shown in Figure 25.1(b). This is the result of the recording medium being fabricated to have an easy axis perpendicular to the disk surface so that it is natural for the recorded bits to assume a vertical position. From a simplistic point of view, it is easy to see why, at high density, perpendicular recording is more stable. With longitudinal recording, at the transition point where magnetization polarity reverses, two like poles are facing each other. The magnetic repelling action between the two domains naturally tends to try to flip each other. On the other hand, with perpendicular recording, opposite poles which attract each other are next to each other on the two sides of a transition.

25.1.1 Write Process, Write Head, and Media

Although the implementation details of perpendicular recording present a different set of challenges from those of longitudinal recording, conceptually, perpendicular recording is not all that different from longitudinal recording; just that magnetization is rotated by 90°. Thus, not surprisingly, the write processes of the two recording methods are quite similar. In fact, the discussion in Chapter 17, Section 17.1.4, on the principle of writing in longitudinal recording is applicable to perpendicular recording if the externally applied magnetization field in the plane of the magnetic medium is replaced by one that is normal to the plane of the magnetic medium. The series of drawings in Chapter 17, Figure 17.6, would then becomes as illustrated in Figure 25.2.

It is theoretically possible to use the ring head described in Chapter 17, Section 17.2.3, to do the writing in perpendicular recording. The vertical component of the trailing edge of its write bubble would provide the magnetic flux to align the grains of the medium whose easy axis is perpendicularly oriented. The current state of the technology is to use a modification of the ring head, called the *single pole head*.[2]

The principle of the single pole head is the same as that of the ring head. However, its geometry, as illustrated in Figure 25.3, is modified to produce a more vertical magnetic field for use in perpendicular recording. To achieve a vertically oriented magnetic flux emanating from the write pole tip and propagating into the magnetic medium, the gap between the two poles of the head is substantially widened from that of the ring head. This gap is considerably larger than the head's flying height. Furthermore, in order to maintain this perpendicular orientation all the way through the medium, the magnetic flux lines should not turn in its return path back to the return pole until it has exited

---

[1] The concept of perpendicular recording is not new. Some people consider that the first magnetic recording was demonstrated over a century ago by Danish scientist Valdermar Poulsen when he recorded sound on a steel wire using a transverse magnetic field as perpendicular recording. However, when RAMAC was designed 50 years ago, longitudinal recording was the logical choice. At low recording density, with low coercivity material and thick medium, longitudinal recording is much more stable. In the 1970s, the potentials of perpendicular recording gained recognition as a result of the research work of Shunichi Iwasaki.

[2] Somewhat of a misnomer, since the head actually still has two poles, but the write action is mainly provided by the vertical trailing pole.

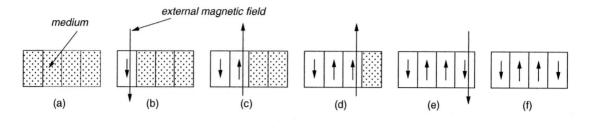

FIGURE 25.2: Write process example for perpendicular recording. (a) Medium before writing. Write magnetic field applied to (b) first compartment, (c) second compartment, (d) third compartment, and (e) fourth compartment. (f) Magnetic pattern in medium after writing.

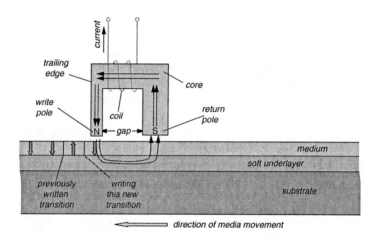

FIGURE 25.3: A single pole head in conjunction with a soft underlayer used in perpendicular recording. How the head is used for writing transitions is also illustrated.

the medium. This is facilitated by adding a relatively thick layer of magnetically soft material underneath the recording medium. This *soft underlayer* (SUL), made of high-permeability material such as CoFeB alloys, allows the flux of the write head to flow freely between the two poles. Therefore, the SUL is, in reality, a part of the head structure, even though physically it is located in the disk platter. The SUL material, thickness, and separation from the write pole must be an integral part of the design of a single pole head for perpendicular recording. An advantageous effect of the SUL is that it acts like a mirror and produces a reflected image of the head on the other side of the medium/SUL interface. This reflection results in doubling the recording field going through the medium.

In addition to having an easy axis normal to the plane of the disk, perpendicular media are thicker than longitudinal media. Materials with a higher coercivity are also used, such as CoPtCr-oxide. This is possible because for the same amount of current, the single pole head in conjunction with the SUL can deliver roughly twice as strong a magnetic field for recording as a ring head. High coercivity improves thermal stability. It is also amenable to having sharper transitions being written, thus supporting higher linear density. Finally, the magnetically soft nature of the SUL material can have a destabilizing effect on the recorded medium. Therefore, a very thin *exchange break layer* (EBL) is placed between the recording layer and the SUL to reduce the magnetic interactions between them.

25.1.2 Read Process and Read Head

Similar to longitudinal recording, perpendicular recording also uses a transition to represent a 1 and the absence of transition to represent a 0. The read process is, therefore, one of detecting transitions. MR, or GMR, heads are also used in perpendicular recording. As discussed in Chapter 17, Section 17.2.3, MR heads are fabricated with an easy axis such that it senses external magnetic field in the vertical direction. With longitudinal recording, the maximum vertical magnetic flux emanating from the medium is at a transition, as shown in Figure 25.4(a). This results in pulses at the transitions in the read-back

signal of the MR head. On the other hand, in the case of perpendicular recording, vertical magnetic flux occurs in between transitions. Thus, the read-back signal from the MR head approximately looks like a square wave, as illustrated in Figure 25.4(b). However, by taking the derivative of this signal, a pulse signal resembling that of the longitudinal recording read-back signal is obtained. Thus, by adding a signal differentiator circuit in the read channel, the rest of the signal detection circuitry can be adapted from longitudinal recording.

25.2 Patterned Media

Perpendicular recording can push the superparamagnetic limit out, perhaps to about 500 Gbits/in^2. To attain higher areal density beyond that, more radical technologies are being explored. One front runner is patterned media [Hughes 2002].

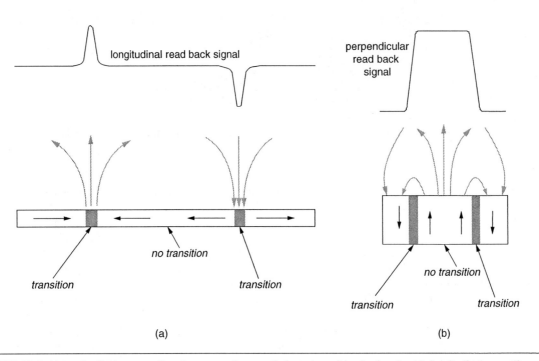

FIGURE 25.4: Magnetic fields emanating from recording medium and read-back signals: (a) longitudinal recording and (b) perpendicular recording.

25.2.1 Fully Patterned Media

In patterned media, each recording domain or bit is physically separated from each other so that the magnetic interaction between neighboring bits can be limited, thus improving thermal stability. The idea is simple: carve a ditch around each square domain to isolate it, as illustrated in Figure 25.5. By creating individual islands of magnetic domains, the bit size will be reduced to just 1 magnetic grain, much smaller than that of traditional continuous recording which typically consists of 100 magnetic grains per bit, and yet still be thermally stable. To turn this idea into practical reality, there are three significant challenges to overcome.

The first challenge is how to make the disk platters and make them cheaply. To create the island features on the surface of a disk, some kind of lithography will likely be used. The feature size for areal densities greater than that of current technology is smaller than what optical lithography, which is what is used for making integrated circuits in the electronics industry, is capable of delivering. For instance, at an areal density of 1 Tbit/in^2, the center-to-center spacing between islands would be 27 nm. Thus, electron beam (e-beam) or ion beam lithography will likely need to be used. A layer of resist material on a stamper substrate will be exposed to an e-beam or ion beam in accordance to the desired pattern. After developing the exposed resist layer and then etching, a stamper having the mirror image of the desired pat-terned media features will be created. The stamper, or mold, can then be used in a process known as nano-imprint lithography (NIL) to mass produce disk platters having the final physical features. This process involves pressing the stamper on a thin layer of soft polymer resist material on the surface of the disk substrate and, at the same time, curing it with ultraviolet light. Finding the right material that will adhere to the disk substrate and yet separate cleanly from the stamper is key to this process. As a final step, magnetic recording material will be deposited on top. Magnetic material, in addition to being deposited on the top of the islands, will unavoidably also end up in the ditches surrounding the islands, but that will have a negligible effect in the recording process since it is further away from the head.

The other two challenges are related to the process of writing and reading those magnetic islands of the patterned media. One of them is tracking. In current conventional recording, tpi is several times smaller than bpi, as discussed in Chapter 19, Section 19.3. In other words, the bits are wider than they are long. With patterned media, the ideal case is to have square bits so as to maximize areal density. This means that tpi will increase much more than bpi if conventional recording is transitioned to patterned media recording. To handle the much narrower tracks, the mechanical servo system will have to be substantially improved over today's in order keep the head on track for both reading and writing.

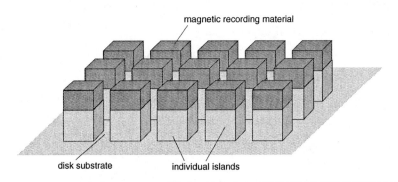

FIGURE 25.5: A conceptual illustration of patterned media recording. Each island, topped with magnetic recording material, is a recordable bit. Each row represents part of a track.

In today's conventional recording, the position of a bit is not predefined. Rather, it is defined by the write head during the write process. Thus, the location of a bit when it is written may not be precisely the same every time. Some small amount of deviation is likely. This is possible because the magnetic recording material is continuous throughout the entire disk surface. Deviations are tolerated and adjusted by the read process as the clocking information as well as the data are written by the same write head. However, with patterned media, the position of a bit is predefined on the disk. To produce a proper magnetic recording, the writing by the head will have to be more precise than conventional recording so that it is synchronized to the individual islands.

While either longitudinal or perpendicular recording can be used in patterned media recording, it is most likely that perpendicular recording will be employed. At extremely high areal densities, perpendicular recording should have better thermal stability.

25.2.2 Discrete Track Media

A halfway step from today's continuous recording to patterned media recording is *discrete track media* recording. Instead of fully patterning every individual recording bit on the media, only individual tracks are patterned. Since only a groove is used to separate tracks from each other, as illustrated in Figure 25.6, instead of ditches around each individual bit, discrete track media should be easier to manufacture, at least during the infancy stage of learning how to pattern disk media. Since recording along each track is still continuous, discrete track recording does not have to solve the write synchronization problem of patterned media.

While discrete track media does not have all the benefits of fully patterned media, the magnetical separation of adjacent tracks provides the following advantages.

- Reduced interference from neighboring tracks will improve signal-to-media noise ratio.
- A stronger write field can be used for writing, resulting in a stronger read-back

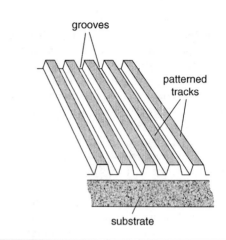

FIGURE 25.6: Discrete track patterned disk. Cross-section view.

signal, thus improving signal-to-electronic noise ratio.

- Write head tolerance can be more relaxed, improving manufacturing yield and efficiency.
- Similar to patterned media, head position servo information can be placed on the media at the time of manufacture of the discrete track media. This would save having to do servo write during the final assembly of the disk drive.

25.3 Thermally Assisted Recording

Another front runner in advanced technologies being researched to further push back the superparamagnetic limit is *thermally assisted recording*, also referred to as *heat-assisted magnetic recording* (HAMR). Magnetic material with higher coercivity is more thermally stable, since more energy is required to reverse its magnetic polarity. Thus, it is desirable to use materials with as high a coercivity as possible for increasing areal density without the problem of thermal instability. However, by its very nature, a stronger magnetic field is required to perform magnetic recording on such materials, perhaps beyond what the write head can deliver. Cranking up the write current being applied to a write head to induce a stronger magnetic field for writing may generate too much heat and damage the head.

The basic idea of thermally assisted recording is based on the principle that coercivity of a magnetic material is temperature-dependent; it goes down as the temperature rises. For some materials, the dependency is small within any practical temperature range. For others, there is a significant decrease in coercivity when the temperature is increased by a few hundred degrees Celsius. In thermally assisted recording, the magnetic recording media will be made of such materials. The temperature of the bit to be written is rapidly raised just before the head is ready to write it. After the bit has been written, it is immediately cooled down so that its coercivity reverts back to its original high value. The resulting recording will then have the good thermal stability advantage of a high-coercivity medium which normally cannot be written with a conventional recording technology.

While the concept is simple, there are clearly several challenges that must be solved.

Material The right material to be used in thermally assisted recording needs to be found. The ideal material should have a coercivity versus temperature dependency that looks

something like that shown in Figure 25.7. First, it should have a rather sharp change in coercivity over a small range of temperature change. Second, this sharp change must occur at a temperature above the normal operating temperature of the drive and yet not be too high so that it can be reached fairly quickly and with practical means. Thus, a range between 100 and 200°C is a good target. Third, its cool temperature coercivity should be high, e.g., 6 KOe, while its hot temperature coercivity should be low, e.g., 1 KOe.

Heating process The heating process for the bit to be written has to be very precise and well controlled. Ideally, only the bit being written should be heated up, and as soon as it has been written, it should be cooled down very rapidly. At a data rate of 100 MB/s, or 1 Gbit/s, a bit is written in 1 ns. Thus, the heating and cooling cycle is required to have a response time in that order of magnitude. A laser light will likely be used to provide the heat source. For this reason, thermally assisted recording is also known as optically assisted recording. In order not to heat up neighboring bits, the spot size of the laser needs to be kept small. At an areal density of 1 Tbit/in^2, for instance, the diameter should not be larger than 27 nm.

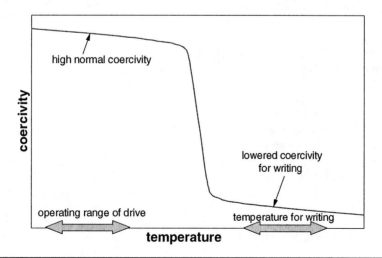

FIGURE 25.7: Coercivity versus temperature characteristic of ideal material for thermally assisted recording.

Recording head A new type of head with an integrated laser and small spot optics will have to be designed. Needless to say, the head-disk interface (HDI) of such new head structures will also have to be studied. The manufacturing process will have to be engineered.

Thermally assisted recording, when ready to move out of laboratories and be deployed in actual disk drive products, will likely be used in conjunction with patterned media. The two techniques together may possibly be able to push the superparamagnetic limit out to beyond tens of terabits per square inch.

25.4 Dual Stage Actuator

The function of the servo system, as discussed in Chapter 18, Section 18.5, is to position the drive's actuator accurately over the track being accessed. As track density increases, the tolerance of the servo system becomes tighter and tighter. This creates two challenges for the traditional actuator. First, there is a limit to how much positioning accuracy can be attained by using the VCM to move the relatively massive comb actuator. Second, in order to maintain the head centered over the track throughout a data access, the servo system needs to monitor the position error signal that gets generated at every servo burst and responds to it by moving the actuator using the VCM. However, the frequency with which adjustments can be made is limited by the mechanical resonance of the VCM actuator. This performance capability of a servo is quantified as the *servo bandwidth*. A tight tolerance means an actuator with high servo bandwidth will be required. For these reasons, current actuator technology will be severely challenged to meet future tpi requirements, such as those introduced by perpendicular recording and patterned media.

One promising approach for increasing the servo bandwidth is the use of a *dual stage actuator* [Semba et al. 1999, Huang et al. 2002, White et al. 2004]. In fact, this technology is starting to appear in some disk drive products being shipped today. As the name implies, the dual stage actuator consists of components that allow positioning to be achieved in two stages. This concept was conceived more than 10 years ago. In the first stage, the traditional VCM driven actuator is used to make a large distance coarse seek from one location of the disk to another, moving the entire E-block comb actuator and all the heads that it carries in the process. In the second stage, a new element in the system will perform the fine positioning of the head. This second stage actuator moves only one of the heads, instead of the entire comb actuator holding all the heads.

Researchers have been looking into three distinctly different approaches and configurations for the second stage actuator:

Moving suspension The first method is to locate the secondary actuator at the junction where the root of the suspension beam meets the end of the actuator arm and swing the whole suspension. By moving the suspension, the slider and the head are moved. Such actuators are typically made using a PZT (piezoelectric transducer).

Moving slider The second method is to insert the secondary actuator in between the suspension and the slider. The slider is moved by the secondary actuator, while the suspension is stationary.

Moving head The third method is to integrate the secondary actuator to the slider and mount the read/write head directly to it. Only the head gets moved.

The locations of these three types of secondary actuators are shown in Figure 25.8. The first method still requires moving a relatively flexible suspension beam, and the maximum servo bandwidth gain will be limited by its resonant modes. The third method has the potential to produce the highest bandwidth gain. However, fabricating such an actuator and integrating it with the magnetic head will be difficult. The second method seems to be the best compromise of offering good bandwidth gain and yet be reasonably

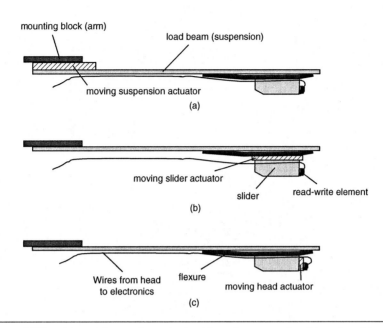

mounting block (arm)
load beam (suspension)
moving suspension actuator
(a)

moving slider actuator
slider
read-write element
(b)

Wires from head
to electronics
flexure
moving head actuator
(c)

FIGURE 25.8: Locations of different types of secondary actuator: (a) moving suspension, (b) moving slider, and (c) moving head.

implementable. Thus, it is currently the preferred approach.

With a dual stage actuator, the servo control circuit shown in Chapter 17, Figure 17.34, needs to be modified. First, a driver circuit needs to be added for the secondary actuator. Second, the servo control logic now needs to coordinate the movements of the primary and secondary actuators. The VCM controls the low-frequency, large-stroke motion, and the secondary actuator controls the high-frequency, small-amplitude motion. The challenge is in handling the mid-frequency hand-off region in a manner such that the two actuators do not interfere destructively. It is important that the secondary actuator does not waste its limited stroke opposing the VCM.

25.4.1 Microactuators

The secondary actuator of the moving slider method is referred to as a *microactuator*. Its small dimension makes it amenable to being fabricated using MEMS (micro-electro-mechanical system) technology. Within the microactuator approach, three distinct technologies are being pursued by various drive vendors and component manufacturers. The differences arise from how electrical power is converted into mechanical power to move the slider.

PZT based With this technology, a U-shaped microactuator with PZTs on either side of its prongs is used to hold and move the slider, as shown in Figure 25.9. When voltage is applied, one of the PZTs expands, while the other contracts as a result of the reverse piezoelectric effect. This causes the prongs to bend, thus moving the slider cradled between them. Reverse the polarity of the voltage applied, and the prongs will bend in the opposite way.

Electromagnetic based Conceptually, this approach is basically to create a miniaturized VCM, possibly fabricated using MEMS technology. Electromagnetic force is generated to move the attached slider by passing current through a coil in the presence of a permanent magnet,

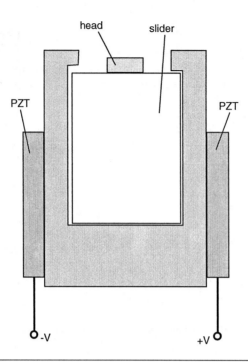

FIGURE 25.9: Conceptual illustration of a PZT-based microactuator, bottom view.

both of which are built in the microactuator. When designing this type of microactuator, care must be taken to ensure that no magnetic field leaks out to interfere with either the read or the write process of the head.

Electrostatic based This type of microactuator is moved using electrostatic force. While varying designs are possible, in the common comb-drive design, teeth on the side of a movable rotor are arranged facing an interlacing set of opposing teeth on a fixed stator. This is illustrated in Figure 25.10(a). With the rotor grounded, and applying a voltage to one of the two stators, the electrostatic attraction between the opposing teeth creates the force for moving the rotor. The slider is thus moved as it is mounted on the rotor. The amount of physical motion is extremely small; the resulting movement of the head is on the order of a few microns.

Apply voltage to the other stator, and the rotor will move in the opposite direction. Rotational motion results if the rotor is suspended in the center. Linear motion results if the rotor is suspended at its corners. Figures 25.10(b) and (c) show a prototype for an electrostatic microactuator.

Microactuators are estimated to have about three to five times the servo bandwidth of traditional single stage actuators. Thus, the dual stage actuator approach should be able to handle several times higher tpi than traditional VCM actuators alone.

25.5 Adaptive Formatting

As areal density goes higher and higher, the head dimension gets smaller and smaller. A tiny variation in manufacturing a head's geometry can result in an

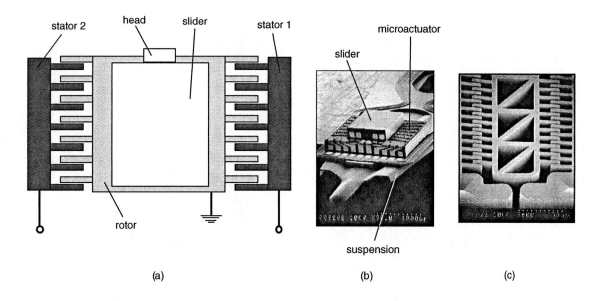

FIGURE 25.10: Electrostatic-based microactuator: (a) conceptual illustration of comb-drive design; (b) photo of a prototype; and (c) close-up view of prototype. (Photos from Hitachi-GST.)

observable variance in performance from the norm. Other parameters such as track width can also be affected. Growth in areal density becomes more and more limited by such variation in head performance and component tolerance. The traditional method for handling heads having different profiles coming off manufacturing lines is to sort the heads and HGAs based on soft error rate performance and track width. Different heads are then allocated to disk drive products with different capacity design points. The logistics plan of using such an approach is complex, making production output difficult to plan and predict.

A technique, invented several years ago, is now starting to become more widely adopted. With this method, heads of different performance characteristics are allowed to co-exist within the same disk drive. Each head operates at the bpi that it is capable of handling, i.e., producing a signal-to-noise ratio such that the net soft error rate falls within the design requirement. Thus, a higher performing head will operate at a higher bpi, and a lower performing head will operate at

a lower bpi. The number of sectors per track, and hence data rate, varies as a result, depending on the head.

In one implementation of this technique, the tpi of all the heads remains the same. This approach is usually adopted by drives using the cylinder mode formatting. Since the number of tracks per surface is constant, the capacity of each disk surface is then dependent on the head. However, all drives need to have the same total capacity. That means a drive with some lower performing heads must be balanced by also having some higher performing heads. A drive with all lower performing heads will not be able to deliver the needed total capacity. Thus, while this approach for adaptive formatting provides a certain degree of leeway in manufacturing, it does not offer 100% flexibility.

In another implementation, the tpi varies along with the bpi from head to head. This technique can only be applied with the banded serpentine formatting, discussed in Chapter 18, Section 18.3.3, and illustrated in Figure 18.5(b). A higher performing head has a wider track width, which is why it gets a stronger signal. Conversely, the track width for a lower performing head is narrower. Thus, higher bpi is coupled with lower tpi, and vice-versa. The product of the two is roughly constant, resulting in the same areal density. The number of tracks within each serpentine band of each surface will depend on the head. The same is true for the number of sectors per track. However, the total number of sectors within a band will be constant, or roughly constant, from surface to surface. For example, one surface may have 90 tracks in one band, with each track holding 1000 sectors. Another surface may have 100 tracks in that same band, but each track only holds 900 sectors. Yet, both surfaces have 90,000 sectors per band. This approach is more flexible, since it can have any mix of heads within the same drive, even all lower performing heads, and still be able to deliver the same total drive capacity.

Hence, adaptive formatting improves manufacturing efficiency. However, the user needs to realize that there may be variance in performance, especially data rate, from head to head and also from drive to drive.

25.6 Hybrid Disk Drive

In 2005, Microsoft submitted to the T13 technical committee for inclusion in the next ATA-8 standard a proposal for a new class of disk drives which incorporate a non-volatile cache inside the drive. To be more precise, the proposal was for a new set of commands for interfacing with such devices. This gives the host machine some control over how the non-volatile cache in the drive is to be used and managed. This new type of storage device is a hybrid disk drive because it will contain two different types of non-volatile memory: the magnetic media and the non-volatile cache.

25.6.1 Benefits

The expected benefits of a disk drive with a non-volatile cache are:

1. **Improved power management** When a drive has been spun down to save power during a period of inactivity, any new write command received from the host can be written to the non-volatile cache without

having to spin up the drive. Such writes are accumulated either until the non-volatile cache is full or when the drive needs to be spun up for other reasons, such as to do a cache-miss read. Since spinning up the drive consumes a considerable amount of power, this is especially beneficial in a mobile system which runs on battery power.

2. **Improved drive reliability** Spinning up and down the drive can add to its wear and tear. By reducing the number of such cycles, the reliability of the drive can be improved. Also, the shock resistance of a drive is much higher when it is spun down and its heads are safely unloaded. In reducing the amount of time the drive is spinning, its exposure to shock damage is reduced.

3. **Faster boot and application loading times** By saving the boot image and the state of the system into the non-volatile cache when a machine is either shut down or put into hibernation, the next machine startup can load from the non-volatile cache without having to wait for the drive to be fully spun up and ready to read, which can take seconds. Similarly, applications that are stored in the nonvolatile memory can be loaded into the system more quickly.

25.6.2 Architecture

The new proposal does not specify the architecture for the new hybrid disk drive, so different designs and implementations are possible. Neither does the proposal specify what technology is to be used for the non-volatile cache. At this point in time, flash memory is the most likely candidate, in part due to its relatively low cost. In the future, other technologies such as MagRAM or MEMS memory [Carley et al. 2000, Albrecht et al. 2004] may be better choices.

The high-level architecture for a flash-based hybrid *Hard Disk Drive* (HDD) will likely look something like that shown in Figure 25.11. The flash memory will be placed on the internal data bus alongside the DRAM buffer/cache. There are several shortcomings with flash memory that the designer needs to be aware of and take into consideration while architecting a hybrid drive.

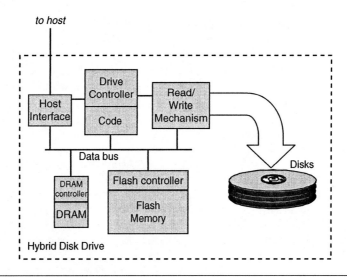

to host

Host Interface

Drive Controller

Code

Read/ Write Mechanism

Data bus

DRAM controller

DRAM

Flash controller

Flash Memory

Disks

Hybrid Disk Drive

FIGURE 25.11: High-level architecture of a hybrid disk drive.

1. **Page write** Writing to flash memory generally has to be done in pages. The page size depends on the flash technology used and the manufacturer.

2. **Erase before write** A block, consisting of multiple pages, must first be erased before it can be written. Erasure time is very slow.

3. **Limited write cycles** Current flash technology has a limited number of cycles that each bit can be written, typically around 100,000 times. There are two general approaches for handling this limit. The first one is wear-monitoring, in which the number of write cycles for each block of flash memory is monitored. A block that has reached its limit will be permanently mapped out and made unavailable for further use. A second approach is wear-leveling, in which all the blocks in the flash memory are managed such that they all get used evenly. This usually means using the flash memory in a circular fashion.

4. **Low data rate** Flash write data rate is about an order of magnitude lower than that of a magnetic disk, read data rate is about one half, and erasure takes milliseconds. Thus,

performance is lower compared to disk access when transferring a large amount of sequential data.

25.6.3 Proposed Interface

The non-volatile memory is used as a cache to the drive, rather than an extension to the drive's address space. The main salient feature of the proposed interface is the definition of a *non-volatile cache pinned set*. The host system can specify to the hybrid drive a set of LBAs that are to be pinned in the cache. An "Add LBAs to pinned set" command is used to add a new range of LBAs to the set, and a companion "Remove LBAs from pinned set" command is to unpin a range of LBAs. Spaces left over in the non-volatile memory are free to be used by the drive for write caching or other internal uses.

An interesting feature of the "Add LBAs to pinned set" command is the "Populate Immediate" flag. If this flag is set in the command, the drive is to prefetch the content of the LBA range from the disk. This usage is envisioned for the pinned set to be used for preloading boot files into the non-volatile cache in preparation for a shutdown and the next reboot. If the flag is not set, then the drive will take no action to fetch data from the disk into those locations. Rather, it is anticipated that the host will send down write data to those LBAs. An example of this usage model is the writing of the hibernation file in preparation for the host system going into hibernation. After either a cold reboot or a wakeup from hibernation, the previously pinned LBAs can be unpinned and freed up for write caching use.

The proposed interface for nonvolatile cache can be found in the draft document "AT Attachment 8—ATA/, ATAPI Command Set (ATA8-ACS)" of the T13 Standard Committee (see www.T13.org). It is expected that the proposal will officially be adopted as part of ATA standard by the end of 2007. Microsoft's new Vista operating system supports hybrid HDDs, although at this time no hybrid HDDs are generally available from any disk manufacturer for evaluation yet.

25.7 Object-Based Storage

A disk drive, like all other digital storage devices, understands that it is being asked to store and retrieve bits of 0's and 1's. A disk drive is not cognizant of the meaning of the data that it is handling. With today's block interface, a drive is asked to read or write blocks of data, with each block being some multiple of its physical sector size. It does not know, or care, whether the block is part of a directory, part of a file, or a complete file. While this paradigm makes the storage device easier to implement and keeps the interface simple, from a system point of view it is not the most efficient.

A more efficient disk architecture would be for the disk drive itself to be cognizant of the space allocation aspect of the file system being used to manage its storage space. With such knowledge, it can perform lookahead prefetch much more intelligently and accurately. This would improve the effectiveness of the disk drive's cache. Furthermore, a user can access his data in the disk more directly without entailing all the file system directory lookup and update traffic going

back and forth between the host and the drive. These and some other benefits can be derived from the proposed *object-based storage device* (OSD[3]) architecture [Mesnier et al. 2003].

In 1999, the OSD Technical Working Group was formed to create a self-managed, heterogeneous, shared storage architecture by moving low-level file storage functions into the storage device itself. The storage device would be accessed using a new object-based standard interface instead of the traditional block-based interfaces of SCSI or ATA. Building on work originating from the Network Attached Storage Devices project of the National Storage Industry Consortium (NSIC) and the Network Attached Secure Disk project at Carnegie Mellon University, the group developed requirements, standard definitions, and prototype demonstrations for OSD storage subsystems. The working group was later adopted by the Storage Networking Industry Association (SNIA), and collaboration with the ANSI T10 technical committee was established in 2000. Since mid-2004, OSD has been a standard extension to SCSI approved by T10.

Because it is defined as a new command set, it can be used on standard SCSI physical interfaces. This also means OSD architecture can be implemented either natively in a disk drive or in some higher level storage controller. So far, OSD exists mostly on paper only. For OSD to be generally adopted and embraced by the storage industry, it will require a massive amount of operating system changes, particularly file systems and databases. New storage devices with the OSD interface implemented will be needed too, naturally. Major software houses are not likely to produce OSD-enabled software until OSD hardware is generally available, while major storage vendors are not likely to manufacture such devices until software is available to use them. Some catalytic event is likely to be needed for OSD to break out of this catch-22 mode.

25.7.1 Object Storage Main Concept

The main idea of OSD is fairly simple. Each piece of user data, e.g., a file or a database record, and its

---

[3]Originally, OBSD.

associated metadata (information describing the data, such as its size) are handled together as one single object. Each object possesses a set of user accessible attributes. An object, instead of a logical block, is the unit of data access between a host and an OSD. A user is allowed to access any number of bytes at any offset within an object. With the traditional block-based interface, a user accesses his data basically using either a "read block" or a "write block" command. In OSD, a user accesses his data using a "read object" or a "write object" command. Additionally, a user directly issues "create object" and "delete object" commands to an OSD. There are also commands available for the user to get and to set the attributes of an object.

The OSD standard allows for a hierarchy of object types. At the top is the root object, kind of analogous to the root directory. There is only one root object per device, and it defines the characteristics of the device. Each root object can hold up to 2^{64} partition objects, kind of analogous to file folders. Each partition object can have its own security and space management characteristics which apply to all objects contained within it. Finally, a partition object can cover up to 2^{64} user objects. Every object has a set of associated attributes, such as object size and timestamp of last access, contained in attribute pages as part of the object.

Data access using an object-based interface is made possible by moving the low-level storage management component of the file system out of the host and into the storage device. As shown in Figure 25.12(a), a file system logically consists of two parts: a component that deals with applications by providing a central point for handling all user requests and a

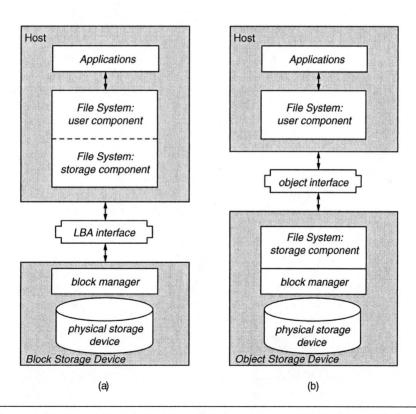

FIGURE 25.12: Storage architectures: (a) today's block-based interface storage and (b) object-based interface storage.

component that takes care of mapping user files to available physical storage space. By migrating the space management and data access functionalities of file management out of the host and into the storage in OSD architecture, the storage can assume the responsibility of mapping user files to its storage space and, in principle, do a much better job at it.

25.7.2 Object Storage Benefits

Theoretically, OSD can provide some significant benefits over today's block-based storage architecture. It also opens the door for more sophisticated functionalities to be added to disk drives as well as storage subsystems.

Performance

The opportunities for improving the performance of a disk drive are much widened when it is aware of the content of the data it is storing. As discussed in Chapter 22, a drive's cache performs lookahead prefetching as a strategy to improve its overall hit ratio. With the current disk drive architecture and interface, lookahead prefetch is no more than a matter of statistics. Without knowing the relationship among data blocks, it can only assume that the next physical block has a high probability statistically of somehow being related to the current block and, therefore, a high probability of being accessed in the near future. This is the basis of spatial locality of access. If it happens that the current block is the end of some user file and the next physical block is the start of another file belonging to a different user, this fact would not be known to the disk drive. The prefetching done would then be a fruitless effort. To allow for the possibility of this scenario, the common strategy used by most disk drives is to abort any prefetching as soon as a new command arrives so as not to delay its execution. However, following such a strategy creates another problem. What if the next physical block, indeed, logically follows the current block and will soon be requested? Accessing that block will then entail a costly mechanical overhead of seek and latency if its prefetch is preempted. Having

the knowledge of the relationship among data blocks as proposed in OSD will solve this dilemma.

As an OSD-enabled disk drive is in charge of allocating storage space to files and databases, it can ensure that such objects are laid down sequentially in the disk. Furthermore, as the relationship of files is also known, the drive can place related files, such as those belonging to the same partition object, close to each other to improve their spatial locality. Data reorganization, as discussed in Chapter 21, Section 21.3, will take on a different form and be more effective. For instance, a new type of ALIS will keep track of hot sequences of file accesses instead of block accesses.

Finally, when a user wants to access a piece of data, the service of the file system manager in the operating system is invoked. A file system needs to look up its directory to find out where this file resides in the disk and where this piece of data is within the file. After the file has been accessed, a record of its access is saved to the directory. As the directory is stored in the disk, there is file system traffic between the host and the disk drive before and after the user's data access for traditional host-based file systems. Such traffic on the I/O bus is simply an overhead cost for a user accessing his data. When the data access portion of a file system is instead located in the disk drive itself, as in OSD, then such directory traffic can be eliminated.

Sector Size

As discussed in Chapter 18, Section 18.1.3, the standard 512-byte sector size in use by all disk drives today is becoming more and more inefficient as stronger ECC is required to deal with ever-increasing areal density. The industry is currently going through a difficult transition to a 4K-byte sector size. Such coordinated transition is necessary because the sector size is a disk drive parameter exposed to the host and its operating system. A change in the definition of the sector size will invariably have a wide ranging impact on a lot of software. If an OSD architecture is used for disk drives, the underlying sector size becomes hidden from the users. As the OSD disk drive controls the mapping from objects to its internal storage space, it is free to use any block size it sees fit. In fact, it can even go back to using variable-size blocks if that is more efficient than fixed-size sectors. This transparency and freedom in choosing the optimal block size to support the technologies in use by a disk drive will be of great benefit to drive manufacturers.

Security

The OSD-enabled device will be able to provide much stronger security of users' data than traditional block-based devices. To access an object, the requester has to supply a "capability" (a sort of security token) as part of the command. The device will validate the correctness of the capability before servicing the command. Thus, a fine-grained data security is provided on a per-object and per-access basis. This is useful in preventing both accidental access by unintentional requests such as from a misconfigured machine and malicious access by unauthorized requests from hackers.

Sharing

The fine-grained security capability of OSD allows non-trusted host machines to be part of the same storage network sharing the same devices. Also, because many of the system-specific storage management functions are moved down to the device, the problem of cross-platform data sharing between heterogeneous systems is simplified.

Scalability

By consolidating the handling of metadata associated with a user's data and pushing that down to the storage device, the processing requirements and overhead of a server are reduced. This frees up the resources of a server to handle a greater number of devices than with a traditional block-based interface. Mixing heterogeneous devices within the same server also becomes easier.

Automation of Storage Management

As the storage device holds information related to the attributes of the data that it is storing, it has the potential to more actively participate in and contribute to the automation of storage management. For instance, an object attribute may specify some data-management policy such as backup frequency, in which case an OSD subsystem can autonomously deliver the object to a backup facility in accordance to the specification, without requiring any operator action. Other issues currently being invested by the OSD Technical Working Group include information lifecycle management (ILM) and quality-of-service (QoS) agreements between OSD initiators (hosts) and targets (disk drives and storage subsystems).

CHAPTER 26

Case Study

Some of the topics discussed in Part III of this book are reviewed in this chapter by means of a case study. The disk drive selected for this case study is the Hitachi Global Storage Technologies Deskstar 7K500. At the time of the writing of this book, this drive was state of the art with an industry leading capacity of 500 GB. Contrasted to the first disk drive IBM RAMAC 350 which had a capacity of 5 MB, this is an increase of 100,000 fold; all that in a package which is smaller by roughly the same order of magnitude. It is a 3.5" form factor drive targeted for desktop machines and entry servers for IT applications, as well as for personal video recorder and gaming applications in the consumer electronics market.

26.1 The Mechanical Components

All the components of the Deskstar 7K500 are basically of conventional designs. Figure 26.1 shows the inside of the disk drive with the cover removed. One main design goal of this drive is to maximize its capacity. Thus, it uses 95-mm disk platters, which is the largest available industry standard size that would fit into the 3.5" form factor. High-end server drives with the same form factor use much smaller diameter disks internally to accommodate higher rpm for performance. Five disks are used in this 500-GB drive. A fluid dynamic bearing (FDB) motor is used to spin the disks at 7200 rpm. Dynamic braking is used to quickly stop the motor.

Each disk platter holds 100 GB of user data, which is the same as contemporary drives in the industry. The capacity of one disk surface is 50 GB. Recording density is 76 Gbits/in.^{2}, with a bpi of 720 Kbit/in. and a tpi of 105. Ten GMR heads on femto sliders are each mounted in an HGA and ganged together to form the HSA. A conventional rotary actuator driven by a VCM, with closed-loop embedded servo control, is used for positioning the heads. Two new design features not available in previous-generation products are added:

Rotational Vibration Safeguard (RVS) External vibration, such as from a neighboring drive in a multi-drive configuration, can cause a disk drive head to move off track. This will interrupt any ongoing reading or writing, negatively impacting performance as the head must reposition itself and retry the operation. Sensors are added to the circuit board in the drive to detect such externally caused vibration. Motion detected by these sensors generates electrical signals that are fed to the servo control system which then anticipatorily adjusts the control of the actuator movement to compensate for such vibration.

New arm design to reduce flutter The disk arm is subject to disturbances caused by the high-speed air flow generated by disk rotation, as illustrated in Figure 26.2. The disturbances manifest in the form of arm bending, swaying, and torsion, collectively called *arm flutter*. Arm flutter negatively impacts the stable operation of a disk drive. The 7K500 incorporates a novel (patent pending) arm design which reduces this arm flutter over previous designs. The main idea is to improve the aerodynamics of the arm so as to calm the air flow to reduce its disturbance.

The net result of all the technologies that go into the Deskstar 7K500 is an areal recording density of

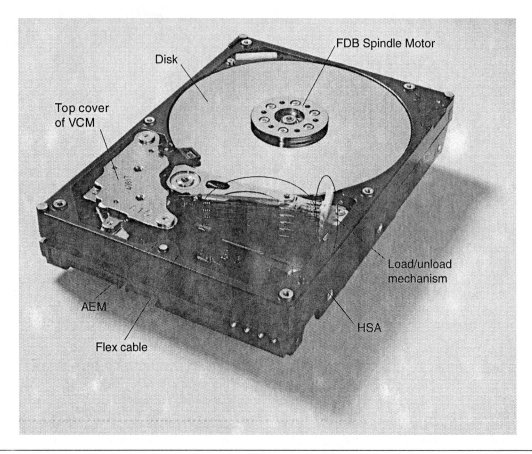

FIGURE 26.1: Hitachi Global Storage Technologies Deskstar(TM) 7K500 with cover removed, showing the internal components.

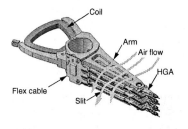

FIGURE 26.2: High speed air flow can cause arm flutter.

76 Gbits/in.^{2}. Its linear density (bpi) is 720 Kbits/in.^{2}, while track density is 105K tpi. Thus, the bit aspect ratio is approximately 7.

26.1.1 Seek Profile

The full stroke (OD to ID, or ID to OD) seek time is specified at 14.7 ms for a read and 15.7 ms for a write. The average seek time is measured as the weighted average of all possible seek combinations, which is the correct method. It is specified at 8.2 ms for a read and 9.2 ms for a write.

The random read whale tail plot data for this drive is taken and shown in Figure 26.3. The seek distance is expressed as the difference between the LBA of a current command and the LBA of its previous command, normalized by the maximum LBA of the drive. As explained in Chapter 23, Section 23.2.4, the bottom outline of the plot is approximately the seek curve. It is approximate because the seek distances

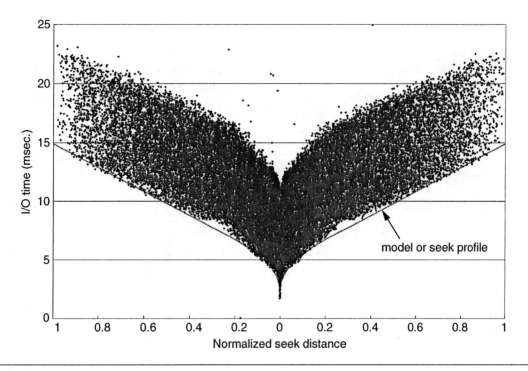

FIGURE 26.3: Whale tail plot for random reads of 7K500 and derived model of the seek profile.

are computed in LBAs, which do not have a fixed relationship to the number of cylinders due to zoned-bit recording.

By selecting a few data points and using trial and error, it is possible to empirically derive a simple mathematical model for the seek profile. Assuming a typical maximum speed control for seeks, as discussed in Chapter 19, Section 19.2.3, the actuator accelerates until it reaches the top speed and then coasts at that speed until it is time to decelerate. The travel time is given by Chapter 19, Equation 19.12. For shorter distance seeks, when the top speed will not be reached, then the actuator accelerates halfway and then decelerates, with the travel time as given by Chapter 19, Equation 19.11. Add the settling time to the travel time and the result is the seek time.

From Figure 26.3, two bottom points are selected where Chapter 19, Equation 19.11, for short seeks probably applies: 6.536 ms at 0.181 and 4.593 ms at

0.050. They can be placed into Chapter 19, Equation 19.11, to form these two equations:

$$seek\ time = 6.536 = settle\ time \\ + 2 \times \sqrt{(0.181/acceleration)} \qquad \textbf{(EQ 26.1)}$$

and

$$seek\ time = 4.593 = settle\ time \\ + 2 \times \sqrt{(0.050/acceleration)} \qquad \textbf{(EQ 26.2)}$$

which can be solved to yield acceleration = 0.043 and settle time = 2.44 ms. Two other bottom points further down the plot are selected where Chapter 19, Equation 19.12, for longer seeks probably applies: 13.803 ms at 0.887 and 10.598 ms at 0.563. They can be put into the following equations:

$$13.803 = settle\ time + T \\ + 0.887/(acceleration \times T) \qquad \textbf{(EQ 26.3)}$$

and

$$10.598 = settle\ time + T$$
$$+ 0.563/(acceleration \times T) \qquad \text{(EQ 26.4)}$$

where T is the time to reach maximum speed. Subtracting Equation 26.4 from Equation 26.3, these two equations can be solved to give (acceleration % T) = 0.098, which results in T = 2.28 ms. From these numbers, it can be determined that the maximum distance covered by bang-bang seek is

$$acceleration \times T^2 = 0.043 \times 2.28^2 = 0.224 \qquad \text{(EQ 26.5)}$$

Thus, a mathematical model of the seek profile is derived from Figure 26.3:

$$seek\ time = \begin{cases} 2.44 \times 2 \cdot \sqrt{d/0.043} & if & d < 0.224 \\ 2.44 + 2.28 + d/0.098 & if & d > 0.224 \end{cases}$$
$$\text{(EQ 26.6)}$$

where d is the normalized LBA seek distance. This model is also graphed in Figure 26.3. The fact that the actual measurement deviates somewhat from the smooth curve of the simple mathematical model is an indication that the operation of the actuator and servo mechanism is more complex than what has been described. Nonetheless, Equation 26.6 should be adequate for most performance modeling studies of this drive, but would not be accurate enough to be used in its actual RPO scheduling. A seek model for writes can be similarly derived using this technique.

As one of the intended applications of the Deskstar 7K500 is DVR (digital video recorder), acoustics is an important feature. One option for reducing the noise generated by the drive is to reduce the speed of actuator movement. This is known as quiet seek, as discussed in Chapter 19, Section 19.2.3. In quiet mode, the average (full stroke) seeks for read and write operations are 19.5 (32.5) and 20.5 (33.5) ms, respectively.

26.2 Electronics

Figure 26.4 is a picture of the electronics card, with a few of its major components annotated. Refer back to Chapter 17, Figure 17.29, for an overview of the logical blocks of a drive's electronics.

HDC, MPU, and Channel The biggest electronic component is a proprietary chip which integrates the hard disk controller, the microprocessor unit, and the read/write channel electronics into a single module. Refer back to Chapter 17, Section 17.3.1, and Figure 17.30 for a more detailed discussion. The MPU executes the firmware of the disk drive. The HDC provides all the hardware for interfacing with the host, the actuator, and the heads and hardware support for caching. For a review of the channel electronics, refer back to Chapter 17, Section 17.3.3.

VCM and Motor Driver This is the control hardware for the acuatator and the spindle motor. These are discussed in detail in Chapter 17, Section 17.3.4, and Figure 17.34.

EEPROM This is where the firmware code of the drive is stored.

Serial Flash This is for downloading patches for the firmware.

DRAM This is mostly used for cache, but a small portion is needed as scratch memory for the MPU.

Resonator It is an oscillator to provide clocking needed for the SATA interface.

Regulator Pass Devices These are for regulating the various voltage levels needed by the drive.

26.3 Data Layout

The Deskstar 7K500 has five disks and ten heads. Conventional cylinder mode formatting is used.[1] According to the spec sheet available for the 7K500, there are 25 distinct recording zones, with the zone boundaries and sectors per track for each zone as shown in Table 26.1. Figure 26.5 is a plot of the sectors per track versus the ID of each zone. It can be seen

---

[1]Its newer sister product, the Deskstar T7K500, uses serpentine formatting.

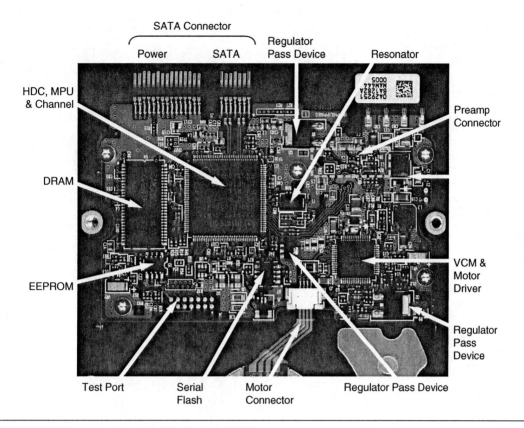

FIGURE 26.4: The electronics card of the Deskstar 7K500.

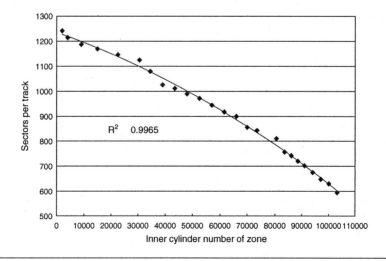

FIGURE 26.5: Plot of sectors per track versus cylinder number at the ID of each zone. The relationship is nonlinear.

that the relationship is not quite linear, but can be fairly well represented by a second order polynomial, with an R-squared value of 0.9965. Thus, bpi is not exactly constant from zone to zone. There are several factors contributing to this:

- The speed of air flow is greater toward the OD of the drive. Greater air speed lifts the flying height of the head higher, which increases the pulse width PW50 and lowers the bpi, as explained in Chapter 17, Section 17.2.8, Equations 17.9 and 17.10.
- The skew angle of the head, inherent in rotary actuators (described in Chapter 17, Section 17.2.5), is worse toward the OD, resulting in lowered signal-to-noise ratio.
- Disk flutter is worse toward the OD.
- Data rate is higher, and thus noise is worse, toward the OD.

The end result of the above factors is that a slightly lower bpi is needed toward the OD in order to achieve a roughly equal soft error rate across the surface of the disk.

The 7K500 uses adaptive formatting, discussed in Chapter 25, Section 25.5. Thus, the sectors per track information of Table 26.1 are only nominal. A head may actually be using more or fewer sectors per track than shown. For example, at zone 0, one may find most heads to have the nominal 1242 sectors per track, while some heads have 1260, and others have 1215. All of these numbers can be determined or verified using the technique given in Chapter 23, Section 23.4.1.

26.3.1 Data Rate

The head switch time T_{HS} and the cylinder switch time T_{CS} for the 7K500 are both specified at 1.5 ms. This is indeed verified in a sample drive using the technique of Chapter 23, Section 23.4.1. Applying these numbers in Chapter 18, Equation 18.14, Table 26.1 can be converted into a table of the sustained data rate for each zone, as shown in Table 26.2.

TABLE 26.1   Zone table of Deskstar 7K500

Zone	Start Cyl. No.	End Cyl. No.	Sectors Per Track
0	0	1999	1242
1	2000	3999	1215
2	4000	8999	1188
3	9000	14999	1170
4	15000	22499	1147
5	22500	30499	1125
6	30500	34499	1080
7	34500	38999	1026
8	39000	43499	1012
9	43500	47999	990
10	48000	52499	972
11	52500	56999	945
12	57000	61499	918
13	61500	65999	900
14	66000	69999	855
15	70000	73499	843
16	73500	80499	810
17	80500	83499	756
18	83500	85999	742
19	86000	88499	720
20	88500	90999	702
21	91000	93999	675
22	94000	96999	648
23	97000	99999	630
24	100000	103182	594

The zone boundaries are also converted into starting and ending physical block addresses. The PBAs are only approximately the same as LBAs, as there are spare sectors sprinkled throughout the drive.[2]

---

[2]The actual maximum LBA for 7K500 is 976,773,167.

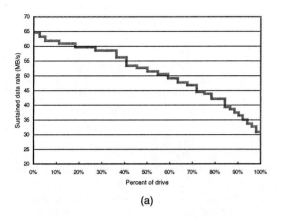 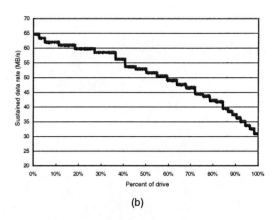

(a)   (b)

FIGURE 26.6: Media data rate for each zone: (a) computed from drive parameters and (b) measurement of an actual sample drive.

Table 26.2 is plotted in Figure 26.6(a), with the PBAs normalized to the maximum capacity of the drive. For verification purposes, the data rate test discussed in Chapter 23, Section 23.2.1, is run on a sample drive and the results are plotted in Figure 26.6(b). It can be seen that the computed data rate for each zone and the zone boundaries match very closely to the actual measurement results.

26.4 Interface

The 7K500 is available in parallel ATA (Model Number HDS725050KLAT80) with an interface data rate of up to 133 MB/s (Ultra DMA Mode 6) and in SATA (Model Number HDS725050KLA360) with a data rate up to 300 MB/s. In both cases, the drive is ATA-7 standard compliant. The SATA drive supports Native Command Queueing. The queued random read performance of this drive is shown in Chapter 23, Figure 23.7.

The 7K500 provides full support of the new *Streaming Command Set,* which has been adopted as part of the ATA-7 standard. Its purpose is for AV (audio-video) applications, where on-time delivery of data to maintain a smooth presentation is more important than delivery of data without errors. A delayed picture frame is much more noticeable to a viewer than a picture frame that has some pixel errors. The main features of the Streaming Command Set are the following:

Error Recovery Procedure Control The standard error recovery procedure when a data error is encountered can be many revolutions long, as explained in Chapter 18, Section 18.9.3. The Streaming Command Set provides controls to set a time limit to stop error recovery. The host AV system, based on its own buffer capacity, can determine how much time can be allotted to each command.

Read and Write Continuous In conjunction with the error recovery control, the new Streaming Read/Write commands support the Read Continuous (RC) or Write Continuous (WC) bit. When used, the drive will complete the command within the specified time limit, doing its best to correct any error condition, but without guarantee. For streaming reads, any uncorrected error is placed in a Read Stream Error Log. Similarly, streaming writes will skip over inaccessible sectors and log the write errors in a Write Stream Error Log.

AV Optimization The new Configure Stream command allows the AV host system to inform

TABLE 26.2 Sustained data rate for each zone

Zone	Start PBA	End PBA	Sustained data rate (MB/s)[a]
0	0	24839999	64.67
1	24840000	49139999	63.26
2	49140000	108539999	61.86
3	108540000	178739999	60.92
4	178740000	264764999	59.72
5	264765000	354764999	58.58
6	354765000	397964999	56.23
7	397965000	444134999	53.42
8	444135000	489674999	52.69
9	489675000	534224999	51.55
10	534225000	577964999	50.61
11	577965000	620489999	49.20
12	620490000	661799999	47.80
13	661800000	702299999	46.86
14	702300000	736499999	44.52
15	736500000	766004999	43.89
16	766005000	822704999	42.17
17	822705000	845384999	39.36
18	845385000	863934999	38.63
19	863935000	881934999	37.49
20	881935000	899484999	36.55
21	899485000	919734999	35.15
22	919735000	939174999	33.74
23	939175000	958074999	32.80
24	958075000	976982019	30.93

[a]Here, MB is defined as 1,000,000 bytes.

the disk drive of how many simultaneous streams will be used and if they are read or write streams. This information allows the drive to optimize its buffer management accordingly.

Handle Stream Error AV applications still have a small amount of metadata such as file system information whose integrity must be guaranteed as any other IT data. The Handle Stream Error (HSE) bit allows an AV host system to do error recovery in multiple steps, interleaved with other streaming data commands between error recovery attempts. When a command is issued with HSE set, the drive will perform error recovery starting at the level of recovery that was reached at the previous try. The command either succeeds or times out. If it times out, the host system, after servicing any time-dependent streaming commands, will retry this HSE command. This continues until the data is correctly recovered.

26.5 Cache

Two DRAM sizes are available for the Deskstar 7K500. The PATA version comes with 8 MB of DRAM, while the SATA version is available with either 8 MB or 16 MB. The controller firmware uses 271 KB of the DRAM space. The remainder is used as the drive's cache space.

The 7K500 uses a circular buffer structure for its cache. See Chapter 22, Section 22.2.3, for a more detailed discussion. In fact, the cache space can optionally be partitioned into two circular buffers, one dedicated to read commands and one dedicated to write commands. A circular buffer architecture means that segments are of variable size. Up to 128 read segments can be created, and there can be up to 63 write segments for caching write data.

26.6 Performance Testing

Results of the Deskstar 7K500 for some of the performance tests described in Chapter 23 are already given in the previous sections. A few more are shown and discussed in this section.

26.6.1 Sequential Access

Figure 26.7 shows the throughput of 7K500 for sequential reads and writes.[3] At block size of one sector (0.5 KB), reads have a higher throughput

---

[3]For consistency with Table 26.2 and Figure 26.6, a MB is 1,000,000 bytes.

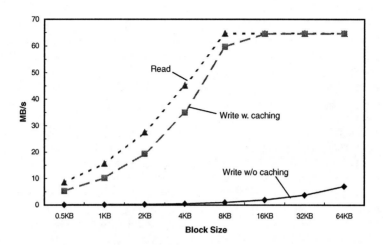

FIGURE 26.7: Sequential performance of the Deskstar 7K500.

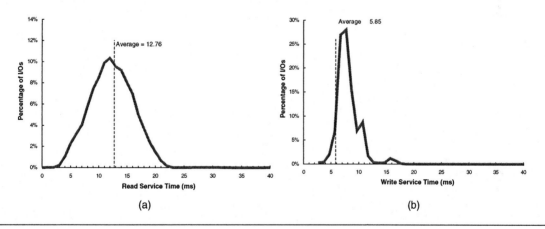

FIGURE 26.8: Distribution of I/O completion time for single sector random accesses: (a) random reads and (b) random writes with write cache enabled.

than writes with write caching on. In fact, the IOPS for reads at one sector block size is 16.7K but only 10.3K for writes. This translates into 60 μs per I/O for reads and 97 μs for writes. The difference of 37 ms is mostly due to the difference in command overheads for handling reads and for handling writes. This delta is maintained as block size is increased until the point is reached when the media data rate becomes the limiting factor, which happens at about 8 KB for reads and 16 KB for writes.

26.6.2 Random Access

Figure 26.8 shows the I/O completion time distributions for random reads and random writes which are computed based on 25,000 I/Os each. The shortest time for a read is about 2 ms according to Figure 26.8(a), which is probably the time for a one or two track seek plus a very small rotational latency. Command overhead also accounts for 0.5 ms, according to the drive's published specifications. The longest time is about 23 ms, which is approximately the sum of the full stroke seek of 14.7 ms and the maximum latency of 8.3 ms. The computed average read service time is 8.2 ms average seek plus 4.17 ms average rotational latency plus 0.5 ms command overhead, totaling 12.87 ms. This compares quite well with the measured average of 12.76 ms. Thus, actual test measurements give good correlation to calcualtions based on the published specification numbers.

The distribution plot of Figure 26.8(b) shows the result of write caching, so the curve no longer has the normal bell shape of Figure 26.8(a). The drive can cache up to 63 writes, which accounts for the 0.3% (63 out of 25,000) of all the I/Os with a completion time less than 1 ms. Once this limit is reached, the next write request that comes in will find the cache full (actually, it is the cache entry table that is full). The drive uses RPO (discussed in Chapter 21, Section 21.2) to select 1 of the 64 possible writes (63 cached write plus the new arrival) to write to disk. This shortest write usually takes about 4 to 5 ms, according to Figure 26.8(b). Because the test is structured so that a new write is sent to the drive as soon as a write command is reported by the drive to be completed, this is the normal scenario for the test after the first 63 initial I/Os. Finally, there is a small distribution, or hump, around 13 ms. This is due to the drive controller selecting a write that turns out to just miss the sector after seek and settling, requiring an extra revolution of 8.3 ms to complete. A small percentage of such "missed revolution" occurrences is expected of a well-tuned RPO implementation, as explained in Chapter 21, Section 21.2.2.

PART IV

Cross-Cutting Issues

Exploring all the options is not the issue. It's making one of them work.

— Brian Eno, on recording

CHAPTER 27

The Case for Holistic Design

Computer system design, in general, and memory hierarchy design, in particular, have reached a point at which it is no longer sufficient to design and optimize subsystems in isolation. A subsystem within a memory hierarchy could be a cache system, a DRAM system, or a disk system, but it could be much more fine-grained, such as a signaling scheme, a resource-management policy, a timing convention, a scheduling algorithm and any associated queue structures, a transaction protocol, a bus organization, a network topology, etc. Each of these items, even taken in isolation, is complex enough that it warrants significant research toward design optimization. When these subsystems are combined into a single, highly complex system, the resulting optimization problem is simply extraordinary.

Because memory systems are so complex, and because their subsystems are so complex, it is now the rule, and not the exception, that the subsystems we thought to be independent actually interact in unanticipated ways. These interactions frequently go undetected until late in the design cycle (e.g., at the time of implementation) and can cause significant cost and inconvenience or even errors of design that propagate into the installed product base.

To combat this problem, one must approach the design of even the smallest subsystem with an eye toward its relationship to the system as a whole and approach all system-level decisions with an understanding of all possible subsystem implications. One must make circuit-design decisions by considering their system-level impact. When designing interface protocols, one must quantify their system-level ramifications. In many cases, process technology issues should enter into the analysis of high-level architectural issues. Today, it has become necessary to take a system-level perspective when designing all aspects of the memory system; it has become necessary to take a forest-level view when designing trees and a tree-level view when designing forests.

This is not an easy task. To do this successfully, several things are required.

1. The designer must have an in-depth understanding of each subsystem in the memory system.

2. The designer must have an extremely detailed and accurate model of the system.

3. The designer must take an architectural approach, i.e., the use of design-space exploration methods, for providing intuition about the interactions of system parameters.

This book provides the breadth and depth necessary for item 1, an in-depth understanding of all the various aspects of the memory hierarchy. In addition, we have provided as a companion to this textbook *DRAMsim*, a detailed and accurate parameter-driven simulator that models performance and energy consumption for components in the DRAM subsystem. This simulator represents (a significant component of) item 2, a model of the memory system that considers low-order details. Last on the list is item 3, the stipulation that a designer use an architectural approach, namely quantitative design-space exploration, a technique championed in the late 1980s and early 1990s by John Hennessy and David Patterson [Hennessy & Patterson 1990]. The widespread adoption and application of this technique in the 1990s revolutionized the design of microprocessors and their cache systems. We believe their approach can do the same for memory systems design.

27.1 Anecdotes, Revisited

The following sections revisit the anecdotes from the "Overview" chapter, discussing them in more detail than previously. These motivate our call-to-arms on holistic design.

27.1.1 Anecdote I: Systemic Behaviors Exist

From 1999–2001, we performed a study of DRAM systems in which we explicitly studied only system-level effects—those that had nothing to do with the CPU architecture, DRAM architecture, or even DRAM interface protocol. Figure 27.1 shows some of the results [Cuppu & Jacob 1999b, 2001; Jacob 2003]. In this study, we held constant the CPU and DRAM architectures and considered only a handful of parameters that would affect how well the two communicate with each other. As shown in the figure, the handful of parameters includes the number of independent DRAM channels in the system, the width of each channel, and the granularity of access (the burst length: 32, 64, or 128 bytes transferred per read or write access).

This study caused us to realize that systemic behaviors exist and that they are significant. The parameters indicated in Figure 27.1 are all seemingly innocuous parameters, certainly not the type that would account for up to 20% of changes in system performance (execution time) if one parameter was increased or decreased by a small amount, which is indeed the case. Moreover, considering the top two graphs, all of the choices represent intuitively "good" configurations; none of the displayed values represent strawmen, machine configurations that one would avoid putting on one's own desktop. All of the configurations represented in the top two graphs, at first glance and in the 1999–2001 time-frame (for example, four independent data channels, each 800 Mbps and 8 bytes wide, using a 32-byte data burst—very close in organization and

behavior to a 4-channel Rambus system), would seem to yield desirable system configurations; yet there is a factor of 2 difference in their resulting execution time. Evidently, despite intuition, they are *not* all desirable system configurations.

When the analysis considers a wider range of bus speeds and burst lengths, the problematic behavior increases. As shown in the bottom graph, the ratio of best-to-worst execution times can be a factor of three, and the local optima are both more frequent and more exaggerated. Systems with relatively low bandwidth (e.g., 100, 200, 400 MB/s) and relatively slow bus speeds (e.g., 100, 200 MHz), if configured well, can equal or better the performance of system configurations with much faster hardware that is poorly configured. For example, a 400-MB/s memory system with a 64-byte burst length and at any bus speed (100, 200 or 400 MHz) can have up to twice the performance of systems that use 800-MHz busses and have 6.4 GB/s total bandwidth (a factor of 16× more bandwidth), but are misconfigured.

The varied parameters in the study also included other relatively innocuous-seeming parameters such as the degree of banking per channel and the size of the memory controller's request queue. Again, none of these parameters would seem to be the type that would account for up to 20% changes in application execution time if one parameter was increased or decreased by a small amount. Intuitively, one would expect the design space to be relatively smooth; as system bandwidth increases, so should system performance. Yet the design space is far from smooth; performance variations of 20% or more can be found in design points that are immediately adjacent to one another; the variations from best-performing to worst-performing design exceed a factor of three across the full space studied; and local minima and maxima abound. Moreover, the behaviors are related—increasing one parameter by a factor of two toward higher expected performance (e.g., increasing the channel width) can move the system off a local optimum, but local optimality can be restored by changing other related parameters to follow suit, such as increasing the burst length and cache block size to match the new channel width. This complex interaction between parameters previously thought to be independent arises because of the complexity

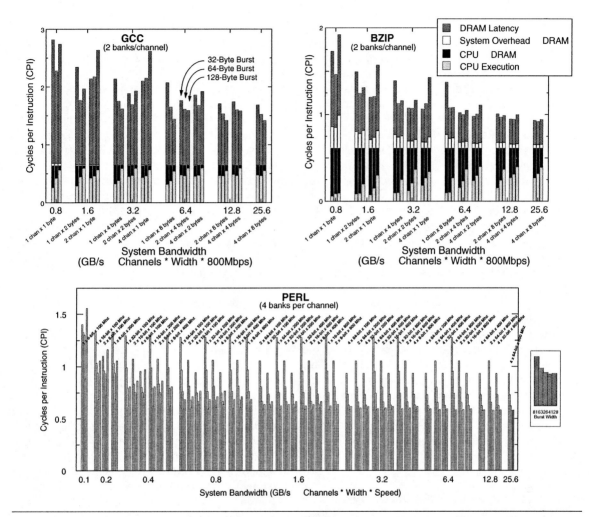

FIGURE 27.1: Execution time as a function of bandwidth, channel organization, and granularity of access. Top two graphs from Cuppu and Jacob [2001] (© 2001 IEEE); bottom graph from Jacob [2003] (© 2003 IEEE).

of the system under study, and so we have named these "systemic" behaviors.[1]

The radical shifts in performance are caused by interactions between parameters. For example, if an atomic burst packet is long and the channel is narrow, requests become backed up in the controller's queue, waiting their turn for system resources. Short bursts in high-bandwidth channels underutilize the channel, failing to amortize the row activation and precharge overheads of the DRAM devices and, therefore, exposing these as a source of overhead. Changing one parameter tends to take the design off a local optimum (a local optimum within the entire design space, but the best achievable design given

---

[1]There is a distinction between this type of behavior and what in complex system theory is called "emergent system" behaviors or properties. Emergent system behaviors are those of individuals within a complex system, behaviors that an individual may perform in a group setting that the individual would never perform alone. In our environment, the behaviors are observations we have made of the design space, which is derived from the system as a whole.

the cost-related design constraints such as maximum data transfer rate, maximum bus width, maximum number of pins per chip, etc.); a designer must make several changes to related parameters to restore the system back to another local optimum. In general, there can be an order-of-magnitude difference between the worst designs and the best designs in the space, and the remaining designs are not clustered near the optimum. A designer that chooses a design without careful analysis will most likely end up at least a factor of two off the optimal design, given the cost constraints.

Note that the behavior is not restricted to the DRAM system. As demonstrated at the end of the "Overview" chapter, we have seen it in the disk system as well, where the variations in performance from one configuration to the next can be even more pronounced.

Recall that this behavior comes from the varying of parameters that are seemingly unimportant in the grand scheme of things, at least they would certainly seem to be far less important than, say, the cache architecture or the number of functional units in the processor core. The bottom line is that, as we have observed, systemic behaviors—unanticipated interactions between seemingly innocuous parameters and mechanisms—cause significant losses in performance, requiring in-depth, detailed design-space exploration to achieve anything close to an optimal design given a set of technologies and limitations.

27.1.2 Anecdote II: The DLL in DDR SDRAM

Figure 27.2(a) illustrates what happens in a DRAM chip, actually *any* chip, when a clock signal enters that chip from the system bus. The clock signal enters through the I/O pads and is sent through a multi-stage amplification process—a series of buffers spread throughout a clock tree—so that the final output signal is strong enough to be distributed across and to drive the entire chip. Each buffer and each segment of wire introduce delay into the signal, so by the time the clock signal reaches the periphery of the chip, where, for example, it will be used to drive data onto the system bus, the signal is out of phase with respect to the original signal. As a result, data exits the chip out of alignment with the system clock, which creates

skew between the data and clock signal, a source of timing uncertainty that increases the difficulty of sampling the data with the clock at some receiver on the bus.

The point of adding a delay-locked loop (DLL) to a DRAM, a technique that was introduced into SDRAM at the DDR1 generation, is to eliminate this source of skew and timing uncertainty (see Figure 27.2(b)). The clock signal, as it enters the chip, is delayed $2\pi - D$, where D is the phase differential between the entering clock signal and the signal *after* going through the multi-stage buffering/amplification process. The added delay brings the phase differential between the two signals up to a full 2π, so the internal clock signal, after buffering and distribution, is exactly in-phase with the original system clock signal (the global clock signal as it immediately comes out of the input buffers).

What does this intentional delay do? It more precisely aligns the DRAM part's output with the system clock. The trade-off is extra latency in the datapath as well as a requirement for higher power and heat dissipation, as the DLL, a dynamic control mechanism, is continuously running. By aligning each DRAM part in a DIMM to the system clock, each DRAM part is effectively de-skewed with respect to the other parts; the DLLs cancel out timing differences due to process variations and thermal gradients.

Thus, the DLL on the DDR SDRAM part performs the following important functions that directly affect the operation of the system:

- The DLL aligns the DRAM's output more closely to the system clock.
- The DLLs on all DRAM parts on a module effectively de-skew the output of those parts relative to each other.

It stands to reason that any mechanism satisfying both of these functions is a potential substitute for the DLL. Moreover, any mechanism that does at least as well as the per-DRAM DLL and provides additional benefits and/or a reduced cost warrants further investigation for potential to be an even better candidate. Regarding this last point, it is important to note that the synchronization performed by

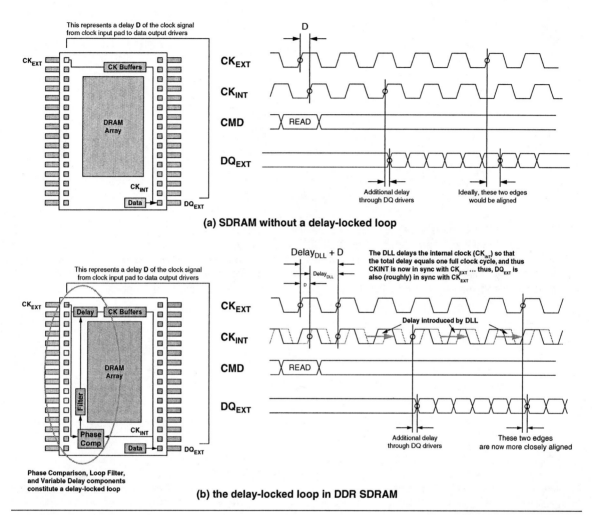

(a) SDRAM without a delay-locked loop

(b) the delay-locked loop in DDR SDRAM

FIGURE 27.2: The use of the DLL in DDR SDRAMs. Figure (a) illustrates the behavior of a DDR SDRAM without a DLL: due to the inherent delays through the clock receiver, multi-stage amplifiers, on-chip wires, output drivers, output pads, bonding wires, etc., the data output (as it appears from the perspective of the bus) occurs slightly delayed with respect to the system clock. Figure (b) illustrates the effect of adding a DLL: the DLL delays the incoming clock signal so that the output of the part is more closely aligned with the system clock. Note that, unless the datapath is running with significant slack, this introduces extra latency into the part's datapath: if the datapath is unable to produce its results D time units sooner, it must be delayed $2\pi - D$.

the on-chip DLL is from the DRAM's perspective: the DRAM synchronizes its own output to its own version of the system clock. Thus, this mechanism fails to cancel any skew between the memory controller and the DRAMs; it also fails to account for process variations that affect the DRAM's internal clock. With all

this in mind, Figure 27.3 illustrates a small handful of alternative solutions. In addition, Figure 27.4 shows the approximate costs and benefits of each scheme (to a *very* rough first-order approximation) in terms of hardware required and the types of timing uncertainty that are addressed.

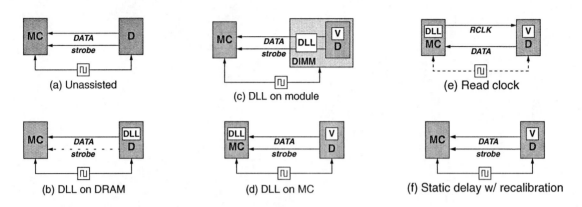

FIGURE 27.3: Several alternatives to the per-DRAM DLL. The figure illustrates six different timing conventions: (a) the scheme in single data rate SDRAM; (b) the scheme chosen for DDR SDRAM; (c) moving the DLL onto the module, with a per-DRAM static delay element (Vernier); (d) moving the DLL onto the memory controller, with a per-DRAM static delay; (e) using a separate read clock per DRAM or per DIMM; and (f) using only a static delay element and recalibrating periodically to address dynamic changes. Each of the last four alternatives is cheaper than (b) and potentially cancels out more timing uncertainty.

SCHEME	COST	EFFECTIVENESS (Uncertainty in read)				
No DLL	0	D_{CLK} +	Xmit +	wire +	Recv +	Clk skew
on DRAM	16 × DLL		Xmit +	wire +	Recv +	Clk skew
on DIMM	2 × DLL 16 × Vernier			wire +	Recv +	Clk skew
on MC	2 × DLL 16 × Vernier			wire +	Recv	
Read CLK	2 × DLL 16 × Vernier			wire +	Recv	
Static	16 × Vernier		Xmit +	wire +	Recv	

FIGURE 27.4: Cost-benefit comparison of various timing schemes for DDR SDRAM. The costs assume a 2-DIMM system with 8 DRAM parts per DIMM, and "cost" applies to both die area and power dissipation. The effectiveness is in terms of sources of timing uncertainty that remain in a DRAM-read operation (i.e., fewer items = better design).

The six alternatives are as follows:

1. **Unassisted source-synchronous operation** This scheme is equivalent to using DDR without a DLL, but using the DQS strobe to capture data. As in all source-synchronous timing schemes, the strobe is routed with the data lines it is meant to synchronize, and therefore it experiences the same skew as the data lines. Thus, it is only marginally out of alignment with respect to the data signal that it accom-

panies. The sources of timing uncertainty that remain using this scheme, assuming a DRAM-read operation, include the delay through the DRAM's internal clock network, jitter in the DRAM's transmitter, wire skew, jitter in the memory controller's receiver circuit, and general clock skew due to the clock signals entering the DRAM and memory controller slightly out of phase with respect to each other.

2. **Put the DLL on the DRAM** This is the mechanism that was chosen by the DRAM

industry. The system uses a global clock to capture data; it does not use source-synchronous clocking. The only source of timing uncertainty that this mechanism eliminates, with respect to the previous scheme, is D_{CLK}—skew due to the delay through the DRAM's internal clock network. In a 2-DIMM system with 8 DRAM chips per DIMM, this scheme uses 16 DLLs, compared to 0 DLLs for the previous scheme.

3. **Put the DLL on the module (DIMM)** Static DRAM-to-DRAM skew is cancelled by the use of a per-DRAM Vernier circuit, each of which is programmed at system initialization. The Vernier introduces a programmable delay that cancels static sources of skew, but not dynamic sources (i.e., jitter). The function of the module-resident DLL is similar to that performed by the DRAM-resident DLL, except that this DLL is closer to the system bus and is therefore in closer alignment with that bus. The mechanism cancels out skew caused by the DRAM's transmitter circuit, but not dynamic jitter. It has a lower DLL cost, and the Vernier costs are relatively low (they are small circuits that do not dissipate significant power relative to a DLL).

4. **Put the DLL on the memory controller** It is easy to make the argument that, because the memory controller (the recipient of the read data) is the benefit of any de-skewing, it should be the memory controller that determines how, when, and to what degree to cancel that skew. The memory controller is arguably the best location for a DLL. In this mechanism, as in the previous, DRAM-to-DRAM skew is cancelled by per-DRAM Vernier circuits. The memory controller maintains a separate DLL per DIMM in the system, so the costs are the same as the previous mechanism, but the scheme can cancel clock skew entirely by virtue of the DLL's placement (it can precisely align the DRAM and module output to align perfectly with the memory

controller's clock, as opposed to aligning output with a local version of the system clock that is skewed with respect to the memory controller's clock).

5. **Use a "read clock" timing scheme** A read clock is a special clock that is used only to time data being driven back to the memory controller on a read. Thus, the DRAMs would use one clock for timing of operations and reading control signals off the bus, but the DRAM's data output would be driven by the read clock which would have some non-zero skew relative to the general clock. Each module would have a separate read clock, and the memory controller would control the phase of each read clock so as to align all DRAM output to its own clock. DRAM-to-DRAM skews would be cancelled by per-DRAM Vernier circuits. Like the previous scheme, this would cancel clock skew because the controlling circuits (the DLLs) would be on the memory controller. It would require an additional per-module wire on the bus, and each DRAM would require an additional pin. Thus, it is a bit more expensive than the previous scheme.

6. **Use static delay with periodic recalibration** In this scheme, each DRAM would be outfitted with a Vernier circuit, which is capable of cancelling out sources of static skew, timing uncertainties due to process variations. However, the Vernier circuit is not capable of cancelling skew due to dynamic variations such as thermal gradients or voltage fluctuations. Temperature gradients tend to occur on millisecond time-frames; thus, it would be possible to recalibrate the Vernier circuits in a system every millisecond and cancel out temperature-related dynamic changes. Voltage fluctuations tend to happen on faster timescales and could not be addressed by this mechanism. In addition, the performance cost of periodically shutting down an entire rank of memory to recalibrate the Verniers could be substantial.

The bottom line is that, despite this being a first-order analysis, it is clear that there are alternatives worth exploring—and a detailed SPICE-level analysis would be invaluable to the community. Several mechanisms are potentially both cheaper *and* better at cancelling skew than the use of a per-DRAM DLL, but they require a system-level approach to design. As it turns out, the DLL is a circuit-level approach to solving what is essentially a system-level problem. Our main point is simply to underscore our design maxim: a system-level perspective and understanding can be extremely valuable for providing insights when evaluating circuit-level design decisions.

27.1.3 Anecdote III: A Catch-22 in the Search for Bandwidth

With every DRAM generation, timing parameters are added. The following timing parameters, shown in Figure 27.5, were added to the DDR specification to address the issues of power and synchronization.

- t_{FAW} (*Four-bank Activation Window*) and t_{RRD} (*Row-to-Row activation Delay*) have been introduced to put a ceiling on the maximum current draw of a single DRAM part. These are protocol-level limitations whose values are chosen to prevent a memory controller from exceeding circuit-related thresholds. As we will later show, these parameters significantly reduce the maximum bandwidth that is available from a DRAM part.

- t_{DQS} is our own name for a system-level timing parameter that does not officially exist. Each device must grab the DQS portion of the system bus for a specific duration of time before it can start driving data over the bus; this is an effective rank-to-rank switching time that has implications only at the system level (i.e., it has no meaning or effect if considering a single-rank DRAM system). By obeying t_{DQS}, one can ensure that a second DRAM rank will not drive the data bus at the same time as a first, when switching from one rank to another for data output.

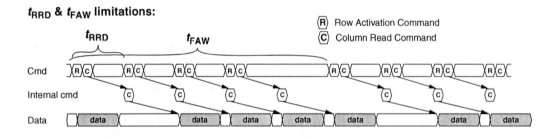

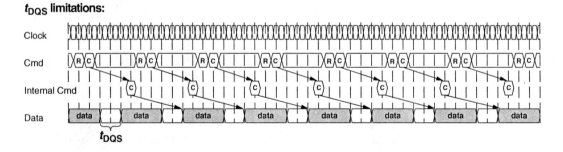

FIGURE 27.5: Some DRAM timing parameters and their effects on system bandwidth.

Its purpose is to ensure that two devices never try to drive the data bus at the same time; its purpose is to counter the effects of a portion of the system's timing uncertainty. Though it does not restrict the bandwidth available from a DRAM device, it can significantly limit the bandwidth available from a DRAM system.

These are per-device timing parameters that were chosen to improve the behavior (current draw, timing uncertainty) of individual devices, and we will show that they do so at the expense of significant system-level performance.

The parameters t_{FAW} and t_{RRD} address the issue of maximum current through a device, which leads to power and heat dissipation. DRAM chips have always run relatively cool; they are not expected to come with heat sinks like so many CPUs and graphics co-processors. However, at the latest speeds they can get hot. Figure 27.6 shows the basic operations that occur in a DRAM read in terms of their current drain. Row activation ("R") is followed by a column read ("C") on the command bus (note: the figure depicts a posted CAS operation). After the column read is finished, the bank is precharged. Below each of these activities is shown the corresponding current-draw profile. Activating the bank is a significant cost, as it comprises driving the row decoders, driving the polysilicon wordline and the several thousand pass-gate transistors it controls, and operating the several thousand corresponding sense amplifiers to detect the signals. Bursting data out the DRAM's pins is a lower cost, but it is proportional to the burst length and thus can extend for a significant length of time. The bank precharge activity is a lower cost than bank activation, but it is still significant. The total current draw for the part is the sum of the current in quiescent mode and the current for each of the active operations.

Modern DDR SDRAMs have four or, above 1 GB density, eight or more banks within each DRAM device. One can imagine what would happen if a memory controller were to activate each bank in a device, one right after the other on successive cycles—a scenario that is certainly possible. The current-draw profiles for each of the bank activations would be superimposed, staggered one cycle in time. The resultant current draw for the entire chip

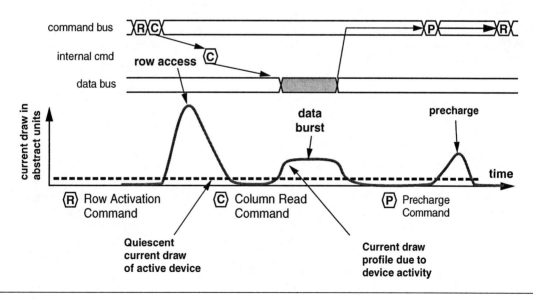

FIGURE 27.6: Current draw of activities in a read operation.

would be far larger than what DRAMs are designed to withstand. To prevent scenarios like this from happening, t_{FAW} and t_{RRD} were added to the DDR specification. Their function is simply to spread out bank activations in time.

- t_{RRD} specifies the minimum time between two successive ACT commands to the same DRAM device (i.e., the same DRAM rank). If the memory controller has two ACT commands destined for the same rank, the second must wait at least this long after the first.

- t_{FAW} represents a sliding window of time during which no more than four ACT commands to the same device/rank may appear. This parameter exists because even obeying t_{RRD}, it is possible to create a relatively large current spike in a DRAM. This parameter spreads activations out even further.

Clearly, these parameters both insert delay and create dead bus cycles. The situation is even worse than that, because the parameters are specified in *nanoseconds* and not bus cycles, which means that their effect on the system will simply worsen over time as bus speeds increase, as illustrated in Figure 27.7. As the data rate increases, t_{FAW} and t_{RRD} fail to scale with it, making bus usage increasingly inefficient. It does not matter how small these parameters are to start with; they will become a problem. They are a function of the DRAM array, not the I/O circuitry; thus, they scale with t_{RC}, not the data rate. Even if their values are small enough at this moment that they are relatively innocuous, the parameters do not scale with the data rate, and unless addressed they will become a critical limitation in the future as data rate increases.

This is shown clearly in Figure 27.8; no matter what configuration is used, at some point (here, it is 1066 Mbps) the system bandwidth hits a ceiling. The figure shows the maximum attainable bandwidth for a single-rank DRAM system. Variations on the configuration include 8 banks or 16 banks; different values for t_{FAW} (either 60 or 30 ns); and a degree of intelligent scheduling in the memory controller, represented by

a per-bank queue depth—0 queue entries represent a simple FIFO controller, a depth of 2 represents a controller of medium-scale complexity and intelligence, and a depth of 4 represents a relatively sophisticated controller. It is important to note that *all* schemes hit the bandwidth ceiling; the sophisticated controller hits the bandwidth ceiling at 1066 Mbps, the medium-complexity controller hits it at 533 Mbps. The main point to understand is that t_{FAW} and t_{RRD} conspire to limit severely the bandwidth coming out of a single rank; at some point determined by t_{FAW} the sustainable bandwidth saturates, and no matter how much faster you run the bus, achievable bandwidth remains fixed.

So the obvious question is why not use a different rank? Why not fill in all of the dead cycles of the bus with data from other ranks? This should bring the system bandwidth back up to maximum. However, the function of t_{DQS} is to prevent exactly this: t_{DQS} is the bus turnaround time, inserted to account for skew on the bus and to prevent different bus masters from driving the bus at the same time. To avoid such collisions, a second rank must wait at least t_{DQS} after a first rank has finished before driving the bus. This is illustrated in the bottom of Figure 27.5.

So we have a catch:

- One set of parameters limits the device-level bandwidth and expects a designer to go to the rank or system level to reclaim performance.
- The other parameter limits rank- and system-level bandwidth and expects a designer to go to the device level to reclaim performance.

The good news is that the problem is solvable (see Chapter 15, Section 15.4.3), but this is nonetheless a very good example of low-level design decisions that create headaches at the system level.

27.1.4 Anecdote IV: Proposals to Exploit Variability in Cell Leakage

Last, but not least, we present an example of a system-level design decision that ignores circuit- and

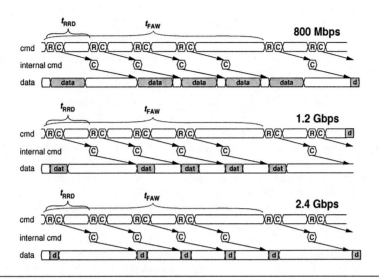

FIGURE 27.7: The effects of t_{FAW} and t_{RRD} as bus speeds increase.

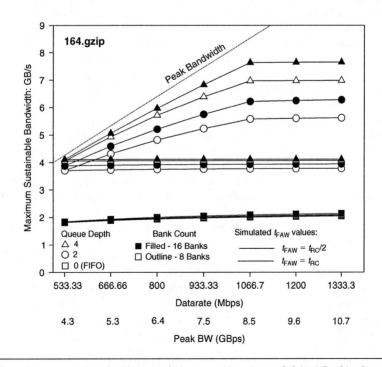

FIGURE 27.8: The effect of t_{FAW} on total attainable bandwidth. $t_{RC} = 60\,ns$, burst of eight, 8 B-wide channel.

device-level implications. Recently, several different groups have proposed exploiting the well-known phenomenon of variability in DRAM cell leakage, with the end result of lowering DRAM power dissipation. The schemes propose treating different rows of a DRAM array differently in terms of the length of time between refresh operations: each row is refreshed as infrequently as possible, given its observed retention characteristics. The problem is that these proposals ignore another, less well-known phenomenon of DRAM cell variability, namely that a cell with a long retention time can suddenly (in the time-frame of seconds) exhibit a *short* retention time. Such an effect would render these power-efficient proposals functionally erroneous.

Ever since DRAM was invented, is has been observed that different DRAM cells exhibit different data retention time characteristics, typically ranging between hundreds of milliseconds to tens of seconds. DRAM manufacturers typically set the refresh requirement conservatively and require that every row in a DRAM device be refreshed at least once every 64 or 32 ms.

Though refresh might not seem a significant concern, in mobile devices researchers have observed that the refresh requirement can consume as much as one-third of the power in otherwise idle systems, prompting action to address the issue. Several recent papers propose moving the refresh function into the memory controller and explicitly refresh a row only when needed. During an initialization phase, the controller would characterize each row in the memory system, measuring DRAM data retention time on a row-by-row (i.e., page-by-page) basis, discarding leaky pages entirely, limiting its DRAM use to only those rows deemed non-leaky, and refreshing once every tens of seconds instead of once every tens of milliseconds.

The problem with these schemes is variable data retention time [Yaney et al. 1987, Restle et al. 1992, Ueno et al. 1998, Kim et al. 2004b]. This phenomenon is well known (the term is *variable retention time* or VRT), and its probability of occurrence in a particular DRAM cell is low but non-zero. Samsung has presented data on a 0.14-um, 256-Mbit DRAM device. At 85°C, three bit cells exhibited bi-modal data retention

time characteristics, where the change in retention time was greater than 50% [Kim et al. 2004b]. When the DRAM device is thermally stressed to 350°C and then retested, *most* of the cells in the same 256-Mbit DRAM device characterized by Samsung show at least some variance between data retention time characteristics [Mori et al. 2001, Kim et al. 2004b].

VRT is caused by subtle defects in the silicon at the p-n junction. These microdefects are necessary but insufficient conditions for the occurrence of VRT; a silicon microdefect has to be the right type and at the right place to serve as an electron-hole generation-recombination (GR) center. The GR center can then conduct current through the p-n junction or not: the current appears as an additional and significant leakage component that can drain electrons from the stored charge in a DRAM cell [Ueno et al. 1998; Mori et al. 2001, 2005; Kim et al. 2004b]. Though steps can be taken by DRAM manufacturers to limit DRAM cell VRT, processes such as ion implantation and dry etching inevitably introduce defects into silicon. It is thus unlikely that VRT can be completely eliminated [Kim et al. 2004b]. Moreover, because VRT is rare and difficult to detect, DRAM manufacturers are not interested in finding and eliminating it—as long as the 64-ms refresh time guarantees that even cells with VRT can pass all tests and retain functional correctness.

Consequently, violating the 64-ms refresh time is a game of rolling the dice, and the correctness of a system that intentionally violates the 64-ms refresh time is questionable. Luckily, there is a straightforward solution to the problem—one that no proposal has actually mentioned. One can increase the refresh period, thereby increasing the error rate due to VRT, provided one uses ECC to catch and correct any errors that occur (see Chapter 30, "Memory Errors and Error Correction," for details on ECC implementation). Assuming VRT does not get much worse in current and future DRAM devices, (64, 72) SECDED ECC should be sufficient to protect against the presence of VRT DRAM cells. Assuming the probability of occurrence is 10^{-8}, the chance that any two cells within the same 72-bit ECC word will both exhibit VRT is circa 10^{-14}. Since there are 4^6 72-bit ECC words in a 256-(288-) Mbit DRAM device, the probability that this DRAM device will have an ECC word with 2 VRT cells with retention time variances of greater than 50% is on the order of 10^{-8}.

27.2 Perspective

To summarize:

Anecdote I Systemic behaviors exist and are significant (they can be responsible for factors of two to three in execution time).

Anecdote II The DLL in DDR SDRAM is a circuit-level solution chosen to address system-level skew.

Anecdote III t_{DQS} represents a circuit-level solution chosen to address system-level skew in DDR SDRAM; t_{FAW} and t_{RRD} are circuit-level limitations that significantly limit system-level performance.

Anecdote IV Several research groups have recently proposed system-level solutions to the DRAM-refresh problem, but fail to account for circuit-level details that might compromise the correctness of the resulting system.

Anecdotes II and III show that the common practice in industry is to design systems by focusing at the level of circuits, and Anecdote IV shows that the common practice in research is to design systems that have circuit-level ramifications, while abstracting away the details of the circuits involved. Anecdote I illustrates that both approaches are doomed to failure in future memory system design.

To reiterate, we argue that it is no longer appropriate to optimize subsystems in isolation: local optima do not yield a globally optimal system, and unilateral changes to the system (e.g., changing one parameter without changing other related parameters to follow suit) tend to bring the system off local optima as well. Both industry and the research community abound with examples where device- and circuit-level decisions are made without considering the system-level implications, as well as system-level designs that fail by not anticipating the device- and circuit-level repercussions. The process of system design has become extremely complex because the subsystems that once were independent or had simple, well-understood interactions now exhibit interactions that are complex, non-intuitive, and not understood at all. In response, system designers must strive to understand details at many levels of the system; we must practice holistic design.

CHAPTER 28

Analysis of Cost and Performance

The characterization of different machine configurations is at the heart of computer system design, and so it is vital that we as practitioners do it correctly. Accurate and precise characterizations can provide deep insight into system behavior, enable correct decision-making, and ultimately save money and time. Failure to accurately and precisely describe the system under study can lead to misinterpretations of behavior, misdirected attention, and loss of time and revenue. This chapter discusses some of the metrics and tools used in computer system analysis and design, from the correct form of combined multi-parameter figures of merit to the philosophy of performance characterization.

28.1 Combining Cost and Performance

The following will be obvious in retrospect, but it quite clearly needs to be said, because all too frequently work is presented that unintentionally obscures information: when combining metrics of both *cost* and *performance* into a single figure of merit, one must take care to treat the separate metrics appropriately. The same reasoning presented in this section lies behind other well-known metric combinations such as energy-delay product and power-delay product.

To be specific, if combining performance and cost into a single figure of merit, one can only divide cost into performance if the choice of metric for performance grows in the opposite direction as the metric for cost. For example, consider the following:

- Bandwidth per pin
- MIPS per square millimeter
- Transactions per second per dollar

Bandwidth is good if it increases, while pin count is good if it decreases. MIPS is good if it increases, while die area (square millimeters) is good if it decreases. Transactions per second is good if it increases, while dollar cost is good if it decreases. The combined metrics give information about the value of the design they represent, in particular, how that design might scale. The figure of merit *bandwidth per pin* suggests that twice the bandwidth can be had for twice the cost (i.e., by doubling the number of pins); the figure of merit *IPC per square millimeter* suggests that twice the performance can be had by doubling the number of on-chip resources; the figure of merit *transactions per second per dollar* suggests that the capacity of the transaction-processing system can be doubled by doubling the cost of the system; and, to a first order, these implications tend to be true.

If we try to combine performance and cost metrics that grow in the same direction, we cannot divide one into the other; we must multiply them. For example, consider the following:

- Execution time per dollar (bad)
- CPI per square millimeter (bad)
- Request latency per pin (bad)

On the surface, these might seem to be reasonable representations of cost performance, but they are not. Consult Table 28.1, which has intentionally vague units of measurement. For example, assume that "performance" is in execution time and that "cost" is in dollars, an example corresponding to the first "bad" bullet item above. Dividing dollars into execution time (performance per cost, fourth column)

TABLE **28.1**

System in Question	Performance	Cost	Performance per Cost	Performance-Cost Product
System A	2 units	2 things	1 unit per thing	4 unit-things
System B	2 units	4 things	1/2 unit per thing	8 unit-things
System C	4 units	2 things	2 units per thing	8 unit-things
System D	4 units	4 things	1 unit per thing	16 unit-things

suggests that systems A and D are equivalent. Yet system D takes twice as long to execute *and* costs twice as much as system A—it should be considered four times *worse* than system A, a relationship that *is* suggested by the values in the last column. Similarly, consider performance as CPI and cost as die area (second bad bullet item above). Dividing die area into CPI (performance per cost, fourth column) suggests that system C is four times worse than system B (its CPI per square millimeter value is four times higher). However, put another way, system C costs half as much as system B, but has half the performance as B, so the two should be equivalent, which is precisely what is shown in the last column.

Using a performance-cost product instead of a quotient gives the results that are appropriate and intuitive:

- Execution-time-dollars
- CPI-square-millimeters
- Request-latency-pin-count product

Note that, when combining multiple atomic metrics into a single figure of merit, one is really attempting to cast into a single number the information provided in a Pareto plot, where each metric corresponds to its own axis. Collapsing a multi-dimensional representation into a single number itself obscures information, even if done correctly, and thus we would encourage a designer to always use Pareto plots when possible. This leads us to the following section.

28.2 Pareto Optimality

This section reproduces part of the "Overview" chapter, for the sake of completeness.

28.2.1 The Pareto-Optimal Set: An Equivalence Class

While it is convenient to represent the "goodness" of a design solution, a particular system configuration, as a single number so that one can readily compare the goodness ratings of candidate design solutions, doing so can often mislead a designer. In the design of computer systems and memory systems, we inherently deal with multi-dimensional design spaces (e.g., encompassing performance, energy consumption, cost, etc.), and so using a single number to represent a solution's value is not really appropriate, unless we assign exact weights to the various metrics (which is dangerous and will be discussed in more detail later) or unless we care about one aspect to the exclusion of all others (e.g., performance at any cost).

Assuming that we do not have exact weights for the figures of merit and that we do care about more than one aspect of the system, a very powerful tool to aid in system analysis is the concept of *Pareto optimality* or *Pareto efficiency*, named after the Italian economist, Vilfredo Pareto, who invented it in the early 1900s.

Pareto optimality asserts that one candidate solution to a problem is better than another candidate solution only if the first *dominates* the second, i.e., if the first is better than or equal to the second in *all* figures of merit. If one solution has a better value in one dimension, but a worse value in another dimension, then the two

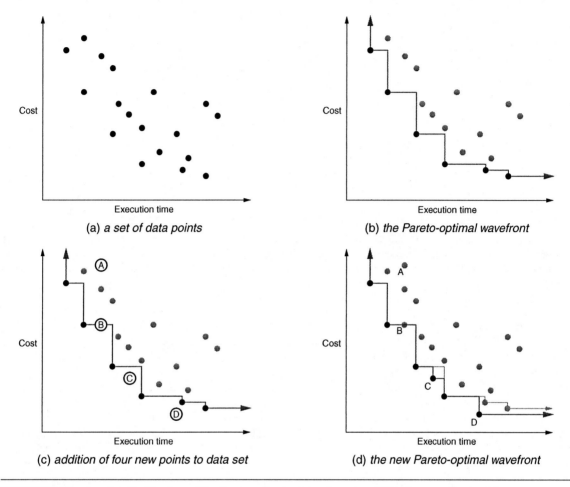

(a) *a set of data points*

(b) *the Pareto-optimal wavefront*

(c) *addition of four new points to data set*

(d) *the new Pareto-optimal wavefront*

FIGURE 28.1: Pareto optimality. Members of the Pareto-optimal set are shown in solid black; non-optimal points are grey.

candidates are Pareto-equivalent. The "best" solution is actually a set of candidate solutions: the set of Pareto-equivalent solutions that are not dominated by any solution.

Figure 28.1(a) shows a set of candidate solutions in a two-dimensional (2D) space that represents a cost/performance metric. In this example, the x-axis represents system performance in execution time (smaller numbers are better), and the y-axis represents system cost in dollars (smaller numbers are better). Figure 28.1(b) shows the Pareto-optimal set in solid black and connected by a line; the line denotes the boundary

between the Pareto-optimal subset and the dominated subset, with points on the line belonging to the dominated set (dominated data points are shown in the figure as grey). In this example, the Pareto-optimal set forms a wavefront that approaches both axes simultaneously. Figures 28.1(c) and 28.1(d) show the effect of adding four new candidate solutions to the space: one lies inside the wavefront, one lies on the wavefront, and two lie outside the wavefront. The first two new additions, A and B, are both dominated by at least one member of the Pareto-optimal set, and so neither is considered Pareto-optimal. Even though B lies on

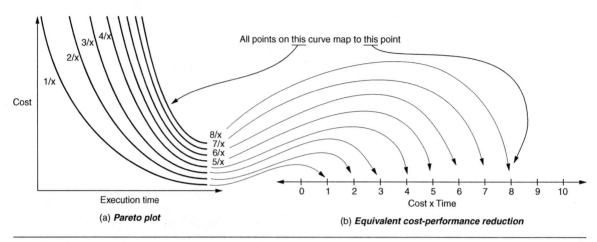

FIGURE 28.2: Combining metrics collapses the Pareto graph. The figure shows two equivalent data sets. (a) is a Pareto plot with 1/x curves drawn on it; (b) is the resulting 1D reduction when the two axes of the Pareto plot are combined into a single figure of merit.

the wavefront, it is not considered Pareto-optimal; the point to the left of B has better performance than B at equal cost, and thus it dominates B.

Point C is not dominated by any member of the Pareto-optimal set, nor does it dominate any member of the Pareto-optimal set; thus, candidate-solution C is added to the optimal set, and its addition changes the shape of the wavefront slightly. The last of the additional points, D, is dominated by no members of the optimal set, but it *does* dominate several members of the optimal set, so D's inclusion in the optimal set excludes those dominated members from the set. As a result, candidate-solution D changes the shape of the wavefront more significantly than does candidate-solution C.

The primary benefit of using Pareto analysis is that, by definition, the individual metrics along each axis are considered independently. Unlike the combination metrics of the previous section, a Pareto graph embodies no implicit evaluation of the relative importance between the various axes. For example, if a 2D Pareto graph presents cost on one axis and (execution) time on the other, a combined cost-time metric (e.g., the *Cost-Execution Time* product) would collapse the 2D Pareto graph into a single dimension, with each value α in the 1D cost-time space corresponding to all points on the curve $y = \alpha/x$ in

the 2D Pareto space. This is shown in Figure 28.2. The implication of representing the data set in a one-dimensional (1D) metric such as this is that the two metrics *cost* and *time* are equivalent—that one can be traded off for the other in a 1-for-1 fashion. However, as a Pareto plot will show, not all equally *achievable* designs lie on a 1/x curve. Often, a designer will find that trading off a factor of two in one dimension (cost) to gain a factor of two in the other dimension (execution time) fails to scale after a point or is altogether impossible to begin with. Collapsing the data set into a single metric will obscure this fact, while plotting the data in a Pareto graph will not, as Figure 28.3 illustrates. Real data reflects realistic limitations, such as a non-equal trade-off between cost and performance. Limiting the analysis to a combined metric in the example data set would lead a designer toward designs that trade off cost for execution time, when perhaps the designer would prefer to choose lower cost designs.

28.2.2 Stanley's Observation

A related observation (made by Tim Stanley, a former graduate student in the University of Michigan's Advanced Computer Architecture Lab) is that requirements-driven analysis can similarly obscure

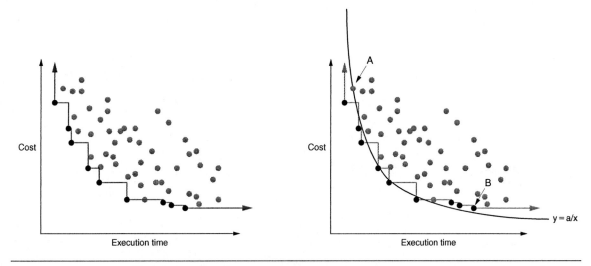

FIGURE 28.3: Pareto analysis versus combined metrics. Combining different metrics into a single figure of merit obscures information. For example, representing the given data-set with a single cost-time product would equate by definition all designs lying on each 1/x curve. The 1/x curve shown in solid black would divide the Pareto-optimal set: those designs lying to the left and below the curve would be considered "better" than those designs lying to the right and above the curve. The design corresponding to data point "A," given a combined-metric analysis, would be considered superior to the design corresponding to data point "B," though Pareto analysis indicates otherwise.

information and potentially lead designers away from optimal choices. When requirements are specified in language such as *not to exceed* some value of some metric (such as power dissipation or die area or dollar cost), a hard line is drawn that forces a designer to ignore a portion of the design space. However, Stanley observed that, as far as design exploration goes, all of the truly interesting designs hover right around that cut-off. For instance, if one's design limitation is *cost not to exceed X*, then all interesting designs will lie within a small distance of cost X, including small deltas beyond X. It is frequently the case that small deltas beyond the cut-off in cost might yield large deltas in performance. If a designer fails to consider these points, he may overlook the ideal design.

28.3 Taking Sampled Averages Correctly

In the opening chapter of the book, we discussed this topic and left off with an unanswered question. Here, we present the full discussion and give closure to the reader. Like the previous section, so that this section can stand alone, we repeat much of the original discussion.

In many fields, including the field of computer engineering, it is quite popular to find a *sampled average*, i.e., the average of a sampled set of numbers, rather than the average of the entire set. This is useful when the entire set is unavailable or difficult to obtain or expensive to obtain. For example, one might want to use this technique to keep a running performance average for a real microprocessor, or one might want to sample several windows of execution in a terabyte-size trace file. Provided that the sampled subset is representative of the set as a whole, and provided that the technique used to collect the samples is correct, the mechanism provides a low-cost alternative that can be very accurate. This section demonstrates that the technique used to collect the samples can easily be incorrect and that the results can be far from accurate, if one follows intuition.

The discussion will use as an example a mechanism that samples the miles-per-gallon performance of an automobile under way. We study an out and back trip with a brief pit stop, shown in Figure 28.4. The automobile follows a simple course that is easily analyzed:

1. The auto will travel over even ground for 60 miles at 60 mph, and it will achieve 30 mpg during this window of time.
2. The auto will travel uphill for 20 miles at 60 mph, and it will achieve 10 mpg during this window of time.
3. The auto will travel downhill for 20 miles at 60 mph, and it will achieve 300 mpg during this window of time.
4. The auto will travel back home over even ground for 60 miles at 60 mph, and it will achieve 30 mpg during this window of time.
5. In addition, before returning home, the driver will sit at the top of the hill for 10 minutes, enjoying the view, with the auto idling, consuming gasoline at the rate of 1 gallon every 5 hours. This is equivalent to 1/300 gallon per minute, or 1/30 of a gallon during the 10-minute respite. Note that the auto will achieve 0 mpg during this window of time.

Let's see how we can sample the car's gasoline efficiency. There are three obvious units of measurement involved in the process: the trip will last some amount of time (minutes), the car will travel some distance (miles), and the trip will consume an amount of fuel (gallons). At the very least, we can use each of these units to provide a space over which we will sample the desired metric.

28.3.1 Sampling Over Time

Our first treatment will sample miles per gallon over time, so for our analysis we need to break down the segments of the trip by the amount of time they take:

- Outbound: 60 minutes
- Uphill: 20 minutes
- Idling: 10 minutes
- Downhill: 20 minutes
- Return: 60 minutes

This is displayed graphically in Figure 28.5, in which the time for each segment is shown to scale. Assume, for the sake of simplicity, that the sampling algorithm samples the car's miles per gallon every minute and adds that sampled value to the running average (it could just as easily sample every second or millisecond). Then the algorithm will sample the value 30 mpg 60 times during the first segment of the trip; it will sample the value 10 mpg 20 times during the second segment of the trip; it will sample the value 0 mpg 10 times during the third segment of the trip; and so on. Over the trip, the car is operating for a total of 170 minutes; thus, we can derive the sampling algorithm's results as follows:

$$\frac{60}{170}30 + \frac{20}{170}10 + \frac{10}{170}0 + \frac{20}{170}300 + \frac{60}{170}30 = 57.5 \text{ mpg}$$

$$\text{(EQ 28.1)}$$

If we were to believe this method of calculating sampled averages, we would believe that the car, at least on this trip, is getting roughly twice the fuel efficiency of traveling over flat ground, despite the fact that the trip started and ended in the same place. That seems

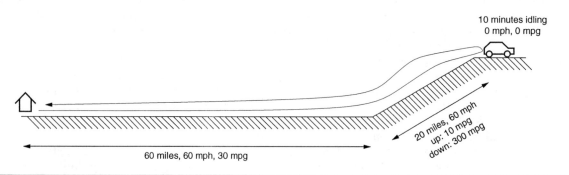

FIGURE 28.4: Course taken by automobile in example.

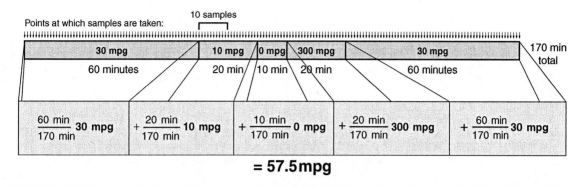

Points at which samples are taken:

10 samples

$$\frac{60 \text{ min}}{170 \text{ min}} 30 \text{ mpg} + \frac{20 \text{ min}}{170 \text{ min}} 10 \text{ mpg} + \frac{10 \text{ min}}{170 \text{ min}} 0 \text{ mpg} + \frac{20 \text{ min}}{170 \text{ min}} 300 \text{ mpg} + \frac{60 \text{ min}}{170 \text{ min}} 30 \text{ mpg}$$

$$= 57.5 \text{mpg}$$

FIGURE 28.5: Sampling mpg over time. The figure shows the trip in time, with each segment of time labelled with the average miles per gallon for the car during that segment of the trip. Thus, whenever the sampling algorithm samples mpg during a window of time, it will add that value to the running average.

a bit suspicious and is due to the extremely high efficiency value (300 mpg) accounting for more than it deserves in the final results: it contributes one-third as much as each of the over-flat-land efficiency values. More importantly, the *amount* that it contributes to the whole is not limited by the mathematics. For instance, one could turn off the engine and coast down the hill, consuming zero gallons while traveling non-zero distance, and achieve essentially infinite fuel efficiency in the final results. Similarly, one could arbitrarily lower the sampled fuel efficiency by spending longer periods of time idling at the top of the hill. For example, if the driver stayed a bit longer at the top of the hill, the result would be significantly different.

$$\frac{60}{220} 30 + \frac{20}{220} 10 + \frac{60}{220} 10 + \frac{20}{220} 300 + \frac{60}{220} 30 = 44.5 \text{ mpg}$$

(EQ 28.2)

Clearly, this method does not give us reasonable results.

28.3.2 Sampling Over Distance

Our second treatment will sample miles per gallon over the distance traveled, so for our analysis we need to break down the segments of the trip by the distance that the car travels:

- Outbound: 60 miles
- Uphill: 20 miles

- Idling: 0 miles
- Downhill: 20 miles
- Return: 60 miles

This is displayed graphically in Figure 28.6, in which the distance traveled during each segment is shown to scale. Assume, for the sake of simplicity, that the sampling algorithm samples the car's miles per gallon every mile and adds that sampled value to the running average (it could just as easily sample every meter or foot or rotation of the wheel). Then the algorithm will sample the value 30 mpg 60 times during the first segment of the trip; it will sample the value 10 mpg 20 times during the second segment of the trip; it will sample the value 300 mpg 20 times during the third segment of the trip; and so on. Note that, because the car does not move during the idling segment of the trip, its contribution to the total is not counted. Over the duration of the trip, the car travels a total of 160 miles; thus, we can derive the sampling algorithm's results as follows:

$$\frac{60}{160} 30 + \frac{20}{160} 10 + \frac{20}{160} 300 + \frac{60}{160} 30 = 61 \text{ mpg}$$

(EQ 28.3)

This result is not far from the previous result, which should indicate that it, too, fails to gives us believable results. The method falls prey to the same problem as before: the large value of 300 mpg contributes significantly to the average, and one can "trick" the

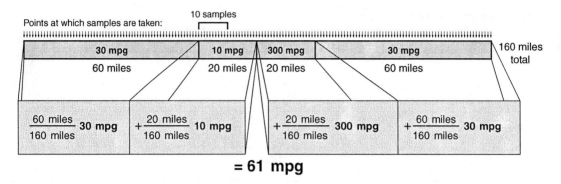

FIGURE 28.6: Sampling mpg over distance. The figure shows the trip in distance traveled, with each segment of distance labelled with the average miles per gallon for the car during that segment of the trip. Thus, whenever the sampling algorithm samples mpg during a window, it will add that value to the running average.

algorithm by using infinite values when shutting off the engine. The one advantage this method has over the previous method is that one cannot arbitrarily lower the fuel efficiency by idling for longer periods of time: idling is constrained by the mathematics to be excluded from the average. Idling travels zero distance, and therefore, its contribution to the whole is zero. Yet this is perhaps too extreme, as idling certainly contributes *some* amount to an automobile's fuel efficiency.

On the other hand, if one were to fail to do a reality check, i.e., if it had not been pointed out that anything over 30 mpg is likely to be incorrect, one might be seduced by the fact that the first two approaches produced nearly the same value. The second result is not far off from the previous result, which might give one an unfounded sense of confidence that the approach is relatively accurate or at least relatively insensitive to minor details.

28.3.3 Sampling Over Fuel Consumption

Our last treatment will sample miles per gallon along the axis of fuel consumption, so for our analysis we need to break down the segments of the trip by the amount of fuel that they consume:

- Outbound: 60 miles @ 30 mpg = 2 gallons
- Uphill: 20 miles @ 10 mpg = 2 gallons
- Idling: 10 minutes at 1/300 gallon per minute = 1/30 gallon

- Downhill: 20 miles @ 300 mpg = 1/15 gallon
- Return: 60 miles @ 30 mpg = 2 gallons

This is displayed graphically in Figure 28.7, in which the fuel consumed during each segment of the trip is shown to scale. Assume, for the sake of simplicity, that the sampling algorithm samples the car's miles per gallon every 1/30 gallon and adds that sampled value to the running average (it could just as easily sample every gallon or ounce or milliliter). Then the algorithm will sample the value 30 mpg 60 times during the first segment of the trip; it will sample the value 10 mpg 60 times during the second segment of the trip; it will sample the value 0 mpg once during the third segment of the trip; and so on. Over the duration of the trip, the car consumes a total of 6.1 gallons. Using this rather than number of samples gives an alternative, more intuitive, representation of the weights in the average: the first segment contributes 2 gallons out of 6.1 total gallons; the second segment contributes 2 gallons out of 6.1 total gallons; the third segment contributes 1/30 gallons out of 6.1 total gallons; etc. We can derive the sampling algorithm's results as follows:

$$\frac{2}{6.1} 30 + \frac{2}{6.1} 10 + \frac{1/30}{6.1} 0 + \frac{1/15}{6.1} 300 + \frac{2}{6.1} 30 = 26.2 \text{ mpg}$$
(EQ 28.4)

This is the first sampling approach in which our results are less than the auto's average fuel efficiency over flat ground. Less than 30 mpg is what we should

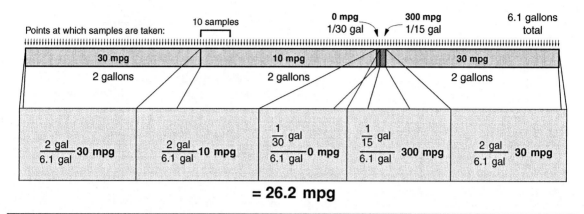

= 26.2 mpg

FIGURE 28.7: Sampling mpg over fuel consumed. The figure shows the trip in quantity of fuel consumed, with each segment labelled with the average miles per gallon for the car during that segment of the trip. Thus, whenever the sampling algorithm samples mpg during a window, it will add that value to the running average.

expect, since much of the trip is over flat ground, and a significant portion of the trip is uphill. In this approach, the large MPG value does not contribute significantly to the total, and neither does the idling value. Interestingly, the approach does not fall prey to the same problems as before. For instance, one cannot trick the algorithm by shutting off the engine: doing so would eliminate that portion of the trip from the total. What happens if we increase the idling time to 1 hour?

$$\frac{2}{6.27}30 + \frac{2}{6.27}10 + \frac{6/30}{6.27}0 + \frac{1/15}{6.27}300 + \frac{2}{6.27}30 = 25.5 \text{ mpg}$$
$$\text{(EQ 28.5)}$$

Idling for longer periods of time affects the total only slightly, as is what one should expect. Clearly, this is the best approach yet.

28.3.4 The Moral of the Story

So what is the real answer? The auto travels 160 miles, consuming 6.1 gallons; it is not hard to find the actual miles per gallon achieved.

$$\frac{160 \text{ miles}}{6.1 \text{ gallons}} = 26.2 \text{ mpg} \qquad \text{(EQ 28.6)}$$

The approach that is perhaps the least intuitive (sampling over the space of *gallons?*) does give the correct answer. We see that, if the metric we are measuring is miles per gallon,

- Sampling over minutes (time) is bad.
- Sampling over miles (distance) is bad.
- Sampling over *gallons* (consumption) is *good.*

Moreover (and perhaps most importantly), in this context, *bad* means "can be off by a factor of two or more."

The moral of the story is that if you are sampling the following metric:

$$\frac{\text{data}}{\text{unit}} \qquad \text{(EQ 28.7)}$$

then you must sample that metric in equal steps of dimension *unit*. To wit, if sampling the metric *miles per gallon*, you must sample evenly in units of *gallon*; if sampling the metric *cycles per instruction*, you must sample evenly in units of *instruction* (i.e., evenly in *instructions committed*, not instructions fetched or executed[1]); if sampling the metric *instructions per*

---

[1]The metrics must match exactly. The common definition of CPI is *total execution cycles divided by the total number of instructions performed/committed* and does not include speculative instructions in the denominator (though it does include their effects in the numerator).

cycle, you must sample evenly in units of *cycle*; and if sampling the metric *cache-miss rate* (i.e., cache misses per cache access), you must sample evenly in units of *cache access*.

What does it mean to sample in units of *instruction* or *cycle* or *cache access*? For a microprocessor, it means that one must have a countdown timer that decrements every unit, i.e., once for every instruction committed or once every cycle or once every time the cache is accessed, and on every epoch (i.e., whenever a predefined number of units have transpired) the desired average must be taken. For an automobile providing real-time fuel efficiency, a sensor must be placed in the gas line that interrupts a controller whenever a predefined unit of volume of gasoline is consumed.

What determines the predefined amounts that set the epoch size? Clearly, to catch all interesting behavior one must sample frequently enough to measure all important events. Higher sampling rates lead to better accuracy at a higher cost of implementation. How does sampling at a lower rate affect one's accuracy? For example, by sampling at a rate of once every 1/30 gallon in the previous example, we were assured of catching every segment of the trip. However, this was a contrived example where we knew the desired sampling rate ahead of time. What if, as in normal cases, one does not know the appropriate sampling rate? For example, if the example algorithm sampled every gallon instead of every small fraction of a gallon, we would have gotten the following results:

$$\frac{2}{6} 30 + \frac{2}{6} 10 + \frac{2}{6} 30 = 23.3 \text{ mpg} \qquad \text{(EQ 28.8)}$$

The answer is off the true result, but it is not as bad as if we had generated the sampled average incorrectly in the first place (e.g., sampling in minutes or miles traveled).

28.4 Metrics for Computer Performance

This section explains what it means to characterize the performance of a computer and discusses what methods are appropriate and inappropriate for the task. The most widely used metric is the performance on the SPEC benchmark suite of programs; currently, the results of running the SPEC benchmark suite are compiled into a single number using the geometric mean. The primary reason for using the geometric mean is that it preserves values across normalization, but, unfortunately, it does not preserve total run time, which is probably the figure of greatest interest when performances are being compared.

Average cycles per instruction (average CPI) is another widely used metric, but using this metric to compare performance is also invalid, even if comparing machines with identical clock speeds. Comparing averaged CPI values to judge performance falls prey to the same problems as averaging normalized values.

Instead of the geometric mean, either the *harmonic* or the *arithmetic* mean is the appropriate method for averaging a set of running times. The arithmetic mean should be used to average times, and the harmonic mean should be used to average rates[2] ("rate" meaning 1/time). In addition, normalized values must never be averaged, as this section will demonstrate.

28.4.1 Performance and the Use of Means

We want to summarize the performance of a computer. The easiest way uses a single number that can be compared against the numbers of other machines. This typically involves running tests on the machine and taking some sort of mean; the mean of a set of

---

[2]A note on rates, in particular, *miss rate*. Even though miss rate is a "rate," it is not a rate in the harmonic/arithmetic mean sense because (a) it contains no concept of time, and, more importantly, (b) the thing a designer cares about is the number of misses (in the numerator), not the number of cache accesses (in the denominator). The oft-chanted mantra of "use harmonic mean to average rates" only applies to scenarios in which the metric a designer really cares about is in the denominator. For instance, when a designer says "performance," he is really talking about time, and when the metric puts time in the denominator either explicitly (as in the case of *instructions per second*) or implicitly (as in the case of *instructions per cycle*), the metric becomes a rate in the harmonic mean sense. For example, if one uses the metric *cache-accesses-per-cache-miss*, this is a *de facto rate*, and the harmonic mean would probably be the appropriate mean to use.

numbers is the central value when the set represents fluctuations about that value. There are a number of different ways to define a mean value, among them the arithmetic mean, the geometric mean, and the harmonic mean.

The *arithmetic mean* is defined as follows:

$$Arithmetic\ Mean\ (a_1, a_2, a_3 \dots , a_N) = \frac{\sum_{i}^{N} a_i}{N} \qquad \text{(EQ 28.9)}$$

The *geometric mean* is defined as follows:

$$Geometric\ Mean\ (a_1, a_2, a_3 \dots , a_N) = \sqrt[N]{\prod_{i}^{N} a_i} \qquad \text{Q 28.10)}$$

The *harmonic mean* is defined as follows

$$Harmonic\ Mean\ (a1, a2, a3, \dots , aN) = \frac{N}{\sum_{i}^{N} \frac{1}{a_i}} \qquad \text{(EQ 28.11)}$$

In the mathematical sense, the geometric mean of a set of *n* values is the length of one side of an *n*-dimensional cube having the same volume as an *n*-dimensional rectangle whose sides are given by the *n* values. It is used to find the average of a set of multiplicative values, e.g., the average over time of a variable interest rate. A side effect of the math is that the geometric mean is unaffected by normalization; whether one normalizes by a set of weights first or by the geometric mean of the weights afterward, the net result is the same. This property has been used to suggest that the geometric mean is superior for calculating computer performance, since it produces the same results when comparing several computers irrespective of which computer's times are used as the normalization factor [Fleming & Wallace 1986]. However, the argument was rebutted by Smith [1988]. In this book, we consider only the arithmetic and harmonic means. Note that the two are inverses of each other:

$$Arithmetic\ Mean\ (a_1, a_2, a_3 \dots)$$
$$= \frac{1}{Harmonic\ Mean\left(\frac{1}{a_1}, \frac{1}{a_2}, \frac{1}{a_3}, \dots\right)} \qquad \text{(EQ 28.12)}$$

28.4.2 Problems with Normalization

Problems arise when we average sets of normalized numbers. The following examples demonstrate the errors that occur. The first example compares the performance of two machines using a third as a benchmark. The second example extends the first to show the error in using averaged CPI values to compare performance. The third example is a revisitation of a recent proposal published on this very topic.

Example 1: Average Normalized by Reference Times

There are two machines, A and B, and a reference machine. There are two tests, Test1 and Test2, and we obtain the following scores for the machines:

Scenario I	Test1	Test2
Machine A	10 s	100 s
Machine B	1 s	1000 s
Reference	1 s	100 s

In scenario I, the performance of machine A relative to the reference machine is 0.1 on Test1 and 1 on Test2. The performance of machine B relative to the reference machine is 1 on Test1 and 0.1 on Test2. Since *time* is in the denominator (the reference is in the numerator), we are averaging *rates*; therefore, we use the harmonic mean. The fact that the reference value is also in units of time is irrelevant. The time measurement we are concerned with is in the denominator; thus, we are averaging rates. The performance results of scenario I:

Scenario I	Harmonic Mean
Machine A	HMean(0.1, 1) = 2/11
Machine B	HMean(1, 0.1) = 2/11

The two machines perform equally well. This makes intuitive sense; on one test, machine A was ten times faster, and on the other test, machine B was ten times faster. Therefore, they should be of equal performance. As it turns out, this line of reasoning is erroneous. Let us consider scenario II, where the only thing that has changed is the reference machine's times (from 100 seconds on Test2 to 10 seconds):

Scenario II	Test1	Test2
Machine A	10 s	100 s
Machine B	1 s	1000 s
Reference	1 s	10 s

Here, the performance numbers for A relative to the reference machine are 1/10 and 1/10, the performance numbers for B are 1 and 1/100, and these are the results:

Scenario II	Harmonic Mean
Machine A	HMean(0.1, 0.1) = 1/10
Machine B	HMean(1, 0.01) = 2/101

According to this, machine A performs about five times better than machine B. If we try yet another scenario, changing only the reference machine's performance on Test2, we obtain the result that machine A performs five times *worse* than machine B.

Scenario III	Test1	Test2	Harmonic Mean
Machine A	10 s	100 s	HMean(0.1, 10) = 20/101
Machine B	1 s	1000 s	HMean(1, 1) = 1
Reference	1 s	1000 s	

The lesson: do not average test results that have been normalized.

Example 2: Average Normalized by Number of Operations

The example extends even further. What if the numbers were not a set of normalized running times, but CPI measurements? Taking the average of a set of CPI values should not be susceptible to this kind of error,

because the numbers are *not* unitless; they are not the ratio of the running times of two arbitrary machines.

Let us test this theory. Let us take the average of a set of CPI values in three scenarios. The units are *cycles per instruction*, and since the time-related portion (cycles) is in the numerator, we will be able to use the arithmetic mean.

The following are the three scenarios, where the only difference between each scenario is the number of instructions performed in Test2. The running times for each machine on each test do not change. Therefore, we should expect the performance of each machine relative to the other to remain the same.

Scenario I	Test1	Test2	Arithmetic Mean
Machine A	10 cycles	100 cycles	AMean(10, 10) = 10 CPI
Machine B	1 cycle	1000 cycles	AMean(1, 100) = 50.5 CPI
Instructions	1 instr	10 instr	**Result:** *Machine A 5x faster*

Scenario II	Test1	Test2	Arithmetic Mean
Machine A	10 cycles	100 cycles	AMean(10, 1) = 5.5 CPI
Machine B	1 cycle	1000 cycles	AMean(1, 10) = 5.5 CPI
Instructions	1 instr	100 instr	**Result:** *Equal performance*

Scenario III	Test1	Test2	Arithmetic Mean
Machine A	10 cycles	100 cycles	AMean(10, 0.1) = 5.05 CPI
Machine B	1 cycle	1000 cycles	AMean(1, 1) = 1 CPI
Instructions	1 instr	1000 instr	**Result:** *Machine B 5x faster*

We obtain the same anomalous result as before: the machines exhibit different relative performances that depend on the number of instructions executed.

So our proposed theory is flawed. Average CPI values are not valid measures of computer performance. Taking the average of a set of CPI values is not inherently wrong, but the result cannot be used to compare performance. The erroneous behavior is due to normalizing the values before averaging them. Again, this example is not meant to imply that average CPI values are meaningless, they are simply meaningless when used to compare the performance of machines.

Example 3: Average Normalized by Both Times and Operations

An interesting mathematical result is that, with the proper choice of weights (weighting by instruction count when using the harmonic mean and weighting by execution time when using the arithmetic mean), the use of both the arithmetic and harmonic means on the very same performance numbers—not the inverses of the numbers—provides the same results. That is,

$$\frac{1}{\sum_i \frac{\omega i_i}{\text{MIPS}_i}} = \sum_i \omega t_i \cdot \text{MIPS}_i \qquad \text{(EQ 28.13)}$$

where the expression on the left is the harmonic mean of a set of values, the expression on the right is the arithmetic mean of the same set, ωi_i is the instruction-count weight, and ωt_i is the execution-time weight, as follows:

$$\omega i_i = \frac{I_i}{\sum I_n} \qquad \omega t_i = \frac{T_i}{\sum T_n} \qquad \text{(EQ 28.14)}$$

I_x is the instruction count of benchmark x, and T_x is the execution time of benchmark x. The fact of this equivalence may seem to suggest that the average so produced is somehow correct, in the same way that the geometric mean's preservation of values across normalization was used as evidence to support its use [Fleming & Wallace 1986]. A recent article does indeed propose this method of normalization for exactly this reason. However, as shown in the sampled

averages section, noting that two roads converge on the same or similar answer is not a proof of correctness; it could always be that both paths are erroneous. Take, for example, the following table, which shows the results for five different benchmarks in a hypothetical suite.

Benchmark	Instruction Count ($\times 10^6$)	Time (s)	Individual MIPS
1	500	2	250
2	50	1	50
3	200	1	200
4	1 000	5	200
5	250	1	250

The overall MIPS of the benchmark suite is 2000 million instructions divided by 10 seconds, or 200 MIPS. Taking the harmonic mean of the individual MIPS values, weighted by each benchmark's contribution to the total instruction count, yields an average of 200 MIPS. Taking the arithmetic mean of the individual MIPS values, weighted by each benchmark's contribution to the total execution time, yields an average of 200 MIPS. This would seem to be a home run. However, let us skew the results by changing benchmark #2 so that its instruction count is 200 times larger than before and its execution time is also 200 times larger than before. The table now looks like this:

Benchmark	Instruction Count (10^6)	Time (s)	Individual MIPS
1	500	2	250
2	10,000	200	50
3	200	1	200
4	1,000	5	200
5	250	1	250

This is the same effect as looping benchmark #2 200 times. However, the total MIPS now becomes roughly 12,000 million instructions divided by roughly 200 seconds, or roughly 60 MIPS—a factor of three lower than the previous value. Thus, though this mechanism is very convincing, it is as easily spoofed as other mechanisms: the problem comes from trying to take the average of normalized values and interpret it to mean *performance*.

28.4.3 The Meaning of Performance

Normalization, if performed, should be carried out *after* averaging. If we wish to average a set of execution times against a reference machine, the following equation holds (which is the ratio of the arithmetic means, with the constant N terms cancelling out):

$$\frac{\dfrac{\sum_i Our\ Time_i}{N}}{\sum_j Ref\ Time_j} \qquad \text{(EQ 28.15)}$$

However, if we say that this describes the performance of the machine, then we implicitly believe that every test counts equally, in that on average it is used the same *number* of times as all other tests. This means that tests which are much longer than others will count more in the results.

Perspective: Performance Is Time Saved

We wish to be able to say, "*this* machine is X times faster than *that* machine." Ambiguity arises because we are often unclear on the concept of performance. What do we mean when we talk about the performance of a machine? Why do we wish to be able to say *this machine is X times faster than that machine*? The *reason* is that we have been using *that* machine (machine A) for some time and wish to know how much time we would save by using *this* machine (machine B) instead.

How can we measure this? First, we find out what programs we tend to run on machine A. These programs (or ones similar to them) will be used as the benchmark suite to run on machine B. Next, we measure how often we tend to use the programs. These values will be used as weights in computing the average (programs used more should count more), but the problem is that it is not clear whether we should use

values in units of time or number of occurrences. Do we count each program the number of times per day it is used or the number of hours per day it is used?

We have an idea about how often we use programs. For instance, every time we edit a source file we might recompile. So we would assign equal weights to the word-processing benchmark and the compiler benchmark. We might run a different set of three or four n-body simulations every time we recompiled the simulator; we would then weight the simulator benchmark three or four times as heavily as the compiler and text editor. Of course, it is not quite as simple as this, but you get the point; we tend to know how often we use a program, independent of how slowly or quickly the machine we use performs it.

What does this buy us? Say, for the moment, that we consider all benchmarks in the suite equally important (we use each as often as the other); all we need to do is total up the times it took the new machine to perform the tests, total up the times it took the reference machine to perform the tests, and compare the two results.

The Bottom Line

It does not matter if one test takes 3 minutes and another takes 3 days on your new machine. If the reference machine performs the short test in less than 1 second (indicating that your new machine is *extremely* slow), and it performs the long test in 3 days and 6 hours (indicating that your new machine is marginally faster than the old one), then the *time saved* is about 6 hours. Even if you use the short program 100 times as often as the long program, the time saved is still 1 hour over the old machine.

The error is that we considered performance to be a value that can be averaged; the problem is our perception that performance is a simple number. The reason for the problem is that we often forget the difference between the following statements:

- On average, the amount of time saved by using machine A over machine B is … .
- On average, the relative performance of machine A to machine B is … .

We usually know what our daily computing needs are; we are interested in how much of that we can get done with *this* computer versus *that* one. In this context, the only thing that matters is how much time is saved by using one machine over another. Performance is, in reality, a specific instance of the following:

- Two machines
- A set of programs to be run on them
- An indication of how important each of the programs is to *us*

Performance is therefore not a single number, but really a collection of implications. It is nothing more or less than the measure of how much time *we* save running *our* tests on the machines in question. If someone else has similar needs to ours, our performance numbers will be useful to them. However, two people with different sets of criteria will likely walk away with two completely different performance numbers for the same machine.

28.5 Analytical Modeling and the Miss-Rate Function

The classical cache miss-rate function, as defined by Stone, Smith, and others, is $M(x) = \beta x^\alpha$ for constants β and negative α and variable cache size x [Smith 1982, Stone 1993]. This function has been shown to describe accurately the shape of a cache's miss rate as a function of the cache's size. However, when used directly in optimization analysis without any alterations to accommodate boundary cases, the function can lead to erroneous results. This section presents the mathematical insight behind the behavior of the function under the Lagrange multiplier optimization procedure and shows how a simple modification to the form solves the inherent problems.

28.5.1 Analytical Modeling

Mathematical analysis lends itself well to understanding cache behavior. Many researchers have used such analysis on memory hierarchies in the past. For instance, Chow showed that the optimum number of

cache levels scales with the logarithm of the capacity of the cache hierarchy [Chow 1974, 1976]. Garcia-Molina and Rege demonstrated that it is often better to have more of a slower device than less of a faster device [Garcia-Molina et al. 1987, Rege 1976]. Welch showed that the optimal speed of each level must be proportional to the amount of time spent servicing requests out of that level [Welch 1978]. Jacob et al. [1996] complement this earlier work and provide intuitive understanding of how budget and technology characteristics interact. The analysis is the first to find a closed-form solution for the size of each level in a general memory hierarchy, given device parameters (cost and speed), available system budget, and a measure of the workload's temporal locality. The model recommends cache sizes that are non-intuitive; in particular, with little money to spend on the hierarchy, the model recommends spending it all on the cheapest, slowest storage technology rather than the fastest. This is contrary to the common practice of focusing on satisfying as many references in the fastest cache level, such as the L1 cache for processors or the file cache for storage systems. Interestingly, it *does* reflect what has happened in the PC market, where processor caches have been among the last levels of the memory hierarchy to be added.

The model provides intuitive understanding of memory hierarchies and indicates how one should spend one's money. Figure 28.8 pictures examples of optimal allocations of funds across three- and four-level hierarchies (e.g., several levels of cache, DRAM, and/or disk). In general, the first dollar spent by a memory-hierarchy designer should go to the lowest level in the hierarchy. As money is added to the system, the size of this level should increase, until it becomes cost-effective to purchase some of the next level up. From that point on, every dollar spent on the system should be divided between the two levels in a fixed proportion, with more *bytes* being added to the lower level than the higher level. This does not necessarily mean that more *money* is spent on the lower level. Every dollar is split this way until it becomes cost-effective to add another hierarchy level on top; from that point on every dollar is split three ways, with more bytes being added to the lower levels than the higher levels, until it becomes cost-effective

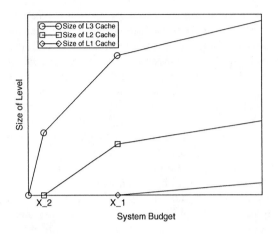
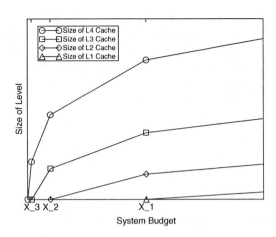

FIGURE 28.8: An example of solutions for two larger hierarchies. A three-level hierarchy is shown on the left; a four-level hierarchy is shown on the right. Between inflection points (at which it is most cost-effective to add another level to the hierarchy) the equations are linear; the curves simply change slopes at the inflection points to adjust for the additional cost of a new level in the hierarchy.

to add another level on top. Since real technologies do not come in arbitrary sizes, hierarchy levels will increase as step functions approximating the slopes of straight lines. The interested reader is referred to the article for more detail and analysis.

28.5.2 The Miss-Rate Function

As mentioned, there are many analytical cache papers in the literature, and many of these use the classical miss-rate function $M(x) = \beta x^{\alpha}$. This function is a direct outgrowth of the 30% Rule,[3] which states that successive doublings of cache size should reduce the miss rate by approximately 30%.

The function accurately describes the shape of the miss-rate curve, which represents miss rate as

a function of cache size, but it does not accurately reflect the values at boundary points. Therefore, the form cannot be used in any mathematical analysis that depends on accurate values at these points. For instance, using this form yields an infinite miss rate for a cache of size zero, whereas probabilities are only defined on the [0,1] range. Caches of size less than one[4] will have arbitrarily large miss rates (greater than unity). While this is not a problem when one is simply interested in the shape of a curve, it can lead to significant errors if one uses the form in optimization analysis, in particular the technique of Lagrange multipliers. This has led some previous analytical cache studies to reach half-completed solutions or (in several cases) outright erroneous solutions.

---

[3]The 30% Rule, first suggested by Smith [1982], is the rule of thumb that every doubling of a cache's size should reduce the cache misses by 30%. Solving the recurrence relation

$$0.7f(x) = f(2x) \qquad \text{(EQ 28.16)}$$

yields a polynomial of the form

$$f(x) = \beta x^{\alpha} \qquad \text{(EQ 28.17)}$$

where α is negative.

[4]Note that this is a perfectly valid region to explore; consider, for example, an analysis in which the unit of cache size measurement is megabytes.

The classical miss-rate function can be used without problem provided that its form behaves well, i.e., it must return values between 1 and 0 for all physically realizable (non-negative) cache sizes. This requires a simple modification; the original function $M(x) = \beta x^{\alpha}$ becomes $M(x) = (\beta x + 1)^{\alpha}$. The difference in form is slight, yet the difference in results and conclusions that can be drawn are very large. The classical form suggests that the ratio of sizes in a cache hierarchy is a constant; if one chooses a number of levels for the cache hierarchy, then all levels are present in the optimal cache hierarchy. Even at very small budget points, the form suggests that one should add money to every level in the hierarchy in a fixed proportion determined by the optimization procedure.

By contrast, when one uses the form $M(x) = (\beta x + 1)^{\alpha}$ for the miss-rate function, one reaches the conclusion that the ratio of sizes in the optimal cache hierarchy is not constant. At small budget points, certain levels in the hierarchy should not appear. At very small budget points, it does not make sense to appropriate one's dollar across every level in the hierarchy; it is better spent on a single level in the hierarchy, until one has enough money to afford adding another level (the conclusion reached in Jacob et al. [1996]).

CHAPTER 29

Power and Leakage

Power dissipation has become a top priority for today's microprocessors. Previously a concern mainly for mobile devices, it has now become extremely important for general-purpose and even high-performance microprocessors, especially with the recent industry emphasis on processor "Performance-per-Watt."

The power dissipated by typical modern circuits can be broken up into three main categories: dynamic or switching power, short circuit power, and leakage power. Dynamic power is due to the charging and discharging parasitic capacitance of transistors during logic transitions. This power is typically expressed in a simplified form:

$$P_{\text{dynamic}} = \alpha C_{\text{tot}} V_{\text{dd}}^2 f \qquad \text{(EQ 29.1)}$$

where α is the average transition probability, C_{tot} is the total load capacitance being switched, V_{dd} is the supply voltage, and f is the operating frequency.

Short circuit power is induced when NMOS and PMOS transistors are conducting simultaneously, causing a short current flowing through from the power supply to the ground. It can be expressed as a function of rise and fall times:

$$P_{\text{short-circuit}} = \frac{t_{\text{r}} + t_{\text{f}}}{2} I_{\text{p}} V_{\text{dd}} f \qquad \text{(EQ 29.2)}$$

where t_{r} and t_{f} are the rise and fall times of the input, respectively. I_{p} is the saturation current of the circuit, and it is directly proportional to the size of the transistors. The primary item to note about this source of power is that, as technology scales and clock speeds increase, the typical waveform gets further and further away from the ideal square wave. As a result,

the time spent in transition between logic high and logic low (i.e., the rise and fall times of the circuit) is becoming a greater proportion of the total cycle time. Thus, even if t_{r} and t_{f} are decreasing with each generation, they are decreasing at a slower rate than f is increasing.

Leakage power is due to leakage current when a transistor's inputs and outputs are not switching. It can be expressed as the product of leakage current and supply voltage:

$$P_{\text{leakage}} = I_{\text{leak}} V_{\text{dd}} \qquad \text{(EQ 29.3)}$$

Dynamic and short circuit power are relatively well-known and well-understood phenomena. Leakage power is less well known and less well understood, and, further, it is becoming the dominant source of power dissipation in modern and future circuits. Thus, this chapter will focus largely on leakage in memory circuits—in particular, understanding the mechanism and measuring the effects.

29.1 Sources of Leakage in CMOS Devices

In the deep submicron regime, as CMOS circuit threshold voltage, channel length, and gate oxide thickness decrease, high leakage current is becoming a significant contributor to power dissipation. Anis [2003] gives a good overview of these leakage currents, as shown in Figure 29.1, and his explanation of these different mechanisms is as follows:

- I_1 is the junction leakage current. It occurs from the source or drain to the substrate

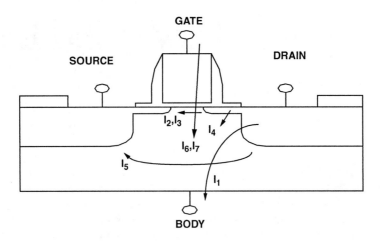

FIGURE 29.1: Typical leakage current mechanisms in a modern MOSFET.

through the reverse-biased diodes when a transistor is OFF. A reverse-biased p/n junction leakage current has two main components: one is the minority carrier diffusion/drift near the edge of the depletion region, and the other is due to electron-hole pair generation in the depletion region. The p/n junction leakage current depends on the area of the drain diffusion and the leakage current density, which is, in turn, determined by the doping concentration. If both n and p regions are heavily doped, band-to-band tunneling dominates the p/n junction leakage.

- I_2 is subthreshold leakage current due to the drain-source current of a transistor operating in a weak inversion region. Unlike the strong inversion region in which the drift current dominates, subthreshold conduction is due to the diffusion current of the minority carriers in the channel of an MOS device. The magnitude of the subthreshold current is a function of temperature, supply voltage, device size, and the process parameters, of which threshold voltage (V_t) plays a dominant role. In current CMOS technologies, the subthreshold leakage current is much larger than other leakage current

components due to the relatively low V_t in modern CMOS devices.

- I_3 represents Drain-Induced Barrier Lowering (DIBL), which occurs when the depletion region of the drain interacts with the source near the channel surface in a a manner that lowers the source's potential barrier (more on this later). The source then injects carriers into the channel surface without the gate playing a role.

- I_4 refers to the Gate-Induced Drain Leakage (GIDL). GIDL current arises in the high electric field under the gate/drain overlap region, causing a deep depletion and effectively thinning out the depletion width of the drain-well p/n junction. Carriers are generated into the substrate and drain by direct band-to-band tunneling, trap-assisted tunneling, or a combination of thermal emission and tunneling. The thinner oxide thickness T_{ox} and higher V_{dd} cause a larger potential difference between the gate and drain, which enhances the electric-field-dependent GIDL.

- I_5 is the channel punch-through which occurs when the drain and source depletion regions approach each other and electrically touch deep within the channel. Punch-through is a space-charge condition that allows the channel current to exist deep in the sub-gate region, causing the gate to lose control of the sub-gate channel.

- I_6 represents oxide leakage tunneling. The gate oxide tunneling current I_{ox} which is a function of the electric field E_{ox} can cause direct tunneling through the gate.

- I_7 is the gate current due to hot carrier injection. Short-channel transistors are more susceptible to the injection of hot carriers (holes and electrons) into the oxide. These charges are a reliability risk and are measurable as gate and substrate currents.

Typically, I_2 and I_3 dominate the off-leakage current,[1] and I_6 dominates the gate leakage.

In previous generations, subthreshold and gate leakage power have not represented a substantial component of the total power. However, as transistor scaling continues, V_t decreases. Logic gate speeds, as measured by the ability to charge and discharge internal capacitances, are dependent on the gate overdrive voltage $V_{gs} - V_t$. Decreasing V_{dd} tends to decrease the speed of the system (even with a decrease in capacitance associated with device scaling), and this is traditionally compensated for by decreasing the threshold voltage to improve the gate overdrive, resulting in an improved current driving capability of the device. Continued device scaling results in a reduction of V_t, and therefore the device off current starts becoming significant, particularly since it is multiplied by the large number of total devices in the entire chip.

Additionally, with this scaling, a certain amount of device gate-to-body capacitance needs to be maintained to retain control of the inversion channel. With the same dielectric material, this requires reduction of the oxide layer thickness, t_{ox}. However, as t_{ox} decreases below 20 Å with continued scaling, the corresponding oxide layer becomes very thin, allowing quantum tunneling effects to become significant. As such, gate leakage effects are becoming substantial.

Indeed, some sources have stated that over recent technology generations, gate leakage has increased more rapidly than subthreshold leakage, and, consequently, gate leakage current may soon become the most dominant component of leakage current.

Many devices and techniques are proposed to reduce leakage power. These include body biased transistors, sleep transistors, and dual threshold voltage CMOS designs, which include Multiple Threshold CMOS (MTCMOS) sleep transistors and domino logic design techniques. In dual and multiple threshold voltage design, NMOS and CMOS devices are constructed with both high and low threshold voltages by selectively adjusting the well depth. This technology can reduce leakage current by an order of magnitude, but also causes performance degradation, increases noise concerns, and complicates power-grid routing. Another phenomenon is that of reverse body bias effects. These occur when I_{dd}, the current through the V_{dd} pin, decreases and saturates as the threshold leakage current becomes negligible compared to the junction leakage or when $I_{bn/p}$, the current through NMOS and PMOS, respectively, increases due to an increase in both surface current and bulk band-to-band junction leakage tunneling current. Keshavarzi [1999] proposed that there exists a unique optimum reverse body bias value for each process technology for which the device's leakage power is very low. Keshavarzi also noted that this value is generally cut in half with each technology generation. While utilization of the reverse body bias value does effectively reduce leakage power, it also increases band-to-band tunneling current and bulk capacitance, thereby increasing dynamic power. Kim [2003] proposed forward biased transistors to target leakage reduction in cache memories. This technique uses high V_t devices to achieve lower standby leakage current and dynamically applies forward body bias to selected portions of the cache for faster read/write capabilities. Dual V_t and sleep transistors utilize dual V_t design which incorporates two different types of transistors,

---

[1]Off-leakage current is typically defined as the device drain-to-source current (IDs) with the gate off (i.e., strong inversion has not been reached, such that no conducting channel exists between the drain and source terminals). Often, this off-current has been associated and is interchanged with the subthreshold current, simply because subthreshold is often the main, dominant factor.

fast/high V_t and slow/low V_t. Sleep transistors employ power gating and can reduce power 1000 times, producing smaller voltage swings which induce IR drops on sleep transistors.

Low-V_t transistors can be used in speed-critical paths of current microprocessors to decrease delay. This usage results in an exponential increase in subthreshold leakage current with reduced V_t for applications that are sometimes idle. As technology scales, this large "off" current in sleep mode represents a significant portion of the total power. MTCMOS has been proposed to reduce standby current. These circuits primarily use low-V_t transistors for fast operation in active mode and high-V_t gain transistors to reduce the off current in sleep mode. In active mode, the high-V_t gating transistors are on, but the virtual ground for the entire circuit is slightly greater than zero, or the virtual power line is slightly less than V_{dd}, as a result of the IR drop across the gating transistors. The gating transistors need to be sized properly to minimize the effect of the IR drop on circuit speed. In sleep mode, the gating transistors are turned off, and all the node voltages in the circuit become approximately V_{dd} or ground, including the virtual ground (for PMOS gating) or virtual supply (for NMOS gating). As a result, the overall leakage is determined by the gating transistor subthreshold voltage and gate

leakage current, with gate leakage being dominant because of the high-V_t but large gate-to-drain voltage in sleep mode.

Multi-supply circuits are used when the chip is divided into multiple blocks. The blocks on the critical path use a higher supply voltage to decrease the circuit's cycle time, while the remaining blocks use a lower supply voltage to decrease power. For blocks at different voltages to communicate accurately, level converters must be implemented on each block; this comes at the expense of area, power, and speed. This method also has the disadvantage that multiple routes for different power supplies are needed.

Most techniques that provide solutions for gate leakage rely on characterizations given by Rao et al. [2003] that describe the behavior of gate leakage with respect to gate-source and drain-source voltages, as shown in Figure 29.2. These studies conclude that, for a given gate bias, gate leakage is minimum if the gate-drain voltage (V_{gd}) is minimum. If possible, gate bias (V_{gs}) should be reduced to minimize gate leakage. In situations where this is not an option, an alternative approach would be to reduce the gate-drain bias (V_{gd}).

Subthreshold leakage current is typically optimized by increasing threshold voltage, either statically or dynamically. DIBL effects that contribute to

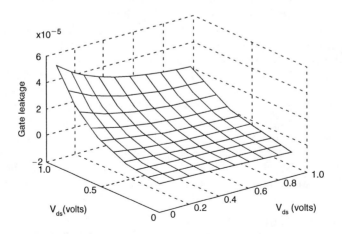

FIGURE 29.2: Gate leakage current for an NMOS as a function of gate-source (V_{gs}) and drain-source (V_{ds}) voltage (figure from Rao et al. [2003]). It shows the highest gate leakage when V_{gs} is max and V_{ds} is zero (making V_{gd} max also).

leakage can be reduced by lowering the drain-source voltage across a transistor in off-state. Gate leakage currents are minimized primarily by reducing the gate bias (V_{gs}) and secondarily by minimizing the gate-drain bias (V_{gd}).

29.2 A Closer Look at Subthreshold Leakage

Subthreshold leakage is an often misunderstood concept in transistor technology. It is frequently associated with deep quantum phenomena like tunneling or even quantum entanglement by some. In fact, it is highly classical in nature and easily grasped in its basics.

To begin with, a formula for I_{off} [Chandrakasan 1996] is the following:

$$I_{off} = \frac{I_o}{W_o} \cdot W \cdot 10^{\frac{V_{gs} - V_1}{S}} \qquad \text{(EQ 29.4)}$$

where I_o/W_o is the saturation current per unit width, W is the width of the device in question, $V_{gs} - V_t$ is the gate overdrive voltage, and S is the subthreshold swing. Leakage increases as the gate overdrive decreases (as V_t increases relative to V_{gs}) and as the subthreshold swing S increases.

S indicates how effectively an MOS device can be turned off with the decrease of gate voltage below threshold voltage. As technology scales, transistor threshold voltage must drop with supply voltage to maintain enough gate overdrive. A higher threshold voltage causes the transistor subthreshold leakage current to increase exponentially: for a typical technology with a subthreshold slope of 100 mV/decade, each 100-mV increase in V_t results in an order of magnitude greater current.

The main issue pertains to the ability of the transistor gate to control the density of mobile charge in the active channel of the transistor—the inversion layer. Reducing the positive bias on the transistor gate, with respect to a usually grounded source, should lower the density of charge (coulombs per cubic centimeter) in the active channel. The current in the active channel is always directly proportional to this charge density. Thus, lowering the gate bias lowers the current.

The gate couples to the active channel mainly through the gate oxide capacitance, but there are other capacitances in a transistor that couple the gate to fixed charge—a charge that cannot move, is present in the bulk, and is not associated with current flow. This is illustrated in Figure 29.3. If these extra capacitances are large (note: they increase with each process generation as physical dimensions shrink), then changing the gate bias merely alters the densities of fixed charge and will not turn the channel off. In this case, the transistor becomes a leaky faucet: it does not turn off, no matter how hard you turn it.

The main parameter describing the impact of subthreshold leakage, the subthreshold swing, S, is given by the following equation:

$$S = \left(\frac{d(\log_{10} I_{ds})}{dV_g} \right)^{-1} = 2.3 \frac{kT}{q} \left(1 + \frac{C_{sc}}{C_{ox}} \right) \qquad \text{(EQ 29.5)}$$

where I_{sc} = source-drain current, V_g = gate voltage, k = Boltzmann's constant, T = temperature, q = charge on the electron, C_{sc} = space-charge capacitance, and C_{ox} = oxide capacitance. This expression is derived in Ning and Taur [Taur & Ning 1998]. Peckerar has shown through his work on radiation-induced interface charge that this expression must be modified to include the interface-state capacitance C_{it} [Peckerar et al. 1979, 1982]. The correct expression is

$$S = 2.3 \frac{kT}{q} \left(1 + \frac{C_{sc} + C_{it}}{C_{ox}} \right) \qquad \text{(EQ 29.6)}$$

Please note that all oxide capacitances are area capacitances, i.e., capacitance per unit area.

As mentioned earlier, S is simply the amount of gate voltage needed to shut off a decade of leakage—to reduce the channel current by an order of magnitude. Typically, the subthreshold swing is 60–70 mV/decade.

The meaning of this expression is intuitively clear. The extra capacitances described above are the space-charge and interface-state capacitances. The gate couples to the bulk fixed charge and to the fixed interface-state charges through these capacitances, diverting control of the inversion charge from the gate. When C_{sc} and C_{it} are large, a larger change in gate bias is needed to get that decade of reduction in the source-drain current.

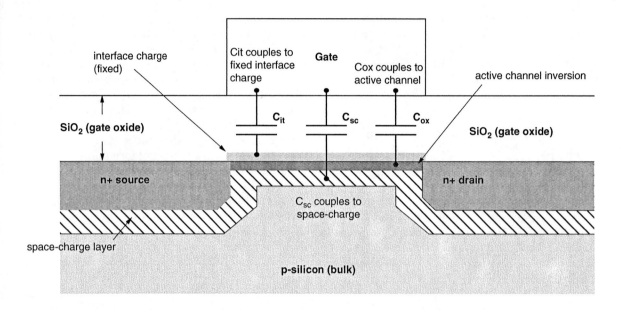

FIGURE 29.3: Gate bias and coupling in a MOSFET. Changing gate bias causes changes in three types of charge: interface-state charge, bulk space charge, and inversion charge. Changes in interface and bulk space charge *do not* change channel current. Only a change in inversion charge affects channel current. Thus, C_{it} and C_{sc} represent "wasted" coupling paths. Note that gate oxide thickness is greatly exaggerated to show the different coupling behaviors.

Ideally, the ratio

$$r = \frac{C_{sc} + C_{it}}{C_{ox}} \qquad \text{(EQ 29.7)}$$

should be small. One would think that in modern VLSI, with its shrinking gate oxide thickness, this would be the case. As we know,

$$C_{ox} = \frac{\varepsilon_{si}}{d_{ox}} \qquad \text{(EQ 29.8)}$$

where d_{ox} is the oxide thickness, and ε_{si} is the dielectric permittivity of silicon. Thus, scaled oxides would have large area capacitances. Unfortunately, r grows as well with technology scaling.

The reason for this is also largely classical, although there may be some quantum component over some range of biases. The source and drain junctions have space-charge layers associated with them. These layers push into the active channel. When the source and drain space charges start to overlap, the potential barrier between the source and drain reduces. Small amounts of bias on the drain will allow direct injection of mobile charge into the drain when this reduction occurs.

This effect is known as DIBL and is illustrated in Figure 29.4. It is eliminated by increasing the substrate doping. Extra doping shrinks the extent of the source-drain space-charge penetration into the active channel, as shown in Figure 29.5. However, it also increases the space-charge capacitance. This is because

$$C_{sc} = \frac{\varepsilon_{si}}{d_{sc}} \qquad \text{(EQ 29.9)}$$

where d_{sc} is the physical extent of the source-drain space charge. It is inversely proportional to the square root of the substrate doping. Thus, to avoid DIBL, r generally increases.

Note the inherent design trade-offs. DIBL-induced leakage can be "cured" by substrate doping, but this

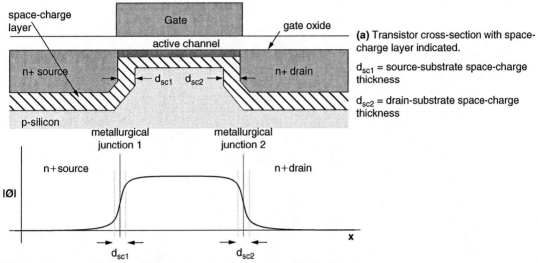

(a) Transistor cross-section with space-charge layer indicated.

d_{sc1} = source-substrate space-charge thickness

d_{sc2} = drain-substrate space-charge thickness

(b) Zero bias potential vs. position plot along semiconductor-oxide interface.

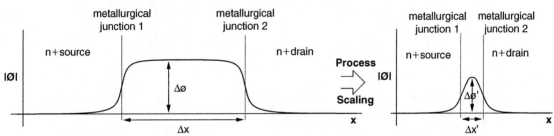

(c) The effect of process scaling, i.e., the effect of overlapping source/drain space charge. As physical dimensions shrink (as $\Delta x'$ becomes much smaller than Δx, i.e. $\Delta x' \ll \Delta x$), the electron-confining barriers ($\Delta \varnothing$) reduce (they become $\Delta \varnothing'$).

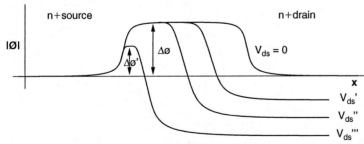

(d) In addition to process scaling effects, drain bias (Vds) can lower the confining barrier, too. $\Delta \varnothing$ goes to $\Delta \varnothing'$ as the potential between drain and source increases. This is called *drain-induced barrier lowering (DIBL)*.

FIGURE 29.4: An illustration of the processes leading to DIBL. As the source injection barrier, $\Delta \varnothing$, lowers (to $\Delta \varnothing'$), more current can be drawn directly from the source by biasing the drain. Drain bias can effectively eliminate the injection barrier, making the transistor conductive even with zero gate bias. The only way to eliminate this is to increase the p-silicon substrate doping, but this increases C_{sc}, thereby raising r.

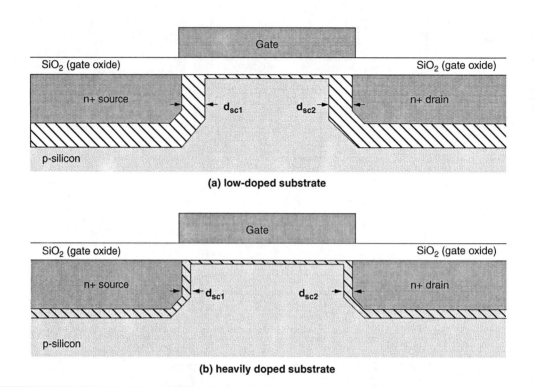

FIGURE 29.5: The effect of substrate doping on the space-charge region. Substrate doping shrinks the space-charge region, thereby lowering DIBL and increasing C_{sc} (which equals $\varepsilon_{si} \div d_{sc}$).

causes the space-charge capacitance to increase, raising r and degrading S. Of course, increasing the substrate doping also increases the transistor threshold, but this is offset naturally by short-channel effects. Here, at least, nature helps!

Even if r did not increase, an increased device count would add to the total channel leakage, and power dissipated is just the leakage current times the source-drain voltage drop. Also, the interface capacitance will increase during use due to voltage stress, creating more interface traps. Ionizing radiation, as encountered in satellite applications, further degrades the interface. Thus, subthreshold power dissipation will increase over time. Furthermore, Equation 29.6 shows the potential for a thermal runaway situation. As the interface-state capacitance grows, the S parameter increases, along with the subthreshold leakage. This, in turn, causes more power dissipation, increasing T, and, by Equation 29.6, S as

well. This further fuels leakage, possibly to the point of component damage.

If, though, the input to logic gates was a true *logic 1* or *logic zero* (V_{dd} or ground), the gates would, in fact, shut off as expected (to the extent that DIBL is controlled). Unfortunately, parasitic resistances and capacitances force the operating biases into the noise margins, and transistors thus operate in what is called the subthreshold region. Here, the inversion charge density is less than the saturation charge, but considerably larger than zero. As the length of a logic chain increases, the gate operates more deeply into its noise margin, creating even larger leakage.

From a component design perspective, the implications are clear. Make r as small as possible, and keep the interface-state densities low. From an architecture perspective, we must keep logic chain lengths as small as possible. As always, broad noise margins are desirable in logic gate design, as this will keep the switching extreme as close to supply voltage and ground as possible.

29.3 υCACTI and Energy/Power Breakdown of Pipelined Nanometer Caches

Cache power dissipation has typically been significant, but the increasing trend of leakage power will have a greater impact on the cache since most of its transistors are inactive (dissipating no dynamic power, only static) during any given access. It is therefore essential to properly account for these leakage effects during the cache design process.

Moreover, microprocessor caches are obviously not designed to exist in a vacuum; they exist to complement the processor by hiding the relatively long latencies of the lower level memory hierarchy. As such, typical caches (specifically, level-1 caches and often level-2) are pipelined and clocked at the same frequency as the core. Explicit pipelining of the cache will involve a non-trivial increase in access time (because of added flop delays) and power dissipation (from the latch elements and the resulting additional clock power), and these effects must be accounted for properly, something which is not currently done by existing publicly available cache design tools.

In this chapter, we use analytical modeling of the cache operation combined with nanometer BSIM3v3/BSIM4 SPICE models [Cao et al. 2000, PTM 2006] to analyze the behavior of various cache configurations. We break down cache energy/power dissipation to show how much energy/power each individual part of a cache consumes and what fraction can be attributed to dynamic (switching) and static (subthreshold leakage and gate tunneling) currents. We explore a three-dimensional cache design space by studying caches with different sizes (16–512 KB), associativities (direct-mapped to 16-way), and process technologies (90, 65, 45, and 32 nm).

Among our findings, we show that cache bitline leakage is increasingly becoming the dominant cause of power dissipation in nanometer technology nodes. We show that subthreshold leakage is the main cause of static power dissipation, but, surprisingly, gate leakage tunneling currents do not become a significant contributor to total cache power even for the deep nanometer nodes. We also show that accounting for cache pipelining overhead is necessary, as power dissipated by the pipeline elements are a significant part of cache power.[2]

29.3.1 Leakage in SRAM Cells

Dynamic power is dissipated by a circuit whenever transistors switch to change the voltage in a particular node. In the process, energy is consumed by charging (or discharging) the node's parasitic capacitive loads and, to a lesser degree, by possible short circuit currents that flow during the small but finite time-window when the transistor pullup and pulldown networks are fully or partially turned "on," providing a low-impedance path from supply to ground.

On the other hand, static power is dissipated by leakage currents that flow even when the device is inactive. Different leakage mechanisms exist for MOS transistors [Anis 2003], but the two most important ones are lumped into the subthreshold leakage current and the gate leakage current. The subthreshold leakage current has been extensively studied [Anis 2003, Borkar 2004, Chen et al. 1998, Rao et al. 2003, Ye et al. 1998]. It is mainly caused by the generational reduction in the transistor threshold voltage to compensate for device speed loss when scaling down the supply voltage, with the consequence of exponentially increasing subthreshold leakage current. The gate leakage current has been less extensively studied because of its relatively smaller value compared to subthreshold leakage for older technologies, but it is increasingly receiving more attention [Hamzaoglu & Stan 2002, Rao et al. 2003] as it is expected to be comparable to

---

[2]Portions reprinted, with permission, from "Energy/Power Breakdown of Pipelined Nanometer Caches (90 nm/65 nm/45 nm/32 nm)," by Samuel V. Rodriguez and Bruce L. Jacob, In *Proc. International Symposium on Low Power Electronics and Design (ISLPED)*, Tegernsee Germany, October 2006. © 2006 IEEE.

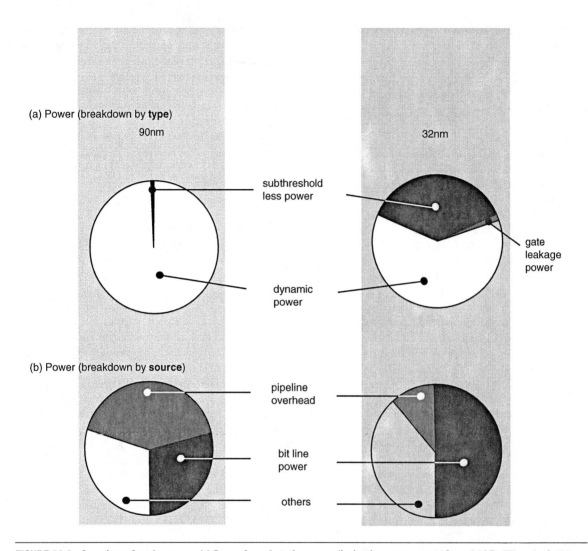

FIGURE 29.6: Overview of cache power. (a) Dynamic and static power dissipation components for a 64 kB-4W cache in 90 nm and 32 nm, (b) major components of power dissipation for a 64 kB-4 way, 90-nm and 32-nm pipelined cache.

the subthreshold leakage current in the deep nanometer nodes. Gate leakage is caused whenever voltages are applied to transistor terminals, producing an electric field across gate oxides that are getting thinner (20 to less than 10 Å), resulting in significant leakage currents due to quantum tunneling effects.

Figure 29.7 shows a typical 6-transistor memory cell (6TMC) and the typical leakage currents involved

for the memory cell idle state (i.e., wordline is off, one storage node is "0," and the other storage node is "1"). Although a sizeable number of transistors in a cache are active for any given access, the vast majority of memory cells are in this inactive state, dissipating static power. Cache designers currently account for subthreshold leakage current (most problematic of which is the bitline leakage since this not only affects power, but also circuit timing and hence functionality), but not much attention is given to gate leakage in the publicly available cache design tools like CACTI [Wilton &

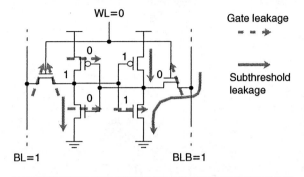

FIGURE 29.7: Memory cell leakage components. An inactive six-transistor memory cell (6TMC) showing the subthreshold leakage and gate leakage currents flowing across the devices.

Jouppi 1996, Reinman & Jouppi 2000, Shivakumar & Jouppi 2001] and eCACTI [Mamidipaka & Dutt 2004]. Our tool considers the gate leakage currents as shown in the 6TMC diagram.

29.3.2 Pipelined Caches

To match the speed of a fast microprocessor core while providing sufficiently large storage capacities, caches are pipelined to subdivide the various delays in the cache into different stages, allowing each individual stage to fit into the core's small clock period. Figure 29.8 shows a typical pipeline diagram for a cache. The given timing diagram shows operations being performed in both phases of the clock. Figure 29.9 shows a possible implementation of a pipeline latch that easily facilitates this phase-based operation.

The major, publicly available, cache analysis tools CACTI and eCACTI use implicit pipelining through

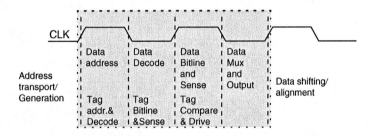

FIGURE 29.8: Cache pipeline diagram. The shaded region shows the part of the pipeline that we model.

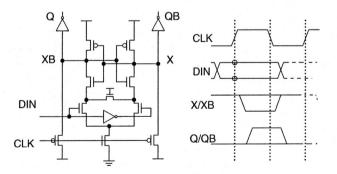

FIGURE 29.9: Pipeline latch. An example of a pipeline latch that can be used to implement the phase-based operations in the cache [Gronowski et al. 1996, Motanaro et al. 1996]. Also shown is the latch's timing diagram.

wave pipelining, relying on regularity of the delay of the different cache stages to separate signals continuously being shoved through the cache instead of using explicit pipeline state elements. Unfortunately, this is not representative of modern designs, since cache wave pipelining is not being used by contemporary microprocessors [Riedlinger & Grutkowski 2002, Weiss et al. 2002]. Although wave pipelining has been shown to work in silicon prototypes [Burleson et al. 1998], it is not ideally suited for high-speed microprocessor caches targeted for volume production which have to operate with significant process-voltage-temperature (PVT) variations. PVT variations in a wave-pipelined cache cause delay imbalances which, in the worst case, lead to signal races that are not possible to fix by lowering the clock frequency. Hence, the risk for non-functional silicon is increased, resulting in unattractive yields. In addition, wave pipelining does not inherently support latch-based design-for-test (DFT) techniques that are critical in the debug and test of a microprocessor, reducing yields even further. On the contrary, it is easy to integrate DFT "scan" elements inside pipeline latches that allow their state to be either observed or controlled (preferably both). This ability facilitates debugging of microprocessor circuitry, resulting in reduced test times that directly translate to significant cost savings. Although not immediately obvious at first, these reasons make it virtually necessary to implement explicit pipelining for high-volume microprocessor caches.

29.3.3 Modeling

Although initially based on CACTI and eCACTI tools, the analysis tool we have developed bears little resemblance to its predecessors. In its current form, it is, to the best of our knowledge, the most

detailed and most realistic (i.e., similar to realistically implementable high-performance caches) cache design-space explorer publicly available. We decided to keep the naming scheme consistent with its roots; the tool is called υCACTI (pronounced "nu-cak-tie").

The main improvements of υCACTI over CACTI/ eCACTI include the following:

- More optimal decode topologies [Amrutur & Horowitz 2001] and circuits [Nambu et al. 1998] along with more realistic device sizing ensures that cache inputs present a reasonable load to the preceeding pipeline stage (at most four times the load of a 1 × strength inverter).[3]
- Accurate modeling of explicit cache pipelining to account for delay and energy overhead in pipelined caches.
- Use of BSIM3v3/BSIM4 SPICE models and equations to perform calculation of transistor drive strengths, transistor RC parasitics, subthreshold leakage, and gate leakage. Simulation characteristics for each tech node are now more accurate.[4]
- More accurate RC interconnect parasitics by using local, intermediate, and global interconnects (as opposed to using the same wire characteristics for all interconnects, as is being done by CACTI and eCACTI), and accurate analytical modeling of these structures. In addition, a realistic BEOL-stack[5] is used for each technology node.

An important note to make when discussing dynamic and static power and/or energy is that it is only possible to combine the two by assuming a specific frequency. Dynamic power describes how much energy is consumed in a single switching event, and

---

[3]Both CACTI and eCACTI produce designs with impractically large first-stage inverters at the cache inputs. This shifts some of the burden of driving the cache decode hierarchy to the circuits preceding the cache, resulting in overly optimistic delay and power numbers.
[4]For delay and dynamic power computations, CACTI and eCACTI use hardcoded numbers based on 0.80-μm technology and use linear scaling to translate power and delay numbers to the desired technology.
[5]The Back-End-Of-Line stack refers to the fabrication steps performed after the creation of the active components. Use of a realistic BEOL-stack results in more accurate modeling of the interconnect. In CACTI and eCACTI, a single interconnect characteristic is assumed.

an assumption of how often that event happens is necessary to convert the energy value into power dissipation (hence, the activity factor and frequency components in standard power equations). On the other hand, static leakage describes the amount of current flow, and hence the instantaneous power, at any given time. Converting this into energy requires an assumption of the amount of time the current is flowing. Table 29.1 shows the values for frequency and supply voltages used for this study, chosen from both historical [TechReport 2006] and projected [SIA 2003, 2005] data.

29.3.4 Dynamic and Static Power

Figure 29.10 shows the power dissipation of the different cache configurations as a function of process technology. Each column of plots represents a specific process technology, while each row represents a specific cache size. Each plot shows the dynamic, subthreshold leakage, gate leakage, and total power as a function of associativity for the given cache size and technology node.

The most basic observation here is that total power is dominated by the dynamic power in the larger technology nodes, but is dominated by static power in the nanometer nodes (with the exception of very highly associative small to medium caches). This parallels the observations in most microprocessors where static leakage currents increase with every die shrink. The phenomenon can be seen from the plots for the 90- and 65-nm nodes, where the dynamic power comprises the majority of the total power. In the 45-nm node, the subthreshold leakage power is significant enough that it becomes the dominant component for some configurations. For small caches of any associativity, dynamic power

typically dominates because there are fewer leaking devices that contribute to subthreshold leakage power. As cache sizes increase, the number of idle transistors that dissipate subthreshold leakage power also increases, making the subthreshold leakage power the dominant component of total power except for the configurations with high associativity (which requires more operations to be done in parallel, dissipating more dynamic power). In the 32-nm node, the subthreshold leakage power is comparable to the dynamic power even for small caches of any associativity, and it starts to become dominant as cache sizes increase, even at high associativities where we expect the cache to burn more dynamic power.

A surprising result that can be seen across all the plots is the relatively small contribution of gate leakage power to the total power. This is surprising given all the attention that gate leakage current is receiving and how it is expected to be one of the dominant leakage mechanisms. It turns out that this is a result of many factors, including the less aggressive gate oxide thickness scaling in the more recent ITRS roadmaps [SIA 2003, 2005], and that V_{dd} scaling and device size scaling both tend to decrease the value of the gate tunneling current. The net effect of a slightly thinner gate oxide (increasing tunneling), slightly lower supply voltage (decreasing tunneling), and smaller devices (decreasing tunneling) from one generation to the next might actually result in an effective decrease in gate leakage from one generation to the next.

Some of the plots in Figure 29.10 (e.g., the 256 and 512K caches for the 45- and 32-nm node) exhibit a sort of "saddle" shape, which shows that increasing cache associativity from direct-mapped to two-way or four-way does not automatically cause an increase

TABLE 29.1 V_{dd} and frequency used for each tech node (T = 50 C)

	250 nm	180 nm	130 nm	90 nm	65 nm	45 nm	32 nm
V_{dd}	2.0 V	1.8 V	1.6 V	1.4 V	1.3 V	1.2 V	1.1 V
Frequency	0.8 GHz	1.5 GHz	1.8 GHz	2.4 GHz	2.6 GHz	2.8 GHz	3.0 GHz

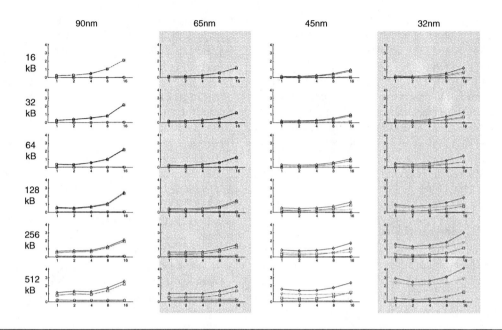

FIGURE 29.10: Power dissipation versus technology node of different cache configurations. The plots show how total power dissipation is broken down into dynamic power and static power (due to subthreshold leakage and gate leakage). Each column of plots represents a single technology node, while a single row represents a specific cache size. Within each plot, the power dissipation is shown in the y-axis, with increasing associativities represented in the x-axis.

in power dissipation, as the internal organization may allow a more power optimal implementation of set-associative caches compared to direct-mapped caches, especially for medium- to large-sized caches.

A final observation for Figure 29.10 is that technology scaling is capable of either increasing or decreasing the total power of a cache. Which direction the power goes depends on which power component is dominant for a particular cache organization. Caches with dominant dynamic power (e.g., small caches/highly associative caches) will enjoy a decrease in cache power as dynamic power decreases because of the net decrease in the CV^2f function, while caches with dominant static power (e.g., large caches/medium-sized, low-associativy caches) will suffer from an increase in cache power as the static power increases.

29.3.5 Detailed Power Breakdown

Figure 29.11 shows a detailed breakdown of cache power for three different cache configurations (16kB-4W, 32kB-4W, and 64kB-4W). Each plot represents a single configuration implemented in the 4-nm nodes. For each of these nodes, total cache power is shown, along with its detailed breakdown. Power dissipation for each component, as shown by each vertical bar in the plot, is also broken down into its dynamic, subthreshold leakage, and gate leakage components.

The first notable point here is that for these cache configurations, going from 90 to 65 nm results in a power decrease, going from 65 to 45 nm results in a smaller power decrease, and, finally, going from 45 to 32 nm causes a significant power decrease. Again, these observations are caused by the intertwined decrease and increase of dynamic and

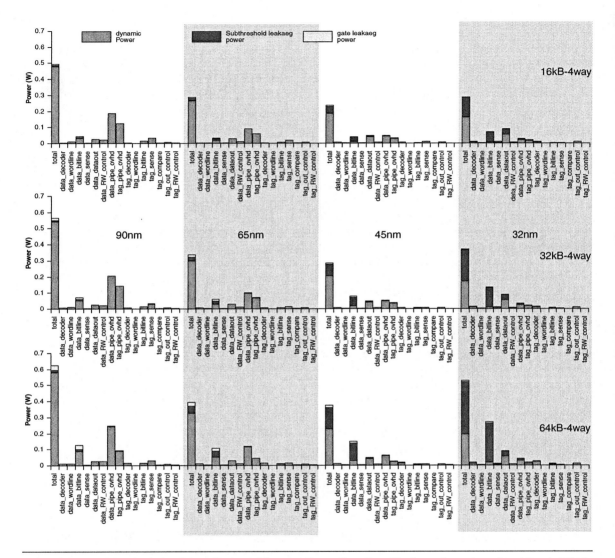

FIGURE 29.11: Detailed power breakdown for three different cache configurations. The figure shows dynamic, subthreshold leakage, and gate leakage power being consumed by different parts of the cache. Each plot shows four sets of values corresponding to different technology nodes, each of which operates at a different frequency. (Note that all three plots use the same scale.)

subthreshold leakage power, respectively, as we go from one technology node to the next.

A second point is that, for most of the plots, the two main contributors to cache power are the bit-lines and the pipeline overhead; the data_dataout component, which accounts for the power in driving the output data busses, is also significant for some configurations. Pipeline overhead, shown in the plots as data_pipe_ovhd and tag_pipe_ovhd, accounts for the power dissipated in the pipeline latches along with the associated clock-tree circuitry. This is an important observation as it shows that the overhead associated with pipelining the cache is often a very significant component of total power and that most of this power is typically dynamic. This can be easily seen in Figure 29.12, which shows the fraction of total power dissipated by pipeline overhead for all the configurations studied. This is especially noteworthy since we model aggressive clock gating where only latches that need to be activated actually see a clock signal. Consequently, we expect the pipeline overhead to be even more significant for circuits that use less aggressive clock gating (ours is essentially oracle based). Finally, it should be noted that since most of the power in the pipeline overhead is dynamic, it should decrease for smaller technology nodes, as seen in Figure 29.11.

Although dynamic power is seen to decrease with each generation—the effect of increased frequency is offset by decreased supply voltage and device capacitances—this is only true for circuits with device-dominated loading (i.e., gate and diffusion capacitances). Circuits with wire-dominated loading may actually see dynamic power go up as we go from one generation to the next, since a wire capacitance decrease due to shorter lengths and slightly smaller coupling area will typically be

offset by the shorter distances between wires that cause significantly increased capacitances. This can be seen in Figure 29.11, where the dynamic power for the data_dataout component increases for all three configurations, mostly since the load for data_dataout is wire-dominated, as it involves only a few high-impedance drivers driving a long wire across the entire cache.

The power breakdown of representative cache configurations in Figure 29.11 shows that most of the power in a pipelined nanometer cache is dissipated in the bitlines, the pipeline overhead, and possibly the data output drivers. To get a better view of the design space, we can lump together similar components. In Figure 29.13, we subdivide total power into five categories: bitline power, pipeline overhead power, decoder power, and data processing power (data/tag sensing, tag comparison, data output muxing, and driving), and lump all remaining blocks into a single component labeled "others." Results for the 65- and 32-nm nodes for all the configurations are then plotted together.

While the power dissipation due to the bitlines monotonically increases as cache size increases for both techology nodes, the power due to the other components does not necessarily do so. For instance, the pipeline power of the 65-nm 128k-16 way and

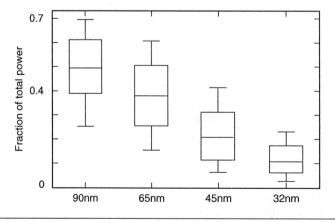

FIGURE 29.12: Pipeline overhead contribution to total cache power. The distribution of data showing the fraction of total power attributed to pipeline overhead for all cache configurations, where each plot shows min, max, median, and quartile information.

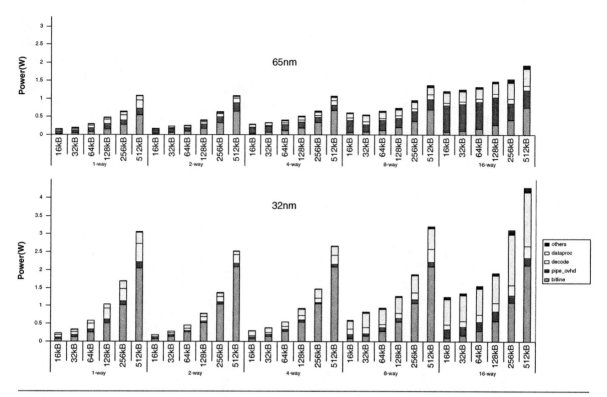

FIGURE 29.13: Detailed breakdown. Power breakdown showing major cache power contributors for the 65- and 32-nm technology nodes for different cache sizes and associativities. Cache operating frequency increases with technology node. (Note that the *y*-axis for both plots uses the same scale.)

256 KB-16 way caches is significantly reduced from one configuration to the next. The reason here is that the bitline power mainly depends on the cache size (assuming static power is the dominant cause of bitline power) and not the cache implementation. The other power components, on the other hand, greatly depend on the particular implementation, so their values may noticeably fluctuate from one implementation to the next, especially if there exist implementations that improve the power of one component at the expense of another. It is important to realize that our scheme optimizes for total power, not component power. As long as a specific implementation has a better power characteristic compared to another, relative values of specific cache components are not considered important.

Figure 29.13 clearly shows that pipeline power (as represented by pipe_ovhd) will typically be a significant contributor to total cache power. Any analysis that fails to account for this pipelining overhead and instead assumes that caches can be trivially interfaced to a microprocessor core will be inaccurate. Although the figure also shows that the contribution of the pipeline overhead to total power is reduced from 65 to 32 nm compared to the contribution of the "dataproc" component (mainly because of the different effect of technology to the dynamic power of the two components), our study modeled conservative scaling of the dielectric constants of the inter-level dielectrics; we did not model aggressively scaled low-K interconnects. If wire delay becomes problematic in future generations, and more aggressive measures are taken to improve the interconnect performance, we can expect the relative contribution of the pipeline overhead to the total power to increase in significance.

A final observation from Figure 29.13 is that increasing cache associativity may not necessarily result in a significant increase in total power, especially for the larger caches at 65 nm and below. The power for these configurations is typically dominated by the bitline leakage, reducing the effect of any increase in dynamic power due to higher associativity. In some cases, the total power dissipation can actually decrease with an increase in associativity, as a particular configuration is able to balance the overall static and dynamic power for all the cache components. This knowledge will be useful in enabling large, high-associativity caches suitable for use in L2 caches (and higher).

CHAPTER 30

Memory Errors and Error Correction

Computers are used for work, entertainment, information distribution, financial services, and numerous other tasks. Different applications exhibit different tolerances for the integrity of the data being processed: for example, a floating -point error in a bank account record is not considered acceptable, whereas a handful of odd-colored pixels in the middle of a video stream might go completely unnoticed by the user and have no effect at all. In data-critical applications such as financial databases or electronic commerce, it is imperative that the data's integrity be assured; otherwise, information can become corrupted silently and propagated widely. Accordingly, server systems used in data-critical applications typically ensure the integrity of their memory at all stages: in the register file, in the caches, in the DRAM system, and in the disk system.

Data failures can be attributed to flaws in the operating system or application software; electronic noises that are transient and unpredictable in nature; electrostatic shock, or electro-mechanical as well as mechanical failures in a subsystem of the computer. Many failures will happen to data words that go unused or are written over before being read. Many failures occur in the low-order bits of large numbers and, even if used in a computation, are not mathematically significant; thus, they do not affect the final result. Nonetheless, systems that must ensure the integrity of their data take the conservative stance of protecting against all possible failures, even if many are actually benign. As has already been seen in previous chapters, such as those on FB-DIMM and RAID systems, modern storage systems implement numerous information-redundant coding schemes to protect their data. Depending on the importance of data integrity and uninterrupted

service, different systems implement algorithms of varying levels of sophistication to detect and recover from localized software and hardware failures.

This chapter deals specifically with failures that occur in memory systems. Typically, transient failures in memory systems are caused by naturally occurring alpha particles or terrestrial neutrons that inject electronic noises into the silicon substrate, and persistent hardware failures can be caused by various causes such as electrostatic shock, thermal cycling, and electro-migration. The chapter examines the causes of the transient errors and some of the causes of persistent hardware failures, and it also examines algorithms that are implemented to detect and recover from transient or persistent failures in memory systems.

30.1 Types and Causes of Failures

Memory storage devices such as DRAM devices are susceptible to both hard failures and soft errors in the same manner that other semiconductor-based electronic devices are susceptible to both hard failures and soft failures. Hard failures are related to the physical breakdown of a device or an interconnect; they can be caused by electro-migration, corrosion, thermal cycling, or electrostatic shock. Soft errors are those in which the physical device remains functional, but random and transient electronic noises corrupt the value of the stored information. In the following sections, the focus is placed on the causes of and solutions to protect against transient soft errors in the context of the overall reliability of the memory system. The discussion it tilted toward

DRAM. SRAM-specific issues are discussed at the end of the chapter.

30.1.1 Alpha Particles

In 1978, abnormally high soft error rates in Intel's 16-Kbit generation of DRAM devices were traced to the presence of a high concentration of relatively low-energy alpha particles. At the time, it was well understood that alpha particles—consisting of two neutrons and two proton nuclei—are emitted as a byproduct from naturally occurring radioactivity, but the source of the alpha particles and the root cause of the relatively higher error rate in the 16-Kbit device as compared to the 4-Kbit device were mysteries to Intel. The source of the alpha particle emissions was ultimately traced to the packaging material of the DRAM devices. As an unfortunate coincidence, the factory that supplied ceramic packaging material for Intel's DRAM devices was built downstream from an old uranium mine. The trace amount of radioactive elements in the contaminated water supply used to manufacture the packaging material was enough to cause elevated soft error rates.

The discovery led to strict controls and careful attention to trace amounts of radioactive elements in semiconductors and their packaging materials. Since the implementation of these controls, DRAM manufacturers now consider soft errors induced by alpha particles an issue largely resolved. Recent studies suggest that most soft errors in modern DRAM devices are caused by terrestrial neutrons, a byproduct of collisions between cosmic rays and the earth's atmosphere.

30.1.2 Primary Cosmic Rays and Terrestrial Neutrons

Cosmic rays exist in space as natural background radiation. Approximately 90% of primary cosmic rays in space are protons; the remainder are composed of mostly alpha particles or heavier nuclei. Some protons, heavy nuclei, and alpha particles in the background radiation of space are relatively high in energy, and their interactions with electronic systems on satellites and spacecraft can wreak havoc in those systems. Fortunately, the earth's atmosphere acts as a shield that partially protects electronic devices on earth from direct interactions with primary cosmic rays. When primary cosmic rays enter earth's atmosphere, they collide with atoms in the atmosphere and generate cascades of high-energy particles such as electrons, protons, and neutrons. These secondary particles then scatter in all directions, and when they interact with electronic equipment on earth, they generate electronic noise. The intensity of the interactions and resulting noise depends primarily on the flux of these high-energy secondary particles at the location of the electronic equipment. The flux, in turn, depends on many different factors, with the primary factor being altitude: the flux of secondary particles is approximately twice as great at 2000 feet of elevation as compared to the flux at sea level; at 40,000 feet of elevation, the flux of the secondary particles is approximately 300 times greater than at sea level.[1]

The secondary particles resulting from the collisions between primary cosmic rays and the earth's atmosphere are often referred to as cosmic rays. However, to distinguish between the causes of noise in electronic systems operating in space from the causes of noise in electronic systems operating in the relative safety of earth's atmosphere, the secondary particles that impact electronic equipment on earth are more properly referred to as *terrestrial neutrons*. The reason that neutrons are singled out in the flux of the secondary particles is because neutrons dominate the effects of soft errors on electronic systems on earth. Unlike relatively low-energy alpha particles from natural occurring background radiation on earth, some high-energy neutrons will penetrate through concrete and nominal shielding. Recent studies indicate that terrestrial neutrons are currently the dominant source of DRAM soft errors, and the soft error rates (SERs) are roughly proportional to the flux of high-energy terrestrial neutrons at a given location.

---

[1]Using a laptop computer on an airplane in flight exposes the electronics in the laptop computer to the higher flux of high-energy particles.

30.1.3 Soft Error Mechanism

Figure 30.1 illustrates the interactions between high-energy alpha particles and neutrons with the silicon lattice. The figure shows that when high-energy alpha particles pass through silicon, the particles leave ionized trails, and the length of those ionized trails depends on the respective energies of the incident particles. The figure also shows that when high-energy neutrons pass through silicon, some neutrons do not collide with atoms in the silicon lattice and thus pass through without affecting operations of the semiconductor device. However, when the neutrons do collide with nuclei in the lattice, the atomic collision can result in the creation of multiple ionized trails as the secondary particles generated in the collision scatter into the silicon lattice. In the presence of an electric field, the ionized trails of electron-hole pairs behave as temporary surges in current or as charges that can change the data values in storage cells. In addition, the charge from the ionized trails of electron-hole pairs can impact the voltage level of bitlines as the value of the stored data is resolved by the sense amplifiers. The SER of a memory device depends on many related factors, including the flux and energy distribution of the incident particles; the process technology of the device; the cross-sectional area of the impact node and, thus, the design of the storage cells; the critical charge at that node and the voltage level of the device; the time period when the critical charge will be placed in that node; the design of the bitlines and sense amplifiers; and even the design of the logic circuits controlling data movement in the device. In DRAM, the area per cell determines the probability of a strike near the cell, and the charge level stored in the cell determines how much incident energy must be imparted to overcome that charge and change the value of the cell. In the context of a bitline, the same issues apply, but the time period of susceptibility is limited to the time right after a DRAM cell has discharged its contents onto the bitline, before the sense amplifier activates and moves the voltage value to one voltage rail or the other.

30.1.4 Single-Bit and Multi-Bit Failures

Recent studies of DRAM devices suggest that the probability and type of soft error depend heavily on the energy of the incident particle. Alpha particles and neutrons with less than 5 MeV of energy typically have insufficient energy to cause errors in laboratory experiments; on the other hand, experiments using high-energy neutrons with energy levels of 300 MeV or greater induce multi-bit errors in DRAM devices. The multi-bit soft error failure mechanism is believed to be limited to collisions between high-energy neutrons and silicon atoms.

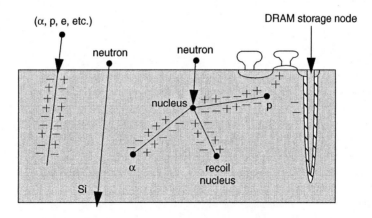

FIGURE 30.1: Generation of electron-hole pairs in silicon by alpha particles and high-energy neutrons.

TABLE 30.1   Frequency of multi-bit and single-bit errors

DRAM Size-Vendor	x4	x8	x16
4 MB-A	7%	7%	—
4 MB-B	16%	16%	24%
16 MB-C	13%	19%	19%
64 MB-D	3%	12%	12%
64 MB-E	13%	18%	18%

Data taken from Dell [1997].

In such an impact event, many electron-hole pairs are generated, and charges can spread to adjacent cells. Fortunately, such high-energy neutrons are a small fraction of the total terrestrial neutron flux; thus, multi-bit failures are less prevalent than single-bit failures. However, as Moore's Law progresses and more transistors are fabricated per unit area, the ratio of multi-bit failures to single-bit failures may change.

Table 30.1 shows the occurrence of multi-bit errors relative to single-bit errors; the data is taken from IBM's paper on chipkill memory, citing data from internal sources within IBM [Dell 1997]. The data is reported for multiple DRAM generations, different device bit-widths, and different DRAM manufacturers. While the data is considered to be preliminary and taken from a very limited sample population, the general trend shows that while multi-bit failures are less common than single-bit failures, multi-bit failures may rise as the industry moves to devices with wider data busses.

In addition to soft errors, the physical handling of memory modules can and does introduce stress fractures into the solder bonds that connect DRAM devices to the memory modules. These stress fractures can develop further with the thermal cycles that computers experience between normal operation and standby or power-down states. In these cases, the stress fracture can cause an interconnect to fail; the loss of a single address, command, or control signal to a given DRAM device can invalidate all of the data bits from that device. Consequently, multi-bit error correction algorithms are needed to protect against both soft, non-persistent failures as well as persistent hardware failures.

30.2 Soft Error Rates and Trends

Table 30.2 shows DRAM SERs reported by IBM, Micron, and Infineon across different generations of DRAM devices. Note that IBM's numbers represent measured or estimated error rates from different manufacturers and not necessarily for its own DRAM devices. The error rates are reported in terms of *failures-in-time* (FIT). One FIT is equivalent to one failure in one billion device-hours.[2]

One generalization that can be made from the data is that different DRAM devices from different DRAM manufacturers can show dramatically different sensitivity to *single event upsets* (SEU). An SEU is simply a change of state caused by incident alpha particles or terrestrial neutrons. The result of the difference in sensitivity to SEU shows up as a wide range of SERs. As an example, IBM reported that one DRAM design with a floating bitline at the 256-Kbit node proved to be exceptionally susceptible to SEU. In contrast, research has also shown that specialized structures that separate active regions of DRAM cells from bulk silicon greatly increase tolerance to SEU and thus reduces SER.

[2]Due to the miniscule SER on a per-device level, SER for DRAM is difficult to quantify. No device can be run for 1 billion hours. Even a carefully controlled setup of 1000 devices cannot reach 1 million hours per device. Thus, SER measurement requires a combination of accelerated testing and statistical extrapolation, and SERs are often reported as a range of values with a specified confidence level (C.L.).

TABLE **30.2**   Reported SER

Reported by	Device Gen	Reported FIT
IBM	256 KB	27,000 ~ 160,000
IBM	1 MB	205 ~ 40,000
IBM	4 MB	52 ~ 10,000
Micron	16 MB	97 ~ ?
Infineon (now Qimonda)	256 MB	11 ~ 900

A second generalization that can be drawn from the data is that, despite the increasing bit density with each generation, the per-device error rate has gradually decreased with each generation of DRAM. The trend is due to the increasing attention paid to the design of SEU-tolerant circuits and the fact that critical cell charge Q_c has remained relatively constant, while cell sizes have shrunk with each process generation. Consequently, the general DRAM SER rate has gradually decreased from the 256-Kbit generation to the 256-Mbit generation. However, the trend of decreasing per-device SER is not a fundamental trend that is guaranteed to continue. Instead, with the demand for faster DRAM devices, lower voltage levels for reduced power dissipation, and smaller DRAM cells with smaller Q_c, future DRAM devices may be more susceptible rather than less susceptible to SEUs than the current generation of DRAM devices.

30.3   Error Detection and Correction

This section examines techniques to detect and, in most cases, to correct single-bit and multi-bit transient soft errors. Though the discussion focuses on DRAM, many of these techniques have been used with SRAM and disk technologies as well.

30.3.1   Parity

One attempt to provide minimal protection for data stored in DRAM memory systems is the use of parity memory; its intent is to provide single-bit error detection capability. Figure 30.2 illustrates the generation of a parity bit for data written to DRAM: parity, indicating

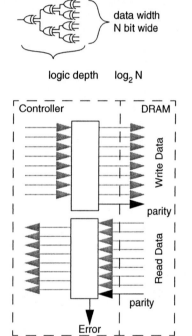

FIGURE 30.2: Parity checking.

either an even or an odd number of "1" bits in the data bit vector, is generated from a recursive application of the exclusive-or function to the bits in the input data. The parity bit is stored into the DRAM memory system along with the input data vector. When the data vector along with the previously computed parity bit is read out from the DRAM system, the parity bit is recomputed from the vector and compared to the retrieved parity bit. If the recomputed parity bit differs from the retrieved parity bit, an odd number of bits must have changed states; a parity checking error is generated and reported by the memory controller.

The parity mechanism is simple and fast. The original IBM PC and subsequent PC clones implemented parity for 8-bit-wide data vectors. For these machines, the parity checking mechanism required the addition of a few exclusive-or gates, and the logic depth for the parity checking mechanism introduced a negligible impact on read latency. The disadvantage of parity checking is that it can only detect an odd number of bit errors, and once an error is detected, the mechanism can neither locate nor correct the error. As a result of the inability to correct errors and the general trend toward wider data bus interfaces, the memory systems of commodity mass market PCs have migrated away from parity checking to forgo error detection and correction altogether or to use more sophisticated mechanisms. In modern computer systems, parity checking mechanisms are still used in places where the data vector to be protected is narrow, and a fast mechanism is needed. For example, cache tags are often protected by simple parity checking.

30.3.2 Single-Bit Error Correction (SEC ECC)

ECC stands for Error Correcting Code; the fundamental idea has deep roots in mathematics. In this chapter, the various ECC algorithms are illustrated without proof of their mathematical validity. Interested readers are encouraged to seek specialized literature that formalizes proofs of the various algorithms.

The basic ECC algorithm is *Single-bit Error Correction (SEC) ECC*. The advantage of SEC ECC is its relatively low cost. The number of storage bits needed for error detection is simply proportional to $\log_2 N$, where N is the number of bits in the data vector. For a 64-bit-wide data vector, N is 64, and the storage cost of SEC ECC is less than that of the 8:1 parity scheme. In SEC ECC, the same basic idea of the recursive application of the exclusive-or function is used. The implementation difference between parity checking and SEC ECC is in the arrangement and utilization of the check bits. In all ECC algorithms, including SEC ECC, redundant parity checking protection of multiple check bits is provided for each data bit. The arrangement of the check bits ensures that the SEC ECC algorithm can detect and locate the faulting bit. Since the data vectors are binary bit vectors, the ability to locate single-bit errors equals the ability to correct those single-bit errors.

SEC ECC maps a given data vector into a longer code word, using superfluous bits to create a non-zero Hamming distance between valid code words. Hamming distance is the number of bits that differ between two binary vectors, so, for example, the Hamming distance between the following eight-bit binary numbers, A and B,

$$A: 0100\ 1011$$
$$B: 0101\ 1001$$

is two: from the left, the fourth bits differ and the seventh bits differ. If one measures "distance" in bit-flips, one would have to flip two bits to transform A to B, and thus, they lie at a distance of two from each other; this is the Hamming distance between them.

In SEC ECC, all valid code words differ from each other by at least three bits; in between each two valid

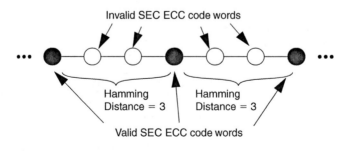

FIGURE 30.3: SEC ECC uses a 3-bit Hamming distance.

code words are two invalid code words. Figure 30.3 illustrates the arrangement. In practical terms, this ensures that any given valid SEC ECC code word can sustain a one-bit error. If any bit in a valid code word is corrupted, the code word is moved a Hamming distance of 1 away from its original place. It becomes an invalid code word, but, more importantly, it becomes an invalid code word at a Hamming distance of 1 from one and only one *valid* code word, which is the original valid code word that was corrupted. Thus, any single-bit error can be corrected by transforming the invalid code word into the nearest valid code word; however, note that a double-bit error creates an invalid code word that lies at a distance of two from the original valid code word, but a distance of one away from a different, totally unrelated valid code word. Thus, a two-bit error will be "corrected" to the wrong value; because of this, and the mechanism is said to be single error correcting.

Figure 30.4 shows an implementation of SEC ECC for an 8-bit-wide data vector. In this example, the encoding phase of the SEC ECC algorithm is implemented by distributing the input data vector throughout the SEC ECC code word. The bits in the input data vector are labelled as D_j, where j goes from 1 to N. The data vector is then distributed into the SEC ECC word R_m, where m goes from 1 to N + ($\log_2$ N) + 1, and m is not an integer power of 2. In bit vector R, all bit positions R_m for which m **is** an integer power of 2 are reserved for the check bits. In this example, each data bit is protected by multiple check bits. The basic idea is that the data bit will be protected by check bits whose indices sum up to the index of the data bit. For example, R_7 is protected by R_1, R_2, and R_4, and R_{10} is protected by R_2 and R_8.

In the SEC ECC algorithm, check bit R_1 is responsible to protect R_3, R_5, R_7, R_9, and R_{11}, and R_1 is computed by the recursive application of the exclusive-or function to R_3, R_5, R_7, R_9, and R_{11}. In this manner, if any single bit in the set $\{R_3, R_5, R_7, R_9, R_{11}\}$ changes value, the stored value of R_1 will be different from the recomputed value of R_1.

Figure 30.5 illustrates the encoding process for an 8-bit data vector into a SEC ECC code word. The process begins by mapping the data in bit vector D into bit positions in vector R where R_m is not a power of 2. The check bits for vector R are then computed and placed into their corresponding power-of-two bit positions.

Single-Bit Error Detection for SEC ECC

Figure 30.6 illustrates the error detection process for an SEC ECC code word. In the figure, bit R_{11} in the SEC ECC code word is corrupt and has changed value from 1 to 0. The error detection process recomputes the check bits for the code word; these are compared to the check bits retrieved with the code word. The bitwise exclusive-or comparison of the stored check bits against the recomputed check bits forms what is called the *ECC syndrome*; in cases that an error exists, the ECC syndrome will be non-zero. Note that R_{11} in Figure 30.6 has changed in value; thus, the recomputed check bits R_1, R_2, and R_8 are different from the original check bits. The ECC syndrome is non-zero and points to the exact bit position of the corrupted bit. In this case, the ECC syndrome has the value 11 and thus fingers bit 11 as the erroneous bit, which then can then be corrected by simply toggling its value.

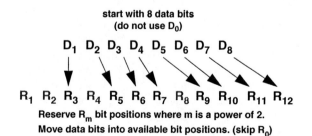

start with 8 data bits
(do not use D_0)

D_1 D_2 D_3 D_4 D_5 D_6 D_7 D_8

R_1 R_2 R_3 R_4 R_5 R_6 R_7 R_8 R_9 R_{10} R_{11} R_{12}

Reserve R_m bit positions where m is a power of 2.
Move data bits into available bit positions. (skip R_0)

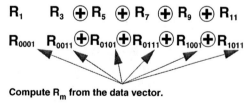

R_1 $R_3 \oplus R_5 \oplus R_7 \oplus R_9 \oplus R_{11}$

R_{0001} $R_{0011} \oplus R_{0101} \oplus R_{0111} \oplus R_{1001} \oplus R_{1011}$

Compute R_m from the data vector.

FIGURE 30.4: Creation of an SEC ECC code word from an 8-bit-wide data vector.

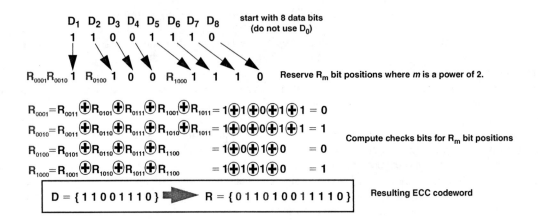

FIGURE 30.5: SEC ECC code word encoding example.

$R = \{ 0\ 1\ 1\ 0\ 1\ 0\ 1\ 0\ 0\ 1\ 1\ 1\ 1\ 0 \}$ **One bit error. Can it be**
$R = \{ 0\ 1\ 1\ 0\ 1\ 0\ 1\ 0\ 0\ 1\ 1\ 1\ 0\ 0 \}$ **detected and corrected?**

Recompute check bits

$R_{0001} = R_{0011} \oplus R_{0101} \oplus R_{0111} \oplus R_{1001} \oplus R_{1011} = 1 \oplus 1 \oplus 0 \oplus 1 \oplus 0 = 1$
$R_{0010} = R_{0011} \oplus R_{0110} \oplus R_{0111} \oplus R_{1010} \oplus R_{1011} = 1 \oplus 0 \oplus 0 \oplus 1 \oplus 0 = 0$
$R_{0100} = R_{0101} \oplus R_{0110} \oplus R_{0111} \oplus R_{1100} \qquad = 1 \oplus 0 \oplus 1 \oplus 0 \qquad = 0$
$R_{1000} = R_{1001} \oplus R_{1010} \oplus R_{1011} \oplus R_{1100} \qquad = 1 \oplus 1 \oplus 0 \oplus 0 \qquad = 0$

XOR old check bits against new check bits

R_{1000}	R_{0100}	R_{0010}	R_{0001}	
1	0	1	0	Old
0	0	0	1	New
1	0	1	1	ECC Syndrome = $1011_2 = 11_{10}$

Syndrome != 0000   Bit position 11 is suspect

FIGURE 30.6: One-bit error detection in SEC ECC code word illustrated.

Two-Bit Error in SEC ECC Code Word

In Figure 30.7 the SEC ECC error detection process is reapplied to the same SEC ECC code word as in Figure 30.6, but here both bits R_9 and R_{10} have been corrupted; this is a multi-bit error. The same verification process as before determines the ECC syndrome is not a zero vector, thus indicating the presence of an error. However, the ECC syndrome now points to bit R_3 as the location of the error. As expected, the SEC ECC algorithm cannot distinguish between a single-bit error and a two-bit error; this is because SEC ECC maps data vectors into a space where valid code words are separated by a Hamming distance of 3 bits. As shown in Figure 30.3, this means that a two-bit corruption of a valid code word is indistinguishable from a one-bit corruption of a different yet equally valid code word. The solution to the two-bit error detection problem is to map the data vector into a space where more than 3 bits of Hamming distance lie between each pair of valid code words.

30.3.3 Single-Bit Error Correction, Double-Bit Error Detection (SECDED ECC)

To distinguish single-bit errors from double-bit errors, an additional check bit is added to the SEC ECC algorithm to create the SECDED ECC algorithm. As Figure 30.8 shows, a parity checking bit is added in the 0th bit position. Bit R_0 provides a quick sanity check to ensure that, in case the ECC syndrome is a non-zero vector and indicates an error, the error is not a double-bit error. In the case of a single-bit error, both the ECC syndrome as well as R_0 will report that an error has occurred. In the case of a double-bit error, R_0 will return the same parity as the original code word, whereas the ECC syndrome will be non-zero. The redundancy of error detection mechanisms enables a memory controller to distinguish between a single-bit error and a double-bit error.

The weakness of the SECDED ECC algorithm is that, though it can distinguish a one-bit error from a two-bit error, it cannot distinguish a one-bit error from a scenario in which an odd number of bits are corrupted (e.g., 3, 5, etc.). The strength of SECDED ECC is that it is able to detect and correct single-bit errors with minimal overhead in storage capacity. For a data bus width of 64 bits (N = 64), the SECDED ECC algorithm requires 8 check bits, which is the same cost as an 8:1 parity checking scheme when applied to a 64-bit-wide data vector. The delay logic of the SECDED ECC algorithm is proportional to $\log_2 N$ and may incur an additional cycle in the read latency depending on the design of the logic circuit.

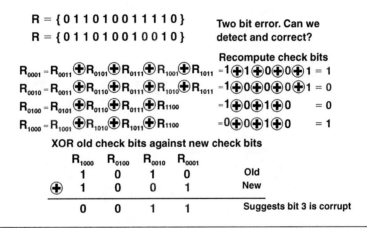

FIGURE 30.7: Error detection in SEC ECC code word with a 2-bit error.

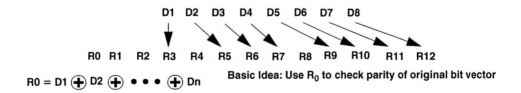

FIGURE 30.8: Addition of parity checking bit for SECDED ECC algorithm.

30.3.4 Multi-Bit Error Detection and Correction: Bossen's b-Adjacent Algorithm

The SEC error detection and correction algorithms described thus far focus on the detection and correction of single-bit errors. However, multi-bit errors can and do occur. The trends associated with the scaling of process technology increase a circuit's sensitivity to SEUs, including the shrinking geometries of basic circuits and the continuing reduction in supply voltage. Thus, multi-bit error detection and correction is increasing in importance. Fortunately, multi-bit error detection and correction algorithms have been developed for systems requiring a high degree of reliability in the memory system.

In a 64-bit data word, a single-bit error can occur in 1 of 64 locations. In the same data word, two randomly located single-bit errors can occur in 2016 different combinations of bit positions. Thus, it is far more difficult to locate and correct two random errors. However, multi-bit errors are usually caused by the same event and thus typically occur in adjacent bit locations. Multi-bit error correction algorithms used in modern computer systems exploit this and focus on detecting and correcting multi-bit errors in adjacent locations.

There are numerous multi-bit error correction algorithms, based on algorithms developed by Hsiao, Carter, Kaneda, Bossen, and others. We illustrate a representative example: Bossen's b-adjacent algorithm [Bossen 1970]. The example describes a 2-adjacent algorithm; the extension to larger values of b is simply asserted and not illustrated.

Bossen's b-adjacent ECC algorithm uses the familiar recursive application of the exclusive-or function to generate parity protection. The difference between 2-adjacent error correction and SEC error correction is in the definition of the basic unit of error detection. The SEC ECC algorithm relies on the redundant parity checking protection of multiple check bits for each data bit. In SEC ECC, the basic unit of error detection—or *symbol size*—is an individual bit. In the b-adjacent ECC algorithm, the basic unit of error detection is a group of b-adjacent bits. As an example, in a 64-bit input data vector, there are 32 groups of 2-adjacent bits, or 32 symbols, with each symbol being 2 bits in size. In this algorithm, each symbol is a basic unit for the error location and correction. Figure 30.9 shows that in 2-adjacent code space, there are 2^2 basic symbols. Formally, 2-bit vectors can be described as elements of a Galois field with 2^2 elements, denoted as $GF(2^2)$. The correction of a single error in $GF(2^2)$ is then equivalent to correcting 2-adjacent bits in the binary field.

The 2-adjacent ECC algorithm can be implemented to correct 2-adjacent bit errors with 8 check bits for 64 data bits, denoted as (64, 72). Figure 30.10 shows the parity check matrix for a single ECC from $GF(2^2)$ transcribed from Bossen's b-adjacent ECC algorithm. In the figure, the symbols 0, 1, α, and α^2 represent the elements in $GF(2^2)$. The matrix can be used to generate 4 check symbols from 32 strings of $GF(2^2)$ elements. That is, each column represents 1 of 32 possible length-four strings of elements in $GF(2^2)$, and each row of the parity check matrix corresponds to 1 of 4 check symbols. The check symbols can detect and locate an error of a single element out of a data vector of 32 elements in $GF(2^2)$. Figure 30.10 shows a transformation applied to the parity check matrix to convert the single error correcting matrix in $GF(2^2)$ to a 2-adjacent error correcting matrix in the binary field. The transformation yields the binary parity check matrix that can generate the necessary check bits to detect and locate 2-adjacent errors out of a data vector of 64 elements in the binary field.

Check bits C_7 through C_0 are generated from the transformed parity check matrix through the recursive application of the exclusive-or function to bit positions indicated by the parity check matrix. As an example, the top row of the parity check matrix shows that check bit C_7 can be generated from the recursive application of the exclusive-or function to $D_0, D_2, D_4, D_7, D_8, D_9, \ldots D_{61}$, and D_{62}.

Table 30.3 shows the *error location table* for th 2-adjacent ECC algorithm; this is taken from the patent filing for Compaq's Advanced ECC algorithm, based on Bossen's 2-adjacent ECC algorithm. When

$$\begin{bmatrix} 0 \\ 0 \end{bmatrix} \quad \begin{bmatrix} 0 \\ 1 \end{bmatrix} \quad \begin{bmatrix} 1 \\ 0 \end{bmatrix} \quad \begin{bmatrix} 1 \\ 1 \end{bmatrix}$$

FIGURE 30.9: Two-bit vectors in 2-adjacent code.

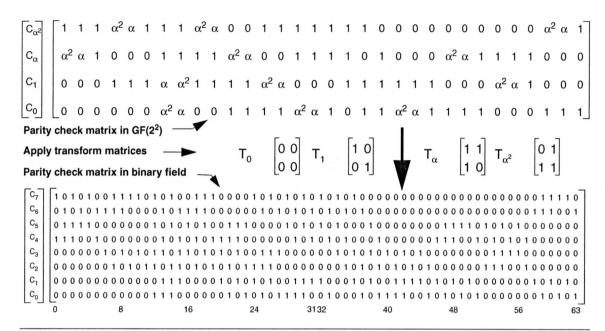

Parity check matrix in GF(2^2)

Apply transform matrices

Parity check matrix in binary field

FIGURE 30.10: Check bit generation for 2-adjacent error detection.

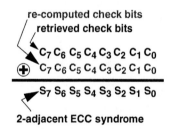

FIGURE 30.11: Recomputed check bits bitwise XOR'ed against retrieved check bits to generate the 2-adjacent ECC syndrome.

an ECC code word is read from memory, the check bits are recomputed from the data bits and compared to the check bits retrieved with the ECC code word. Figure 30.11 shows that, just as in the SEC ECC algorithm, the bitwise comparison of the original check bits against the recomputed check bits is used to generate the ECC syndrome, denoted as S_7 through S_0 in the figure. The ECC syndrome is used as an index into the error location table to determine the type and location of the error.

Figure 30.12 illustrates how both single-bit errors and double-bit errors that occur on even-bit boundaries can be located with 2-adjacent error correction.

In the first matrix, bit 32 of a 64-bit block has been corrupted while stored in memory. The first matrix in Figure 30.12 shows that check bits C_7, C_5, and C_1 would be affected by this. Note that bit 32 in the block is the only bit that would affect these check bits and only these check bits. A comparison of the retrieved check bits against the recomputed check bits results in the ECC syndrome bit vector of 10100010. A check of Table 30.3 shows that an ECC syndrome of 10100010 indicates bit 32 as being corrupt.

In the second example, assume bits 32 and 33 are both corrupted. As a result, check bits C_7, C_6, C_5, C_4, C_1, and C_0 are affected. A comparison of the retrieved check bits against the recomputed check bits results in the ECC syndrome 11110011. Using this as an index into the error location table identifies bits 32 and 33 as corrupted.

30.3.5 Bit Steering and Chipkill

The 2-adjacent ECC algorithm can detect single bit and two adjacent bit errors. The limitation on

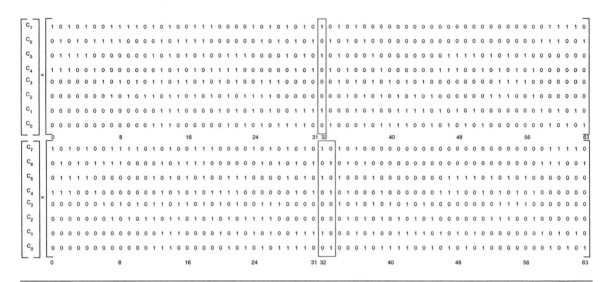

FIGURE 30.12: Locating a single bit and 2-adjacent bit errors in a 64-bit word.

detecting adjacent two-bit errors, and only if they start at an even-bit address, is a notable drawback. This is the nature of the algorithm, as it is a binary representation of $GF(2^2)$. For example, a two-bit error in bit positions 32 and 33 is, in reality, a single symbol error in $GF(2^2)$. Consequently, 2-adjacent ECC cannot properly locate a 2-adjacent bit error that occurs across symbol boundaries (e.g., errors in bit positions 31 and 32), and it cannot locate 2 non-adjacent bit errors with arbitrary bit addresses.

For the cases of DRAM device failures, *chipkill memory* is a concept pioneered and promoted by IBM. The basic idea for chipkill memory is to design the memory system in such a manner as to tolerate the complete failure of a DRAM device and continue to provide valid data for each request. In Compaq's Advanced ECC algorithm, to provide this level of reliability, the 2-adjacent ECC algorithm is used in combination with *bit steering*: the data bits of a single DRAM device are "steered" to two different ECC words to provide two-bit error correction and device failure protection for ×4 devices. Figure 30.13 illustrates: the data bus output of each ×4 device is divided[3] into 2-bit-wide groups sent to two separate 72-bit-wide ECC code words. Physically adjacent data bits from the same DRAM device are routed to different ECC words. In the case where a single DRAM device suffers a catastrophic failure, multiple ECC words in the same system will sustain, at most, one or two bits of error, and such errors can be corrected by the 2-adjacent ECC algorithm.

---

[3]Note that the bit steering concept is superficially incompatible with the use of source-synchronous reference strobes. In modern DRAM memory systems such as DDR SDRAM, source-synchronous strobes are sent along with small groups of data signals. In the case where the data bits are steered to different locations, the timing of the data signals cannot be synchronized with respect to the source-synchronous strobe and still retain the matching load and topology between each of the data signals and the data strobe signal. However, the data strobe signals are only needed for data transport between different chips on the system board. Therefore, one solution is to steer the data to different ECC words only after the data has been received by the memory controller. That is, bit steering occurs in datapaths located inside of the memory controller rather than on the system board.

TABLE **30.3**   Error location table for the 2-adjacent error correction algorithm, taken from US Patent #5,490,155 (Compaq's Advanced ECC implementation)

					S7: 0	0	0	0	0	0	0	0	1	1	1	1	1	1	1	1
					S6: 0	0	0	0	1	1	1	1	0	0	0	0	1	1	1	1
s3	s2	s1	s0		s5: 0	0	1	1	0	0	1	1	0	0	1	1	0	0	1	1
					s4: 0	1	0	1	0	1	0	1	0	1	0	1	0	1	0	1
0	0	0	0			C4	C5		C6	5	3	1	C7		4	2		2,3	0,1	4,5
0	0	0	1		C0	51	49	47	63	33			61		28		59			30,31
0	0	1	0		C1	46	50	48	58	31			62		32		60			28,29
0	0	1	1			48,49	46,47	50,51	60,61	29			58,59				62,63			32,33
0	1	0	0		C2	57	52	54,55	11	35			9	19			7	17		
0	1	0	1		45	39	23	21	37											
0	1	1	0		43								24							12,13
0	1	1	1		41										14		26,27			
1	0	0	0		C3	55	56	52,53	6		16		10		34		8		18	
1	0	0	1		40				27											14,15
1	0	1	0		44	20	38	22					36							
1	0	1	1		42												24,25			
1	1	0	0			53	54	56,57	8,9			18,19	6,7			16,17	10,11			34,35
1	1	0	1		42,43				25							12				
1	1	1	0		40,41				15				26							
1	1	1	1		44,45	22,23	20,21	38,39									36,37			

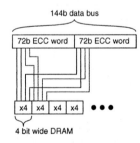

144b data bus

| 72b ECC word | 72b ECC word |

x4 x4 x4 x4 •••

4 bit wide DRAM

FIGURE 30.13: Bit steering in Compaq's Advanced ECC.

The move from ×4 to ×8, ×16, and ×32 DRAM devices means that in case of the failure of a DRAM device, or the failure of a single connection to the address, command, or control bus of the DRAM device, the wide multi-errors would be more difficult to contain. In such a case, 8, 16, or 32 bits of data would fail concurrently, and this is a non-trivial problem to solve. Note that Compaq's Advanced ECC algorithm provides chipkill functionality for the failure of 4-bit DRAM devices in a memory system with a 144-bit data bus. Using the same algorithm with x8 parts would require a 288-bit bus and so forth for systems with even wider DRAM devices.

30.3.6 Chipkill with ×8 DRAM Devices

High-end computer servers that make use of DDR and DDR2 SDRAM memory systems have more-or-less standardized on the use of ×4 DRAM devices to obtain the maximum capacity in each rank of memory, largely because ×4 chipkill algorithms such as the one just described easily contain the most single point failures in the memory system. However, due to the dynamics of the commodity DRAM market, a price premium is now attached to ×4 devices relative to ×8 devices of the same capacity. Moreover, this price premium is projected to grow larger as the price delta forces memory system architects and design engineers to use the less expensive ×8 devices; consequently, memory system architects are actively exploring new ECC algorithms that work with ×8 devices.

In his b-adjacent error correction paper, Bossen notes that a class of error-correction mechanisms can be implemented from the generic b-adjacent algorithm. This class of useful b-adjacent error locating and correcting algorithm can be described as a 2-redundant, b-adjacent algorithm where b numbers of b-adjacent symbols can be protected with the redundancy of two b-bit-wide symbols. In practical terms, this class of algorithms means that eight 8-bit symbols can be protected with the redundancy of two 8-bit symbols. That is, an 8-adjacent ECC algorithm can be implemented for a 64-bit data block using 16 check bits to protect against the failure of 8 aligned, adjacent bits (64, 80). The drawbacks are that the algorithm requires the data bus to increase from 72 to 80 bits, and the storage overhead of error correction increases from 1:8 to 1:4. Consequently, the (64, 80) 8-adjacent algorithm is considered unacceptable for use in modern memory systems. However, note that the overhead ratio of the 2-redundant b-adjacent algorithm decreases with larger values of b; for b = 16, only two 16-bit symbols are needed to protect sixteen 16-bit symbols. The overhead ratio of 256 data bits to 32 check bits suggests that the algorithm is compatible with existing infrastructure of 72-bit data busses.

Figure 30.14 shows that 18 DRAM devices, each with an 8-bit-wide data bus, can be connected together to form a single rank of DRAM devices for a memory system with a 144-bit-wide data bus. A memory controller implementing the 2-redundant, 16-adjacent algorithm can take two 144-bit data blocks over 2 consecutive cycles and treat this as a single 288-bit-wide ECC word containing sixteen 16-bit data symbols with two 16-bit check symbols. In this configuration, the loss of any single $\times 8$ DRAM device would result in the loss of a 16-bit symbol in the 288-bit-wide ECC word, and the lost data can be reconstructed by the memory controller from the two 16-bit check symbols.

The implementation of the 2-redundant, 16-adjacent error correction algorithm is rather expensive in terms of hardware complexity. Moreover, the implementation illustrated in Figure 30.14 is still lacking: in the failure of a $\times 8$ device, the error detection and correction capability is completely expended to correct for the loss of data from the $\times 8$ device, and the memory controller can no longer detect single-bit soft errors. That is, in the case where a single $\times 8$ DRAM device fails, the memory controller must read out and reconstruct the data from the failed memory device and then place the data in a different location. Since the memory system of a high-availability computer system must continue to service requests to other ranks of memory of the same channel, the memory controller is then limited to reading out all of the data contained in the failed rank of memory in an opportunistic fashion, and the process can potentially occur over tens of seconds. Consequently, for these types of highly reliable memory systems, it may be desirable to detect

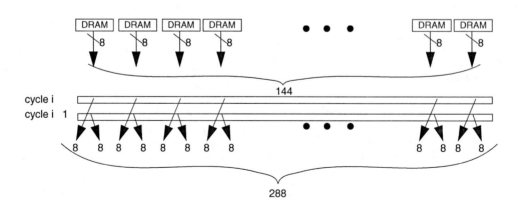

FIGURE 30.14: Using 2-redundant, 16-adjacent error correction algorithm to provide chipkill functionality for x8 devices.

the occurrence of a single-bit soft error even after the failure of a ×8 device.

Figure 30.15 illustrates one possible implementation of the 2-redundant, 16-adjacent error correction algorithm where each 4-bit half of the 8-bit data bus from every ×8 DRAM device is steered to a different ECC word. A 16-bit symbol from a given DRAM device is then constructed over *four* consecutive cycles. In this configuration, two 288-bit-wide ECC words are constructed over four cycles, with each ECC word consisting of sixteen 16-bit data symbols and two 16-bit check symbols. In the case where a ×8 DRAM device fails, the two ECC words would both report the failure of a single symbol in the same symbol location. In the case where a single-bit error occurs in addition to the failure of a ×8 DRAM device, the two ECC words would report the failure of different symbols, indicating that two separate errors had occurred. In this manner, multi-error failures can be detected, but not corrected. Finally, the 16-adjacent, 2-redundant algorithm is a relatively old algorithm; newer and more efficient algorithms now exist to encode and protect for ×8 device failure.

30.3.7 Memory Scrubbing

One method that has been deployed in the quest to ensure DRAM memory system reliability is the concept of *memory scrubbing*, which addresses the fact that while single-bit and b-adjacent bit errors are correctable by the various multi-bit ECC algorithms, non-adjacent multi-bit errors are not correctable. In the case where two cosmic ray events impact the same DRAM row and generate multiple errors in different parts of the same DRAM row, or in the case where a soft error impacts a memory location in a rank of memory that subsequently suffers the failure of a DRAM device, these multi-failure errors cannot be corrected. One solution to the randomly distributed multi-bit error problem is for the DRAM controller to constantly cycle through data in the memory system through the error correction circuitry, relying upon the low probability of simultaneous errors to correct any single bit or a group of b-adjacent bits before another failure occurs in the memory system. The constant cycling of data through the error correction circuitry is referred to as *scrubbing*.

Active memory scrubbing consumes significant power and bandwidth, since the error detecting

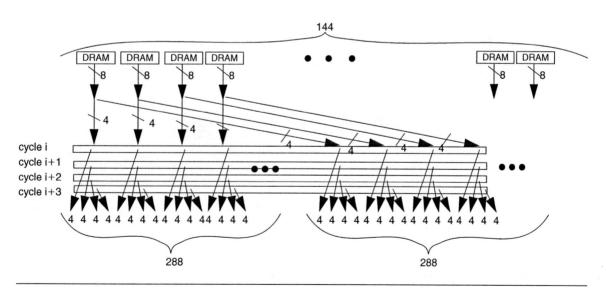

FIGURE 30.15: Using 2-redundant, 16-adjacent error correction algorithm and bit steering to provide single-bit soft error detection capability in addition to chipkill functionality for ×8 devices.

and correction circuitry is contained in the DRAM controller. To scrub the memory system, data is transported from DRAM devices to the memory controller. Fortunately, due to the relatively low SERs of modern DRAM devices, memory controllers that perform scrubbing are presently only found on high-end servers that demand as close to absolute reliability as practicable. Memory systems that operate in extreme environments, or future memory systems with significantly higher error rates, may require the deployment of scrubbing as an active defense against uncorrectable multi-failure errors.

30.3.8 Bullet Proofing the Memory System

High-availability systems require no unscheduled system downtime. The requirement therefore is for absolutely reliable memory systems that can tolerate a hardware DRAM device failure and still correct soft errors. Combined with the relatively low cost of DRAM memory, servers designed for reliable operations are now incorporating more advanced DRAM protection such as RAID-like mirroring of memory data, on-line spare memory, and hot sparing.

30.4 Reliability of Non-DRAM Systems

In general, the error-correcting concepts described in this chapter are generic and can be applied to different memory systems. The primary difference then is the failure mechanism and failure rates for different memory systems. In this section, a brief overview is provided for a few different types of memory systems whose reliability characteristics are notably different from the reliability characteristics of DRAM memory systems.

30.4.1 SRAM

SRAM device error rates historically tracked DRAM devices until the 180-nm process generation. Due to the combination of reduced supply voltage and reduced critical cell charge, SRAM SERs have climbed dramatically for the 180- and 130-nm process generations. In a recent publication, Monolithic System

Technology, Inc. (MoSys) claims that, for the 250-nm process generation, SRAM SERs are in the range of 100 FITs per megabit, while SERs for the 130-nm process generation are in the range of 100,000 FITs per megabit. The generalized trend is expected to continue to increase as the demand for low power dissipation forces a continued reduction in supply voltage and reduced critical charge per cell.

Due to SRAM's extreme sensitivity to SEU, modern processors now ship with parity and SECDED ECC protection for the SRAM caches. Typically, the tag arrays are protected by parity, whereas the data arrays are protected by the SECDED ECC algorithm. More sophisticated multi-bit ECC algorithms are typically not deployed for on-chip SRAM caches in modern processors since the addition of sophisticated computation circuitry can add to the die size and causes significant delay relative to the timing demands of the on-chip caches. Moreover, caches typically store copies of data held in main memory, and in case an uncorrectable error is detected, a processor simply has to refetch the data from memory. In this sense, it is usually unnecessary to detect and correct multi-bit errors; it is sufficient simply to detect multi-bit errors.

30.4.2 Flash

The issues relating to flash reliability differ from the issue of DRAM reliability and SRAM reliability. While DRAM and SRAM devices must contend with cosmic ray neutron-induced soft errors, flash memories must contend with the problem of a limited number of write cycles in flash memory cells. Due to the fact that a flash cell can fail after a limited number of read-write cycles (in the 10K–100K range), writes to flash cells cannot be taken for granted. Instead, sophisticated algorithms must be deployed to verify that the data written to the cells is correctly stored in flash cells. In some cases, ECC logic circuits are built into the flash devices.

30.4.3 MRAM

Similar to the ferrite core memories of yesteryear, Magnetic RAM (MRAM) cells operate on the principle of magnetics and not on the storage of electrical charges. This subtle difference means that MRAM devices are immune to the effects of incident alpha particles or cosmic ray neutrons. However, since they are based on the storage of a magnetic field in the bit cells, MRAM cells are more susceptible to electromagnetic fields. Moreover, the issue of device failure will exist for MRAM devices, just as it does for other devices. Consequently, system-level reliability considerations must be considered for MRAM devices just as they are for DRAM devices.

30.5 Space Shuttle Memory System

Liberally quoted and edited from *Second Generation Computers FAQ*:

> *All of the flight-critical software on the space shuttle is executed on five IBM AP-101 General Purpose Computers (GPCs). The crew may use commercially available laptop computers and programmable calculators for non-critical applications. By modern standards, the AP-101 is incredibly slow. The original shuttle computers, AP-101B, were replaced in 1991 by an upgraded version, the AP-101S. The amount of memory available in the AP-101B is 212,992 16-bit words. The AP-101S holds up to 524,288 words. These numbers do not include error detection bits. The memory in the original AP-101B was ferrite core. Since core memory is non-volatile, a GPC can be turned off and turned on later without losing its mind. The AP-101S uses normal RAM with battery backup to achieve the same result. Ferrite core memory was originally selected for the GPCs because little was known about the effects of radiation on the high-density solid state RAM which is now used in almost all digital computer hardware.*
>
> *The AP101S uses a solid state CMOS memory with battery backup. Because the CMOS memory can be altered by radiation which the Shuttle encounters in orbit, the memory was designed with error detection and correction (EDAC) logic. Whenever the GPC is powered, a hardware process called "scrub" continually checks the GPC's memory for alterations. Scrub is capable of detecting and correcting single bit errors. Multi-bit errors can be detected, but not corrected. Scrub checks all of the GPC's memory in 1.7 seconds. Each memory location is also checked by EDAC prior to being executed by the GPC. With the non-volatile memory of the old AP101B, the crew would configure one GPC for De-orbit and Entry, then shut off its power. With the AP101S, the crew configures one GPC with software for the De-orbit and Entry phases of Shuttle flight then puts the GPC to "Sleep." Sleep is a reduced power mode in the GPC which uses only 10% of its rated power. This reduced power mode reduces the amount of electricity which must be generated by the Orbiter's Fuel Cell system, but allows the EDAC logic to continually scrub the GPC's memory.*

CHAPTER 31

Virtual Memory

Virtual memory is one technique for managing the resource of physical memory, including the caches, main memory, and the disk subsystem. It was originally invented to provide to software the illusion of a very large amount of main memory [Kilburn et al. 1962]. Though administrators today typically purchase enough main memory that nearly all code and data needed by software is actually in main memory (i.e., virtual memory has outlived its original purpose), the mechanism is nonetheless the most popular front-end for the memory system today, in general-purpose systems and, to an increasing degree, embedded systems as well.

The basic functions of virtual memory are well known [Denning 1970]. One is to create a virtual-machine environment for every process, which among other things allows text, data, and stack regions to begin at statically known locations in all processes without fear of conflict. Another is demand-paging—setting a finer granularity for process residence than an entire address space, thereby allowing a process to execute as long as a single page is memory resident. Today's expectations of virtual memory extend its original semantics and now include additional features such as virtual-address aliasing (enabling different processes to map shared objects at different virtual addresses), protection aliasing (enabling different processes to map shared objects using different protections), and support for virtual caches.

In general-purpose systems, the virtual memory system is the primary client of the memory system, in that a user process is not aware of physical memory and does not access it directly. All user-level accesses to the main memory system are made indirectly through the virtual memory system. The operating system's mapping from virtual space to physical space determines the access pattern seen by the physical memory system (including caches, DRAMs, and, to an extent, disks). Thus, it is no exaggeration to say that the structure and organization of the virtual memory system largely determine the way the memory system is used. Chief advantages of using virtual memory today include the following:

1. It provides an intuitive framework on which an operating system can implement multitasking. Virtual memory allows each process to act as if it "owns" all of the available hardware resources, and the mechanism ensures that no process can directly affect the resources belonging to another process.

2. It supports the execution of processes only partially resident in memory. In a virtual memory system, only the most-often used portions of a process's address space actually occupy physical memory; the rest of the address space is stored on disk until needed.

Most operating systems support virtual memory through a *page table*, an in-memory database of translation information that indicates where in the memory system each virtual page can be found. Virtual memory underlies nearly all academic and experimental operating systems, most Unix systems including SCO and Solaris, and many Unix-based or Unix-influenced systems such as Mac OSX (which is based on Mach [Accetta et al. 1986], itself an emulation of BSD Unix), Windows NT through to XP, OS/2, and Spring [Custer 1993, Deitel 1990, Hamilton & Kougiouris 1993,

Mitchell et al. 1994]. Virtual memory is also playing an increasingly significant role in embedded systems, found in such real-time operating systems as Windows CE and Inferno.

Most processors support virtual memory through a hardware *memory-management unit* (MMU) that translates virtual addresses to physical addresses. The classic MMU design, as seen in the GE 645, DEC VAX, and Intel x86 architectures [Organick 1972, Clark & Emer 1985, Intel 1993], is composed of two parts: the *translation lookaside buffer* (TLB) and a finite state machine. The TLB is an on-chip memory structure that caches the page table; it holds only page table entries, and its only purpose is to speed address translation and permissions checking. If the necessary translation information is on-chip in the TLB, the system can translate a virtual address to a physical address without requiring an access to the page table. If the translation information is not found in the TLB (an event called a *TLB miss*), one must search the page table for the translation and insert it into the TLB before processing can continue. Early designs provided a hardware state machine to perform this activity; in the event of a TLB miss, the state machine would walk the page table, locate the translation information, insert it into the TLB, and restart the computation. All modern general-purpose microprocessors support virtual memory through some form of MMU, and an increasing number of embedded processors[1] have MMUs as well.

Because of the cache hierarchy's potentially non-trivial interaction with the virtual memory system, the choice of cache organization and architecture (which would otherwise seem a simple enough decision to make) provides a designer the ability to target either hardware or the operating system to bear the brunt of run-time activity and/or design complexity. Physical caches require no explicit operating system support, but place more burden on hardware for acceptable performance. In comparison, virtual caches can require less hardware activity (for example, they allow the TLB access to be pushed further out), but, in turn, place a heavier burden on the operating system in the form of explicit cache management. This was discussed in detail in Chapter 4, "Management of Cache Consistency." A system that provides virtual memory must typically also provide support for precise interrupts. This design problem scales with the complexity of the processor's pipeline organization—in sequential processors, providing support for precise interrupts is straightforward; in more complex machines, it is anything but. The difficulty of guaranteeing precise interrupts is exacerbated by a cache hierarchy, because a cache system is expected to provide instantaneous access to data for load and store instructions while also acting as non-permanent storage, even though it is generally implemented in a technology that fails to support "undo" operations easily.

31.1 A Virtual Memory Primer

In the virtual addressing model, processes execute in imaginary address spaces that are mapped onto physical memory by the operating system. Processes generate instruction fetches and loads and stores using imaginary or "virtual" names for their instructions and data. The ultimate home for the process's address space is the *backing* or *permanent store*, e.g., a disk drive. This is where the process's instructions and data come from and where all of its permanent changes go to. Every hardware memory structure between the CPU and the backing store is a cache for the instructions and data in the process's address space. This includes main memory: main memory is really nothing more than a cache for a process's virtual-address space, a space that can range from gigabytes to exabytes in size. Everything in the address space initially comes from the program file stored on disk or is created on demand and defined to be zero.

The following sections provide a brief overview of the mechanics of virtual memory.[2] A more detailed

---

[1]Even as far back as the mid- to late 1990s, the move to use virtual memory in embedded systems was well underway. For instance, National Semiconductor abandoned several years' worth of development on their Pentium-class embedded processor largely due to customer dissatisfaction with the processor's lack of an MMU [Turley 1998a].

[2]Portions reprinted, with permission, from "Virtual memory: Issues of implementation," by Bruce Jacob and Trevor Mudge, *IEEE Computer*, vol. 31, no. 6, pp. 33–43, June 1998. © 1998 IEEE.

treatment of the topic can be found on-line [Jacob & Mudge 1998a, 1998b, 1998c].

31.1.1 Address Spaces and the Main Memory Cache

Just as hardware caches can have many different organizations, so can the main memory cache, including a spectrum of designs from direct-mapped to fully associative. Figure 31.1 illustrates a few choices. Note that virtual memory was invented at a time when physical memory was expensive and typical systems had very little of it. A fully associative organization was chosen so that the operating system could place a virtual page into any available slot in physical memory, thus ensuring that no space would go unused (a guarantee that could not be made for a direct-mapped or set-associative organization). This design reduced contention for main memory as far as possible, but at the cost of making the act of accessing main memory more complex and perhaps more time-consuming.

This design decision has never been seriously challenged by later systems, and the fully associative organization is still in use. However, there have been proposals to use set-associative designs to solve specific problems. Taylor describes a hardware caching mechanism (the *TLB slice*) used in conjunction with a speculative TLB lookup to speed up the access time of the TLB [Taylor et al. 1990]. Taylor suggests that restricting the degree of set associativity when locating pages in main memory would increase the hit rate of the caching mechanism. It should be noted that if the hardware could impose a set-associative main memory organization on the operating system, the caching mechanism described in the paper would be superfluous, i.e., the speculative TLB lookup would work just as well without the TLB slice. Chiueh and Katz [1992] suggest a set-associative organization for main memory to move the TLB lookup off the critical path to the physically indexed Level-1 processor cache and

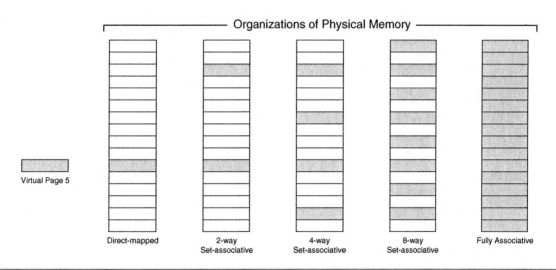

Organizations of Physical Memory

Virtual Page 5

Direct-mapped | 2-way Set-associative | 4-way Set-associative | 8-way Set-associative | Fully Associative

FIGURE 31.1: Associative organizations of main memory. These diagrams illustrate the placement of a virtual page (page 0x05) within aphysical memory of 16 pages. If the memory is organized as a direct-mapped cache, the page can only map to one location. If the memory is 2-way set-associative, the page can map to two locations. If the memory is 4-way set-associative, the page can map to four locations, etc. A fully associative organization allows the page to map to any location—this is the organization used most often in today's operating systems, though set-associative organizations have been suggested before to solve cache-coherence problems and to speed TLB access times.

to allow the cache to be larger than the page size times the cache's associativity. Similarly, the SunOS operating system, to eliminate the possibility of data corruption, aligns virtual-address aliases on boundaries at least as large as the largest virtual cache [Cheng 1987]. Kessler and Hill [1992] propose a similar mechanism to be used in conjunction with optimizing compilers so that the compiler's careful placement of code and data objects is not accidentally undermined by the virtual memory system. The consistency of virtual caches is described in more detail in Chapter 4.

31.1.2 Address Mapping and the Page Table

Mapping information is organized into *page tables*, which are collections of *page table entries* (PTEs). Each PTE typically maintains information for only one page at a time. At the minimum, a PTE indicates whether its virtual page is in memory, on disk, or unallocated. Over time, virtual memory evolved to handle additional functions, including address space protection and page-level protection, so a typical PTE now contains additional information such as whether the page holds executable code, whether it can be modified, and, if so, by whom. Most operating systems today, including Windows XP, Linux, and other variations of UNIX, support address space and page-level protection in this way. From a PTE, the operating system must be able to determine

- The ID of the page's owner (the *address-space identifier*, sometimes called an *access key*)
- The virtual page number (VPN)
- Whether the PTE contains valid translation information (a *valid* bit)
- The page's translation information: its location in memory (page frame number or PFN) or location on disk (for example, a disk block number or an offset into a swap file)
- The page's protection information, such as whether it is read-write, read-only, write-only, etc.
- Whether the page has been written recently
- Whether the page was recently accessed (to aid in making replacement decisions).

The operating system uses the *reference* and *modify* bits to implement an approximation to a least-recently used page-replacement policy. The operating system periodically clears the reference bits of all mapped pages to measure page usage. The modify bit indicates that a replaced page either is clean and can simply be discarded or is dirty and must be written back to disk before replacement.

It is rare to see all of this information stored explicitly in each PTE; careful organization of the page table may allow some items to be implicit. For instance, most implementations do not need both the VPN and the PFN; one or the other can often be deduced from the PTE's location in the table. Also, the address-space identifier is unnecessary if every process has its own page table or if there is another mechanism besides address-space identifiers that differentiates the virtual addresses generated by unrelated processes. One such example is paged segmentation, in which virtual addresses are translated to physical addresses in two steps: the first is at a segment granularity, and the second is at a page granularity. Other items such as disk-block information can be placed in secondary tables. The net result is that a PTE can often be made to fit within a 32- or 64-bit word.

A generation ago, when address spaces were much smaller, a single-level table of mapping information, called a *direct table*, mapped an entire address space and was small enough to be maintained entirely in hardware. As address spaces grew larger, the table size grew to the point that system designers were forced to move it into memory. They preserved the illusion of a large table held in hardware by caching portions of this page table in a hardware TLB and by automatically refilling the TLB from the page table on a TLB miss. The search of the page table, called *page table walking*, is therefore a large component of handling a TLB miss. Accordingly, today's designers take great care to construct page table organizations that minimize the performance overhead of table walking. Searching the table can be simplified if PTEs are organized contiguously so that a VPN or PFN can be used as an offset to find the appropriate PTE. This leads to two primary types of page table organization: the *forward-mapped* or *hierarchical page table*, indexed by the VPN, and the *inverse-mapped* or *inverted page table*, indexed by the PFN. The page table's structure dictates several things,

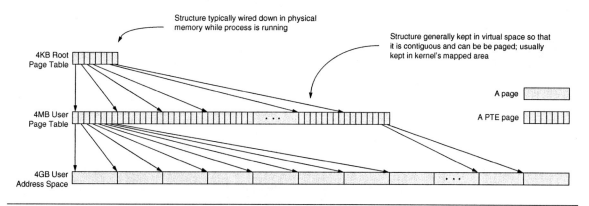

FIGURE 31.2: Classic two-level hierarchical page table for a 32-bit address space.

including efficiency in space (how much of main memory the table requires) and efficiency in time (how long it takes to find the mapping for a particular page).

31.1.3 Hierarchical Page Tables

The classical hierarchical page table, depicted in Figure 31.2, comes from the self-similar idea that a large space can be mapped by a smaller space, which can, in turn, be mapped by an even smaller space. If we assume 32-bit addresses and 4-KB pages, the 4-GB address space is composed of 1,048,576 (2^{20}) pages. If each of these pages is mapped by a 4-byte PTE, we can organize the PTEs into a 4-MB linear structure. This is rather large, and since it is likely that not all the user's pages will be mapped (much of the 4-GB virtual-address space might never be touched), why *wire down*[3] the entire 4-MB array of PTEs if most will be empty? Why not map the page table itself—place the array into virtual space and allow *it* to be paged just like "normal" virtual memory? A 4-MB linear structure occupies 1024 (2^{10}) pages, which can be mapped by 1024 PTEs. Organized into a linear array, they occupy 4 KB—a reasonable amount of memory to wire down for a running process. As address spaces grow to 64 bits, so does the size of the hierarchical page table, in particular, the number of levels in the

table. Figure 31.3 shows the page table structure used by both OSF/1 and OpenVMS on the 64-bit Alpha architecture [Sites 1992]. The page table structure is limited to three tiers to reduce the cost of TLB refill.

There are two ways to perform a lookup in the hierarchical page table: *top-down* (also *forward-mapped*) or *bottom-up*. A top-down lookup uses physical addresses for the components of the hierarchical page table, while a bottom-up strategy uses virtual addresses.

Top-Down Traversal

Figure 31.4 shows the steps in the top-down hierarchical page table access for a 32-bit architecture. First, the top 10 bits index the 1024-entry root page table, whose base address is typically stored in a hardware register. The referenced PTE gives the physical address of a 4-KB PTE page or indicates that the PTE page is on disk or unallocated. Assuming the page is in memory, the next 10 bits of the virtual address index this PTE page. The selected PTE gives the PFN of the 4-KB virtual page referenced by the faulting virtual address. The bottom 12 bits of the virtual address index the physical data page to access the desired byte.

If at any point in the algorithm a PTE indicates that the desired page (which could be a PTE page) is paged out or does not yet exist, the hardware raises a page-fault exception. The operating system must

---

[3]To "wire down" a region of virtual memory is to reserve space for it in physical memory and not allow it to be paged to disk. Thus, the space cannot be used for any other purpose.

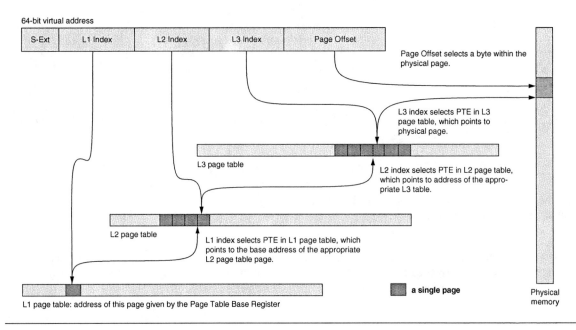

FIGURE 31.3: The Alpha three-level page table used in both OSF/1 and OpenVMS.

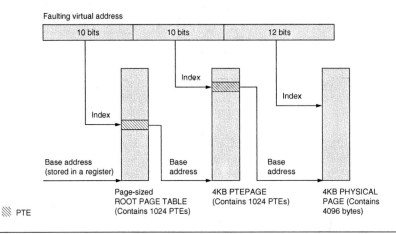

FIGURE 31.4: Top-down/forward-mapped access method for the hierarchical page table. The top 10 bits identify a PTE in the root page table that maps the PTE page; the middle 10 bits identify within that PTE page the single PTE that maps the data page; and the bottom 12 bits identify a byte within the 4-KB data page.

then retrieve the page from disk (or create a new page, or signal the process) and place its mapping into the page table and possibly the TLB.

Many of the early hierarchical page tables were traversed in this way, so the term *forward-mapped*

page table is often used to mean a hierarchical page table accessed top-down. Due to its simplicity, this algorithm is often used in hardware table-walking schemes, such as the one in Intel's IA-32 architecture.

Bottom-Up Traversal

Note that the top-down traversal requires as many memory references as there are table levels, plus one more to get the actual data, and this number grows as the virtual address grows (as depicted in the Alpha's table, Figure 31.3). Alternatively, one can use a bottom-up traversal of the page table and often incur a single memory access to get the mapping information, reducing the total (which includes the access for the mapping and then the access for the requested data) to two in the case where the virtual load succeeds and using a top-down approach only if the virtual load fails.

In a bottom-up traversal, the top bits of the virtual address are used as a *virtual* offset into the user page table, which is contiguous in virtual space (refer back to Figure 31.2). Knowing the virtual address of the start of the user page table (*PTbase*) and the faulting page number (*BadVPN*), one can easily construct a virtual address for the PTE; as suggested by Figure 31.2, the virtual address for the PTE is given by the following:

$$\text{address} = PTbase + (BadVPN * \text{sizeof(PTE)}) \qquad \textbf{(EQ 31.1)}$$

The pseudo-code in Figure 31.5 briefly illustrates the steps. Figure 31.5 shows the bottom-up method for a 32-bit architecture. In step 1, the top 20 bits of a faulting virtual address are concatenated with the virtual offset of the user page table. The bottom bits of the address are zero, because a PTE is usually a power of two size in bytes and aligned. The virtual page number of the faulting address is equal to the PTE index in the user page table. Therefore, this virtual address points to the appropriate user PTE. If a load using this address succeeds, the user PTE is placed into the TLB and can translate the faulting virtual address.

The user PTE load can, however, cause a TLB miss of its own. In step 2, the system generates a second address when the user PTE load fails. The mapping

```
/* user code executing ... */
load X /* load misses TLB, invokes TLB-miss handler: */
    construct virtual address for PTE (in user page table)
    load user PTE /* possibly misses TLB, invokes TLB-miss handler: */
        construct physical address for PTE (in root page table)
        load root PTE /* cannot cause TLB miss -- physical address */
        put root PTE into TLB
        jump to faulting instruction
    load user PTE /* this time, load succeeds */
    put user PTE into TLB
    jump to faulting instruction
load X /* this time, load succeeds */
```

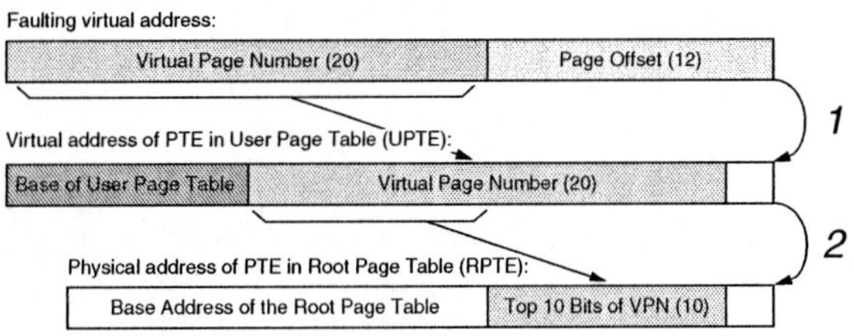

FIGURE 31.5: The bottom-up method for accessing the hierarchical page table. The algorithm typically accesses memory only once to translate a virtual address. It resorts to a top-down traversal if the initial attempt fails.

PTE for this load is an entry in the root page table, and the index is the top 10 bits of the faulting address's VPN, just as in the top-down method. These 10 bits are concatenated with the root page table's base address to form a physical address for the appropriate root PTE. Unlike a virtual address, using this physical address cannot cause another TLB miss. The system loads the root PTE and inserts it into the TLB to map the page containing the user PTE. When the root PTE is loaded into the TLB, the root table handler ends, and the user PTE load is retried. Once this user PTE is loaded into the TLB, the user table handler ends and the faulting user-level load or store is retried. Usually, however, the first PTE lookup—the user PTE lookup—succeeds and then a TLB miss only requires one memory reference to translate the faulting user address. Architectures that use the bottom-up approach include MIPS and Alpha. Section 31.2 will go into more detail on how the mechanism is implemented.

31.1.4 Inverted Page Tables

The classical inverted page table, pictured in Figure 31.6, has several advantages over the hierarchical table. Instead of one entry for every virtual page belonging to a process, it contains one entry for every physical page in main memory. Thus, rather than scaling with the size of the virtual space, it scales with the size of the physical space. This is a distinct advantage over the hierarchical table when one is concerned with 64-bit address spaces. Depending on the implementation, it can also have a lower average number of memory references to service a TLB miss than a typical hierarchical page table. Its compact size (there are usually no unused entries wasting space) makes it a good candidate for a hardware-managed mechanism that requires the table to be wired down in memory.

The structure is said to be *inverted* because the index of the PTE in the page table is the PFN, not the VPN. However, one typically uses the page table to *find* the PFN for a given VPN, so the PFN is not readily available. Therefore, a hashing scheme is used; to locate a PTE, the VPN is hashed to index the table. Since different VPNs might produce identical hash values, a collision-chain mechanism is used to allow different virtual mappings to exist in the table simultaneously. When a collision occurs, a different slot in the table is chosen, and the new entry is added to the end of the chain. Thus, it is possible to chase a long list of pointers while servicing a single TLB miss. Collision chains in hash tables are well researched. To keep the average chain length short, one can increase the size of the hash table. However, by changing the inverted page table's size, one loses the ability to index the table

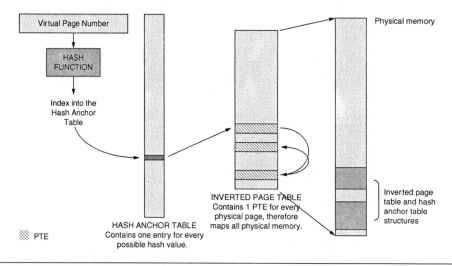

FIGURE 31.6: Classical inverted page table structure.

by the PFN. Therefore, a level of indirection is used; the *hash anchor table* (HAT) points to the chain head for every hash value. Every doubling of the HAT size reduces the average chain length by half, so the number of entries in the HAT is generally several times larger than that of the inverted page table.

This lookup mechanism is relatively expensive in that it requires at least two memory references to find a PTE; modern inverted tables (e.g., in the PA-RISC and PowerPC architectures) reduce this to one. PA-RISC systems typically use a variant of the inverted page table called the *hashed page translation table* [Huck & Hays 1993], pictured in Figure 31.7. It is similar to the canonical inverted page table, but it removes the HAT. The table is also unlike the inverted page table in that it can hold more entries than physical pages in the system, and the collision chain can be held in the page table itself or in a separate structure called the *collision resolution table*. This means that the PFN cannot be deduced from an entry's location in the hashed page translation table, so each table entry must explicitly record this information: a table entry contains both the VPN and the PFN of the mapped page. The lookup algorithm is simpler than the canonical table's lookup algorithm, as the initial

HAT lookup is gone. The primary difference is that the PFN comes directly from the page table entry itself, not from its location within the table, so the page table entry is a bit larger than the canonical form. The trade-off is space for speed, and the form supports shared memory by allowing multiple mappings to the same physical page to co-exist in the table.

The PowerPC hashed page table is pictured in Figure 31.8 [Weiss & Smith 1994, IBM & Motorola 1993]. It has no HAT, which reduces the minimum number of memory references by one, and the PTE group takes the place of the collision chain. The table is eight PTEs wide, and if more than eight VPNs hash to the same location, the extra PTEs are simply left out. On a TLB miss, the hardware loads an entire PTE group at once and searches through the PTEs for a matching virtual address. This happens even if the PTE group contains no valid PTEs. The PowerPC can perform an optional second lookup to a different PTE group based on a secondary hash value. The second lookup is identical to the first: an entire PTE group is loaded and searched. Each table entry is large—like the PA-RISC table, this is unavoidable because the location of a PTE in the table bears no relation to either the VPN or the PFN in the mapping, and thus

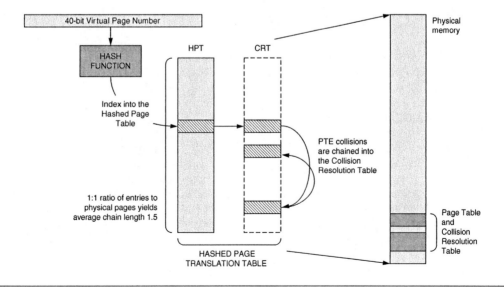

FIGURE 31.7: The PA-RISC hashed paged translation table.

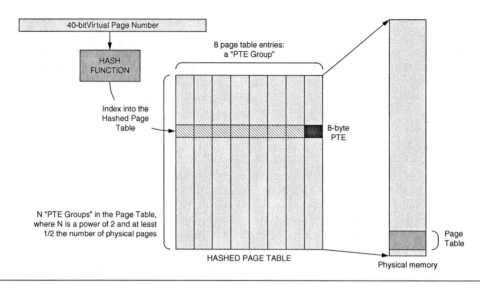

FIGURE 31.8: The PowerPC hashed page table structure.

both values need to be stored in the PTE. For 32-bit PowerPC implementations, the PTE is 8 bytes wide; for 64-bit implementations, it is 16 bytes wide.

31.1.5 Comparison: Inverted vs. Hierarchical

When a designer implements a virtual memory system on a real-world memory system, subtle problems surface. The choice between hierarchical and inverted page tables is not an obvious one; there are many trade-offs between performance and memory usage. Implementations of shared memory can vary widely in performance, especially with different hardware support. For instance, shared memory on virtual caches requires more consistency management than shared memory on physical caches [Chao et al. 1990], and shared memory's interactions with different page table organizations can yield significant variations in TLB performance. The address-space protection scheme is also heavily dependent on hardware support and has a great impact on the shared memory implementation.

The first hierarchical tables were accessed top-down. The most common complaint against this design is that its support for large address spaces and sparse address spaces is inefficient. The top-down access variant wastes time because it requires more than two tiers to cover a large address space, and each tier requires a memory reference during table-walking. The bottom-up variant, popularized by the MIPS processor, is more efficient. Although it also may require more than two tiers to map a large address space, the bottom-most tier is probed first, using an easily constructed virtual address. The user PTEs needed for mapping the user address space will likely be found in the cache, often requiring just a single memory reference to cover a TLB miss.

Both access variants can waste memory, because space in the table is allocated by the operating system an entire page at a time. A process-address space with a single page in it will require one full PTE page at the level of the user page table. If the process adds to its address space virtual pages that are contiguous with the first page, they might also be mapped by the existing PTE page, since the PTEs that map the new pages will be contiguous with the first PTE and will likely fit within the first PTE page. If instead the process adds to its address space another page that is distant from the first page, its mapping PTE will be distant from the first PTE and will likely not lie within the first PTE page. A second PTE page will be added to the user page table, doubling the amount of memory required to map the address space. Clearly, if the address space is very sparsely populated—if it is composed of many individual virtual pages spaced far apart—most of the entries in a given PTE page will be unused, but will consume memory nonetheless. Thus, the organization can degrade to using as many PTE pages as there are mapped virtual pages.

The inverted table was developed, in part, to address the potential space problems of hierarchical tables. No matter how sparsely populated the virtual-address space, the inverted page table wastes no memory because the operating system allocates space in the table one PTE at a time. Since the size of the table is proportional to the number of physical pages available in the system, a large virtual address does not affect the number of entries in the table.

However, the inverted organization does have drawbacks. Because the table only contains entries for virtual pages actively occupying physical memory, an alternate structure is required to maintain information for pages on disk in case they are needed again. The organization of this backup page table could potentially negate the space-saving benefit the inverted organization offers. The PowerPC and PA-RISC tables address this issue by removing the size restriction of the table. These organizations may hold more mappings than pages in physical memory, which decreases the pressure on a backup table. Nonetheless, unlike hierarchical tables, these inverted tables cannot guarantee the presence of a desired mapping, and so they do not remove the need for a backup table entirely.

Because the classical inverted table contains one and only one entry for each page frame in the system, it cannot simultaneously hold mappings for different virtual pages mapped to the same physical location. This is pictured in Figure 31.9. If virtual page 1 in Process A's address space and virtual page 3 in Process B's address space are mapped to the same page frame, thereby allowing A and B to share memory, both mappings cannot reside in the table at the same time. If the processes are using the memory for communication, the operating system could potentially service two page faults for every message exchange. The PA-RISC and PowerPC variants solve

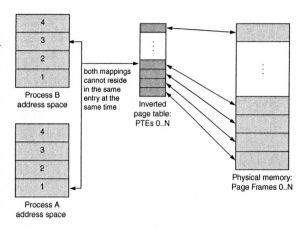

FIGURE 31.9: Inverted page table and shared memory.

the problem by eliminating the requirement that there exist a one-to-one mapping between PTEs and physical pages in the system.

Like the bottom-up table, inverted tables can be accessed quickly. With a large HAT, each lookup averages just over two memory references. By their elimination of the HAT, the PowerPC and PA-RISC reduce this by one. The technique has mixed results. It reduces the minimum number of memory references by one, but it increases the page table's size, requiring the PTE to contain both the VPN and the PFN; this increases bandwidth needs and cache needs because fewer PTEs fit in a single cache block than before.

31.1.6 Translation Lookaside Buffers, Revisited

When a process attempts to load from or store to a virtual address, the hardware searches the TLB for the address's mapping. If the mapping exists in the TLB, the hardware can translate the reference without using the page table. This translation also gives the page's protection information, which is often used to control access to the on-chip instruction and data caches; this is done instead of maintaining protection information in the cache for each resident block. If the mapping does not exist in the TLB, the hardware does not have immediate access to the protection information, and it conservatively denies the process access to the cache. Even if the data is present in the cache, the process is blocked until the TLB is filled with the correct mapping information.

When placed in this perspective, the TLB is clearly seen to function as a tags array for the main memory cache as well as the actual cache hierarchy fronting main memory. The TLB's advantage is that, since it is typically situated on-CPU, it has a fast access time. It is therefore also used to map the contents of the on-chip and off-chip processor caches; it provides protection information and performs the function of a tags array for physically indexed caches. However, when used as a tags array for main memory as well as large off-chip caches, its disadvantage is that its *reach*—notionally, the total memory the TLB can map at once, given by the product of the number of TLB entries and the amount of space each entry maps [Talluri & Hill 1994]—fails to scale with the cache and main memory sizes. While increasing the size of main memory is as simple as buying more DRAM, and increasing the size of an off-chip cache is often just as easy (for a system designer), it is usually not possible to increase the size of the TLB for a given physical CPU chip. Moreover, for reasons of power dissipation, TLB sizes have not increased dramatically over the previous decade, whereas cache and main memory sizes have: the MIPS R2000 TLB in 1990 held 64 entries, compared with the Intel Core processor of 2006, which has 256 entries (128 in each of the I- and D-TLBs). This represents a factor of four increase. In contrast, modern workstations routinely have several megabytes of L2 or L3 cache and one or more gigabytes of DRAM, both of which are two to three orders of magnitude larger than the typical sizes in the early 1990s.

The fact that the TLB reach is effectively decreasing as time goes on is a problem, but it is a problem that could be addressed by exploring unorthodox system organizations and architectures. The page table can require from 0.1 to 10% of main memory [Talluri et al. 1995]. Note that this figure does not include the information required to map those pages held on disk at the moment; it is simply the size of that portion of the page table currently mapping main memory. This amount of main memory is reserved for the page tables and cannot be used for general-purpose data. It is essentially the tags array portion of the main memory cache (which is itself cached by the TLB). An organization potentially just as effective as this could instead use that memory as an *explicit* hardware tags array. This would accomplish the same purpose: it would map the data array portion of the main memory cache. The advantage would be a potentially simpler and faster addressing scheme, which would reduce the performance cost of taking a TLB miss. The disadvantage would be a potentially higher degree of contention for space in main memory if main memory did not remain fully associative, but, in the age of cheap memory, this can be offset by simply increasing the amount of DRAM, assuming that the resulting power dissipation problems can be solved.

Either the operating system or the hardware can refill the TLB when a TLB miss occurs. With a hardware-managed TLB, a hardware state machine walks the page table; there is no interrupt or interaction with the instruction cache. With a software-managed TLB, the general interrupt mechanism invokes a software TLB-miss handler—a primitive in the operating system usually 10–100 instructions long. If the handler code is not in the instruction cache at the time of the TLB miss exception, the time to handle the miss can be much longer than in the hardware-walked scheme. In addition, the software-managed TLB's use of the interrupt mechanism adds to the cost by flushing the pipeline, possibly removing many instructions from the reorder buffer; this could amount to hundreds of cycles [Jacob & Mudge 1998c]. However, the software-managed TLB design allows the operating system to choose any organization for the page table, while the hardware-managed scheme defines a page table organization for the operating system. The flexibility afforded by the software-managed scheme can outweigh the potentially higher per-miss cost of the design [Nagle et al. 1994].

Software-managed TLBs are found in MIPS, SPARC, Alpha, and PA-RISC architectures. PowerPC and ×86 architectures use hardware-managed TLBs. The PA-7200 uses a hybrid approach, implementing the initial probe of its hashed page table in hardware [Huck & Hays 1993], and, if this initial probe fails, walking the rest of the page table in software.

If the hardware provides no form of address space protection mechanism (for example, address-space identifiers or segmentation), then the TLB must be flushed on every process context switch. With hardware support for protection, flushing is typically only required when the operating system reassigns an address-space identifier or segment identifier to a new process, such as at process creation or whenever there are fewer address-space identifiers than currently active processes (a scenario that necessitates a temporary ID remapping). Flushing is also required if the protection mechanism goes unused, as is often the case for the segmentation mechanism provided by the $\times 86$ architecture. Generally, one need not empty the entire TLB of its contents; one need only flush those entries tagged with that address-space identifier. However, whereas most instruction sets provide an instruction to invalidate a single TLB entry with a specified VPN and address-space identifier, most do not provide an instruction that invalidates all TLB entries matching an address-space identifier. As a result, the operating system must often invalidate the entire TLB contents or individually invalidate each entry that matches the address-space identifier. Typically, it is cheaper to invalidate the entire TLB contents than to maintain a list of entries to be flushed on context switch, as this list can be large and expensive to maintain.

When one views the entire memory hierarchy as a virtual memory cache for the disk system, new design opportunities become apparent that can exploit the advantages of virtual caches in different ways. For instance, one can have a memory hierarchy that is entirely physically addressed (as is the case with many older architectures such as the VAX and $\times 86$), one can have a memory hierarchy that is partially physically addressed and partially virtually addressed (as is the case with virtually indexed cache systems of today), or one can have a memory hierarchy that is entirely virtually addressed. These organizations are pictured in Figure 31.10. The only conceptual difference between the designs is the point at which the address translation is performed. One must translate addresses before the point at which the hierarchy becomes physically addressed. If most of the hierarchy is physically addressed (e.g., the MIPS R3000 had a physically addressed L1 processor cache, and all subsequent levels in the hierarchy including any

L2 cache and physical memory would be addressed physically as well), translation will be required frequently, perhaps on every memory reference, and thus, it is necessary that the act of translating incur a low overhead. If the translation point is moved downward in the hierarchy (toward the backing store), more of the hierarchy is virtually addressed, and the act of translating can be less efficient since it will happen less often, assuming that caches have better global hit rates as one moves further from the processor. It is clear to see that at some point the usefulness of the hardware MMU may decline to where it is actually more trouble than it is worth.

31.1.7 Perspective: Segmented Addressing Solves the Synonym Problem

Earlier chapters have described in some detail the problems that arise when the virtual memory system meets the cache system (see, for example, Chapter 2, Section 2.4, "Virtual Addressing and Protection," and Chapter 4, Section 4.2, "Consistency with Self"). The traditional purported weakness of virtual caches is their inability to support shared memory. Many implementations of shared memory are at odds with virtual caches. For instance, ASID aliasing and virtual-address aliasing can cause false cache misses and/or give rise to data inconsistencies in a virtual cache, but they are necessary features of many virtual memory implementations. Despite their inherent potential for problems, virtually indexed caches are quite popular due to their speed and power dissipation (no need for a TLB).

By appropriately using a segmented architecture, one can solve these problems and use a virtual cache without significant trouble; the need to flush virtual caches can be eliminated, and virtual cache consistency management can be eliminated. Though it might seem obvious that segmentation can solve the problems of a virtual cache organization, we note that several contemporary microarchitectures use segmented addressing mechanisms, including PA-RISC [Hewlett-Packard 1990], PowerPC [IBM & Motorola 1993], POWER2 [Weiss & Smith 1994], and $\times 86$ [Intel 1993], while only two of the four (PA-RISC and POWER2) take advantage of a virtual cache.

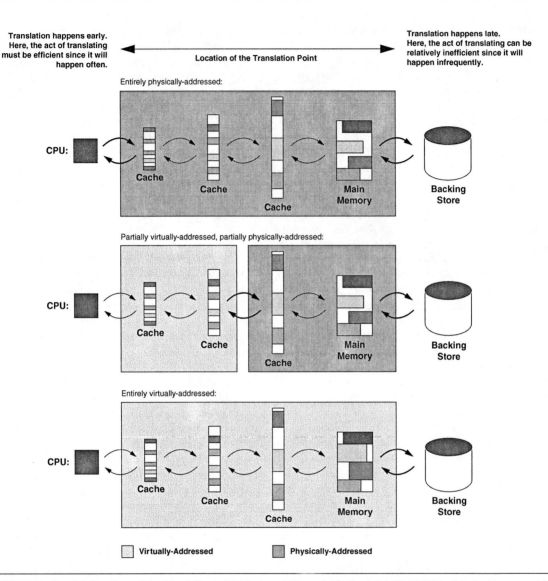

Translation happens early. Here, the act of translating must be efficient since it will happen often.

Location of the Translation Point

Translation happens late. Here, the act of translating can be relatively inefficient since it will happen infrequently.

Entirely physically-addressed:

CPU:

Cache

Cache

Cache

Main Memory

Backing Store

Partially virtually-addressed, partially physically-addressed:

CPU:

Cache

Cache

Cache

Main Memory

Backing Store

Entirely virtually-addressed:

CPU:

Cache

Cache

Cache

Main Memory

Backing Store

☐ Virtually-Addressed   ▨ Physically-Addressed

FIGURE 31.10: Possible locations of the translation point. The translation point is the point at which the virtual address must be translated to a physical address to reference a memory location. The point is shown in each diagram by using thick lines to represent the transfer of data between cache level the point moves toward the backing store (which will always require a translation, since the disk subsystem typically uses a different naming scheme from that of main memory or process address spaces), the act of translating can become less efficient since translation will be needed less frequently.

Management of the virtual cache can be avoided entirely if sharing is implemented through the global segmented space. This gives the same benefits as single address space operating systems (SASOS): if virtual-address aliasing (allowing processes to us different virtual addresses for the same physical data) is eliminated, then so is the virtual cache synonym problem. Thus, consistency management of the virtual cache can be eliminated by a simple operating system organization. The advantage of a segmented approach as opposed to a pure SASOS approach is that by mapping virtual addresses to physical addresses in two steps, virtual aliasing and the synonym problem are divided into two orthogonal issues. Thus, applications can map physical memory at multiple locations within their address spaces—they can use virtual-address aliasing, something a SASOS does not support—*without* creating a synonym problem in the virtual cache.

Segmented Architectures

Traditional virtual memory systems provide a mapping between process address spaces and physical memory. SASOS designs place all processes in a single address space and map this large space onto physical memory. Both can be represented as a single level of mapping, as shown in Figure 31.11. These organizations manage a single level of indirection between virtual and physical memory; they combine into a single mechanism the two primary functions of virtual memory: that of providing a virtual operating environment and that of demand-paging on a small (page-sized) granularity. Segmentation allows one to provide these two distinct functions through two distinct mechanisms: two levels of indirection between the virtual-address space and main memory. The first level of indirection supports the virtual operating environment and allows processes to locate objects at arbitrary segment-aligned addresses. The second level of indirection provides movement of data between physical memory and the backing store at the granularity of pages.

This organization is shown in Figure 31.12. Processes operate in the top layer. A process sees a contiguous address space that stretches from 0×00000000 to $0 \times FFFFFFFF$, inclusive (we will restrict ourselves to using 32-bit examples in this report for the purposes of brevity and clarity). The process-address space is transparently mapped onto the middle layer at the granularity of hardware segments, identified by the top bits of the user address. The segments that make up a user-level process may, in actuality, be scattered throughout the global space and may very well not

be contiguous. Note that the addresses generated by the process do not reach the cache; they are mapped onto the global space first. The cache and TLB see global addresses only. Therefore, there is no critical path between address generation and a virtual cache lookup except for the segmentation mechanism, and if the segment size is larger than the L1 cache size, the segment bits are not used in the cache lookup. Thus, the segmentation mechanism can run in parallel with the cache access.

Segmented systems have a long history. Multics, one of the earliest segmented operating systems, used a segmented/paged architecture, the GE 645 [Organick 1972]. This architecture is similar to the Intel Pentium memory-management organization [Intel 1993] in that both the GE 645 and the Intel Pentium support segments of variable size. An important point

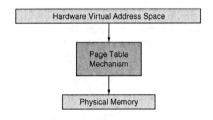

FIGURE 31.11: The single level of indirection of traditional memory-management organizations.

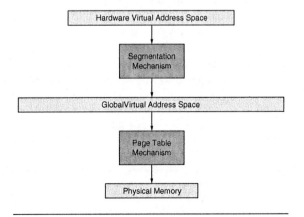

FIGURE 31.12: Multiple levels of indirection in a segmented memory-management organization.

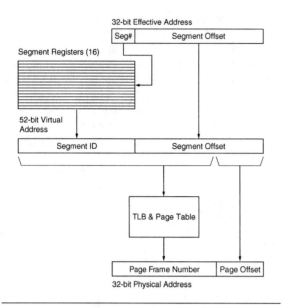

FIGURE 31.13: The PowerPC segmentation mechanism. Segmentation extends a 32-bit user address into a 52-bit global address. The global address can be used to index the caches.

is that the Pentium's global space is no larger than an individual user-level address space, and there is no mechanism to prevent different segments from overlapping one another in the global 4-GB space.

In contrast, the IBM 801 [Chang & Mergen 1988] introduced a fixed-size segmented architecture that continued through to the POWER and PowerPC architectures [IBM & Motorola 1993, May et al. 1994, Weiss & Smith 1994], shown in Figure 31.13. The PowerPC memory-management design maps user addresses onto a global flat address space much larger than each per-process address space. It is this extended virtual address space that is mapped by the TLBs and page table.

Segmented architectures need not use address-space identifiers; address space protection is guaranteed by the segmentation mechanism.[4] If two processes have the same segment identifier, they share that virtual segment by definition. Similarly, if a process has a given segment identifier in several of its segment registers, it has mapped the segment into its address space at multiple locations. The operating system can enforce inter-process protection by disallowing shared segment identifiers, or it can share memory between processes by overlapping segment identifiers.

The "Virtue" of Segmentation

One obvious solution to the synonym and shared memory problems is to use global naming, as in a SASOS implementation, so that every physical address corresponds to exactly one virtual location. This eliminates redundancy of PTEs for any given physical page, with significant performance and space savings. However, it does not allow processes to map objects at multiple locations within their address spaces; all processes must use the same name for the same data, which can create headaches for an operating system, as described earlier in "Perspective on Aliasing."

A segmented architecture avoids this problem; segmentation divides virtual aliasing and the synonym problem into two orthogonal issues. A one-to-one mapping from global space to physical space can be maintained—thereby eliminating the synonym problem—while supporting virtual aliases by independently mapping segments in process-address spaces onto segments in the global space. Such an organization is illustrated in Figure 31.14. In the figure, three processes share two different segments and have mapped the segments into arbitrary segment slots. Two of the processes have mapped the same segment at multiple locations in their address spaces. The page table maps the segments onto physical memory at the granularity of pages. If the mapping of global

---

[4]Page-level protection is a different thing entirely. Whereas address space protection is intended to keep processes from accessing each other's data, page-level protection is intended to protect pages from misuse. For instance, page-level protection keeps processes from writing to text pages by marking them read-only, etc. Page-level protection is typically supported through a TLB, but could be supported on a larger granularity through the segmentation mechanism. However, there is nothing intrinsic to segments that provide page-level protection, whereas address space protection *is* intrinsic to their nature.

pages to physical pages is one-to-one, there are no virtual cache synonym problems.

When the synonym problem is eliminated, there is no longer a need to flush a virtual cache or a TLB for consistency reasons. The only time flushing is required is when virtual segments are remapped to new physical pages, such as when the operating system runs out of unused segment identifiers and needs to reuse old ones. If there is any data left in the caches or TLB tagged by the old virtual address, data inconsistencies can occur. Direct Memory Access (DMA) also requires flushing of the affected region before a transaction, as an I/O controller does not know whether the data it overwrites is currently in a virtual cache.

The issue becomes one of segment granularity. If segments represent the granularity of sharing and data placement within an address space (but not the granularity of data movement between memory and disk), then segments must be numerous and small. They should still be larger than the L1 cache to keep the critical path between address generation and cache access clear. Therefore, the address space should be divided into a large number of small segments, for instance, 1024 4-MB segments, 4096 1-MB segments, etc.

Disjunct Page Table

Figure 31.15 illustrates an example mechanism. The segmentation granularity is 4 MB. The 4-GB address space is divided into 1024 segments. This simplifies the design and should make the discussion clear. A 4-byte PTE can map a 4-KB page, which can, in turn, map an entire 4-MB segment. The "disjunct" page table organization uses a single global table to map the entire 52-bit segmented virtual-address space yet gives each process-address space its own addressing scope. Any single process is mapped onto 4 GB of this global space, and so it requires 4 MB of the global table at any given moment (this is easily modified to support MIPS-style addressing in which the user process owns only half the 4 GB [Kane & Heinrich 1992]). The page table organization is pictured in Figure 31.16. It shows the global table as a 4-TB linear structure at the top of the global virtual-address space, composed of 2^{30} 4-KB PTE pages that each map a 4-MB segment. If each user process has a 4-MB address space, the user space can be mapped by 1024 PTE pages in the global page table. These 1024 PTE pages make up a *user page table*, a disjunct set of virtual pages at the top of the global address space. These 1024 pages can be mapped by 1024 PTEs—a collective structure small enough to wire down in physical memory for every running process (4 KB, if each is 4 bytes). This structure is termed the *per-user root page table* in Figure 31.16. In addition, there must be a table for every process containing 1024 segment IDs and per-segment protection information.

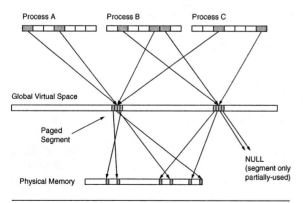

FIGURE 31.14: The use of segments to provide virtual-address aliasing.

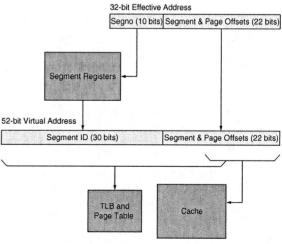

FIGURE 31.15: Segmentation mechanism used in discussion.

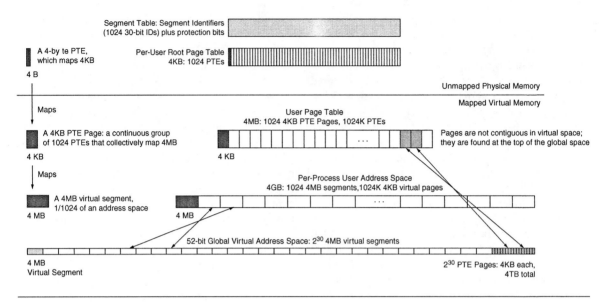

FIGURE 31.16: The disjunct page table.

Figure 31.17 depicts the algorithm for handling misses in the last-level cache. Processes generate 32-bit effective addresses that are extended to 52 bits by segmentation, replacing the top 4 bits of the effective address. In step 1, the VPN of a 52-bit failing global virtual address becomes an index into the global page table to reference the PTE mapping the failing data (the UPTE), similar to the concatenation of *PTEBase* and VPN to index into the MIPS user page table. The bottom bits of the address are 0's, according to the PTE size (e.g., 4 bytes here). The top ten bits of the address are 1's since the table is at the very top of the global space.

If this reference misses in the L2 cache, the operating system takes a recursive cache-miss exception. At this point, we must locate the mapping PTE in the user root page table. This table is an array of PTEs that cannot be indexed by a global VPN. It mirrors the structure of the user's perceived address space, not the structure of the global address space, and thus it is indexed by a portion of the original 32-bit effective address. The top 10 bits of the effective address index 1024 PTEs that map a 4-MB user page table, which, in turn, map a 4-GB address space. These 10 bits index the array of 1024 PTEs in the user root page table. In

step 2, the operating system builds a physical address for the appropriate PTE in the user root page table (the URPTE), a 52-bit virtual address whose top 20 bits indicate physical+cacheable. It then loads the user root PTE, which maps the user PTE that missed the cache at the end of step 1. When control is returned to the miss handler in step 1, the user PTE load retry will complete successfully.

The page table provides a simple scheme for sharing. Since PTEs in the root page table correspond directly to 4-MB segments in the virtual-address space, two processes need only duplicate information in their root PTEs to share a 4-MB segment. In Figure 31.18, two processes are shown, each with text, data, and stack regions. The two processes share their text regions by duplicating information in their root PTEs (shown in a darker color). This duplication means that one of the PTE pages in the disjunct table overlaps between the two user page tables, enabling the two address spaces to intersect at a 4-MB region.

Processes map objects at arbitrary segment-aligned addresses in their address spaces and can map objects at multiple locations if they wish. Processes can also map objects with different protections, as long as the segmentation mechanism supports protection bits

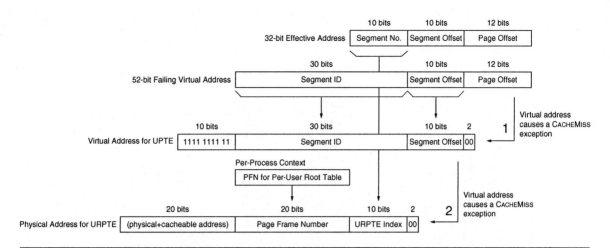

FIGURE 31.17: An example cache-miss algorithm. Step 1 is the result of a user-level L2 cache miss; the operating system builds a virtual address for a PTE in the global page table. If this PTE is not found in the L1 or L2 cache, a root PTE is loaded, shown in step 2. One special requirement is a register holding the initial failing address. Another required hardware structure, the per-process context register, points to the process control block of the active process.

for each segment. As we have described, the global page table maintains a one-to-one mapping between global pages and physical page frames; therefore, the virtual cache synonym problem disappears. The virtual memory fragmentation problem is also solved by this organization. There is no restriction on where an object is placed in the global space, and there is no restriction on where an object is placed in a process-address space.

31.1.8 Perspective: A Taxonomy of Address Space Organizations

Different architectures provide support for operating system features in very different ways. One of the fundamental differences is their treatment of address spaces; it is important to understand the hardware's view of an address space because the operating system's mechanisms for shared memory, multi-threading, fine-grained protection, and address space protection are all derived from the hardware's definition of an address space. This section presents a taxonomy describing the architectural organization and protection of an address space. The *Owner* portion of the classification characterizes the organization of the hardware address space, and the *ID* portion characterizes the hardware

protection mechanism. The address space available to the application can be owned by a *single* process or shared among *multiple* processes. The hardware can provide a *single* protection identifier per process and page, *multiple* identifiers per process and/or per page, or *no* identifiers whatsoever. Table 31.1 describes these characteristics.

A *single-owner* space is one in which the entire range of hardware addressability is owned by one process at a time. A single-owner system must provide some sort of protection mechanism (ignoring the use of software protection mechanisms [Wahbe et al. 1993]), or else virtually addressed structures such as the TLB must be flushed on context switch.

A *multiple-owner* space is divided among many processes. This is not the same as dividing the address space into kernel and user regions as in the MIPS architecture. It instead implies a difference between the addresses generated by processes (private addresses) and the addresses seen by the TLB or virtual caches (global addresses). It is also not the same thing as ASIDs. While it is possible to imagine a global 38-bit address space formed by the concatenation of a 6-bit ASID with a 32-bit per-process virtual address, it is simply an alternate way to look at ASIDs. It is not the same thing as a multiple-owner address

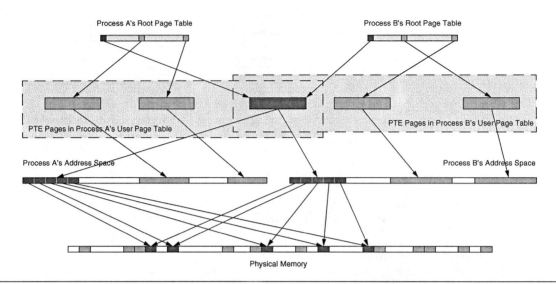

Process A's Root Page Table

Process B's Root Page Table

PTE Pages in Process A's User Page Table

PTE Pages in Process B's User Page Table

Process A's Address Space

Process B's Address Space

Physical Memory

FIGURE 31.18: Simple sharing mechanism in a hierarchical page table. The structure of the hierarchical page table allows for a simple sharing mechanism, by duplicating information in two or more root page tables. When root PTEs are duplicated, the virtual pages in the user page tables are then mapped to the same physical page and therefore allow two address spaces to overlap. In the figure, two processes are each composed of a text, data and stack region (each less than 4 MB in size), and they share their text regions by sharing a page in their user page tables. Since the text regions are composed of five virtual pages, the shared PTE page contains only five valid PTEs. The shared regions are identical in size (as they must be, since the region is shared), but the other regions (data and stack) need not be and, in the figure, are not.

space. Figure 31.19 illustrates the difference between the two. An ASID mechanism is useful for *protecting* address spaces; it is not useful for *organizing* address spaces.

The mechanism typically used to provide a multiple-owner address space, hardware segmentation, is also an implicit protection mechanism. A process address space is a set of segments. If the address spaces of two processes have a null intersection, the processes are protected from each other. For example, Process 4 in Figure 31.19(b) has a null intersection with every other address space. Therefore, Process 4 is protected from all other processes, and they are protected from Process 4. When the intersection is non-null, only the segments in the intersection are unprotected. Therefore, further protection mechanisms are, in principle, unnecessary. However, they do become necessary if user-level processes are allowed to modify the contents of the segment registers, which would allow a process to address arbitrary virtual segments.

A *single-identifier* architecture associates a single protection ID with every process and every page in its address space. This is synonymous with an ASID mechanism, pictured in Figure 31.19(a). Every process is confined to its own virtual address space, and every extended virtual address identifies the address space to which it belongs. The implication is that the only way to share pages is to circumvent the protection mechanism—to make pages globally available by marking them with a special flag that turns off protection on a page-by-page basis. For example, this is seen in the GLOBAL bits of the MIPS and Alpha TLB designs.

A *multiple-identifier* architecture is designed to support sharing of pages across address spaces by associating more than one ID with every process and/or every page. Therefore, address spaces can belong to multiple protection domains, and pages can belong to multiple process-address spaces. There is no need for a GLOBAL bit mechanism, and the multiple-ID mechanism goes beyond the all-or-nothing sharing of the single-ID mechanism. A multiple-ID mechanism supports finite

TABLE **31.1** Characteristics of the owner/ID taxonomy

Owner	Identifier
Single (S)	Single (S)
In a single-owner address space, the application owns the entire range of hardware addressability. For instance, if the hardware's maximum virtual address is 32 bits wide, applications generate 32-bit pointers. The implication is that the hardware supports a virtual machine environment in which every process "owns" the hardware's address space. Therefore, a protection mechanism is necessary to prevent multiple processes from treading on each other's data. Examples: Alpha, MIPS, Pentium, SPARC	A single-identifier architecture uses a single value to distinguish one process from another. This is typically called an address-space identifier or something similar. Each context is tagged with a single ID, and each virtual page is tagged with a single ID. Examples: Alpha, MIPS, SPARC
Multiple (M)	Multiple (M)
In a multiple-owner address space, the range of hardware addressability is shared by all processes on the machine. The addresses generated by individual processes are not directly seen by the TLB or a virtual cache. This is typically done by mapping process-address spaces onto a global space at the granularity of hardware segments. Examples: PA-RISC, Pentium, PowerPC	A multiple-identifier architecture allows processes or pages to associate with themselves multiple protection identifiers. This can be done with multiple ASIDs per context and/or multiple protection IDs per virtual page. Examples: PA-RISC
	None (N)
	This architecture does not use any explicit hardware identifiers to distinguish between different processes or different virtual pages. Examples: Pentium, PowerPC

group ownership, where a shared page can be accessed by a small, well-defined group of processes but not by processes outside the group. Note that we have made the deliberate choice to place segmentation mechanisms into the organization category (*owner*) and not into the protection category (*identifier*), though they could be appropriately placed in the latter.

A *no identifier* architecture provides no hardware protection IDs of any kind. The operating system must provide protection by flushing virtually indexed structures (for example, TLBs and virtually indexed caches) on context switch and/or by using software protection mechanisms.

The various schemes are the following:

- **Single-Owner, No ID** This architecture makes the entire range of hardware addressability available to the application but does not distinguish between addresses generated by different processes. Therefore, any structure that is dependent on virtual addresses, e.g., the TLB and any virtually addressed cache, must be flushed on context switch. Also, pages must be shared through the page tables; the hardware offers no explicit support for sharing. One possible implementation of the class is shown in Figure 31.20.

- **Single-Owner, Single-ID** Most microarchitectures today fall into this category. The user-level application generates virtual addresses that, augmented by a single ASID, are used to address all virtual structures, including caches and TLBs. Processes are protected from each other by identifiers, and an entry in a TLB or a line in a cache explicitly identifies its owner. When

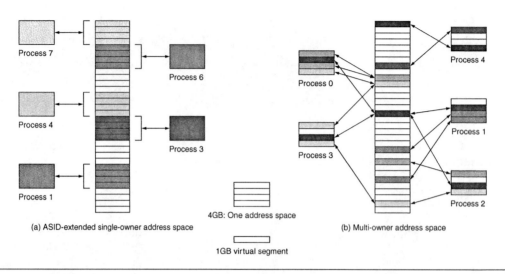

(a) ASID-extended single-owner address space

4GB: One address space

1GB virtual segment

(b) Multi-owner address space

FIGURE 31.19: The difference between ASIDs and a multiple-owner address space. This example compares a 35-bit multiple-owner address space and a 32-bit single-owner address space extended by a 3-bit ASID. In (a) the ASID-extended space is shown. It is organized into eight regions, each of which corresponds to exactly one process as determined by the process ASID. In (b) the multiple-owner space is shown. It is seen as an array of 1-GB virtual segments, each of which can be mapped into any number of process-address spaces, at any location (or multiple locations) within the address space. For example, the second and fourth segments in the address space of Process 0 are mapped to the same virtual segment. Note that the number of processes in scenario (a) is limited by the size of the ASID (case, a limit of eight processes), while there is no limit to the number of processes in scenario (b) unless shared memory is strictly disallowed, in which case the maximum number of processes equals the number of segments (a segment is the minimum size of a process).

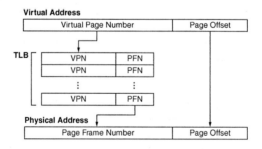

FIGURE 31.20: An implementation of a single-owner, no ID architecture.

a process generates an address, the ASID match guarantees that the correct datum is read or written. The disadvantage is that the protection method makes sharing difficult. When all references are tagged with a single owner, the system implicitly requires multiple mappings to the same shared physical page. Intuitively, this reduces the effectiveness of the TLB; Khalidi and Talluri have shown that it doubles the TLB miss rate [1995]. Solutions to this problem have been to subvert the protection mechanism using GLOBAL bits in the TLB, or to vary the structure of the inverted page table, like

PA-RISC's table or the 8-way PTE cache of the PowerPC architecture. One possible implementation of the class is shown in Figure 31.21.

- **Single-Owner, Multiple-ID** This architecture is not segmented but has multiple protection IDs associated with each process and/or each page. The PA-RISC can be used in this manner. If multiple IDs are associated with each page, each TLB entry could be shared by all the processes with which the page is associated. A TLB entry would have several available slots for protection IDs, requiring more chip area but alleviating the problem of multiple TLB entries per physical page. Alternatively, if there were multiple IDs associated with each process and not with each page (this is like the scheme used in PA-RISC), a different ID could be created for every instance of a

shared region, indicating the "identity" of the group that collectively owns the region. One possible implementation of the class is shown in Figure 31.22.

- **Multiple-Owner, No ID** This is the basic segmented architecture that maps user addresses onto a global address space at the granularity of segments. This is how the PowerPC architecture is designed, and it is how the Pentium segmentation mechanism *can* be used. If the Pentium's 4-GB linear address space were treated as a global space to be shared a segment at a time, the segmentation mechanism would be an effective protection mechanism, obviating the need to flush the TLB on context switch. If the segment registers are protected from modification by user-level processes, no protection identifiers are necessary. One possible implementation of the class is shown in Figure 31.23.

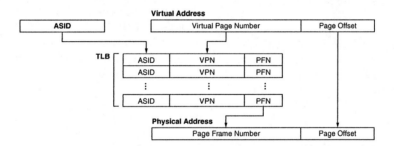

FIGURE 31.21: An implementation of a single-owner, single-ID architecture. The ASID acts as a process ID.

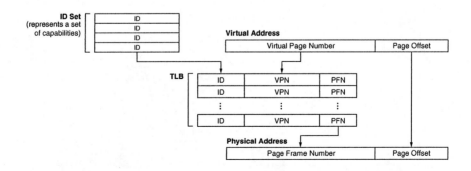

FIGURE 31.22: An implementation of a single-owner, multiple-ID architecture. Each ID in the ID set is compared against every ID in the TLB to find a match. If any match succeeds, the result is a TLB hit.

- **Multiple-Owner, Single-ID** This is an extension of the previous architecture by a single protection ID, producing multiple global spaces—each multiple owner, and each protected from each other. Each process would have a window onto a larger multiple-owner address space. There is no reason that a single process would require a unique ID. Several processes could share the same ID and still be protected from each other by the segmentation mechanism. Alternatively, multiple threads within a process could co-exist safely in a single multiple-owner address space, all identified by the same ASID. One possible implementation of the class is shown in Figure 31.24.
- **Multiple-Owner, Multiple-ID** The PA-RISC is an example of this architecture. It defines a global shared virtual-address space and multiple protection IDs as well. In the case of the PA-RISC, the protection IDs are necessary because the PA-RISC segmentation mechanism (space registers) allows a user-level process to modify segment registers and organize its own address space. One could also use this mechanism with secure segmentation, supporting a hierarchy of address spaces with each process-address

space mapped onto a global address space, of which many would exist simultaneously. This could be used for maintaining process hierarchies and/or supporting many threads within large address spaces. The difference between this and the previous architecture is that this allows each process-address space to span many different global address spaces at once. One possible implementation of the class is shown in Figure 31.25.

31.2 Implementing Virtual Memory

A system's interrupt mechanism, memory map, and page table/TLB combination comprise the heart of a typical virtual memory system, one of the most fundamental services that a modern operating system provides. Any in-depth look at these facilities exposes the interaction between operating-system-level software and specialized control hardware (e.g., control registers and TLBs, as opposed to instruction-execution hardware) and, in particular, highlights the operating system's use of and response to precise interrupts, arguably the fundamental building block of today's multi-tasking systems. This section presents a definition for a base in-order pipeline and then adds support for nested interrupts and virtual

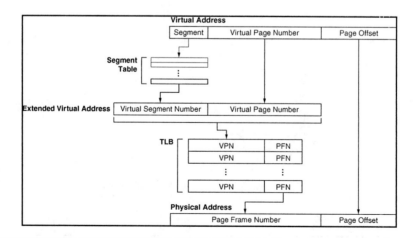

FIGURE 31.23: An implementation of a multiple-owner, no ID architecture. Note that the segment table could be implemented as a direct table-like an SRAM or register file, or it could have tags and be probed for a hit just as a cache is.

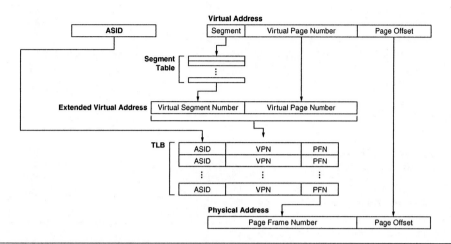

FIGURE 31.24: An implementation of a multiple-owner, single-ID architecture. The ASID acts as a process ID. Note that the segment table could be implemented as a direct table like an SRAM or register file, or it could have tags and be probed for a hit just as a cache is.

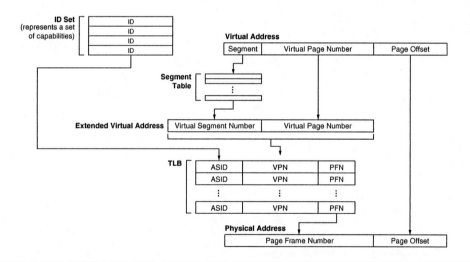

FIGURE 31.25: An implementation of a multiple-owner, multiple-ID architecture. Each ID in the ID set is compared against every ID in the TLB to find a match. If any match succeeds, the result is a TLB hit. Note that the segment table could be implemented as a direct table like an SRAM or register file, or it could have tags and be probed for a hit just as a cache is.

memory management via a MIPS-like memory map, page table, and TLB. This example has been used at the University of Maryland since Fall 2000 to teach precise interrupts and operating-system interactions. The instruction set itself is largely immaterial to the discussion (the pipeline organization is compatible

with nearly any instruction set), and the interested reader is directed to our on-line companion document for details not covered in the chapter.

The implementation illustrates the operating system's perspective of the memory system, which is unique because the operating system must use both physical and virtual addresses to reference the memory system. We will see that even an extremely simple example such as this requires a complex and carefully orchestrated arrangement of data structures in memory, values in hardware registers, pipeline extensions, and supporting details in the instruction set that tie everything together.

31.2.1 The Basic In-Order Pipe

The basic RiSC-16[5] in-order pipeline is shown in Figure 31.26. It is very similar to the five-stage DLX/MIPS pipeline described in both Hennessy and Patterson and Patterson and Hennessy. Though the pipeline is largely independent of instruction-set details, a few ISA-specific details remain:

- The example pipeline supports zero-, one-, two-, and three-operand instructions, including those with immediate values.
- The base three-operand instruction format is shown below. If an instruction writes to the register file, rA identifies the target register. Instructions that do not write to the register file (e.g., store instructions) can use the rA field to denote a read operand (thus, MUX_{s2}).

op	rA	rB		rC

- The architecture is word-addressed, not byte-addressed, thus the '+1' in the PC-update path and not '+2.'
- Like MIPS/DLX, register 0 is read as zero and non-writable. Thus, a write enable control signal for the register file is implicit in the register specifier in the write-back stage.

In Figure 31.26, shaded boxes represent clocked storage (e.g., registers), thick lines represent word-width busses, thin lines represent smaller datapaths; and dotted lines represent control paths. The pipeline register contents, control logic, and control signals are presented in detail in the on-line companion document. The salient points for this discussion center on the handling of control-flow changes. In particular, on detecting a jump instruction or a mispredicted branch instruction, the ID stage sets a "stomp" signal such that the instruction currently being fetched will not be latched in the IF/ID register (i.e., it will be stomped upon), and the IF/ID register will instead latch a NOP instruction.

The problem to solve is that of providing precise interrupts[6] which, as mentioned, are the cornerstone of many operating-system facilities such as multitasking and address space protection. A precise interrupt guarantees a clean boundary between those instructions that have completely finished execution and those that have effectively not even started. Having a precise interrupt allows an operating system to halt execution in the middle of a program, do something else, and cleanly return to the point where execution was left off. The only information required to restart program execution is the machine state (i.e., register file contents) and an indication of which instruction is next-to-execute (i.e., a return address).

The difficulty in implementing precise interrupts is to guarantee that no instruction following an "exceptional" instruction can modify permanent state. Caches are effectively permanent state: without hardware support such as *speculative-dirty* bits per cache block, it is difficult to un-write data that has been written to cache, and all data written to cache is ultimately supposed to find its way to main memory. Out-of-order machines solve the problem by exploiting the *reorder buffer* [Smith & Pleszkun 1985, 1988], a mechanism designed specifically for the purpose. In-order machines solve the problem by monitoring the state of the pipeline and disallowing memory access when exceptions are observed.

Interrupts are handled at the time of instruction commit. This requires recognizing that an exceptional situation has occurred, holding that information with the instruction state (i.e., in the pipeline registers), propagating the information down the pipeline with the instruction, and acting on it during the write-back

---

[5]The 16-bit *Ridiculously Simple Computer*.
[6]Notionally, a precise interrupt is one in which a clear line separates instructions that have completely committed state from those that have not affected the system at all. An in-depth treatment is given in papers by Smith and Pleszkun [1985, 1988].

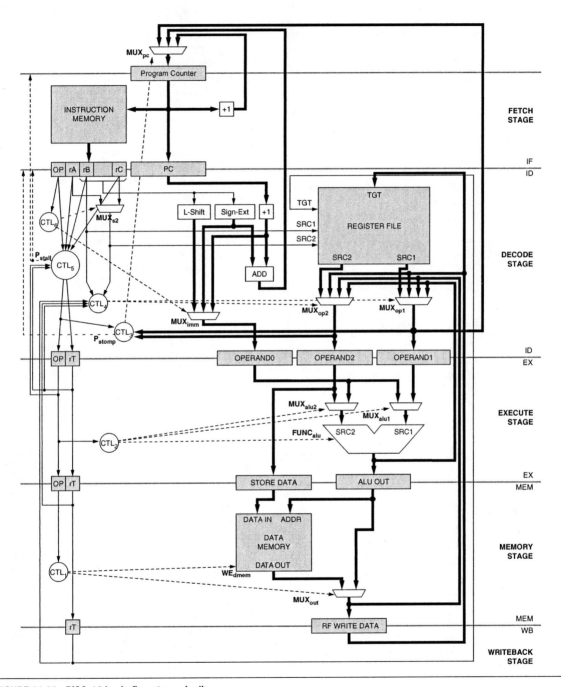

FIGURE 31.26: RiSC-16 basic five-stage pipeline.

stage—and *only* in the write-back stage. This addresses the case of back-to-back instructions causing exceptions out of order with respect to one another in different stages of the pipeline (e.g., a load instruction that generates an invalid-address exception followed by an instruction with an invalid opcode). This is illustrated in the figure below. If an exceptional instruction is flagged as such at the moment the exception is detected, it is safe to handle that exceptional condition during write-back, because all previous instructions by that time have finished execution and committed their state to the machine.

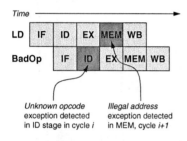

Time

| LD | IF | ID | EX | MEM | WB | |
| BadOp | | IF | ID | EX | MEM | WB |

Unknown opcode exception detected in ID stage in cycle *i*

Illegal address exception detected in MEM, cycle *i+1*

Why exceptions must be handled in program order.

31.2.2 Precise Interrupts in Pipelined Computers

This section builds upon the previous section and presents a full working pipeline implementation.

Pipeline Modifications

A RiSC-16 pipeline that handles interrupts and exceptions precisely is shown in Figure 31.27. Note that a solid square represents concatenation in the figure. The pipeline diagram reflects the following visible modifications:

1. Support for detecting and handling exceptions and interrupts has been added by the creation of an exception register (labeled *EXC* in the figure) in pipeline registers IF/ID through MEM/WB. Also, the instruction's PC is maintained all the way to the MEM/WB register. If a stage's incoming *EXC* register is non-zero, the corresponding instruction is interpreted as

having caused an exception. The pipeline uses these values to ensure that all instructions following an exceptional instruction become NOPs: if there is an exception in the write-back stage, all other instructions in the pipe should be squashed. If a stage detects a non-zero *EXC* value, the associated instruction is disabled (its corresponding *OP* value is turned into something without side effects, like ADD, and its target register *rT* is set to be non-writable).

2. TLB access has been added to instruction-fetch and data access stages. The choice of a single TLB versus split I- and D-TLBs does not affect the substance of the implementation. Note, however, that the write-back stage must be able to distinguish between an I-TLB miss and a D-TLB miss for purposes of generating the PTE address (this is similar to the MIPS mechanism [Kane & Heinrich 1992] and is described later). This can be done with a 16-bit register in MEMWB to hold the faulting address (which holds either *EXMEM.aluout* if the D-TLB causes a miss or EXMEM.pc otherwise) or a simple status bit in MEMWB which would be set similarly.

Each pipeline stage must suspend normal operation if its instruction has caused an exception and the pipeline stage modifies machine state (for example, the memory stage must not write to memory if the instruction caused a privilege violation in a previous stage). Each stage must forward the incoming exception code on to the following pipeline stage if it is a non-zero code. If the instruction has not already caused an exception, but does so during the stage in question, the *EXC* field in the following pipeline register must be set appropriately. Finally, any stage must suspend normal operation if there is an exceptional instruction in the write-back stage, and if "normal" operation can modify state. For example, if the *MEMWB.exc* register is non-zero, indicating an exceptional instruction in the write-back stage, the memory stage must not allow read or write access to the memory system by the instruction in the memory stage. Otherwise, pipeline operation is as normal. In the simplest form of an exceptional condition, when an exceptional

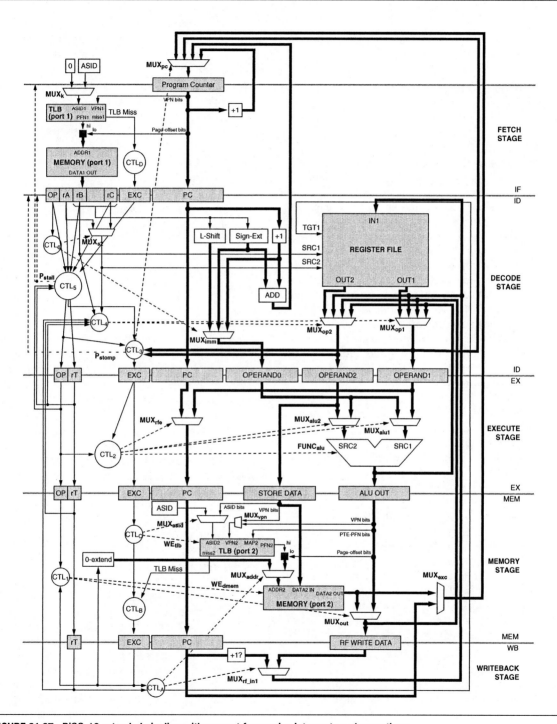

FIGURE 31.27: RiSC-16 extended pipeline with support for precise interrupts and exceptions.

instruction reaches the write-back stage, the following steps are performed by the hardware:

1. Either the PC of the exceptional instruction or the PC of the instruction *after* the exceptional instruction (PC+1) is saved in a safe place, for instance, a control register built for just such a purpose, typically called something like the *exceptional PC* (EPC) register. The choice of which value to save is based on the opcode of the exceptional instruction and the type of exception raised: some exception-raising instructions should be retried at the end of a handler's execution (e.g., a load or store instruction that causes a TLB miss), while others should be jumped over (e.g., TRAP instructions that invoke the operating system—jumping back to a TRAP instruction would simply re-invoke the trap and would cause an endless loop). If the exceptional instruction should be retried, the handler returns to PC; if the exceptional instruction should not be re-executed or retried, the handler returns to PC + 1.

2. The exception type is used as an index into the *interrupt vector table* (IVT), located at a known physical address, and the vector corresponding to the exception type is loaded into the program counter. This is known as *vectoring* to the exception/interrupt handler.

3. Some exceptions cause the hardware to perform additional steps before vectoring to the handler. For instance, when handling a TLB-miss exception, before vectoring to the handler, the hardware might create an address for the handler to use in searching the page table. Most architectures that use software-managed TLBs provide such a feature, and ours is described in detail later.

The general form of an exception/interrupt handler, a short piece of software deep in the operating system, looks like the following (note that, in this architecture,

hardware places the machine into a privileged operating mode and saves the previous operating mode):

1. Save the EPC in a safe location. This is done in case another exception or interrupt occurs before the handler has completed execution, which would cause the EPC register to be overwritten.
2. Handle the exception/interrupt.
3. Reload the EPC.
4. Return the processor to the previous operating mode, e.g., user or privileged, and jump to the EPC.

Most architectures have a facility ("return-from-exception," or similar name) that performs step 4 in an atomic manner.

System-Level Instruction-Set Extensions

To do this, we need the system-level facilities found in microarchitectures that support operating systems and privileged mode. We must protect the operating system from user processes; we must distinguish between processes; we must translate virtual addresses; we need an exception-handling facility; the operating system needs some control registers and would do well to have a set of general-purpose registers that it can use without disturbing user processes (otherwise, it would have to save/restore the entire register state on every exception, interrupt, or trap); etc. Briefly, the extensions to the base pipeline include the following:

- Addition of a privileged kernel mode that is activated upon handling an exception or interrupt or upon handling a TRAP instruction, which raises an exception.
- Addition of a TLB to translate addresses. The TLB should have the same number of ports as the number of memory ports: i.e., if there is a separate instruction-fetch port that is distinct from the data read/write port, then there should be two TLB ports. The trade-off is cost for speed. Fewer ports in both the TLB and memory access translates to a less expensive implementation, but it can also translate to a

significant overhead in time spent waiting for a port to free up. Clearly, this choice would be made through an architectural design study.

- The ability for software to enter an exceptional state directly, for example, via *trap* instructions. Note some "exceptions" that hardware supports are actually privileged instructions that the machine handles at the time of instruction execution, instead of vectoring to a software handler routine. This includes TLB handling routines, mode instructions (e.g., sleep, doze), etc. Table 31.2 gives examples of both instructions ("sys") and system-level instructions such as TLB-write and return-from-exception.

- Addition of control registers available in privileged mode, e.g., those shown in Figure 31.28. "GPR" refers to a general-

purpose register, of which there may be several. The *processor status register* (PSR) contains mode bits that directly influence processor operation. The *interrupt service register* (ISR) indicates interrupts that have been received by the processor. The *interrupt mask register* (IMR) allows software to ignore selected interrupts. The *exceptional program counter* (EPC) register is filled by hardware when vectoring to a handler and indicates the return address for the exceptional instruction. Even if using a shadow register file of the same size as the user-visible register file while in kernel mode, access to the GPR file may still be possible through special *register-move* instructions.

- The definition of a *memory map* that delineates portions of the virtual space as being

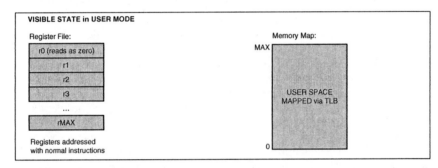

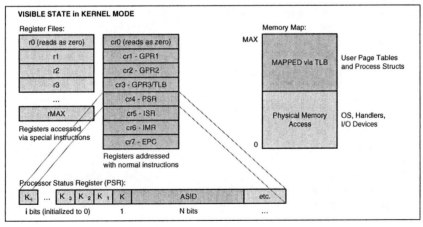

FIGURE 31.28: The extended CPU state visible in privileged kernel mode.

TABLE **31.2** System-level instructions added to the instruction set

Assembly Code Format	Meaning
tlbw regA, regB	Write TLB entry (held in regA and regB) to the TLB: regA holds the page table entry, and thus the bottom bits of regA contain the PFN; by construction, regB contains both the ASID and VPN (see discussion for details); all other bits in regA and regB are ignored
rfe regA, regB or rfe regA	Return from exception: waits until write-back stage to jump (without link) through a register; simultaneously returns processor to previously stored K mode **Note:** the pipeline may also place a return value into the user-visible register file; this can represent the result of a system call, for example
sys class	Cause exceptional condition of specified class (inserts the value of "class" directly into IDEX.exc); implements TRAP instructions and can be used for testing and debugging if allowed to insert all classes of exceptions (**note:** must authenticate against privilege mode first)

mapped through the TLBs, accessible in kernel mode only, etc. This is also illustrated in Figure 31.28; the illustrated map resembles both MIPS and VMS architectures. For the example architecture, in user mode all of the address space is mapped through the TLB. All virtual addresses are first translated by the TLB before being used to reference memory locations. Note that this implies that all virtual addresses are valid in user mode. This is similar to VMS, but unlike many other operating systems. In kernel mode, the top half of the address space is mapped through the TLB, and the bottom half is not. This means that addresses in this region, while the computer is in privileged kernel mode, will be sent directly to the memory system without first being translated. This is MIPS-like in design.

- Addition of the concept of an address-space identifier. The ASID distinguishes different processes that run on the machine, and its use allows state from many different processes to reside in the TLB and cache at the same time (otherwise, the TLB and potentially the cache as well would have to be flushed on context switches). In this architecture, ASID 0 is interpreted by the hardware to indicate the kernel executing

in privileged mode. When the processor is in kernel mode (i.e., when the K bit in the processor status register is set), instruction fetch must use ASID 0; this overrides whatever value may be in the ASID portion of the processor status register. In contrast, data memory access in the memory stage will use whatever ASID is in the PSR. This last mechanism allows the operating system to read and write locations within different user address spaces (i.e., "masquerade" as different processes), but it prevents the operating system from executing instructions belonging to unprivileged processes, which might otherwise constitute a security hole.

- Creation of memory-management constructs including the user page table organization. Having hardware define this structure is beneficial in that the hardware can quickly generate the address that the TLB-miss handler needs to locate the PTE. Though this could limit flexibility by having the hardware dictate a page table format to the operating system, software can always ignore this address (treat it as a "hint" that need not be followed) to implement whatever page table it wants. However, it would then have to generate its own PTE addresses.

Exceptions and Interrupts

Following Motorola's terminology, we will distinguish two classes of exceptional conditions: those stemming from internal actions (exceptions) and those stemming from external actions (interrupts). Another type of exception (another class of internally generated exceptional condition) is a trap or syscall. Trap instructions implement various operating system routines, because the trap type is interpreted by the hardware to indicate a particular vector, just like each exception and interrupt type has a separate vector. Each of the trap vectors is operating-system defined (e.g., TRAP 1 can mean read or write or open or close ...); the hardware simply vectors to the corresponding handler, so the operating system can attach arbitrary semantics to each of the trap handlers. Most architectures implement only one vector: all system calls are vectored through the same exception, and the user code first places the trap type into a user-visible register or known memory location for the operating system to read once the handler runs. The most noticeable effect of offering more than one trap vector is to reduce the register file pressure in handling system calls, which may be important in architectures with small instruction footprints and thus small register files. Table 31.3 describes various exception codes and/or privileged instructions that one could implement.

Control Registers, Generally

The control registers are those extra registers that are visible only in kernel mode:

```
cr0 - Reads as 0, read-only
cr1 - For general-purpose use
cr2 - For general-purpose use
cr3 - For general-purpose use and TLB interface
cr4 - Processor Status Register
cr5 - Interrupt Status Register
cr6 - Interrupt Mask Register
cr7 - EPC Register
```

These additional registers perform two separate functions. First, they provide the operating system access to mode-control information such as the PSR and ISR; facilities similar to these are found in nearly every processor architecture in existence and are necessary for most system-level software. The second function served is a small set of *shadow registers* not visible to user-level processes. While not necessary for implementing most system-level software, shadow registers—such as those found in processors as diverse as the Alpha, SPARC, PA-RISC, Xscale, and M-CORE architectures—provide the operating system a safe haven in which to operate. These registers do not need to be saved when moving to and from privileged mode, as would be necessary if the operating system shared the same register file as user-level code. For instance, the MIPS R2000 architecture has only one space of registers, and the kernel, to avoid having to save and restore user-level registers, claims two of the registers as its own; the assembler and compiler assure that user-level code does not access these registers, and they are not saved or restored on interrupts or system calls and traps. The disadvantage of having shadow registers is either ensuring that data can be moved between the two sets of registers (e.g., by providing a larger register specifier in some or all privileged-mode instructions, or by providing a special data-move operation whose sole function is to move data between register namespaces) or ensuring that such a scenario is never needed.

In the RiSC-16 architecture, **cr0–cr7** are the default registers when kernel mode is active, i.e., when the K-mode bit in the processor status register contains a '1' value. Thus, when the operating system performs instructions like the following:

```
# kernel mode is on
add  r1, r0, r4
```

the operand values are read from control registers. The result is written to a control register. This example moves the contents of the processor status register into **cr1**.

Processor Status Register

The PSR is the heart of a machine, as it contains some of the most important state information in a processor. See Figure 31.28 for a relatively minimal example PSR. It includes three pieces of information: (1) the ASID of the executing process, (2) the

Table 31.3   Example values targeting the EXC registers in the modified RiSC-16 pipeline

Code/Instruction	Semantics
MODE_RUN	Normal mode—ignore (equivalent to JALR)
MODE_SLEEP	Low-power doze mode, awakened by interrupt
MODE_HALT	Halt machine (useful for simulators)
TLB_READ	Probe TLB for PTE matching VPN in rB
TLB_WRITE	Write contents of rB to TLB (random)
TLB_CLEAR	Clear contents of TLB
MOVE_SPECIAL	Moves a value to/from the control registers from/to the general-purpose registers
SYS_RFE	*Return From Exception:* JUMP (without link) to address held in rB (a control register), and right-shift (zero-fill) the kmode history vector
EXC_GENERAL	General exception vector
EXC_TLBUMISS	User address caused TLB miss
EXC_TLBKMISS	Kernel address caused TLB miss
EXC_INVALIDOPCODE	Opcode the execute stage does not recognize
EXC_INVALIDADDR	Memory address is out of valid range
EXC_PRIVILEGES	Decoded privileged instruction in user mode
INT_IO	General I/O interrupt
INT_CLOCK	Used to synchronize with external real-time clock
INT_TIMER	Raised by a watchdog timer
TRAP_GENERAL	General operating system TRAP vector
TRAP_1	OS-definable TRAP vector
TRAP_2	OS-definable TRAP vector
...	...

kernel-mode bit that enables the privileged *kernel mode*, and (3) a bit array that represents a history of previous *kernel-mode* bit values.

1. The *address-space identifier* (ASID) identifies the process currently active on the CPU. This is used to extend the virtual address when accessing the TLB (see Section 31.1.8

for more details on how address-space identifiers work).

2. The K *(kernel-mode)* bit indicates whether the processor is in privileged mode or user mode. Privileged instructions are only allowed to execute while the processor is in privileged mode. They cause an exception otherwise (EXC_PRIVILEGES).

3. The K_1 through K_i bits make up a shift register that maintains the previous i modes of operation; every time an exception or interrupt is handled, the kernel mode bit is left-shifted into this array (which is itself shifted to the left to accommodate the incoming bit), and the kernel mode is set appropriately (usually turned on). Every invocation of the *return-from-exception* instruction right-shifts the bit array (while zero-filling from the left) and places the rightmost bit of the array into the kernel-mode bit. To simplify operating system software, this sub-array should be available as read-only to the kernel.

This implementation of maintaining previous history bits allows the hardware to handle *nested interrupts*, a facility that is extremely important in modern processors and operating systems. A nested interrupt is a situation where the hardware handles an exception or interrupt while in the middle of handling a completely different exception or interrupt. In our implementation of virtual memory, the ability to handle nested interrupts will be of crucial importance.

Concrete Example: RiSC-16 TLB and Page Table Organization

The RiSC-16 is a 16-bit, word-addressed architecture. The page size is 256 bytes; the 64-bit space is divided into 256 pages; and a 16-bit address is divided into an 8-bit page number and an 8-bit page offset. This is a simple architecture, and it serves as a good example largely because very little appears in the literature describing how virtual memory can be done in short-word embedded architectures, even though virtual memory use in these architectures is becoming increasingly popular.

The RiSC-16 architecture uses a software-managed TLB, which simply means that the operating system, and not the hardware, is responsible for handling *TLB refill*, the act of walking the page table on a TLB miss to find the appropriate PTE and inserting it into the TLB. When the TLB fails to find a given VPN for a mappable virtual address, the TLB raises an exception, invoking the operating system. If the address being translated is a user address (i.e., if the CPU was in user mode at the time of the exception), then the exception raised is a "user miss," i.e., EXC_TLBUMISS. If the CPU is in kernel mode, and the top bit of the virtual address to be translated is a '1,' then a "kernel miss," or EXC_TLB-KMISS, is raised. If in kernel mode, and the top bit of the address is '0,' the address cannot cause an exception because it is not translated through the TLB, but instead is mapped directly onto physical memory.

The page table format is very similar to that used in the MIPS architecture and is illustrated in Figure 31.29 (note the difference in scale between the user page table and the user address space). The full address space contains 256 pages, which requires 256 PTEs to map it. Each PTE is a single word, and 256 PTEs can thus fit in a single page. Therefore, a single page of PTEs can map the entire user space. The kernel keeps

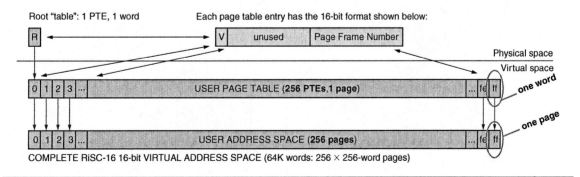

FIGURE 31.29: RiSC-16 page table organization. Vertical grey arrows indicate a mapping function.

a set of pages in its virtual space, each of which holds one user page table. There are 64 of these tables (there are 64 unique ASIDs; the ASID is 6 bits wide), and the corresponding user tables are held in the top 64 virtual pages of the kernel's address space. These are, in turn, mapped by root PTEs that are held in the top 64 words of page frame 0. Thus, the VPN of the user page table is equal to the physical address of the root PTE that maps it.

The kernel's use of the virtual space is shown in Figure 31.30; the top quarter of the address space is dedicated to the user page tables. The ASID is 6 bits, and thus there are 64 tables, each one page in size. When the TLBUMISS exception handler runs, its job is to find the user PTE corresponding to the page that missed the TLB. The (virtual) location of the PTE, given the ASID of the current user process and the VPN of the address that caused the TLB miss, is computed as follows:

$$\text{ADDRpte} = 0\times\text{C000} + (\text{ASID} << 8) + \text{VPN}$$

To aid in the handling of the exception, the construction of this address is performed by hardware. This is similar to the memory-management facilities offered by MIPS and UltraSPARC processors. Because all of the values in question (number of unique ASID values, number of unique VPNs) are powers of two, the additions in the equation above become ordinary concatenations of bit-fields, illustrated on the left half (the *User Mode* to *UMISS* transition) of Figure 31.31, which shows the locations in the register file and formats of the various data that are placed into the

register file by hardware when vectoring to a TLB-miss handler. At this time, the address is placed into **cr3**, control register 3. In addition, the return address (EPC) is saved in **cr7**. Afterwards, the hardware vectors to the UMISS handler. When the handler runs, it will use the virtual address in **cr3** to reference the PTE. When the PTE is loaded (the format is shown at the top of Figure 31.29), the handler obtains the PFN. The handler then performs a **tlbw** (TLB-write) instruction to move the loaded mapping into the TLB.

Note that the handler loads the PTE into the processor using a virtual address. Thus, it is possible for the handler itself to cause a TLB miss. This invokes the KMISS handler. When handling a kernel-level TLB miss, the page table needed is the kernel's own page table that maps the top half of the address space (the kernel's virtual space). This page table is 128 PTEs in length, as it maps 128 pages; it is located at address 128 in physical memory and extends to address 255. This is shown in Figure 31.32. The top half of this page table (addresses 192–255) maps the user page tables referenced by the user TLB-miss handler. By construct, because the user page tables begin at virtual address $0\times\text{C000}$, their VPNs range from $0\times\text{C0}$ to $0\times\text{FF}$—in decimal, the range is 192–255. Therefore, by construction, the VPN of the virtual address for the user PTE that the UMISS handler loads equals the physical address of the kernel PTE that maps the user page table. Before vectoring to the KMISS handler, the hardware places this VPN (which, as described, is equal to the physical address required by the KMISS handler)

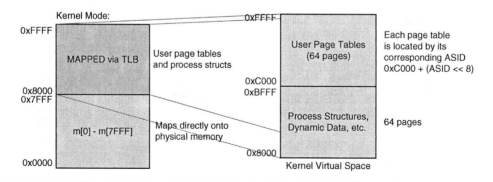

FIGURE 31.30: The kernel's virtual space.

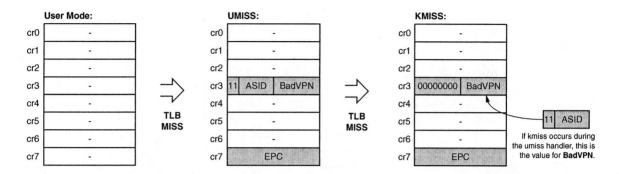

FIGURE 31.31: Hardware steps in the nested TLB-miss exceptions. In the RiSC-16, like in many architectures that use software-managed TLBs, hardware provides to the operating system not only the address of the faulting instruction (EPC), but the addresses of the faulting user-level and root-level PTEs as well. Upon vectoring to a UMISS or KMISS handler, the hardware places the EPC into control register 7 and the address of the faulting PTE in control register 3. Note that providing the PTE addresses assumes a certain page table organization as well as virtual and physical memory maps (location in virtual space of the user-level page table; location in physical space of the root-level table). The operating system is free to use this information or disregard it and use a different table organization.

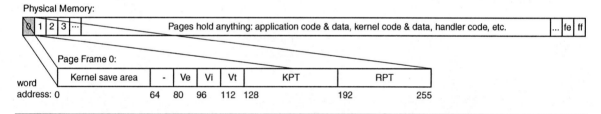

FIGURE 31.32: The first page of physical memory. The first page of physical memory contains important information, such as the interrupt vector table (Ve, Vi, and Vt), the kernel page table that maps the kernel's 64 pages of virtual space, and the root page table that maps the 64 user page tables (also in virtual space). In this architecture, we have reserved a small kernel save area at the very bottom 64 words of physical space; this provides access to known memory locations through the load/store instructions' immediate offset (7 sign-extended bits).

into **cr3**, control register 3, as well as saving the return address (EPC) in **cr7**. This is shown on the right half of Figure 31.31 (the *UMISS* to *KMISS* transition).

Once the desired PTE has been loaded, generating the TLB entry is straightforward: the handler must verify the validity of the PTE and then write it to the TLB. The TLB-write instruction, **tlbw**, takes three operands:

1. The faulting VPN (the page that caused the TLB miss)

2. The faulting page's corresponding PFN, i.e., the contents of the PTE just loaded

3. The ASID of the process causing the TLB miss

Note that, by construction of the page table, items #1 and #3 taken together are the same as the address used to load the PTE, which the hardware stored into **cr3** at the time of vectoring to the handler. See the value of **cr3** in Figure 31.31. Thus, the TLB-write instruction can easily compact the three operands into two register operands:

1. The PTE, loaded into a register by the operating system
2. The ASID and VPN, loaded into a register by the hardware and used by the operating system to load the PTE

When the **tlbw** instruction executes, hardware takes the appropriate bits from the register operands and ignores all else. TLB update can be accomplished with the following instructions. Assume that the load address is in **r2** and the PTE is in **r1**.

```
lw r2, r2, 0          # get the PTE
lui r3, 0×8000        # will be used to test top bit
nandr3, r3, r1        # r3 = 0 × 7fff => valid;
                      # r3 = 0 × ffff => invalid
beq  r3, −1, invalid
tlbw r1, r2           # writes r1 + r2 to TLB,
                        sets 'v' bit in TLB entry


invalid:
sys  PAGE_FAULT       # bring in the big guns
```

The steps that the UMISS and KMISS handlers go through are very similar. Note that this is not a complete handler. For example, the beginnings of the handlers are missing (in which register contents are saved and the PTE is loaded), the ends of the handlers are missing (in which register contents are restored from memory), and return-from-exception is missing. These details are where the UMISS and KMISS handlers differ.

Page Zero and Interrupt Vector Table

Figure 31.32 illustrates numerous things, among them the layout of physical page 0, a very important page to the operating system. The *kernel save area* is used to save/restore state during handler execution. The *Ve*, *Vi*, and *Vt* regions contain vector addresses for *exceptions*, *interrupts*, and *traps*, respectively,

which are typically numbered to facilitate easy indexing into the array. The *kernel page table* (KPT) maps the region of memory in which process structures and associated data are held. The *root page table* (RPT) contains the mappings for the various user page tables that occupy the top quarter of the virtual-address space. It is no accident that the RPT is placed in the top quarter of page frame 0; as mentioned earlier, the result is that the VPN of any kernel virtual address can be used directly as a physical address to obtain the appropriate root-level PTE.

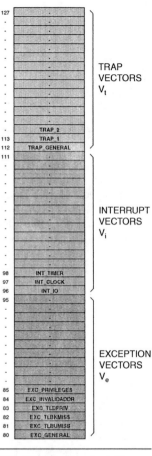

RiSC-16 interrupt vector table.

The interrupt vector table, also part of physical page 0 in this architecture, has a simple format: for every exceptional condition that the hardware recognizes (including exceptions, interrupts, and/or traps), there must be an address in the table that points to a handler routine. The RiSC-16 table is located at physical address 80 in memory and has 48 entries (16 exception types, 16 interrupt types, and 16 trap types). The exception codes happen to correspond exactly to their addresses in the table. The table is illustrated in the figure above.

References

S. G. Abraham, R. A. Sugumar, D. Windheiser, B. R. Rau, and R. Gupta. 1993. "Predictability of load/store instruction latencies." In Proc. 26th Ann. Int. Symp. on Microarchitecture (MICRO 1993), pp. 139–152, Austin, TX, December 1993.

M. Accetta, R. Baron, W. Bolosky, D. Golub, R. Rashid, A. Tevanian, and M. Young. 1986. "Mach: A new kernel foundation for UNIX development." In USENIX Technical Conference Proceedings, 1986.

M. Adiletta, M. Rosenbluth, D. Bernstein, G. Wolrich, and H. Wilkinson. 2002. "The next generation of Intel IXP Network processors." *Intel Technol. J.*, 6(3), Aug. 2002. http://developer.intel.com/technology/itj/2002/volume06issue03/.

S. V. Adve, A. L. Cox, S. Dwarkadas, R. Rajamony, and W. Zwaenepoel. 1996. "A comparison of entry consistency and lazy release consistency implementations." In Proc. Second High Performance Computer Architecture Symp. (HPCA 2), pp. 26–37, San Jose, CA, February 1996.

A. Agarwal, J. Hennessy, and M. Horowitz. 1989. "An analytical cache model." *ACM Trans. Comput. Syst.*, 7(2), 184–215, May 1989.

A. Agarwal et al. 2003. "A single-Vt low-leakage gated-ground cache for deep submicron." *IEEE J. Solid-State Circuits*, 38(2), 319–328, Feb. 2003.

A. V. Aho, R. Sethi, and J. D. Ullman. 1988. *Compilers: Principles, Techniques, and Tools.* Addison-Wesley, Reading, MA, 1988.

A. Aiken and A. Nicolau. 1988. "A development environment for horizontal microcode." *IEEE Trans. Software Eng.*, 14(5), 584–594, May 1988.

J. Alakarhu. 2002. "A comparison of precharge policies with modern DRAM architectures." Proc. 9th Int. Conf. Eletronics, Circuits and Systems, vol. 2, pp. 823–826, Sept. 2002.

K. Albayraktaroglu, A. Jaleel, X. Wu, M. Franklin, B Jacob, C. Tseng, and D. Yeung. 2005. "BioBench: A benchmark suite of bioinformatics applications." In Proc. 2005 IEEE Int. Symp. Performance Analysis of Systems and Software (ISPASS 2005). Austin, TX, March 2005.

T. R. Albrecht, J. U. Bu, M. Despont, E. Eleftheriou, and T. Hirano. 2004. Chapter 6: MEMS in mass storage systems. In Baltes, H., Brand, O., Fedder, G. K., Hierold, C., Korvink, J. G., and Tabata, O., Eds., *Enabling Technologies for MEMS and Nanodevices.* John Wiley & Sons, Hoboken, NJ, 2004.

T. Alexander and G. Kedem. 1996. "Distributed predictive cache design for high performance memory systems." In Second Int. Symp. High-Performance Computer Architecture (ISCA 1996), pp. 254–263, February 1996.

A. Allara, C. Brandolese, W. Fornaciari, F. Salice, and D. Sciuto. 1998. "System-level performance estimation strategy for SW and HW." In Int. Conf. Computer Design (ICCD 1998), Austin, TX, October 1998.

B. Amrutur and M. Horowitz. 1994. "Techniques to reduce power in fast wide memories." in Dig. Tech. Papers 1994 Symp. Low Power Electronics, 1994, pp. 92–93.

B. Amrutur and M. Horowitz. 1998. "A replica technique for wordline and sense control in low-power SRAMs." *IEEE J. Solid State Circuits*, 33, 1208–1219, Aug. 1998.

B. Amrutur and M. Horowitz. 2000. "Speed and power scaling of SRAMs." *IEEE J. Solid-State Circuits*, 35(2), Feb. 2000.

B. Amrutur and M. Horowitz. 2001. "Fast low-power decoders for RAMs." *IEEE J. Solid State Circuits*, 36(10), 1506–1515, Oct. 2001.

Analog Devices. 1996. ADSP-21xx 16-bit DSP Family. http://www.analog.com/processors/processors/ADSP/index.html.

Analog Devices. 2001. SHARC ADSP-21160M 32-bit Embedded CPU. http://www.analog.com/processors/processors/sharc/index.html.

Analog Devices. 2004. TigerSharc ADSP-TS201S 32-bit DSP. Revised Jan. 2004. http://www.analog.com/processors/processors/tigersharc/index.html.

D. Anderson, F. Sparacio, and R. Tomasulo. 1967. "The IBM System/360 Model 91: Machine philosophy and instruction-handling." *IBM J. Res. Dev.*, vol. 11, no. 1, pp. 8–24, Jan. 1967.

D. Anderson, J. Dykes, and E. Riedel. 2003. "More than an interface—SCSI vs. ATA." In Proc. 2nd Ann. Conf. File and Storage Technology (FAST), San Francisco, CA, 2003.

T. Anderson, H. M. Levy, B. N. Bershad, and E. D. Lazowska. 1991. "The interaction of architecture and operating system design." In Proc. Fourth Int. Conf. Architectural Support for Programming Languages and Operating Systems (ASPLOS-4), pp. 108–120, 1991.

F. Angiolini, L. Benini, and A. Caprara. 2003. "Polynomial-time algorithm for on-chip scratchpad memory partitioning." In Proc. 2003 Int. Conf. Compilers, Architectures, and Synthesis for Embedded Systems (CASES 2003), pp. 318–326. ACM Press, New York, 2003.

F. Angiolini, F. Menichelli, A. Ferrero, L. Benini, and M. Olivieri. 2004. "A postcompiler approach to scratchpad mapping of code." In Proc. 2004 Int. Conf. Compilers, Architecture, and Synthesis for Embedded Systems (CASES 2004), pp. 259–267. ACM Press, New York, 2004.

M. Anis. 2003. "Subthreshold leakage current: Challenges and solutions." In Proc. 15th Int. Conf. on Microelectronics (ICM 2003), pp. 77–80, 2003.

A. W. Appel. 1987. "Garbage collection can be faster than stack allocation." Inf. Process. Lett., 25(4), 275–279, June 1987.

A. W. Appel. 1989. "Simple generational garbage collection and fast allocation." *Software—Practice and Experience,* 19(2), 171–183, Feb. 1989.

A. W. Appel and K. Li. 1991. "Virtual memory primitives for user programs." In Proc. Fourth Int. Conf. Architectural Support for Programming Languages and Operating Systems (ASPLOS-4), pp. 96–107, 1991.

Apple Computer, Inc. 1992. *Technical Introduction to the Macintosh Family, 2nd Edition.* Addison-Wesley Publishing Company, Reading, MA, 1992.

J. Archibald and J. Baer. 1986. "Cache coherence protocols: Evaluation using a multiprocessor simulation model." *ACM Trans. Comput. Syst.* 4(4), 273–298, Sept. 1986.

ARM 2004. ARM968E-S 32-bit Embedded Core. Arm, Revised March 2004. http://www.arm.com/products/CPUs/ARM968E-S.html.

K. G. Ashar. 1997. *Magnetic Disk Drive Technology.* IEEE Press, New York, 2004.

Atmel. 2004. AT91C140 16/32-bit Embedded CPU. Atmel, Revised May 2004. http://www.atmel.com/dyn/resources/prod documents/doc6069.pdf.

O. Avissar, R. Barua, and D. Stewart. 2001. "Heterogeneous memory management for embedded systems." In Proc. ACM 2nd Int. Conf. Compilers, Architectures, and Synthesis for Embedded Systems (CASES), November 2001.

O. Avissar, R. Barua, and D. Stewart. 2002. "An optimal memory allocation scheme for scratch-pad based embedded systems." *ACM Trans. Embedded Systems (TECS)*, 1(1), Sept. 2002.

J. Y. Babonneau, M. S. Achard, G. Morisset, and M. B. Mounajjed. 1977. "Automatic and general solution to the adaptation of programs in a paging environment." In Proc. Sixth ACM Symp. Operating Systems Principles (SOSP '77), West Lafayette, IN, November 16–18, 1977. ACM Press, New York, 109–116, 1977.

M. J. Bach. 1986. *The Design of the UNIX Operating System.* Prentice Hall, Inc., Englewood Cliffs, NJ, 1986.

J.-L. Baer and T.-F. Chen. 1991. "An effective on-chip preloading scheme to reduce data access penalty." In Proc. 1991 ACM/IEEE Conf. Supercomputing (ICS 1991), pp. 176–186, Albuquerque, NM, November 1991.

J.-L. Baer and G. R. Sager. 1976. "Dynamic improvement of locality in virtual memory systems." *IEEE Trans. Software Eng.*, 2(1), 54–62. Mar. 1976.

R. J. Baker, H. W. Li, and D. E. Boyce. 1998. *CMOS: Circuit Design, Layout, and Simulation.* IEEE Press, New York, 1998.

J. Baker. 2002. Personal communication.

R. J. Baker. 2005. *CMOS: Circuit Design, Layout, and Simulation, 2nd Ed.* IEEE Press and Wiley-Interscience, New York, 2005.

H. E. Bal, M. F. Kaashoek, and A. S. Tanenbaum. 1992. "Orca: A language for parallel programming of distributed systems." *IEEE Trans. Software. Eng.*, 18(3), 190–205, Mar. 1992.

K. Bala, M. F. Kaashoek, and W. E. Weihl. 1994. "Software prefetching and caching for translation lookaside buffers." In Proc. First USENIX Symp. Operating Systems Design and Implementation (OSDI-1), pp. 243–253, November 1994.

R. Balan and K. Gollhardt. 1992. "A scalable implementation of virtual memory HAT layer for shared memory multiprocessor machines." In USENIX Technical Conference Proceedings, 1992.

S. R. Ball. 1996. *Embedded Microprocessor Systems: Real World Design.* Newnes, Butterworth–Heinemann, Boston, MA, 1996.

R. Banakar, S. Steinke, B.-S. Lee, M. Balakrishnan, and P. Marwedel. 2002. "Scratchpad memory: A design alternative for cache on-chip memory in embedded systems." In Tenth Int. Symp. Hardware/Software Codesign (CODES), pp. 73–78, Estes Park, Colorado, May 2002.

D. Barrett and B. Zorn. 1993. "Using lifetime predictors to improve memory allocation performance." SIGPLAN'93—Conference on Programming Language Design and Implementation, pp. 187–196, Albuquerque, New Mexico, June 1993.

L. A. Barroso et al. 1998. "Memory system characterization of commercial workloads." Int. Symp. Computer Architecture (ISCA-25) 3–14, June 1998.

K. Baynes, C. Collins, E. Fiterman, C. Smit, T. Zhang, and B. Jacob. 2000. "The performance and energy consumption of embedded real-time operating systems." Tech. Rep. UMD-SCA-2000-4, U. Maryland Systems & Computer Architecture Group, November 2000.

K. Baynes, C. Collins, E. Fiterman, B. Ganesh, P. Kohout, C. Smit, T. Zhang, and B. Jacob. 2001. "The performance and energy consumption of three embedded real-time operating systems." In Proc. Int. Conf. Compilers, Architecture, and Synthesis for Embedded Systems (CASES 2001), pp. 203–210, Atlanta, GA, November 2001.

K. Baynes, C. Collins, E. Fiterman, C. Smit, T. Zhang, and B. Jacob. 2003. "The performance and energy consumption of embedded real-time operating systems." *IEEE Trans. Computers,* 52(11), 1454–1469, Nov. 2003.

H. Becker. 2002. Personal communication.

L. A. Belady. 1966. "A study of replacement algorithms for virtual storage." *IBM Syst. J.,* 5(2), 78–101, 1996.

T. Bell, I. H. Witten, and J. G. Cleary. 1989. "Modeling for text compression." *ACM Comput. Surv.,* 21(4), 557–591, Dec. 1989.

L. Benini and G. D. Micheli. 1998. "System-level power optimization: Techniques and tools." In Int. Symp. Low Power Electronics and Design (ISLPED), pp. 288–293, Monterey CA, August 1998.

J. K. Bennett, J. B. Carter, and W. Zwaenepoel. 1990a. "Adaptive software cache management for distributed shared memory architectures." In Proc. 17th Int. Symp. Computer Architecture (ISCA), pp. 148–159, May 1990.

J. K. Bennett, J. B. Carter, and W. Zwaenepoel. 1990b. "Adaptive software cache management for distributed shared memory architectures." In Proc. 17th Annal Int. Symp. Computer Architecture (ISCA'90), pp. 125–135, 1990.

J. K. Bennett, J. B. Carter, and W. Zwaenepoel. 1990c. "Munin: Distributed shared memory based on type-specific memory coherence." In Proc. 2nd ACM Symp. Principles and Practice of Parallel Programming (PPoPP), pp. 168–177, March 1990.

A. Bensoussan, C. T. Clingen, and R. C. Daley. 1972. "The Multics virtual memory: Concepts and design." *Commun. ACM,* 15(5), 308–318, May 1972.

B. Bershad and M. Zekauskas. 1991. Shared Memory Parallel Programming with Entry Consistency for Distributed Memory Multiprocessors, CMU Technical Report CMU-CS-91-170, September 1991.

B. Bershad, M. Zekauskas, and W. Sawdon. 1993. "The Midway distributed shared memory system." In Proc. IEEE CompCon Conference, 1993.

B. Bershad, D. Lee, T. Romer, and J. Chen. 1994a. "Avoiding conflict misses dynamically in large direct-mapped caches." In Proc. Sixth Int. Conf. Architectural Support for Programming Languages and Operating Systems (ASPLOS'94), pp. 158–170, San Jose, CA, 1994.

B. Bershad, C. Chambers, S. Eggers, C. Maeda, D. McNamee, P. Pardyak, S. Savage, and E. Sirer. 1994b. SPIN—An Extensible Microkernel for Application-Specific Operating System Services, Technical Report 94-03-03, University of Washington, 1994.

H. N. Bertram. 1994. *Theory of Magnetic Recording.* Cambridge University Press, Cambridge, UK, 1994.

A. Bestavros, R. L. Carter, M. E. Crovella, C. R. Cunha, A. Beddaya, and S. A. Mirdad. 1990. "Application-level document caching in the internet." In Proc. Second Int. Workshop on Services in Distributed and Networked Environments (SDNE)'95, pp. 125–135, 1990.

D. Bhandarkar and J. Ding. 1997. "Performance characterization of the Pentium Pro processor." Int. Symp. High Performance Computer Architecture (HPCA-3), pp. 288–297, February 1997.

S. S. Bhattacharyya, P. K. Murthy, and E. A. Lee. 1996. *Software Synthesis from Dataflow Graphs*. Kluwer Academic, Dordrecht/Norwell, MA, 1998.

S. S. Bhattacharyya, P. K. Murthy, and E. A. Lee. 1998. "Synthesis of embedded software from synchronous dataflow specifications (invited paper)." *J. VLSI Signal Processing*, 1998.

B. Bhushan, M. Dominiak, and J. P. Lazzari. 1992. "Contact-start-stop studies with silicon planar head sliders against thin-film disks." *IEEE Trans. Magnetics*, 28(5), 2874–2876, 1992.

L. Birkedal, M. Tofte, and M. Vejlstrup. 1996. "From region inference to von neumann machines via region representation inference." In Proc. 23rd ACM SIGPLAN-SIGACT Symp. Principles of Programming Languages, pp. 171–183, ACM Press, New York, 1996.

K. Birman and T. Joseph. 1987. "Exploiting virtual synchrony in distributed systems." In Proc. Eleventh ACM Symp. Operating Systems Principles (SOSP '87), Austin, Texas, United States, November 08–11, 1987, pp. 123–128, ACM Press, New York, 1987.

B. Blanchet. 1998. "Escape analysis: Correctness proof, implementation and experimental results." In Proc. 25th ACM SIGPLAN-SIGACT Symp. Principles of Programming Languages, pp. 25–37, ACM Press, New York, 1998.

B. Blanchet. 1999. "Escape analysis for object-oriented languages: Application to Java." In Proc. 14th ACM SIGPLAN Conf. Object-Oriented Programming, Systems, Languages, and Applications, pp. 20–34, ACM Press, New York, 1999.

M. Blaum, J. Brady, J. Bruck, and J. Menon. 1995. "EVENODD: An optimal scheme for tolerating double disk failures in RAID architecture." *IEEE Trans. Computers*, 44(2), 192–201, 1995.

L. Bloom, M. Cohen, and S. Porter. 1962. "Considerations in the design of a computer with high logic-to-memory speed ratio." In Gigacycle Computing Systems, Proc. Sessions on Gigacycle Computing Systems Presented

at the AIEE Winter General Meeting, pp. 53–63. New York, January 1962.

S. Blumson, P. Honeyman, T. E. Ragland, and M. T. Stolarchuk. 1993. AFS Server Logging, Tech. Rep. CITI-93-10, University of Michigan, November 1993.

Bochs. 2006. The Bochs IA-32 Emulator Project. http://bochs.sourceforge.net.

E. M. Boehm and T. B. Steel, Jr. 1959. "The Share 709 System: Machine implementation of symbolic programming." *J. ACM (JACM)*, 6(2), 134–140, April 1959.

S. Borkar. 2004. "Circuit techniques for subthreshold leakage avoidance, control and tolerance." *IEDM* 2004.

D. Bossen. 1970. "b-Adjacent error correction." *IBM J. Res. Dev.*, July 1970.

N. Bowman et al. 1997. "Evaluation of existing architectures in IRAM systems." Workshop on Mixing Logic and DRAM, June 1997.

D. Brash. 2002. The ARM architecture Version 6 (ARMv6). ARM Ltd., January 2002. White Paper.

H. Bratman and I. V. Boldt, Jr. 1959. "The Share 709 System: Supervisory control." *J. ACM (JACM)*, 6(2), 152–155, April 1959.

A. Braunstein, M. Riley, and J. Wilkes. 1989. "Improving the efficiency of UNIX file buffer caches." In Proc. Twelfth ACM Symp. Operating Systems Principles (SOSP), pp. 71–82, December 1989.

B. S. Brawn, F. G. Gustavson, and E. S. Mankin, 1970. "Sorting in a paging environment." *Commun. ACM*, 13(8), 483–494, Aug. 1970.

J. M. Bray, V. P. Nelson, P. A. D. de Maine, and J. D. Irwin. 1985. "Data-compression techniques ease storage problems." *Computer Design*, 1985.

L. Breuer and D. Baum. 2006. *An Introduction to Queueing Theory and Matrix-Analytic Methods*. Springer, Berlin, 2006.

F. Briggs, M. Cekleov, K. Creta, M. Khare, S. Kulick, A. Kumar, L. Looi, C. Natarajan, S. Radhakrishnan, and L. Rankin. 2002. "Intel 870: A building block for cost-effective, scalable servers." *IEEE Micro*, 22(2), Mar. 2002.

R. A. Bringmann. 1995. "Compiler-Controlled Speculation." PhD thesis, University of Illinois, Urbana, IL, Department of Computer Science, 1995.

D. Brooks and M. Martonosi. 1999. "Dynamically exploiting narrow width operands to improve processor power and performance." In Proc. 5th Int. Symp. High Performance Computer Architecture (HPCA), pp. 13–22, Orlando, FL, January 1999.

D. M. Brooks, P. Bose, S. E. Schuster, H. Jacobson, P. N. Kudva, A. Buyuktosunoglu, J.-D. Wellman, V. Zyuban, M. Gupta, and P. W. Cook. 2000a. "Power-aware microarchitecture: Design and modeling challenges for next-generation microprocessors." *IEEE Micro*, 20(6), 26–44, November/December 2000.

D. Brooks, V. Tiwari, and M. Martonosi. 2000b. "Wattch: A framework for architectural-level power analysis and optimizations." In Proc. 27th Annal International Symposium on Computer Architecture (ISCA'00), pp. 83–94, Vancouver BC, June 2000.

D. Brooks and M. Martonosi. 2000. "Value-based clock gating and operation packing: Dynamic strategies for improving processor power and performance." *ACM Trans. Comput. Syst.*, 18(2), 89–126, 2000.

W. R. Bryg, K. K. Chan, and N. S. Fiduccia. 1996. "A high-performance, low-cost multiprocessor bus for workstations and midrange servers." *The Hewlett-Packard J.*, 47(1), February 1996.

D. Burger et al. 1996a. "Memory bandwidth limitations of future microprocessors." In. Proc. Int. Symp. Computer Architecture (ISCA) 23, 78–89, May 1996.

D. Burger, J. R. Goodman, and A. Kagi. 1996b. "Memory bandwidth limitations of future microprocessors." In Proc. 23rd Annual Int. Symp. Computer Architecture (ISCA'96), pp. 78–89, Philadelphia, PA, May 1996.

D. Burger and T. M. Austin. 1997. The SimpleScalar Tool Set, version 2.0, Tech. Rep. CS-1342, University of Wisconsin-Madison, June 1997.

W. P. Burleson et al. 1998. "Wave-pipelining: A tutorial and research survey," *IEEE Trans. VLSI Systems*, 6(5), Sept. 1998.

M. Burrows, C. Jerian, B. Lampson, and T. Mann. 1992. "On-line data compression in a log-structured file system." In Proc. Fifth Int. Conf. Architectural Support For Programming Languages and Operating Systems (ASPLOS-V), pp. 2–9, Boston, Massachusetts, October 1992), R. L. Wexelblat, Ed., ACM Press, New York, 1992.

J. A. Butts and G. S. Sohi. 2000. "A static power model for architects." In Proc. 33rd Ann. Int. Symp. Microarchitecture (MICRO-33), pp. 191–201, Monterey, CA, December 2000.

B. Calder and D. Grunwald. 1995. "Next cache line and set prediction." In Proc. 22nd Ann. Int. Symp. Computer Architecture (ISCA '95), S. Margherita Ligure, Italy, June 22–24, 1995, pp. 287–296, ACM Press, New York, 1995.

B. Calder, C. Krintz, S. John, and T. Austin. 1998. "Cache-conscious data placement." In Proc. Eighth Int. Conf. Architectural Support for Programming Languages and Operating Systems (ASPLOS'98), pp. 139–149, San Jose, CA, 1998.

D. Callahan, K. Kennedy, and A. Porterfield. 1991. "Software prefetching." In Proc. 4th Int. Conf. Architectural Support for Programming Languages and Operating Systems (ASPLOS), pp. 40–52, April 1991.

P. Cao, E. W. Felten, and K. Li. 1994a. "Application-controlled file caching policies." In Proc. USENIX Summer 1994 Technical Conf., pp. 171–182, Boston, MA, June 1994.

P. Cao, E. W. Felten, and K. Li. 1994b. "Implementation and performance of application-controlled file caching." In Proc. 1st USENIX Symp. Operating Systems Design and Implementation (OSDI), pp. 165–178. Monterey, CA, November 1994.

P. Cao, E. W. Felten, A. R. Karlin, and K. Li. 1995. "A study of integrated prefetching and caching strategies." In Proc. 1995 ACM SIGMETRICS Joint Int. Conf. Measurement and Modeling of Computer Systems SIGMETRICS '95/PERFORMANCE '95, (Ottawa, Ontario, Canada, May 15–19, 1995, B. D. Gaither, Ed., pp. 188–197, ACM Press, New York, 1995.

P. Cao, E. W. Felten, A. R. Karlin, and K. Li. 1996. "Implementation and performance of integrated application-controlled file caching, prefetching, and disk scheduling." *ACM Trans. Comput. Syst.*, 14(4), 311–343, Nov. 1996.

Y. Cao et al. 2000. "New paradigm of predictive MOSFET and interconnect modeling for early circuit design." Proc. of CICC, pp. 201–204, 2000.

L. R. Carley, G. R. Ganger, and D. F. Nagle. 2000. "Mems-based integrated-circuit mass-storage systems." *Commun. the ACM*, 43(11), 73–80, 2000.

M. C. Carlisle and A. Rogers. 1996. "Software caching and computation migration in Olden." *J. Parallel Distributed Computing*, 38(2), 248–255, 1996.

R. W. Carr and J. L. Hennessy. 1981. "WSCLOCK—A simple and effective algorithm for virtual memory management." In Proc. Eighth ACM Symp. Operating

Systems Principles (SOSP-8), pp. 87–95, Pacific Grove, CA, December 1981.

S. Carr. 1993. "Memory-Hierarchy Management." PhD thesis, Rice University, 1993.

S. Carr, K. S. McKinley, and C. Tseng. 1994. "Compiler optimizations for improving data locality." In Proc. Sixth Int. Conf. Architectural Support for Programming Languages and Operating Systems (ASPLOS'94), pp. 252–262, San Jose, CA, 1994.

J. B. Carter, J. K. Bennett, and W. Zwaenepoel. 1991. "Implementation and performance of Munin." In Proc. 13th ACM Symp. Operating Systems Principles (SOSP), pp. 152–164, October 1991.

J. Carter, W. Hsieh, L. Stoller, M. Swanson, L. Zhang, E. Brunvand, A. Davis, C. Kuo, R. Kuramkote, M. Parker, L. Schaelicke, and T. Tateyama. 1999. "Impulse: Building a smarter memory controller." In Proc. Fifth Int. Symp. High Performance Computer Architecture (HPCA'99), pp. 70–79, Orlando, FL, January 1999.

B. Case. 1994a. "AMD unveils first superscalar 29K core." *Microprocessor Rep.*, 8(14), 1994.

B. Case. 1994b. "x86 has plenty of performance headroom." *Microprocessor Rep.*, 8(11), 1994.

F. Catthoor, S. Wuytack, E. De Greef, F. Franssen, L. Nachtergaele, and H. De Man. 1998. "System-level transformations for low power data transfer and storage." In A. Chandrakasan and R. Brodersen, Eds., *Low Power CMOS Design*. IEEE Press, New York, pp. 609–618, 1998.

K. K. Chan, C. C. Hay, J. R. Keller, G. P. Kurpanek, F. X. Schumacher, and J. Zheng. 1996. "Design of the HP PA7200 CPU." *Hewlett-Packard J.*, 47(1), 25–33, February 1996.

A. P. Chandrakasan and R. W. Brodersen. 1995. *Low Power Digital CMOS Design*. Kluwer Academic, Dordrecht/ Norwell, MA, 1995.

A. Chang and M. F. Mergen. 1988. "801 storage: Architecture and programming." *ACM Trans. Computer Syst.*, 6(1), February 1988.

P. P. Chang and W. W. Hwu. 1988. "Trace selection for compiling large C application programs to microcode." In Proc. 21st Ann. Workshop on Microprogramming and Microarchitecture, San Diego, California, United States, November 28 to December 02, 1988, International. Symposium on

Microarchitecture, pp. 21–29, IEEE Computer Society Press, Los Alamitos, CA, 1988.

C. Chao, M. Mackey, and B. Sears. 1990. "Mach on a virtually addressed cache architecture." In USENIX Mach Workshop, 1990.

T. Chappell et al. 1991. "A 2-ns cycle, 3.8-ns access 512-kb CMOS ECL SRAM with a fully pipelined architecture." *IEEE J. Solid-State Circuits*, 26, 1577–1585, Nov. 1991.

H. R. Charney and D. L. Plato. 1968. "Efficient partitioning of components." In Proc. 5th Ann. Workshop on Design Automation (DAC '68), Washington, D. C., United States, July 15–18, 1968, ACM Press, New York, 16.1–16.21, 1968.

M. J. Charney and A. P. Reeves. 1995. Generalized Correlation Based Hardware Prefetching, Technical Report EE-CEG-95-1, Cornell University, February 1995.

M. Charney, P. Coteus, P. Emma, J. Rivers, and J. Rogers. 1999. Private communication.

J. S. Chase, H. M. Levy, M. Baker-Harvey, and E. D. Lazowska. 1992a. How to Use a 64-bit Virtual Address Space, Technical Report 92-03-02, University of Washington, 1992.

J. S. Chase, H. M. Levy, E. D. Lazowska, and M. Baker-Harvey. 1992b. Lightweight Shared Objects in a 64-bit Operating System, Technical Report 92-03-09, University of Washington, 1992.

W. Y. Chen, S. A. Mahlke, P. P. Chang, and W. Mei W. Hwu. 1991. "Data access microarchitectures for superscalar processors with compiler-assisted data prefetching." In Proc. 24th Int. Symp. Microarchitecture (MICRO), 1991.

T. F. Chen and J. L. Baer. 1992. "Reducing memory latency via non-blocking and prefetching cache." In the 5th Int. Conf. Architectural Support for Programming Languages and Operating Systems (ASPLOS), pp. 51–61, October 1992.

J. B. Chen, A. Borg, and N. P. Jouppi. 1992. "A simulation based study of TLB performance." In Proc. 19th Ann. Int. Symp. Computer Architecture (ISCA-19), 1992.

W. Y.-W. Chen, Jr. 1993. "Data Preload for Superscalar and VLIW Processors." PhD thesis, University of Illinois at Urbana-Champaign, Department of Electrical Engineering, August 1993.

P. M. Chen, E. K. Lee, G. A. Gibson, R. H. Katz, and D. A. Patterson. 1994. "RAID: High-performance, reliable secondary storage." *ACM Computing Surveys*, 26(2), 145–185, 1994.

Z. Chen, M. Johnson, L. Wei, and K. Roy. 1998. "Estimation of standby leakage power in CMOS circuits considering accurate modeling of transistor stacks." In Proc. Int. Symp. Low Power Electronics and Design (ISLPED), 1998.

B. M. Chen, T. H. Lee, K. Peng, and V. Venkataramanan. 2006. *Hard Disk Drive Servo Systems.* Springer, London, 2006.

R. Cheng. 1987. "Virtual address cache in UNIX." In Proc. Summer 1987 USENIX Technical Conference, 1987.

D. R. Cheriton, G. A. Slavenburg, and P. D. Boyle. 1986. "Software-controlled caches in the VMP multiprocessor." In Proc. 13th Ann. Int. Symp. Computer Architecture (ISCA-13), 1986.

D. R. Cheriton, A. Gupta, P. D. Boyle, and H. A. Goosen. 1988. "The VMP multiprocessor: Initial experience, refinements and performance evaluation." In Proc. 15th Ann. Int. Symp. Computer Architecture (ISCA-15), 1988.

D. R. Cheriton, H. A. Goosen, and P. D. Boyle. 1989. "Multi-level shared caching techniques for scalability in VMP-MC." In Proc. 16th Ann. Int. Symp. Computer Architecture (ISCA-16), 1989.

B. S. Cherkauer and E. G. Friedman, 1995. "A unified design methodology for CMOS tapered buffers." *IEEE J. Solid-State Circuits*, 3, 99–111, Mar. 1995.

T. M. Chilimbi, M. D. Hill, and J. R. Larus. 1999. "Cache-conscious structure layout." In Proc. ACM SIGPLAN '99 Conference on Programming Language Design and Implementation (PLDI), Atlanta, GA, ACM, May 1999.

D. Chiou, P. Jain, L. Rudolph, and S. Devadas. 2000. "Application-specific memory management in embedded systems using software-controlled caches." In Proc. 37th Design Automation Conference (DAC), June 2000.

Z. Chishti, M. Powell, and T. N. Vijaykumar. 2003. "Distance associativity for high-performance energy-efficient non-uniform cache architectures." In Proc. 36th Ann. Int. Symp. Microarchitecture (MICRO), pp. 55–66, San Diego, CA, December 2003.

T. Chiueh and R. H. Katz. 1992. "Eliminating the address translation bottleneck for physical address caches." In Proc. Fifth Int. Conf. Architectural Support for Programming Languages and Operating Systems (ASPLOS-5), 1992.

J.-D. Choi, M. Gupta, M. Serrano, V. C. Sreedhar, and S. Midkiff. 1999. "Escape analysis for java." In Proc. 14th ACM SIGPLAN Conf. Object-oriented Programming, Systems, Languages, and Applications (OOPSLA), pp. 1–19, ACM Press, New York, 1999.

H.-T. Chou and D. J. DeWitt. 1985. "An evaluation of buffer management strategies for relational database systems." In Proc. 11th Int. Conf. Very Large Data Bases, Stockholm, Sweden, August 21–23, pp.127–141 1985.

C. K. Chow. 1974. "On optimization of storage hierarchies." *IBM J. Res. Dev.*, 194–203, May 1974.

C. K. Chow. 1976. "Determination of cache's capacity and its matching storage hierarchy." *IEEE Trans. Computers*, 25(2), 157–164, Feb. 1976.

D. W. Clark and J. S. Emer. 1985. "Performance of the VAX-11/780 translation buffer: Simulation and measurement." *ACM Trans. Computer Systems*, 3(1), 1985.

E. G. Coffman and P. J. Denning. 1973. *Operating System Theory.* Prentice Hall, Englewood Cliffs, NJ, 1973.

D. Colarelli, D. Grunwald, and M. Neufeld. 2002. "The case for massive arrays of idle disks." In Proc. 2002 FAST, Monterey, CA, 2002.

C. Collins, E. Fiterman, T. Zhang, and B. Jacob. 2000. SimBed: Accurate Microarchitecture-level Simulation of Embedded Real-Time Operating Systems, Tech. Rep. UMD-SCA-2000-1, University of Maryland Systems & Computer Architecture Group, April 2000.

C. M. Collins. 2000. "An evaluation of embedded system behavior using full-system software emulation." Master's thesis, University of Maryland at College Park, May 2000.

J. Collins, S. Sair, B. Calder, and D. Tullsen. 2002. "Pointer cache assisted prefetching." In Proc. 35th Ann. IEEE/ACM Int. Symp. Microarchitecture (MICRO), November 2002.

R. Colwell, R. Nix, J. O'Donnell, D. Papworth, and P. Rodman. 1987. "A VLIW architecture for a trace scheduling compiler." In Proc. Second Int. Conf. Architectural Support for Programming Languages and Operating Systems (ASPLOS-2), pp. 180–192, 1987.

L. W. Comeau. 1967. "A study of the effect of user program optimization in a paging system." In Proc. First ACM

Symp. Operating System Principles (SOSP '67), J. Gosden and B. Randell, Eds., pp. 4.1–4.7, ACM Press, New York, 1967.

Compaq. New Challenges Drive Compaq Advanced Memory Protection Strategy, Compaq Computer Corporation, Whitepaper.

J. P. Considine and J. J. Myers. 1969. "Establishment and maintenance of a storage hierarchy for an on-line data base under TSS/360." In Proc. Fall Joint Computer Conference, pp. 433–440, November 1969.

J. P. Considine and J. J. Myers. 1977. "MARC: MVS archival storage and recovery program." *IBM Systems J.*, 16(4), 378–397, 1977.

T. M. Conte, K. N. Menezes, P. M. Mills, and B. A. Patel. 1995. "Optimization of instruction fetch mechanisms for high issue rates." In Proc. 22nd Ann. Int. Symp. Computer Architecture (ISCA), pp. 333–344. Santa Margherita Ligure, Italy, June 1995.

R. Cooksey, S. Jourdan, and D. Grunwald. 2002. "A stateless, content-directed data prefetching mechanism." In Proc. Int. Conf. Architectural Support for Programming Languages and Operating System (ASPLOS), 2002.

K. D. Cooper and T. J. Harvey. 1998. "Compiler-controlled memory." In Architectural Support for Programming Languages and Operating Systems (ASPLOS), pp. 2–11, San Jose, CA, Oct. 1998.

F. J. Corbato. 1968. A Paging Experiment with the Multics System, MIT Project -MAC Report MAC-M-384, May 1968.

G. V. Cormack. 1985. "Data compression on a database system." *Commun. ACM*, 28(12), 1336–1342, Dec. 1985.

D. W. Cornell and P. S. Yu. 1989. "Integration of buffer management and query optimization in relational database environment." In Proc. Fifteenth Int. Conf. Very Large Data Bases, August 22–25, Amsterdam, The Netherlands, pp. 247–255, 1989.

S. L. Coumeri and D. E. Thomas. 1998. "Memory modeling for system synthesis." In Proc. 1998 Int. Symp. Low Power Electronics and Design (ISLPED '98), Monterey, California, United States, August 10–12, 1998, ACM Press, New York, pp. 179–184, 1998.

R. Crisp. 1997. "Direct Rambus technology: The new main memory standard." *IEEE Micro*, 17(6), 18–28, Nov. 1997.

V. Cuppu and B. Jacob. 1999a. The Performance of Next-Generation DRAM Architectures, Tech. Rep. UMD-SCA-TR-1999-1, University of Maryland Systems and Computer Architecture Group, March 1999.

V. Cuppu and B. Jacob. 1999b. Organizational Design Trade-offs at the DRAM, Memory Bus, and Memory Controller Level: Initial Results, Tech. Rep. UMD-SCA-1999-2, University of Maryland Systems & Computer Architecture Group, November 1999.

V. Cuppu, B. Jacob, B. Davis, and T. Mudge. 1999. "A performance comparison of contemporary DRAM architectures." In Proc. 26th Ann. Int. Symp. Computer Architecture (ISCA'99), pp. 222–233. Atlanta, GA, May 1999.

V. Cuppu and B. Jacob. 2001. "Concurrency, latency, or system overhead: Which has the largest impact on uniprocessor dram-system performance?" In Proc. 28th Ann. Int. Symp. Computer Architecture (ISCA'01), pp. 62–71, Göteborg, Sweden, June 2001.

V. Cuppu, B. Jacob, B. Davis, and T. Mudge. 2001. "High performance DRAMs in workstation environments." *IEEE Trans. Computers*, 50(11), 1133–1153, Nov. 2001. (Special issue on High-Performance Memory Systems)

H. Custer. 1993. Inside Windows/NT, Technical report, Microsoft Press.

Z. Cvetanovic and D. Bhandarkar. 1994. "Characterization of Alpha AXP performance using TP and SPEC workloads." Int. Symp. Computer Architecture (ISCA-21), pp. 60–70, April 1994.

Z. Cvetanovic and R. E. Kessler. 2000. "Performance analysis of the Alpha 21264-based Compaq ES40 system." In Proc. 27th Ann. Int. Symp. Computer Architecture (ISCA'00), pp. 192–202, Vancouver, BC, June 2000.

W. Dally and J. Poulton. 1998. *Digital Systems Engineering*. Cambridge University Press, Cambridge, UK, 1998.

R. Das, M. Uysal, J. Saltz, and Y.-S. Hwang. 1994. "Communication optimizations for irregular scientific computations on distributed memory architectures." *J. Parallel Distributed Computing*, 22(3), 462–479, Sept. 1994.

M. Das. 2000. "Unification-based pointer analysis with directional assignments." In Proc. SIGPLAN '00 Conf. Program Language Design and Implementation (PLDI), pp. 35–46, Vancouver, BC, June 2000.

B. Davis, T. Mudge, and B. Jacob. 2000a. The New DRAM Interfaces: SDRAM, RDRAM and Variants. In M. Valero,

K. Joe, M. Kitsuregawa, and H. Tanaka, Editors, *High Performance Computing, Lecture Notes in Computer Science*, Vol. 1940, pp. 26–31, Springer Publishing, Tokyo, Japan, 2000.

B. Davis, T. Mudge, V. Cuppu, and B. Jacob. 2000b. "DDR2 and low-latency variants." In Proc. Workshop on Solving the Memory Wall Problem, Held in conjunction with ISCA-27, pp. 15–29, Vancouver, BC, June 2000.

P. A. D. de Maine and B. A. Marron. 1966. "The SOLID System I: A method for organizing and searching files." In G. Schecter, Editor, *Information Retrieval—A Critical View* (Based on the Third Annal National Colloquium on Information Retrieval, Philadelphia PA, May 1966), Thompson Book Co., Washington, DC, pp. 243–282, 1967.

H. Deitel. 1990. *Inside OS/2*. Addison-Wesley, Reading, MA.

V. Delaluz, M. Kandemir, N. Vijaykrishnan, A. Sivasubramaniam, and M. Irwin. 2001. "Hardware and software techniques for controlling DRAM power modes." In Seventh Int. Symp. High-Performance Computer Architecture (HPCA'01), January. 2001.

T. Dell. 1997. A White Paper on the Benefits of Chipkill-Correct ECC for PC Server Main Memory. IBM Microelectronics Division, November 1997. White Paper.

P. J. Denning. 1967. "The working set model for program behavior." In Proc. First ACM Symp. Operating System Principles (SOSP 1), pp. 15.1–15.12, 1967.

P. J. Denning. 1968. "The working set model for program behavior." *Commun. ACM*, 11(5), 323–333, 1968.

P. J. Denning. 1970. "Virtual memory." *Computing Surveys*, 2(3), 153–189, 1970.

P. J. Denning. 1972. "On modeling program behavior." In Proc. AFIPS Spring Joint Computer Conference, pp. 937–944, 1972.

P. J. Denning. 1980. "Working sets past and present." *IEEE Trans. Software Eng.*, 6(1), 64–84, 1980.

J. B. Dennis. 1965. "Segmentation and the design of multiprogrammed computer systems." *J. ACM*, 12(4), 589–602, Oct. 1965.

Design & Test Roundtable. 1997. "Hardware-software codesign." *IEEE Design Test Computers*, 14(1), 75–83, January–March 1997.

R. P. Dick, G. Lakshminarayana, A. Raghunathan, and N. K. Jha. 2000. "Power analysis of embedded operating systems." In 37th Design Automation Conference (DAC), Los Angeles CA, pp. 312–315, June 2000.

Digital. 1994. DECchip 21064 and DECchip 21064A Alpha AXP Microprocessors Hardware Reference Manual. Digital Equipment Corporation, Maynard, MA.

Digital. 1996. Digital Semiconductor 21164 (366 MHz Through 433 MHz) Alpha Microprocessor Hardware Reference Manual. Digital Equipment Corporation, Maynard, MA.

Digital. 1997. DIGITAL FX!32. Digital Equipment Corp., http://www.digital.com/info/semiconductor/amt/fx32/fx.html.

V. J. DiGri and J. King. 1959. "The Share 709 System: Input-output translation." *J. ACM (JACM)*, 6(2), 141–144, April 1959.

C. Ding and K. Kennedy. 1999. "Improving cache performance in dynamic applications through data and computation reorganization at run time." In Proc. ACM SIGPLAN 1999 Conf. on Programming Language Design and Implementation (PLDI 1999), pp. 229–241, Atlanta, GA, May 1999.

B. Dipert. 2000. "The slammin, jammin, DRAM scramble." *EDN*, 2000(2), 68–82, Jan. 2000.

A. Dominguez, S. Udayakumaran, and R. Barua. 2005. "Heap data allocation to scratch-pad memory in embedded systems." *J. Embedded Computing (JEC)*, 1(4), 2005. IOS Press, Amsterdam, Netherlands.

F. Douglis. 1993. "The compression cache: Using on-line compression to extend physical memory." In Proc. Usenix Winter 1993 Technical Conference, pp. 519–529, San Diego, CA, January 1993.

B. Doyle et al. 2002. "Transistor elements for 30 nm physical gate lengths and beyond." *Intel Technol. J.* 6, 42–54, May 2002.

A. L. Drapeau and R. H. Katz. 1993. "Striped tape arrays." In Proc. 1993 IEEE Symp. on Mass Storage Systems, pp. 1993. 257–265.

P. Druschel and L. L. Peterson. 1993. "Fbufs: A high-bandwidth cross-domain transfer facility." In Proc. Fourteenth ACM Symp. on Operating Systems Principles (SOSP-14), pp. 189–202, December 1993.

R. Duncan, C. Petzold, A. Schulman, M. S. Baker, R. P. Nelson, S. R. Davis, and R. Moote. 1994. *Extending*

DOS—A Programmer's Guide to Protected-Mode DOS, 2nd Edition. Addison-Wesley, Reading, MA, 1994.

J. DuPreez. 2002. Personal communication.

C. P. Earnest, K. G. Balke, and J. Anderson. 1972. "Analysis of graphs by ordering of nodes." *J. ACM,* 19(1), 23–42, Jan. 1972.

K. Ebcioglu. 1987. "A compilation technique for software pipelining of loops with conditional jumps." In Proc. 20th Ann. Workshop on Microprogramming (MICRO-20), pp. 69–79, Colorado Springs, CO, December 1987.

K. Ebcioglu. 1988. "Some design ideas for a VLIW architecture for sequential natured software." In *Parallel Processing* (Proc. IFIP WG 10.3, Working Conference on Parallel Processing), M. Cosnard, M. Barton, and M. Vanneschi, Eds., pp. 3–21, 1988.

K. Ebcioglu and E. R. Altman. 1997. "DAISY: Dynamic compilation for 100% architectural compatibility." In Proc. 24th Ann. Int. Symp. on Computer Architecture (ISCA-24), pp. 26–37, Denver, CO, 1997.

C. H. Edwards, Jr. and D. E. Penney. 1982. *Calculus and Analytic Geometry.* Prentice Hall, Englewood Cliffs, NJ, 1982.

J. R. Ellis. 1985. *Bulldog: A Compiler for VLIW Architectures.* The MIT Press, Cambridge, MA. 1985. (Ellis's Ph.D. Thesis, Yale, 1984).

C. Ellis. 1999. "The case for higher-level power management." In Workshop on Hot Topics in Operating Systems, 1999.

Y. Endo, Z. Wang, J. B. Chen, and M. Seltzer. 1996. "Using latency to evaluate interactive system performance." In Proc. 1996 Symp. on Operating System Design and Implementation (OSDI-2), October 1996.

D. Engler, R. Dean, A. Forin, and R. Rashid. 1994. "The operating system as a secure programmable machine." In Proc. 1994 European SIGOPS Workshop, 1994.

ESDRAM. 1998. Enhanced SDRAM 1M x 16. Enhanced Memory Systems, Inc., http://www.edram.com/products/datasheets/16M_esdram0298a.pdf.

Etch. 1998. Memory System Research at the University of Washington. The University of Washington, http://etch.cs.washington.edu/.

A. Eto et al. 1998. "Impact of Neutron Flux on Soft Error in MOS Memories" In. Proc. Int'l. Electron Devices Meeting (IEDM), pp. 367–370. Dec. 1998.

A. Eustace and A. Srivastava. 1994. ATOM: A Flexible Interface for Building High Performance Program Analysis Tools, Technical Report WRL-TN-44, DEC Western Research Laboratory.

K. Farkas, P. Chow, N. Jouppi, and Z. Vranesic. 1997. "Memory-system design considerations for dynamically-scheduled processors." In Proc. 24th Ann. Int. Symp. on Computer Architecture (ISCA), 1997.

A. H. Farrahi, G. E. Téllez, and M. Sarrafzadeh. 1995. "Memory segmentation to exploit sleep mode operation." In Proc. 32nd ACM/IEEE Conf. on Design Automation (DAC '95), pp. 36–41, San Francisco, California, United States, June 12–16, 1995, ACM Press, New York, 1995.

R. R. Fenichel, and J. C. Yochelson. 1969. "A LISP garbage-collector for virtual-memory computer systems." *Commun. ACM,* 12(11), 611–612, Nov. 1969.

D. Ferrari. 1973. "A tool for automatic program restructuring." In Proc. Ann. Conf. (ACM '73), Atlanta, Georgia, United States, August 27–29, 1973), pp. 228–231, ACM Press, New York, 1973.

D. Ferrari. 1974. "Improving locality by critical working sets." *Commun. ACM,* 17(11), 614–620, Nov. 1974.

D. Ferrari. 1976. "The improvement of program behavior." *IEEE Computer,* 9(11), Nov. 1976.

J. A. Fisher. 1980. "2n-way jump microinstruction hardware and an effective instruction binding method." In Proc. 13th Ann. Workshop on Microprogramming (MICRO-13), pp. 64–75, November 1980.

J. Fisher. 1981. "Trace scheduling: A technique for global micro-code compaction." *IEEE Trans. Computers,* 30(7), 478–490, July 1981.

J. A. Fisher. 1983. "Very long instruction word architectures and the ELI-512." In Proc. 10th Ann. Int. Symp. on Computer Architecture (ISCA-10), pp. 140–150, June 1983.

J. A. Fisher, J. R. Ellis, J. C. Ruttenberg, and A. Nicolau. 1984. "Parallel processing: A smart compiler and a dumb machine." In Proc. ACM SIGPLAN '84 Symp. on Compiler Construction, SIGPLAN Notices, 19(6), 37–47, June 1984.

K. Flautner, S. Reinhardt, and T. Mudge. 2001. "Automatic performance-setting for dynamic voltage scaling." In 7th Conf. on Mobile Computing and Networking (MOBICOM'01), Rome, Italy, July 2001.

J. Flinn and M. Satyanarayanan. 1999. "Powerscope: A tool for profiling the energy usage of mobile applications." In Workshop on Mobile Computing Systems and Applications, pp. 2–10, February 1999.

J. Fotheringham. 1961. "Dynamic storage allocation in the Atlas computer, including an automatic use of a backing store." *Commun. ACM*, 4(10), 435–436, Oct. 1961.

M. Franklin and M. Smotherman. 1994. "A fill-unit approach to multiple instruction issue." In Proc. 27th Ann. Int. Symp. on Microarchitecture (MICRO-27), pp. 162–171, San Jose, CA, November 1994.

R. Fromm, S. Perissakis, N. Cardwell, C. Kozyrakis, B. McGaughy, D. Patterson, T. Anderson, and K. Yelick. 1997. "The energy efficiency of IRAM architectures." In Proc. 24th Ann. Int. Symp. on Computer Architecture (ISCA'97), pp. 327–337, Denver, CO, June 1997.

J. W. Fu and J. H. Patel. 1991. "Data prefetching in multiprocessor vector cache memories." In Proc. 18th Ann. Int. Symp. on Computer Architecture (ISCA 1991), pp. 54–63, Toronto, Ontario, May 1991.

D. M. Gallagher, W. Y. Chen, S. A. Mahlke, J. C. Gyllenhaal, and W. mei W. Hwu. 1994. "Dynamic memory disambiguation using the memory conflict buffer." In Proc. Sixth Int. Conf. on Architectural Support for Programming Languages and Operating Systems (ASPLOS-6), San Jose, CA, 1994.

B. Ganesh, A. Jaleel, D. Wang, and B. Jacob. 2007. "Fully-Buffered DIMM memory architectures: Understanding mechanisms, overheads and scaling." In Proc. 13th Int. Symp. on High Performance Computer Architecture (HPCA 2007), Phoenix, AZ, February 2007.

G. Ganger, B. Worthington, and Y. Patt. 2006. The DiskSim Simulation Environment Version 2.0 Reference Manual, http://www.pdl.cmu.edu/DiskSim/. 2006.

J. G. Ganssle. 1994. "An OS in a can." *Embedded Systems Programming*, January 1994.

J. G. Ganssle. 1997. "The challenges of real-time programming." *Embedded Systems Programming*, 11(7), 20–26, July 1997.

J. Ganssle. 2000a. "Conspiracy theory." *The Embedded Muse Newsl.*, no. 46, March 3, 2000.

J. Ganssle. 2000b. "Conspiracy theory, take 2." *The Embedded Muse Newsl.*, No. 47, March 22, 2000.

H. Garcia-Molina, A. Park, and L. R. Rogers. 1987. "Performance through memory." In Proc. 1987 ACM Sigmetrics Conference. on Measurement and Modeling of Computer Systems, pp. 122–131, 1987.

W. E. Garrett, R. Bianchini, L. Kontothanassis, R. A. McCallum, J. Thomas, R. Wisniewski, and M. L. Scott. 1992. Dynamic Sharing and Backward Compatibility on 64-bit Machines, Technical Report TR 418, University of Rochester.

W. E. Garrett, M. L. Scott, R. Bianchini, L. I. Kontothanassis, R. A. McCallumm, J. A. Thomas, R. Wisniewski, and S. Luk. 1993. "Linking shared segments." In USENIX Technical Conference Proceedings, pp. 13–27, January 1993.

J.-L. Gassée. 1996. "CoffeeBean." *Be Newsletter*, Issue 52, December 4, 1996.

R. Geist and S. Daniel. 1987. "A continuum of disk scheduling algorithms." *ACM Trans. Comput. Syst.*, 5(1), 77–92, 1987.

P. Gelsinger. 2001. "Microprocessors for the new millenium: Challenges, opportunities, and new frontiers," *ISSCC*, 22–5, 2001.

L. Geppert. 2004. "A Static RAM says goodbye to data errors." *IEEE Spectrum*, February 2004.

K. Gharachorloo, D. Lenoskj, J. Laudon, P. Gibbons, A. Gupta, and J. Hennessy. 1990. "Memory consistency and event ordering in scalable shared-memory multiprocessors." In Proc. 17th Ann. Int. Symp. on Computer Architecture (ISCA), pp. 15–26, May 1990.

N. Gloy, T. Blackwell, M. D. Smith, and B. Calder. 1997. "Procedure placement using temporal ordering information." In Proc. 30th Ann. IEEE/ACM Int. Symp. on Microarchitecture (MICRO), pp. 303–313, December 1997.

R. Gonzalez and M. Horowitz. 1996. "Energy dissipation in general purpose microprocessors." *IEEE J. Solid-State Circuits*, 31(9), 1277–1284, Sept. 1996.

J. R. Goodman. 1987. "Coherency for multiprocessor virtual address caches." In Proc. Second Int. Conf. on Architectural Support for Programming Languages and Operating Systems (ASPLOS-2), pp. 72–81, 1987.

B. Goodman. 2002. Personal communication.

K. Govil, E. Chan, and H. Wasserman. 1995. "Comparing algorithms for dynamic speed-setting of a low-power CPU." In Proc. First ACM Int. Conf. on Mobile Computing and Networking, Berkeley, CA, November 1995.

M. K. Gowan, L. L. Biro, and D. B. Jackson. 1998. "Power considerations in the design of the Alpha 21264 microprocessor." In 35th Design Automation Conference (DAC). 1998.

I. D. Greenwald and M. Kane. 1959. "The Share 709 System: Programming and modification." *J. ACM (JACM)*, 6(2), 128–133, April 1959.

J. Griffioen and R. Appleton. 1994. "Reducing file system latency using a predictive approach." In Proc. 1994 Summer USENIX Conf., pp. 197–207, Boston, MA, June 1994.

P. Gronowski et al. 1996. "A 433-MHz 64-b quad-ussue RISC microprocessor." *JSSC*, 31(11), 1687–1696, Nov. 1996.

A. Grove. 2002. "Changing Vectors of Moore's Law." Presented at International. Electron Devices Meeting (IEDM), December 2002.

D. Grunwald, B. Zorn, and R. Henderson. 1993. "Improving the cache locality of memory allocation." In R. Cartwright, Ed., Proc. ACM SIGPLAN 1993 Conf. on Programming Language Design and Implementation (PLDI '93), pp. 177–186, Albuquerque, New Mexico, United States, June 21–25, 1993, ACM Press, New York, 1993.

D. Grunwald, P. Levis, C. B. M. III, M. Neufeld, and K. I. Farkas. 2000. "Policies for dynamic clock scheduling." In Proc. Fourth USENIX Symp. on Operating Systems Design and Implementation (OSDI 2000), pp. 73–86, San Diego, CA, October 2000.

S. Gurumurthi, A. Sivasubramaniam, M. Kandemir, and H. Franke. 2003. "DRPM: Dynamic speed-control for power management in server class disks," In Proc. 30th Int. Symp. on Computer Architecture (ISCA 2003), pp. 169–179, June 2003.

L. Gwennap. 1994a. "MIPS R10000 uses decoupled architecture." *Microprocessor Rep.*, 8(14), 1994.

L. Gwennap. 1994b. "PA-8000 combines complexity and speed." *Microprocessor Rep.*, 8(15), 1994.

L. Gwennap. 1995a. "Intel's P6 uses decoupled superscalar design." *Microprocessor Rep.*, 9(2), 1995.

L. Gwennap. 1995b. "PA-8000 stays on track (sidebar in Integrated PA-7300LC powers HP midrange)." *Microprocessor Rep.*, 9(15), 1995.

L. Gwennap. 1995c. "Intel's P6 uses decoupled superscalar design." Microprocessor Rep., 9(2), Feb. 1995.

L. Gwennap. 1996. "Digital 21264 sets new standard." *Microprocessor Rep.*, 10(14), October 1996.

L. Gwennap. 1998a. "Alpha 21364 to ease memory bottleneck." *Microprocessor Rep.*, 12(14), 12–15, Oct. 1998.

L. Gwennap. 1998b. "New processor paradigm: V-IRAM." *Microprocessor Rep.*, 12(3), 17–19, March 1998.

J. Haas and P. Vogt. 2005. "Fully-buffered DIMM technology moves enterprise platforms to the next level." *Technology@Intel Magazine*, March 2005.

E. Hagersten, A. Landin, and S. Haridi. 1992. "DDM—A cacheonly memory architecture." *IEEE Computer*, 25(9), 44–54, Sept. 1992.

S. Hall, G. Hall, and J. McCall. 2000. *High-Speed Digital System Design—A handbook of Interconnect Theory and Design Practices*, Wiley-Interscience, New York, 2000.

N. Hallenberg, M. Elsman, and M. Tofte. 2002. "Combining region inference and garbage collection." In Proc. ACM SIGPLAN 2002 Conf. on Programming Language Design and Implementation (PLDI) pp. 141–152, ACM Press, New York, 2002.

G. Hallnor and S. K. Reinhardt. 2000. "A fully associative software-managed cache design." In Proc. 27th Int. Symp. on Computer Architecture (ISCA), Vancouver, BC, Canada, June 2000.

J. P. Halter and F. Najm, 1997. "A gate-level leakage power reduction method for ultra-low-power CMOS circuits." In Proc. IEEE Custom Integrated Circuits Conf., 1997.

G. Hamilton and P. Kougiouris. 1993. "The Spring nucleus: A microkernel for objects." In USENIX Technical Conference Proceedings, 1993.

F. Hamzaoglu and M. R. Stan. 2002. "Circuit-level techniques to control gate-leakage for sub-100nm CMOS." *ISLPED*, August 2002.

R. Hank, S. Mahlke, R. Bringmann, J. Gyllenhaal, and W. Hwu. 1993. "Superblock formation using static program analysis." In 26th Int. Symp. on Microarchitecture (MICRO), pp. 247–256, IEEE Press, New York, December 1993.

W. J. Hansen. 1969. "Compact list representation: Definition, garbage collection, and system implementation." *Commun. ACM*, 12(9), 499–507, Sep. 1969.

J. M. Harker, D. W. Brede, R. E. Pattison, G. R. Santana, and L. G. Taft. 1981. "A quarter century of disk file innovation." *IBM J.* Res. Dev., 25(5), 677–689, 1981.

S.J. Hartley. 1988. "Compile-time program restructuring in multiprogrammed virtual memory systems." *IEEE Trans. Software Eng.*, 14 (11), 1640–1644, Nov. 1988.

D.J. Hatfield and J. Gerald. 1971. "Program restructuring for virtual memory." *IBM Systems J.* 10(3), 168–192, 1971.

S. Haykin. 2002. *Adaptive Filter Theory, 4th Ed.*, Prentice Hall, Upper Saddle River, NJ.

R. Heald and J. Hoist. 1993. "A 6-ns cycle 256-kb cache memory and memory management unit." *IEEE J. Solid-State Circuits*, 28, 1078–1083, Nov. 1993.

J. Heinrich, editor. 1995. MIPS R10000 Microprocessor User's Manual, version 1.0. MIPS Technologies, Inc., Mountain View, CA.

J. Hennessy and M. Heinrich. 1996. "Hardware/software codesign of processors: Concepts and examples." In G. De Micheli and M. Sami, Eds., *Hardware/Software Co-Design*, Kluwer Academic, San Mateo, CA, pp. 29–44, 1996.

J. L. Hennessy and D. A. Patterson. 1990. *Computer Architecture: A Quantitative Approach*. Morgan Kaufmann, San Mateo, CA, 1990.

J. L. Hennessy and D. A. Patterson. 1996. *Computer Architecture: A Quantitative Approach, 2nd Ed.*, Morgan Kaufmann, San Mateo, CA, 1996.

J. L. Hennessy and D. A. Patterson. 2003. *Computer Architecture: A Quantitative Approach, 3rd Ed.*, Morgan Kaufmann, San Mateo, CA, 2003.

D. S. Henry. 1994. Adding Fast Interrupts to Superscalar Processors, Tech. Rep. Memo-366, MIT Computation Structures Group, December 1994.

D. Henry, B. Kuszmaul, G. Loh, and R. Sami. 2000. "Circuits for wide-window superscalar processors." In Proc. 27th Ann. Int. Symp. on Computer Architecture (ISCA'00), pp. 236–247, Vancouver, BC, June 2000.

Hewlett-Packard. 1990. PA-RISC 1.1 Architecture and Instruction Set Reference Manual. Hewlett-Packard Company.

M. D. Hill, S. J. Eggers, J. R. Larus, G. S. Taylor, G. Adams, B. K. Bose, G. A. Gibson, P. M. Hansen, J. Keller, S. I. Kong,

C. G. Lee, D. Lee, J. M. Pendleton, S. A. Ritchie, D. A. Wood, B. G. Zorn, P. N. Hilfinger, D. Hodges, R. H. Katz, J. K. Ousterhout, and D. A. Patterson. 1986. "Design decisions in SPUR." *IEEE Computer,* 19(11), Nov. 1986.

G. Hinton, D. Sager, M. Upton, D. Boggs, D. Carmeanand, A. Kyker, and P. Roussel. 2001. "The microarchitecture of the Pentium 4 Processor." *Intel Technol. J.*, First Quarter, 2001.

T. Hirose et al. 1990. "A 20-ns 4-Mb CMOS SRAM with hierarchical word decoding architecture." *IEEE J. Solid-State Circuits*, SC-25(5), 1068–1074, Oct. 1990.

J. D. Hiser and J. W. Davidson. 2004. "Embarc: an efficient memory bank assignment algorithm for retargetable compilers." In Proc. 2004 ACM SIGPLAN/SIGBED Conf. on Languages, Compilers, and Tools for Embedded Systems (LCTES), pp. 182–191, ACM Press, New York, 2004.

Hitachi/Renesas. 1999. SH7050 32-bit CPU. Hitachi/Renesas, Revised Sep. 1999. http://documentation.renesas.com/eng/products/mpumcu/e602121 sh7050.pdf.

Hitachi/Renesas. 2004. M32R-32192 32-bit Embedded CPU. Revised July 2004. http://documentation.renesas.com/eng/products/mpumcu/rej03b0019 32192ds.pdf.

A. S. Hoagland. 2003. "History of magnetic disk storage based on perpendicular magnetic recording." *IEEE Trans. Magnetics*, 39(4), 1871–1875, 2003.

H. Hohnson and M. Graham. 1993. *High-Speed Digital Design—A Handbook of Black Magic*, Prentice Hall PTR, Upper Saddle River, NJ, 1993.

N. Honda, K. Ouchi, and S. Iwasaki. 2002. "Design consideration of ultrahigh-density perpendicular magnetic recording media." *IEEE Trans. Magnetics*, 38(4), 1615–1621, 2002.

S. I. Hong, S. A. McKee, M. H. Salinas, R. H. Klenke, J. H. Aylor, and W. A. Wulf. 1999. "Access order and effective bandwidth for streams on a Direct Rambus memory." In Proc. Fifth Int. Symp. on High Performance Computer Architecture (HPCA'99), pp. 80–89, Orlando, FL, January 1999.

M. Horowitz, T. Indermaur, and R. Gonzalez. 1994. "Low-power digital design." In IEEE Symp. on Low Power Electronics, pp. 8–11, October 1994.

M. Horowitz, M. Martonosi, T. C. Mowry, and M. D. Smith. 1995. Informing Loads: Enabling Software to Observe and React to Memory Behavior, Technical Report CSL-TR-95-673, Stanford University, Stanford, CA.

T. R. Hotchkiss, N. D. Marschke, and R. M. McColsky. 1996. "A new memory system design for commercial and technical computing products." *The Hewlett-Packard J.*, 47 (1), Feb. 1996.

H. Hsiao and D. DeWitt. 1993. "A performance study of three high availability data storage strategies." *J. Distributed Parallel Databases*, 1(1), 53–80, 1993.

W. W. Hsu and A. J. Smith. 2004. "The real effect of i/o optimizations and disk improvements." *IBM J. Res. Dev.*, 48(2), 255–289, 2004.

W. W. Hsu, H. C. Young, and A. J. Smith. 2005. "The automatic improvement of locality in storage systems." *ACM Trans. Computers*, 23(4), 424–473, 2005.

Z. Hu, S. Kaxiras, and M. Martonosi. 2002. "Timekeeping in the memorysystem: Predicting and optimizing memory behavior." In 29th Int. Symp. on Computer Architecture (ISCA), May 2002.

Z. Hu, M. Martonosi, and S. Kaxiras. 2003. "Tag correlating prefetchers." In 9th Int. Symp. on High-Performance Computer Architecture (HPCA), February 2003.

A. S. Huang, G. Slavenberg, and J. P. Shen. 1994. "Speculative disambiguation: A compilation technique for dynamic memory disambiguation." In Proc. 21st Ann. Int. Symp. on Computer Architecture (ISCA-21), Chicago, IL, 1994.

F. Y. Huang, M. T. White, and T. Semba. 2002. "Single vs dual stage actuator—why and when." In Proc. ASME/STLE Int. Joint Tribology Conference, pp. 27–30, Cancun, Mexico, 2002.

J. Huck and J. Hays. 1993. "Architectural support for translation table management in large address space machines." In Proc. 20th Ann. Int. Symp. on Computer Architecture (ISCA'93), pp. 39–50, May 1993.

J. Huck. 1996. Personal communication.

C. J. Hughes. 2000. "Prefetching linked data structures in systems with merged DRAM-logic." Master's thesis, University of Illinois at Urbana-Champaign, May 2000. Technical Report UIUCDCS-R-2001-2221.

G. F. Hughes. 2002. "Patterned media recording systems—The potential and the problems." In Magnetics Conference, 2002. INTERMAG Europe 2002. Digest of Technical Papers, page GA6, Amsterdam, The Netherlands.

J. Huh and T. Chang. 2003. "Hierarchical disk cache management in RAID 5 controller." *J. Computing Sciences in Colleges Archive*, 19(2), 47–59, Dec. 2003.

A. Hume. 1988. "The File Motel—An incremental backup system for Unix." In Proc. Summer 1988 USENIX Conference, pp. 61–72, June 1988.

C. Huneycutt and K. Mackenzie. 2002. "Software caching using dynamic binary rewriting for embedded devices." In Proc. Int. Conf. on Parallel Processing, pp. 621–630, 2002.

I. Hur and C. Lin. 2004. "Adaptive history-based memory schedulers." In Proc. 37th Int. Symp. on Microarchitecture (MICRO), December 2004.

J. Huynh. 2003. The AMD Athlon MP Processor with 512KB L2 Cache: Technology and Performance Leadership for x86 Microprocessors. AMD White Paper, May 2003.

W. W. Hwu and P. P. Chang. 1989. "Achieving high instruction cache performance with an optimizing compiler." In Proc. 16th Ann. Int. Symp. on Computer Architecture (ISCA), pp. 242–251, Jerusalem, Israel, April 1989.

W.-M. Hwu and Y. N. Patt. 1986. "HPSm, a high performance restricted data flow architecture having minimal functionality." In Proc. 13th Ann. Int. Symp. on Computer Architecture (ISCA-13), 1986.

W.-M. W. Hwu and Y. N. Patt. 1987. "Checkpoint repair for out-of-order execution machines." In Proc. 14th Ann. Int. Symp. on Computer Architecture (ISCA-14), 1987.

P. Ibanez, V. Vinals, J. Briz, and M. Garzaran. 1998. "Characterization and improvement of load/store cache-based prefetching." In Int. Conf. on Supercomputing, pp. 369–376, July 1998.

IBM and Motorola. 1993. PowerPC 601 RISC Microprocessor User's Manual. IBM Microelectronics and Motorola.

IBM and Motorola. 1994. PowerPC 604 RISC Microprocessor User's Manual. IBM Microelectronics and Motorola.

IBM. 1981. Information Management System: Programming Reference Manual, 9th Ed., IBM, 1981.

IBM. 1998a. EDO DRAM 4M x 16 Part No. IBM0165165PT3C. http://www.chips.ibm.com/products/memory/88H2011/88H2011.pdf.

IBM. 1998b. SDRAM 1M x 16 x 4 Bank Part No. IBM0364164. http://www.chips.ibm.com/products/memory/19L3265/19L3265.pdf.

IBM. 2002a. The PowerPC 405 Embedded Processor Family. IBM Inc. Microelectronics, 2002. http://www306.ibm.com/chips/products/powerpc/processors/.

IBM. 2002b. The PowerPC 440 Embedded Processor Family. IBM Inc. Microelectronics, 2002. http://www306.ibm.com/chips/products/powerpc/processors/.

IBM. 2002c. IBM Power4 System Architecture White Paper, 2002. http://www1.ibm.com/servers/eserver/pseries/hardware/whitepapers/power4.html.

Infineon. 2001. XC-166 16-bit Embedded Family. Revised Jan. 2001. http://www.infineon.com/cmc upload/documents/036/812/c166sv2um.pdf.

J. Inouye, R. Konuru, J. Walpole, and B. Sears. 1992. The Effects of Virtually Addressed Caches on Virtual Memory Design and Performance, Technical Report CS/E 92-010, Oregon Graduate Institute.

K. Inoue, K. Kai, and K. Murakami. 1999. "Dynamically variable line-size cache exploiting high on-chip memory bandwidth of merged DRAM/logic LSIs." In Proc. Fifth Int. Symp. on High Performance Computer Architecture (HPCA'99), pp. 218–222, Orlando, FL, January 1999.

Intel. 1993. Pentium Processor User's Manual. Intel Corporation, Mt. Prospect, IL.

Intel. 1995. Pentium Pro Family Developer's Manual, Volume 3: Operating System Writer's Guide. Intel Corporation, Mt. Prospect, IL.

Intel. Intel 875P Chipset: Intel 82875P Memory Controller Hub (MCH) Datasheet. http://www.intel.com.

K. Ishibashi. 1990. "An alpha-immune 2-V supply voltage SRAM using a polysilicon PMOS load cell." *IEEE J. Solid-State Circuits*, SC-25(1), 55–60, Feb. 1990.

S. Iwasaki. 1980. "Perpendicular magnetic recording." *IEEE Trans. Magnetics*, 16(1), 71–76, 1980.

S. Iwasaki. 1984. "Perpendicular magnetic recording—Evolution and future." *IEEE Trans. Magnetics*, 20(5), 657–662, 1984.

S. Iwasaki. 2002. "Perpendicular magnetic recording focused on the origin and its significance." *IEEE Trans. Magnetics*, 38(4), 1609–1641, 2002.

A. Iyengar. 1996. "Design and performance of a general purpose software cache." *J. Parallel Distributed Computing*, 38(2), 248–255, 1996.

B. Jacob. 1994. Optimization of Storage Hierarchies," Tech. Rep. CSE-TR-228-95, University of Michigan, May 1994.

B. Jacob. 1997. "Software-Oriented Memory-Management Design." PhD Thesis, The University of Michigan, July 1997.

B. Jacob. 1998. "Software-managed caches: Architectural support for real-time embedded systems." In Proc. Int. Workshop on Compiler and Architecture Support for Embedded Systems (CASES'98), Washington, DC, December 1998.

B. Jacob. 2002a. "Virtual memory." In R. Flynn, Editor, *Computer Sciences.* Macmillan Reference USA: Farmington Hills, MI, 2002.

B. Jacob. 2002b. "Virtual memory systems and TLB structures." In V. Oklobdzija, Editor, *The Computer Engineering Handbook,* CRC Press, Boca Raton, FL, pp. 5:55–5:65, 2002.

B. Jacob. 2003. "A case for studying DRAM issues at the system level." *IEEE Micro,* 23(4), 44–56, July/Aug. 2003.

B. Jacob and S. Bhattacharyya. 2000. Real-Time Memory Management: Compile-Time Techniques and Run-Time Mechanisms that Enable the Use of Caches in Real-Time Systems, Technical Report UMIACS-TR-2000-60, University of Maryland Institute for Advanced Computer Studies (UMIACS) September 2000.

B. Jacob and S. Bhattacharyya, Editors. 2002. "Embedded systems: The memory resource." Special (and inaugural) issue of *ACM Trans. Embedded Computing Systems,* 1(1), November 2002 (continued as vol. 2, no. 1 in February 2003).

B. Jacob, P. Chen, S. Silverman, and T. Mudge. 1996. "An analytical model for designing storage hierarchies." *IEEE Trans. Computers,* 45(10), 1180–1194, Oct. 1996.

B. Jacob, P. Chen, S. Silverman, and T. Mudge. 1997. "A comment on 'An analytical model for designing memory hierarchies.'" *IEEE Trans. Computers,* 46(10), 1151, Oct. 1997.

B. Jacob and T. Mudge. 1996. Specification of the PUMA Memory Management Design, Technical Report CSE-TR-314-96, University of Michigan.

B. Jacob and T. Mudge. 1997. "Software-managed address translation." In Proc. Third IEEE Int. Symp. High Performance Computer Architecture (HPCA 1997), pp. 156–167, San Antonio, TX, February 1997.

B. Jacob and T. Mudge. 1998a. "A look at several memory-management units, TLB-refill mechanisms, and page table organizations." In Proc. Eighth Int. Conf. on

Architectural Support for Programming Languages and Operating Systems (ASPLOS'98), pp. 295–306, San Jose, CA, 1998.

B. Jacob and T. Mudge. 1998b. "Virtual memory in contemporary microprocessors." *IEEE Micro*, 18(4), 60–75, 1998.

B. Jacob and T. Mudge. 1998c. "Virtual memory: Issues of implementation." *IEEE Computer*, 31(6), 33–43, 1998.

B. Jacob and T. Mudge. 2001. "Uniprocessor virtual memory without TLBs." *IEEE Transactions on Computers*, 50(5), 482–499, May 2001.

V. Jacobson, R. Braden, and D. Borman. 1992. TCP Extensions for High Performance—Network Working Group Request for Comments 1323. May 1992.

D. Jacobson and J. Wilkes. 1991. Disk Scheduling Algorithms Based on Rotational Position, Technical Report HPCLCSP-91-7, HP Labs, Palo Alto, CA.

R. C. Jaeger. 1975. "Comments on 'An optimized output stage for MOS integrated circuits.'" *IEEE J. Solid-State Circuits*, SC-10, 185–186, June 1975.

A. Jaleel and B. Jacob. 2001a. "In-line interrupt handling for software-managed TLBs." In Proc. 19th IEEE Int. Conf. on Computer Design (ICCD 2001), pp. 62–67, Austin, TX, September 2001.

A. Jaleel and B. Jacob. 2001b. "Improving the precise interrupt mechanism of software-managed TLB miss handlers." In *High Performance Computing, Lecture Notes in Computer Science*, 2228, 282–293, 2001; B. Monien, V. Prasanna, and S. Vajapeyam, Editors, Springer Publishing, Berlin, Germany, 2001.

A. Jaleel and B. Jacob. 2005. "Using virtual load/store queues (VLSQs) to reduce the negative effects of reordered memory instructions." In Proc. 11th IEEE Int. Symp. on High Performance Computer Architecture (HPCA 2005), pp. 191–200, San Francisco, CA, February 2005.

Aamer Jaleel, Matthew Mattina, and Bruce Jacob. 2001. "Last-level cache (LLC) performance of data-mining workloads on a CMP—A case study of parallel bioinformatics workloads." In Proc. 12th International Symposium on High Performance Computer Architecture (HPCA 2006). PP. 88–98. Austin TX, February 2006.

Aamer Jaleel and Bruce Jacob. 2006. "In-line interrupt handling and lock-up free translation lookaside buffers

(TLBs)." IEEE Transactions on Computers, vol. 55, no. 5, pp. 559–574. May 2006.

J. Janzen. 2001. "Calculating memory system power for DDR SDRAM." *Micron Designline*, 10(2), 1–12, 2Q, 2001.

J. Janzen. 2004. "Calculating memory system power for DDR2." *Micron Designline*, 13(1), 1Q, 2004.

L. K. John. 2004. "More on finding a single number to indicate overall performance of a benchmark suite." *SIGARCH Computer Architectre News*, 32(1), pp. 3–8, Mar. 2004.

M. Johnson. 1991. *Superscalar Microprocessor Design*. Prentice Hall, New York, 1991.

T. L. Johnson and W.-M. W. Hwu. 1997. "Run-time adaptive cache hierarchy management via reference analysis." In Proc. 24th Ann. Int. Symp. on Computer Architecture (ISCA-24), pp. 315–326, Denver, CO, 1997.

D. Joseph and D. Grunwald. 1997. "Prefetching using Markov predictors." In Proc. 24th Int. Symp. on Computer Architecture (ISCA 1997), pp. 252–263, Denver, CO, June 1997.

N. P. Jouppi. 1990. "Improving direct-mapped cache performance by the addition of a small fully-associative cache and prefetch buffers." In Proc. 17th Ann. Int. Symp. on Computer Architecture (ISCA-17), pp. 364–373, Seattle, WA, May 1990.

N.P. Jouppi. 1993. "Cache write policies and performance." In Proc. Int. Symp. Computer Architecture (ISCA), 191–201, 1993.

T. Juan, T. Lang, and J.J. Navarro. 1997. "Reducing TLB power requirements." In Proc. 1997 IEEE Int. Symp. Low Power Electronics and Design (ISLPED'97), pp. 196–201, Monterey, CA, August 1997.

E. Jul, H. Levy, N. Hutchinson, and A. Black. 1988. "Fine-grained mobility in the Emerald system." *ACM Trans. Computer Systems*, 6(1), 109–133, 1988.

D. R. Kaeli and P. G. Emma. 1991. "Branch history table prediction of moving target branches due to subroutine returns." In Proc. 18th Ann. Int. Symp. on Computer Architecture (ISCA), 34–42, 1991.

D. Kalinsky. 1999. "A survey of task schedulers." In Embedded Systems Conf. 1999, San Jose, CA, September 1999.

H. Kalter, J. Barth, J. Dilorenzo, C. Drake, J. Fifield, W. Hovis, G. Kelley, S. Lewis, J. Nickel, C. Stapper, and J. Yankosky,

1990a. "A 50 ns 16 Mb DRAM with a 10 ns data rate." In 37th IEEE Int. Solid-State Circuits Conf. (ISSCC), pp. 232–233, San Francisco, CA, February 1990.

H. L. Kalter, C.H. Stapper, J.E. Barth, Jr., J. DiLorenzo, C.E. Drake, J.A. Fifield, G.A. Kelley, Jr., S.C. Lewis, W.B. van der Hoeven, and J.A. Yankosky. 1990b. "A 50-ns 16-Mb DRAM with a 10-ns data rate and on-chip ECC." *IEEE J. Solid-State Circuits,* 25(5), 1118–1128, Oct. 1990.

M. Kandemir, J. Ramanujam, M. J. Irwin, N. Vijaykrishnan, I. Kadayif, and A. Parikh. 2001. "Dynamic management of scratch-pad memory space." In Proc. 38th Conf. on Design Automation (DAC 2001), pp. 690–695, 2001.

G. Kane. 1996. *PA-RISC 2.0 Architecture.* Prentice Hall PTR, Upper Saddle River, NJ, 1996.

G. Kane and J. Heinrich. 1992. *MIPS RISC Architecture.* Prentice Hall, Englewood Cliffs, NJ, 1992.

C. Karabotsos. 2002. Personal communication.

M. Karlsson, F. Dahlgren, and P. Stenstrom. 2000. "A prefetching technique for irregular accesses to linked data structures." In Proc. 6th Int. Conf. on High Performance Computer Architecture (HPCA), pp. 206–217, Toulouse, France, January 2000.

K. Karplus and A. Nicolau. 1985. "Efficient hardware for multiway jumps and pre-fetches." In Proc. 18th Ann. Workshop on Microprogramming (MICRO-18), pp. 11–18, Pacific Grove, CA, December 1985.

V. Kathail, M. S. Schlansker, and B. R. Rau. 2000. HPL-PD Architecture Specification: Version 1.1, HP Laboratories Technical Report HPL-93-80(R.1), Palo Alto, CA, February 2000.

S. Kaxiras, Z. Hu, and M. Martonosi. 2001. "Cache decay: Exploiting generational behavior to reduce cache leakage power." In Proc. 28th Int. Symp. on Computer Architecture (ISCA-28), pp. 240–251, Göteborg, Sweden, June 2001.

K. Keeton et al. 1998. "Performance characterization of a quad Pentium Pro SMP using OLTP workloads." In Proc. Int. Symp. Computer Architecture (ISCA), 25, June 1998, pp. 15–26.

P. Keleher, A. L. Cox, and W. Zwaenepoel. 1992. "Lazy release consistency for software distributed shared memory." In Proc. 19th Ann. Int. Symp. on Computer Architecture (ISCA), pp. 13–21, May 1992.

P. Keleher, S. Dwarkadas, A. Cox, and W. Zwaenepoel. 1994. "TreadMarks: Distributed shared memory on standard workstations and operating systems." In Proc. 1994 Winter Usenix Conf., pp. 115–131, January 1994.

M. Kellogg. 2002. Personal communication.

C. N. Keltcher. 2002. "The AMD Hammer Processor Core." Presentation given at HotChips 14. August 2002.

R. E. Kessler and M. D. Hill. 1992. "Page placement algorithms for large real-indexed caches." *ACM Trans. Comput. Syst,* 10(4), 338–359, Nov. 1992.

Y. A. Khalidi, M. Talluri, M. N. Nelson, and D. Williams. 1993. "Virtual memory support for multiple page sizes." In Proc. Fourth Workshop on Workstation Operating Systems, 1993.

Y. A. Khalidi and M. Talluri. 1995. Improving the Address Translation Performance of Widely Shared Pages, Technical Report SMLI TR-95-38, Sun Microsystems.

T. Kilburn, D. B. G. Edwards, M. J. Lanigan, and F. H. Sumner. 1962. "One-level storage system." *IRE Trans. Electronic Computers,* EC-11(2), 223–235, April 1962.

M. V. Kim. 1986. "Synchronized disk interleaving." *IEEE Trans. Computers,* C-35 (11), 978–988, November 1986.

C. Kim, D. Burger, and S.W. Keckler. 2002. "An adaptive, non-uniform cache structure for wire-delay dominated on-chip caches." In Proc. Int. Conf. Architectural Support for Programming Languages and Operating Systems (ASPLOS-10), pp. 211–222, San Jose, CA, December 2002.

N. S. Kim et al. 2004a. "Circuit and microarchitectural techniques for reducing cache leakage power." *IEEE J. Solid-State Circuits,* 12(2), 167–184, Feb. 2004.

Y. I. Kim, K. H. Yang, and W. S. Lee. 2004b. "Thermal degradation of DRAM retention time: Characterization and improving techniques." In Proc. 42nd Ann. Int. Reliability Physics Symposium, pp. 667–668, 2004.

N. S. Kim et al. 2004c. "Circuit and microarchitectural techniques for reducing cache leakage power." *IEEE J. Solid-State Circuits,* 12(2), 167–184, Feb. 2004.

J. Kin, M. Gupta and W. Mangione-Smith. 1997. "The filter cache: An energy efficient memory structure." In Proc. 30th Ann. Int. Symp. on Microarchitecture (MICRO'97), pp. 184–193, Research Triangle Park, NC, December 1997.

J. Kin, M. Gupta, and W. H. Mangione-Smith. 2000. "Filtering memory references to increase energy efficiency." *IEEE Trans. Computers,* 49(1), 1–15, Jan. 2000.

D. B. Kirk. 1989. "SMART (strategic memory allocation for real-time) cache design." In Proc. IEEE Symp. on Real-Time Systems (RTSS), pp. 229–237, December 1989.

A. C. Klaiber and H. M. Levy. 1991. "An architecture for software-controlled data prefetching." In Proc. 18th Int. Symp. on Computer Architecture (ISCA), pp. 43–53, Toronto, Canada, May 1991.

L. Kleinrock. 1975. *Queueing Systems Volume 1: Theory*. John Wiley & Sons, Hoboken, NJ, 1975.

J. Knight. 1976. "CASHEW—A proposed permanent data storage system." Computer Center Report, Lawrence Berkeley Laboratory, May 1976.

D. E. Knuth. 1963. "Computer-drawn flowcharts." *Commun. ACM*, 6(9), 555–563, Sep. 1963.

D. E. Knuth. 1973. *The Art of Computer Programming—Volume 3 (Sorting and Searching)*. Addison-Wesley, Reading, MA, 1973.

U. Ko, P. T. Balsara, and A. K. Nanda. 1998. "Energy optimization of multilevel cache architectures for RISC and CISC processors." *IEEE Trans. Very Large Scale Integr. Syst*, 6(2), 299–308, June 1998.

P. Kohout, B. Ganesh, and B. Jacob. 2003. "Hardware support for real-time operating systems." In Proc. First IEEE/ACM/IFIP Int. Conf. on Hardware/Software Codesign and System Synthesis (CODES+ISSS 2003), pp. 45–51, Newport Beach, CA, October 2003.

K. Korner. 1990. "Intelligent caching for remote file service." In Proc. Tenth Int. Conf. on Distributed Computer Systems, pp. 220–226, IEEE Press, New York, 1990.

D. F. Kotz and C. S. Ellis. 1990. "Prefetching in file systems for MIMD multiprocessors." *IEEE Trans. Parallel Distributing Syst*. 1(2), 218–230. Apr. 1990.

D. Koufaty and J. Torrellas. 1998. "Comparing data forwarding and prefetching for communication-induced misses in shared-memory MPs." In Int. Conf. on Supercomputing, pp. 53–60, July 1998.

C. Kozyrakis, S. Perissakis, D. Patterson, T. Anderson, K. Asanovic, N. Cardwell, R. Fromm, J. Golbus, B. Gribstad, K. Keeton, R. Thomas, N. Treuhaft, and K. Yelick. 1997. "Scalable processors in the billion-transistor era: IRAM." *IEEE Computer*, 30(9), 75–78, Sept. 1997.

T. M. Kroeger and D. D. E. Long. 1996. "Predicting file system actions from prior events." In Proc. USENIX 1996 Technical Conference, pp. 319–328, San Diego, CA, January 1996.

D. Kroft. 1981. "Lockup-free instruction fetch/prefetch cache organization." In Proc. 8th Int. Symp. on Computer Architecture (ISCA), pp. 81–87, May 1981.

A. Kumar. 1996. "The HP PA-8000 RISC CPU: A high performance out-of-order processor." In Hot Chips 8: A Symp. on High-Performance Chips, Stanford, CA. http://infopad.eecs.berkeley.edu/HotChips8/.

J. J. Labrosse. 1999. *MicroC/OS-II: The Real-Time Kernel*. R&D Books (Miller Freeman, Inc.), Lawrence, KS, 1999.

A. Lai, C. Fide, and B. Falsafi. 2001. "Dead-block prediction and dead-block correlating prefetchers." In The 28th Int. Symp. on Computer Architecture (ISCA), pp. 144–154, June 2001.

L. Lamport. 1979. "How to make a multiprocessor computer that correctly executes multiprocess programs." *IEEE Trans. Computers*, C-28(9), 690–691, 1979.

D. Landskov, S. Davidson, B. Shriver, and P. W. Mallett. 1980. "Local microcode compaction techniques." *ACM Computing Surveys*, 12(3), 261–294. Sept. 1980.

P. Lapsley, J. Bier, A. Shoham, and E. A. Lee. 1994. *DSP Processor Fundamentals: Architectures and Features*. Berkeley Design Technology, Inc., Berkeley, CA, 1994.

P. Lapsley, J. Bier, A. Shoham, and E. A. Lee. 1997. *DSP Processor Fundamentals*. IEEE Press, Piscataway, NJ, 1997.

E. Larson and T. Austin. 2000. "Compiler controlled value prediction using branch predictor based confidence." In Proc. 33th Ann. Int. Symp. on Microarchitecture (MICRO-33), IEEE Computer Soc., Los Alamitos, CA, December 2000.

E. Larson, S. Chatterjee, and T. Austin. 2001. "The MASE Microarchitecture Simulation Environment" 2001 IEEE Int. Symp. Performance Analysis of Systems and Software (ISPASS-2001), June 2001.

T. Laskodi, B. Eifrig, and J. Gait. 1988. "A UNIX file system for a write-once optical disk." In Proc. Summer 1988 USENIX Conf., pp. 51–60, June 1988.

LCTES Panel. 2003. "Compilation challenges for network processors." Industrial Panel, ACM Conf. Languages, Compilers and Tools for Embedded Systems (LCTES), June 2003.

F. F. Lee. 1960. "Study of 'look aside' memory." *IEEE Trans. Computers*, 18(11), 1062–1064, Nov. 1960.

J. Lee and A. J. Smith. 1984. "Branch prediction strategies and branch target buffer design." *IEEE Computer,* 17(1), 6–22, Jan. 1984.

E. A. Lee and D. G. Messerschmitt. 1987. "Synchronous dataflow." *Proc. IEEE,* 75(9), 1235–1245, 1987.

C. C. Lee, I. C. Chen, and T. Mudge. 1997a. "The bi-mode branch predictor." In Proc. 30th Ann. Int. Symp. on Microarchitecture (MICRO-30), pp. 4–13, Research Triangle Park, NC, December 1997.

C. Lee, M. Potkonjak, and W. Mangione-Smith. 1997b. "MediaBench: A tool for evaluating and synthesizing multimedia and communications systems." In Proc. 30th Ann. Int. Symp. on Microarchitecture (MICRO'97), pp. 330–335, Research Triangle Park, NC, December 1997.

H.-H. Lee and G. Tyson. 2000. "Region-based caching: An energy-delay efficient memory architecture for embedded processors." In Proc. Int. Conf. on Compilers, Architectures, and Synthesis for Embedded Systems (CASES 2000), pp. 120–127, San Jose, CA, November 2000.

T. Lee. 2002. Personal communication.

S. J. Leffler, M. K. McKusick, M. J. Karels, and J. S. Quarterman. 1989. *The Design and Implementation of the 4.3BSD UNIX Operating System.* Addison-Wesley, Reading, MA, 1989.

C. Lefurgy, P. Bird, I.-C. Chen, and T. Mudge. 1997. "Improving code density using compression techniques." In Proc. 30th Ann. Int. Symp. on Microarchitecture (MICRO 1997), pp. 194–203, Research Triangle Park, NC, December 1997.

K. Li and P. Hudak. 1986. "Memory coherence in shared virtual memory systems." In Proc. Fifth Ann. ACM Symp. on Principles of Distributed Computing, Calgary, Alberta, Canada, August 11–13, 1986.

K. Li and P. Hudak. 1989. "Memory coherence in shared virtual memory systems." *ACM Trans. Comput. Syst.,* 7(4), 321–359, Nov. 1989.

Y. Li, M. Potkonjak, and W. Wolf. 1997. "Real-time operating systems for embedded computing." In Int. Conf. on Computer Design (ICCD), Austin, TX, October 1997.

J. Liedtke. 1993. "Improving IPC by kernel design." In Proc. Fourteenth ACM Symp. on Operating Systems Principles (SOSP-14), pp. 175–187, 1993.

J. Liedtke. 1995a. "Address space sparsity and fine granularity." *ACM Operating Systems Rev.,* 29(1), 87–90, 1995.

J. Liedtke. 1995b. "On micro-kernel construction." In Proc. Fifteenth ACM Symp. on Operating Systems Principles (SOSP-15), 1995.

J. Liedtke and K. Elphinstone. 1996. "Guarded page tables on MIPS R4600." *ACM Operating Systems Rev.,* 30(1), 4–15, 1996.

C. Liema, F. Nacabal, C. Valderrama, P. Paulin, and A. Jerraya. 1997. "System-on-a-chip cosimulation and compilation." *IEEE Design Test Computers,* 14(2), 16–25, April–June 1997.

W. Lin, S. Reinhardt, and D. Burger. 2001. "Reducing DRAM latencies with an integrated memory hierarchy design." In Proc. 7th Int. Symp. on High-Performance Computer Architecture (HPCA), January 2001.

F. J. List. 1986. The Static Noise Margin of SRAM Cells, ESSCIRC Dig. Tech. Papers, Sept. 1986, pp. 16–18, 1986.

J. W. S. Liu. 2000. *Real-Time Systems.* Prentice Hall, Upper Saddle River, NJ, 2000.

J. Lohstroh, E. Seevinck, and J. de Groot. 1983. "Worst-case static noise margin criteria for logic circuits and their mathematical equivalence." *IEEE J. Solid-State Circuits,* SC-18(6), 803–807, Dec. 1983.

T. C. Lowe. 1968. "The influence of data base characteristics and usage on direct access file organization." *J. ACM,* 15(4), 535–548, Oct. 1968.

T. C. Lowe. 1969. "Analysis of Boolean program models for time-shared, paged environments." *Commun. ACM,* 12(4), 199–205, April 1969.

T. C. Lowe. 1970. "Automatic segmentation of cyclic program structures based on connectivity and processor timing." *Commun. ACM,* 13(1), 3–6, Jan. 1970.

E. S. Lowry and C. W. Medlock. 1969. "Object code optimization." *Commun. ACM,* 12(1), 13–22, Jan. 1969.

C.-K. Luk and T. C. Mowry. 1996. "Compiler-based prefetching for recursive data structures." In Proc. Seventh Int. Conf. on Architectural Support for Programming Languages and Operating Systems (ASPLOS), pp. 222–233, Cambridge, MA, October 1996.

C.-K. Luk and T. C. Mowry. 1998. "Cooperative instruction prefetching in modern processors." In Proc. 31st Ann.

ACM/IEEE Int. Symp. on Microarchitecture (MICRO), pp. 182–194, November 30–December 2, 1998.

A. Luotonen and K. Altis. 1994. "World-wide Web proxies." *Computer Networks ISDN Systems*, 27(2), 147–154, November 1994.

J. E. MacDonald and K. L. Sigworth. 1975. "Storage hierarchy optimization procedure." *IBM J. Res. Dev.*, 133–140, March 1975.

J. Macri. 2002. Personal communication.

K. Mai et al. 1998. "Low-power SRAM design using half-swing pulse-mode techniques." *IEEE J. Solid-State Circuits*, 33(11), 1659–1670, November 1998.

A. Malik, B. Moyer, and D. Cermak. 2000. "A low power unified cache architecture providing power and performance flexibility." In Proc. Int. Symp. on Low Power Electronics and Design (ISLPED), pp. 241–243, Rapallo, Italy, June 2000.

M. Mamidipaka and N. Dutt. 2004. eCACTI: An Enchanced Power Estimation Model for On-Chip Caches, Center for Embedded Computer Systems, Technical Report TR 04-28, Oct. 2004.

A. A. Mamun, G. Guo, and B. Chao. 2006. *Hard Disk Drive*. CRC Press, Boca Raton, FL, 2006.

B. A. Marron and P. A. de Maine. 1967. "Automatic data compression." *Commun. ACM*, 10(11), 711–715, Nov. 1967.

R. E. Matick and S. E. Schuster. 2005. "Logic-based eDRAM: Origins and rationale for use." *IBM J. Res. Dev.*, 49(1), 145–165, 2005.

Matlab 6.1. 2001. The Math Works, Inc., 2001. http://www.mathworks.com/products/matlab/.

R. L. Mattson, J. Gecsei, D. R. Slutz, and I. L. Traiger. 1970. "Evaluation techniques for storage hierarchies." *IBM Syst. J.*, 9(2), 78–117, 1970.

R. Mattson and S. Ng. 1992. "Maintaining good performance in disk arrays during failure via uniform parity group distribution." In Proc. 1st Int. Symp. on High Performance Distributed Commmputing, pp. 260–269, Syracuse, NY, 1992.

R. L. Mattson and S. Ng. 1993. Method and Means for Managing DASD Array Accesses when Operating in Degraded Mode. US Patent No. 5265098. U.S. Patent and Trademark Office.

T. May and M. Woods. 1978. "A new physical mechanism for soft errors in dynamic memories." In Proc. Sixteenth Int. Reliability Physical Symp., April 1978.

C. May, E. Silha, R. Simpson, and H. Warren, Editors. 1994. *The PowerPC Architecture: A Specification for a New Family of RISC Processors*. Morgan Kaufmann, San Francisco, CA, 1994.

J. McCalpin. 2000. "An industry perspective on performance characterization: Applications vs benchmarks." Keynote address at Third Ann. IEEE Workshop on Workload Characterization, Austin TX, September 16, 2000.

J. McCalpin. STREAM: Sustainable Bandwidth in High Performance Computers. http://www.cs.virginia.edu/stream/.

J. McCarthy. 1960. "Recursive functions of symbolic expressions and their computation by machine, Part I." *Commun. ACM*, 3(4), 184–195, Apr. 1960.

S. McFarling. 1989. "Program optimization for instruction caches." In Proc. Third Int. Conf. on Architectural Support for Programming Languages and Operating Systems (ASPLOS-1989), pp. 183–191, 1989.

S. McFarling. 1991. Cache Replacement with Dynamic Exclusion, WRL Technical Note TN-22, Digital Western Research Laboratory, November 1991. (Note: later published in ISCA, see McFarling [1992].)

S. McFarling. 1992. "Cache replacement with dynamic exclusion." In Proc. 19th Ann. Int. Symp. on Computer Architecture (ISCA '92), pp. 191–200, Queensland, Australia, May 19–21, 1992, ACM Press, New York, 1992. DOI= http://doi.acm.org/10.1145/139669.139727.

S. McKee. 1994. Dynamic Access Ordering: Bounds on Memory Bandwidth, Technical Report CS-94-38, University of Virginia, October 1994.

S. A. McKee and W. A. Wulf. 1995. "Access ordering and memory-conscious cache utilization." In Proc. Int. Symp. on High Performance Computer Architecture (HPCA'95), pp. 253–262, Raleigh, NC, January 1995.

S. McKee et al. 1996a. "Design and evaluation of dynamic access ordering hardware." In Proc. Int. Conf. on Supercomputing, May 1996.

S. McKee, A. Aluwihare, B. Clark, R. Klenke, T. Landon, C. Oliver, M. Salinas, A. Szymkowiak, K. Wright, W. Wulf, and J. Aylor. 1996b. "Design and evaluation of dynamic access ordering hardware." In Proc. Int. Conf. on Supercomputing, Philadelphia, PA, May 1996.

W. McKee et al. 1996c. "Cosmic ray neutron induced upsets as a major contributor to the soft error rate of current and future generation DRAMs." In Proc. Int. Reliability Physical Symp., 1996.

Mcore. 1997. M-CORE Reference Manual. Motorola Literature Distribution, Denver, CO, 1997.

Mcore. 1998. M-CORE MMC2001 Reference Manual. Motorola Literature Distribution, Denver, CO, 1998.

C. D. Mee and E. D. Daniel, Editors. 1996. *Magnetic Recording Technology*. McGraw-Hill, New York, 1996.

J. Mellor-Crummey, D. Whalley, and K. Kennedy. 1999. "Improving memory hierarchy performance for irregular applications." In Proc. 13th Int. Conf. on Supercomputing (ICS '99), pp. 425–433, Rhodes, Greece, June 20–25, 1999, ACM Press, New York, 1999.

S. W. Melvin, M. C. Shebanow, and Y. N. Patt. 1988. "Hardware support for large atomic units in dynamically scheduled machines." In Proc. 21st Ann. Int. Symp. on Microarchitecture (MICRO-21), pp. 60–63, San Diego, CA, November 1988.

J. M. Menon, R. L. Mattson, and S. Ng. 1993. Method and Means for Distributed Sparing in DASD Arrays. US Patent No. 5258984. U.S. Patent and Trademark Office.

M. Mesnier, G. R. Ganger, and E. Riedel. 2003. "Object-based storage." *IEEE Commun.* Magazine, 41(8), 84–90, 2003.

Micron. 1995. 1 Gbit DDR2 SDRAM Device Datasheet, Micron Inc.

Micron. 2005. *240-Pin 512MB/1GB/2GB DDR2 SDRAM FBDIMM (DR FB x72) Features*, April 2005.

Micron. 2006. *1Gb: x4,x8,x16 DDR SDRAM Features*, January 2006.

M. A. Milne. 1971. "CLUSTR: A program for structuring design problems." In Proc. 8th Workshop on Design Automation (DAC '71), Atlantic City, New Jersey, United States, June 28–30, 1971, 242–249, ACM Press, New York, 1971.

O. Minato et al. 1987. "A 42 ns 1Mb CMOS SRAM." *ISSCC Dig. Tech. Papers*, Feb., 260–261, 1987.

J. Mitchell, J. Gibbons, G. Hamilton, P. Kessler, Y. Khalidi, P. Kougiouris, P. Madany, M. Nelson, M. Powell, and S. Radia. 1994. "An overview of the Spring system." In Proc. IEEE Compcon, 1994.

N. Mitchell, L. Carter, and J. Ferrante. 1999. "Localizing non-affine array references." In Proc. Int. Conf. on Parallel Architectures and Compilation Techniques, Newport Beach, LA, October 1999.

O. Mock and C. J. Swift. 1959. "The Share 709 system: Programmed input-output buffering." *J. ACM (JACM)*, 6(2), 145–151, April 1959.

J. C. Mogul. 1996. "Hinted caching in the Web." In Proc. Seventh ACM SIGOPS European Workshop, pp. 103–108, Connemara, Ireland, September 1996.

J. Montanaro et al. 1996. "A 160-MHz, 32-b, 0.5-W CMOS RISC microprocessor." *JSSC*, 31(11), 1703–1714, Nov. 1996.

Y. Mori, R.-I. Yamada, S. Kamohara, M. Moniwa, K. Ohyu, and T. Yamanaka. 2001. "A new method for predicting distribution of DRAM retention time." In Proc. 39th Ann. Int. Reliability Physics Symposium, pp. 7–11, 2001.

Y. Mori, K. Ohyu, K. Okonogi, and R.-I. Yamada. 2005. "The origins of variable retention time in DRAM." In Int. Electron Devices Meeting Technical Digest, pp. 1057–1060, 2005.

C. A. Moritz, M. Frank, and S. Amarasinghe. 2000. "FlexCache: A framework for flexible compiler generated data caching." In The 2nd Workshop on Intelligent Memory Systems, Boston, MA, November 12, 2000.

J. E. B. Moss. 1992. "Working with persistent objects: To swizzle or not to swizzle." *IEEE Trans. Software Eng.*, 18(8), 657–673, Aug. 1992.

Motorola/Freescale. 2002a. Coldfire MCF5206E 32-bit CPU. Motorola/Freescale, Revised 2002. http://www.freescale.com/files/dsp/doc/fact sheet/CFPRODFACT.pdf.

Motorola/Freescale. 2002b. MPC500 32-bit MCU Family. Motorola/Freescale, Revised July 2002. http://www.freescale.com/files/-microcontrollers/doc/fact sheet/MPC500FACT.pdf.

Motorola/Freescale. 2003. Dragonball MC68SZ328 32-bit Embedded CPU. Motorola/Freescale, Revised April 2003. http://www.freescale.com/files/32bit/doc/fact sheet/MC68SZ328FS.pdf.

M. Moudgill and S. Vassiliadis. 1996. "Precise interrupts." *IEEE Micro*, 16(1), 58–67, Feb. 1996.

T. Mowry and A. Gupta. 1991. "Tolerating latency through software-controlled prefetching in shared-memory multiprocessors." *J. Parallel Distributed Computing,* 12(2), 87–106, June 1991.

T. Mowry, M. Lam, and A. Gupta. 1992. "Design and evaluation of a compiler algorithm for prefetching." In Proc. 5th Int. Conf. on Architectural Support for Programming Languages and Operating Systems (ASPLOS-V), pp. 62–73, Boston, MA, October 1992.

T. C. Mowry. 1994. Tolerating Latency Through Software-Controlled Data Prefetching, PhD Thesis. Technical report, Stanford University, Stanford, CA, March 1994.

T. Mowry. 1998. "Tolerating latency in multiprocessors through compiler-inserted prefetching." *Trans. Comput. Syst.,* 16(1), 55–92, Feb. 1998.

F. Mueller. 1995. "Compiler support for software-based cache partitioning." In Proc. ACMSIGPLAN 1995 Workshop on Languages, compilers, & Tools for Real-Time Systems, pp. 125–133, ACM Press, New York, 1995.

J. M. Mulder, N. T. Quach, and M. J. Flynn. 1991. "An area model for on-chip memories and its application." *IEEE J. Solid-State Circuits,* 26(2), 98–106, 1991.

J. E. Mulford and R. K. Ridall. 1971. "Data compression techniques for economic processing of large commercial files." In Proc. 1971 Int. ACM SIGIR Conf. on Information Storage and Retrieval (SIGIR '71), pp. 207–215, College Park, Maryland, April 01–02, 1971, ACM Press, New York, 1971.

R. B. Mulvany and L. H. Thompson. 1981. "Innovations in disk file manufacturing." *IBM J.* Res. Dev., 25(5), 663–675, 1981.

C. D. Murta, V. Almeida, and W. Meira, Jr. 1998. "Analyzing performance of partitioned caches for the WWW." Proc. 3rd Int. WWW Caching Workshop, June 1998.

D. Nagle. 1995. Personal communication.

D. Nagle, R. Uhlig, T. Stanley, S. Sechrest, T. Mudge, and R. Brown. 1993. "Design tradeoffs for software-managed TLBs." In Proc. 20th Ann. Int. Symp. on Computer Architecture (ISCA-20), 1993.

D. Nagle, R. Uhlig, T. Mudge, and S. Sechrest. 1994. "Optimal allocation of on-chip memory for multiple-API operating systems." In Proc. 21st Ann. Int. Symp. on Computer Architecture (ISCA-1994), pp. 358–369, 1994.

R. Nair. xprof/xtrace —An RS/6000 Xwindows-Based Tracing and Profiling Package, Technical report, IBM T. J. Watson Research Lab.

R. Nair. 1996. "Profiling IBM RS/6000 applications." *Int. J. Computer Simulation,* 6(1), 101–112, 1996.

R. Nair and M. E. Hopkins. 1997. "Exploiting instruction level parallelism in processors by caching scheduled groups." In Proc. 24th Ann. Int. Symp. on Computer Architecture (ISCA-24), pp. 13–25, Denver, CO, 1997.

K. Nakamura. 1997. "A 500-MHz 4-Mb CMOS pipeline-burst cache SRAM with point-to-point noise reduction coding I/O." *IEEE J. Solid-State Circuits,* 32(11), 1758–1765, Nov. 1997.

H. Nambu et al. 1998a. "A 1.8-ns access, 550MHz, 4.5-Mb CMOS SRAM." *IEEE J. Solid-State Circuits,* 33(11), 1650–1658, Nov. 1998.

H. Nambu et al. 1998b. "A 1.8 ns access, 550 MHz 4.5 Mb CMOS SRAM." In 1998 IEEE Int. Solid State Circuits Conf. Dig. *Tech. Papers,* pp. 360–361, 1998.

C. Natarajan, B. Christenson, and F. Briggs. 2004. "A study of performance impact of memory controller features in multi-processor server environment." In Proc. 3rd Workshop on Memory Performance Issues (WMPI-2004), 2004.

B. Nayfeh et al. 1996a. "Evaluation of design alternatives for a multiprocessor microprocessor." Int. Symp. on Computer Architecture (ISCA-23), pp. 67–77, May 1996.

B. A. Nayfeh et al. 1996b. "The impact of shared-cache clustering in small-scale shared-memory multiprocessors." Int. Symp. High Performance Computer Architecture (HPCA-2), pp. 74–84, February 1996.

M. Nelson, B. Welch, and J. Ousterhout. 1988. "Caching in the Sprite Network File System." *ACM Trans. Comput. Syst.,* 6(1), 134–154, Feb. 1988.

S. Ng. 2006. Personal communication.

S. Ng. 1986. "Reliability and availability of duplex systems: Some simple models." *IEEE Trans. Reliability, R-,* 35(3), 295–300, 1986.

S. Ng. 1987. "Reliability availability and performance analysis of duplex disks systems." In Proc. IASTED Int. Symp. on Reliability and Control, pp. 5–9, Paris, France, 1987.

S. Ng. 1989. "Some design issues of disk arrays." In CompCon Spring89, pp. 137–142, San Francisco, CA, 1989.

R. Ng, C. Faloutsos, and T. Sellis. 1991. "Flexible buffer allocation based on marginal gains." In Proc. 1991 ACM SIGMOD Int. Conf. on Management of Data (SIGMOD '91), pp. 387–396, Denver, Colorado, United States, May 29–31, 1991, J. Clifford and R. King, Eds., ACM Press, New York, 1991.

S. Ng. 1991. "Improving disk performance via latency reduction." *IEEE Trans. Computers,* 40(1), 22–30, 1991.

S. Ng. 1994a. "Crosshatch disk array for improved reliability and performance." In Proc. 21st Int. Symp. on Computer Architecture (ISCA), pp. 255–264, Chicago, IL, 1994.

S. Ng. 1994b. Method and Means for Optimally Accessing Data Residing on Dual Actuator DASDs. US Patent No. 5341351. U.S. Patent and Trademark Office.

S. Ng. 1994c. "Sparing for redundant disk arrays." *Distributed Parallel Databases,* 2(2), 133–149, 1994.

S. Ng. 1995. Two-Dimensional Disk Array. US Patent No. 5412661. U.S. Patent and Trademark Office.

S. Ng. 1998. "Advances in disk technology: Performance issues." *Computers,* pp. 75–81, 1998.

S. Ng. 1999. System for Handling Missed Revolution in a Disk Drive by Aborting the Execution of Primary Command and Executing Secondary Command if a Missed Revolution Occurs. US Patent No. 5991825. U.S. Patent and Trademark Office.

S. Ng. 2001a. Method of System for Determining the Data Layout Geometry of a Disk Drive. US Patent No. 6237070. U.S. Patent and Trademark Office.

S. Ng. 2001b. Method of System for Determining the Data Layout Geometry of a Disk Drive. US Patent No. 6253279. U.S. Patent and Trademark Office.

S. Ng. and R. Mattson. 1994. "Uniform parity group distribution in disk arrays with multiple failures." *IEEE Trans. Computers,* 43(4), 501–506, 1994.

S. Ng. 2006. Personal communcation.

A. Nicolau. 1989. "Run-time disambiguation: Coping with statically unpredictable dependencies." *IEEE Trans. Computers,* 38(5), 663–678, 1989.

J. Nievergelt. 1965. "On the automatic simplification of computer programs." *Commun. ACM,* 8(6), 366–370, June 1965.

K. Noda et al. 1998. "A 1.9 um2 loadless CMOS four-transistor SRAM cell in a 0.18um2 logic technology." *IEDM Tech. Dig.,* 847–850, 1998.

Y. Nunomura et al. 1997. "M32R/D—Integrating DRAM and microprocessor." *IEEE Micro,* 17(6), 40–48, Nov. 1997.

NVIDIA. Technical Brief: NVIDIA nForce Integrated Graphics Processor (IGP) and Dynamic Adaptive Speculative Pre-Processor (DASP). http://www.nvidia.com/.

E. I. Organick. 1972. *The Multics System: An Examination of Its Structure.* The MIT Press, Cambridge, MA, 1972.

K. Osada et al. 2001. "Universal-Vdd 0.65-2.0V 32-kB cache using a voltage-adapted timing-generation scheme and a lithographically symmetrical cell." *IEEE J. Solid-State Circuits,* 36(111), 1738–1744, Nov. 2001.

R. Oswald. 1974. "Design of a disk file head-positioning servo." *IBM J. Res. Dev.,* 18, 506–512, 1974.

N. K. Ouchi. 1978. System for Recovering Data Stored in Failed Memory Unit. US Patent No. 4092732. U.S. Patent and Trademark Office.

A. O'Donnell. 2002. Personal communication.

C. W. Padgett and F. L. Newman. 1974. Memory Clocking System. US Patent Number 3,943,496. U.S. Patent and Trademark office, Submitted on September 9, 1974.

V. N. Padmanabhan and J. C. Mogul. 1996. "Using predictive prefetching to improve World Wide Web latency." *Computer Commun. Rev.,* 26(3), 22–39, July 1996.

S. Palacharla and R. Kessler. 1994. "Evaluating Stream Buffers as a Secondary Cache Replacement." In The 21st Int. Symp. on Computer Architecture (ISCA), pp. 24–33, April 1994.

S. Palacharla, N. P. Jouppi, and J. E. Smith. 1996. Quantifying the complexity of superscalar processors, Technical Report CS-TR-96-1328, university of Wisconsin, Madison November 19, 1996.

P. R. Panda, N. D. Dutt, and A. Nicolau. 2000. "On-chip vs. off-chip memory: The data partitioning problemin embedded processor-based systems." *ACM Trans. Design Automation Electronic Systems,* 5(3), July 2000.

H. C. Park et al. 1998. "A 833-Mb/s 2.5-V 4-Mb double-date-rate SRAM," In 1998 IEEE Int. Solid State Circuits Conf. Dig. Tech. Papers, pp. 356–357, 1998.

Y. Park and B. Goldberg. 1992. "Escape analysis on lists." In Proc. ACM SIGPLAN1992 Conf. on Programming

Language Design and Implementation (PLDI), pp. 116–127, ACM Press, New York, 1992.

D. Patterson, G. Gibson, and R. H. Katz. 1988. "A case for redundant arrays of inexpensive disks (RAID)." In Proc. ACM SIGMOD Conf. pp. 109–116, Chicago, IL, 1988.

R. H. Patterson, G. Gibson, E. Ginting, D. Stodolsky, and J. Zelenka. 1995. "Informed prefetching and caching." In Proc. 15th Symp. on Operating Systems Principles (SOSP), pp. 79–95, Copper Mountain, CO, December, 1995.

M. Pechura. 1982. "File archival techniques using data compression." *Commun. ACM*, 25(9), 605–609, Sept. 1982.

M. Peckerar, R. Fulton, P. Blaise, and D. Brown. 1979. "Radiation effects in MOS devices caused by X-ray and e-beam lithography," *J. Vacuum Science Technology*, 16(6), 1658–1661, November–December 1979.

M. C. Peckerar, C. M. Dozier, D. B. Brown, and D. Patterson. 1982. "Radiation effects introduced by X-ray lithography in MOS devices." *IEEE Trans. Nuclear Science*, 29(6), 1697–1701, Dec. 1982.

A. Peleg and U. Weiser. 1995. Dynamic Flow Instruction Cache Memory Organized around Trace Segments Independent of Virtual Address Line. US Patent No. 5,381,533, U.S. Patent Office.

T. Pering and R. Broderson. 1998. "The simulation and evaluation of dynamic voltage scaling algorithms." In Proc. Int. Symp. on Low-Power Electronics and Design (ISLPED'98), June 1998.

T. Pering, T. Burd, and R. Brodersen. 1998. "Dynamic voltage scaling and the design of a low-power microprocessor system." In Power Driven Microarchitecture Workshop, attached to ISCA98, 1998.

T. Pering, T. Burd, and R. Broderson. 2000. "Voltage scheduling in the lpARM microprocessor system." In Proc. Int. Symp. on Low-Power Electronics and Design (ISLPED'00), pp. 96–101, July 2000.

K. Pettis and R. C. Hansen. 1990. "Profile guided code positioning." In Proc. ACM SIGPLAN 1990 Conf. on Programming Language Design and Implementation (PLDI '90), pp. 16–27; White Plains, New York, ACM Press, New York, 1990.

P. J. Fleming and J. J. Wallace. 1986. "How not to lie with statistics: The correct way to summarize benchmark results." *CACM*, 29(3), 218–221, March 1986.

J. E. Pierce. 1995. "Cache behavior in the presence of speculative execution: the benefits of misprediction." Doctoral Thesis. The University of Michigan.

J. Pierce and T. Mudge. 1996. "Wrong-path instruction prefetching." In Proc. 29th Ann. ACM/IEEE Int. Symp. on Microarchitecture Paris, France, December 02–04, 1996, pp. 165–175, Int. Symp. on Microarchitecture (MICRO), IEEE Computer Society, Washington, DC, 1996.

E. Pinheiro, W.-D. Weber, and L. A. Barroso. 2007. "Failure trends in a large disk-drive population." In Proc. Fifth USENIX Conf. on File and Storage Technoligies (FAST 2007), San Jose, CA, February 2007.

A. R. Pleszkun, J. R. Goodman, W.-C. Hsu, R. T. Joersz, G. Bier, P. Woest, and P. B. Schechter. 1987. "WISQ: A restartable architecture using queues." In Proc. 14th Ann. Int. Symp. on Computer Architecture (ISCA-14), 1987.

S. Podlipnig and L. Böszörményi. 2003. "A survey of Web cache replacement strategies." *ACM Computing Surveys*, 35(4), 374–398, 2003.

F. J. Pollack, K. C. Kahn, and R. M. Wilkinson. 1981. "The iMAX-432 object filing system." In Proc. Eighth ACM Symp. on Operating Systems Principles (SOSP '81), pp. 137–147, Pacific Grove, CA, December 14–16, 1981, ACM Press, New York, 1981.

J. Pomerene, T. Puzak, R. Rechtschaffen, and F. Sparacio. 1989. Prefetching System for a Cache Having a Second Directory for Sequentially Accessed Blocks. US Patent 4,807,110. U.S. Patent office, February 1989, filed April 1984.

M. A. Postiff and T. Mudge. 1999. Smart Register Files for High-Performance Microprocessors, Technical Report no. CSE-TR-403-99, University of Michigan.

J. Poulton. 1999. "Signaling in High Performance Memory Systems," Tutorial presented at ISSCC, San Francisco, CA, February 1999.

M. Powell et al. 2000. "Gated-Vdd: A circuit technique to reduce leakage in deep-submicron cache memories," in Proc. IEEE/ACM Int. Symp. on Low Power Electronics and Design (ISLPED), pp. 90–95, 2000.

F. Prein. 2002. Personal communication.

D. Pricer. 2002. Personal communication.

B. Prince. 1997. *Semiconductor Memories, 2nd Ed.* John Wiley & Sons Ltd., New York, 1997.

B. Prince. 1999. *High Performance Memories*. John Wiley & Sons Ltd., New York, 1999.

B. Prince. 2000. *High Performance Memories*. John Wiley & Sons, West Sussex, England, 2000.

S. Przybylski. 1990. *Cache and Memory Hierarchy Design: A Performance-Directed Approach*. Morgan Kaufmann, San Mateo, CA, 1990.

S. Przybylski. 1996. *New DRAM Technologies: A Comprehensive Analysis of the New Architectures*. MicroDesign Resources, Sebastopol, CA, 1996.

PTM. 2006. Predictive technology model. http://www.eas.asu.edu/~ptm

W. Pugh. 1990. "Skip Lists: A probabilistic alternative to balanced trees." *Commun. ACM*, 33(6), June 1990.

X. Qiu and M. Dubois. 1999. "Tolerating late memory traps in ILP processors." In Proc. 26th Ann. Int. Symp. on Computer Architecture (ISCA'99), pp. 76–87, Atlanta, GA, May 1999.

S. Quinlan. 1991. "A cached WORM file system." *Software—Practice and Experience*, 21(12), 1289–1299, Dec. 1991.

C. V. Ramamoorthy. 1965. "Analysis of computational systems: Discrete Markov analysis of computer programs." In Proc. 1965 20th Natl. Conf., pp. 386–392, Cleveland, Ohio, August 24–26, 1965, L. Winner, Ed., ACM Press, New York, 1965.

C. V. Ramamoorthy. 1966. "The analytic design of a dynamic look ahead and program segmenting system for multiprogrammed computers." In Proc. 1966 21st Natl. Conf. ACM Press, New York, pp. 229–239, 1966.

C. V. Ramamoorthy and K. M. Chandy. 1970. "Optimization of memory hierarchies in multiprogrammed systems." *J. ACM*, 17(3), 426–445, July 1970.

Rambus. 1994. Rambus Memory: Enabling Technology for PC Graphics. Tech. Rep., Rambus Inc., Mountain View, CA, October 1994.

Rambus. 1995. 64-Megabit Rambus DRAM Technology Directions. Tech. Rep., Rambus Inc., Mountain View, CA, September 1995.

Rambus. 1996a. Comparing RDRAM and SGRAM for 3D Applications. Tech. Rep., Rambus Inc., Mountain View, CA, October 1996.

Rambus. 1996b. Memory Latency Comparison. Tech. Rep., Rambus Inc., Mountain View, CA, September 1996.

Rambus. 1998a. 16/18Mbit & 64/72Mbit Concurrent RDRAM Data Sheet. Rambus, http://www.rambus.com/docs/Cnctds.pdf.

Rambus. 1998b. Direct RDRAM 64/72-Mbit Data Sheet. Rambus. http://www.rambus.com/docs/64dDDS.pdf.

Rambus. 2000. Direct RDRAM 256/288-Mbit Data Sheet. Rambus. http://www.rambus.com/developer/downloads/rdram.256s.0060-1.1.book.pdf.

A. Ramirez, L. A. Barroso, K. Gharachorloo, R. Cohn, J. Larriba-Pey, P. G. Lowney, and M. Valero. 2001. "Code layout optimizations for transaction processing workloads." In Proc. 28th Ann. Int. Symp. on Computer Architecture (ISCA '01), pp. 155–164, Göteborg, Sweden, June 30–July 04, 2001, ACM Press, New York, 2001.

S. Ranade. 1991. *Mass Storage Technologies*. Meckler Publishing, Westport, CT, 1991.

B. Randell and C. J. Kuehner. 1967. "Dynamic storage allocation systems." In Proc. First ACM Symp. on Operating System Principles (SOSP '67), pp. 9.1–9.16, J. Gosden and B. Randell, Eds., ACM Press, New York, 1967.

P. Ranganathan et al. 1998. "Performance of database workloads on shared-memory systems with out-of-order processors." In Proc. Int. Conf. Architectural Support for Programming Languages and Operating Systems (ASPLOS-8), pp. 307–318, October 1998.

R. M. Rao, J. L. Burns and R.B. Brown. (2003) "Circuit techniques for gate and subthreshold leakage minimization in future CMOS technologies," ESSCIRC '03. Proc. 29th European Solid-State Circuits Conf., 2003.

R. Rashid, A. Tevanian, M. Young, D. Young, R. Baron, D. Black, W. Bolosky, and J. Chew. 1988. "Machine-independent virtual memory management for paged uniprocessor and multiprocessor architectures." *IEEE Trans. Computers*, 37(8), 896–908, 1988.

E. S. Raymond. 1997. The On-line Hacker Jargon File, version 4.0.0. The MIT Press. http://www.ccil.org/jargon/.

R. Rechstschaffen. 1983. "Cache miss history table." *IBM Technical Disclosure Bulletin*, 25(11B), 5978–5980, April 1983.

S. L. Rege. 1976. "Cost, performance and size trade-offs for different levels in a memory hierarchy." *IEEE Computer*, 19, 43–51, April 1976.

S. Reinhardt, M. Hill, J. Larus, A. Lebeck, J. Lewis, and D. Wood. 1993. "The Wisconsin Wind Tunnel: Virtual prototyping of parallel computers." In Proc. ACM

SIGMETRICS Conf. on Measurement and Modeling of Computer Systems '93, 1993.

G. Reinman and N. Jouppi. 2000. CACTI 2.0: An Integrated Cache Timing and Power Model, WRL Research Report 2000/7, Feb. 2000.

P. J. Restle, J. W. Park, and B. F. Lloyd. 1992. "DRAM variable retention time." *In International. Electron Devices Meeting Technical Digest*, pp. 807–810, 1992.

D. Rhoden. 2002. Personal communication.

R. Riedlinger and T. Grutkowski. 2002. "The high-bandwidth 256 kB 2nd level cache on an Itanium microprocessor," In ISSCC, 2002.

S. A. Ritchie. 1985. "TLB for Free: In-Cache Address Translation for a Multiprocessor Workstation," Technical Report UCB/CSD 85/233, University of California.

J. A. Rivers and E. S. Davidson. 1996. "Reducing conflicts in direct-mapped Caches with a temporality based design." In Proc. 1996 Int. Conf. on Parallel Processing (ICPP 1996), Volume 1: Architecture, pp. 154–163, Bloomingdale, IL, August 1996.

J. A. Rivers, E. S. Tam, G. S. Tyson, E. S. Davidson, and M. Farrens. 1998. "Utilizing reuse information in data cache management." In Proc. 12th Int. Conf. on Supercomputing (ICS '98), pp. 449–456. Melbourne, Australia, 1998.

S. Rixner, W. Dally, U. Kapasi, P. Mattson, and J. Owens. 2000. "Memory access scheduling." In Proc. 27th Int. Symp. on Computer Architecture (ISCA), June 2000.

S. Rixner. 2004. "Memory controller optimizations for Web servers." In Proc. 37th Int. Symp. on Microarchitecture (MICRO), December 2004.

N. Robertson, H. Hu, and C. Tsang. 1997. "High performance write head using NiFe 45/55." *IEEE Trans. Magnetics*, 33(5), 2818–2820, 1997.

T. Roscoe. 1994. "Linkage in the Nemesis single address space operating system." *ACM Operating Syst. Rev.*, 28(4), 48–55, 1994.

T. Roscoe. 1995. The Structure of a Multi-Service Operating System, PhD thesis, Queens' College, University of Cambridge.

M. Rosenblum, E. Bugnion, S. A. Herrod, E. Witchel, and A. Gupta. 1995. "The impact of architectural trends on operating system performance." In Proc. Fifteenth ACM Symp. on Operating Systems Principles (SOSP-15), December 1995.

M. Rosenblum and J. K. Ousterhout. 1992. "The design and implementation of a log-structured file system." *ACM Transactions on Computer Systems*, 10(1), 26–52, 1992.

E. Rotenberg, S. Bennett, and J. E. Smith. 1996. "Trace cache: A low latency approach to high bandwidth instruction fetching." In Proc. 29th Ann. ACM/IEEE Int. Symp. on Microarchitecture (MICRO-29), pp. 24–35, Paris, France, December 1996.

A. Roth, A. Moshovos, and G. Sohi. 1998. "Dependence based prefetching for linked data structures." In The 8th Int. Conf. on Architectural Support for Programming Languages and Operating Systems (ASPLOS), pp. 115–126, October 1998.

A. Roth and G. S. Sohi. 1999. "Effective jump-pointer prefetching for linked data structures." In Proc. 26th Int. Symp. on Computer Architecture (ISCA), Atlanta, GA, May 1999.

K. Roy and M. C. Johnson. 1996. "Software design for low power." In NATO Advanced Study Institute on Low Power Design in Deep Submicron Electronics (ISGA), Ciocco, Lucca, Italy, August 1996.

C. Ruemmler and J. Wilkes. 1994. "An introduction to disk drive modeling." *Computer*, 27(3), 17–28, 1994.

J. Russell and M. Jacome. 1998. "Software power estimation and optimization for high performance, 32-bit embedded processors." In Int. Conf. on Computer Design (ICCD), Austin, TX, October 1998.

K. Ryan. 2002. Personal communication.

G. M. Sacco and M. Schkolnick. 1982. "A mechanism for managing the buffer pool in a relational database system using the hot set model." In Proc. 8th Int. Conf. on Very Large Data Bases, pp. 257–262, Mexico City, Mexico, September 1982.

S. Sair and M. Charney. 2000. "Memory behavior of the SPEC 2000 Benchmark Suite." *IBM Research Report*, October, 2000.

Samsung. 1998. FPM DRAM 4M x 16 Part No. KM416V4100C. Samsung Semiconductor. http://www.usa.samsungsemi.com/products/prodspec/dramcomp/KM416V40(1)00C.PDF.

K. Sasaki et al. 1988. "A 15-ns 1-Mbit CMOS SRAM." *IEEE J. Solid-State Circuits*, 23(5), 1067–1072, Oct. 1988.

K. Sasaki et al. 1989. "A 9-ns 1-Mbit CMOS SRAM." *IEEE J. Solid-State Circuits*, 24(5), 1219–1225, Oct. 1989.

K. Sasaki et al. 1990. "A 23-ns 4-Mb CMOS SRAM with 0.2-uA standby current." *IEEE J. Solid-State Circuits*, 25(5), 1075–1081, Oct. 1990.

I. Sase et al. 1997. "Multimedia LSI accelerator with embedded DRAM." *IEEE Micro*, 17(6), 49–54, Nov. 1997.

H. Sato et al. 1999. "A 500-MHz pipeline burst SRAM with improved SER immunity." *IEEE J. Solid-State Circuits*, SC-34(11), 1571–1579, Nov. 1999.

A. Saulsbury, F. Pong, and A. Nowatzyk. 1996. "Missing the memory wall: The case for processor/memory integration." In Proc. 23rd Ann. Int. Symp. on Computer Architecture (ISCA'96), pp. 90–101, Philadelphia, PA, May 1996.

Y. Sazeides and J. E. Smith. 1997. "The predictability of data values." In Proc. 30th Ann. Int. Symp. on Microarchitecture (MICRO 1997), pp. 248–258, Research Triangle Park, NC, December 1997.

C. Scheurich and M. Dubois. 1998. "Concurrent miss resolution in multiprocessor caches." In Proc. 1988 Int. Conf. on Parallel Processing, 1998.

I. Schoinas, B. Falsafi, A. R. Lebeck, S. K. Reinhardt, J. R. Larus, and D. A. Wood. 1994. "Fine-grain access control for distributed shared memory." In Proc. Sixth Int. Conf. on Architecture Support for Programming Languages and Operating Systems (ASPLOS), pp. 297–306, 1994.

M. D. Schroeder. 1971. "Performance of the GE-645 associative memory while Multics is in operation." In Proc. ACM SIGNOPS Workshop on System Performance Evaluation, pp. 227–245. Cambridge, MA, April 1971.

D. M. Schuler and E. G. Ulrich. 1972. "Clustering and linear placement." In Proc. 9th Workshop on Design Automation (DAC '72), pp. 50–56, June 26–28, 1972, ACM Press, New York, 1972.

R. C. Schumann. 1997. "Design of the 21174 memory controller for DIGITAL personal workstations." *Digital Technical J.*, 9(2), 57–70, 1997.

S. Schuster et al. 1986. "A 15-ns CMOS 64K RAM." *IEEE J. Solid-State Circuits*, SC-21(5), 704–712, Oct. 1986.

W. D. Schwaderer and A. W. Wilson, Jr. 1996. *Understanding I/O Subsystems*. Adaptec, Milpitas, CA, 1996.

T. Schwarz and W. Burkhard. 1995. "Reliability and performance of RAIDs." *IEEE Trans. Magnetics*, 31(2), 1161–1166, 1995.

M. L. Scott, T. J. LeBlanc, and B. D. Marsh. 1988. "Design rationale for Psyche, a general-purpose multiprocessor operating system." In Proc. 1988 Int. Conf. on Parallel Processing, August 1988.

J. Scott, L. Lee, A. Chin, J. Arends, and B. Moyer. 1999. "Designing the M.CORE M3 CPU architecture." In Int. Conf. on Computer Design, Austin, TX, October 1999.

M. L. Seidl and B. G. Zorn. 1998. "Segregating heap objects by reference behavior and lifetime." In Proc. Eighth Int. Conf. on Architectural Support For Programming Languages and Operating Systems (ASPLOS-VIII), pp. 12–23, San Jose, CA, October 02–07, 1998, ACM Press, New York, 1998.

M. Seltzer, P. Chen, and J. Ousterhout. 1990. "Disk scheduling revisited." In Winter USENIX 1990, pp. 313–324, Washington, DC, 1990.

T. Semba, T. Hirano, J. Hong, and L. Fan. 1999. "Dual-stage servo controller for hdd using mems microactuator." *IEEE Trans. Magnetics*, 35(5), 2271–2273, 1999.

S. M. Shahrier and J. C. Liu. 1997. "On the design of multiprogrammed caches for hard real-time systems." In Proc. IEEE Int. Performance, Computing and Communications Conference (IPCCC'97), pp. 17–25, February 1997.

D. L. Shell. 1959. "The Share 709 System: A cooperative effort." *J. ACM (JACM)*, 6(2), 123–127, April 1959.

T. Sherwood, S. Sair, and B. Calder. 2000. "Predictor-directed stream buffers." In The 33rd Int. Symp. on Microarchitecture (MICRO), pp. 42–53, December 2000.

N. Shirle and D. Lieu. 1996. "History and trends in the development of motorized spindles for hard disk drives." *IEEE Trans. Magnetics*, 32(3), 1703–1708, 1996.

W. Shiue and C. Chakrabarti. 1999. "Memory exploration for low power, embedded systems." In Proc. 36th ACM/IEEE Conf. on Design Automation (DAC '99), pp. 140–145, New Orleans, Louisiana, June 21–25, 1999, M. J. Irwin, Ed., ACM Press, New York, 1999.

P. Shivakumar and N. Jouppi . 2001. CACTI 3.0: An Integrated Cache Timing, Power and Area Model, WRL Research Report 2001/2, Aug. 2001.

B. Shriver and B. Smith. 1998. *The Anatomy of a High-Performance Microprocessor: A Systems Perspective.* IEEE Comput. Soc., Los Alamitos, CA, 1998.

SIA. 2003. *Int. Technology Roadmap for Semiconductors 2003 Edition*. Semiconductor Industry Association. http://public.itrs.net.

SIA. 2005. *Int. Technology Roadmap for Semiconductors 2005 Edition*. Semiconductor Industry Association. http://public.itrs.net.

H. M. Sierra. 1990. *An Introduction to Direct Access Storage Devices*. Academic Press, San Diego, CA, 1990.

SimOS. 1998. SimOS: The Complete Machine Simulator. Stanford University. http://simos.stanford.edu/.

R. L. Sites, Editor. 1992. *Alpha Architecture Reference Manual*. Digital Equipment Corporation, Maynard, MA.

R. Sites. 1996. "It's the memory, stupid!" *Microprocessor Rep.*, 10(10), Aug. 1996.

J. Sjodin, B. Froderberg, and T. Lindgren. 1998. "Allocation of global data objects in on-chip RAM." Compiler and Architecture Support for Embedded Computing Systems (CASES '98), December 1998.

J. Sjodin and C. Von Platen. 2001. "Storage allocation for embedded processors." Compiler and Architecture Support for Embedded Computing Systems (CASES), November 2001.

M. Slater. 1994. "AMD's K5 designed to outrun Pentium." *Microprocessor Rep.*, 8(14), Oct. 1994.

SLDRAM. 1998. 4M x 18 SLDRAM Advance Datasheet. SLDRAM, Inc. http://www.sldram.com/Documents/corp400b.pdf.

A. J. Smith. 1977. "Two methods for the efficient analysis of memory address trace data." *IEEE Trans. Software Eng.*, 3(1), 94–101, Jan. 1977.

A. J. Smith. 1981a. "Long term file migration: Development and evaluation of algorithms." *Commun. ACM*, 24(8), 521–532, Aug. 1981.

J. E. Smith. 1981. "A study of branch prediction strategies." In Proc. 8th Ann. Symp. on Computer Architecture (ISCA-8), pp. 135–148, Minneapolis, MN, May 1981.

A. J. Smith. 1982. "Cache memories." *Computing Surveys*, 14(3), 473–530, Sept. 1982.

A. J. Smith, 1985a. "Disk cache: Miss ratio analysis and design considerations." In Proc. 5th Ann. Symp. on Computer Architecture, pp. 242–248, April 1985.

A. J. Smith. 1985b. "Disk cache-miss ratio analysis and design considerations." *ACM Trans. Comput. Syst.*, 3(3), 161–203, Aug. 1985.

J. E. Smith and A. R. Pleszkun. 1985. "Implementation of precise interrupts in pipelined processors." In Proc. 12th Ann. Int. Symp. on Computer Architecture (ISCA'85), pp. 36–44, Boston, MA, June 1985.

J. E. Smith. 1988. "Characterizing computer performance with a single number." *CACM*, 31(10), 1202–1206, Oct. 1988.

J. E. Smith, G. E. Dermer, and M. A. Goldsmith. 1988. Computer System Employing Virtual Memory. US Patent No. 4,774,659. U.S. Patent Office.

J. E. Smith and A. R. Pleszkun. 1988. "Implementing precise interrupts in pipelined processors." *IEEE Trans. Computers*, 37(5), 1988.

M. J. Smith. 1997. *Application-Specific Integrated Circuits*. Addison-Wesley, Reading, MA, 1997.

G. S. Sohi and S. Vajapeyam. 1987. "Instruction issue logic for high-performance, interruptable pipelined processors." In Proc. 14th Ann. Int. Symp. on Computer Architecture (ISCA'87), June 1987.

Y. Solihin, J. Lee, and J. Torrellas. 2002. "Using a user-level memory thread for correlation prefetching." In 29th Int. Symp. on Computer Architecture (ISCA), May 2002.

Y. Solihin, J. Lee, and J. Torrellas. 2003. "Correlation prefetching with a user-level memory thread." *IEEE Trans. Parallel Distributed Systems*, June 2003.

J. A. Solworth and C. U. Orji. 1990. "Write-only disk caches." In Proc. 1990 ACM SIGMOD Int. Conf. on Management of Data (SIGMOD '90, pp. 123–132, Atlantic City, New Jersey, May 23–26, 1990, SIGMOD '90. ACM Press, New York, 1990.

S. W. Son and M. Kandemir, 2006. "Energy-aware data prefetching for multi-speed disks." In Proc. 3rd Conf. on Computing Frontiers (CF '06, pp. 105–114, Ischia, Italy, May 03–05, 2006, ACM Press, New York, 2006.

S. Srinivasan, V. Cuppu, and B. Jacob. 2001. "Transparent data-memory organizations for digital signal processors." In Proc. Int. Conf. on Compilers, Architecture, and Synthesis for Embedded Systems (CASES 2001), pp. 44–48, Atlanta, GA, Nov. 2001.

A. Srivastava and A. Eustace. 1994. ATOM: A System for Building Customized Program Analysis Tools,

Technical Report WRL-RR-94/2, DEC Western Research Laboratory.

Staktek. 2006. Personal communication.

J. W. Stamos. 1984. "Static grouping of small objects to enhance performance of a paged virtual memory." *ACM Trans. Comput. Syst.*, 2(2), 155–180, May 1984.

Standard Performance Evaluation Corp. 1993. SPEC Newsletter, December 1993.

B. Steensgaard. 1996. "Points-to analysis in almost linear time." In Symp. on Principles of Programming Languages (POPL), St. Petersburg Beach, FL, January 1996.

S. Steinke, L. Wehmeyer, B. Lee, and P. Marwedel. 2002a. "Assigning program and data objects to scratchpad for energy reduction." In Proc. of the Conf. on Design, Automation and Test in Europe (DATE), p. 409, IEEE Comput. Soc., Los Alamitos, CA, 2002.

S. Steinke, N. Grunwald, L. Wehmeyer, R. Banakar, M. Balakrishnan, and P. Marwedel. 2002b. "Reducing energy consumption by dynamic copying of instructions onto onchip memory." In Proc. 15th Int. Symp. on System Synthesis (ISSS '02), pp. 213– 218, Kyoto, Japan, October 02–04, 2002, ACM Press, New York, 2002.

L. D. Stevens. 1981. "The evolution of magnetic storage." IBM J. Res. Dev. 25(5), 663–675, 1981.

L. Stevens. 1998. "Data storage on magnetic disks." In E. Daniel, C. Mee, and M. Clark, Editors, *Magnetic Recording: The First 100 years.* IEEE Press, New York, 1988.

H. S. Stone. 1993. *High Performance Computer Architecture.* Addison-Wesley, Reading, MA, 1993.

M. Stonebreaker. 1981. "Operating system support for database management." *Commun. ACM*, 24(7), 412–418, July 1981.

A. Stoutchinin, J. N. Amaral, G. R. Gao, J. C. Dehnert, S. Jain, and A. Douillet. 2001. "Speculative pointer prefetching of induction pointers." In Compiler Construction 2001, European Joint Conferences on Theory and Practice of Software, Genova, Italy, April 2001.

STREAM. 1997. STREAM: Measuring Sustainable Memory Bandwidth in High Performance Computers. The University of Virginia. http://www.cs.virginia.edu/stream/.

C. Su and A. M. Despain. 1995. "Cache design trade-offs for power and performance optimization: A case study." In Proc. 1995 Int. Symp. on Low Power Design (ISLPED '95), pp. 63–68, Dana Point, California, April 23–26, 1995, ACM Press, New York, 1995.

Sun. 1995. The UltraSPARC Processor. Sun Technology, November 1995. White Paper.

Sun. 1997. Wabi 2.2 Product Overview. Sun Microsystems. http://www.sun.com/solaris/products/wabi/.

H. Sussman. 2002. Personal communication.

I. E. Sutherland and R. F. Sproull. 1991. "Logical effort: Designing for speed on the back of an envelope." *Advanced Res. VLSI*, 1–16, 1991.

I. E. Sutherland et al. 1999. *Logical Effort: Designing Fast CMOS Circuits, 1st Ed., Morgan Kauffman*, San Mateo, CA, 1999.

S. Suzuki and S. Iwasaki. 1982. "Magnetization transitions in perpendicular magnetic recording." *IEEE Trans. Magnetics*, 18(2), 771–769, 1982.

M. Swanson, L. Stoller, and J. Carter. 1998. "Increasing TLB reach using superpages. backed by shadow memory." In Proc. 25th Ann. Int. Symp. on Computer Architecture (ISCA'98), pp. 204–213, Barcelona, Spain, June 1998.

Synopsys. 2002. DesignWare DW8051 MacroCell Databook. Synopsys, December 2002.

Systems Performance Evaluation Cooperative. SPEC Benchmarks. http://www.spec.org.

C. D. Tait and D. Duchamp. 1991. "Detection and exploitation of file working sets." In 11th Int. Conf. on Distributed Computing Systems (Cat. No. 91CH2996-7), pp. 2–9, 20–24, Arlington, TX, IEEE, Press, New York, May 1991.

M. Talluri, S. Kong, M. D. Hill, and D. A. Patterson. 1992. "Tradeoffs in supporting two page sizes." In Proc. 19th Ann. Int. Symp. on Computer Architecture (ISCA-19), 1992.

M. Talluri and M. D. Hill. 1994a. "Surpassing the TLB performance of Superpages with less operating system support." In Proc. Sixth Int. Conf. on Architectural Support for Programming Languages and Operating Systems (ASPLOS-6), San Jose, CA, 1994.

M. Talluri and M. D. Hill, 1994b. "Surpassing the TLB performance of superpages. with less operating system support." In Proc. Sixth Int. Conf. on Architectural Support for Programming Languages and Operating Systems (ASPLOS), 1994.

M. Talluri, M. D. Hill, and Y. A. Khalidi. 1995. "A new page table for 64-bit address spaces." In Proc. Fifteenth ACM Symp. on Operating Systems Principles (SOSP-15). December 1995.

Y. Tan and V. Mooney. 2003. "A prioritized cache for multi-tasking real-time systems." In Proc. 11th Workshop on Synthesis and System Integration of Mixed Information technologies (SASIMI), pp. 168–175, April 2003.

Y. Taur and T. Ning. 1998. *Fundamentals of Modern VLSI Devices*. Cambridge University Press, Cambridge, England, 1998.

G. Taylor, P. Davies, and M. Farmwald. 1990. "The TLB slice—A low-cost high-speed address translation mechanism." In Proc. 17th Ann. Int. Symp. on Computer Architecture (ISCA '90), pp. 355–363, Seattle, Washington, May 28–31, 1990, ACM Press, New York, 1990.

TechReport. 2006. The Tech Report. http://techreport.com/cpu/.

Texas Instruments. TMS320C6000 peripherals reference guide, TI Inc. http://www-s.ti.com/sc/psheets/spru190d/spru190d.pdf.

A. Thomasian and M. Blaum. 2006. "Mirrored disk organization reliability analysis." *IEEE Trans. Computers*, 55(12), 1640–1644, 2006.

A. Thomasian and C. Liu. 2002. "Disk scheduling policies with lookahead." *ACM SIGMETRICS Performance Evaluation Rev.*, 30(2), 31–40, 2002.

A. Thomasian. 2006. "Multi-level RAID for very large disk arrays." *ACM SIGMETRICS Performance Rev. — SPECIAL ISSUE: Design Implementation and Performance of Storage Systems*, 33(4), 17–22, 2006.

J. E. Thornton. 1970. *Design of a Computer: The Control Data 6600*. Scott, Foresman and Co., Glenview, IL, 1970.

V. Tiwari, S. Malik, and A. Wolfe. 1994. "Power analysis of embedded software: A first step towards software power minimization." *IEEE Trans. VLSI Syst.*, 2(4), 1277–1284, Dec. 1994.

V. Tiwari and M. T.-C. Lee. 1998. "Power analysis of a 32-bit embedded microcontroller." *VLSI Design J.*, 7(3), 1998.

R. M. Tomasulo. 1967. "An efficient algorithm for exploiting multiple arithmetic units." *IBM J. Res. Dev.*, 11(1), 25–33, 1967.

H. C. Torng and M. Day. 1993. "Interrupt handling for out-of-order execution processors." *IEEE Trans. Computers*, 42(1), 122–127, Jan. 1993.

J. Torrellas, A. Gupta, and J. Hennessy. 1992. "Characterizing the caching and synchronization performance of a multiprocessor operating system." In Proc. Fifth Int. Conf. on Architectural Support for Programming Languages and Operating Systems (ASPLOS), 1992.

J. D. Touch and D. J. Farber. 1994. "An experiment in latency reduction." In Proc. IEEE Infocom, pp. 175–181, Toronto, June 1994.

C. Tsang, R. Fontana, T. Lin, D. Heim, V. Speriosu, B. Gurney, and M. Williams. 1994. "Design fabrication and testing of spin-valve read heads for high density recording." *IEEE Trans. Magnetics*, 24(6), 3801–3806, 1994.

C. Tsang, M. Chen, T. Yogi, and K. Ju. 1997. "Gigabit density recording using dual-element mr/inductive heads on thin-film disks." *IEEE Trans. Magnetics*, 26(5), 2271–2276, 1997.

J. L. Turley. 1995. "Thumb squeezes ARM code size." *Microprocessor Rep.*, 9(4), 1–5, March 27, 1995.

J. Turley. 1997a. "M.Core shrinks code, power budgets." *Microprocessor Rep.*, 11(14), 12–15, Oct. 1997.

J. Turley. 1997b. "TI's new 'C6x DSP screams at 1,600 MIPS." *Microprocessor Rep.*, 11(2), 14–18, 1997.

J. Turley. 1998a. "MCore: Does Motorola need another processor family?" *Embedded Systems Programming*, July 1998.

J. Turley. 1998b. "M.Core for the portable millenium." *Microprocessor Rep.*, 12(2), 15–18, Feb. 1998.

J. Turley. 1998c. "National kills in-house embedded x86 work." *Microprocessor Rep.*, 12(2), 10, Feb. 1998.

G. Tyson, M. Farrens, J. Matthews, and A. R. Pleszkun. 1995. "A modified approach to data cache management." In Proc. 28th Ann. Int. Symp. on Microarchitecture (MICRO-28), pp. 93–103, Ann Arbor, MI, 1995.

S.-Y. Tzou and D. P. Anderson. 1991. "The performance of message-passing using restricted virtual memory remapping." *Software—Practice and Experience*, 21(3), 251–267, 1991.

K. Uchiyama et al. 1991. "Design of a second-level cache chip for shared-bus multimicroprocessor systems." *IEEE J. Solid-State Circuits*, 26(4), 566–571, Apr. 1991.

S. Udayakumaran and R. Barua. 2003. "Compiler-decided dynamic memory allocation for scratchpad based embedded systems." In Proc. Int. Conf. on Compilers, Architectures and Synthesis for Embedded Systems (CASES), pp. 276–286, ACM Press, New York, 2003.

S. Ueno, T. Yamashita, H. Oda, S. Komori, Y. Inoue, and T. Nishimura. 1998. "Leakage current observation on irregular local Pn junction forming the tail distribution of DRAM retention time characteristics." In International Electron Devices Meeting Technical Digest (IEDM), pp. 153–156, 1998.

R. Uhlig, D. Nagle, T. Mudge, and S. Sechrest. 1994. "Trap-driven simulation with Tapeworm-II." In Proc. Sixth Int. Conf. on Architectural Support for Programming Languages and Operating Systems (ASPLOS-6), San Jose, CA, 1994.

O. S. Unsal, R. Ashok, I. Koren, C. M. Krishna, and C. A. Moritz. 1990. "Coolcache for hot multimedia." In Proc. Int. Symp. on Microarchitecture (MICRO), pp. 274–283, 1990.

M. Upton. 1997. Personal communication.

A. Vahdat, A. Lebeck, and C. Ellis. 2000. "Every joule is precious: The case for revisiting operating system design for energy efficiency." In SIGOPS European Workshop, Kolding, Denmark, September 2000.

A. Varma and Q. Jacobson. 1998. "Destage algorithms for disk arrays with nonvolatile caches." *IEEE Trans. Comput.* 47(2), 228–235, Feb. 1998.

A. Varma, B. Ganesh, M. Sen, S. R. Choudhary, L. Srinivasan, and B. Jacob. 2003. "A control-theoretic approach to dynamic voltage scaling." In Proc. Int. Conf. on Compilers, Architectures, and Synthesis for Embedded Systems (CASES 2003), pp. 255–266, San Jose, CA, October 2003.

R. K. Venkatesan, S. Herr, and E. Rotenberg. 2006. "Retention-aware placement in DRAM (RAPID): Software methods for quasi-non-volatile DRAM." In Proc. 12th Int. Symp. on High Performance Computer Architecture (HPCA), pp. 157–167, 2006.

M. Verma, L. Wehmeyer, and P. Marwedel. 2004. "Cache-aware scratchpad allocation algorithm." In Proc. Conf. on Design, Automation and Test in Europe (DATE), IEEE Comput. Soc., Los Alamitos, CA, 2004.

N. Vijaykrishnan, M. Kandemir, M. Irwin, H. Kim, and W. Ye. 2000. "Energy-driven integrated hardware-software optimizations using simplepower." In Proc. 27th Ann. Int. Symp. on Computer Architecture (ISCA'00), pp. 95–116, Vancouver, BC, June 2000.

M. A. Viredaz and D. A. Wallach. 2003. "Power evaluation of a handheld computer." *IEEE Micro,* 23(1), 66–74, Jan./Feb. 2003.

F. Vivien and M. Rinard. 2001. "Incrementalized pointer and escape analysis." In Proc. ACM SIGPLAN 2001 Conf. on Programming Language Design and Implementation (PLDI), pp. 35–46, ACM Press, New York, 2001.

P. Vogt. 2004a. "Fully buffered DIMM (FB-DIMM) server memory architecture: Capacity, performance, reliability, and longevity." Intel Developer Forum, Session OSAS008, February 2004.

P. Vogt. 2004b. "Fully buffered DIMM (FB-DIMM) Architecture." Denali MemCon, Westford, MA, May 2004.

R. Wahbe, S. Lucco, T. E. Anderson, and S. L. Graham. 1993. "Efficient software-based fault isolation." In Proc. Fourteenth ACM Symp. on Operating Systems Principles (SOSP-14), pp. 203–216, 1993.

W. Walker and H. G. Cragon. 1995. "Interrupt processing in concurrent processors." *IEEE Computer,* 28(6), June 1995.

A. Walker. 2002. Personal communication.

W.-H. Wang, J.-L. Baer, and H. M. Levy. 1989. "Organization and performance of a two-level virtual-real cache hierarchy." In Proc. 16th Ann. Int. Symp. on Computer Architecture (ISCA-16), pp. 140–148, 1989.

S. X. Wang and A. M. Taratorin. 1999. *Magnetic Information Storage Technology.* Academic Press, San Diego, CA, 1999.

D. Wang, B. Ganesh, N. Tuaycharoen, K. Baynes, A. Jaleel, and B. Jacob. 2005. "DRAMsim: A memory-system simulator." *SIGARCH Computer Architecture News,* 33(4), 100–107. Sept. 2005.

D. L. Weaver and T. Germand, Editors. 1994. *The SPARC Architecture Manual Version 9.* PTR Prentice Hall, Englewood Cliffs, NJ, 1994.

C. F. Webb. 1988. "Subroutine call/return stack." *IBM Technical Disclosure Bulletin,* 30(11), April 1988.

L. R. Wechsler. 1973. "The effect of look-ahead paging in a virtual memory system as determined by simulation." In Proc. 1st Symp. on Simulation of Computer Systems, pp. 234–241, (Gaithersburg, Maryland, June 19–20, 1973, H. J. Highland, Ed., Ann. Simulation Symposium. IEEE Press, Piscataway, NJ, 1973.

L. Wehmeyer, U. Helmig, and P. Marwedel. 2004. "Compiler-optimized usage of partitioned memories." In Proc.

3rd Workshop on Memory Performance Issues (WMPI2004), 2004.

M. Weiser, B. Welch, A. Demers, and S. Shenker. 1994. "Scheduling for reduced CPU energy." In Proc. First USENIX Symp. on Operating Systems Design and Implementation (OSDI'94), pp. 13–23, Monterey, CA, November 1994.

S. Weiss and J. E. Smith. 1984. "Instruction issue login in pipelined supercomputers." *IEEE Trans. Computers*, 33(11), 1984.

S. Weiss and J. E. Smith. 1994. *POWER and PowerPC*. Morgan Kaufmann, San Francisco, CA, 1994.

D. Weiss, J. J. Wuu, and V. Chin. 2002. "An on-chip 3MB subarray-based 3rd level cache on an Itanium microprocessor." In Proc. Int'l. Solid-State Circuits Conference (ISSCC) 2002.

T. A. Welch. 1978. "Memory hierarchy configuration analysis." *IEEE Trans. Computers*, 27(5), 408–413, May 1978.

M. Wells. 1972. "File compression using variable length encodings." *The Computer J.*, 15(4), 308–313, Nov. 1972.

B. Wheeler and B. N. Bershad. 1992. "Consistency management for virtually indexed caches." In Proc. Fifth Int. Conf. on Architectural Support for Programming Languages and Operating Systems (ASPLOS-5), pp. 124–136, October 1992.

M. White, P. Hingwe, and T. Hirano. 2004. "Comparison of a mems microactuator and a pzt milliactuator for high-bandwidth hdd servo." In American Control Conference 2004, pp. 541–546, Boston, MA, 2004.

K. Wilcox and S. Manne. 2001. "Alpha Processors: A History of Power Issues and A Look to the Future." Compaq Computer Corporation, 2001.

M. V. Wilkes. 1965. "Slave memories and dynamic storage allocation." *IEEE Trans. Electronic Computers (Short Notes)*, EC-14, 270–271, April 1965.

M. V. Wilkes. 1971. "Slave memories and segmentation." *IEEE Trans. Computers (Short Notes)*, C-20(6), 674–675, June 1971.

R. Williams. 1997. *Data Powers of Ten*. Center for Advanced Computing Research, Caltech, Pasadena CA. http://www.cacr.caltech.edu/ roy/dataquan/.

S. Williams, M. Abrams, C. R. Standridge, G. Abdulla, and E. A. Fox. 1996. "Removal policies in network caches for World-Wide Web documents." In Proc. ACM SIGCOMM '96 Conf. on Applications, Technologies,

Architectures, and Protocols for Computer Communications, pp. 293–305, Stanford, CA, August 1996.

R. Wilson. 1997. "MoSys tries synthetic SRAM." EE Times Online, July 15, 1997. http://www.eetimes.com/news/98/1017news/tries.html.

K. M. Wilson, K. Olukotun, and M. Rosenblum. 1996. "Increasing cache port efficiency for dynamic superscalar microprocessors." In Proc. 23rd Ann. Int. Symp. on Computer Architecture (ISCA '96), pp. 147–157, Philadelphia, Pennsylvania, May 22–24, 1996, ACM Press, New York, 1996.

P. R. Wilson. 1991. "Pointer swizzling at page fault time: Efficiently supporting huge address spaces on standard hardware." *ACM Computer Architecture News*, June, 6–13, 1991.

S. Wilton and N. Jouppi. 1994. An Enhanced Access and Cycle Time Model for On-chip Caches, WRL Research Report 93/5, DEC Western Research Laboratory, 1994.

S. J. Wilton and N. P. Jouppi. 1996. "CACTI: An enhanced cache access and cycle time model." *IEEE JSSC*, 31(5), May 1996.

M. S. Wojtyna and P. A. de Maine. 1988. "SOLID: A high-speed data- and question-independent information management system." In Proc. 1988 ACM Sixteenth Ann. Conf. Computer Science (CSC '88), PP. 652–657, Atlanta, Georgia, ACM Press, New York, 1988.

M. E. Wolf and M. S. Lam. 1991. "A data locality optimizing algorithm." In Proc. SIGPLAN Conf. on Programming Language Design and Implementation (PLDI), ACM, New York, June 1991.

O. Wolf and J. Bier. 1998. "StarCore launches first architecture: Lucent and Motorola disclose new VLIW-based approach." *Microprocessor Rep.*, 12(14), 22–55, 1998.

A. Wolfe and A. Chanin. 1992. "Executing compressed programs on an embedded RISC architecture." In Proc. 25th Ann. Int. Symp. on Microarchitecture (MICRO 1992), pp. 81–91, Portland, OR, December 1992.

M. Wolfe. 2005. "How compilers and tools differ for embedded systems." Keynote address, International Conference on Compilers, Architecture, and Synthesis for Embedded Systems (CASES 2005), San Francisco, CA, September 2005.

D. A. Wood, S. J. Eggers, G. Gibson, M. D. Hill, J. M. Pendleton, S. A. Ritchie, G. S. Taylor, R. H. Katz, and D. A. Patterson. 1986. "An in-cache address translation mechanism." In Proc. 13th Ann. Int. Symp. on Computer Architecture (ISCA-13), 1986.

D. A. Wood. 1990. "The design and evaluation of in-cache address translation." PhD thesis, University of California at Berkeley, 1990.

B. Worthington, G. Ganger, and Y. Patt. 1994. "Scheduling algorithms for modern disk drives." In Proc. 1994 ACM SIGMETRICS Joint Int. Conf. on Measurement and Modeling of Computer Systems, pp. 241–251, Nashville, TN, 1994.

B. Worthington, G. Ganger, Y. Patt, and J. Wilkes. 1995. "On-line extraction of SCSI disk drive parameters." In Proc. 1995 ACM SIGMETRICS Joint Int. Conf. on Measurement and Modeling of Computer systems, pp. 146–156, Ottawa, Canada, 1995.

W. A. Wulf and S. A. McKee. 1995. "Hitting the memory wall: Implications of the obvious." *ACM Computer Architecture News*, 23(1), pp. 20–24, March 1995.

S. Wuytack, J. Diguet, F. V. Catthoor, and H. J. De Man. 1998. "Formalized methodology for data reuse exploration for low-power hierarchical memory mappings." *IEEE Trans. Very Large Scale Integr. Syst.*, 6(4), 529–537, Dec. 1998.

D. S. Yaney, C. Y. Lu, R. A. Kohler, M. J. Kelly, and J. T. Nelson. 1987. "A Meta-Stable Leakage Phenonmenon in DRAM Charge Storage—Variable Hold Time." In International. Electron Devices Meeting Technical Digest (IEDM), pp. 336–338, 1987.

C.-L. Yang and A. R. Lebeck. 2000. "Push vs. pull: Data movement for linked data structures." In Int. Conf. on Supercomputing, pp. 176–186, May 2000.

Y. Ye, S. Borkar and V. De. 1998. "A new technique for standby leakage reduction in high-performance circuits." In Symp. on VLSI Circuits Dig. Tech. Papers, 1998.

K. C. Yeager. 1996. "The MIPS R10000 superscalar microprocessor." *IEEE Micro,* 16(2), 28–40, April 1996.

T.-Y. Yeh and Y. N. Patt. 1991. "Two-level adaptive training branch prediction." In Proc. 24th Ann. Int. Symp. Microarchitecture (MICRO-24), pp. 51–61. 1991. DOI= http://doi.acm.org/10.1145/123465.123475

T. Yeh and Y. N. Patt. 1992. "Alternative implementations of two-level adaptive branch prediction." In Proc. 19th Ann. Int. Symp. Computer Architecture (ISCA '92), pp. 124–134. Queensland, Australia, May 19–21, 1992, ACM Press, New York, 1992.

T. Yeh, D. T. Marr, and Y. N. Patt. 1993. "Increasing the instruction fetch rate via multiple branch prediction and a branch address cache." In Proc. 7th Int. Conf. on Supercomputing (ICS), pp. 67–76, Tokyo, Japan, July 1993.

Y. C. Yeo et al. 2000. "Direct tunneling gate leakage current in transistorswith ultrathin nsilicon nitride gate dielectric." *IEEE Electron Device Letters*, Nov. 2000.

M. Yoshimoto et al. 1983. "A divided word-line structure in the static RAM and its application to a 64K full CMOS RAM," *IEEE J. Solid-State Circuit*s, SC-18(5), 479–485, Oct. 1983.

S. Zarandioon and A. Thomasian. 2006. "Optimization of online disk scheduling algorithms." ACM SIGMETRICS Performance Evaluation Review - SPECIAL ISSUE: Design implementation and performance of storage systems, 33(4), 42–46, 2006.

M. J. Zekauskas, W. A. Sawdon, and B. N. Bershad, 1994. Software Write Detection for a Distributed Shared Memory, Proceedings of the First Symposium on Operating Systems Design and Implementation (OSDI), 1994.

Z. Zhang and J. Torrellas. 1995. "Speeding up irregular applications in shared-memory multiprocessors: Memory binding and group prefetching." In 22nd Int. Symp. Computer Architecture (ISCA), pp. 188–199, June 1995.

C. Zhang and S. McKee. 2000. "Hardware-only stream prefetching and dynamic access ordering." In Proc. 14th Int. Conf. on Supercomputing, 2000.

Z. Zhang, Z. Zhu, and X. Zhang, 2000. "A permutation-based page interleaving scheme to reduce row-buffer conflicts and exploit data locality." In Proc. 33rd IEEE/ACM Int. Symp. on Microarchitecture (MICRO), pp. 32–41, Dec. 2000.

L. Zhang, Z. Fang, M. Parker, B. Mathew, L. Schaelicke, J. Carter, W. Hsieh, and S. McKee. 2001. "The impulse memory controller." *IEEE Trans. Computers* 50(11), Nov. 2001.

T. Zhang. 2001. "RTOS performance and energy consumption analysis based on an embedded system testbed." Master's thesis, University of Maryland at College Park, May 2001.

Z. Zhang, Z. Zhu, and X. Zhang. 2002a. "Breaking address mapping symmetry at multi-levels of memory hierarchy to reduce DRAM row-buffer conflicts." The *J. Instruction-Level Parallelism*, 3, 2002.

Y. Zhu and Y. Hu. 2002. "Can large disk built-in caches really improve system performance?" In Proc. ACM SIGMETRICS 2002 (extended abstract), pp. 284–285, Marina Del Rey, CA, June 15–19, 2002.

Z. Zhu, Z. Zhang, and X. Zhang. 2002. "Fine-grain priority scheduling on multi-channel memory systems."

In Proc. 8th Int. Symp. on High Performance Computer Architecture (HPCA), February 2002.

Z. Zhu and Z. Zhang. 2005. "A performance comparison of DRAM memory system optimizations for SMT processors." In Proc. 11th Int. Symp. High-Performance Computer Architecture (HPCA), February 2005.

J. Ziegler et al. 1998. "IBM experiments in soft fails in computer electronics." *IBM J. Res. Dev.*, 40(1), 1998.

Index